TELECOMMUNICATIONS

Telecommunications

AN INTRODUCTORY TEXTBOOK FOR ENGINEERING STUDENTS

(In S.I. Units)

By W. FRASER, M.Sc.(Eng.), F.I.E.E.

Senior Lecturer, Department of Electronic and Electrical Engineering, University of London, King's College

With a foreword by

SIR ARCHIBALD J. GILL, B.Sc.(Eng.), F.I.E.E., F.I.R.E.

Past President, Institution of Electrical Engineers

Formerly Engineer-in-Chief

G.P.O. London

Second Edition

CBS PUBLISHERS & DISTRIBUTORS PVT. LTD

New Delhi • Bangalore • Pune • Cochin • Chennai (India)

ISBN : 81-239-0983-7

First Indian Edition : 1985
Reprint : 1997, 1999, 2000, 2002, 2003

This edition has been published in India by arrangement with Macdonald & Company (Publishers) Ltd., UK

Published by Satish Kumar Jain and produced by V.K. Jain for
CBS Publishers & Distributors Pvt. Ltd.,
CBS Plaza, 4819/XI Prahlad Street, 24 Ansari Road, Daryaganj,
New Delhi - 110002, India. • Website: www.cbspd.com
e-mail: delhi@cbspd.com, cbspubs@vsnl.com, cbspubs@airtelmail.in
Ph.: 23289259, 23266861, 23266867 • Fax: 011-23243014

Branches:

- ***Bangalore:*** Seema House, 2975, 17th Cross, K.R. Road, Bansankari 2nd Stage, Bangalore - 560070 Ph.: 26771678/79 Fax: 080-26771680 • e-mail: bangalore@cbspd.com
- ***Pune:*** Bhuruk Prestige, Sr. No. 52/12/2+1+3/2, Narhe, Haveli (Near Katraj-Dehu Road by Pass), Pune-411051 Ph.: +91-20-32404169 • Fax: 020-24464059 e-mail: pune@cbspd.com
- ***Cochin:*** 36/14, Kalluvilakam, Lissie Hospital Road, Cochin - 682018, Kerala • e-mail: cochin@cbspd.com Ph.: 0484-4059061-65 • Fax: 0484-4059065
- ***Chennai:*** 20, West Park Road, Shenoy Nagar, Chennai - 600030 e-mail: chennai@cbspd.com Ph.: 044-26260666-26202620 Fax: 044-45530020

Printed at :
Nikunj Print Process, Delhi

FOREWORD

When one considers the changes and increased amenities which have been put at the disposal of the public by engineers during the last half-century certain developments stand out prominently, such as, for example, the motor-car, the aeroplane, the widespread availability of electric power and the improvements in telecommunications.

Many of these advances have been due to gradual improvements in materials and methods. The motor-car of to-day is not fundamentally different from that of fifty years ago, and the steam turbine of today does not differ from that in use then—it merely uses steam at higher temperatures and pressures which new materials have made possible.

In the field of telecommunications the greatest changes which have taken place stem from a fundamental discovery: the amplifying properties of the thermionic valve. The three-electrode valve which Lee de Forest invented and patented in 1906 was not a very reliable article—I can vouch for this, having used a number for wireless reception—and it was not until the period of the First World War that the reasons for its imperfections became known and means for eliminating them established.

Before this was done long-distance telephony was limited to about 400 miles, using open wire lines with very heavy conductors; picture-telegraphy was impracticable; radio-telephony, apart from a few experimental installations using arcs or alternators, was non-existent, and broadcasting and television unthought of.

With the three-electrode valve it became possible to generate continuous oscillations on medium and short waves, and to modulate them by speech or other signals. Receivers of high sensitivity and high output power became possible and broadcasting practicable.

Various developments such as picture-telegraphy, television, radar and other navigational aids such as echo-sounders followed in due course.

In the case of line telephony the valve made it possible to introduce intermediate amplifiers (or repeaters, as they are generally called) in trunk lines, and also made possible carrier current working, which, although patented by Squiers as far back as 1910, could not be applied in practice until reliable valves became available. This practice has now reached the stage where more than 1,000 conversations can be carried on one pair of conductors simultaneously. The culminating achievement in this direction has been the laying and bringing into successful operation of the transatlantic telephone cables with their numerous intermediate repeaters submerged in the depths of the ocean.

The foregoing developments have been the work of engineers in many countries of which Britain has borne a not inconspicuous part. The recent discoveries of the travelling wave tube in this country and of the transistor in the U.S.A. makes it reasonable to assume that the rate of development in telecommunications will, instead of relaxing, be speeded up in order to take the fullest advantage of these devices as quickly as possible.

Although many, if not most, of the developments have received adequate notice individually in the proceedings of professional institutions, there have been published in recent years in this country few books of a comprehensive character covering the whole field of telecommunications and of a standard suitable for students and engineers.

Mr. Fraser's experience both as a practising engineer and as a teacher makes him eminently suitable as the author of a work of this kind, and this book with its wide scope and copious treatment of every branch of telecommunications will, I believe, meet a definite need.

A. J. GILL.

PREFACE TO THE FIRST EDITION

THIS book has been written primarily to meet the needs of engineering students. It covers the range of the subject required of students reading for the University of London Engineering Degree and should also be suitable for Higher National Certificate work. It should be useful for candidates preparing for the examinations in Radio and Line Communication of the Institution of Electrical Engineers, and for the higher grades of examination in Telecommunications Principles held by the City and Guilds of London Institute.

Although it has not been possible to provide exhaustive references to the literature, a selection has been made of those which describe outstanding developments; others have been chosen, either to extend the text, or because they are reviews. References to more specialised works, for further reading, have been included.

London, 1957 W.F.

PREFACE TO THE SECOND EDITION

IN THIS edition the section on transistors has been rewritten and enlarged in a chapter on semiconductor devices; subsequent chapters have been rewritten to take account of the uses of these devices. I have also expanded the treatment of noise and put it in a separate chapter. Further new material has been incorporated and the layout of some sections modified.

London, 1967 W.F.

NOTE TO THE REVISED IMPRESSION OF THE SECOND EDITION

THE occasion of a further printing has been used to change the units employed. SI units are now used throughout the text. Some small changes have been made as aid to clarity and further examination questions have been added.

PREFACE TO THE FIRST EDITION

This book has been written primarily to meet the needs of engineering students. It covers the range of the subject required of students reading for the University of London Engineering Degree and should also be suitable for Higher National Certificate work. It should be useful for candidates preparing for the examinations in Radio and Line Communications of the Institution of Electrical Engineers and for the higher grades of examinations in Telecommunications Principles held by the City and Guilds of London Institute.

Although it has not been possible to provide exhaustive references to the literature, a selection has been made of those which describe outstanding developments; others have been chosen, either to extend the treatment or because they are reviews. References to more specialized works for further reading have been included.

London, 1957 W.F.

PREFACE TO THE SECOND EDITION

In this new edition the section on transistors has been rewritten and enlarged in a chapter on semiconductor devices; subsequent chapters have been rewritten to take account of the uses of these devices. I have also expanded the treatment of noise and put it in a separate chapter. Further new material has been incorporated and the layout of some sections modified.

London, 1967 W.F.

NOTE TO THE REVISED IMPRESSION OF THE SECOND EDITION

The occasion of a further printing has been used to change the units employed. SI units are now used throughout the text. Some small changes have been made as aid to clarity and further examination questions have been added.

ACKNOWLEDGEMENTS

THE help of a number of organisations—in particular Messrs. Creed & Co., E.M.I., G.E.C., Muirhead & Co., Mullard, Post Office Engineering Department, Siemens Bros. and Standard Telephones & Cables—in supplying descriptive material and illustrations is gratefully acknowledged.

Appreciation is also expressed to the Board of Editors of the *Post Office Electrical Engineers Journal* for permission to reproduce a number of illustrations and some text material, particularly extracts (which have been used in Chapter 20) from *A Survey of Modern Radio Valves*.

Figures 17.10–14 and 17.27 are based on diagrams contained in *Post Office Engineering Department Courses in Telecommunications Engineering*.

I wish to thank the Senate of London University and also the Council of the Institution of Electrical Engineers for permission to include examples from examination papers.

For help with the manuscript I am grateful to B. R. Bettridge, F. C. Caish, A. B. Ewen (who also checked the diagrams), Dr. A. S. Gladwin, H. T. Prior, P. R. Thomas, Dr. G. W. Sutton, and Dr. G. Smith.

W.F.

ACKNOWLEDGEMENTS

The help of a number of organisations—in particular Messrs. Creed & Co., E.M.I., G.E.C., Muirhead & Co., Mullard, Post Office Engineering Department, Siemens Bros. and Standard Telephones & Cables—in supplying descriptive material and illustrations is gratefully acknowledged.

Appreciation is also expressed to the Board of Editors of the *Post Office Electrical Engineers Journal* for permission to reproduce a number of illustrations and some text material, particularly extracts (which have been used in Chapter 20) from *A Survey of Modern Radio Valves*. Figures 17.10–14 and 17.3 are based on diagrams contained in *Post Office Engineering Department Course in Telecommunications Engineering*.

I wish to thank the Senate of London University and also the Council of the Institution of Electrical Engineers for permission to include examples from examination papers.

For help with the manuscript I am grateful to J. R. Betteridge, P. C. Caleb, A. B. Ewen (who also checked the diagrams), Dr. A. S. Gladwin, H. E. Holman, P. R. Thomas, Dr. G. W. Sutton, and Dr. G. Smith.

W. F.

CONTENTS

1

INTRODUCTION

THE name *telecommunications* is applied to the branches of electrical engineering and applied physics which concern themselves with the electrical communication of information. This definition normally excludes those applications which involve measurements of physical quantities, and so *radio direction finding*, and radio detection and ranging, i.e. *radar*, are excluded and are not discussed in their own right in the present volume.

Historically, the three main divisions of the subject were telegraphy, telephony, and radio transmission. The distinction between telegraphy and telephony was, and still is, in terms of the type of signals encountered. At first, transmission was by overhead lines and cables, as opposed to the subsequent development of radio transmission by electromagnetic waves in free space. Nowadays, the diversity of techniques employed tends to make such subdivisions of the subject rather arbitrary. The communication engineer is thus concerned with all branches of the subject. It is hoped that this book, which is concerned with the underlying circuit theory and an illustration of the principles involved, will form an introduction to the extensive and often very specialised literature of the subject.

THE COMMUNICATION SYSTEM

It is worth while emphasising, at the outset, the essential features of a communication system as compared with, say an electrical power system. The first point is that the communication engineer designs systems to convey *information* between the terminal points. The message, originating from an information source, whether it be speech from an individual or numerical data from a computer, can be regarded as a selection or choice of one particular message from a much wider set of possible messages. No information is transmitted if the outcome is known in advance.

Arising from this, a communication system always involves a spectrum or band of frequencies, and so the question of *bandwidth* is an important feature. Depending on the application, the bandwidth may vary from about 100 cycles per second, as in some forms of telegraphy, to several million cycles per second for television purposes. Frequency is measured in *hertz* (with the abbreviation Hz) rather than cycles per second. Large values are commonly expressed in terms of kHz, MHz or GHz corresponding to 10^3 Hz, 10^6 Hz and 10^9 Hz.

Another feature is the wide range of powers used in communication systems. Radio transmitters may have power outputs of the order of 100 kW. On the other hand the signal power in line telephony is usually of the order of a milliwatt. In satellite systems, the signal power input to the receiver may be a very small fraction of a microwatt. If the power level is low, it is imperative that the transfer from one circuit to another should be optimised, i.e. there should be maximum power transfer. The idea of *impedance matching* is thus important. Another contrast with an electrical power supply system is that in the power case the voltage is substantially constant, whereas in a communication system the transmitted signal may vary a great deal. The level at the receiving end may be small compared with that sent from the transmitter and so calculations of permissible loss or *attenuation* are often a significant feature of system design.

In the course of transmission the signal may be modified by the introduction of *electrical noise*. This will have the effect of introducing some ambiguity or uncertainty at the receiver. The effect produced will depend upon the levels of signal and noise, and clearly will be most significant when the signal level is low. Noise in fact often sets a definite limit to the sensitivity of a system. Distortion may have the same effect as noise. If, in transmission, the signal is changed due to non-linearity or some other cause, errors may be produced at the receiver. *Signal/noise ratio* and *distortion level* are often important parameters in communication system design.

THE BASIC FEATURES OF A COMMUNICATION SYSTEM

The previous section has indicated some general features of communication systems. Any consideration of their operation is best handled in terms of the individual units. The most natural sub-division gives a block schematic diagram of three blocks, namely the transmitter, the transmission path or circuit and the receiver as indicated in Fig. 1.1.

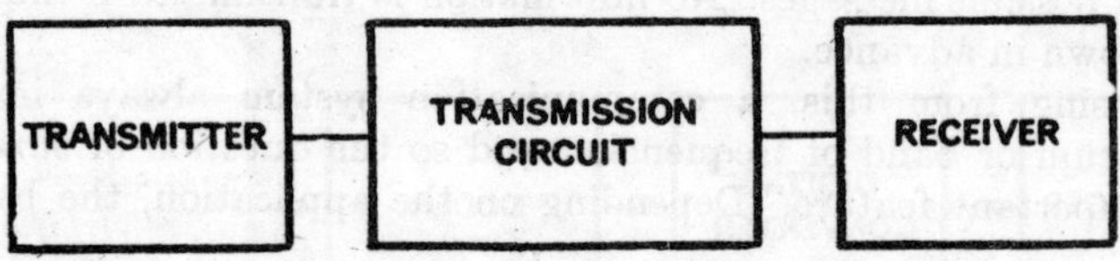

Fig. 1.1. Simple diagram of a communication system.

The transmission circuit, linking the transmitter and receiver, is associated with distance and is distributed in space.

The Transmitter

The block schematic diagram of Fig. 1.1. shows the transmitter as one unit. Normally there are a number of sub-units. First of all there is the information source which provides the message. This is followed by a device known as a *transducer*. The function of such a device is to convert the physical quantity, in which the information is presented, into a corresponding electrical quantity. The commonest example is probably the carbon microphone used in telephony. The pressure variations in sound waves set up by the speaker's voice are converted by the microphone into electrical voltages of the same waveform. A television camera is another example of a transducer. An electrical waveform is produced which corresponds to the light and shade of the picture scanned by a camera.

It is convenient to refer to the output from the transducer as the *signal*. This may then be modified further at the transmitter, by amplification or frequency translation as required, before connection to the transmission circuit. Signals may be classified into two types, *analogue* or *digital*. The first type is produced when the signal output from the transducer is a continuous time function, i.e. a smooth curve which is an analogue of the original physical variation at the transducer input. The continuous signals of speech and music are analogue signals. Digital signals on the other hand are not continuous but discrete as in telegraphy. The signal then consists of pulses arranged in some particular form of code.

Communication systems may also be classified as being either analogue or digital. It does not always follow that analogue systems are best for analogue signals. In some cases analogue signals are converted to digital form and then transmitted through a digital system. In such a case the transmitter might be sectionalised as shown in Fig. 1.2.

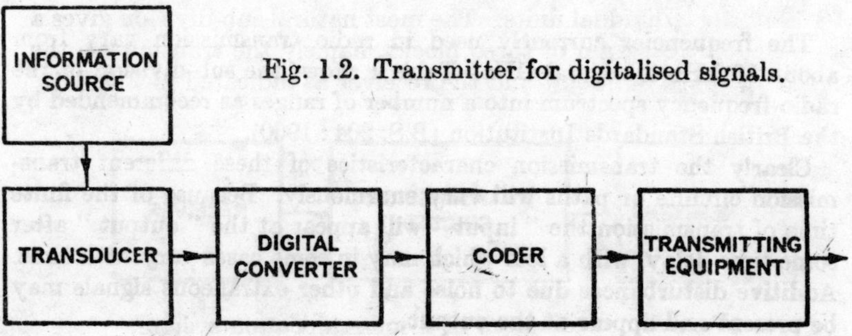

Fig. 1.2. Transmitter for digitalised signals.

The Transmission Circuit

The output from the transmitter is passed to the transmission circuit which in turn supplies the input to the receiver. In all cases the energy is transmitted in terms of travelling electric and magnetic fields, i.e. by electromagnetic waves. These waves may travel unbounded through space to the receiver or they may be guided to their destination by a system of conductors and insulators. In this second category the circuit may consist of a length of overhead open-wire transmission line or one of many forms of land or undersea cable. The length may vary from short distances to a few thousand km. Intermediate amplifiers or *repeaters* and other auxiliary equipment is used when the distance is appreciable. The spacing of the repeaters depends on the attenuation and this, in turn, depends on the form of transmission line and the type of signals transmitted. In land cables, spacings of about 5–80 km are encountered. The higher end of this range is used for submerged repeaters in transoceanic cable systems.

Alternatively a *waveguide* may be used in place of a transmission line. The waveguide is essentially of hollow metallic tube, of either rectangular or circular cross-section, and functions by confining the electromagnetic field to its internal volume.

When radio transmission is involved, the transmission " circuit " is, of course, not a circuit at all but simply the path taken by the radio waves. These waves of electromagnetic radiation travel through free space with the velocity of light, i.e. at 3×10^8 metres per second. The radiation may be discussed in terms of frequency or wavelength. If a single sine wave is considered for convenience, the wavelength λ is the distance between corresponding points on the waveform, for example between consecutive maxima. The velocity of propagation is given by the product of the wavelength and the number of wavelengths sent out from the source in each second, i.e. the product of λ and f where f is the frequency in hertz. Hence the wavelength of any particular radiation is given by

$$\lambda = 3 \times 10^8/f \text{ metres}$$

The frequencies currently used in radio transmission vary from about 16 kHz to several GHz. Table 1 shows the sub-division of the radio-frequency spectrum into a number of ranges as recommended by the British Standards Institution (B.S. 204 : 1960).

Clearly the transmission characteristics of these different transmission circuits or paths will vary enormously. Because of the finite time of transmission the " input " will appear at the " output " after some time delay, with a loss which may in some cases vary with time. Additive disturbances due to noise and other extraneous signals may be present and appear at the output.

TABLE 1. Classification of Radio Waves

Range	Frequency	Wavelength
Very-low frequency (V.L.F.)	below 30 kHz	above 10,000 m
Low-frequency (L.F.)	30–300 kHz	10,000–1,000 m
Medium-frequency (M.F.)	300–3,000 kHz	1,000–100 m
High-frequency (H.F.)	3–30 MHz	100–10 m
Very-high frequency (V.H.F.)	30–300 MHz	10–1 m
Ultra-high frequency (U.H.F.)	300–3,000 MHz	100–10 cm
Super-high frequency (S.H.F.)	3–30 GHz	10–1 cm
Extra-high frequency (E.H.F.)	30–300 GHz	1–0.1 cm

The Receiver

The functions of a receiver tend to be the inverse of those of the transmitter. The signal from the transmission circuit may be amplified and possibly have its frequencies changed. A transducer is usually necessary to present the information in the desired form. In telephony this means sound waves audible to the listener, or in television a steady picture for the viewer.

THE COMMUNICATION CHANNEL

The previous section has considered the link between the transmitter and receiver as a transmission circuit. The word " channel " is often used in this context. A channel is defined as " a means of a communication from a source to a receiver ", i.e. a means of one-way communication. Depending on the application there may be a difference between a transmission circuit and a channel.

Single-channel Operation

The simplest case to consider is the interconnection of two telephone subscribers. Over short distances they are commonly connected by a pair of wires. These function as a transmit channel in one direction and as a receiver channel in the other direction. When the subscribers are many miles apart, it is usually preferable to operate with two pairs of wires; each pair of wires transmits in one direction only. Thus for single-channel operation no distinction need be made between a transmission circuit and a channel.

Multi-channel Operation

As the cost of conductors in a long-distance telephone system may be a significant part of the total cost, the conductors are used to transmit more than one message simultaneously. In one common system the speech from twelve subscribers is arranged for transmission over a single pair of wires, a different frequency band being used for the speech from each subscriber. Modern practice makes extensive use of this process of multi-channel operation. An internationally agreed system involves 2,700 speech channels transmitted over a single co-axial cable.

Multi-channel operation is not confined to telephony. A television channel may be combined with a number of speech channels. Alternatively telegraph and speech channels may be combined and transmitted over a common circuit. The number of possible channels is decided by the bandwidth of each and the overall bandwidth of the system.

INTERNATIONAL AGREEMENT

Long-distance communication circuits which cross national boundaries are obviously only possible if there is a measure of international agreement, and if the systems of the various countries are compatible. The first international organisation in the sphere of electrical communication was the *International Telegraph Union*, created in Paris in 1865, to obtain some agreement on international telegraph operation. In 1903 an international conference was held in Berlin to discuss radio communication; the *International Radiotelegraph Union* emerged from the suggestions of a second conference in 1906. A single body dealing with telegraphy and telephony was created in 1932. The word *telecommunication* was coined to cover the activities of the new organisation, the *International Telecommunication Union*.

The task of achieving agreement in international communication practice is the business of consultative committees of the International Telecommunication Union, now a specialised agency of the United Nations Organisation. The committees which include representatives from practically all the world's communication administrations, meet periodically and issue recommendations on standards to be adhered to in international working. There is a committee concerned with telegraphy and telephony, the International Telegraph and Telephone Consultative Committee (CCITT). The committee dealing with radio transmission is the *Comité Consultatif International Technique des Communications Radioelectriques*, and has the abbreviation CCIR. It is also concerned with satellite systems for space communication.

2

NETWORK THEOREMS

INTRODUCTION

THE CURRENT in any part of an electrical circuit or network can be calculated for any given applied voltage by the two well known laws of Kirchhoff, which state that

(1) At any point in a circuit the algebraic sum of the currents flowing towards the point is zero.

(2) In any closed mesh the algebraic sum of the potential drops across the circuit elements composing the mesh is equal to the algebraic sum of the electromotive forces in that mesh.

As the number of meshes increases the application of the second law may become increasingly difficult. In such multi-mesh networks, the necessary simultaneous equations are best set up by the use of Maxwell's method of cyclic currents. Each of these currents is associated with a particular mesh in which it is assumed to circulate ; all such currents satisfy Kirchhoff's first law at any point as any one circulating current brings as much current towards the point as it takes away from it. Fig. 2.1 shows a bridge network with four meshes in which four arbitrary circulating currents I_1, I_2, I_3, and I_4 are assumed to flow. By the application of Kirchhoff's second law to each mesh, four simultaneous equations are obtained. The value of the currents in the various meshes can then be obtained from the solution of the set of simultaneous equations.

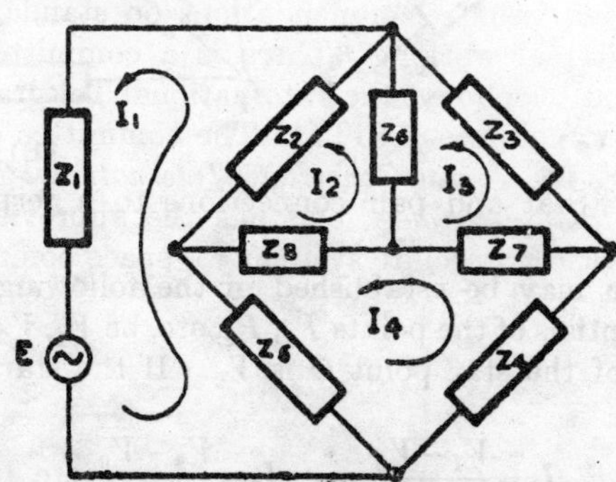

Fig. 2.1. Maxwell's cyclic currents applied to a bridge network.

All electrical networks containing lumped impedances may be solved by this means, but the work is often lengthy. The complexity of the calculation can often be reduced, either by the direct replacement of the given network by a simpler equivalent, or by the use of certain network theorems which have been developed from the simple fundamental laws. Some of these theorems will now be stated.

ROSEN'S THEOREM

This useful theorem may be stated as follows, "A network which is composed of impedances Z_1, Z_2, Z_3 . . . Z_N, joining the points P_1, P_2, P_3 . . . P_N to a star point O may be replaced by a network of impedances Z_{12}, Z_{13} . . . joining all the pairs of points P, if the suffixes show the points connected, and

$$Z_{12} = Z_1 Z_2 \Sigma 1/Z$$

$$Z_{13} = Z_1 Z_3 \Sigma 1/Z \text{ etc.}$$

where $\Sigma 1/Z = 1/Z_1 + 1/Z_2 + \ . \ . \ . \ + 1/Z_N$"

By means of the theorem a star connected network may be replaced by a pair connected network, as shown in Fig. 2.2.

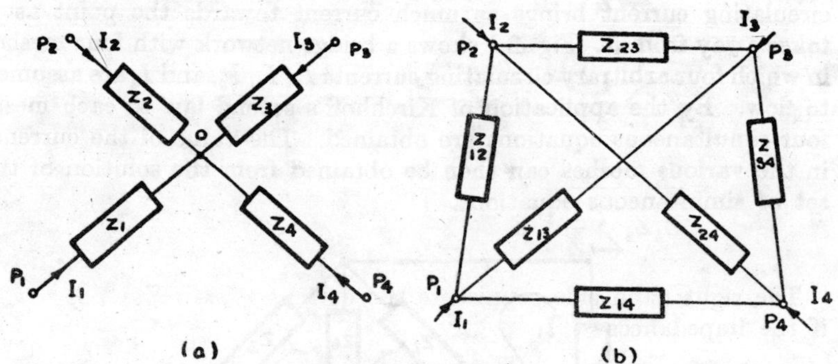

Fig. 2.2. Star and pair connections to n terminals ($n = 4$).

The theorem may be established in the following manner.

Let the potentials of the points P_1, P_2, etc. be V_1, V_2 etc. and suppose the potential of the star point O is V_0. If the star currents are I_1, I_2, etc. then

$$I_1 = \frac{V_1 - V_0}{Z_1}, \qquad I_2 = \frac{V_2 - V_0}{Z_2} \text{ etc.}$$

and from Kirchhoff's first law $I_1 + I_2 + I_3 + I_4 = 0$

$$\therefore \sum \frac{V_1 - V_0}{Z_1} = 0$$

$$\therefore \left(\frac{V_1}{Z_1} + \frac{V_2}{Z_2} \text{ etc.}\right) - V_0\left(\frac{1}{Z_1} + \frac{1}{Z_2} \text{ etc.}\right) = 0$$

$$\therefore V_0 = \frac{\left(\frac{V_1}{Z_1} + \frac{V_2}{Z_2} + \text{etc.}\right)}{\frac{1}{Z_1} + \frac{1}{Z_2} + \text{etc.}}$$

$$\text{Hence } I_1 = \frac{V_1}{Z_1} - \frac{1}{Z_1} \frac{\left(\frac{V_1}{Z_1} + \frac{V_2}{Z_2} + \text{etc.}\right)}{\left(\frac{1}{Z_1} + \frac{1}{Z_2} + \text{etc.}\right)}$$

$$\text{If } \sum \frac{1}{Z} = \frac{1}{Z_1} + \frac{1}{Z_2} + \text{etc.}$$

$$\text{Then } I_1 = \frac{1}{Z_1 \sum \frac{1}{Z}} \left\{ V_1 \sum \frac{1}{Z} - \left[\frac{V_1}{Z_1} + \frac{V_2}{Z_2} \text{ etc.}\right]\right\}$$

$$= \frac{1}{Z_1 \sum \frac{1}{Z}} \left\{ \frac{V_1 - V_2}{Z_2} + \frac{V_1 - V_3}{Z_3} + \text{etc.} \right\}$$

$$= \frac{V_1 - V_2}{Z_1 Z_2 \sum \frac{1}{Z}} + \frac{V_1 - V_3}{Z_1 Z_3 \sum \frac{1}{Z}} + \text{etc.} \qquad 2.1$$

The right hand side represents the current that would flow to P_1 if the impedances

$$Z_1 Z_2 \sum \frac{1}{Z}, \; Z_1 Z_3 \sum \frac{1}{Z}, \text{ etc.}$$

were connected between P_1 and P_2, P_1 and P_3 etc. The same treatment may be adopted for the other currents. If the external currents I_1, I_2 etc. are to be the same in the two cases then impedances of the above kind must be connected between all pairs of points. The two networks will then be equivalent. This equivalence will hold only at the one frequency at which the impedances are calculated.

It should be noted that networks are said to be equivalent when one is indistinguishable from the other as far as externally connected loads and generators are concerned.

Rosen has pointed out that any star network of impedances may be replaced by an equivalent mesh, but the transformation from a mesh to a star is indeterminate when more than three elements are involved.

EQUIVALENT OF T AND π NETWORKS

When a network has three elements these may be arranged as a **T** section (Fig. 2.3a) or a π section (Fig. 2.3b). Provided certain relations hold, a **T** arrangement can be replaced by an equivalent π (this is a particular case of Rosen's theorem) and conversely a π network can be replaced by an equivalent **T**.

The Replacement of a T Network by an equivalent π

If the π network is to be an equivalent for the **T** (Fig. 2.3) then the values of the π arms may be determined in terms of the **T** values by the application of Rosen's theorem.

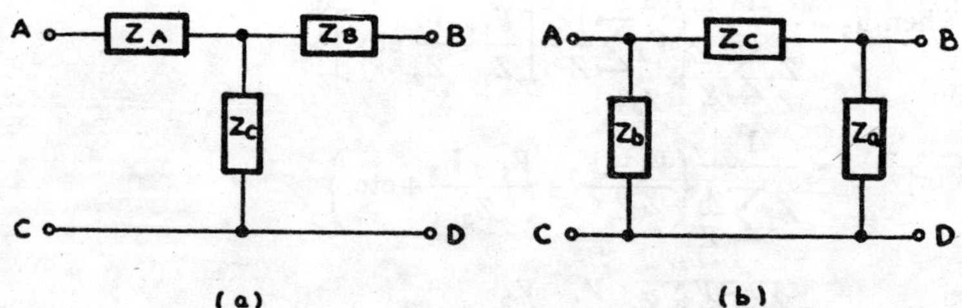

Fig. 2.3. **T** and π networks.

$$Z_a = Z_B Z_C \sum \frac{1}{Z} = Z_B Z_C \left(\frac{1}{Z_A} + \frac{1}{Z_B} + \frac{1}{Z_C} \right)$$

$$= \frac{Z_B Z_C + Z_A Z_C + Z_A Z_B}{Z_A} \quad . \quad . \quad . \quad . \quad . \quad . \quad 2.2$$

also $$Z_b = \frac{Z_B Z_C + Z_A Z_C + Z_A Z_B}{Z_B} \quad . \quad . \quad . \quad . \quad . \quad . \quad 2.3$$

and $$Z_c = \frac{Z_B Z_C + Z_A Z_C + Z_A Z_B}{Z_C} \quad . \quad . \quad . \quad . \quad . \quad . \quad 2.4$$

By means of these relations the values of the equivalent π arms can be calculated for given values of the **T** arms.

The Replacement of a π Network by an equivalent T

If **T** and π networks are to be equivalent then the impedances viewed in any pairs of terminals with the third terminal free must be the same in either structure. By the use of this fact, the following relations are obtained from Fig. 2.3.

$$Z_{AC} = Z_A + Z_C = \frac{Z_b(Z_c + Z_a)}{Z_a + Z_b + Z_c} \qquad 2.5$$

$$Z_{BC} = Z_B + Z_C = \frac{Z_a(Z_b + Z_c)}{Z_a + Z_b + Z_c} \qquad 2.6$$

$$Z_{AB} = Z_A + Z_B = \frac{Z_c(Z_a + Z_b)}{Z_a + Z_b + Z_c} \qquad 2.7$$

subtracting 2.6 from 2.5 gives

$$Z_A - Z_B = \frac{Z_bZ_c - Z_aZ_c}{Z_a + Z_b + Z_c} \qquad 2.8$$

adding 2.7 and 2.8 gives

$$Z_A = \frac{Z_bZ_c}{Z_a + Z_b + Z_c} \qquad 2.9$$

similarly $$Z_B = \frac{Z_aZ_c}{Z_a + Z_b + Z_c} \qquad 2.10$$

and $$Z_C = \frac{Z_aZ_b}{Z_a + Z_b + Z_c} \qquad 2.11$$

In this case the values of the equivalent **T** arms can be calculated for given values of the π arms.

It should be noted that the conditions determined above for the **T** and π networks have been derived for the case where the networks are isolated. To show that the conditions of equivalence are independent of the external connections it is necessary to consider the two networks connected to identical generators and identical loads, and to evaluate the external currents in both cases. It is left as an exercise for the reader to show that if a π network is replaced by an equivalent **T** the generator and load currents are the same as those for the π network, whatever the value of the load or generator impedance.

SIMPLIFICATION OF A COMPLEX NETWORK

The fact that a π network of impedances can be replaced by an equivalent **T** network may be used to simplify complex networks.

The simplification is obtained because the number of meshes is reduced by one each time that a π network is replaced by a **T** arrangement. A simple example is shown in Fig. 2.4a. In this case the π network of impedances Z_2, Z_3 and Z_4 in the bridge is replaced by a **T** of Z_2', Z_3' and Z_4' (Fig. 2.4b). This network can then be redrawn and simplified further, as in Fig. 2.4c.

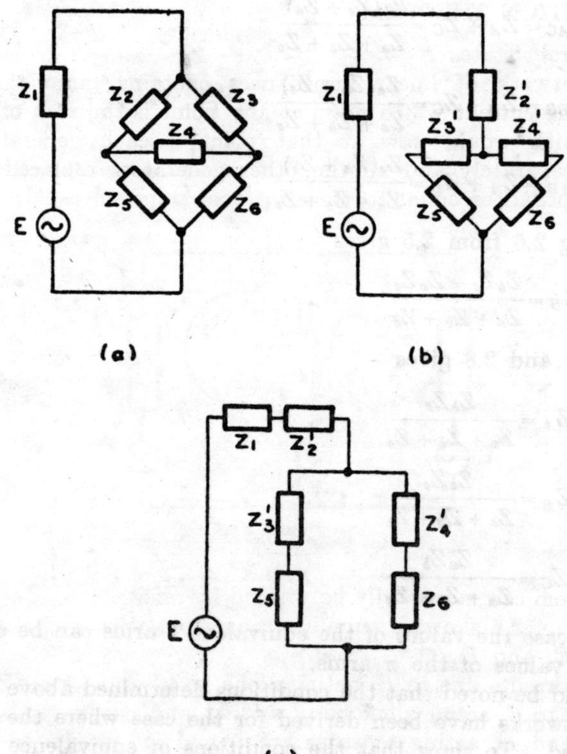

Fig. 2.4. Network simplification.

By successive applications of the mesh-star transformation any complex network can be reduced to a single π or **T** which will be equivalent at a single frequency.

The values of the equivalent π (or **T**) may be determined experimentally if three independent measurements are possible. If the given network has four terminals, four measurements can be made and three of them used to obtain the three desired unknown values. The four measurements on the network that are possible are (1) input impedance with the output terminals open-circuited, (2) input impedance with the output terminals short-circuited, (3) output impedance with the input terminals short-circuited, and (4) output impedance with the input terminals open-circuited. Three of the values of impedance so obtained can be compared with those for the equivalent **T** (or π) and the values of the arms of the latter calculated.

SUPERPOSITION THEOREM

This theorem states :—

"If a network of linear impedances contains more than one generator, the current which flows at any point is the sum of all the currents which would flow at that point if each generator was considered separately and all the other generators replaced at the time by impedances equal to their internal impedances."

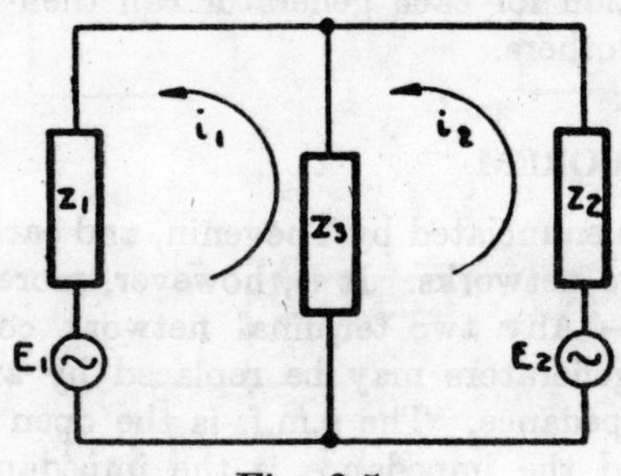

Fig. 2.5.

The theorem can most easily be verified by reference to a particular network. Fig. 2.5 shows a simple arrangement with two generators of e.m.f's, E_1 and E_2.

Let the currents due to E_1 acting alone be i_1' and i_2' and also the currents due to E_2 acting alone be i_1'' and i_2'', and suppose the currents due to E_1 and E_2 acting together are i_1 and i_2.

Then when E_1 is considered to act alone, the application of Kirchhoff's second law to each mesh,

$$i_1'(Z_1+Z_3)-i_2'Z_3=E_1 \quad . \quad . \quad . \quad 2.12$$

$$\text{and } i_2'(Z_2+Z_3)-i_1'Z_3=0 \quad . \quad . \quad . \quad 2.13$$

and when E_2 is considered alone

$$i_1''(Z_1+Z_3)-i_2''Z_3=0 \quad . \quad . \quad 2.14$$

$$i_2''(Z_2+Z_3)-i_1''Z_3=E_2 \quad . \quad . \quad . \quad 2.15$$

When both e.m.f's are applied simultaneously

$$i_1(Z_1+Z_3)-i_2Z_3=E_1 \quad . \quad . \quad 2.16$$

$$\text{and } i_2(Z_2+Z_3)-i_1Z_3=E_2 \quad . \quad 2.17$$

By the addition of equations 2.12 and 2.14

$$(i_1' + i_1'')(Z_1 + Z_3) - (i_2' + i_2'')Z_3 = E_1 \quad . \quad . \quad . \quad 2.18$$

and the addition of equations 2.13 and 2.15 gives

$$(i_2' + i_2'')(Z_1 + Z_3) - (i_1' + i_1'')Z_3 = E_2 \quad . \quad . \quad . \quad 2.19$$

It can be seen that equation 2.18 and 2.19 are identical with 2.16 and 2.17 respectively if $i_1 = i_1' + i_1''$ and $i_2 = i_2' + i_2''$ which must then be true.

The principle of superposition is important and simplifies network calculations when several generators are present. The solution obtained by use of the superposition theorem is not necessarily shorter than by other methods but is usually simpler, as each generator can be allowed to act independently and its component of current calculated. This is especially useful when generators of different frequencies are present as a solution for each generator can then be obtained independently of the others.

THÉVENIN'S THEOREM

This theorem as enunciated by Thévenin, and earlier by Helmholtz, applied to resistive networks. It is, however, more general and may be stated thus:—"Any two terminal network consisting of linear impedances and generators may be replaced by an e.m.f. acting in series with an impedance. The e.m.f. is the open circuit voltage at the terminals, and the impedance is the impedance viewed at the terminals when all the generators in the network have been replaced by impedances equal to their internal impedances."

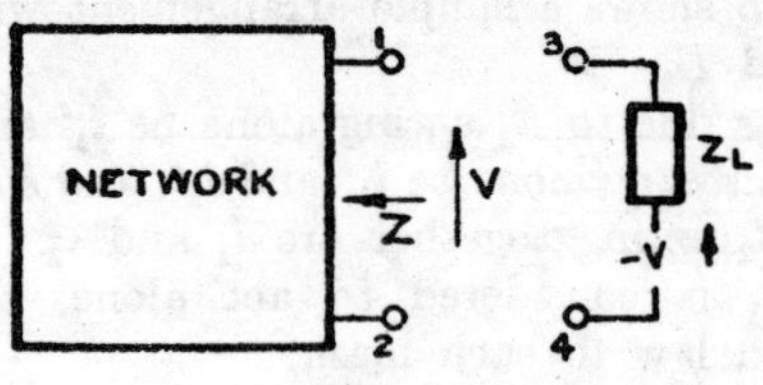

Fig. 2.6.

This may be shown easily by considering Fig. 2.6. in which the terminals 1 and 2 represent the output terminals of a network of impedances and generators.

Suppose that the open circuit voltage at the terminals 1,2 is V and that the impedance Z_{12} is Z when the internal generators have stopped generating.

If now an e.m.f. of $-V$ is connected in series with an impedance Z_L across the terminals then no current will flow when the terminals

1 and 3 and 2 and 4 are connected. By the superposition principle this zero current can be regarded as the sum of two equal and opposite currents circulated by the internal generators and by $-V$. The current circulated by $-V$ is

$$-V/[Z+Z_L]$$

and so the current which would be circulated by the connection of Z_L at the terminals 1,2 would be

$$V/[Z+Z_L]$$

Thus the network acts as though it was a simple series circuit e.m.f. V and internal impedance Z.

Alternatively, the theorem may be established by making use of the fact that a network may be reduced to an equivalent **T**, and the given network reduced to that shown in Fig. 2.7. If more than one generator is present they can be treated separately by the principle of superposition.

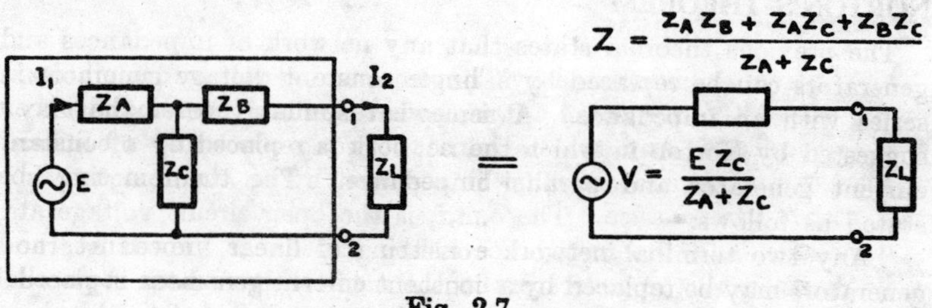

Fig. 2.7.

From Fig. 2.7.

$$I_1 = \frac{E}{Z_A + \dfrac{Z_C(Z_B+Z_L)}{Z_C+Z_B+Z_L}} \quad \text{and } I_2 = \frac{I_1 Z_C}{Z_C+Z_B+Z_L}$$

By substitution for I_1

$$I_2 = \frac{EZ_C}{Z_AZ_C+Z_AZ_B+Z_AZ_L+Z_CZ_B+Z_CZ_L}$$

$$= \frac{EZ_C}{Z_AZ_C+Z_AZ_B+Z_CZ_B+Z_L(Z_A+Z_C)}$$

$$= \frac{E\dfrac{Z_C}{Z_A+Z_C}}{\dfrac{Z_AZ_C+Z_AZ_B+Z_CZ_B}{Z_A+Z_C}+Z_L}$$

This is the current that would flow in any value of load impedance Z_L, if Z_L was connected to a generator of e.m.f.

$$E\frac{Z_C}{Z_A+Z_C} \quad \text{and internal impedance} \quad Z=\frac{Z_AZ_C+Z_AZ_B+Z_CZ_B}{Z_A+Z_C}$$

The voltage which would appear at the terminals 1,2 is

$$V=\frac{EZ_C}{Z_A+Z_C}$$

and if E is short-circuited, then $Z_{12}=Z_B+\dfrac{Z_AZ_C}{Z_A+Z_C}$

$$=\frac{Z_AZ_C+Z_AZ_B+Z_CZ_B}{Z_A+Z_C}$$

which establishes the theorem.

NORTON'S THEOREM

The previous theorem states that any network of impedances and generators can be replaced by a single constant voltage generator in series with an impedance. A somewhat similar theorem has been suggested by Norton in which the network is replaced by a constant current generator and parallel impedance. The theorem may be stated as follows:—

"Any two terminal network consisting of linear impedances and generators may be replaced by a constant current generator in parallel with an impedance Z, if the generated current is equal to the short circuit current at the two terminals and if Z is the internal impedance of the network viewed from the two terminals when all the generators have been replaced by their internal impedances."

The equivalent circuits as obtained by Thévenin's and Norton's theorems give the same current in, and voltage across a load impedance.

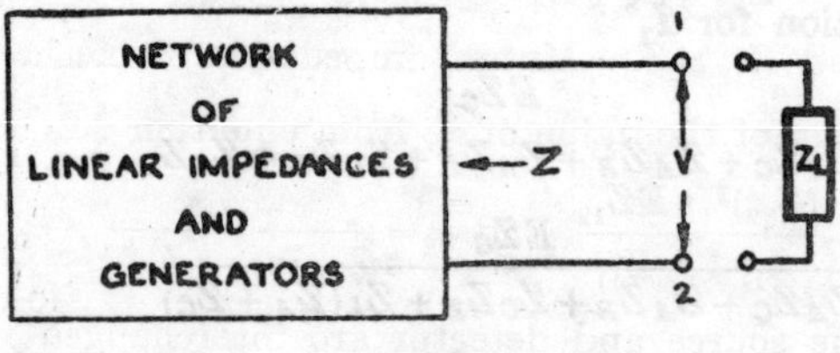

Fig. 2.8.

Consider the network shown in Fig. 2.8 in which the open-circuit voltage is V. If Norton's theorem applies the short-circuit current

$I_{S/C}$ is given by $I_{S/C} = \frac{V}{Z}$ and the current in the load Z_L is given by

$$I_L = \frac{Z}{Z_L + Z} \cdot I_{S/C}.$$

The current in the load is then $I_L = \frac{V}{Z + Z_L}$ . . . 2.20

and the voltage across the load, $V_L = \frac{Z_L}{Z + Z_L} \cdot V$ . . 2.20a

Equations 2.20 and 2.20a are the results which would be obtained from the application of Thévenin's theorem. Thus either theorem may be applied to any given network and the choice in a particular case is one of convenience.

RECIPROCITY THEOREM

"If an e.m.f. applied in one mesh of a network of linear impedances produces a certain current in any second mesh, then the same e.m.f. acting in the chosen second mesh will provide the same current in the first mesh."

The theorem can be verified by considering the arrangement shown in Fig. 2.9 in which a **T** network is inserted between a generator and a load.

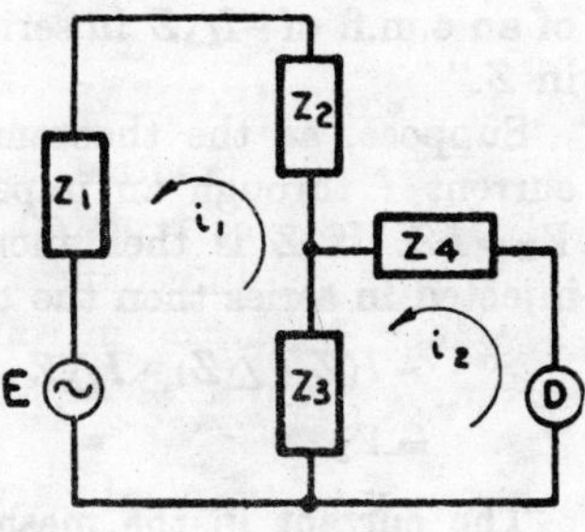

Fig. 2.9.

The application of Kirchhoff's second law to the two meshes gives

$$i_1 Z_{11} - i_2 Z_{12} = E \quad . \quad . \quad . \quad . \quad 2.21$$

and $i_2 Z_{22} - i_1 Z_{12} = 0$ 2.22

where $Z_{11} = Z_1 + Z_2 + Z_3 =$ Self impedance of mesh 1

$Z_{22} = Z_3 + Z_4$ = ,, ,, ,, 2

and $Z_{12} = Z_3 =$ Mutual impedance of meshes 1 and 2.

By insertion of the value of i_1, from equation 2.21 in equation 2.22

$$i_2 Z_{22} - i_2 \frac{(Z_{12})^2}{Z_{11}} = \frac{E Z_{12}}{Z_{11}} \text{ and } i_2 = \frac{E Z_{12}}{Z_{11} Z_{22} - (Z_{12})^2} \quad . \quad . \quad 2.23$$

If now the source and detector are interchanged then

$$i_1 Z_{11} - i_2 Z_{12} = 0$$

and $i_2 Z_{22} - i_1 Z_{12} = E$

from which

$$i_1 Z_{11} - \frac{i_1(Z_{12})^2}{Z_{22}} = \frac{EZ_{12}}{Z_{22}} \text{ and } i_1 = \frac{EZ_{12}}{Z_{11}Z_{22} - (Z_{12})^2} \qquad 2.24$$

It is obvious from either equation 2.23 or 2.24 that the transposition of the source and detector, which in this case is the same as interchanging Z_{11} and Z_{22}, will leave the result unaltered.

It should be noted, however, that the source and detector impedances cannot be interchanged except in the special case when they are equal.

COMPENSATION THEOREM

This theorem may be stated as follows :—

"If any network of impedances and generators is changed by a change of impedance $\triangle Z$ in one branch, the change in the currents in all other branches is that which would be caused by the introduction of an e.m.f. of $-I\triangle Z$ in series with the modified Z if I is the current in Z."

Suppose, as the theorem states, one mesh in the network has a current I through an impedance Z. Then the voltage across Z is $V_Z = IZ$. If Z is then increased to $Z + \triangle Z$ and an e.m.f. of $-I\triangle Z$ injected in series then the terminal voltage is V_Z'

$$= I(Z + \triangle Z) - I\triangle Z$$

$$= V_Z.$$

The current in the mesh containing Z is the same as before and the currents in the other meshes are unchanged.

The theorem offers a useful means of calculating the effect on the network of a change in a branch and obviates the necessity for an entire re-calculation for the network.

It should be noted that Z need not be restricted to a self impedance but may be a mutual impedance connecting two meshes. If Z carries two currents I_1 and I_2 then an increase in Z to $Z + \triangle Z$ will change the network currents in the same way as the introduction of two e.m.f.'s of value $-I_1\triangle Z$ and $-I_2\triangle Z$ into the two meshes concerned.

MAXIMUM POWER TRANSFER THEOREM

This theorem, which applies to all branches of electrical engineering, is particularly important in communication work, and may be stated as follows, "Any two terminal network will absorb maximum power from a generator if the load impedance is the conjugate of the internal impedance of the generator."

In Fig. 2.10 the generator impedance is $Z_G\underline{/\phi} = R_G + jX_G$ where $\tan \phi = X_G/R_G$. The load impedance is assumed to be $Z_L\underline{/\theta} = R_L + jX_L$ where $\tan \theta = X_L/R_L$. The power P, in the load is $\overline{I^2 R_L}$ and so

$$P = \frac{E^2 R_L}{(R_L + R_G)^2 + (X_L + X_G)^2}$$

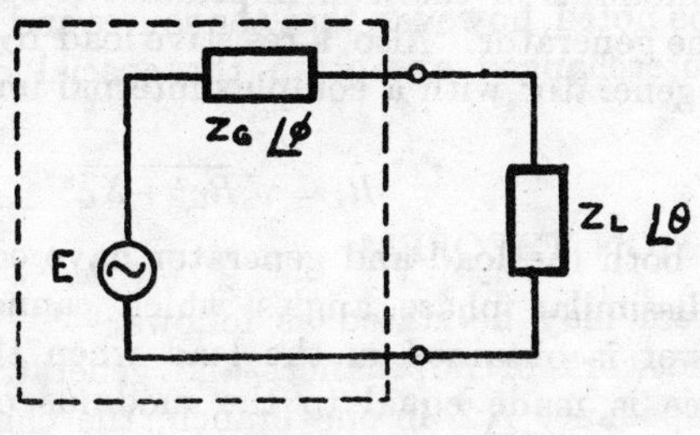

Fig. 2.10.

An inspection of this expression shows that as far as variation in the value of X_L is concerned, the power will be a maximum when X_L had the special value $-X_G$. If this condition applies, then

$$P = \frac{E^2 R_L}{(R_L + R_G)^2}$$

As far as variation of R_L is concerned, the value of R_L which makes P a maximum will be that which makes dP/dR_L zero.

$$\text{Now } \frac{dP}{dR_L} = \frac{E^2(R_L + R_G)^2 - E^2 R_L(2R_L + 2R_G)}{(R_L + R_G)^4}$$

Hence P will be a maximum for the value of R_L which satisfies the relation

$$(R_L + R_G)^2 - 2R_L^2 - 2R_G R_L = 0$$

$$\text{i.e. when } R_L = R_G$$

The power absorbed by the load is thus a maximum when the resistive component of the load impedance is equal to the resistive component of the generator impedance, and the reactance of the load is opposite in sign to the reactance of the generator, i.e. when the load impedance is the conjugate of the internal impedance of the generator.

The value of the maximum power P is then given by

$$P = I^2 R_L = \frac{E^2 R_L}{(2R_L)^2} = \frac{E^2}{4R_L}$$

When the load impedance is a complex quantity, $R_L + jX_L$, and the generator has an internal impedance which is a pure resistance R_G, it can be shown by an argument similar to that used above that the condition for maximum power obtains when

$$\sqrt{R_L^2 + X_L^2} = R_G \quad . \quad . \quad 2.25$$

i.e. when the modulus of the load impedance is equal to the internal resistance of the generator. Also, a resistive load R_L absorbs maximum power from a generator with a complex internal impedance $R_G + jX_G$, when

$$R_L = \sqrt{R_G^2 + X_G^2} \quad . \quad . \quad 2.26$$

Finally, when both the load and generator have complex impedances which have dissimilar phase angles which cannot be altered, the maximum power is obtained in the load when the modulus of the load impedance is made equal to the modulus of the internal impedance of the generator. A transformer or other impedance changing device should thus be employed to make

$$\sqrt{R_L^2 + X_L^2} = \sqrt{R_G^2 + X_G^2} \quad . \quad . \quad 2.27$$

NON-LINEAR CIRCUITS

The networks discussed have consisted of linear elements, the values of which are assumed to be independent of current or voltage, and of time. Non-linear circuit elements are often encountered in practical work. Thermionic valves, iron-cored coils and transistors are examples of elements which have an impedance which varies with the value of the applied voltage ; the carbon microphone discussed in chapter 16 is a device which has a resistance which varies with time.

If a network contains, say a non-linear resistor (i.e. one which does not obey Ohm's law) and if the resistance is a function of the current passing through it, so that $R = \phi(i)$, then in any mesh equation formulated, a term $i\phi(i)$ will appear, and the equation will thus not be linear. The value of the resistor cannot be specified until the value of the current is known, and the value of the current may be the desired quantity.

In non-linear circuits, the principle of superposition does not apply, and harmonic currents and voltages appear. The general mathematical method of solution becomes complicated and in some cases, depending on the network, an exact solution may not be possible. Approximations with varying degrees of accuracy can sometimes be made by assuming the element to be linear ; in other cases the terminal voltage/current characteristic must be used and represented by some mathematical series. Graphical and step by step methods of analysis are commonly employed.

WORKED EXAMPLE

In a "bridged-T" method of measuring the inductance and effective resistance of a coil at radio frequency, the coil under test is shunted across the two condensers of capacitance C constituting the series arms of a symmetrical T-network, the shunt arm being a non-reactive resistance R. In a particular measurement at 10 MHz the conditions of balance, i.e. zero voltage at the output terminals of the T, is obtained with $C = 211$ micro-microfarads, and $R = 4{,}750$ ohms. Calculate, after deriving the necessary relations, the inductance and effective resistance of the coil.

(I.E.E. Radio Comm. April, 1947)

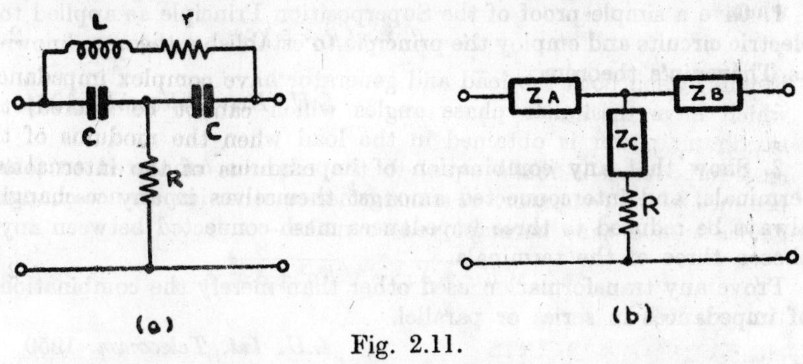

Fig. 2.11.

Fig. 2.11a shows the original arrangement. If the network of the coil and the two capacitors is replaced by the equivalent T the circuit is that shown in Fig. 2.11b. It will be seen that the output will be zero if the shunt impedance, $Z_C + R$, is equal to zero.

$$\text{Now } Z_C = \frac{Z_a Z_b}{Z_a + Z_b + Z_c} \quad \text{(equation 2.11)}$$

where $Z_a = 1/j\omega C$, $Z_b = 1/j\omega C$, and $Z_c = r + j\omega L$

$$\therefore Z_C = \frac{\left(\dfrac{1}{j\omega C}\right)^2}{\dfrac{2}{j\omega C} + r + j\omega L} = \frac{1}{2j\omega C - \omega^2 C^2 r - j\omega^3 C^2 L}$$

Hence for the shunt impedance to be zero

$$Z_C + R = 0 \text{ or } 1 + 2j\omega CR - \omega^2 C^2 rR - j\omega^3 C^2 LR = 0$$

$$\therefore r = \frac{1}{\omega^2 C^2 R} \text{ and } \omega^2 = \frac{2}{LC}$$

If the values given are inserted, it will be found that $r = 1{\cdot}21$ ohms and $L = 2{\cdot}4$ μH.

References for Further Reading

RICHARDSON, D. E.: *Electrical Network Calculations* (D. Van Nostrand Co. Inc., 1946).

GUILLEMIN, E. A.: *Introductory Circuit Theory* (Chapman & Hall, 1954).

EXAMPLES

1. Give a simple proof of the Superposition Principle as applied to electric circuits and employ the principle to establish a theorem known as Thévenin's theorem.

L.U. Ext. Telecomm. 1944

2. Show that any combination of impedances connected to four terminals, and interconnected amongst themselves in any way, can always be reduced to three impedances mesh-connected between any chosen three of the terminals.

Prove any transformation used other than merely the combination of impedances in series or parallel.

L.U. Int. Telecomm. 1950

3. Show that if a high frequency generator, of e.m.f. E, can be regarded as having an internal resistance R, and as being shunted by a condenser of capacitance C, it can also be regarded as a generator of e.m.f. E' and internal impedance Z', where E' and Z' are independent of the load. Find E' and Z' in terms of E, R, and C.

L.U. Int. Telecomm. 1945

4. State the Thévenin or Helmholtz theorem. A source of alternating power, of frequency 796 kHz has an internal resistance of 20 ohms. It is connected to the sending end of a transmission line, which may be represented as a resistance of 80 ohms with a capacitance of 0·001 microfarad shunted across the receiving end. Across this a coil of inductance 1 millihenry and resistance 50 ohms is connected. Calculate the current in the coil when the source e.m.f. is 10 volts.

L.U. Int. Telecomm. 1949

5. A "twin-T" or parallel-T circuit has input terminals A and B, and output terminals C and D. B and D are common. Between A and C are two parallel circuits, one consisting of two 5,000 ohms resistors in series, and the other of two 0·05 microfarad capacitors in series. A 0·1 microfarad capacitor is connected between B and

the junction of the two resistors, and a 2,500 ohm resistor is connected between B and the junction of the two capacitors. Calculate the frequency at which the output is zero with a finite input voltage.

***L.U. Int. Telecomm.* 1950**

6. A source of alternating e.m.f. E has an internal impedance $R_1 + jX_1$ and is connected to a load of impedance $R + jX$, of which both R and X are variable. Derive the conditions for maximum power output. What is then the ratio of power generated to power output? Plot to a logarithmic base the ratio of the actual power output to the maximum possible power output as the ratio R/R_1 is varied from 0·1 to 1·0 and X is adjusted for the maximum power in each case. Four points will be sufficient.

***L.U. Int. Telecomm.* 1952**

3

CIRCUIT THEORY

INTRODUCTION

ELECTRICAL networks may be classified as active or passive, depending on whether they contain generators or not. The generators used in communication work usually incorporate either thermionic valves or transistors, which are discussed in later chapters. Passive networks may contain resistive, inductive, and capacitive elements, and the coupling between circuits may be effected by electrostatic or electromagnetic means, or by the use of common impedances. A detailed consideration of the design and practical form of the various components is beyond the scope of this book, but some of the main features of such components will be mentioned very briefly before dealing with the resonant circuits in which they may be employed. As quartz, and other piezo-electric material, is widely used as, or in conjunction with, resonant circuits, the chapter concludes with a brief consideration of such resonators.

CIRCUIT COMPONENTS

Resistors

The resistors in general use may be classified as (a) wire-wound or (b) " composition " types. The fixed-value resistors employed in communication equipment are normally of the composition variety, and the use of wire-wound types is confined to measuring equipment.

(a) Wire-wound Resistors. These are made from wire of high resistivity and low temperature coefficient. Nickel-copper and nickel-chrome are two materials used.

In order that their inductance should be small, such resistors are wound non-inductively. If the winding occupies a number of slots on a bobbin, the wire may be wound in different directions in adjacent slots, alternatively a bifilar winding may be used ; in the latter case, the wire is doubled back on itself before winding, to give the effect of two wires side by side carrying currents in opposite directions. By this means the inductance of the winding is kept fairly low. The self-capacitance between the terminals of a bifilar winding tends to be relatively high, and can only be reduced if the winding is split up into two or more sections. As a first approximation, the sub-division of a winding reduces the self-capacitance by a factor of n^2, where n is the number of sections into which the winding is subdivided; this arises from the fact that the self-capacitance of a coil or loop of wire is proportional to its length; subdivision into a number of sections in series then produces a number of self-capacitances in series. Thus for an n-section winding as indicated in Fig. 3.1, each section has a capacitance $1/n$ times that of a resistor wound entirely in one section. The voltage applied to any subsection is $1/n$ of the terminal voltage, and so the capacitive current is reduced by a factor of n^2. This approximation is less valid as the frequency is increased, and the use of wire-wound resistors of high value is restricted to frequencies having an upper limit in the region of 10–50 kHz. The shunting effect of self-capacitance is less serious with low values of resistance, and such wire resistors wound on very thin card operate satisfactorily up to frequencies of about 30 MHz.

(b) Composition Resistors. Such resistors are made from a mixture of carbon particles and an insulating binding medium. The material is used in the form of solid rods, or is employed as a coating on an insulating support, such as a glass rod. Alternatively carbon in a hard crystalline form may be used in a variety of ways[1]. Composition resistors have an extremely low inductance and self-capacitance; the effect of residual inductance is only significant with low values of resistance at very high frequencies while the effect of self-capacitance may be important with high values of resistance at high frequencies.

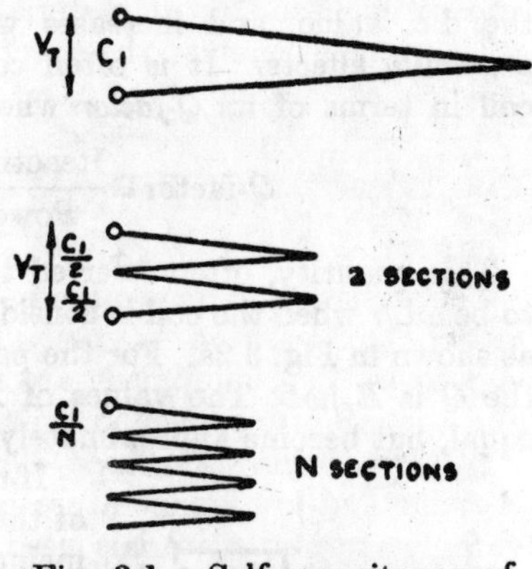

Fig. 3.1. Self-capacitance of a sectionalised winding.

Composition type resistors have, in general, a larger temperature coefficient and poorer long term stability of resistance value as com pared with the wire-wound variety.

Inductors

Communication circuits employ inductors of all types ranging from small air-cored coils in radio-frequency tuned circuits, having an inductance of a fraction of a micro-henry, to the iron-cored coils as used in low-frequency filters and smoothing circuits, when the inductance may perhaps be as large as 100 henrys.

Inductors may be air-cored, or they may have a core of magnetic material. At power and audio frequencies iron laminations may be used. Alternatively, magnetic powder cores may be used. Such cores consist essentially of ferromagnetic particles, coated with insulating material, and compacted to form a solid mass ; at audio frequencies, relatively large particles and small amounts of insulation may be used, while at higher frequencies smaller particles and larger amounts of insulation are used. A group of materials in common use as magnetic cores are the *ferrites*; the most interesting property of this class of materials is their extremely high resistivity, which produces a very low eddy current loss. They are used for inductor and transformer cores in communication circuits.

Coils, or inductors, are made from copper wire, either solid, or in the form of twisted and insulated filaments. Air-cored coils may be represented by an inductance L and a resistance to represent the losses, either as a low value r, in series with L, or as a high value R_p, in parallel with L. The losses consist of the a.c. resistance of the wire, together with any dielectric losses in the former on which the coil is wound. The a.c. resistance of the conductor is greater than the d.c. value, and increases with frequency because of *skin* and *proximity* effects. It is often convenient to express the losses in a coil in terms of its *Q-factor* where this quantity is defined as,

$$Q\text{-factor} = \frac{\text{Reactive volt-amperes in } L}{\text{Power dissipated in coil}}$$

This quantity, often referred to as the Q of the coil, can be shown to be $\omega L/r$ when the coil is considered as having a series loss resistance as shown in Fig. 3.2a. For the parallel loss representation of Fig. 3.2b the Q is $R_p/\omega L$. The values of L in the two representations are not equal, but become approximately so in low-loss, or high-Q, coils.

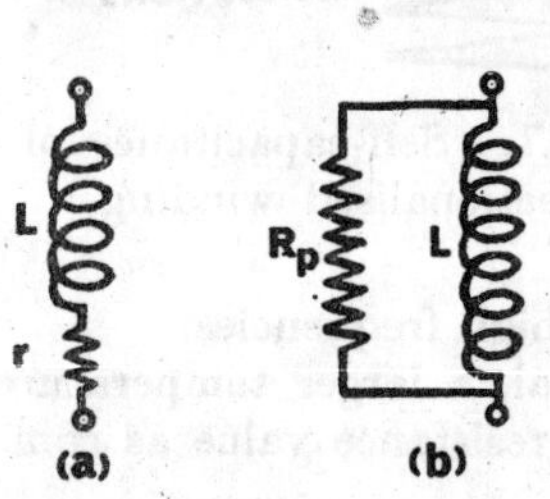

Fig. 3.2. Equivalent circuits for an inductor.

If the coil has a magnetic core the value of the loss resistance must be amended to include the effect of core losses; the value of the resistance may then vary with the current flowing in the coil.

In addition to inductance and resistance, practical inductors have some self-capacitance due to capacitance between turns and also between layers when multi-layer windings are used. The presence of self-capacitance causes the apparent value of the inductance and resistance to vary with frequency, and the inductor has an anti-resonant frequency. In a well designed inductor, the anti-resonant frequency should be very much higher than the highest operating frequency.

Capacitors

The losses associated with a practical capacitor arise from the resistance of the connections to the plates and power losses in the dielectric, and may be represented in two ways, either as a low value of resistance r in series with the capacitor (as shown in Fig. 3.3a), or as a high value of resistance R in parallel with the capacitor (Fig. 3.3b).

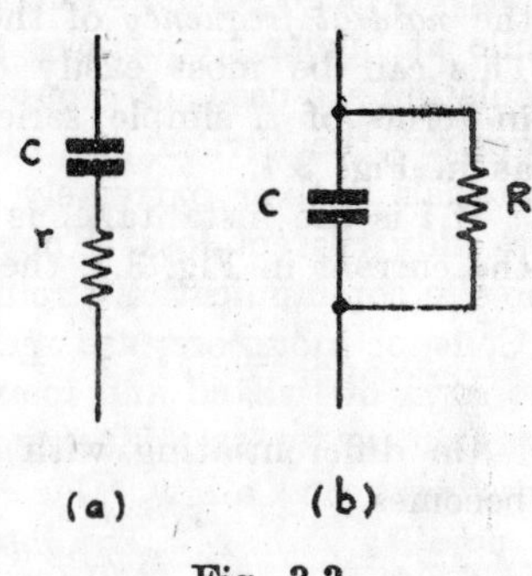

Fig. 3.3.

Continuously variable capacitors have an air dielectric, the series loss resistance is very small, and the phase angle of such capacitors can normally be considered to be 90°. The choice of dielectric in a fixed capacitor depends upon the value of the capacitance required, the applied voltage, and the frequency of operation. Capacitors with mica as the dielectric have a very small power factor, and the loss resistance is usually ignored. Because of this and their high stability, mica capacitors are widely used in precision equipment for values of capacitance which would make an air capacitor inconveniently large. For relatively small values of capacitance a deposit of silver may be bonded directly on to the surface of the mica ; ceramic material is also used as a dielectric, with properties roughly of the same order as for mica. Polystyrene film is now widely used as a dielectric for capacitors.

For capacitors of larger sizes, up to about 10–20μF depending on the working voltage, impregnated paper is used as a dielectric ; the power factor is higher, and the dielectric strength is not so great as for mica or porcelain dielectrics. When large values of capacitance are required, as in power supply smoothing circuits, electrolytic capacitors are generally used as they provide an attractive economy in space. This is possible because of the extreme thinness of the dielectric which is an insulating film built up by an electrolytic process on one of the electrodes. The film has a high resistance with one polarity of applied voltage, and behaves as a dielectric ; if the polarity of the applied voltage is reversed, however, the film behaves as a relatively low resistance, and if the voltage is high enough a large current is passed and the film breaks down. The electrolytic capacitor in its simple form is thus a polarised element which cannot be used in alternating current circuits.

CONDITION FOR OSCILLATION IN AN LCR CIRCUIT

A passive circuit containing inductance, capacitance, and resistance, may, if disturbed, give rise to a sinusoidal oscillation with an exponential

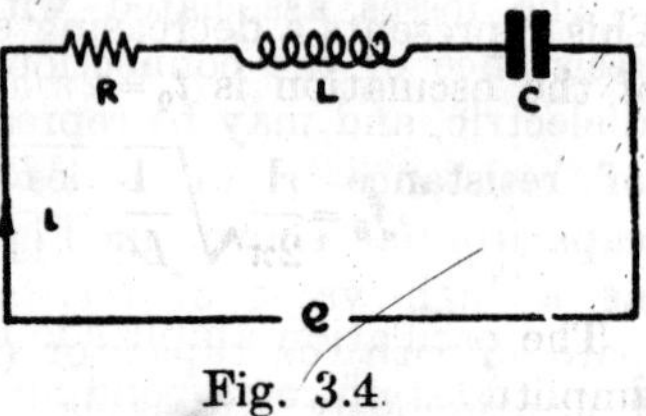

Fig. 3.4.

decay, if the resistance is less than a certain critical value; the frequency of the oscillation is termed the *natural frequency* of the circuit. This can be most easily discussed in terms of a simple series circuit as in Fig. 3.4.

If i is the instantaneous value of the current in Fig. 3.4, then

$$L\frac{di}{dt}+Ri+\frac{1}{C}\int i\,dt=e \qquad 3.1$$

On differentiating with respect to time, and dividing by L this becomes

$$\frac{d^2i}{dt^2}+\frac{R}{L}\frac{di}{dt}+\frac{1}{LC}i=\frac{1}{L}\frac{de}{dt} \qquad 3.2$$

If e is constant, then $\frac{de}{dt}=0$ and the equation becomes

$$\left(p^2+\frac{R}{L}p+\frac{1}{LC}\right)i=0$$

where $p\equiv\frac{d}{dt}$. The solution is given by $i=Ae^{m_1t}+Be^{m_2t}$

where A and B are constants determined by the initial conditions, and

$$m_1=-\frac{R}{2L}+\sqrt{\frac{R^2}{4L^2}-\frac{1}{LC}} \text{ and } m_2=-\frac{R}{2L}-\sqrt{\frac{R^2}{4L^2}-\frac{1}{LC}}$$

If $\frac{R^2}{4L^2}>\frac{1}{LC}$, m_1 and m_2 are entirely real. On the other hand, if $\frac{R^2}{4L^2}<\frac{1}{LC}$, both m_1 and m_2 become complex, and may be expressed as

$$m_1=-\frac{R}{2L}+j\omega_0 \text{ and } m_2=-\frac{R}{2L}-j\omega_0$$

$$\text{where } \omega_0=\sqrt{\frac{1}{LC}-\frac{R^2}{4L^2}}$$

The solution to equation 3.2 then becomes

$$i=Ae^{\left(-\frac{R}{2L}+j\omega_0\right)}+Be^{\left(-\frac{R}{2L}-j\omega_0\right)t}$$

If the initial conditions are such that $i=0$ at $t=0$, then it will be seen that $B=-A$

and so $$i=Ae^{-\frac{R}{2L}t}\left(e^{j\omega_0t}-e^{-j\omega_0t}\right)=2jAe^{-\frac{R}{2L}t}\sin\omega_0t \qquad 3.3$$

This represents a decreasing sinusoidal oscillation in which the period of the oscillation is $t_0 = 2\pi/\omega_0$ and the natural frequency

$$f_0 = \frac{1}{2\pi}\sqrt{\frac{1}{LC} - \frac{R^2}{4L^2}} \quad . \quad . \quad . \quad . \quad . \quad 3.4$$

The oscillation amplitude decreases with time and the ratio of the amplitudes of corresponding points in adjacent cycles is given by

$$e^{\frac{R}{2L}t} = e^{\frac{\pi R}{\omega_0 L}} \quad . \quad . \quad . \quad . \quad . \quad 3.5$$

The logarithm of this ratio namely $\pi R/\omega_0 L$ is referred to as the *logarithmic decrement.*

Equation 3.3. shows how the amplitude of the oscillation produced depends on the value of R; if R is positive the amplitude decays; if, however, R is zero, the oscillation will have a fixed amplitude, whilst a negative value for R will give rise to an oscillation which increases in amplitude with time. It therefore follows that the *limiting condition* for the maintenance of continuous oscillations is that R shall be zero. If this is so, the coefficient of the $\frac{di}{dt}$ term (sometimes called the damping term) is zero in equation 3.2, and the frequency of the oscillation is then $\frac{1}{2\pi}$ ($\sqrt{\text{coefficient of } i \text{ in equation 3.2}}$)

i.e. $f = \dfrac{1}{2\pi\sqrt{LC}}$

These results are completely general and any circuit in which the current/time relationship is of the form

$$\frac{d^2i}{dt^2} + P\frac{di}{dt} + Qi = 0$$

will give rise to continuous oscillation if $P = 0$. The frequency of the oscillation f, is then given by $\omega^2 = Q$ where $\omega = 2\pi f$.

RESONANCE

A circuit is said to be *resonant* when a sinusoidal e.m.f. with a frequency equal to the natural frequency, is applied to the circuit.

A number of other definitions of resonance exist in practice,[2] apart from the definition given above. A circuit is sometimes said to be resonant when,

1. The reactive component of the impedance is zero and the circuit behaves as a pure resistance.

2. The impedance is a minimum (for a series circuit) or a maximum (for a parallel circuit).

3. The inductive reactance is equal to the magnitude of the capacitive reactance, i.e. when $\omega L = 1/\omega C$.

All three definitions give the same value for the resonant frequency in a series circuit. This value is different from the natural frequency of equation 3.4 if R is large, but not if R is vanishingly small compared with the values of the reactive components. For parallel circuits the three definitions listed above will give different values for the differently defined resonant frequencies. These values approach one another as R decreases and all the definitions become identical in the ideal case of dissipationless components, i.e. when $R=0$. This is also true when the coil is represented with a parallel loss resistance R_P. For these reasons it is useful to define *resonant frequency* as the frequency of the ideal case. Hence, the resonant frequency will be subsequently denoted by f_R, where

$$f_R = \frac{1}{2\pi\sqrt{LC}} \qquad . \quad . \quad . \quad . \quad . \qquad 3.6$$

From equations 3.4 and 3.6, the ratio of the natural frequency to the resonant frequency is

$$\frac{f_0^2}{f_R^2} = \frac{\dfrac{1}{LC} - \dfrac{R^2}{4L^2}}{\dfrac{1}{LC}} = 1 - \frac{CR^2}{4L} = 1 - \frac{R^2}{4\omega_R^2 L^2}$$

as $\omega L = 1/\omega C$ at the resonant frequency, and so $C/L = 1/\omega_R^2 L^2$. If, between the natural and the resonant frequency, the change in value of R can be ignored, then the quantity $R/\omega_R L$ may be written as $1/Q_R$, i.e. the reciprocal of the Q-factor at the resonant frequency, and so

$$\frac{f_0^2}{f_R^2} = 1 - \frac{1}{4Q_R^2}.$$

$$\text{and } f_0 = f_R\sqrt{1 - \frac{1}{4Q_R^2}} \simeq f_R\left(1 - \frac{1}{8Q_R^2}\right) \qquad . \quad . \quad . \qquad 3.7$$

It will be seen from equation 3.7 that if $Q>4$, the resonant and natural frequencies differ by less than 1%.

SERIES RESONANCE

In a series circuit containing resistance, capacitance, and inductance, as shown in Fig. 3.5 the terminal impedance Z is given by

$$Z = R + j(\omega L - 1/\omega C)$$

where R represents the total series resistance. The reactive component will be inductive or capacitive, depending on whether ωL is greater or less than $1/\omega C$ at the frequency at which Z is calculated. The current is given by

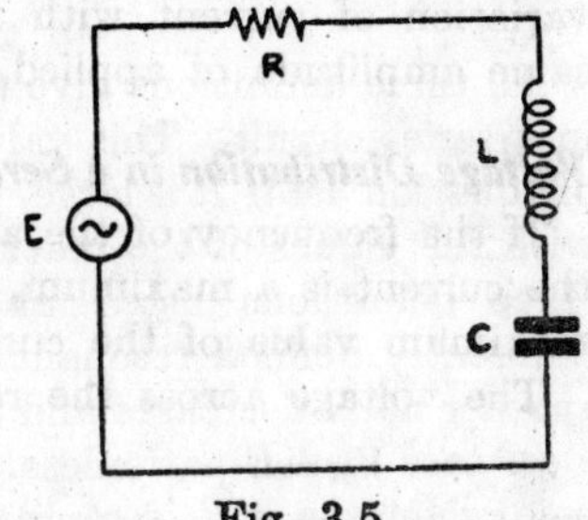

Fig. 3.5.

$$I = \frac{E}{\sqrt{R^2 + (\omega L - 1/\omega C)^2}} \quad . \quad . \quad . \quad 3.8$$

If the frequency of the applied voltage is varied, or alternatively the value of the capacitor or the inductor is varied so that

$$\omega L = 1/\omega C \quad . \quad . \quad . \quad . \quad . \quad 3.9$$

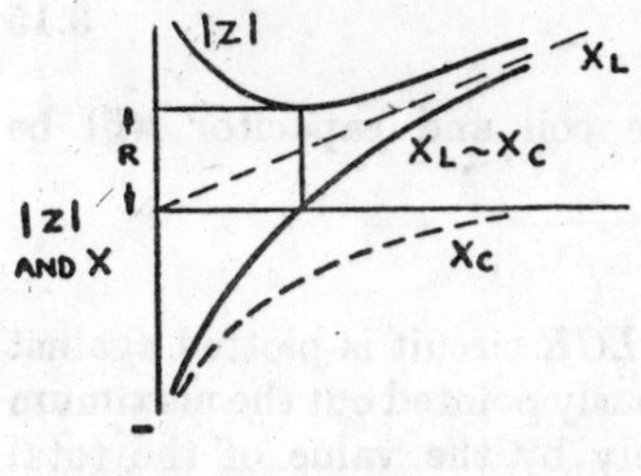

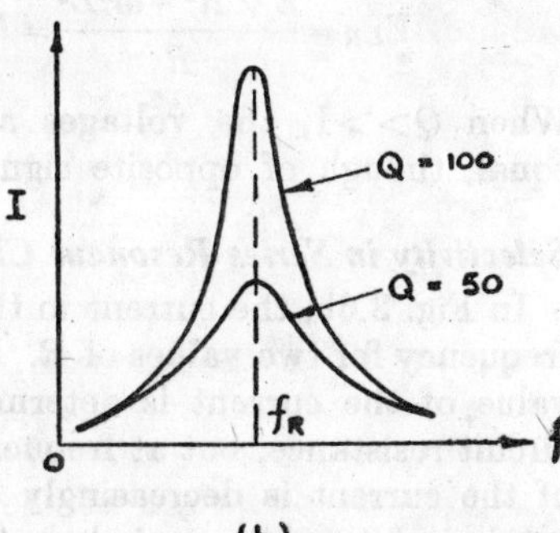

Fig. 3.6. (a) Variation of impedance and reactance with frequency for a series circuit.
(b) Variation of current with frequency in a series circuit.

then the circuit impedance is a minimum, and reduces to

$$Z = R \quad . \quad . \quad . \quad . \quad . \quad 3.10$$

The circuit is said to be ***series-resonant***, and the resonant frequency, f_R, is of course determined from equation 3.9,

$$\text{i.e. } \omega_R^2 = 1/LC, \text{ and } f_R = 1/(2\pi\sqrt{LC}) \quad . \quad . \quad . \quad 3.11$$

Fig. 3.6a shows the variation of impedance and reactance with frequency for such a circuit, whilst Fig. 3.6b shows the corresponding variation of current with frequency for two values of R (for the same amplitude of applied voltage).

Voltage Distribution in a Series Resonant Circuit

If the frequency of the applied voltage on Fig. 3.5 is varied until the current is a maximum, this will occur when $\omega L = 1/\omega C$, and the maximum value of the current will be E/R.

The voltage across the resistance R will be

$$V_R = E \qquad 3.12$$

The voltage across the capacitor will be

$$V_C = E/\omega CR, \text{ or } E.Q \qquad 3.13$$

The voltage across the inductance L will be,

$$V_L = E\omega L/R, \text{ or } E.Q \qquad 3.14$$

If L and R represent the inductance and resistance of a coil, then the voltage at the coil terminals will be

$$V_{LR} = \frac{E\sqrt{R^2 + \omega^2 L^2}}{R} = E\sqrt{1 + Q^2} \qquad 3.15$$

When $Q >> 1$, the voltages across the coil and capacitor will be equal, though of opposite sign.

Selectivity in Series Resonant Circuits

In Fig. 3.6b, the current in the series LCR circuit is plotted against frequency for two values of R. As previously pointed out the maximum value of the current is determined solely by the value of the total circuit resistance, but at frequencies far from resonance the amplitude of the current is decreasingly dependent on R. In cases where the total circuit resistance is low, the curve of current against frequency has a sharp peak and such a circuit is said to be sharply resonant or highly *selective*. If, on the other hand, the resistance of the circuit is high, or if the generator has a high value of internal resistance, the *selectivity* is poor and the peak is not pronounced. Series circuits which are to be sharply resonant should thus be energised from a low-impedance generator.

In order to compare the selectivity of one circuit with another it is necessary to consider the band of frequencies between limits at which the current is reduced by a specified amount. It is convenient to specify as limits the frequencies at which the current has fallen to $1/\sqrt{2}$ of its maximum value of E/R. This occurs when the circuit impedance is increased by $\sqrt{2}$, i.e. when

$$\omega L - 1/\omega C = \pm R \qquad 3.16$$

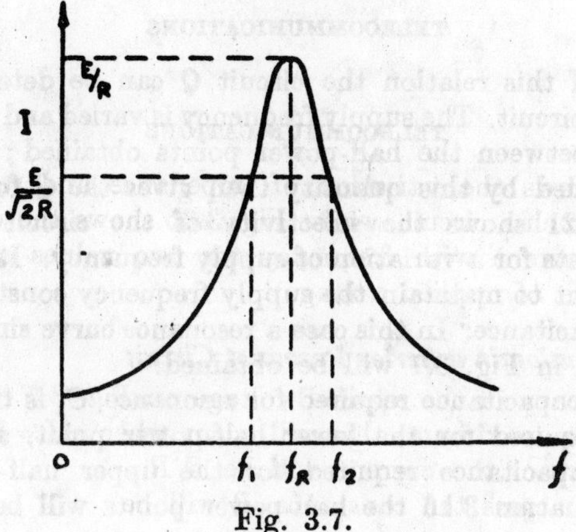

Fig. 3.7.

Thus there are two requencies (f_1 and f_2 in Fig. 3.7) between which $I > E/(\sqrt{2}R)$. At the frequencies f_1 and f_2 the power dissipation is half of the maximum value; these points on the response curve (Fig. 3.7) are referred to as *half-power points*.

From equation 3.16, f_1 and f_2 are $(\omega_R \pm \omega')/2\pi$ if

$$(\omega_R \pm \omega')L - \frac{1}{(\omega_R \pm \omega')C} = \pm R \quad . \quad . \quad . \quad 3.17$$

Now $\omega_R L = 1/\omega_R C$, and so $C = 1/\omega_R^2 L$

Hence by substitution of this value for C in equation 3.17

$$R = (\omega_R + \omega')L - \frac{\omega_R^2 L}{\omega_R + \omega'} = \omega_R L + \omega' L - \frac{\omega_R L}{1 + \omega'/\omega_R}$$

If, as is usually the case, $\omega_R >> \omega'$, then

$$\left(1 + \frac{\omega'}{\omega_R}\right)^{-1} = 1 - \omega'/\omega_R \quad \text{and so} \quad R = 2\omega' L \quad \therefore \omega' = R/2L$$

$$\text{Now } f_1 = \frac{\omega_R - \omega'}{2\pi} = f_R - \frac{R}{4\pi L} \quad . \quad . \quad . \quad . \quad . \quad 3.18$$

$$\text{and } f_2 = \frac{\omega_R + \omega'}{2\pi} = f_R + \frac{R}{4\pi L} \quad . \quad . \quad . \quad . \quad . \quad 3.19$$

$$\text{Hence } f_2 - f_1 = \Delta f \quad = \frac{R}{2\pi L} \quad . \quad . \quad . \quad . \quad . \quad 3.20$$

If the Q-factor is given by $Q = \dfrac{\omega_R L}{R}$ then from equation 3.20

$$\frac{f_R}{\Delta f} = Q \quad . \quad . \quad . \quad 3.21$$

By means of this relation the circuit Q can be determined for a constant LCR circuit. The supply frequency is varied and the difference in frequency between the half-power points obtained; the resonant frequency divided by this quantity then gives the Q for the circuit.

Equation 3.21 shows the selectivity of the circuit in terms of half-power points for a variation of supply frequency. It is sometimes more convenient to maintain the supply frequency constant and vary the tuning capacitance. In this case a resonance curve similar in shape to that shown in Fig. 3.7 will be obtained.

If C_R is the capacitance required for resonance, C_1 is the increase in capacitance required for the lower half-power point, and C_2 is the decrease in capacitance required for the upper half-power point. Then from equation 3.16 the half-power points will be given by

$$\omega_R L - \frac{1}{\omega_R(C_R+C_1)} = R \qquad . \quad . \quad . \quad . \quad . \quad 3.22$$

$$\text{and} \quad \frac{1}{\omega_R(C_R-C_2)} - \omega_R L = R \qquad . \quad . \quad . \quad . \quad . \quad 3.23$$

Hence by the addition of these two equations

$$\frac{(C_R+C_1)-(C_R-C_2)}{\omega_R(C_P-C_2)(C_R+C_1)} = 2R$$

$$\text{and} \quad \frac{C_1+C_2}{\omega_R(C_R+C_1)(C_R-C_2)} = 2R$$

Then if C_1 and C_2 are small and approximately equal,

$$(C_R+C_1)(C_R-C_2) = C_R^2 \quad \text{and} \quad C_1+C_2 = 2\Delta C$$

$$\text{then} \quad 2\Delta C/\omega C_R^2 = 2R$$

Now $\dfrac{1}{\omega_R C_R} = \omega_R L$ and hence

$$\frac{C_R}{\Delta C} = Q \qquad . \quad . \quad . \quad . \quad 3.24$$

If the self-capacitance of the inductors is an appreciable part of the tuning capacitance, the value of C_R will have to be amended, otherwise an error will arise in the application of equation 3.24.

PARALLEL RESONANCE

In a two branch circuit such as that shown in Fig. 3.8a, the generator current I_G will lead or lag on the applied voltage depending on whether the impedance of the capacitive branch is smaller or larger than that of the inductive branch. At a certain frequency the generator current

will be in phase with the applied voltage ; the amplitude of the current is then relatively small and the circuit behaves as a high resistance. This resonant condition of the parallel circuit is often termed *anti-resonance* to distinguish it from series resonance.

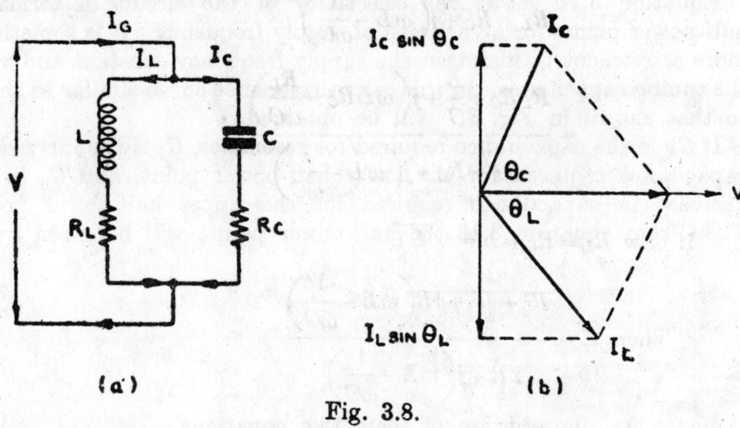

Fig. 3.8.

From the vector, or phasor, diagram it will be seen that the circuit will behave as a resistance if

$$|I_C| \sin \theta_C = |I_L| \sin \theta_L \quad . \quad . \quad . \quad 3.25$$

This equation may be used to obtain the frequency for this condition in terms of R_L, R_C, C and L, by re-writing as

$$\frac{V}{\sqrt{R_C^2+\left(\frac{1}{\omega C}\right)^2}} \cdot \frac{1}{\omega C} \cdot \frac{1}{\sqrt{R_C^2+\left(\frac{1}{\omega C}\right)^2}} = \frac{V}{\sqrt{R_L^2+(\omega L)^2}} \cdot \frac{\omega L}{\sqrt{R_L^2+(\omega L)^2}}$$

$$\therefore \frac{1}{\omega C} \cdot \frac{1}{R_C^2+\left(\frac{1}{\omega C}\right)^2} = \frac{\omega L}{R_L^2+(\omega L)^2}$$

$$\therefore R_L^2+(\omega L)^2 = \omega^2 LC\left[R_C^2+\left(\frac{1}{\omega C}\right)^2\right]$$

$$\therefore \omega^2(L^2 - LCR_C^2) = \frac{L}{C} - R_L^2$$

$$\text{and } \omega^2 = \frac{L-CR_L^2}{L^2C - LC^2R_C^2}$$

from which the frequency at which the circuit is non-reactive is

$$f = \frac{1}{2\pi}\sqrt{\frac{1}{LC}\left(\frac{L-CR_L^2}{L-CR_C^2}\right)} \quad . \quad 3.26$$

An interesting case arises from this result. If $R_L = R_C = \sqrt{L/C}$ the impedance of the circuit becomes independent of frequency. This can be shown as follows.

The impedance of the circuit of Fig. 3.8 is given by

$$Z = \frac{(R_L + j\omega L)(R_C - j/\omega C)}{R_L + R_C + j\left(\omega L - \frac{1}{\omega C}\right)} \quad . \quad . \quad . \quad . \quad 3.27$$

$$= \frac{R_L R_C + \frac{L}{C} + j\left(\omega L R_C - \frac{R_L}{\omega C}\right)}{R_L + R_C + j\left(\omega L - \frac{1}{\omega C}\right)}$$

If now $R_L = R_C = R = \sqrt{L/C}$

$$\text{Then } Z = \frac{R^2 + R^2 + jR\left(\omega L - \frac{1}{\omega C}\right)}{2R + j\left(\omega L - \frac{1}{\omega C}\right)}$$

$$\therefore Z = R \quad . \quad . \quad . \quad . \quad . \quad . \quad . \quad . \quad 3.28$$

The circuit impedance is thus resistive *at all frequencies*. This condition will only hold, however, if R_L and R_C maintain their desired value of $\sqrt{L/C}$.

The impedance of the general circuit when $R_L \neq R_C$ can be obtained by referring to the vector diagram of Fig. 3.8b. If the circuit is non-reactive then the supply current will be given by

$$I = I_C \cos\theta_C + I_L \cos\theta_L = \frac{VR_C}{R_C^2 + \frac{1}{\omega^2 C^2}} + \frac{VR_L}{R_L^2 + \omega^2 L^2}$$

Now from equation 3.26

$$\omega^2 L^2 = \frac{L}{C}\left(\frac{L - CR_L^2}{L - CR_C^2}\right) \quad \text{and} \quad \frac{1}{\omega^2 C^2} = \frac{L}{C}\left(\frac{L - CR_C^2}{L - CR_L^2}\right)$$

If these values are substituted in the expression for I, then

$$I = \frac{VR_C C(L - CR_L^2)}{L^2 - C^2 R_C^2 R_L^2} + \frac{VR_L C(L - CR_C^2)}{L^2 - C^2 R_C^2 R_L^2}$$

$$= \frac{VC(R_C + R_L)(L - CR_L R_C)}{L^2 - C^2 R_C^2 R_L^2}$$

The admittance Y of the circuit $=\frac{I}{V}$,

$$\text{and so } Y=\frac{C(R_C+R_L)(L-CR_LR_C)}{L^2-C^2R_C^2R_L^2}=\frac{C(R_C+R_L)}{L+CR_LR_C}=\frac{C(R_C+R_L)}{L\left(1+\frac{C}{L}R_CR_L\right)}$$

Hence the impedance of the circuit is given by

$$Z=\frac{L\left(1+\frac{C}{L}R_CR_L\right)}{C(R_C+R_L)} \quad . \quad . \quad . \quad . \quad 3.29a$$

If $\omega^2L^2>>R_L^2$, and $1/\omega^2C^2>>R_C^2$, then $\frac{C}{L}R_CR_L<<1$, and the impedance reduces to

$$Z=\frac{L}{C(R_C+R_L)} \quad . \quad . \quad . \quad . \quad . \quad 3.29b$$

Parallel Resonance with Resistance in the Inductive Arm Only

The circuit shown in Fig. 3.9a is encountered more frequently than the general circuit considered above, because of the small power losses in capacitors.

Case I. Circuit to be Non-reactive. The admittance of the circuit, Y is given by

$$Y=1/Z=G+jB$$

where G is the conductance, and B the susceptance.

Now if an impedance Z is expressed as

$$Z=R+jX \text{ then } G=\frac{R}{R^2+X^2} \text{ and } B=\frac{-X}{R^2+X^2}$$

In the circuit of Fig. 3.9a, the conductance of the inductive branch is $\frac{R}{R^2+\omega^2L^2}$, and for the capacitive branch it is zero. Hence the total conductance of the circuit is

$$G=\frac{R}{R^2+\omega^2L^2}$$

The susceptance of the inductive branch is $-\omega L/(R^2+\omega^2L^2)$, and for the capacitive branch it is ωC. Hence the total susceptance of the circuit is

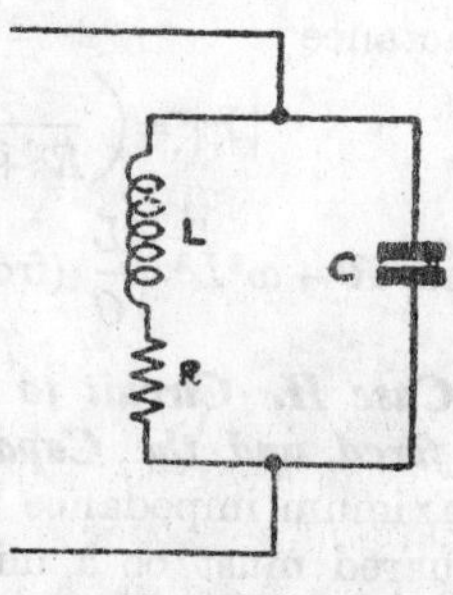

Fig. 3.9a.

$$B = \omega C - \frac{\omega L}{R^2 + \omega^2 L^2}$$

The magnitude $|Y|$ of the admittance is expressed as

$$|Y|^2 = \left(\frac{R}{R^2 + \omega^2 L^2}\right)^2 + \left(\omega C - \frac{\omega L}{R^2 + \omega^2 L^2}\right)^2 \quad . \quad . \quad 3.30$$

If the circuit is to be non-reactive then the susceptance must be zero, and so this gives

$$\omega C = \frac{\omega L}{R^2 + \omega^2 L^2} \text{ or } C = \frac{L}{R^2 + \omega^2 L^2} \quad . \quad . \quad . \quad 3.31$$

The frequency at which the circuit is non-reactive is then

$$\omega^2 = \frac{1}{LC} - \frac{R^2}{L^2} \text{ or } f = \frac{1}{2\pi}\sqrt{\frac{1}{LC} - \frac{R^2}{L^2}} \quad . \quad . \quad . \quad 3.32$$

This result could have been obtained from the more general case previously dealt with, and equation 3.32 could be obtained from equation 3.26 if $R_C = 0$.

The ratio of the frequency of equation 3.32 to the resonant frequency f_R is given by

$$\frac{f^2}{f_R^2} = \frac{\frac{1}{LC} - \frac{R^2}{L^2}}{\frac{1}{LC}} = 1 - \frac{C}{L}R^2$$

$$\text{again } \frac{C}{L} = \frac{1}{\omega_R^2 L^2} \text{ and so } \frac{f^2}{f_R^2} = 1 - \frac{R^2}{\omega_R^2 L^2}$$

$$\text{and } f = f_R\sqrt{1 - \frac{1}{Q_R^2}} \simeq f_R\left(1 - \frac{1}{2Q_R^2}\right) \quad . \quad . \quad . \quad 3.33$$

The impedance of the circuit, when the capacitor is adjusted for zero reactance, is given by equations 3.30 and 3.31; i.e. for zero reactance

$$|Y|^2 = \left(\frac{R}{R^2 + \omega^2 L^2}\right)^2 + 0$$

$$\text{and } R^2 + \omega^2 L^2 = \frac{L}{C} \text{ (from equation 3.31) } \therefore Z = \frac{L}{CR} \quad . \quad . \quad 3.34a$$

Case II. Circuit to have Maximum Impedance when the Frequency is fixed and the Capacitance varied. If the circuit is to have its maximum impedance then the admittance and hence the admittance squared must be a minimum. This condition can be obtained from equation 3.30.

Differentiating with respect to C

$$2Y\frac{dY}{dC}=2\omega\left[\omega C-\frac{\omega L}{R^2+\omega^2L^2}\right]$$

then equating the numerator of $\frac{dY}{dC}$ to zero gives

$$\omega^2C=\frac{\omega^2L}{R^2+\omega^2L^2} \quad \text{and } C=\frac{L}{R^2+\omega^2L^2}$$

This result is identical with equation 3.31, and so the frequency at which the parallel circuit is non-reactive is also the frequency which makes the impedance a maximum provided that in the latter case the variable is the capacitance C.

The maximum value of impedance is exactly that given in equation 3.34a, i.e. $|Z|_{max}=\frac{L}{CR}=\frac{\omega L}{\omega CR}=Q\omega L \text{ or } Q\frac{1}{\omega C}$ . . . 3.34b

When the capacitance is adjusted to make the circuit impedance a maximum, the maximum value obtained is resistive in character, and is sometimes referred to as the *dynamic resistance* of the circuit. It should be noted that this quantity is proportional to the L/C ratio of the circuit.

Case III. Circuit to have Maximum Impedance when the Components are fixed and the Frequency is variable. The assumption in this case is that one works with a given circuit and it is then desired to find the particular frequency at which the circuit has its maximum impedance.

This condition can also be obtained from equation 3.30.

Differentiating with respect to ω

$$2Y\frac{dY}{d\omega}=2\left[\frac{-2\omega L^3R^2}{(R^2+\omega^2L^2)^3}\right]$$
$$+2\left[\omega C-\frac{\omega L}{R^2+\omega^2L^2}\right]\left[C-\frac{L(R^2+\omega^2L^2)-2\omega^2L^3}{(R^2+\omega^2L^2)^2}\right]$$

If this is multiplied throughout by $(R^2+\omega^2L^2)^3$ and the numerator of $\frac{dY}{d\omega}$ equated to zero then it can be shown that the frequency at which the impedance is a maximum is given by

$$f=\frac{1}{2\pi}\sqrt{\frac{1}{LC}\sqrt{1+\frac{2CR^2}{L}}-\frac{R^2}{L^2}} \quad . \quad . \quad . \quad 3.35$$

The ratio of this frequency to the resonant frequency f_R can be obtained from equations 3.6 and 3.35 as

$$\frac{f^2}{f_R^2}=\frac{\frac{1}{LC}\sqrt{1+\frac{2CR^2}{L}-\frac{R^2}{L^2}}}{\frac{1}{LC}}=\sqrt{1+\frac{2CR^2}{L}-\frac{CR^2}{L}}$$

substituting $\frac{1}{\omega_R^2 L^2}$ for $\frac{C}{L}$, as in previous cases, gives

$$f=f_R\sqrt{\sqrt{1+\frac{2}{Q_R^2}-\frac{1}{Q_R^2}}}\simeq f_R\left(1-\frac{1}{4Q_R^4}\right) \quad . \quad . \quad 3.36$$

This frequency is slightly different from that of Cases I and II However, if $Q>10$, the difference is less than ½%.

Case IV. Circuit to have Maximum Impedance when the Frequency is fixed and the Inductance varied. This case may be treated in a manner similar to that for Case II. It will then be found that the maximum impedance occurs at a frequency f where

$$f=\frac{1}{2\pi}\sqrt{\frac{1}{LC}+\frac{R^2}{L^2}} \quad . \quad . \quad . \quad . \quad . \quad 3.37$$

and the ratio of this frequency to the resonant frequency is then

$$f\simeq f_R\left(1+\frac{1}{2Q_R^2}\right) \quad . \quad . \quad . \quad . \quad . \quad 3.38$$

This result is obtained on the assumption that the value of R does not change as L is varied.

Parallel Resonance with Shunt Loss Resistance

If the circuit of Fig. 3.9b is considered rather than Fig. 3.9a, then the resonant condition is given by $\omega_R L=1/\omega_R C$. The circuit then has its maximum (resistive) impedance $|Z|_{max}$ which has the value R_P. The value of the Q-factor at resonance is given by

$$Q=R_P/\omega_R L=\omega_R C R_P=R_P/\sqrt{L/C}$$

Selectivity in Parallel Resonant Circuits

The circuit of Fig. 3.9a has an impedance Z, given by

$$Z=\frac{(R+j\omega L)1/j\omega C}{R+j(\omega L-1/\omega C)}$$

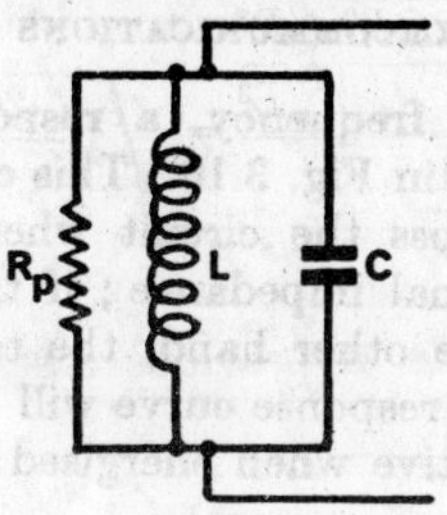

Fig. 3.9b.

If $\omega L >> R$, then

$$Z = \frac{L/C}{R + j(\omega L - 1/\omega C)} = \frac{L/CR}{1 + j\frac{\omega_R L}{R}\left(\frac{\omega}{\omega_R} - \frac{\omega_R}{\omega}\right)} \text{ as } LC = 1/\omega_R^2.$$

Now $$\frac{\omega}{\omega_R} - \frac{\omega_R}{\omega} = \frac{\omega^2 - \omega_R^2}{\omega\omega_R} = \frac{(f - f_R)(f + f_R)}{ff_R}$$

Suppose now that $f = f_R + \delta f$, then the quantity

$$\frac{\omega}{\omega_R} - \frac{\omega_R}{\omega} = \frac{\delta f(2f_R + \delta f)}{f_R(f_R + \delta f)}$$

If δf is always restricted in value so that it is small compared with f_R, then this quantity is approximately equal to $2\delta f/f_R$, and the impedance of the circuit at some frequency δf away from f_R is given by

$$Z = \frac{\frac{L}{CR}}{1 + jQ_R\frac{2\delta f}{f_R}}$$

When δf is zero, the impedance of the circuit has its maximum value

$$|Z|_{max} = \frac{L}{CR}$$

The impedance falls on either side of f_R as δf increases. The magnitude of the impedance is given by

$$|Z| = \frac{\frac{L}{CR}}{\sqrt{1 + \left(Q_R\frac{2\delta f}{f_R}\right)^2}} \quad . \quad . \quad . \quad . \quad . \quad 3.39a$$

If $|Z|$ is plotted against frequency, a response curve is obtained which has the form shown in Fig. 3.10. This curve will also represent the voltage variation across the circuit when it is connected to a generator of infinite internal impedance; if the generator has a low internal impedance on the other hand, the terminal voltage will be fairly constant, and so the response curve will be flat. Parallel circuits are thus only highly selective when energised from a high impedance source.

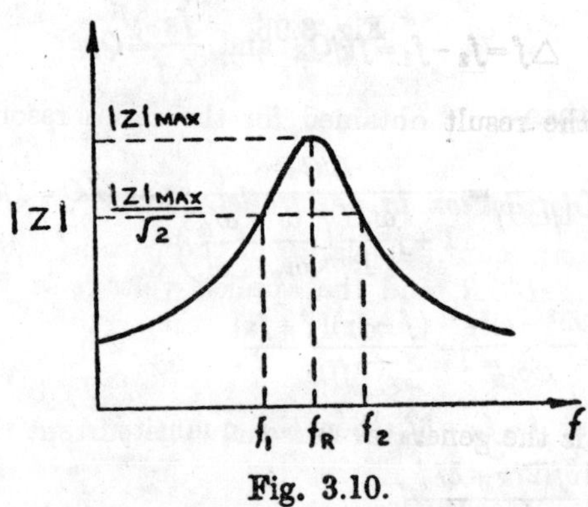

Fig. 3.10.

For the circuit of Fig. 3.9b the impedance at any frequency is given by

$$\frac{1}{Z}=\frac{1}{R_P}+\frac{1}{j\omega L}+j\omega C$$

$$\therefore \quad Z=\frac{R_P}{1+j\omega_R CR_P\left(\dfrac{\omega}{\omega_R}-\dfrac{\omega_R}{\omega}\right)}$$

Again, at frequencies close to resonance $\omega/\omega_R-\omega_R/\omega$ is approximately equal to $2\delta f/f_R$, and $Q_R=\omega_R CR_P$, hence

$$Z=\frac{R_P}{1+jQ_R 2\delta f/f_R}$$

$$\therefore \quad |Z|=\frac{R_P}{\sqrt{1+\left(Q_R\dfrac{2\delta f}{f_R}\right)^2}} \quad . \quad . \quad . \quad 3.39b$$

As indicated by equations 3.39a or b, $|Z|$ will be $1/\sqrt{2}$ of $|Z|_{max}$ when δf is such

$$Q_R\frac{2\delta f}{f_R}=1 \quad \text{i.e. when } \delta f=f_R/2Q_R$$

Hence if the frequencies for which this relation is true (i.e. the frequencies of the half-power points) are f_1 and f_2, then

$$f_1 = f_R - \frac{f_R}{2Q_R} = f_R\left(1 - \frac{1}{2Q_R}\right) \quad . \quad . \quad . \quad 3.40a$$

$$\text{and } f_2 = f_R + \frac{f_R}{2Q_R} = f_R\left(1 + \frac{1}{2Q_R}\right) \quad . \quad . \quad . \quad 3.40b$$

The bandwidth, $\triangle f$, between the half-power points in either case is then

$$\triangle f = f_2 - f_1 = f_R/Q_R \text{ and } \frac{f_R}{\triangle f} = Q_R \quad . \quad . \quad . \quad 3.41$$

which is the result obtained for the series resonant circuit.

Current Distribution in a Parallel Circuit

If the maximum impedance of the parallel LRC circuit of Fig. 3.9a is taken as L/CR, and the applied voltage is V, then

$$V = I_G \cdot \frac{L}{CR} \quad . \quad . \quad . \quad . \quad . \quad . \quad . \quad 3.42$$

where I_G is the generator current. The current through the capacitor is I_C and

$$I_C = V\omega C$$

and so, by substitution for V from equation 3.42,

$$I_C = \frac{I_G L\omega C}{CR} = QI_G \quad . \quad . \quad . \quad . \quad . \quad . \quad 3.43$$

If the Q of the coil is large, then the current I_L in the coil will be approximately

$$I_L = QI_G \quad . \quad . \quad . \quad . \quad . \quad . \quad 3.44$$

PHASE SHIFT IN RESONANT CIRCUITS

(a) Series Circuits

A series LRC circuit will produce a phase shift between the voltage applied to the terminals and the current taken from the generator. The circuit will be capacitive for frequencies less than the resonant value and so the circuit current will lead on the applied voltage by an angle θ, where

$$\theta = \tan^{-1} \frac{X_C - X_L}{R} \quad . \quad . \quad . \quad . \quad . \quad 3.45$$

As the frequency is raised the phase shift will decrease to zero at the resonant value. For frequencies beyond this the circuit is inductive and takes a lagging current. Fig. 3.11 shows phase shift plotted against

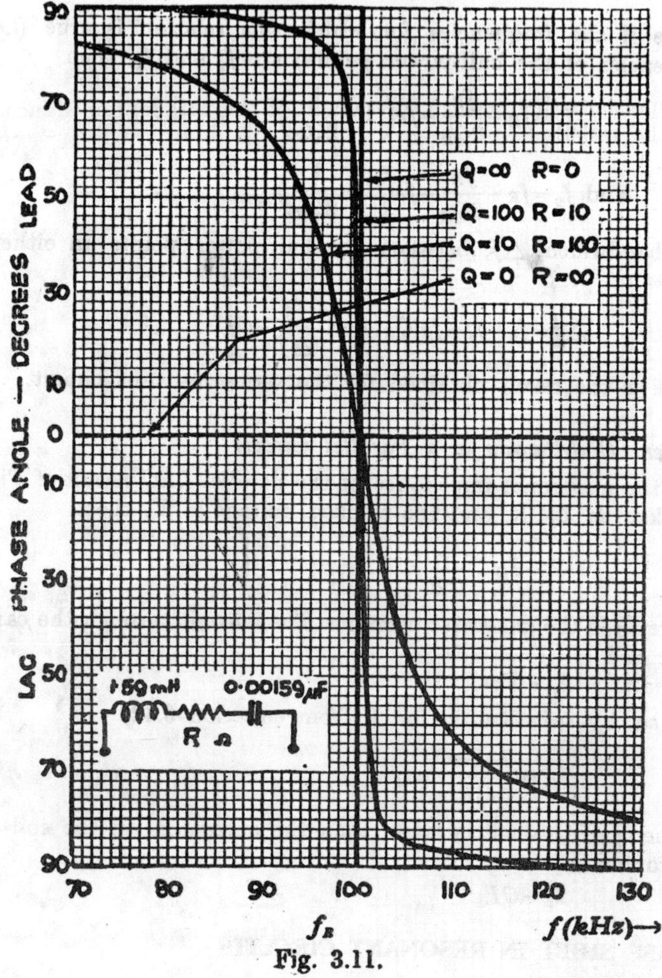

Fig. 3.11.

frequency for two values of resistance in the series circuit shown. In addition the limiting cases of $R=\infty$ and $R=0$ are drawn. In the last case the phase shift is 90°; leading up to the resonant frequency then 90° lagging thereafter.

(b) Parallel Circuits

A parallel resonant circuit also gives rise to a phase shift between the voltage across the circuit terminals and the generator current flowing to the circuit. The phase shift is given by

$$\theta = \tan^{-1}\frac{X'}{R'}$$

where X' represents the reactive component of the parallel impedance and R' is the resistive component.

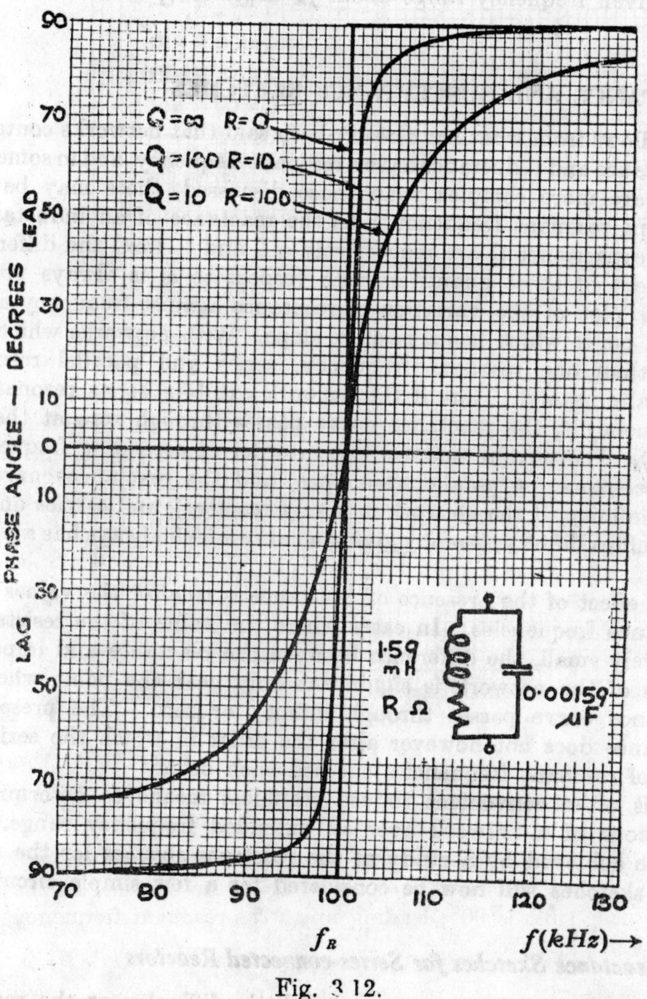

Fig. 3.12.

Fig. 3.12 shows the phase shift for two values of R in the parallel circuit. If these curves are compared with the equivalent series cases it will be seen that the phase shift is nearly the same except that when the series circuit leads, the parallel circuit lags, and vice versa.

Phase shift is of importance in frequency-modulated circuits where non-linearity of phase shift produces distortion. It can be seen from Figs. 3.12 and 3.13 that the linearity of the phase characteristics for a given frequency range about f_R depends upon the value of Q.

REACTANCE AND SUSCEPTANCE SKETCHES

It follows from what has already been said that networks containing capacitance and inductance have a resonant frequency, and in some cases which are more complex than those discussed, there may be more than one resonant frequency. As the reactance of an inductance L and a capacitance C are respectively ωL and $-1/\omega C$ the differential coefficient of these quantities with respect to ω is always positive, hence a plot of the variation of reactance against frequency always gives a curve which has a positive slope. With networks which have more than one resonant frequency, series and parallel resonance occur alternately. Thus if the network exhibits series resonance at a frequency f_1 the reactance curve passes through zero at that frequency. The next resonant effect in order of ascending frequency is anti-resonance, or parallel resonance, and the reactance curve rises up to infinity (if the network is purely reactive), and carries on again from minus infinity, thereby giving a curve which always has a positive slope.

The effect of the presence of resistance is to alter the values of the resonance frequencies. In cases where the value of the resistance is relatively small, the difference between the reactance and impedance curves of the network is significant only near the point where the reactance curve passes through infinity or zero. The presence of resistance does not however alter the order in which the series and parallel resonant frequencies succeed each other.

It is often convenient to use graphical means to determine the behaviour of a network over an extended frequency range. This can be achieved by a study of the *reactance sketches* for the circuit. Such sketches will now be considered for a few simple circuits.

(a) Reactance Sketches for Series-connected Reactors

Series-connected reactors present little difficulty as the reactance curve for the whole network is simply the sum of the separate curves for the component reactors. Any series connection of reactors may be simplified to the series LC circuit of Fig. 3.13a. The reactance curve is then the full line curve of Fig. 3.13b which is obtained from the addition of the two dotted curves.

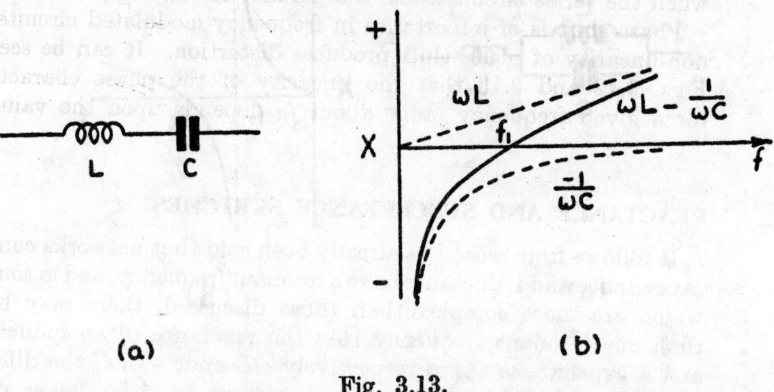

Fig. 3.13.

Series resonance occurs at the frequency f_1 where the reactance curve passes through zero.

(b) Reactance Sketches for Parallel-connected Reactors

In the case of parallel-connected reactors the reactance curve can be obtained as the reciprocal of the susceptance curve, which is simply the sum of the separate susceptance curves for the parallel reactors. Any number of inductors and capacitors connected in parallel can be reduced to the parallel *LC* circuit of Fig. 3.14a. The corresponding susceptance curve is that of Fig. 3.14b.

(It should be remembered that the susceptance of an inductance is $-1/\omega L$ and the susceptance curve is similar to the reactance curve of a capacitance; the susceptance curve of a capacitance is $+\omega C$ and the susceptance curve is similar in form to the reactance curve of an inductance.)

The reactance curve for the parallel *LC* circuit is the reciprocal of the susceptance curve and is shown in Fig. 3.14c.

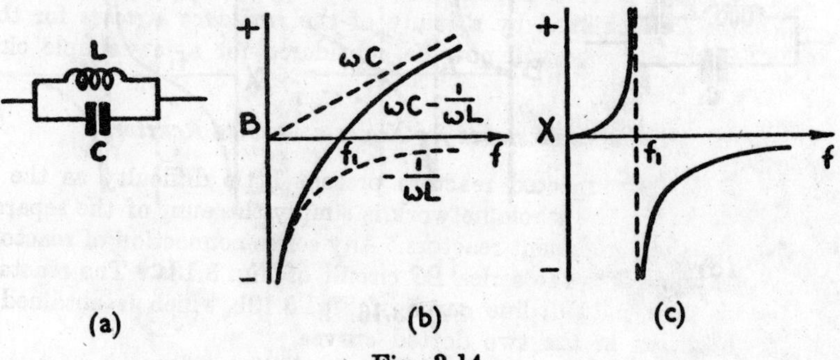

Fig. 3.14.

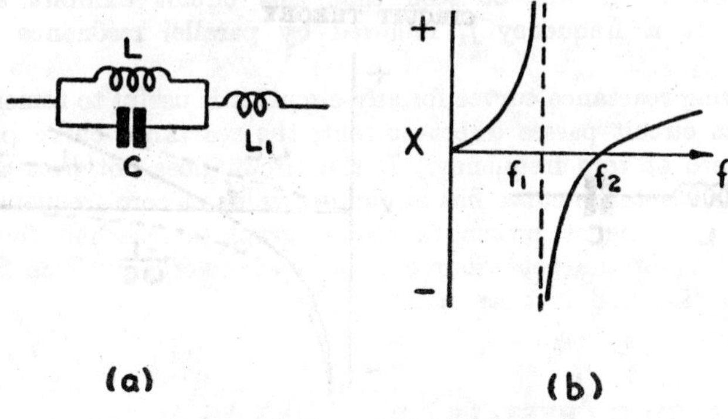

Fig. 3.15.

(c) *Reactance Sketches for Series-Parallel-Connected Reactors*

The circuit of Fig. 3.15a has a reactance curve as shown in Fig. 3.15b. This curve is obtained by the addition of the curve for L_1 to the curve for the parallel LC circuit (Fig. 3.14c).

The sketch shows that at low frequencies the circuit has an inductive reactance which increases in value up to the frequency f_1 at which the circuit is parallel resonant (or anti-resonant). At frequencies immediately above this value the circuit has a capacitance reactance which diminishes as the frequency increases, until the frequency f_2 is reached when series resonance occurs; at frequencies in excess of f_2 the circuit has an inductive reactance.

The circuit of Fig. 3.16a has a susceptance curve as indicated by the full line curve of Fig. 3.16b. This curve is obtained by the addition of the curve for the capacitor C_1 to the curve for the series combination of L and C.

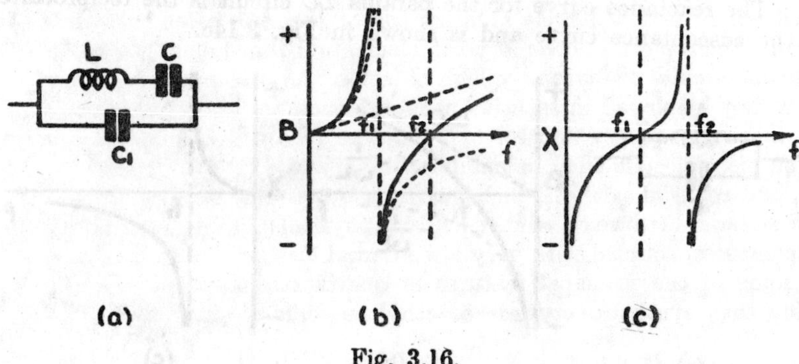

Fig. 3.16.

The reciprocal of the susceptance curve gives the reactance curve of Fig. 3.16c. It will be seen that this circuit exhibits series resonance at a frequency f_1 followed by parallel resonance at a frequency f_2.

In drawing reactance curves for any circuit it is useful to remember that if the circuit passes direct current, the reactance curve passes through zero at zero frequency. If the circuit does not pass direct current the reactance curve has an infinite value at zero frequency.

Reactance sketches present a useful graphical method for the determination of the behaviour of reactive networks such as filters which are discussed in chapter 5.

PIEZO-ELECTRIC CRYSTALS

It has been found that certain natural crystalline materials exhibit what is known as the *piezo-electric* effect. If a section is cut in a particular direction from a piezo-electric crystal and a metallic film applied to two opposite faces, so that the arrangement can function as a capacitor, the application of a potential difference to the electrodes produces a mechanical strain in the crystal material; if the polarity of the applied voltage is reversed the strain is also reversed. On the other hand the application of a suitable mechanical force releases an electric charge from the material.

If an element of piezo-electric material is subjected to an alternating voltage, alternating mechanical strains are produced in the element and cause it to execute forced vibrations. When the frequency of the applied alternating voltage is equal to the natural frequency of the element, mechanical resonance occurs and the amplitude of the vibration increases enormously. This relatively large amplitude of vibration produces at the electrodes a large alternating electric charge which reacts on the source of the applied voltage. The resonant frequency of the element is determined by its linear dimensions, density and the value of the elastic constant concerned in the particular mode of vibration, and is largely independent of the associated electrical circuit. Such piezo-electric crystal elements behave electrically as resonant circuits of extremely high Q-factor. As a consequence, they are widely employed in reactive networks such as filters (chapter 5) and in the frequency control of oscillators (chapter 11).

The piezo-electric effect is exhibited by crystals of quartz, tourmaline, and rochelle salt, of which quartz is by far the most commonly used material because of its chemical and physical stability at ordinary temperatures, coupled with very low internal losses. Before considering some of the principal features of quartz resonators it is worth noting that synthetic crystals of ethylene diamine tartrate (EDT) and dipotassium tartrate (DKT) are used as substitutes for quartz in highly selective networks.

Quartz Crystals

Quartz vibrators are obtained as sections cut from natural quartz crystals, which consist mainly of silicon dioxide but contain small amounts of impurities. In shape the crystal consists ideally, of a prism of hexagonal form, terminated at each end by hexagonal pyramids (Fig. 3.17). The crystal may assume one of two forms which are the mirror image of each other.

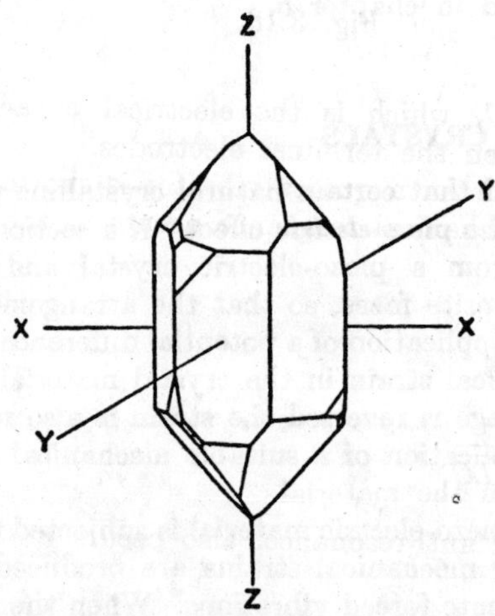

Fig. 3.17.

The electrical (X) and mechanical (Y) axes lie in planes perpendicular to the Z axis and occur alternately at 30° intervals. Each electrical axis is parallel to two crystal faces, while each mechanical axis is perpendicular to two crystal faces.

Equivalent Electrical Circuit of Quartz Vibrator

At frequencies close to resonance a quartz vibrator may be replaced, as far as the associated electrical circuits are concerned, by the equivalent electrical circuit of Fig. 3.18a. The inductance is the electrical equivalent of the vibrating mass† of the element, C is the electrical equivalent of the mechanical compliance, while R represents the electrical equivalent of mechanical friction. In addition to the electrical equivalents of the mechanical quantities there is a

† The electrical equivalents of mechanical quantities are discussed in Chapter 16.

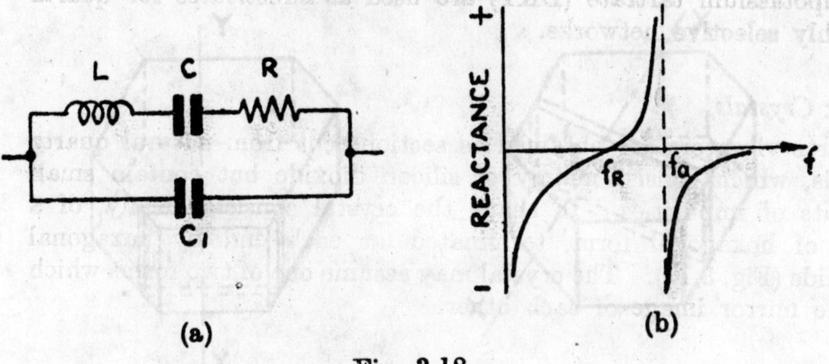

Fig. 3.18.

parallel capacitance C_1 which is the electrical capacitance of the quartz element between the terminal electrodes.

The reactance sketch for a quartz vibrator is shown in Fig. 3.18b (assuming $R=0$). Mechanical resonance occurs at the frequency f_R, at which

$$\omega_R L = \frac{1}{\omega_R C}$$

$$\text{i.e. } f_R = \frac{1}{2\pi\sqrt{LC}}$$

Parallel resonance, or anti-resonance, also occurs at a frequency f_a given by

$$f_a = \frac{1}{2\pi\sqrt{L\dfrac{CC_1}{C+C_1}}}$$

$$= f_R\sqrt{1+\frac{C}{C_1}}$$

It can be shown[3] that the ratio C_1/C normally has a value of at least 125, and so the anti-resonant frequency f_a lies very close to the resonant frequency.

Quartz Vibrator Cuts

(a) *X and Y Cuts.* The simplest types of cut to consider for quartz vibrators are the X and Y cuts shown in Fig. 3.19. The crystal is first cut by two planes normal to the Z axis. Plates cut from this slab in a direction normal to an X axis are then referred to as X plates. Y plates are cut normal to a Y axis.

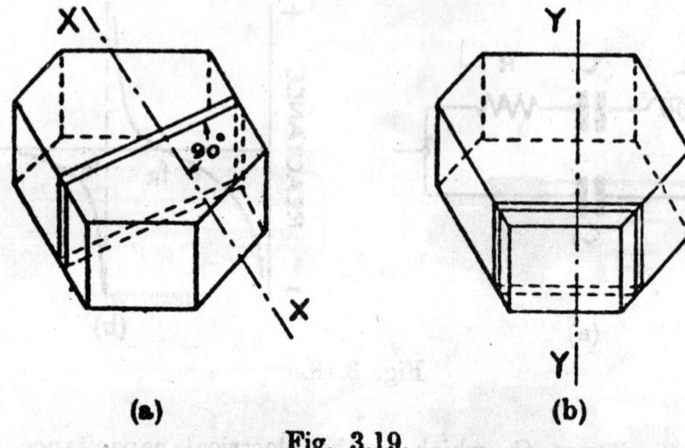

Fig. 3.19.

X cut plates have two principal modes of oscillation. The higher frequency vibration, given by the thickness mode, is determined by the thickness of the plate in the direction of the *X* axis. Longitudinal vibrations of the plate give a lower frequency oscillation which is dependent on the width of the element in the direction of the *Y* axis. The *Y* cut plate also exhibits thickness and longitudinal modes of oscillation.

Both *X* and *Y* cut vibrators suffer a defect referred to as " stepping ". This defect arises from the coupling of two modes of oscillation, as, for example, coupling between the fundamental thickness vibration and some harmonic of the width vibration. As a consequence subsidiary resonances appear, while the frequency/temperature characteristic exhibits discontinuities.

(b) *Inclined Angle Cuts.* *X* and *Y* cut plates have relatively large frequency/temperature coefficients, and this together with their liability to " stepping " has made them obsolescent for a number of applications. A large variety of cuts are now employed for particular purposes. Some of these elements are plates cut with the longest dimension parallel to the *X* axis but with their largest surface inclined at an acute angle to the *ZX* plane. Other elements are cut at an inclination to all three crystal axes.

Quartz Vibrator Mounting

In modern practice quartz vibrators have their two major surfaces coated with a fine metallic film. Connecting wires are then fused to this film at nodal points and the element is enclosed in an evacuated glass bulb in the same way as the electrode structure of a thermionic valve. Operation in a vacuum in this way has the advantage that air damping is removed and the *Q*-factor of the vibrator increased. Fig. 3.20 shows a selection of quartz crystal units.

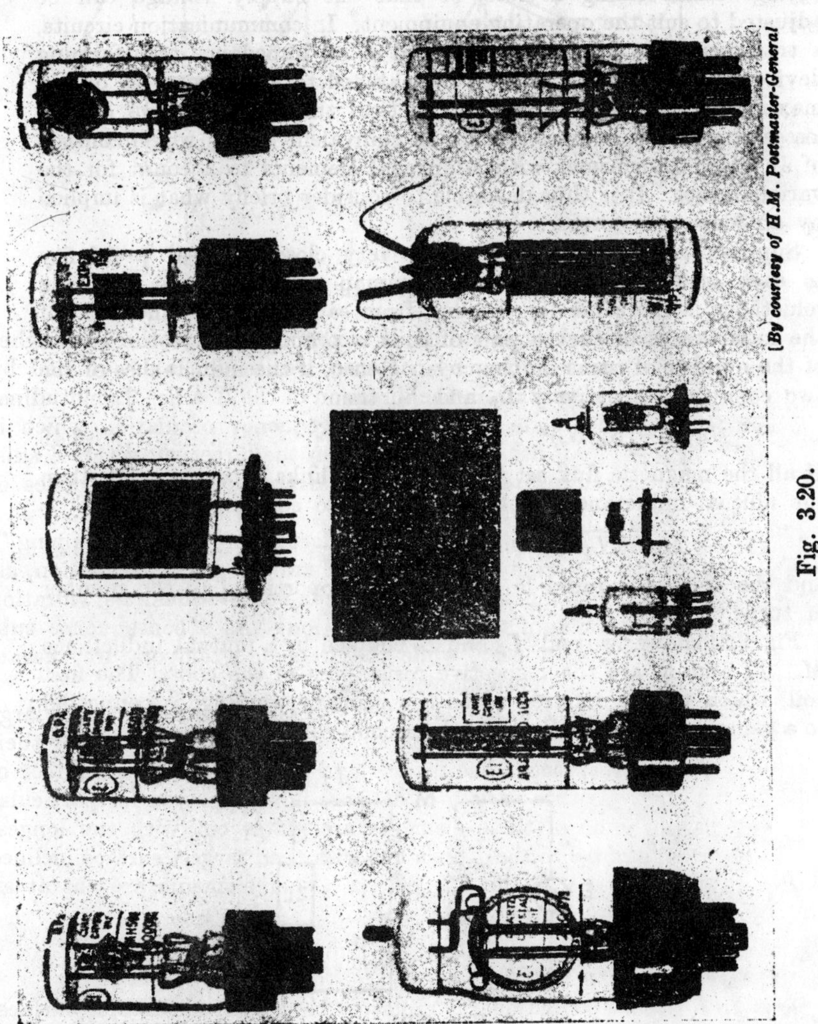

[By courtesy of H.M. Postmaster-General

Fig. 3.20.

THE IDEAL TRANSFORMER

In electrical power circuits, transformers are normally employed as voltage transforming devices, so that the supply voltage can be adjusted to suit the operating equipment. In communication circuits, a transformer is more often regarded as an impedance transforming device which enables a load to be matched to a generator to obtain maximum power in the load. Practical transformers have certain losses, and can be represented by an equivalent circuit which consists of an ideal transformer with additional elements to account for the various losses. It is thus desirable to consider briefly what is implied by an ideal transformer.

Suppose two coils are wound in very close physical proximity to each other, or wound on a common magnetic core, and the reluctance is the same for the flux from each coil, then the ratio of the inductances of such a pair of coils is proportional to the square of the number of turns on the coils. Hence, if the inductances of the two coils are respectively L_p and L_s, then

$$L_p/L_s = (N_p/N_s)^2 \qquad . \quad . \quad . \quad . \quad . \quad . \qquad 3.46$$

If all the magnetic flux set up by one coil links with the other then the mutual inductance M, between the two coils is given by,

$$M = \sqrt{L_p L_s} \qquad . \quad . \quad . \quad . \quad . \quad . \qquad 3.47$$

and the voltage induced in each coil is proportional to the number of turns.

Fig. 3.21 shows two coils L_p and L_s coupled by a mutual inductance M. R_p and R_s are the respective resistances of the coils. The first coil, which will be referred to as the primary winding, is connected to a generator of e.m.f. E, while the second coil, or secondary winding,

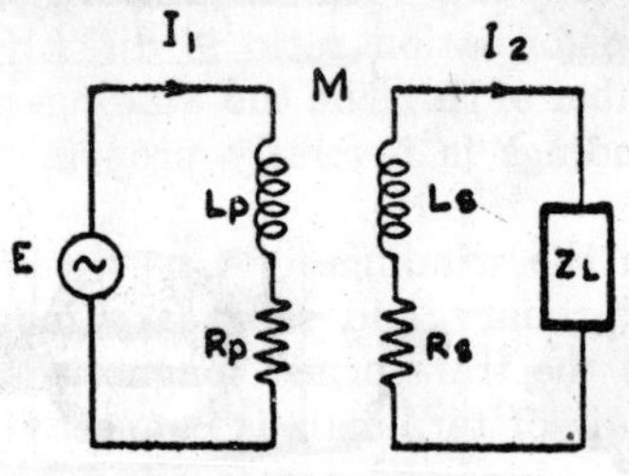

Fig. 3.21.

is connected to an impedance Z_l. The application of Kirchhoff's second law to the two meshes then gives,

$$E = (R_p + j\omega L_p)I_1 - j\omega M I_2$$

and $0=(R_s+j\omega L_s+Z_l)\ I_2-j\omega MI_1$

Substitution of the value of I_2, obtained from the second equation, into the first equation gives,

$$E=I_1[R_p+j\omega L_p+\omega^2M^2/(R_s+j\omega L_s+Z_l)]$$

and so the impedance, viewed at the primary terminals, is

$$\frac{E}{I_1}=R_p+j\omega L_p+\frac{\omega^2M^2}{R_s+j\omega L_s+Z_l} \quad . \quad . \quad . \quad 3.48a$$

If the resistance is small compared with the inductance of the winding so that it can be neglected, then the impedance at the primary terminals, i.e. the impedance viewed by the generator, is

$$Z=\frac{-\omega^2L_pL_s+j\omega L_pZ_l+\omega^2M^2}{j\omega L_s+Z_l}$$

Now $M=\sqrt{L_pL_s}$, and so $Z=\dfrac{j\omega L_pZ_l}{j\omega L_s+Z_l}=\dfrac{Z_l}{L_s/L_p+Z_l/j\omega L_p}$

If the value of the primary inductance L_p is very large, so that $j\omega L_p>>Z_l$, then

$$Z=(L_p/L_s)Z_l=(N_p/N_s)^2Z_l \quad . \quad . \quad . \quad 3.48b$$

If the above assumptions are valid, then the two coils will behave as an ideal transformer. Such a transformer thus has the following properties.

1. A coefficient of coupling equal to unity, i.e. $M=\sqrt{L_pL_s}$.
2. The voltage transformation ratio is directly proportional to the ratio of the number of turns on the windings; the ratio of the currents in the windings is inversely proportional to the turns ratio.
3. No resistance in the windings.
4. Infinitely large primary and secondary inductances. As a consequence of this the transformer magnetising current is zero, no matter which pair of terminals is connected to the supply.
5. An impedance Z_l connected across the secondary winding is equivalent to an impedance $(N_p/N_s)^2Z_l$ connected across the primary winding; when Z_l is infinite, i.e. if the terminals of the secondary winding are free, the impedance at the primary terminals is infinitely large. Also, an impedance Z_l connected across the primary terminals is equivalent to an impedance $(N_s/N_p)^2Z$ connected across the secondary terminals.

TRANSFORMER LOSSES

Any practical transformer gives rise to some loss. If it has a core of iron or some other magnetic material, then the losses may be classified as follows :—

(a) *Eddy Current Loss.* This arises from the circulation of eddy currents which are induced in the core material. These currents cause a power dissipation which appears as heat in the core.

(b) *Hysteresis Loss.* This arises from the cyclic magnetisation of the core, and causes a power loss in the core material.

(c) *Magnetising Current.* If the winding connected to the supply, normally called the primary winding, has not an infinite inductance there will be some reactive current flowing into the primary winding when the latter is connected to a generator, even though the secondary winding is open-circuited. This does not consume power but affects the transformer current ratio when a load is connected to the secondary winding.

(d) *Copper Loss.* The resistance of the windings gives rise to a power dissipation ; the total copper loss is normally divided fairly equally between the two windings.

(e) *Flux Leakage.* The flux produced by any one winding does not link entirely with the other winding, and a certain amount of leakage takes place. The flux produced by the primary which does not link with the secondary is called the *primary leakage flux ; secondary leakage flux* is that flux produced by the secondary which does not link with the primary. Under such conditions, the mutual inductance between the windings is related to the inductance of the windings by $M = k\sqrt{L_p L_s}$, where k is the *coefficient of coupling.* The effect of flux leakage is to cause a voltage drop in the transformer.

(f) *Self Capacitance of Windings.* Each winding of a transformer has a certain amount of self capacitance, due to the inter-turn and inter-layer capacitances. In addition, capacitance exists between every pair of windings. Self capacitance is not important at power frequencies, but may cause resonant effects at higher frequencies.

EQUIVALENT CIRCUITS FOR A TRANSFORMER

Iron-cored transformers may be represented by the equivalent circuit shown in Fig. 3.22.

In this diagram, the resistance in series with the primary winding represents the resistance of that winding, while the series inductance represents the effect of primary leakage flux. The capacitance C_p represents the capacitance associated with the primary winding. The primary inductance L_p is shown in parallel with a resistance R_0 which accounts for the power loss in the core material. The terminals

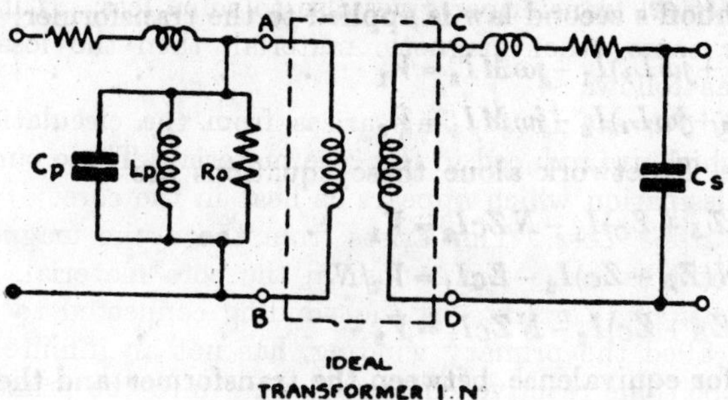

Fig. 3.22.

AB are connected to *CD* through an ideal transformer. This changes the voltage applied to it in the ratio of number of turns on the primary and secondary, so that

$$V_{CD} = NV_{AB}$$

The inductance in series with the secondary winding represents the effect of secondary leakage flux, and is connected in series with a resistance which is of course the resistance of the secondary winding. C_s is the capacitance associated with the secondary winding.

In communication work, transformers are often air-cored and have smaller coupling coefficients than power frequency transformers. It is then often more convenient to treat the transformer as a coupled circuit and use other variations of the equivalent circuit of Fig. 3.22. The actual transformer may be represented by a *T* section of impedances plus an ideal transformer, or a π section plus the ideal transformer.

If the *T* arrangement is considered, the transformer of Fig. 3.23a may be represented by the circuit of Fig. 3.23b.

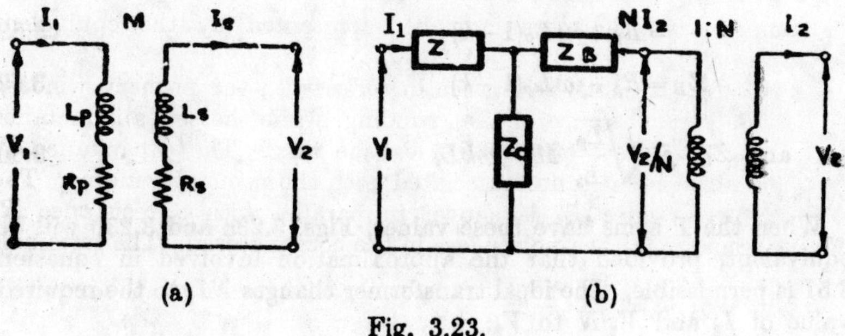

Fig. 3.23.

If Kirchhoff's second law is applied to the transformer,

$$(R_p + j\omega L_p)I_1 - j\omega M I_2 = V_1 \quad . \quad . \quad . \quad . \quad 3.49$$

and $(R_s + j\omega L_s)I_2 - j\omega M I_1 = V_2$ 3.50

For the T network alone these equations are

$$(Z_A + Z_C)I_1 - N Z_C I_2 = V_1 \quad . \quad . \quad . \quad . \quad . \quad 3.51$$

and $N(Z_B + Z_C)I_2 - Z_C I_1 = V_2/N$

$$\therefore N^2(Z_B + Z_C)I_2 - N Z_C I_1 = V_2 \quad . \quad . \quad . \quad . \quad . \quad . \quad 3.52$$

Hence for equivalence between the transformer and the T network

$$Z_A + Z_C = R_p + j\omega L_p$$

$$N^2(Z_B + Z_C) = R_s + j\omega L_s$$

$$Z_C = j\omega M/N$$

from which $Z_A = R_p + j\omega L_p - j\omega M/N$ 3.53

$$Z_B = (R_s + j\omega L_s)/N^2 - j\omega M/N \quad . \quad . \quad . \quad . \quad 3.54$$

$$Z_C = j\omega M/N \quad . \quad . \quad . \quad . \quad . \quad . \quad . \quad 3.55$$

If the T network is to be symmetrical so that $Z_A = Z_B$ then from equations 3.53 and 3.54

$$R_p + j\omega L_p - j\omega M/N = (R_s + j\omega L_s)/N^2 - j\omega M/N$$

$$\therefore N = \sqrt{\frac{R_s + j\omega L_s}{R_p + j\omega L_p}} \quad . \quad . \quad . \quad 3.56$$

If now $R_s << \omega L_s$ and $R_p << \omega L_p$ then $N = \sqrt{L_s/L_p}$. 3.57
and so under these conditions the values of the arms of the T network become

$$Z_A = R_p + j\omega\left(L_p - \sqrt{\frac{L_p}{L_s}} \cdot M\right)$$

$$= R_p + j\omega L_p\left(1 - \frac{M}{\sqrt{L_p L_s}}\right)$$

$$= R_p + j\omega L_p(1 - k) \quad . \quad . \quad . \quad . \quad . \quad . \quad 3.58$$

$$Z_B = R_p + j\omega L_p(1 - k) \quad . \quad . \quad . \quad . \quad . \quad 3.59$$

and $Z_C = j\omega\sqrt{\frac{L_p}{L_s}}\, M = j\omega k L_p$ 3.60

When the T arms have these values, Figs. 3.23a and 3.23b will be equivalent, provided that the approximation involved in equation 3.57 is permissible. The ideal transformer changes NI_2 to the required value of I_2 and V_2/N to V_2.

If a load of Z_L is applied to the secondary then Fig. 3.24 will be an equivalent circuit for the transformer.

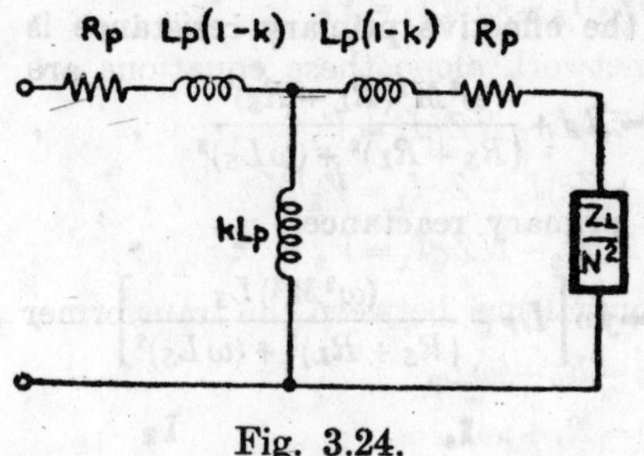

Fig. 3.24.

INDUCTIVELY-COUPLED CIRCUITS

In the foregoing discussion of the transformer, mention has been made of circuits coupled by mutual inductance. It is often convenient to treat transformers as such, especially when the coefficient of coupling is small.

If the general circuit of Fig. 3.21 is considered, the secondary load Z_L can have any value of impedance. As shown in equation 3.48a the equivalent primary impedance is

$$=Z_P+(\omega^2M^2)/Z_S \quad . \quad . \quad . \quad . \quad . \quad 3.61$$

where Z_S = total secondary impedance

and so the effect of the secondary circuit has been to increase the primary impedance by the quantity $(\omega^2M^2)/Z_S$ which is called the *coupled* impedance. Physically the primary induces a voltage in the secondary which then causes a current to flow in the secondary if closed, and this current in the secondary winding then induces an e.m.f. in the primary in opposition to the applied voltage. This effect is then dealt with by considering that the primary impedance has been increased by the presence of the coupled impedance.

All the conditions may be derived directly from equation 3.48a, but it is convenient for purposes of discussion to treat the various values of Z_L separately, and this will now be done.

Case I. Inductively-Coupled Circuits with a Resistive Load on the Secondary

The circuit is shown in Fig. 3.25 and the application of Kirchhoff's second law to the two circuits gives

$$E=(R_P+j\omega L_P)I_1-j\omega MI_2 \quad . \quad . \quad . \quad 3.62$$

$$0=(R_S+R_L+j\omega L_S)I_2-j\omega MI_1 \quad . \quad . \quad . \quad 3.63$$

from which the effective primary impedance is

$$= Z_P + \omega^2 M^2 / Z_S$$

as before, and the effective primary resistance is

$$= R_P + \frac{\omega^2 M^2 (R_L + R_S)}{(R_S + R_L)^2 + (\omega L_S)^2} \quad . \quad . \quad . \quad . \quad 3.64$$

The effective primary reactance

$$= j\omega \left[L_P - \frac{(\omega^2 M^2) L_S}{(R_S + R_L)^2 + (\omega L_S)^2} \right] \quad . \quad . \quad . \quad 3.65$$

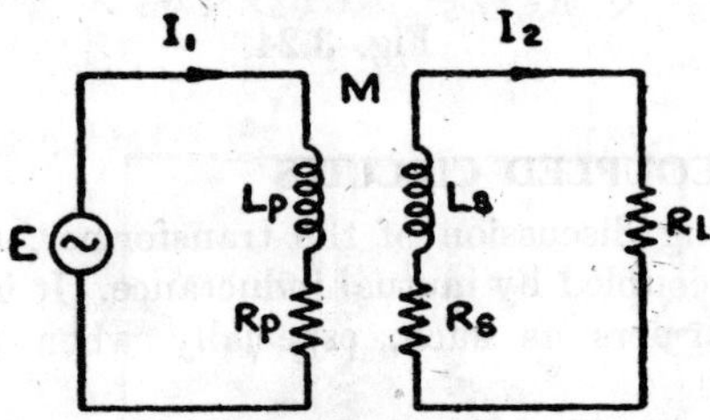

Fig. 3.25.

Equations 3.64 and 3.65 show that the presence of the load on the secondary has increased the effective primary resistance and decreased the effective primary reactance.

R_L may represent a load resistor. Alternatively, the secondary circuit may represent a metallic conductor adjacent to the primary coil carrying the current I_1, in which case I_2 is an eddy current flowing in a path of resistance $(R_L + R_S)$ and reactance $j\omega L_S$, coupled to the primary coil by a mutual inductance M.

Case II. Mutual Inductively-Coupled Circuits with a Resonant Secondary

The circuit in this case is shown in Fig. 3.26. The equation corresponding to 3.62 and 3.63 are thus,

$$E = (R_P + j\omega L_P) I_1 - j\omega M I_2 \quad . \quad . \quad . \quad . \quad 3.66$$

$$\text{and } 0 = \left[R_S + j\left(\omega L_S - \frac{1}{\omega C} \right) \right] I_2 - j\omega M I_1 \quad . \quad . \quad . \quad 3.67$$

From these equations the effective primary impedance is

$$R_P + j\omega L_P + (\omega^2 M^2) / Z_S \quad . \quad . \quad . \quad . \quad 3.68$$

where Z_S = total series impedance of the secondary.

In this case the coupled impedence has a maximum value of

$(\omega^2 M^2)/R_S$ at the resonant frequency of the secondary circuit when $\omega L_S = \dfrac{1}{\omega C}$. At frequencies on either side of this resonant point the value of the coupled impedance decreases and the curve of impedance against frequency, for the coupled impedance has the same general form as a parallel LCR circuit.

If, when $\omega L_S = \dfrac{1}{\omega C}$, and $(R_P + j\omega L_P) << \dfrac{\omega^2 M^2}{R_S}$

then the impedance viewed from the primary terminals

$$\simeq \frac{\omega^2 M^2}{R_S} = \frac{M^2}{L_S C R_S} = \left(\frac{L_S}{C R_S}\right)\frac{M^2}{L_S^2} \simeq \left(\frac{L_S}{C R_S}\right)\left(\frac{k N_P}{N_S}\right)^2 \quad . \quad . \quad 3.69$$

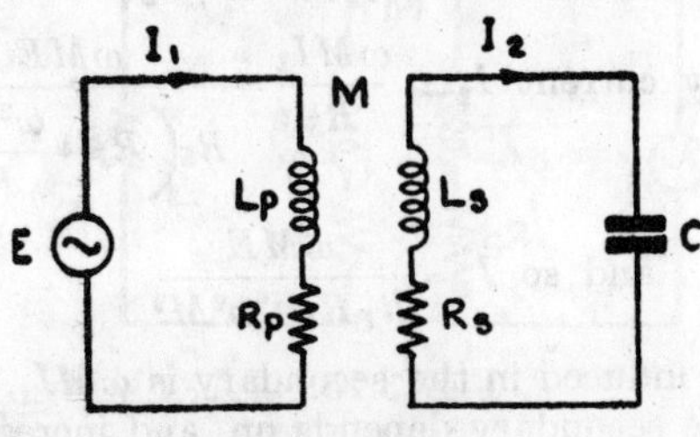

Fig. 3.26.

It will be seen from this result that a coil coupled to a tuned LCR circuit gives an impedance approximately equal to the dynamic impedance (L_S/CR_S) of the tuned circuit, multiplied by the square of the effective transformation ratio, where this is defined as

$$k^2\left(\frac{N_P}{N_S}\right)^2$$

Case III. Inductively-Coupled Circuits under Resonant Conditions

The circuit for this case is shown in Fig. 3.27.

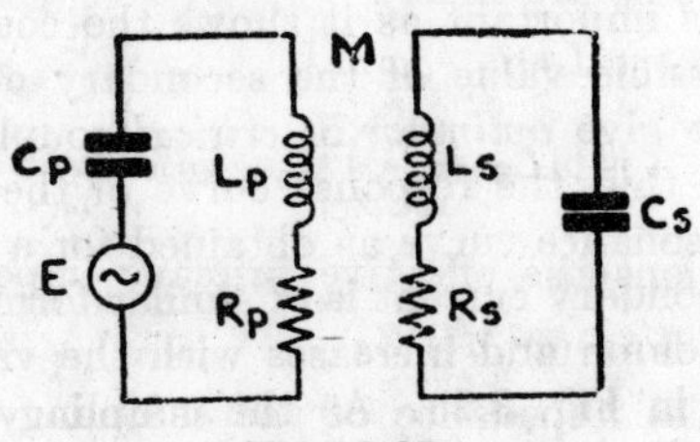

Fig. 3.27.

The effective primary impedance is given by

$$Z = R_P + j\left(\omega L_P - \frac{1}{\omega C_P}\right) + \frac{\omega^2 M^2}{R_S + j\left(\omega L_S - \frac{1}{\omega C_S}\right)} \qquad . \quad 3.70$$

If the coupling between the two circuits is small enough each can be considered independently and can be assumed to resonate as though the other circuit was absent. If this condition is assumed and the circuits tuned to a common angular frequency ω, so that

$$\omega L_P = \frac{1}{\omega C_P} \text{ and also } \omega L_S = \frac{1}{\omega C_S}$$

then the primary current $I_1 = \dfrac{E}{R_P + \omega^2 M^2 / R_S}$

The secondary current $I_2 \simeq \dfrac{\omega M I_1}{R_S} = \dfrac{\omega M E}{R_S\left(R_P + \dfrac{\omega^2 M^2}{R_S}\right)}$

$$\text{and so } I_2 = \frac{\omega M E}{R_P R_S + \omega^2 M^2} \qquad . \quad . \quad . \quad 3.71$$

As the voltage induced in the secondary is $\omega M I_1$, the amplitude of the current in the secondary depends on, and increases with increase in coupling up to a maximum value. This maximum value for I_2 can be found by differentiating equation **3.71** with respect to (ωM) and equating to zero.

$$\text{Thus } \frac{dI_2}{d(\omega M)} = \frac{(R_S R_P + \omega^2 M^2)E - \omega M E(2\omega M)}{(R_P R_S + \omega^2 M^2)^2}$$

and for a maximum

$$(R_P R_S + \omega^2 M^2)E = 2\omega^2 M^2 E$$

$$\text{or } \omega^2 M^2 = R_P R_S \qquad . \quad . \quad . \quad . \quad . \quad . \quad 3.72$$

The fact that this is a maximum may be checked by substituting values of $\omega^2 M^2$ slightly greater and slightly less than $R_P R_S$ in equation **3.71**. It will be found that $\omega M = \sqrt{R_P R_S}$ makes I_2 a maximum.

Equation **3.72** is important as it shows the coupling necessary for the maximum possible value of the secondary current. This value of $\omega^2 M^2$ is said to give *optimum* or *critical* coupling. For values of coupling less than this, the response curve of the primary current is a single peaked resonance curve as obtained for a single circuit. The response of the secondary current is of similar form and the amplitude of the peak depends on and increases with the value of ωM. These curves are shown in Fig. 3.28. As the coupling is increased to the optimum value each circuit begins to affect the other. The coupled

impedance reduces the peak in the primary current curve and small peaks occur on either side of the resonant frequency, while the secondary current increases and reaches its absolute maximum value. If the coupling is then increased further it will be found that the primary current decreases at the common resonant frequency but develops " humps " on either side. The secondary current also exhibits the same effect; the frequency interval between the humps increases with an increase in the coupling. This last condition is shown with the others in Fig. 3.28.

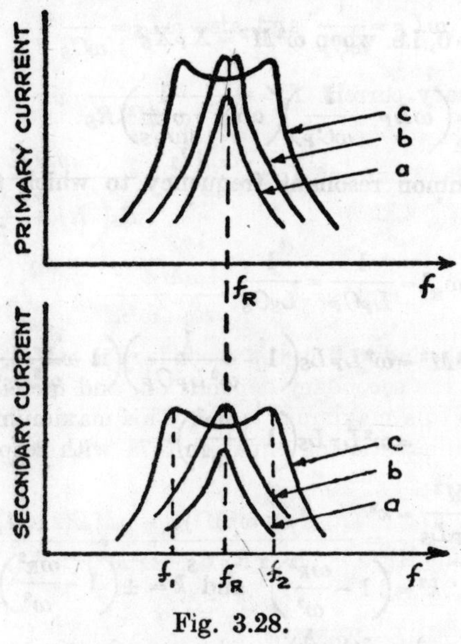

Fig. 3.28.

(a) Coupling < optimum
(b) Coupling = optimum
(c) Coupling > optimum

The frequencies at which the humps occur, namely of f_1 and f_2, can be found by considering the primary impedance. This will have a minimum value at frequencies which make the reactive component zero,

i.e. when $$X_P - \frac{\omega^2 M^2}{Z_S^2} X_S = 0 \qquad 3.73$$

At these frequencies the primary current will have a maximum value.

If now f_1 and f_2 are sufficiently remote from f_R the common resonant frequency, that

$$R_S << \left(\omega L_S - \frac{1}{\omega C_S}\right) \text{ and } R_P << \left(\omega L_P - \frac{1}{\omega C_P}\right)$$

$$\text{then } Z_S^2 = \left(\omega L_S - \frac{1}{\omega C_S}\right)^2$$

and the primary impedance will be zero when

$$X_P - \frac{\omega^2 M^2}{X_S} = 0, \text{ i.e. when } \omega^2 M^2 = X_P X_S$$

$$= \left(\omega L_P - \frac{1}{\omega C_P}\right)\left(\omega L_S - \frac{1}{\omega C_S}\right)$$

If f_R the common resonant frequency to which the circuits are tuned is

$$\frac{\omega_R}{2\pi} \text{ so that } \omega_R^2 = \frac{1}{L_P C_P} = \frac{1}{L_S C_S}$$

$$\text{then } \omega^2 M^2 = \omega^2 L_P L_S \left(1 - \frac{1}{\omega^2 L_P C_P}\right)\left(1 - \frac{1}{\omega^2 L_S C_S}\right)$$

$$= \omega^2 L_P L_S \left(1 - \frac{\omega_R^2}{\omega^2}\right)^2$$

$$\text{Now } \frac{M^2}{L_P L_S} = k^2$$

$$\therefore k^2 = \left(1 - \frac{\omega_R^2}{\omega^2}\right)^2 \text{ and } k = \pm\left(1 - \frac{\omega_R^2}{\omega^2}\right)$$

$$\therefore \omega_R^2 = \omega^2(1 \pm k)$$

$$\left.\begin{aligned} \text{from which } f_1 &= \frac{f_R}{\sqrt{1+k}} \\ \text{and } f_2 &= \frac{f_R}{\sqrt{1-k}} \end{aligned}\right\} \quad . \quad . \quad . \quad . \quad . \quad . \quad 3.74$$

A pair of overcoupled resonant circuits will thus act as a form of bandpass filter in as much as they will transmit frequencies between f_1 and f_2 with little loss (Fig. 3.28), whereas frequencies outside this range will be subject to attenuation.

The bandwidth between the peaks $\Delta f = f_2 - f_1$ may be determined from equation 3.74

$$\text{for } f_2^2 - f_1^2 = f_R^2\left(\frac{1}{1-k} - \frac{1}{1+k}\right) = f_R^2\left(\frac{2k}{1-k^2}\right)$$

then if $k<<1$

$$f_2^2 - f_1^2 \simeq 2kf_R^2$$

$$\text{or } (f_2+f_1)(f_2-f_1) \simeq 2kf_R^2$$

$$\text{or } 2f_R(f_2-f_1) \simeq 2kf_R^2$$

$$\therefore \Delta f = f_2 - f_1 \simeq kf_R \quad . \quad . \quad . \quad . \quad . \quad 3.75$$

If optimum coupling is considered $\omega^2 M^2 = R_P R_S$

$$\text{and } k^2 = \frac{M^2}{L_P L_S} = \frac{\omega^2 M^2}{\omega L_P \omega L_S}$$

$$\therefore k^2 = \frac{R_P R_S}{\omega L_P \omega L_S} = \frac{1}{Q_P Q_S}$$

$$\text{and so } k = \frac{1}{\sqrt{Q_P Q_S}} \quad . \quad . \quad . \quad . \quad . \quad 3.76$$

Under this condition the bandwidth Δf becomes

$$\Delta f \simeq \frac{f_R}{\sqrt{Q_P Q_S}}$$

$$\text{or } \frac{f_R}{\Delta f} \simeq \sqrt{Q_P Q_S} \quad . \quad . \quad . \quad . \quad . \quad 3.77$$

It must be remembered that Δf in this case is the bandwidth between the peaks.

COUPLED CIRCUITS NOT CONTAINING MUTUAL INDUCTANCE

Although mutual inductance is the most common method of circuit coupling, many other methods are employed for special purposes. Two general possibilities are shown in Fig. 3.29. Fig. 3.29a shows direct coupling in which the coupling impedance is connected in series between the two circuits, whilst a shunt coupling impedance arrangement is shown in 3.29b.

Occasionally more than one form of coupling is used between the two circuits which are then said to have " mixed coupling ".

IMPEDANCE MATCHING

It is usually desirable that a load should absorb the maximum power when connected to a generator, and it was shown in chapter 2 that this is so when the load impedance is the conjugate of the generator impedance, or in the special case when the generator and load impedance are resistances, these should be equal in value to each other. In considering the transformer it was seen that with certain reservations the transformer was able to change a load

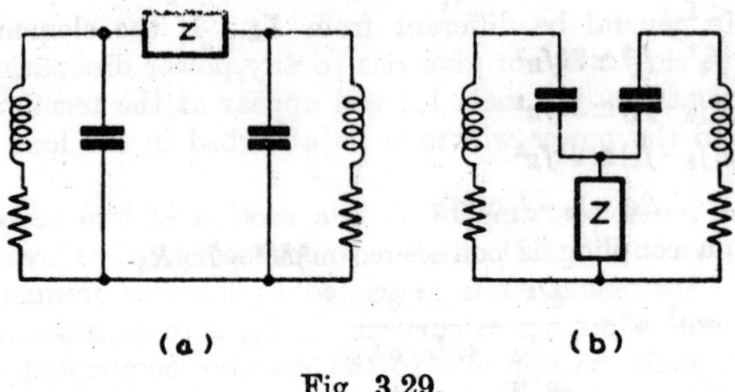

Fig. 3.29.

impedance Z_L to Z_L/N^2 where N is the transformation ratio, and so the transformer can act as a device which can change the magnitude but not the phase angle of a load impedance. The methods by which an impedance may be transformed to some other value are :—

1. By a transformer.
2. By a network of reactances.
3. By a network of resistances.
4. By a quarter wave transmission line of low loss.

The transformer has already been considered. It has the advantage over the other arrangements (except the third method) that it is possible to match the impedances over a fairly wide range of frequencies. Impedance matching by resistances involves a power loss. A transmission line a quarter of a wavelength long has an impedance transforming property under certain conditions, as discussed in chapter 19.

Impedance Transformation by a Network of Reactances

If an impedance Z_L is connected to a network of reactive elements as shown in Fig. 3.30 then the input impedance Z_{12} of the composite

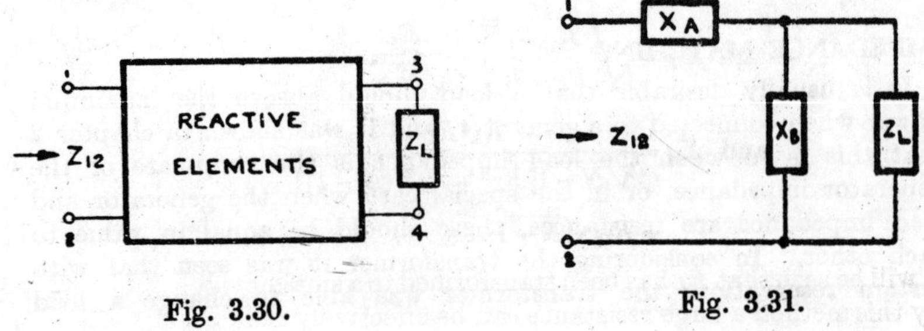

Fig. 3.30. Fig. 3.31.

network will in general be different from Z_L. If the elements are entirely reactive they will not give rise to any power dissipation and energy received at the terminals 1,2 will appear at the terminals 3,4 without loss and the power will then be absorbed in the load Z_L as required.

The simplest possible arrangement is a section of two reactances arranged as shown in Fig. 3.31. This is sometimes called a " reactance transformer ". Its operation is restricted to the one frequency at which the element values are calculated. If Z_{12} is to be resistive then the sign of X_A must be opposite to the reactive component of the parallel combination of X_B and Z_L.

Suppose Z_L is a resistance R_L which it is desired to convert to another value of resistance, R_{12} such that

$$\frac{R_L}{R_{12}}=N$$

where N is greater than unity.

In this case, for Z_{12} to be resistive, X_A and X_B must be reactances of opposite sign. As Z_L is also resistive it is immaterial whether X_A or X_B is positive, i.e. the arrangement will operate successfully in this case if X_A represents a capacitor and X_B a low loss coil, or alternatively X_A may represent the low loss coil and X_B the capacitor. Suppose X_A is negative and X_B is positive.

The impedance of X_B in parallel with R_L

$$=\frac{jX_BR_L}{R_L+jX_B}=\frac{R_LX_B^2+jR_L^2X_B}{R_L^2+X_B^2}$$

If as required, Z_{12} is to be resistive

$$\text{then } |X_A|=\left|\frac{R_L^2X_B}{R_L^2+X_B^2}\right|$$

$$Z_{12} \text{ then becomes } R_{12}=\frac{R_LX_B^2}{R_L^2+X_B^2} \qquad 3.78$$

$$\therefore R_{12}R_L^2+R_{12}X_B^2=R_LX_B^2$$

$$\text{and } X_B=\sqrt{\frac{R_{12}R_L^2}{R_L-R_{12}}}=\frac{R_L}{\sqrt{N-1}} \qquad 3.79$$

$$\text{and } X_A=\frac{R_L^2R_L}{\sqrt{N-1}[R_L^2+R_L^2/(N-1)]}$$

$$=R_{12}\sqrt{N-1} \qquad 3.80$$

It will be seen that R_L has been transformed to a smaller value R_{12}, and so by this method a large resistance can be effectively reduced in value.

Although a special case has been considered where Z_L and Z_{12} are both resistances the method can be applied for any angle of Z_L and Z_{12}.

The converse of the above procedure may be applied to change a small value of Z_L to a larger value. In this case the arrangement is that shown in Fig. 3.32.

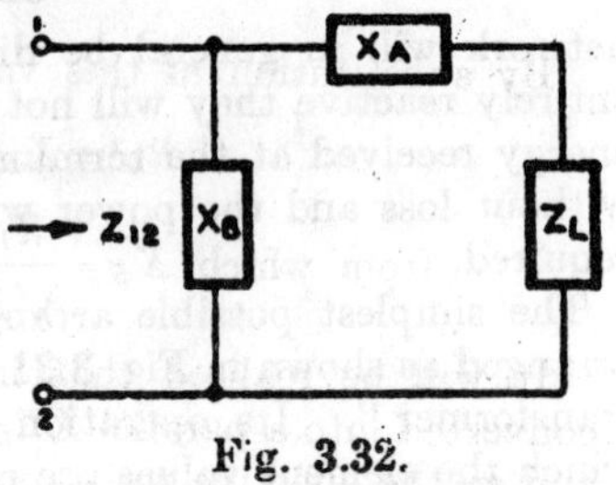

Fig. 3.32.

Suppose Z_L is again a resistance R_L, and that Z_{12} is required to be a resistance R_{12}, such that

$$\frac{R_{12}}{R_L} = M$$

where M is greater than unity. If X_A is arbitrarily made a positive reactance then X_B must be some value of negative reactance in order that Z_{12} shall be resistive.

$$\text{The impedance } Z_{12} = \frac{(R_L + jX_A)(-jX_B)}{R_L + j(X_A - X_B)}$$

$$= \frac{(X_A X_B - jR_L X_B)[R_L - j(X_A - X_B)]}{R_L^2 + (X_A - X_B)^2}$$

$$= \frac{R_L X_B^2 + j(X_A X_B^2 - X_A^2 X_B - R_L^2 X_B)}{R_L^2 + (X_A - X_B)^2}$$

If Z_{12} is to be non-reactive

$$X_A X_B^2 - X_A^2 X_B - R_L^2 X_B = 0$$

$$\text{and } R_L^2 = X_A X_B - X_A^2 \quad . \quad . \quad . \quad . \quad 3.81$$

Under this condition,

$$Z_{12} = R_{12} = \frac{R_L X_B^2}{R_L^2 + (X_A - X_B)^2} = \frac{R_L X_B}{X_B - X_A}$$

$$\text{and } \therefore R_{12} X_B - R_{12} X_A = R_L X_B$$

$$\therefore X_B = \left(\frac{R_{12}}{R_{12} - R_L}\right) X_A \quad . \quad . \quad . \quad . \quad 3.82$$

If this value for X_B is now substituted in equation 3.81

$$R_L^2 = X_A^2\left(\frac{R_{12}}{R_{12} - R_L} - 1\right)$$

$$\text{from which } X_A = \pm\sqrt{R_{12} R_L - R_L^2} = \pm R_L \sqrt{M - 1} \quad . \quad 3.83$$

By substitution of this value for X_A in equation 3.81

$$R_L^2 = X_B R_L \sqrt{M-1} - R_L^2(M-1)$$

$$\text{from which } X_B = \frac{R_L \cdot M}{\sqrt{M-1}} \quad . \quad . \quad . \quad . \quad 3.84$$

It will be realised that in this case the resistance R_L has been converted into a parallel LR_LC circuit operating at unity power factor and so the effective resistance of the circuit at the terminals 1,2, has been increased from R_L to $MR_L = R_{12}$. Z_L need not necessarily be a resistance, but if it is not, then the reactance of X_B must be of such a sign and magnitude as to neutralise the reactive component in the arm containing X_A and X_L, if Z_{12} is required to be resistive.

The arrangement shown in Figs. 3.31 and 3.32 can be used to match a load to a source at the particular frequency for which the values of the reactances X_A and X_B are calculated. At any other frequency the matching will not be correct. Such networks may however suffice in radio-frequency work where the range of operating frequencies is a small fraction of an octave.

In some applications the impedance matching network is also required to function as a filter, and for such cases T and π sections of reactances are used.

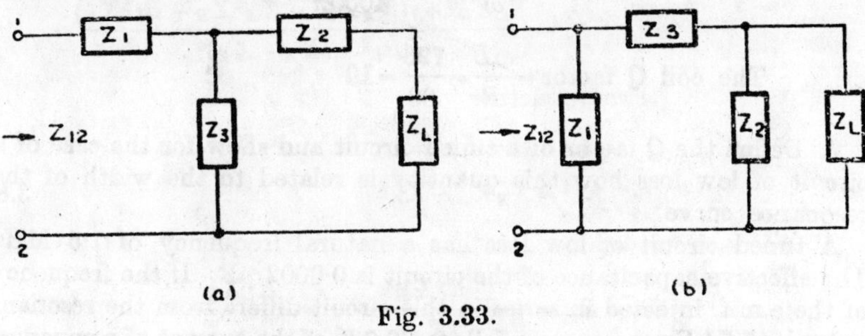

Fig. 3.33.

In either case the input impedance Z_{12} (Fig. 3.33) is clearly not necessarily Z_L, but varies with the values chosen for Z_1, Z_2 and Z_3. This will be dealt with at greater length when such structures are considered as filters.

WORKED EXAMPLES

1. What is meant by the Q of a coil ?

Give examples illustrating where you consider a coil with a high Q would be beneficial. A coil is placed in series with a standard capacitor of 0·1 μF and negligible power factor, and an oscillator is connected across the two. At resonance, as shown by a milliammeter in the circuit, the oscillator frequency is 2000 Hz and the milliammeter reads 10 mA. The voltage across the coil and condenser is measured by means of a valve voltmeter and is 0·8 V. Calculate the inductance of the coil and its Q.

I.E.E. Line Comm. April, 1948.

As will be seen in later chapters, coils of high Q factor are beneficial in valve oscillators, filters and various tuning circuits in some radio receivers and transmitters.

At resonance the circuit impedance

$$Z = R$$

The voltage measured by the valve voltmeter

$$= V = IZ = IR$$

$$\text{Hence } 0{\cdot}8 = 10^{-2}R \quad \therefore R = 80\ \Omega$$

$$\text{The coil reactance } \omega L = \frac{1}{\omega C} = \frac{10^6}{2\pi \times 2000 \times 0{\cdot}1} = 796\ \Omega$$

$$\text{The coil inductance} = \frac{796}{\omega}\text{ H} = \frac{796 \times 10^3}{4000\pi}\text{ mH} = 63{\cdot}5\text{ mH}$$

$$\text{The coil } Q \text{ factor} = \frac{\omega L}{R} = \frac{796}{80} = 10$$

2. Define the Q factor of a tuned circuit and show for the case of a circuit of low loss how this quantity is related to the width of the resonance curve.

A tuned circuit of low loss has a natural frequency of 1·5 MH[illegible] The effective capacitance of the circuit is 0·0002 μF. If the frequenc[illegible] of the e.m.f. injected in series in this circuit differs from the resonant value by 7·5 kHz the current falls to 70·7% of the current of resonance. Calculate the Q factor and the parallel resonant impedance of the circu[illegible].

I.E.E. Radio Comm. Oct. 1946.

The Q factor of a series tuned circuit is the Q factor of the coil if the condenser is assumed to be loss free.

In a low loss tuned circuit the resonant frequency is given by $f_R = \frac{1}{2\pi\sqrt{LC}}$ and the derivation of equation 3.21 shows that for the series tuned case $f_R/\Delta f = Q$, where Δf is the bandwidth between the half-power points. The same result is true for parallel circuits (equation 3.41).

The natural frequency of the circuit is 1·5 MHz. As the circuit is a low loss one the natural and resonant frequencies may be assumed to coincide, and so $f_R = 1{\cdot}5$ MHz

Also $f_R - f_1 =$ or $f_2 - f_R = 7{\cdot}5$ kHz. Hence $f_2 - f_1 = \Delta f = 15$ kHz

$$\text{Now} \frac{f_R}{\Delta f} = Q \quad \therefore \frac{1{\cdot}5 \times 10^6}{15 \times 10^3} = Q \text{ and so } Q = 100.$$

With a Q factor of this order the parallel resonant impedance can be taken as L/CR.

$$\text{Parallel resonant impedance} = \frac{L}{CR} = \frac{\omega_R L}{\omega_R CR} = Q \cdot \frac{1}{\omega_R C}$$

$$\text{Now } \frac{1}{\omega_R C} = \frac{10^6}{6{\cdot}28 \times 1{\cdot}5 \times 10^6 \times 0{\cdot}0002} = 532\ \Omega$$

Parallel resonant impedance $= 100 \times 532 = 53{,}200\ \Omega$

3. An oscillator has an output impedance of $600 + j50$ ohms. Calculate the turns-ratio of an ideal transformer necessary to match the oscillator to a load of $65 + j30$ ohms for maximum transference of power. Prove any formula used.

L.U. Ext. Telecomm. 1941.

The source and load in this case are impedances the angles of which are dissimilar. For this case maximum power is delivered to the load when the modulus of the load impedance is equal to the modulus of the source, i.e.

$$|Z_G| = |Z_L|$$

The method of impedance matching to be used is an ideal transformer and so a step down transformer of ratio

$$N = \sqrt{|Z_G| / |Z_L|}$$

should be used.

$$|Z_G| = \sqrt{(600)^2 + (50)^2} = 50\sqrt{145}$$

$$|Z_L| = \sqrt{(65)^2 + (30)^2} = 71{\cdot}6$$

Hence the required transformer ratio is

$$N = \sqrt{\frac{50\sqrt{145}}{71{\cdot}6}} = 2{\cdot}9$$

4. It was found that the output of a certain oscillator was 50V when on open circuit, but fell to 30V when a resistance of 1000 ohms was connected across its terminals. Find the internal impedance (which is known to be purely resistive) of the oscillator. The oscillator is now required to supply as much power as possible to a load having an admittance of $0{\cdot}1 + j0{\cdot}2$ mho. What should be the turns ratio of the transformer ? Explain your solution.

I.E.E. Radio Comm. Oct. 1949.

The information given about the oscillator output can be formulated as

$$E = 50 \text{———————} \text{(a)}$$

$$E - RI = 30 \text{———————} \text{(b)}$$

$$1000\ I = 30 \text{———————} \text{(c)}$$

if E is the oscillator open circuit voltage,

R „ „ internal resistance of the oscillator,

I „ „ current flowing when the output is loaded with 1000 Ω.

From equation (c) $I = {\cdot}03$

and equation (b) gives $50 - R({\cdot}03) = 30$

$$\therefore R = \mathbf{667}\ \Omega.$$

If the oscillator is to be transformer coupled to a load then the maximum power will be obtained in the load when its modulus is equal to the resistance of the oscillator (chapter 2, equation 2.25).

The modulus of the load impedance $|Z_L| = 1/|Y_L|$

$$\text{and so } |Z_L| = \frac{1}{\sqrt{(0{\cdot}1)^2 + (0{\cdot}2)^2}} = \frac{10}{\sqrt{5}}$$

Hence the turns-ratio of the transformer required will be

$$N = \sqrt{\frac{2000 \times \sqrt{5}}{3 \times 10}} = \mathbf{12{\cdot}2}$$

5. A coil of 100 μH inductance and a variable condenser form a parallel resonant circuit, across which a p.d. of 1000V at a frequency of $10^7/2\pi$ Hz is applied. Coupled to the coil is a second coil of 50 μH inductance, across which is a resistance of 500 ohms. The mutual inductance between the coils is 20 μH. Find the value of the capacitance which will make the current from the supply come into phase with the applied p.d. Find the value of this current and the power in the 500 ohm load. Losses in coils and condenser are negligible.

I.E.E. Radio Comm. Oct. 1949.

From the information given

$$\omega = 10^7$$
$$L_P = 10^{-4}$$
$$L_S = 5 \times 10^{-5} \qquad \omega L_S = 5 \times 10^2$$
$$M = 2 \times 10^{-5} \quad \omega^2 M^2 = 4 \times 10^4 \qquad R_L = 500$$

and $\dfrac{\omega^2 M^2}{R_L^2 + (\omega L_S)^2} = \dfrac{4 \times 10^4}{(500)^2 + (500)^2} = 8 \times 10^{-2}$

The effective primary resistance $= R_P + \dfrac{\omega^2 M^2 (R_L + R_S)}{(R_S + R_L)^2 + (\omega L_S)^2}$

If R_P and R_S are neglected this is then

$$= 0 + 8 \times 10^{-2} \times 500 = 40\ \Omega.$$

The effective primary reactance, neglecting R_S

$$= j\omega\left[L_P - \frac{\omega^2 M^2 L_S}{R_L^2 + (\omega L_S)^2}\right]$$
$$= j10^7[10^{-4} - 8 \times 10^{-2} \times 5 \times 10^{-5}] = j960.$$

If the condenser C is in parallel with the primary coil the parallel

$$\text{impedance} = \frac{(40 + j960)\dfrac{-j}{\omega C}}{40 + j\left(960 - \dfrac{1}{\omega C}\right)}$$

$$= \frac{\left(\dfrac{960}{\omega C} - \dfrac{j40}{\omega C}\right)\left[40 - j\left(960 - \dfrac{1}{\omega C}\right)\right]}{(40)^2 + \left(960 - \dfrac{1}{\omega C}\right)^2}$$

$$= \frac{\dfrac{40}{\omega^2 C^2} + j\left(\dfrac{960}{\omega^2 C^2} - \dfrac{(960)^2}{\omega C} - \dfrac{1600}{\omega C}\right)}{(40)^2 + \left(960 - \dfrac{1}{\omega C}\right)^2}$$

This will be non-reactive if $\dfrac{960}{\omega^2 C^2} - \dfrac{(960)^2}{\omega C} - \dfrac{1600}{\omega C} = 0$

i.e. if $\omega C \neq 0$

$$\frac{960}{\omega C} = (960)^2 + 1600$$

and $C = \dfrac{1}{10^7(960 + 1{\cdot}7)}$ F $= 104\ \mu\mu$F and so the value of parallel capacitance required to make the circuit operate at unity power factor is **104** μμF.

Under these conditions the circuit impedance viewed from the supply terminals

$$= L/CR$$

where $L = 960/\omega = 960 \times 10^{-7}$

$C = 104 \times 10^{-12}$ μμF

$R = 40\ \Omega$

$$\therefore \text{Circuit impedance} = \frac{960 \times 10^{-7} \times 10^{12}}{104 \times 40} = 23{,}100\ \Omega.$$

$$\text{The supply current is then } \frac{1000}{23{,}100} \times 10^3 \text{ mA.} = \mathbf{43{\cdot}3} \text{ mA.}$$

The current through the primary coil is given by $I = 1000/Z$ where Z is the effective coil impedance, $40 + j960$

$$\text{As } (40)^2 << (960)^2,\ Z = 960 \text{ and so } I = \frac{1000}{960} = 1{\cdot}04 \text{ A.}$$

$$\text{The voltage induced in the secondary circuit} = j\omega MI = 2 \times 10^2 \times 1{\cdot}04 = 208\text{V}$$

$$\text{The current in the secondary} = \frac{\omega MI}{\sqrt{R_L^2 + (\omega L_S)^2}} = \frac{208}{\sqrt{(500)^2 + (500)^2}}$$

$$\text{The power dissipated in } R_L = I_S^2 R_L = \frac{(208)^2 \times 500}{(500)^2 \times 2} = 43{\cdot}3 \text{ W.}$$

The power dissipated in the 500 Ω load is thus 43·3 W.

This could have been obtained directly from the supply current and voltage, as the circuit operates at unity power factor and R_L is considered to be the only power dissipating element.

6. Two identical tuned circuits of high Q value are inductively coupled. Show that each circuit exhibits two resonant frequencies, one above and one below the natural frequency of each circuit alone.

Calculate the resonant frequencies of two coupled circuits to which the following data apply :—

$$L_1 = L_2 = 500\ \mu\text{H};\ C_1 = C_2 = 200\ \mu\mu\text{F};\ M = 30\ \mu\text{H}.$$

L.U. Ext. Telecomm. **1945.**

In coupled circuits of high Q the two resonant frequencies are given by

$$f_1 = f_R\sqrt{1-k}$$
$$\text{and } f_2 = f_R\sqrt{1+k}$$
$$\text{where } f_R = \frac{1}{2\pi\sqrt{L_1C_1}}$$
$$\text{and } k = M/\sqrt{L_1L_2}$$
$$f_R = \frac{1}{2\pi\sqrt{\dfrac{500\times 200}{10^{18}}}} = \frac{10^9}{2\pi\times 316{\cdot}2} = 503 \text{ kHz}$$
$$\text{and } k = 0{\cdot}06$$

Hence the lower resonant frequency $= 503\sqrt{1-0{\cdot}06}$ kHz

$= 488$ kHz

The upper resonant frequency $= 495\sqrt{1+0{\cdot}06}$ kHz

$= 518$ kHz

References

[1] COURSEY, P. R.: "Fixed Resistors in Communication Equipment", *Proc. I.E.E.*, 96, Part III, p. 169 (1949).

[2] BOYLAND, H. J.: "Resonance in Series and Parallel Circuits", *Experimental Wireless and the Wireless Engineer*, p. 4, 675 (1927).

[3] VIGOUREUX, P., and BOOTH, C. F.: *Quartz Vibrators and their Applications* (H.M.S.O., 1950).

Reference for Further Reading

WELLARD, C. L.: *Resistance and Resistors* (McGraw Hill, 1960).
DUMMER, G. W.: *Fixed and Variable Capacitators* (McGraw Hill, 1960).
VIGOUREUX, P., and BOOTH, C. F.: *Quartz Vibrators and their Applications* (H.M.S.O., 1950).

EXAMPLES

1. Discuss very briefly the various types of resonance that may occur between a single coil and a condenser.

A coil of inductance 100 micro-henries and 60 Ω effective resistance is connected in parallel with a condenser of 100 $\mu\mu$F and the resonant circuit so formed is excited from an alternating current source. The frequency of this source is varied until the maximum impedance of the circuit is obtained.

Determine, as accurately as you can, the frequency of the generator when this occurs. Any formula you use must be proved.

I.E.E. Line Comm. April, 1950.

2. A parallel circuit, consisting of a loss free condenser of capacitance C shunted by a coil of resistance R and inductance L has three characteristic frequencies, viz.:

(1) frequency of damped oscillations when the circuit is "shock excited";

(2) frequency of forced oscillation at which the circuit impedance is purely resistive;

(3) frequency of forced oscillation at which the circuit impedance has a maximum value.

Derive an expression for any one of these frequencies, and show by what percentage it differs in the case of a circuit described by $C = 500\ \mu\mu\text{F}$, $R = 100\ \Omega$, $L = 2$ mH, from the resonant frequency of forced oscillation of the same components connected in series.

L.U. Ext. Telecomm. 1949.

3. Define the Q-factor of a tuned circuit. Determine after deriving the necessary expression, the Q-factor and parallel resonant impedance of a circuit tuned to a frequency of 1·5 MHz and having an effective capacitance of 0·00015 μF in which the current falls to 70·7% of its resonant value when the frequency of an e.m.f. of constant magnitude injected in series with the circuit deviates from the resonant frequency by 5 kHz.

L.U. Ext. Telecomm. 1947.

4. What is meant by the Q-factor of a tuned circuit? The tuning capacitance of a circuit of high Q consists of two condensers of capacitance C_1 and C_2 connected in series. The Q-factor of the circuit of a series resonant circuit is 150 at the resonant frequency of 10 MHz, the tuning capacitors being $C_1 = 0{\cdot}0002\ \mu$F and $C_2 = 0{\cdot}0001\ \mu$F. Determine approximately the impedance presented by the circuit as a parallel resonant circuit (a) across the coil, and (b) across the condenser C_2. Assume the condition of resonance to be that at which the circuit presents a purely resistive impedance.

I.E.E. Radio Comm. April, 1947.

5. An inductance L is connected in series with a capacitance C, each being shunted by a non-reactive resistance R. Show that there

is a particular value of R for which the impedance between the terminals of such a circuit would be equivalent at all frequencies to a fixed resistance. Describe briefly any applications of this principle.

L.U. Int. Telecomm. 1941.

6. Show that the two pure reactance networks given present identically equivalent impedances between terminals at all frequencies if the following conditions are satisfied:

$$C_A = \frac{C_2^2}{C_1 + C_2},\ C_B = \frac{C_1 C_2}{C_1 + C_2},\ L_A = L_1\left(1 + \frac{C_1}{C_2}\right)^2$$

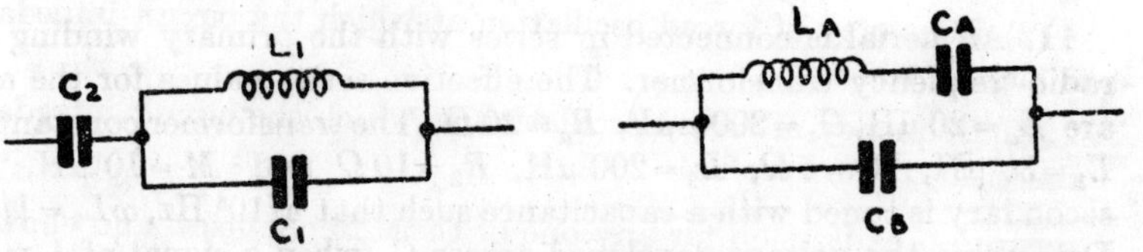

C2 L1 C1 LA CA CB

Fig. 3.34.

Sketch curves showing the variation of reactance with frequency and the position of the resonant frequencies.

L.U. Ext. Telecomm. 1947.

7. What are the special properties which render the piezo crystal useful as a resonator in electric circuits ? Explain how, for calculation purposes, the crystal may be replaced by a purely electrical circuit. Illustrate by an example the application of crystals in filter networks.

L.U. Ext. Telecomm. 1945.

8. Derive an expression for the " coupled impedance " transferred from one circuit to another by a mutual inductance coupling.

A primary coil of inductance 7 μH and resistance 8 Ω is coupled by a mutual inductance of 1·5 μH to a closed secondary circuit of inductance 2 μH and resistance 75 Ω. Evaluate the resistance and reactance coupled from the secondary circuit into the primary at a frequency of $50/2\pi$ MHz, and also the effective Q-factor of the primary coil at this frequency.

L.U. Ext. Telecomm. 1950.

9. Deduce an expression for the effective resistance and reactance of a circuit when a second closed circuit containing resistance and reactance is coupled to it by a mutual inductance.

A circuit consists of a transformer with tuned primary and untuned secondary. The inductance of each winding is 1 millihenry, and the mutual inductance between them is 0·4 millihenry. The primary winding was tuned to resonance at 470 kHz with the secondary circuit open. Calculate the change in tuning capacitance necessary to restore the resonance at 470 kHz when the secondary is closed. The resistance of the windings is negligible.

L.U. Int. Telecomm. 1950.

10. Show that a chain of tuned circuits coupled by mutual inductance has a band-pass characteristic.

L.U. Ext. Telecomm. 1939.

11. An aerial is connected in series with the primary winding of a radio-frequency transformer. The effective series values for the aerial are $L_a = 20$ μH, $C_a = 200$ μμF, $R_a = 20\ \Omega$. The transformer constants are $L_1 = 30$ μH, $R_1 = 5\ \Omega$, $L_2 = 200$ μH, $R_2 = 10\ \Omega$ and $M = 10$ μH. The secondary is tuned with a capacitance such that at 10^6 Hz, $\omega L_2 = 1/\omega C_2$. Determine the voltage developed across C_2 when a signal of 1 mV at 10^6Hz is induced in the aerial.

L.U. Int. Telecomm. 1955.

12. Define the term *Q*-factor as applied to a tuned circuit. The circuit diagram represents a resonant circuit of high *Q*-factor with the input tapped across a portion of the coil. Determine, on the assumption of zero loss, the ratio of the voltage, at resonance, across the condenser to the input voltage and apply this result to calculate approximately the impedance presented to the supply if the *Q*-factor of the circuit is 40. Assume the condition of resonance to be that at which the impedance between the terminals is purely resistive.

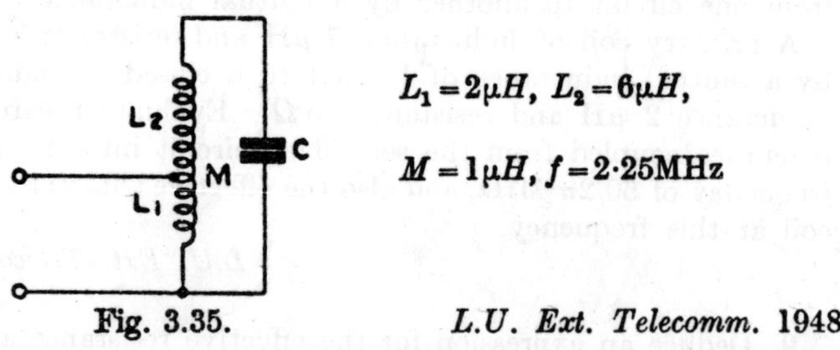

$L_1 = 2\mu H$, $L_2 = 6\mu H$,

$M = 1\mu H$, $f = 2{\cdot}25$MHz

Fig. 3.35.

L.U. Ext. Telecomm. 1948.

13. The diagram shows the circuit of a reactance transformer for coupling an aerial to a feeder. Determine the respective reactances of *L* and *C* to be used in a transformer to couple a feeder of 75 Ω

resistance and negligible reactance to an aerial. The impedance of the aerial may be considered as a capacitance of 150 Ω reactance in series with a resistance of 200 Ω.

L.U. Int. Telecomm. 1952.

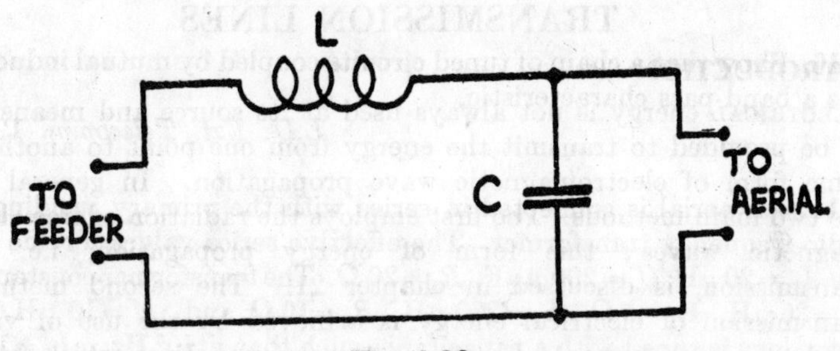

Fig. 3.36.

14. The inductance of a canned inductor is sometimes adjusted during manufacture by deforming the can with a suitable tool, the periphery of the can in the neighbourhood of the central section of the winding being reduced by a controllable amount. Explain the principle underlying the method.

A coil, of inductance 3 mH, supplied with current at 500 kHz is brought near to a short-circuited coil of inductance 1 mH and a Q-factor of 30 at this frequency. Calculate the change in effective inductance of the 3 mH coil if the coupling coefficient between the coils is 0.1.

L.U. Ext. Telecomm. 1955.

4

TRANSMISSION LINES

INTRODUCTION

ELECTRICAL energy is not always used at its source and means have to be provided to transmit the energy from one point to another by some form of electromagnetic wave propagation. In general there are two main methods. The first employs the radiation of free electromagnetic waves; this form of energy propagation, i.e. radio transmission, is discussed in chapter 21. The second method of transmission of electrical energy is achieved by the use of various conductor arrangements known as ***transmission lines*** which may be regarded as "guides" for the electromagnetic waves.

In a transmission line system, the presence of the conductors imposes boundary conditions on the electric and magnetic fields, and so limits the possible configuration of these fields. This in turn determines the particular mode (or modes) of propagation which is possible. It is important to realise that the propagation of energy is a consequence of the propagation of the electric and magnetic fields for which the conductors act as guides, while the amount of power transmitted depends on the intensities of the fields. The transmission lines considered in this chapter convey power by a mode known as the *principal mode* of propagation. This has the electric and magnetic fields disposed at right angles to the direction of propagation, which is along the length of the line; this mode of propagation is thus associated with a transverse electromagnetic (TEM) wave. Other modes are mentioned in chapter 19 which deals with high-frequency lines.

The operation of a transmission line may be analysed by the solution of Maxwell's field equations. Alternatively, the method of ordinary lumped circuit theory may be used. In the first method, the field intensities have to be determined in three dimensions, so that three space variables are involved in addition to the time variable; in the second method, the effects of the electric and magnetic fields are considered in terms of the circuit parameters, i.e. the resistance, inductance, conductance, and capacitance of the conductors, and the analysis is then reduced to the solution of a problem which involves only one space variable and a time variable.

For purposes of voltage and current calculations, it is preferable to treat a transmission line from the standpoint of circuit theory rather than field theory, and circuit theory analysis will be used in this chapter.

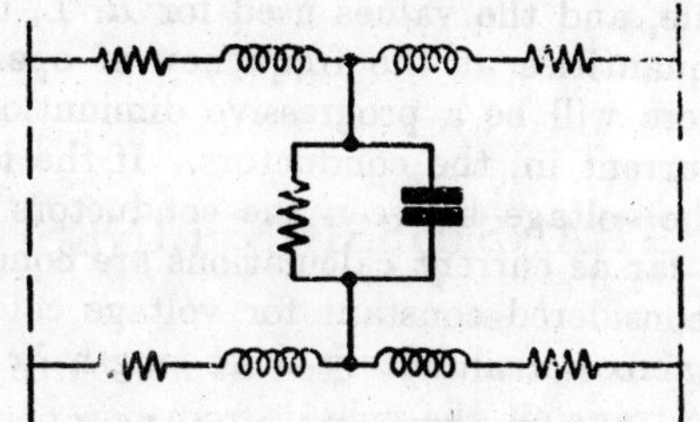

Fig. 4.1. Representation of a short section of transmission line.

The four parameters, or *primary constants*, of the line, namely resistance, inductance, conductance, and capacitance, are distributed along its length, and a short section of line may be represented as shown in Fig. 4.1.

BASIC LINE EQUATIONS

The simplest form of transmission line consists of a pair of parallel conducting wires spaced a small distance apart in air. The basic equations for the current and voltage at any point along the line may be deduced from a consideration of a short section of line, as indicated in Fig. 4.2.

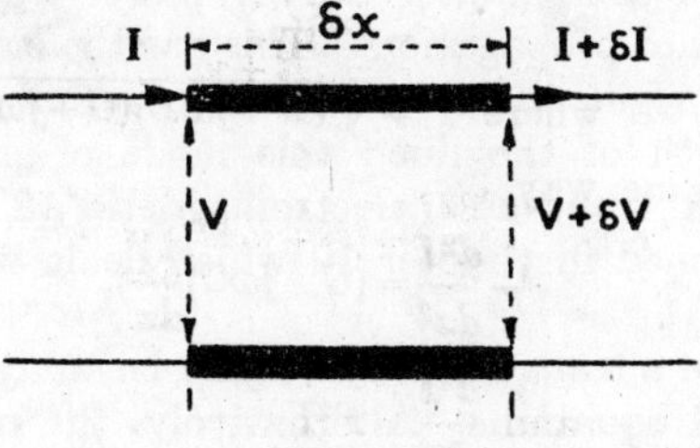

Fig. 4.2.

If the length of the short section of line is δx units, then the voltages at the input and output of the section are respectively

$$V, \text{ and } V + \delta V$$

The corresponding values of currents are,

$$I, \text{ and } I + \delta I$$

Suppose now that R and L represent respectively the loop resistance and loop inductance per unit length of line, and also that G and C represent the shunt conductance and capacitance respectively for unit length of the line. (The unit of length is usually taken as a kilometre or a mile, and the values used for R, L, G, and C are the values of these quantities at the frequency of operation.) In any section of line there will be a progressive diminution of the voltage across, and the current in, the conductors. If the length δx is very short, however, the voltage between the conductors can be assumed to be constant as far as current calculations are concerned, while the current may be considered constant for voltage calculations, and so the voltage drop across an infinitely short length δx is given by,

$$V-(V+\delta V)=R\delta xI+j\omega L\delta xI \qquad 4.1$$

$$\therefore -\frac{dV}{dx}=(R+j\omega L)I \qquad 4.2$$

The rate of decrease of current with distance due to the shunt admittance over the length δx is

$$I-(I+\delta I)=VG\delta x+Vj\omega C\delta x \qquad 4.3$$

$$\therefore \quad -\frac{dI}{dx}=(G+j\omega C)V \qquad 4.4$$

Differentiation of equation 4.2 with respect to x then gives

$$-\frac{d^2V}{dx^2}=(R+j\omega L)\frac{dI}{dx}$$

$$\text{or} \quad \frac{d^2V}{dx^2}=(R+j\omega L)(G+j\omega C)V$$

$$=P^2V \qquad 4.5$$

$$\text{where } P=\sqrt{(R+j\omega L)(G+j\omega C)} \qquad 4.6$$

In exactly the same way

$$-\frac{d^2I}{dx^2}=(G+j\omega C)\frac{dV}{dx}$$

$$\text{and} \quad \frac{d^2I}{dx^2}=P^2I \qquad 4.7$$

Equations 4.5 and 4.7 have solutions of the form

$$V=Ae^{-Px}+Be^{+Px} \qquad 4.8$$

$$\text{and } I=Ce^{-Px}+De^{+Px} \qquad 4.9$$

where the constants A, B, C and D are arbitrary, although there are relations between A and B and C and D. Their values depend on the conditions existing at the ends of the line.

If the expression for P is considered it will be seen to be a complex quantity, and if

$$P = \alpha + j\beta$$

then the equations for V and I become

$$V = Ae^{-\alpha x} \cdot e^{-j\beta x} + Be^{\alpha x} \cdot e^{j\beta x} \quad . \quad 4.10$$

$$\text{and } I = Ce^{-\alpha x} \cdot e^{-j\beta x} + De^{\alpha x} \cdot e^{j\beta x} \quad . \quad 4.11$$

The first term in these equations represents a voltage (or current) component of a travelling wave which decays exponentially in the positive direction for x (which is away from the source) and suffers a phase shift of β radians per unit length of line. The second term represents a wave ..milar to the first but travelling towards the source.

THE INFINITE LINE

An important te minal condition is covered by the case of a hypothetical line of infinite length. If such a line is considered, the current and voltage will diminish to zero at an infinite distance from any selected reference point. If at $x=0$ (when x is measured from the sending end)

$$V = V_S$$

then from equation 4.8

$$V_S = A + B$$

and from the same equation if $V \to 0$ as $x \to \infty$, then the constant must be zero,

$$\text{and } V = V_S e^{-Px} = V_S e^{-\alpha x} \cdot e^{-j\beta x} \quad . \quad . \quad . \quad . \quad 4.12$$

The corresponding expression for the current for this particular case may be obtained from equation 4.2.

$$\text{i.e. } -\frac{dV}{d} = (R + j\omega L)I$$

$$\therefore I = (PV_S e^{-Px})/(R + j\omega L) = \frac{V_S e^{-Px}}{\sqrt{\dfrac{R + j\omega L}{G + j\omega C}}}$$

$$= \frac{V_S}{Z_0} e^{-Px} = \frac{V_S}{Z_0} e^{-\alpha x} \cdot e^{-j\beta x} \quad . \quad 4.13$$

$$\text{where } Z_0 = \sqrt{\frac{P + j\omega L}{G + j\omega C}} \quad . \quad . \quad . \quad 4.14$$

Equation 4.13 shows that the current entering the infinite line at the sending-end is V_S/Z_0, and so Z_0 is the input impedance presented by the infinite line. This quantity is called the *characteristic impedance* of the line. In general, the characteristic impedance of any line may be defined as the impedance at the input terminals of an infinite length of the line concerned.

Equations 4.12 and 4.13 show that voltage and current phasors diminish in magnitude as x increases, and at a distance x from the

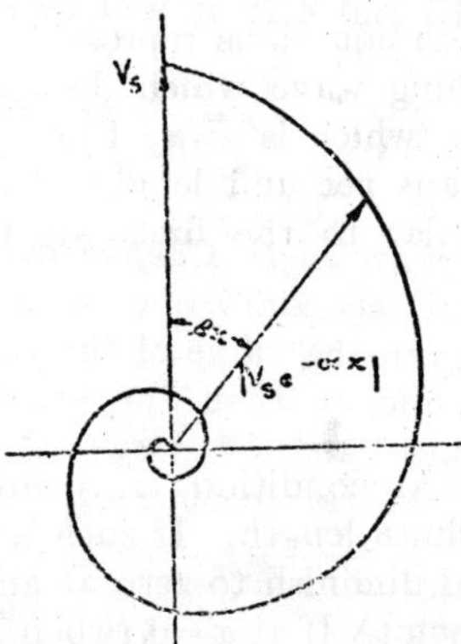

Fig. 4.3. Phasor (Vector) voltage for an infinite line.

sending-end the phasors have a magnitude which is $e^{-\alpha x}$ times that of V_S and I_S. Another effect is that the voltage and current phasors along the line are continuously retarded in phase with respect to the appropriate sending-end phasor. If phasors are drawn to represent the voltage and current at increasing distances from the sending-end, the tips of such phasors will then form a logarithmic spiral. Fig. 4.3 shows this for the voltage along the line.

Secondary Line Coefficients

The real part α of the propagation coefficient P determines the reduction in magnitude for the current or voltage along a line and is called the *attenuation coefficient*. β, the imaginary part of P, is called the *wavelength coefficient*. The special value of the distance x which makes $\beta x = 2\pi$ is called the *wavelength* (λ) of the propagation and so

$$\lambda = \frac{2\pi}{\beta} \qquad . \quad . \quad . \quad . \qquad 4.15$$

i.e. the wavelength is the distance in which the phase changes by 2π radians.

P, α, and β, together with the characteristic impedance Z_0, are known as the *secondary coefficients* of the line.

Phase Velocity

The velocity of a point which denotes the location in space of a definite phase of a periodic wave is the phase velocity V_P,

$$\text{and } V_P = \lambda f \quad . \quad . \quad . \quad . \qquad 4.16$$

because the wave moves with a velocity of one wavelength per cycle and hence λf wavelengths per second, if f is the frequency in hertz. From equations 4.15 and 4.16 it will be seen that

$$V_P = \frac{\omega}{\beta} \quad . \quad . \quad . \quad . \quad . \qquad 4.17$$

Attenuation and Wavelength Coefficients in terms of Primary Line Constants. The four secondary line coefficients all tend to vary with frequency. If, however, the value of the primary coefficients is known at a particular frequency then the secondary coefficients for that frequency can be calculated.

The complex propagation coefficient P is given in equation 4.6 as

$$P = \sqrt{(R + j\omega L)(G + j\omega C)} = \alpha + j\beta \quad . \quad . \quad . \qquad 4.18$$

$$\text{and so } \alpha^2 + 2j\alpha\beta - \beta^2 = RG - \omega^2 LC + j(\omega LG + \omega RC)$$

and by separation of the real and imaginary parts

$$\alpha^2 - \beta^2 = RG - \omega^2 LC \quad . \quad . \quad . \qquad 4.19$$

$$\text{and } 2\alpha\beta = \omega LG + \omega RC \quad . \quad . \quad . \qquad 4.20$$

If the phasor magnitudes of equation 4.18 are equated to each other,

$$\alpha^2 + \beta^2 = \sqrt{R^2 + \omega^2 L^2} \, . \, \sqrt{G^2 + \omega^2 C^2} \quad . \qquad 4.21$$

and the addition of equations 4.19 and 4.21 gives

$$\alpha = \sqrt{\tfrac{1}{2}[\sqrt{(R^2 + \omega^2 L^2)(G^2 + \omega^2 C^2)} + (RG - \omega^2 LC)]} \qquad 4.22$$

Subtraction of 4.19 from 4.21 gives

$$\beta = \sqrt{\tfrac{1}{2}[\sqrt{(R^2 + \omega^2 L^2)(G^2 + \omega^2 C^2)} - (RG - \omega^2 LC)]} \qquad 4.23$$

In practice approximations can be made to yield simplified expressions for all the secondary coefficients under particular conditions. In some paper-insulated telephone cables the conductors are relatively small in diameter and are close together. The inductance and leakage are small, and at audio frequencies, $R >> \omega L$ and $\omega C >> G$

$$\text{and so } P \simeq \sqrt{j\omega CR} = |\sqrt{\omega CR}| \underline{/45^\circ} \quad . \quad . \quad . \qquad 4.24$$

$$= \sqrt{\omega CR} \cos 45^\circ + j\sqrt{\omega CR} \sin 45^\circ$$

$$\text{hence } |\alpha| = |\beta| \simeq \sqrt{\frac{\omega CR}{2}} \quad . \quad . \quad . \quad . \qquad 4.25$$

For such a case the characteristic impedance Z_0 reduces to

$$Z_0 \simeq \sqrt{\frac{R}{\omega C}} \angle -45^\circ \quad . \quad . \quad . \quad . \quad . \quad 4.26$$

Lines used for the transmission of high frequencies, such as coaxial cables, have $\omega L >> R$ and $\omega C >> G$. With these assumptions other simple expressions can be obtained for P and Z_0. These are considered for high-frequency lines in chapter 19.

REFLECTION IN THE FINITE TERMINATED LINE

Practical transmission lines are not of infinite length and in addition are required to deliver power to a terminal load or to a second line. If the terminating impedance is equal to the characteristic impedance of the line then measurements made at the input to the line will be unable to distinguish between the terminated line and one of infinite length. The line is then said to be *correctly terminated*. This condition is important because it avoids power loss due to unwanted reflections in the line.

If the value of the terminal impedance is not Z_0, then a discontinuity exists at the end of the line, and a reflected wave, which travels back towards the sending-end, is set up.

This reflection (which occurs in all cases of travelling waves meeting a discontinuity of medium) appears because the ratio of the electric and magnetic fields on both sides of the terminal boundary must be the same under all conditions. This condition can only be complied with by the addition of a reflected wave to the incident wave. As far as incident energy is concerned, some is reflected back towards the source, and some is transmitted or absorbed in the load. The extreme cases of mis-termination occur when the line is either open- or short-circuited at its far end.

When the incident wave reaches the open-circuit at the end of the line the magnetic field collapses as the current must become zero. This collapsing of the magnetic field produces an electric field which is added to the existing electric field so that the voltage at the open-circuited end is increased. This extra voltage gives rise to a wave which travels back to the source; the reflected wave has the same magnitude and phase as the initial incident wave at the termination as there is nothing present at the open-circuited end to absorb energy. Voltage doubling is thus said to occur with open-circuited lines. The phase of the reflected current wave, however, is in opposition to that of the incident wave and the sum of the two is zero.

In the case of a line which is short-circuited at its far end the electric field collapses on the shorting conductor, the charge on the line is reversed at the short circuit and a reflected wave is again set up. At the front of the reflected wave current doubling is found, whilst the voltage is zero.

The above conditions can be put in general mathematical form as follows. Suppose a transmission line has a characteristic impedance Z_0 and is connected to a second line of characteristic impedance Z_R which is correctly terminated. Reflection will take place at the junction of the two lines

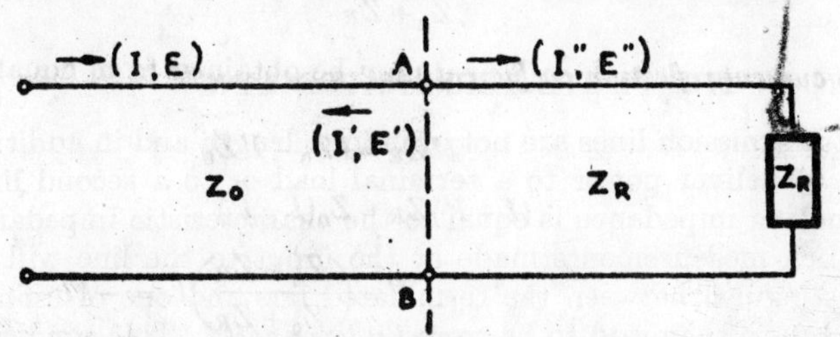

Fig. 4.4. Reflection at a discontinuity in a transmission line.

If, as shown in Fig. 4.4, E and I are the voltage and current associated with the incident wave, E' and I' apply to the reflected wave, and E'' and I'' apply to the transmitted wave, then,

$$I'' = I + I' \qquad 4.27$$

$$\text{and } E'' = E + E' \qquad 4.28$$

also $I = E/Z_0$, $I'' = E''/Z_R$, and $I' = -E'/Z_0$

(The reflected current is taken as negative, because a reflected voltage if considered positive, will circulate a current in the opposite direction to the current I.)

Equation 4.27 may be rewritten as

$$\frac{E''}{Z_R} = \frac{E - E'}{Z_0} \qquad 4.29$$

$$\therefore E'' Z_0 = (E - E') Z_R$$

$$\therefore (E + E') Z_0 = (E - E') Z_R$$

$$\therefore E' = \left(\frac{Z_R - Z_0}{Z_0 + Z_R}\right) E = kE \qquad 4.30$$

The *voltage reflection coefficient* k is thus

$$\frac{Z_R - Z_0}{Z_0 + Z_R}$$

From equation 4.28

$$E'' = E\left(1 + \frac{Z_R - Z_0}{Z_0 + Z_R}\right)$$

$$= \left(\frac{2Z_R}{Z_0 + Z_R}\right)E \quad . \quad . \quad 4.31$$

The *voltage transmission coefficient* is thus

$$\frac{2Z_R}{Z_0 + Z_R}$$

The *current reflection coefficient* may be obtained from equation 4.28, as

$$I''Z_R = IZ_0 - I'Z_0$$

$$\therefore (I + I')Z_R = Z_0(I - I')$$

$$\therefore I' = \left(\frac{Z_0 - Z_R}{Z_0 + Z_R}\right)I \; = -kI \qquad 4.32$$

The *current transmission coefficient* may then be shown to be

$$\frac{2Z_0}{Z_0 + Z_R}$$

GENERAL SOLUTION OF A LINE TERMINATED WITH ANY IMPEDANCE

The general line equations of 4.8 and 4.9 have been applied to the infinitely long line, and it has already been stated that the current and voltage relations obtained for that case also apply to a line which is terminated in its characteristic impedance. If the terminal

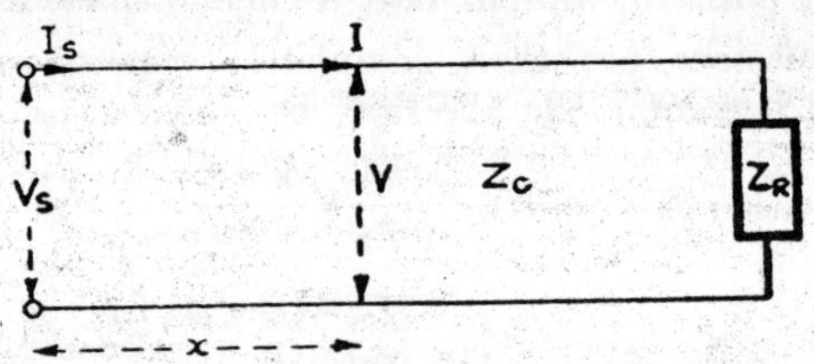

Fig. 4.5.

impedance at the end of the line is not equal to the Z_0 of the line then the general current and voltage equations must be used.

Equations 4.8 and 4.9 give

$$V = Ae^{-Px} + Be^{+Px} \text{ and } I = Ce^{-Px} + De^{+Px}$$

$$\text{also } -\frac{dV}{dx} = (R + j\omega L)I \qquad \text{(from equation 4.2)}$$

$$\therefore -[-PAe^{-Px} + PBe^{+Px}] = (R + j\omega L)I$$

$$\text{and so } I = \frac{P}{R + j\omega L}[Ae^{-Px} - Be^{+Px}] \quad . \quad 4.33$$

$$\text{Now } \cosh Px = (e^{Px} + e^{-Px})/2$$

$$\text{and } \sinh Px = (e^{Px} - e^{-Px})/2$$

and so the voltage equation may be rewritten as

$$V = A(\cosh Px - \sinh Px) + B(\cosh Px + \sinh Px)$$

$$= (A + B) \cosh Px - (A - B) \sinh Px \quad . \quad . \quad 4.34$$

and from equation 4.33

$$I = \frac{P}{R + j\omega L}[A(\cosh Px - \sinh Px) - B(\cosh Px + \sinh Px)]$$

$$= \frac{1}{Z_0}[(A - B) \cosh Px - (A + B) \sinh Px] \quad . \quad . \quad . \quad 4.35$$

Now when $x = 0$, $\sinh Px = 0$ and $\cosh Px = 1$

also when $x = 0$, $V = V_S$ and $I = I_S$

$$\therefore V_S = A + B \text{ and } I_S = (A - B)/Z_0$$

If these substitutions are made, the equations for voltage and current then become

$$V = V_S \cosh Px - I_S Z_0 \sinh Px \quad . \quad . \quad . \quad 4.36$$

$$\text{and } I = I_S \cosh Px - (V_S/Z_0) \sinh Px \quad . \quad . \quad . \quad 4.37$$

These equations are then completely general solutions for the voltage and current along the line, before any boundary conditions are applied. They can be utilised to determine the input impedance for a line with any termination.

THE INPUT IMPEDANCE OF A LINE TERMINATED WITH ANY IMPEDANCE Z_R

The voltage across terminal load $Z_R = V_R = I_R Z_R$

$$\therefore I_R = V_R / Z_R \quad . \quad . \quad . \quad . \quad . \quad 4.38$$

If the line has a propagation coefficient P and is of length l, then

$$V_R = V_S \cosh Pl - I_S Z_0 \sinh Pl \quad . \quad . \quad . \quad 4.39$$

$$\text{and } I_R = I_S \cosh Pl - (V_S/Z_0) \sinh Pl \quad . \quad . \quad . \quad 4.40$$

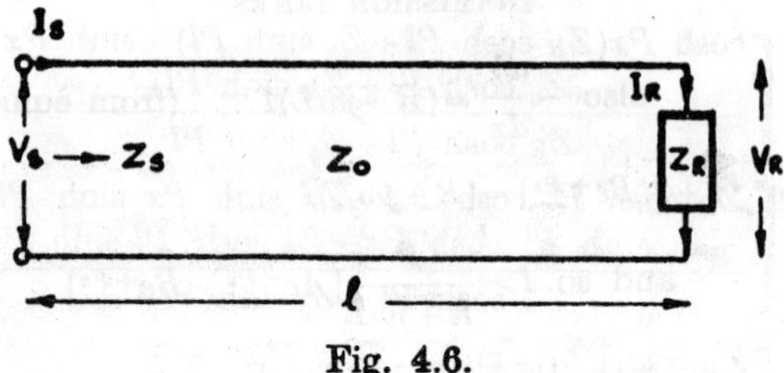

Fig. 4.6.

By substitution of these values for V_R and I_R in equation 4.38

$$\frac{V_S}{Z_R}\cosh Pl-\frac{I_S Z_0}{Z_R}\sinh Pl=I_S\cosh Pl-(V_S/Z_0)\sinh Pl$$

$$\therefore I_S(Z_0 Z_R\cosh Pl+Z_0^2\sinh Pl)=V_S\,(Z_0\cosh Pl+Z_R\sinh Pl)$$

$$\therefore I_S=\frac{V_S\,(Z_0\cosh Pl+Z_R\sinh Pl)}{Z_0\,(Z_R\cosh Pl+Z_0\sinh Pl)}$$

Now the sending-end impedance as viewed by the generator is

$$Z_S=V_S/I_S$$

and so the sending-end impedance

$$Z_S=Z_0\left(\frac{Z_R\cosh Pl+Z_0\sinh Pl}{Z_0\cosh Pl+Z_R\sinh Pl}\right)\quad . \quad . \quad . \quad 4.41$$

The result is important because it is completely general and applies to all uniform lines and terminations. In special cases it can be simplified. It should be noted that if $Z_R=Z_0$ then Z_S reduces to Z_0 as would be expected.

VOLTAGE AND CURRENT AT ANY POINT IN A LINE

The general solutions to the line equations have already been given as

$$V=V_S\cosh Px-I_S Z_0\sinh Px$$

$$\text{and } I=I_S\cosh Px-(V_S/Z_0)\sinh Px.$$

The disadvantage of such forms is that they involve I_S, the current at the sending end. This cannot be determined unless Z_S, the input impedance of the line, is known. This disadvantage can be removed by replacing I_S by V_S/Z_S and making use of the expression for Z_S.

The voltage equation for a line of length l, when terminated by an impedance Z_R, is then

$$V=V_S\cosh Px-Z_0\sinh Px\left\{\frac{V_S}{Z_0}\left[\frac{Z_0\cosh Pl+Z_R\sinh Pl}{Z_R\cosh Pl+Z_0\sinh Pl}\right]\right\}$$

$$= V_S \left[\frac{\cosh Px(Z_R \cosh Pl + Z_0 \sinh Pl) - \sinh Px\,(Z_0 \cosh Pl + Z_R \sinh Pl)}{Z_R \cosh Pl + Z_0 \sinh Pl} \right]$$

$$= V_S \left[\frac{Z_R \cosh Pl \cosh Px - Z_R \sinh Px \sinh Pl + Z_0 \sinh Pl \cosh Px - Z_0 \cosh Pl \sinh Px}{Z_R \cosh Pl + Z_0 \sinh Pl} \right]$$

$$= V_S \left[\frac{Z_R \cosh P(l-x) + Z_0 \sinh P(l-x)}{Z_R \cosh Pl + Z_0 \sinh Pl} \right] \quad . \quad . \quad . \quad 4.42$$

In the same way the current equation becomes

$$I = \frac{V_S}{Z_0} \left[\frac{Z_0 \cosh P(l-x) + Z_R \sinh P(l-x)}{Z_R \cosh Pl + Z_0 \sinh Pl} \right] \quad . \quad . \quad . \quad 4.43$$

These equations now give the voltage and current at any distance x measured from the sending end in a line of length l.

Open-Circuited Line

If a transmission line is open-circuited at its far end, the input impedance can be obtained from the general expression for Z_S in equation 4.41. If this is divided throughout by Z_R the value of Z_S is then given by

$$Z_S = Z_0 \left\{ \frac{\cosh Pl + (Z_0/Z_R) \sinh Pl}{(Z_0/Z_R) \cosh Pl + \sinh Pl} \right\}$$

then if Z_R is infinite, as in an open circuit, the terms containing Z_0/Z_R can be neglected,

$$\text{and } Z_S = Z_{0/c} = Z_0 \coth Pl \quad . \quad . \quad . \quad . \quad . \quad 4.44$$

If the line is very long, or the value of P is relatively large as in a line with high losses, so that Pl is large, then $\coth Pl \to 1$ and $Z_{0/c} = Z_0$.

The voltage and current along the open-circuited line may be obtained from equations 4.42 and 4.43 as,

$$V = \frac{V_S \cosh P(l-x)}{\cosh Pl} \quad . \quad . \quad . \quad . \quad . \quad 4.45$$

$$\text{and } I = \frac{V_S \sinh P(l-x)}{Z_0 \cosh Pl} \quad . \quad . \quad . \quad . \quad . \quad 4.46$$

Short-Circuited Line

The input impedance of a line in which $Z_R = 0$ is obtained by substitution of this value in the general expression of 4.41 and so,

$$Z_{S/C} = Z_0 \tanh Pl \quad . \quad . \quad . \quad . \quad . \quad . \quad 4.47$$

For a long, or high-loss line this also approaches the value Z_0. The voltage and current along such a line are given by putting $Z_R = 0$ in equations 4.42 and 4.43,

$$\text{i.e. } V = \frac{V_S \sinh P(l-x)}{\sinh Pl} \qquad 4.48$$

$$\text{and } I = \frac{V_S \cosh P(l-x)}{Z_0 \sinh Pl} \qquad 4.49$$

EQUIVALENT NETWORKS FOR THE TRANSMISSION LINE

Equivalent T Circuit

It is sometimes convenient to replace a length of transmission line by an equivalent circuit, such as a T section of impedances. Such an arrangement will only represent the line exactly at the one frequency at which the impedance values of the T section are calculated.

Suppose the T section in Fig. 4.7 is to be an equivalent for a line of length l and propagation coefficient P.

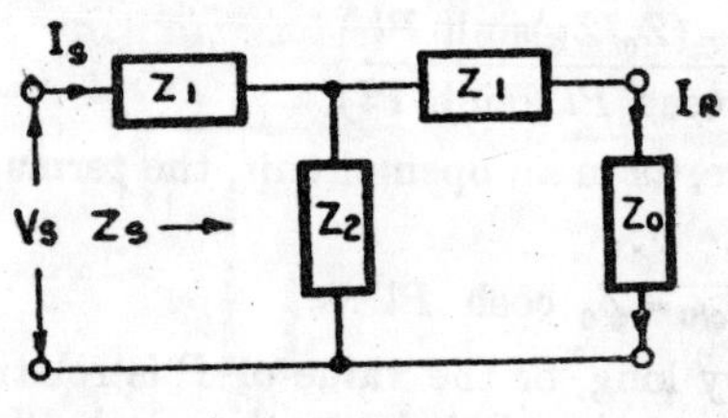

Fig. 4.7.

From Fig. 4.7

$$Z_S = Z_1 + \frac{Z_2(Z_1 + Z_0)}{Z_1 + Z_2 + Z_0}$$

If the T section is to be an equivalent to the line then Z_S must equal Z_0,

$$\text{and so } Z_0 = Z_1 + \frac{Z_2(Z_1 + Z_0)}{Z_1 + Z_2 + Z_0} \qquad 4.50$$

$$\text{but } I_R = \left(\frac{Z_2}{Z_1 + Z_2 + Z_0}\right) I_S$$

$$\text{and for the line } \frac{I_R}{I_S} = e^{-Pl} \quad \therefore \frac{Z_2}{Z_1 + Z_2 + Z_0} = e^{-Pl} \qquad 4.51$$

Substitution in equation 4.50 gives

$$Z_0 = Z_1 + e^{-Pl}(Z_1 + Z_0) \quad . \quad . \quad . \quad . \quad 4.52$$

$$\therefore Z_0(1 - e^{-Pl}) = Z_1(1 + e^{-Pl})$$

$$\therefore Z_1 = Z_0\left(\frac{1 - e^{-Pl}}{1 + e^{-Pl}}\right)$$

$$= Z_0\left(\frac{e^{\frac{Pl}{2}} - e^{-\frac{Pl}{2}}}{e^{\frac{Pl}{2}} + e^{-\frac{Pl}{2}}}\right) = Z_0 \tanh \frac{Pl}{2} \quad . \quad . \quad 4.53$$

Also equations 4.51 and 4.52 give

$$Z_0 = Z_0\left(\frac{1 - e^{-Pl}}{1 + e^{-Pl}}\right) + Z_2(1 - e^{-Pl})$$

$$\therefore Z_0\left(1 - \frac{1 - e^{-Pl}}{1 + e^{-Pl}}\right) = Z_2(1 - e^{-Pl})$$

$$\therefore Z_2 = Z_0\left(\frac{2e^{-Pl}}{1 - e^{-2Pl}}\right) = \frac{Z_0}{\sinh Pl} \quad . \quad . \quad . \quad 4.54$$

The equivalent T section for the line closed in its characteristic impedance Z_0 is then as shown in Fig. 4.8a.

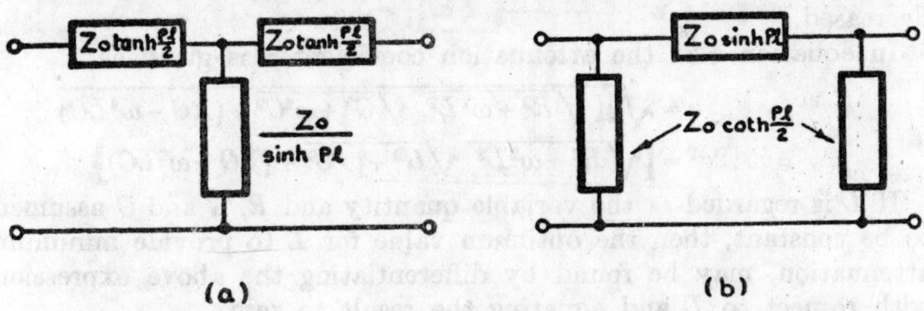

Fig. 4.8. Equivalent T and π sections for a transmission line.

By following a similar process it is possible to show that the equivalent π section for such a line is that shown in Fig. 4.8b.

The networks shown in Fig. 4.8 are exact equivalents for the transmission line. Approximate representations are possible, such as the nominal T and nominal π sections shown in Fig. 4.9.

In the nominal T and π circuits shown the values of R, L, G and C are the total quantities involved for the line considered. If the length of the line is short and l is so small that

$$\sinh Pl \rightarrow Pl$$
$$\text{and } \tanh Pl \rightarrow Pl$$

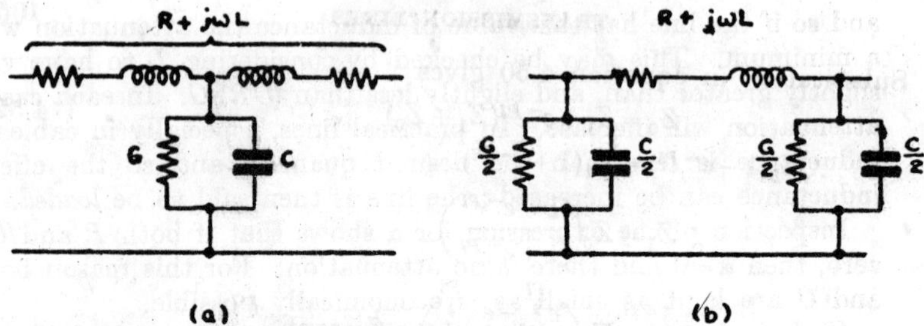

Fig. 4.9. Nominal T and π circuits for a transmission line.

then the impedances in the equivalent circuit reduce to those of the nominal circuits.

DISTORTIONLESS LINE

Reference to the expression for the attenuation and wavelength coefficients (equations 4.22 & 4.23) shows that these quantities are functions of frequency, hence if the voltage applied to the line at the sending-end has several components of frequency, i.e. if the voltage is complex, the various components are attenuated unequally, and travel with different phase velocities. The voltage at the receiving-end then differs from the applied voltage, and the line is said to produce *amplitude and phase distortion.* Heaviside[1] pointed out that if the inductance of the line could be increased the distortion would be decreased.

In equation 4.22 the attenuation coefficient α is given as

$$\alpha = \sqrt{\tfrac{1}{2}[\sqrt{R^2+\omega^2L^2}\ \sqrt{G^2+\omega^2C^2}+(RG-\omega^2LC)]}$$

$$\therefore 2\alpha^2 = \left[\sqrt{R^2+\omega^2L^2}\ \sqrt{G^2+\omega^2C^2}+(RG-\omega^2LC)\right]$$

If L is regarded as the variable quantity and R, G and C assumed to be constant, then the optimum value for L to provide minimum attenuation, may be found by differentiating the above expression with respect to L and equating the result to zero

$$4\alpha\frac{d\alpha}{dL} = \left[\frac{\omega^2L(G^2+\omega^2C^2)}{\sqrt{(R^2+\omega^2L^2)(G^2+\omega^2C^2)}}-\omega^2C\right]$$

and for a minimum

$$\frac{\omega^2L(G^2+\omega^2C^2)}{\sqrt{(R^2+\omega^2L^2)(G^2+\omega^2C^2)}}=\omega^2C$$

$$\therefore L^2(G^2+\omega^2C^2)^2 = C^2(R^2+\omega^2L^2)(G^2+\omega^2C^2)$$

$$\therefore L^2G^2+\omega^2L^2C^2 = C^2R^2+\omega^2L^2C^2$$

$$\therefore L = \frac{CR}{G} \quad . \quad . \quad . \quad . \quad 4.55$$

and so if the line has this value of inductance the attenuation will be a minimum. This may be checked by considering L to have values slightly greater than, and slightly less than $(CR)/G$. In each case the attenuation will increase. In practical lines, especially in cables, the inductance is less than the desired quantity and so the effective inductance can be increased ; the line is then said to be *loaded.*

Inspection of the expression for α shows that if both R and G are zero, then $\alpha=0$ and there is no attenuation. For this reason both R and G are kept as small as is economically possible.

If L is increased so that $LG=CR$, the attenuation becomes a minimum. In addition, the distortion is reduced. This may be shown as follows.

$$P^2=(R+j\omega L)(G+j\omega C)$$

$$=RG\left(1+\frac{j\omega L}{R}\right)\left(1+\frac{j\omega C}{G}\right)$$

If $LG=CR$

$$\text{then } P^2=RG\left(1+\frac{j\omega L}{R}\right)^2 \text{ or } RG\left(1+\frac{j\omega C}{G}\right)^2$$

$$\text{and so } P=\alpha+j\beta=\sqrt{RG}\left(1+\frac{j\omega L}{R}\right)$$

$$\text{and hence } \alpha=\sqrt{RG} \quad . \quad . \quad . \quad . \quad 4.56$$

$$\text{and } \beta=\omega\sqrt{LC} \quad . \quad . \quad . \quad . \quad 4.57$$

The attenuation coefficient is now independent of frequency if R and G are invariable.

The phase velocity of propagation, V_P = frequency × wavelength.

The wavelength (from equation 4.15) is $\lambda=2\pi/\beta$

$$\text{and so } V_P=\frac{2\pi f}{\beta}=\frac{\omega}{\beta} \text{ and for } LG=CR,\ \beta=\omega\sqrt{LC}$$

Hence for this condition, the phase velocity

$$V_P=\frac{1}{\sqrt{LC}} \quad . \quad . \quad . \quad . \quad . \quad 4.58$$

This is also independent of frequency so that all components of a complex wave will travel with the same velocity, and the output waveform will be similar to that applied to the line.

In addition to amplitude and phase distortion occurring in the line itself, a variation of Z_0 with frequency will cause a distortion of the received signal, as the reflection will vary with frequency.

$$Z_0 = \sqrt{(R+j\omega L)/(G+j\omega C)}$$

$$= \sqrt{\frac{R}{G}}\sqrt{\left(1+\frac{j\omega L}{R}\right)\Big/\left(1+\frac{j\omega C}{G}\right)}$$

and if $LG = CR$, or

$$\frac{L}{R} = \frac{C}{G}$$

$$\text{then } Z_0 = \sqrt{\frac{R}{G}}\,\underline{/0^\circ} \text{ or } \sqrt{\frac{L}{C}}\,\underline{/0^\circ}$$

The characteristic impedance is then independent of frequency, and is resistive. A line which has $LG = CR$ may thus be terminated correctly for all frequencies. $LG = CR$ is called the *distortionless condition.*

LOADED LINES

M. I. Pupin[2] showed that practical transmission lines could be improved by the insertion of lumped inductances, or " loading coils " at intervals along the line provided that the distance between such coils was not too large. A distinctive feature of such a lump-loaded line is that it exhibits a " cut-off " frequency and behaves as a low-pass filter (see chapter 5).

Such lines may be treated by replacing the actual line by a chain of equivalent T sections with the loading coils interposed between the sections. The arrangement can then be regarded as in Fig. 4.10 which is referred to as a chain of " half coil sections ", as each section begins and ends with half a coil. Fig. 4.10 shows the total loading impedance inserted in one conductor, whereas in practice it is divided evenly between the two conductors. (See Fig. 4.13.)

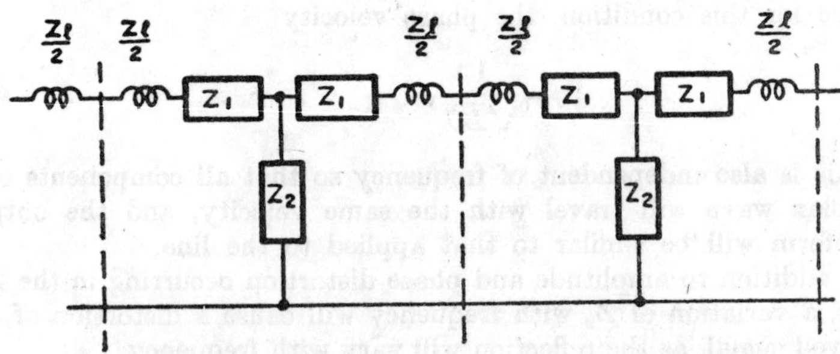

Fig. 4.10. Loaded line—Half coil sections.

In the T section, $Z_1 = Z_0 \tanh \frac{Pd}{2}$

and $Z_2 = Z_0/\sinh Pd$

where d is the distance between the loading coils.

If the equivalent T section for the line alone is considered then

$$\frac{Z_1}{Z_2} = \tanh \frac{Pd}{2} \sinh Pd = \frac{\sinh \frac{Pd}{2} \sinh Pd}{\cosh \frac{Pd}{2}}$$

$$= \frac{\sinh^2 \frac{Pd}{2} \sinh Pd}{\cosh \frac{Pd}{2} \sinh \frac{Pd}{2}} = \cosh Pd - 1$$

and so if θ $(=Pd)$ is the propagation coefficient for the section

$$\cosh \theta = 1 + \frac{Z_1}{Z_2} \quad . \quad . \quad . \quad . \qquad 4.59$$

If the complete half coil section is considered, the propagation coefficient for the section θ' will evidently be given by

$$\cosh \theta' = 1 + \frac{Z_1'}{Z_2'}$$

$$\text{where } Z_1' = Z_0 \tanh \frac{Pd}{2} + \frac{Z_l}{2} \text{ and } Z_2' = Z_0 \sinh Pd$$

$$\text{hence } \cosh \theta' = 1 + \left[\frac{Z_0 \tanh \frac{Pd}{2} + Z_l/2}{Z_0}\right] \sinh Pd$$

$$= 1 + \tanh \frac{Pd}{2} \sinh Pd + \frac{Z_l}{2Z_0} \sinh Pd$$

In deriving equation 4.59 it was seen that

$$\tanh \frac{Pd}{2} \sinh Pd = \cosh Pd - 1$$

hence

$$\cosh \theta' = \cosh Pd + \left(\frac{Z_l}{2Z_0}\right) \sinh Pd \quad . \quad . \qquad 4.60$$

This equation was first derived by G. A. Campbell[8] and is referred to as Campbell's formula. On further examination, this expression shows that the loaded line has the frequency response of a low-pass filter. There is a small attenuation from zero frequency up to the "cut-off" value, after which the attenuation increases rapidly. To show this it is convenient to consider the line between the loading coils as being loss free. Such a line will have R and $G=0$ and so $P=j\omega\sqrt{LC}$ and $Z_0=\sqrt{L/C}$.

If the actual resistance of the loading coils is neglected, Campbell's formula becomes

$$\cosh \theta' = \cosh (j\omega\sqrt{LC})d + \frac{j\omega(L_l)}{2}\sqrt{\frac{C}{L}} \sinh (j\omega\sqrt{LC})d$$

$$= \cos \omega\sqrt{LC} \,.\, d - \frac{\omega L_l}{2}\sqrt{\frac{C}{L}} \sin \omega\sqrt{LC} \,.\, d \qquad 4.61$$

θ' is a complex quantity and may be expressed as

$$\theta' = \alpha' + j\beta'$$

where α' and β' refer to the loaded line.
Hence $\cosh \theta'$ may be expanded as

$$\cosh \theta' = \cosh \alpha' \cos \beta' + j \sinh \alpha' \sin \beta' \quad . \quad . \qquad 4.62$$

If the real and imaginary parts of equations 4.61 and 4.62 are equated then,

$$\cosh \alpha' \cos \beta' = \cos \omega\sqrt{LC} \,.\, d - \frac{\omega L_l}{2}\sqrt{\frac{C}{L}} \sin \omega\sqrt{LC} \,.\, d \qquad 4.63$$

and $\sinh \alpha' \sin \beta' = 0$ 4.64

α' can be zero provided that

$$\cos \beta' = \cos \omega\sqrt{LC} \,.\, d - \frac{\omega L_l}{2}\sqrt{\frac{C}{L}} \sin \omega\sqrt{LC} \,.\, d$$

In practice the distance between loading coils is such that $\omega\sqrt{LC}\,.\,d$ is a small angle, so that

$$\cos \omega\sqrt{LC} \,.\, d \simeq 1 \quad \text{and} \quad \sin \omega\sqrt{LC} \,.\, d \simeq \omega\sqrt{LC} \,.\, d$$

with this approximation,

$$\cos \beta' = 1 - \frac{\omega^2 L_l C d}{2} \quad . \quad . \quad . \quad . \quad . \qquad 4.65$$

$\cos \beta'$ can vary between $+1$ and -1, and so equation 4.65 will hold for values of ω from zero up to a value such that

$$-1 = 1 - \frac{\omega^2 L_l C d}{2}$$

$$\text{i.e. } \omega' = \frac{2}{\sqrt{L_l C d}} \quad . \quad . \quad . \quad . \quad . \quad . \qquad 4.66$$

For values of ω greater than this, attenuation is present in the loaded line, even though the unloaded line is loss free.

For frequencies much less than the "cut-off" frequency, ω' θ' and Pd are small angles and approximations may be made for the hyperbolic quantities in Campbell's formula, which then becomes,

$$1+\frac{(\theta')^2}{\underline{/2}}=1+\frac{P^2d^2}{\underline{/2}}+\frac{Z_l}{2Z_0}Pd$$

$$\therefore\left(\frac{\theta'}{d}\right)^2=P^2+\frac{Z_l}{d}\frac{P}{Z_0}=(R+j\omega L)(G+j\omega C)+\frac{Z_l}{d}(G+j\omega C)$$

If P' represents the propagation constant per unit length

$$\text{i.e. } P'=\frac{\theta'}{d}=\sqrt{\left(R+j\omega L+\frac{Z_l}{d}\right)(G+j\omega C)} \quad . \quad . \quad 4.67$$

This result shows that the propagation constant for a lump loaded line may be obtained by using the formula for an unloaded line, provided that the loading coil impedance is assumed to be spread uniformly along the line.

If the loading coil inductance L_l is written as $L_l=L'd$, L' then represents the increase in inductance per unit length. If L is now used to denote the new total inductance per unit length (of which the natural inductance is a small part) then equation 4.66 for the "cut-off" frequency ω' may be rewritten as

$$\omega'=\frac{2}{d\sqrt{LC}} \text{ or } d=\frac{2}{\omega'\sqrt{LC}} \quad . \quad . \quad . \quad 4.68$$

The wavelength constant for the loaded line is $\beta'=\omega\sqrt{LC}$, and so the wavelength for the loaded line is,

$$\lambda'=\frac{2\pi}{\beta'}=\frac{2\pi}{\omega'\sqrt{LC}}=\pi d \qquad \text{(from equation 4.68)}$$

$$\therefore d=\frac{\lambda'}{\pi} \quad . \quad . \quad . \quad . \quad . \quad 4.69$$

In other words d, the spacing of the loading coils, must be such that there are at least π coils per smoothed wavelength. As the number of coils is increased beyond the value π, the attenuation decreases, whereas it increases steeply if there are π, or less than π coils in a smoothed wavelength of line.

An examination of equation 4.66 shows that for a given spacing of loading coils, the "cut-off" frequency is inversely proportional to the square root of the loading coil inductance, and so the cut-off frequency decreases as the size of the loading coils is increased. This effect is shown graphically in Fig. 4.11.

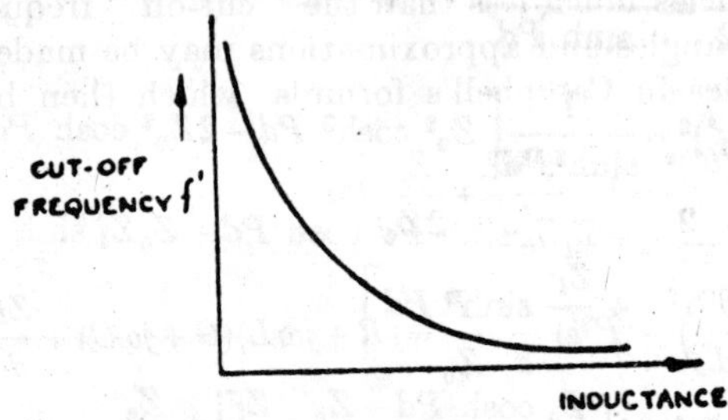

Fig. 4.11. Variation of cut-off frequency with loading coil inductance for fixed spacing of coils.

Characteristic Impedance for a Lump Loaded Line with Half-Coil Termination

The characteristic impedance for a lump-loaded line can be obtained by considering the characteristic impedance of a single section as shown between the dotted lines in Fig. 4.10. The characteristic impedance for a long line, so loaded, will then be the same as that of the section when both are terminated with this impedance.

It is convenient to consider first of all the characteristic impedance of an equivalent T section for an unloaded line when terminated in Z_0. The arrangement will be that shown in Fig. 4.7 and as the T section is to be equivalent to the line, then input impedance must be equal to Z_0.

Hence from equation 4.50,

$$Z_0 = Z_1 + \frac{Z_2(Z_1 + Z_0)}{Z_1 + Z_2 + Z_0}$$

$$\therefore Z_0^2 + Z_0(Z_1 + Z_2) = Z_1^2 + Z_1Z_2 + Z_0(Z_1 + Z_2) + Z_1Z_2$$

$$\therefore Z_0 = \sqrt{Z_1^2 + 2Z_1Z_2} \qquad 4.70$$

The characteristic impedance of the loaded line will by analogy with this result be,

$$Z_0' = \sqrt{Z_1'^2 + 2Z_1'Z_2'}$$

$$\text{where } Z_1' = Z_0 \tanh \frac{Pd}{2} + \frac{Zl}{2}$$

$$\text{and } Z_2' = Z_0/\sinh Pd$$

$$\therefore (Z_1')^2 = \left[Z_0\left\{\frac{\cosh Pd - 1}{\sinh Pd}\right\} + \frac{Z_l}{2}\right]^2$$

as $\tanh \dfrac{Pd}{2} = \dfrac{\cosh Pd - 1}{\sinh Pd}$

$$\therefore (Z_1')^2 = \frac{1}{\sinh^2 Pd}\Big[Z_0^2 \cosh^2 Pd - 2Z_0^2 \cosh Pd + Z_0^2 + Z_lZ_0 \sinh Pd \cosh Pd - Z_0Z_l \sinh Pd + \frac{Z_l^2}{4} \sinh^2 Pd\Big]$$

$$2Z_1'Z_2' = 2\left[\frac{Z_0 \cosh Pd - Z_0}{\sinh Pd} + \frac{Z_l}{2}\right]\frac{Z_0}{\sinh Pd}$$

$$= \frac{1}{\sinh^2 Pd}[2Z_0^2 \cosh Pd - 2Z_0^2 + Z_lZ_0 \sinh Pd]$$

and so

$$(Z_0')^2 = \frac{1}{\sinh^2 Pd}\Big[Z_0^2 \cosh^2 Pd - Z_0^2 + Z_0Z_l \sinh Pd \cosh Pd + \frac{Z_l^2}{4} \sinh^2 Pd\Big]$$

$$\text{and } Z_0' = Z_0\sqrt{1 + \frac{Z_l^2}{4Z_0^2} + \frac{Z_l}{Z_0} \coth Pd} \quad . \quad . \quad 4.71$$

This expression gives accurate values for Z_0'. If the spacing between the coils is small so that $\coth Pd$ may be replaced by $1/Pd$ then,

$$Z_0' = \sqrt{Z_0^2 + (Z_0Z_l)/Pd + Z_l^2/4}$$

and if it is possible to neglect $Z_l^2/4$,

$$Z_0' = \sqrt{\frac{R + j\omega L}{G + j\omega C} + \frac{Z_l}{d} \cdot \frac{1}{G + j\omega C}} = \sqrt{\frac{R + j\omega L + Z_l/d}{G + j\omega C}} \quad . \quad 4.72$$

This result shows that, to a fair approximation, the characteristic impedance for a lump loaded line can be calculated as for an unloaded line if the loading coil impedance Z_l is assumed to be distributed uniformly along the line.

The propagation coefficient P' and the characteristic impedance Z_0' have been derived for a half-coil termination, i.e. the terminal section ends in half a loading coil as shown in Fig. 4.10. If the loaded line is regarded as a series of sections which have one loading coil and a line of length $d/2$ on either side an identical expression for P' will be obtained. The characteristic impedance is altered, but if the quantity Pd can be considered to be so small that cosh $Pd = 1$, an approximate expression is obtained which is identical with equation 4.72.

Methods of Loading

Loading of a line may be carried out by the insertion of loading coils at definite intervals, or by what is known as continuous loading. This has been used mainly with submarine cables, and the process consists of wrapping the conductors with a tape of iron alloy in a continuous spiral. By increasing the permeability of the medium surrounding the conductors in this way, it is possible to increase the cable inductance by a substantial amount. This method of loading has the advantage that the attenuation increases smoothly with frequency and does not exhibit the cut-off effect experienced with coil loading. Continuous loading is, however, very costly, is expensive to repair, and is now much less important because of the higher frequencies at present in use and because of the possibility of using submerged repeaters.

For lumped loading, the coils used are required to have,

1. A low effective resistance which should be fairly uniform over the transmitted frequency range.
2. A high stability with time and temperature, i.e. the inductance of the coil should not change with age or with the passage of normal operating current.
3. The material of the core should have a low loss.
4. The crosstalk or interference between coils of adjacent circuits should be small.

The coils are wound on toroidal cores made from an iron alloy dust material which when mixed with a binding medium can be pressure-moulded to the appropriate shape. The toroidal core reduces magnetic leakage and so reduces crosstalk between adjacent coils. The winding is divided into equal parts so that half the inductance can be inserted into each limb of the circuit. The coils are separately screened and the requisite number mounted in a steel case for protection and further screening.

The introduction of "carrier" working (see chapter 17) at relatively high frequencies has made loading much less important, and indeed undesirable in view of the high value of cut-off frequency which such systems demand. While it may be useful on cables where the traffic does not justify the introduction of carrier working, loading is now much less important than it was in the early days of telegraphy and telephony, because of the widespread use of amplifiers and equaliser circuits.

PHANTOM WORKING

A physical speech circuit involves two conductors between the near and distant points. It is possible to provide additional circuits without extra conductors by an arrangement known as "phantom" working, the connections for which are shown in Fig. 4.12.

Fig. 4.12. Phantom circuit.

It will be seen that two physical circuits have been arranged to provide three circuits. The two wire-circuits are referred to as "side" circuits whilst the third is called the "phantom" circuit. It is possible to transmit speech on the phantom circuit without interference to either side-circuit because speech current arriving at the centre tap of the secondary of the line transformer in side-circuit 1, divides equally along the two lines of that circuit which then forms one effective conductor for the phantom circuit. The two currents produce no resultant flux in the cores of the line transformers (provided these have balanced windings) and so none of the phantom speech is heard in side-circuit 1. In the same way the two conductors of the side-circuit 2 complete the phantom circuit. Such circuits have an increased capacitance compared with physical circuits but their resistance is halved.

Loading coil arrangements for a phantom and two side-circuits are shown in Fig. 4.13. Each side-circuit is loaded in the normal fashion and one coil is shown for each circuit (C_1 and C_2). Such coils add resistance but no inductance to the phantom circuit as the two equal phantom currents in the conductors produce equal and opposite magnetic fluxes. The phantom coil (C_3) adds no inductance to the side-circuits, as the currents in each pair of conductors, due to speech in the side-circuits, produce no flux in this core.

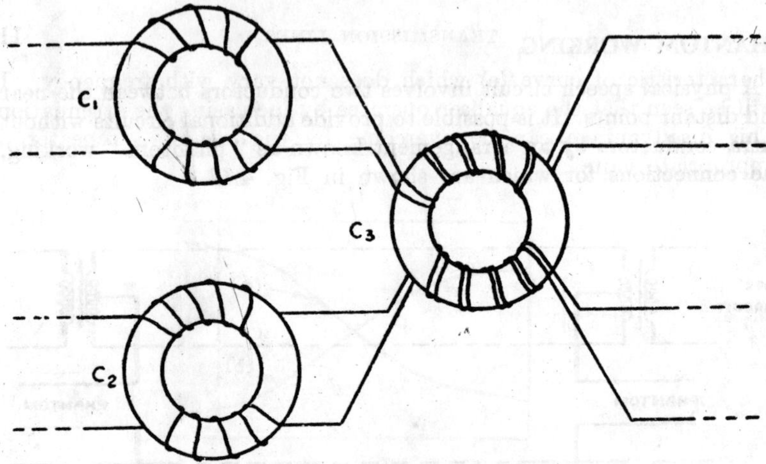

Fig. 4.13. Phantom loading.

Additional circuits may be provided by utilising pairs of phantom circuits to produce other phantom circuits. The limit to this process depends on the type of cable or line used and upon the permissible level of interference between circuits.

EQUALISERS

A complex signal will in general suffer distortion (see chapter 9 for definitions of distortion) in its transmission through a line or cable The various component frequencies will be attenuated unequally and will suffer phase shifts relative to each other. Ideally, all frequency components should be attenuated by the same amount and the transmission times of all frequencies in passing through the system should be equal. An approach to the ideal state of affairs can be made by the insertion of equalising networks into the system. Such networks are now very widely used in telephone and telegraph practice. In conjunction with amplifiers or repeaters they can give predetermined overall characteristics to a transmission system involving lines or cables.

Amplitude or Attenuation Equalisers

Loaded and unloaded cables have an attenuation/frequency characteristic which increases with frequency. If such cables have a characteristic as shown by curve (a) in Fig. 4.14 for a certain frequency range, the connection of an ideal equaliser which has the inverse attenuation/frequency characteristic curve (b) will give the overal characteristic of curve (c) which does not vary with frequency. It will be seen that the equaliser operates by increasing the attenuation. This disadvantage can be overcome by the use of a repeater of appropriate gain.

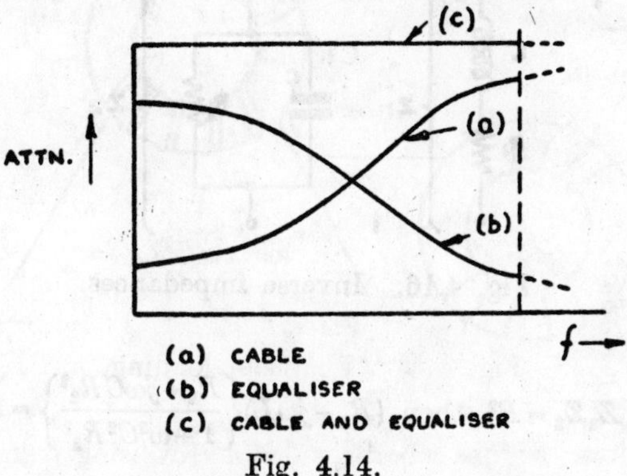

Fig. 4.14.

In audio-frequency circuits and in cases where the attenuation in the line is low and the range of frequencies employed is fairly small, a simple two-terminal network of the form shown in Fig. 4.15 may be used. If this is inserted between the line and repeater it will be seen that a shunt loss is introduced which varies with frequency. If L and C are arranged to resonate at a frequency slightly higher than the highest operating frequency the shunt loss will be a minimum at this frequency. For frequencies below this the value of the terminal impedance will fall and the shunt loss increase as the frequency decreases.

A disadvantage of this elementary type of equalisation is that the impedance of the network varies with frequency and this causes a varying reflection loss. Because of this, four-terminal equalisers which present a constant impedance (usually resistive) have been designed; with such types of equaliser there is no reflection loss when the design impedance is made equal to the terminating impedance for the line. Attention can then be confined to the required attenuation/frequency characteristic.

Fig. 4.15.

Four-terminal equalisers make use of *inverse impedances*. Two impedances may be defined as being inverse when their geometric mean is a real number. Thus, if two impedances Z_1 and Z_2 are such that

$$Z_1 Z_2 = R^2$$

where R is a resistance, Z_1 and Z_2 are then said to be inverse impedances. Two such impedances are shown in Fig. 4.16.

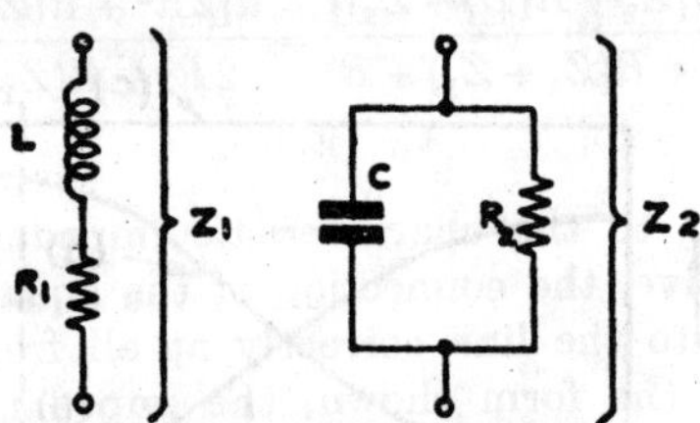

Fig. 4.16. Inverse impedances.

$$\text{If } Z_1 Z_2 = R^2, \text{ then } (R_1 + j\omega L)\left\{\frac{R_2 - j\omega C R_2^2}{1 + \omega^2 C^2 R_2^2}\right\} = R^2$$

$$\therefore \frac{R_1 R_2 + \omega^2 LCR_2^2 + j(\omega LR_2 - \omega CR_2^2 R_1)}{1 + \omega^2 C^2 R_2^2} = R^2$$

the reactive component must then be zero

$$\text{i.e. } \omega LR_2 = \omega CR_2^2 R_1 \quad \text{or} \quad \frac{L}{C} = R_2 R_1 \qquad 4.73$$

If this relation applies for the components of Z_1 and Z_2 they will then be inverse impedances.

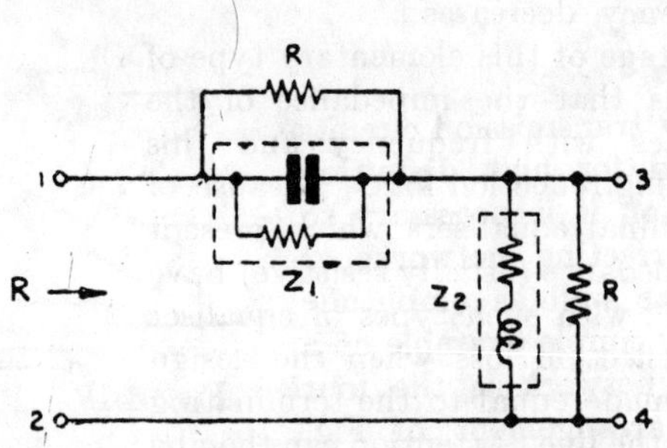

Fig. 4.17. Simple equaliser.

A simple type of fixed equaliser is shown in Fig. 4.17 where Z_1 and Z_2 are the inverse impedances of Fig. 4.16.

The input impedance at the terminals 1 and 2 is given by

$$Z_{12}=\frac{Z_1R}{Z_1+R}+\frac{Z_2R}{Z_2+R}=\frac{Z_1R(Z_2+R)+Z_2R(Z_1+R)}{Z_1Z_2+Z_2R+Z_1R+R^2}$$

$$=\frac{R[2Z_1Z_2+R(Z_1+Z_2)]}{Z_1Z_2+R(Z_1+Z_2)+R^2}=\frac{R[2R^2+R(Z_1+Z_2)]}{2R^2+R(Z_1+Z_2)}$$

$$=R.$$

If R is made equal to the characteristic impedance of the line, assuming this is resistive, the connection of the equaliser network of Fig. 4.17 will terminate the line correctly at all frequencies.

If Z_1 and Z_2 have the form shown, the impedance between the terminals 1 and 3 will decrease, whilst the impedance between the terminals 3 and 4, will rise, with increase in frequency. The equaliser then has an attenuation/frequency characteristic of the general form of curve (b) in Fig. 4.14.

The output voltage V_O is thus a fraction of the input voltage V_I depending on the ratio of the impedance at the input terminals to the impedance at the output terminals.

$$\text{i.e. } \frac{Z_{12}}{Z_{34}}=\frac{V_I}{V_O}=\frac{R}{\dfrac{RZ_2}{R+Z_2}}$$

$$\therefore \frac{V_I}{V_O}=1+\frac{R}{Z_2}=1+\frac{Z_1}{R} \qquad 4.74$$

as $Z_1Z_2=R^2$

In practice, particularly when a large amount of attenuation is to be equalised, more complex equalisers are employed.

Phase Equalisation

In high quality transmission circuits such as are used for high definition picture transmission it is necessary to employ phase correcting networks or *phase equalisers* as well as amplitude equalisers. A very simple example of a phase equalising network is the four terminal lattice arrangement of Fig. 4.18.

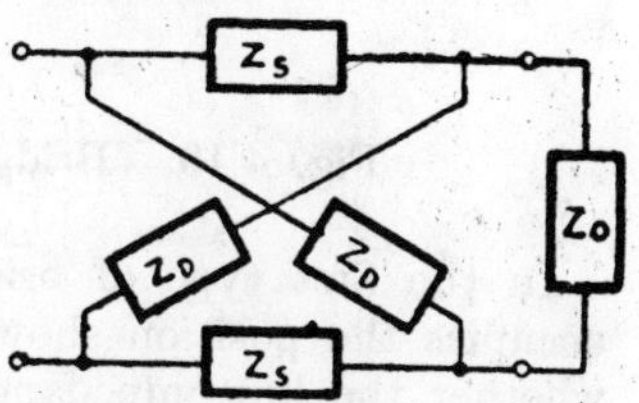

Fig. 4.18. Phase shift network.

This network is considered in chapter 5, where it is shown (equation 5.15) that if Z_S and Z_D are inverse impedances such that $Z_S \cdot Z_D=R^2$, the characteristic impedance of such a section when correctly terminated is

$$Z_0=\sqrt{Z_S \cdot Z_D}=R$$

In addition it is shown that if Z_S and Z_D are pure reactances of unlike sign the network has zero attenuation at all frequencies and a phase shift which depends upon the network of Z_S.

LINE MEASUREMENTS

(1) Determination of Primary and Secondary Line Constants by A.C. Bridge Method

If the input impedance of a transmission line is measured with the far end first open-circuited, then short-circuited, the propagation coefficient and characteristic impedance may be calculated from the two measurements. The attenuation and wavelength coefficients together with the primary constants R, L, G and C can then be computed from the values obtained for Z_0 and P.

The impedance measurements may be made with either of the bridges shown in Fig. 4.19.

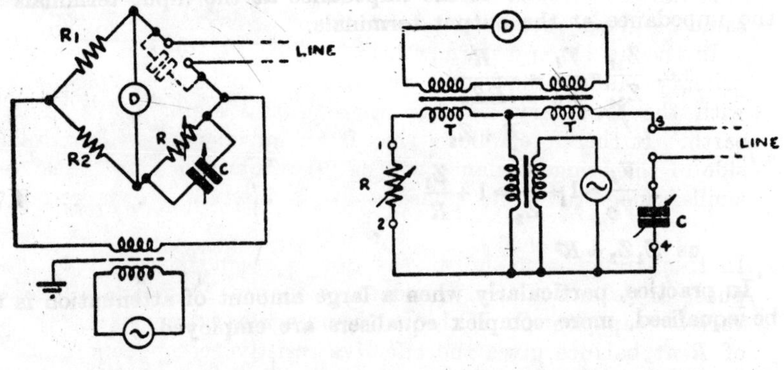

Fig. 4.19. Bridges for impedance measurement.

In the first type of bridge (Fig. 4.19a) the variable capacitor C occupies the position shown by the full or dotted lines according to whether the line impedance has a negative or positive phase angle respectively. R_1 and R_2 are resistive ratio arms which are usually made equal in value.

If the impedance of the line is $X + jY$ then at balance, with $R_1 = R_2$

$$X + jY = \frac{\dfrac{-jR}{\omega C}}{R - \dfrac{j}{\omega C}}$$

$$\therefore X + jY = \frac{R - j\omega C R^2}{1 + \omega^2 C^2 R^2}$$

$$\text{hence } X = \frac{R}{1 + \omega^2 C^2 R^2} \quad . \quad . \quad . \quad 4.75$$

$$\text{and } Y = \frac{-\omega C R^2}{1 + \omega^2 C^2 R^2} \quad . \quad . \quad . \quad 4.76$$

$$\text{thus } |Z| = \sqrt{X^2 + Y^2} = \frac{\sqrt{R^2 + \omega^2 C^2 R^4}}{1 + \omega^2 C^2 R^2}$$

$$= \frac{R}{\sqrt{1 + \omega^2 C^2 R^2}} \quad . \quad . \quad 4.77$$

$$\text{also } \phi = \tan^{-1} \frac{Y}{X} = \tan^{-1} (-\omega C R) \quad . \quad . \quad 4.78$$

If the capacitor is connected across the line the value of Z is the same as given above, but $\phi = \tan^{-1} \omega C R$, a positive angle.

In the hybrid transformer bridge of Fig. 4.19b, the halves of the primary winding marked T are arranged to have identical coupling with the secondary detector winding and similar capacitances to earth. It therefore follows that if an impedance is inserted in one side of the bridge, balance will only be obtained if an impedance of similar magnitude and phase angle is inserted on the other side.

$$(Z_{12} \equiv Z_{34})$$

In the arrangement shown, the line is assumed to have a positive phase angle and is then tuned to resonance by means of the series variable capacitor C. If the two windings have unity ratio the value of R at balance gives the effective resistive component of the line impedance directly. If the line has a negative phase angle the condenser C must be transferred to the opposite arm and either connected in series or in parallel with R depending on the value of the reactive component of the line impedance.

Let the measured line impedances be $|Z_{S/C}| \angle \phi_{S/C}$ and $|Z_{O/C}| \angle \phi_{O/C}$ when the far end is first short-circuited and then open-circuited.

Then from equations 4.44 and 4.47

$$Z_O = \sqrt{(Z_{S/C})(Z_{O/C})} = \sqrt{|Z_{S/C}||Z_{O/C}|} \cdot \angle \tfrac{1}{2}(\phi_{S/C} + \phi_{O/C}) \quad 4.79$$

$$\text{and } \tanh Pl = \sqrt{\frac{Z_{S/C}}{Z_{O/C}}} = \sqrt{\frac{|Z_{S/C}|}{|Z_{O/C}|}} \angle \tfrac{1}{2}(\phi_{S/C} - \phi_{O/C}) \quad 4.80$$

Equation 4.79 gives the value of Z_O fairly directly. The *RHS* of equation 4.80 gives a complex number, say $M + jN$

$$\therefore \tanh (\alpha + j\beta) l = M + jN \quad . \quad 4.81$$

the problem then is to obtain α and β in terms of M and N.

If equation 4.81 is true then

$$\tanh(\alpha - j\beta)l = M - jN \qquad 4.82$$

is also true

$$\text{now } \tanh 2\alpha l = \tanh[(\alpha + j\beta)l + (\alpha - j\beta)l]$$

$$= \frac{(M+jN)+(M-jN)}{1+(M+jN)(M-jN)}$$

$$\text{because } \tanh[(\alpha+j\beta)l+(\alpha-j\beta)l] = \frac{\tanh[(\alpha+j\beta)l]+\tanh[(\alpha-j\beta)l]}{1+\tanh[(\alpha+j\beta)l]\tanh[(\alpha-j\beta)l]}$$

$$\therefore \tanh 2\alpha l = \frac{2M}{1+M^2+N^2}$$

$$\text{and } 2\alpha l = \tanh^{-1}\left[\frac{2M}{1+M^2+N^2}\right] \qquad 4.83$$

In the same way

$$2\beta l = \tan^{-1}\left[\frac{2N}{1-M^2-N^2}\right] \qquad 4.84$$

The value of α may be determined from the expression in equation 4.83. The equation for β will give a value, say $X°$. In general, however, β is given by $2\beta l = X° \pm n\pi$ where n is zero or a positive integer

$$\therefore 2\beta l = \frac{\pi X}{180} \pm n\pi \text{ radians}$$

$$\therefore \beta = \frac{\pi X}{360 l} \pm \frac{n\pi}{2l} \text{ radians/unit length.}$$

In order to determine the value of n it is necessary to know the approximate value for β.

The primary constants can be found as follows :—

$$Z_0 = \sqrt{\frac{R+j\omega L}{G+j\omega C}} \text{ and } P = \sqrt{(R+j\omega L)(G+j\omega C)}$$

$$\therefore Z_0 P = R + j\omega L \qquad 4.85$$

$$\text{and } \frac{P}{Z_0} = G + j\omega C \qquad 4.86$$

hence by taking the real and imaginary parts of Z_0P and P/Z_0 the values of all four primary constants can be found at the frequency of measurement.

(2) Location of Faults by means of an A.C. Bridge

A wide variety of faults can occur in an overhead line or underground cable and many of them may be located by simple d.c. loop tests. A general method of fault detection is by means of impedance measurements with an a.c. bridge.

If alternating current is sent into the line some of the electrical energy will be reflected back to the sending end from the fault whilst the remainder will travel to the distant end where it will be absorbed if the line is correctly terminated. The reflected current or voltage at any given frequency f_1 will have travelled a distance $2x$ when it returns to the sending-end and differ in phase by an angle

$$\theta = 2\beta_1 x + \phi_1 \qquad 4.87$$

where x = distance of fault from sending end.

ϕ_1 = change in phase produced at fault.

β_1 = wavelength constant of the line at the frequency f_1.

If now the frequency of the supply is continually varied from a low value the phase angle θ will change continuously so that the reflected wave will pass through inphase and antiphase conditions. Any measurement of impedance at the sending-end will then show maximum and minimum points at regular intervals; successive points of maximum (or minimum) impedance will be separated by a phase of 2π radians.

If two successive maximum points are found at f_1 and f_2 in an impedance frequency curve on a faulty pair, the phase difference between the reflected waves at f_1 and f_2 will be given by

$$(2\beta_2 x + \phi_2) - (2\beta_1 x + \phi_1) = 2\pi$$

$$\text{and so } x = \frac{\pi + \frac{1}{2}(\phi_2 - \phi_1)}{\beta_2 - \beta_1}$$

Generally ϕ_1 and ϕ_2 (the change in phase at the fault at frequencies f_1 and f_2 respectively) are small and nearly equal and their difference may be neglected

$$\text{and thus } x = \frac{\pi}{\beta_2 - \beta_1} \qquad 4.88$$

If β_1 and β_2 are known the distance to the fault may then be determined.

The impedance/frequency characteristic may be determined by either of the bridges of Fig. 4.19, and it is sufficient to plot variation in the resistive component of the input impedance, rather than the calculated value of the modulus of the impedance.

UNITS OF ATTENUATION—THE DECIBEL AND NEPER

It has been stated that in passing along a terminated line a signal is reduced in amplitude and retarded in phase. The extent to which this takes place depends on the magnitude of α the attenuation coefficient, and β the wavelength coefficient. The value of β gives the phase shift in radians per unit length. To find the attenuation represented by α it is necessary to consider the units of attenuation.

Historically, attenuation was first of all defined in terms of the attenuation produced by a standard reference cable. A circuit was then said to have an attenuation of so many miles of standard cable (M.S.C.). The fundamental objection to this unit was the fact that the attenuation of the standard cable varied with frequency. With the introduction of systems operating over different frequency ranges it became necessary to define a unit of attenuation which was independent of frequency. The unit selected for this purpose was the bel, but in practice a submultiple, the *decibel*, is more commonly used.

If P_S represents the power supplied to a network and P_R is the output power from a network, then the attenuation of the network

$$= \log_{10} \frac{P_S}{P_R} \text{ bels}$$

$$\text{or } = 10 \log_{10} \frac{P_S}{P_R} \text{ decibels}$$

If the power is developed in the same value of impedance for the two cases, then the attenuation may be expressed as

$$= 20 \log_{10} \frac{I_S}{I_R} \text{ or } 20 \log_{10} \frac{V_S}{V_R}$$

where the subscript S refers to the input quantity and the subscript R refers to the output quantity.

It will be seen that the decibel is defined as a ratio of powers and so cannot by itself be used to express an absolute level of power. Power levels may, however, be expressed in terms of some arbitrary reference level, a common value of which is 1 mW in a resistive load of 600 Ω. Using this datum, a power of 3·98 mW in a 600 Ω resistive circuit could then be expressed as +6dB (rel. to 1 mW) as the power ratio in this case is

$$= 10 \log_{10} \frac{3{\cdot}98}{1} = 6 \text{ dB}.$$

Attenuation may alternatively be quoted in terms of the *neper*. This is a unit based on a natural logarithm of a current ratio.

A network which has an input current I_S and an output current I_R has an attenuation of

$$\log_e \frac{I_S}{I_R} \text{ nepers.}$$

If the currents are measured in identical impedances the attenuation may be expressed as

$$\tfrac{1}{2} \log_e \frac{P_S}{P_R} \text{ nepers.}$$

The relationship between the two units can be obtained by considering a network which has $P_S/P_R = A$.

$$\text{The attenuation in decibels} = 10 \log_{10} A$$

$$\text{The attenuation in nepers} = \tfrac{1}{2} \log_e A$$

$$\text{and } \log_{10} A = \log_e A/2{\cdot}3026$$

$$\text{hence 1 neper} = \frac{20}{2{\cdot}3026} \text{dB} = 8{\cdot}686 \text{ dB}$$

$$\text{and 1 dB} = 0{\cdot}115 \text{ neper.}$$

It will be seen from the foregoing that the attenuation coefficient gives the attenuation for a line in nepers per unit length.

The decibel and the neper are both logarithmic units. This is particularly useful in communication equipment as the gain or loss of apparatus connected in cascade can be found by a process of addition or subtraction rather than by the multiplication or division which would be necessary with a linear system of units.

Another reason for the preference of logarithmic units is that the human senses, such as hearing and vision, perceive changes in logarithmic rather than a linear fashion. This arises from the fact that any change in level, such as the change in brightness of a screen or the output from telephones, is judged in relation to the level already existing. If, for example, the output of a loudspeaker is changed from 50 to 100 mW the ear would perceive this as a greater change than one from 100 to 150 mW.

WORKED EXAMPLES

1. An underground cable is 20 km long, and has the following distributed constants all per mile loop, at a frequency of 1000 Hz. $R = 90\,\Omega$, $L = 0{\cdot}001$ H, $C = 0{\cdot}062$ μF, and $G = 1{\cdot}5$ micro-mhos.

If the line is terminated in its characteristic impedance and supplied with an input power at the sending of 6 mW, calculate (1) the characteristic impedance, (2) the magnitude of the received current,

(3) the phase difference between the received and sent currents, (4) the power received, (5) wavelength, and (6) velocity of propagation.

$$\omega = 2\pi f = 6283$$

$$R + j\omega L = 90 + j6283 \times 0{\cdot}001 = 90{\cdot}2\underline{/3°59'}$$

$$G + j\omega C = 1{\cdot}5 \times 10^{-6} + j6283 \times 0{\cdot}062 \times 10^{-6}$$

$$= 390 \times 10^{-6}\underline{/89°47'}$$

Hence the characteristic impedance, Z_0

$$= \sqrt{\frac{R + j\omega L}{G + j\omega C}} = \sqrt{\frac{90{\cdot}2\underline{/3°59'}}{390 \times 10^{-6}\underline{/89°47'}}}$$

$$= 481\overline{\backslash 43°} \quad (1)$$

The input power $= P_S = V_S I_S \cos \phi_S$

where ϕ_S is the angle of Z_0

Now $I_S = V_S / Z_0$

$$\therefore P_S = \frac{V_S^2 \cos \phi_S}{Z_0}$$

$$\therefore V_S^2 = \frac{0{\cdot}006 \times 481}{0{\cdot}7325}$$

$$\therefore V_S = 1{\cdot}98 \text{ V}$$

and so $I_S = \dfrac{1{\cdot}98 \times 1000}{481}$ mA $= 4{\cdot}12$ mA

The propagation coefficient $P = \sqrt{(R + j\omega L)(G + j\omega C)}$

$$\therefore P = \sqrt{(90{\cdot}2\underline{/3°59'})(390 \times 10^{-6}\underline{/89°47'})}$$

$$= \sqrt{0{\cdot}0352\underline{/93°46'}} = 0{\cdot}187\underline{/46°53'}$$

$$= 0{\cdot}187 \cos 46°53' + j\, 0{\cdot}187 \sin 46°53'$$

$$= 0{\cdot}128 + j0{\cdot}137$$

now $P = \alpha + j\beta$

$$\therefore \alpha = 0{\cdot}128 \text{ nepers/km}$$

and $\beta = 0{\cdot}137$ radians/km.

For a line of n km when terminated in the characteristic impedance

$$\frac{I_R}{I_S} = e^{-\alpha n}$$

$$\therefore 2{\cdot}303 \log_{10} \frac{I_S}{I_R} = n\alpha$$

$$\therefore \quad \log_{10} \frac{4{\cdot}12}{I_R} = \frac{20 \times 0{\cdot}128}{2{\cdot}303} = 1{\cdot}11$$

$$\therefore \quad \frac{4{\cdot}12}{I_R} = 12{\cdot}91$$

$$\therefore \quad I_R = \frac{4{\cdot}12}{12{\cdot}91} = 0{\cdot}32 \text{ mA} \quad (2)$$

Phase per shift km $= \beta = 0{\cdot}137$ radian

hence the phase shift over the whole line

$$= 20 \times 0{\cdot}137 \text{ radians} = 157° \quad (3)$$

The ratio $\frac{I_S}{I_R}$ was seen to be 12·91

$$\therefore \frac{E_S}{E_R} = 12{\cdot}91$$

$$E_R = \frac{1{\cdot}98}{12{\cdot}91} = 0{\cdot}153 \text{ V.}$$

The received power $= P_R = E_R I_R \cos \phi_R$ and for the terminated line $\phi_R = \phi_S$

$$\therefore P_R = 0{\cdot}153 \times 0{\cdot}32 \times 0{\cdot}7325 \text{ mW}$$

$$= 0{\cdot}037 \text{ mW} \quad (4)$$

The wavelength of the propagation λ is given by

$$\lambda = \frac{2\pi}{\beta} = \frac{6{\cdot}283}{0{\cdot}137} = 45{\cdot}9 \text{ km} \quad (5)$$

The velocity of the propagation along the line is given by

$$V = \lambda f = 45{\cdot}9 \times 1000 = 45{,}900 \text{ km/s} \quad (6)$$

2. Derive an expression for the current at any point along a uniform telephone transmission line in terms of the sending-end voltage and current and the characteristic impedance of the line.

A line, 20 miles long, has a characteristic impedance $Z_0 = 600 \angle 0°$ ohms, an attenuation of 0·1 neper per mile and a wavelength coefficient of 0·05 radian per mile.

Determine the magnitude and phase angle of *(a)* the sending-end voltage and *(b)* the receiving-end current when the sending-end current is $50 \angle 0°$ mA and the receiving end is short-circuited.

***L.U. Telecomm. Part III.* 1962**

Equation 4·37 gives

$$I_x = I_S \cosh Px - (V_S/Z_0) \sinh Px$$

while for a short-circuited line of length l the equations for voltage and current at the receiving-end of the line are,

$$O = V_S \cosh Pl - I_S Z_0 \sinh Pl$$

$$\text{and } I_R = I_S \cosh Pl - (V_S/Z_0) \sinh Pl$$

$$\text{Hence } I_R = I_S \cosh Pl - I_S \sinh^2 Pl/\cosh Pl$$

$$= I_S/\cosh Pl \quad . \quad . \quad . \quad . \quad . \quad . \quad (1)$$

$$\text{also } V_S = I_S Z_0 \sinh Pl/\cosh Pl \quad . \quad . \quad . \quad . \quad . \quad (2)$$

$$\text{Now } \cosh Pl = \cosh[20(0{\cdot}1 + j0{\cdot}05)] = \cosh(2 + j1)$$

$$= \cosh 2 \cdot \cos 57{\cdot}3^0 + j\sinh 2 \cdot \sin 57{\cdot}3^0$$

$$= (3{\cdot}76 \times 0{\cdot}54) + j(3{\cdot}63 \times 0{\cdot}8415)$$

$$= 2{\cdot}032 + j3{\cdot}055 = 3{\cdot}66 \underline{|56{\cdot}3^0}$$

$$\sinh Pl = \sinh(2 + j1)$$

$$= \sinh 2 \cdot \cos 57{\cdot}3^0 + j\cosh 2 \cdot \sin 57{\cdot}3^0$$

$$= (3{\cdot}63 \times 0{\cdot}54) + j(3{\cdot}76 \times 0{\cdot}8415)$$

$$= 1{\cdot}96 + j3{\cdot}165 = 3{\cdot}72 \underline{|58{\cdot}3^0}$$

The sending-end voltage V_S is thus

$$= \frac{50 \times 10^{-3} |0^0 \times 600 |0^0 \times 3{\cdot}72 |58{\cdot}3^0}{3{\cdot}66 |56{\cdot}3^0} = \underline{30{\cdot}5 |2^0 \text{ volts (a)}}$$

Also the receiving-end current I_R is $= \dfrac{50 |0^0}{3{\cdot}66 |56{\cdot}3^0} = \underline{13{\cdot}65 | -56{\cdot}3^0 \text{ mA(b)}}$

3. Show from the general solution of the equations of the transmission line that the characteristic impedance of a uniform line may be determined from a knowledge of the impedance of any length of the line measured

(a) with the far end short circuited.

(b) with the far end open circuited.

The sending end impedance of a ten mile length of line measured with the far end open is 348 $\underline{/32°}$ Ω, and measured with the far end shorted is 1775 $\underline{/-45°}$ Ω. Determine (a) the magnitude and phase angle of the characteristic impedance, and (b) the propagation constant of the line.

L.U. Ext. Telecomm. 1945.

It has been shown that in the open circuit case

$$Z_{o/c} = Z_0 \coth Pl$$

while in the short circuit case

$$Z_{s/c} = Z_0 \tanh Pl$$

hence $Z_0^2 = (Z_{o/c})(Z_{s/c})$

and $\tanh Pl = \sqrt{Z_{s/c}/Z_{o/c}}$

$$\therefore Z_0 = \sqrt{348 \times 1775} \quad \frac{/32° - 45°}{2} = \underline{785 \,/-6° \; \Omega}$$

$$\text{Tanh } Pl = \sqrt{\frac{1775}{348}} \frac{/-45° - 32°}{2} = \underline{2{\cdot}26 /-38{\cdot}5°}$$

By reference to Kennelly's tables of hyperbolic functions it will be found that

$$Pl = \underline{1{\cdot}9 /80°} \text{ and so } \underline{P = 0{\cdot}19 /80}$$

Alternatively P may be found by using equations 4.83 and 4.84.

o

4. Deduce an expression for the cut-off frequency of a coil loaded line, assuming the resistance and leakance to be negligible. A telephone cable has a resistance of 40 Ω and a capacitance of 0·06 μF per loop mile, the inductance and leakance being negligible. Loading coils, each having a resistance of 15 Ω and an inductance of 80 mH, are inserted at intervals of 1·2 miles. Find (a) the approximate value of the cut-off frequency, and (b) the attenuation in nepers per mile at a frequency of 5/2π kHz assuming the cable to be terminated by its characteristic impedance.

L.U. Ext. Telecomm. 1945.

Equation 4.66 gives the cut-off frequency for a coil loaded line as

$$f' = 1/\pi\sqrt{L_l C d}$$

where L_l is the coil inductance, C is the capacitance per mile of the line, and d is the separation in miles of the coils.
Hence

$$f' = \frac{1}{\pi\sqrt{80 \times 10^{-3} \times 6 \times 10^{-8} \times 1{\cdot}2}} = \underline{4210 \text{ Hz.}}$$

The frequency of 5000/2π hertz is much lower than the cut-off frequency and the inductance can be regarded as that due to the loading coils, uniformly distributed over the length of the line.

The inductance per loop mile can thus be taken as 80/1·2 = 66·7 mH/mile.

The resistance per loop mile is $= 40 + 15/1{\cdot}2$

$$= 52{\cdot}5\ \Omega$$

The series impedance per loop mile

$$= 52{\cdot}5 + j5000 \times 66{\cdot}7 \times 10^{-3} = 337\underline{/81°3'}$$

The shunt impedance per loop mile

$$= 0 + j5000 \times 0{\cdot}06 \times 10^{-6} = 3 \times 10^{-4}\underline{/90°}$$

The propagation coefficient P is then given by

$$P = \sqrt{(337\underline{/81°3'})(3 \times 10^{-4}\underline{/90°})} = 0{\cdot}317\underline{/85°31'}$$

Hence α the attenuation per mile at this frequency is given by

$$\alpha = 0{\cdot}317 \cos 85°31' = 0{\cdot}025 \text{ neper/mile}$$

References

[1] Heaviside, O.: *Electromagnetic Theory*, Vol. 1 (The Electrician Publishing Co., 1893).

[2] Pupin, M. I.: "Wave Transmission over Non-Uniform Cables and Long Distance Air-Lines", Transactions of the American I.E.E., 17, p. 445 (1900).

[3] Campbell, G. A.: "On Loaded Lines in Telephonic Transmission", *Philosophical Magazine*, 5, p. 313 (1903).

References for Further Reading

Guillemin, E. A.: *Communication Networks*, Vol. 2 (Chapman & Hall, 1935).

Everitt, W. L.: *Communication Engineering* (McGraw-Hill, 1937).

Skilling, H. H.: *Electric Transmission Lines* (McGraw-Hill, 1951).

EXAMPLES

1. Explain what is meant by attenuation constant, wavelength constant, and characteristic impedance of a telephone line.

Find these quantities and the velocity of propagation for a frequency of 800 Hz in the case of a line having a resistance of 10 Ω, negligible leakance, a capacitance of 0·02 μF and an inductance of 5 mH, all per loop mile.

L.U. Ext. Telecomm. 1950.

2. A telephone line, 10 miles long, has the following constants per mile loop: $R = 20\ \Omega$, $L = 3$ mH, $C = 0{\cdot}06\ \mu$F, and $G = 10$ micromhos. Calculate the value of the impedance that would correctly terminate the line at a frequency of $5000/2\pi$Hz. Calculate also the corresponding values of

(a) the velocity of propagation along the line, (b) the attenuation of the line in decibels and (c) the phase difference between the voltage at the receiving end and that at the sending end.

L.U. Ext. Telecomm. 1956.

3. Explain what is meant by the attenuation of a line. A magneto bell is so arranged as to terminate smoothly a line having a characteristic impedance of 2,000 $\angle -45°$ Ω, and it is known that 1 mA in this circuit is required just to ring the bell. It is found that 75 V is measured at the transmitting end of the line when the bell is just ringing. Calculate the attenuation of the line. What would be the voltage measured half-way along the line?

I.E.E. Line Comm. April, 1948.

4. Define (a) the decibel, (b) the decineper, and deduce the relationship between the two units.

A telephone cable, 20 miles long, has the following constants per loop mile; resistance 50 Ω; capacitance 0·06 μF; inductance and leakance negligible. The line is closed by an impedance equal to the characteristic impedance of the line, and a p.d. of 4 V having a frequency of $5/2\pi$ kHz is applied at the sending end.

Calculate (a) the attenuation of the line in decibels and in decinepers and (b) the currents at the sending and receiving ends. Represent vectorially the voltages and currents at the sending and receiving ends.

L.U. Ext. Telecomm. 1945.

5. The propagation constant of a telephone line 200 miles long is $0{\cdot}008 + j0{\cdot}029$ per mile; its characteristic impedance is 750 $\angle -15°$ Ω and the impedance of the receiving apparatus is 400 $\angle 45°$ Ω. Find (i) the current through the receiving apparatus when the p.d. at the sending end is 10 V, (ii) the phase angle between the two.

L.U. Int. Telecomm. 1947.

6. Explain what is meant by (a) the characteristic impedance and (b) the attenuation constant of a transmission line.

A telephone line 10 miles long, is terminated by its characteristic impedance. At a frequency of 800 Hz the attenuation of the line is 6 dB and the p.d. at the receiving end lags 44° behind that at the sending end. If the sending end voltage is $10\angle 0°$ V, find (a) the value of the receiving end voltage, and (b) the value and the phase of the voltage half-way along the line. Also find the propagation constant per loop mile and the velocity of propagation.

L.U. Ext. Telecomm. 1946.

7. A telephone line, 20 miles long, has the following smoothed constants per loop mile: resistance 30 Ω; inductance 20 mH; capacitance 0·05 μF; and leakance 3 micromhos. A P.D. of 40 V having a frequency of $5000/2\pi$ Hz, is applied to the sending end. Calculate (a) the P.D. at the receiving end and its phase relative to the sending end voltage when the line is on open circuit, and (b) the value and the phase of the current at the receiving end when the line is short-circuited.

L.U. Ext. Telecomm. 1944.

8. A telephone line, 10 miles long, has a characteristic impedance of 640 $\underline{/-8^\circ}$ Ω and a propagation constant of 0·18 $\underline{/80^\circ}$ at a certain frequency (per loop mile). A p.d. of 10 V at that frequency is applied at the sending end, and the line is short circuited at the receiving end. Calculate the currents at the sending end and at the short-circuited end, and draw a phasor diagram representing the voltage and the two currents.

L.U. Ext. Telecomm. 1944.

9. A telephone line, 20 miles long, is open circuited at the far end. When a sinusoidal voltage of 10 V having a frequency of 800 Hz is applied at the sending end, the p.d. at the receiving end is 9·14 V, lagging 60° behind the sending end voltage. Calculate the attenuation constant of the line and the speed of propagation.

L.U. Ext. Telecomm. 1944.

10. Explain the causes and effects of attenuation and phase distortion in audio-frequency cables.

A cable is 20 miles long and has the following distributed constants per loop mile; $R = 40\ \Omega$, $L = 1$ mH, $C = 0{\cdot}06\ \mu$F. Shunt conductance can be neglected. Calculate the value of the characteristic impedance at 10 kHz. If the cable is terminated with this impedance, calculate for a 10 kHz signal (*a*) the wavelength and (*b*) the velocity of propagation. Calculate also the gain in dB of a repeater, inserted at the mid-point of the cable, to provide zero loss over the cable length.

L.U. Telecomm. Part III 1963.

11. A signal is sent along a line and is reflected from the further end. Describe in terms of the incident and reflected pulses the conditions existing near the further end,

(a) on open circuit, (b) on short circuit.

The current vector distribution along a line of length l and short circuited at the end is

$$I_x = \frac{V_s}{Z_0} \frac{\cosh P(l-x)}{\sinh Pl}$$

By expressing this function as a sum of exponential terms, interpret the result as a wave system.

L.U. Int. Telecomm. 1945.

12. A transmission line of characteristic impedance 600 Ω is terminated in a resistance of 400 Ω, and alternating current is passed down the line. Under steady-state conditions what is the amplitude of the reflected wave compared with the initial wave ? An oscillograph connected across the line would show only one wave present. Show mathematically why this is so.

I.E.E. Line Comm., October, 1948.

13. Show that the attenuation constant of a loaded cable can be expressed approximately by the expression

$$\alpha = \frac{R}{2}\sqrt{\frac{C}{L}} + \frac{G}{2}\sqrt{\frac{L}{C}}$$

State the assumption made in deriving the expression and discuss the limitations as to its use.

L.U. Int. Telecomm. 1947.

14. What is meant by the equivalent circuit of a transmission line ? To what extent can such a circuit be physically realised ?

Derive the equivalent T circuit of l miles of transmission line of characteristic impedance Z_0 and propagation constant P per mile.

L.U. Int. Telecomm. 1948.

15. Deduce expressions for the series and shunt elements of an equivalent T network for a transmission line, l miles long, having a characteristic impedance Z_0 ohms and a propagation constant P per loop mile.

With the aid of these expressions, calculate the resistance and inductance (or capacitance) of the series and shunt elements of a network equivalent to 10 miles of a line having a characteristic impedance of $280 \underline{/-30°}\ \Omega$ and a propagation constant of $0{\cdot}08 \underline{/40°}$ per loop mile at a frequency of $5{,}000/2\pi$ Hz.

L.U. Ext. Telecomm. 1946.

16. Calculate the value of the impedances required to construct a T network equivalent to a 40 mile long line having the following smoothed constants per mile :

$R = 60\ \Omega$ $\qquad$ $L = 20$ mH

G is negligible $\qquad$ $C = 0{\cdot}05\ \mu$F.

The frequency is $5{,}000/2\pi$ hertz

Prove any formula used apart from the general expressions for current and voltage in a line with uniformly distributed constants.

L.U. Ext. Telecomm. 1939.

17. If a uniform line has a characteristic impedance Z_0 and a propagation constant P, show that a length l of such a line can be represented by a T network having a series and shunt elements of impedance Z_1 and Z_2 respectively, where:

$$Z_1 = Z_0 \tanh \frac{Pl}{2} \text{ and } Z_2 = Z_0/\sinh Pl$$

If the series elements of a T network, which is equivalent to 5 miles of uniform line at a frequency of $5{,}000/2\pi$ Hz each has a resistance of 175 Ω and an inductance of 10 mH and the shunt element consists of a 0·2 μF condenser in series with a 270 Ω resistor, derive the characteristic impedance and the propagation constant of the line.

L.U. Ext. Telecomm. 1950.

18. Derive an expression for the characteristic impedance of a uniform transmission line in terms of its primary constants. How is the input impedance of a line affected by variation of the terminating impedance?

Bridge measurements on a particular line at 800 Hz gave the following results:

Open circuit—Resistance of 379 Ω in series with capacitance, 1·755 μF.

Short circuit—Resistance of 396·8 Ω in series with capacitance, 20·2 μF.

Calculate the characteristic impedance of the line.

I.E.E. Line Comm. April, 1949.

19. A cable pair is known to be short-circuited 10 miles from one end. Determine the impedance which will be measured from the free end under the following conditions:—

Attenuation coefficient, 0·616 dB/mile

Phase coefficient, 1·4 rad/mile

Characteristic impedance $52{\cdot}55 \angle -3{\cdot}1^\circ\ \Omega$

I.E.E. Line Comm. October, 1947.

20. Using the general expressions for the characteristic impedance and propagation coefficient of a line show that when $R/G = L/C$ transmission is distortionless. Discuss the effect of trying to achieve this condition by "lumped" inductance loading.

L.U. Ext. Telecomm. 1956.

21. Describe methods used for loading telephone cables and compare their relative advantages and disadvantages.

The primary constants per loop mile of a certain cable are: resistance 20 Ω; capacitance 0·05 μF; leakance and inductance negligible. The cable is loaded with coils, each having a resistance of 12 Ω and an inductance of 120 mH. Estimate the approximate value of the spacing of the coils to give a cut-off frequency of 4,000 Hz. For that spacing, calculate the attenuation constant in nepers per loop mile and the velocity of propagation for a frequency of 796 Hz.

Show that the attenuation constant and the velocity of propagation are practically independent of the frequency for the audio range necessary to transmit speech.

L.U. Ext. Telecomm. 1946.

22. A telephone cable has a resistance of 30 Ω and a capacitance of 0·06 μF, each per loop mile, the inductance and leakance being negligible. Estimate the spacing of loading coils, each having an inductance of 60 mH and a resistance of 5 Ω to give a cut-off frequency of about $40/2\pi$ kHz. Justify briefly the expression employed.

For the spacing determined above, calculate the attenuation coefficient for a frequency of the order of $5/2\pi$ kHz.

L.U. Ext. Telecomm. 1950.

23. A fault has occurred on a submarine cable. On taking an impedance frequency run on the cable, peaks are observed at 10 kHz intervals, two occurring at 10 kHz and 20 kHz. Calculate the distance to the fault.

The constants of the cable per nautical mile at 10 kHz and 20 kHz may for the purpose of this example be assumed to be

$L = 0{\cdot}576$ mH $\qquad C = 0{\cdot}203$ μF

$G = 16$ micromhos $\qquad R = 5{\cdot}45$ Ω.

I.E.E. Line Comm. October, 1946.

24. A uniform telephone cable has the primary coefficients per loop mile $C = 0{\cdot}06$ μF, $L = 1$ mH, $R = 100$ Ω. The conductance is negligible. Calculate the frequency at which the angle of the characteristic impedance is $-22{\cdot}5°$. What additional distributed inductance per mile is required to reduce this frequency to 300 Hz?

If this inductance is provided by the insertion of loading coils at regular intervals to produce a nominal cut-off frequency of 4 kHz, estimate: (i) the spacing between adjacent coils, and (ii) the inductance of each coil.

L.U. Telecomm. Part III. 1966.

5

ATTENUATORS AND FILTERS

Attenuators and filters are some particular examples of four-terminal, or *two-port*, networks. It is convenient to consider some of the characteristics of such networks in their general form before dealing with particular types which are used as attenuating or filtering networks.

DEFINITIONS FOR FOUR-TERMINAL NETWORKS

The transmission line may be regarded as a two-port network, and as such may be replaced by an equivalent T or π network as discussed in chapter 4. Such equivalent networks are " symmetrical ", in that the input and output ports may be interchanged without affecting the transmission in any way.

The equivalent networks for the line were defined by two parameters, namely the characteristic impedance Z_0, and the propagation coefficient P. Four-terminal networks need not, however, necessarily be symmetrical. With asymmetric arrangements, the impedances viewed from the two ends differ, and the ratio of input and output currents is not the same as the ratio of the input and output voltages. As a result of this, additional parameters are used for asymmetrical networks and these will now be defined.

Image Impedances

These are a pair of impedances such that if one of them is connected to one pair of terminals of the network, the other is the input impedance

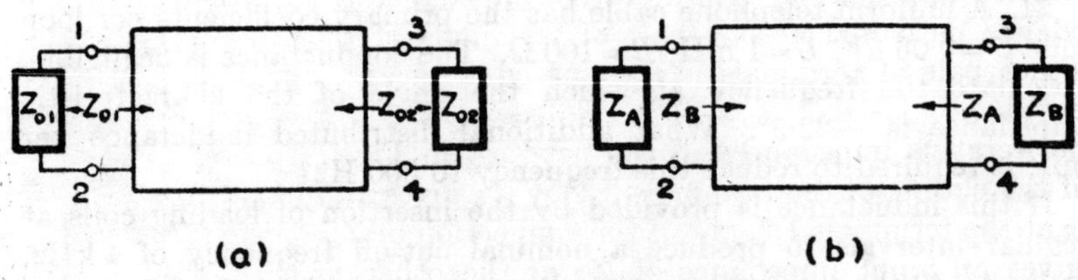

Fig. 5.1. (a) Image impedances.
(b) Iterative impedances.

at the other pair of terminals; when the two image impedances are equal their common value is the characteristic impedance of the network.

In Fig. 5.1a, if the terminals 3,4 are closed by Z_{02}, the impedance viewed at the terminals 1,2 is then Z_{01}. Likewise, if the terminals 1,2 are closed by Z_{01} the impedance viewed at the terminal 3,4 is Z_{02}. The image impedances of the network are thus Z_{01} and Z_{02}. It will be seen that when terminated in its image impedances, the impedance at any pair of terminals is the same when viewed in either direction.

Image-Transfer Coefficient

If a four-terminal network is terminated in its image impedances, and V_S and I_S are respectively the complex input voltage and current at the input terminals, while V_R and I_R are the corresponding output quantities, then the image-transfer coefficient θ, is given by

$$\theta = \tfrac{1}{2} \log_e \frac{V_S I_S}{V_R I_R} \quad . \quad . \quad . \quad 5.1$$

Generally, the voltages and currents are complex quantities, so that θ is a complex quantity, and

$$\theta = A + jB \quad . \quad . \quad . \quad . \quad 5.2$$

where A is the ***image attenuation coefficient,***
and B is the ***image phase-change coefficient.***

If natural logarithms are used, A is given in nepers, and B in radians.

When the network is symmetrical,

$$\theta = \log_e \frac{V_S}{V_R} \text{ or } \log_e \frac{I_S}{I_R} \quad . \quad . \quad . \quad 5.3$$

and θ then becomes the same as the propagation coefficient.

Iterative Impedances

In recurrent networks it is sometimes convenient to work in terms of iterative impedances. The iterative impedance is the value of the impedance measured at one pair of terminals of the network when the other pair of terminals is terminated with an impedance of the same value.

The iterative impedances of the network in Fig. 5.1b are Z_A and Z_B, if the closing of the terminals 3,4 by Z_B gives an input impedance of Z_B at the terminals 1,2, and if the connection of Z_A to the terminals 1,2 gives an input impedance of Z_A at the other pair of terminals. If the network is symmetrical, the iterative impedances are equal and their common value is the characteristic impedance of the network.

Iterative Propagation Constant

If a network is terminated on an iterative basis at both ends (as it would be if it were one section in a chain of recurrent sections), the iterative propagation coefficient P_I is defined as

$$P_I = \log_e \frac{I_S}{I_R} \quad . \quad . \quad . \quad . \quad . \quad 5.4$$

where I_S is the input current to the network,
and I_R is the output current from the network.

Open and Short-circuit Impedances. If the output terminals of a network are free, the impedance presented at the input terminals is then referred to as the open-circuit impedance ($Z_{O/C}$). In the same way if the output terminals are short-circuited, the input impedance under this condition is the short-circuit impedance ($Z_{S/C}$). These quantities are important as their geometric mean gives the characteristic impedance for a symmetrical section or the image impedances for an asymmetrical section.

LADDER NETWORKS

Communication equipment often involves a train of repeated sections, or a recurrent network. A common form is the ladder network shown in Fig. 5.2.

The form (a) is said to be *unbalanced* and is used with equipment in which one side is earthed or at earth potential. The *balanced* form

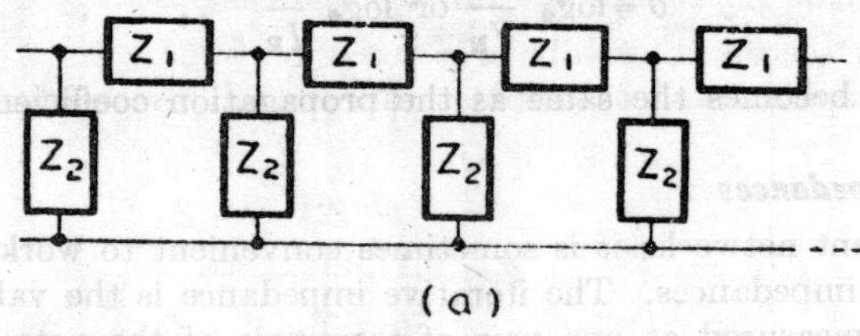

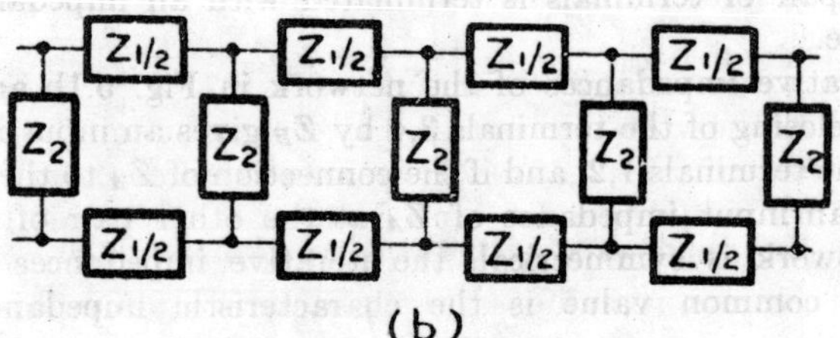

Fig. 5.2. Ladder network.

in Fig. 5.2b is used with line equipment or in other cases where both sides are balanced with respect to earth. These balanced and unbalanced sections have identical transmission properties provided there is no external impedance between the input and output terminals.

An inspection of the ladder networks of Fig. 5.2 show that they may be considered as a chain of T sections, or of π sections, or half-sections. These alternatives are shown in Fig. 5.3 for the unbalanced case.

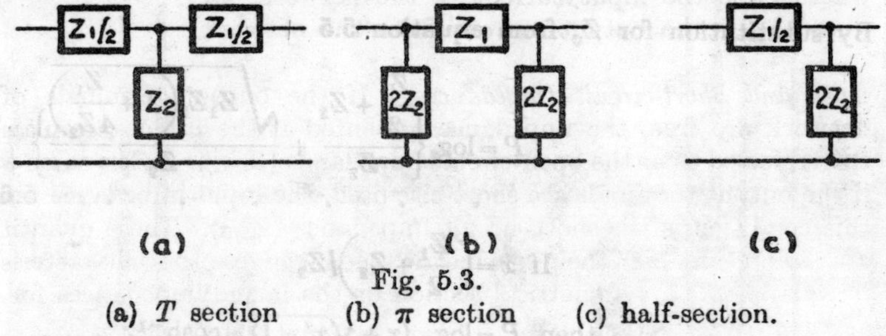

Fig. 5.3.
(a) T section (b) π section (c) half-section.

Such sections are not equivalent to each other, but are three ways of considering the given ladder network. It is also possible to consider the network as consisting of a chain of asymmetrical T or π sections.

The T and π sections shown above are symmetrical and so have a characteristic impedance and propagation constant, whereas the half-section is asymmetrical and has image and iterative impedances, an mage-transfer coefficient and an iterative propagation constant.

Characteristic Impedance and Propagation Coefficient of a T Section

If the T section shown above is closed in its characteristic impedance Z_0, the impedance at the input terminals will be equal to this value, and so

$$Z_0 = \frac{Z_1}{2} + \frac{Z_2\left(\frac{Z_1}{2} + Z_0\right)}{\frac{Z_1}{2} + Z_2 + Z_0}$$

$$\therefore Z_0^2 + Z_0\left(\frac{Z_1}{2} + Z_2\right) = \frac{Z_1^2}{4} + Z_1Z_2 + \frac{Z_0Z_1}{2} + Z_2Z_0$$

$$\therefore Z_0^2 = \frac{Z_1^2}{4} + Z_1Z_2$$

and Z_{0T} the value of Z_0 for the T section is given by

$$Z_{0T} = \sqrt{Z_1Z_2\left(1 + \frac{Z_1}{4Z_2}\right)} \quad . \quad . \quad 5.5$$

If P is the propagation coefficient for the section terminated in Z_0

$$\text{then } P = \log_e \frac{I_S}{I_R} = \log_e \frac{\frac{Z_1}{2} + Z_2 + Z_0}{Z_2}$$

$$\text{as } I_R = \frac{Z_2}{\frac{Z_1}{2} + Z_2 + Z_0} \cdot I_S$$

By substitution for Z_0 from equation 5.5

$$P = \log_e \left\{ \frac{\frac{Z_1}{2} + Z_2}{Z_2} + \frac{\sqrt{Z_1 Z_2 \left(1 + \frac{Z_1}{4Z_2}\right)}}{Z_2} \right\} \qquad 5.6$$

$$\text{If } x = \left(\frac{Z_1}{2} + Z_2\right) / Z_2$$

$$\text{then } P = \log_e \left(x + \sqrt{x^2 - 1}\right) = \cosh^{-1} x$$

and so P may be defined by

$$\cosh P = 1 + \frac{Z_1}{2Z_2} \qquad 5.7$$

Open and Short-circuit Impedances of a T Section

The T section of Fig. 5.4 has an open circuit impedance given by

$$Z_{O/C} = \frac{Z_1}{2} + Z_2 \text{ and } Z_{S/C} = \frac{Z_1}{2} + \frac{\left(\frac{Z_1}{2}\right) Z_2}{\frac{Z_1}{2} + Z_2}$$

$$\therefore (Z_{O/C})(Z_{S/C}) = Z_1 Z_2 \left(1 + \frac{Z_1}{4Z_2}\right) = Z_{OT}^2$$

$$\therefore Z_{OT} = \sqrt{Z_{O/C} \cdot Z_{S/C}} \qquad 5.8$$

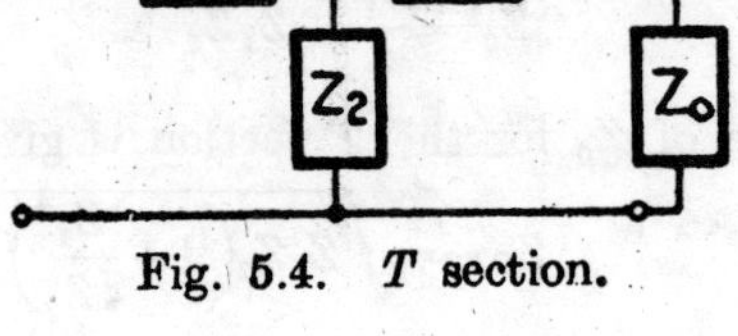

Fig. 5.4. T section.

As previously stated, this result is true for all symmetrical sections.

Characteristic Impedance and Propagation Coefficient of a π Section

As in the case of the T section, the input impedances of a symmetrical π section, when terminated in Z_0 will be equal to Z_0.

Hence for the π section shown in Fig. 5.5.

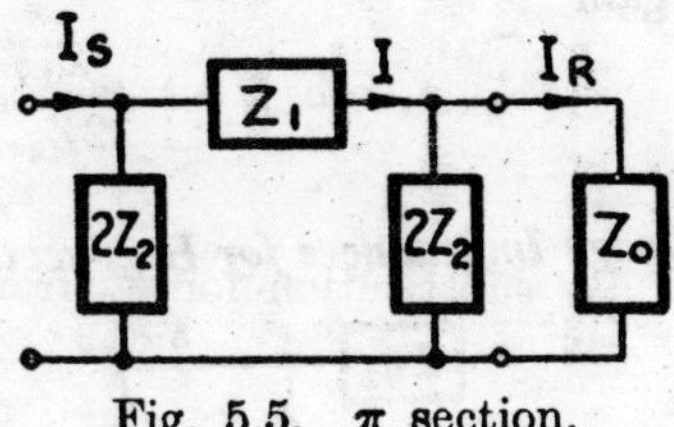

Fig. 5.5. π section.

$$Z_0 = \frac{2Z_2\left(Z_1 + \dfrac{2Z_2Z_0}{2Z_2 + Z_0}\right)}{2Z_2 + Z_1 + \dfrac{2Z_2Z_0}{2Z_2 + Z_0}}$$

Simplification of this expression gives

$$Z_0^2 = \frac{Z_1Z_2}{1 + \dfrac{Z_1}{4Z_2}}$$

and so the characteristic impedance for the π section is

$$Z_{0\pi} = \sqrt{\frac{Z_1Z_2}{1 + \dfrac{Z_1}{4Z_2}}} \quad . \quad . \quad . \quad 5.9$$

As in the case of the T section, the propagation coefficient for the correctly terminated section is given by

$$P = \log_e \frac{I_S}{I_R}$$

$$\text{In this case } I_R = \frac{2Z_2}{2Z_2 + Z_0} \cdot I$$

$$\text{and } I = \left(\frac{2Z_2}{Z_1 + 2Z_2 + \dfrac{2Z_2Z_0}{2Z_2 + Z_0}}\right) I_S$$

$$\therefore \frac{I_S}{I_R} = \frac{(2Z_2 + Z_0)\left(Z_1 + 2Z_2 + \dfrac{2Z_2Z_0}{2Z_2 + Z_0}\right)}{4Z_2^2}$$

$$\text{and so } P = \log_e\left\{\frac{(2Z_2 + Z_0)(Z_1 + 2Z_2) + 2Z_2Z_0}{4Z_2^2}\right\}$$

$$= \log_e\left\{\frac{4Z_2^2 + 2Z_1Z_2}{4Z_2^2} + Z_0\left(\frac{Z_1 + 4Z_2}{4Z_2^2}\right)\right\}$$

By substitution for Z_0 from equation 5.9 and re-arrangement

$$P=\log_e\left\{\left(1+\frac{Z_1}{2Z_2}\right)+\frac{\sqrt{Z_1Z_2\left(1+\frac{Z_1}{4Z_2}\right)}}{Z_2}\right\} \quad . \quad 5.10$$

It will be seen that this is identical with equation 5.6 and so once again

$$\cosh P=1+\frac{Z_1}{2Z_2} \quad . \quad . \quad . \quad . \quad . \quad . \quad 5.11$$

Image Impedances for Half-section

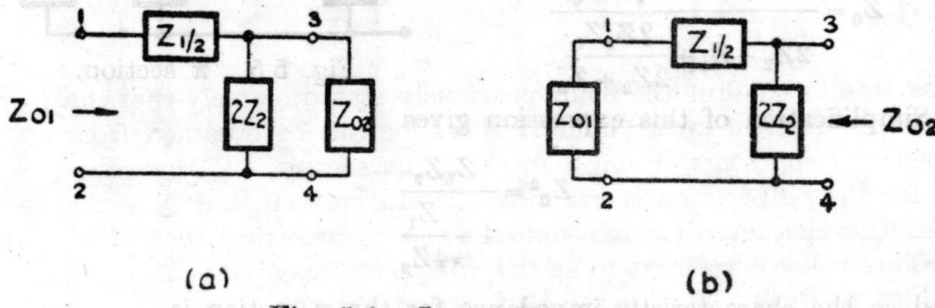

Fig. 5.6. Image impedances.

It will be seen from Fig. 5.6 that the image impedances for the half-section shown are

$$Z_{01}=\frac{Z_1}{2}+\frac{2Z_2Z_{02}}{2Z_2+Z_{02}} \text{ and } Z_{02}=\frac{2Z_2\left(\frac{Z_1}{2}+Z_{01}\right)}{\frac{Z_1}{2}+2Z_2+Z_{01}}$$

Substitution of the expression for Z_{02} in the first equation enables Z_{01} to be obtained. It will then be found that

$$Z_{01}=\sqrt{Z_1Z_2\left(1+\frac{Z_1}{4Z_2}\right)} \quad . \quad . \quad . \quad . \quad 5.12$$

$$\text{and } Z_{02}=\sqrt{\frac{Z_1Z_2}{1+\frac{Z_1}{4Z_2}}} \quad . \quad . \quad . \quad . \quad . \quad 5.13$$

Open and Short-circuit Impedances for a Half-section

If in Fig. 5.6a the terminals 3,4 are open-circuited then short-circuited, the impedances at the terminals 1,2 are respectively,

$$Z_{O/C}=\frac{Z_1}{2}+2Z_2 \text{ and } Z_{S/C}=\frac{Z_1}{2}$$

$$\therefore Z_{O/C} \cdot Z_{S/C} = Z_1 Z_2\left(1 + \frac{Z_1}{4Z_2}\right) = (Z_{01})^2$$

In the same way the corresponding impedances at the terminals 3,4 are

$$Z_{O/C} = 2Z_2 \text{ and } Z_{S/C} = \frac{\dfrac{2Z_2 Z_1}{2}}{2Z_2 + \dfrac{Z_1}{2}}$$

$$\therefore Z_{O/C} \cdot Z_{S/C} = \frac{Z_1 Z_2}{1 + \dfrac{Z_1}{4Z_2}} = (Z_{02})^2$$

These results confirm the point previously stated, namely that the image impedances of an asymmetrical section can be obtained from the open and short-circuit impedances of the section. If the value of Z_{01} for the half-section is examined it will be seen that it is the same as the characteristic impedance for a symmetrical T section (Z_{OT}). This value is referred to as the *mid-series* image impedance of the ladder network. Z_{02} for the half-section has the same value as the characteristic impedance for the symmetrical π section ($Z_{O\pi}$) and this is referred to as the *mid-shunt* image impedance for the ladder network. The half-section may thus be used to match a T section to a π section.

Image-transfer Coefficient for Half-section

If a voltage V_S is applied to the terminals 3,4 in Fig. 5.6b, the input current I_S will be V_S/Z_{02} as the input impedance of the terminated section is Z_{02}.

$$\therefore V_S I_S = V_S^2/Z_{02}$$

The voltage across the terminals 1,2 will then be

$$V_R = \frac{V_S Z_{01}}{Z_{01} + \dfrac{Z_1}{2}}$$

and the current through $Z_{01} = I_R = \dfrac{V_S}{Z_{01} + \dfrac{Z_1}{2}}$

and so $V_R I_R = \dfrac{V_S^2 Z_{01}}{\left(Z_{01} + \dfrac{Z_1}{2}\right)^2}$

By definition the image-transfer coefficient θ, for a network terminated in its image impedances is given by

$$\theta = \tfrac{1}{2}\log_e \frac{V_S I_S}{V_R I_R} = \tfrac{1}{2}\log_e\left\{\frac{Z_{01}}{Z_{02}}\left(\frac{Z_{01}+Z_1/2}{Z_{01}}\right)^2\right\}$$

then by substitution of the values for Z_{01} and Z_{02} (equations 5.12 and 5.13)

$$\theta = \tfrac{1}{2}\log_e\left\{\left(1+\frac{Z_1}{2Z_2}\right)+\frac{\sqrt{Z_1Z_2\left(1+\dfrac{Z_1}{4Z_2}\right)}}{Z_2}\right\} \qquad 5.14$$

This same value for θ will be obtained if transmission is considered to take place in the opposite direction through the network.

If equation 5.14 is compared with equations 5.6 and 5.10 (for the T and π sections) it will be seen that the value of θ in the half-section is half the value of P for the T or π section, as would be expected. The half-section may thus be regarded as the basic form, and if a ladder network is made up of half-sections which have their image impedances matched at their junctions, the network will then have image impedances equal to the open end image impedances of the terminating half-sections. The image-transfer coefficient of the ladder network will be given by the value for a half-section multiplied by the number of half-sections involved.

LATTICE SECTIONS

Another arrangement often used, particularly in crystal filters, is the lattice section shown in Fig. 5.7. The most general form has all four impedances unequal but only the simple symmetrical section will be considered.

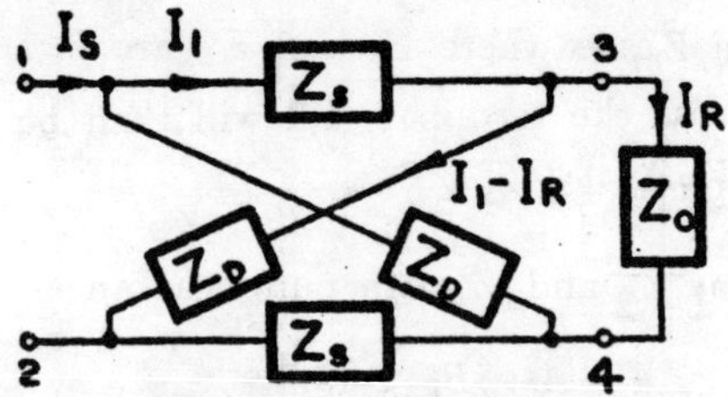

Fig. 5.7. Lattice section.

Characteristic Impedance and Propagation Coefficient of a Symmetrical Lattice Section

A symmetrical section has a characteristic impedance equal in value to the geometric mean of the open and short circuit impedances.

This idea may be used to find the Z_0 for the lattice section shown.

If the terminals 3,4 are first open-circuited then short-circuited, the respective input impedances at 1,2 are given by

$$Z_{O/C} = \tfrac{1}{2}(Z_S + Z_D) \text{ and } Z_{S/C} = \frac{2Z_S Z_D}{Z_S + Z_D}$$

$$\therefore Z_0 = \sqrt{Z_{O/C} \,.\, Z_{S/C}} = \sqrt{Z_S Z_D} \qquad . \quad . \qquad 5.15$$

This result may be confirmed by connecting an impedance Z_0 across the output terminals and then calculating the ratio V_S/I_S $(=Z_0)$ for an applied voltage of V_S at the input terminals.

To determine the propagation coefficient for the section it is necessary to find the ratio of the input and output currents (I_S/I_R). This may be found by supposing a voltage V_S to be applied at the terminals 1,2 which then gives rise to a distribution of currents as shown.

The application of Kirchhoff's second law to the mesh 1342 gives

$$V_S = I_1 Z_S + I_R Z_0 + (I_S - I_1 + I_R) Z_S$$
$$= I_S Z_S + I_R (Z_0 + Z_S)$$

now the input impedance is Z_0 and so $V_S = I_S Z_0$

$$\therefore I_S(Z_0 - Z_S) = I_R(Z_0 + Z_S)$$

$$\therefore \frac{I_S}{I_R} = \frac{Z_0 + Z_S}{Z_0 - Z_S} \text{ and } P = \log_e \frac{Z_0 + Z_S}{Z_0 - Z_S} \qquad . \quad . \qquad 5.16$$

$$\text{alternatively } e^P \; \frac{Z_0 + Z_S}{Z_0 - Z_S}$$

$$\therefore \frac{Z_S}{Z_0} = \frac{e^P - 1}{e^P + 1} = \frac{e^{\frac{P}{2}} - e^{-\frac{P}{2}}}{e^{\frac{P}{2}} + e^{-\frac{P}{2}}} \therefore \tanh \frac{P}{2} = \frac{Z_S}{Z_0} = \sqrt{Z_S/Z_D} \qquad . \qquad 5.17$$

In the special case where Z_S and Z_D are *inverse impedances* such that $Z_S \,.\, Z_D = R^2$

$$\text{then } \tanh \frac{P}{2} = \sqrt{Z_S/Z_D} = \frac{Z_S}{\sqrt{Z_S \,.\, Z_D}} = \frac{Z_S}{R}$$

If, in addition, Z_S and Z_D are pure reactances, jX_S and jX_D then

$$P = A + jB = 2 \tanh^{-1} \frac{jX_S}{R}$$

$$\therefore A + jB = 2j \tan^{-1} \frac{X_S}{R}$$

This result shows that such a network, if realised, has zero attenuation at all frequencies and a phase shift which depends on the reactance variation of X_S.

BRIDGED-T SECTION

A third network arrangement is the bridged-T section, the symmetrical unbalanced version of which is shown in Fig. 5.8.

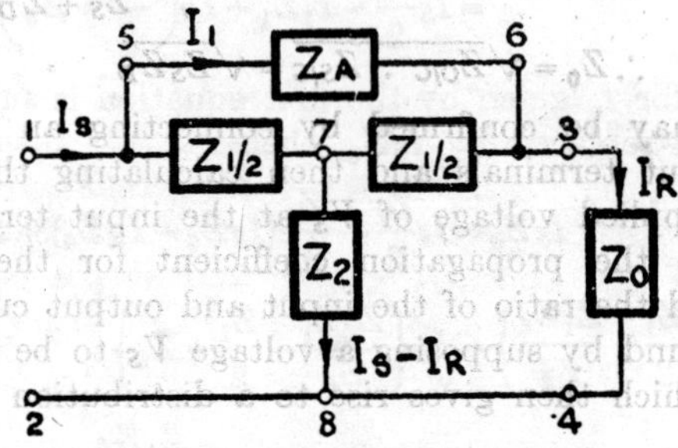

Fig. 5.8. Bridged-T section.

The section is symmetrical, and so $Z_0 = \sqrt{Z_{O/C} \cdot Z_{S/C}}$

$$\text{Now } Z_{O/C} = Z_2 + \frac{\frac{Z_1}{2}\left(\frac{Z_1}{2} + Z_A\right)}{Z_1 + Z_A}$$

$$= \frac{Z_1Z_2 + Z_2Z_A + \frac{Z_1^2}{4} + \frac{Z_1Z_A}{2}}{Z_1 + Z_A}$$

$$\text{and } Z_{S/C} = \frac{Z_A\left(\frac{Z_1}{2} + \frac{\frac{Z_1}{2}Z_2}{\frac{Z_1}{2} + Z_2}\right)}{Z_A + \frac{Z_1}{2} + \frac{\frac{Z_1}{2}Z_2}{\frac{Z_1}{2} + Z_2}} = \frac{Z_AZ_1^2/4 + Z_AZ_2Z_1}{\frac{Z_AZ_1}{2} + Z_AZ_2 + \frac{Z_1^2}{4} + Z_1Z_2}$$

$$\therefore Z_0 = \sqrt{\frac{\frac{Z_AZ_1^2}{4} + Z_AZ_2Z_1}{Z_1 + Z_A}} = \sqrt{\frac{Z_AZ_1(Z_1 + 4Z_2)}{4(Z_1 + Z_A)}} \quad . \quad . \quad 5.18$$

The propagation coefficient of the section may be obtained as before from the ratio of I_S/I_R.

If a voltage V_S is applied at the terminals 1,2 and the current distribution is as shown in Fig. 5.8, then the application of Kirchhoff's second law to the mesh 1563482 and 173482 respectively gives

$$V_S = I_1 Z_A + I_R Z_0$$

$$\text{and } V_S = (I_S - I_1)\frac{Z_1}{2} - (I_1 - I_R)\frac{Z_1}{2} + I_R Z_0$$

$$= I_S\frac{Z_1}{2} - I_1 Z_1 + I_R\left(\frac{Z_1}{2} + Z_0\right)$$

If the value for I_1 given by the first equation is substituted in the second, and V_S replaced by $I_S Z_0$, then

$$I_S Z_0 = I_S\frac{Z_1}{2} - \frac{Z_1}{Z_A}(I_S Z_0 - I_R Z_0) + I_R\left(\frac{Z_1}{2} + Z_0\right)$$

$$\therefore I_S\left\{Z_0 - \frac{Z_1}{2} + \frac{Z_1 Z_0}{Z_A}\right\} = I_R\left\{\frac{Z_0 Z_1}{Z_A} + \frac{Z_1}{2} + Z_0\right\}$$

$$\therefore \frac{I_S}{I_R} = \frac{Z_0 Z_1 + Z_0 Z_A + \dfrac{Z_1 Z_A}{2}}{Z_0 Z_1 + Z_0 Z_A - \dfrac{Z_1 Z_A}{2}}$$

$$\text{and thus } P = \log_e\left\{\frac{Z_0(Z_1 + Z_A) + \dfrac{Z_1 Z_A}{2}}{Z_0(Z_1 + Z_A) - \dfrac{Z_1 Z_A}{2}}\right\} \qquad 5.19$$

The Conversion of a Symmetrical Network to an Equivalent Lattice Structure

Ladder, lattice, and bridged-T networks have so far been considered. Of these, the lattice is the most general in that the ladder and bridged-T networks may be converted to the lattice form, while converse transformation from the lattice form is not always possible.

It is sometimes convenient to deal with the lattice equivalent rather than the original network. All symmetrical networks may be converted to the equivalent lattice arrangement by means of a theorem known as Bartlett's bisection theorem.[1] This states, in effect, that any network which can be divided into two mirror image halves can be reduced to an equivalent lattice network. The series arms of the equivalent lattice contain an impedance equal to the input impedance of one half of the network when all the cut wires of the network are short circuited; the diagonal arms of the equivalent lattice contain the impedance obtained at the input terminals of one half of the network when all the cut wires are open circuited.

As an illustration of the theorem, consider the bridged-T section of Fig. 5.8. When bisected, this appears as shown in Fig. 5.9a. The input impedance when the terminals 5,6,7, are short circuited is given by,

$$\frac{\dfrac{Z_1 Z_A}{4}}{\dfrac{Z_1}{2}+\dfrac{Z_A}{2}}=\frac{Z_1 Z_A}{2(Z_1+Z_A)}$$

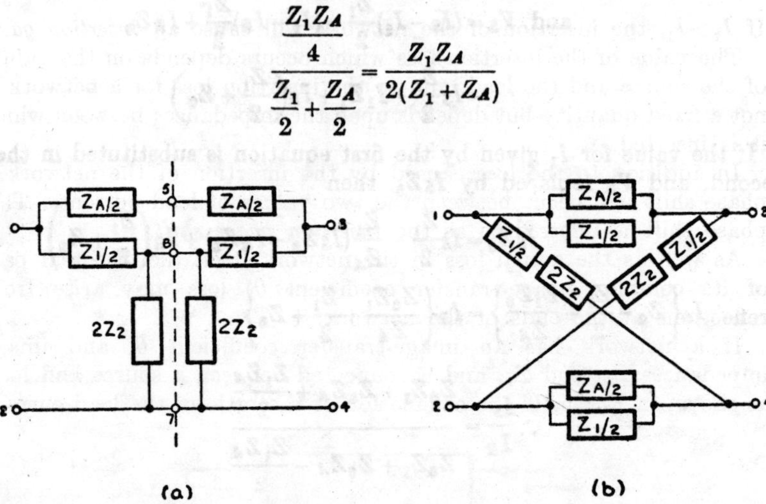

Fig. 5.9. Conversion of a bridged-T to a lattice section.

The input impedance with the terminals 5,6,7 open circuited is given by,

$$\frac{Z_1}{2}+2Z_2$$

It then follows from the theorem that the equivalent lattice is that of Fig. 5.9b. If the characteristic impedance of this equivalent lattice is calculated it will be found to have the value given by equation 5.18 for the original bridged-T section.

Insertion Loss

If a network is inserted between a generator and its load there will, in general, be a reduction in the power received in the load, and the load current will be decreased. The loss produced by the insertion of the network is referred to as the *insertion loss*. If the load current without the network is I_1 and the load current with the network inserted is I_2, then the insertion loss is equal to

$$\left.\begin{array}{l} 20\log_{10}\dfrac{|I_1|}{|I_2|}\ \text{dB} \\ \text{or } \log_e\dfrac{|I_1|}{|I_2|}\ \text{nepers} \end{array}\right\} \quad . \quad . \quad . \quad 5.20$$

If $I_2 > I_1$, the insertion of the network will cause an *insertion ga*

The value of the insertion loss which occurs depends on the valu of the source and the load, and so the insertion loss for a network not a fixed quantity but depends upon the impedances between whi it is inserted.

In addition to the loss caused by the insertion of the network phase shift will occur between the two values of load current. Tl phase shift is referred to as the *insertion phase shift.*

As well as the actual loss in the network itself (i.e. the real pa of its complex image-transfer coefficient θ) loss may arise fro reflections at the ends of the network.

If a network has an image-transfer coefficient θ, and ima impedances Z_{01} and Z_{02} and is connected between a source and lo as shown in Fig. 5.10, the calculation of the ratio of the load curre

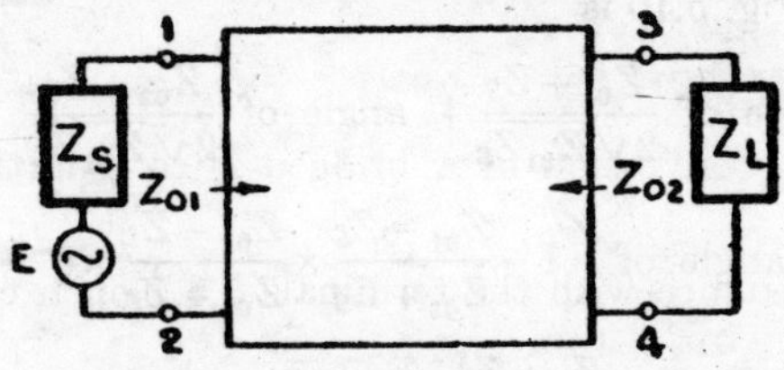

Fig. 5.10.

with the network (I_2) to the load current in the absence of the networl (I_1) can be shown to give

$$\frac{I_2}{I_1} = \frac{2\sqrt{Z_{01}Z_S}}{Z_{01}+Z_S} \times \frac{2\sqrt{Z_{02}Z_L}}{Z_{02}+Z_L} \times \left(1 - \frac{Z_{01}-Z_S}{Z_{01}+Z_S} \times \frac{Z_{02}-Z_L}{Z_{02}+Z_L} \times e^{-2\theta}\right)^{-1}$$

$$\times \frac{Z_S+Z_L}{2\sqrt{Z_SZ_L}} \times e^{-\theta} \quad . \quad . \quad . \quad . \quad . \quad . \quad 5.21$$

The first factor represents the reflection factor between Z_{01} and Z_S whilst the second factor is the reflection factor between Z_{02} and Z_L The third factor represents the interaction factor and accounts fo the loss of energy when a mismatch occurs at each end of the network. The fourth factor is the reciprocal of the reflection factor between Z_S and Z_L, whilst the last factor represents the loss occurring in the network 1234.

The complete insertion loss for the network 1234 when insertec between impedances Z_S and Z_L as in Fig. 5.10 is thus

$$L = 20 \log_{10} \frac{I_1}{I_2} \text{ dB}$$

$$\left[20 \log_{10}\left|\frac{Z_{01}+Z_S}{2\sqrt{Z_{01}Z_S}}\right| + 20 \log_{10}\left|\frac{Z_{02}+Z_L}{2\sqrt{Z_{02}Z_L}}\right|\right.$$

$$+20 \log_{10}\left|1-\frac{Z_{01}-Z_S}{Z_{01}+Z_S}\times\frac{Z_{02}-Z_L}{Z_{02}+Z_L}\times e^{-2\theta}\right|$$

$$\left.-20 \log_{10}\left|\frac{Z_S+Z_L}{2\sqrt{Z_SZ_L}}\right| + A\right] \text{ decibels} \quad . \quad . \quad . \quad 5.22$$

If the network is matched to the source, i.e. $Z_{01}=Z_S$, the first and third terms disappear. If $Z_{02}=Z_L$ the second and third terms disappear. The third term may become vanishingly small if the value of θ for the network is large. If all four impedances are equal to each other the insertion loss is simply the attenuation A occurring in the network 1234.

The complete insertion phase shift for the network inserted between Z_S and Z_L in Fig. 5.10 is

$$=\left[\text{angle of } \frac{Z_{01}+Z_S}{2\sqrt{Z_{01}Z_S}} + \text{angle of } \frac{Z_{02}+Z_L}{2\sqrt{Z_{02}Z_L}}\right.$$

$$+\text{ angle of }\left(1-\frac{Z_{01}-Z_S}{Z_{01}+Z_S}\times\frac{Z_{02}-Z_L}{Z_{02}+Z_L}\times e^{-2\theta}\right)$$

$$\left.-\text{angle of } \frac{Z_S+Z_L}{2\sqrt{Z_SZ_L}} + B\right] \text{ radians} \quad . \quad . \quad . \quad 5.23$$

ATTENUATORS

Attenuators are usually resistive networks designed for the purpose of introducing a given loss when inserted between specified impedances. An attenuator is normally a four terminal network, either symmetrical or asymmetrical in form. Symmetrical types have a characteristic impedance which is resistive and referred to as the *characteristic resistance.*

No phase shift is involved in attenuators and so the propagation coefficient and image-transfer coefficient for such networks are entirely real quantities.

The decibel is the most commonly used unit of attenuation and the loss introduced by any network is given by

$$\text{Loss} = 10 \log P_S/P_R \text{ dB}$$

where P_S = Power Input

P_R = Power Output

For a symmetrical section, inserted between matched terminations the loss may be written as

$$= 20 \log_{10} N \text{ dB}$$

$$\text{or} = \log_e N \text{ nepers}$$

$$\text{where } N = I_S/I_R$$

For asymmetrical arrangements the loss can be written as

$$= 20 \log_{10} N^1 \text{ dB}$$

$$\text{where } N^1 = \sqrt{P_S/P_R}$$

Symmetrical T Section Attenuator

When an attenuator is to be designed the characteristic resistance and the desired attenuation are the quantities which are known; it is then necessary to calculate the values for the elements in terms of these quantities.

The values of the arms of a symmetrical T section attenuator may be obtained by referring to the equivalent T section for a transmission line (Fig. 4.8a) as the arms are specified in terms of the characteristic impedance Z_0 and propagation coefficient P, of the line. The equivalent T section has series arms which have the value

$$Z_0 \tanh Pl/2$$

while the value of the shunt arm is given by

$$Z_0/\sinh Pl$$

hence in Fig. 5.11, R_1 will be equivalent to $Z_0 \tanh \frac{Pl}{2}$ and R_2 will be equivalent to $Z_0/\sinh Pl$.

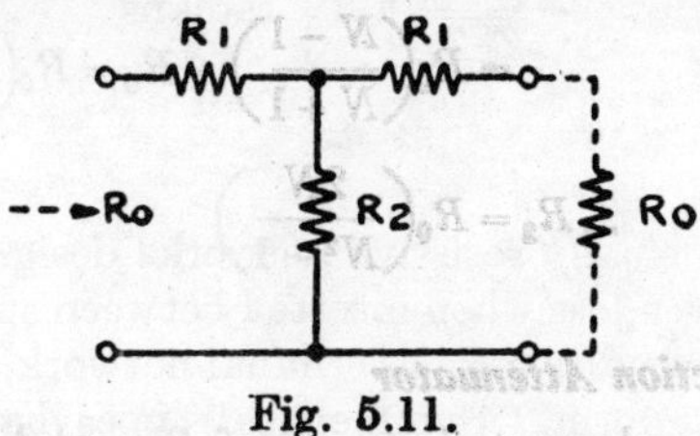

Fig. 5.11.

In the attenuator, Z_0 becomes R_0, and $I_S/I_R = e^\alpha = N$.

$$\therefore R_1 = R_0 \tanh \frac{\alpha}{2} = R_0\left(\frac{e^{\frac{\alpha}{2}} - e^{-\frac{\alpha}{2}}}{e^{\frac{\alpha}{2}} + e^{-\frac{\alpha}{2}}}\right) = R_0 \frac{e^\alpha - 1}{e^\alpha + 1}$$

$$\therefore R_1 = R_0\left(\frac{N-1}{N+1}\right) \quad . \quad . \quad . \quad . \quad 5.24$$

$$\text{also } R_2 = \frac{R_0}{\sinh \alpha} = \frac{2R_0}{e^\alpha - e^{-\alpha}} = \frac{2R_0 e^\alpha}{e^{2\alpha} - 1}$$

$$R_2 = R_0\left(\frac{2N}{N^2 - 1}\right) \quad . \quad . \quad . \quad . \quad 5.25$$

These results may be derived directly from a consideration of the terminated section. If the section is correctly terminated in R_0, the input impedance will be R_0 and so from Fig. 5.11

$$R_0 = R_1 + \frac{R_2(R_1 + R_0)}{R_1 + R_2 + R_0}$$

but it will be seen that

$$\frac{R_2}{R_1 + R_2 + R_0} = \frac{I_R}{I_S} = \frac{1}{N} \quad . \quad . \quad . \quad . \quad 5.26$$

$$\therefore R_0 = R_1 + \frac{R_1 + R_0}{N}$$

$$\therefore R_0(N-1) = R_1(N+1)$$

$$\therefore R_1 = R_0\left(\frac{N-1}{N+1}\right)$$

which agrees with the result of equation 5.24. Equation 5.26 may be used to confirm the value for R_2,

$$\text{as } \frac{R_2}{R_1 + R_2 + R_0} = \frac{1}{N}$$

$$R_2(N-1) = R_1 + R_0$$

$$= R_0\left(\frac{N-1}{N+1}\right) + R_0 = R_0\left(\frac{2N}{N+1}\right)$$

$$\therefore R_2 = R_0\left(\frac{2N}{N^2-1}\right)$$

Symmetrical π Section Attenuator

The values of the elements in terms of R_0 and N may be determined as for the T section. The equivalent π section for a transmission line of characteristic impedance Z_0 and propagation coefficient P has a series arm of $Z_0 \sinh Pl$ and shunt arms $Z_0 \coth Pl/2$. In the case of the π section attenuator shown in Fig. 5.12

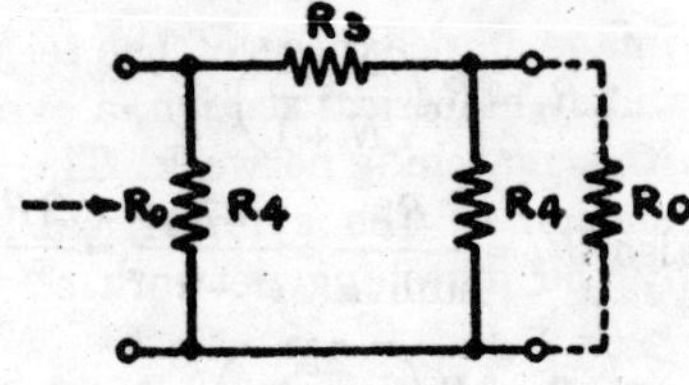

Fig. 5.12.

$$R_3 = Z_0 \sinh Pl = R_0 \sinh \alpha \text{ and } R_4 = Z_0 \coth \frac{Pl}{2} = R_0 \coth \frac{\alpha}{2}$$

and as before, $\alpha = \log_e \dfrac{I_S}{I_R} \quad \therefore e^{\alpha} = \dfrac{I_S}{I_R} = N$

$$\therefore R_3 = R_0 \frac{e^{\alpha} - e^{-\alpha}}{2} = R_0 \frac{e^{2\alpha} - 1}{2e^{\alpha}} = R_0\left(\frac{N^2 - 1}{2N}\right) \quad . \quad . \quad . \quad 5.27$$

$$R_4 = R_0 \frac{e^{\frac{\alpha}{2}} + e^{-\frac{\alpha}{2}}}{e^{\frac{\alpha}{2}} - e^{\frac{-\alpha}{2}}} = R_0 \frac{e^{\alpha} + 1}{e^{\alpha} - 1}$$

$$\therefore R_4 = R_0\left(\frac{N + 1}{N - 1}\right) \quad . \quad . \quad . \quad . \quad . \quad . \quad 5.28$$

These results may be confirmed in the same way as was shown for the T section.

A T section may be interchanged with a π section of the same characteristic resistance and the same attenuation. The choice between the two types in any given case becomes one of convenience for the particular value of attenuation desired. In the T type the shunt arm becomes small whilst the series arm in the π section becomes large, when the attenuation is high. (See worked example No. 1.)

Attenuation between Unequal Impedances

If an attenuator is required to work between two impedances of unequal value an asymmetrical T or π section may be designed to have image impedances equal to the given impedances. The values of the arms can be calculated for the values of the two image impedances and the relation for the attenuation, when the N of the symmetrical sections is replaced by N^1,

$$\text{where } N^1 = \sqrt{\frac{P_S}{P_R}} = \frac{I_S}{I_R}\sqrt{\frac{R_S}{R_R}}$$

h R_S and R_R are the image impedances of the section.

As an alternative to an asymmetrical section, a symmetrical section may be used together with a matching network. The total attenuation will then be the attenuation of the symmetrical section plus the attenuation produced by the matching network.

***L* Section.** The L section of two resistors is the simplest type of matching section. Fig. 5.13 shows such a section for use between equipment which has impedances R_{01} and R_{02}.

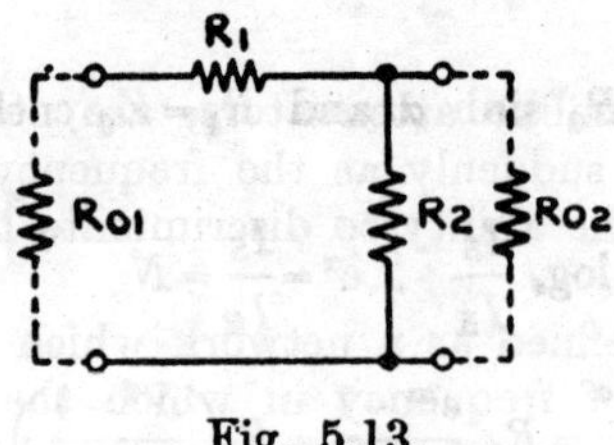

Fig. 5.13.

The matching section is then required to have image impedances R_{01} and R_{02}. Values for these quantities may be obtained from the open and short-circuit impedances of the section,

$$\text{and so } R_{01}=\sqrt{(R_1+R_2)R_1} \quad \therefore (R_{01})^2=R_1{}^2+R_1R_2 \quad . \quad 5.29$$

$$\text{also } R_{02}=\sqrt{R_2\left(\frac{R_1R_2}{R_1+R_2}\right)} \quad \therefore (R_{02})^2=\frac{R_1R_2{}^2}{R_1+R_2} \quad . \quad . \quad 5.30$$

Equation 5.29 gives

$$R_2=[(R_{01})^2-R_1{}^2]/R_1$$

and so substitution of this value in equation 5.30 gives

$$(R_{02})^2=\frac{[(R_{01})^2-R_1{}^2]^2}{R_1\left(R_1+\dfrac{(R_{01})^2-R_1{}^2}{R_1}\right)}$$

$$\therefore (R_{01})^2-R_1{}^2=(R_{01})(R_{02})$$

$$\therefore R_1=\sqrt{R_{01}(R_{01}-R_{02})} \quad . \quad . \quad . \quad 5.31$$

Substitution of this value for R_1 in equation 5.29 gives

$$R_2=\sqrt{\frac{R_{01}(R_{02})^2}{R_{01}-R_{02}}} \quad . \quad . \quad . \quad 5.32$$

If R_1 and R_2 have the values given by equations 5.31 and 5.32 the image impedances will then be R_{01} and R_{02} and the section will match the two dissimilar networks as required without reflection loss. The attenuation produced by the values of the arms required for matching purposes can then be calculated by considering the current distribution for the circuit shown in Fig. 5.13.

FILTERS

Electrical filters, unlike attenuators, are networks in which the attenuation changes suddenly as the frequency is varied. Because of this, filters have the ability to discriminate between signals which differ in frequency.

A filter may be defined as a network which in its ideal form has at least one range of frequency in which the attenuation is zero, and at least one other range of frequency in which the attenuation is infinite. A range in which the attenuation is zero is called a *pass-band* whilst a range of frequencies subject to attenuation is called an *attenuation-band*. Frequencies which separate a pass and an attenuation band are called *cut-off frequencies*.

Whereas attenuators are built up of combinations of resistors, ideal filters are composed of pure reactors. Practical filters fall short of the ideal however, because of the presence of resistance in reactive components. This results in a finite (but usually small) loss in the pass-band, a finite loss in the attenuation-band, and a poorly-defined cut-off frequency. Another source of loss in a practical filter assembly is due to terminal reflections when the image impedances of the filter depart from their desired value.

Determination of Pass and Attenuation-Bands

If a network is composed of components which are pure reactances the open and short circuit impedances of all such networks are pure reactances. This is proved in a general reactance theorem[3] but can be confirmed in an elementary fashion by considering the open and short-circuit impedances of a T section to which any network can be reduced. If the arms of a T section consist of reactances jX_1, jX_2 and jX_3 where X_1, X_2 and X_3 are real numbers it will be found that the open and short-circuit impedances are entirely reactive.

It follows that an ideal filter composed entirely of pure reactances has an image or characteristic impedance which is the geometric mean of a pair of reactances $\pm jX_{O/C}$ and $\pm jX_{S/C}$. It will be seen that for all possible combinations of these two values the image or characteristic impedance will be either wholly real or wholly imaginary. Now a network of pure reactances is incapable of dissipating power and so if the input impedance of a filter is real, power will be absorbed from a source but none of it will be expended in the filter. The power output will be the same as the power input and this will correspond to a pass-band. If, on the other hand, the input impedance of the filter is wholly reactive, no power will be absorbed from a source connected to the input terminals, and this condition will correspond to an attenuation-band.

The character of the input impedance of a filter may thus be used as a means for determining pass and attenuation bands. Cut-off frequencies will occur when the input impedance changes from a resistive to a reactive value, or vice versa. Reactance sketches may also be used to determine the variation of the input impedance with frequency.

Alternatively, the behaviour of the filter may be found from a consideration of its propagation coefficient or image-transfer coefficient.

Constant-K Ladder Type Filters

If a ladder type network (Fig. 5.2) has a series impedance Z_1 and a shunt impedance Z_2 such that

$$Z_1Z_2=R^2$$

the component T, π or half sections are said to be *constant-K* sections with a design impedance R.

The characteristic impedances for symmetrical T and π sections were found to be

$$Z_{0T}=\sqrt{Z_1Z_2\left(1+\frac{Z_1}{4Z_2}\right)} \quad \text{(equation 5.5)}$$

$$\text{and } Z_{0\pi}=\sqrt{\frac{Z_1Z_2}{1+\frac{Z_1}{4Z_2}}} \quad \text{(equation 5.9)}$$

It can be seen that $Z_{0T} \cdot Z_{0\pi}=Z_1Z_2=R^2 \quad \therefore Z_{0T}=\dfrac{R^2}{Z_{0\pi}}$. 5.33

and so Z_{0T} and $Z_{0\pi}$ must be either real or imaginary together. A T section, as shown in Fig. 5.14a, will thus have the same pass-band and the same cut-off frequency as the π section of 5.14b.

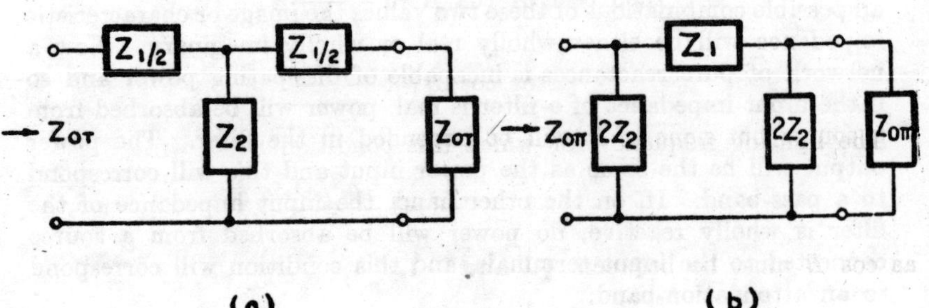

Fig. 5.14.

Low-Pass Constant-K Filter Section

(a) T Section. If in Fig. 5.14a, $Z_1 = j\omega L$ and $Z_2 = -j/\omega C$

then $Z_1 Z_2 = R^2 = L/C$ 5.34

and $Z_{0T} = \sqrt{Z_1 Z_2 \left(1 + \frac{Z_1}{4Z_2}\right)} = R\sqrt{1 - \frac{\omega^2 LC}{4}}$. 5.35

this will be resistive for frequencies from zero up to the point where

$$\omega^2 LC/4 = 1$$

and the limiting value of ω is thus ω_c

$$\text{where } \omega_c = 2/\sqrt{LC}$$

The arrangement will thus function as a low-pass filter and transmit frequencies from zero up to the cut-off frequency, f_c

$$\text{where } f_c = \frac{1}{\pi\sqrt{LC}} \quad . \quad . \quad . \quad 5.36$$

This may be confirmed by considering the propagation coefficient P

$$\text{where } \cosh P = 1 + \frac{Z_1}{2Z_2} = 1 - \frac{\omega^2 LC}{2}$$

and so $\cosh A \cos B + j \sinh A \sin B = 1 - \frac{\omega^2 LC}{2}$

$$\therefore \cosh A \cos B = 1 - \frac{\omega^2 LC}{2}$$

$$\text{and } \sinh A \sin B = 0$$

This last condition will be satisfied if

$A = 0$ (which makes $\cosh A = 1$ and $B \neq 0$)

or if $B = 0$ (which makes $\cos B = 1$ and $A \neq 0$)

or if $B = \pi$ (which makes $\cos B = -1$ and $A \neq 0$)

If a pass-band is considered, i.e. $A = 0$

$$\text{then } \cosh A \cos B = 1 - \frac{\omega^2 LC}{2}$$

$$\text{or } \cos B = 1 - \frac{\omega^2 LC}{2} \quad 5.37$$

The limiting frequency for which this condition holds will be

$$-1 = 1 - \frac{\omega^2 LC}{2}$$

as $\cos B$ must lie between $+1$ and -1.

The limiting value for ω is given by ω_c, where

$$\omega_c = \frac{2}{\sqrt{LC}}$$

and the cut-off frequency f_c is

$$f_c = \frac{1}{\pi\sqrt{LC}}$$

which agrees with the result obtained by considering the characteristic impedance of the section.

If the value for ω_c is inserted in equation 5.37 and $\omega = x\omega_c$

then $\cos B = 1 - 2x^2$

and $B = \cos^{-1}(1 - 2x^2)$ radians 5.38

This result gives the phase shift occurring in the pass-band as x varies from zero to unity at cut-off.

If the attenuation-band is considered, i.e. $A \neq 0$

then $B = \pi$ and $\cos B = -1$

$$\therefore -\cosh A = 1 - \frac{\omega^2 LC}{2}$$

$$= 1 - 2x^2$$

if $\omega = x\omega_c$

and so $A = \cosh^{-1}(2x^2 - 1)$ nepers . . 5.39

This result gives the value of the attenuation in the attenuation-band as x increases from unity to infinity.

The characteristic impedance of the T section is by equation 5.35.

$$Z_{0T} = R\sqrt{1 - \frac{\omega^2 LC}{4}} = R\sqrt{1 - x^2} \quad . \quad . \quad . \quad . \quad 5.40$$

as $LC/4 = 1/\omega_c^2$

The expression shows how the impedance of the section varies with frequency.

The results obtained above are summarised in Fig. 5.15a.

(b) π Section. As $\cosh P = 1 + \dfrac{Z_1}{Z_2}$ is true for the π section of Fig. 5.14b. as well as the T section of Fig. 5.14a, it follows that the results obtained for the T section will apply equally well for the π section with the exception of the characteristic impedance.

For the π section

$$Z_{0\pi} = \sqrt{\frac{Z_1 Z_2}{1 + \frac{Z_1}{4Z_2}}} \quad \text{(equation 5.9)}$$

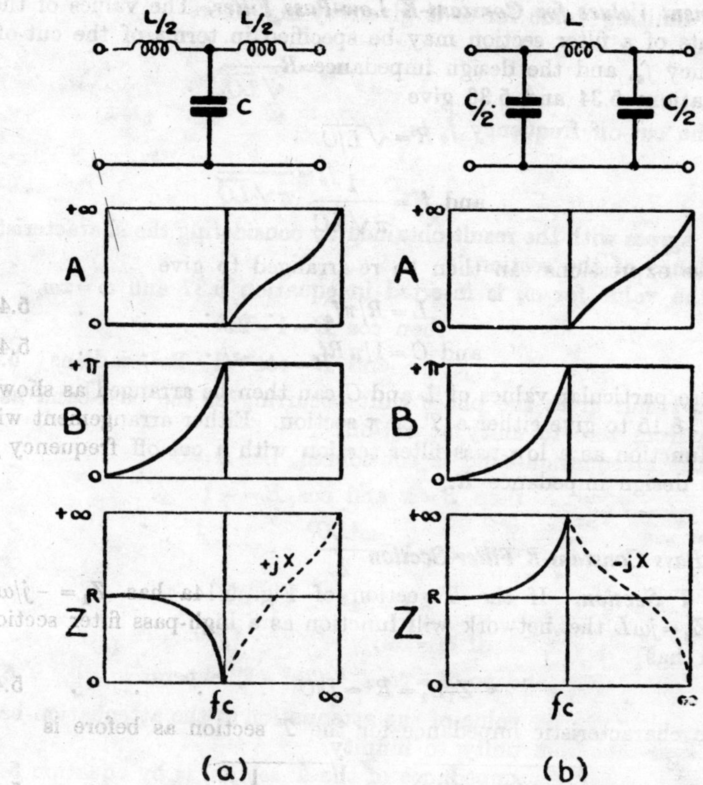

Fig. 5.15. Properties of ideal low-pass constant-K filter sections.

$$= \frac{R}{\sqrt{1-\frac{\omega^2 LC}{4}}} = \frac{R}{\sqrt{1-x^2}} \quad . \quad . \quad . \quad . \quad . \quad 5.41$$

if $\omega_c = \dfrac{2}{\sqrt{LC}}$ and $\omega = x\omega_c$

The behaviour of a π section as a low-pass filter is shown in Fig. 5.15b.

It will be noticed that both the T and π sections have impedances which vary over the pass-band. This is an undesirable feature which gives rise to reflection losses, and is a fundamental objection to a simple constant-K section and as a result more complicated structures, free from this defect, are commonly employed.

Element Values for Constant-K Low-Pass Filter. The values of the elements of a filter section may be specified in terms of the cut-off frequency f_c, and the design impedance R.

Equations 5.34 and 5.36 give

$$R = \sqrt{L/C}$$

$$\text{and } f_c = \frac{1}{\pi\sqrt{LC}}$$

These expressions can then be re-arranged to give

$$L = R/\pi f_c \quad . \quad . \quad . \quad . \quad 5.42$$

$$\text{and } C = 1/\pi R f_c \quad . \quad . \quad . \quad . \quad 5.43$$

These particular values of L and C can then be arranged as shown in Fig. 5.15 to give either a T or π section. Either arrangement will then function as a low-pass filter section with a cut-off frequency f_c and a design impedance R.

High-Pass Constant-K Filter Section

(a) T Section. If the T section of Fig. 5.14a has $Z_1 = -j/\omega C$ and $Z_2 = j\omega L$ the network will function as a high-pass filter section which has

$$Z_1 Z_2 = R^2 = L/C \quad . \quad . \quad . \quad . \quad 5.44$$

The characteristic impedance for the T section as before is

$$Z_{OT} = \sqrt{Z_1 Z_2\left(1 + \frac{Z_1}{4Z_2}\right)} = R\sqrt{1 - \frac{1}{4\omega^2 LC}} \quad . \quad . \quad . \quad 5.45$$

This impedance will be real provided that $1/4\omega^2 LC$ is less than unity and the limiting condition is that $4\omega^2 LC = 1$

The limiting value for ω is then given by ω_c where

$$\omega_c = \frac{1}{2\sqrt{LC}}$$

$$\text{The cut-off frequency } f_c = \frac{1}{4\pi\sqrt{LC}} \quad . \quad . \quad . \quad . \quad 5.46$$

This result may also be obtained from a consideration of the propagation coefficient P. For such a section

$$\cosh P = 1 + Z_1/2Z_2$$

$$\therefore \cosh A \cos B + j \sinh A \sin B = 1 - \frac{1}{2\omega^2 LC}$$

The left-hand side must thus be real, and so sinh A sin $B=0$.

If in the pass band $A=0$ then cosh A cos $B=1-\frac{1}{2\omega^2LC}$

$$\therefore \cos B=1-\frac{1}{2\omega^2LC} \quad . \quad . \quad . \quad 5.47$$

The limiting value of ω over which this expression can hold is thus from $\omega=\infty$ to $1-\frac{1}{2\omega^2LC}=-1$

ω must then lie between ∞ and ω_c

$$\text{where } \omega_c=\frac{1}{2\sqrt{LC}}$$

and the section thus has a pass-band for frequencies from f_c upwards

$$\text{where } f_c=\frac{1}{4\pi\sqrt{LC}}$$

This agrees with equation 5.46. Equation 5.47 shows that

$$\cos B=1-\frac{1}{2\omega^2LC}=1-\frac{2\omega_c^2}{\omega^2}=1-\frac{2}{x^2} \text{ if } \omega=x\omega_c$$

$$\therefore B=\cos^{-1}\left(1-\frac{2}{x^2}\right) \text{ radians} \quad . \quad 5.48$$

This last result gives the phase shift in the pass-band as x varies from 1 to ∞ as the frequency varies from cut-off to infinity. For frequencies below cut-off $B=-\pi$. In this latter region, the attenuation is given by

$$A=\cosh^{-1}\left(\frac{2}{x^2}-1\right) \text{ nepers} \quad . \quad 5.49$$

This result can be deduced in the same way as equation 5.39. The impedance of the T section is given by equation 5.45 as

$$Z_{OT}=R\sqrt{1-\frac{1}{4\omega^2LC}}$$

If the substitutions of $\omega=x\omega_c$ and $1/2\sqrt{LC}=\omega_c$ are made

$$Z_{OT}=R\sqrt{1-\frac{1}{x^2}} \quad . \quad . \quad . \quad 5.50$$

which shows that such a section, even in its idealised form of pure reactances, has an impedance variation from zero at cut-off ($x=1$) to its value R at an infinitely high frequency.

The variation of impedance, attenuation and phase shift for the T section considered are shown in Fig. 5.16a.

(b)* π *Section. **The corresponding π section of Fig. 5.14b has the identical value of propagation coefficient as the *T* section considered above, and so the variation of attenuation and phase shift with frequency is identical.**

The impedance of a π section is

$$Z_{0\pi} = \sqrt{\frac{Z_1 Z_2}{1+\dfrac{Z_1}{4Z_2}}} \quad \text{(equation 5.9)}$$

$$= \frac{R}{\sqrt{1-\dfrac{1}{4\omega^2 LC}}} = \frac{R}{\sqrt{1-\dfrac{1}{x^2}}} \quad . \quad . \quad 5.51$$

The properties of the π section are shown in Fig. 5.16b.

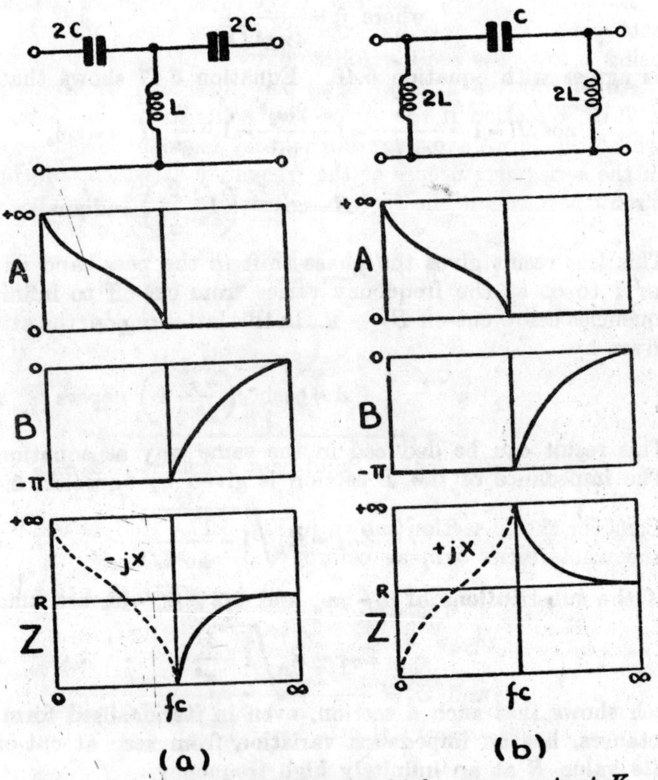

Fig. 5.16. Properties of ideal high-pass constant-*K* filter sections.

Element Values for Constant-K High-Pass Filter. The values of the elements in a constant-K high-pass filter section may be determined in terms of the cut-off frequency and the design impedance from equations 5.44 and 5.46 which give

$$R=\sqrt{\frac{L}{C}} \text{ and } f_c=\frac{1}{4\pi\sqrt{LC}}$$

From these relations

$$L=\frac{R}{4\pi f_c} \quad \ldots \quad 5.52$$

$$\text{and } C=\frac{1}{4\pi f_c R} \quad \ldots \quad 5.53$$

Band-Pass Constant-K Filter Section

Band-pass filters transmit a certain range of frequencies and attenuate all others, and so a band-pass effect may be secured by using a low-pass section followed by a high-pass section.

An alternative form of band-pass filter can be obtained either as a T or π section if the series arm contains a series resonant circuit whilst the shunt arms contain parallel resonant circuits ; if resonance in the series arm occurs at the frequency at which the shunt parallel circuit is resonant the section will have a band-pass characteristic.

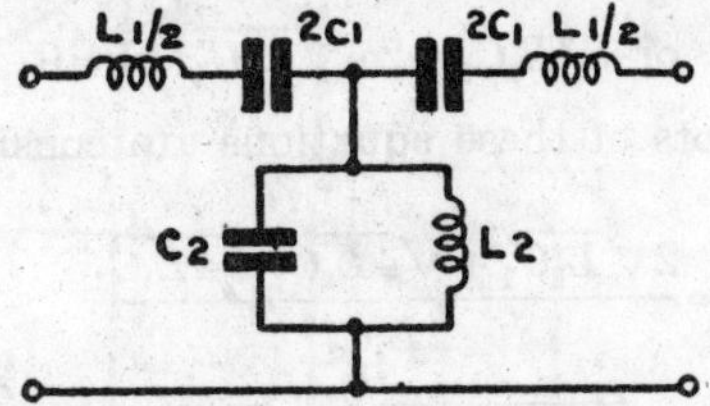

Fig. 5.17. Band-pass constant-K filter.

Consider the T section shown in Fig. 5.17. If Z_1 is the impedance of the whole series arm as before

$$Z_1=j\left(\omega L_1-\frac{1}{\omega C_1}\right)=j\frac{(\omega^2L_1C_1-1)}{\omega C_1}$$

$$\text{and } Z_2=\frac{L_2/C_2}{j\left(\omega L_2-\dfrac{1}{\omega C_2}\right)}=\frac{\omega L_2}{j(\omega^2L_2C_2-1)}$$

$$\therefore Z_1Z_2=\frac{L_2}{C_1}\left[\frac{\omega^2L_1C_1-1}{\omega^2L_2C_2-1}\right]=\frac{L_2}{C_1} \text{ if } L_1C_1=L_2C_2$$

If this condition is complied with, the arrangement will be a constant-K section which has

$$R^2 = \frac{L_2}{C_1} = \frac{L_1}{C_2} \quad . \quad . \quad . \quad . \quad . \quad 5.54$$

The characteristic impedance of the section is

$$Z_{0T} = \sqrt{Z_1 Z_2 \left(1 + \frac{Z_1}{4Z_2}\right)}$$

$$= R\sqrt{1 - \frac{(\omega^2 L_1 C_1 - 1)(\omega^2 L_2 C_2 - 1)}{4\omega^2 L_2 C_1}}$$

This quantity will be real if

$$\frac{(\omega^2 L_1 C_1 - 1)(\omega^2 L_2 C_2 - 1)}{4\omega^2 L_2 C_1} < 1$$

now as $L_1C_1 = L_2C_2$ this can be re-written as $\dfrac{(\omega^2 L_1 C_1 - 1)^2}{4\omega^2 L_2 C_1} < 1$

and this will be true if $-1 < \dfrac{\omega^2 L_1 C_1 - 1}{2\omega\sqrt{L_2 C_1}} < +1$

The limiting values of ω are then defined by $\omega^2 L_1 C_1 - 1 = \pm 2\omega\sqrt{L_2 C_1}$

$$\text{i.e. } \omega^2 L_1 C_1 - 2\omega\sqrt{L_2 C_1} - 1 = 0$$

$$\text{or } \omega^2 L_1 C_1 + 2\omega\sqrt{L_2 C_1} - 1 = 0$$

If the positive roots of these equations are considered respectively as ω_2 and ω_1

$$\text{then } \omega_2 = \frac{2\sqrt{L_2 C_1} + \sqrt{4L_2 C_1 + 4L_1 C_1}}{2L_1 C_1}$$

$$= \frac{\sqrt{L_2 C_1 + L_1 C_1} + \sqrt{L_2 C_1}}{L_1 C_1} \quad . \quad . \quad . \quad 5.55$$

$$\text{and } \omega_1 = \frac{\sqrt{L_2 C_1 + L_1 C_1} - \sqrt{L_2 C_1}}{L_1 C_1} \quad . \quad . \quad . \quad 5.56$$

The cut-off frequencies for the section are thus

$$f_1 = \frac{1}{2\pi}\left[\frac{\sqrt{L_2 C_1 + L_1 C_1} - \sqrt{L_2 C_1}}{L_1 C_1}\right] \quad . \quad . \quad 5.57$$

$$\text{and } f_2 = \frac{1}{2\pi}\left[\frac{\sqrt{L_2 C_1 + L_1 C_1} + \sqrt{L_2 C_1}}{L_1 C_1}\right] \quad . \quad . \quad 5.58$$

From equations 5.55 and 5.56

$$\omega_1 \cdot \omega_2 = \frac{L_2C_1 + L_1C_1 - L_2C_1}{(L_1C_1)^2} = \frac{1}{L_1C_1} = \frac{1}{L_2C_2} = \omega_m^2$$

where ω_m is the midband frequency to which the series and shunt arms are separately tuned.

In the section considered, $L_1C_1 = L_2C_2$. Suppose now that the element values are related by a constant n, such that

$$\left.\begin{aligned} L_1 = L/n \text{ and } C_1 = nC \\ \text{and also } L_2 = nL \text{ and } C_2 = C/n \end{aligned}\right\} \qquad 5.59$$

$$\text{then } L_1C_1 = LC = L_2C_2 = \frac{1}{\omega_m^2} \qquad 5.60$$

$$\text{and also } \frac{L_2}{C_1} = \frac{L_1}{C} = \frac{L}{C} = R^2 \qquad 5.61$$

$$\text{Then } Z_1 = j\frac{(\omega^2 L_1C_1 - 1)}{\omega C_1} = j\frac{(\omega^2 LC - 1)}{\omega nC} \qquad 5.62$$

$$\text{and } Z_2 = \frac{\omega L_2}{j(\omega^2 L_2C_2 - 1)} = \frac{\omega nL}{j(\omega^2 LC - 1)} \qquad 5.63$$

The propagation coefficient P, for the section is expressed by

$$\cosh P = 1 + \frac{Z_1}{2Z_2} = 1 - \frac{(\omega^2 LC - 1)^2}{2\omega^2 n^2 LC}$$

$$= 1 - \frac{(x^2 - 1)^2}{2n^2x^2} \qquad 5.64$$

if $\omega = x\omega_m$

The values of x for the two cut-off frequencies may be determined from equations 5.55 and 5.56. Using the relations of 5.59, and inserting them in 5.56,

$$\omega_1 = (\sqrt{n^2+1} - n)\omega_m$$

$$\text{or } x_1 = \sqrt{n^2+1} - n, \text{ if } \omega_1 = x_1\omega_m$$

Operating on equation 5.55 in the same way gives

$$\omega_2 = (\sqrt{n^2+1} + n)\omega_m$$

$$\text{or } x_2 = \sqrt{n^2+1} + n, \text{ if } \omega_2 = x_2\omega_m$$

from these results $x_2 - x_1 = 2n$ 5.65

Equation 5.64 may then be re-written as

$$\cosh P = 1 - 2\left[\frac{x^2 - 1}{x(x_2 - x_1)}\right]^2 \qquad 5.66$$

The variation of x from zero to infinity in equation 5.66 enables the attenuation and phase shift to be determined for the section.

For frequencies below f_1, i.e. when $0<x<x_1$ cosh P lies between $-\infty$ and -1

$$\text{and } A=\cosh^{-1}\left[\frac{(x^2-1)^2}{2n^2x^2}-1\right]\text{nepers} \quad . \quad . \quad . \quad 5.67$$

while $B=-\pi$.

For frequencies above f_2, i.e. when $x_2<x<\infty$, cosh P lies between -1 and $-\infty$

$$\text{and again } A=\cosh^{-1}\left[\frac{(x^2-1)^2}{2n^2x^2}-1\right]\text{ nepers} \quad . \quad . \quad 5.68$$

whilst $B=+\pi$.

For frequencies in the pass band, i.e. when $x_1<x<x_2$ cosh P lies between -1 and $+1$

and $A=0$

$$\text{whilst } B=\cos^{-1}\left[1-\frac{(x^2-1)^2}{2n^2x^2}\right]\text{ radians} \quad . \quad . \quad 5.69$$

The characteristic impedance of the T section is

$$Z_{OT}=\sqrt{Z_1Z_2\left(1+\frac{Z_1}{4Z_2}\right)}=R\sqrt{1-\frac{(\omega^2LC-1)^2}{4\omega^2n^2LC}}$$

if the relations of 5.59 are used.

Bearing in mind that $LC=1/\omega_m^2$ and substituting $x\,\omega_m$ for ω

$$Z_{OT}=R\sqrt{1-\frac{(x^2-1)^2}{4n^2x^2}} \quad . \quad . \quad . \quad . \quad . \quad 5.70$$

The characteristic impedance for the π section is

$$Z_{0\pi}=\sqrt{\frac{Z_1Z_2}{1+\dfrac{Z_1}{4Z_2}}}$$

$$=\frac{R}{\sqrt{1-\dfrac{(x^2-1)^2}{4n^2x^2}}} \quad . \quad . \quad 5.71$$

The variation of attenuation, phase shift and impedance for the two sections are shown in Fig. 5.18.

Element Values for Constant-K Band-Pass Filter. The values of the elements may be calculated in terms of the two cut-off frequencies and the design impedance.

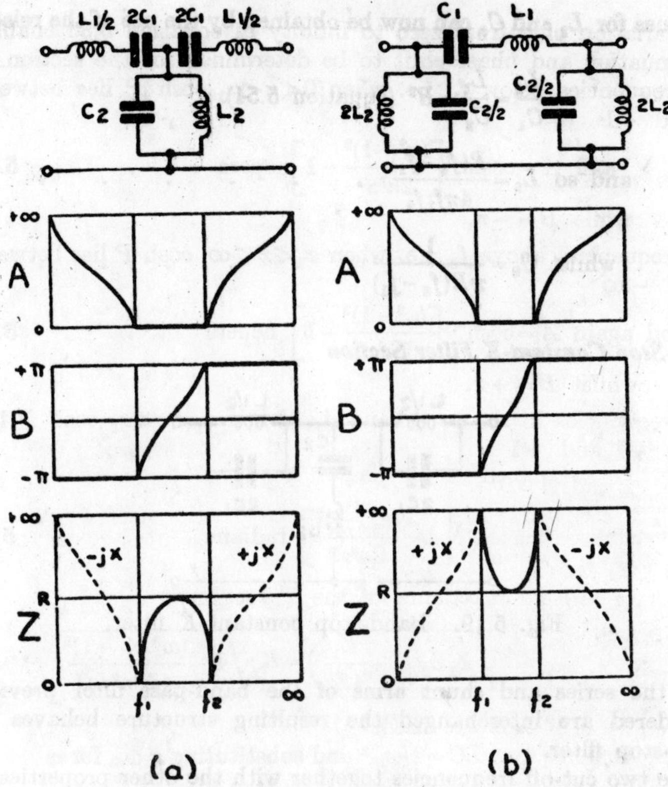

Fig. 5.18. Properties of ideal band-pass constant-K filter section.

It has been shown that $\omega_1 \,.\, \omega_2 = \omega_m{}^2 = 1/L_1C_1 = 1/L_2C_2$

$$\therefore C_1 = \frac{1}{\omega_m{}^2 L_1} = \frac{1}{\omega_1\omega_2 L_1} \quad . \quad . \quad . \quad . \quad . \quad 5.72$$

Equation 5.55 and 5.56 show that

$$\omega_2 - \omega_1 = \frac{2\sqrt{L_2C_1}}{L_1C_1} = \frac{2R}{L_1} \quad \therefore f_2 - f_1 = \frac{R}{\pi L_1}$$

$$\text{and so } L_1 = \frac{R}{\pi(f_2 - f_1)} \quad . \quad . \quad . \quad . \quad . \quad . \quad 5.73$$

$$\text{and } C_1 = \frac{1}{\omega_1\omega_2 L_1} = \frac{f_2 - f_1}{4\pi f_1 f_2 R} \quad . \quad . \quad . \quad . \quad 5.74$$

Values for L_2 and C_2 can now be obtained by the use of the relationship

$$\frac{L_2}{C_1}=\frac{L_1}{C_2}=R^2 \text{ (equation 5.54)}$$

$$\text{and so } L_2=\frac{R(f_2-f_1)}{4\pi f_1 f_2} \quad . \quad . \quad . \quad . \quad . \quad . \quad 5.75$$

$$\text{whilst } C_2=\frac{1}{\pi R(f_2-f_1)} \quad . \quad . \quad . \quad . \quad . \quad 5.76$$

Band-Stop Constant-K Filter Section

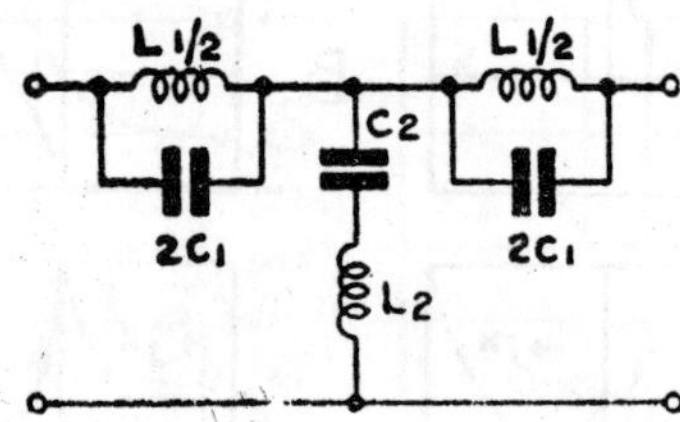

Fig. 5.19. Band-stop constant-K filter.

If the series and shunt arms of the band-pass filter previously considered are interchanged the resulting structure behaves as a band-stop filter.

The two cut-off frequencies together with the other properties may be deduced in a manner analogous to the band-pass case. The variation of impedance, attenuation, and phase shift for both T and π band-stop sections is shown in Fig. 5.20.

The values of the four elements, which may be arranged as a T or π section as in Fig. 5.20, have values in terms of the cut-off frequencies, f_1 and f_2, and the design impedance R as follows,

$$L_1=\frac{(f_2-f_1)R}{\pi f_1 f_2} \quad . \quad . \quad . \quad . \quad 5.77$$

$$C_1=\frac{1}{4\pi(f_2-f_1)R} \quad . \quad . \quad . \quad . \quad 5.78$$

$$L_2=\frac{R}{4\pi(f_2-f_1)} \quad . \quad . \quad . \quad . \quad 5.79$$

$$\text{and } C_2=\frac{f_2-f_1}{\pi f_1 f_2 R} \quad . \quad . \quad . \quad . \quad 5.80$$

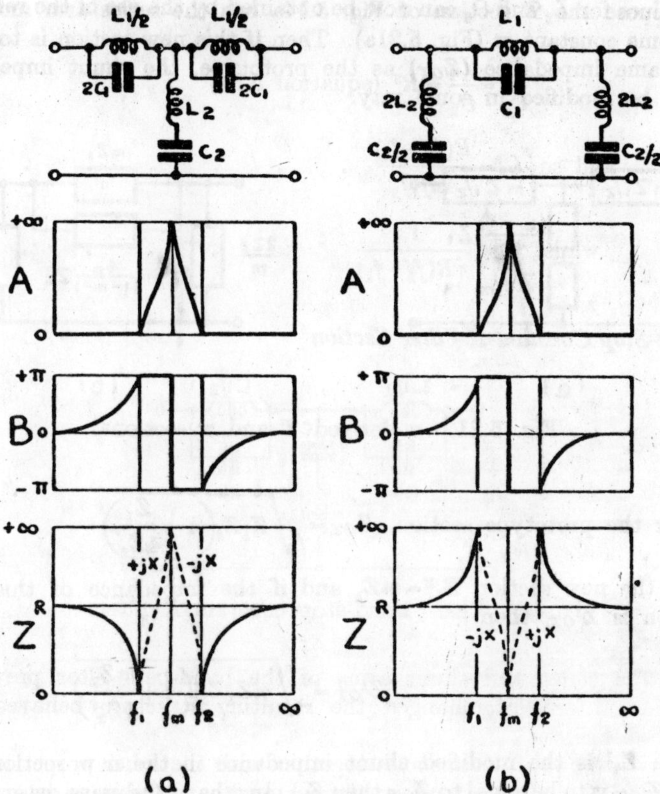

Fig. 5.20. Properties of ideal band-stop constant-K section.

m-Derived Filter Sections

If the characteristics of the various type of constant-K filter sections are examined, it will be seen that even in their idealised form (when they are considered to be composed of pure reactances) the characteristics are by no means ideal. The attenuation does not increase rapidly beyond the cut-off frequencies and in the pass-band the characteristic impedance varies widely from the desired value, namely the design impedance R. A high degree of attenuation just beyond cut-off, or a constant impedance in the pass-band, demands a more complicated structure. If the constant-K section is regarded as the prototype, it is possible to design a section to have the same impedance and hence the same pass and attenuation bands, but with a different degree of attenuation outside the pass-band. This may be done in the following manner.

Suppose the T section of Fig. 5.14a has the series arm modified by some constant m (Fig. 5.21a). Then if this new section is to have the same impedance (Z_{OT}) as the prototype, the shunt impedance must be modified in some way.

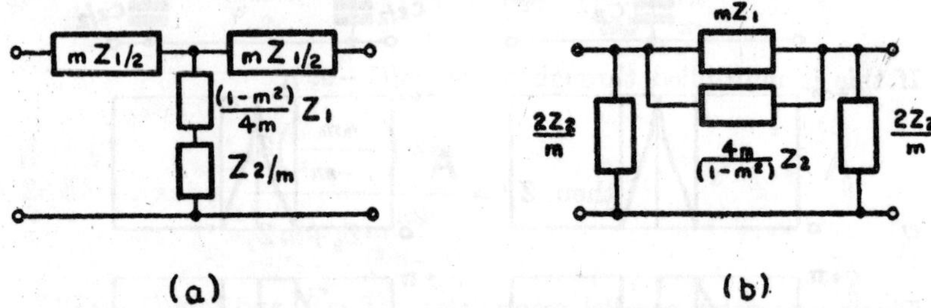

Fig. 5.21. m-derived T and π sections.

For the prototype section, $Z_{OT}=\sqrt{Z_1Z_2\left(1+\dfrac{Z_1}{4Z_2}\right)}$

In the new section $Z_1{}^1=mZ_1$ and if the impedance of this new section is $Z^1{}_{OT}$, then

$$Z^1{}_{OT}=\sqrt{mZ_1Z_2{}^1\left(1+\frac{mZ_1}{4Z_2{}^1}\right)}$$

where $Z_2{}^1$ is the modified shunt impedance in the new section.

If $Z^1{}_{OT}$ is to be equal to Z_{OT} then $Z_2{}^1$ must have the value determined by

$$Z_1Z_2\left(1+\frac{Z_1}{4Z_2}\right)=mZ_1Z_2{}^1\left(1+\frac{mZ_1}{4Z_2{}^1}\right)$$

$$\text{i.e. } Z_2{}^1=\frac{Z_2}{m}+\frac{(1-m^2)}{4m}Z_1 \quad . \quad . \quad 5.81$$

and so the derived T section, as shown in Fig. 5.21a has the same impedance as the prototype T section.

The same technique can be applied to the π section. If the shunt arms are reduced by the factor $1/m$ then to make $Z_{0\pi}$ for the prototype section equal to $Z^1{}_{0\pi}$ for the derived section, the series arm has to be modified.

$$\text{Now } Z_{0\pi}=\sqrt{\frac{Z_1Z_2}{1+\dfrac{Z_1}{4Z_2}}}=Z^1{}_{0\pi}=\sqrt{\frac{Z_1{}^1Z_2/m}{1+\dfrac{mZ_1{}^1}{4Z_2}}}$$

$$\therefore Z_1^1\left(\frac{Z_2}{m}+\frac{Z_1}{4m}\right)=Z_1Z_2+Z_1^1\left(\frac{mZ_1}{4}\right)$$

$$\therefore Z_1^1=\frac{Z_1Z_2}{\dfrac{Z_2}{m}+\dfrac{Z_1}{4m}(1-m^2)}=\frac{mZ_1 4Z_2}{4Z_2+Z_1(1-m^2)}$$

If this is multiplied throughout by $m/(1-m^2)$

$$\text{then } Z_1^1=\frac{mZ_1\left(\dfrac{4m}{1-m^2}\right)Z_2}{\dfrac{4m}{(1-m^2)}Z_2+mZ_1} \quad . \quad . \quad 5.82$$

This represents a parallel combination of mZ_1 and $[4m/(1-m^2)]Z_2$ and so the derived π section is that shown in Fig. 5.21b.

The T and π sections derived above are called m-derived sections. They are physically realisable if $0<m<1$.

The effect of m-derivation on the various prototype sections will now be considered.

m-Derived Low-Pass Sections

If the T and π sections of Fig. 5.15 are regarded as constant-K prototypes, the corresponding m-derived sections are then those shown in Fig. 5.22.

An examination of the m-derived T section shows that if the shunt arm is resonant it will have zero impedance ; the output will then be

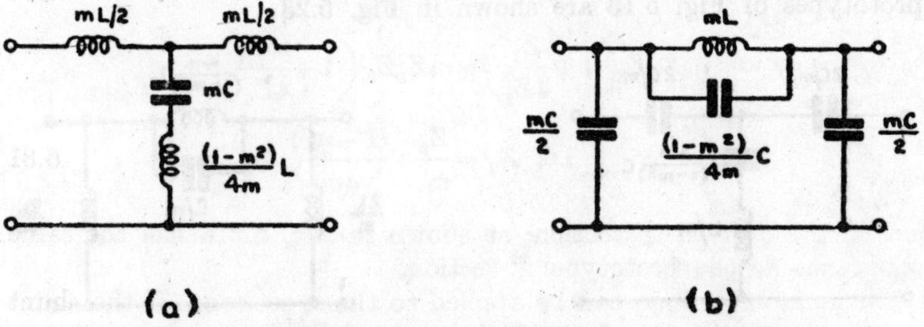

Fig. 5.22. m-derived T and π low-pass sections.

zero, and this will correspond to infinite attenuation at this particular frequency.

An inspection of the π section reveals that the series arm will be resonant and have an infinite impedance at the frequency of resonance of the shunt arm in the T section. Both sections will thus have infinite attenuation at the same frequency.

The shunt arm in the T section will have zero impedance when

$$\frac{1}{m\omega C}=\frac{(1-m^2)}{4m}\omega L \quad \text{i.e. when } \omega^2=\frac{4}{(1-m^2)LC}$$

and so the frequency of infinite attenuation, f_∞ is given by

$$f_\infty=\frac{1}{\pi\sqrt{LC}\sqrt{1-m^2}}$$

f_c the cut-off frequency for the prototype section is given by

$$f_c=\frac{1}{\pi\sqrt{LC}} \text{ (equation 5.36)} \quad \therefore f_\infty=\frac{f_c}{\sqrt{1-m^2}}$$

$$\text{i.e. } 1-m^2=\left(\frac{f_c}{f_\infty}\right)^2 \text{ and } m=\sqrt{1-\left(\frac{f_c}{f_\infty}\right)^2} \qquad . \quad . \quad 5.83$$

This result shows that if the cut-off frequency, and the frequency of infinite attenuation are specified the necessary value of m may then be evaluated.

The values of the elements of the m-derived section can then be calculated for any value of design impedance from the appropriate relations for the prototype section (equations 5.42 and 5.43). Equation 5.83 shows that the smaller the value of m the nearer f_∞ comes to f_c, and so for a sharp cut-off m should be small.

m-Derived High-Pass Sections

The m-derived high-pass sections based on the constant-K prototypes of Fig. 5.16 are shown in Fig. 5.23.

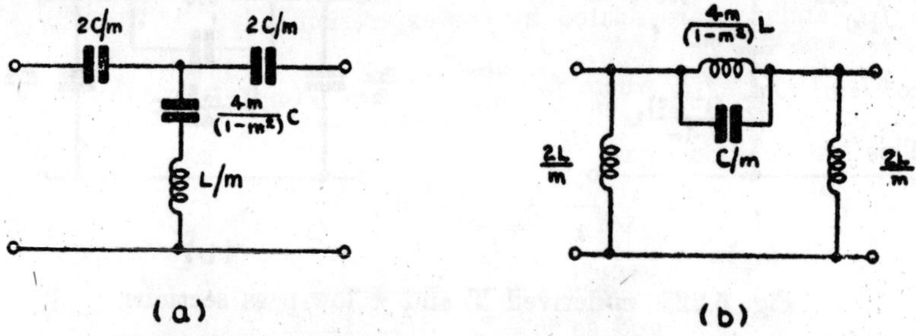

Fig. 5.23. m-derived T and π high-pass sections.

In this case infinite attenuation will occur when

$$\frac{\omega L}{m}=\frac{(1-m^2)}{4m\omega C} \quad \text{i.e. when } \omega^2=\frac{1-m^2}{4LC}$$

$$\text{and } f_\infty = \frac{1}{2\pi}\sqrt{\frac{1-m^2}{4LC}} = \frac{\sqrt{1-m^2}}{4\pi\sqrt{LC}}$$

The cut-off frequency for the prototype is given by

$$f_c = \frac{1}{4\pi\sqrt{LC}} \quad \text{(equation 5.46) and so } f_\infty = \sqrt{1-m^2}\cdot f$$

$$\therefore m = \sqrt{1-\left(\frac{f_\infty}{f_c}\right)^2} \quad . \quad . \quad 5.84$$

As in the low pass case, the element values for an m-derived high-pass section can be calculated if f_∞, f_c and R are known.

m-Derived Band-Pass and Band-Stop Sections

If the prototype band-pass and band-stop sections of Figs. 5.18 and 5.20 respectively are treated in accordance with Fig. 5.21 which has been used to obtain m-derived low and high-pass sections, the resulting structures will be m-derived band-pass and band-stop sections.

The T section in each case will have a shunt impedance

$$\frac{Z_2}{m} + \left[\frac{1-m^2}{4m}\right]Z_1$$

where Z_1 and Z_2 refer to the values of the prototype sections.

Infinite attenuation will occur when

$$\frac{Z_2}{m} + \left[\frac{1-m^2}{4m}\right]Z_1 = 0 \quad . \quad . \quad . \quad 5.85$$

If in the case of the band-pass section the values of Z_1 and Z_2 are inserted in equation 5.85, it will be found that two positive values of frequency $f_{1\infty}$ and $f_{2\infty}$ satisfy the equation.

$f_{1\infty}$ and $f_{2\infty}$ are related by the expression

$$(f_{1\infty})(f_{2\infty}) = f_m^2 = f_1 f_2 \text{ where } f_m = \frac{\omega_m}{2\pi} \text{ and } f_{2\infty} - f_{1\infty} = \frac{f_2 - f_1}{\sqrt{1-m^2}}$$

This last relation gives

$$\sqrt{1-m^2} = \frac{f_2 - f_1}{f_{2\infty} - f_{1\infty}}$$

$$\text{and so } m = \sqrt{1-\left(\frac{f_2-f_1}{f_{2\infty}-f_{1\infty}}\right)^2} \quad . \quad . \quad 5.86$$

This expression together with a knowledge of the design impedance R enables the element values of the m-derived band-pass section to be calculated if the cut-off frequencies and $f_{1\infty}$ and $f_{2\infty}$ are specified.

The solution of equation 5.85 for the band-stop case gives two frequencies $f_{1\infty}$ and $f_{2\infty}$ related so that,

$$(f_{1\infty})\ (f_{2\infty}) = f_m^2 = f_1 f_2 \text{ and } f_{2\infty} - f_{1\infty} = (f_2 - f_1)\sqrt{1-m^2}$$

In this case $\sqrt{1-m^2} = \dfrac{f_{2\infty} - f_{1\infty}}{f_2 - f_1}$ and $m = \sqrt{1 - \left(\dfrac{f_{2\infty} - f_{1\infty}}{f_2 - f_1}\right)^2}$ 5.87

The frequency/attenuation characteristic of the m-derived sections for the four kinds of filter considered are shown in Fig. 5.24.

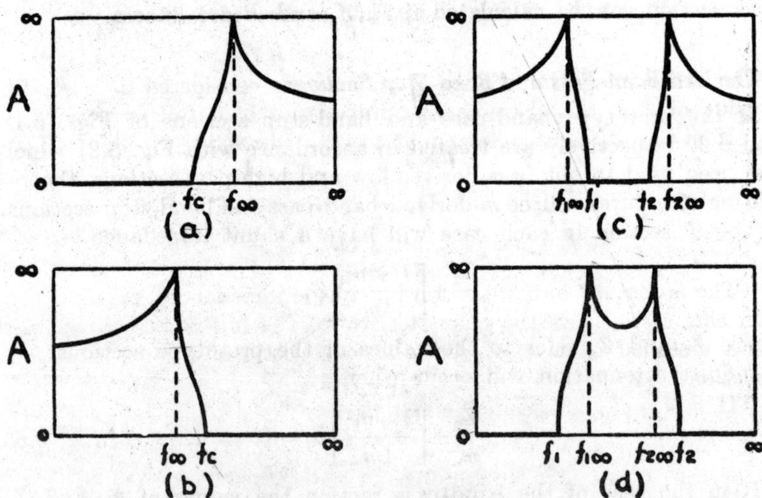

Fig. 5.24. Attenuation characteristics of m-derived sections.
(a) Low-pass (c) Band-pass
(b) High-pass (d) Band-stop

Impedance Characteristics of m-Derived Filter Sections

In the consideration of m-derived filter sections attention has so far been confined to the attenuation/frequency characteristics. m-derivation can, however, be used to obtain greater constancy of impedance in the pass-band. It is convenient in dealing with this effect to consider the basic half-sections. These are obtained by bisection of the full T and π sections, and are shown in Fig. 5.25.

The half-section of Fig. 5.25a is an m-derived half T section. It is sometimes called a series derived half-section. Fig. 5.25b shows an m-derived half π section, otherwise referred to as a shunt derived half-section.

The m-derived half T section has image impedances Z_{OT} and $Z_{O\pi m}$ where Z_{OT} is the characteristic impedance of the prototype full section.

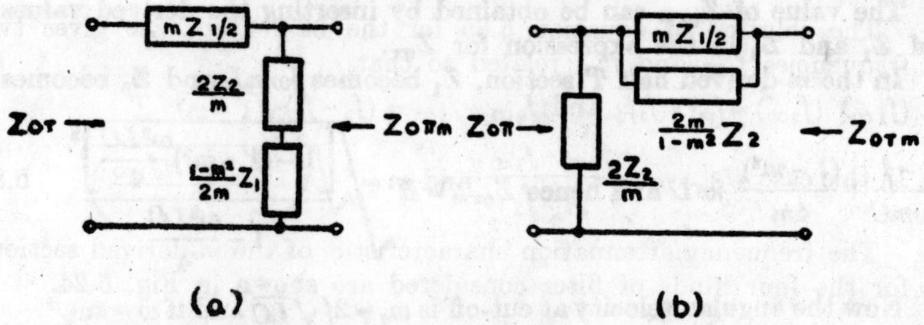

Fig. 5.25. Series and shunt m-derived half-sections.

The other image impedance $Z_{0\pi m}$ may be considered as a modified value of $Z_{0\pi}$, the characteristic impedance of a full π section.

If $m=1$, $Z_{0\pi m}$ becomes equal to $Z_{0\pi}$ where

$$Z_{0\pi}=\sqrt{\frac{Z_1Z_2}{1+\frac{Z_1}{4Z_2}}}$$

The m-derived half π section has image impedances $Z_{0\pi}$ and Z_{OTm}. In this case $Z_{0\pi}$ is the characteristic of the full π section and Z_{OTm} is a modified value of Z_{OT}, the characteristic impedance of a full T section.

If $m=1$, Z_{OTm} becomes equal to Z_{OT}

$$\text{where } Z_{OT}=\sqrt{Z_1Z_2\left(1+\frac{Z_1}{4Z_2}\right)}$$

The effect of the m-derivation on the pass-band impedance can most easily be seen by choosing a particular example. The low-pass section will be discussed but the treatment may be applied to the other types in the same way.

The Impedance-Frequency Characteristic of m-Derived Low-Pass Filter Half-Sections

(a) Series Derived Half-Section. For the half-section shown in Fig. 5.26a the impedance at the terminals 1,2 is

$$Z_{OT}=\sqrt{Z_1Z_2\left(1+\frac{Z_1}{4Z_2}\right)}$$

where Z_1 and Z_2 refer to the prototype section,

$$\text{and } Z_{OT}=R\sqrt{1-x^2} \quad \text{(equation 5.40)}$$

The impedance at the terminals 3,4 is $Z_{0\pi m}$.

The value of Z_{0Tm} can be obtained by inserting the derived values of Z_1 and Z_2 in the expression for Z_{0T}.

In the m-derived half T section, Z_1 becomes $j\omega mL$ and Z_2 becomes

$$\frac{-j}{\omega mC}+\frac{(1-m^2)}{4m}\,j\omega L \text{ and hence } Z_{0Tm}=R\sqrt{\frac{\left[1-(1-m^2)\frac{\omega^2LC}{4}\right]^2}{1-\frac{\omega^2LC}{4}}}$$

Now the angular velocity at cut-off is $\omega_c=2/\sqrt{LC}$ and if $\omega=x\omega_c$ then $\omega^2LC/4=x^2$ where x is a quantity which varies from 0 to 1 as the frequency varies from zero to cut-off.

$$\text{and so } Z_{0Tm}=\frac{R[1-x^2(1-m^2)]}{\sqrt{1-x^2}} \qquad 5.88$$

If $m=1$, this reduces to

$$\frac{R}{\sqrt{1-x^2}}=Z_{0T} \quad \text{(equation 5.41)}$$

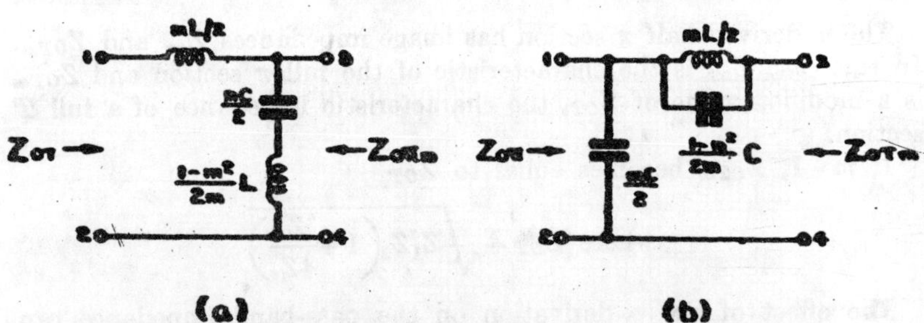

Fig. 5.26. Series and shunt m-derived low-pass half-sections.

(b) Shunt-Derived Half-Section. For the half-section of Fig. 5.26b the impedance at the terminals 1,2

$$Z_{0\pi}=\sqrt{\frac{Z_1Z_2}{1+\frac{Z_1}{4Z_2}}}$$

where Z_1 and Z_2 refer to the prototype section and $Z_{0\pi}=\dfrac{R}{1-x^2}$

The impedance at the terminals 3,4 is $Z_{0\pi m}$, the value of which can be obtained by insertion of the derived values of Z_1 and Z_2 in the expression for $Z_{0\pi}$.

In the shunt derived half-section Z_1 becomes

$$\frac{\dfrac{4mL}{C}}{j\omega L(1-m^2)+\dfrac{4}{j\omega C}}=\frac{4m\dfrac{L}{C}(j\omega C)}{4-\omega^2LC(1-m^2)}$$

and Z_2 becomes $1/jwmC$

If these values for Z_1 and Z_2 are inserted in the expression for Z_{OT}

$$\text{then } Z_{OTm}=R\sqrt{\frac{1}{1-\dfrac{\omega^2LC}{4}(1-m^2)}\left[\frac{4-\omega^2LC(1-m^2)-m^2\omega^2LC}{4-\omega^2LC(1-m^2)}\right]}$$

$$=\frac{R\sqrt{1-x^2}}{1-x^2(1-m^2)} \quad . \quad . \quad . \quad . \quad . \quad 5.89$$

if x has the same significance as in equation 5.88.

If $m=1$, Z_{OTm} reduces to $R\sqrt{1-x^2}=Z_{OT}$

Equation 5.89 has been used to calculate the variation of Z_{OTm} as x varies from zero to unity, for various values of m, as shown in Fig. 5.27. It can be seen very clearly that when $m=0{\cdot}6$ the impedance

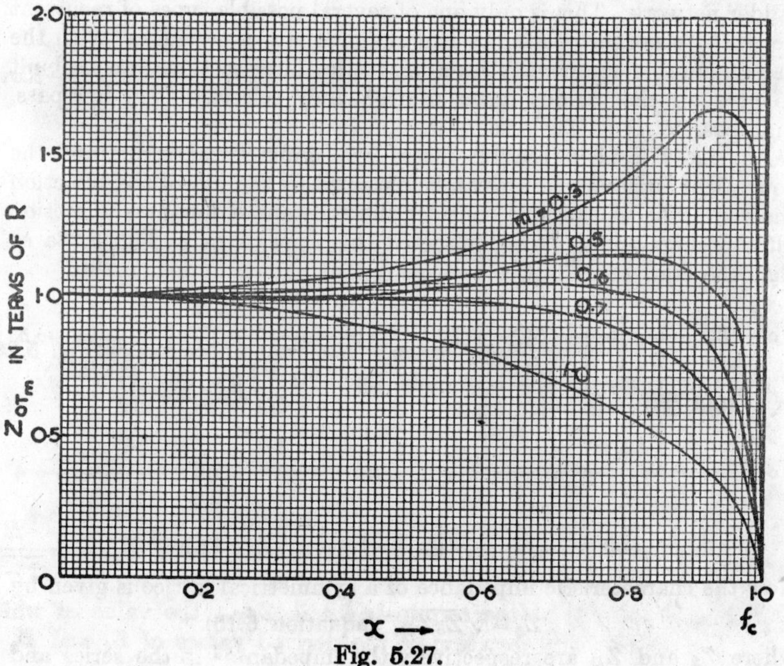

Fig. 5.27.

variation is less than 5% over more than 80% of the pass-band. The same is true for the series derived impedance $Z_{0\pi m}$.

This effect is used in practical filters by building a composite filter with, say, one or more constant-K prototype sections terminated at each end with a 0·6 m-derived half-section. The arrangement then has an attenuation given by the sum of the separate sections, and an impedance characteristic which is equal to that of the 0·6 m-derived section at each end.

mm′ Derivation

Occasionally where the impedance requirements are such that the variation of impedance of a filter must be small, double derivation is used. In this case sections known as mm' sections, are derived from m-derived sections. A filter terminated with mm' derived sections has a smaller impedance variation in the pass-band than the m-derived sections discussed above.

LATTICE FILTER SECTIONS

The various filters which have been discussed have all been either T or π sections, that is to say sections of what has been termed a ladder network. This is only one of several possible types of recurrent network. Another possibility is a chain of lattice sections. With the use of suitable component reactors, lattice filter sections can be built to give all the various forms of frequency selection (e.g. low-pass, high-pass, etc.) so far discussed.

As the T and π section filters are symmetrical structures the equivalent lattice structure can be obtained by the use of the bisection theorem. As an example consider the constant-K low-pass T section filter of Fig. 5.15a. When bisected this appears as in Fig. 5.28a so that the equivalent lattice section is that shown in Fig. 5.28b.

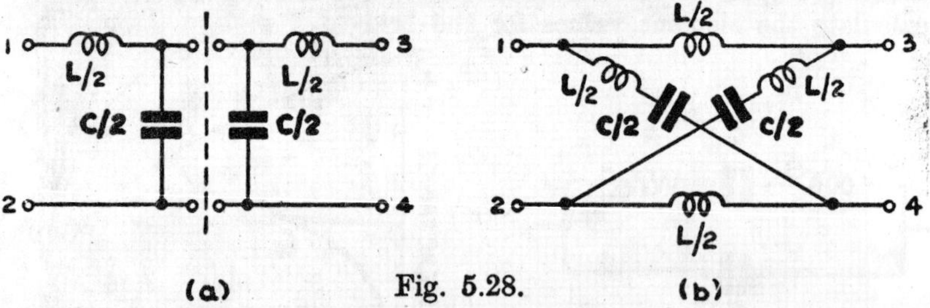

Fig. 5.28.

Now the characteristic impedance of a symmetrical lattice is given by

$$Z_0 = \sqrt{Z_S Z_D} \quad \text{(equation 5.15)}$$

where Z_S and Z_D are respectively the impedances in the series and diagonal arms.

For the lattice section of Fig. 5.28b,

$$Z_S = j\omega L/2 \text{ and } Z_D = \frac{1}{j}\left(\frac{2}{\omega C} - \frac{\omega L}{2}\right)$$

$$\text{Hence, } Z_0 = \sqrt{\frac{j\omega L}{2} \cdot \frac{1}{j}\left(\frac{2}{\omega C} - \frac{\omega L}{2}\right)}$$

$$= \sqrt{\frac{L}{C}}\sqrt{1 - \frac{\omega^2 LC}{4}}$$

This corresponds with the value given by equation 5.35 for the T section. The lattice arrangement shown will thus function, as the T section, as a low-pass filter and transmit frequencies from zero up to the cut-off frequency f_c,

$$\text{where } f_c = \frac{1}{\pi\sqrt{LC}}$$

The lattice equivalent of a low-pass T section has thus been obtained. If the same technique is applied to any other T or π section (prototype or m-derived) the equivalent lattice section can readily be found.

Bridged-T Filter Sections

Bridged-T networks of reactors may be employed as filters. The detailed form of such filters will not be discussed as the element values may be obtained with the help of the bisection theorem from the corresponding lattice section; the impedance of the series arm of the lattice section will give the input impedance of half of the bridged-T section when the "bisected" terminals are short-circuited; the impedance of the diagonal arms of the lattice section will give the input impedance of half of the bridged-T section when the "bisected" terminals are open-circuited. These two conditions can then be used to calculate the element values for the bridged-T section.

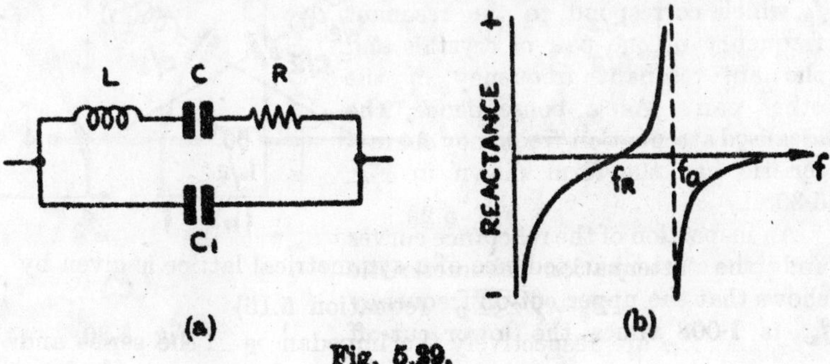

Fig. 5.29.

Crystal Filters

Piezo-electric crystals (see Chapter 3) have very large reactance/resistance ratios and as a consequence are ideal elements for filters in which a rapid change of attenuation is required. The equivalent circuit and corresponding reactance curve for quartz elements have already been discussed, and are reproduced again in Fig. 5.29 for convenience.

It will be seen that the crystal element functions as a two terminal impedance which changes the sign of its reactance between the resonant frequency, f_R, and the anti-resonant frequency, f_a. With quartz the ratio of C_1/C is such that

$$f_a/f_R = 1{\cdot}004$$

If a pair of similar crystals are used as the series elements of a lattice section and another pair of crystals used as the diagonal elements as shown in Fig. 5·30a, the section will have band-pass characteristics, provided that the series resonant frequency of one pair coincides with the anti-resonant frequency of the other. The reactance sketches of the series arms (X_S) and the diagonal arms (X_D) are shown in Fig. 5·30b.

The characteristic impedance of such section is given by,

$$Z_0 = \sqrt{Z_S Z_D} = \sqrt{(\pm jX_S)(\pm jX_D)}$$

when the presence of resistance is ignored.

For Z_0 to be resistive X_S and X_D must have opposite signs. Fig. 5.30b shows that this occurs between f_1 and f_2 which correspond to the resonant frequency of one pair of crystals and the anti-resonant frequency of the other pair. As a consequence, the idealised attenuation/frequency characteristic has the form shown in Fig. 5·30c.

An inspection of the reactance curves and the attenuation characteristic shows that the upper cut-off frequency f_2, is 1·008 times the lower cut-off

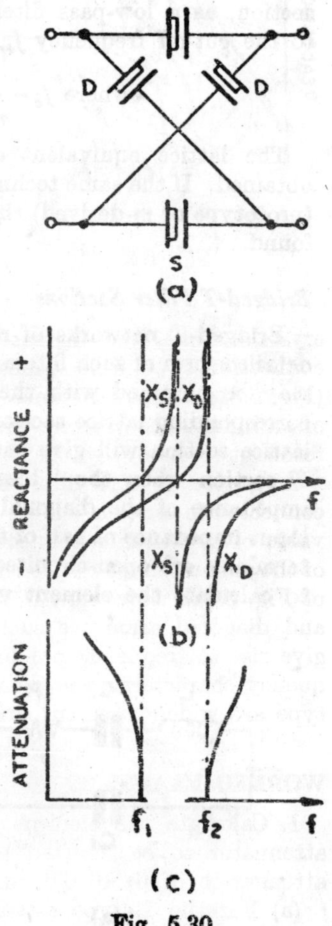

Fig. 5.30.

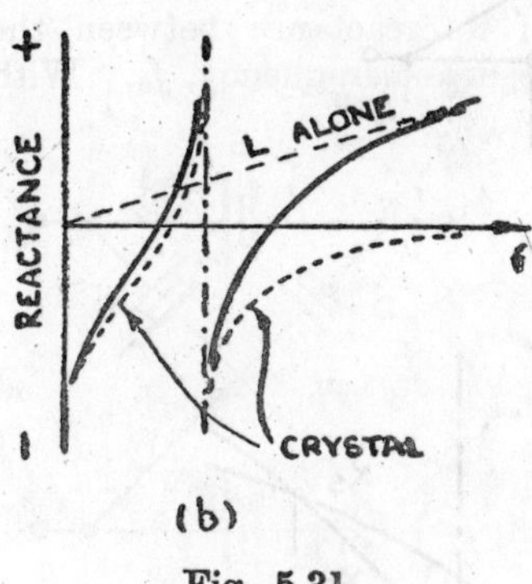

Fig. 5.31.

frequency f_1, on the assumption that the ratio of f_a/f_R for the crystal elements is 1·004. The bandwidth of such a filter, i.e. $f_2 - f_1$, is thus approximately 0·8% of the midband frequency.

If the bandwidth required is narrower than that provided by the crystals alone, the decreased bandwidth can be obtained by the connection of suitable values of capacitance across each crystal. Capacitance in parallel with the crystal increases the value of C_1 in the equivalent circuit (Fig. 5.29); this has the effect of lowering the value of the anti-resonant frequency f_a while leaving the resonant frequency unchanged, so that the frequency interval $f_a - f_R$ is diminished.

If the bandwidth required is broader than that provided by the crystals alone, the increased bandwidth can be obtained by the connection of suitable values of inductance in series with the crystals (Fig. 5.31a). The reactance curves of Fig. 5.31b show that the effect of an inductance in series with the crystal is to lower the value of the resonant frequency so that the frequency interval $f_a - f_R$ is increased.

A lattice crystal filter in which the crystals have inductance connected in series is shown in Fig. 5.32a. The crystals have a small value of capacitance connected in parallel to provide for adjustment of the anti-resonant frequencies. The corresponding reactance sketches of Fig. 5.32b show that if the reactance characteristics of the series and diagonal arms are such that they intersect, such intersections give rise to frequencies of infinite attenuation. The attenuation/frequency characteristic is then as shown in Fig. 5.32c. Filters of this type are widely used in carrier telephony.

WORKED EXAMPLES

1. Calculate the element values for (a) a T and (b) a π type attenuator to be inserted between $600\underline{/0^\circ}$ ohm impedances for an attenuation of (i) 10 dB, and (ii) 60 dB.

(a) For the T type attenuator the element values are given by equations 5.24 and 5.25. The value of the series resistance R_1, is given by

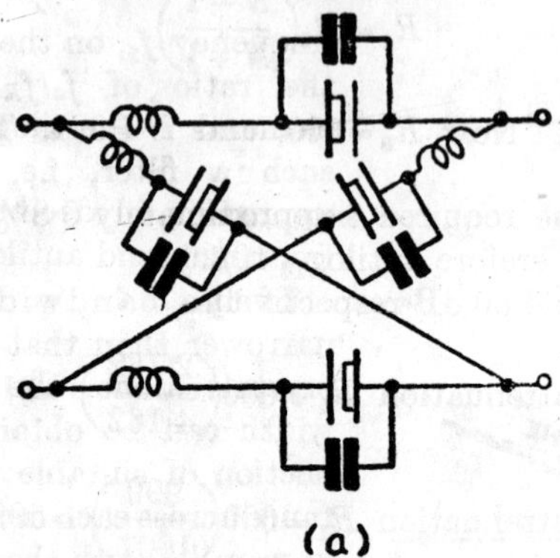

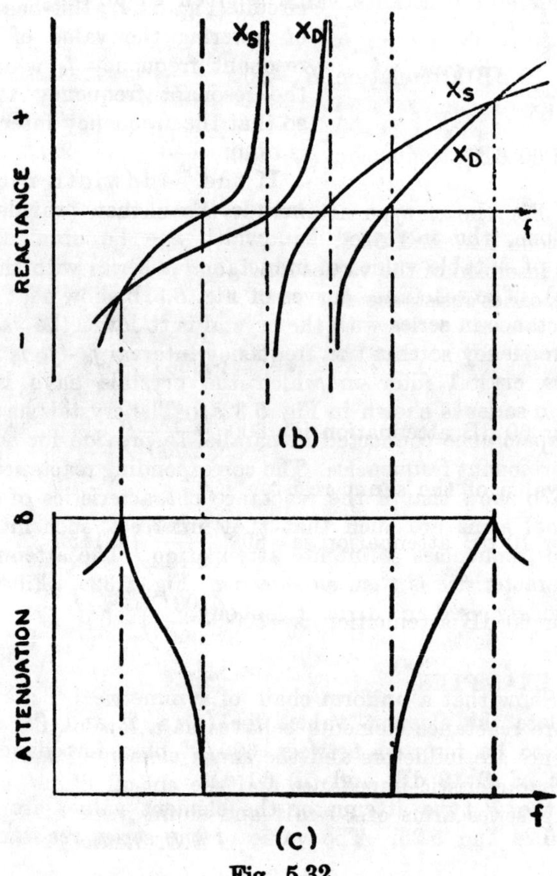

Fig. 5.32.

$$R_1 = R_0\left(\frac{N-1}{N+1}\right)$$

$$\text{Now } R_0 = 600, \text{ and } N = \text{antilog}_{10}\frac{D}{20}$$

where D is the required attenuation in decibels. The values of N required are therefore antilog_{10} 10/20, and antilog_{10} 60 /20 for attenuations of 10, and 60 dB respectively.

$$\therefore \text{For 10 dB attenuation } R_1 = 600\left(\frac{2{\cdot}162}{4{\cdot}162}\right) = 312\ \Omega$$

$$\text{For 60 dB attenuation } R_1 = 600\left(\frac{999}{1001}\right) = 599\ \Omega$$

$$\text{The shunt resistance value is given by } R_2 = R_0\left(\frac{2N}{N^2-1}\right)$$

$$\therefore \text{For 10 dB attenuation } R_2 = 600\left(\frac{6{\cdot}324}{9}\right) = 422\ \Omega$$

$$\text{For 60 dB attenuation } R_2 = 600\left(\frac{2000}{10^6-1}\right) = 1{\cdot}2\ \Omega$$

(b) For the π type attenuator the element values are given by equations 5.27 and 5.28.

By insertion of the values for R_0 and N it will be found that the value of the series resistance R_3,

$$\text{for 10 dB attenuation is} = 600\left(\frac{10-1}{6{\cdot}324}\right) = 853\ \Omega$$

$$\text{for 60 dB attenuation is} = 600\left(\frac{10^6-1}{2000}\right) = 300{,}000\ \Omega$$

The value of the shunt resistor R_4

$$\text{for 10 dB attenuation is} = 600\left(\frac{4{\cdot}162}{2{\cdot}162}\right) = 1155\ \Omega$$

$$\text{for 60 dB attenuation is} = 600\left(\frac{1001}{999}\right) = 601\ \Omega$$

2. Show that a uniform chain of symmetrical T-sections composed of pure reactance elements behaves as a low pass filter if the series elements are inductors and the shunt elements capacitors. Calculate the characteristic impedance and the cut-off frequency for the filter having series arms of 30 mH and shunt arms of 0·176 μF.

I.E.E. Radio Comm. Oct., 1947.

The characteristic impedance for a chain of T-sections is

$$Z_{OT}=\sqrt{Z_1Z_2\left(1+\frac{Z_1}{4Z_2}\right)} \quad \text{(equation 5.5)}$$

For a low pass filter as considered in the question

$$Z_{OT}=R\sqrt{1-\frac{\omega^2LC}{4}} \quad \text{where } R=\sqrt{L/C}$$

As no frequency has been specified Z_{OT} will be considered at zero frequency, and so

$$Z_{OT}=R=\sqrt{\frac{L}{C}}=\sqrt{\frac{2\times30\times10^{-3}}{0{\cdot}176\times10^{-6}}}=585\ \Omega$$

The cut-off frequency is given by $f_c=\dfrac{1}{\pi\sqrt{LC}}$ (equation 5.36)

$$=\frac{1}{\pi\sqrt{2\times30\times10^{-3}\times0{\cdot}176\times10^{-6}}}=3100\text{ Hz}$$

3. Derive an expression for the cut-off frequency of a T-type high pass filter and employ this expression to calculate the values of the shunt and series elements of a high pass filter having a cut-off frequency of 10,000 Hz suitable for insertion in a transmission line having a characteristic impedance of $600\underline{/0^\circ}$ ohms. Assume the elements to be non-dissipative.

L.U. Ext. Telecomm. 1945.

Equation 5.46 gives the cut-off frequency as $f_c=\dfrac{1}{4\pi\sqrt{LC}}$

$$\therefore \omega_c=\frac{1}{2\sqrt{LC}}=6{\cdot}28\times10^4$$

$$\therefore LC=\left(\frac{1}{2\times6{\cdot}28\times10^4}\right)^2$$

Now $L/C=R^2=(600)^2$ and hence $L^2=\left(\dfrac{600}{2\times6{\cdot}28\times10^4}\right)^2$

$$\text{and } L=\frac{600}{2\times6{\cdot}28\times10^4}\text{H}=4{\cdot}78\text{ mH}$$

$$\therefore \frac{4{\cdot}78\times10^{-3}}{C}=600^2 \text{ and } C=\frac{4{\cdot}78\times10^6}{36\times10^4\times10^3}=0{\cdot}0133\ \mu\text{F}$$

The required T-section thus consists of a shunt inductance of 4·78 mH with series arms each containing a capacitor of 0·0266 μF.

4. Each of the two series elements of a T-type low-pass filter consists of an inductance of 30 mH having negligible resistance, and a shunt element having a capacitance of 0·2 μF. Calculate the cut-off frequency and determine the iterative impedances at frequencies of (a) 1000 Hz and (b) 5000 Hz. Also find the ratio of, and the phase difference between, the input and output voltages for one section of the filter at 1000 Hz and at 5000 Hz.

L.U. Ext. Telecomm. 1946.

The cut-off frequency is given by

$$f_c = \frac{1}{\pi\sqrt{LC}} = \frac{1}{\pi\sqrt{60\times10^{-3}\times0{\cdot}2\times10^{-6}}} = 2910 \text{ Hz}$$

The section is symmetrical and the iterative impedance is the same as the characteristic impedance which is given by

$Z_{0T} = R\sqrt{1-x^2}$ (equation 5.40) where $R=\sqrt{L/C}$ and $x = f/f_c$

Hence at 1000 Hz, $Z_{0T} = \sqrt{\dfrac{60\times10^{-3}}{0{\cdot}2\times10^{-6}}}\cdot\sqrt{1-\left(\dfrac{1}{2{\cdot}91}\right)^2} = 515\ \Omega$

At 5000 Hz, $Z_{0T} = \sqrt{\dfrac{60\times10^{-3}}{0{\cdot}2\times10^{-6}}}\cdot\sqrt{1-\left(\dfrac{5}{2{\cdot}91}\right)^2} = j765\ \Omega$

The frequency of 1000 Hz is less than the cut-off value and so lies in the pass-band where the attenuation is zero (in the absence of dissipation in the elements). The phase shift in the pass-band is given by

$$B = \cos^{-1}(1-2x^2) \text{ radians} \quad \text{(equation 5.38)}$$

In this case $x = 1000/2910$

$$\therefore B = \cos^{-1} 0{\cdot}763 \quad \therefore B = 40{\cdot}15°$$

The frequency of 5000 Hz lies in the attenuation band in which $B=\pi$. The attenuation is given by $A = \cosh^{-1}(2x^2-1)$ nepers (equation 5.39)

$= \cosh^{-1} 4{\cdot}92$ nepers $= 2{\cdot}27$ nepers.

Thus the voltage ratio, $V_{in}/V_{out} = e^{2{\cdot}27} = 9{\cdot}68$

Hence at 1000 Hz, $V_{in}/V_{out} = 1$, $B = 40°\ 15'$

and at 5000 Hz, $V_{in}/V_{out} = 9{\cdot}68$, $B = 180°$

References

[1] BARTLETT, A. C.: " An Extension of a Property of Artificial Lines ", Philosophical Magazine, 4, p. 902 (1927).

[2] FOSTER, R. M.: " A Reactance Theorem ", Bell System Technical Journal, 3, p. 259 (1924).

References for Further Reading

SCOWEN, F.: *Electric Wave Filters* (Chapman & Hall, 1950).

STARR, A. T.: *Electric Circuits and Wave Filters* (Pitman, 1938).

MOLE, J. H.: *Filter Design Data for Communication Engineers* (E. & F. N. Spon, 1952).

EXAMPLES

1. Distinguish between *iterative impedance* and *image impedance* of a network and give examples of the application of these impedances in circuit design. Calculate the iterative and image impedances at the terminals 1 1 and 2 2 of the network shown.

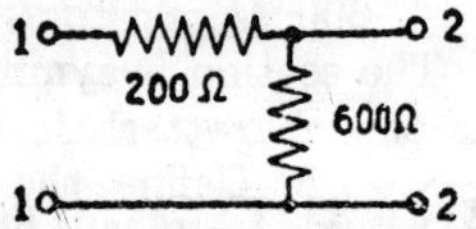

L.U. Ext. Telecomm. 1956.

2. Obtain formulae for the characteristic resistance and attenuation constant of a symmetrical H type attenuator section in terms of its series and shunt resistances. Calculate the values of these components for a section whose characteristic resistance is 600 Ω and whose attenuation is equal to 15 dB.

L.U. Int. Telecomm. 1939.

3. Find the appropriate resistances for the resistive T units of an attenuator which will give an attenuation of 20 dB with an iterative impedance of 600 Ω.

L.U. Int. Telecomm. 1949.

4. Define the decibel and give the main reasons for the adoption of a logarithmic unit for the measurement of losses in communication networks.

An attenuator is composed of symmetrical T-sections having series arms each of 175 Ω and shunt arm of 350 Ω. Derive expressions for, and calculate the characteristic impedance of this network and the attenuation per section.

L.U. Ext. Telecomm. 1947.

5. Design a symmetrical T-pad to operate between 600 Ω impedances (non-reactive) and to have an insertion loss of 6 dB. What would be the error in the pad if the shunt arm were 10% low?

I.E.E. Line Comm., October, 1948.

6. For what purpose is an attenuator commonly employed? A T-type attenuator is to be inserted in a line having a characteristic impedance of $500 \angle 0^\circ \ \Omega$ to give an attenuation of 15 dB, the line being correctly terminated. Calculate, after deriving the necessary expressions, the values of the shunt and series elements of the attenuator.

L.U. Ext. Telecomm. 1945.

7. Determine the equivalent primary shunt inductance of a transformer in order that the transmission loss at 50 Hz may not be greater than the loss at 200 Hz by more than 1 dB. The ratio of the transformer is 1 : 1 and the loss should be determined between 600 Ω resistors.

I.E.E. Line Comm. October, 1947.

8. Define the decibel and give the reasons for the employment of a unit of this type for the measurement of transmission efficiency in telecommunication networks.

A network which may be represented by a symmetrical T is inserted in a transmission channel having a total series impedance of $1000+j0 \ \Omega$. At a point of insertion the loop impedance towards the source is $600+j0 \ \Omega$ and towards the receiver $400+j0 \ \Omega$. The series arms of the T are each resistances of 150 Ω and the shunt arm at the frequency of operation is a reactance of $-j300 \ \Omega$. Calculate the insertion loss in dB produced by the T network.

L.U. Ext. Telecomm. 1944.

9. Show that the iterative impedance Z_0 of a chain of T-sections each having series arms Z_1 and a shunt arm Z_2 is given by $Z_0 = \sqrt{(Z_1^2+2Z_1Z_2)}$.

Explain the physical significance of (a) a resistive value of Z_0 when Z_1 and Z_2 are resistive, (b) a resistive value of Z_0 when Z_1 and Z_2 are purely reactive and (c) a purely reactive value of Z_0 when Z_1 and Z_2 are purely reactive.

Derive the limiting frequencies of the pass band of such a chain in which arms Z_1 are coils of inductance 96 mH and arms Z_2 are condensers of capacitance 0·53 μF, all being loss-free. Sketch a curve showing how Z_0 varies with frequency in the pass band.

L.U. Ext. Telecomm. 1952.

10. Explain carefully what is meant by the terms *pass band*, *attenuation band* and *cut-off frequency* as applied to a filter network. Point out the effect of losses in the inductors and condensers on the filter characteristics.

Prove, by consideration of a representative T or π section, that the attenuation is zero in the frequency band for which the characteristic impedance of an *ideal* filter is resistive, and that the attenuation is finite in the frequency band for which the characteristic impedance is reactive.

L.U. Ext. Telecomm. 1953.

11. Derive from the network equations an expression for (a) the characteristic impedance and (b) the cut-off frequency of a low pass filter. Employ the relations obtained to calculate element values for a low pass filter having a characteristic impedance of 600 Ω and a cut-off frequency of 3 kHz.

I.E.E. Radio Comm. October, 1946.

12. A low pass filter is composed of π sections having a series arms of 63·6 mH inductance and shunt arms of 0·088 μF each. Determine, either by deriving the necessary formula, or by the direct application of the simple circuit theory (a) the cut-off frequency, (b) the attenuation per section at a frequency of 5000 Hz. Assume that the filter is terminated in its characteristic impedance and that the elements are loss free.

L.U. Ext. Telecomm. 1948.

13. Show how the pass and attenuate bands of a ladder-type filter may be determined from a knowledge of the ratio of the impedance of the series and shunt arms.

A filter, composed of T-sections, has series arms of 0·035 H inductance and shunt arms of 0·04 H in series with a capacitance of 0·196 μF. Determine the cut-off frequency of this filter and the frequency of infinite attenuation.

L.U. Int. Telecomm. 1943.

14. A ladder network has series arms of 0·2 H inductance and shunt arms of 0·275 μF capacitance. Assuming the network to be terminated in its characteristic impedance and neglecting the effect of dissipation, calculate the phase shift per section at a frequency of 500 Hz.

State, indicating briefly the reasons for the answer given, whether the frequency of 500 Hz lies in a pass or an attenuation band.

L.U. Ext. Telecomm. 1944.

15. Derive an expression for the characteristic impedance, Z_K, of a symmetrical T-section, in terms of Z_1, the total series impedance, and Z_2, the shunt impedance.

Considering a low-pass, prototype (constant-k) filter composed of pure reactances as an example, show that Z_K is a pure resistance over the pass band.

Find the attenuation in decibels produced by one section of such a filter at a frequency which is twice the cut-off frequency.

The equation $\cosh \gamma = 1 + Z_1/2Z_2$ may be assumed, where γ is the propagation coefficient.

L.U. Telecomm. Part III, 1959.

16. Give a simple proof of the frequency discriminative properties of the ladder-type network composed of pure reactance elements and terminated in its characteristic impedance. Use the relationship derived to determine the pass band of a filter composed of T sections in which each of the series arms consists of a 35 mH inductance in series with an 8 μF condenser and each of the shunt arms consists of a 0·16 μF condenser.

L.U. Int. Telecomm. 1941.

17. Design a low pass filter having a cut-off frequency of 3000 Hz. To give a sharp cut-off it should include one section giving a frequency of infinite attenuation at 3100 Hz. The filter should be arranged to give a very low reflection loss when operating between apparatus of $600\angle 0^\circ\ \Omega$.

I.E.E. Line Comm. April, 1946.

18. Explain what is meant by the term "*m*-derived" as applied to symmetrical T filter sections. State the relations connecting the element values of the *m*-derived section with those of the prototype in the case of a simple low-pass filter, and show that they satisfy the required conditions.

I.E.E. Radio Comm. April, 1948.

19. The elements of a band-pass filter consist of an inductance and a condenser in series, and a condenser in shunt. Deduce expressions for the cut-off frequencies.

If the coils available have an inductance of 10 mH, determine the capacitances of the condensers to give cut-off frequencies of $20{,}000/2\pi$ and $40{,}000/2\pi$ hertz. How will resistance and losses modify the shape of the attenuation-frequency curve ?

L.U. Int. Telecomm. 1948.

20. Show from first principles that in a symmetrical T network the attenuation in the stop band is given by $\cosh \alpha = 1 + Z_1/2Z_2$ and hence show that for an "m" derived low-pass section

$$\cosh \alpha = 1 - \frac{\dfrac{2f^2m^2}{f_c^2}}{1 - \dfrac{f^2}{f_c^2}\left(1 - m^2\right)}$$

where f_c is the cut-off frequency.

L.U. Int. Telecomm. 1956.

21. Each of the series arms of a symmetrical T type low-pass filter section consists of an inductor of 18 mH having negligible resistance while the shunt arm is a 0·1 μF capacitor. Indicate how the characteristic impedance varies with frequency and calculate its value at 1 kHz and 8 kHz. Derive any formulae used.

What are the limitations of such a filter section? Indicate how the performance can be improved.

L.U. Telecomm. Part III. 1963.

6

THERMIONIC VALVES

THIS chapter is concerned in the main with the characteristics of the more common forms of thermionic valve, and also contains an introduction to the cathode ray tube.

Electron Emission

Electrons are emitted from the surfaces of metals if sufficient energy is transferred to them, so that they can overcome the restraining surface forces. It is also necessary that the electrons have a certain freedom of movement within the conductor in order to pass from the interior to the surface, to replace those ejected into the surrounding space. The necessary energy can be absorbed from incident electromagnetic radiation. When the radiation is in the form of visible light, the alkaline earth metals exhibit the effect, which is called *photoelectric* emission. This phenomenon is utilised in the operation of photoelectric cells. Energy may also be transferred to surface electrons in a conductor by the impact of high-velocity electrons from some other source; in this case, the primary electrons impinging on the surface give rise to a secondary emission, an effect used in devices known as electron multipliers. Alternatively, electron emission from a conductor can be achieved by the application of heat. Emission by this means is utilised in thermionic valves. The rate of electron emission increases with temperature in accordance with Richardson's equation[1]

$$i = AT^2 e^{-b/T} \quad . \quad . \quad . \quad . \quad . \quad . \quad . \quad 6.1$$

where A and b are constants depending on the material, and T is the absolute temperature of the emitting material.

It is found that if, say, a tungsten wire is heated to a temperature of the order of 2000°K, electrons will acquire sufficient energy to leave the wire surface; some electrons return due to the attractive force exerted by the wire which becomes positively charged, and also because of the repelling effect of the cloud of negatively charged electrons around the wire. This electron cloud in the vicinity of the emitting surface is known as a *space charge.*

If a second electrode with a positive potential is present, electrons will be attracted from the space charge and will move to the positive electrode. If the emitting wire and collecting electrode are enclosed in an evacuated glass envelope, oxidation of the emitting surface is prevented and an electron stream is obtained which leaves the emitting surface, or *cathode,* and travels to the positively charged *anode.* The direction of the conventional electric current in passing through a thermionic valve is thus from the anode to the cathode.

The Diode

The diode is the simplest form of thermionic valve, and has two electrodes, namely an anode and a cathode. The latter may be directly or indirectly heated, and such valves are represented diagrammatically as in Fig. 6.1. In the indirectly heated valve the heating and emitting functions are separated; the cathode is heated by an insulated "heater" wire through which either direct or alternating current is passed. The anode is commonly in the form of a cylinder around the cathode.

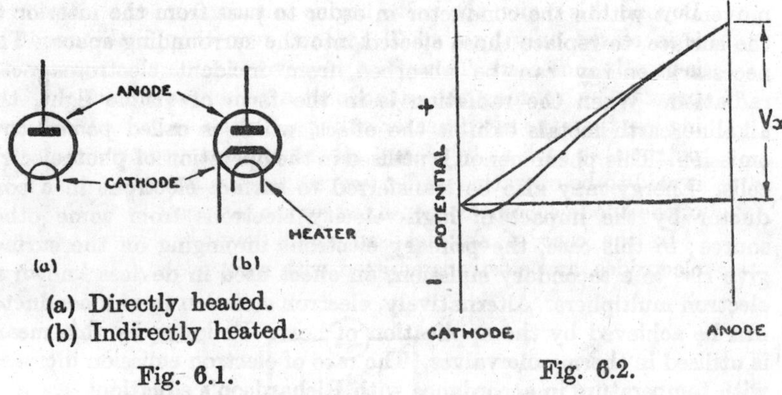

(a) Directly heated.
(b) Indirectly heated.

Fig. 6.1.

Fig. 6.2.

The cathodes of large valves are usually made of thoriated tungsten wire; the cathode material used for small receiving-type valves is a mixture of barium and strontium oxides on a base of nickel alloy.

If the anode is made positive with respect to an unheated cathode by an amount V_x the potential distribution between the electrodes will be linear (Fig. 6.2). If the cathode is heated and a space charge is present the distribution of potential will be as shown in the lower curve of Fig. 6.2. It will be seen that a potential minimum exists near the cathode.

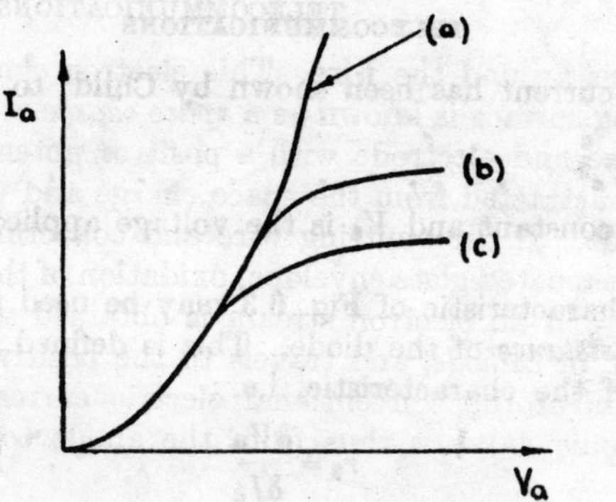

(a) Heater voltage normal
(b) Heater voltage 60% normal
(c) Heater voltage 50% normal

Fig. 6.3.

The characteristic curves for a diode are shown in Fig. 6.3 and may be obtained by means of the circuit shown in Fig. 6.4. It can be seen that the anode current at first increases with increase in anode voltage. Under this condition the current is said to be *space-charge-limited*. Beyond this region the valve begins to saturate, i.e. the anode current is increased only by a small amount even though the anode voltage is greatly increased. This effect, however, can only be demonstrated in practice by running the cathode at a reduced temperature by applying less than the rated heater voltage. In this second region, the anode potential is such as to attract all the emitted electrons, and the valve is said to be operating under *temperature-limited conditions*. The value of the anode current is then fixed by the temperature of the cathode.

In the case of an idealised diode having infinite parallel plane electrodes, and electrons emitted with zero velocity, the space-charge-

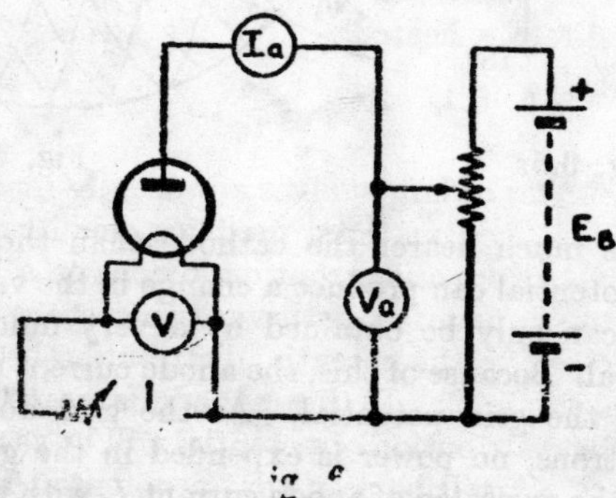

limited anode current has been shown by Child[2] to be given by the equation

$$I_a = K^1 V_a^{\frac{3}{2}} \qquad . \quad . \quad . \quad . \quad . \quad . \quad . \qquad 6.2$$

where K^1 is a constant and V_a is the voltage applied between anode and cathode.

The static characteristic of Fig. 6.3 may be used to determine the *slope* or *a.c. resistance* of the diode. This is defined as the reciprocal of the slope of the characteristic, i.e.

$$r_a = \frac{\delta V_a}{\delta I_a} \qquad . \quad . \quad . \quad . \qquad 6.3$$

The Triode

The triode valve has three electrodes, an anode and cathode as in a diode, and a third electrode in the form of a grid of fine wire interposed. The arrangement is represented diagrammatically in Fig. 6.5.

Electrons emitted from the cathode pass through the meshes of the grid on their way to the anode and the flow is controlled by the combined effect of the electrostatic fields due to the grid and anode. The anode current is a function of the anode and grid potentials and can be represented by a surface, part of which is shown in Fig. 6.6.

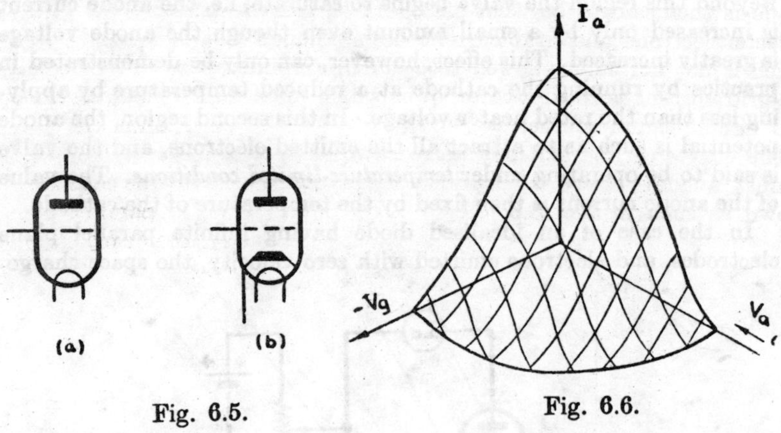

Fig. 6.5. Fig. 6.6.

As the grid is much nearer the cathode than the anode, a small change in grid potential can produce a change in the value of the anode current, which can only be obtained by a very much larger change in anode potential. Because of this, the anode current can be controlled by variation of the grid potential. As the grid does not normally collect any electrons, no power is expended in the grid circuit. The general form of the variation of anode current I_a with the grid potential V_g is shown in Fig. 6.7 for three arbitrary values of anode voltage.

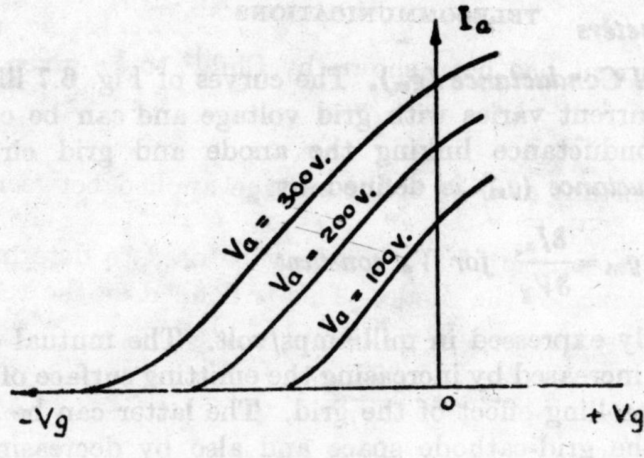

Fig. 6.7.

The curves shown may be regarded as intersections of the surface in Fig. 6.6 with various $I_a V_g$ planes corresponding to different values of anode voltage. It should be noted that all voltages are measured from the cathode, or from the negative end of the filament in a directly-heated valve.

The curves show that if the grid is made sufficiently negative with respect to the cathode, the anode current is reduced to zero, and the anode is then said to be "cut-off". If V_g is made positive the grid collects electrons and grid current flows, though this is a condition which is not normally allowed to occur in amplifiers, as the effect of the grid current is to dissipate power which must be supplied by the grid circuit signal source.

The curves of Fig. 6.7 may be redrawn as curves of anode current against anode voltage for various values of grid voltage, and are shown as such in Fig. 6.8.

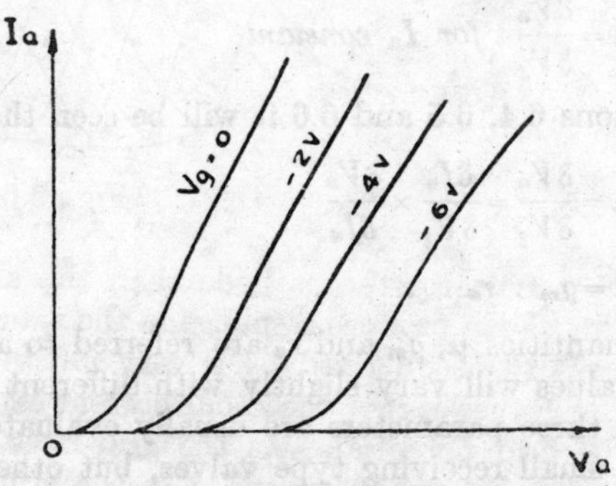

Fig. 6.8.

Valve Parameters

(a) Mutual Conductance (g_m). The curves of Fig. 6.7 illustrate how the anode current varies with grid voltage and can be considered to represent conductance linking the anode and grid circuits. The *mutual conductance* (g_m) is defined by

$$g_m = \frac{\delta I_a}{\delta V_g} \text{ for } V_a \text{ constant} \quad . \quad . \quad . \quad . \quad 6.4$$

and is usually expressed in milliamps/volt. The mutual conductance of a valve is increased by increasing the emitting surface of the cathode and the controlling effect of the grid. The latter can be achieved by decreasing the grid-cathode space and also by decreasing the pitch of the winding of the grid wire.

(b) A.C. Resistance, or Slope Resistance (r_a). The reciprocal of the slope of the anode current/anode voltage characteristics gives the *a.c. resistance* for the triode exactly as for the diode, and so

$$r_a = \frac{\delta V_a}{\delta I_a} \text{ for } V_g \text{ constant} \quad . \quad . \quad . \quad 6.5$$

It should be noted that the value so obtained will be different from the value obtained for the quotient V_a/I_a at any point. This latter value is termed the *d.c. resistance,* but is seldom used.

(c) Amplification Factor (μ). As far as the value of the anode current is concerned, the grid exerts a much greater effect than the anode for a given potential change. If the anode current is reduced by making the grid more negative, the anode current can be restored to its former value by increasing the anode voltage. A quantity called the *amplification factor* (μ) is defined by

$$\mu = \frac{\delta V_a}{\delta V_g} \text{ for } I_a \text{ constant} \quad . \quad . \quad . \quad . \quad 6.6$$

From equations 6.4, 6.5 and 6.6 it will be seen that

$$\mu = \frac{\delta V_a}{\delta V_g} = \frac{\delta I_a}{\delta V_g} \times \frac{\delta V_a}{\delta I_a}$$

$$\text{or } \mu = g_m \,.\, r_a \quad . \quad . \quad . \quad . \quad . \quad . \quad . \quad 6.7$$

The three quantities μ, g_m and r_a are referred to as *valve constants,* though their values will vary slightly with different values of supply voltages. The three parameters are usually evaluated at $V_a = 100$ V and $V_g = 0$ for small receiving type valves, but other values may be used, depending on the application of the valve.

Measurement of Valve Characteristics

The valve parameters may be obtained if a family of mutual characteristics or a set of anode characteristics are available. Both sets of characteristics may be measured by means of the circuit shown in Fig. 6.9. Characteristics so obtained are referred to as *static* characteristics as opposed to *dynamic* characteristics. The latter are obtained when the valve is used with a load in a circuit with an alternating signal present.

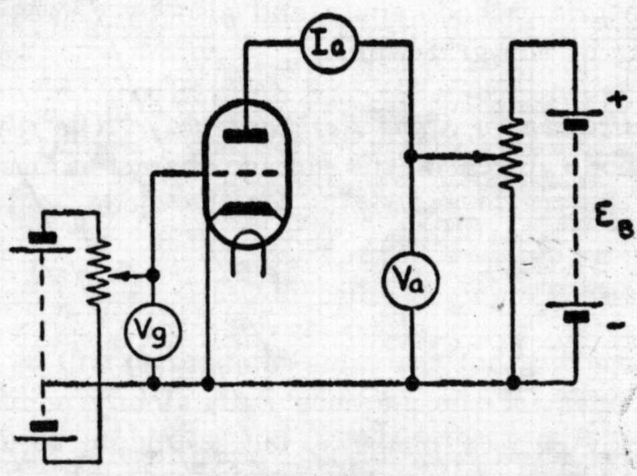

Fig. 6.9.

In order to obtain the mutual characteristics the anode voltage is first adjusted to some convenient figure, say 100 V, and kept constant at this value. V_g is then varied from a large negative to a small positive value and the corresponding values of the anode current observed. By repeating this procedure for other values of anode voltage, a family of mutual characteristics will be obtained as in Fig. 6.7. The anode characteristics are obtained by variation of the anode voltage with the grid voltage fixed. If either set of curves is available, the other set may be derived from them, and so all three parameters may be derived from either the mutual or anode characteristics.

Derivation of Valve Parameters from Static Characteristics

The static anode current/grid voltage characteristics of a medium impedance triode are shown in Fig. 6.10.

The figure shows that for an anode voltage of 100 V, the anode current is 9·2 mA, when the grid voltage is zero, and then falls to 7·3 mA, for a grid voltage of −1 volt.

$$\text{Thus } g_m = \frac{\delta I_a}{\delta V_g} = \frac{AC}{BC} = \frac{9{\cdot}2 - 7{\cdot}3}{1} = 1{\cdot}9 \text{ mA/V}$$

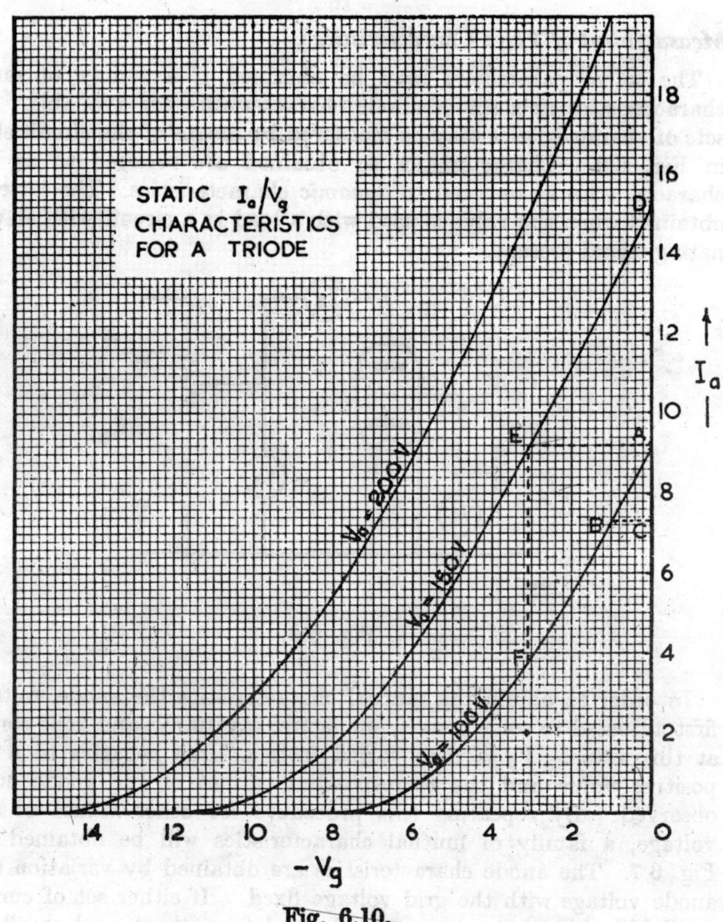

Fig. 6.10.

If, on the other hand, the grid voltage is maintained at zero and the anode voltage is changed from 100 V to 150 V, the anode current increases from point A to point D, and thus

$$r_a = \frac{\delta V_a}{\delta I_a} = \frac{50}{\dfrac{15 \cdot 1 - 9 \cdot 3}{1000}} = 8500\ \Omega$$

An anode voltage of 100 V and grid voltage of zero give the point A. The same value of anode current is obtained on the $V_a = 150$ V curve at the point E. This corresponds to a grid voltage of $-3 \cdot 1$ V and thence the amplification factor

$$\mu = \frac{\delta V_a}{\delta V_g} = \frac{50}{3 \cdot 1} = 16 \cdot 2$$

This agrees with the product of $g_m \cdot r_a = 1 \cdot 9 \times 10^{-3} \times 8500 = 16 \cdot 2$.

As an alternative, the three constants evaluated above may be determined from a set of anode current/anode voltage characteristics as shown in Fig. 6.11.

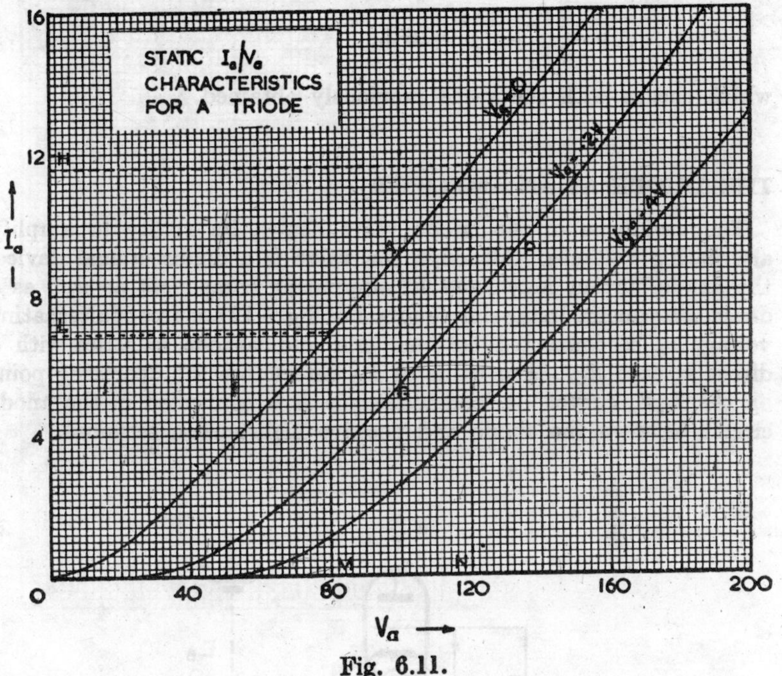

Fig. 6.11.

In this case the point A represents an anode voltage of 100 V and zero grid volts. For the same anode voltage, the anode current falls to the point G when the grid voltage is 2 V negative, and so

$$g_m = \frac{\delta I_a}{\delta V_g} = \frac{AG}{2} = \frac{9 \cdot 2 - 5 \cdot 4}{2} = 1 \cdot 9 \text{ mA/V}.$$

A change in anode voltage from 120 V to 80 V when the grid voltage is maintained at zero gives an anode current change of 11·6 mA to 6·9 mA, and so

$$r_a = \frac{\delta V_a}{\delta I_a} = \frac{NM}{HL} = \frac{40}{4 \cdot 7} = 8500 \ \Omega$$

At the original point A the anode current is 9·2 mA. This is also obtained at the point P. The latter point, however, represents an anode voltage of 132·4 V and a grid voltage of −2 V, or in terms of the incremental changes

$$\delta V_a = 132{\cdot}4 - 100 = 32{\cdot}4 \text{ V}$$

$$\text{and } \delta V_g = 0 - (-2) = 2 \text{ V}$$

$$\therefore \mu = \frac{\delta V_a}{\delta V_g} = \frac{32{\cdot}4}{2} = 16{\cdot}2.$$

which checks with the value previously obtained.

THE TRIODE AS AN AMPLIFIER

The usefulness of the triode valve lies in its ability to amplify alternating voltages. Although the valve is a unidirectional device, the anode current may have an alternating component as well as a direct component. In the simple circuit of Fig. 6.12 a source of alternating voltage v_g, is connected between grid and cathode in series with a direct voltage E_C. The value of E_C determines the operating point on the I_a/V_g curve. A load resistance R is connected in the anode circuit between the anode and positive high-tension terminal.

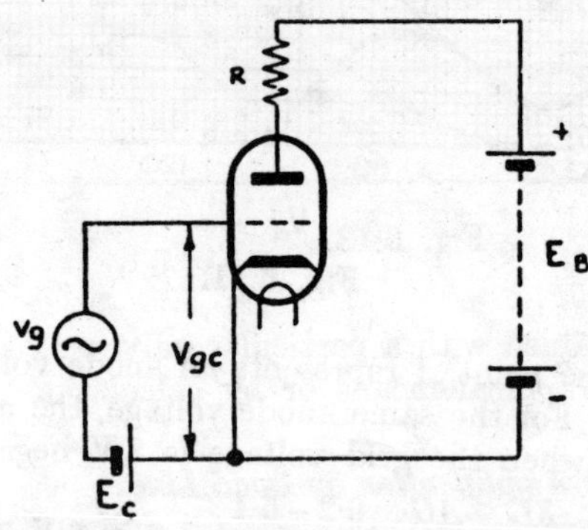

Fig. 6.12. Simple triode amplifier.

The application of the alternating voltage v_g causes the anode current to vary and so the resultant anode current can be thought of as an alternating current, superimposed on a direct current. The former gives rise to an alternating voltage across the load resistance R. The amplification obtained is then the ratio of the alternating voltage across R to the alternating input voltage v_g. In the case where v_g is sinusoidal the corresponding variation in anode current and anode voltage are shown in Fig. 6.13, which shows that there is a phase reversal in the valve. As the grid voltage increases positively the anode current increases. This increase in anode current gives rise to an increased ohmic drop in R, and so the potential of the anode falls. In the absence of the alternating voltage v_g the anode current has the value I_B and the anode potential is $E_B - I_B R$.

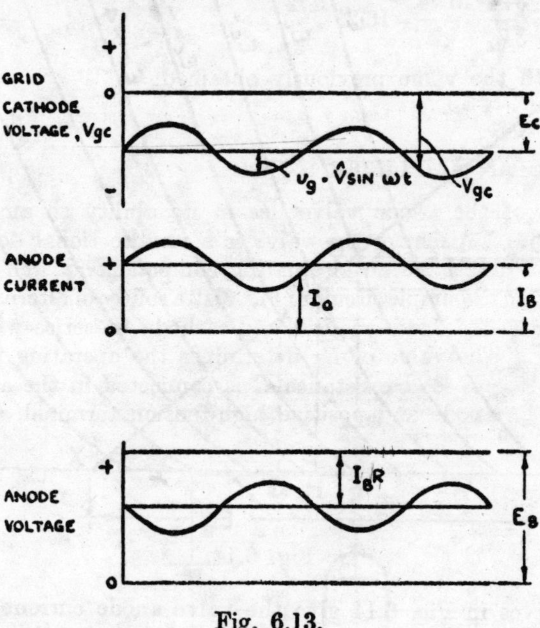

Fig. 6.13.

The amplification obtained with a particular valve and load can be determined either by graphical means or by calculation.

Determination of Voltage Amplification by Load Line

The amplification obtained with the circuit of Fig. 6.12 may be determined for any value of load resistance if the anode current/anode voltage characteristics for the valve are available. (Fig. 6.14.)

The presence of the load resistance R causes a voltage drop so that the potential of the anode (V_a) is no longer E_B, but

$$V_a = E_B - I_a R \qquad . \quad . \quad . \quad . \quad . \quad . \qquad 6.8$$

This determines the voltage at the anode for any value of anode current, and so for any given value of R the actual voltage at the anode may be determined. When I_a is zero, $V_a = E_B$. and when V_a is zero, $I_a = E_B/R$. These conditions give the extremities of the straight line XY in Fig. 6.14, and other intermediate points can be determined by equation 6.8. The line XY is called a *load line* and represents the locus of the values of the anode current and anode voltage for a particular value of R.

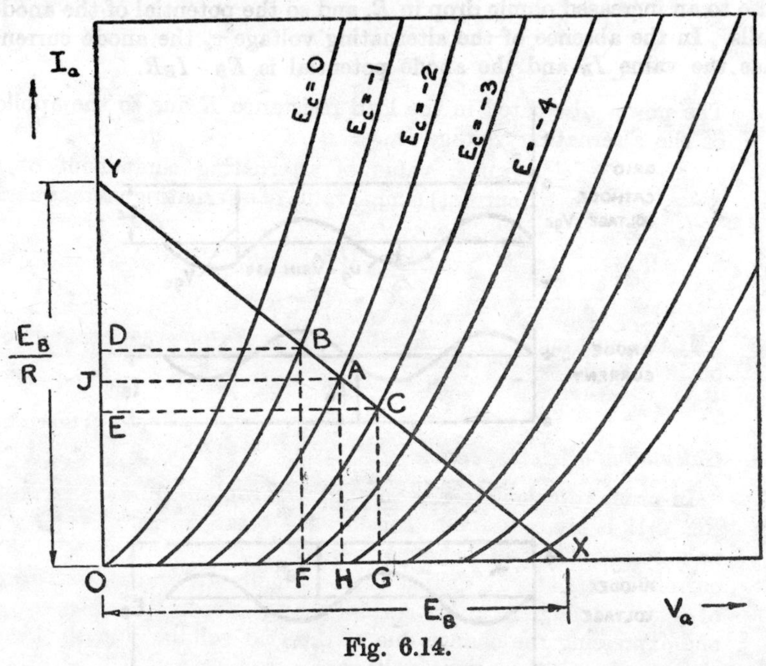

Fig. 6.14.

The curves in Fig. 6.14 give the valve anode current for various values of the grid bias voltage E_c. It follows that for a particular grid voltage and load resistance R, the anode current has the value given by the intersection of the appropriate grid voltage curve with the load line. If, for example, the steady grid voltage is -2 V, then in the absence of an alternating voltage the operating point will be the point A. Under these conditions the anode current will be OJ and the voltage across the valve will be OH. If an alternating voltage of 1 V peak is applied as in Fig. 6.12 the line of operation will be $ABCA$. The actual anode voltage will vary between the values represented by the points F and G, whilst the anode current will vary between the values represented by D and E.

The *voltage amplification* (A_v) obtained is defined as

$$A_v = \frac{\text{Output voltage}}{\text{Input voltage}}$$

FG represents the peak to peak output voltage and so the peak value of the output voltage is $FG/2$, for an input voltage of 1 V peak. In general, if the input alternating voltage is an r.m.s. voltage v_g, the voltage amplification will be,

$$A_v = \frac{FG}{2\sqrt{2} \cdot v_g} \quad . \quad . \quad . \quad . \quad . \quad 6.9$$

The power dissipated in the load resistance R due to the application of the alternating voltage is,

$P =$ (r.m.s. value of alternating component of anode current) (r.m.s. value of alternating voltage across R)

$$= \frac{DE}{2\sqrt{2}} \times \frac{FG}{2\sqrt{2}} = \frac{DE \cdot FG}{8} \quad . \quad . \quad . \quad . \quad 6.10$$

If the current scale is in milliamperes the power so calculated will be in milliwatts.

Calculation of Amplification

In order to calculate the amplification obtained with the circuit of Fig. 6.12 it is necessary to consider the total change in anode current as a consequence of a change in grid voltage. Any change in anode current itself causes a change in anode voltage because of the presence of R and so the total anode current change is represented by two terms, one expressing the change due to the grid voltage, and the other the change due to the anode voltage.

Suppose the grid voltage changes by an amount δv_g and the resulting anode current change is δi_a with a change in anode voltage of δv_a

$$\text{Then } \delta i_a = \left(\frac{\partial i_a}{\partial v_g}\right)\delta v_g + \left(\frac{\partial i_a}{\partial v_a}\right)\delta v_a \quad . \quad . \quad . \quad . \quad 6.11$$

$$= g_m \delta v_g + \frac{1}{r_a}\,\delta v_a = \frac{\mu}{r_a}\delta v_g + \frac{1}{r_a}\,(-\delta i_a R)$$

The minus sign is necessary in the second term because an increase in anode current causes a decrease in the value of the anode voltage

$$\text{Hence } \delta i_a\left(1 + \frac{R}{r_a}\right) = \frac{u}{r_a}\,\delta v_g$$

$$\therefore \delta i_a = \frac{\mu \delta v_g}{r_a + R}$$

If alternating quantities are considered in place of small changes then

$$i_a = \frac{\mu v_g}{r_a + R} \quad . \quad . \quad . \quad . \quad . \quad 6.12$$

and the voltage across the load resistance R is

$$v_a = -i_a R = -\frac{\mu v_g R}{r_a + R} \quad . \quad . \quad . \quad . \quad 6.13$$

The voltage amplification obtained is then the ratio of the voltages v_a and v_g

$$\text{i.e. Voltage amplification} = -\frac{\mu R}{r_a + R} \quad . \quad . \quad . \quad . \quad 6.14$$

Equation 6.14 shows that for fixed values of μ and r_a the voltage amplification increases with the value of R and becomes asymptotic to the value μ as shown in Fig. 6.15. The value of R used in practice is limited by the value of the high-tension supply as the voltage at the anode of the valve is less than this by the amount of the IR drop.

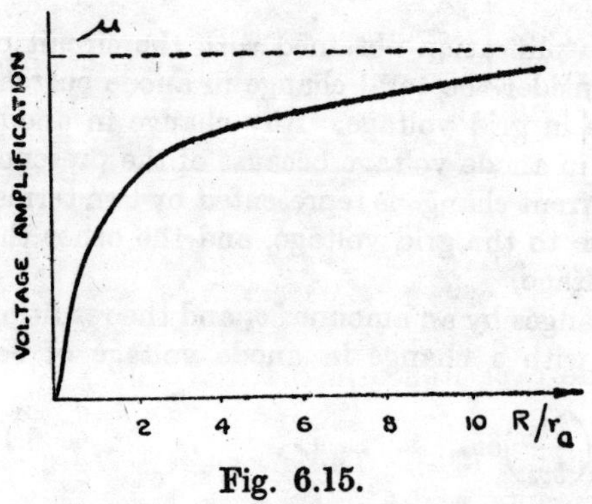

Fig. 6.15.

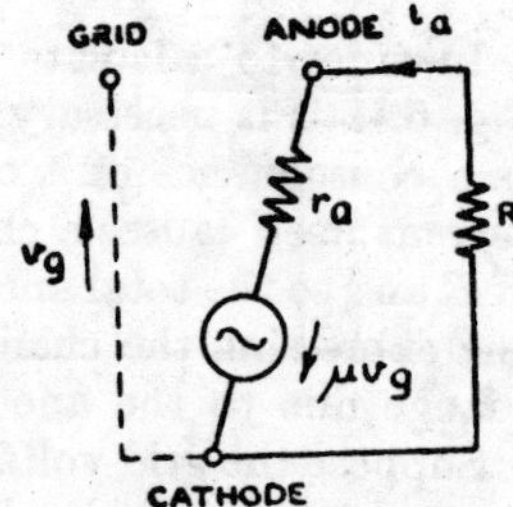

Fig. 6.16. Equivalent circuit for simple triode amplifier of Fig. 6.12.

Equation 6.14 is important as it enables the amplification to be calculated for any value of load when the valve constants are known. The load need not necessarily be a resistance but may in general be any impedance, provided it has a direct current path.

Equivalent Circuit for a Triode

Equation 6.12 gives the alternating component of current flowing in the anode circuit of a triode valve. This is the current which would flow in the series circuit of r_a and R where the emf. is μv_g, and so the equivalent circuit is as shown in Fig. 6.16.

This equivalent circuit applies to alternating components of voltage and current, and is valid as long as operation is restricted to the linear region of the valve characteristics.

Interelectrode Capacitance

Capacitance exists between every pair of electrodes, and depends on their size and disposition. In the triode there are three electrode capacitances.

1. The grid to cathode capacitance (C_{gk}). This is shunted across the applied voltage, and so reduces the input impedance of the valve.

2. The anode to cathode capacitance (C_{ak}). This is shunted across the output voltage which appears across the load impedance Z (Fig. 6.17a). (It should be noted that as far as alternating currents are concerned the points A and B in Fig. 6.17a are at the same potential if the H.T. source has zero impedance.) The effect of this capacitance is to reduce the amplification at high frequencies.

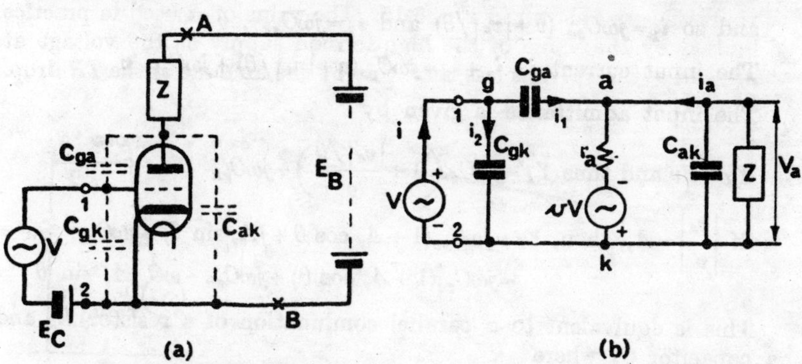

Fig. 6.17. Interelectrode capacitance in a triode valve.

3. The grid to anode capacitance (C_{ga}). This provides a coupling between the grid and anode circuits, and a fraction of the amplified voltage at the anode is fed back to the grid. This effect is of importance at high frequencies. If the voltage fed back is of sufficient magnitude and is in phase with the applied grid voltage, the valve may cease to function as an amplifier and become a generator, or oscillator; the amplifier is then said to be *unstable*, and the output is independent of the input.

Although the effect of the C_{ga} coupling may be eliminated by providing a second feedback path, which "neutralises" the effect of the first, high-frequency amplification by triode valves is not often employed in the manner shown and tetrode or pentode valves are used instead.

Input Impedance of a Triode—Miller Effect

The input impedance of a triode amplifier is the impedance measured between the grid input terminals. If it is assumed that there is no grid current it would seem that the input impedance would be simply the reactance of C_{gk}. The anode circuit however is coupled to the grid circuit by C_{ga} and alters the grid-cathode impedance; this is known as the "Miller Effect".[3] The equivalent circuit for alternating currents is that shown in Fig. 6.17b. As the anode load is complex the voltage across the anode load may be considered as $v_a\underline{|\theta}$ where θ is the angle between the grid and anode voltages.

Suppose the input voltage at the terminals 1,2 is v, then from Fig. 6.17b the voltage across $C_{ga} = v + |v_a|\angle\theta$

and so $i_1 = j\omega C_{ga}\ (v + |v_a|\angle\theta)$ and $i_2 = j\omega C_{gk}\ .\ v$

The input current $i = i_1 + i_2 = j\omega C_{ga}(v + |v_a|\angle\theta) + j\omega C_{gk}.\ v$

The input admittance is given by

$$Y_I = i/v \text{ and thus } Y_I = j\omega C_{ga}\left(1 + \frac{|v_a|\angle\theta}{v}\right) + j\omega C_{gk}$$

$$\text{if } \left|\frac{v_a}{v}\right| = A_v, \text{ then, } Y_I = j\omega C_{ga}(1 + A_v \cos\theta + jA_v \sin\theta) + j\omega C_{gk}$$
$$= j\omega C_{ga}(1 + A_v \cos\theta) + j\omega C_{gk} - \omega C_{ga}A_v \sin\theta$$

This is equivalent to a parallel combination of a resistor R_I and a capacitor C_I where

$$C_I = \text{input capacitance} = C_{ga}\ (1 + A_v \cos\theta) + C_{gk} \quad . \qquad 6.15$$

$$\text{and } R_I = \text{input resistance} = \frac{-1}{\omega C_{ga}\ A_v \sin\theta} \quad . \quad . \quad . \qquad 6.16$$

The voltage amplification A_v is usually large compared with unity and so the input capacitance depends mainly on the grid to anode capacitance. (C_{ga} and C_{gk} are very approximately equal.)

In tetrode and pentode valves (see below) C_{ga} is very small and for such valves the input capacitance is substantially C_{gk}.

In cases where θ is positive (i.e. for inductive anode loads) the input impedance of a triode valve consists of a capacitance in parallel with a negative resistance. This implies that some of the output power is fed back to the grid circuit with a phase relation such that there is a component of input current 180° out of phase with the input voltage. This effect may cause the total grid circuit resistance to be zero or negative and this causes the amplifier to be unstable.

THE TETRODE

This valve was introduced to overcome the difficulties of high-frequency amplification with triode valves. In order to diminish the anode to grid capacitance, an extra electrode is interposed between the grid and anode with the object of forming an electrostatic screen between them. The most effective screening is obtained by surrounding the grid with a metallic plate and then connecting the latter to a point at earth potential. Although a solid plate is not possible the desired screening properties are not greatly reduced if the extra electrode is made in the form of a wire mesh from a helix of wire. The electrode used has this form and is commonly called a screen grid or "screen". If the latter is connected directly to earth or cathode, the steady potential distribution in the valve is such that emitted electrons are not then attracted sufficiently strongly towards the anode, and the current through the valve is small. This objection is overcome by connecting the screen grid to a source of steady positive potential, comparable with that applied to the anode. At the same time the screen is arranged to be dynamically at earth potential. This second condition is met by the connection between the screen grid and earth of a capacitor, the reactance of which is low at the operating frequency. (Fig. 6.18.)

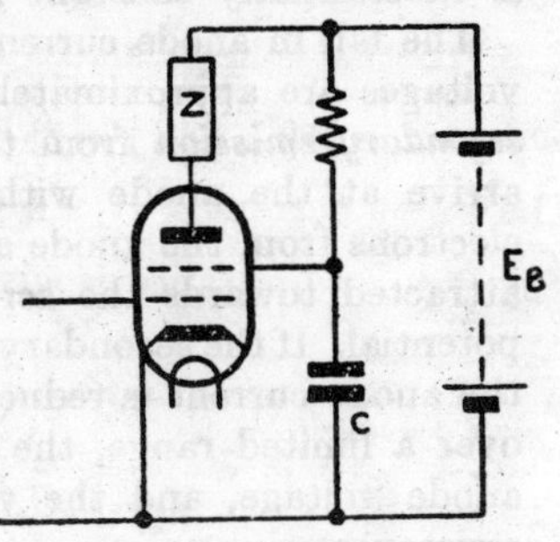

Fig. 6.18. The tetrode valve.

The presence of the screen grid reduces the anode to grid capacitance to something of the order of 0·01 μμF or less, as compared with the value of 2 – 5 μμF in the case of the triode.

Tetrode Characteristics

The static characteristics of a tetrode may be obtained by means of the circuit shown in Fig. 6.19a.

The anode current/grid voltage characteristics are similar in form to those of the triode. The anode current/anode voltage curves have the general form shown in Fig. 6.19b. The curves shown are for a constant voltage of V_s on the screen grid.

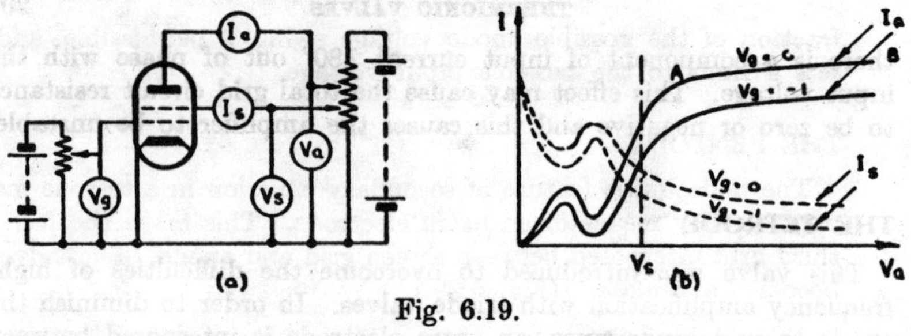

Fig. 6.19.

It will be seen that the anode current first of all increases rapidly with increase in anode voltage, then decreases when the latter has a value which approaches that of the screen voltage. As the anode voltage is increased further the anode current again rises, rapidly at first, and then remains fairly constant. The screen current varies in an inverse manner to the anode current, so that the total cathode current is substantially constant for all values of anode voltage.

The fall in anode current in the region where the anode and screen voltages are approximately equal may be explained on the basis of *secondary emission* from the anode. The primary emitted electrons arrive at the anode with sufficient velocity to dislodge secondary electrons from the anode surface. These secondary electrons are then attracted towards the screen when this is at the same or a higher potential. If the secondary emission exceeds the primary bombardment the anode current is reduced and the screen current increased. Thus, over a limited range, the anode current decreases for an increase in anode voltage, and the valve behaves as though it had a *negative* resistance.

This property of the tetrode is utilised to form an oscillator circuit (see the *dynatron* oscillator in chapter 11).

When the anode potential exceeds that of the screen the secondary electrons return to the anode, and the anode current then increases with anode voltage. The working range of the characteristic is the linear portion *AB*, the gradient of which is very small, so that the anode slope resistance is very high. The anode current is substantially independent of the anode voltage but depends upon the voltage applied to the screen.

Because of the high value of r_a the amplification factor for a tetrode is very much higher than that of a triode. Unfortunately, however, it is not possible to make use of this high value of amplification with the tetrode unless the input voltage is kept small. The reason for this is that the voltage swing at the anode must be restricted to the linear portion *AB* in order to avoid distortion due to the kink in the characteristics. For normal supply voltages this means that only a fraction of the possible anode voltage swing is permissible, and this sets a limit to the possible input voltage.

THE PENTODE

The undesirable feature of secondary emission in a tetrode may be overcome by means of an extra electrode. This takes the form of a third grid interposed between screen grid and anode. The valve then becomes a *pentode*. (Fig. 6.20.)

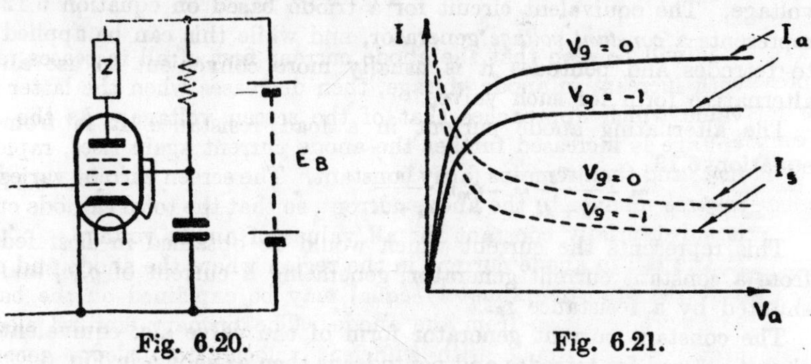

Fig. 6.20. Fig. 6.21.

The extra grid is known as a *suppressor* grid, and is connected to the cathode. The electrons produced at the anode by secondary emission are prevented from travelling to the screen by the negative potential gradient set up by the suppressor grid when the latter is at zero potential.

The static characteristics of a pentode may be obtained by the circuit of Fig. 6.19a. The anode current/grid voltage characteristics are similar to those of a triode or tetrode, and the anode characteristics have the form shown in Fig. 6.21.

The pentode has a high value of r_a and hence a high amplification factor which can be more fully utilised than in the case of the tetrode because of the absence of the kink in the anode characteristics.

The Beam Tetrode

The pentode valve eliminates the effect of secondary emission in the normal screened grid or tetrode valve by means of the presence of the suppressor grid. An alternative method is used in a valve known as the *beam tetrode*. In this type of valve the actual electrode structure is arranged so that the electron stream is concentrated into a beam. This is done by alignment of the control and screen grids, and by the presence of two beam forming rods, or small plates, which are kept at cathode potential, and placed between the screened grid and the anode. A dense space charge is formed and a potential minimum occurs in the screen-anode space and secondary electrons are repelled back to the anode. The anode current/anode voltage characteristic of such valves is similar to that of the pentode except that the "knee" of the curve is sharper and closer to the current axis.

Equivalent Circuit for a Tetrode or Pentode

Tetrodes and pentodes behave as *constant current* generators in as much as the anode current is substantially independent of the anode voltage. The equivalent circuit for a triode based on equation 6.12 represents a *constant voltage* generator, and while this can be applied to tetrodes and pentodes it is usually more convenient to use an alternative form for such valves.

The alternating anode current in a load resistance R is from equation 6.13

$$= -\frac{\mu v_g}{r_a + R} = -g_m v_g \frac{r_a}{r_a + R} \quad . \quad . \quad . \quad . \quad 6.17$$

This represents the current which would be obtained in R if fed from a constant current generator, generating a current of $g_m v_g$ and shunted by a resistance r_a.

The constant current generator form of the valve a.c. equivalent circuit as used for tetrodes and pentodes is then as shown in Fig. 6.22.

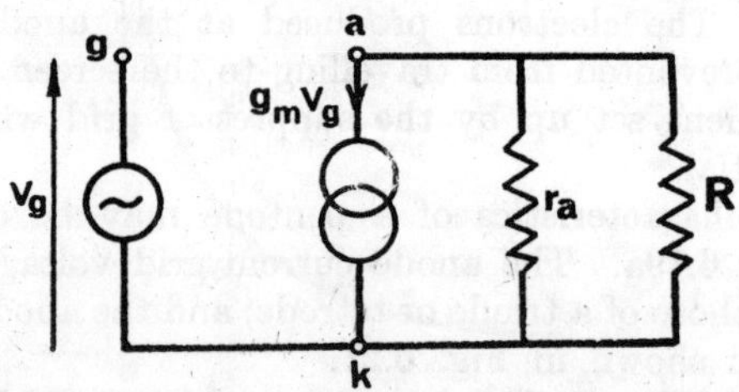

Fig. 6.22. A.C. equivalent circuit for tetrode or pentode valve.

The voltage across the load resistance R is

$$= -g_m v_g \frac{r_a R}{r_a + R}$$

and hence the amplification (A_v) is $= \frac{|v_a|}{|v_g|} = -g_m \frac{r_a R}{r_a + R}$. 6.18

If the load is small compared with r_a,

$$A_v = -g_m \frac{r_a R}{r_a + R} = -g_m \frac{R}{1 + \frac{R}{r_a}}$$

$$\simeq -g_m R \quad . \quad . \quad . \quad . \quad . \quad . \quad 6.19$$

This result applies to most cases where pentode valves are used for voltage amplifiers, as the slope resistance of such valves is usually of the order of 1 MΩ while the load impedance is often appreciably less than this.

Variable Mu Valves

The valves so far considered have anode current/grid voltage curves which are substantially linear, except in the region of cut-off. Such valves have a constant value of g_m over the operating range. There is another type which has a grid voltage/anode current curve which exhibits fairly constant curvature. Such a characteristic is shown in Fig. 6.23 where it will be seen that the slope of the characteristic decreases as the grid is made increasingly negative. The utility of such a characteristic is that the amplification obtained depends on the operating point chosen. The amplification is greatest when the negative bias is small and decreases as the bias is made increasingly negative. The *variable mu*, or remote cut-off valve as it is sometimes called, thus finds application in circuits where a variable gain is required.

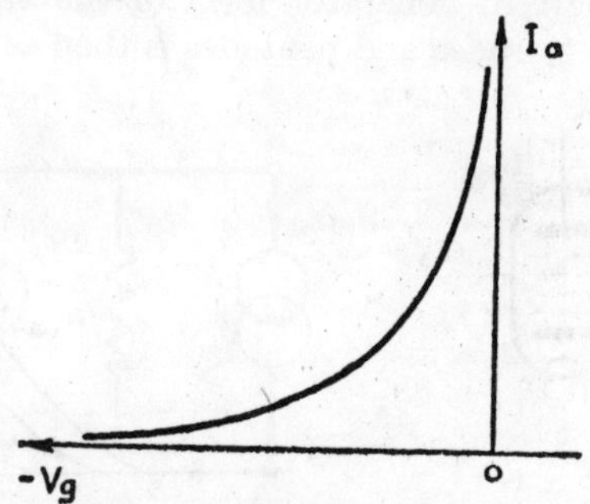

Fig. 6.23. Variable *mu* characteristic.

The desired curvature in the characteristics is obtained by varying the pitch of the control grid winding. A valve which has a closely wound grid has a fairly high mutual conductance whereas when the grid is "openly" wound the g_m is low. With zero or a small negative bias the close wound section of the grid is the effective part which determines the value of the anode current. With a large negative bias the anode current flows in the open mesh regions and the mutual conductance is low.

The curvature of the characteristic causes distortion if large input voltages are applied, and so variable *mu* valves are employed in the early stages of amplifiers where the signal voltage is small.

Multiple Valve Assemblies

A variety of valve types have been evolved for special purposes, There are, for example, double diodes and double triodes. These consist of two electrode structures in a common envelope. Sometimes all the electrodes are separate and in other cases the cathode is common. Double diode triode and diode pentode assemblies are also widely used. In addition to special requirements such multiple valve assemblies often present a useful economy in space and wiring. The double triode is frequently used where two input channels are connected to a single amplifier, or when an input is required to be balanced with respect to earth.

FREQUENCY-CHANGING VALVES

One type of valve employed as a frequency-changer has two control grids and the anode current is a function of two signal voltages. Such a valve is shown in Fig. 6.24a where the control grids are G_1 and G_3. G_2 and G_4 form a screen and prevent interaction between the circuits connected to G_1 and G_3. In the absence of G_3 such a valve would function as a normal tetrode. If, however, a negative potential is

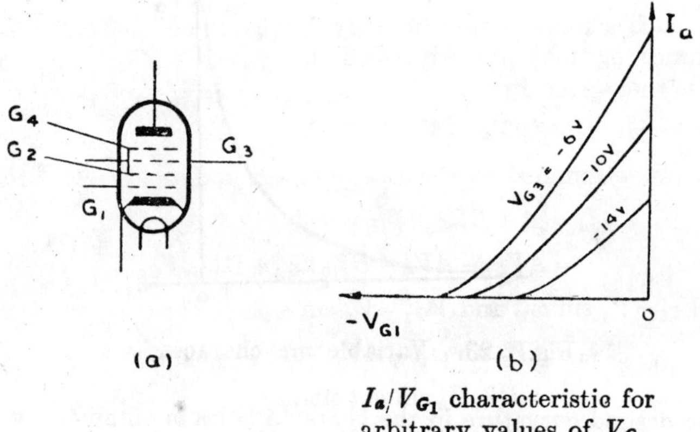

I_a/V_{G1} characteristic for arbitrary values of V_{G3}.

Fig. 6.24. Valve with two control grids.

applied to G_3 this will have the effect of modifying the potential distribution in the valve so that the anode current is reduced. The extent to which this occurs will depend on the magnitude of the potential applied to G_3, and the controlling effect is small when G_3 is near zero potential with respect to the cathode. Fig. 6.24b shows the characteristics of such a valve and it will be seen that the mutual conductance of G_1 depends on the voltage applied to G_3.

The frequency-changing properties of such a valve may be considered in a simple fashion by supposing the static mutual characteristics of V_{G1} for such a valve to be represented by straight lines as shown in Fig. 6.25.

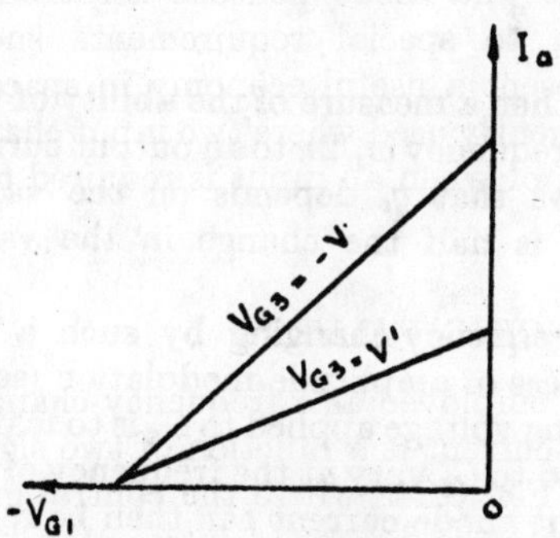

Fig. 6.25. Idealised static mutual characteristics for a valve with two control grids.

With such characteristics it may be assumed that the mutual conductance g_m may be expressed by $g_m = A + BV_{G3}$; the anode current is then given by

$$i_a = g_m(V_{G1} - V_0)$$

where V_0 is determined by the steady screen and anode potentials.

Thus,

$$\begin{aligned} i_a &= (A + BV_{G3})(V_{G1} - V_0) \\ &= AV_{G1} - AV_0 - BV_0V_{G3} + BV_{G1}V_{G3} \end{aligned}$$

then if $V_{G1} = V_1 \sin \omega_1 t$ and $V_{G3} = V_3 \sin \omega_3 t$

$$\begin{aligned} i_a &= AV_1 \sin \omega_1 t - AV_0 - BV_0V_3 \sin \omega_3 t \\ &\quad + BV_1V_3 \sin \omega_1 t \sin \omega_3 t \\ &= AV_1 \sin \omega_1 t - AV_0 - BV_0V_3 \sin \omega_3 t \\ &\quad + \frac{B}{2}V_1V_3[\cos (\omega_1 - \omega_3)t - \cos (\omega_1 + \omega_3)t] \end{aligned}$$

The first and third terms in this expression represent components of anode current which vary at the frequency of the voltages applied to G_1 and G_3 respectively. The last two terms represent components of anode current having frequencies equal to the difference, and the sum of the original input frequencies. If the difference-frequency component is selected, then

$$i_{a_{(\omega_1 - \omega_3)t}} = \frac{B}{2}V_1V_3 \cos (\omega_1 - \omega_3)t$$

If the quotient of the difference-frequency current and the input voltage at G_1 is represented as the *conversion* conductance, (g_c), then

$$g_c = \frac{BV_3}{2} \quad . \quad . \quad . \quad . \quad 6.20$$

The value of g_c is then a measure of the ability of the valve to change an input voltage of frequency $\omega_1/2\pi$ to an output current of $(\omega_1 - \omega_3)/2\pi$. Equation 6.20 shows that g_c depends on the value of the voltage applied to G_3, and is half the change in the value of the mutual conductance g_m.

The process of frequency-changing by such a valve can also be considered as a process of amplitude-modulation (see chapter 12). The effect of an alternating voltage applied to G_3 is to make the amplification of the voltage applied to G_1 vary at the frequency of the voltage applied to G_3, and the output anode current can then be regarded as a current of frequency ω_1 varying in amplitude at a frequency of ω_3.

The *triode-hexode* (Fig. 6.26a) is a valve commonly used as a frequency-changer. The triode section is used to generate a voltage of the desired frequency which is injected into the hexode section. The hexode has the signal to be converted applied to its control grid G_1 and the output then contains sum and difference products.

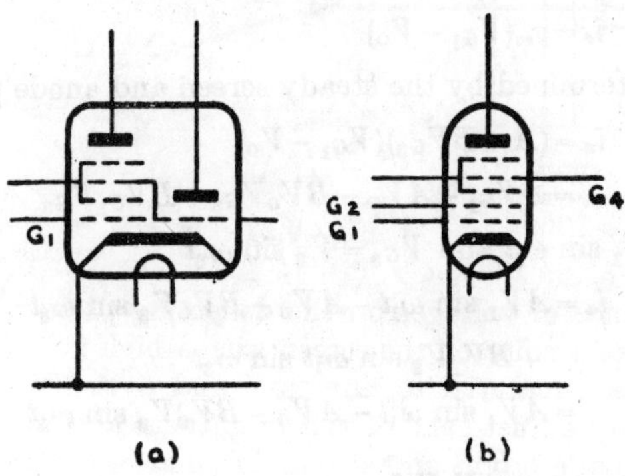

Fig. 6.26 (a) Triode-hexode
(b) Pentagrid

The addition of a suppressor grid converts the valve to a *triode heptode*. The *pentagrid* (Fig. 6.26b) is also used as a frequency-changer, and may be regarded as a tetrode with two additional grids G_1 and G_4 to which the alternating input voltages are applied; if a suppressor grid is incorporated the valve is called an *octode*.

THE CATHODE RAY TUBE

The cathode ray tube may be regarded as a thermionic valve designed for the special purpose of giving a visual picture of an electrical quantity. It can be used to examine voltage and current waveforms and the various phase relationships in a circuit. It is especially useful, when used with auxiliary circuits, for the examination of transient phenomena. The delineation of the waveform is presented by the deflection of an electron beam, or " cathode ray " which has negligible inertia.

One form of cathode ray tube is illustrated diagrammatically in Fig. 6.27. The electrode structure consists of an indirectly heated cathode, a grid, and then three anodes and two pairs of deflecting plates. The intensity of the electron beam is controlled by the negative potential on the grid; the three anodes function as an electrostatic lens system, and by varying the potential of the intermediate anode the focal length of the electric lens may be adjusted so as to focus the beam on the screen on the end of the tube.

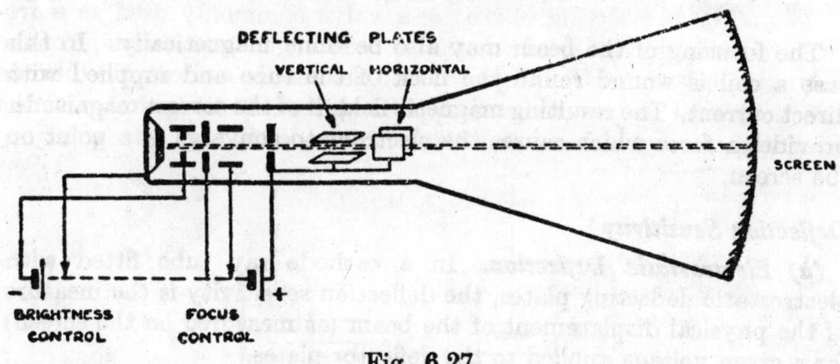

Fig. 6.27.

In the absence of voltages on the deflecting plates the electrons in the beam strike a point on the screen with a high velocity and thereby cause the screen material to fluoresce, and a visible spot is seen on the screen. By adjustment of the brightness and focus controls the spot may be made bright and sharp. If an alternating voltage is then applied to the horizontal deflecting plates the beam is deflected from side to side and the spot is drawn out into a line, the length of which is proportional to the peak to peak amplitude of the deflecting voltage. In the same way an alternating voltage applied to the vertical deflecting plates causes the spot to describe a vertical line. If both the horizontal and vertical deflecting plates are connected to the same source of alternating voltage the spot traces out a line at 45° to the horizontal. If there is a phase difference between the two voltages the spot traces out an ellipse.

Deflection of the beam may be accomplished by electromagnetic rather than by electrostatic means. The electromagnetically deflected tube has two pairs of coils positioned on the neck of the tube. In this case the direction of the beam deflection is at right angles to the direction of the axis of the pair of coils considered. (Fig. 6.28.)

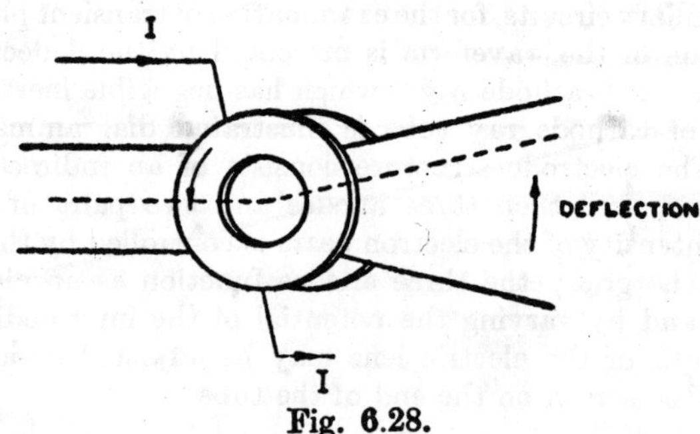

Fig. 6.28.

The focusing of the beam may also be done magnetically. In this case a coil is wound round the neck of the tube and supplied with direct current. The resulting magnetic field, if of the correct magnitude, provides a force which causes the electrons to converge at a point on the screen.

Deflection Sensitivity

(a) Electrostatic Deflection. In a cathode ray tube fitted with electrostatic deflecting plates, the deflection sensitivity is the measure of the physical displacement of the beam (as measured on the screen) for a given voltage applied to the deflector plates.

The deflection sensitivity may be calculated provided certain simplifying assumptions are made, namely that the electric field between the plates is uniform and confined to the space between them, and is unaffected by the passing of the electrons. In addition, it will be assumed that the electrons are emitted from the cathode with zero velocity, and that the forces on a single electron will be the forces applied to the beam.

If the potential applied between the cathode and final anode is V_a then in traversing the cathode to anode space an electron will encounter a potential difference of V_a as a result of which it will acquire kinetic energy. If the potential and kinetic energies are equated, then for an electron of charge e and rest mass m

$$eV_a = \tfrac{1}{2}mv^2$$

$$\therefore v = \sqrt{\frac{2eV_a}{m}} \qquad \ldots \qquad 6.21$$

This result gives the velocity of an electron in passing through the final anode. Equation 6.21 will apply for velocities in which the mass m remains constant (i.e. for velocities well below that of light).

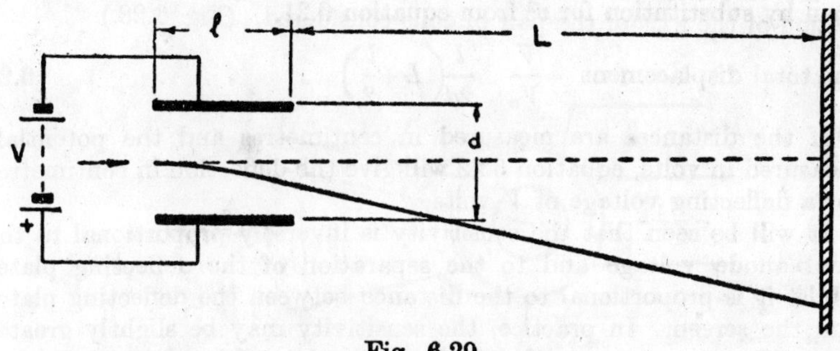

Fig. 6.29.

The electron will thus enter the electric deflecting field with a velocity v directed towards the centre of the screen. It will then encounter a constant deflecting force (downward in Fig. 6.29) while it travels between the plates. As a result of this the electron will traverse a parabolic path between the plates.

For the arrangement shown in Fig. 6.29, the transverse acceleration

$$=\text{Transverse Force/Mass}$$

$$=\left(\frac{eV}{d}\right)\frac{1}{m}$$

The time taken to pass the distance $l=\frac{l}{v}$ and so the transverse displacement on leaving the deflecting field

$$=\frac{1}{2}\left(\frac{eV}{d}\right)\frac{1}{m}\left(\frac{l}{v}\right)^2$$

The transverse velocity on leaving the deflecting field

$$=\left(\frac{eV}{d}\right)\frac{1}{m}\left(\frac{l}{v}\right)$$

This transverse velocity will give rise to a transverse displacement or a distance L

$$=\frac{eV}{d}\cdot\frac{1}{m}\cdot\frac{l}{v}\cdot\frac{L}{v}$$

The total transverse displacement on the screen is then

$$=\frac{eV}{d}\frac{1}{m}\frac{l}{v^2}\left(L+\frac{l}{2}\right)$$

then by substitution for v^2 from equation 6.21,

$$\text{the total displacement } =\frac{V}{V_a}\cdot\frac{l}{2d}\left(L+\frac{l}{2}\right) \quad . \quad . \quad . \quad . \quad 6.22$$

If the distances are measured in centimetres and the potentials measured in volts, equation 6.22 will give the deflection in centimetres for a deflecting voltage of V volts.

It will be seen that the sensitivity is inversely proportional to the final anode voltage and to the separation of the deflecting plates whilst it is proportional to the distance between the deflecting plates and the screen. In practice, the sensitivity may be slightly greater than that given by equation 6.22 as the edge effect of the deflecting field has been ignored. The extension of the deflecting field beyond the plates tends to increase the deflection.

(b) Magnetic Deflection. Deflection sensitivity in this case refers to the deflection of the beam for a given current applied in the deflecting coil system. As the magnetic field produced by a coil system depends on the physical arrangement of the coils, and also on the magnetic core (if one is used), it is not possible to develop a general expression for the deflection in terms of the deflecting current. A simple expression, however, may be obtained in terms of the deflecting magnetic field.

Suppose the effect of the deflecting coils is to set up a uniform magnetic field of density B extending over a distance l. If an electron enters this field with a velocity v, as defined by equation 6.21, the electron of charge e will then be moving perpendicularly to the magnetic field. There will be a force on the electron at right angles to the direction of the field and to the direction of motion. As the force is perpendicular to the direction of motion, no work will be done on the electron. Its speed in the direction of the screen will be unaltered and it will travel along an arc.

The deflecting force will equal Bev and hence the transverse acceleration equals Bev/m. The electron will be subject to the magnetic field for a time l/v and so the transverse displacement on leaving the field will be

$$\frac{1}{2}\frac{Bev}{m}\cdot\left(\frac{l}{v}\right)^2$$

It will have a transverse velocity $\dfrac{Bev}{m}\cdot\dfrac{l}{v}$ and so the total displacement at an external distance L from the coil system will be

$$\frac{Bev}{m}\frac{l}{v^2}\left(L+\frac{l}{2}\right)=\frac{Bl}{\sqrt{2V_a}}\sqrt{\frac{e}{m}}\left(L+\frac{l}{2}\right) \qquad 6.23$$

This will then be the displacement recorded on the screen due to the application of a deflecting magnetic field which has a flux density B.

References

[1] Richardson, O. W.: "On the Negative Radiation from Hot Platinum", *Proceedings of the Cambridge Philosophical Society*, 11, p. 286 (1901).

[2] Child, C. D.: "Discharge from Hot CaO", *Physical Review* 32, p. 492 (1911).

[3] Miller, J. M.: "Dependence of the Input Impedance of a Three Electrode Vacuum Tube upon the Load in the Anode Circuit", Scientific Paper 351, U.S. Bureau of Standards.

References for Further Reading

Parker, P.: *Electronics* (Edward Arnold, 1950).

EXAMPLES

1. Explain with relation to a simple diode, the meanings of the terms "emission limited" and "space charge limited" anode current. Give a simple derivation of the relation connecting anode current and anode voltage under space charge limited conditions assuming zero initial velocity of emission.

L.U. Ext. Telecomm. 1945.

2. What is secondary emission in a valve? Show how it affects the operation and characteristic of a tetrode valve, and describe the steps taken in a pentode valve to reduce its effects.

L.U. Int. Telecomm. 1949.

3. The screen grid in a tetrode is said to reduce the capacitance between the control grid and the anode. Explain precisely what is meant by such a statement.

Derive an expression showing how, in an amplifier, the effective capacitance between the control grid and the cathode of a triode is influenced by the inter-electrode capacitance between the anode and the control grid.

Describe a method other than the use of a screen grid, for minimising feed-back from the anode to the control-grid circuit.

L.U. Ext. Telecomm. 1946.

4. Describe briefly the physical principles underlying the action of a thermionic triode, demonstrating the control of the grid by means of sketches of electrostatic field configuration in the absence of space charge. Explain the effect of space charge, assuming unlimited emission and zero initial velocity. Sketch typical characteristic curves for a triode. Define with relation to the characteristics, Mutual Conductance, Anode Slope Resistance and Amplification Factor and show the relationship connecting the three quantities.

L.U. Ext. Telecomm. **1946.**

5. Justify the use of an equivalent generator to represent, for calculation purposes, a triode valve operating within the linear range of its static characteristics. The static characteristics of a triode are given in the accompanying table.

$V_g=0$		$V_g=-20$ V		$V_g=-40$ V	
V_a volts	I_a mA	V_a volts	I_a mA	V_a volts	I_a mA
60	26	140	15	240	15
80	45	160	28	260	27
100	67	180	44	280	43

This valve operating as a power amplifier, feeds by transformer coupling a load which may be treated as a pure resistance of 100 Ω. The ratio of primary turns to secondary turns of the transformer is 5 : 1. Treating the transformer as " ideal ", calculate the power output of the stage when the grid driving voltage is 20 V peak.

I.E.E. Radio Comm. April, **1948.**

6. The characteristics of a certain triode are given in the table below.

E_a volts		40	80	120	160	200	240	280	320	360	400
I_a	E_g 0	12	30	49	67						
	−4	3	15	30	47	65					
	−8		3	14	29	45					
	−12			5	13	26	42				
	−16				4	12	24	30			
	−20					3	11	22	36		
	−24						4	11	21	32	
	−28						1	6	12	19	28
	−32								5	11	18

Maximum permissible anode dissipation is 10 watts.

This valve is used in the output stage of an amplifier supplying a loudspeaker, the impedance of which may be assumed to be a pure resistance of 15 Ω. The anode supply voltage is 250 V.

Draw a suitable load line and estimate the maximum output which can be obtained without appreciable distortion and the input grid voltage which this would require. Specify the cathode biasing resistance and the turns ratio of the output transformer.

I.E.E. Radio Comm. October, 1948.

7. What is the Miller effect? Show that the input admittance between the grid a... cathode of a triode amplifier with grounded cathode is given by

$$Y \simeq j\omega C_{ga}\left[1+\frac{\mu Z}{(Z+r_a)}\right]+j\omega C_{gk}$$

where C_{ga} = grid-to-a...de capacitance,
C_{gk} = grid-to-cathode capacitance,
Z = anode load impedance.

Discuss the conditions under which oscillation can occur when the anode load is purely inductive.

L.U. Electronics & Telecomm. Part II. 1966.

8. State briefly the limitations of the triode, both in audio- and in radio-frequency amplifiers, which gave rise to the development of the tetrode and the pentode. Explain with the aid of characteristic curves, the effect of introducing the additional electrodes into the structure of the triode.

L.U. Ext. Telecomm. 1951.

9. Sketch typical static characteristics for a frequency changer valve of the hexode type. Describe the internal structure of such a valve and explain, from a consideration of the electron trajectories in the valve, why the static characteristics have the form shown.

I.E.E. Radio Comm. April, 1946.

10. Explain what is meant by " conversion conductance " of a frequency changer and describe how this quantity can be pre-determined from the static characteristics or measured directly by experiment.

L.U. Ext. Telecomm. 1944.

11. Develop an expression for the deflectional sensitivity of a cathode-ray tube employing magnetic deflection. What alteration in sensitivity will result from a 100% increase in final accelerator voltage, and why is this alteration less than that which would be obtained with electrostatic deflection ?

***I.E.E. Radio Comm. April,* 1946.**

12. Compare the uses of magnetic and electric fields for the deflection of the beam of a cathode ray tube. Show that the path of the beam while in a transverse electric field is parabolic. Also derive an expression for the distance moved by the spot on the fluorescent screen, per volt of deflecting potential, given the length of the deflecting plates, their distance from the screen, and the potential of the final anode, relative to the cathode.

***L.U. Int. Telecomm.* 1949.**

7

SEMICONDUCTOR DEVICES

INTRODUCTION

In communication systems, and in most applications of electronics the transistor is now the most important active circuit element. Before discussing circuit applications of such semiconductor devices however it is necessary to consider some of the elementary concepts relating to electrical conduction in solid materials.

Atomic Structure

Atoms, once thought to be indivisible, are now known to consist of a large number of elementary particles. Of these, the three most important are the positively charged proton, the uncharged neutron and the negatively charged electron. The electrical charges of the proton and the electron, although of opposite sign, have the same magnitude, namely $1{\cdot}6 \times 10^{-19}$ coulomb. The protons and neutrons (when present) form the relatively heavy nucleus or centre core of the atom. At large distances from the nucleus the electrons are disposed in circular or elliptical orbits; in three dimensions one may regard these orbits as shells. In the normal state the number of electrons is equal to the number of protons. Electrons moving in orbits close to the nucleus are subjected to stronger forces of attraction compared with electrons in orbits further from the nucleus. The electrons in the outermost orbit, referred to as *valence electrons* can thus be detached most easily from the atom, which then has a net positive charge and is said to be *ionised*.

It is necessary to emphasise at this point that the idea of electrons as minute particles which traverse particular orbits is a very much simplified concept which certainly does not explain many of the observed properties of electrons. Instead, one must accept the idea that electrons have a dual type of behaviour; in the free state they can be considered as particles; in interactions with matter they exhibit the properties of waves. Such electron waves have a wavelength λ given by

$$\lambda = h/mv \qquad . \quad . \quad . \quad . \qquad 7.1$$

where m is the mass corresponding to the velocity v and h is a constant, namely Planck's constant $= 6{\cdot}6 \times 10^{-34}$ joule-second.

Electron Energy

The most important point concerning the orbital motion of electrons is that only a definite set of orbits (or shells) is possible for a given isolated atom. The energy of a given orbit or state is fixed, hence the energy of an electron can have only certain precisely defined values. As a consequence, the position of an electron in an atom may be specified by naming its particular shell, or alternatively by stating its energy level. It should be noted that each of these levels can only contain up to two electrons. It may be helpful to think of the partial correspondence with the orbits of satellites round the earth. To place a satellite in a particular orbit requires that it be given a certain energy. An orbit of greater height requires extra energy. Whereas a satellite can occupy any orbit if given the corresponding correct amount of energy, an electron can only occupy certain discrete orbits. If an electron is to be moved from one orbit to the next one further from the nucleus, a definite amount, or quantum, of energy is required to produce this change; conversely if an electron falls from an orbit to the next possible inner one a definite quantum of energy is released, as the electrons in outer orbits have more energy than those in inner orbits.

In each instance the energy is in the form of a packet of electromagnetic radiation, namely a photon. One jump always involves one photon, but the frequency of the radiation in the packet is proportional to the energy difference between the initial and final orbits, and so

$$\triangle E = hf \qquad . \quad . \quad . \quad . \qquad 7.2$$

where $\triangle E$ is the energy change, f is the frequency of the radiation emitted or absorbed, and h is Planck's constant. It follows then that an atom with a limited number of allowed orbits with energy levels E_1, E_2, E_3, etc., can emit radiation only at frequencies corresponding to the various energy jumps, i.e. $E_1 - E_2$, $E_1 - E_3$, $E_2 - E_3$, etc. These frequencies are characteristic of a particular type of atom.

Covalent Bonds

Metallic conductors, and the common semiconductor materials, germanium and silicon have a crystalline structure. Such a structure is a fixed array of atoms, set in a regular pattern, or three dimensional lattice arrangement, having an atom at each crossing point. The interatomic bonds which hold the atoms together are represented by the links between the crossing points. These are referred to as *covalent bonds.*

Atoms of silicon have 14 protons in the nucleus (and also 14 neutrons) and 14 electrons, of which 4 are valence electrons. Silicon (like germanium) is thus said to be *tetravalent.* Each covalent bond links two atoms and is composed of two electrons, one from each atom, which is thus linked by 4 covalent bonds to 4 neighbouring atoms. At absolute zero temperature none of the electrons is free to act as an electrical conductor and so material such as germanium or silicon at this temperature implies a perfect insulator. At temperatures above absolute zero, some of the electrons forming covalent bonds are liberated to form conduction electrons. The space left in the covalent bond due to this liberation is known as a *hole* and is capable in suitable circumstances of trapping another conduction electron. This process is referred to as electron-hole combination. At any particular ambient temperature there is an equilibrium between the electrons liberated from the covalent bonds giving rise to holes, and electrons recombining with the holes.

Energy Bands

It has been mentioned that the electrons in isolated atoms have distinct energy levels. An energy level diagram for such an atom would then correspond, in principle, to the diagram of Fig. 7.1a, in which the horizontal lines represent the different possible levels. The presence of interatomic forces in solid material produces interactions which cause splitting of each energy level into a series of levels, so that energy bands are produced (Fig. 7.1b). The spreading of a line into a band has the effect of narrowing the width of the forbidden energy zones.

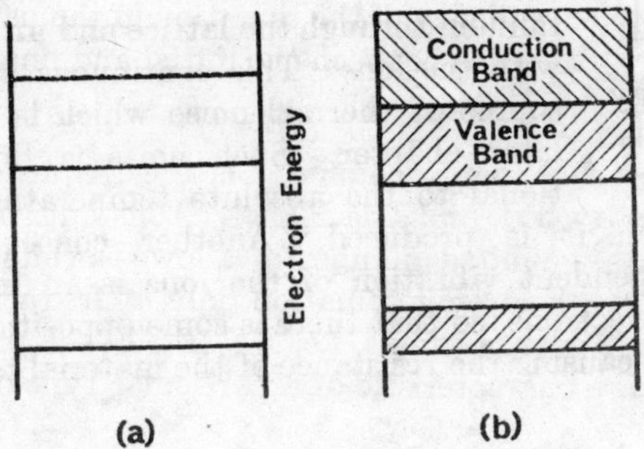

Fig. 7.1. (a) Electron energy levels
(b) Energy bands.

The transition of electrons between bound and free states as mentioned previously may be expressed by an energy band diagram such as Fig. 7.1b. Electrons in covalent bonds occupy energy levels in the valence band. At higher energies there are one or more conduction bands which may be empty or only partially occupied. If electrons in the valence band are supplied with energy they may jump to a conduction band and become available as charge carriers.

The energy band concept is very useful. It must not, however, be interpreted as indicating positions through which holes or electrons move; it indicates energy levels in which conduction is or is not permissible.

Conductors

Solid conductors are normally metals, having a crystalline structure. In the case of copper, which has a resistivity of about 10^{-6} ohm-cm, the single valence electron is so loosely bound that it can readily escape and is then free to move throughout the crystal lattice. An electric current is thus produced with the application of an electric field of any magnitude.

The high conductivity of copper may be explained in terms of energy bands. The concentration of atoms in the material produces a valence band which overlaps the conduction band as shown in Fig. 7.2. The valence band is never filled, the conduction band is normally vacant, and so it is easy to raise electrons to the conduction band at all temperatures. At absolute zero temperature the atomic nuclei, or ions are at rest. As the temperature is raised from zero, the nuclei undergo thermal vibration about their lattice points, while the conduction electrons move at random through the lattice and undergo collisions with the ions. This continuous agitation is the source of thermal noise which is discussed in a later chapter. Such noise is directly proportional to the absolute temperature of the conductor in which it is produced. Another consequence of the temperature dependent vibration of the ions is an increased interaction with the electrons, so that there is some opposition to their free movement, thus causing the resistance of the material to increase with temperature.

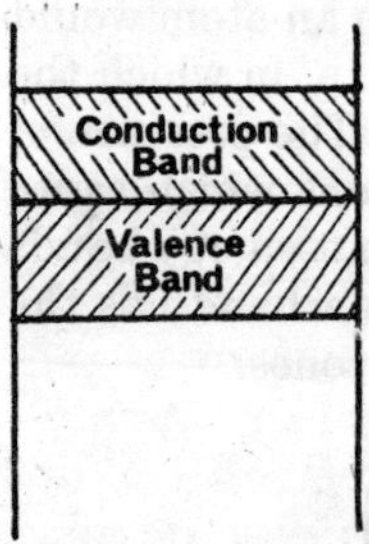

Fig. 7.2. Energy bands in metals.

Insulators

Practical insulating materials such as glass or mica have resistivities of the order of 10^{14} ohm-cm. The main features of the band structure for an insulator is shown in Fig. 7.3. There are as many valence electrons as there are energy levels in the valence band. Consequently no valence electron in the full valence band can absorb the energy given by an electric field unless another electron takes a lower place and so cancels the current due to the first electron. While there is an upper empty conduction band above, the relatively large gap of a few electron volts is such that moderate values of electric field strength do not provide enough energy to move the electrons across the gap. Thus insulators do not conduct, at least not until the applied voltage is sufficiently large to force the electrons across the energy gap, when the material then breaks down.

An increase in temperature, if great enough, will cause sufficient thermal agitation for some electrons to cross the gap to the upper empty band. This process is known as thermal excitation. In general the conductivity of insulators tends to increase with temperature.

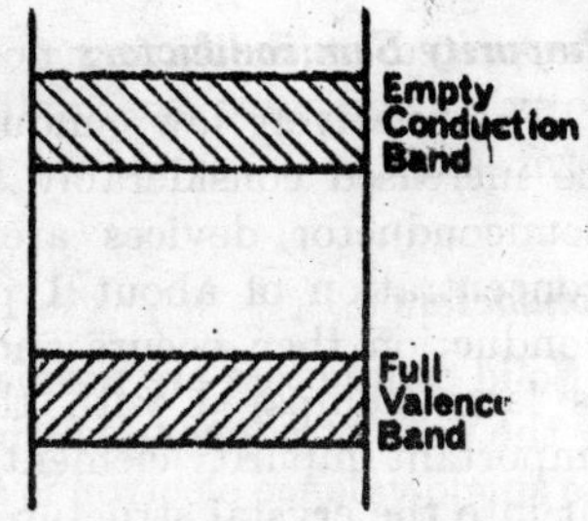

Fig. 7.3. Energy bands in insulators.

SEMICONDUCTORS

Intrinsic Semiconductors

As one would expect, semiconductors have conductivities intermediate between conductors and insulators. In terms of energy gaps, the most common materials, namely germanium and silicon, have energy gaps which are respectively 0·72 and 1·1 electron volts. Such material when pure, behaves as an insulator and is said to be an *intrinsic* semiconductor. Purity in this connection implies an impurity level of less than 1 part in 10^{-10}, a level which is far too small to be detected by chemical means and has to be deduced from measurements of electrical conductivity.

As a result of thermal excitation, electrons are raised to the conduction band and contribute to electrical conduction. At any given temperature materials with small energy gaps conduct more readily; the conductivity of germanium at room temperature is thus very much greater than that of silicon. A second consequence of the elevation of electrons from the valence to the conduction band is that the valence band is then no longer completely filled. Some valence electrons can gain energy from an applied electric field to occupy levels left vacant by those electrons that have moved to the conduction band. This in effect is the movement of positive holes in the valence band. Conduction in the material is thus in terms of negative and positive charge carriers, i.e. electrons and holes, in equal numbers.

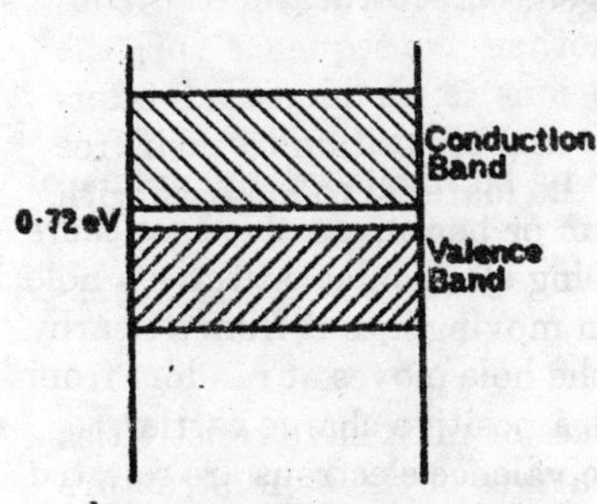

Fig. 7.4. Energy band for germanium.

Impurity Semiconductors

The relatively low conductivity of an intrinsic semiconductor may be increased considerably by the introduction of impurities. Many semiconductor devices are made of material having an impurity concentration of about 1 part in 10^7 or 10^8. Impurity or extrinsic conduction then occurs and this, at normal operating temperatures, is large compared with the intrinsic conduction component. The important impurity elements have the property that their atoms nearly fit into the crystal structure of the semiconductor.

N-Type Semiconductors

If a pentavalent impurity element such as arsenic or antimony is introduced into, say, a germanium crystal, then only four of the five valence electrons in each atom are used in forming covalent bonds with the nearby germanium atoms. The fifth electron at even relatively low temperatures acquires sufficient energy for it to break away and raise it into the conduction band, when it can move freely and increase the conductivity.

Atoms of impurity elements with five valence electrons are referred to as *donors* because they donate electrons to the crystal. The semiconductor is then said to be *n*-type. In such material the electrons are thus the majority carriers as opposed to the thermally-liberated holes which are minority carriers. It should be noted that in *n*-type material the impurity atoms become positive ions which are not free to move. Thus donor atoms provide fixed positively charged ions and an equal number of electrons which move about in the crystal. The material as a whole is electrically neutral or uncharged.

P-Type Semiconductors

The intrinsic semiconductor atoms may be displaced by atoms of trivalent elements such as indium, gallium or boron. In this case there is an incomplete valence band. The missing electron constitutes a hole which may be neutralised by an electron moving into it from a nearby bond. In the absence of external forces the hole moves at random from one covalent bond to another and acts as a positive charge carrier.

Atoms of impurity elements with three valence electrons are referred to as *acceptors* because they accept electrons from the adjacent germanium (or silicon) atoms. The semiconductor is then said to be *p*-type. The holes are the majority carriers as their number is very large compared with the thermally-liberated electrons which are minority carriers. Each trivalent atom of impurity material with four covalent bonds complete has a net negative charge (i.e. four electrons of charge $-4e$ combined with a nucleus of $+3e$) and is not free to move.

Acceptor atoms thus provide fixed negative ions and an equal number of moveable holes. The material as a whole is uncharged.

The P-N Junction

A *p-n* junction refers to a boundary between the two types of semiconductor in such a way that the material is in effect a single crystal with the lattice structure matched throughout the junction area. Such an interface may be produced in a variety of ways, commonly by alloying or diffusion processes.

The formation of the *p-n* junction causes some holes from the *p* material and some electrons from the *n* material to diffuse towards each other and combine. This process does not continue, however, but occurs only momentarily in the immediate area of the junction. This is because near the junction the fixed positive donor ions in the *n*-type material and the fixed negative acceptor ions in the *p*-type material are left uncompensated. This positive charge on the *n* side and negative charge on the *p* side of the junction is thus a *potential barrier* and may be represented by a battery connected across the junction as shown in Fig. 7.5.

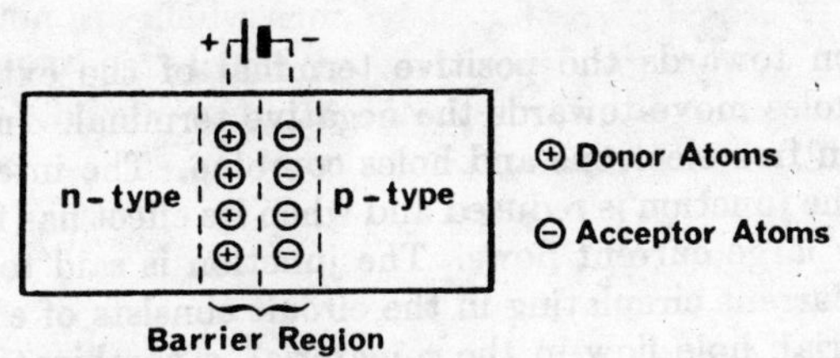

Fig. 7.5. *p-n* junction.

The difference of potential and hence electric field established across the junction is such as to prevent further movement of both holes and electrons. The initial combination of electrons and holes at the junction thus gives rise to a depletion of these charge carriers at the junction. The space charge region is then referred to as the *depletion layer* or barrier region.

Reverse Bias

If metallic connections are made to the *p* and the *n* material and an external voltage applied with the polarity shown in Fig. 7.6a, the depletion layer width is increased. The electrons are attracted towards the positive terminal and away from the junction, while the holes are attracted towards the negative terminal. This again is away from the unction. When the barrier potential is increased in this way the unction is said to have *reverse bias* applied.

Forward Bias

Suppose that the external voltage has the polarity as shown in Fig. 7.6b. The electrons in the *n*-type material are now urged across

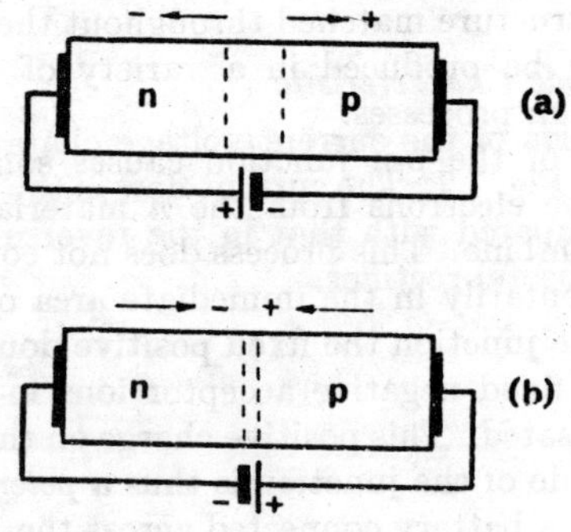

Fig. 7.6. (a) Reverse bias
(b) Forward bias.

the junction towards the positive terminal of the external battery, while the holes move towards the negative terminal. In the region of the junction free electrons and holes combine. The internal potential barrier at the junction is reduced and when its effect has been overcome a relatively large current flows. The junction is said to have *forward bias*. The current circulating in the circuit consists of electron flow in the *n*-material, hole flow in the *p*-material, a combination of the two in the neighbourhood of the junction and electron flow outside the semiconductor material.

Junction Capacitance

The thin depletion layer at the junction, due to the separation of the majority carriers, gives a charge distribution which makes it equivalent to a capacitance. As the depletion layer increases in width with increase of applied reverse voltage, the capacitance is voltage dependent. It is inversely proportional to a fractional index of the applied voltage, the exact value depending on the form of the charge distribution at the junction.

In practice the *p-n* junction, or junction diode usually has greater impurity concentration in the *p*-type material than in the *n*-type material. The forward current is carried by holes injected into the *n*-region. If the polarity of the external supply is then reversed the diode does not instantly assume a high resistance because of the minority carrier holes in the *n*-region. Some recombination occurs but most of the holes diffuse back to the junction where they are swept across by the negative potential. The current so constituted decays exponentially with time as the holes disappear. The effect can be represented as a further junction capacitance called the ***storage*** or ***diffusion capacitance.***

The Junction Diode Characteristic

The general form of the current/voltage characteristic of a junction diode is shown in Fig. 7.7. The current flow in the forward (+) direction is very large compared with that in the reverse direction and such a device is a very useful rectifier.

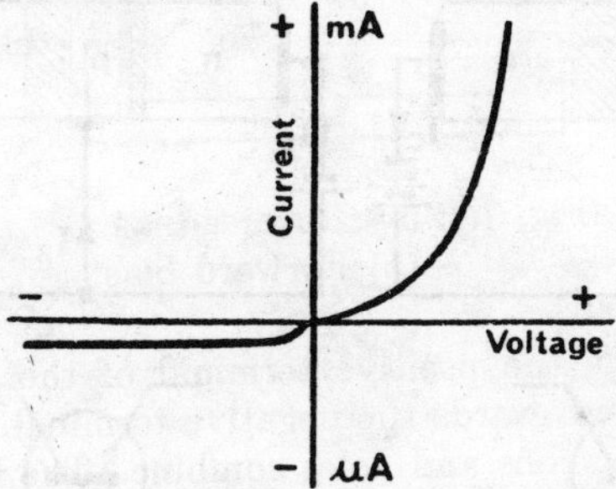

Fig. 7.7. Static characteristic of a junction diode.

The reverse current through the diode varies greatly with temperature and with the semiconductor material used. If the reverse voltage is sufficiently large (greater than indicated in Fig. 7.7), the reverse current increases sharply and reverse voltage breakdown occurs.

It follows from the above discussion that the equivalent circuit of a junction diode is an ideal rectifier shunted by a parallel combination of capacitance and resistance.

THE JUNCTION TRANSISTOR

Transistor Action

The simplest conception of the transistor is to regard it as a composite pair of *p-n* junctions arranged back to back. A *p-n* junction with forward bias has a low resistance and, conversely, a high resistance with reverse bias. If then the first junction is forward biased and a signal current introduced in this circuit, then assuming this current can be transferred to the high resistance junction, it appears as a current in a high impedance source. If the magnitude of the currents in the two diodes is substantially the same, the available power output from the reverse biased junction exceeds the input power. There is thus a power gain. This, of course, is a simplification which takes no account at all of the external circuits.

Two junctions " back-to-back " imply three connections, and the transistor is thus a device with three terminals. Generally two of them are arranged as input terminals while one of them with the third functions as a pair of output terminals. With suitable external connections, *current, voltage* or *power amplification* is possible. Obviously a pair of *p-n* junctions may be arranged in two ways, with either the *n* or *p* material common, and so there are two general types of transistor, namely *p-n-p* or *n-p-n*. If the junctions are to have bias as mentioned above, then the external supplies must be arranged as shown in Fig. 7.8.

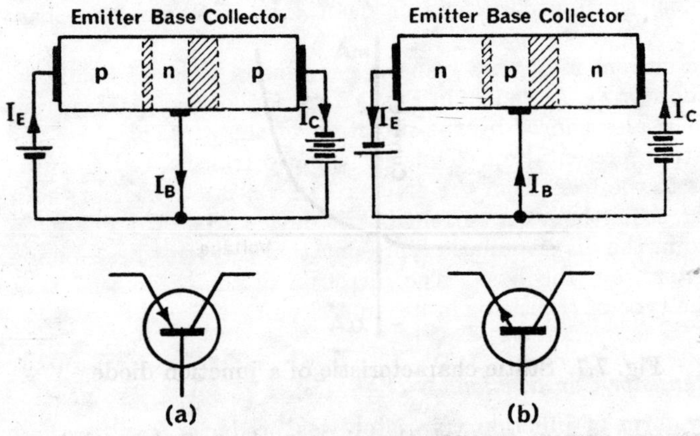

Fig. 7.8. (a) *p-n-p* transistor
(b) *n-p-n* transistor.

In Fig. 7.8a the left side *p-n* junction is forward biased while the right hand one is reverse biased. The same condition for the *n-p-n* transistor of Fig. 7.8b requires that the external bias supplies have the opposite polarity. The corresponding circuit representations are also shown in Fig. 7.8.

The three regions of the transistor are given the names *emitter*, *base* and *collector*, as shown in the diagram. As might be expected there are two depletion layers (shown shaded), one between emitter and base and the other between base and collector. Reference to the *p-n-p* transistor indicates that in the absence of emitter current I_E, there should be no collector current I_C, except for the small component I_{CBO}, due to thermally generated minority carriers. If emitter current flows as indicated then in the *p*-material of the emitter this current can be thought of as arising from the emission of holes into the material from the forward bias battery. These holes enter the base and diffuse through it to the collector junction where they are swept across it by the field existing there and become majority carriers in the *p*-type collector region.

In practice, some of the holes from the emitter in passing through the base combine with electrons there. Others reach the base terminal and produce a base current I_B. To secure effective transistor action, a very high proportion (90–99%) of the holes from the emitter must reach the collector. To achieve this the base is made extremely thin. Nearly all the injected holes are then extracted by the collector and very few are lost by recombination. The situation is further improved by making the emitter and collector impurity concentrations substantially greater than that of the *n*-type base material.

The main current in a *p-n-p* transistor is thus in terms of hole flow. The directions for I_E, I_B and I_C in Fig. 7.8 are for conventional current flow, which is also shown by the direction of the arrowhead on the diagrammatic representation. Thus for a *p-n-p* transistor the arrowhead points to the base from the emitter. In a *n-p-n* transistor, indicated in Fig. 7.8b, the main current in the device arises from electron flow, and so in the diagrammatic representation the arrowhead points to the emitter from the base. The direction of the arrowhead thus indicates the type of transistor in use in a circuit.

Junction Transistor Construction

The early form of junction transistor was produced from a semiconductor crystal, usually germanium, to which impurity materials were added while the material was in a molten state. This crystal growing method permits the production of either single impurity material, or under suitable conditions, multiple layers of different impurities.

Alloy Transistor

This form of transistor indicated in Fig. 7.9, is in widespread use. A thin wafer of *n*-type germanium about 0·1 mm thick has a pellet of indium (*p*-type impurity) placed on either side. The assembly is then heated to a temperature above the melting point of the indium. On cooling the alloy of indium and germanium recrystallises and takes up the same molecular structure as the wafer material. Hence germanium contaminated with indium is produced at the alloy-germanium interface. Leads are soldered to the indium and the *n*-region to provide external connections. (An important point is that it is not possible to make direct contact to the active part of the *n*-region.) The assembly is hermetically sealed in an opaque capsule to exclude moisture and light. The pellet used for the collector is normally about three times the size of that used for the emitter. This permits more effective collection of the current carriers which diffuse outwards through the base. Also the heat dissipated at the collector-base junction is usually greater than that at the emitter-base junction.

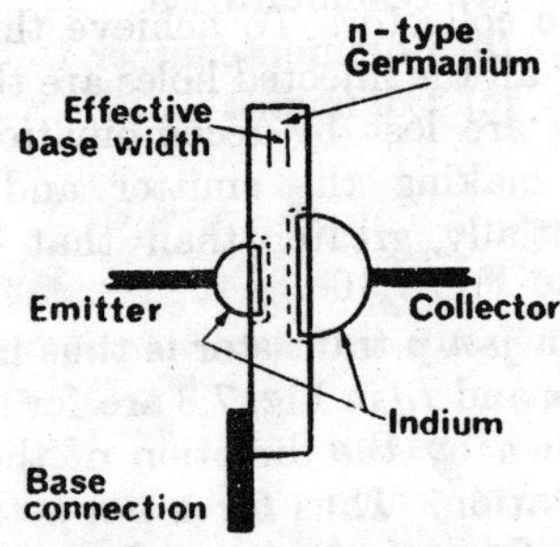

Fig. 7.9. Alloyed *p-n-p* transistor.

Transistors are produced in a variety of ways, so that a range of types with different operating characteristics is available. The processes of diffusion and epitaxial growth are most often used. In a diffusion process strips of intrinsic semiconductor material are heated with the necessary impurity element to a temperature just below the melting point of the semiconductor and set up an impurity concentration in it, which decreases with depth of penetration from the surface. Epitaxial growth involves heating of the semiconductor to a temperature below its melting point in the presence of vapour of the same material. Some of the vapour is then deposited on the solid material which thus grows and continues its crystal configuration.

Transistor Arrangements

The circuit configuration so far discussed has the base terminal common to the input and output connections. This arrangement (Fig. 7.10a) is referred to as a *common-base* or sometimes a *grounded-base* circuit. The collector current is slightly less than the emitter current and when used as an amplifier this circuit does not give current gain, although voltage and power gain is possible.

Fig. 7.10b shows an arrangement in which the emitter is the common terminal. This *common-emitter* circuit is the one most frequently used

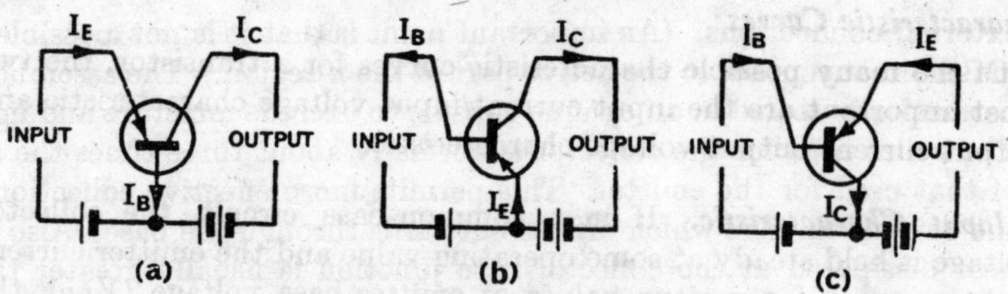

Fig. 7.10. Circuit arrangements
(a) Common-base
(b) Common-emitter
(c) Common-collector.

in amplifiers. Current as well as voltage gain is possible. The third arrangement shown in Fig. 7.10c, is the *common-collector* circuit. This can produce a current gain but the output voltage is less than the input voltage.

It should be noted in passing that the triode valve may also be connected in three ways which are shown in Fig. 7.11. Fig. 7.11b indicates the most common arrangement which has been considered as an amplifier in the previous chapter. This *common-cathode* circuit corresponds to the common-emitter circuit. With the common-grid circuit of Fig. 7.11a, the input is applied to the cathode. This arrangement corresponds to the common-base configuration for the transistor.

The common-anode circuit of Fig. 7.11c corresponds to the common-collector configuration, and like it, gives a voltage gain which is less than unity.

The common-anode circuit is known as a *cathode-follower*. Triode valves have been shown in Fig. 7.11, but the three arrangements are also possible for pentodes.

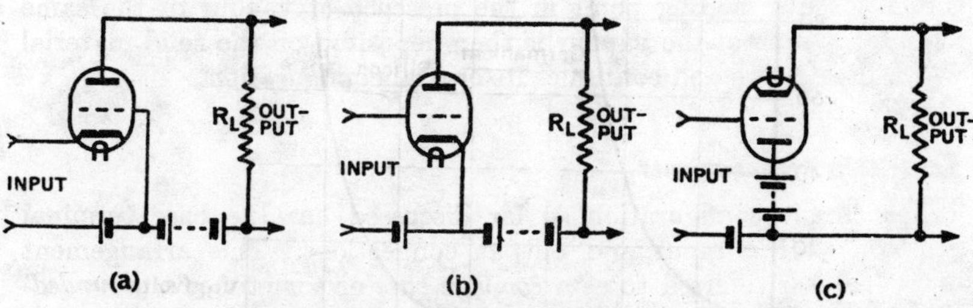

Fig. 7.11. Triode circuits
(a) Common-grid
(b) Common-cathode
(c) Common-anode.

Characteristic Curves

Of the many possible characteristic curves for a transistor, the two most important are the input current/input voltage characteristic and output current/output voltage characteristic.

Input Characteristic. If in a common-base circuit, the collector voltage is held steady at some operating value and the emitter current (I_E) measured for various values of emitter-base voltage (V_{EB}), the curve shown in Fig. 7.12a is obtained. It will be noted that for the same emitter current the emitter-base voltage is about 0·4 V. greater for silicon. The curves are approximately exponential in shape as in a

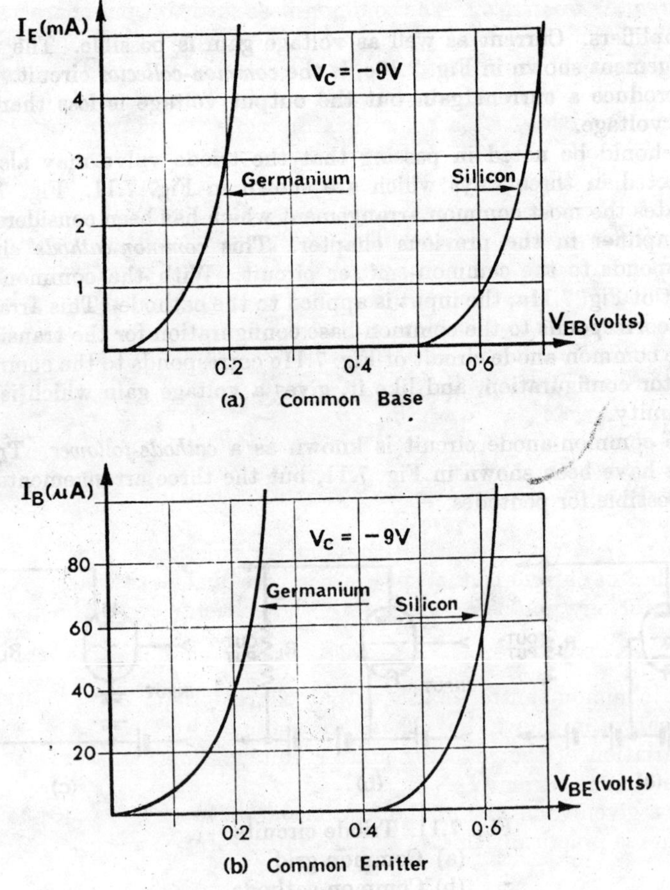

Fig. 7.12. Input characteristics.

forward biased diode. Fig. 7.12b shows the corresponding input characteristics when the common-emitter circuit is used. The curves have the same general form as for common-base, except that I_E, measured in milliamperes in the common-base connection, is replaced by I_B, measured in microamperes, for the common-emitter.

The reciprocal of the incremental gradient of the input characteristic gives the input resistance between emitter and base at the operating point chosen, i.e. at the particular value of I_E or I_B. The input resistance for the common-base connection may be something less than 100 Ω, while the common-emitter value is very roughly of the order of 1 kΩ.

The input characteristic depends to a small extent on the collector-base voltage as this affects the collector depletion layer which in turn alters the effective base width.

Output Characteristic. The common-base static output characteristic has the form shown in Fig. 7.13a. These curves are obtained by measurement of the collector current, I_C for variation of the collector-base voltage, V_{CB}, with various fixed values of the emitter current I_E. The curves of Fig. 7.13a show that the collector current varies little with the collector-base voltage. For any particular value of this voltage, I_C is substantially proportional to I_E. The ratio I_C/I_E, without regard to the leakage current I_{CBO}, is the direct current common-base short-circuit gain (α). In amplifier circuits, the small signal alternating current gain, namely the change of collector current ($\triangle I_C$) for a given small change of emitter current ($\triangle I_E$) is an important quantity and this is substantially the same as the direct current gain. Hence the *short-circuit current gain* or the *current amplification factor*, α, for the common-base circuit is

$$\alpha = \left(\frac{\triangle I_C}{\triangle I_E}\right) V_{CB} \text{ constant} \quad . \quad . \quad . \qquad 7.3$$

The quantity α is always less than unity, but is commonly greater than 0·95.

When I_E is zero, i.e. when the emitter junction is open-circuited, the collector current consists of the small residual leakage current I_{CBO}. Hence for any non-zero value of I_E, the collector current is given by

$$I_C = I_{CBO} + \alpha I_E \quad . \quad . \quad . \quad . \qquad 7.4$$

The common-emitter static output characteristic curves have the form shown in Fig. 7.13b. These are obtained by measurement of I_C for variation of the collector-emitter voltage V_{CE} with various fixed values of base current I_B.

For a given value of V_{CE} the relationship between collector and base currents is practically linear, and the ratio $\triangle I_C/\triangle I_B$ is referred to as

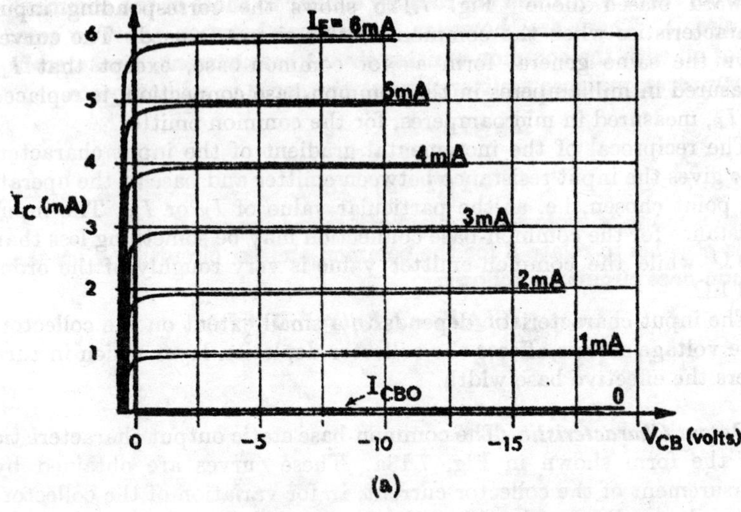

(a)

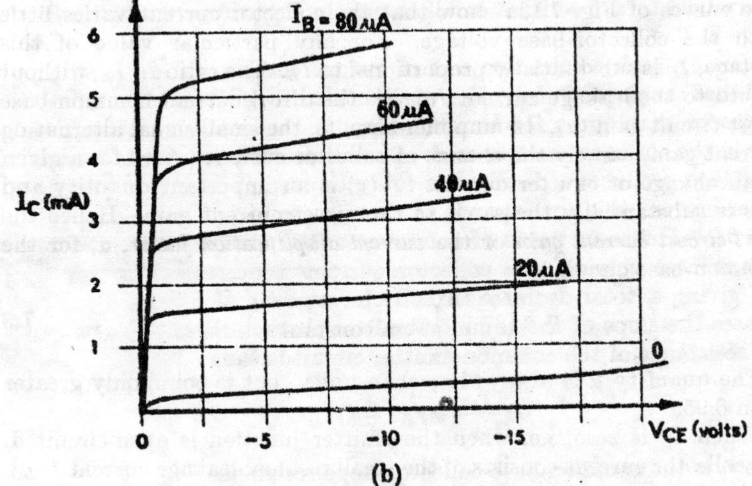

(b)

Fig. 7.13. Static output characteristics
(a) Common-base
(b) Common-emitter.

the *short-circuit current gain* or the *current amplification factor*, β, or h_{fe}, for the common-emitter circuit. Thus

$$\beta = \left(\frac{\Delta I_C}{\Delta I_B}\right) V_{CE} \text{ constant} \qquad 7.5$$

The curves of Fig. 7.13b are roughly similar to those of the common-base circuit. There are, however, differences between the two sets. First of all with the common-emitter circuit base current, measured in microamperes, replaces emitter current measured in milliamperes.

$$\begin{aligned} I_B &= I_E - I_C \\ &= I_E - (I_{CBO} + \alpha I_E) \\ &= I_E(1-\alpha) - I_{CBO} \end{aligned} \qquad 7.6$$

With a value of α close to unity both terms are small.

It is possible to relate β for the common-emitter circuit to α for the common-base circuit, as follows:

$$\alpha = \Delta I_C / \Delta I_E = \Delta I_C / (\Delta I_C + \Delta I_B)$$

$$\therefore \quad 1/\alpha = 1 + 1/\beta$$

$$\therefore \quad \alpha = \frac{\beta}{1+\beta} \qquad 7.7a$$

$$\text{or} \quad \beta = \frac{\alpha}{1-\alpha} \qquad 7.7b$$

If $\alpha = 0{\cdot}98$ then $\beta = 49$. A small change in α produces a much larger change in β.

Referring back to the two sets of output characteristics, it will be noted that the slopes $\Delta I_C/\Delta V_{CE}$ of the common-emitter characteristics are steeper than those for common-base, i.e. the output resistance is lower in the common-emitter case. A small decrease in α with decreasing voltage produces a decrease in collector current δI_C. For constant emitter current this corresponds to an increase in the base current of value δI_C. Hence in terms of common-emitter characteristics having constant base current, the collector current is decreased further by $\beta\delta I_C$, giving a total decrease in collector current of $\delta I_C(1+\beta)$. This increases the slope of the common-emitter characteristic. The output slope resistance of the common-emitter circuit is thus

$$\frac{r_c}{1+\beta} = r_c(1-\alpha)$$

where r_c is the common-base collector slope resistance.

Assuming r_c and β are respectively 1 MΩ and 49 respectively, the common-emitter slope resistance is $10^6/(1+49)$ or 20 kΩ.

Reference to equation 7.6 shows that I_B is zero when I_E has the value I_E' given by

$$I_E' = I_{CBO}/(1-\alpha)$$

This condition of zero base current makes the emitter and collector currents equal and so the value of I_C for $I_B = 0$, namely I_{CEO} is given by

$$I_{CEO} = I_{CBO}/(1-\alpha) \simeq \beta I_{CBO} \qquad 7.8$$

hence on the common-emitter characteristic the collector current for $I_B = 0$ is larger than the collector current in the common-base circuit when $I_E = 0$.

THE COMMON-EMITTER AMPLIFIER

The simplest arrangement of a *p-n-p* transistor used as an amplifier with a resistive load R_L is indicated in Fig. 7.14.

The signal source of e.m.f. e_s and internal resistance R_S is inserted between the base and emitter while the load resistor R_L is connected to the collector. The a.c. operation of the circuit is controlled by the base current. When the input signal voltage swings positive with respect to earth it decreases the base-emitter voltage and decreases the base-current. This decreases the collector current so that the voltage drop across R_L is thus diminished and the voltage at the collector terminal thus approaches the negative terminal of the collector supply voltage V_{CC}.

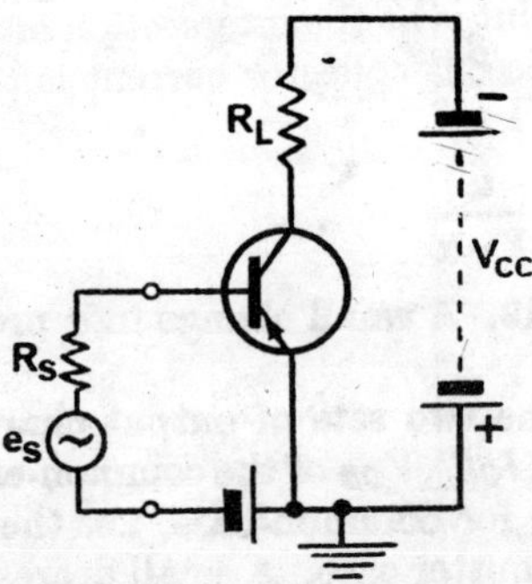

Fig. 7.14. Simple common-emitter amplifier.

The converse is true when the input signal voltage reverses its polarity. For a sinusoidal signal voltage there is thus a corresponding output voltage swing across R_L. The ratio of this voltage to that of the signal input is the voltage gain. With this circuit a phase shift of 180° is produced by the transistor so that the input and output voltages are in anti-phase.

Graphical Determination of Transistor Gain. It was shown in the previous chapter that it was possible to determine the gain, or amplification, of a triode by means of a load line drawn on the output characteristics. Exactly the same procedure can be followed for the transistor amplifier shown in Fig. 7.14. The output characteristics of a common-emitter amplifier with a collector supply voltage (V_{CC})

of 12 V are shown in Fig. 7.15. Assuming a 2 kΩ resistive load, the load line is located on the characteristics by determining its terminal points. Thus when the collector current is zero, the collector voltage is clearly the same as $V_{CC} = 12$ V, as there is no voltage drop across R_L. For zero collector-emitter voltage, the whole of V_{CC} would be applied across R_L with a corresponding current in it of $12/2000 = 6$ mA. Hence the co-ordinates $V_{CE} = 0$, $I_C = 6$ mA give the second terminal point of the load line. The straight line through the terminal points then gives the required load line.

Fig. 7.15 gives no information about the input circuit. If it is assumed that the steady base current in the absence of the alternating signal is 40 μA, then the quiescent operating point is the point 0 on the diagram, as this point is at the intersection of the 40 μA curve with the load line. The quiescent collector current is then approximately 3 mA

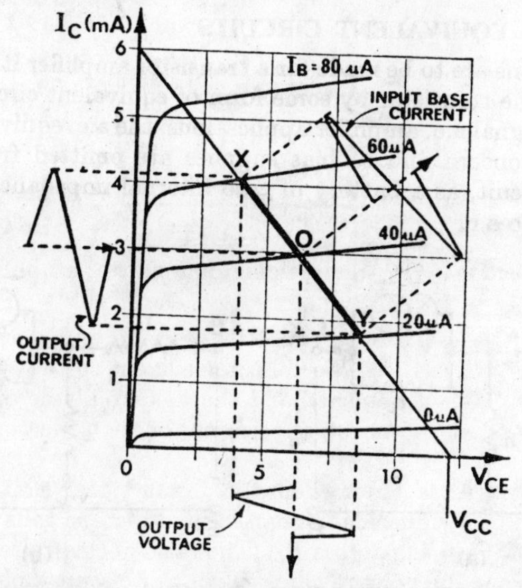

Fig. 7.15. Output characteristics and load line for common-emitter amplifier

and the corresponding value of V_{CB} is 6·2 V, i.e. about half the collector voltage V_{CC}. Suppose the base-emitter input a.c. resistance is 1 kΩ, and that the alternating signal voltage applied to the base produces a maximum change in base current of 20 μA. The base current will thus vary between 20 and 60 μA over the signal cycle, i.e. over the range XY of the load line.

Horizontal projection through the points X and Y to the current axis gives the total change in I_C; vertical projection to the voltage axis gives the total change in V_{CE}.

The current gain A_i is thus given by

$$A_i = \frac{\Delta I_C}{\Delta I_B} = \frac{(4{\cdot}12 - 1{\cdot}8) \times 10^{-3}}{40 \times 10^{-6}} = 58$$

The voltage gain A_v is given by

$$A_v = \frac{\Delta V_{CE}}{\Delta V_{BE}} = \frac{8{\cdot}5 - 6}{40 \times 10^{-6} \times 10^3} = 62{\cdot}5$$

The value of ΔV_{BE} is obtained from the product of 40 μA current change in 1 kΩ.

The power gain is given by $A_i \times A_v = 58 \times 62{\cdot}5 = 3626 = 36$ dB.

TRANSISTOR EQUIVALENT CIRCUITS

If calculations are to be made for a transistor amplifier it is necessary to represent the transistor by some form of equivalent circuit.

For small-signal a.c. amplifier applications, the a.c. equivalent circuit is the main concern and so bias supplies are omitted from such an equivalent circuit, as a battery of zero internal impedance presents a short-circuit to a.c.

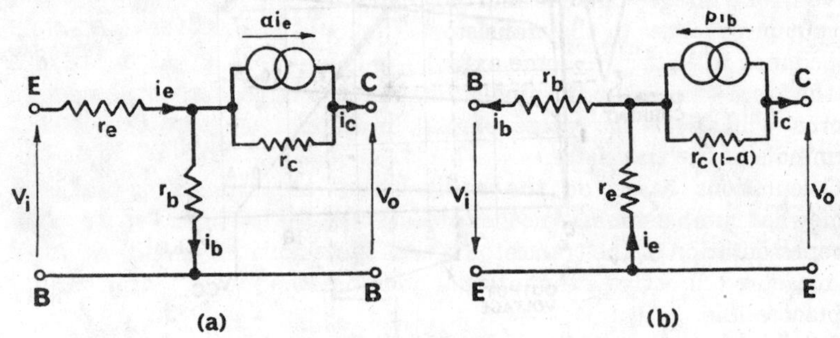

Fig. 7.16. Equivalent-T circuits
(a) Common-base
(b) Common-emitter.

A confusingly large number of a.c. equivalent circuits for transistors are possible. One of the earliest is the equivalent-T version which is drawn in Fig. 7.16 for the common-base and common-emitter configurations.

It will be seen from the diagram that the output circuit contains a constant current generator in shunt with a resistor. If desired this may be replaced with a constant voltage generator in series with the resistor. The value of the voltage can be shown to be the current value multiplied by the resistor value. Thus for Fig. 7.16a, the parallel combination shown would be replaced by a generator of e.m.f. $\alpha i_e r_c$ in series with r_c.

In Fig. 7.16 the quantity r_e is the incremental resistance of the forward biased emitter-base diode. This, as Fig. 7.12 indicates, is a function of I_E, and is given approximately by

$$r_e \simeq kT/qI_E \quad . \quad . \quad . \qquad 7.9$$

where k is Boltzmann's constant $= 1{\cdot}38 \times 10^{-23}$ joule/°K

T is the temperature °K

q is the electronic charge $= 1{\cdot}6 \times 10^{-19}$ coulomb

and so at room temperatures, $r_e = 25/I_E$ ohms, where I_E is measured in milliamperes.

The quantity r_b is the ohmic resistance of the base contact and base region. Values encountered for r_b range from several hundred ohms down to tens of ohms. The quantity r_c is the incremental resistance of the collector junction. Its value as stated previously is of the order of 1 MΩ.

The performance of the transistor as a low-frequency amplifier may thus be calculated by connecting a signal source to the input and an a.c. load to the output terminals. The complete circuit may then be solved for voltage, current and power gains, and also for input and output impedances of the transistor. It should be noted that the load impedance will affect to some extent the value of the input impedance at the transistor input terminals; likewise the impedance of the signal source will affect the value of the impedance seen at the output terminals of the transistor.

Calculations based on the equivalent-T are straightforward but somewhat cumbersome. Another objection to the use of the equivalent-T representation of the transistor is that the quantities r_e and r_b cannot be measured directly as the internal node (i.e. the junction of r_e and r_b) is inaccessible.

A transistor may be regarded as a four-terminal network having two terminals common. Any four-terminal, or two-port, network may be described by a system of parameters. The three systems most commonly used are, the open-circuit impedance or z parameters, the short-circuit admittance or y parameters, or a combination of these two, namely the hybrid or h parameters. These three systems are set out in Appendix A. The hybrid parameters are most commonly used for representation of a transistor. They are the easiest set to measure. The z parameters are determined by open-circuit a.c. measurements which can be awkward, particularly for the high-impedance output circuit. The y parameters are determined by short-circuit a.c. measurements, which may be difficult for the low-impedance input circuit, at least at low frequencies.

These difficulties are avoided with the h parameters which are defined in Appendix A. For the general four-terminal network the small-signal equations are

$$v_1 = h_i i_1 + h_r v_2 \quad . \quad . \quad . \quad . \quad 7.10$$

$$\text{and} \quad i_2 = h_{fi_2} + h_o v_2 \quad . \quad . \quad . \quad . \quad 7.11$$

Where i_1 and i_2 are the input and output currents respectively; v_1 and v_2 are the input and output voltages.

When applied to a transistor the hybrid parameters have a second subscript added (b, e or c) according to the transistor configuration under discussion. Hence applied to a common-base circuit, Equations 7.10 and 7.11 become

$$v_{eb} = h_{ib} i_e + h_{rb} v_{cb} \quad . \quad . \quad . \quad . \quad 7.12$$

$$\text{and} \quad i_c = h_{fb} i_e + h_{ob} v_{cb} \quad . \quad . \quad . \quad . \quad 7.13$$

Applied to the common-emitter circuit of Fig. 7.17a they become

$$v_{be} = h_{ie} i_b + h_{re} v_{ce} \quad . \quad . \quad . \quad . \quad 7.14$$

$$\text{and} \quad i_c = h_{fe} i_b + h_{oe} v_{ce} \quad . \quad . \quad . \quad . \quad 7.15$$

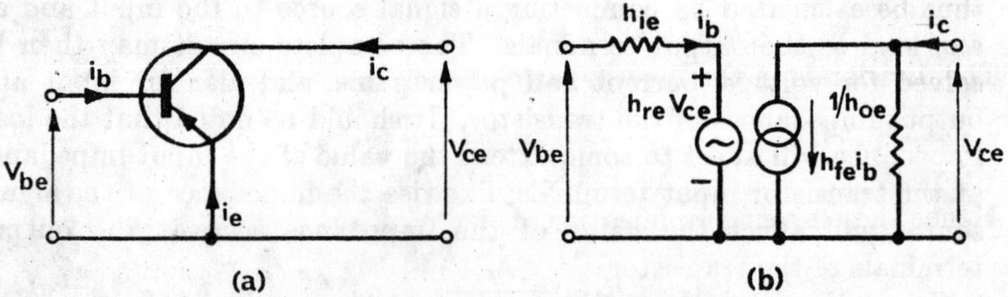

Fig. 7.17 (a) Common-emitter configuration
(b) Corresponding hybrid equivalent circuit.

From the equivalent circuit of Fig. 7.17b the input impedance is approximately h_{ie} (or exactly so when v_{ce} is zero, i.e. when the output voltage is short-circuited to a.c.) The value of h_{ie}, as indicated previously is of the order of 1–2 kΩ. The quantity h_{re} is a ratio sometimes called the voltage feedback factor and has a value between 10^{-3} and 10^{-4}. *The term $h_{re}v_{ce}$ can often be neglected; the a.c. equivalent circuit and calculations are then much simpler*. The quantity h_{fe} corresponds to β and this ratio for the common-emitter configuration may commonly lie in the range from 20 to 100. The fourth h parameter is the output *conductance* h_{oe} and this may often have a value of about 50 μmhos.

Common-Emitter Amplifier Calculations

If a common-emitter amplifier has a resistive load R_L and is driven by a signal source of e.m.f. E_s and source resistance R_s, the equivalent a.c. circuit is as shown in Fig. 7.18.

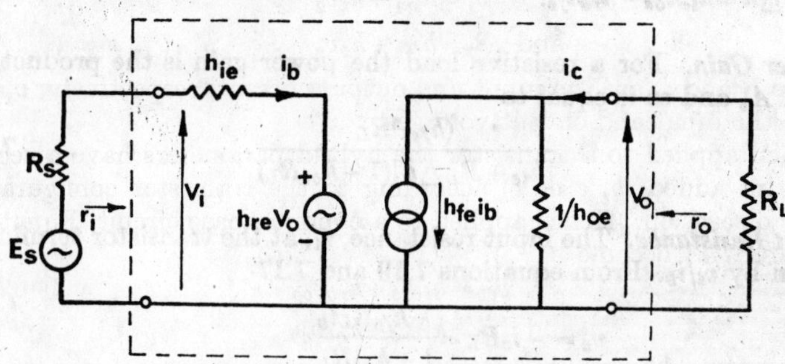

Fig. 7.18. A.c. equivalent circuit for common-emitter amplifier.

Current Amplification. The current, $h_{fe}i_b$, supplied by the current generator in the output circuit divides into two parts so that

$$h_{fe}i_b = h_{oe}v_o + i_c \qquad 7.16$$

The division is in the inverse ratio of their resistances and thus

$$i_c = h_{fe}i_b\left[\frac{1/h_{oe}}{R_L + 1/h_{oe}}\right]$$

Hence the current amplification A_i is given by

$$A_i = i_c/i_b = \frac{h_{fe}}{1 + h_{oe}R_L} \qquad 7.17$$

Voltage Amplification. The transistor input voltage v_i is given by

$$v_i = h_{ie}i_b + h_{re}v_o \qquad 7.18$$

Substitution of the value for i_b from equation 7.17 gives

$$v_i = \frac{h_{ie}i_c(1 + h_{oe}R_L)}{h_{fe}} + h_{re}v_o$$

The load current $\quad i_c = -v_o/R_L. \qquad 7.19$

and so $\quad v_i = v_o\left[\frac{-h_{ie}(1 + h_{oe}R_L) + h_{fe}h_{re}}{h_{fe}R_L}\right]$

Hence the voltage amplification,

$$A_v = v_o/v_i$$

$$= \frac{-h_{fe}R_L}{h_{ie} + R_L(h_{ie}h_{oe} - h_{fe}h_{re})} \qquad 7.20$$

The negative sign indicates 180° phase shift between the input and output voltages. As would be expected the voltage amplification approaches zero at low values of load resistance. For high values of R_L on the other hand, the voltage amplification approaches $A_v \simeq -h_{fe}/\Delta h$ where $\Delta h = h_{ie}h_{oe} - h_{re}h_{fe}$.

Power Gain. For a resistive load the power gain is the product of A_i and A_v and so is equal to

$$\frac{(h_{fe})^2 R_L}{[h_{ie} + R_L\Delta h](1 + h_{oe}R_L)} \qquad 7.21$$

Input Resistance. The input resistance, r_i, at the transistor terminals is given by v_i/i_b. From equations 7.19 and 7.17

$$v_o = -i_c R_L = \frac{-h_{fe}R_L i_b}{1 + h_{oe}R_L}$$

Substitution of this value in equation 7.18 gives

$$v_i = h_{ie}i_b - \frac{h_{re}h_{fe}R_L i_b}{1 + h_{oe}R_L}$$

hence

$$r_i = h_{ie} - \frac{h_{re}h_{fe}R_L}{1 + h_{oe}R_L} \qquad 7.22$$

It will be seen that the input resistance has its maximum value when $R_L = 0$, and is then equal to h_{ie}; r_i has a minimum value when R_L is very large so that $h_{oe}R_L \gg 1$. The value of r_i is then given by

$$r_i = h_{ie} - \frac{h_{re}h_{fe}}{h_{oe}} = \Delta h/h_{oe}. \qquad 7.23$$

Output Resistance. When the applied signal voltage E_s is zero, the input circuit equation is

$$(R_s + h_{ie})i_b = h_{re}v_o \qquad 7.24$$

$$\therefore \quad i_b = h_{re}v_o/(R_s + h_{ie})$$

By substitution of this value in equation 7.16

$$\frac{h_{fe}h_{re}v_o}{R_s + h_{ie}} = h_{oe}v_e + i_c$$

$$\therefore \quad \frac{v_o}{i_c} = \frac{R_s + h_{ie}}{R_s h_{oe} + \Delta h} \qquad 7.25$$

For large values of source resistance ($R_s \gg h_{ie}$)

$$r_o \simeq 1/h_{oe}$$

while for $R_s = 0$, $\quad r_o = h_{ie}/\Delta h$

THE FIELD EFFECT TRANSISTOR

The field effect transistor (FET) is based on different principles from the junction transistor discussed so far.

Junction Gate Type. **The principle of operation of the field effect transistor may be illustrated by reference to Fig. 7.19. The body of the device may be assumed to consist of a minute strip of *n*-type material having ohmic (or non-rectifying) contacts called the *source* and *drain* at the two ends. With a direct voltage applied to these terminals, as shown in Fig. 7.19, electrons flow from source to drain. A third terminal, referred to as the *gate*, is connected to *p*-type material alloyed or diffused on to the *n*-type material, which is commonly silicon.**

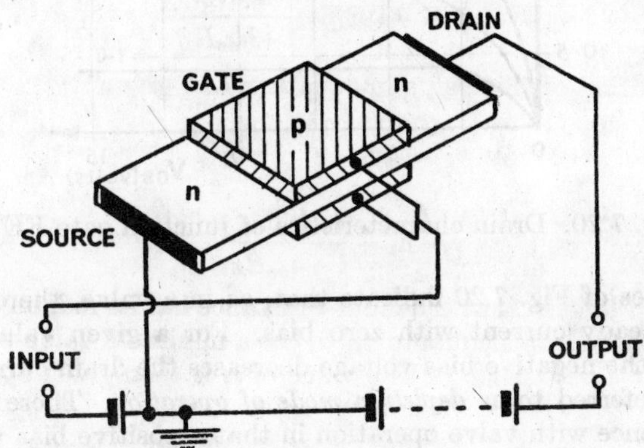

Fig. 7.19. Junction gate field effect transistor.

When this gate is biased negatively it repels some of the electrons flowing in the material and forces them into a narrower path, thereby increasing the resistance of the current channel. In effect an increase in the reverse bias of the junction broadens the depletion layer within which there are no free carriers, and by constriction of the conducting channel reduces the longitudinal current; the transverse electric *field* of the gate voltage has the *effect* of modulating the resistivity of the current path.

The drain current I_D depends on the value of the drain-source voltage V_{DS} and on the gate source voltage V_{GS}. The drain current increases rapidly with V_{DS} when the latter is small, but at larger values the drain current increases very little. This arises because as the drain voltage is increased the body of the material is made more

positive with respect to the source, the gate bias is thereby increased, and the flow of current restricted.

The general form of the output or drain, characteristic is shown in Fig. 7.20. It will be seen that the curves are similar in shape to those of a pentode valve. Also the linear portions of the curves indicate that the device has a high output resistance. As the input to the FET is through a reverse biased *p-n* junction, the input resistance is very high. This is a distinguishing feature of field effect transistors.

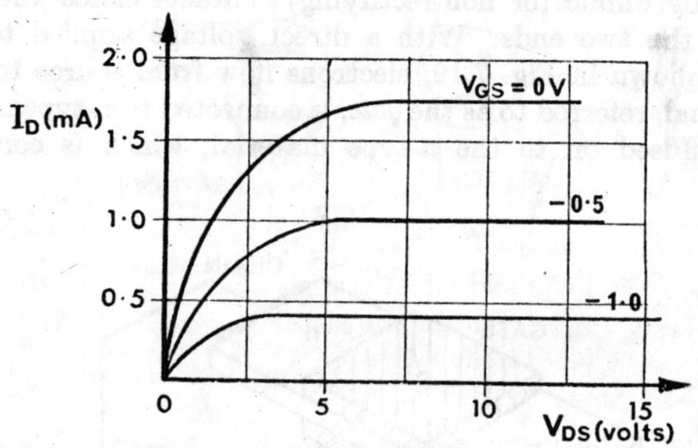

Fig. 7.20. Drain characteristics of junction gate FET.

The curves of Fig. 7.20 indicate that, as in a valve, there is a considerable steady current with zero bias. For a given value of V_{DS}, increase of the negative bias voltage decreases the drain current. This feature is referred to as *depletion mode of operation*. There is further correspondence with valve operation in that a positive bias voltage on the gate junction produces an input current (and low input resistance) just as a positive voltage on the grid of a valve with respect to its cathode causes it to draw grid current.

The field effect transistor may be arranged as an amplifier, the gate acting in similar fashion to the grid of a valve in that it controls the flow of current through the device. By analogy, the mutual conductance g_m of the FET relates the change in drain current δI_D to the change in gate source voltage δV_{GS} for defined values of V_{GS} and V_{DS}, and so

$$g_m = \delta I_D / \delta V_{GS} \quad . \quad . \quad . \quad 7.26$$

The discussion so far has related to an *n*-channel device. As might be expected, *p*-channel devices, operating with opposite polarities of supply voltages, are also possible.

The graphical symbol for an FET is shown in Fig. 7.21, which also indicates the correspondence as far as terminals are concerned, between the FET, junction transistor and valve.

The direction of the arrowhead in the graphical symbol for the FET in Fig. 7.21a is used to indicate the channel material. The direction shown indicates n-channel material. A p-channel device has the direction reversed and the drain voltage negative with respect to the source.

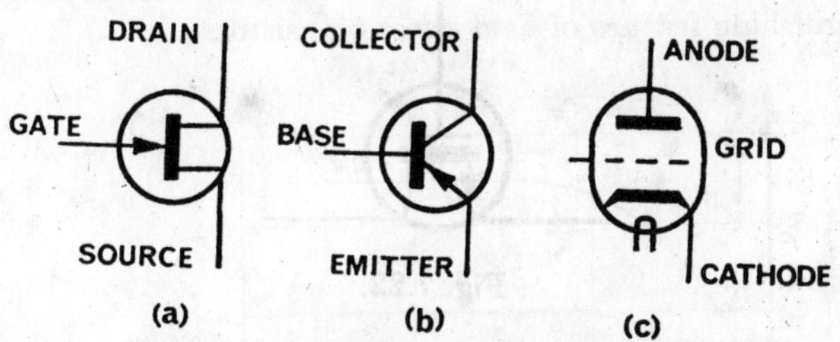

Fig. 7.21 (a) Field effect transistor
(b) Junction transistor
(c) Triode valve.

Insulated Gate Type. The form of field effect transistor discussed has the control gate separated from the main channel by a reversed biased diode. There is a second category in which the gate is isolated from the remainder of the device by a thin layer of insulation. The metallic gate contact surface functions as one electrode of a capacitor while the other electrode is the underlying silicon channel. The insulation film forming the dielectric of the effective capacitor is usually a fine layer of silicon dioxide. If a positive charge is produced on the gate terminal by the application of a positive voltage, then a negative charge is induced in the silicon material close to the surface. If the material is originally p-type, then for a sufficiently large charge on the gate, the p-type surface becomes n-type by induction and thus a junction is formed below the surface. Such a channel is connected at both ends to n-type regions which are used as contacts, that is as the source and drain.

Insulated gate type devices have the advantage of an extremely high input resistance, irrespective of the polarity of the bias voltage. Depending on the polarity of the materials involved, an insulated gate transistor can be used in the depletion mode mentioned above, or it may be arranged to produce *enhancement mode of operation.*

In the depletion mode of operation the device has, with zero bias, a fairly large standing current. This is then reduced as the bias is increased as in the case of a valve. Enhancement operation, on the other hand, involves an arrangement in which the standing current is small or zero. In use such a device is " biased on ", as with a junction transistor, and an increase of bias increases the steady current. The graphical symbol for an insulated gate transistor is shown in Fig. 7.22.

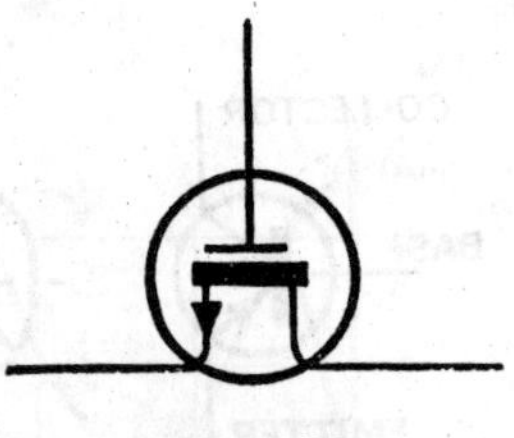

Fig. 7.22.

OTHER SEMICONDUCTOR DEVICES

Transistors are now manufactured in a variety of ways. The differences of construction lead to marked differences in operating characteristics so that the user is thus able to select the form most suited for any particular application, whether this be switching, high-frequency operation, or some other consideration. Three devices are mentioned below, but for further information the reader should consult the references given at the end of this chapter.

The Junction Tetrode. This is one of many devices which have more than three terminals. The high-frequency performance of a junction transistor may be improved by the addition of a second base contact opposite the first. A voltage applied between the two base contacts causes the normally forward biased emitter to be "biased off" over most of its area except for a small region near one of the base contacts. The effective cross-sectional area of the base is thereby reduced so that the collector-base capacitance is reduced; the distance of the active base region from the base contact is also reduced. Both of these effects improve the device performance at high frequencies.

The Tunnel Diode. Of the many special types of diode available, the tunnel diode is one of the most important and finds widespread application at ultra-high frequencies, either in oscillator, amplifier or high-speed switching circuits.

A tunnel diode differs from other *p-n* junction diodes in that the impurity or "doping" levels used are very much higher, a thousand times or more, and consequently the depletion layer is narrowed to about 10^{-6} cm. The tunnel diode is so called because it involves the phenomenon of *electron tunnelling* through the ultra-thin barrier when a small forward bias is applied, so that the current/voltage characteristic has the form shown in Fig. 7.23. Increase in forward bias leads to a decrease in the tunnel component of current. In this region the current decreases with increase of applied voltage and so the slope resistance is negative.

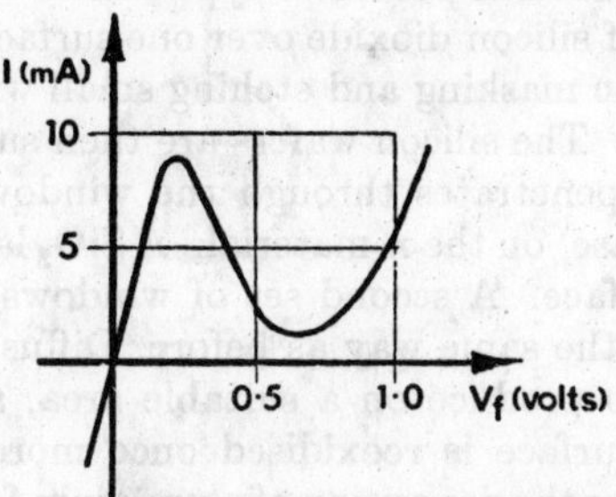

Fig. 7.23. Tunnel diode characteristic.

At higher forward voltages the current rises again, along a curve similar to that of the ordinary junction diode. The tunnel diode operated in the negative slope region has a very low resistance. The low negative resistance is made use of in amplifier and other circuits, usually by reducing the effect of normal (positive) resistance. The fact that the tunnel diode is a two-terminal device complicates the construction of cascaded stages.

The Thermistor. As the temperature of a semiconductor rises the thermal generation of electron-hole pairs increases and lowers the resistance of the material. This property is made use of in thermal resistors, or thermistors. These are semiconductor resistors having a large and accurately controlled negative coefficient of resistance with a rise in temperature. The change in temperature may be produced by external means such as a change in air temperature, or internally by the current flowing through the device.

MICROELECTRONICS

Evolution in electronic equipment is in the direction of decreasing size and weight. In general terms it would seem that as devices are invented and become familiar with use, they are then produced in physically smaller sizes. This trend is often reinforced by a growth in circuit complexity, with possible increase in number of components, due to more sophisticated requirements in the performance specification;

there is a desire to limit the size of the equipment and so the size of the individual components has to be reduced. This process of miniaturisation has been carried out with thermionic valves and their associated components. Transistors have carried the process a step further. The planar *n-p-n* transistor is produced in a way that illustrates further developments.

In a planar construction process *n*-type silicon wafers are oxidised to form a thin layer of silicon dioxide over one surface and by a combination of photographic masking and etching small windows are produced in the SiO_2 surface. The silicon wafers are then subject to diffusion by boron which only penetrates through the windows. This produces a *p*-type layer (the base) on the *n*-material. A SiO_2 layer is then produced over the entire surface. A second set of windows is then produced in this oxide layer in the same way as before. Diffusion with phosphorus is then arranged to produce on a suitable area, an *n*-type layer (the emitter) and the surface is reoxidised once more. Finally areas are cleared to provide for the deposition of aluminium for electrical contacts. The resulting structure has the form indicated in Fig. 7.24. The steps outlined briefly above may be performed on up to a thousand or so transistors at once on a single slice of material which is subsequently divided. The transistor is protected by a glass-like layer of SiO_2, with the junctions formed beneath this surface.

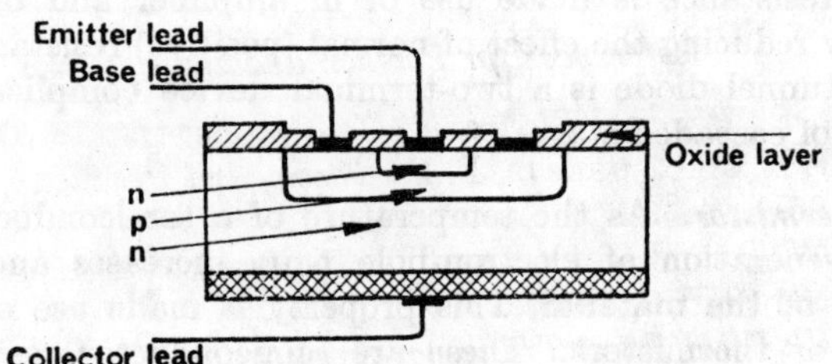

Fig. 7.24. Planar Transistor.

Such a form of construction leads to high reliability and long life.

The association of such active devices with miniature components leads to circuits of minute size. Microelectronics has, however, developed a stage further beyond miniaturisation because of the need for reliability and low cost, neither of which is easy to achieve when interconnecting wires and soldered joints are involved. Microelectronic units may be achieved by thin film techniques or by integrated circuits.

Thin Film Technology. This technique involves the deposition of thin films, in vacuum, on a thin glass plate to produce, say, a combination of resistors and capacitors. The resistor material can be one of many resistive metals; the capacitors are made by depositing metal, then the dielectric then metal again. The necessary diodes or transistors (in miniaturised form) and the wires to lead to other circuits, are soldered on at the appropriate points. The resulting thin film circuit is finally encapsulated in resin and is then ready for use.

Integrated Circuits. The term integrated circuit here refers to a collection of components joined together to serve a particular function, say, an amplifier or an oscillator. All the circuit components form an integral part of a piece of bulk semiconductor material, usually silicon. Often it may not be possible to identify discrete components as such. A chip of silicon may be etched, have suitably doped material deposited and the process continued until all the necessary resistors, capacitors, diodes and transistors are produced. Inter connections may not be necessary when the components are adjacent. Other interconnections, as demanded by the function of the circuit, may be arranged in the form of conducting films. The final wafer so produced may have a volume of a few cubic millimetres.

The advent of microelectronics, capable of producing standard functional circuits in large quantities demands fresh thinking on the part of circuit designers. Indeed the division between component manufacturer and circuit designer may well become much less definite than in the past.

References for Further Reading

ALFREY, G. F.: *Physical Electronics* (D. Van Nostrand Co. Ltd., 1964).

TILLMAN, J. R. and ROBERTS, F. F.: *Theory and Practice of Transistors* (Pitman, 1961).

BURFORD, W. B. and GREY VERNIER, H.: *Semiconductor Junctions and Devices* (McGraw Hill, 1965).

GOSLING, W.: *Field Effect Transistor Applications* (Temple Press Books Ltd., 1964).

SEVIN, L. J.: *Field Effect Transistors* (McGraw Hill, 1965).

GENTILE, S. P.: *Basic Theory and Application of Tunnel Diodes* (D. Van Nostrand Co., Inc., 1962).

Dummer, G. W. A. and Granville, J. W.: *Miniature and Microminiature Electronics* (Pitman, 1961).

KHAMBATA, A. J.: *Introduction to Integrated Semiconductor Circuits* (John Wiley & Sons, Inc., 1963).

WARNER, R. M. and FORDEMWALT, J. N.: *Integrated Circuits* (McGraw Hill, 1965).

8

LOW-FREQUENCY AMPLIFIERS

Transistors and Valves. Low-frequency amplifiers may commonly be defined as types which operate up to a frequency of about 20 kHz. This figure is arbitrary, but is convenient in that interelectrode capacitances can often be ignored below this frequency but have to be taken into account at higher frequencies.

The function of an amplifier is to increase the level of the voltage, current, or power. The amount of this increase is then referred to as the amplifier *gain*. A *voltage*, or a *current amplifier* does not necessarily provide any appreciable power output, whereas a *power amplifier* does.

An amplifier may contain valves, or alternatively transistors may be used. Transistors have the obvious advantage over valves that no heater is necessary. They are also much smaller in size and require lower operating voltages. As a result, transistors have displaced valves in most amplifiers, especially in low-level circuits, i.e. where the signal voltage or current to be amplified is small. The operating characteristics of transistors are, however, much more temperature dependent and this has always to be borne in mind in the design of a transistor amplifier. Another difference between valves and transistors is that whereas valves are voltage controlled devices, transistors are basically current controlled. Valves have a high input impedance and this is independent (if Miller effect can be ignored) of the output voltage or current. This isolation between input and output simplifies circuit calculations. Some transistors, however, have a low input impedance, require input current and a certain amount of input power. Also the value of the input impedance is affected by the output voltage, and so transistor circuit calculations tend to be more complicated than for valves. Field effect transistors do, however, provide an exception to this generalisation.

The present chapter deals with the common forms of low frequency voltage and power amplifiers, for both valves and transistors. High-frequency amplifiers are discussed in chapter 10.

OPERATING CONDITIONS FOR A SIMPLE VALVE AMPLIFIER

If an amplifier is to give an output voltage which is a faithful replica of a complex input voltage, the valve operation must be restricted to the linear region of its characteristics. In this connection it is necessary to study the dynamic anode current/grid voltage curve for the particular load considered. The dynamic I_a/V_g curve for any load is obtained from the intersection of the I_a/V_a characteristic with the load line. Fig. 8.1b shows that the dynamic grid characteristic is less steep and also straighter than the static grid characteristic.

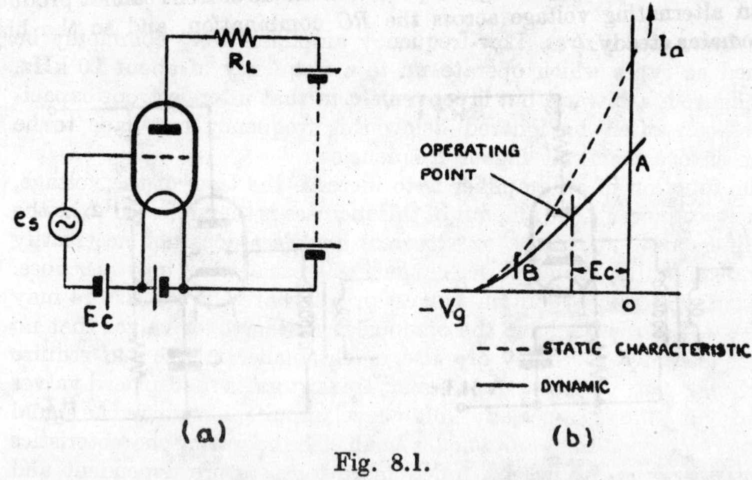

Fig. 8.1.

If the simple amplifier of Fig. 8.1a is to meet the required conditions of linearity it follows that only the linear part *AB* of the dynamic characteristic can be used. This is achieved by correct choice of the value of *negative* grid bias, and by limitation of the input voltage. Thus the bias voltage (E_c in Fig. 8.1a) must be such as to give the required operating point, and the peak value of the input voltage must not exceed the value of E_c. The valve is then said to be working under class *A* conditions.

Bias Circuits

In the simple amplifier the grid has been kept at the requisite negative potential or " bias " with respect to the cathode by means of a battery E_c. In practice, batteries are only used in battery-operated equipment.

Cathode Bias. With indirectly heated valves, the negative bias for the grid is obtained by the method shown in Fig. 8.2a. A resistor *R* is inserted between the cathode and H.T. negative terminals. The current taken by the valve then flows through this resistor from the cathode to H.T. –. The cathode of the valve is thereby made positive with respect to the H.T. – point by the ohmic drop in R. The grid (in the absence of grid current) has the same potential as the H.T. negative terminal and so the grid is at a potential which is negative with respect to the cathode. The function of the capacitor C is to keep the cathode bias voltage constant when an alternating input signal is applied. If the reactance of C is very small (ideally zero) at the lowest operating frequency, the alternating component of anode current cannot produce an alternating voltage across the RC combination, and so the bias remains steady.

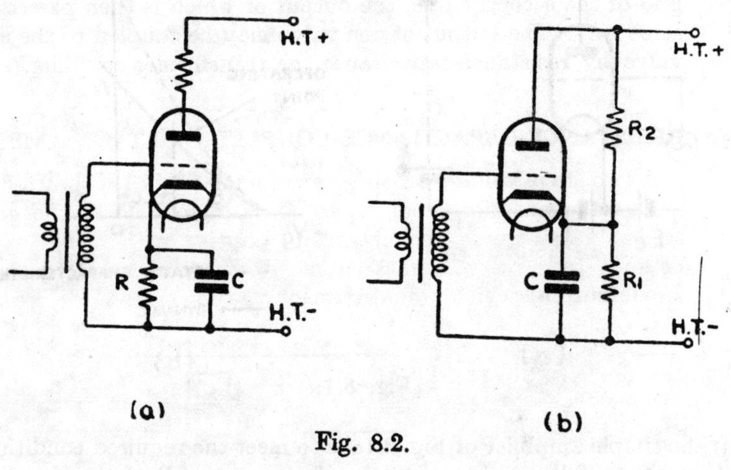

Fig. 8.2.

H.T. Supply Bias. If a large negative bias is required, the arrangement shown in Fig. 8.2b may be used. The cathode is connected to a potential divider chain connected across the H.T. supply. The grid then has a negative bias equal to the voltage drop in the resistor R_1 which carries the valve and divider chain currents. R_1 is then shunted by the bypass capacitor C.

The two bias circuits shown have a conducting path between the grid and cathode. This is essential as *a few* of the emitted electrons may accumulate on the grid. In the absence of a conducting path the grid will then acquire an additional negative charge which will upset the operating conditions. If the input voltage source does not provide a conducting path it is necessary to connect a resistor between the grid and H.T. – terminals. This resistor is normally of a high value to avoid shunting the signal source, and is referred to as a "grid leak".

MULTISTAGE AMPLIFIERS

Where high values of amplification are required, more than valve or " stage " of amplification may be necessary. If too hig degree of amplification is attempted in one stage the amplifier tend to be unstable because of coupling between the input and out circuits. For this reason the maximum gain per stage is usuall the order of 100. Where several stages of amplification are used, output voltage at the anode of the first valve is connected to grid of the second valve, the output of which is then passed on in same way. The output of one valve may be coupled to the succee valve by resistance-capacitance, or transformer-coupling.

RESISTANCE-CAPACITANCE-COUPLED VOLTAGE AMPLIFIE

A two stage voltage amplifier employing triodes is shown in Fig. Direct connection from R_3 to R_4 is impossible as the grid of second valve would then be made positive with respect to its cathode by a very large amount. This would give rise to a l anode current which would damage the second valve. The pres

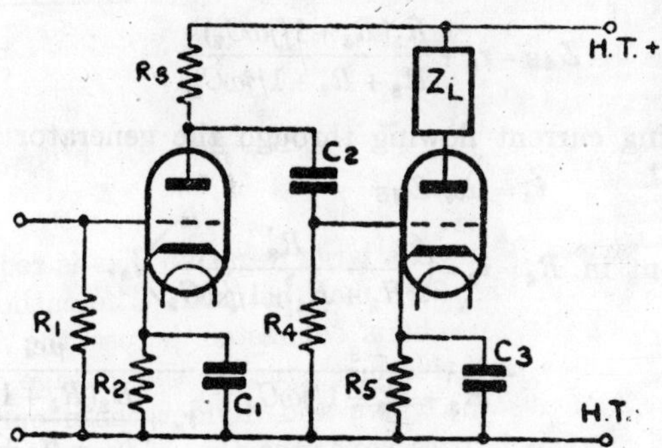

Fig. 8.3. Two stage triode amplifier.

R_1 is the grid leak for V_1
R_2 is the bias resistor for V_1
R_3 is the anode load for V_1
R_4 is the grid leak for V_2
R_5 is the bias resistor for V_2
C_1 is the bias decoupling capacitor for V_1
C_2 is the coupling capacitor
C_3 is the bias decoupling capacitor for V_2
Z_L is the output load.

of the coupling capacitor prevents the application of this direct potential to the second grid but couples the alternating voltage across R_3 to R_4.

The equivalent circuit for the first stage is shown in Fig. 8.4a with an input voltage of e_s.

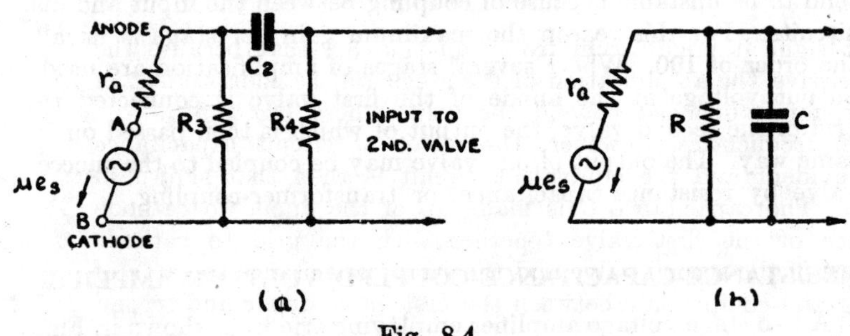

Fig. 8.4.

The amplification at any frequency can be calculated from the equivalent circuit of Fig. 8.4a.

The impedance at the generator terminals AB is

$$Z_{AB} = r_a + \frac{R_3(R_4 + 1/j\omega C_2)}{R_3 + R_4 + 1/j\omega C_2}$$

the alternating current flowing through the generator is then

$$i_a = \mu e_s / Z_{AB}$$

The current in $R_4 = i_0 = \left(\dfrac{R_3}{R_3 + R_4 + 1/j\omega C_2}\right) i_a$

$$= \frac{R_3}{R_3 + R_4 + 1/j\omega C_2} \cdot \frac{\mu e_s}{r_a + \dfrac{R_3(R_4 + 1/j\omega C_2)}{R_3 + R_4 + 1/j\omega C_2}}$$

$$= \frac{\mu e_s R_3}{r_a R_3 + r_a R_4 + r_a/j\omega C_2 + R_3 R_4 + R_3/j\omega C_2}$$

The output voltage across $R_4 = V_0 = i_0 R_4$ and so the magnitude of the voltage amplification from the grid of the first valve to the grid of the second is given by

$$|A_v| = \left|\frac{V_0}{e_s}\right| = \frac{\mu R_3 R_4}{\sqrt{\{r_a(R_3 + R_4) + R_3 R_4\}^2 + (r_a + R_3)^2/\omega^2 C_2^2}} \qquad 8.1$$

This expression will give exact results for any frequency of operation for which the circuit of Fig. 8.4a applies. For frequencies at which

$1/\omega C_2 << R_4$ the equivalent circuit may be simplified by the omission of C_2. Under such conditions the load for the valve becomes a resistance R, which is the parallel combination of R_3 and R_4. Equation 8.1 then reduces to

$$|A_v| = \frac{\mu R}{R + r_a} = \frac{\mu R_3 R_4}{r_a(R_3 + R_4) + R_3 R_4} \quad . \quad . \quad 8.2$$

At first sight it might seem from equation 8.2 that because the load is resistive the amplification of the stage will be independent of frequency, for frequencies beyond the value where $1/\omega C_2 \ll R_4$.

At high frequencies, however, the effect of circuit capacitance becomes evident and the equivalent circuit is then that shown in Fig. 8.4b. The capacitance C is made up of the anode to cathode capacitance of the first valve together with the grid to cathode capacitance of the second valve and the stray capacitance to earth of the wiring and components between the first valve anode and second valve grid.

The alternating anode current in this case is given by

$$i_a = \frac{\mu e_s}{r_a + \dfrac{R}{1 + j\omega CR}}$$

and the output voltage is then

$$V_0 = \frac{\mu e_s}{r_a + \dfrac{R}{1 + j\omega CR}} \cdot \frac{R}{1 + j\omega CR} = \frac{\mu e_s R}{r_a + R + j\omega CRr_a}$$

The magnitude of the amplification is then given by

$$|A_v| = \left|\frac{V_0}{e_s}\right| = \frac{\mu R}{\sqrt{(r_a + R)^2 + (\omega CRr_a)^2}} \quad . \quad . \quad . \quad 8.3$$

The general form of the gain/frequency characteristic of a conventional resistance coupled amplifier is shown in Fig. 8.5. The characteristic feature is that a level response is obtained over a wide range of frequencies. (Such amplifiers are reconsidered as video amplifiers with a bandwidth of several megahertz, in chapter 10.) For a large value of amplification the effective load resistance should be high compared with the anode slope resistance. To maintain the gain at low frequencies, the reactance of the coupling capacitor should be small compared with the value of the grid leak for the succeeding stage. (R_4 in Fig. 8.3.)

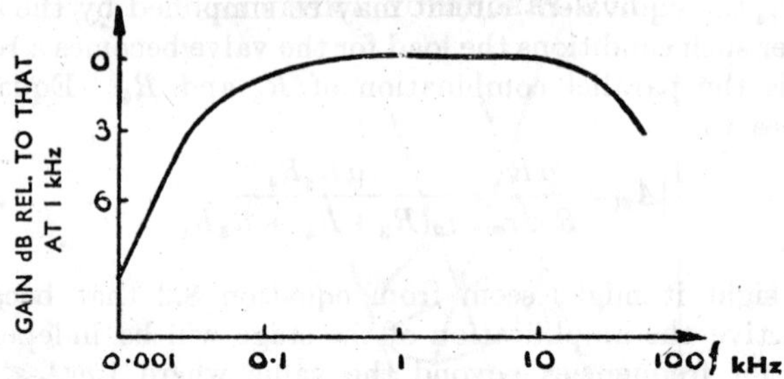

Fig. 8.5. Response curve for resistance-capacitance-coupled amplifier.

Choke-capacitance-coupled Voltage Amplifier

If the load resistance (R_3) in the amplifier stage previously discussed is replaced by an inductor, the stage is then said to be choke-capacitance-coupled.

If the inductor has an inductance L and a resistance r the voltage amplification at any frequency can be obtained from equation 8.1 if R_3 is replaced by $r+j\omega L$. The amplification obtained with choke-capacitance-coupling falls off at low, and at high frequencies, because of the presence of the coupling capacitor, and the stray capacitance. The drop in amplification at low frequencies is accentuated by the fact that the impedance of the inductive load also decreases.

With choke-capacitance-coupling the alternating voltage across the anode load, and the current through it, are no longer in phase and so the load line is not a straight line but a closed curve. This is true for all complex loads including the resistive case when the reactance of the coupling capacitor cannot be ignored. The load line for an inductive load is shown in Fig. 8.6.

If the phase angle of the anode load is zero (i.e. if the load is purely resistive) the load line is a straight line. At the other extreme, if the phase angle of the load is 90°, the load line becomes a circle. For loads which have a phase angle between 0 and 90° the load line is some form of ellipse as shown in Fig. 8.6.

When the load has a reactive component the instantaneous anode voltage may swing above the HT + supply voltage of E_B, a phenomenon which is impossible with a purely resistive load. The line XY represents a " d.c. load line ", or static load line as it is sometimes called, for the resistive component of the load impedance. This line has a slope of $-1/r$ and passes through the point $I_a=0$, $V_a=E_B$. It intersects the ellipse at points where the tangent to the ellipse is horizontal; at such points the current is a maximum or a minimum, the rate of change of current is then zero and the induced e.m.f. in the inductance L is zero.

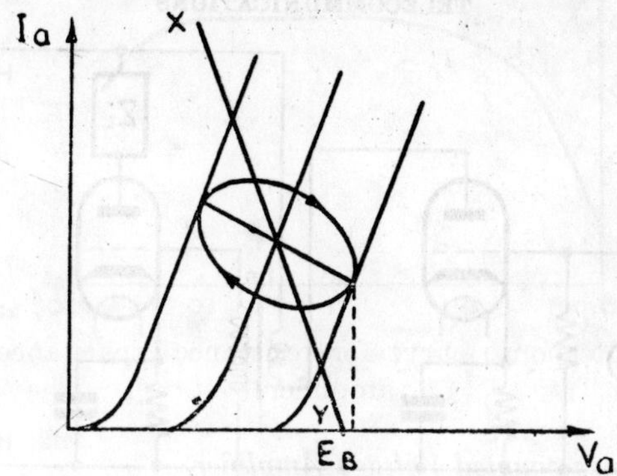

Fig. 8.6.

Transformer Coupling

An alternative form of intervalve coupling is by means of a transformer as shown in Fig. 8.7a.

If the secondary winding of the transformer is connected to the grid and cathode of a voltage amplifying valve in which no grid current flows, the secondary winding will then be open circuited and the equivalent circuit is that shown in Fig. 8.7b.

The voltage across the primary winding is

$$V_P = \frac{\mu e_s(r_1 + j\omega L_1)}{r_a + r_1 + j\omega L_1}$$

$$= \frac{\mu e_s j\omega L_1}{r_a + j\omega L_1} \text{ if } r_1 << \omega L_1$$

The voltage induced in the secondary winding is $j\omega M i_a$

where $i_a = \mu e_s/(r_a + j\omega L_1)$, and so the secondary voltage is

$$V_s = \frac{j\omega M \mu e_s}{r_a + j\omega L_1}$$

This is M/L_1 times the primary voltage and if the ratio M/L_1 is equal to n, the output or secondary voltage is equal to

$$\frac{\mu e_s n j\omega L_1}{r_a + j\omega L_1}$$

The magnitude of the amplification, $|A_v|$, is then

$$|A_v| = \frac{\mu n\omega L_1}{\sqrt{r_a^2 + (\omega L_1)^2}} \quad . \quad . \quad . \quad . \quad . \quad 8.4$$

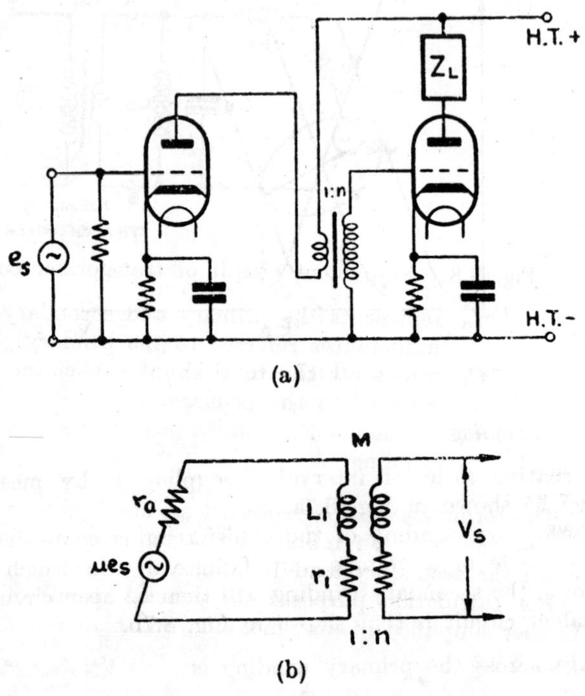

Fig. 8.7.

This result shows that the gain is directly proportional to the step-up ratio n.

Limits are placed on the value of n however, if a level response over a wide range of frequencies is required. If n is increased by an increase in the number of secondary turns the self-capacitance of the secondary winding increases. This capacitance resonates with the leakage inductance and gives rise to a peak in the response curve around the resonant frequency. The limit to the alternative method of increasing n (by decreasing the number of turns on the primary winding) is set by the fact that the amplification is also proportional to the value of the primary inductance. If this is not greater than r_a the amplification falls sharply at low frequencies. Because of these restrictions the step-up ratio in intervalve transformers is not usually greater than 5 : 1 if wideband operation is required.

A simplified equivalent circuit for a practical transformer* coupled stage (as opposed to the idealised version of Fig. 8.7b) is shown in Fig. 8.8.

* See Chapter 3.

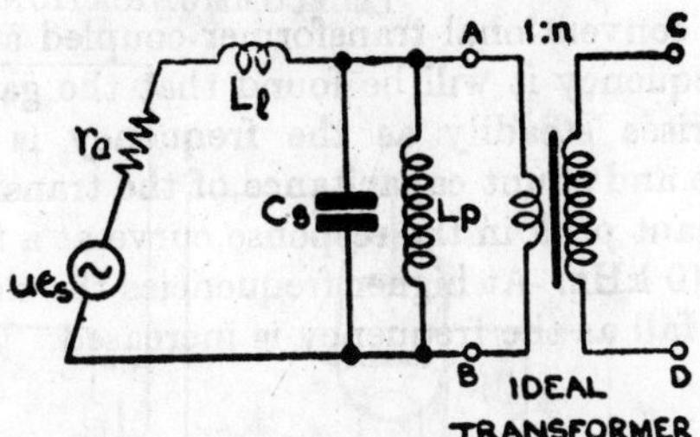

Fig. 8.8. Equivalent circuit of transformer coupled stage.

L_l represents the primary and secondary leakage inductances referred to the primary.

C_s represents the total shunt capacitance referred to the primary.

L_p represents the inductance of the primary winding.

The terminals $ABCD$ represent an ideal transformer of turns ratio $1 : n$, and with an infinite input impedance at the terminals AB when the secondary load is infinite.

For calculation purposes the general circuit of Fig. 8.8 may be further simplified at low, medium, and high frequencies as shown in Fig. 8.9.

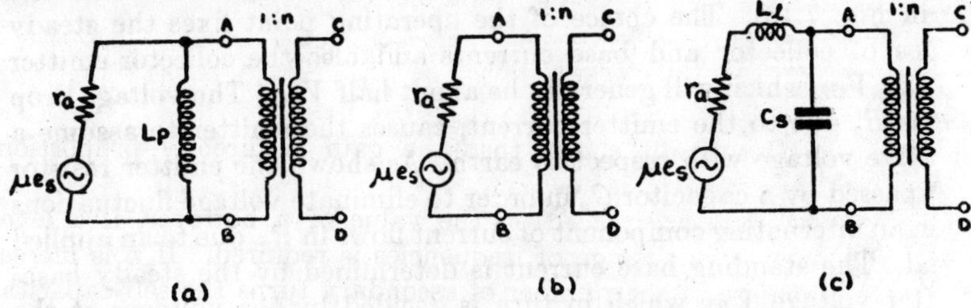

Fig. 8.9. Equivalent circuits for transformer coupling.

(a) Low frequency circuit.
(b) Medium frequency circuit.
(c) High frequency circuit.

The three circuits of Fig. 8.9 are self-explanatory. At low frequencies the leakage inductance can be ignored but the primary inductance L_p is important. At medium frequencies L_p can also be ignored as the shunting effect decreases with rise in frequency. At high frequencies the effect of leakage inductance and stray capacitance have to be considered.

f the gain of a conventional transformer-coupled amplifier stage is ttted against frequency it will be found that the gain is low at low quencies, but rises steadily as the frequency is increased; the age inductance and shunt capacitance of the transformer windings e rise to a resonant peak in the response curve at a frequency in the ghbourhood of 10 kHz. At higher frequencies the shunt capacitance ses the gain to fall as the frequency is increased.

todes in Low-Frequency Amplifiers

Pentode valves have displaced triodes to a large extent in voltage plifiers, because of their greater gain. All the circuits so far conered may be used with pentode valves. Modern practice utilises todes in resistance-capacitance-coupled stages which provide level ponse over a wide range of frequencies with a large value of amplition. As a result, the use of chokes and transformers in voltage plifiers is restricted to special purposes.

ERATING CONDITIONS FOR A CE TRANSISTOR AMPLIFIER

A simple common-emitter amplifier stage with a resistive load is wn in Fig. 8.10. The operating point is chosen by drawing a load corresponding to a suitable value of R_L on the output characteristics in Fig. 7.15). The choice of the operating point fixes the steady ues of collector and base currents and also the collector-emitter age V_{CE} which will generally be about half V_{CC}. The voltage drop oss R_3 due to the emitter current, causes the emitter to assume a ative voltage with respect to earth. As shown the emitter resistor ypassed by a capacitor C_2 in order to eliminate voltage fluctuations en an alternating component of current flows in R_3, due to an applied ial. The standing base current is determined by the steady basetter voltage V_{BE} which in turn is decided by the voltages at the e and the emitter terminals. The capacitors C_1 and C_3 are d.c. king components at the input and output respectively. These acitors affect the low-frequency response so that their values are ided by the frequency characteristic required. It should be noted t the value of C_1 has to be sufficiently large for its reactance to be ch lower than the relatively low value of input impedance at the est frequency of operation.

D.C. Stabilisation. It will be seen from Fig. 8.10 that the bias ngement is slightly more complicated than that of the corresponding valve circuit. The stabilisation of the operating point is important h transistors because of the variation of the leakage current with

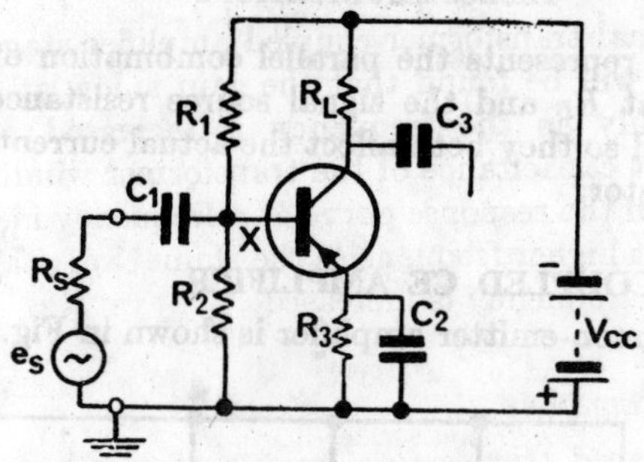

Fig. 8.10. Common-emitter amplifier.

temperature. There may also be substantial variations in the parameter β and in the leakage current between supposedly identical transistors. The circuit shown in Fig. 8.10 provides a measure of stabilisation. If the voltage at the point X at the junction of R_1 and R_2 is V_X, then

$$V_X = V_{BE} + I_E R_3 = V_{BE} + (I_B + I_C) R_3$$

I_C is much larger than I_B and so to a high degree of approximation

$$V_X = V_{BE} + I_C R_3$$

If R_1 and R_2 constitute a relatively low-resistance path, the voltage V_X is fixed. Hence for a fixed value of R_3, the variables in the above relation are V_{BE} and I_C. If now I_C increases due to a temperature rise the voltage across R_3 increases and causes V_{BE} to fall. This causes a decrease in I_B and consequently a decrease in I_C. To provide a high degree of stabilisation the voltage V_X must remain constant which implies that the current through R_1 and R_2 should be large compared with the base current I_B. From the viewpoint of an a.c. signal R_1 and R_2 are in parallel and form a shunt on the input signal, so that there is a lower limit for the values of R_1 and R_2.

The capacitors and steady voltage supply V_{CC} are all (ideally) short-circuits as far as a.c. is concerned. Hence the circuit of Fig. 8.10 may be redrawn to give the a.c. version shown in Fig. 8.11.

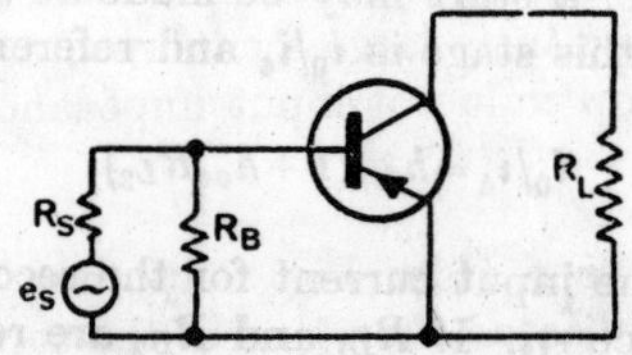

Fig. 8.11. A.C. circuit of common-emitter amplifier.

In Fig. 8.11, R_B represents the parallel combination of R_1 and R_2. It will be seen that R_B and the signal source resistance R_S form a voltage divider, and so they both affect the actual current and voltage input to the transistor.

TWO-STAGE RC-COUPLED CE AMPLIFIER

A two-stage common-emitter amplifier is shown in Fig. 8.12.

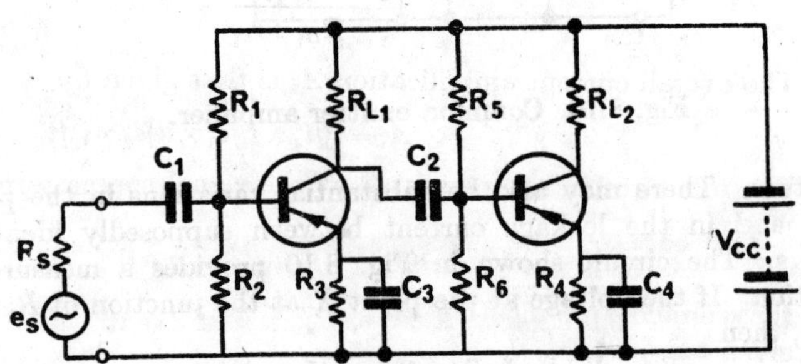

Fig. 8.12. Two-stage CE amplifier.

The corresponding equivalent circuit is shown in Fig. 8.13. R_{B1} and R_{B2} represent the parallel combination of R_1 and R_2 and R_5 and R_6 respectively.

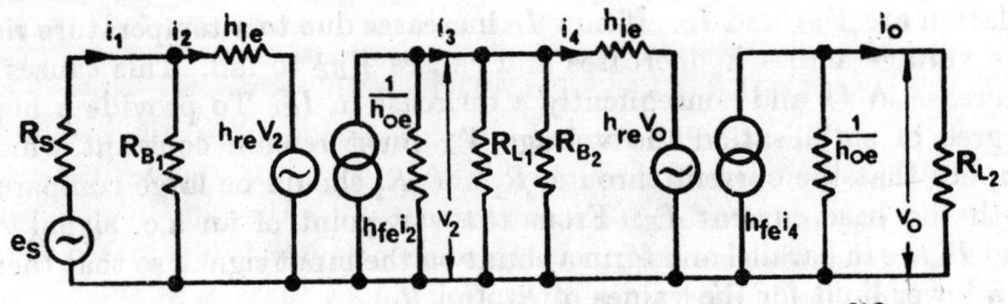

Fig. 8.13. A.C. equivalent circuit of two-stage amplifier.

The starting point for gain calculations is the second stage. (If however the voltage feedback terms are sufficiently small to ignore, as they commonly are, a start may be made at the input terminals.) The current gain for this stage is i_0/i_4 and reference to equation 7.17 shows that

$$i_0/i_4 = h_{fe}/(1 + h_{oe}R_{L2})$$

The current i_4 is the input current for the second transistor which has an input resistance r_{i2}. If R_{L1} and R_{B2} are replaced by the equivalent value R, then

$$i_4/i_3 = R/(R + r_{i2})$$

The current gain for the first transistor is i_3/i_2 and so

$$\frac{i_3}{i_2} = \frac{h_{fe}}{1 + h_{oe}R'}$$

Where R' is the value of R and r_{i_2} in parallel. The current i_2 is the input current to the first transistor which has an input resistance r_{i1}, hence

$$\frac{i_2}{i_1} = \frac{R_{B1}}{R_{B1} + r_{i1}}$$

The overall current amplification A_i is thus given by

$$A_i = i_0/i_4 \times i_4/i_3 \times i_3/i_2 \times i_2/i_1$$

The input resistance presented at the signal source terminals is R_{IN}, where

$$R_{IN} = R_{B1}r_{i1}/(R_{B1} + r_{i1})$$

the voltage amplification and power gain of the amplifier are thus given by

$$A_v = A_i R_{L2}/R_{IN} \text{ and } G_P = (A_i)^2 R_{L2}/R_{IN}$$

These quantities so far determined are ratios. To determine, say, the output voltage, it is necessary to determine i_1, which involves the signal source. The output current is then known and hence the output voltage for the given output load R_{L_2}.

AMPLIFIER CLASSIFICATION IN TERMS OF BIAS CONDITIONS

Class A. The valve and transistor amplifiers so far considered have been biased in such a way that with, say, sinusoidal excitation the rise and the fall in output current (i.e. either anode or collector current) on successive half cycles have been equal. When biased in this way, the device is said to be operating under Class A conditions. In Class A operation, which is normal for small signal amplifiers, the output current flows throughout the whole of the 360° of the signal cycle.

Class B and AB. If a transistor or valve is so biased that with no input signal, the standing output current is zero, the device is said to be operating under Class B conditions. Output current then flows for half, or 180° of the signal cycle. A condition in which the no-signal standing current is small rather than zero, so that the angle of flow is slightly greater than 180°, is referred to as Class AB.

Class C. If the bias condition in the amplifier stage causes the angle of current flow to be appreciably less than 180°, Class C operation is involved.

Class B (or AB) and C conditions of bias are normally restricted to those stages of amplifiers designed to produce a relatively large output of power.

POWER AMPLIFIERS

Although all valves produce a certain power in their anode loads the term *power amplifier* is restricted to cases where power output is the chief consideration, as opposed to a voltage amplifier in which gain is the only consideration.

Valves in the output stage of an amplifier which drives a power actuated device are chosen for their power handling capabilities, and the circuit is designed to feed the maximum power to the load for a given input voltage. To provide large power a high value of anode current and large anode voltage are required.

In general, the actual load impedance differs from the optimum load required by the valve, and so power amplifiers usually have the load coupled to the valve through a transformer. The case of a resistive load is shown in Fig. 8.14. If the shunting effect of the transformer primary can be ignored together with the effects of magnetic leakage and shunt capacitance, the load presented to the valve is then R/n^2 (Fig. 8.14b). When R is small, n is less than unity.

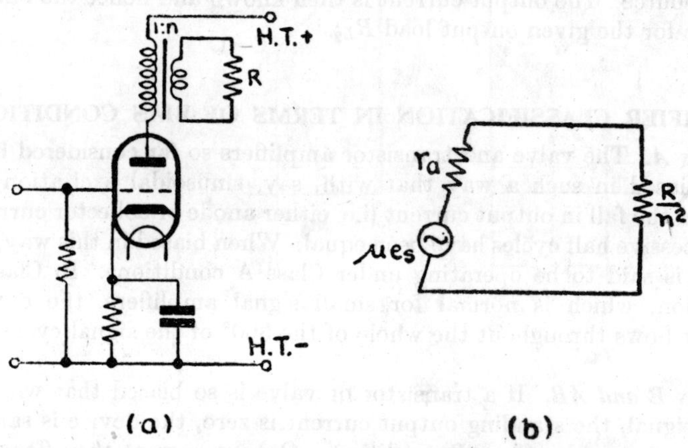

Fig. 8.14. Transformer coupled load.

Optimum Load for a Triode Class A Amplifier Stage

If a triode valve is used under class A conditions, the operation is restricted to the linear regions of its characteristics. Such a restriction affects the conditions for maximum power output. The maximum undistorted power output obtainable depends on the input voltage e_s and the load resistance R, on the ***assumption that the high-tension supply voltage is fixed.*** The maximum permissible input voltage is determined by the extent of the linearity of the dynamic characteristic. The limits are presented by curvature towards cut-off and the curvature at the top of the characteristic due to the presence of grid current. For the distortion to be small, operation will be restricted to the range AB of the dynamic characteristic shown in Fig. 8.15a. The working range of grid voltage is then that represented by CD. This corresponds to the maximum peak-to-peak voltage for e_s the input voltage, and clearly the steady bias voltage should have the value $CD/2 = E_c$. With the maximum input voltage fixed in this way, it is only necessary to find how the output power varies with the value of the load, R_L, presented to the valve. This may be achieved by considering the anode current/anode voltage characteristics of the valve, and the load line corresponding to R_L (Fig. 8.15b). If the load is transformer-coupled, as indicated in Fig. 8.14, then

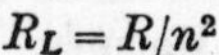

$$R_L = R/n^2$$

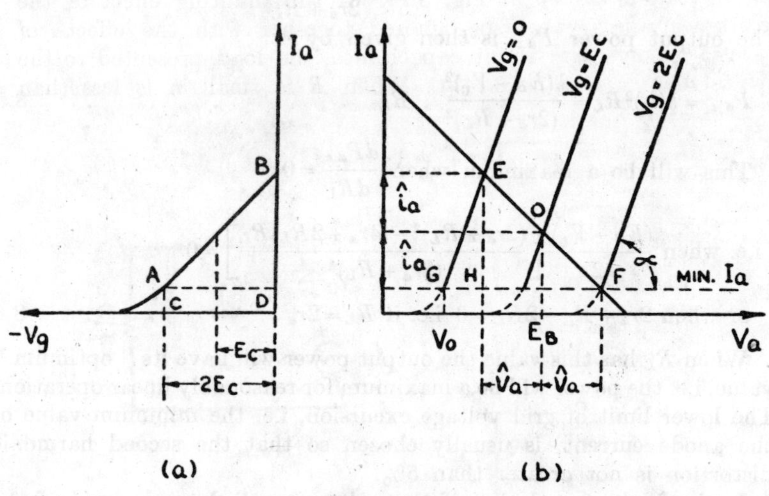

Fig. 8.15.

If the d.c. resistance of the primary winding of the transformer is ignored, and the operating point on the characteristics is O, then this point gives the steady value of anode current for an anode supply voltage of E_B; the straight line EOF, drawn through the operating point O with a slope of $-1/R_L$, is the *a.c.* or *dynamic* load line for the load R_L. If now the input grid voltage is an alternating quantity which has a peak value equal to the bias voltage E_c, then the anode-current will have an alternating component of peak value $\hat{\imath}_a$; this will produce an alternating component of anode voltage with a peak value of $\hat{v}_a$, where

$$\hat{v}_a = \hat{\imath}_a R_L$$

and so the anode voltage will vary between $E_B + \hat{v}_a$, and $E_B - \hat{v}_a$.

If the limits of grid excursion are fixed as above, the operating portion of the a.c. load line is EF. The point E represents the minimum value of the anode voltage for one limit of the grid swing whilst F represents the other limit when the grid has its maximum negative value.

If the reasonable approximation is made that the I_a/V_a curves are parallel straight lines above the minimum value of anode current and have a slope given by $\cot\alpha = r_a$ then from Fig. 8.15b,

$$GH = EH \cot\alpha$$

$$\text{and } E_B - V_0 = \hat{v}_a + 2\hat{\imath}_a r_a = \hat{\imath}_a R_L + 2\hat{\imath}_a r_a$$

$$\therefore \hat{\imath}_a = \frac{E_B - V_0}{2r_a + R_L}$$

The output power $P_{a.c.}$ is then given by

$$P_{a.c.} = \tfrac{1}{2}(\hat{\imath}_a)^2 R_L = \frac{\tfrac{1}{2}(E_B - V_0)^2}{(2r_a + R_L)^2} \cdot R_L \quad . \quad . \quad . \quad . \quad . \quad 8.5$$

This will be a maximum when $\dfrac{dP_{a.c.}}{dR_L} = 0$

$$\text{i.e. when } \frac{(E_B - V_0)^2}{2}\left[\frac{(2r_a + R_L)^2 - (4r_a + 2R_L)R_L}{(2r_a + R_L)^4}\right] = 0$$

or when $2r_a + R_L - 2R_L = 0$ i.e. if $R_L = 2r_a$ 8.6

When R_L has this value the output power will have its " optimum " value, i.e. the power will be a maximum for reasonably linear operation. The lower limit of grid voltage excursion, i.e. the minimum value of the anode current, is usually chosen so that the second harmonic distortion is not greater than 5%.

It should be noted that if the voltage applied to the grid of the valve is smaller than that considered, and the only variable is the magnitude of the anode load, then the variation of the anode load will give a maximum power output when the anode load is equal to the valve anode resistance, which is in agreement with the maximum power transfer theorem. This particular value of maximum power, however, is less than the absolute maximum which depends on the magnitude of the grid voltage swing.

If the transformer which couples the actual load R to the valve has a transformation ratio n, then for the optimum load (R_L') for the valve

$$n=\sqrt{\frac{\text{Actual Load Resistance }(R)}{\text{Optimum Load Resistance }(R_L')}} \qquad 8.7$$

If R_L' is made equal to twice r_a then equation 8.5 gives the power output as

$$P_{a.c.}=\frac{\frac{1}{2}(E_B-V_0)^2 2r_a}{16r_a^2}\simeq\frac{E_B^2}{16r_a} \qquad . \quad . \quad . \qquad 8.8$$

if $E_B>>V_0$. This will be true when the initial curvature in the characteristics is small compared with the operating range.

Optimum Load for a Pentode Class A Power Amplifier

The treatment applied above to obtain the best load for a triode may also be applied to a pentode, or tetrode, although variations arise because of the difference in form of the I_a/V_a characteristics. The problem in the case of the pentode is further complicated by the fact that the anode characteristics are not so evenly spaced for equal increments of grid voltage (Fig. 8.16), and are spaced closer together as the grid voltage is made increasingly negative.

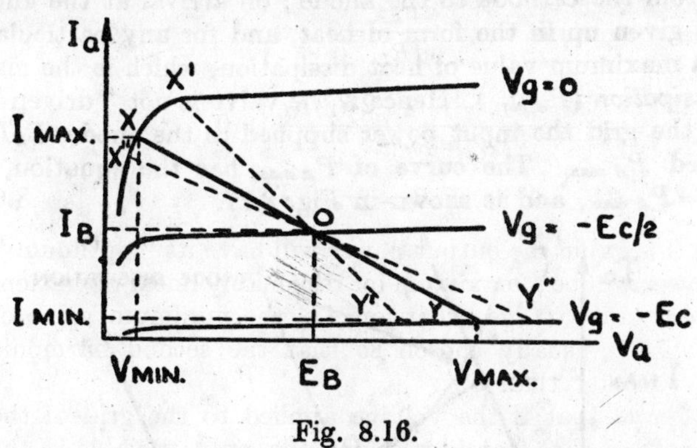

Fig. 8.16.

In Fig. 8.16, O is the operating point, determined by the H.T. supply voltage E_B and a value of bias E_C approximately midway between the zero bias and the value which causes curvature in the dynamic mutual characteristic.

Load lines are drawn through O corresponding to various values of a.c. load. The load line chosen is that which gives approximately equal changes in anode current and anode voltage (i.e. $OX \simeq OY$).

If the difference between the positive and negative excursion of the grid is still too large to be tolerated, the input voltage swing at the grid must then be reduced until the difference between the two half cycles gives a permissible value of distortion.

Unlike the triode, the optimum load for a pentode with a transformer coupled load is usually less than r_a, and may be of the order of $0{\cdot}1r_a$

Anode Dissipation

In discussing the maximum power obtainable from a valve it was assumed that the high-tension supply voltage was fixed. This value is decided by the maximum anode dissipation and the maximum permissible anode voltage.

If the high-tension supply has a value of E_B, and the steady anode current, in the absence of an input voltage at the grid, is I_B, then the power supplied by the high-tension source is $E_B I_B$. If the load is coupled to the valve through a transformer, the only resistance to the direct current is the negligibly small resistance of the primary winding of the transformer, and so all power supplied by the high-tension source is dissipated by the valve. The power supctrds is equal to the kinetic energy gained per second by the eleponlie in passing from the cathode to the anode ; on arrival at the anode this energy is given up in the form of heat, and for any particular valve there is a maximum value of heat dissipation, which is the maximum *anode dissipation* ($P_{A\,max}$). Hence if the valve is not "driven" by an input at the grid the input power supplied to the anode, $E_B I_B$, must not exceed $P_{A\,max}$. The curve of $P_{A\,max}$ has the equation, $I_a V_a =$ constant $= P_{A\,max}$, and is shown in Fig. 8.17.

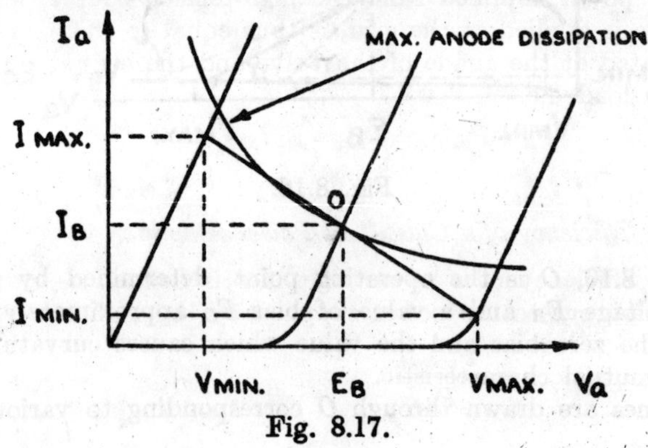

Fig. 8.17.

If an alternating voltage is applied to the grid of the valve, the anode current and anode voltage alternate in antiphase, i.e. the current is a maximum when the anode potential is at its lowest point, and the anode current is a minimum when the anode voltage has its maximum value ; under this condition, the average kinetic energy of all the electrons reaching the anode is lower than would be the case if the applied grid voltage was absent. The application of an input to the grid of the valve thus decreases the power dissipation at the anode. This can be confirmed in mathematical terms as follows.

If an alternating voltage is applied to the grid, the anode current and anode voltage will contain an alternating component, and may be expressed as

$$i_a = (I_B + \hat{i}_a \sin \omega t)$$

$$\text{and } v_a = [E_B + \hat{v}_a \sin (\omega t + \pi)]$$

where $\hat{i}_a$ and $\hat{v}_a$ are the maximum values of the alternating components of the anode current and anode voltage respectively. The instantaneous power (p) dissipated by the valve is then given by

$$p = v_a i_a = (I_B + \hat{i}_a \sin \omega t)[E_B + \hat{v}_a \sin (\omega t + \pi)]$$

$$= (I_B + \hat{i}_a \sin \omega t)(E_B - \hat{v}_a \sin \omega t)$$

$$= E_B I_B - \frac{\hat{v}_a \hat{i}_a}{2} + [\hat{i}_a E_B \sin \omega t - \hat{v}_a I_B \sin \omega t + (\hat{i}_a \hat{v}_a \cos 2\omega t)/2]$$

The terms in the square brackets have a mean value which is zero, if taken over a whole cycle, and so the mean value of power (P) dissipated by the valve is

$$P = E_B I_B - \frac{\hat{v}_a \hat{i}_a}{2}$$

which shows that the power dissipated by the valve is smaller when an input voltage is supplied at the grid.

The power supplied from the high-tension source, when an input voltage is applied at the grid, is thus equal to the sum of the power dissipated at the anode of the valve and the output power delivered to the load, i.e.

$$P_A + P_{output} = P_{d.c.} = E_B I_B$$

Anode Efficiency of a Class "A" Power Amplifier

The efficiency of a power amplifier is defined as the ratio of the power output to the power supplied by the high tension source, i.e.

$$\eta = \frac{P_{output}}{P_{d.c.}}$$

It will be seen in Fig. 8.17 that the output power due to an alternating voltage at the grid is given by

$$P_{output} = \frac{(I_{max.} - I_{min.})(V_{max.} - V_{min.})}{8}$$

if $V_{max.} - V_{min.} = 2(E_B - V_{min.})$

and $I_{max.} - I_{min.} = 2(I_B - I_{min.})$

$$\text{then } P_{output} = \tfrac{1}{2}(I_B - I_{min.})(E_B - V_{min.})$$

$$= \frac{E_B I_B}{2}\left(1 - \frac{I_{min.}}{I_B}\right)\left(1 - \frac{V_{min.}}{E_B}\right)$$

and the efficiency is then

$$= \frac{1}{2}\left(1 - \frac{I_{min.}}{I_B}\right)\left(1 - \frac{V_{min.}}{E_B}\right) \quad . \quad . \quad 8.9$$

In the extreme case if $I_{min.}$ and $V_{min.}$ are each equal to zero the efficiency is 50%.

This efficiency is achieved if the load is coupled to the valve through a transformer; if the load is a resistor connected directly in the anode circuit the voltage of the anode is then always less than the supply voltage E_B, and the efficiency can be shown to have a maximum value of 25%.

If the pentode is compared with the triode, it will be seen that V_{min} (the anode potential when the current has its maximum value) is smaller for the pentode than for the triode, and so the pentode has the higher efficiency.

VALVES IN PARALLEL

In some applications, the power delivered by a single valve may be insufficient. In the absence of a valve capable of handling an increased power, two or more valves may be used in parallel, i.e. with the corresponding electrodes connected to each other. A combination of n similar valves connected in parallel will thus have an anode current n times that of a single valve. The anode voltage swing will be the same as for a single valve. The parallel connected valves will thus function as an equivalent single valve which has n times the current and an anode resistance $1/n$th of one valve. The combination will then be able to deliver n times the power of a single valve to a load which is $1/n$ that for a single valve. The performance of the whole stage can be deduced from the I_a/V_a curves for one valve merely by multiplying the anode current scale by the number of valves it is proposed to use.

VALVES IN PUSH-PULL

As an alternative to parallel connection, valves may be used in *push-pull.* Fig. 8.18 shows two valves connected in this way (V_2 and V_3). These valves are fed from the previous stage (V_1) by means of a transformer which has the centre tap of its secondary winding connected to earth. Each of the push-pull valves receives half of the available voltage across the secondary of the input transformer, the voltages at the grids of the two valves being in anti-phase.

The anode currents in the two valves have a phase difference of 180° and are added together by passing them through the two halves of the output transformer in opposite directions. The voltage induced in the secondary of the output transformer thus arises from the difference of the two anode currents flowing through the primary windings.

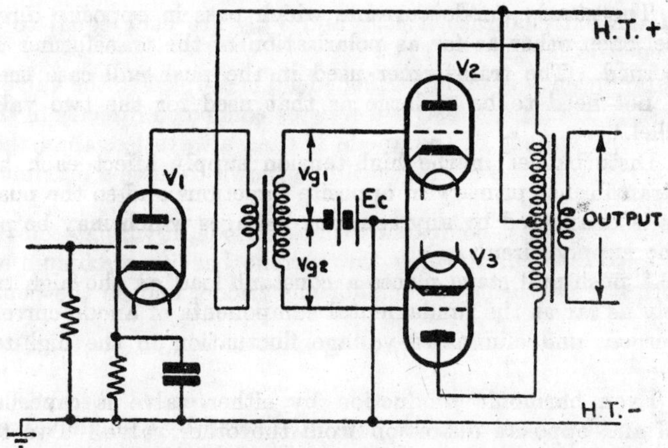

Fig. 8.18. Push-pull stage with transformer input.

If two similar valves are used and the anode current is expressed in terms of a power series of the grid voltage, then

$$i_a = av_g + bv_g^2 + cv_g^3 + dv_g^4 + \ldots \text{ etc.}$$

The current flowing in the output transformer is

$$I_a = I_{a1} - I_{a2}$$

and if an alternating voltage is applied to the input so that

$$v_g = V \sin \omega t$$

$$\text{then } v_{g1} = V \sin \omega t$$

$$\text{and } v_{g2} = -V \sin \omega t$$

$$\text{and hence } I_a = (aV \sin \omega t + bV^2 \sin^2 \omega t + cV^3 \sin^3 \omega t + \ldots)$$
$$- (-aV \sin \omega t + bV^2 \sin^2 \omega t - cV^3 \sin^3 \omega t + \ldots)$$
$$= 2aV \sin \omega t + 2cV^3 \sin^3 \omega t$$
$$= (2aV + \tfrac{3}{2}cV^3) \sin \omega t - \frac{cV^3}{2} \sin 3\omega t$$

The secondary current and voltage then contain odd powers of ωt and so the push-pull arrangement contains only odd harmonics of the applied voltage in the output, provided that the two valves have similar characteristics.

Compared with the parallel arrangement the push-pull connection has the following advantages :—

1. The steady anode currents which pass in opposite directions cancel each other as far as polarisation of the transformer core is concerned. The transformer used in the push-pull case therefore does not need to be as large as that used for the two valves in parallel.
2. Disturbances in the high-tension supply affect each half of the transformer primary in opposite directions and so the push-pull stage is unaffected by any spurious voltages which may be present in the supply circuit.
3. A push-pull stage places a constant load on the high tension supply as far as the fundamental components of anode current are concerned, and eliminates voltage fluctuation in the high-tension source.
4. Even harmonic production by either valve is cancelled by equal and opposite distortion from the other valve. Two triodes will thus give a larger undistorted output when connected in push-pull than they would if connected in parallel. In pentodes where the distortion is mainly third harmonic (see chapter 9) this advantage does not apply.

An additional point is that the push-pull stage offers a balanced input with respect to earth which may be an advantage, in some cases where the voltage to be amplified is so balanced.

Power Output and Load Line for a Push-Pull Stage

The equivalent circuit of the push-pull stage of Fig. 8.18 is shown in Fig. 8.19a, if the load connected to the secondary winding is a resistance R. If both valves are matched so that $i_{a_1} = i_{a_2} = i_a$, no current flows in the branch ab and this connection may be omitted, so that

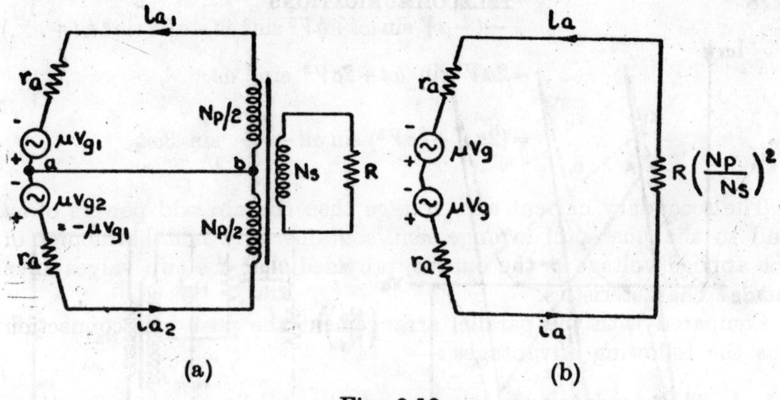

Fig. 8.19.

the equivalent circuit may be simplified to that of Fig. 8.19b assuming the output transformer to be ideal.

If v_g is the r.m.s. value of the alternating grid voltage then the r.m.s. value of the alternating component of anode current is given by,

$$\frac{2\mu v_g}{2r_a + \left(\frac{N_p}{N_s}\right)^2 R}$$

and the power output P is expressed by

$$P = \frac{4\mu^2 v_g^2}{\left[2r_a + \left(\frac{N_p}{N_s}\right)^2 R\right]^2} \cdot \left(\frac{N_p}{N_s}\right)^2 R$$

If $N_p/N_s = 2n$, then

$$P = \frac{16\mu^2 v_g^2 n^2 R}{[2r_a + 4n^2 R]^2} = \frac{\mu^2 v_g^2 n^2 R}{[r_a/2 + n^2 R]^2} \quad . \quad . \quad 8.10$$

The power output of the push-pull stage may also be considered by treating the stage in terms of the equivalent single valve. It is then necessary to deal with the *composite* characteristics. These are obtained by reversing one set of the valve characteristics, both horizontally and vertically, so that at the two operating points O_1 and O_2 the values of the steady anode voltage coincide. (Fig. 8.20a.)

The composite characteristics are obtained by substracting the values of one set of curves from those of the other, and are then the characteristics of the equivalent single valve, as the difference between the anode currents of the two valves corresponds to the anode current of the equivalent single valve.

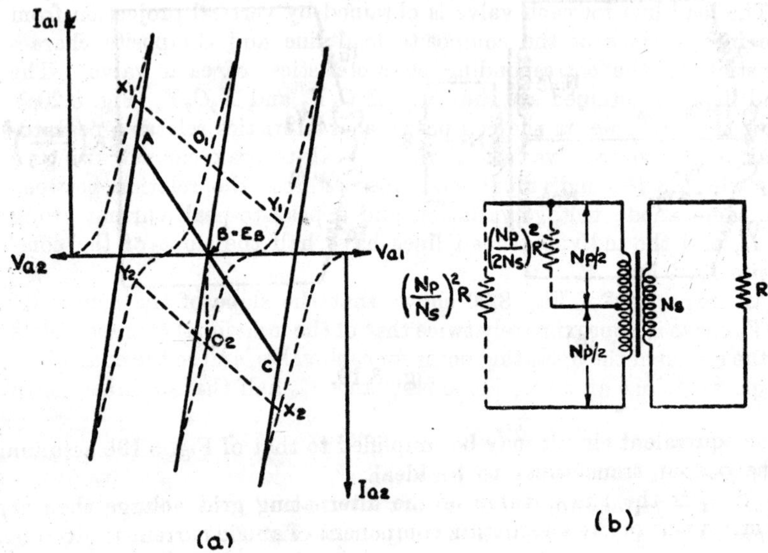

Fig. 8.20. Composite characteristics for a push-pull stage.

The magnetic flux in the transformer core is proportional to the load current I_L which is the difference in the anode currents of the valves. As this difference varies periodically it is equivalent to an alternating current in the primary winding of the transformer and gives rise to a potential difference across each half of the primary of V_L where

$$V_L = I_L R_L$$

when R_L is the impedance seen at each half of the primary winding; this impedance is $(N_p/2N_s)^2 R$.

The load line drawn on the composite characteristics must thus have a slope corresponding to R_L, and so is equivalent to the load presented by one half of the primary winding.

The composite load line AC shown in Fig. 8.20a will then have a slope of $1/R_L$. The co-ordinates of the composite operating point are the H.T. supply voltage E_B and zero anode current (if the two valves are matched).

The anode-to-anode load, i.e. the load viewed across the whole of the primary is

$$= \left(\frac{N_p}{N_s}\right)^2 R = 4R_L$$

and so the composite load for the equivalent single valve is one quarter of the anode-to-anode load.

The load line for each valve is obtained by vertical projection from the intersections of the composite load line and composite characteristics, to the corresponding characteristics, of each valve. The load lines so obtained are shown at $X_1O_1Y_1$ and $X_2O_2Y_2$ (Fig. 8.20a). Now the load line on the composite characteristics relates a peak-to-peak anode voltage variation with a peak-to-peak current swing of $2I_a$ whereas the individual load lines express the relation between the same anode voltage variation and a peak-to-peak current swing of I_a, and the individual load lines have half the slope of the composite load line *AC*.

An inspection of Fig. 8.20 shows that the slope of the composite I_a/V_a curve is approximately twice that of the individual characteristics in the region of the operating point for each valve, and so the equivalent single valve has an anode slope resistance r_{as} half that of either valve

$$\text{i.e. } r_{as} \simeq r_a/2$$

If the grid voltage applied to the equivalent single valve is the same as the voltage applied to one of the push-pull valves, the equivalent single valve has the equivalent circuit of Fig. 8.21.

If the output current may be assumed to be sinusoidal, and to have a maximum value of $2I_a$, then the output power, P, is

$$P = (I^2_{r.m.s.})R_L$$

$$= \frac{\mu^2 v_g^2}{(r_a/2 + R_L)^2} \cdot R_L$$

now $R_L = (N_p/2N_s)^2 R = n^2 R$, and so

$$P = \frac{\mu^2 v_g^2 n^2 R}{(r_a/2 + n^2 R)^2} \quad . \quad . \quad . \quad . \quad . \quad 8.11$$

which is identical with the result obtained in equation 8.10.

The circuit of Fig. 8.21 is in effect the equivalent circuit for two valves in parallel and only represents the push-pull stage as far as the power output is concerned.

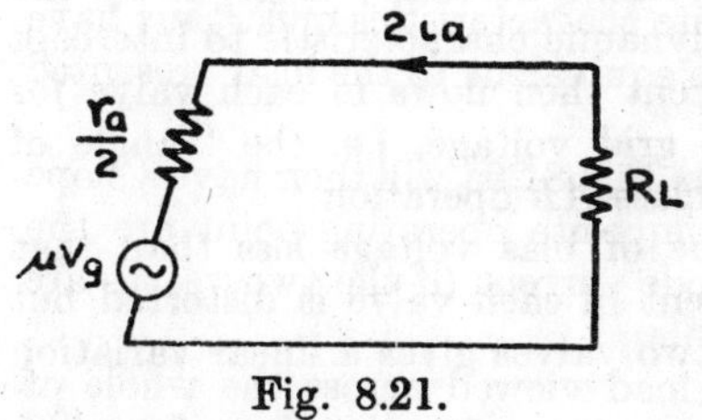

Fig. 8.21.

Class B Amplifiers

It has been mentioned earlier in this chapter that amplifiers may be classified according to their operating conditions. All the amplifiers so far discussed have been Class *A* amplifiers. The steady bias voltage has had a value so that the valves take some anode current over the whole cycle of the applied grid voltage, whilst the input has been restricted to the linear region of the characteristic.

In Class *B* operation the valves are biased at or near their "cut-off" point so that in the absence of an applied grid voltage, the anode current is zero or some small value. The application of an input voltage then causes a rise in the value of the mean anode current. (This variation of anode current with signal amplitude prohibits the use of a cathode bias resistor, and the appropriate grid bias voltage must be obtained from some other source.)

Because of the small standing current under quiescent conditions, a Class *B* amplifier stage has a greater anode efficiency than a corresponding Class *A* stage. A Class *C* amplifier, in which the valve is biased beyond "cut-off", has a still higher anode efficiency, but its use is restricted to tuned high-frequency amplifiers, which are discussed in chapter 10.

If the amplifier output is to be a reproduction of the input voltage waveform, as in speech frequency amplifiers, then Class *B* operation can only be employed in a push-pull arrangement.

Class B Push-Pull

Suppose a pair of valves are set up in the same circuit as was used for class *A* push-pull (Fig. 8.18). If the bias voltage E_c is such that it reduces the anode current to zero, the dynamic characteristics will be as shown in Fig. 8.22a. It will be seen that this gives rise to distortion because of the curvature in the characteristics and a sinusoidal input voltage produces a non-sinusoidal anode current.

This defect in the class *B* stage may be eliminated if the bias voltage E_c is reduced in value so that there is a small steady current in each valve. (The actual value of bias voltage necessary is given by the projection of the linear part of the dynamic characteristic to intercept the grid voltage axis). Anode current then flows in each valve for slightly more than half a cycle of grid voltage, i.e. the "angle of flow" is greater than 180°. This is class *AB* operation.

It can be seen that with a value of bias voltage less than that required for cut-off, the anode current in each valve is distorted but the composite characteristic of the two valves gives a linear variation of anode current with grid voltage.

If the grid bias is adjusted as for Fig. 8.22b the composite anode current anode voltage characteristics for the class *AB* push-pull stage are then as shown in Fig. 8.23. It will be seen that, unlike the corresponding class *A* characteristics, the slope is the same as that of the individual valves over a wide range. This, of course, arises from the

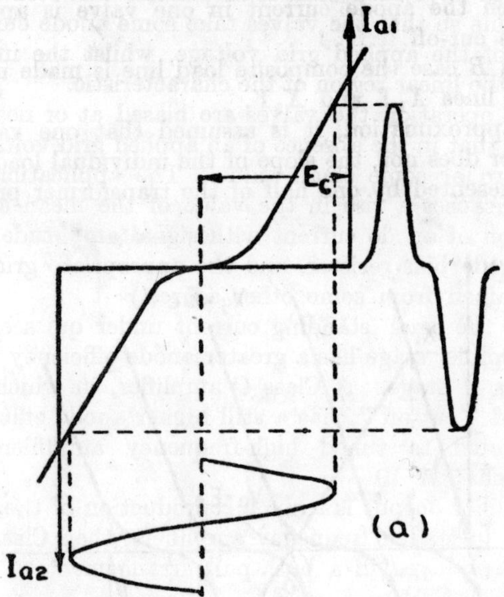

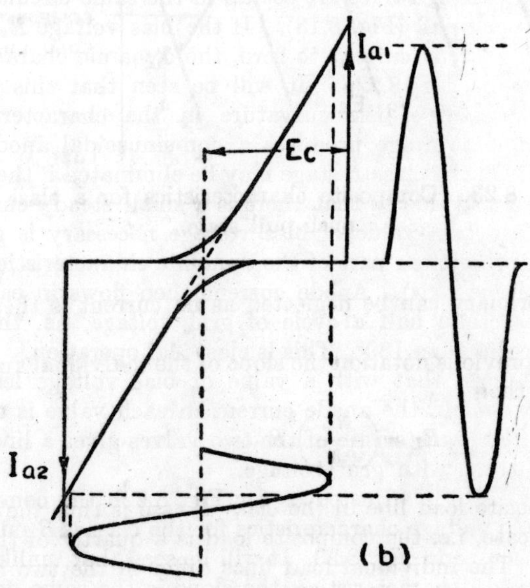

Fig. 8.22.

fact that when the anode current in one valve is appreciable the other valve is cut-off.

In the class *B* case the composite load line is made up of the two separate load lines X_1Y and X_2Y.

If, as an approximation, it is assumed that one valve conducts while the other does not, the slope of the individual load lines is that of the load presented by one half of the transformer primary. (The

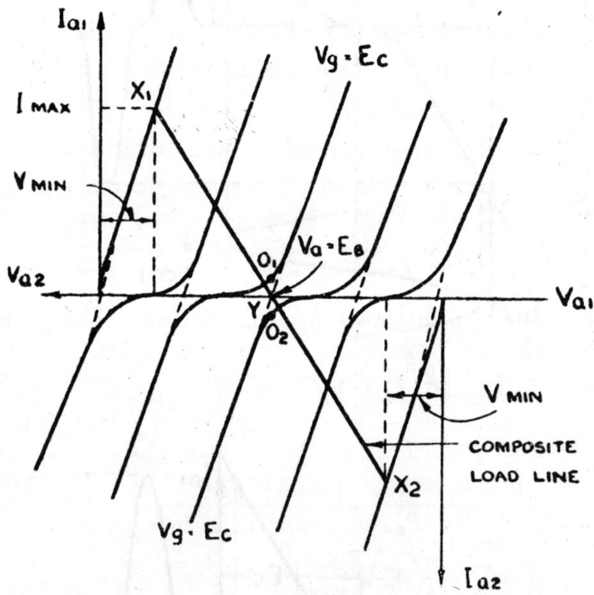

Fig. 8.23. Composite characteristics for a class *AB* push-pull stage.

other half primary can be neglected as no current is then flowing in it.)

With the previous notation the slope of the individual and composite load lines is then

$$R_L = \left(\frac{N_p}{2N_s}\right)^2 R$$

The composite load line in the class *B* case is thus the same as for the class *A* case, i.e. the composite load is a quarter of the anode-to-anode load. The individual load lines differ in the two cases as can be seen by comparing Figs. 8.20a and 8.23.

Anode Efficiency of a Class B Amplifier Stage

The power output from an amplifier when subjected to an alternating input is

$$P_{output} = \frac{1}{2} \text{ (Peak Anode Voltage Swing)} \times \text{(Peak Anode Current Swing)}$$

The load line X_1YX_2 in Fig. 8.23 has a peak anode voltage swing of $E_B - V_{min.}$ and a peak anode current swing of $I_{max.}$

$$\therefore P_{output} = \frac{1}{2} I_{max.} (E_B - V_{min.})$$

The power supplied by the high-tension source

$$P_{d.c.} = 2I_BE_B$$

where I_B = mean current of each valve.

If the approximation is made that the valves have anode currents which consist of half sine waves spaced by a half period, then

$$I_B = \frac{1}{\pi} I_{max.}$$

(as the mean value of a sine wave over half a period is $2/\pi$ times the maximum value).

$$\therefore P_{d.c.} = \frac{2}{\pi} I_{max.} E_B$$

and hence the anode efficiency of the stage is given by

$$\eta = \frac{P_{output}}{P_{d.c.}} = \frac{\frac{1}{2} I_{max.} (E_B - V_{min.})}{2/\pi \ I_{max.} E_B}$$

$$= \frac{\pi}{4}\left(1 - \frac{V_{min.}}{E_B}\right) \quad . \quad . \quad . \quad . \quad 8.12$$

In the extreme case, if $V_{min.}/E_B$ approaches zero, the anode efficiency approaches 78·5%.

The increased efficiency obtained by class *B* operation and the consequent saving in power supplied by the high-tension source may be of no consequence in low power amplifiers. In high-power amplifiers such as modulators for high-power radio transmitters, the question of cost may become important.

TRANSISTOR POWER AMPLIFIERS

The previous sections have dealt with power amplifiers incorporating thermionic valves, but the discussion may also be applied to circuits containing transistors. Thus in place of the valve anode dissipation, the transistor has a collector dissipation. Any particular type has a maximum collector power dissipation $P_{c\ max}$, which is fixed for any

particular ambient temperature. A maximum power hyperbola, given by

$$P_{c\ max} = I_c V_c$$

may be drawn on the output characteristics as in Fig. 8.17. The permissible working region is then the area contained by the hyperbola and collector current and voltage axes. Transistor manufacturers specify in addition a maximum value for collector voltage and for collector current. Thermal stability is important as an increase in temperature causes an increase in leakage current with further increase of temperature which may cause *thermal runaway* and destruction of the junction. *Heat sinks* in good thermal contact with the transistor are commonly used to improve the dissipation of heat.

Class A Stage. The simplest form of Class A power amplifier, with a transformer-coupled load is shown in Fig. 8.24. In the absence of an input signal, the collector voltage is that of the supply, V_{cc}, because of the low resistance of the output transformer primary winding. The maximum value of input signal then produces a peak collector voltage swing of nearly V_{cc}, so that the collector voltage varies from a small value to nearly twice V_{cc}. The collector current then varies from near zero to about twice the no-signal value. As in the corresponding valve circuit, the maximum theoretical efficiency is 50%.

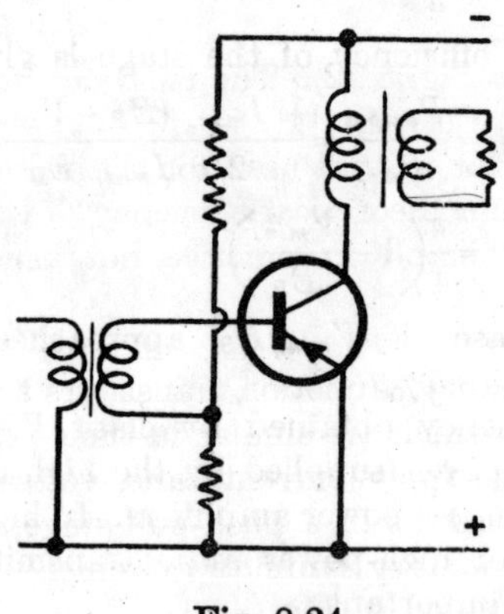

Fig. 8.24.

If a resistive load connected directly to the collector is used the steady (i.e. no-signal collector voltage is half V_{cc}. An alternating signal can then produce a peak swing of $V_{cc}/2$, to give a maximum theoretical efficiency of 25%.

Two transistors may be used in a Class A push-pull circuit with a transformer-coupled load. In practice because of the relatively large standing dissipation it is more usual to employ a Class B push-pull stage.

Class B Stage. A common form of Class B stage is shown in Fig. 8.25 which also shows the preceding driver stage. A pair of matched transistors are always preferable. There is then no resultant flow due to direct current in the output transformer, although a small forward bias is commonly applied to the base-emitter junctions to eliminate

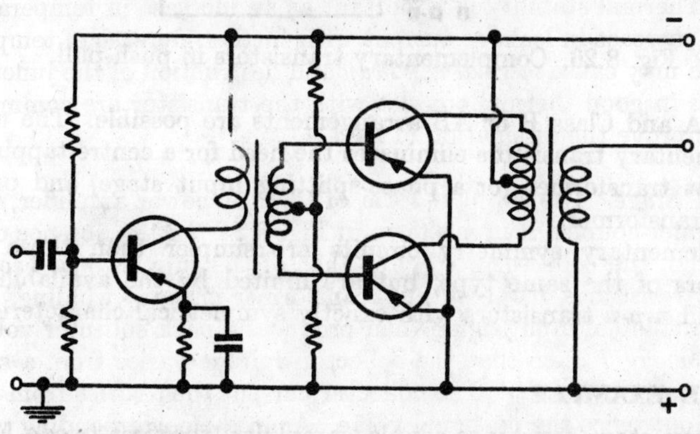

Fig. 8.25. Push-pull circuit with driver stage.

crossover distortion (see Fig. 8.22). The push-pull stage then operates in Class AB rather than Class B.

By an argument similar to that used for the valve circuit it can be shown that the maximum theoretical efficiency of the Class B stage is 78·5%. The value attainable in practice not usually greater than 60–70%.

Complementary Symmetry. Junction transistors are available either as *p-n-p* or *n-p-n* types which are similar in their principles and characteristics, except that supply currents and voltages differ in sign. When both types are used, as in a push-pull stage, the connection is referred to as a complementary symmetry circuit.

The principle is illustrated in Fig. 8.26. If the two transistors are connected as shown, the current in one transistor conducts (or increases) while the other is non-conducting (or decreases) as the signal that produces forward bias in one transistor gives reverse bias on the other. On the positive half cycle of an alternating input signal, the *n-p-n* transistor in Fig. 8.26 is forward biased and will thus conduct. Reversal of the input polarity will cause the *p-n-p* transistor to conduct.

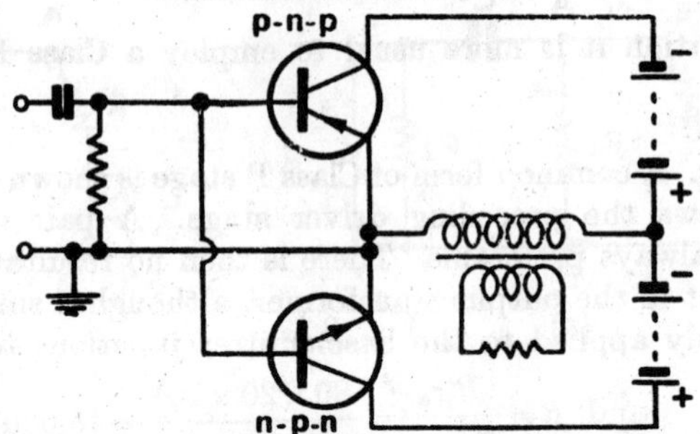

Fig. 8.26. Complementary transistors in push-pull.

Class A and Class B or AB arrangements are possible. The use of complementary transistors eliminates the need for a centre-tapping on the input transformer (or a phase-splitting input stage) and on the output transformer.

Complementary symmetry circuits are simpler than those with transistors of the same type, but are limited by the availability of *p-n-p* and *n-p-n* transistors with exactly symmetrical characteristics.

WORKED EXAMPLE

In a two-stage resistance-coupled amplifier, the first triode has an amplification factor of 25 and a slope resistance of 20,000 ohms. A non-inductive load resistance of 80,000 ohms is connected in its anode circuit.

If the coupling condenser and grid leak resistance have values of 0·1 μF and 200,000 ohms respectively, calculate the magnitude of the voltage applied to the grid of the second valve for 1 V at a frequency of 100 Hz applied to the grid of the first valve. Assume the valve to be operated within the linear range of its characteristics.

L.U. Ext. Telecomm. 1945.

The equivalent circuit for the first valve is shown in Fig. 8.27a. The problem is thus the calculation of the output voltage for a known value of applied grid voltage. The direct calculation from the equivalent circuit is quite straightforward. A considerable simplification can be made if Thévenin's theorem is applied to the circuit to the left of the terminals *AB*. The modified equivalent circuit then becomes that of Fig. 8.27b.

With the values given $E = 25$ V, and so

$$E' = \frac{ER_1}{R_1 + r_a} = \frac{25 \times 80 \times 10^3}{(80+20) \times 10^3} = 20 \text{ V}$$

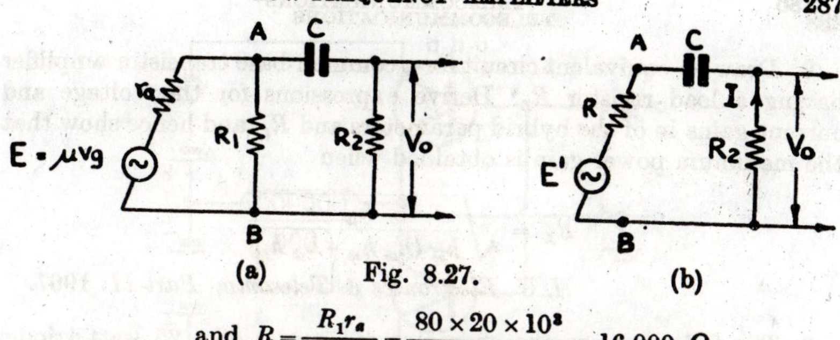

Fig. 8.27.

$$\text{and } R=\frac{R_1 r_a}{R_1+r_a}=\frac{80\times 20\times 10^3}{(80+20)\times 10^3}=16{,}000\ \Omega$$

At 100 Hz, $1/j\omega C=-j10^6/(6{\cdot}28\times 100\times 0{\cdot}1)=-j0{\cdot}01593\times 10^6$

Hence the current I in Fig. 8.20b is given by

$$I=\frac{20}{(0{\cdot}216\times 10^6)-j(0{\cdot}01593\times 10^6)}$$

and the output voltage V_0 is thus

$$V_0=\frac{20\times 2\times 10^5}{(0{\cdot}216\times 10^6)-j(0{\cdot}01593\times 10^6)}=18{\cdot}5$$

The voltage applied to the second valve at 100 c/s is thus = 18·5 V.

EXAMPLES

1. The values of the collector current I_C in an *n-p-n* transistor for a range of collector-emitter voltages V_{CE} and base currents I_B, when connected in the common-emitter configuration are shown below. Plot these characteristics and determine the value of load resistor required, if the steady base current is 80 μA and the corresponding collector-emitter voltage is 4 V when used with a collector supply of 8 V.

V_{CE} (V)	Values of I_C (mA) for I_B (μA) = 40	60	80	100	120
1	1·8	2·8	3·8	4·8	5·7
2	1·9	3·0	4·0	5·0	6·0
4	2·2	3·3	4·3	5·4	6·5
6	2·5	3·6	4·6	5·8	7·0
8	2·8	3·9	5·0	6·2	7·5

Determine the current gain, the maximum and minimum values of the collector voltage, and the r.m.s output voltage for an input signal current (μA) of

$$i_s = 30 \sin \omega t - 10 \sin 3\omega t.$$

L.U. Electronics & Telecomm. part II. 1969.

2. Draw an equivalent circuit for a common-base transistor amplifier having a load resistor R_L. Derive expressions for the voltage and current gains in of the hybrid parameters and R_L, and hence show that the maximum power gain is obtained when

$$R_L = \sqrt{\frac{h_{ib}}{h_{ob}\,(h_{ib}\,h_{ob} - h_{rb}\,h_{fb})}}$$

L.U. Electronics & Telecomm. Part II. 1967.

3. The following are the characteristic curves of a 25 watt triode.

$V_g = 0$	V_a (volts)	24	60	100	150	180
	i_a (mA)	10	30	68	120	154
$V_g = -10{\cdot}7$	V_a	123	150	200	250	
	i_a	10	25	66	120	
$V_g = -21$	V_a	220	250	300	350	
	i_a	10	27	67	119	
$V_g = -32$	V_a	312	350	400		
	i_a	10	29	68		

This valve delivers power to a resistive load by a choke-condenser coupling. Separate grid-bias voltage is provided. It may be assumed that the reactance of the choke is infinite and that of the condenser zero at the operating frequency. The anode supply voltage available is 300 V.

Plot the characteristic curves and determine graphically :—

(a) The value of load resistance in which the maximum power may be developed with as little distortion as possible and the approximate value of that power.

(b) A suitable resistance for the choke.

Indicate by shaded areas on the graph the power dissipated in the load, in the choke, and at the anode of the valve.

L.U. Ext. Telecomm. 1948.

4. Sketch a two-stage common-emitter RC-coupled amplifier and explain simple biasing and interstage coupling arrangements.

Calculate the voltage gain of the second stage if the collector load resistor is 10 kΩ and the transistor has the following parameters: small-signal current gain, $h_{fe} = 60$; input resistance, $h_{ie} = 2$ kΩ; voltage feedback ratio, $h_{re} = 3{\cdot}6 \times 10^{-4}$; and output conductance, $h_{oe} = 12{\cdot}5$ μmho.

The effect of the biasing and coupling components may be ignored.

L.U. Electronics & Telecomm. Part II. 1966.

5. Draw a circuit diagram for a two-stage *RC*-coupled common-emitter amplifier. The transistors in such an amplifier have the following hybrid parameters: $h_{ie} = 1500\Omega$, $h_{fe} = 80$, $h_{oe} = 100\ \mu S$ and h_{re} is negligible.

A $1{\cdot}5\ k\Omega$ load resistor is used for each stage. Draw the a.c. equivalent circuit for frequencies at which the reactance of the coupling capacitor is negligible (the presence of the base bias resistors can also be ignored). Hence calculate the overall current gain if the amplifier is connected to a signal generator having an open-circuit e.m.f. of 5 mV and an internal resistance of 500 Ω. Determine also the corresponding voltage gain.

L.U. Electronics & Telecomm. Part II 1969.

9

DISTORTION AND FEEDBACK IN AMPLIFIERS

This chapter is concerned with a brief consideration of some of the forms of distortion encountered in amplifiers and the modification of amplifier characteristics which may be produced by the application of negative feedback. The amplifiers are assumed to be of low-frequency range, but the ideas involved may often be applied to other forms of amplifier.

DISTORTION IN AMPLIFIERS

Distortion is the name given to the change in waveform which occurs between the input and output of an amplifier (or any electrical transmission system). A distorted output waveform may contain frequency components not present in the input, and if the input is represented by a complex wave, the output may have the various component frequencies altered in amplitude or phase with respect to each other.

Attenuation Distortion

If the input to an amplifier consists of a complex wave, representing either a fundamental frequency and its harmonics, or a number of components of different frequencies, then for all such components to be amplified to the same extent, the amplification must be independent of frequency. If this condition is not met, the amplifier is said to produce *attenuation distortion*, which may thus be defined briefly as distortion due to variation of loss or gain with frequency. Normally most amplifiers have a gain characteristic which varies with frequency, because of the presence of reactive components. This may be diminished if the effect of the reactance is made small over the operating range of frequencies. For amplifiers of narrow bandwidth this is a relatively simple matter, but in wideband amplifiers complex equalising networks may be required. Alternatively, the attenuation distortion may be reduced by the use of negative feedback.

Phase Distortion

If a complex non-sinusoidal signal is to be amplified satisfactorily, the relative phases of the various components must be unaltered by the process of amplification. If this is not so, *phase distortion* is said to be present in the amplifier. Distortion of this nature will occur in the amplifier if the plot of the overall phase shift against frequency is not a straight line which passes through zero on the phase shift axis or through a point which is an integral multiple of π radians. Phase distortion, like attenuation distortion, is caused by the presence of reactive and resistive elements in the amplifier circuits. Phase distortion is relatively unimportant in audio-frequency amplifiers, as the ear is insensitive to moderate changes in phase. In picture transmission however, careful attention has to be paid to the phase characteristic over the operating range of frequency. It should be noted that a single stage of amplification causes a phase shift of 180°, neglecting phase change due to the load, and hence an amplifier with an odd number of stages has an overall phase shift of approximately 180°, while an even number of stages will give zero phase shift.

Non-Linear Distortion

If the gain of an amplifier varies with the instantaneous magnitude of the input signal, *non-linear* distortion is present. It is customary to define[1] sub-divisions of this form of distortion as *amplitude* distortion, *harmonic* distortion, and *intermodulation* distortion. Amplitude distortion is the name given to the lack of constancy of the ratio of the r.m.s. value of the output to that of the input at different amplitudes of the input; it is measured under steady-state conditions with a sine-wave input, and when the output contains other frequencies, the r.m.s. value of the output refers to the fundamental alone. Harmonic distortion refers to the production of harmonic frequencies in the output when a sinusoidal input is applied; it is measured as the ratio of the total r.m.s. voltage of all harmonics in the output to the total r.m.s. voltage at the output. Intermodulation distortion is the production of combination tones in the output when two or more sinusoidal voltages are applied at the input; if the two inputs applied have frequencies f_1 and f_2, the combination tones may be second-order $(f_1 \pm f_2)$, or third-order $(f_1 \pm 2f_2$, or $2f_1 \pm f_2)$, etc.

Non-linear distortion may be caused by curvature in the *dynamic* characteristics of valves or transistors; it may also be caused by the overloading of one (or more) of the stages of an amplifier so that operation extends beyond the linear region of the characteristics. Distortion may also be caused by the use of iron-cored inductors or transformers which have a non-linear flux/current characteristic. In this case if direct current is absent from the windings, and the applied alternating voltage is of sufficient magnitude to cause saturation in the magnetic core, then the peaks of both the negative and positive half-cycles will be flattened, and odd-order harmonics, mainly third, produced ; if there is a steady component of flux in the core, then saturation may only occur on one peak of each cycle of the applied voltage and even order harmonics will be produced.

Non-linear distortion may also arise in valve circuits from the flow of grid current at some point in the operating cycle. Grid current starts to flow as the potential of the grid approaches that of the cathode, and so even in a class *A* amplifier a small amount of grid current may flow on the "positive" peak of the applied voltage, when the grid is only slightly negative with respect to the cathode. This grid current flowing through the external grid-cathode impedance gives rise to a varying unidirectional voltage, a varying load is place on the signal source, and this leads to distortion. This can be diminished by reducing the amplitude of the input voltage, and by decreasing the external grid-cathode impedance.

Distortion due to Curvature in Dynamic I_a V_g Valve Characteristics

(a) Triode Valve. The dynamic anode current/grid voltage curve of a valve is seldom strictly linear. Triode valves have a characteristic of the form shown in Fig. 9.1.

The triode characteristic can be represented to a fair degree of approximation by the equation,

$$I_a = a + bV_g + cV_g^2 \quad . \quad . \quad . \quad . \quad . \quad . \quad 9.1$$

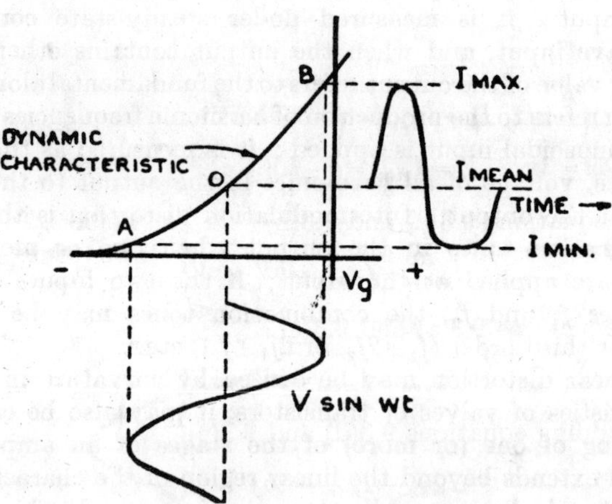

Fig. 9.1. Distortion produced by curvature in dynamic characteristics of a triode valve.

where a is the value of the anode current in the absence of a signal, and b and c are constants.

If $V_g = V \sin \omega t$

then $I_a = a + bV \sin \omega t + cV^2 \sin^2 \omega t$

$$= a + bV \sin \omega t + (cV^2/_2)(1 - \cos 2\omega t)$$

$$= (a + cV^2/_2) + bV \sin \omega t + (cV^2/_2)[\sin(2\omega t - \pi/_2)] \quad . \quad . \quad 9.2$$

Thus with the application of a signal the steady component of anode current has increased by $cV^2/_2$ and in addition to the wanted signal there is a term $(cV^2/_2)[\sin(2\omega t - \pi/_2)]$. This term represents a second harmonic displaced by 45° from the fundamental. The change in the value of the direct component of the anode current can be taken as an indication of the presence of an even harmonic.

If the percentage of *second harmonic* distortion is taken as

$$\frac{\text{Amplitude 2nd Harmonic}}{\text{Amplitude of Fundamental}} \times 100\% \text{ this equals } \frac{cV^2/_2 \times 100}{bV} = \frac{100cV}{2b}\%$$

If the constants b and c are unknown the percentage distortion can be calculated if the maximum, mean and minimum values of the current are obtainable for the conditions of operation. Thus from Fig. 9.1

when $\omega t = 0,\ I_a = I_{mean} = a$ . . . . . . 9.3(a)

and when $\omega t = \pi/2,\ I_a = I_{max.} = a + bV + cV^2$ . . . . 9.3(b)

and at $\omega t = 3\pi/2,\ I_a = I_{min.} = a - bV + cV^2$ . . . 9.3(c)

Then from equations 9.3(a) and 9.3(b)

$$I_{max.} - I_{mean} = bV + cV^2 \quad . \quad . \quad 9.3(d)$$

Also from equations 9.3(a) and 9.3(c)

$$I_{mean} - I_{min.} = bV - cV^2 \quad . \quad . \quad . \quad 9.3(e)$$

Hence by adding equations 9.3(d) and 9.3(e)

$$I_{max.} - I_{min.} = 2bV \quad . \quad . \quad . \quad . \quad 9.3(f)$$

Subtracting equation 9.3(e) from 9.3(d)

$$I_{max.} + I_{min.} - 2I_{mean} = 2cV^2 \quad . \quad . \quad . \quad . \quad 9.3(g)$$

$$\therefore \frac{I_{max.} + I_{min.} - 2I_{mean}}{2(I_{max.} - I_{min.})} = \frac{cV}{2b} \quad . \quad . \quad . \quad . \quad 9.3(h)$$

The percentage second harmonic distortion is thus given by

$$\frac{I_{max.} + I_{min.} - 2I_{mean}}{2(I_{max.} - I_{min.})} \times 100\%$$

for cases where the anode load current is related to the applied grid voltage by equation 9.1. This equation is assumed to represent the dynamic characteristic but may be applied to the static characteristic provided that the anode load is small compared with the slope resistance of the valve.

(b) Pentode Valve. The dynamic grid voltage/anode current characteristic for a pentode is usually of the form shown in Fig. 9.2. This curve has a point of inflection and the curvature increases as the load resistance is increased.

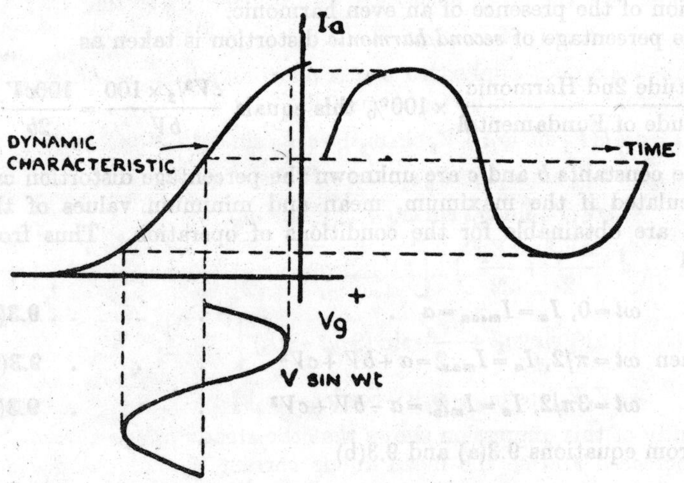

Fig. 9.2. Distortion produced by curvature in dynamic I_a/V_g characteristic for a pentode valve.

The dynamic valve characteristic can be represented by the equation,

$$I_a = a + bV_g + cV_g^2 - dV_g^3 \quad . \quad . \quad . \quad . \quad . \quad 9.4$$

If $V_g = V \sin \omega t$ then

$$I_a = a + bV \sin \omega t + cV^2 \sin^2 \omega t - dV^3 \sin^3 \omega t$$

$$= a + bV \sin \omega t + (cV^2/2)[1 - \cos 2\omega t]$$

$$- (dV^3/4)[3 \sin \omega t - \sin 3\omega t]$$

$$= (a + cV^2/2) + (bV - 3dV^3/4) \sin \omega t$$

$$+ (cV^2/2) \sin (2\omega t - \pi/2) + (dV^3/4) \sin 3\omega t \quad . \quad . \quad 9.5$$

In contrast with the triode case both halves of the input waveform are treated similarly and third harmonic distortion is produced. There is also some second harmonic present but the amplitude of this is small, as the value of c is usually small.

By the use of a technique similar to that adopted for the triode, the distortion may be expressed in terms of the anode current for particular points on the input waveform, though in this case four such points are required.

Intermodulation

In considering non-linearity in the characteristics of a valve it has been seen that the effect is to produce harmonics when the input voltage consists of a single frequency.

Suppose now the input consists of two frequencies so that

$$V_s = V_1 \sin \omega_1 t + V_2 \sin \omega_2 t$$

If this voltage is applied to the triode previously considered, th anode current will then be (equation 9.1.)

$$\begin{aligned} I_a &= a + b(V_1 \sin \omega_1 t + V_2 \sin \omega_2 t) + c(V_1 \sin \omega_1 t + V_2 \sin \omega_2 t)^2 \\ &= a + bV_1 \sin \omega_1 t + bV_2 \sin \omega_2 t + cV_1^2 \sin^2 \omega_1 t \\ &\quad + 2cV_1 V_2 \sin \omega_1 t \sin \omega_2 t + cV_2^2 \sin^2 \omega_2 t \\ &= \left(a + \frac{cV_1^2}{2} + \frac{cV_2^2}{2}\right) + \left[bV_1 \sin \omega_1 t + \frac{cV_1^2}{2} \sin(2\omega_1 t - \pi/_2)\right] \\ &\quad + \left[bV_2 \sin \omega_2 t + \frac{cV_2^2}{2} \sin(2\omega_2 t - \pi/_2)\right] \\ &\quad + cV_1 V_2[\cos(\omega_1 - \omega_2)t - \cos(\omega_1 + \omega_2)t] \qquad 9.6 \end{aligned}$$

A study of this expression shows that the steady anode current has been increased and so the mean anode current in the presence of a signal will be greater than the steady value of anode current when the signal is absent. In addition to the two original frequencies, second harmonics of each frequency are present, while the terms in the last square bracket of equation 9.6 show that there are components of anode current which have frequencies equal to the difference, and the sum of the original frequencies. These components are combination tones and are sometimes referred to as ***intermodulation products***, as they arise from the process of intermodulation in which one frequency "modulates" the other (see chapter 12).

FEEDBACK IN AMPLIFIERS

In any amplifier, or stage of an amplifier, some of the output signal may be fed back to the input. If connected in such a way as to increase the input signal, the amplification will be increased, and the feedback is said to be *positive*; with *negative* feedback, the voltage derived from the output is fed back in antiphase to the input, and the gain is decreased. There are, however, several advantages to be obtained by applying negative feedback. The amplification can be made independent of reasonable changes in supply voltages, or the condition of the valves or transistors; distortion and phase shift in the amplifier may be diminished; the input and output impedances may be modified.

The Effect of Negative Feedback on Amplifier Gain

Consider an amplifier (Fig. 9.3), the gain of which without feedback is A. Now suppose a network be connected from the output to the input. If the output is E and the fraction of the output fed back is β, the voltage at the input terminals will then be seen from Fig. 9.3 to be $e_s + \beta E$.

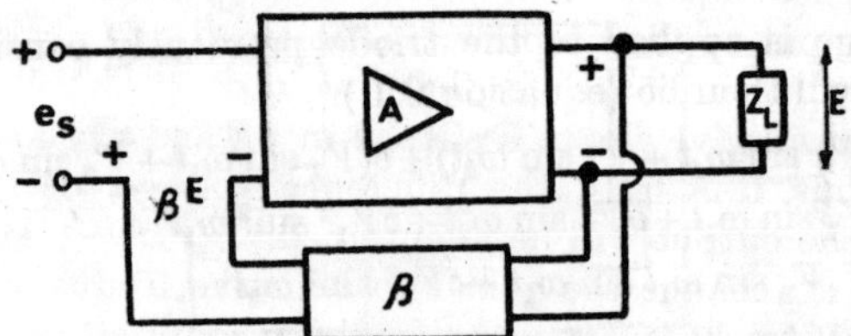

Fig. 9.3. Application of negative feedback to an amplifier.

Thus
$$A(e_s + \beta E) = E, \quad \text{or} \quad E(1 - A\beta) = Ae_s$$
$$\therefore \quad E = Ae_s/(1 - A\beta)$$

The effective amplification

$$E/e_s = \frac{A}{1 - A\beta} \qquad 9.7$$

The loop gain, (i.e. the gain around the loop formed by the amplifier and feedback network) must be negative if negative feedback is desired. Hence the quantity $A\beta$ must be negative. Often A is a real quantity, as for example in the mid-frequency range of an *RC*-coupled amplifier, and if β is entirely real (as in Fig. 9.6) then either A must be negative and β positive, or the converse must apply. A will normally be negative and may be complex, while β will normally be positive and may also be complex.

If A is negative and β positive, then the amplification will change with the application of negative feedback from

$$-A \text{ to } \frac{-A}{1 + A\beta}$$

If the quantity $A\beta$ is large compared with unity, the amplification with negative feedback approaches $A_{FB} = 1/\beta$.

Example. Suppose an amplifier has $A = 10^5$ and $\beta = 10^{-2}$. Then the gain with feedback $= A_{FB} = \dfrac{A}{1 + A\beta} = 100.$

If the value of A falls to 10^3 due to a defect in the amplifier, such as a drop in the supply voltages,

$$\text{then } A_{FB} = \frac{10^3}{1+10} = 90{\cdot}9$$

If the value of A drops still further, to say, 10^2 then $A_{FB} = 10^2/2 = 50$ i.e. due to the effect of negative feedback an initial drop of 60 dB in the amplifier itself has resulted in the output falling by only 6 dB. The amplification can thus be said to be independent of supply voltages, transistor, or valve constants, as β may be determined solely by circuit components, which are independent of these quantities.

This independence of gain on supply conditions arises from the fact that the actual input to the amplifier is the small difference between the signal voltage (e_s) and the feedback voltage (βE). A change in amplification (A) will give rise to a change in βE and so the difference will change. Thus, if A falls, the difference voltage, or input, will increase and so the output will be maintained.

If it is desired to change the gain in a negative feedback amplifier the gain control must be outside the feedback loop, otherwise it will be inoperative. An attenuator or potential divider at the input terminals may be used if it is placed before the feedback connection. Alternatively, if β is varied the overall gain will vary. This, however, is not always convenient, as a large change in β will change the input or output impedances and may give rise to instability.

The Effect of Negative Feedback on Distortion

Distortion generated in an amplifier may be reduced with respect to the output signal by the application of negative feedback. Suppose an amplifier has an input signal e_s, and a gain A before the application of feedback (Fig. 9.4a). If the magnitude of the distortion produced in the amplifier is represented by D, the output will be $Ae_s + D$.

Suppose the desired output with feedback is E, and the distortion is d the output will be $E + d$ (Fig. 9.4b).

Then assuming all the distortion occurs in the output stage, as is usually the case,

$$Ae_s + D - A\beta(E + d) = E + d$$

$$\therefore \; E(1 + A\beta) + d(1 + A\beta) = Ae_s + D$$

$$\therefore \qquad E + d = \frac{Ae_s}{1 + A\beta} + \frac{D}{1 + A\beta}$$

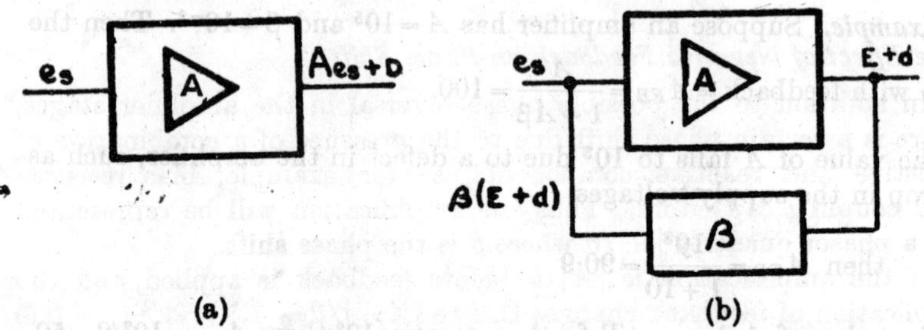

Fig. 9.4. The effect of negative feedback on distortion.

The percentage distortion without feedback is $100D/Ae_s$, with feedback it is $100d/E$, and so the ratio of distortion with and without feedback is

$$=\frac{100d}{E}\times\frac{Ae_s}{100D}$$

$$=\frac{100D}{E(1+A\beta)}\cdot\frac{Ae_s}{100D}=\frac{Ae_s}{E(1+A\beta)} \quad . \quad . \quad . \qquad 9.8$$

For a true comparison the output must be the same in the two cases, i.e. Ae_s must equal E. Now the effect of negative feedback has been to reduce the gain which means a reduced output for the same input voltage. If the output with negative feedback applied is to be the same as the output without feedback, the input level must be increased in the feedback case. This can be achieved by additional voltage amplification at the input. If this extra stage (or stages) of amplification do not contribute to the distortion, then it will be seen that the distortion is reduced in the same ratio as the gain, namely $1/(1+A\beta)$. In practice it is relatively easy to secure distortionless amplification of small voltages.

The effect of noise in an amplifier will also be reduced, provided always that the noise is generated in the amplifier in a part of the circuit within the feedback loop.

The Effect of Negative Feedback on Frequency Response

The presence of reactive components, such as coupling capacitors, inductors, or stray capacitance, causes the gain to vary with frequency. The application of negative feedback has the effect of decreasing this attenuation distortion and gives a more uniform frequency response. This, of course, is obtained at the expense of gain. Again the improvement will only be achieved insofar as the cause is within the feedback loop; the response of say, an input transformer outside the loop will remain unchanged.

The Effect of Negative Feedback on Phase Shift

In addition to the possible phase reversal in the amplifier stages, there is a certain phase shift due to the presence of a combination of resistive and reactive components, as for example, bias resistors and coupling capacitors. Thus the amplification will be represented by a phasor quantity $|A|\underline{/\theta}$ where θ is the phase shift.

If the amplification is $|A|\underline{/\theta}$ before feedback is applied, and the application of feedback changes this to $|A_{FB}|\underline{/\theta_{FB}}$

$$\text{then } |A_{FB}|\underline{/\theta_{FB}} = \frac{|A|\underline{/\theta}}{1+\beta|A|\underline{/\theta}} = \frac{|A|\underline{/\theta}}{X+jY}$$

$$\text{where } X = 1+\beta|A|\cos\theta \text{ and } Y = \beta|A|\sin\theta$$

$$\text{and so } |A_{FB}|\underline{/\theta_{FB}} = \frac{|A|}{\sqrt{X^2+Y^2}}\underline{\Big/\theta - \tan^{-1}\frac{Y}{X}}$$

The reduction of phase shift due to the feedback is

$$\tan^{-1}\frac{Y}{X} = \tan^{-1}\frac{\beta|A|\sin\theta}{1+\beta|A|\cos\theta} \qquad . \quad . \quad . \quad . \quad . \qquad 9.9$$

If $\beta|A|\cos\theta >> 1$, then $\tan^{-1}\frac{Y}{X} = \tan^{-1}\tan\theta$ and $\theta_{FB} = 0°$

Feedback Circuits

Either voltage or current feedback may be employed. In the former case a fraction of the output voltage is fed back to the input, whereas for current feedback a voltage proportional to the output current is fed back. The voltage due to feedback may be connected in series or in parallel with the original input signal. Fig. 9.5 shows four possible arrangements.

The properties of negative feedback previously discussed apply irrespective of whether the feedback is due to voltage or current, series or parallel.

The effective output impedance of the amplifier, however, depends on whether voltage or current feedback is used. The output impedance is decreased in the former case and increased in the latter. The effective input impedance depends on the method of connection. With series connected feedback the input impedance is increased, whilst the opposite is true for parallel feedback. In practice, a combination of arrangements may be employed. By using a mixture of voltage and current feedback the output impedance of an amplifier can be made to match any particular load.

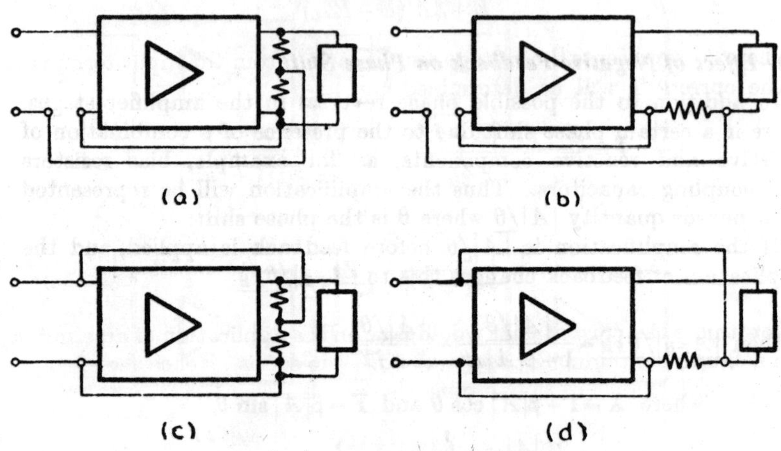

Fig. 9.5. Feedback connections.

(a) Series voltage feedback
(b) Series current feedback
(c) Parallel voltage feedback
(d) Parallel current feedback

The Effect on the Output Impedance of Series Voltage Negative Feedback

In this case the arrangement is as shown in Fig. 9.5a. If, by the use of Thévenin's theorem, the output of the amplifier before the application of feedback is represented as a voltage generator in series with a resistance r_o, the effective output impedance with feedback may be deduced from Fig. 9.6.

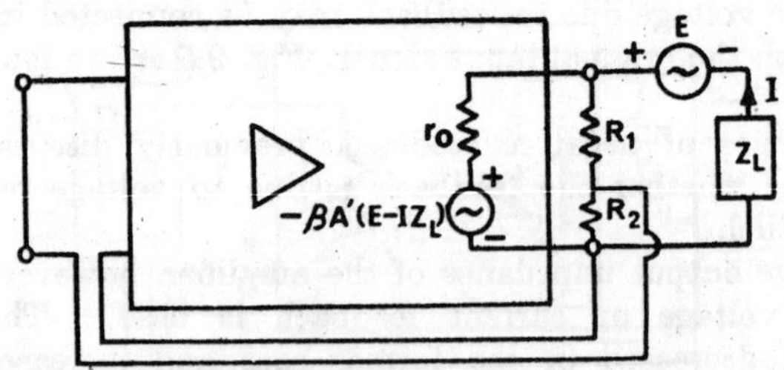

Fig. 9.6. Output impedance with series voltage negative feedback.

Suppose a generator of e.m.f. E is connected so that a current I flows in the output circuit as shown. Then if Z_L represents the load, and the presence of R_1 and R_2 is neglected, the voltage acting in the output circuit, with the input terminals short-circuited will be equal to

$$E + \beta A'(E - IZ_L)$$

where A′ represents the voltage amplification from the input terminals. The current I will be determined by

$$I = \frac{E + \beta A'(E - IZ_L)}{r_o + Z_L} = \frac{E(1 + \beta A')}{r_o + Z_L(1 + \beta A')}$$

$$= \frac{E}{\dfrac{r_o}{1 + \beta A'} + Z_L}$$

Now this is the current that would flow on the application of an e.m.f. E in a circuit containing Z_L and $r_o/(1 + \beta A')$ in series. Hence the effective output impedance of the amplifier is

$$Z_{FB} = \frac{r_o}{1 + \beta A'} \quad . \quad . \quad . \quad . \qquad 9.10$$

The output impedance without feedback is r_o bearing in mind that the shunting effect of R_1 and R_2 has been neglected,

$$\therefore \frac{Z_{FB}}{r_o} = \frac{1}{1 + \beta A'}$$

i.e. the effect of the feedback has been a reduction in the value of the output impedance in the ratio $1/(1 + \beta A')$.

The Effect on the Output Impedance of Series Current Negative Feedback

If r represents the resistance which gives rise to the feedback, the arrangement will be as shown in Fig. 9.7.

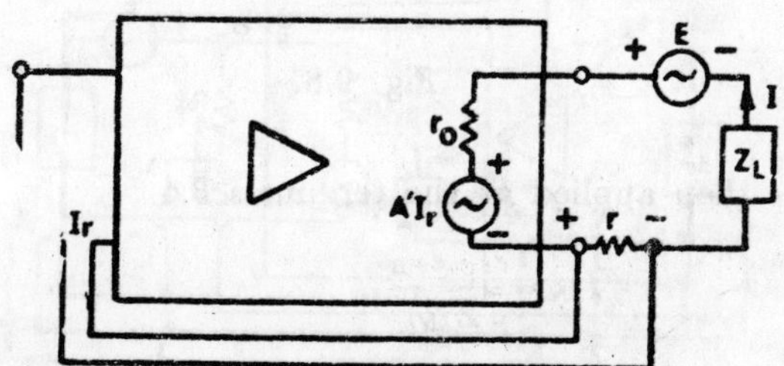

Fig. 9.7. Output impedance with negative current feedback.

As in the previous case assume a generator of e.m.f. E is connected in the output circuit and let the resultant current be I as shown. Then the e.m.f. acting in the output circuit will be $E - A'Ir$

$$\text{and } I = \frac{E - A'Ir}{Z- + r_o + r}$$

$$= \frac{E}{Z_L + r_o + r(1 + A')}$$

This is the current that would flow in a series circuit of Z_L, r_o, and $r(1 + A')$. Hence the output impedance of the amplifier is $r_o + r(1 + A')$. Before the application of feedback the output impedance at the amplifier terminals on open circuit was $r_o + r$. Thus feedback in this case has increased the output impedance in the ratio

$$\frac{r_o + r(1 + A')}{r_o + r} = 1 + A'\beta \text{ where } \beta \text{ is defined as } \frac{r}{r_o + r}$$

The Effect on the Input Impedance of Series (Current or Voltage) Negative Feedback

The feedback voltage e_{FB} will oppose the input signal e_s (Fig. 9.8). If e_{FB} is zero and the terminals 3,4, are short circuited then the input impedance of the amplifier at the terminals 1,2, will be

$$Z_{IN} = \frac{e_s}{I_{IN}} \quad \text{or} \quad I_{IN} = \frac{e_s}{Z_{IN}}$$

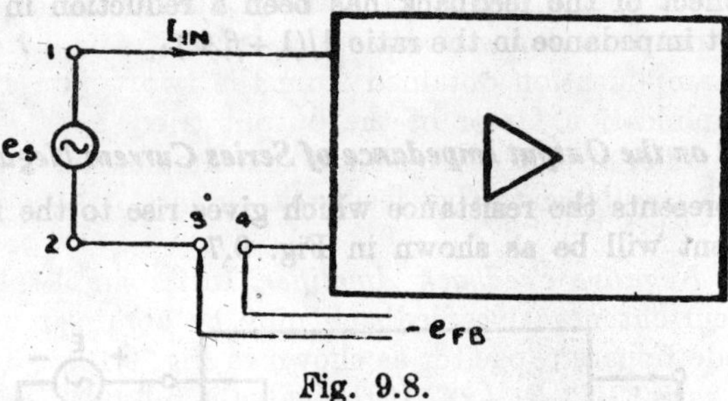

Fig. 9.8.

If $-e_{FB}$ is then applied at the terminals 3,4

$$I_{IN} = \frac{e_s - e_{FB}}{Z_{IN}}$$

and so the input current will be reduced by the factor $(e_s - e_{FB})/e_s$, and the input impedance increased.

Voltage Negative Feedback Amplifier. **Fig. 9.9 shows a three-stage amplifier with feedback applied from the last stage back to the first grid circuit.**

If the reactance of the capacitor C is sufficiently small over the working range for its presence to be neglected, the results of the general arrangement shown in Fig. 9.6 can be applied.

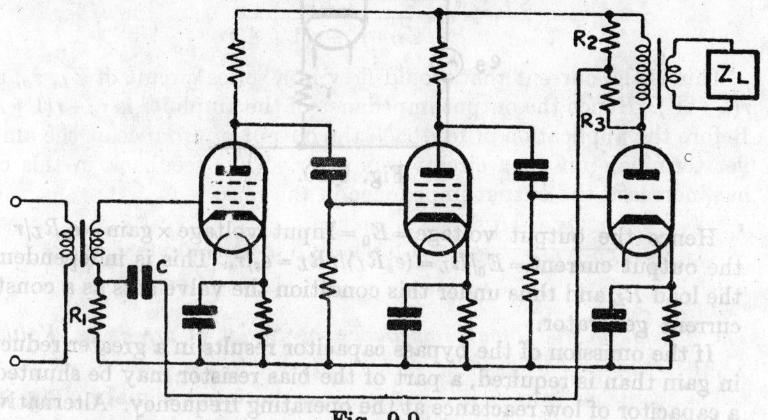

Fig. 9.9.

In this case, $\beta = \dfrac{R}{R+R_3}$ where $R = \dfrac{R_1 R_2}{R_1 + R_2}$

while the gain (from equation 9.7) is $A_v/(1+A_v\beta)$ where A_v is the overall gain of the amplifier in the absence of the feedback connection.

The output impedance (from equation 9.10) is $r_a/(1+\mu A'\beta)$ where A' is the amplification obtained from the two pentode valves and μ is the amplification factor of the output triode.

The amplifier circuit of Fig. 9.9 is one simple example from a large number of possible negative feedback circuits.

Current Negative Feedback Amplifier. In its simplest form a single stage of current negative feedback may be obtained by omission of the cathode bypass capacitor as shown in Fig. 9.10.

In this case $\beta = r/(R_L + r)$. If the valve is fully decoupled, i.e. there is no feedback applied, then $A = -\mu R_L/(R_L + r_a)$

With feedback, $A_{FB} = \dfrac{A}{1 + A\beta} = \dfrac{-\mu R_L}{r_a + R_L + \mu R_L \beta}$

and if $\beta = \dfrac{r}{R_L + r} \simeq r/R_L \quad A_{FB} = \dfrac{-\mu R_L}{r_a + R_L + \mu r} \simeq -R_L/r.$ 9.11

if $\mu r >> r_a + R_L$

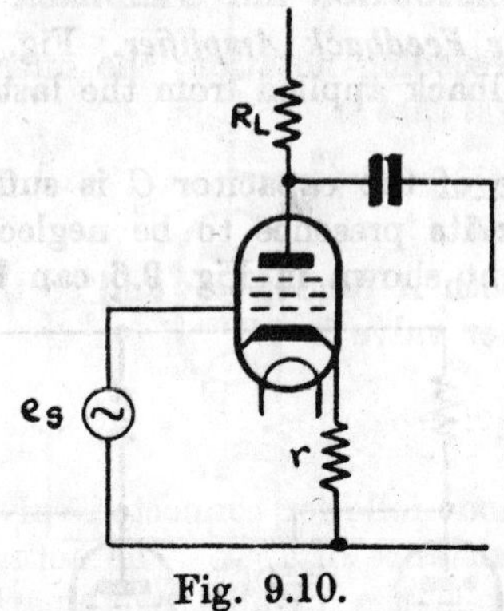

Fig. 9.10.

Hence the output voltage $= E_0 =$ Input voltage $\times$ gain $= e_s R_L / r$ and the output current $= E_0 / R_L = (e_s R_L) / r R_L = e_s / r$. This is independent of the load R_L and thus under this condition the valve acts as a constant current generator.

If the omission of the bypass capacitor results in a greater reduction in gain than is required, a part of the bias resistor may be shunted by a capacitor of low reactance at the operating frequency. Alternatively, for increased feedback, an additional resistor can be inserted between cathode and the H.T. negative point. Conversely, in a normal amplifier insufficient decoupling of the cathode bias resistor will produce negative feedback and reduce the gain.

The Cathode Follower

The cathode follower is an amplifier stage which has the load connected in the cathode circuit, whilst the anode is decoupled to earth. It can be thought of as a single stage of voltage negative feedback, in which the whole of the output voltage is fed back to the grid circuit. Thus $\beta = 1$.

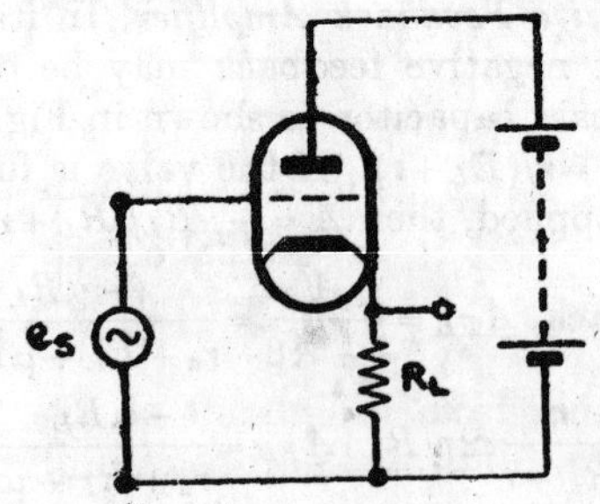

Fig. 9.11. The cathode follower.

With the preceding notation, the output impedance of the valve from the general case is

$$\frac{r_a}{1+\mu A'\beta}$$

In this case both A' and $\beta=1$, and so the output impedance of the cathode follower valve is

$$=\frac{r_a}{1+\mu}\simeq\frac{1}{g_m} \quad . \quad . \quad . \quad . \quad . \quad . \quad 9.12$$

Thus the cathode follower connected valve behaves as though it had an internal resistance of $1/g_m$. The actual output impedance at the load terminals is the parallel combination of the valve and load resistance. The output impedance is thus

$$Z_0=\frac{\dfrac{r_aR_L}{1+\mu}}{R_L+\dfrac{r_a}{1+\mu}}=\frac{r_aR_L}{r_a+(1+\mu)R_L} \quad . \quad . \quad . \quad . \quad . \quad 9.13$$

The amplification $A_{FB}=A/(1+A)$ where $A=\mu R_L/(r_a+R_L)$. It will be seen that the amplification of the cathode follower stage is less than unity, which is approached as A is increased, i.e. as R_L is increased.

The above results have been obtained from the general case of a voltage NFB amplifier. They may of course be obtained directly from the cathode follower (or common-anode) circuit.

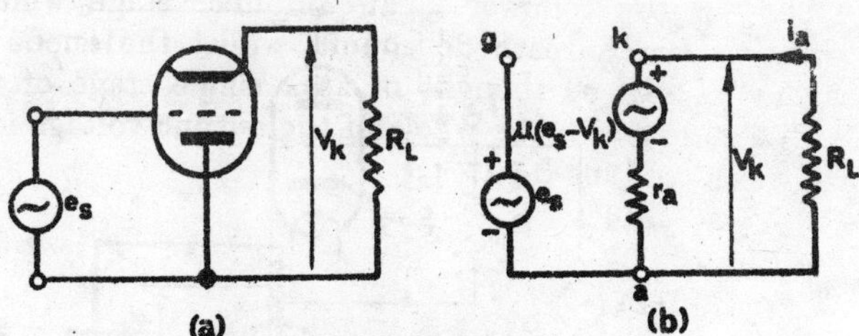

Fig. 9.12 Cathode follower

(a) Actual circuit
(b) A.c. equivalent circuit

Thus, either from the circuit of Fig. 9.11 or the redrawn version shown in Fig. 9.12a (both of which omit d.c. bias),

$$V_k=\mu(e_s-v_k)+r_ai_a \quad . \quad . \quad . \quad 9.14$$

$$\text{and} \quad v_k=-R_Li_a$$

Hence the voltage amplification is given by, v_k/e_s,

$$=\mu R_L/[r_a+R_L(1+\mu)]$$

$$=\frac{\frac{\mu}{\mu+1}R_L}{\frac{r_a}{\mu+1}+R_L}\simeq\frac{\mu}{\mu+1}$$

if $R_L \gg r_a/(\mu+1)$

The output impedance at the valve terminals may be obtained by short-circuiting the signal voltage e_s. Equation 9.14 then becomes

$$v_k=-\mu v_k+r_a i_a$$

and so $\quad v_k/i_a=r_a/(\mu+1)\simeq 1/g_m$

The output impedance of the whole circuit, including R_L, is as given by equation 9.13.

The Input Impedance of a Cathode Follower Stage

The cathode follower circuit is one which uses series voltage feedback. As a consequence of this the input impedance is high whereas the output impedance is low, especially for valves with a high value of mutual conductance. The cathode follower has thus the property of impedance transformation and is often used to match a high impedance circuit to a low impedance.

The input impedance of the cathode follower stage may be deduced by considering the circuit of Fig. 9.13.

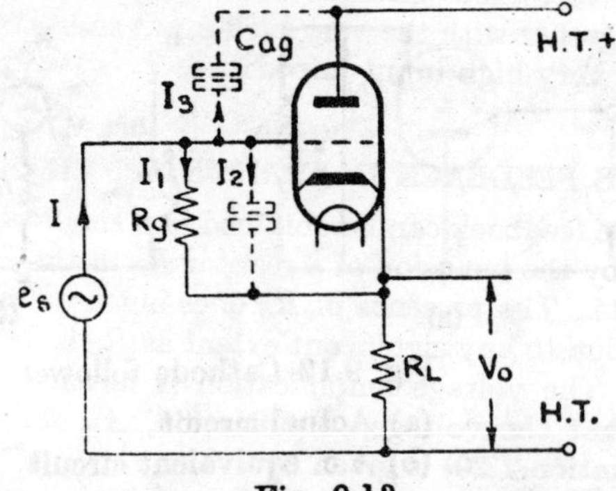

Fig. 9.13.

If R_g is a grid leak connected as shown, the voltage across it is then the difference between the applied signal voltage e_s and the output voltage V_0 and so

$$I_1=(e_s-V_0)/R_g$$

If the output load is resistive as shown, the two voltages e_s and V_0 are in phase and I_1 is the resistive component of the input current I. In this case the input resistance, R_I is

$$R_I = \frac{e_s}{I_1} = \frac{R_g e_s}{e_s - V_0} = \frac{R_g}{1-A} \quad . \quad . \quad . \quad . \quad . \quad . \quad 9.15$$

where $A = V_0/e_s$ the amplification of the stage.

The effect of changing the load from the anode to the cathode has thus been to increase the input resistance of the stage by the factor $1/(1-A)$ which increases as m approaches unity.

The input reactance of the cathode follower is determined by the values of C_{ak} and C_{gk}. The voltage applied across C_{ag} is equal to e_s (if zero impedance exists between the H.T. + and H.T. – terminals), whilst the voltage applied to C_{gk} is $e_s - V_0$.

The total reactive input current is then

$$= I_2 + I_3 = j\omega C_{ag} e_s + j\omega C_{gk}(e_s - V_0)$$

$$= j\omega e_s \left[C_{ag} + C_{gk}\left(1 - \frac{V_0}{e_s}\right) \right]$$

and so the input capacitance C_I

$$= C_{ag} + C_{gk}(1-A) \quad . \quad . \quad . \quad . \quad . \quad 9.16$$

In many cases A is nearly equal to unity and the input capacitance is substantially C_{ag}. If equation 9.16 is compared with the corresponding expression for the input capacitance of a normal amplifier (equation 6.15) it will be seen that the input capacitance of the cathode follower is very much smaller.

This, together with the very high input resistance, gives the cathode follower a very high input impedance.

NEGATIVE FEEDBACK IN TRANSISTOR CIRCUITS

Negative feedback can be obtained in a single-stage common-emitter amplifier by the inclusion of a resistor R_E in the emitter lead as shown in Fig. 9.14. The presence of R_E does not normally affect the current amplification to any significant extent as R_E is usually small compared with R_L. The voltage amplification is however reduced. It will be recalled that the voltage amplification, A_v, for the common-emitter stage (equation 7.20) is given by

$$A_v = \frac{-h_{fe} R_L}{h_{ie} + \triangle h R_L}$$

The feedback factor, β_v, is approximately R_E/R_L and so the voltage amplification with negative feedback is given by

$$A_{v_{FB}} \simeq \frac{-h_{fe}R_L/(h_{ie}+\triangle hR_L)}{1+h_{fe}R_LR_E/R_L(h_{ie}+\triangle hR_L)}$$

$$\simeq \frac{-h_{fe}R_L}{h_{ie}+\triangle hR_L+h_{fe}R_E} \quad . \quad . \quad . \quad . \quad 9.17$$

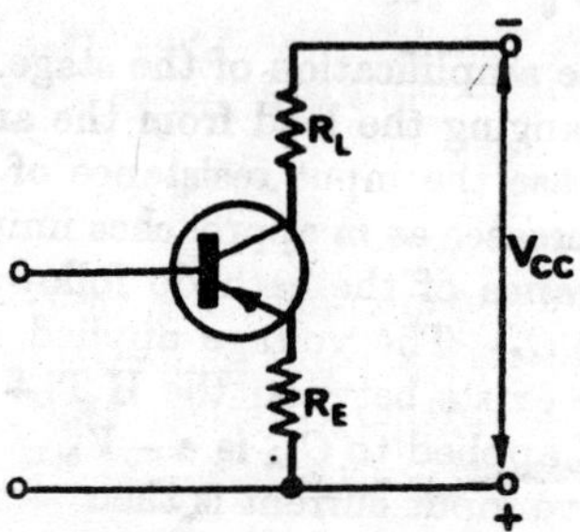

Fig. 9.14. Emitter feedback.

If $h_{fe}R_E \gg h_{ie}+\triangle hR_L$ the amplification is approximately R_L/R_E (as in the corresponding valve case), and relatively independent of the transistor.

As might be expected, the input resistance is increased because of the series connection at the input, while the output resistance is increased to a small extent.

The connection of a resistor between the collector and base is another simple way in which negative feedback can be applied. If, in Fig. 9.15, $R \gg R_L$ the voltage amplification is not affected nearly so much

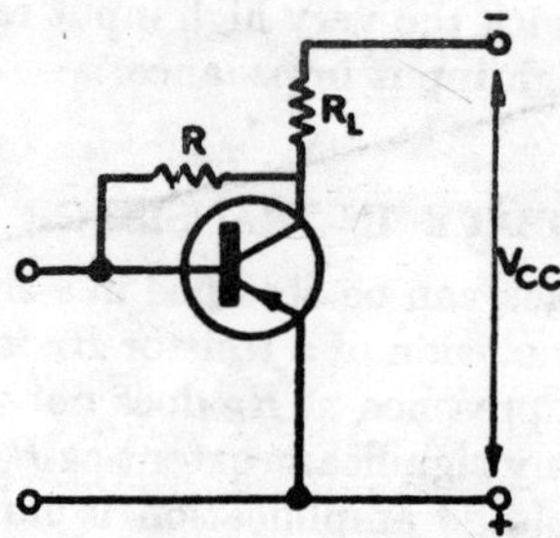

Fig. 9.15. Collector to base feedback.

as the current amplification. The ratio, β_i, of the current fed back to the load current is R_L/R, the current amplification is (equation 7.17)

$$A_i = \frac{h_{fe}}{1+h_{oe}R_L}$$

Hence $$A_{i_{FB}} = \frac{h_{fe}/(1+h_{oe}R_L)}{1+h_{fe}R_L/(1+h_{oe}R_L)R} = \frac{h_{fe}}{1+h_{oe}R_L+h_{fe}R_L/R} \qquad 9.18$$

With this circuit the feedback path is in parallel with the input and output, and the input and output resistances are decreased.

The Emitter Follower

The basic form of the common-collector, or emitter follower, stage is shown in Fig. 9.16a and its a.c. equivalent circuit drawn in Fig. 9.16b.

The relation between the currents, for the directions shown in Fig. 9.16b is

$$v_e h_{oe} = i_e + i_b(1+h_{fe}) \qquad 9.19$$

and for the input circuit

$$v_b = h_{ie}i_b - h_{re}v_e + v_e$$

$$\therefore \quad i_b = \frac{v_b - v_e(1-h_{re})}{h_{ie}} \qquad 9.20$$

while in the output circuit

$$v_e = -i_e R_L \qquad 9.21$$

by elimination of i_e and i_b from equation 9.19

$$A_v = \frac{v_e}{v_b} = \frac{1+h_{fe}}{h_{ie}h_{oe} + h_{ie}/R_L + (1-h_{re})(1+h_{fe})}$$

$$= \frac{(1+h_{fe})R_L}{R_L[\Delta h + 1 + h_{fe} - h_{re}] + h_{ie}} \qquad 9.22$$

where $\Delta h = h_{ie}h_{oe} - h_{re}h_{fe}$.

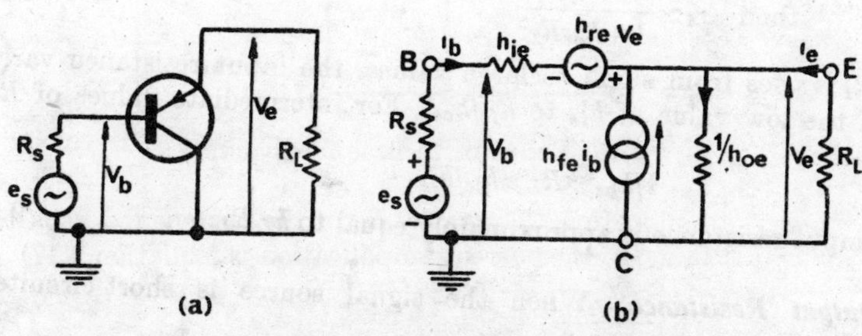

Fig. 9.16. Emitter follower
(a) Actual circuit
(b) A.C. equivalent circuit

As $h_{fe} \gg 1 + \Delta h - h_{re}$ the voltage amplification becomes

$$A_v \simeq \frac{R_L}{R_L + h_{ie}/h_{fe}} \quad . \quad . \quad . \quad . \quad 9.23$$

The voltage amplification thus depends on R_L and varies from nearly zero for very low values of R_L to a maximum which approaches unity.

From equations 9.19 and 9.21

$$-i_e R_L h_{oe} = i_e + i_b(1 + h_{fe})$$

$$\text{hence} \quad A_i = \frac{i_e}{i_b} = \frac{-(1 + h_{fe})}{1 + R_L h_{oe}} \quad . \quad . \quad . \quad . \quad 9.24a$$

$$\simeq \frac{-h_{fe}}{1 + R_L h_{oe}} \quad . \quad . \quad . \quad . \quad . \quad 9.24b$$

and for small values of R_L

$$\simeq -h_{fe} \quad . \quad . \quad . \quad . \quad . \quad . \quad 9.24c$$

The emitter follower, like the cathode follower, is often used as an impedance transforming stage because of its high input resistance and low output resistance.

Input Resistance. From equations 9.19 and 9.21

$$v_e = \frac{i_b(1 + h_{fe})R_L}{1 + h_{oe}R_L}$$

thence by substitution in equation 9.20

$$i_b = \frac{v_b - i_b(1 + h_{fe})R_L(1 + h_{re})/(1 + h_{oe}R_L)}{h_{ie}}$$

$$\text{and so} \quad r_i = v_b/i_b = \frac{h_{ie} + R_L(\Delta h + 1 + h_{fe} - h_{ve})}{1 + h_{oe}R_L}$$

If $h_{fe} \gg \Delta h + 1 - h_{re}$

$$\text{then} \quad r_i \simeq \frac{h_{ie} + h_{fe}R_L}{1 + h_{oe}R_L} \quad . \quad . \quad . \quad . \quad 9.25$$

As R_L varies from small to large values, the input resistance varies from the low value of h_{ie} to h_{fe}/h_{oe}. For intermediate values of R_L, such that

$$1/h_{oe} \gg R_L \gg h_{ie}/h_{fe}$$

the input resistance is approximately equal to $h_{fe}R_L$. . . 9.26

Output Resistance. When the signal source is short-circuited,

$$v_b = -R_s i_b.$$

Inserting this relation in equation 9.19 gives

$$v_e h_{oe} = i_e - v_b(1 + h_{fe})/R_s$$

Equation 9.20 may be rearranged to give

$$v_b = v_e(1 - h_{re})R_s/(R_s + h_{ie})$$

Substitution of this expression for v_b in the previous expression and simplification gives

$$r_o = v_e/i_e = \frac{R_s + h_{ie}}{1 + h_{fe} - h_{re} + \triangle h + h_{oe}R_s}$$

Again, if $h_{fe} \gg 1 + \triangle h - h_{re}$,

$$r_o \simeq \frac{R_s + h_{ie}}{L_{fe} + h_{oe}R_s} \quad . \quad . \quad . \quad . \quad . \quad . \quad 9.27a$$

When the transistor is fed from a signal source of insignificant internal resistance

$$r_o \simeq h_{ie}/h_{fe} \quad . \quad . \quad . \quad . \quad . \quad . \quad . \quad 9.27b$$

Alternatively when energised from a very high resistance source

$$r_o \simeq 1/h_{oe} \quad . \quad . \quad . \quad . \quad . \quad . \quad . \quad 9.27c$$

For a range of intermediate values of source resistance

$$r_o \simeq R_s/h_{fe} \quad . \quad . \quad . \quad . \quad . \quad . \quad . \quad 9.27d$$

INSTABILITY IN NEGATIVE FEEDBACK AMPLIFIERS

It has been shown that the effect of the application of negative feedback to an amplifier is to reduce the gain from A without feedback to $A/(1 + A\beta)$ with feedback ; the amplification A is a vector quantity $|A|\angle\theta$, in which the phase shift represented by the angle θ is usually fairly small. Phase shift at low frequencies is caused by the reactance of coupling capacitors (when these are used) or by the low reactance of chokes and transformers ; at high frequencies the phase shift is normally due to the shunting effect of circuit capacitance in parallel with the load. Now although θ is small within the operating frequency range of the amplifier, it may well be that at very high or very low frequencies θ approaches or exceeds $\pm\pi$. Now, $\beta A/\angle \pm\pi = -\beta A/\angle 0$, and at frequencies where this is so the feedback will become positive, and instability may result. If the phase shift amounts to 180°, at a certain frequency, then oscillation will occur if the loop gain is equal to or greater than unity. To avoid this instability the phase shift must be kept smaller than 180° at very high and very low frequencies. The rate of fall of amplifier gain with frequency at the extremes of the pass-band (as a consequence of the presence of reactive components) is related to the maximum phase shift through the amplifier.[3]

WORKED EXAMPLES

1. A certain valve has a parabolic anode current/grid voltage characteristic and gives an anode current of 30 mA with zero grid

potential. A sine wave e.m.f. applied to the grid causes the anode current to rise to a maximum value of 41 mA and fall to a minimum value of 21 mA. Assuming that the external anode load is small compared with the internal resistance of the valve, calculate the percentage harmonic distortion of the output current. Prove any formula employed.

L.U. Int. Telecomm. 1939

As the load is small compared with the internal resistance of the valve equation 9.1 can be applied. The output will then contain a fundamental and a second harmonic component. The harmonic distortion will thus be second harmonic distortion. From the application of equation 9.3 the percentage harmonic distortion is given by

$$\frac{I_{max.} + I_{min.} - 2I_{mean}}{2(I_{max.} - I_{min.})} \times 100\%$$

$$= \frac{41 + 21 - 2 \times 30}{2(41 - 21)} \times 100\% \quad = \underline{5\%}$$

2. Derive expressions for the output voltage and the internal impedance of a cathode follower stage. A cathode follower stage employs a triode having an amplification factor of 40 and a differential anode resistance of 11,000 Ω. Determine the internal impedance of the stage and the ratio of the alternating output voltage to the input voltage for a cathode load of 5,000 Ω.

L.U. Int. Telecomm. 1943

It has been shown that the amplification with feedback, $A_{FB} = \dfrac{A}{1+A}$ for the cathode follower, where $A = \dfrac{\mu R_L}{r_a + R_L}$

$$\therefore A_{FB} = \frac{\mu R_L}{r_a + R_L(1+\mu)}$$

If the input voltage is V the output voltage V_0 will be given by

$$V_0 = \frac{\mu R_L V}{r_a + R_L(1+\mu)}$$

The internal impedance of the cathode follower is given by $r_a/(1+\mu)$.

Hence internal impedance $= 11{,}000/41 = \underline{268\Omega}$

The ratio of the output to input voltage $= \dfrac{\mu R_L}{r_a + R_L(1+\mu)} = \underline{0{\cdot}925.}$

3. An amplifier has a voltage gain of 100 before negative feedback is applied. Under these conditions, with a certain input voltage, the distortion products generated in the valve and measured at the output are 40 dB below the fundamental. One tenth of the output voltage is then fed back to the input. With the same output voltage, what will now be the relation between the distortion products and the output voltage?

I.E.E. Line Comm. April, 1948

If the output voltage is maintained constant as in this case, and all the distortion is assumed to be generated in the output stage, the effect of feedback is to reduce the distortion by the factor $1/(1+A\beta)$.

Now $1/(1+A\beta)=1/11$

Hence the reduction in level of the distortion products by $20 \log_{10} 11$ dB

$$=20\times 1{\cdot}041=20{\cdot}8 \text{ dB}$$

Thus with feedback the level of the distortion products will be 60·8 dB below the fundamental.

References

[1] British Standard 204: 1960. Glossary of Terms Used in Telecommunications (British Standards Institution).

[2] BODE, H. W.: " Relations between Attenuation and Phase in Feedback Amplifier Design ", Bell System Technical Journal, 19, p. 421 (1940).

References for Further Reading

BODE, H. W.: *Network Analysis and Feedback Amplifier Design* (D. Van Nostrand, 1945).

EXAMPLES

1. Discuss the factors which determine the most suitable load impedance for a pentode.

A certain pentode has the following characteristics when operated with a screen voltage of 200 V.

Anode volts	50	100	200	300
Grid volts	anode current i_a			
0	55	64	68	70
−5	41	47	50	51·5
−10	28	31	33	34

Find the amplification factor, the anode slope resistance and the mutual conductance when the grid bias is -5 V and the anode voltage is 200 V.

If the peak value of the sinusoidal voltage applied to the control grid be 5 volts, calculate the output power and the second harmonic distortion when the load resistance is 5,000 Ω, the H.T. voltage being 400 V.

L.U. Ext. Telecomm. 1944

2. If the phase displacement between the output voltage and the input voltage of an amplifier stage varies with frequency, what requirements must be satisfied if wave-form distortion is to be avoided? Explain simply the justification for these requirements.

Plot a curve of phase shift against frequency for the range 30 to 300 Hz for an *RC* amplifier stage employing a tetrode having a mutual conductance of 3 mA/V and an anode slope resistance of 0·5 MΩ. The anode load resistance is 25,000 Ω, the capacitance of the coupling condenser 0·01 μF and the resistance of the grid leak of the next stage 0·5 MΩ. Comment on the performance of the stage in regard to phase distortion.

L.U. Ext. Telecomm. 1947

3. Give a simple analysis to show the nature of the distortion produced by an amplifier having a slightly non-linear output/input relationship when the input signal contains component voltages of several different frequencies. Explain the factors that may give rise to non-linear distortion in a class A power amplifier stage having an iron-cored output transformer and deriving its input signal from a source of appreciable internal resistance.

L.U. Ext. Telecomm. 1953

4. What advantages are to be gained from the application of negative feedback to an amplifier? Derive an expression for the factor by which the amplification without feedback must be multiplied to give the amplification in the presence of feedback and show that with certain assumptions, which are justified in practice, the harmonic distortion present in the output is reduced in the same ratio.

In a particular 2-stage amplifier the actual voltage amplification of each stage is 100. From a potentiometer connected across the output 1/1000 of the output voltage is fed back in anti-phase to the input. Calculate the overall amplification obtained in a frequency range in which the phase changes throughout the amplifier are negligible and repeat the calculation for the condition in which the gain per stage has dropped to 80% of its normal value.

L.U. Int. Telecomm. 1941

5. Derive an expression for the voltage amplification of an amplifier when a fraction of its output p.d. is fed back and combined with the input p.d.

Determine the effective gain of a feedback amplifier having an amplification without feedback of $-200-j300$ if the feedback circuit adds to the input signal a p.d. which is 0·5% of the output p.d. and lags a quarter of a cycle behind it in phase. Explain whether the feedback in this case is positive or negative.

***L.U. Ext. Telecomm.* 1950**

6. State the advantages gained from the application of negative feedback to an amplifier. Derive an expression for the factor by which the amplification without feedback must be multiplied to give the amplification in the presence of feedback. Show that, with certain assumptions, the harmonic distortion present in the output is reduced in the same ratio.

Discuss the effect of negative feedback on noise introduced into (a) the input, (b) the output stage, or an amplifier.

A certain amplifier has 1/5000th part of its output fed back in anti-phase to the input, the gain of the amplifier itself (without feedback) being 55,000.

Calculate the percentage reduction in the amplification if the overall amplification without feedback falls to 40,000.

***L.U. Telecomm. Part III.* 1959**

7. Explain why a valve operated as a cathode follower presents a relatively high input impedance compared with that of a normal amplifier stage. Deduce an expression for the output impedance of such a stage.

***L.U. Int. Telecomm.* 1950**

8. An amplifier has a gain m and an output impedance R_0. Derive expressions for the effective gain and output impedance of this amplifier when a fraction β of the output voltage is added, in anti-phase, to the input voltage. Discuss the effect of negative feedback on the frequency response characteristic of the amplifier. What other beneficial results may be expected from its use ?

***L.U. Ext. Telecomm.* 1949**

9. Develop a simple theory to show that the application of negative feedback will reduce the harmonic distortion generated in an amplifier. What assumptions are made in the theory given ?

An amplifier is required to give an overall voltage amplification of 1000 with the harmonic content not exceeding 2% at full output. If

the harmonic content obtained without feedback is 10% estimate how much feedback must be applied and what additional amplification will be required.

L.U. Ext. Telecomm. 1945

10. In a single valve negative feedback amplifier the output transformer has a turns ratio of 6:1 and operates into a load impedance of 600 $\underline{/0°}\ \Omega$. One tenth of the anode winding voltage is fed back to the grid input exactly 180° out of phase with the input voltage.

Assuming that the limits of mutual conductance on the valve are 1·65 and 2·75 mA/V, calculate the change in gain of the amplifier over this range, (a) without feedback applied, (b) with feedback applied.

I.E.E. Line Comm. October, 1945

11. Outline the advantages of feeding back into the input circuit of an amplifier a voltage which is proportional to (a) the output voltage and (b) the output current. A fraction $\beta\ \underline{/0°}$ of the output voltage of an amplifier whose gain is $A\ \underline{/180° + \theta}$ is inserted in series with the normal input in such a direction as to reduce the gain. Show that the amplifier phase shift is reduced by

$$\tan^{-1}\frac{A\beta \sin\theta}{1 + A\beta\cos\theta}$$

L.U. Int. Telecomm. 1953

12. What are the special properties of a triode connected as a cathode follower. Describe a practical application of this device and show how these special properties are employed. The anode slope resistance of a triode is 15 kΩ and its amplification factor is 30. Its cathode is connected to the earth line by a resistor of 10 kΩ. Calculate the output impedance of the stage. The effect of stray capacitances may be neglected in this calculation. Derive any formula used.

L.U. Ext. Telecomm. 1954

13. The anode resistor of a triode valve is 50,000 Ω and so also is the resistor connecting its cathode to the negative terminal of the high tension supply and earth. The grid is so biased that the anode slope may be taken to be 10,000 Ω, and the amplification factor of the valve 25. Calculate the approximate values of the internal resistance of (a) the anode circuit, and (b) the cathode circuit, when each is used to drive a subsequent stage of amplification. The input voltage of the triode is applied between grid and earth.

L.U. Ext. Telecomm. 1947

14. Give a simple theory to illustrate the advantages resulting from the application of negative feedback to amplifiers.

Negative feedback is applied to one stage of an amplifier by the inclusion of an unbypassed resistance in the cathode lead of the valve, which is a pentode having a mutual conductance of 5 mA/V and an anode slope resistance of 200,000 Ω. The anode load is 10,000 Ω and the resistance between cathode and negative H.T. lead is 500 Ω. The input signal is applied between the control grid and the negative H.T. terminal. Determine the approximate reduction in amplification due to feedback.

L.U. Ext. Telecomm. July, 1946

15. A triode valve connected as a cathode follower to a load resistance of 4 kΩ has the following characteristics: anode slope resistance, 8 kΩ; mutual conductance, 2·5 mA/V; anode-grid capacitance 3 pF; and grid-cathode capacitance 2·5 pF. Calculate from first principles the stage gain, the internal output impedance and the input shunt capacitance.

L.U. Int. Telecomm. 1953

16. Differentiate between current-controlled and voltage-controlled negative feedback, using a circuit diagram to illustrate an example of each. Explain why a large measure of negative feedback may give rise to instability in an amplifier, and what steps, other than reducing the feedback, may be taken to prevent oscillation.

L.U. Ext. Telecomm. 1955

17. Derive an expression for the output impedance of a negative feedback amplifier in terms of the constants of the output valve, the preceding amplification, and the feedback factor β, if the feedback is proportional to the output voltage.

An amplifier has two pentode stages with a total gain of 900 and a triode output valve with a mutual conductance of 5 mA/V and an anode slope resistance of 4,000 Ω. If the load at the output terminals is 6,000 $\underline{/0°}$ Ω in parallel with a high-resistance potential-divider which gives 4% negative feedback, calculate the overall gain and the output impedance of the amplifier.

L.U. Telecomm. Part III. 1962.

10

HIGH-FREQUENCY AMPLIFIERS

WIDEBAND AMPLIFIERS

THE WIDEBAND amplifiers considered in chapter 8 are representative of the basic circuits in which frequencies in the audio range, extending from a few hertz to 10–20 kilohertz, are to be amplified. In high-definition picture transmission the range of frequencies to be amplified extends from the same lower limit of a few hertz upwards to several megahertz. When used in television transmission circuits, such amplifiers are referred to as vision frequency, or video, amplifiers.

The design of video amplifiers demands a study of the response to transients as well as steady state signals, coupled with a compromise between the conflicting quantities of gain and large bandwidth. The simple aspects of gain and bandwidth in such amplifiers, operating under class A conditions will now be considered.

The basic circuit of a resistance-capacitance-coupled amplifier stage using a pentode valve is shown in Fig. 10.1.

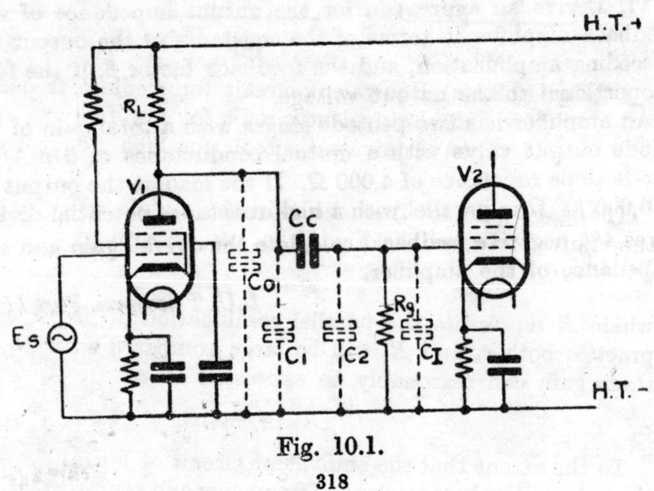

Fig. 10.1.

R_L is the load resistor for V_1
R_g is the grid resistor for V_2
C_c is the coupling capacitance
C_0 is the output capacitance of V_1
C_I is the input capacitance of V_2
C_1 and C_2 represent stray capacitance due to wiring and components
For frequencies where C_c is negligibly small
$C = C_0 + C_I + C_1 + C_2$ is the total shunt capacitance.

In dealing with the gain/frequency response of such an amplifier it is convenient to divide the frequency range into three parts. There is a mid-frequency range in which the effect of both the coupling capacitor and the shunt capacitance can be neglected. At lower frequencies the shunt capacitance can still be neglected but the presence of the coupling capacitor has to be taken into account. Finally, at high frequencies the presence of the shunt capacitance has to be considered. The equivalent circuits for alternating currents for the first valve and its load for the three frequency ranges are then as shown in Fig. 10.2.

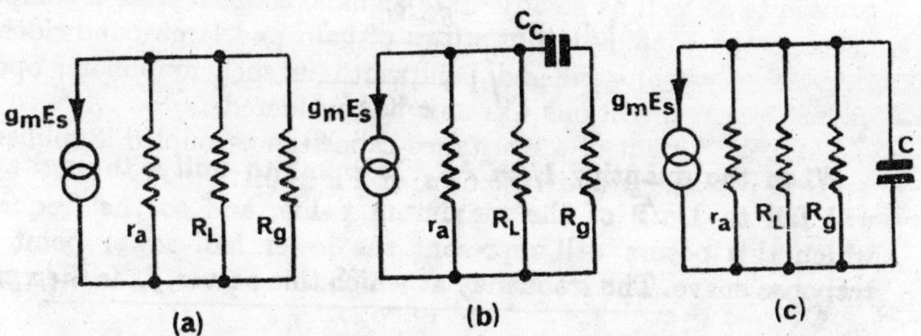

Fig. 10.2. (*a*) Equivalent circuit for medium frequencies.
(*b*) Equivalent circuit for low frequencies.
(*c*) Equivalent circuit for high frequencies.

The stage gain for frequencies in the middle range, A_m for which the equivalent circuit is Fig. 10.2a, can be seen to be

$$A_m = -g_m R$$

where R represents the parallel combination of R_L, r_a and R_g. In practice both r_a and R_g will be large compared with R_L and so the stage gain can reasonably be expressed as

$$|A_m| = -g_m R_L \quad . \quad . \quad . \qquad 10.1$$

To the extent that the equivalent circuit of Fig. 10.2a is applicable, the gain will be independent of frequency and represents the maximum value of stage gain as the effect of the coupling capacitor and shunt capacitance is to reduce the gain at the low and high frequency ends of the gain/frequency response curve.

The phase shift of the stage is 180°, which is the phase shift due to the valve alone.

At low frequencies the equivalent circuit is that of Fig. 10.2b and it will be seen that the current flowing in R_g is a fraction of the current through the valve. If r_a is neglected as being large compared with R_L the current in R_g

$$= -g_m E_s \left(\frac{R_L}{R_L + R_g + \dfrac{1}{j\omega C_c}} \right)$$

the output voltage is then

$$= -g_m E_s \left(\frac{R_L R_g}{R_L + R_g + \dfrac{1}{j\omega C_c}} \right)$$

If R_L is small compared with R_g, the stage gain at such frequencies, A_l, can then be expressed by

$$|A_l| = \frac{-g_m R_L}{\sqrt{1 + \dfrac{1}{\omega^2 C_c^2 R_g^2}}} \quad . \quad . \quad . \quad . \quad 10.2$$

When the quantity $1/\omega^2 C_c^2 R_g^2$ is equal to unity, the voltage gain will fall to $1/\sqrt{2}$ of the maximum value, and so the frequency at which this occurs will represent the lower half-power point on the response curve. The frequency at which this occurs, f_1, is then given by

$$\omega_1^2 C_c^2 R_g^2 = 1$$

$$\therefore f_1 = \frac{1}{2\pi C_c R_g} \quad . \quad . \quad . \quad . \quad 10.3$$

By means of this result equation 10.2 may then be rewritten as

$$|A_l| = \frac{-g_m R_L}{\sqrt{1 + (f_1/f)^2}} \quad . \quad . \quad . \quad . \quad 10.4$$

for any frequency f,

The effect of the coupling capacitor is to cause the output voltage to lead on the voltage across R_L by an angle $\tan^{-1} 1/\omega C_c R_g$

$$= \tan^{-1} f_1/f$$

and so the phase shift over the stage in this range is given by

$$\phi_l = 180° + \tan^{-1} f_1/f \quad . \quad . \quad . \quad . \quad 10.5$$

As the frequency f is decreased the phase shift increases and becomes asymptotic to 270°.

In the high frequency range the impedance presented to the valve is equal to

$$\frac{R}{1 + j\omega CR}$$

where R again represents the effective parallel resistance, and C is the total shunt capacitance.

The stage gain at these frequencies A_h may thus be expressed as

$$A_h = \frac{-g_m R}{\sqrt{1 + \omega^2 C^2 R^2}} \quad . \quad . \quad . \quad 10.6$$

At the frequency at which $\omega^2 C^2 R^2$ is equal to unity, the gain will fall to $1/\sqrt{2}$ of the maximum value. The frequency of the upper half-power point, f_2, is thus given by

$$\omega_2^2 C^2 R^2 = 1$$

$$\text{i.e. } f_2 = \frac{1}{2\pi CR} \quad . \quad . \quad . \quad . \quad 10.7$$

$$\text{and so } |A_h| = \frac{-g_m R}{\sqrt{1 + \left(\frac{f}{f_2}\right)^2}} \quad \text{for any frequency } f$$

$$\simeq \frac{-g_m R_L}{\sqrt{1 + \left(\frac{f}{f_2}\right)^2}} \quad . \quad . \quad . \quad . \quad . \quad 10.8$$

The phase shift over the stage for this range of frequency is

$$\phi_h = 180° - \tan^{-1} f/f_2 \quad . \quad . \quad . \quad . \quad . \quad 10.9$$

As the frequency increases the phase shift decreases and ϕ_h becomes asymptotic to 90°.

The general form of the amplitude and phase characteristics of the amplifier shown in Fig. 10.1 are as shown in Fig. 10.3.

The bandwidth between half-power points is $\Delta f = f_2 - f_1$. If f_1 is of the order of 100 Hz or so, and f_2 approximately 1 MHz, or more, the bandwidth may be taken as f_2.

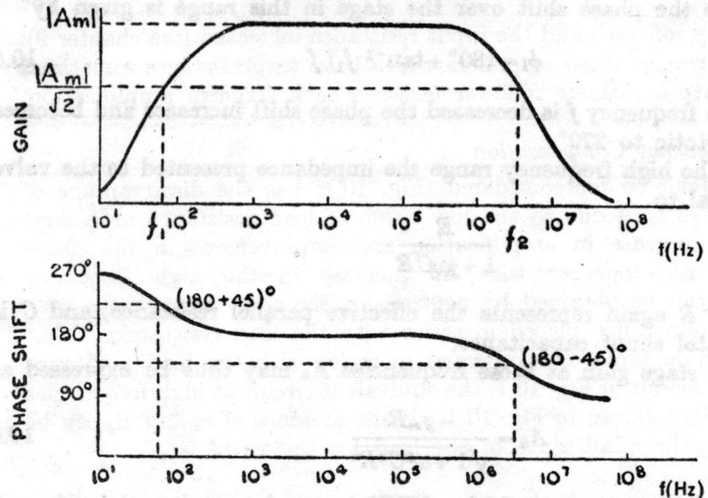

Fig. 10.3. Amplitude and phase characteristics of wideband amplifier.

If a reasonable gain is required together with a large bandwidth, the *gain bandwidth product* must be as large as possible. The maximum value of the gain is g_mR and so the gain bandwidth product

$$= g_mR \; . \; \triangle f \simeq g_mRf_2$$

$$= \frac{g_m}{2\pi C} \quad . \quad . \quad . \quad . \quad 10.10$$

As the sum of the valve output capacitance (C_0) and the valve input capacitance (C_1) form an appreciable fraction of the total shunt capacitance C, it will be seen that the gain bandwidth product is determined largely by the type of valve used. Unfortunately, the requirements of a high value of g_m and low input capacitance are fundamentally opposed to one another. The quantity $g_m/(C_0+C_I)$ is referred to as the figure of merit for valves used in wideband amplifiers.

Equation 10.7 shows that if the upper half-power frequency, f_2, is to be high the quantity CR must be small. If the shunt capacitance C is fixed by the valve used, the bandwidth can only be increased by a decrease in the value of R, and so wideband amplifiers, such as video amplifiers, are characterised by low values of anode load (and hence low stage gain) compared with audio amplifiers.

The shunt capacitance of the stage is reduced if the input capacitance of the following valve is reduced. If the second valve is connected as a cathode follower, the input capacitance will be materially reduced, and the input resistance increased (see chapter 9). For this reason video amplifiers which have several stages sometimes incorporate a cathode follower between each stage of amplification.

High-Frequency Compensation

The circuit so far considered (Fig. 10.1) has the disadvantage of a low stage gain due to the low value of load resistance necessary. A slight increase in amplification and improvement in the phase characteristic together with an increase in the high frequency response can be obtained by neutralising the stray capacitance with a small inductance placed in series with the load resistance.

If an inductance L is inserted in series with the load resistance R_L in the circuit of Fig. 10.1, the equivalent circuit at high frequencies becomes that shown in Fig. 10.4. If the presence of r_a and R_g can be neglected, the admittance of the load for the valve is

$$Y = \frac{R_L}{R_L^2 + \omega^2 L^2} + j\left(\omega C - \frac{\omega L}{R_L^2 + \omega^2 L^2}\right)$$

The susceptance will be zero, and the circuit will be non-reactive if

$$\omega C = \omega L / [R_L^2 + \omega^2 L^2]$$

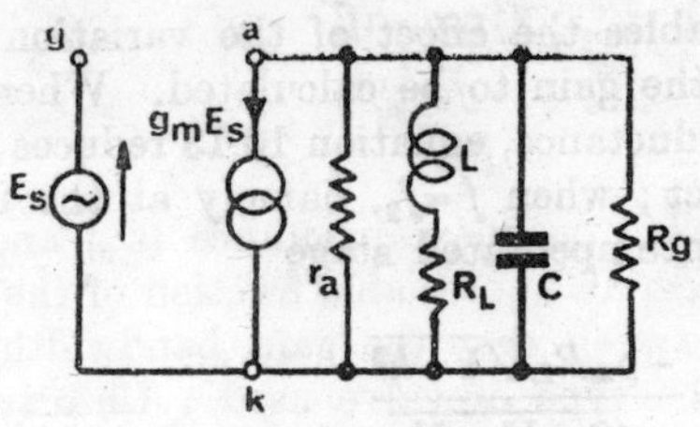

Fig. 10.4.

If the added inductance is small, so that $R_L^2 >> \omega^2 L^2$, the susceptance will be zero at the frequency given by

$$\omega C = \omega L / R_L^2$$

i.e. when $L = CR_L^2$ 10.11

The voltage gain of the compensated stage at high frequencies is given by,

$$A_h = -g_m/Y = \frac{-g_m(R_L^2 + \omega^2 L^2)}{R_L + j\omega C(R_L^2 + \omega^2 L^2) - j\omega L}.$$

$$\text{and } |A_h| = \frac{-g_m\sqrt{R_L^2+\omega^2L^2}}{\sqrt{1+\omega^2C^2(R_L^2+\omega^2L^2)-2\omega^2LC}}$$

$$= \frac{-g_mR_L\sqrt{1+\omega^2L^2/R_L^2}}{\sqrt{1+\omega^2C^2R_L^2(1+\omega^2L^2/R_L^2)-2\omega^2LC}} \quad . \quad 10.12$$

If f_2 is the upper half-power frequency of the uncompensated stage, $C=1/2\pi f_2R_L$, and if this substitution is made for C, then

$$|A_h| = \frac{-g_mR_L\sqrt{1+\omega^2L^2/R_L^2}}{\sqrt{1+\left(\frac{f}{f_2}\right)^2[1+\omega^2L^2/R_L^2]-\frac{2\omega^2L}{\omega_2R_L}}}$$

If now, the added inductance is such that $L=hCR_L^2$, where h is a constant, then $\omega^2L^2=h^2\omega^2C^2R_L^4$, and so,

$$|A_h| = \frac{-g_mR_L\sqrt{1+\left(\frac{f}{f_2}\right)^2h^2}}{\sqrt{1+\left(\frac{f}{f_2}\right)^2+h^2\left(\frac{f}{f_2}\right)^4-2h\left(\frac{f}{f_2}\right)^2}} \quad . \quad . \quad 10.13$$

This expression enables the effect of the variation of the value of the inductance on the gain to be calculated. When $h=0$, i.e. when there is no added inductance, equation 10.13 reduces to equation 10.8, as one would expect; when $f=f_2$, namely at the upper half-power frequency of the uncompensated stage

$$|A_h| = \frac{-g_mR_L\sqrt{1+h^2}}{\sqrt{2+h^2-2h}} \quad . \quad . \quad . \quad . \quad . \quad 10.14$$

In the special case when $h=0{\cdot}5$, i.e. $L=0{\cdot}5\ CR^2$, the gain at f_2 is

$$|A_h| = -g_mR_L$$

which is the maximum value of the voltage gain, as obtained in the medium-frequency range. Thus the effect of this particular amount of inductance compensation has been to increase the voltage gain at the upper half-power frequency by a factor of $\sqrt{2}$. It is found that values of h in excess of 0·5 give rise to an undesirable peak in the response curve, and so the inductance L is generally made approximately equal to 0·5 CR^2.

Bandwidth in a Multi-stage Amplifier

An amplifier of wide bandwidth, for use as a video or pulse amplifier, may be achieved by a number of RC-coupled stages. The characteristic feature is that the values of anode load resistor R are low; the value of the shunt circuit capacitance C in parallel with the load is also kept to a low value so that with a small value of RC an appropriately high value for the upper half-power point (or -3 dB frequency) is obtained. If there is no inductance compensation, equation 10.7 indicates that the upper half-power frequency f_2 is given by

$$f_2 = 1/2\pi RC$$

and this may reasonably be taken as the bandwidth of the stage. The low value of load resistor however means that the amplification of each stage is low and so a number of stages are commonly needed. If identical stages are used the overall bandwidth is less than that of a single stage. This may be shown as follows.

The gain of a pentode amplifier stage is approximately $g_m Z$ where Z is the effective load impedance. Hence for n such stages the overall gain A_n is given by

$$A_n = (A)^n = (g_m Z)^n$$

The overall -3 db point occurs when

$$|A_n| = A^n/\sqrt{2} = (g_m Z)^n/\sqrt{2}$$

The maximum value of the gain at mid-band frequencies is given by $g_m R$, i.e.

$$A_{max} = g_m R$$

and in general

$$|A| = \frac{g_m R}{\sqrt{1+x^2}}$$

where x is a frequency dependent parameter, which has a value $x = \omega CR$ for a single stage (equation 10.6). For an n stage amplifier the magnitude of the gain is

$$|A_n| = \frac{g_m{}^n R^n}{(1+x^2)^{n/2}} \qquad . \quad . \quad . \quad 10.15$$

while the maximum gain at mid-band is $(g_m R)^n$. Hence from equation 10.10 the overall upper half-power frequency will occur when

$$(1+x^2)^{n/2} = \sqrt{2}$$

i.e. when

$$x = \sqrt{2^{1/n} - 1}$$

The half-power frequency of a single stage occurs when $x = 1$, and so the bandwidth of n stages is equal to $\sqrt{2^{1/n} - 1}$ times that of a single stage.

This result has ignored the effect of the multi-staging on the lower half-power frequency. It may be shown by a similar argument that the overall lower half-power frequency is given by $f_1/\sqrt{2^{1/n}-1}$. The overall bandwidth is thus

$$f_2\sqrt{2^{1/n}-1} - f_1/\sqrt{2^{1/n}-1}$$

$$= \frac{f_2[2^{1/n}-1]-f_1}{\sqrt{2^{1/n}-1}} \quad . \quad . \quad . \quad . \quad 10.16$$

TRANSISTORS AT HIGH FREQUENCIES

The parameters of the junction transistor begin to take a complex form at the upper end of the audio frequency range. Their high-frequency performance is limited because of several factors which have been neglected in the low-frequency amplifiers considered previously. The most important of these factors are the collector-base capacitance, the emitter-base capacitance, the frequency variation of the current amplification factor, and the transit time of current carriers in passing from the emitter to the collector.

Collector Capacitance. The collector-base capacitance, due to the depletion layer at the collector junction, is proportional to the junction area and inversely proportional to the square root of the voltage across the junction in an alloy transistor; in the diffused transistor, having a graded junction, the collector capacitance is inversely proportional to the cube root of the voltage.

Emitter Capacitance. This consists of two components, namely the depletion layer capacitance and the diffusion capacitance. The latter component is a function of the base width, increasing with it, and is dependent on the actual value of the emitter current. At small values of emitter current, the diffusion component is insignificant, whereas at high values of emitter current as in forward biasing, the diffusion capacitance predominates over the depletion capacitance.

Variation of Current Amplification Factor. The magnitude of the current amplification factor α for the common-base circuit and β (or h_{fe}) for the common-emitter circuit varies with frequency due to the distributed nature of the base resistance and junction capacitance. The current amplification factor thus becomes a complex quantity at high frequencies as opposed to being entirely real at low frequencies, and so α has to be regarded as frequency dependent, i.e.

$$\alpha = \frac{\alpha_0}{1+jf/f_\alpha}$$

where α_o is the low-frequency value and f_a denotes the *alpha cut-off frequency*. At this frequency α has fallen by 3 dB from the low-frequency value. It has been shown that $\beta = \alpha/(1-\alpha)$, and for low frequencies $\beta_o = \alpha_o/(1-\alpha_o)$. Hence at high frequencies,

$$\beta = \frac{\alpha_o/(1+jf/f_a)}{1-\dfrac{\alpha_o}{1+jf/f_a}}$$

$$= \frac{\alpha_o/(1-\alpha_o)}{1+jf/f_a(1-\alpha_o)} = \frac{\beta_o}{1+jf/f_a(1-\alpha_o)}$$

Alternatively if f_β is the -3 dB frequency for the common-emitter circuit, it will be seen that

$$\beta = \frac{\beta_o}{1+jf/f_\beta}$$

$$\text{where} \quad f_\beta = f_a(1-\alpha_o)$$

Hence for a transistor with $\alpha_o = 0{\cdot}98$ and $f_a = 1$ MHz, f_β will then be 20 kHz. Instead of using the cut-off frequency f_a or f_β an alternative parameter f_T is sometimes used; f_T is defined as the frequency at which the common-emitter current gain factor has fallen to unity.

Transit Time. The flow of minority current carriers by diffusion across the base region involves a finite time proportional to a function of the width of the base region. This factor alone limits the frequency of operation to a value such that the transit time is equal to half the period of the signal frequency.

Transistor Equivalent Circuits at High Frequency

The two equivalent circuits so far mentioned, namely the T-equivalent and the h-parameter circuits, are unsuitable for use over an extended frequency range. While the T-circuit may be modified by the inclusion of suitable capacitances, the resulting circuit, with a frequency dependent generator is cumbersome and may involve large approximations; all the h-parameters are frequency sensitive and thus each should be available in complex form. These difficulties may be overcome by the use of the hybrid-π circuit, which is discussed in Appendix B. The hybrid-π a.c. equivalent circuit for the transistor can be used for wideband and high-frequency circuits and is shown in Fig. 10.5.

Single Stage RC-coupled Wideband Amplifier

An RC-coupled amplifier stage, as indicated in Fig. 10.6a can have a wide bandwidth if the load resistor is small. The resistances $r_{b'c}$ and

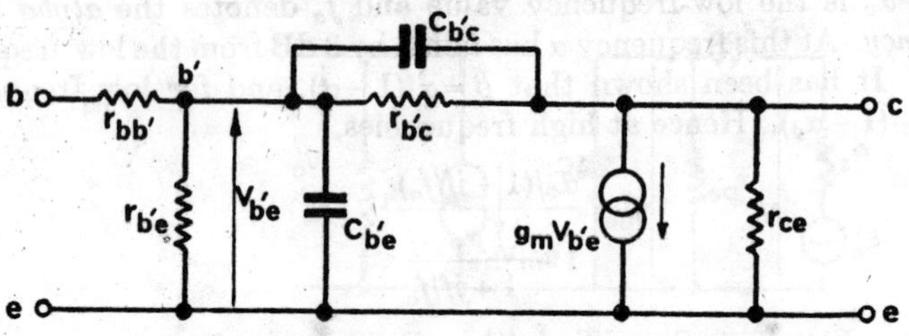

Fig. 10.5. Hybrid-π equivalent circuit.

r_{ce} are then very large compared with R_L and so the equivalent circuit of such a stage may be simplified to that shown in Fig. 10.6b if, for the moment, the presence of C_c and the input resistance of the following stages, R_{IN} is neglected.

It will be seen from the circuit of Fig. 10.6b that the voltage applied across $C_{b'c}$ is $V_{b'e} + g_m V_{b'e} R_L$ and so the current in $C_{b'c}$ is

$$V_{b'e} \omega C_{b'e}(1 + g_m R_L)$$

This is the current that would flow in a capacitor $(1 + g_m R_L) C_{b'c}$ connected across the voltage $V_{b'e}$, and so the circuit can conveniently be redrawn as in Fig. 10.7, where $C = C_{b'e} + (1 + g_m R_L) C_{b'c}$. This enhancement of the value of the input capacitance due to the presence of feedback capacitance corresponds to Miller Effect in a triode valve (see equation 6.15).

As far as the frequency response of the circuit of Fig. 10.7 is concerned, it will be seen to be the same as that of an RC circuit in which the equivalent R is given by

$$R = \frac{r_{b'e}(R_s + r_{bb'})}{r_{b'e} + R_s + r_{bb'}}$$

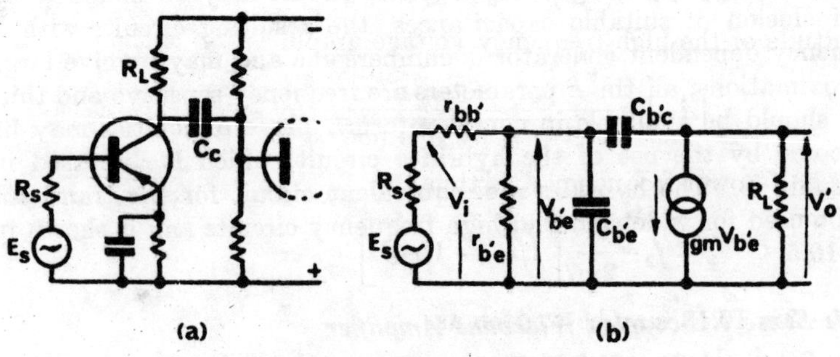

Fig. 10.6 (a) Actual circuit
(b) A.C. equivalent circuit.

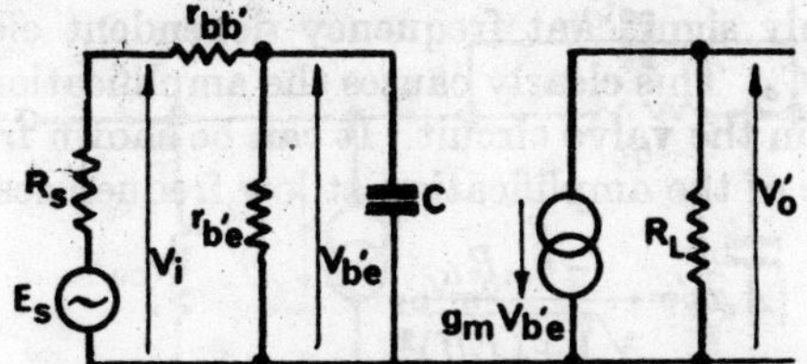

Fig. 10.7. Simplified equivalent circuit.

At mid-band frequencies, when the presence of C and the coupling capacitor C_c can be ignored, and R_L is assumed to include the input resistance of the following stage R_{IN}, in parallel, then

$$V_{b'e}/V_i = r_{b'e}/(r_{bb'} + r_{b'e})$$

while $\quad V_o' = -g_m V_{b'e} R_L$

and so in this frequency range the voltage amplification of the stage A_v is given by

$$A_v = V_o'/V_i = \frac{-g_m R_L r_{b'e}}{r_{bb'} + r_{b'e}}$$

and if $r_{b'e} > r_{bb'}$, $\quad A_v \simeq -g_m R_L$ . . . 10.17

At high frequencies, when the shunting effect of the input capacitance C can no longer be neglected

$$\frac{V_{b'e}}{V_i} = \frac{\dfrac{r_{b'e}}{1 + j\omega C r_{b'e}}}{r_{bb'} + \dfrac{r_{b'e}}{1 + j\omega C r_{b'e}}}$$

while $\quad \dfrac{V_o'}{V_i} = \dfrac{-g_m R_L r_{b'e}}{(1 + j\omega C r_{b'e}) r_{bb'} + r_{b'e}}$

The magnitude of the high-frequency voltage amplification is thus

$$|A_{vh}| = \frac{-g_m R_L}{\sqrt{(1 + r_{bb'}/r_{b'e})^2 + (\omega C r_{bb'})^2}} \quad . \quad . \quad 10.18$$

The upper half-power frequency f_2 is thus

$$f_2 = \frac{1}{2\pi C}\left[1/r_{b'e} + 1/r_{bb'}\right]$$

and so equation 10.18 may be written as

$$|A_{vh}| = \frac{-g_m R_L}{\sqrt{1 + (f/f_2)^2}} \quad . \quad . \quad . \quad . \quad 10.19$$

which corresponds with equation 10.8 for the pentode stage. At low frequencies, the only significant frequency dependent element is the coupling capacitor C_c. This clearly causes the amplification to decrease with frequency, as in the valve circuit. It can be shown from Fig. 10.8 that the magnitude of the amplification at low frequencies is given by

$$|A_{vl}| = \frac{-g_m R_L}{\sqrt{1+(f_1/f)^2}} \quad . \quad . \quad . \quad . \quad 10.20$$

where f_1 is the lower half-power frequency.

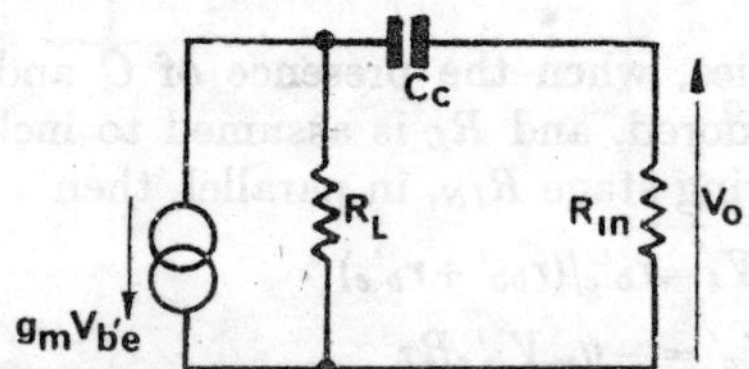

Fig. 10.8. Low-frequency circuit.

In the transistor circuit the value of C_c required for a given low frequency response is very much larger than that needed for the valve circuit as the value of the input resistance R_{IN} is relatively low.

An extension of the high-frequency end of the response curve may be obtained by means of inductance compensation. As in the valve circuit, a suitable value of inductance is inserted in series with the load resistor.

The remarks on the effect of multi-staging on the bandwidth of an amplifier were made with respect to a valve amplifier, but apply also to a multi-stage transistor amplifier. The result of equation 10.16 may thus be applied to either type.

TUNED VOLTAGE AMPLIFIERS

It is often necessary to amplify a single frequency, or a narrow range of frequencies where the bandwidth is small compared with the midband frequency. In such cases, tuned amplifiers incorporating resonant circuits are used.

VALVE TUNED AMPLIFIERS

The Tuned Anode Circuit

The simplest arrangement is that shown in Fig. 10.9a where the anode load of the valve is a parallel tuned circuit, in which the stray

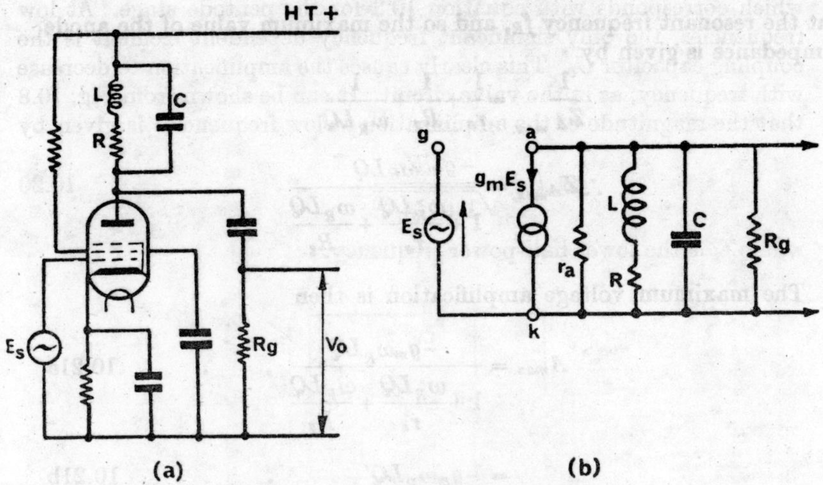

Fig. 10.9. Simple tuned anode circuit.

circuit and valve capacitance is in parallel with, and forms part of, the tuning capacitance C.

With a pentode valve, the anode resistance r_a is larger than the dynamic resistance of the circuit when resonant. If the succeeding grid resistance is also large compared with the maximum impedance of the tuned circuit, the amplification obtained with the stage will vary with the impedance of the resonant circuit, and so a curve of amplification against frequency will then be substantially the same as the impedance/frequency curve for the LCR circuit. The presence of the coupling capacitance can be ignored as the reactance is negligibly small over the operating range. It can be seen from the equivalent circuit of Fig. 10.9b that the voltage amplification, A, is given by,

$$A = \left|\frac{V_0}{E_s}\right| = -g_m Z_A$$

where Z_A is the total anode impedance.

Z_A has its maximum value when the tuned circuit is resonant. If resonance is achieved by adjustment of the capacitance C, the tuned circuit impedance is

$$\frac{L}{CR} = \omega_R LQ \quad \text{(equation 3.34b)}$$

at the resonant frequency f_R, and so the maximum value of the anode impedance is given by

$$\frac{1}{Z_{A\,max.}} = \frac{1}{r_a} + \frac{1}{R_g} + \frac{1}{\omega_R LQ}$$

$$\therefore Z_{A_{max.}} = \frac{\omega_R LQ}{1 + \frac{\omega_R LQ}{r_a} + \frac{\omega_R LQ}{R_g}}$$

The maximum voltage amplification is then

$$A_{max.} = \frac{-g_m\omega_R LQ}{1 + \frac{\omega_R LQ}{r_a} + \frac{\omega_R LQ}{R_g}} \quad . \quad . \quad . \quad 10.21a$$

$$= -g_m\omega_R LQ' \quad . \quad . \quad . \quad . \quad 10.21b$$

where Q' is the equivalent Q-factor for the total anode impedance, as opposed to the Q-factor for the LCR circuit alone. Thus the effect of r_a and R_g is to reduce the value of Q to Q' and thereby decrease the selectivity of the anode circuit. If a pentode valve is used, the shunting effect of r_a is negligibly small and can be neglected. If this is also true for the grid leak resistor R_g the maximum voltage amplification is then

$$A_{max.} = -g_m\omega_R LQ \quad . \quad . \quad . \quad . \quad 10.22$$

It will be seen that *if the Q-factor of the coil is sensibly constant over a range of frequencies*, the stage gain obtained is proportional to the value of the resonant frequency used.

Equation 10.22 gives the gain obtained at the resonant frequency f_R. For any other frequency $\omega/2\pi$, the gain is given by,

$$|A| = -g_m|Z|$$

If the coil of the tuned circuit is expressed as having a parallel loss resistance R_p (as shown in Fig. 3.2b), rather than the series resistance R as considered above, then from equation 3.39b the impedance of the tuned circuit at a small separation δf from the resonant value, is given by

$$Z \simeq \frac{R_p}{1 + jQ2\delta f/f_R}$$

and so the gain at any frequency is

$$A \simeq \frac{-g_m R_p}{1 + jQ2\delta f/f_R} \quad . \quad . \quad . \quad . \quad 10.23a$$

or in terms of magnitudes

$$|A| \simeq \frac{g_m R_p}{\sqrt{1+(Q2\delta f/f_R)^2}} \quad . \quad . \quad . \quad . \quad 10.23b$$

If any resistance is present in parallel with R_p, such as the anode slope resistance of the pentode valve, or a following grid leak, the results of equations 10.23a or 10.23b may be used if the value of R_p is suitably modified.

The ratio of the amplification at any frequency f to the maximum value of the amplification at the resonant frequency is

$$\frac{A}{A_{max.}} \simeq \frac{1}{1+jQ2\delta f/f_R} \quad . \quad . \quad . \quad . \quad 10.24a$$

or in terms of magnitudes

$$\frac{|A|}{|A_{max.}|} \simeq \frac{1}{\sqrt{1+(Q2\delta f/f_R)^2}} \quad . \quad . \quad . \quad . \quad 10.24b$$

The Transformer Coupled Tuned Circuit

An alternative to the tuned anode circuit considered above has the tuned circuit replaced by a high-frequency transformer with the secondary circuit tuned to resonance (i.e. to maximum impedance) by adjustment of C.

The impedance at the terminals of the primary winding is

$$R_1 + j\omega L_1 + \omega^2 M^2/Z_S^2 \quad \text{(equation 3.68)}$$

If the secondary circuit is tuned to resonance so that $\omega L = 1/\omega C$ and the transferred impedance of the secondary is large compared with

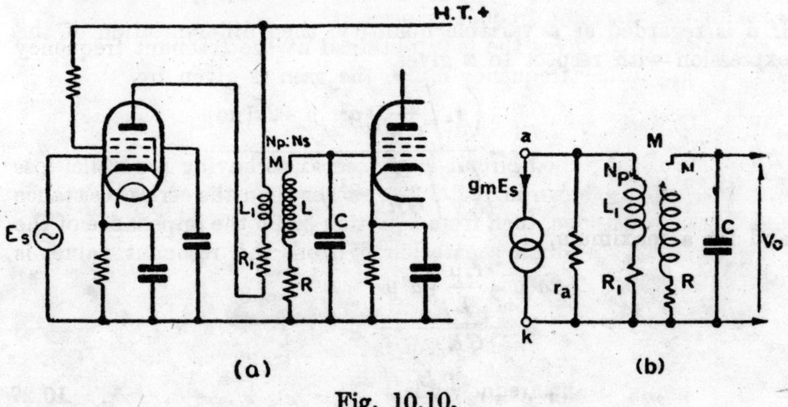

Fig. 10.10.

the impedance of the primary winding, then the impedance presented as an anode load for the valve is

$$\frac{L}{CR}\left(k\frac{N_p}{N_s}\right)^2 \text{ (equation 3.69)}$$

where k is the coefficient of coupling between the two windings. The alternating current in the primary winding is then given by

$$i_p = g_m E_s \,.\, r_a/(r_a + a^2 L/CR)$$
$$\text{where } a = kN_p/N_s,$$

and so the voltage at the primary terminals is given by

$$g_m E_s \frac{r_a \,.\, a^2 \dfrac{L}{CR}}{r_a + a^2 \dfrac{L}{CR}} \quad . \quad . \quad 10.25$$

The secondary circuit is resonant, and has an impedance R, hence the secondary current is $j\omega Mi_p/R$, and the output voltage V_0, across the capacitor is

$$\frac{j\omega Mi_p}{R} \,.\, \frac{1}{j\omega C} = \frac{M}{CR} i_p = g_m E_s \frac{r_a M/L}{CRr_a/L + a^2}$$

$$\text{now } M/L = k\sqrt{L_1 L}/L = k\sqrt{L_1/L} = a$$

$$\therefore \text{Output voltage } V_0 = \frac{\mu E_s a}{CRr_a/L + a^2}$$

and the voltage amplification of the stage is thus

$$A = \frac{-\mu a}{r_a\Big/\dfrac{L}{CR} + a^2} \quad . \quad . \quad . \quad . \quad 10.26$$

If a is regarded as a variable quantity, then differentiation of this expression with respect to a gives,

$$\frac{dA}{da} = \frac{\left(r_a\Big/\dfrac{L}{CR} + a^2\right)\mu - 2a(\mu a)}{\left(r_a\Big/\dfrac{L}{CR} + a^2\right)^2}$$

and for a maximum,

$$2a^2\mu = \frac{r_a \mu}{\dfrac{L}{CR}} + a^2\mu$$

$$\text{or } a^2 = r_a\Big/\frac{L}{CR} \quad . \quad . \quad . \quad . \quad 10.27$$

This result shows that the voltage amplification will be a maximum when the value of a is adjusted so that the impedance at the primary terminals of the transformer is equal to the anode slope resistance of the valve. If the valve is a pentode, r_a may well be greater than L/CR, which implies that for such a case a must be greater than unity for maximum amplification, i.e. a "step-down" transformer with $N_p > N_s$ must be used.

In practice, a step-up transformer, with a less than unity is often employed in the interests of stability. If the gain is very high the alternating anode voltage may circulate sufficient current through the residual anode to grid capacitance of the valve to cause the stage to be unstable. Equation 10.25 shows that the alternating anode voltage is

$$= -g_m E_s \frac{a^2 \dfrac{L}{CR}}{1 + a^2 \dfrac{L}{CRr_a}} = -g_m E_s\, a^2 \frac{L}{CR} \text{ if } r_a >> a^2 \frac{L}{CR}$$

The alternating anode voltage is thus reduced by a factor a^2 compared with the tuned anode case. The amplification on the other hand is

$$A = \frac{-g_m \,.\, r_a \,.\, a\, \dfrac{L}{CR}}{r_a + a^2\, \dfrac{L}{CR}} = -g_m \,.\, a\, \frac{L}{CR}, \text{ if } r_a >> a^2 \frac{L}{CR}$$

and this is reduced from that for the tuned anode case by the factor a.

The tuned anode circuit thus gives a larger amount of amplification than the transformer coupled arrangement. If, however, it is necessary to limit the stage gain, the step up transformer circuit achieves this and decreases the possibility of instability, by reducing the alternating voltage at the valve anode.

The expression for the voltage amplification in equation 10.26 is the amplification obtained when the secondary circuit is resonant. At frequencies on either side of the resonant value the amplification falls and the gain/frequency characteristic is substantially that of the impedance/frequency characteristic of the transformer secondary circuit.

High-Frequency Transformer with Tuned Primary and Tuned Secondary

The two types of tuned amplifier so far described have a gain/frequency curve which has a maximum when the tuned circuit has its maximum impedance. On either side of this frequency the gain falls away and so such circuits cannot provide uniform amplification over even a narrow bandwidth.

If uniform amplification over a band is desired, it is necessary to use some form of band pass filter. A simple form of this is the transformer with tuned primary and tuned secondary. The circuit arrangement for this is shown in Fig. 10.11. The bandwidth obtained

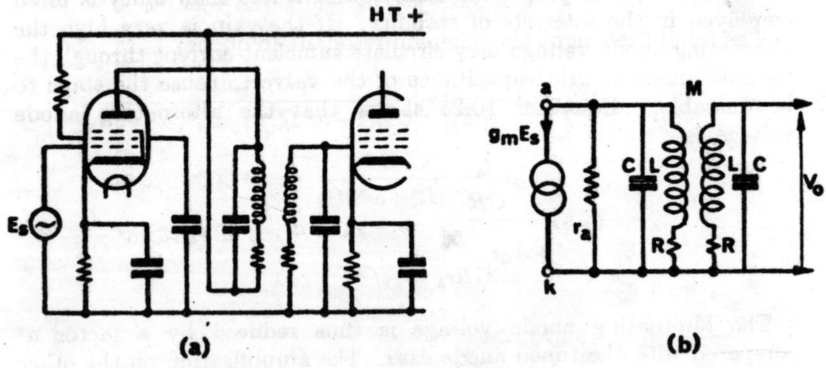

Fig. 10.11.

depends on the magnetic coupling between the two coils (see chapter 3) and increases as the coupling increases beyond the critical value.

This tuned coupling arrangement in its most common form has identical primary and secondary circuits, and this will be assumed so that each coil has an inductance L, and a resistance R, whilst the tuning capacitance in both cases is C, which is assumed to be loss free.

If a pentode valve is used the anode resistance r_a will be shunted across the primary as shown in the equivalent circuit of Fig. 10.11b. It is reasonable to neglect the presence of r_a as being large compared with the primary input impedance of the coupled circuit. With this assumption the current in the primary coil i_p is then a fraction of the current g_mE_s

i.e. $$i_p = g_mE_s\left[\frac{1/j\omega C}{\dfrac{1}{j\omega C}+R+j\omega L+\dfrac{\omega^2M^2}{R}}\right]$$

as the impedance at the primary coil terminals is $\left(R+j\omega L+\dfrac{\omega^2M^2}{R}\right)$ when the secondary circuit is resonant.

$$\therefore\ i_p = \frac{g_mE_sR}{R+j\omega CR^2-\omega^2LCR+j\omega C\omega^2M^2}$$

The voltage induced in the secondary coil is $j\omega M i_p$, and the secondary current is $(j\omega M i_p)/R$. The output voltage across the capacitor in the

$$\text{secondary circuit} = V_0 = \frac{j\omega M i_p}{j\omega CR} = \frac{M}{CR} i_p$$

$$\therefore V_0 = \frac{g_m E_s M}{CR + j\omega C^2 R^2 - \omega^2 LC^2 R + j\omega C^2 \omega^2 M^2}$$

The amplification at the common resonant frequency f_R is then

$$A = \left|\frac{V_o}{E_s}\right| = \left|\frac{g_m M}{CR(1-\omega^2 LC) + j\omega C^2(R^2+\omega^2 M^2)}\right|$$

$$= \frac{g_m M}{\omega C^2(R^2+\omega^2 M^2)} \quad \text{as } \omega^2 LC = 1$$

$$\text{or } A = \frac{g_m \omega M}{\omega^2 C^2 \omega^2 L^2\left(\dfrac{1}{Q^2}+k^2\right)}$$

$$\text{as } \frac{\omega^2 L^2}{R^2} = Q^2,\ \omega^2 M^2 = k^2 \omega^2 L^2, \text{ and } \omega M = k\omega L$$

$$\therefore \quad A = \frac{g_m k\omega L}{\dfrac{1}{Q^2}+k^2} \qquad . \quad . \quad . \quad . \quad . \qquad 10.28$$

This result thus gives the voltage amplification at the common resonant frequency of the two circuits. If the coefficient of coupling has its critical value of $1/Q$ (equation 3.76) then for this special case the voltage amplification has its maximum amplification which is

$$A_{max.} = \tfrac{1}{2} g_m\ \omega LQ \qquad . \quad . \quad . \quad . \quad . \qquad 10.29$$

If this result is compared with equation 10.22 it will be seen that the pair of critically coupled circuits produce a maximum value of amplification which is half that for a single circuit alone. The selectivity in the coupled circuit case, however, is much greater.

The bandwidth between the peaks in the response in the coupled circuit case is

$$\Delta f = \frac{f_R}{Q} \text{ (equation 3.77)}$$

if, as has been assumed $Q_p = Q_s = Q$.

TRANSISTOR TUNED AMPLIFIERS

The various types of tuned amplifier described above may have the valves replaced by transistors. Often the main difference arises from the low input impedance of the transistor as compared with the valve, and so the coupling circuit between the two transistors has to be arranged to match the fairly high output impedance of the first to the low input impedance of the second. Fig. 10.12 shows a simple form of tuned amplifier in which the collector load is a single tuned circuit, transformer coupled to the second transistor. The transformation ratio n is chosen such that

$$n = \sqrt{R_o/R_{in}}$$

where R_o is the output resistance of the first stage and R_{in} is the input resistance of the second.

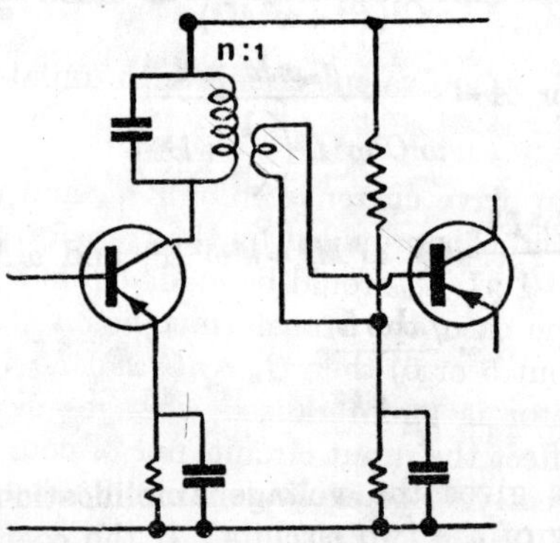

Fig. 10.12. Simple tuned amplifier stage.

Unilateralisation

A study of the hybrid-π equivalent circuit shows that internal feedback in the transistor exists by virtue of the presence of the components $r_{b'c}$ and $C_{b'c}$. The input impedance depends on the output load impedance so that the resonant frequencies of tuned circuits at the input and output terminals of the transistor are interdependent. This makes the process of tuning a multi-stage amplifier very difficult. The internal feedback may be eliminated, over a restricted range of frequency, by applying external feedback, equal in magnitude and opposite in phase. When the input is isolated from the output in this way, the transistor is said to be *unilateralised*, i.e. it now transmits energy in one direction only. If the resistance $r_{b'c}$ is very large and its feedback effect thus insignificant, feedback results from the presence of $C_{b'c}$. Feedback can then be eliminated by an external capacitor alone. In this case the process is referred to as *neutralisation*.

The hybrid-π circuit of Fig. 10.5 may be redrawn as in Fig. 10.13 with the feedback elements $r_{b'c}$ and $C_{b'c}$ replaced by their respective equivalent series values R and C. The unilateralising components are R_u and C_u.

It should be noted that Fig. 10.13 is a π-equivalent circuit having a current generator related to the input voltage V_i. The necessary phase

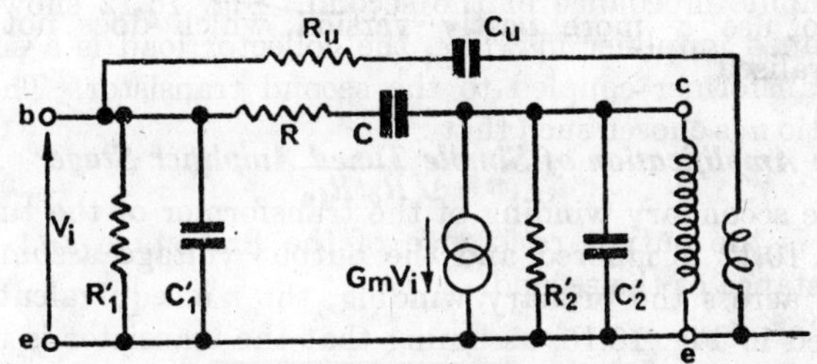

Fig. 10.13. π-equivalent circuit with unilateralisation.

reversal of voltage to drive current through R_u and C_u in opposition to the current in R and C is provided by the transformer. If the transformer had a ratio of 1 : 1, C_u would be made equal to C and R_u to R. If, as is normally the case, the transformer has a step-down ratio of $n : 1$ (where n is about 5 or 6) then $C_u = nC$ and $R_u = R/n$.

When the transistor is unilateralised, changes in the output load impedance do not affect the input circuit, nor of course does the input affect the output directly. The equivalent circuit then simplifies to the form shown in Fig. 10.14.

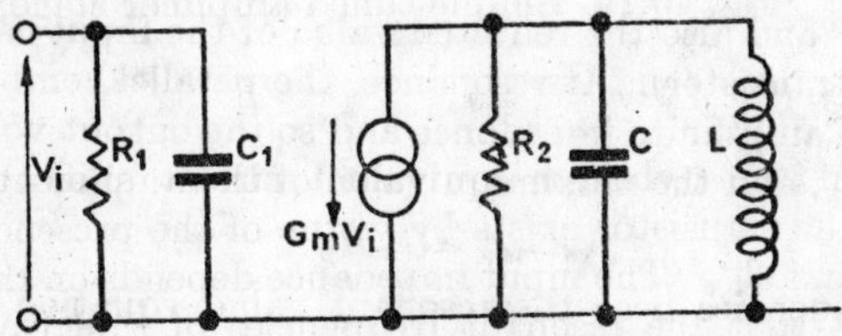

Fig. 10.14. Simplified equivalent circuit of a unilateralised transistor.

R_u and C_u are in parallel with the input circuit and so the parallel equivalent values of these components, R_u' and C_u' respectively contribute to the values of R_1 and C_1. In the output circuit, the effect of R_u' and C_u' is seen at the transistor terminals of the transformer and they thus appear to have the values n^2R_u' and C_u'/n^2. These latter values thus form part of R_2 and C_2.

The question of whether a transistor is unilateralised or not depends on the type of transistor and the frequency at which it is to be used. The construction may be such that the internal feedback is insignificant and unilateralisation unnecessary. Alternatively it may be more economic to unilateralise a cheaper, relatively low-frequency type, than to use a more costly version which does not need to be unilateralised.

Voltage Amplification of Simple Tuned Amplifier Stage

If the secondary winding of the transformer of the tuned amplifier of Fig. 10.12 is ignored and the output voltage assumed to be the voltage across the primary winding, the a.c. equivalent circuit is as indicated in Fig. 10.15, assuming that the transistor is unilateralised.

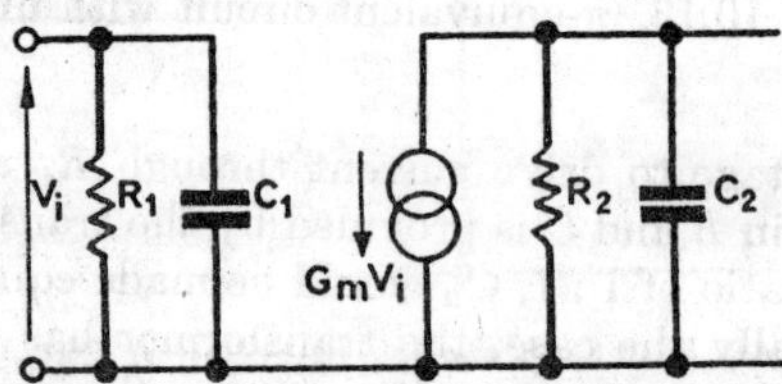

Fig. 10.15. Equivalent circuit for tuned amplifier stage.

If the tuning coil L is treated as having a parallel loss resistance R_p, this can be represented as shown and can include the value of R_2 in Fig. 10.14. The tuning capacitance C also includes the value of C_2 in Fig. 10.14 (and also the reflected value of the input capacitance of the following transistor). At resonance, the parallel combination of L and C presents an infinite impedance and so the output voltage V_o is equal to $G_m V_i R_p$, and the maximum value of the amplification

$$A_{max} = G_m R_p \qquad 10.30$$

For frequencies near the resonant value, equation 10.23a indicates that the magnitude of the amplification is

$$A \simeq \frac{G_m R_p}{\sqrt{1 + (Q2\delta f/f_R)^2}} \qquad 10.31$$

The maximum amplification of the stage when a step-down transformer of ratio $n : 1$ is used will be $G_m R_p/2n$ if the secondary winding is loaded with a resistance of matching value.

Multi-stage Tuned Amplifiers

Two stages of a tuned amplifier, with unilateralisation applied to each stage, are shown in Fig. 10.16. Depending on the bandwidth required, the collector may be connected to a tapping on the primary coil. This decreases the loading on the circuit to give a narrower bandwidth.

The third transistor in Fig. 10.16 is shown coupled to the second by a double tuned circuit, i.e. resonant primary and resonant secondary.

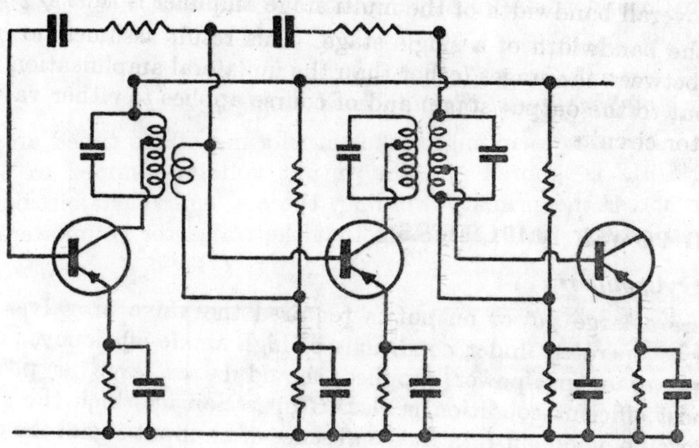

Fig. 10.16. Two stages of a tuned amplifier.

When this is employed the following transistor is connected to a tapping on the secondary winding.

Bandwidth of a Multi-stage Tuned Amplifier

In a multi-stage tuned amplifier the overall bandwidth is less than that of any individual stage. Suppose for simplicity that all the stages are identical, that each stage has a single parallel resonant circuit, and that they are all tuned to the same resonant frequency; the amplifier is then said to be *synchronously tuned*. At frequencies close to resonance it has been shown that the magnitude of the amplification for a single stage is given by

$$|A| = \frac{g_m R_P}{\sqrt{1+(Q2\delta f/f_R)^2}} \quad \text{(equation 10.23b)}$$

and so for n identical stages

$$|A_n| = \frac{(g_m R_P)^n}{(1+x^2)^{n/2}}$$

$$\text{where} \quad x = Q2\delta f/f_R$$

The overall -3 dB frequencies are then defined by the value of δf which makes

$$|A_n| = |A_{max}|/\sqrt{2}$$

i.e. when $(1+x^2)^{n/2}=\sqrt{2}$ or when $x=\sqrt{2^{1/n}-1}$. The -3 dB bandwidth of a single stage $\Delta f = 2\delta f$ is defined by

$$\Delta f = 2\delta f = f_R/Q$$

i.e. when $x = 1$.

The overall bandwidth of the multi-stage amplifier is thus $\sqrt{2^{1/n}-1}$ times the bandwidth of a single stage. This result assumes no interaction between the stages (other than the unilateral amplification from the input to the output stage) and of course applies to either valve or transistor circuits.

TUNED POWER AMPLIFIERS

Class C Amplifiers

Where a large power output is required the valve or valves used should be operated under conditions of high anode efficiency, i.e. the ratio power output/power supplied should be as large as possible. The most efficient condition is class *C* operation in which the grid is biased well beyond cut-off. In the absence of an input signal the anode current is zero. The application of a signal between grid and cathode causes anode current to flow for that part of the signal voltage cycle which makes the grid voltage less than the cut-off value. The anode current then consists of a series of pulses. Such non-linear operation would give gross distortion if the anode load was a resistor, as the output voltage would bear little resemblance to the applied grid voltage.

If the signal voltage is a single frequency it is possible to use a parallel resonant circuit as an anode load. If this circuit is tuned to the frequency of the applied signal in the grid circuit, it will present a high impedance to that frequency, and a low impedance to other (harmonic) frequencies. It is thus possible to operate a tuned amplifier under class *C* conditions with a relatively small amount of distortion in the output. Such amplifiers are used in radio transmitters and in other cases where a large power output is required.

The circuit arrangement is shown in Fig. 10.17.

It might at first sight seem preferable to use a pentode rather than a triode valve, but it must be remembered that class *C* operation is used where the amount of power handled is large. This means that the anode dissipation of the valve must be high. The anode can be kept to a safe temperature by a water cooling system whereas the heating of the screen in a tetrode or pentode cannot be so limited. This means that the size of a tetrode or pentode valve may be limited by heating of the screen. Triodes are free from this limitation and can be constructed and used to give much larger outputs.

The effect of unwanted feedback through the anode to grid capacitance

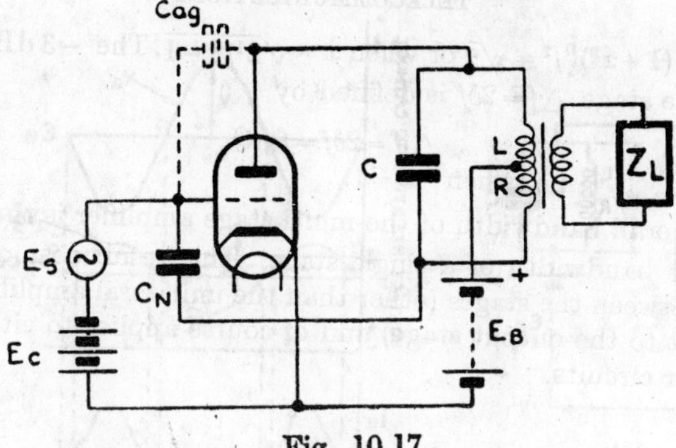

Fig. 10.17.

of the triode is eliminated by the use of a neutralising circuit. If the coil in the output tuned circuit is centre tapped as shown, the connection of the neutralising capacitor C_N will give rise to feedback in phase opposition to that due to C_{ag}. If the size of C_N is correctly adjusted the stage will then be stable.

The tuned anode circuit is inductively coupled to the load impedance Z_L. If this is a resistance then its effect will be to reduce the Q factor of the coil in the resonant circuit, i.e. the value of R will be increased. A reactive component in Z_L will necessitate adjustment of the anode tuning capacitor C to make the anode circuit resonant to the signal frequency applied to the grid.

Voltages and Currents in a Class C Tuned Amplifier

If the neutralising circuit is omitted, the basic circuit is that shown in Fig. 10.18a, whilst the corresponding currents and voltages are as shown in Fig. 10.18b.

When the anode tuning capacitor C is varied, the anode circuit becomes non-reactive at the setting which gives the anode load impedance its maximum value. The anode load is then said to be correctly tuned and the valve then has a resistive anode load ; the anode voltage variation is sinusoidal (provided the anode circuit has a large Q-factor) and is in phase opposition to the grid voltage. The anode current consists of a series of pulses, the length of which depends on θ, the " angle of current flow " where

$$\theta = 2\left(90° - \sin^{-1}\frac{E_c - E_{cut\text{-}off}}{\hat{E}_s}\right) \quad . \quad . \quad 10.32$$

Grid current flows in the form of a series of pulses if the grid voltage is driven positive, as is normally the case. The angle of grid current flow is less than θ as grid current starts to flow when the

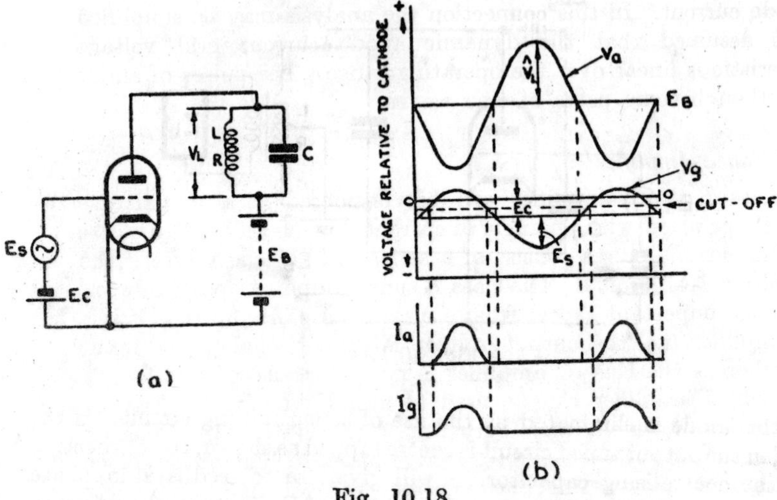

Fig. 10.18.

grid is slightly negative with respect to the cathode, and not necessarily at the anode current cut off point. (The grid and anode currents are not shown to the same scale Fig. 10.18b.)

Power Output and Anode Efficiency of a Class C Tuned Amplifier

The power output of a Class *C* tuned amplifier is given by

$$P_o = \frac{\hat{V}_L}{\sqrt{2}} \times \frac{\hat{I}_{a1}}{\sqrt{2}} \quad . \quad . \quad . \quad . \quad 10.33$$

where $\hat{I}_{a1}$ is the maximum value of the fundamental component of the anode alternating current and $\hat{V}_L$ is the maximum value of the alternating voltage across the anode load.

The power supplied to the valve is the product of the mean anode voltage and the mean value of the anode current. The mean value of the anode voltage is E_B, the voltage of the supply, and if I_B represents the mean value of anode current, the power supplied to the anode is

$$P_{d.c.} = E_B I_B \quad . \quad . \quad . \quad . \quad . \quad 10.34$$

and the anode efficiency is

$$= \frac{\hat{V}_L \hat{I}_{a1}}{2E_B I_B} \quad . \quad . \quad . \quad . \quad 10.35$$

To obtain the fundamental component of anode current I_{a_1} and also the mean value I_B it is necessary to carry out a Fourier analysis of the anode current. In this connection the analysis may be simplified if it is assumed that the dynamic anode current grid voltage characteristic is linear over the operating range. The pulses of anode current then become parts of sine waves.

Class B Tuned Amplifier

The class *B* tuned amplifier can be considered as a special case of class *C* operation with an angle of current flow of 180°. In this case the anode current pulses consist of a series of half sine waves if the input voltage is sinusoidal. The class *B* tuned amplifier does, however, differ in one important aspect from a class *C* amplifier, in that it is a linear amplifier (i.e. the output voltage is proportional to the input signal) whereas the class *C* amplifier is not. Because of this fact, a class *B* tuned amplifier can be used to amplify modulated signals, the amplitude of which varies with time (see chapter 12). Consider the application of such a signal to a valve biased to cut off as shown in Fig. 10.19. If the dynamic anode current/grid voltage characteristic is assumed to be linear then a signal voltage applied as shown will

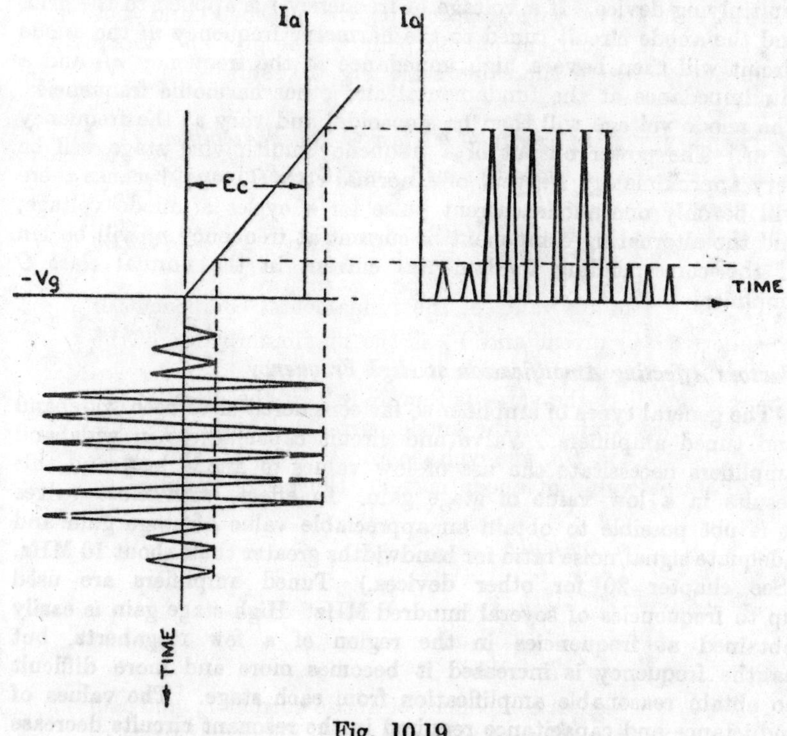

Fig. 10.19.

give rise to pulses of anode current. The envelope waveform of these pulses is the same as the envelope of the applied grid voltage. If now the anode load is a circuit tuned to the high-frequency component of the signal the output voltage at the anode will have the same waveform as the input.

If the valve had been biased to say twice the value of cut-off it is clear that the envelope waveform of the resulting anode current would not correspond to the envelope waveform of the input.

In practice, the dynamic anode current/grid voltage characteristic of a valve is curved, particularly near the cut-off point. The distortion in a class *B* tuned amplifier due to this cause can be reduced if the valve is biased to a value slightly less than cut-off (i.e. to projected cut-off, as mentioned in connection with class *B* audio frequency push-pull amplifiers in chapter 8).

Frequency Multiplier Amplifiers

In cases where a frequency is to be multiplied by a factor n (where n is a small integer) a class *C* amplifier can be used as the frequency multiplying device. If a voltage of frequency f is applied to the grid, and the anode circuit tuned to the harmonic frequency nf the anode circuit will then have a high impedance at the frequency nf, and a low impedance at the fundamental and other harmonic frequencies. The anode voltage will then be sinusoidal and vary at the frequency of nf. The power output of a frequency multiplying stage will be very approximately $1/n$ that of a normal class *C* stage, because there will be only one anode current pulse for n cycles of anode voltage, and the alternating component of current at frequency nf will be $1/n$ of the corresponding fundamental current in the normal class *C* amplifier.

Factors Affecting Amplification at High Frequency

The general types of amplifier so far considered have been wideband and tuned amplifiers. Valve and circuit capacitances in wideband amplifiers necessitate the use of low values of anode load and this results in a low value of stage gain. In effect, with most valves it is not possible to obtain an appreciable value of stage gain and adequate signal/noise ratio for bandwidths greater than about 10 MHz. (See chapter 20 for other devices.) Tuned amplifiers are used up to frequencies of several hundred MHz. High stage gain is easily obtained at frequencies in the region of a few megahertz, but as the frequency is increased it becomes more and more difficult to obtain reasonable amplification from each stage. The values of inductance and capacitance required in the resonant circuits decrease in value and the impedance of such circuits decreases; the gain falls as a consequence. Other, and more important limitations arise from the behaviour of the valves.

VALVE PERFORMANCE AT HIGH FREQUENCIES

There are two effects in a valve which diminish the gain at high frequencies. The first is the transit time of the electrons in their passage through the valve from cathode to anode. It has been assumed implicitly that the change of anode current which results from a change of grid voltage is an instantaneous effect, whereas the electrons do in fact have a finite time of travel, known as the *transit time*. This has to be taken into account when the electron transit time ceases to be a negligible fraction of the time for one cycle of the applied signal. The most important aspect of this effect is that it causes the input resistance between grid and cathode to be decreased.[1,2] The second effect which causes a reduction of gain at high frequencies is the presence of inductance in the cathode lead. This also causes a decrease in the input resistance between grid and cathode of the valve. These effects are not significant at frequencies lower than say, about 30 MHz, but become increasingly important at higher frequencies and eventually set a limit to the usefulness of conventional type valves as amplifiers or oscillators.

(a) Transit Time Effect

A detailed consideration of this effect is beyond the scope of this book but the phenomenon can be treated in an approximate fashion as follows:

Let g_m = mutual conductance of the valve,

t_g = time occupied by electrons in traversing the distance between the cathode and grid,

and t_a = the time occupied by electrons in traversing the distance between the grid and the anode.

Suppose now that a sinusoidal voltage is applied to the grid, so that

$$V_g = V \sin \omega t$$

then the current flowing towards the grid is given by

$$i = g_m V \sin \omega(t - t_g)$$

and the current flowing towards the anode i_a, is given by

$$i_a = g_m V \sin \omega(t - t_g - t_a)$$

now the grid current

$$i_g = i - i_a$$

$$= g_m V[\sin \omega(t - t_g) - \sin \omega(t - t_g - t_a)]$$
$$= 2g_m V \cos \omega(t - t_g - t_a/2) \sin (\omega t_a/2)$$

This can be expressed as

$$i_g = 2g_m V \sin (\omega t_a/2)\{\cos \omega t \cos \omega(t_g + t_a/2) + \sin \omega t \sin \omega(t_g + t_a/2)\}$$

There are thus two components of grid current, one

$$[2g_m V \sin (\omega t_a/2) \sin \omega(t_g + t_a/2)] \sin \omega t$$

is in phase with the applied grid voltage, while the other

$$[2g_m V \sin (\omega t_a/2) \cos \omega(t_g + t_a/2)] \cos \omega t$$

leads the applied grid voltage by 90°. If ωt_g and $\omega t_a/2$ are relatively small quantities, so that with a fair degree of approximation,

$$\sin \omega t_a/2 = \omega t_a/2,$$
$$\sin \omega(t_g + t_a/2) = \omega(t_g + t/_a2),$$
$$\text{and } \cos \omega(t_g + t_a/2) = 1,$$

then the in-phase component of grid current is given, very approximately, by

$$g_m V \omega^2(t_g t_a + t_a^2/2)$$

and the capacitance component of grid current is approximately

$$g_m V \omega t_a$$

Thus the effect of transit time is to cause the valve to have an apparent complex input impedance consisting of a resistance and capacitance in parallel. The resistive component R_I is given by

$$R_I = \frac{K}{g_m f^2} \quad . \quad . \quad . \quad . \quad . \quad . \quad . \quad 10.36$$

where K is a constant for a given valve under particular operating conditions. The input capacitance C_I is given by

$$C_I = g_m t_a \quad . \quad . \quad . \quad . \quad . \quad . \quad . \quad . \quad 10.37$$

The increase of input capacitance due to transit time is not usually important. The effective damping of the external circuit connected between the grid and cathode terminals on the other hand, is serious in that it decreases the impedance of the external circuit connected to the valve. Another disadvantage of finite electron transit time is that the mutual conductance of the valve is decreased in magnitude and is made a complex quantity by the introduction of a phase angle varying with frequency and with changes in the applied voltages. A third disadvantage of transit time is that it reduces the anode efficiency realisable in a power amplifier or oscillator, when the output power is limited by the permissible anode dissipation ; in such circuits anode efficiencies up to about 80% are obtainable at frequencies at which transit time is negligible, because anode current flows only at times when the anode voltage is near its minimum value. Finite transit time upsets this relationship at high frequencies ; the anode efficiency is decreased and the output will be further diminished if the H.T. voltage has to be reduced to keep the anode dissipation constant.

(b) Valve Capacitances and Lead Inductances

At low frequencies a valve may often be regarded as a voltage amplifying device added to, or connected across, an external tuned circuit ; in very high frequency amplifiers the unavoidable capacitances and inductances within the valve envelope may form major portions of the tuned circuits, thus introducing serious problems in the design of inter-stage couplings. In the limiting case the circuit tends to vanish inside the valve. The internal capacitances and self-inductances of a triode are shown in Fig. 10.20(a) while Fig. 10.20(b) indicates

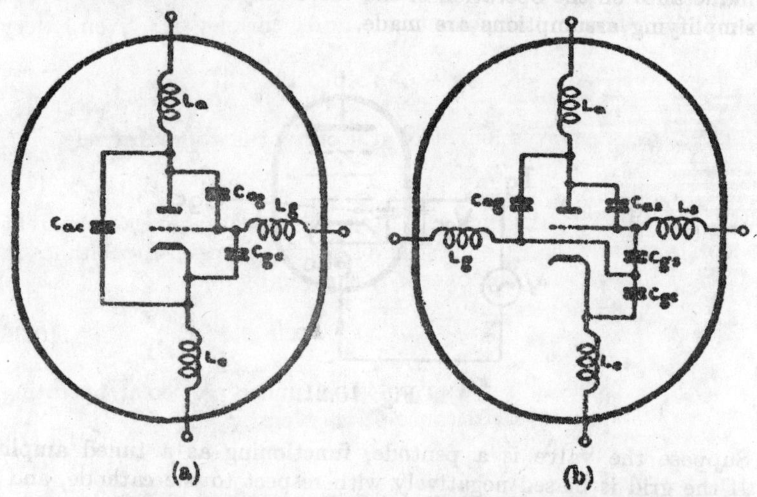

[By permission of the P.O.E.E. Journal

Fig. 10.20. Self-inductances and internal capacitances of
(a) A triode valve
(b) A tetrode valve.

some of the more important capacitances of a tetrode valve. Mutual inductance between leads have also to be considered in a full analysis of the operation of many very high frequency valves.

Low input and output capacitances in a valve are of importance not only in ensuring reasonable circuit size at very high frequencies, but also on account of their influence on the maximum stage gain and bandwidth realisable as discussed above (see equation 10.10). Because of transit time limitations, it is impossible to reduce capacitances in very high frequency valves by increasing inter-electrode spacings, and capacitance between the active sections of adjacent electrodes can be reduced only by decreasing their areas. Stray capacitances between leads and supports make no useful contribution to the operation of the valve, and it is particularly important that they should be as small as possible. As a very high frequency valve often forms the main tuning capacitance, reasonably close tolerances on input and output capacitances are most desirable if interchangeability is to be ensured.

In addition to the effect of lead inductances on circuit size, individual leads may be of special importance in particular circuits. For example, in the case of an amplifier valve with the cathode as the "earthy" electrode, the self-inductance is important. The effect of the self-inductance on the operation of the valve may be considered if certain simplifying assumptions are made.

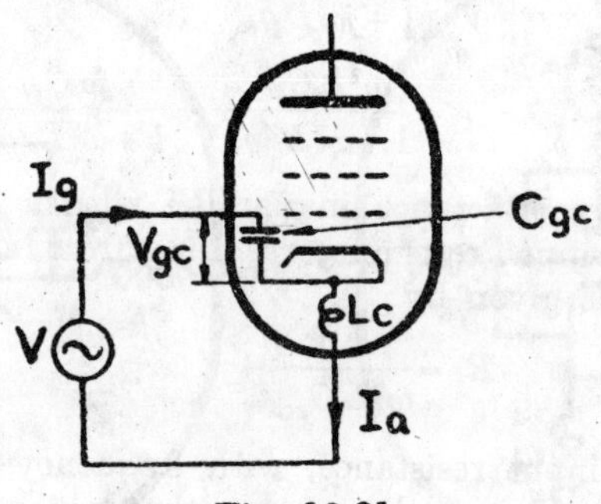

Fig. 10.21.

Suppose the valve is a pentode, functioning as a tuned amplifier. If the grid is biased negatively with respect to the cathode, and the effect of transit time is neglected, the alternating anode current will be in phase with the grid voltage provided that the phase shift due to the self-inductance of the cathode lead (L_c in Fig. 10.21) may be neglected. To a fair degree of approximation, the cathode current may be considered to consist of the anode current only, i.e. the screen current is neglected. With these assumptions the externally applied voltage V, (Fig. 10.21) is equal to V_{gc} together with the voltage drop in L_c, i.e.

$$V = V_{gc} + j\omega L_c(I_a + I_g)$$

Now $I_a = g_m V_{gc}$ and $I_a >> I_g$

$$\therefore V = V_{gc}(1 + j\omega L_c g_m) \quad . \quad . \quad . \quad 10.38$$

$$\therefore \frac{V_{gc}}{V} = \frac{1}{1 + j\omega L_c g_m} \quad . \quad . \quad . \quad . \quad 10.39$$

The voltage V_{gc} which drives current through the valve and load is thus less than the applied voltage V, so that there is a negative feedback effect due to the cathode lead inductance which reduces the voltage amplification of the valve.

As the diagram shows,

$$V_{gc} = \frac{I_g}{j\omega C_{gc}}$$

hence equation 10.38 may be expressed as

$$V = \frac{I_g}{j\omega C_{gc}}(1 + j\omega L_c g_m)$$

The input admittance of the valve is

$$\frac{I_g}{V} = \frac{j\omega C_{gc}}{1 + j\omega L_c g_m}$$

$$= \frac{\omega^2 L_c C_{gc} g_m}{1 + \omega^2 L_c^2 g_m^2} + \frac{j\omega C_{gc}}{1 + \omega^2 L_c^2 g_m^2}$$

This represents a conductance in parallel with a susceptance. If $\omega^2 L_c^2 g_m^2 << 1$ the input resistance resulting from the inductance of the cathode lead is given by

$$R_I = \frac{1}{\omega^2 L_c C_{gc} g_m} \quad . \quad . \quad . \quad . \quad 10.40$$

This variation of input resistance, with frequency and the mutua conductance of the valve, is the same as that which occurs in transit time, and the two effects are not easily distinguishable.

Cathode lead inductance can be minimised by the use of short connections of large surface area. A limit is set however as the glass-metal seal must be at a lower temperature than the cathode itself. For fixed frequency operation, L_c can be eliminated by series tuning, and in many cases a correct choice of the cathode resistor by-pass capacitance is all that is required.

Unwanted Feedback

The phenomenon of unwanted feedback of energy from anode to grid in high frequency amplifiers has already been mentioned. In early triode amplifiers it was countered by "neutralisation" and it led to the development of tetrode and pentode valves. By the use of a close-mesh screen electrode, reasonably wide spacings, and adequate external shielding, the anode to grid capacitance can be reduced sufficiently to allow satisfactory results up to frequencies of 10–30 MHz. At higher frequencies, wide spacings are barred by transit time troubles, a close mesh screen leads to high screen current, and the inductance of the screen lead prevents proper earthing of the screen electrode so that the efficiency of the screening is reduced.

On account of the difficulty of producing satisfactory transmitting tetrodes or pentodes at frequencies of the order of 100–300 MHz triodes have been extensively used in power amplifiers. Satisfactory neutralisation is not, however, easy to achieve.

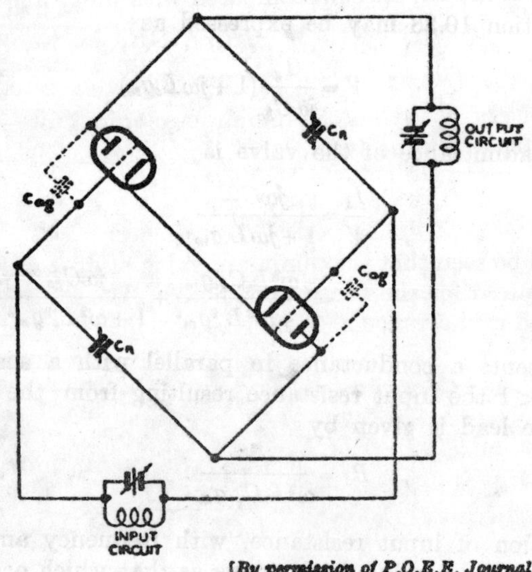

[By permission of P.O.E.E. Journal

Fig. 10.22. Typical neutralising arrangement for a push-pull triode amplifier stage operating in the range 1–30 MHz.

Although the capacitance bridge arrangement shown in Fig. 10.22 is satisfactory at say 5 MHz, a more complex arrangement, such as that shown in Fig. 10.23, is generally necessary at say 200 MHz.

Unless the inductances of the grid and cathode leads are small, they will have to be series tuned by capacitances C_g and C_c in addition to adjustment of the normal bridge balancing capacitances C_n. As these adjustments are to some extent inter-dependent, correct neutralisation can be quite difficult.

This can then be expressed as

$$R_1 r_a - \omega^2 L_1 L + \frac{L}{C} = \frac{\mu M}{C} - \omega^2 M^2 \quad . \quad . \quad . \quad . \quad 11.11$$

and $$\omega L_1 r_a + \omega L R_1 - \frac{r_a}{\omega C} = 0 \quad . \quad . \quad . \quad . \quad 11.12$$

Equation 11.11 can be written as

$$CR_1 r_a - \omega^2 L_1 LC + L = \mu M - \omega^2 M^2 C$$

and if the grid circuit is resonant so that

$$\omega^2 L_1 C \simeq 1$$

$$\text{then } CR_1 r_a = \mu M - \frac{M^2}{L_1} = \mu M\left(1 - \frac{M}{\mu L_1}\right)$$

In general $M/\mu L_1$ is small compared with unity and so

$$M = \frac{CR_1 r_a}{\mu} = \frac{CR_1}{g_m} \quad . \quad . \quad . \quad . \quad 11.13a$$

This value of M is thus the minimum required for the maintenance of oscillation, or alternatively,

$$g_m \geq \frac{CR_1}{M} \quad . \quad . \quad . \quad . \quad . \quad 11.13b$$

It will be seen that the minimum value of M is slightly smaller than that required for the tuned anode case. The frequency generated by the tuned grid arrangement may be obtained from equation 11.12.

$$\omega L_1 r_a + \omega L R_1 = \frac{r_a}{\omega C}$$

$$\text{i.e. } \omega^2 L_1 C r_a + \omega^2 LCR_1 = r_a$$

$$\therefore \omega^2 = \frac{r_a}{L_1 C r_a + LCR_1}$$

$$\therefore \frac{\omega}{2\pi} = \frac{1}{2\pi\sqrt{L_1 C\left(1 + \dfrac{LR_1}{L_1 r_a}\right)}}$$

$$\text{and } f = f_R\left(1 - \frac{LR_1}{2L_1 r_a}\right) \quad . \quad . \quad . \quad 11.14$$

$$\text{where } f_R = \frac{1}{2\pi\sqrt{L_1 C}}$$

The frequency generated in this case is thus slightly lower than that of the resonant frequency of the circuit connected between the grid and cathode of the valve.

The Hartley Oscillator

In this case a single tapped coil is used in place of the two separate coils used in the previous oscillators. Two forms of circuit arrangement are shown in Fig. 11.6. In each circuit the total tuned circuit inductance L, is equal to L_1+L_2+2M.

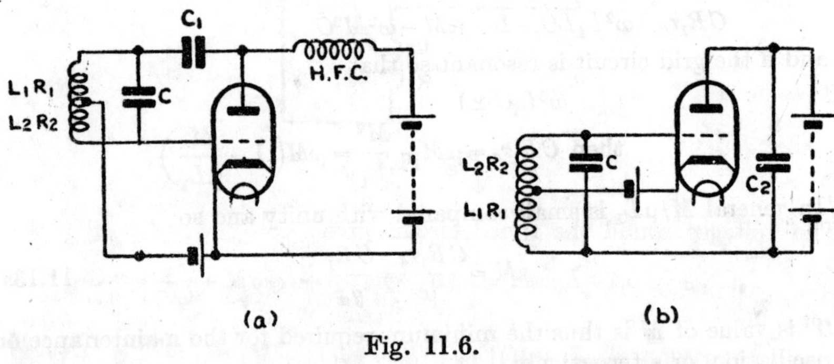

Fig. 11.6.

(a) Shunt fed circuit. (b) Series fed circuit.

In the shunt fed circuit the valve and tuned circuit are in parallel with the high tension source. Because of this it is necessary to insert an impedance between the anode and H.T. + terminals in order to avoid short-circuiting the valve to alternating currents by the low impedance of the H.T. source. The inductance, or high frequency choke shown, is included for this purpose. In addition it is necessary to block the direct potential from the grid. This is achieved by the inclusion of the capacitor C_1. It will be seen that the other form of the Hartley circuit has the tuned circuit, valve and H.T. source connected in series, so that the oscillatory current flows through the H.T. source. For this reason the latter is shunted by a capacitor (C_2) of low reactance.

If the presence of the capacitors C_1 and C_2 and the high frequency choke are ignored, the simplified equivalent circuit for the two arrangements is that of Fig. 11.7. From the equivalent circuit

$$\mu v_g = I_a r_a + I_1(R_1 + j\omega L_1) + I_2 j\omega M$$

$$v_g = I_2(R_2 + j\omega L_2) + I_1 j\omega M$$

$$\text{and } I_a = I_1 - I_2$$

From these relations

$$I_1[r_a + R_1 + j\omega(L_1 - \mu M)] = I_2[r_a + \mu R_2 + j\omega(\mu L_2 - M)]$$

$$\therefore I_1 = \frac{I_2[r_a + \mu R_2 + j\omega(\mu L_2 - M)]}{r_a + R_1 + j\omega(L_1 - \mu M)} \qquad 11.15$$

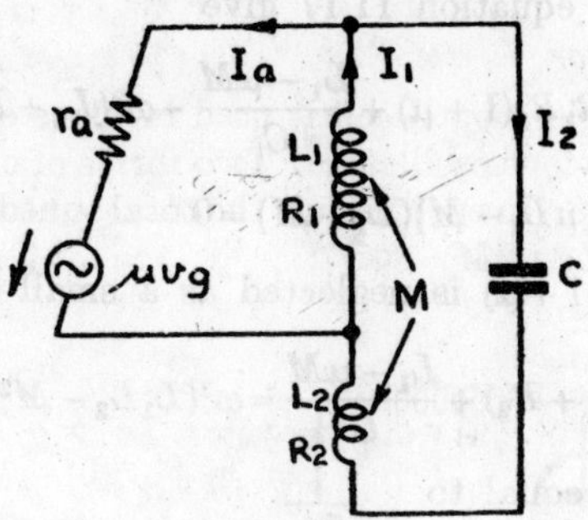

Fig. 11.7.

The voltages round the tuned circuit give

$$I_1(R_1+j\omega L_1)+I_2 j\omega M+I_2(R_2+j\omega L_2)+I_1 j\omega M+\frac{I_2}{j\omega C}=0$$

$$\text{i.e. } I_1[R_1+j\omega(L_1+M)]+I_2\left[R_2+j\omega(L_2+M)+\frac{1}{j\omega C}\right]=0 \qquad 11.16$$

If the value of I_1 given by equation 11.15 is inserted in this equation

$$I_2\left[\{r_a+\mu R_2+j\omega(\mu L_2-M)\}\{R_1+j\omega(L_1+M)\}\right.$$
$$\left.+\left\{R_2+j\omega(L_2+M)+\frac{1}{j\omega C}\right\}\{r_a+R_1+j\omega(L_1-\mu M)\}\right]=0 \qquad 11.17$$

If the circuit is to be oscillatory $I_2\neq 0$, and so the quantity in the square bracket must be zero. If this quantity is separated into real and imaginary parts, the relation between the real terms gives the condition for maintenance of oscillation while the frequency generated is expressed by the relation between the imaginary terms.

The imaginary terms give

$$\omega^2[r_a(L_1+M+L_2+M)+L_1(1+\mu)R_2+L_2(1+\mu)R_1]=\frac{r_a+R_1}{C}$$

If $L_1(1+\mu)R_2$ and $L_2(1+\mu)R_1$ are small compared with $r_a\,(L_1+L_2+M)$

$$\text{then } \omega\simeq\sqrt{\frac{r_a+R_1}{Cr_a(L_1+L_2+2M)}}$$

$$\text{and so } f\simeq f_R\left(1+\frac{R_1}{2r_a}\right) \quad . \quad . \quad . \quad . \qquad 11.18$$

$$\text{where } f_R=\frac{1}{2\pi\sqrt{(L_1+L_2+2M)C}}$$

The real terms of equation 11.17 give

$$r_a(R_1+R_2)+R_1R_2(1+\mu)+\frac{L_1-\mu M}{C}-\omega^2(L_2+M)(L_1-\mu M)$$

$$-\omega^2(\mu L_2-M)(L_1+M)=0$$

If the term $R_1R_2(1+\mu)$ is neglected as a small quantity, then

$$r_a(R_1+R_2)+\frac{L_1-\mu M}{C}=\omega^2(L_1L_2-M^2)(1+\mu) \quad . \quad 11.19$$

ω^2 is very nearly equal to

$$\frac{1}{(L_1+L_2+2M)C}$$

and if this value is inserted in equation 11.19,

$$\frac{L_1-\mu M}{C}=\frac{(L_1L_2-M^2)(1+\mu)}{C(L_1+L_2+2M)}-r_a(R_1+R_2)$$

from which

$$\mu=\frac{L_1+M}{L_2+M}+\frac{Cr_a(R_1+R_2)(L_1+L_2+2M)}{(L_1+M)(L_2+M)} \quad . \quad 11.20$$

If the resistance of the coil is neglected this simplifies to

$$\mu=\frac{L_1+M}{L_2+M}$$

The circuit can thus be adjusted for oscillation by alteration of the tapping point on the coil.

The Colpitts Oscillator

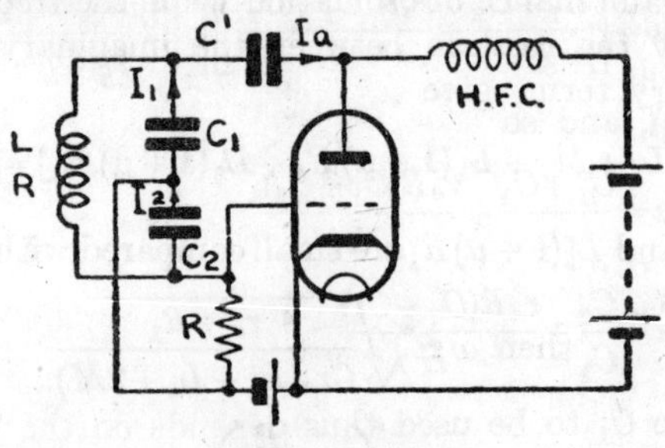

Fig. 11.8.

This form of oscillator is shown in Fig. 11.8. It will be seen to be of the same form as the Hartley circuit, the only change being that the cathode is connected to a tapping point on the capacitor instead of the coil. As there is no conducting path between the grid and cathode of the valve, it is essential to provide a grid leak resistor (R). In addition a low reactance capacitor C' is required to block the direct potential of the anode from the grid. A high frequency choke is also necessary as the circuit is shunt fed. If the effect of these extra components can be neglected, the simplified equivalent circuit is similar to that for the Hartley circuit, Fig. 11.7.

For the Colpitts oscillator,

$$\mu v_g = I_a r_a + \frac{I_1}{j\omega C_1}$$

$$v_g = I_2/j\omega C_2$$

$$I_a = I_1 - I_2$$

and $I_1/j\omega C_1 + I_2(R + j\omega L + 1/j\omega C_2) = 0$

From these equations it can be shown that the frequency of oscillation f, is given by

$$f = f_R\sqrt{1 + \left(\frac{C_2}{C_1 + C_2}\right)\frac{R}{r_a}} \quad . \quad . \quad . \quad . \quad 11.21$$

where f_R is the resonant frequency of the tuned circuit,

$$\text{i.e. } f_R = \frac{1}{2\pi\sqrt{L\left(\frac{C_1 C_2}{C_1 + C_2}\right)}}$$

The condition for the circuit to be oscillatory may be obtained from the current and voltage equations given above, and is given by

$$1 + \mu = \left[\frac{C_1 + C_2}{C_1} + \frac{r_a R(C_1 + C_2)}{L}\right]\left[1 + \frac{RC_2}{r_a(C_1 + C_2)}\right]$$

$RC_2 << r_a(C_1 + C_2)$, and so

$$1 + \mu = \frac{C_1 + C_2}{C_1} + \frac{r_a R(C_1 + C_2)}{L}$$

$$\therefore \mu = \frac{C_2}{C_1} + \frac{r_a R(C_1 + C_2)}{L} \quad . \quad . \quad . \quad . \quad . \quad 11.22$$

The ratio of C_2 to C_1 to be used thus depends on the parameters of the particular valve chosen.

Oscillator Self-Bias

In dealing with the four types of oscillator above, the valve was shown as having a fixed bias voltage, and was considered to have

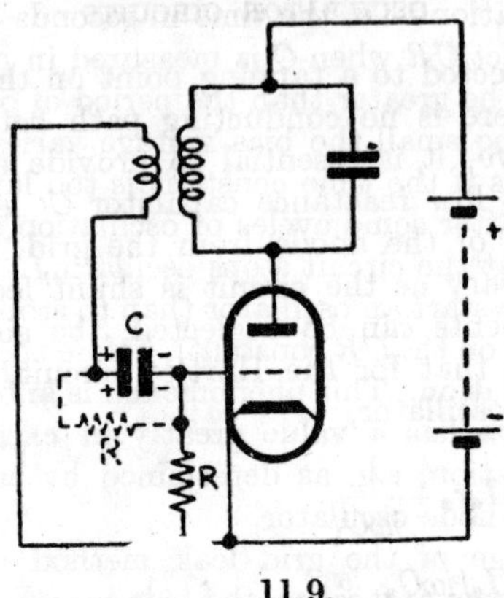

11.9.

linear characteristics, so that such circuits may be regarded as class *A* oscillators. It is more usual, however, to provide what is known as " grid leak bias ". This utilises a capacitor *C* and grid leak resistor *R*. The arrangement may be applied to all forms of oscillator, and Fig. 11.9 shows the circuit for a tuned anode oscillator. An alternative connection for *R* is shown dotted.

The capacitor, resistor, and grid and cathode of the valve function as a diode detector system, as discussed in chapter 13. This arrangement develops a direct voltage, proportional to the peak value of the applied alternating voltage.

The initial bias on the valve is zero, but as soon as the oscillation starts the grid becomes positive with respect to the cathode for a fraction of each cycle. This causes a grid current to flow so that the capacitor acquires a charge with the polarity shown. This charge can only leak away through the conducting path across the capacitor plates, i.e. through the resistor *R*. The charge on the capacitor causes the potential of the grid to become negative with respect to the cathode; if the amplitude of oscillation increases the mean value of grid current increases and the greater is the negative potential of the grid.

Such a bias arrangement will thus regulate the amplitude of oscillation. If the oscillatory amplitude increases, the bias will increase and operate to reduce the anode current and so cause the amplitude of oscillation to decrease again. In the same way a decrease in the amplitude of oscillation will be offset by a reduced value of bias and a consequent increase in the power delivered to the anode circuit. If the feedback coupling is sufficient the bias developed across *C*, and hence across *R*, will reach a value similar to that for a class *C* amplifier, and the oscillator will operate under class *C* conditions.

If the grid bias arrangement is to function correctly the reactance of *C* should be low at the frequency of operation, and the time constant of the CR combination—i.e. the time in seconds corresponding to the value of the product CR when C is measured in microfarads and R in megohms—should be greater than the period of oscillation. If the CR time constant is too small the bias voltage varies during the cycle of oscillation, whereas if the time constant is too large, the oscillation is not continuous. After some cycles of oscillation a large negative bias is developed so that the circuit stops oscillating. Now a smaller value of bias is needed to start an oscillator than to stop it, and so some time elapses (depending on the CR constant), before the " cut off " oscillator recommences oscillation. This phenomenon is known as " squegging ". It also occurs if g_m has a value greatly in excess of the minimum required for oscillation, e.g. as determined by equation 11.5b in the case of the tuned anode oscillator.

One disadvantage of the grid leak method of biasing is that if oscillation ceases from any cause, the bias becomes zero and the anode current increases correspondingly. If this causes the anode dissipation to be exceeded the valve will be damaged. To safeguard against this a small amount of fixed bias is sometimes provided, either by a battery or by cathode bias. Such fixed bias will not affect the amplitude of oscillation. When the fixed bias is added the total bias will be increased and the oscillation amplitude will then decrease correspondingly and cause a fall in the value of the grid leak bias. The total bias will then settle down to the original equilibrium value of the grid leak bias alone, and the amplitude of oscillation will have its initial value.

Valve Limitation of Amplitude of Oscillation

In deriving the relation of the circuit constants necessary for oscillation to be maintained it was assumed that the valve was a linear device. It must be pointed out, however, that in fact the non-linearity of the valve characteristics is responsible for the stable operation of the oscillator.[2] In the types of oscillator considered, continuous oscillation will take place if the mutual conductance of the valve has a certain critical minimum value which is determined by the relations between the circuit elements. Thus in the tuned anode case, the circuit is oscillatory if

$$g_m \geq \frac{CR}{M} + \frac{L}{Mr_a} \text{ (equation 11.5b).}$$

(The maintenance equations for the Hartley and Colpitts circuits are not expressed directly in this fashion, but such circuits also depend on the valve having a certain minimum value of mutual conductance.)

If the valve characteristics were linear and g_m had a constant value there would be no limit to the amplitude of the oscillation and a stable state (of oscillation) would not be obtained. (This compares with the voltage generated by a d.c. shunt generator. Because of the non-linearity of the magnetisation characteristic the machine builds up its voltage to a value dependent on the resistance of the shunt field. If the magnetisation characteristic was linear the voltage generated would increase indefinitely.)

In practice the dynamic valve characteristic is only approximately linear between two limiting values, namely the cut-off value and an upper limit at which the valve saturates. (The anode current does not increase linearly in the positive grid region as the presence of grid current robs the anode of a fraction of the total cathode current.)

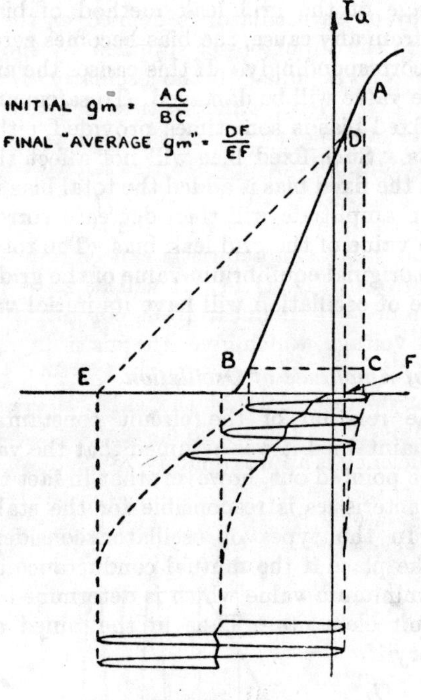

Fig. 11.10.

The valve will start off with zero bias, if grid leak biasing is used. If the anode to grid coupling is sufficient, the oscillatory amplitude will increase, while the grid potential will increase negatively. This process will continue until the " average mutual conductance " has decreased to a value just sufficient to maintain oscillation whilst supplying the circuit losses. In this connection the " average mutual conductance " of the valve is taken as the change in anode current resulting from a given peak to peak grid voltage. Fig. 11.10 shows how the mutual conductance decreases from its maximum value in the region of zero bias to a smaller value when the bias increases.

When the grid bias reaches a value such that the "average mutual conductance" is just sufficient to maintain oscillation, the oscillatory amplitude will remain fixed as long as the circuit conditions remain unchanged. It should be noted that the actual amplitude obtained with any given circuit will depend on the value of steady anode voltage used.

Anode Efficiency of a Tuned Anode Oscillator

The anode efficiency of an oscillator is defined as the ratio of the useful output power to the input power supplied by the high tension source. The input power supplied to the oscillator depends on the mean value of the anode current, which in turn depends on the value of grid-bias. The anode efficiency therefore depends on the value of grid-bias with which the oscillator operates (as is also true in the case of power amplifiers).

An estimation of the anode efficiency for the tuned anode oscillator can be obtained if the valve characteristic can be represented by the approximate form shown in Fig. 11.11. It will be seen that the valve anode current is assumed to be linear from cut off up to a certain positive value of grid voltage, which gives the maximum or saturation value.

When the oscillator operates so that the valve is biased to cut-off and the grid voltage runs the anode current up to the saturation value I_s, the anode efficiency is approximately 75%. This can be shown as follows.

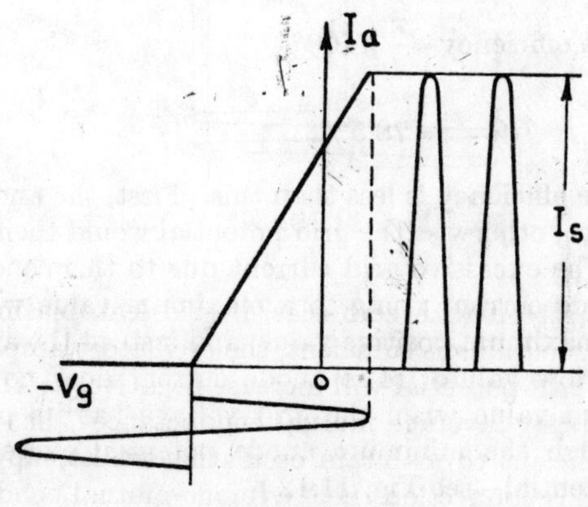

Fig. 11.11.

The tuned circuit in the valve anode has an impedance at resonance equal to $\frac{L}{CR}$. The power supplied to this circuit, P_0, may be expressed as

$$P_0 = (\text{r.m.s. value of anode current})^2 \frac{L}{CR}$$

$$= \frac{I^2_s}{4} \frac{L}{CR} \quad . \quad . \quad . \quad . \quad . \quad . \quad 11.23$$

on the assumption that the anode current consists of a series of half sine waves. If the voltage of the high tension source is E_B the maximum possible value of the anode voltage swing, V_a, will have a value equal to E_B. The anode potential will then vary between

$$E_B + V_a \text{ and } E_B - V_a$$

i.e. from $2E_B$ to zero.

$$\text{Now } V_a = I_s\left(\frac{L}{CR}\right) = E_B \quad . \quad . \quad . \quad . \quad . \quad 11.24$$

By equations 11.23 and 11.24 the output power

$$P_0 = \frac{E_B I_s}{4} \quad . \quad . \quad . \quad . \quad . \quad . \quad . \quad 11.25$$

The power input to the oscillator from the high tension source is

$$P_{D.C.} = E_B \text{ (mean value of anode current)}$$

$$= \frac{E_B I_s}{\pi}$$

Hence the anode efficiency $= \frac{\pi}{4} \times 100\%$

$$= 78{\cdot}5\%.$$

In practice the efficiency is less than this. First, the anode potential cannot fall to zero, otherwise the grid potential would then exceed that of the anode. The excessive grid current due to this condition would prevent the anode current rising to a maximum value when the grid voltage had its maximum positive value, and instead the anode current would fall to a low value. (The anode current does not necessarily have a maximum value when the grid voltage has its peak positive value even though the minimum anode potential exceeds the peak positive grid potential—see Fig. 11.12.)

Current and Voltage Waveforms of a Power Oscillator

A power oscillator in which the angle of flow is 180° or less will clearly have an anode current which consists of a series of pulses, and so will consist of a fundamental and various harmonic components of current. Because of the selective action of the resonant circuit, however, the anode voltage variation is usually sinusoidal. Fig. 11.12 shows the form of the variation of the anode voltage, anode current and grid current over part of an oscillatory cycle for a 100 kW triode valve. It will be seen that grid current flows in a series of pulses which have a smaller angle of flow than the anode current, and that the anode current is reduced from its maximum value when grid current flows.

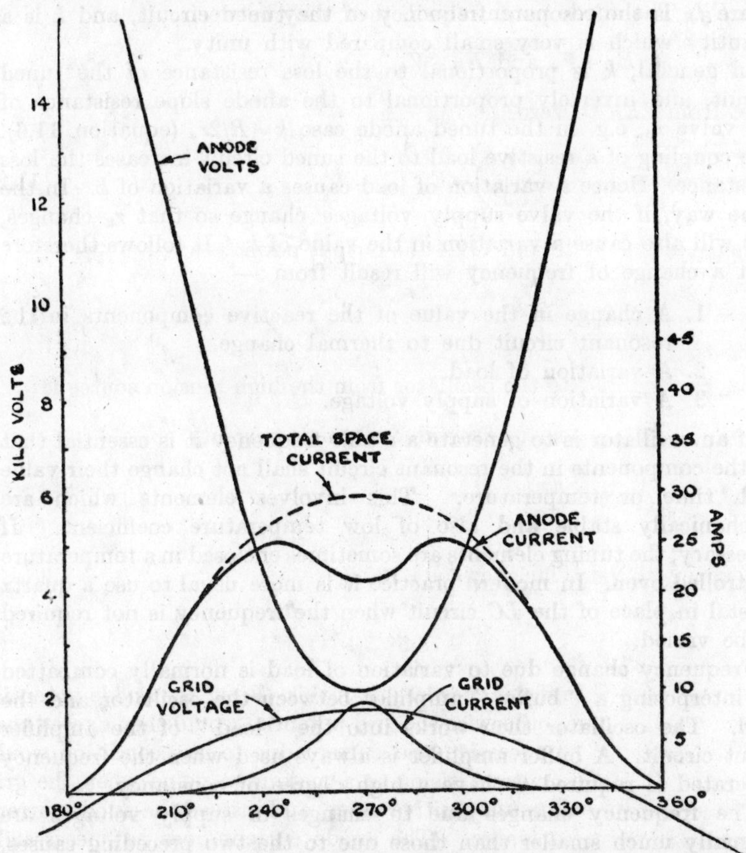

[*By permission of the Research Laboratories of The General Electric Co., Wembley, England*

Fig. 11.12.

Oscillator Frequency Stability

In the oscillators so far considered it will be seen that the frequency generated is substantially the same as the resonant frequency of the tuned circuit employed. It follows that if the frequency variation of the generated waveform is to be small, i.e. the oscillator is to generate a stable frequency, the variation of the reactances in the tuned circuit, due to thermal or other changes, should be small.

In all cases the frequency f, which is generated is given by an expression of the form

$$f = f_R(1 + k)$$

where f_R is the resonant frequency of the tuned circuit, and k is a quantity which is very small compared with unity.

In general, k is proportional to the loss resistance of the tuned circuit, and inversely proportional to the anode slope resistance of the valve r_a, e.g. in the tuned anode case $k = R/2r_a$ (equation 11.6). The coupling of a resistive load to the tuned circuit increases the loss resistance. Hence a variation of load causes a variation of k. In the same way, if the valve supply voltages change so that r_a changes, this will also cause a variation in the value of k. It follows therefore that a change of frequency will result from :—

1. A change in the value of the reactive components in the resonant circuit due to thermal change.
2. A variation of load.
3. A variation of supply voltage.

If an oscillator is to generate a stable frequency it is essential that all the components in the resonant circuit shall not change their value with time or temperature. This involves elements which are mechanically stable and also of low temperature coefficient. If necessary, the tuning elements are sometimes enclosed in a temperature controlled oven. In modern practice it is more usual to use a quartz crystal in place of the LC circuit when the frequency is not required to be varied.

Frequency change due to variation of load is normally combatted by interposing a " buffer " amplifier between the oscillator and the load. The oscillator then works into the " load " of the amplifier input circuit. A buffer amplifier is always used when the frequency generated is required to have a high degree of constancy.

The frequency changes due to changes in supply voltages are normally much smaller than those due to the two preceding causes, but in extreme cases voltage stabilisation is used.

It has been found that the presence of harmonic frequencies gives rise to a small decrease of the fundamental frequency, and for this reason, master oscillators of high stability are normally operated so that the oscillatory amplitude is small. Additional amplification is then used to bring the power level up to the required value.

It should be noted that the presence of grid current has been ignored in the discussion of the frequency generated by any particular circuit. This can be remedied to a certain extent by supposing that the grid and cathode terminals of the valve are closed by a resistance, the value of which is equal to the grid dissipation divided by the mean square value of the grid current. If the effect of grid current is represented in this way, it will be found that the frequency generated is very slightly lower than that obtained by supposing that the grid to cathode resistance is infinite.

Electron-Coupled Oscillator

It is convenient at this stage to mention an arrangement in which a single valve is used as an oscillator and a buffer amplifier. This is the electron-coupled oscillator, and one form employing a pentode valve is shown in Fig. 11.13. As far as the oscillator part is concerned, the grid and screen operate as the grid and anode of a triode, which

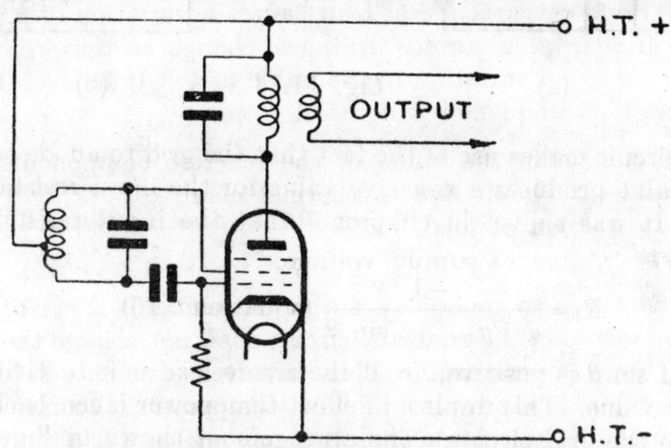

Fig. 11.13. Electron-coupled oscillator.

functions as a Hartley oscillator. The oscillatory voltage between cathode and grid causes the anode current to flow in a series of pulses, and an oscillatory output is produced in the impedance connected in the anode circuit. As changes in anode load do not effect the screen current, reasonable variations in load do not affect the oscillator circuit ; the output circuit is then virtually isolated from the oscillator circuit.

A pentode valve and Hartley oscillator circuit have been illustrated. The principle of the electron-coupled oscillator however permits of many variations. Any valve with more than one grid may be employed, and any of the forms of triode oscillator may be used.

Crystal Controlled Oscillator

Where a high degree of frequency stability is required, it is common practice to make use of quartz crystal, or other piezoelectric material, as a resonating element. The frequency generated by such an oscillator is much more stable than that obtained when a coil and capacitor combination is employed.

One of the simplest and earliest arrangements which utilises a quartz crystal is shown in Fig. 11.14a.

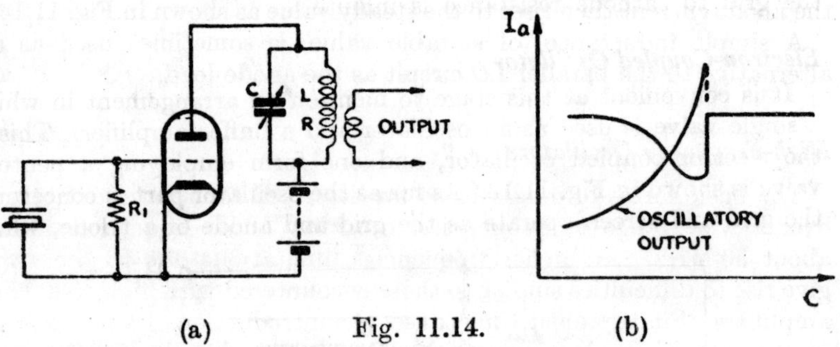

(a) Fig. 11.14. (b)

This circuit makes use of the fact that the grid to anode capacitance of the valve produces a negative value for the input resistance of the valve. It was shown in chapter 7 that the input resistance R_I, is given by,

$$R_I = \frac{-1}{\omega \, Cg_a \, . \, A \, . \sin \theta} \quad \text{(equation 6.16)}$$

and so if $\sin \theta$ is positive, i.e. if the anode load is inductive, R_I has a negative value. This implies in effect that power is fed back from the anode to the grid circuit. The arrangement shown in Fig. 11.16 will thus oscillate when sufficient energy is fed back to the grid circuit to supply the losses.

The required inductive anode load is obtained in this case by a parallel *LC* circuit, tuned to a frequency slightly above that of the mechanical resonant frequency of the crystal. Variation of the capacitor *C* in the anode circuit has practically no effect on the value of the frequency generated, but affects the amplitude of the output. If the circuit is set up with a very small value of anode tuning capacitance, so that the anode tuned circuit resonates at a frequency very much greater than that of the crystal, the amplification of the valve at the crystal frequency is small and R_I has a large value, and the circuit does not oscillate. As the value of *C* is increased the energy fed back to the grid circuit increases; the circuit then oscillates when R_I has a sufficiently small value.

The combination of the equivalent series capacitance of the crystal together with the grid resistor R acts as a grid leak bias arrangement. As a result of this, the grid bias increases negatively with increase of oscillation amplitude. After oscillation has commenced, a further increase in the value of C causes an increase in the oscillatory amplitude which then gives rise to a fall in the mean value of the anode current. This process is progressive until the anode-tuned circuit becomes resonant at the crystal resonant frequency. At this point the anode load is no longer inductive and oscillation ceases. The mean value of the anode current then rises to the steady value as shown in Fig. 11.14b.

A simple inductance, of suitable value, is sometimes used as an alternative to the parallel LC circuit as the anode load.

High-Frequency Oscillators

The basic forms of oscillator so far described function satisfactorily over a wide range of frequencies, from low audio frequencies up to about 30 MHz. At higher frequencies, limitations due to the valve give rise to difficulties similar to those encountered with high-frequency amplifiers. Finite transit time causes the introduction of a phase angle in the mutual conductance, and also causes a decrease in the grid-cathode input resistance. The effect of valve inter-electrode capacitance and lead inductance tends to restrict the form of the oscillatory circuit.

An oscillator arrangement which utilises the feedback arising from the anode to grid capacitance is shown in Fig. 11.15a. As the two coils are coupled by C_{ag}, mutual inductance is unnecessary. The more general form of this arrangement is shown in Fig. 11.15b, in which the grid bias and H.T. sources have been omitted. C_1 includes the grid to cathode capacitance of the valve, the self capacitance of L_1, and any additional tuning capacitance. C_2 represents the anode to cathode capacitance of the valve and all other capacitances connected across L_2. Such a circuit is referred to as a tuned anode-tuned grid oscillator. (The particular form of crystal controlled oscillator previously mentioned belongs to this class of oscillator.)

The circuit of Fig. 11.15b may be redrawn as shown in Fig. 11.15c. X_1 and X_2 represent the reactances of the parallel circuits L_1C_1 and L_2C_2 respectively. If the circuit is to act as a resonant circuit oscillator, either X_1 or X_2 must be inductive to provide the necessary resonant circuit. Again if either X_1 or X_2 is inductive, the other must also be inductive in order to give a feedback voltage to the grid in the correct phase. The circuit may accordingly be redrawn as in Fig. 11.15d, which is that of a Hartley oscillator. Hence at the frequency of oscillation, the circuit of Fig. 11.15a, or the tuned anode-tuned grid oscillator, corresponds to the Hartley oscillator. (In passing, it should

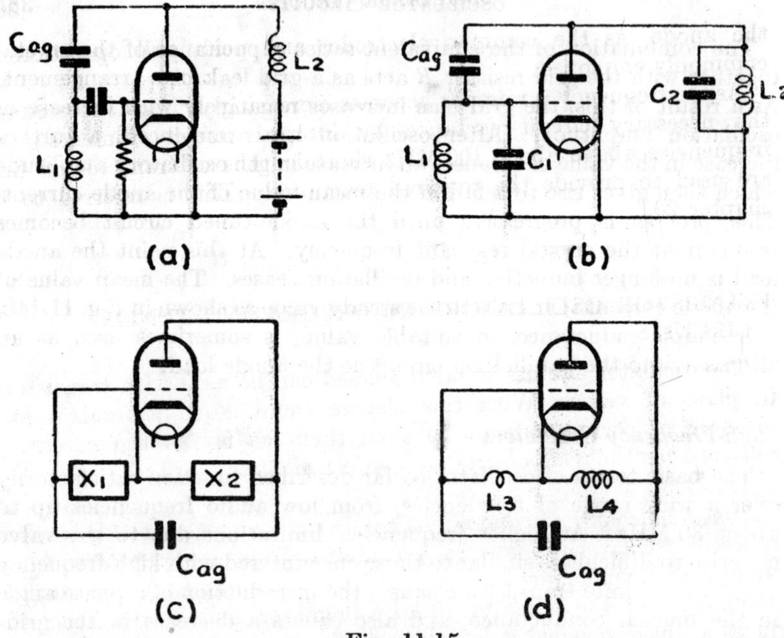

Fig. 11.15.

be noted that the general circuit diagram for all forms of feedback oscillator is obtained if, in Fig. 11.15c, C_{ag} is replaced by a reactance X_3. The conditions for oscillation then are that X_1 and X_2 should have the same sign, and X_3 should be of opposite sign. If, for example, X_3 is inductive, then X_1 and X_2 must be capacitive; this gives the Colpitts oscillator of Fig. 11.8.)

The fact that the tuned circuits L_1C_1 and L_2C_2 are required to be inductive at the frequency of oscillation means that the resonant frequencies of these circuits must be greater than the frequency of oscillation, i.e. the system oscillates at a frequency which is less than the lower resonant frequency. If the two circuits L_1C_1 and L_2C_2 have resonant frequencies which differ appreciably, the circuit tuned to the lower frequency controls the frequency generated, while the other circuit affects the amplitude of the feedback voltage. The values of effective inductance, i.e. the values of L_3 and L_4, must also satisfy the normal relations for a Hartley oscillator. Thus to a first approximation, L_4 must be equal to μL_3, where μ is the amplification factor of the valve.

The oscillators of Fig. 11.15a and 11.15b have the two tuned circuits connected to the cathode, as far as high frequency currents are concerned. Other variations of this class of oscillator utilise either the grid, or the anode, as the common electrode, and push pull operation is commonly employed.

As the frequency is raised it becomes increasingly difficult to produce the necessary circuit-reactance by lumped circuit elements; at frequencies above about 100 MHz short lengths of transmission line are used to provide the required reactance. This is referred to in chapter 20.

TRANSISTOR OSCILLATORS INCORPORATING TUNED CIRCUITS

The oscillator circuits so far discussed can be used with transistors in place of valves. With this change there is, in general, a fair measure of correspondence between them as far as the necessary relations for the components are concerned.

Tuned-collector Oscillator. The basic common-emitter tuned-collector oscillator is shown in Fig. 11.16a. This circuit, with suitable changes of components, can be used from low audio frequencies up to frequencies of the order of 10 MHz or more. As the transistor produces a phase reversal it is necessary to ensure that the voltage fed back to the base has a phase reversal with respect to the collector.

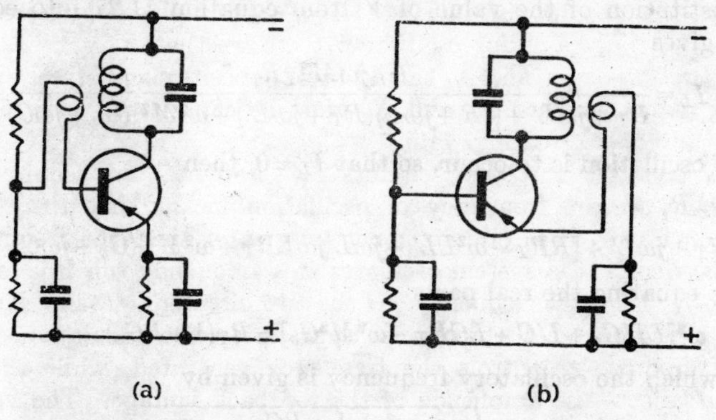

Fig. 11.16 (a) Common-emitter tuned-collector oscillator
(b) Common-base tuned-collector oscillator.

Fig. 11.16b shows a common-base tuned-collector circuit. In this arrangement there is no phase reversal from emitter to collector and so the sense of the feedback winding must be opposite to that of Fig. 11.16a.

N

If the input and output capacitances of the transistor are assumed to be included in the tuning capacitance C the a.c. equivalent circuit for the oscillator of Fig. 11.16a may be represented as shown in Fig. 11.17, and the current in the coil L is thus given by

$$I_L = \frac{G_m V/(G_o + j\omega C)}{1/(G_o + j\omega C) + Z_L} = \frac{G_m V}{1 + Z_L(G_o + j\omega C)} \quad . \quad . \quad 11.26$$

$$= \frac{G_m V}{1 + [R + j\omega L + \omega^2 M^2/(R_T + j\omega L')](G_o + j\omega C)}$$

where

$$R_T = R' + R_1$$

also $\quad V = j\omega M I_L R_1/(R_T + j\omega L') \quad . \quad . \quad . \quad . \quad . \quad . \quad 11.27$

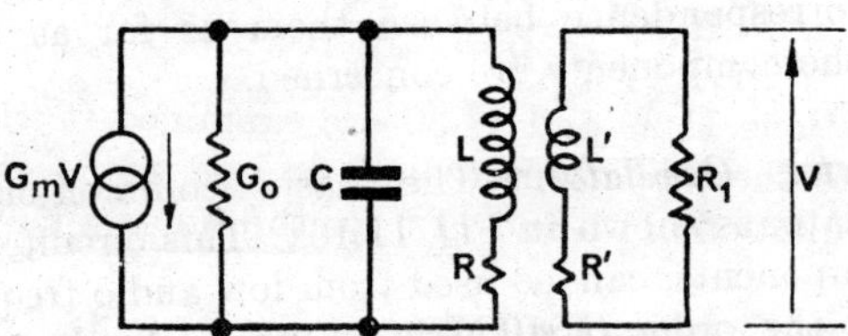

Fig. 11.17. A.C. equivalent circuit of tuned-collector oscillator.

Substitution of the value of V from equation 11.27 into equation 11.26 gives

$$I_L = \frac{G_m j\omega M I_L R_1}{R_T + j\omega L' + [(R + j\omega L)(R_T + j\omega L') + \omega^2 M^2](G_o + j\omega C)}$$

and if oscillation is to occur, so that $I_L \neq 0$, then

$$j\omega M G_m R_1 = R_T + j\omega L' + [RR_T - \omega^2 LL' + j\omega L' j\omega L R_T + \omega^2 M^2](G_o + j\omega C) \quad 11.28$$

Hence equating the real parts

$$\omega^2[LL'G_o + L'C + LCR_T - \omega^2 M^2 G_o] = R_T(1 + RG_o)$$

from which the oscillatory frequency is given by

$$f = f_R \sqrt{\frac{1 + RG_o}{1 + \left[\frac{L'G_o}{C} + \frac{L'}{L} - \frac{M^2 G_o}{LC}\right]/R_T}} \quad . \quad . \quad 11.29$$

where $\quad f_R = 1/2\pi\sqrt{LC}$

Equating the imaginary parts of equation 11.28 gives

$$j\omega M G_m R_1 = j\omega L' + j\omega CRR_T - j\omega^3 CLL' + j\omega^3 CM^2 + j\omega L'G_o + j\omega LR_T G_o$$

$$\therefore \quad MG_mR_1 = L' + CRR_T - \omega^2CLL' + \omega^2CM^2 + L'G_o + LR_TG_o$$

If the coils L and L' are closely coupled so that $M = \sqrt{LL'}$, then

$$MG_mR_1 = L' + CRR_T + L'G_o + LR_TG_o$$

and hence

$$M = \frac{LR_TG_o + CRR_T + L'(1+G_o)}{G_mR_1}$$

$$= \frac{LG_o + CR}{G_mR_1/R_T} + \frac{L'(1+G_o)}{G_mR_1}$$

If G_o is replaced by $1/R_o$ and $R_1 \gg R'$

$$M = \frac{L + CRR_o}{G_mR_o} + \frac{L'(R_o+1)}{G_mR_1R_o}$$

This is the minimum value for M and so the maintenance condition is that

$$M \geqslant \frac{L + CRR_o}{G_mR_o} + \frac{L'}{G_mR_1} \quad . \quad . \quad . \quad . \quad . \quad 11.30$$

If equations 11.29 and 11.30 are examined it will be seen tnat for R_T infinite these relations reduce, as one would expect, to the same form as equations 11.5 and 11.6 for the tuned anode oscillator.

Hartley and Colpitts Oscillators

An inspection of the Hartley and Colpitts circuits shows that they are examples of a generalised three-impedance circuit, having three terminals connected to the active device. For the transistor case the basic a.c. circuit, omitting bias and supply voltages, is shown in Fig. 11.18.

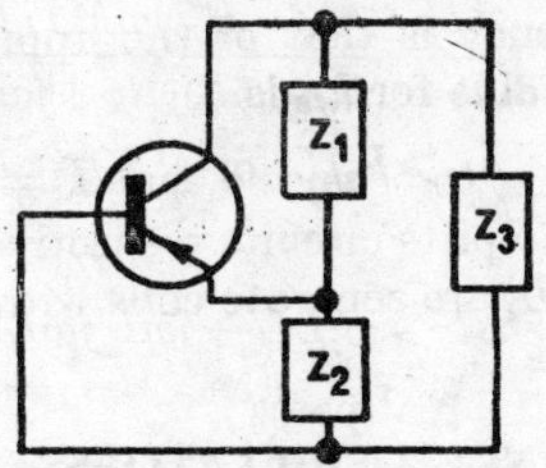

Fig. 11.18.

The transistor may be replaced by the h-parameter equivalent circuit for low-frequency oscillators. The equivalent oscillator circuit is then as indicated in Fig. 11.19a. This circuit may be simplified. First the impedance Z_1 can usually be assumed to be sufficiently small that the voltage V across it makes the quantity $h_{re}V$ small and insignificant; in the same way the presence of the conductance h_{oe} can be neglected.

If the current generator is replaced by the equivalent voltage generator the resulting simplified circuit is that of Fig. 11.19b. From this circuit it will be seen that

$$i = \frac{h_{fe}Z_1 i_b}{Z_2 h_{ie}/(Z_2 + h_{ie}) + Z_3 + Z_1} \quad \text{and} \quad i_b = -Z_2 i/(h_{ie} + Z_2)$$

so that
$$i = \frac{-h_{fe}Z_1 Z_2 i}{Z_2 h_{ie} + (Z_2 + h_{ie})(Z_1 + Z_3)} \qquad . \quad . \quad . \quad . \quad 11.31$$

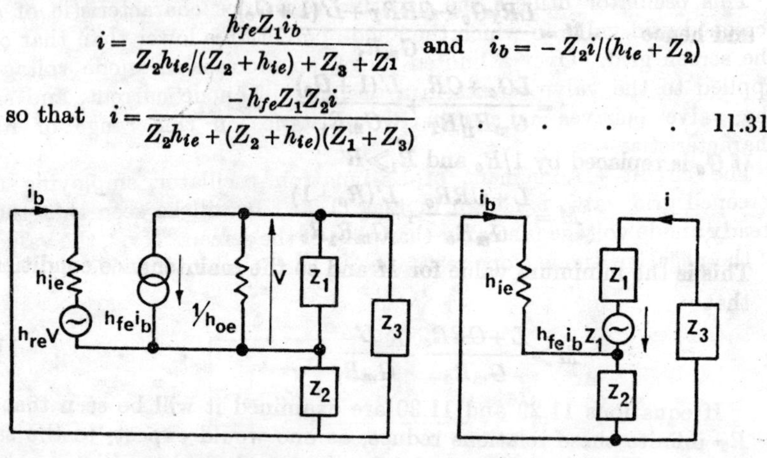

Fig. 11.19 (a) Equivalent a.c. circuit
(b) Simplified circuit.

By substitution of the appropriate values for Z_1, Z_2, and Z_3 the frequency of oscillation and the maintenance condition may be obtained. If the presence of resistance in the three impedances is ignored, the oscillation frequency is that of the appropriate resonant circuit, while the minimum value for h_{fe} is

$$h_{fe} \geqslant L_2/L_1 \text{ or } C_1/C_2$$

for the Hartley and Colpitts circuits respectively, assuming that in the Hartley case L_1 and L_2 are separate coils without mutual inductance.

NEGATIVE RESISTANCE OSCILLATORS

The oscillators so far considered have involved some coupling arrangement whereby energy is fed back from the output circuit to the input circuit. In the negative resistance type of oscillator no such coupling is used and oscillatory conditions are obtained by virtue of the fact that the valve is so operated as to present a negative resistance between a pair of electrodes. This type of oscillator is thus able to generate oscillations in a two terminal circuit. This is often a convenience when tests have to be made on a coil which is screened and inaccessible apart from its terminal connections.

Dynatron Oscillator

This oscillator utilises the negative resistance characteristic of a screened grid valve in which the anode potential is lower than that of the screen grid. Over a limited range, an increase in anode voltage applied to the valve results in a decrease in anode current, and so the valve behaves as a negative resistance in this range of its characteristics.

The circuit arrangement of a dynatron oscillator employing a screened grid valve is shown in Fig. 11.20. It will be seen that the steady anode voltage is smaller than that of the screen. If r_a', the value of the negative anode slope resistance, is such that $r_a' \leqslant L/CR$

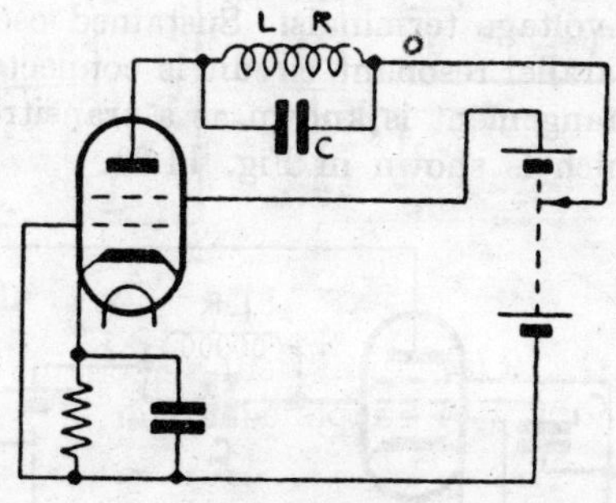

Fig. 11.20.

continuous oscillation will be produced in the *LCR* circuit. This result can be obtained from the differential equation which applies to the equivalent circuit for alternating currents, ignoring the steady potentials. This equivalent circuit consists simply of the parallel *LCR* circuit in shunt with the negative resistance r_a'. The frequency of the oscillation produced will be found to be

$$f=\frac{1}{2\pi}\sqrt{\frac{1}{LC}\left(1-\frac{R}{r_a'}\right)} \quad . \quad . \quad . \quad . \quad . \quad 11.31$$

The actual static potentials required must be determined from an inspection of the valve characteristics, as the actual value of the negative resistance (i.e. the negative gradient of the I_a/V_a curve) obtained varies with the control grid bias.

Amplitude Limitation in the Dynatron Oscillator. If a dynatron oscillator is set up and the anode resistance is less than the critical value, oscillation will take place. The amplitude of oscillation will then increase until the whole of the negative resistance region is traversed. When the amplitude exceeds this value the valve will begin to operate in a range where the valve behaves as a positive resistance. The amplitude of oscillation will then stabilise itself at a value such that the average negative resistance" presented by the valve is equal to the dynamic resistance $\left(\frac{L}{CR}\right)$ of the resonant circuit.

The Transitron Oscillator

The curve relating screen current with screen potential in a pentode valve has a negative gradient over part of the range if the suppressor grid is connected dynamically to the screen grid. The valve then behaves as though it has a negative resistance between its screen and screen supply voltage terminals. Sustained oscillation can thus be produced if a parallel resonant circuit is connected between these terminals. The arrangement is known as a transitron oscillator, the basic circuit of which is shown in Fig. 11.21.

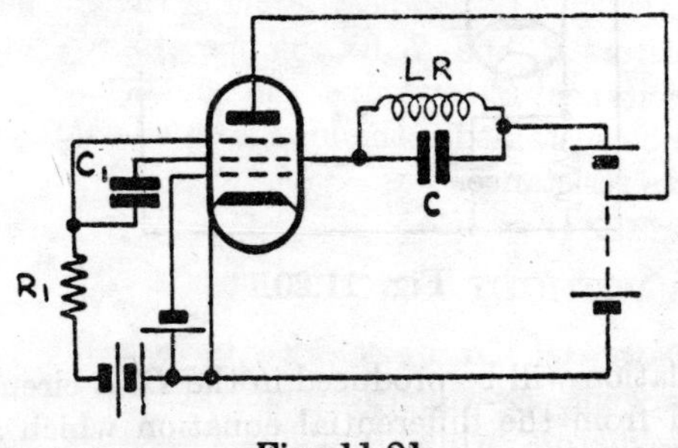

Fig. 11.21.

It will be seen that the suppressor grid is connected to the screen grid through the capacitor C_1. The capacitance of C_1 must be such that the suppressor potential can follow that of the screen grid without appreciable amplitude change or time lag. Any variation in screen grid potential will then be accompanied by a corresponding variation in suppressor grid potential.

In the absence of the capacitor C_1 a fall in screen voltage would result in a decrease in screen current. The effect of C_1 however is to cause a corresponding drop in the potential of the suppressor grid. This has the effect of turning back a number of electrons which would otherwise have continued towards the anode. Because of this there is an increase in screen current. In the same way an increase in screen and suppressor potentials will produce a decrease in screen current.

If the resonant circuit is connected as shown, continuous oscillation can be produced, as in the case of the dynatron oscillator.

Tunnel Diode Oscillator

The tunnel diode (referred to briefly in chapter 7) has a negative resistance over a restricted range of forward bias (at approximately

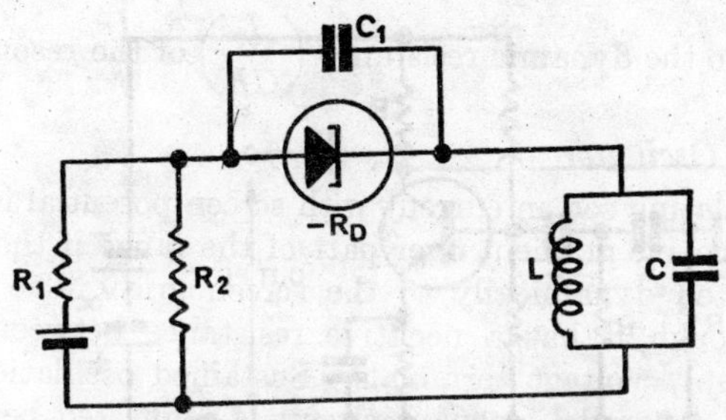

Fig. 11.22. Tunnel diode oscillator.

0·25 V). This negative resistance characteristic may be used as the previous circuits. Fig. 11.22 indicates one of several possible arrangements. The resistors R_1 and R_2 fix the operating point for the diode, while the capacitance C_1 swamps the smaller diode capacitance. Oscillations can be sustained if the load is equal to or greater than the effective negative resistance.

OSCILLATORS WITHOUT LC CIRCUITS

All the oscillators so far dealt with have made use of resonant circuits, or arrangements which are equivalent to *LC* circuits. Two examples of oscillators which employ resistance and capacitance networks in place of tuned circuits will now be considered.

Phase Shift Oscillators

It was pointed out at the beginning of this chapter that if feedback exists in an amplifier the arrangement will oscillate at the frequency at which the loop phase shift is zero, provided that the gain round the loop is at least equal to unity.

The simplest form of such an oscillatory circuit would contain a single stage amplifier with the output and input terminals connected by a network having a phase shift of 180°, and an attenuation equal to or less than the amplification of the valve or transistor.

The resistance capacitance oscillator (shown in Fig. 11.23) is an illustration of this principle. In this case the transistor produces a phase shift of approximately 180° between base and collector. (The phase shift is not exactly 180° because the effective load has a capacitance component.) The *RC* network has thus to provide a phase shift somewhat more than 180° at the frequency at which it is desired that the circuit should oscillate. It can be seen that the required phase shift is provided by three stages of resistance and capacitance, each of which is arranged to give a phase shift of approximately 60° at the desired frequency.

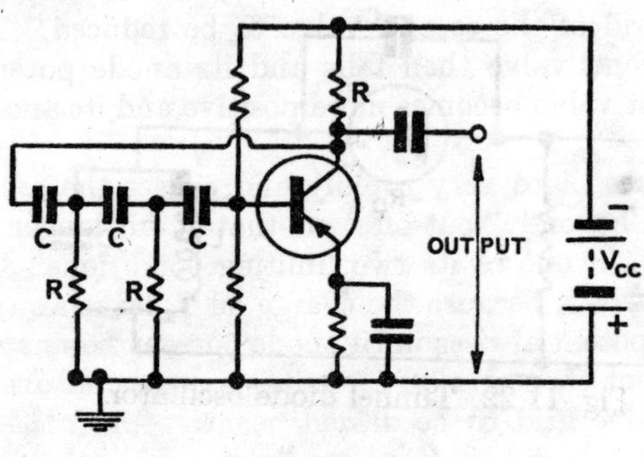

Fig. 11.23.

The waveform generated is substantially sinusoidal if the gain produced by the transistor is only slightly greater than the attenuation produced by the *RC* network at the frequency of oscillation.

The *RC* oscillator has the obvious advantage that no inductances are necessary. This is particularly useful at low frequencies which would otherwise necessitate the use of relatively large iron cored coils.

The Multivibrator

The multivibrator belongs to a class of oscillator in which the circuit conditions change or relax cyclically between two unstable limiting states. For this reason the name relaxation oscillator has been applied to the multivibrator and other oscillators which behave on similar lines. The basic arrangement is that of Fig. 11.24 which shows that the circuit is essentially a two stage resistance capacitance coupled amplifier in which the output is connected to the input.

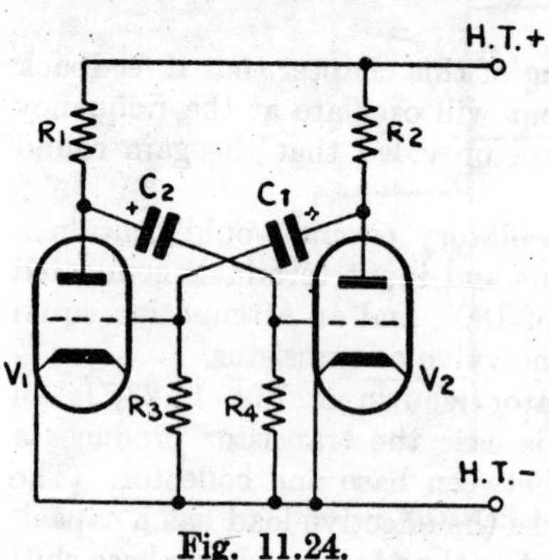

Fig. 11.24.

Initially, when the supplies are connected it can be assumed that both valves have zero grid bias so that they conduct. The coupling capacitors C_1 and C_2 then acquire a charge as shown. Suppose now the grid potential of one valve rises slightly, due to some random cause, the anode current of that valve then increases. This causes the potential of the anode to fall because of the potential drop in the anode resistor. This means that the voltage applied across the associated coupling capacitor and grid leak is reduced, and so this causes the potential of the grid of the second valve to be reduced. The anode current of the second valve then falls and its anode potential rises. The grid of the first valve becomes more positive and its anode current increases.

This process takes place very rapidly and causes the second valve grid to be driven beyond " cut-off " so that it no longer conducts. The circuit is then in one of its two limiting conditions. This is an unstable state, however, because the charge on C_2 leaks away, and the second valve grid potential rises until anode current flows again. This rise of anode current then sets off a similar sequence of events which causes the first valve grid to be driven negative until that valve is cut off. This is the second limiting condition. The whole process is then repeated.

If one valve is cut off, the subsequent change is governed by the exponential discharge of the associated coupling capacitor. This is a relatively slow process compared with the rapid change which occurs immediately the " cut-off " valve conducts and drives the other valve to its non-conducting state.

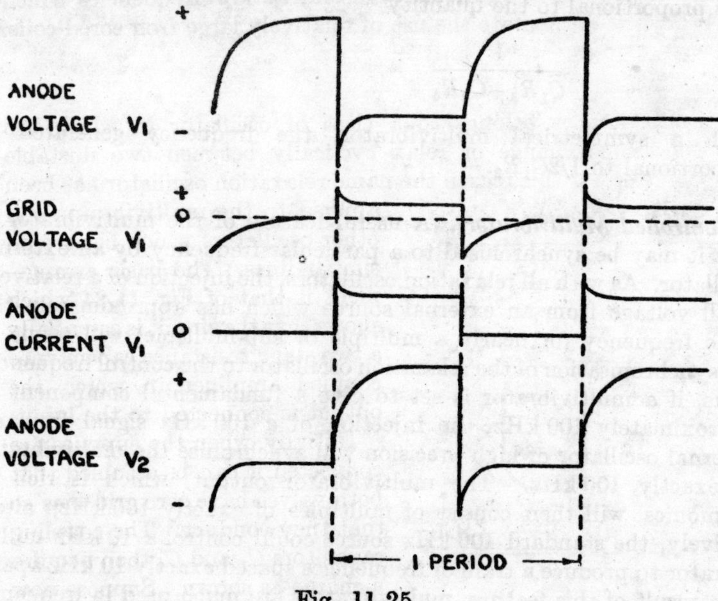

Fig. 11.25.

If the two valves are similar, $C_1 = C_2$, $R_1 = R_2$, and $R_3 = R_4$, the arrangement is a symmetrical multivibrator and the waveform generated is that shown in Fig. 11.25.

Frequency Generated by a Multivibrator. An examination of the multivibrator output shows that the period of oscillation is decided by the times necessary for the valves to return to the conducting state after they have been cut off, i.e. the period of oscillation is the sum of the " recovery " times for the two valves. The recovery time of V_1 depends on the discharge time constant of the capacitor C_1, which has a discharge path which consists of R_3 the H.T. source and R_2, with the anode slope resistance of the conducting valve V_2 bridged across the series combination of the capacitor and R_3. If it is assumed that the H.T. source impedance consists of a capacitor, which is large compared with C_1, then the discharge time constant T_1 is approximately C_1R_3, provided that R_3 is much larger than R_2 and the anode slope resistance of V_2, as is often true. In the same way the discharge time constant T_2 for the capacitor C_2 is approximately C_2R_4. The period of oscillation T is thus proportional to

$$C_1R_3 + C_2R_4$$

and the frequency of oscillation f, with the foregoing assumptions, is thus proportional to the quantity

$$\frac{1}{C_1R_3 + C_2R_4}$$

With a symmetrical multivibrator, the frequency generated is proportional to $1/2C_1R_3$.

Controlled Multivibrators. A useful feature of the multivibrator is that it may be synchronised to a particular frequency by an external oscillator. As with all relaxation oscillators, the injection of a relatively small voltage from an external source which has approximately the same frequency (or nearly a multiple or sub-multiple) will result in the synchronisation of the relaxation oscillator to the control frequency. Thus, if a multivibrator is set to give a fundamental component of approximately 100 kHz, the injection of a 100 kHz signal from an external oscillator of high precision will synchronise the multivibrator to exactly 100 kHz. The multivibrator output, which is rich in harmonics, will then consist of multiples of exactly 100 kHz; alternatively, the standard 100 kHz source could control a 10 kHz multivibrator to produce a train of frequencies spaced exactly 10 kHz apart. As a result of this feature, multivibrators are much used in frequency measuring equipment.

WORKED EXAMPLES

1. A tuned pentode amplifier stage operating at 100 kHz is provided with positive retroaction (insufficient to cause oscillation) by means of a loose inductive coupling to the grid circuit. The effective inductance of the tuned anode circuit is 3 mH and the Q-factor of the circuit is 50. The mutual inductance from anode coil to grid coil is 6 μH. Calculate the voltage amplification which will be obtained with a valve having a mutual conductance of 5 mA/V and an anode slope resistance of 250,000 Ω.

I.E.E. Radio Comm. October, 1945.

The effective impedance of the tuned circuit at resonance is a resistance with a value given by

$$Q\omega L = 50 \times 2\pi \times 10^5 \times 3 \times 10^{-3} = 94{,}200\,\Omega$$

This impedance is in parallel with the anode slope resistance of the valve, so that the total anode impedance Z is given by

$$Z = \frac{250{,}000 \times 94{,}200}{344{,}200} = 68{,}600\ \Omega$$

The gain in the absence of feedback is

$$= g_m Z = 5 \times 10^{-3} \times 68{,}600 = 343$$

As the input impedance of the valve is infinite the voltage fed back to

the grid is $\qquad = \dfrac{M}{L} \times (\text{Anode Voltage})$

i.e. the feedback factor is $M/L = 1/500$. The gain with positive feedback

is given by $\qquad \dfrac{A}{1 - A\beta}$

where A is the gain without feedback $= 343$

and β is the feedback factor $\qquad = 1/500$

$\therefore$ Voltage amplification with positive feedback

$$= \frac{343}{1 - \dfrac{343}{500}} = \underline{1090}$$

2. Deduce the critical condition for oscillations to take place with a triode having the oscillatory circuit in series with the anode and the grid inductively coupled. Explain the effect of (a) varying the anode

voltage, (b) varying the coupling between the grid and anode coils, and (c) inserting a relatively large condenser shunted by a relatively large resistor in the grid circuit.

The frequency of oscillations of a reaction oscillator of the above type is found to be 160 kHz. The anode coil has an inductance of 3·5 mH and is shunted by a condenser having a capacitance of 300 $\mu\mu$F and the anode a.c. resistance of the triode is 1,200 Ω. Estimate the Q of the oscillatory circuit.

L.U. Ext. Telecomm. 1944.

The reader is referred to the text for the answer to the descriptive part of the question. The numerical part of the question can be solved by the formula for the frequency generated by a tuned anode oscillator. It has been shown that the frequency generated by such an oscillator is given by

$$f=\frac{1}{2\pi}\sqrt{\frac{1}{LC}\left(1+\frac{R}{r_a}\right)}$$

In the present case this expression can be used to find the value of R, the resistance of the coil in the oscillatory circuit. Inserting values,

$$2\pi\times 160\times 10^3=\sqrt{\frac{10^{15}}{3{\cdot}5\times 300}\left(1+\frac{R}{1200}\right)}$$

$$\therefore\ 4\pi^2\times 2{\cdot}56\times 10^{10}=\frac{10^{15}}{3{\cdot}5\times 300}\left(1+\frac{R}{1200}\right)$$

$$\therefore\qquad 1+\frac{R}{1200}=\frac{4\pi^2\times 2{\cdot}56\times 10{\cdot}5}{10^3}=1{\cdot}06$$

$$\therefore\qquad R=72\Omega$$

Now $\qquad \omega L=2\pi\times 160\times 10^3\times 3{\cdot}5\times 10^{-3}=3520\Omega$

Hence the Q of the coil is $\dfrac{3520}{72}=\underline{49.}$

References

[1] NYQUIST, H.: "Regeneration Theory", Bell System Technical Journal, 11, p. 126 (1932).

[2] GILLIES, A. W.: "Electrical Oscillations", Wireless Engineer, 30, p. 143 (1953).

References for Further Reading

THOMAS, H. A.: *Theory and Design of Valve Oscillators* (Chapman & Hall, 1951).

EDSON, W. A.: *Vacuum-Tube Oscillators* (Chapman & Hall, 1953).

EXAMPLES

1. A simple oscillator system consists of a tuned circuit connected between the grid and cathode of a triode valve, and coupled to the anode circuit by mutual inductance.

Give a physical explanation of the mechanism of the operation of the oscillator and derive from first principles an expression for the minimum value of the mutual inductance required for the inception of oscillations.

Discuss briefly the factors which influence the frequency stability of such an oscillator.

L.U. Telecomm. Part III. 1959.

2. Derive by means of a simple theory a criterion determining the conditions under which an amplifying system will, with feedback, become self-oscillatory. Show that the criterion involves considerations of phase as well as magnitude.

The parallel resonant impedance of the tuned anode circuit of a pentode amplifier stage is 7000 Ω. The mutual conductance of the valve is 5·0 mA/V. Determine the approximate magnitude, expressed as a fraction of the alternating anode voltage, and the phase of the voltage which, if fed back to the grid, would produce self-oscillation.

I.E.E. Radio Comm. April, 1947.

3. What are the essential parts of an oscillator? Explain by reference to one particular type, the mechanism of operation, stressing the physical principles underlying the process. Derive, from first principles, the equation governing the inception of oscillations for the circuit chosen.

L.U. Int. Telecomm. 1954.

4. A triode tuned-anode oscillator has an anode coil of inductance L and series resistance R. This coil is coupled to the grid coil by mutual inductance M. The valve has a mutual conductance g_m and an anode slope resistance r_a. Show from first principles that there is a minimum value of M to maintain oscillation, and hence show that the approximate minimum value of g_m to maintain oscillation is given by

$$g_m = \frac{1}{M}\left[\frac{R}{\omega^2 L} + \frac{L}{r_a}\right].$$

Such an oscillator has a coil of 80 μH with a Q of 100 and is tuned by a capacitor which can be varied from 50 to 550 pF. The mutual inductance is 3 μH and the anode slope resistance is 10 kΩ. Determine the minimum value of mutual conductance of the valve to maintain oscillation over the entire tuning range.

L.U. Electronics & Telecomm. Part II. 1965.

5. A triode, having a mutual conductance of 1·4 mA/V, is to be used as an H.F. oscillator. The tuned grid-circuit may be taken to have an equivalent series resistance of 30 Ω and a total capacitance of 120 $\mu\mu$F. Calculate the minimum value of mutual inductance between the untuned anode-coil and the grid-coil which will maintain oscillations.

Prove any formulae used.

***L.U. Ext. Telecomm.* 1949.**

6. Describe briefly two possible circuit arrangements for the maintenance of continuous oscillations in an oscillatory circuit by a triode valve, and derive the necessary initial conditions for continual increase of oscillation amplitude in one of them. How is the amplitude of oscillation limited by the characteristics of the valve ?

***L.U. Int. Telecomm.* 1948.**

7. Determine the conditions for oscillation of a Hartley oscillator. Describe two advantages that this circuit possesses over the tuned-anode oscillator for the production of low audio frequencies.

***L.U. Int. Telecomm.* 1955.**

8. Discuss the factor which governs the stability of a linear network containing amplifying valves. Show how the general criterion may be applied to determine the frequency and the necessary back-coupling for a triode oscillator of the Colpitts type.

***L.U. Int. Telecomm.* 1943.**

9. Give the circuit arrangement of a single-valve triode oscillator suitable for operation at frequencies up to several megacycles per second, and sketch typical waveforms of anode voltage, anode current, grid voltage and grid current for such an oscillator when in normal adjustment.

Describe the action of the grid leak and grid condenser. Explain with the aid of the anode voltage and anode current waveforms, how energy conversion efficiencies approaching 80% are obtainable with such oscillators.

***I.E.E. Radio Comm.* October, 1945.**

10. Explain, with the aid of a circuit diagram, any method by which a triode may be used in the generation of high frequency oscillations. Find for the current described, an expression for the necessary relationship between the circuit and valve constants for oscillation to commence, and an expression for the frequency of oscillations produced. What influence have the inter-electrode capacitances of the valve upon the values found from these expressions ?

***L.U. Int. Telecomm.* 1950.**

11. Draw a circuit diagram of a high-power tuned-anode oscillator having self-bias in the grid circuit. Sketch typical waveforms for the anode and grid voltages, and the anode and grid currents. Give reasons for these waveforms.

The anode current pulse in a class-C oscillator, plotted as a current/time curve, has an "area" of 2·4 microcoulombs per cycle. The fundamental component of the current has a peak amplitude of 0·79 A at a frequency of 200 kHz. If the anode voltage varies sinusoidally with an amplitude of 9 kV about a mean value of 10 kV, determine the anode efficiency.

L.U. Telecomm. Part III. 1962.

12. Describe, with a circuit diagram, one method by which continuous oscillations can be maintained in a circuit containing resistance capacitance, and valves, but no inductance. Explain the conditions necessary for the maintenance of oscillations.

L.U. Int. Telecomm. 1949.

13. Draw the connection diagram for a dynatron oscillator and deduce the condition for oscillations to take place.

Discuss the factors that determine (a) the amplitude of the oscillations, (b) the frequency, and (c) the waveform.

***L.U. Ext. Telecomm.* 1945.**

14. Draw a circuit diagram of a multivibrator and explain its operation. Discuss the factors that determine the recurrence frequency and the waveform of the p.d. between the anode and cathode.

State two applications of the multivibrator.

***L.U. Ext. Telecomm.* 1945.**

12

MODULATION

INTRODUCTION

In any electrical communication system, the information to be transmitted is first of all transformed into an electrical time varying quantity, e.g. a current or voltage, which comprises the " signal ". In some cases the waveform of the signal is transmitted directly to the receiving point, in other cases the signal is used to " modulate " the output of a high-frequency generator, so that some property of the high-frequency wave is altered in accordance with the signal. Transmission then takes place by means of the modulated high-frequency wave. At the receiving point the wave is subjected to a demodulation process, which enables the original modulating signal to be obtained.

The high-frequency wave is spoken of as the " carrier ", and after modulation is referred to as a " modulated carrier ".

Modulation may, at first sight, seem an unnecessary complication in a transmission system. Often, however, the modulation process is essential, when for example the transmission medium does not transmit the original frequency spectrum efficiently, if at all. In such a case it is clearly necessary that the component frequencies of the signal be translated so that they occupy a frequency range acceptable to the transmission system. An illustration of this is provided by radio transmission ; the efficiency of transmission is negligible at speech frequencies, but increases rapidly as the frequency is raised. Efficient radio transmission of low-frequency signals, such as speech, can be secured if the signal is arranged to modulate a carrier of higher frequency. Alternatively, if two or more signals occupy the same frequency band (e.g. speech from separate sources), transmission by a common circuit is possible if each signal is arranged to modulate a separate high-frequency carrier. The separation of signals at the receiver then becomes a question of separating the carriers. Modulation thus enables communication to be carried on at frequencies which differ from those of the original modulating signal.

It should be noted that no " message " or information is transmitted by the passage of a steady current (or voltage) between two points, or by the passage of a continuous invariable tone, i.e. an alternating voltage or current of constant amplitude and fixed frequency. Information can only pass between the points if the steady current or tone is varied in some way.

The carrier used may be continuous, or discontinuous in the form of recurrent pulses, and commonly consists of a high-frequency sinusoidal wave of the form,

$$A \sin (\omega_c t + \phi)$$

where A is the amplitude of the carrier,

f_c is the carrier frequency $= \omega_c/2\pi$, and

ϕ is the phase angle of the carrier relative to some datum.

If the carrier frequency is maintained constant and the amplitude is varied in accordance with the modulating signal, the carrier is said to be *amplitude modulated.* Alternatively, the amplitude may be kept constant and the argument of the sine function varied in accordance with the signal. *Pulse modulation* exists when the carrier is made discontinuous and some characteristic of the pulses is varied in accordance with the modulating signal.

For any given system of modulation the characteristics of the modulated wave are the same, irrespective of the circuits which have been used to produce such a waveform. It is therefore convenient to consider the broad aspects of the modulation process first and defer the discussion of the various circuits to the following chapter.

AMPLITUDE MODULATION

Suppose a sinusoidal carrier current of constant amplitude and fixed frequency is represented at any instant by

$$i = A \sin (\omega_c t + \phi) \qquad . \quad . \quad . \quad . \quad . \quad . \qquad 12.1$$

If this carrier is to be amplitude modulated by a signal which is some function of time, $g(t)$, the amplitude of the carrier will be given by

$$[A + g(t)]$$

The instantaneous value of the amplitude-modulated carrier current is then

$$i = [A + g(t)] \sin \omega_c t \qquad . \quad . \quad . \quad . \quad . \quad . \qquad 12.2$$

if the reference phase is chosen so that $\phi = 0°$.

Amplitude Modulation by a Single Sine Wave

In general, the waveform of the modulating signal will be complex and in the case of speech will have a large number of component frequencies together with their harmonics. If the signal is assumed to have its simplest form and consist of a single sine wave, of a frequency low compared with the carrier, then for such a signal, represented by say, $B \sin \omega_s t$, equation 12.2 becomes

$$i = [A + B \sin \omega_s t] \sin \omega_c t \qquad . \quad . \quad . \quad . \quad . \qquad 12.3$$

A carrier modulated in this way is shown in Fig. 12.1. It will be seen that the amplitude of the carrier when modulated varies between

$$A+B \text{ and } A-B.$$

The ratio of B/A is known as the degree or *depth of modulation* If $B=k_aA$ then $k_a \times 100$ is referred to as the percentage modulation. It will be seen that the carrier will be modulated to its greatest extent when k_a is equal to unity. The amplitude will then vary between twice the unmodulated value and zero, and the carrier is said to be fully modulated. If through any cause the modulation percentage exceeds 100, the modulated wave is no longer represented by equation 12.3. This " over-modulation " gives rise to distortion in the received signal, and because of this the circuits are normally arranged to limit the maximum depth of modulation to slightly less than 100%.

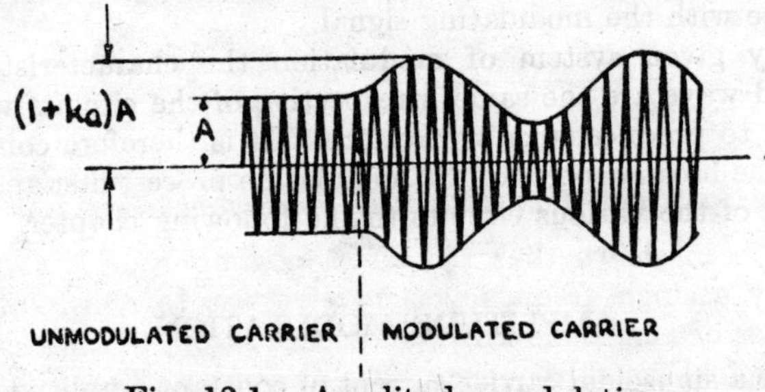

Fig. 12.1. Amplitude modulation.

Equation 12.3 shows that the modulated carrier is expressed as a wave of constant frequency, varying in amplitude about a datum displaced from zero by the unmodulated amplitude. The modulated waveform may however be expressed alternatively as

$$i=A \sin \omega_c t+k_aA(\sin \omega_s t \sin \omega_c t)$$

$$=A \sin \omega_c t+\frac{k_aA}{2} \cos (\omega_c-\omega_s)t-\frac{k_aA}{2} \cos (\omega_c+\omega_s)t \qquad 12.4$$

where $k_a=B/A$

This result shows that the single constant frequency, amplitude-modulated wave may be considered as three separate waves of constant frequency. The amplitude of the carrier frequency component is independent of the degree of modulation while the other components have amplitudes which vary directly with the degree of modulation.

Amplitude Modulation by a Complex Wave

The modulating signal rarely consists of a single continuous sine wave (except for test purposes) and so it is necessary to consider briefly the effect of more than one frequency component in the modulating signal. Suppose, for the sake of simplicity, the signal consists of two sine wave components

$$B \sin \omega_{s_1}t \text{ and } C \sin \omega_{s_2}t$$

The amplitude variation will then be expressed by

$$(B \sin \omega_{s_1}t + C \sin \omega_{s_2}t)$$

and the modulated waveform is given by

$$i = (A + B \sin \omega_{s_1}t + C \sin \omega_{s_2}t) \sin \omega_c t$$

This can be expressed in the form of equation 12.4 when it will be found that there are now four frequency components in addition to the carrier.

The depth of modulation in this case is given by the peak value of the quantity

$$\frac{B \sin \omega_{s_1}t + C \sin \omega_{s_2}t}{A}$$

Frequency Spectrum of an Amplitude-Modulated Wave

It has been shown that the effect of amplitude modulation of a carrier by a single frequency is to give rise to a pair of sinusoidal frequencies of amplitude $k_a A/2$ and spaced from the carrier frequency by the original signal frequency. The presence of these side frequencies can be confirmed experimentally by passing the modulated wave through highly selective measuring equipment, when each component can be separated and identified.

If the carrier is modulated by a complex signal, and the system is linear, each frequency component in the signal will give rise to a pair of side frequencies. If a carrier is modulated by n frequencies, $f_1, f_2, f_3, \ldots f_n$ there will be $2n$ side frequencies.

One band of side frequencies, or *sideband*, will exist over the range $f_c - (f_1, f_2, \ldots f_n)$. This is referred to as the lower sideband. The upper sideband then extends over the range $f_c + (f_1, f_2, \ldots f_n)$. This is shown in Fig. 12.2. It will be seen that the bandwidth occupied by

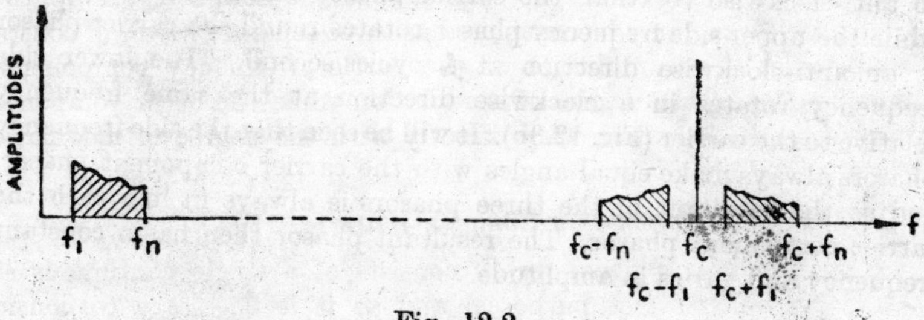

Fig. 12.2.

the amplitude-modulated wave is twice the bandwidth of the original signal.

Phasor Representation of an Amplitude-Modulated Wave

The phasor representation of an amplitude-modulated wave can be illustrated if the modulating signal is assumed to have a simple form, and consists of say, a single sine wave of constant frequency and fixed amplitude. The phasor representing equation 12.3 is thus a rotating phasor which rotates at f_c times per second, and varies in amplitude f_s times per second between the amplitude limits of $A(1 + k_a)$ and $A(1 - k_a)$. An observer attached to a similar rotating phasor of the same angular frequency as the carrier, would then see the carrier phasor stationary in position but varying in length (Fig. 12.3a).

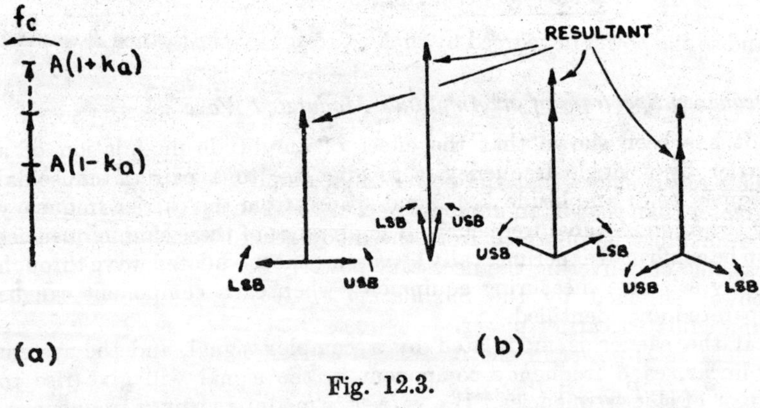

Fig. 12.3.

If the modulated wave is considered as a fixed amplitude carrier with two side frequencies, three rotating phasors are involved. If the carrier frequency is subtracted from all three phasors, and it is borne in mind that the accepted positive direction of frequency corresponds to anti-clockwise rotation, the carrier phasor will appear stationary while the upper side frequency phasor rotates round the carrier phasor in an anti-clockwise direction at f_s cycles/second. The lower side frequency rotates in a clockwise direction at the same frequency relative to the carrier (Fig. 12.3b). It will be seen that the side frequency phasors always make equal angles with the carrier component phasor, and so the resultant of the three phasors is always in line with the carrier component phasor. The resultant phasor then has a constant frequency and varies in amplitude.

Power in an Amplitude-Modulated Wave

The mean power dissipated in any circuit is given by

$$P = I^2 R$$

where I is the r.m.s. value of the current and R is the circuit resistance. The r.m.s. value of a complex current (or voltage) is obtained from the square root of the sum of the squares of the r.m.s. values of the various components. The r.m.s. value of the modulated current of equation 12.4 is thus given by

$$I_{r.m.s.} = \sqrt{\frac{A^2}{2} + \frac{k_a{}^2 A^2}{8} + \frac{k_a{}^2 A^2}{8}}$$

$$= \frac{A}{\sqrt{2}} \sqrt{1 + \frac{k_a{}^2}{2}}$$

and so the power developed by such a current in a resistance R would be

$$P = \frac{A^2}{2}\left(1 + \frac{k_a{}^2}{2}\right) R \quad . \quad . \quad . \quad . \quad . \quad . \quad 12.5$$

This result shows that the power in an amplitude-modulated wave is greater than that in an unmodulated wave when $k_a = 0$. The additional power must be obtained from the modulating source which must be capable of delivering the necessary power. For 100% modulation the power supplied by the modulating source must be 50% of the unmodulated carrier power.

The total power in the modulated carrier, P_{total} is thus given by

$$P_{total} = P_{carrier} + P_{sidebands} \quad . \quad . \quad . \quad . \quad . \quad . \quad 12.6$$

The ratio of power in the sidebands to total power can be seen from equation 12.5 to be

$$\frac{P_{sideband}}{P_{total}} = \frac{\dfrac{k_a{}^2}{2}}{1 + \dfrac{k_a{}^2}{2}} = \frac{k_a{}^2}{2 + k_a{}^2} \quad . \quad . \quad . \quad . \quad . \quad . \quad 12.7$$

Fig. 12.4 shows the percentage of total power in both sidebands, and in the carrier, plotted against different depths of modulation. It will be seen that when the percentage modulation is less than 20% the power in one sideband is less than 1% of the total power. In practice the power in the sidebands does not remain constant but varies from instant to instant in accordance with the variation of the signal waveform with time.

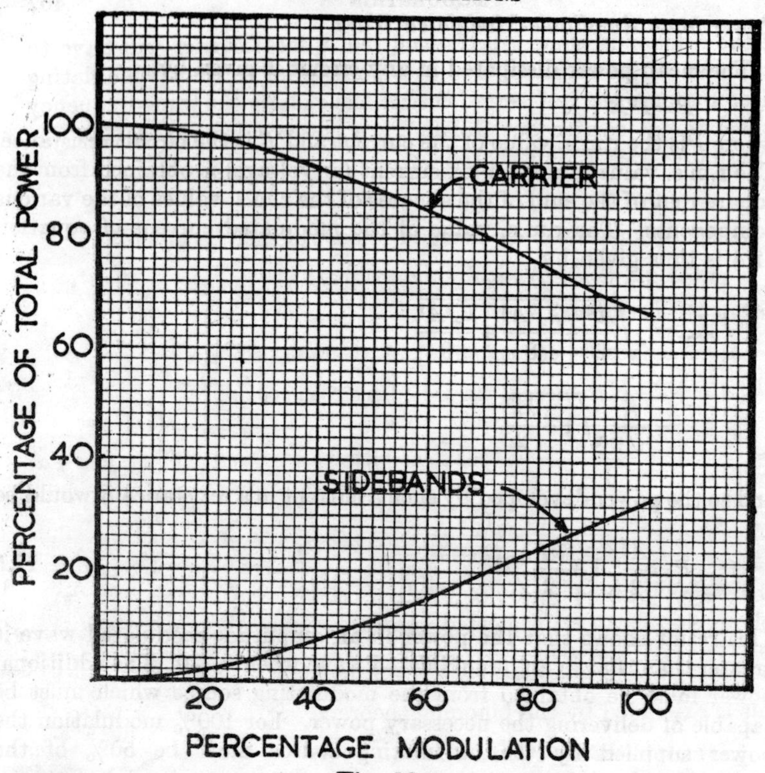

Fig. 12.4.

SUPPRESSED CARRIER TRANSMISSION

In a practical amplitude-modulated transmission system the circuits are arranged so that the peak modulation depth does not exceed 100%, so as to avoid distortion. As a result the mean value of the modulation depth is low in cases where the modulating signal is such that the ratio of peak to mean value is appreciable. With this low mean value of modulation most of the power resides in the carrier component which contains no information whatsoever. If the carrier is suppressed at the sending end, and the sidebands transmitted alone, a large saving in transmitter power results. Demodulation at the receiving end with such a system can be obtained by re-inserting a local carrier. While such a system is possible, troubles arise in practice from the stringent requirements which the re-inserted carrier has to meet. This may be shown in a simple way by considering the transmission of a modulating signal which is a single sine wave. As before, the modulated wave is represented by

$$i = A \sin \omega_c t + k_a A \sin \omega_s t \sin \omega_c t$$

If the sidebands alone are transmitted, a local carrier will have to be supplied at the receiving end at a point prior to the demodulating device. Suppose the re-inserted carrier has exactly the same frequency as the original carrier but differs by a phase angle θ, so that the re-inserted carrier is represented by

$$A \sin (\omega_c t+\theta)$$

The waveform presented for demodulation will then be given by

$$i = A \sin (\omega_c t+\theta) + k_a A \sin \omega_s t \sin \omega_c t$$

This can be written as,

$$\begin{aligned} i &= A[\sin \omega_c t \cos \theta + \cos \omega_c t \sin \theta] + k_a A \sin \omega_s t \sin \omega_c t \\ &= [A \cos \theta + k_a A \sin \omega_s t] \sin \omega_c t + [A \sin \theta] \cos \omega_c t \\ &= \left[\sqrt{A^2 + \frac{k_a^2 A^2}{2} - \frac{k_a^2 A^2}{2} \cos 2\omega_s t + 2k_a A^2 \cos \theta \sin \omega_s t}\right] \sin (\omega_c t+\alpha) \end{aligned}$$

where $\alpha = \tan^{-1}\left[\dfrac{\sin \theta}{\cos \theta + k_a \sin \omega_s t}\right]$

If the depth of modulation is small so that $k_a << 1$, and the terms involving $k_a^2 A^2$ can be neglected compared with A^2,

then $\quad i \simeq \left[A\sqrt{1+2k_a \cos \theta \sin \omega_s t}\right] \sin (\omega_c t+\alpha)$

If this is expanded by the binomial theorem

$$i \simeq A(1+k_a \cos \theta \sin \omega_s t) \sin (\omega_c t+\alpha) \qquad . \quad . \quad . \quad 12.8$$

If now $\theta = 0$

$$i = A(1+k_a \sin \omega_s t) \sin (\omega_c t)$$

and the result is an amplitude-modulated waveform as desired.

If on the other hand, the re-inserted carrier has not exactly the correct phase, the depth of the modulation is changed from the original value.

If $\theta = 90°$

$$i = A \sin (\omega_c t+\alpha)$$

and in this special case the modulation is entirely suppressed. In general, as θ varies from zero to quadrature the depth of modulation is diminished from its correct value to zero. For values of θ greater than 90° the modulation appears with its sense reversed, and at $\theta = 180°$ the waveform has again its original depth of modulation but with the sense reversed.

The disappearance of the modulation, for a small depth of modulation, when the re-inserted carrier is in quadrature, can be shown by considering the phasors involved. Fig. 12.5 shows that for a quadrature carrier the resultant phasor oscillates through a small angle and has only a small amplitude change. The oscillation of the carrier phasor about its unmodulated position implies that the carrier frequency is changing, and in fact Fig. 12.5 would represent an angle-modulated phasor with a very small amount of amplitude modulation present. For pure angle-modulation the resultant phasor would have a constant magnitude and oscillate over an arc.

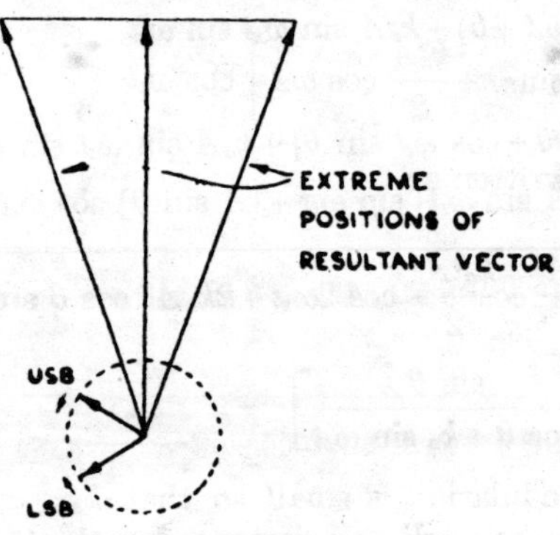

Fig. 12.5.

A simple suppressed carrier system is not used, as the frequency of the re-inserted carrier must be exactly equal to the original carrier, otherwise the phase will vary continuously.

SINGLE SIDEBAND TRANSMISSION

Although double sideband suppressed carrier transmission is not employed, *single sideband* systems are utilised. In this case the carrier and one sideband (either upper or lower) are suppressed at the sending end after the modulation has taken place. The remaining single sideband is then transmitted to the received point where a local carrier is introduced so that demodulation can take place.

If the received sideband is assumed to be the lower one, and the modulation is of a simple sinusoidal nature, then with the previous notation the received sideband will be represented by

$$\frac{k_a A}{2} \cos (\omega_c - \omega_s)t$$

If the re-inserted carrier has a phase displacement θ from its correct value, the voltage waveform available for demodulation is then

$$e = A \sin (\omega_c t + \theta) + \frac{k_a A}{2} \cos (\omega_c - \omega_s)t$$

On expansion this becomes

$$e = A \sin \omega_c t \cos \theta + A \cos \omega_c t \sin \theta$$

$$+ \frac{k_a A}{2} [\cos \omega_c t \cos \omega_s t + \sin \omega_c t \sin \omega_s t]$$

$$= \left[A \cos \theta + \frac{k_a A}{2} \sin \omega_s t \right] \sin \omega_c t$$

$$+ \left[A \sin \theta + \frac{k_a A}{2} \cos \omega_s t \right] \cos \omega_c t$$

This can be re-written as

$$e = \left[\sqrt{A^2 \cos^2 \theta + k_a A^2 \cos \theta \sin \omega_s t + \frac{k_a{}^2 A^2}{4} \sin^2 \omega_s t + + A^2 \sin^2 \theta + k_a A^2 \sin \theta \cos \omega_s t + \frac{k_a{}^2 A^2}{4} \cos^2 \omega_s t} \right] \sin (\omega_c t + \alpha)$$

$$\text{where} \quad \alpha = \tan^{-1} \left[\frac{\sin \theta + \frac{k_a}{2} \cos \omega_s t}{\cos \theta + \frac{k_a}{2} \sin \omega_s t} \right]$$

and so, on simplifying

$$e = \left[\sqrt{A^2 + \frac{k_a{}^2 A^2}{4} + k_a A^2 \sin (\omega_s t + \theta)} \right] \sin (\omega_c t + \alpha)$$

If the depth of modulation is small so that $k_a < 1$ and the $k_a{}^2 A^2$ term is neglected in comparsion with A^2

$$e = [A^2 + k_a A^2 \sin (\omega_s t + \theta)]^{\frac{1}{2}} \sin (\omega_c t + \alpha)$$

If the quantity in the square brackets is expanded by the binomial theorem,

$$e \simeq \left[A + \frac{k_a A}{2} \sin (\omega_s t + \theta) \right] \sin (\omega_c t + \alpha)$$

This result shows that the effect of a variation of θ is to cause a phase shift of the modulating signal from its correct position, and so if the phase angle varies slowly the effect is to cause the phase of the modulation to vary correspondingly.

A consideration of the phasors in this case (Fig. 12.6) shows that angle modulation is present in addition to the desired amplitude modulation.

The amplitude of the re-inserted carrier must be such as to make $k_a < 1$ at the receiver, otherwise the envelope amplitude will no longer be represented by

$$A + \frac{k_a A}{2} \sin (\omega_s t + \theta)$$

and harmonics of the modulating signal will appear in the receiver output, and so cause distortion. This can be avoided if the amplitude of the re-inserted carrier is made large compared with the received sideband.

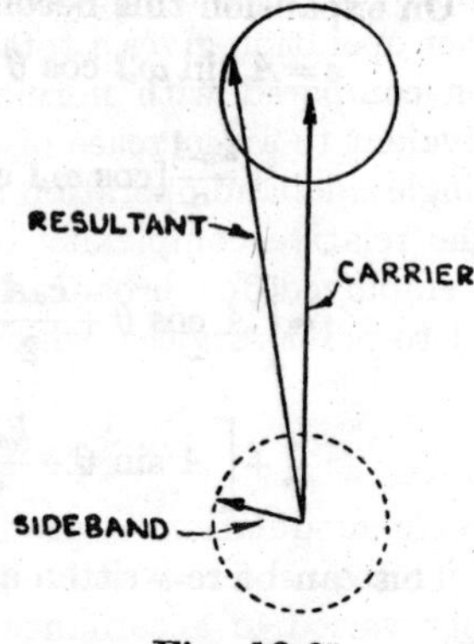

Fig. 12.6.

The question of the phase shift of the modulation in the single sideband suppressed carrier system has been considered for simplicity for the case where the modulation consists of a single sine wave. This is misleading to some extent, as the same waveform will be produced when the carrier is re-inserted, whatever the phase of the carrier, i.e. the waveform envelope is always of sinusoidal form. If, however, the modulating signal has several frequency components, the waveform after demodulation will not be the same as the modulating signal in so far as the relative phases of the various components are altered. If the ultimate destination of the demodulated signal is the human ear this phase distortion will be relatively unimportant because of the insensitivity of the ear to phase shift. If the inserted carrier differs very slightly in frequency from its correct value the result is to change the frequencies comprising the demodulated signal by that amount.

It is often customary, however, to transmit a " pilot " carrier at a low level compared with the original. The pilot carrier is then amplified at the receiving position to function as the inserted carrier for demodulation. This then avoids trouble due to lack of synchronisation of the local carrier at the receiving point.

Advantages of Single Sideband Transmission

Single sideband transmission offers advantages over double sideband transmission, and as a result is widely used in carrier systems of line communication. The bandwidth required is halved, and as a consequence twice as many channels can be used on a multi-channel circuit, as compared with double sideband operation.

A further advantage of single sideband suppressed carrier operation over normal double sideband transmission is that the signal/noise ratio is improved. This is discussed in chapter 14. Single sideband suppressed carrier operation gives a total improvement in signal/noise ratio of 9dB when compared with normal double sideband transmission ; this is equivalent to an increase of eight times in the transmitter power.

Single sideband operation is also used in radio transmission. Because of the relative complexity in the receiving equipment however, it is not employed for broadcast operation, and its use is restricted to point-to-point services, which are discussed in chapter 22.

ANGLE MODULATION

Angle modulation is produced when the amplitude of the carrier wave remains fixed and either the frequency or the phase of the carrier varied in accordance with the signal. As the frequency and phase are not independent a change in one means that the other quantity is also changing. One advantage of such modulation arises from the resulting fixed amplitude of the modulated wave. This permits class C operation, with a consequent increase in efficiency, of the output stages of the transmitter.

Frequency Modulation

In frequency modulation the amplitude of the modulating signal is used to change the carrier frequency from its unmodulated value, so that the instantaneous frequency deviation is proportional to the amplitude of the signal. This is illustrated in Fig. 12.7 (b) which shows a carrier frequency modulated by a square wave signal. (Note the frequency is not drawn to scale.)

To take a numerical example, suppose a carrier of 1 MHz is to be frequency modulated and assume that for every 10 V of modulation signal the frequency change is 10 kHz. Then modulation of the carrier by a sine wave voltage of 10 V peak value and a frequency of 400 Hz will cause the carrier frequency to vary from 1·01 to 0·99 MHz. This variation will then take place 400 times per second. If the amplitude of the modulating signal is increased to 30 V peak the carrier frequency will vary from 1·03 to 0·97 MHz.

Suppose the carrier consists of a high-frequency sinusoidal voltage, represented by

$$e = A \sin \theta = A \sin (\omega_c t + \phi) \qquad 12.9$$

where A, ω_c, and ϕ have the same significance as before. If this carrier is to be frequency modulated, the expression for its instantaneous frequency must contain a term with a waveform similar to that of the modulating signal. Now the instantaneous frequency of a frequency-modulated wave, represented by

$$A \sin \theta'$$

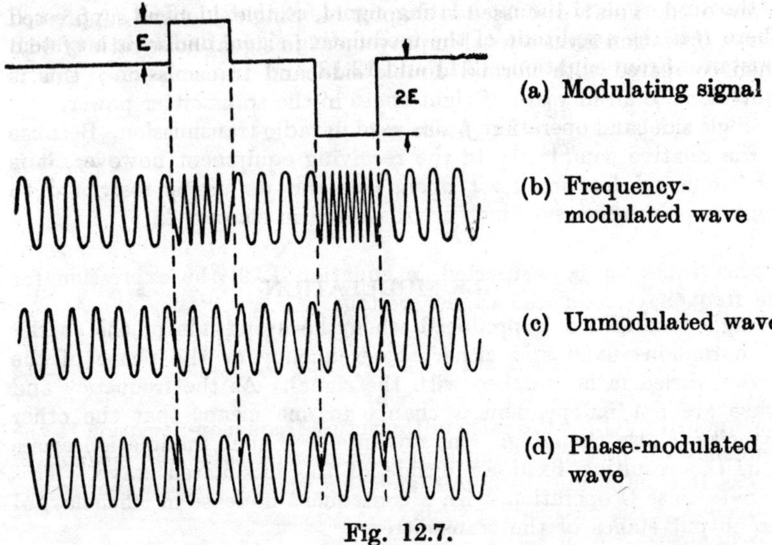

Fig. 12.7.

may be defined as

$$f' = \frac{1}{2\pi}\frac{d\theta'}{dt} \quad . \quad . \quad . \quad . \quad . \quad . \quad 12.10a$$

and the instantaneous angular frequency is then,

$$\omega' = \frac{d\theta'}{dt} \quad . \quad . \quad . \quad . \quad . \quad . \quad 12.10b$$

The instantaneous frequency of the carrier wave represented by equation 12.9 is then,

$$f = \frac{1}{2\pi}\frac{d}{dt}(\omega_c t + \phi) = \frac{\omega_c}{2\pi} + \frac{1}{2\pi}\frac{d\phi}{dt} \quad . \quad . \quad 12.11$$

By definition, ω_c is a constant quantity, hence the effect of frequency modulation must be to vary the quantity $d\phi/dt$. If the modulating signal is assumed to be sinusoidal, the instantaneous frequency will be,

$$f = \frac{\omega_c}{2\pi} + \Delta f_c \sin \omega_s t \quad . \quad . \quad . \quad . \quad 12.12$$

and so there is a cyclic variation in frequency having a peak value when $\sin \omega_s t = \pm 1$. Δf_c is called the *frequency deviation*. It should be remembered, however, that the frequency deviation itself is proportional to the amplitude of the modulating signal, so that in effect, $\triangle f_c = k_1 B$ where B is the amplitude of the modulating signal and k_1 is a system constant. From equations 12.11 and 12.12

$$\frac{d\phi}{dt} = 2\pi \triangle f_c \sin \omega_s t$$

$$\text{and } \phi = \frac{-\triangle f_c \cos \omega_s t}{f_s}$$

If this value for ϕ is inserted in equation 12.9, the expression for the frequency-modulated carrier voltage is

$$e = A \sin \left(\omega_c t - \frac{\triangle f_c}{f_s} \cos \omega_s t \right) \quad . \quad . \ 12.13$$

The quantity $\triangle f_c / f_s$, the ratio of the actual frequency deviation to the frequency of the modulating signal, is referred to as the *modulation index*. It is important to note that it is inversely proportional to the frequency of the modulating signal.

A quantity, the *deviation ratio* k_f, is used to relate the actual frequency deviation produced by a particular modulating signal to the maximum possible frequency deviation corresponding to the largest amplitude of modulating signal permitted in a given system. The deviation ratio corresponds to the modulation depth k_a in an amplitude modulation system, and is also often quoted as a percentage. When k_f has its maximum value of 100%, $\triangle f_c = \triangle f_{cmax}$. Practical systems are arranged so that $\triangle f_{cmax} / f_c$ is always small compared with unity.

Phase Modulation

In phase modulation the amplitude of the modulating signal is used to change the carrier phase from the value it would have if unmodulated. The phase angle of the carrier is thus advanced or retarded by some angle which is proportional to the instantaneous amplitude of the signal, irrespective of the signal frequency. Fig. 12.7 (d) shows a wave which is phase modulated by a square wave modulating signal. The illustration shows that for an amplitude of E volts of modulation in a positive sense, the phase of the carrier is retarded by 90°. When the modulating voltage is zero the carrier has the same phase as it would have had if no modulation had occurred. $2E$ volts of modulation in a negative sense cause the phase of the carrier to be increased by 180° with respect to the unmodulated value.

If the sinusoidal carrier voltage is represented by

$$e = A \sin \theta$$

then for a sinusoidal modulating voltage, the angle θ will differ sinusoidally from its unmodulated value, and will in fact be expressed by,

$$\theta = \omega_c t + k_2 B \sin \omega_s t$$

hence the phase-modulated wave may be expressed by the equation,

$$e = A \sin (\omega_c t + m_p \sin \omega_s t) \quad . \quad . \quad . \quad 12.14$$

where the quantity $m_p(=k_2 B)$ is called the modulation index and is the maximum phase shift produced by the modulating signal, being the angle in radians through which the phase of the carrier is displaced from the unmodulated value; B is proportional to the amplitude of the modulating signal but independent of its frequency, and k_2 is a system constant.

It should be noted that at points of maximum phase displacement the rate of change of phase is zero and so the frequency of the phase-modulated wave at this point is that of the unmodulated wave. On the other hand when the phase displacement has its maximum rate of change the frequency deviation is a maximum. As a result of this the higher the modulating signal frequency the higher is the resultant rate of change of phase, or the greater is the frequency deviation. In consequence, with phase modulation the quantity, frequency deviation/signal frequency, remains constant, unlike frequency modulation in which $\triangle f_c$ is fixed for a given amplitude of modulating signal, so that $\triangle f_c/f_s$ varies as f_s varies.

Frequency Spectrum of an Angle-Modulated Wave

An amplitude modulated wave has two sidebands for each modulating frequency. Equation 12.13, which gives the instantaneous value of a frequency-modulated wave, may be expanded and expressed as a series of Bessel functions representing a carrier and infinite number of sidebands spaced from the carrier by frequencies $\pm f_s$, $\pm 2f_s$, $\pm 3f_s$, etc.; a phase-modulated wave has also a theoretically infinite number of sidebands for each modulating frequency. (In both cases the odd-numbered sideband vector $f_c \pm f_s$, $f_c \pm 3f_s$, etc. have a resultant which is at right angles to the carrier vector, while the even numbered sidebands have a resultant in line with the carrier vector.)

Although angle modulation gives rise in theory to an infinite number of side frequencies, the actual number which have significant amplitudes depends on the modulation index. In frequency modulation a low ratio $\triangle f_c/f_s$ results in a small number of side frequencies of appreciable amplitude. This number increases as the quantity $\triangle f_c/f_s$ increases. If a sinusoidal modulating signal causes the same angular departure from the unmodulated condition in either type of modulation the frequency spectrum is the same in both cases. For more complex modulating signals there may be appreciable difference between the spectra of frequency and phase-modulated waves.

It should be pointed out that the frequency spectrum for either type of modulated wave is never less than approximately twice the value of the frequency deviation $\triangle f_c$, or the maximum value of the modulating signal f_s, whichever is the larger.[1] Thus if $\triangle f_c/f_{s\,max}$ is less than unity the necessary bandwidth is determined by the value of $f_{s\,max}$. For wide frequency deviation in which $\triangle f_c > f_{s\,max}$ the bandwidth is determined by the value of $\triangle f_c$.

Phasor Representation of an Angle-Modulated Wave

(a) Frequency Modulation

If a high-frequency carrier is frequency modulated by a sinusoidal modulating signal, and the unmodulated carrier is represented by a stationary phasor, the modulated wave will be represented by a phasor which travels at a velocity which varies cyclically about zero. This phasor will then oscillate through an angle α about the unmodulated position (Fig. 12.8a). The magnitude of the angle α which is swept out will depend on the velocity of the phasor and the time of oscillation. Now the phasor velocity depends on the frequency deviation $\triangle f_c$ while the time for one complete oscillation over the path *AOBOA* is the time for one cycle of the modulating signal, i.e. $1/f_s$ seconds.

From this it is apparent that the angle of travel of the phasor is dependent on the ratio $\triangle f_c/f_s$. $\triangle f_c$ is fixed by the amplitude of the modulating signal and it follows from this that if the frequency of the modulating signal is decreased and the amplitude maintained constant the angle α will increase. If the carrier is modulated by a frequency f_s the angle α will be increased to α' as shown in Fig. 12.8a, if f_s is replaced by another modulating signal of lower frequency.

(b) Phase Modulation

If a high-frequency carrier is phase modulated by a sinusoidal modulating signal then the modulated wave will be represented by a phasor which travels at a velocity which again varies cyclically about the unmodulated value ; if the unmodulated carrier is represented by a stationary phasor, the modulated wave will be represented by a phasor which oscillates through some angle about the unmodulated position (Fig. 12.8b). In this case, however, it will be remembered that m_p is a constant quantity and so the angle described will be constant for all frequencies of modulating signals which have the

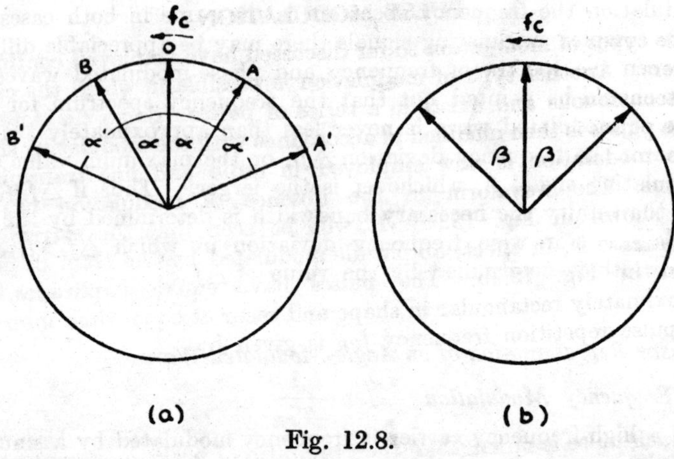

Fig. 12.8.

same peak amplitude. The frequency deviation is directly proportional to the frequency of the modulating signal, and so high modulation frequencies produce large frequency deviations.

Power in an Angle-Modulated Wave

By definition the amplitude of an angle-modulated wave is invariant. It follows that if the modulation of a high-frequency carrier results in the production of sidebands, the power in the carrier component must decrease in order that the total power shall remain constant. This transfer of energy from the carrier to the sideband depends on the modulation index, so that the amplitude of the carrier component depends on the modulation index.

Noise Reduction in a Frequency-Modulated System

Amplitude modulation was the first and is still by far the most widely used method of modulation. As a result of investigations in the nineteen-thirties it was realised that frequency and phase modulation offered the advantage of an improved signal/noise ratio under certain conditions. Because of this, frequency modulation has since been used and in some cases is preferred to amplitude modulation. Phase modulation has not been quite so widely used although some practical systems are, in fact, a combination of frequency and phase modulation.

If a frequency-modulation system is compared with an amplitude-modulation system of the same total bandwidth, the ratio of noise power in the outputs will be as 1 : 3 (see chapter 14) provided that the noise is due to fluctuation noise uniformly distributed throughout the frequency spectrum involved.

PULSE MODULATION

The types of modulation so far discussed have employed continuous carriers. Another type of modulation is possible in which the carrier is discontinuous and exists in a series of pulses. Some characteristic of the pulses is then modified in accordance with the modulating signal. Pulse modulation is now employed in radio and line transmission systems. The waveform in the absence of modulation has the form shown in Fig. 12.9a. It will be seen that the carrier used in this case is, in effect, amplitude modulated by the train of pulses shown in Fig. 12.9b. The pulses have equal amplitudes, are approximately rectangular in shape and recur at equal time intervals. The pulse repetition frequency f_{PR} is given by

$$f_{PR} = \frac{1}{T_{PR}}$$

If each pulse is of length T then the ratio of peak to average power (over a long period) is given by T_{PR}/T.

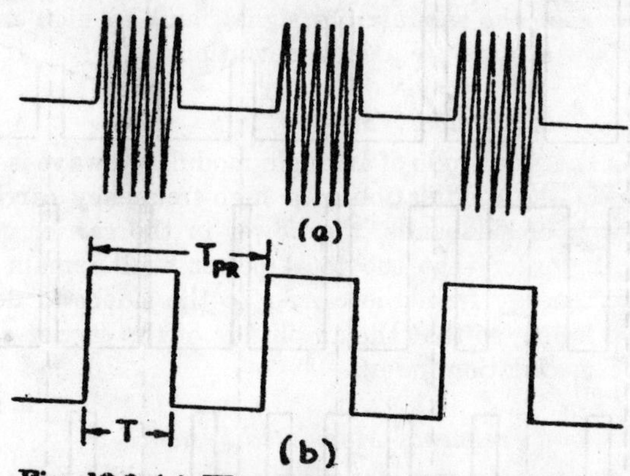

Fig. 12.9 (a) Waveform of pulsed carrier
(b) Unmodulated pulse waveform.

Modulation consists, as has been suggested, in varying some characteristic of the pulses. There is a large number of ways in which this may be done, but only a few are of practical importance.

Pulse-Modulation Systems

Three types of pulse modulation are shown in Fig. 12.12. They are:

(a) Pulse Amplitude Modulation
(b) Pulse Width Modulation
(c) Pulse Position Modulation

o

If the signal to be transmitted, i.e. the quantity so far called the modulating signal, has its amplitude "sampled" at regular intervals in accordance with the sampling theorem (see chapter 15) so that the time interval between samples is not more than half the period of the highest signal frequency, a series of pulses of constant width but varying amplitude is obtained (Fig. 12.10b). This constitutes pulse-amplitude-modulation as the amplitude is proportional to the amplitude of the modulating signal.

In pulse-width-modulation Fig. 12.10c, the width of the pulses is made to vary in accordance with the modulation. The pulse amplitude, and mean pulse repetition frequency are maintained constant.

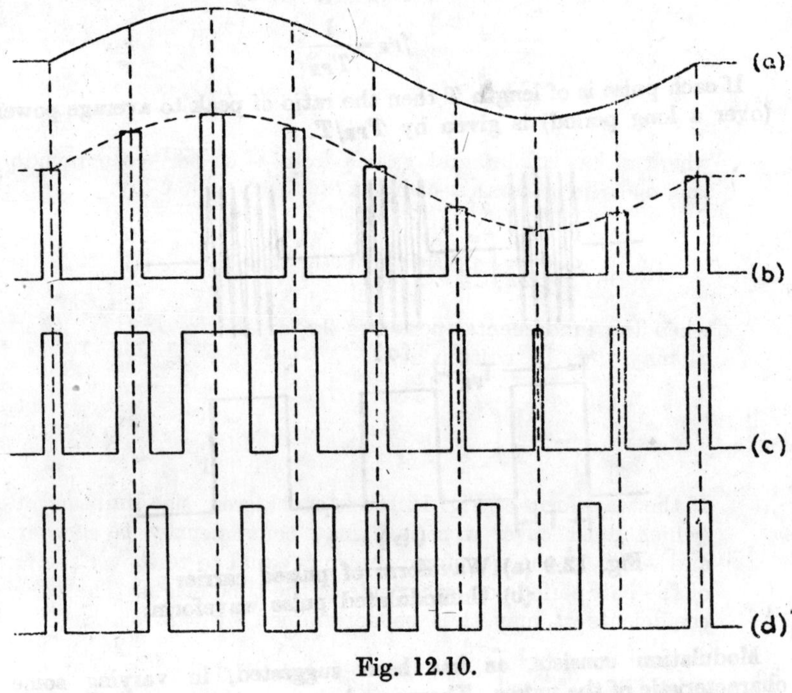

Fig. 12.10.

With pulse-position-modulation the pulse amplitude and width are kept constant, also the mean pulse repetition frequency, but the position of the pulse is varied in accordance with the amplitude of the modulating signal. In practice timing pulses (not shown in Fig. 12.10d) are used in this particular system so that the variation in position of the signal pulses can be ascertained.

The modulating signal has been considered as a simple sine wave. This of course has only been used for illustration purposes, and in practice the nature of the modulating signal will vary according to the information to be transmitted. The modulating signal itself may consist of pulses, if the information to be transmitted is a telegraphic code such as morse.

Frequency Spectrum of Rectangular Pulses

Consider a periodic rectangular pulse, which when described as a function of time has the form shown in Fig. 12.11. It will be seen that the pulse lasts for a time δ, and is repeated after a time T so that the frequency of repetition, or repetition frequency, is defined as $1/T$. Now it is shown in Appendix E that a periodic function of time $f(t)$, may be expressed in the form of a complex Fourier series, i.e.,

$$f(t) = \sum_{n=-\infty}^{n=+\infty} a_n . e^{jn\omega t} \quad . \quad . \quad . \quad . \quad . \quad . \quad 12.15$$

where n has all integral values from $-\infty$ to $+\infty$, including zero and a_n is in general a complex quantity given by

$$a_n = \frac{1}{2\pi}\int_{-\pi}^{\pi} f(t)e^{-jn\omega t}d(\omega t) \quad . \quad . \quad . \quad . \quad . \quad 12.16$$

when the fundamental period is 2π, so that $\omega = 2\pi/T$. The value of a_n may thus be written as,

$$a_n = \frac{1}{T}\int_{-\frac{\pi}{\omega}}^{+\frac{\pi}{\omega}} f(t)e^{-jn\omega t}dt$$

If the waveform of Fig. 12.13a is considered, the limits of integration (which must cover a period) may conveniently be chosen as $+\delta/2$ and $-\delta/2$, as the waveform shown is equal to zero over the remainder of the half periods on either side of the time origin. The values of the coefficients a_n may thus be determined by the relation,

$$a_n = \frac{1}{T}\int_{-\frac{\delta}{2}}^{+\frac{\delta}{2}} E \,.\, e^{-jn\omega t}dt$$

$$= \frac{E}{T}\left[\frac{e^{-jn\omega t}}{-jn\omega}\right]_{-\frac{\delta}{2}}^{+\frac{\delta}{2}} = \frac{2E}{Tn\omega}\sin\frac{n\omega\delta}{2} \quad . \quad . \quad . \quad 12.17$$

The " curve " obtained by plotting the values of a_n against $n\omega$ is thus a graph which indicates the amplitudes of the various frequency components of the waveform plotted against the various values of

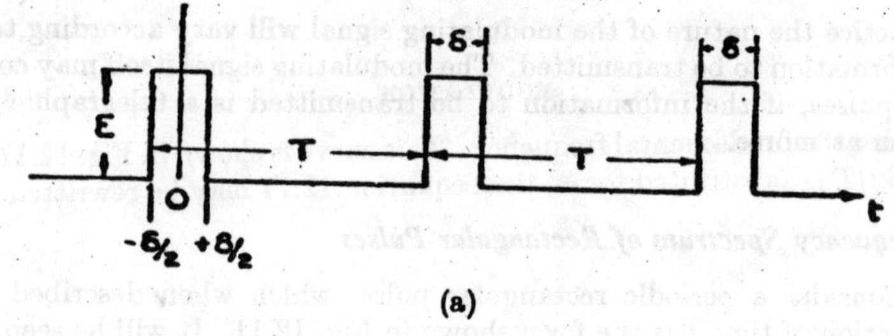
δ
δ
E
T
T
O
t
-δ/2 +δ/2

(a)

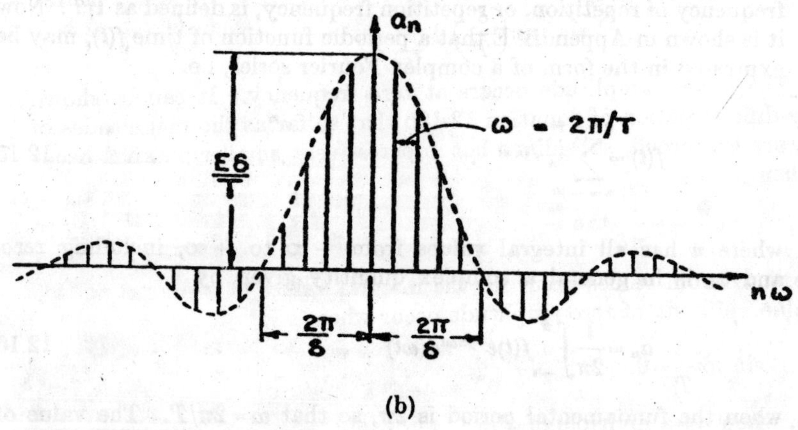
a_n
ω = 2π/T
Eδ/T
nω
2π/δ
2π/δ

(b)

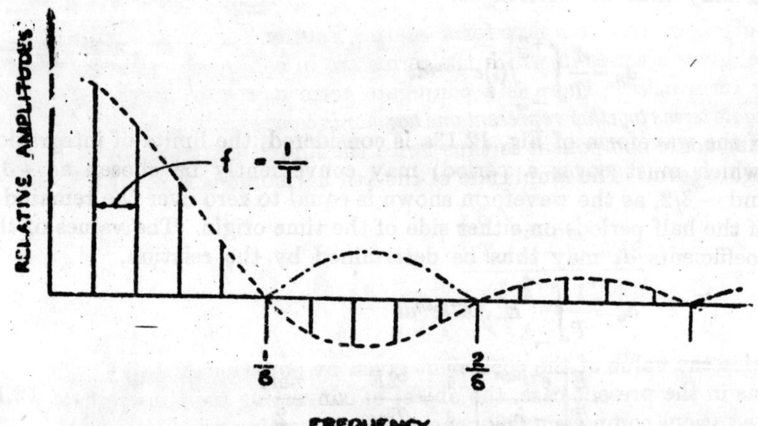
RELATIVE AMPLITUDES
f = 1/T
1/δ
2/δ
FREQUENCY

(c)

Fig. 12.11.

2π times the fundamental frequency. This curve is shown in Fig. 12.11b.

If $2\pi/T$ is substituted for ω, then equation 12.17 may be rewritten as

$$a_n = \frac{E}{n\pi} \sin n\pi\left(\frac{\delta}{T}\right) \quad . \quad . \quad . \quad . \quad 12.18\text{a}$$

$$\text{or } a_n = E\left(\frac{\delta}{T}\right) \frac{\sin n\pi\left(\frac{\delta}{T}\right)}{n\pi\left(\frac{\delta}{T}\right)} \quad . \quad . \quad . \quad . \quad 12.18\text{b}$$

The largest amplitude occurs at zero frequency. It can be shown by differentiation of equation 12.18b that as far as the magnitudes of a_n are concerned, subsidiary but progressively smaller maxima occur when

$$n = \frac{T}{\pi\delta} \tan \frac{n\pi\delta}{T} \quad . \quad . \quad . \quad . \quad 12.19$$

i.e. maximum values occur for the integral values of n nearest to this value. Minima of zero amplitude occur when

$$\sin \pi n \frac{\delta}{T} = 0 \quad . \quad . \quad . \quad . \quad . \quad . \quad 12.20$$

i.e. when $n =$ a multiple of T/δ.

The use of the complex form of the Fourier series, as employed above, gives a series in which the terms are in conjugate pairs, i.e. for every term $a_n \cdot e^{jn\omega t}$ there is a conjugate term $a_n \cdot e^{-jn\omega t}$. *Each pair of conjugate terms together represent one harmonic component*; the amplitude of a harmonic component is thus twice the amplitude given by either conjugate term. The amplitude of the kth harmonic is thus

$$\frac{2E\delta}{T} \frac{\sin k\pi\left(\frac{\delta}{T}\right)}{k\pi\left(\frac{\delta}{T}\right)}$$

i.e. twice the value of the coefficient given by equation 12.18b.

If, as in the present case, the object of converting the time function into its various component frequencies is to determine which amplitudes of the frequency components are significant, attention can be confined to the positive values of n, as in Fig. 12.11c. It can be seen that the amplitudes of the harmonic components have positive and negative values; the negative values indicate that such components pass through a maximum negative value instead of a maximum positive value at time $t = 0$. As far as magnitudes are concerned, the negative portions of the envelope may be replaced by the chain dotted line.

Variation of the Pulse Repetition Frequency

Equation 12.18b shows that the amplitudes of the frequency components of the waveform are inversely proportional to T, hence a decrease in the repetition frequency will cause a reduction in the amplitudes of the components; in addition the fundamental frequency will be decreased, so that the frequency interval between the components will be reduced, and they will lie closer together. Fig. 12.12a shows the form of the frequency spectrum for a rectangular periodic pulse in which the ratio T/δ is equal to 10.

Frequency Spectrum of a Single Rectangular Pulse

A non-periodic function such as a single rectangular pulse can be regarded as the equivalent of a periodic pulse with an infinitely long repetition period. When T approaches an infinitely large value, so that only a single pulse exists, the fundamental frequency component approaches zero frequency and the frequency interval between the harmonic components becomes vanishingly small. In the limit, when T is infinite, the frequency spectrum becomes continuous rather than an assembly of discrete ordinates.

Variation of the Pulse Width

If the repetition frequency is maintained constant, variation of the pulse width has the effect of varying the position of the zeros in the spectrum envelope and altering the amplitudes of the component frequencies. If a rectangular pulse of width δ, and repetition period T has the ratio $T/\delta = 10$, the frequency spectrum is as shown in Fig. 12.12a. If the pulse width is halved the frequency spectrum becomes that of Fig. 12.12b. A further halving of the pulse width gives the spectrum of Fig. 12.12c ; if the pulse width is made infinitely small, the spectrum has a constant though indefinitely small amplitude as indicated in Fig. 12.12d.

As long as the pulse width δ is finite, the frequency spectrum has an amplitude variation similar to that of a damped sine wave as shown in Fig. 12.12a.

A study of the diagrams of Fig. 12.12 indicates that a decrease in the time duration of the pulse causes an increase in the frequency spectrum of the waveform. This phenomenon is sometimes referred to as ***reciprocal spreading***, the extreme example of which is the indefinitely short pulse with an infinitely wide frequency spectrum ; the other extreme case is a steady-state sine wave which exists for all values of time, and has an infinitely narrow frequency spectrum.

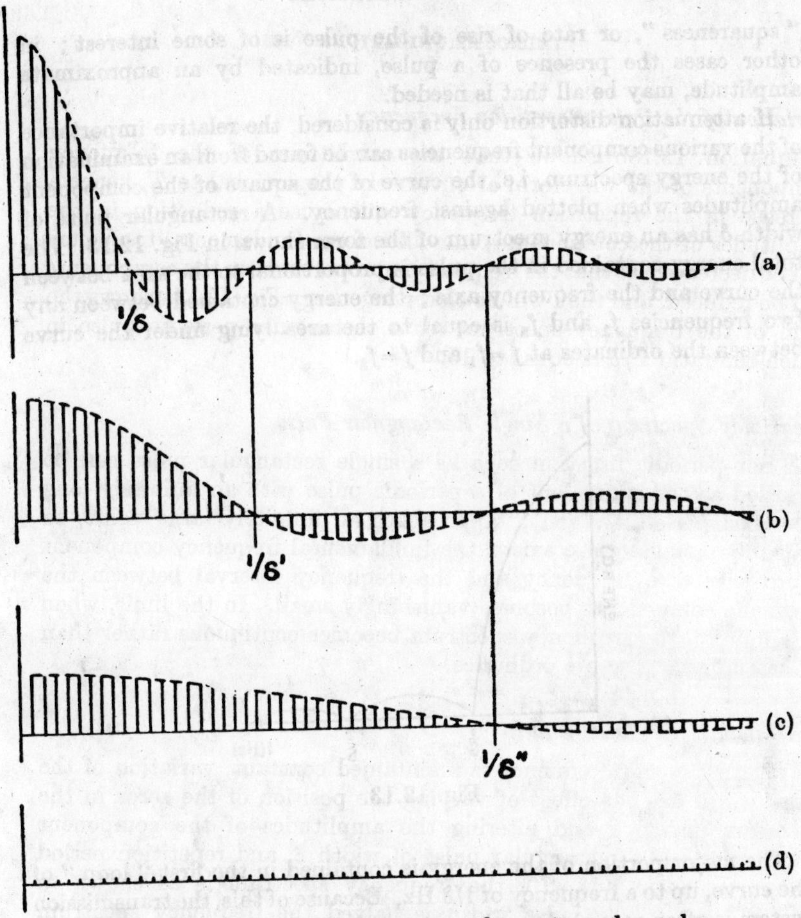

Fig. 12.12. Frequency spectrum of a rectangular pulse

(a) $T/\delta = 10$
(b) $T/\delta' = 20$
(c) $T/\delta'' = 40$
(d) $T/\delta = \infty$

Bandwidth Required for the Transmission of a Pulse

If a single pulse of short time duration, is to be transmitted, the bandwidth of the transmission system should ideally be infinite. In practice some distortion has to be tolerated, and the question arises how much distortion ? The answer to this depends on the duty which the pulse fulfils at the receiving terminal ; in a picture system the

" squareness ", or rate of rise of the pulse is of some interest ; in other cases the presence of a pulse, indicated by an approximate amplitude, may be all that is needed.

If attenuation distortion only is considered, the relative importance of the various component frequencies can be found from an examination of the energy spectrum, i.e. the curve of the square of the component amplitudes when plotted against frequency. A rectangular pulse of width δ has an energy spectrum of the form shown in Fig. 12.13. The total energy contained in the pulse is proportional to the area between the curve and the frequency axis ; the energy contained between any two frequencies f_1 and f_2 is equal to the area lying under the curve between the ordinates at $f = f_1$ and $f = f_2$.

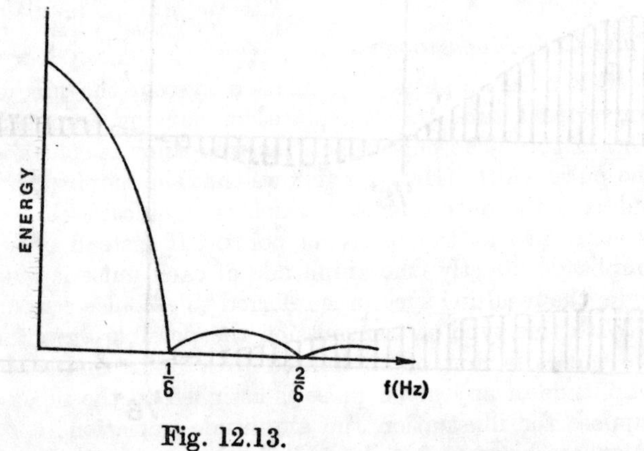

Fig. 12.13.

The major portion of the energy is contained in the first " loop " of the curve, up to a frequency of $1/\delta$ Hz. Because of this, the transmission system is often regarded as adequate, as far as bandwidth is concerned, if it is capable of transmitting frequencies up to a value of $1/\delta$ Hz ; the system then operates in the fashion of a low-pass filter with a cut-off frequency,

$$f_c = \frac{1}{\text{time of duration of pulse}}$$

If modulation of a carrier is involved the bandwidth required of the system will be at least twice the value of the cut-off frequency. (In many cases a lower value of cut-off frequency may be satisfactory.) Operation with this bandwidth will certainly give rise to distortion in that the received pulse will differ, and in general not be so sharp as the transmitted pulse. It must be remembered however that although an increased bandwidth will increase the energy content of the received pulse, the extra bandwidth will increase the fluctuation noise in the receiving equipment and the resultant effect may be that the signal/noise ratio will decrease.

Non-Rectangular Pulses

The pulses so far discussed have been assumed, for purposes of illustration, to be of rectangular form. The discussion need not however be limited to this type of pulse ; if pulses of any other shape are encountered the frequency spectrum involved may be examined by the use of the technique employed above for the case of rectangular pulses.

Pulse-Code-Modulation

In a pulse-amplitude-modulation system the modulating signal is converted into a train of pulses of varying amplitude as shown in Fig. 12.10b. The pulse repetition frequency is constant and so also is the pulse width. Hence it follows that the amplitude variation of the pulses is the only quantity which is significant as far as intelligence is concerned at the receiving point. If instead of transmitting the amplitude directly, the amplitude of each pulse is indicated by some code, the resulting system is referred to as pulse-code-modulation.[a]

With this type of transmission the possible amplitude variation of the pulses is first of all limited to a finite number of levels. The amplitude of any given pulse is assigned to the nearest level. Thus, suppose for illustration the amplitude variation of a signal can lie anywhere between 0 and 7 volts with respect to some reference level. This might then be split up into seven different levels of 1 volt each. Then a pulse of amplitude between 0·5 and 1·5 V would be considered as having an amplitude of the first level. An amplitude between 1·5 and 2·5 V would belong to the second level, and so on. This finite number of levels is then coded, usually by a binary code which is the simplest. In a binary system numbers are designated as in the table below.

Decimal Number	Equivalent Binary Number
1	1
2	10
3	11
4	100
5	101
6	110
7	111
8	1000

etc.

It will be seen that seven levels can be represented by three binary digits, so that a system of three pulses could be used as a code to indicate (by the presence or absence of any one, two or three pulses) any level from 1 to 7. Thus, suppose in terms of the numerical values used above, the amplitude of a particular pulse obtained from a signal was 5·2 V. This is nearest to the fifth step of amplitude and would then be coded in binary notation as 101. The original amplitude would then be transmitted as a train of three pulses in which the middle pulse was absent. (The absence of a coding pulse in the train carries as much significance as the presence of a pulse.) All that is required of the receiving equipment is that it should examine each train of coding pulses and be able to determine which particular pulses are present and which are absent. The level of amplitude of the original pulse is then determined to the nearest level.

Fig. 12.14 shows a binary coding system operating with 16 levels

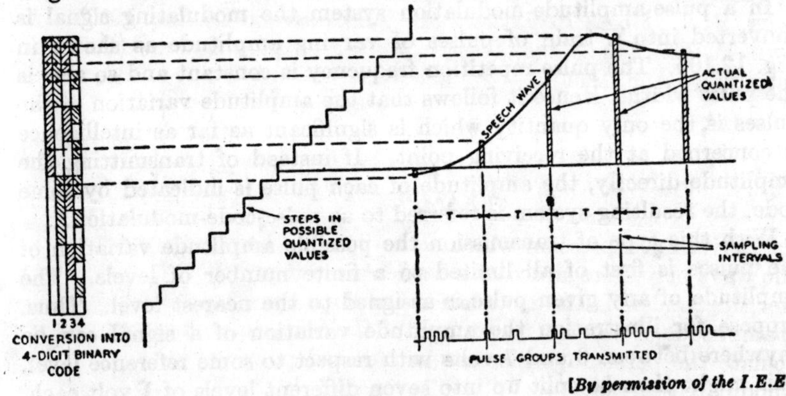

[By permission of the I.E.E

Fig. 12.14.

and employing up to four coding pulses. It should be noted that zero amplitude counts as the first level.

If there are M levels of amplitude provided for the signal variation, excluding the zero level, then the number of binary digits (or coding pulses) required to indicate these levels is

$$\log_2(1 + M)$$

Thus for $M(=15)$ levels as in Fig. 12.14 the number of coding pulses required is

$$\log_2(1 + 15) = \log_2(2^4) = 4$$

Pulse-code-modulation thus requires $\log_2(1 + M)$ as many pulses as pulse amplitude modulation if a binary code is used.

The advantage gained in using pulse-code-modulation is that the signal/noise ratio is increased.

References

[1] CROSBY, M. G.: "Carrier and Side-Frequency Relations with Multi-Tone Frequency or Phase Modulation", *R.C.A. Review*, 3, p. 103 (1938-39).

[2] GOODALL, W. M.: "Telephony by Pulse Code Modulation", *Bell System Technical Journal*, 26, p. 395 (1947).

References for Further Reading

GOLDMAN, S.: *Frequency Analysis Modulation and Noise* (McGraw-Hill, 1948).
TUCKER, D. G.: *Modulators and Frequency Changers* (Macdonald & Co., 1953).
BLACK, H. S.: *Modulation Theory* (D. Van Nostrand Co. Inc. 1953).
ROWE, H. E.: *Signals and Noise in Communication Systems* (D. Van Nostrand Co. Inc. 1966).

EXAMPLES

1. Derive an expression which shows how an amplitude-modulated radio wave may be regarded as a carrier wave together with upper and lower sidebands. If the modulation envelope consists of a sine wave, the amplitude of which is 50 per cent of the unmodulated carrier wave, calculate the percentage increase in radiated power over that of the unmodulated carrier.

L.U. Ext. Telecomm. 1951.

2. Show that when a sinusoidal carrier is amplitude modulated by another sine wave of lower frequency the resultant wave may be resolved into the carrier and two sidebands. Derive from this analysis a graph giving the relationship between the output power of a radio transmitter, and the percentage modulation, for values of the latter between 10 per cent and 100 per cent.

L.U. Ext. Telecomm. 1951.

3. What is meant by the terms "carrier wave" and "sidebands" as used in connection with radio-telephony? Give a theoretical justification of the terms. Explain carefully how it is possible to receive good telephonic signals when only one "sideband" is radiated.

L.U. Int. Telecomm. 1950.

4. An amplitude-modulated e.m.f. is induced in a resonant circuit tuned to the carrier frequency. The modulating frequency f_m is very small compared with the carrier frequency f_c. Show that, for the voltage developed across the capacitor, the attenuation of the modulation compared with that of the injected e.m.f. is given by the expression

$$10 \log_{10}\left\{1+\left(\frac{2Qf_m}{f_c}\right)^2\right\} \text{ decibels}$$

L.U. Int. Telecomm. 1952.

5. Show that a sinusoidally amplitude-modulated carrier wave is compounded of the carrier wave and two side-bands. Deduce that the effect of retarding or advancing the phase of the carrier by $\pi/2$ radians practically replaces amplitude modulation by frequency modulation.

L.U. Int. Telecomm. 1955.

6. Describe the single side-band system of radio-telephony and discuss fully its advantages.

L.U. Int. Telecomm. 1955.

7. Discuss the distinguishing features of amplitude, frequency and phase modulation.

L.U. Ext. Telecomm. 1943.

8. What is meant by the "frequency deviation" of a frequency-modulated carrier wave? Illustrate by a vector diagram, how the angle of phase advance and of retardation of the carrier vector depends upon the frequency deviation and the modulation frequency, and give an expression for a frequency modulated wave. Explain briefly how the characteristics of frequency modulation may be advantageous in obtaining a high signal/noise ratio.

I.E.E. Radio Comm. April, 1946.

9. Explain what is meant by *pulse code modulation.* State the form of coding normally employed and discuss the advantages of such a system.

Indicate the essential features of the equipment at the transmitting and receiving terminals for the transmission of two speech channels over a cable by pulse code modulation.

L.U. Telecomm. Part III. 1963.

10. The periodic pulse train shown in Figure 12.15 can be expressed by the Fourier series

$$f(t) = E\left[\frac{1}{6} + \frac{1}{\pi}\cos(2\pi \times 10^4 t) + \sum_{n=2}^{n=\infty} \frac{2}{\pi n}\sin\left(\frac{n\pi}{6}\right)\cos(2\pi n \times 10^4 t)\right].$$

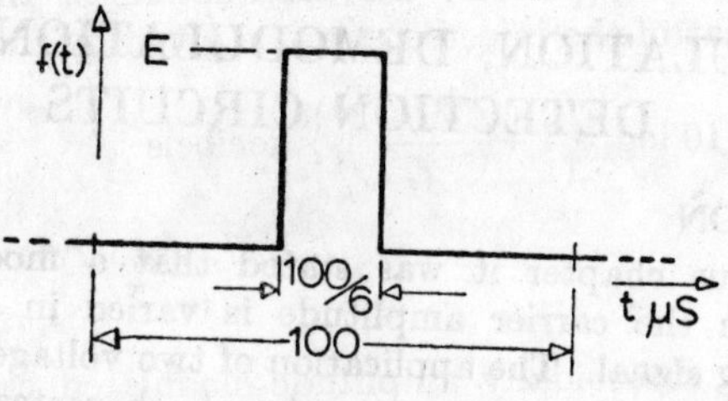

Fig. 12.15.

Deduce the corresponding series when the pulse train is amplitude modulated to a depth of 50% by a sinusoidal signal with a frequency of 3 kHz. Indicate the main components of the frequency spectrum produced.

Calculate the r.m.s. value and sketch the waveform of the voltage at the output of (*a*) a low-pass filter with a cut-off frequency at 4 kHz, and (*b*) a band-pass filter with cut-off frequencies at 30 kHz ± 4 kHz, when the modulated pulse train is applied to the input and E = 12 V.

L.U. Telecomm. Part III. 1963.

13

MODULATION, DEMODULATION, AND DETECTION CIRCUITS

INTRODUCTION

In the previous chapter it was stated that a modulated wave is obtained when the carrier amplitude is varied in accordance with the modulating signal. The application of two voltages to a non-linear impedance which has an asymmetrical characteristic about the operating point, produces currents which have an amplitude dependent on the product of the two voltages, and modulation can be produced by a circuit which contains such an impedance (Fig. 13.1a). Appreciable depth of modulation will only occur in a circuit of this sort if the non-linear impedance is large compared with the total (linear) impedance of the remainder of the circuit.

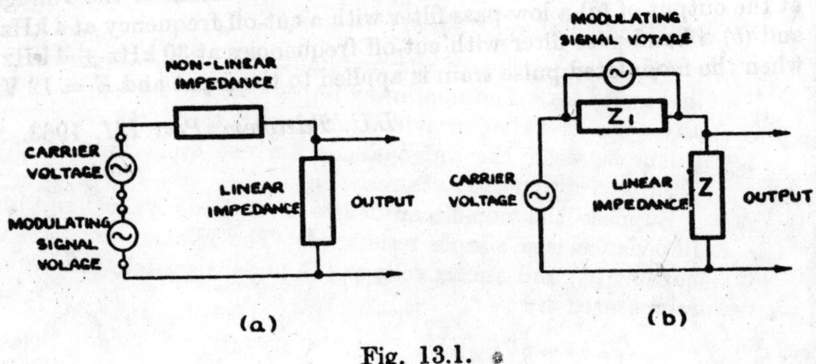

Fig. 13.1.

Another general system of modulation is referred to as "impedance modulation". In this case the impedance of a circuit element is varied by the modulating signal. Fig. 13.1b shows a circuit in which a series impedance Z_1 is assumed to vary by the application of the modulating signal voltage. If the modulating signal voltage source is arranged to have an impedance which is *large compared with* Z_1 at the carrier frequency, then the carrier current will flow through Z_1, and the output carrier voltage across the linear impedance Z will vary with the variation of the impedance Z_1. Alternatively, the variable impedance element may be connected in shunt across the carrier voltage source. (An impedance which varies with the applied voltage is necessarily non-linear, and so it is to some extent rather arbitrary to distinguish between non-linear and impedance modulators.)

The output of an oscillator, and also a class C amplifier depends upon the potential applied to the valve anode. If the modulating voltage is inserted in series with the anode supply, modulation is obtained in both cases.

AMPLITUDE MODULATION CIRCUITS

The various methods of modulation will now be considered in detail but before doing so it is worth noting that the process of modulation is similar in many ways to the process of frequency changing. Circuits which produce modulation (modulators) always have at least two input voltages which differ in frequency, while the output voltage is different from the input voltages. These remarks also apply to frequency changing circuits.

Modulators Using a Non-Linear Impedance

(a) *Diode Valve*

The basic circuit of the non-linear impedance modulator is shown in Fig. 13.1 a. The non-linear impedance used may take the form of any type of valve, provided always that the required non-linearity exists between the valve anode current and the applied voltage; alternatively, transistors may be used.

Suppose the non-linear device is a diode valve, and the output impedance is a simple resistance. The relation between the anode current (i_a) and anode voltage (V) under dynamic conditions may be represented by

$$i_a = bV + cV^2$$

where b and c are constants.

If the carrier voltage, $E_c \sin \omega_c t$, is applied in series with the modulating voltage, $E_m \sin \omega_m t$, then,

$$V = E_c \sin \omega_c t + E_m \sin \omega_m t$$

and $i_a = b(E_c \sin \omega_c t + E_m \sin \omega_m t)$

$$+ c[E_c^2 \sin^2 \omega_c t + 2E_c E_m \sin \omega_c t \sin \omega_m t + E_m^2 \sin^2 \omega_m t]$$

$$= \left[\left(1 + \frac{2cE_m}{b} \sin \omega_m t\right) bE_c \sin \omega_c t\right]$$

$$+\frac{c}{2}\left(E_c^2+E_m^2\right)+\frac{c}{2}E_c^2\sin\left(2\omega_c t-\frac{\pi}{2}\right)$$

$$+\frac{c}{2}E_m^2\sin\left(2\omega_m t-\frac{\pi}{2}\right)+bE_m\sin\omega_m t \quad . \quad . \quad 13.1$$

The first term, enclosed between the square brackets, indicates that there is a component of current which represents amplitude modulation ; the other terms indicate the presence of direct current, together with harmonics of the modulating signal and the carrier. The original modulating voltage is also present.

Fig. 13.2a shows the current waveform when the output impedance, or load, is resistive. If the voltage across the load is applied to a filter which passes the carrier and the two sidebands, and rejects all other components, the output voltage obtained from the filter is the normal waveform of an amplitude-modulated voltage. (Fig. 13.2b.)

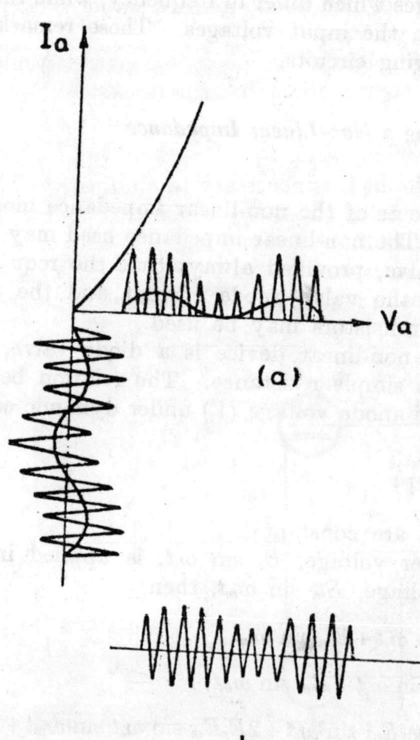

Fig. 13.2.

(b) *Triode Valve*

An alternative arrangement is to use a triode valve rather than a diode. The triode is biased negatively, so that no grid current flows, and at a point where the I_a/V_g characteristic is non-linear. Such a circuit is known as a van der Bijl, or *square law modulator*. The method of operation is the same as for the diode circuit, except of course that the carrier and modulating voltages are applied to the grid input terminals. It should be noted that if the modulating signal has more than one frequency component the output contains the sum and difference components of every pair of components of the applied signal voltage. The anode efficiency of the modulator is also low. Because of these disadvantages, the square law type of modulator is normally only used in low power systems in which the depth of modulation required is small. It is however an improvement over the diode modulator inasmuch as the input impedance of the valve is higher (the grid has a steady negative potential). Also, because of the amplification produced, the triode gives a larger output for the same values of applied voltage.

Multi-electrode valves may also be used as square law modulators provided that the I_a/V_g characteristic has the necessary curvature.

(c) *The Balanced Modulator*

In single sideband systems it is necessary to eliminate or reduce the level of the carrier. The basic circuit by which this is achieved is the *balanced modulator* (Fig. 13.3), sometimes called a Carson modulator.

Two valves (or two transistors) are used. The modulating voltage is applied to the two valves in anti-phase, or push-pull, while the carrier

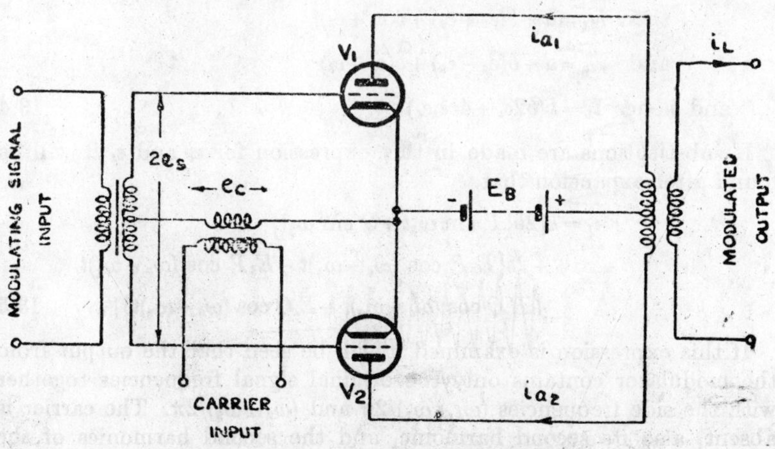

Fig. 13.3. Balanced modulator.

is applied in phase. Triode valves are shown but the circuit will function with any pair of similar non-linear impedances. Each half of the circuit may be regarded as a square law modulator.

Let the carrier voltage be sinusoidal so that the carrier is represented at any instant by

$$e_c = E_c \sin \omega_c t \quad . \quad . \quad . \quad . \quad . \quad . \quad 13.2$$

Suppose also that the signal consists of two frequencies so that the signal voltage is represented by

$$e_s = P \sin \omega_1 t + Q \sin \omega_2 t \quad . \quad . \quad . \quad . \quad . \quad . \quad 13.3$$

If the signal and carrier voltages are assumed to be additive for the valve V_1, then the voltages appearing at the grids of the two valves will be $V_{g1} = e_c + e_s$

and $V_{g2} = e_c - e_s$

The anode currents of the two valves flow in opposite directions through the two halves of the primary winding of the output transformer, so that the output load current i_L in the secondary will be proportional to the difference between the anode currents of the two valves,

i.e. $i_L = k(i_{a1} - i_{a2})$

where k is a constant of proportionality.

If both valves are similar and have I_a/V_g characteristics such that

$$i_a = a + bV_g + cV_g^2$$

then $i_{a1} = a + b(e_c + e_s) + c(e_c + e_s)^2$

and $i_{a2} = a + b(e_c - e_s) + c(e_c - e_s)^2$

and hence $i_L = k(b2e_s + 4ce_s e_c) \quad . \quad . \quad . \quad . \quad . \quad 13.4$

If substitutions are made in this expression for e_c and e_s it will be found after expansion that

$$\begin{aligned} i_L = k[2b\{&P \sin \omega_1 t + Q \sin \omega_2 t\} \\ &+ 2c\{E_c P \cos (\omega_c - \omega_1)t - E_c P \cos (\omega_c + \omega_1)t \\ &+ E_c Q \cos (\omega_c - \omega_2)t - E_c Q \cos (\omega_c + \omega_2)t\}] \ldots \quad 13.5 \end{aligned}$$

If this expression is examined it will be seen that the output from the modulator contains only the original signal frequencies together with the side frequencies $(\omega_c \pm \omega_1)/2\pi$ and $(\omega_c \pm \omega_2)/2\pi$. The carrier is absent, also its second harmonic, and the second harmonics of the modulating signal voltages ; the components corresponding to the sum and differences of the two signal frequencies are also suppressed.

In practice the suppression of the carrier and other components is not complete, due to dissimilarity in the valve characteristics, and because of slight unbalances in the two halves of the input and output transformers.

Variable Impedance Modulators

(a) *The Cowan Modulator*

The modulator circuit of Fig. 13.4a is a form of balanced modulator. It is normally used with four semiconductor diodes connected as shown. It will be recalled from chapter 7 that such rectifiers present a low impedance when a voltage of one polarity is applied, and a high impedance when a voltage of opposite polarity is applied.

If, in the circuit of Fig. 13.4a, the carrier voltage is large compared with the signal voltage, the behaviour of the rectifiers will be determined by the carrier voltage. Thus when the carrier voltage is such that terminal 1 is positive with respect to terminal 2, all four rectifiers will conduct. The rectifier combination will then appear as a low impedance across the signal path (Fig. 13.4b). Reversal of the polarity of the carrier voltage will polarise the rectifiers so that they are (ideally) non-conducting. The rectifier combination will then have no effect on the signal path (Fig. 13.4c). In simple terms, the signal voltage is cyclically short-circuited at a frequency corresponding to that of the carrier. This produces an alternating waveform of carrier

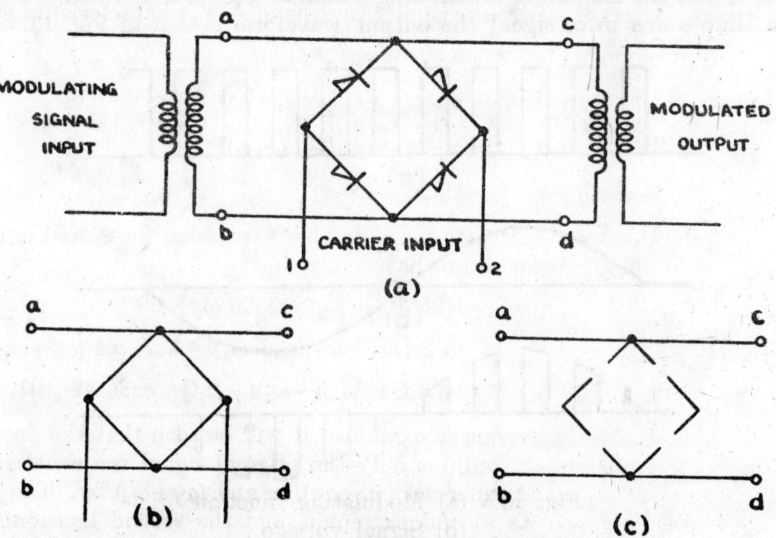

Fig. 13.4. The Cowan Modulator.

frequency which varies in amplitude at the signal frequency, although it contains no carrier component.

Analysis of Modulator Output. In the Cowan and similar forms of modulator the function of the rectifier combination is to provide a modulated output. It is convenient to regard the rectifier operation as a function of time $\phi(t)^1$. This modulating function $\phi(t)$ can thus be defined as " that function which when multiplied by the signal gives the modulated output ". The modulating function is a quantity which varies with time as the rectifier resistance alters with the time varying carrier-voltage.

Because of the non-linear characteristic of the rectifiers, the determination of the exact form of the modulating function is a matter of some difficulty, and is beyond the scope of this book. (The waveform of the modulating function depends on the actual characteristic of the rectifiers used, and an analytical expression for it involves some assumption as to the law for the resistance variation with voltage.)

A simplification is possible, however, if the rectifiers are regarded as ideal, i.e. they are assumed to have zero forward resistance and infinite reverse resistance, the change being made instantaneously when the applied carrier voltage changes polarity.

With these assumptions, the signal voltage e_s can be considered to be short-circuited every alternate half cycle of the carrier voltage. This causes the modulator output to alternate between zero and e_s at carrier frequency ; the output can thus be regarded as the product of e_s and the simplified modulating function $\phi(t)$ of Fig. 13.5a. For a simple sine wave signal the output waveform is that of Fig. 13.5c

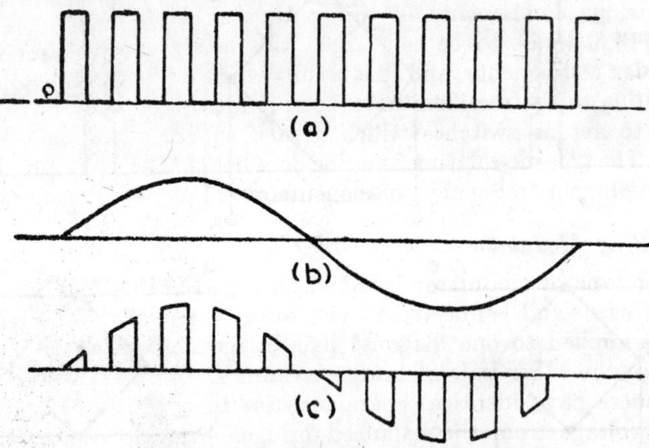

Fig. 13.5 (a) Modulating function
(b) Signal voltage
(c) Output voltage.

The modulating function can be expressed as a Fourier series,

$$\phi(t) = \tfrac{1}{2} + \frac{2}{\pi}[\sin \omega_c t + \tfrac{1}{3} \sin 3\omega_c t + \tfrac{1}{5} \sin 5\omega_c t + \ldots\ldots]$$

as the fundamental alternating component is that of the carrier.

If the signal voltage e_s is sinusoidal so that

$$e_s = E_s \sin \omega_s t$$

the modulator output will be $[E_s \sin \omega_s t]\phi(t)$

$$= E_s \sin \omega_s t\left[\tfrac{1}{2} + \frac{2}{\pi}\{\sin \omega_c t + \tfrac{1}{3} \sin 3\omega_c t + \tfrac{1}{5} \sin 5\omega_c t + \ldots\ldots\}\right]$$

$$= \tfrac{1}{2}E_s \sin \omega_s t + \frac{E_s}{\pi}[\cos (\omega_c - \omega_s)t - \cos (\omega_c + \omega_s)t]$$

$$+ \frac{E_s}{3\pi}[\cos (3\omega_c - \omega_s)t - \cos (3\omega_c + \omega_s)t]$$

$$+ \frac{E_s}{5\pi}[\cos (5\omega_c - \omega_s)t - \cos (5\omega_c + \omega_s)t] + \ldots\ldots \quad 13.6$$

It will be seen from this result that the output contains the signal frequency $\omega_s/2\pi$, together with the corresponding upper and lower side frequencies of the carrier. In addition there are an infinite number of components which have frequencies of the form $nf_c \pm f_s$, where n is an odd integer.

Practical rectifiers have a modulating function which has a more rounded waveform. Because of this, in any given case the amplitude of the various components in the modulator output, predicted by equation 13.6, tends to be too large, this is especially true for the higher order components, and is a result which might be expected, as all losses due to the rectifiers have been ignored, and they have been assumed to act as switches which give a square wave modulating function. The true modulating function does not change instantaneously so that the higher frequency components are of smaller amplitude.

(b) *The Ring Modulator*

Another type of modulator is shown in Fig. 13.6a. Four rectifiers are again used and connected in the form of a bridge. The signal voltage is applied to one diagonal pair of terminals and the output taken from the other pair of bridge terminals. It follows that if all four rectifiers have identical characteristics there will be no output of signal voltage from the balanced bridge. The modulator is also arranged to balance out the carrier. As a consequence neither the modulating signal nor the carrier appear in the output, and the circuit is known as a *double balanced modulator*. The bridge arrangement of rectifiers is sometimes drawn in the lattice form of Fig. 13.6b.

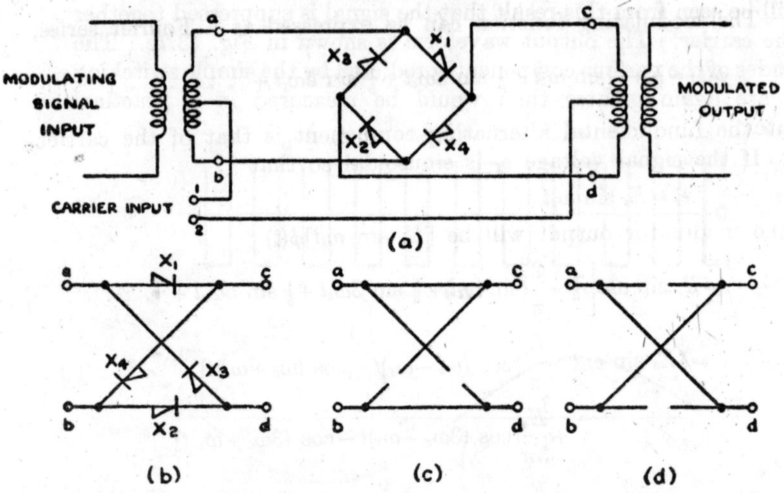

Fig. 13.6. The ring modulator.

If the carrier voltage is large compared with the signal voltage, the rectifiers are controlled by the carrier voltage. When the carrier input is such that terminal 1 is positive with respect to terminal 2, the series rectifiers X_1 and X_2 conduct while the diagonal rectifiers X_3 and X_4 do not. If as an approximation the rectifiers are assumed to be ideal the circuit will be as shown in Fig. 13.6c; reversal of the carrier voltage will give the circuit of Fig. 13.6d.

The rectifier system behaves as a reversing switch operating on the modulating signal voltage e_s at carrier frequency, so that the output alternates between $+e_s$ and $-e_s$. The modulating function thus has the waveform of Fig. 13.7a, and when expressed as a Fourier series is given by

$$\phi(t)=\frac{4}{\pi}\{\sin \omega_c t+\tfrac{1}{3}\sin 3\omega_c t+\tfrac{1}{5}\sin 5\omega_c t+\ldots\ldots\}$$

For a signal voltage $e_s=E_s \sin \omega_s t$

the modulator output will be $[E_s \sin \omega_s t]\phi(t)$

$$=\frac{2E_s}{\pi}[\cos(\omega_c-\omega_s)t-\cos(\omega_c+\omega_s)t]$$

$$+\frac{2E_s}{3\pi}[\cos(3\omega_c-\omega_s)t-\cos(3\omega_c+\omega_s)t]$$

$$+\frac{2E_s}{5\pi}[\cos(5\omega_c-\omega_s)t-\cos(5\omega_c+\omega_s)t]+\ldots\ldots \quad 13.7$$

It will be seen from this result that the signal is suppressed together with the carrier. The output waveform is shown in Fig. 13.7c. The amplitudes of the various components predicted by the simple switching theory are again greater than would be measured in a practical modulator.

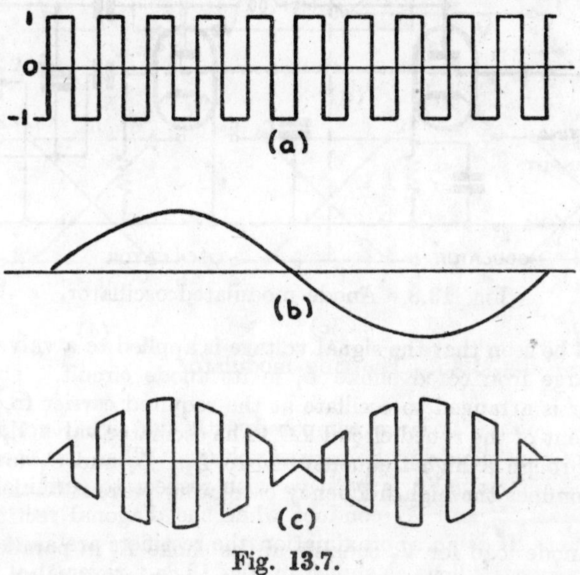

Fig. 13.7.

Both the Cowan and ring type modulator produce a spectrum of frequencies even when the signal voltage consists of a single sine wave. As such modulators are mainly used in single sideband systems of carrier telephony the modulator is normally followed by a filter which rejects all components except the desired sideband. The combination of modulator and filter is sometimes referred to as a *linear modulator*.

The Modulated Oscillator

The output from a valve oscillator is approximately proportional to the steady value of anode voltage applied. If the modulating signal voltage is connected in series with the direct voltage applied to the valve anode the oscillatory output will vary in accordance with the applied signal voltages and the output waveform will be amplitude-modulated. Fig. 13.8 shows an arrangement which provides for anode modulation of an oscillator in this way. This circuit is sometimes referred to as Heising, or " choke " modulation.

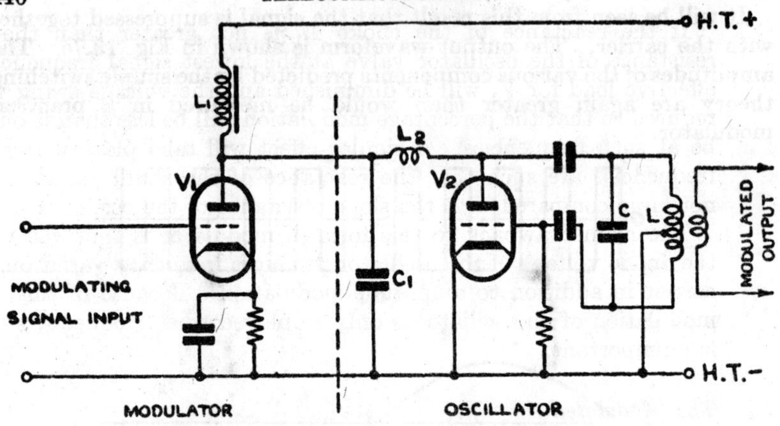

Fig. 13.8. Anode modulated oscillator.

It will be seen that the signal voltage is applied to a valve V_1 which has a large iron cored choke L_1 in its anode circuit. The Hartley oscillator is arranged to oscillate at the required carrier frequency by adjustment of the tuned circuit LC. The oscillator valve V_2 is coupled to V_1 through a high frequency choke L_2. L_2 and C_1 form a filter which confines the high-frequency oscillatory current to the oscillator section.

The anode load for V_1 consists of the choke L_1 in parallel with the oscillator valve. (The reactance of L_2 is negligible at the signal frequencies while the reactance of C_1 is infinite, in the ideal case.) If the reactance of the iron cored choke L_1 is large at all signal frequencies compared with the r_a of the oscillator valve the effective anode load for V_1 is then simply the r_a of the oscillator valve V_2. The modulating signal voltage applied to V_1 is thus developed across V_2.

In the absence of any signal at the grid of V_1 the mean anode voltage of the oscillator valve is constant, and the output consists of a high-frequency carrier of constant amplitude. The application of an alternating voltage to the grid of V_1 causes the anode potential of both valves to vary together so that an output is obtained which is amplitude-modulated in accordance with the applied signal voltage.

It should be noted that a change of voltage at the grid of V_1 leads to a change of current through V_1 in phase with the grid voltage, while the anode voltage changes in anti-phase. Thus suppose the grid voltage of V_1 increases in a positive direction; the anode current of V_1 will increase and the anode voltage will decrease. This decrease of anode voltage will cause a decrease of current in V_2 so that as the current in V_1 increases the current in V_2 decreases.

To produce full modulation in this way it is necessary to swing the anode voltage of the oscillator from twice its mean value to zero.

If the reactance of the choke L_1 is not greater than the slope resistance of the oscillator valve at the lowest signal frequency, the effective load for V_1 will be diminished and the voltage swing will be reduced so that the percentage modulation will be less than it ought to be at such frequencies. A similar effect will take place if the signal frequencies are such that the reactance of the shunt capacitor C_1 is not large compared with the slope resistance of the oscillator valve.

The main drawback to this form of modulator is that variation of the anode voltage of the oscillator produces frequency variation of the carrier in addition to amplitude-modulation. Because of this, anode modulation of an oscillator is only employed when frequency stability is unimportant.

The Modulated Amplifier

In radio transmitters (see chapter 22) it is customary to generate the carrier frequency by a master oscillator of good frequency stability. The output is then amplified and modulated at some amplifying stage. As a result an improvement in frequency stability of the carrier is obtained compared with direct modulation of the oscillator. Modulation is usually obtained by variation of the anode voltage applied to the amplifier in the same way as for anode modulation of an oscillator. It should be noted in this connection however that modulation will only be obtained if the amplifier is operating under class *B* or class *C* conditions. (No modulation can be obtained by varying the anode voltage of a class *A* amplifier. This results from the fact that a valve operating under class *A* conditions has characteristics which are parallel straight lines ; a change of the operating (anode) voltage does not give rise to a change of output and so a modulated output is not obtained.)

(a) Anode Modulation of a Class C Amplifier

For reasons of efficiency the carrier amplifying stages are usually operated under class C conditions. Such a stage may be modulated by applying the signal voltage in series with the steady anode voltage as shown in Fig. 13.9. It will be seen that the principle involved is the same as that for anode modulation of an oscillator.

V_2 is the carrier amplifier valve which is arranged to operate so that the steady grid bias is about twice the cut-off value. The input and output *LC* circuits are adjusted to be resonant to the carrier frequency. (In practice if V_2 is a triode valve as shown, some form of neutralising is essential. This has been omitted from the diagram for purposes of clarity.) L_1 is a high-frequency choke which serves to prevent the high-frequency current from flowing through the modulating circuit. It has a high reactance at the carrier frequency, and a negligible

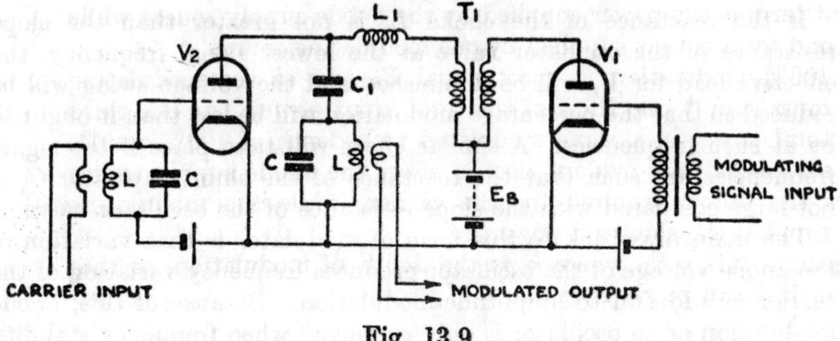

Fig. 13.9.

reactance at the frequencies used for modulation. The blocking capacitor C_1 has a low reactance at the carrier frequency but a very high reactance at the highest modulating frequency. Under these conditions the load across the secondary of the modulation transformer T_1 is the slope resistance of the carrier amplifier valve.

The anode current and output voltage of a class C amplifier are approximately proportional to the total applied anode voltage. As a result the class C amplifier appears as a load resistance

$$R_B = \frac{E_B}{I_B} \quad . \quad . \quad . \quad . \quad . \quad . \quad . \quad 13.8$$

where E_B is the anode supply voltage and I_B is the mean value of anode current in the absence of modulation.

The use of a modulation transformer rather than a choke has two advantages. First, it permits the load presented by V_2 to be matched to the modulator valve V_1; secondly the direct currents of the two valves can be arranged to produce anti-phase magnetisation of the core, so that troubles due to magnetic saturation, resulting from the steady components of anode current, are diminished.

The power input to the anode of the class C amplifier is obtained from two sources, namely the anode supply source and the modulating source. If the modulating signal voltage is sinusoidal and is represented by $e_s = E_s \sin \omega_s t$

the average power input to the class C stage is then

$$P_{input} = \frac{1}{2\pi}\int_0^{2\pi} \frac{(E_B + E_s \sin \omega_s t)^2}{R_B} d(\omega_s t)$$

where R_B is defined by equation 13.8.

$$\therefore P_{input} = \frac{E_B{}^2}{R_B} + \frac{E_s{}^2}{2R_B} \quad . \quad . \quad . \quad . \quad . \quad 13.9$$

The first term is the power supplied by the anode supply source while the second term is that supplied by the modulating source.

For 100% modulation E_s must equal E_B and so the modulating source must supply one third of the total input power. As one third of the total power in a wave modulated to a depth of 100% resides in the sidebands, it is evident that in effect the anode supply source delivers the power required for the carrier, while the modulating source supplies the sideband power.

In general $k_aE_s = E_B$ where k_a is the depth of modulation, so that equation 13.9 can be rewritten as

$$P_{input} = \frac{E_B{}^2}{R_B}\left(1 + \frac{k_a{}^2}{2}\right) \quad . \quad . \quad . \quad . \quad . \quad . \quad 13.10$$

This is the power supplied to the class C amplifier and is equal to the power output plus the loss in the valve. It follows from equation 13.10 that the anode supply and modulating sources must provide for the power loss in the amplifier valve; in the absence of modulation the anode supply source provides for the output power and all the power loss in the valve.

It should be noted that the modulator valve may have to have a considerably greater anode dissipation than the carrier amplifier valve. This point is best illustrated by a numerical example. Suppose the class C amplifier delivers an unmodulated output of 400 watts and has an anode efficiency of $66\frac{2}{3}$%, the input power from the anode supply source in the absence of modulation is then 600 watts. If now a modulating signal is applied so that 100% modulation is produced the power output will be increased by 50%, to 600 watts. If the anode efficiency remains unchanged at $66\frac{2}{3}$% the power input required will be 900 watts. Of this, 600 watts are supplied by the high tension source so that the modulator valve must provide an output of 300 watts. If the modulator valve is operating under class A conditions with an anode efficiency of 25% the input to the modulator valve must then be 1200 watts, so that the anode dissipation of the modulator will be 900 watts. Now the modulation will vary and may even be zero for short periods so that the modulator output will then be zero. Under this condition the modulator valve must withstand a dissipation of 1200 watts at its anode. The anode dissipation of the carrier amplifier valve has a maximum value of 300 watts when fully modulated. This is all that the valve is required to dissipate as the carrier input is maintained all the time that the stage is operative. On the figures assumed, it will be seen that the anode dissipation of the modulator valve must be four times that of the carrier amplifier valve.

The modulator valve has been regarded as operating under class A conditions. In practice two valves in push pull, operating under class B conditions, are often employed.

(b) Alternative Modulation of a Class C Amplifier

A class C amplifier can be grid modulated by connecting the modulating signal voltage in series with the carrier in the grid circuit of the amplifier, so that the grid bias is varied by the modulating signal. With this arrangement the amplitude of the applied carrier is usually made slightly less than the value of steady bias employed. Grid modulation has the advantage that it requires less power from the modulating source. On the other hand the output of modulated power from the valve is smaller. It is also difficult to obtain distortionless modulation because of the varying load caused by changing grid current of the amplifier.

Tetrode and pentode valves cannot be modulated conveniently by variation of the anode voltage because in such valves the anode current is nearly independent of the anode voltage. Modulation may however be secured by the injecting of the modulating voltage in series with the screen grid supply. In the case of the pentode, modulation can be achieved by applying the modulating signal to the suppressor grid. This arrangement is preferable to screen grid modulation and normally gives less distortion.

DEMODULATION OF AMPLITUDE-MODULATED VOLTAGES

The term *demodulator* is applied to a circuit arranged to deliver the original modulating signal voltage as the output. The term *detector* is also applied to such a circuit and the two names are often used indiscriminately. Generally, the name " demodulator " is applied to circuits which produce the desired output from two inputs, namely the modulated input and the carrier voltage. The term " detector " is normally applied to circuits which produce the original modulating signal from the modulated input alone.

The circuits used for modulation may be used for demodulation, with the exception of the modulated oscillator and modulated amplifier. In particular the ring and Cowan modulators could be used as demodulators.

If a single sideband system is considered and the upper sideband is assumed to be transmitted, the inputs to the demodulator will then be

$$e_s = E_s \sin (\omega_c + \omega_s)t$$

and $$e_c = E_c \sin \omega_c t$$

where $\omega_c/2\pi$ is the carrier frequency and $\omega_s/2\pi$ is the original modulation frequency.

It can easily be shown that if these voltages are applied as the input to a non-linear device with an asymmetrical characteristic about the operating point, the output will contain a term of frequency $\omega_s/2\pi$ which is the wanted signal output. It will be found that if the re-inserted carrier differs slightly in frequency from its correct value, the output signal frequency will be changed by a corresponding amount. As was pointed out in chapter 12, a double sideband suppressed carrier system has to meet stringent requirements; commonly one sideband only is transmitted, with or without, a reduced level of carrier.

DETECTION OF AMPLITUDE-MODULATED VOLTAGES

Square Law Detection

If a device has a non-linear, current/voltage characteristic which is a symmetrical it may be used as a detector to produce the desired modulation as an output. All thermionic devices exhibit curvature at some point in their characteristics, and may accordingly be used, if desired, as square law detectors ; semi-conductors and all metal rectifiers also possess asymmetrical non-linearity and may also be used as detectors. When the signal voltage to be detected is large a form of linear detector is employed ; with small signal voltages, of the order of a fraction of a volt or less, the detector usually functions as a square law device.

Suppose for simplicity that the detector has a resistive load connected in series and that the combination gives a dynamic current/voltage characteristic which can be expressed accurately by the relation

$$I = a + bV + cV^2$$

where I is the current through the detector and load and V is the applied voltage.

If the applied voltage is modulated by a single sine wave, then with the notation used previously, the voltage at the input to the detector can be expressed as

$$V = E_c \sin \omega_c t + \frac{k_a E_c}{2} \cos (\omega_c - \omega_s)t - \frac{k_a E_c}{2} \cos (\omega_c + \omega_s)t$$

The complete expression for the load current will obviously be obtained by inserting the value for V in the relation for the detector characteristic. The term which gives rise to demodulation is the squared term (cV^2) and so the current I' due to this term is given by

$$I' = c\left[E_c^2 \sin^2 \omega_c t + k_a E_c^2 \sin \omega_c t \{\cos (\omega_c - \omega_s)t - \cos (\omega_c + \omega_s)t\} \right.$$
$$\left. + \frac{k_a^2 E_c^2}{4} \cos^2 (\omega_c - \omega_s)t + \frac{k_a^2 E_c^2}{4} \cos^2 (\omega_c + \omega_s)t \right.$$

$$-\frac{k_a^2 E_c^2}{2} \cos (\omega_c - \omega_s)t \cos (\omega_c + \omega_s)t \Big]$$

The terms

$$E_c^2 \sin^2 \omega_c t, \frac{k_a^2 E_c^2}{4} \cos^2 (\omega_c - \omega_s)t, \frac{k_a^2 E_c^2}{4} \cos^2 (\omega_c + \omega_s)t$$

give the second harmonic of the carrier and the two sidebands together with direct components. The remaining terms give a current I'', where

$$I'' = ck_a E_c^2 \sin \omega_c t[\cos (\omega_c - \omega_s)t - \cos (\omega_c + \omega_s)t]$$

$$-\frac{ck_a^2 E_c^2}{2} \cos (\omega_c - \omega_s)t \cos (\omega_c + \omega_s)t$$

This can be rewritten as

$$I'' = \tfrac{1}{2} ck_a E_c^2 [\sin (2\omega_c - \omega_s)t + \sin \omega_s t + \sin \omega_s t - \sin (2\omega_c + \omega_s)t]$$

$$-\frac{ck_a^2 E_c^2}{4} (\cos 2\omega_c t + \cos 2\omega_s t) \quad . \quad . \quad . \quad 13.11$$

It will be seen from this result that in addition to direct components the input frequencies, and second harmonics of the input frequencies, the output of the square law detector contains sum and difference terms which have frequencies of $(2\omega_c - \omega_s)/2\pi$, $\omega_s/2\pi$, $2\omega_s/2\pi$ and $(2\omega_c + \omega_s)/2\pi$.

The first point of interest is that there are two terms of frequency $\omega_s/2\pi$, the wanted modulation frequency. One is derived from each sideband and they add together in phase in the output. This shows that both sidebands are not essential for the production of the original modulating signal at the output of the detector.

A second point of interest is that the terms of frequency $\omega_s/2\pi$ have an amplitude proportional to the square of the carrier voltage.

The total current at this frequency is

$$\tfrac{1}{2} ck_a E_c^2 (\sin \omega_s t + \sin \omega_s t) = ck_a E_c^2 \sin \omega_s t$$

The second harmonic of the modulation frequency has an amplitude of $ck_a^2 E_c^2/4$. Hence the ratio of the second harmonic term to the fundamental is $k_a/4$. The distortion is thus proportional to the depth of modulation.

The various components of current in the load have been considered for the case of a modulated wave in which the modulation consists of a single sine wave. If more than one modulation frequency is present the output will be found to contain components which have frequencies equal to the sums and differences of the modulation frequencies.

The Diode Detector

The basic circuit of a diode detector, otherwise referred to as a *linear* or an *envelope* detector, is shown in Fig. 13.10a. The alternative arrangement of Fig. 13.10b is sometimes used, but this has the disadvantage that the high frequency voltage is developed across the load resistor R, and is passed on to the succeeding circuits. In both circuits the capacitor C is arranged to have a low reactance at carrier frequency so that the whole of the carrier voltage is applied to the diode.

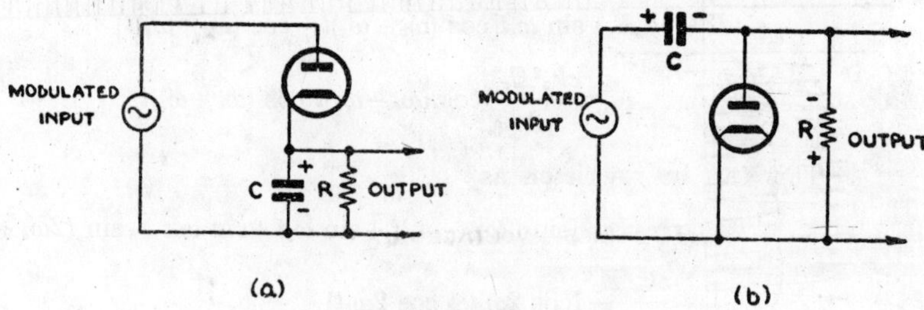

Fig. 13.10 (a) Series diode circuit
(b) Shunt diode circuit.

If, to begin with, the load resistor R is absent from the circuit of, say, Fig. 13.10a, the application of a high frequency carrier voltage will cause the diode to charge the capacitor C when the anode is positive with respect to the cathode. This action will produce a direct voltage across C so that the anode is made negative with respect to the cathode. If the carrier has a constant amplitude, this process will continue until a point is reached where the voltage across the capacitor C attains the peak value of the applied voltage, when the diode will cease to conduct. The capacitor will then maintain this value of direct voltage, as no discharge path exists.

In the actual detector circuit, the presence of the load resistor permits the capacitor to discharge. If the voltage, v_c, across the capacitor, is less than the peak value of the high frequency carrier, the diode will conduct. The " angle of flow ", or time during which the diode conducts, is dependent on the rate of discharge of the capacitor, i.e. upon the value of the time constant of CR; the current flows in a series of pulses which recharge the capacitor. A direct voltage, nearly equal to the peak value of the constant amplitude carrier, then exists across the C and R combination. This condition obtains if the time constant CR is long compared with the period of the carrier, so that C does not discharge to any appreciable extent between the periods of conduction.

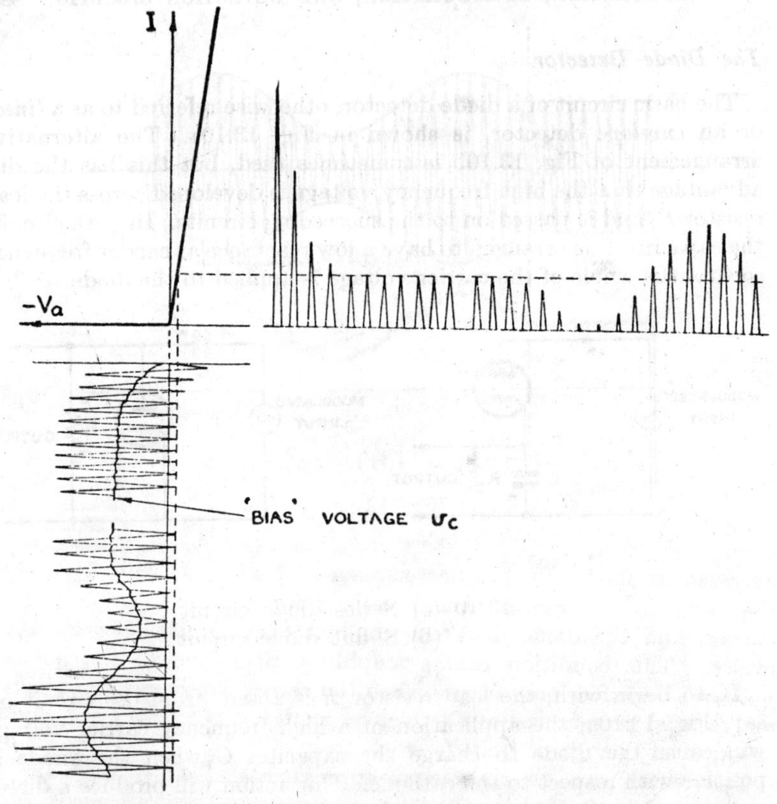

Fig. 13.11.

If the CR constant is also short compared with the period of the modulating voltage, the output voltage across C and R will be able to follow variations in the carrier amplitude at the modulating frequency. This is shown in Fig. 13.11. In this diagram the current/voltage curve for the diode is shown as a linear relation for simplicity. The actual operation is thus modified by the curvature which exists in a practical diode characteristic. If the applied carrier voltage is modulated as shown in Fig. 13.12a, the output voltage obtained from the detector circuit will have the waveform shown in Fig. 13.12b. The "ripples" in this voltage are due to the small discharge of the capacitor between succeeding "positive" half cycles of the carrier voltage.

If the CR time constant is long compared with the period of modulation, the voltage across the capacitor will not decrease sufficiently rapidly to follow the modulation waveform, and will

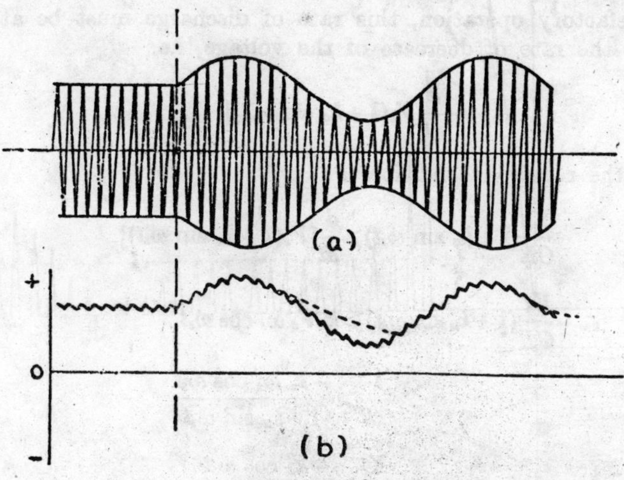

Fig. 13.12.

decrease as shown by the dotted curve of Fig. 13.12b. In effect, the capacitor voltage is then greater than the peak value of the carrier, and the diode does not conduct even on the positive half cycles. This condition causes amplitude distortion of the output voltage ; the effect only occurs when the carrier voltage is decreasing, and is most pronounced at the highest modulation frequencies, where the rate of change of voltage is greatest.

This effect can be considered approximately as follows. If a capacitor C is to discharge through a resistor R, the voltage across the capacitor is given by,

$$v_c = Ve^{-\frac{t}{CR}}$$

where V is the voltage across the capacitor at the start of the discharge, and t is the time measured from the beginning of the discharge. The rate of discharge is,

$$-\frac{dv_c}{dt} = \frac{V}{CR}e^{-\frac{t}{CR}} = \frac{v_c}{CR}$$

so that the rate of discharge when the voltage is v_c', is given by v_c'/CR. If a sinusoidally-modulated carrier is applied, the voltage across the capacitor should have the form

$$v_c = V_c(1 + k_a \sin \omega_s t)$$

in order to reproduce the envelope of the input waveform. The rate of discharge will thus be

$$V_c (1 + k_a \sin \omega_s t)/CR$$

For satisfactory operation, this rate of discharge must be at least equal to the rate of decrease of the voltage, i.e.

$$-\frac{d}{dt}[V_c(1+k_a \sin \omega_s t)]$$

so that the required condition is

$$-\frac{V_c}{CR}(1+k_a \sin \omega_s t) \geqslant \frac{d}{dt}[V_c(1+k_a \sin \omega_s t)]$$

$$\therefore -\frac{V_c}{CR}(1+k_a \sin \omega_s t) \geqslant k_a V_c \omega_s \cos \omega_s t$$

$$\therefore \frac{1}{CR} \geqslant \frac{-k_a \omega_s \cos \omega_s t}{1+k_a \sin \omega_s t}$$

$$\text{or } \frac{X_c}{R} \geqslant \frac{-k_a \cos \omega_s t}{1+k_a \sin \omega_s t} \quad . \quad . \quad . \quad . \quad 13.12$$

as $X_c = 1/\omega_s C$.

The right hand side of this inequality varies with time and the limiting value of X_c/R must at least equal the largest value. Now,

$$\frac{-k_a \cos \omega_s t}{1+k_a \sin \omega_s t} = \frac{-k_a}{\sec \omega_s t + k_a \tan \omega_s t}$$

This quantity will be a maximum when the denominator is a minimum, which can be shown to occur when

$$\sin \omega_s t = -k_a$$

The limiting value for X_c/R is thus defined by the insertion of this value for t in the inequality 13.12, i.e.

$$\frac{X_c}{R} \geqslant \frac{k_a\sqrt{1-k_a^2}}{1-k_a^2}$$

$$\geqslant \frac{k_a}{\sqrt{1-k_a^2}} \quad . \quad . \quad . \quad . \quad 13.13$$

This relationship must hold for the highest modulation frequency to be encountered by the detector. If 100% modulation is employed, so that $k_a = 1$, the relationship of 13.13 breaks down. This might be expected, because under such circumstances, the output voltage is required to fall to zero in every period of the modulation cycle, whereas the time required for the complete discharge of a capacitor is infinitely great.

Diode Detection Efficiency

It has been shown that the application of an unmodulated carrier to a diode detector circuit gives a direct voltage across the load resistor R. The ratio

$$\frac{\text{Output voltage across load}}{\text{Peak voltage applied}}$$

is known as the detection efficiency, and is represented by the symbol η.

An approximate expression for η may be derived reasonably simply, if the diode characteristic is assumed to be that of an ideal rectifier, as shown in Fig. 13.13. The I_a/V_a curve for positive input voltages is then a straight line given by

$$I_a = \frac{V_a}{R_d}$$

where R_d is the diode conduction resistance, i.e. the reciprocal of the slope of the I_a/V_a characteristic. The error involved in this assumption is largest when the signal input is small, but decreases as the input is increased. A second assumption, necessary for the derivation of the detector efficiency, is that the output voltage across C and R is considered as a direct voltage, v_c. This ignores the small ripples in the true output voltage v_c', but the error involved is small in the practical case when the CR time constant is long compared with the period of the carrier voltage.

If the input is taken as a cosinusoidal voltage, $E_{max} \cos \omega t$, for convenience, and the assumptions stated above apply, the diode will conduct when

$$E_{max} \cos \omega t = v_c$$

$$\text{i.e. when } \omega t = \theta = \cos^{-1} \frac{v_c}{E_{max}}$$

The anode current then consists of a series of cosinusoidal pulses as shown in Fig. 13.13.

The mean value of the anode current is given by,

$$I_{mean} = \frac{1}{2\pi} \int_{-\pi}^{+\pi} I_a d(\omega t)$$

As the diode does not conduct outside the range $+\theta$ to $-\theta$,

$$I_{mean} = \frac{1}{2\pi} \int_{-\theta}^{+\theta} I_a d(\omega t) = \frac{1}{\pi} \int_{0}^{\theta} I_a d(\omega t)$$

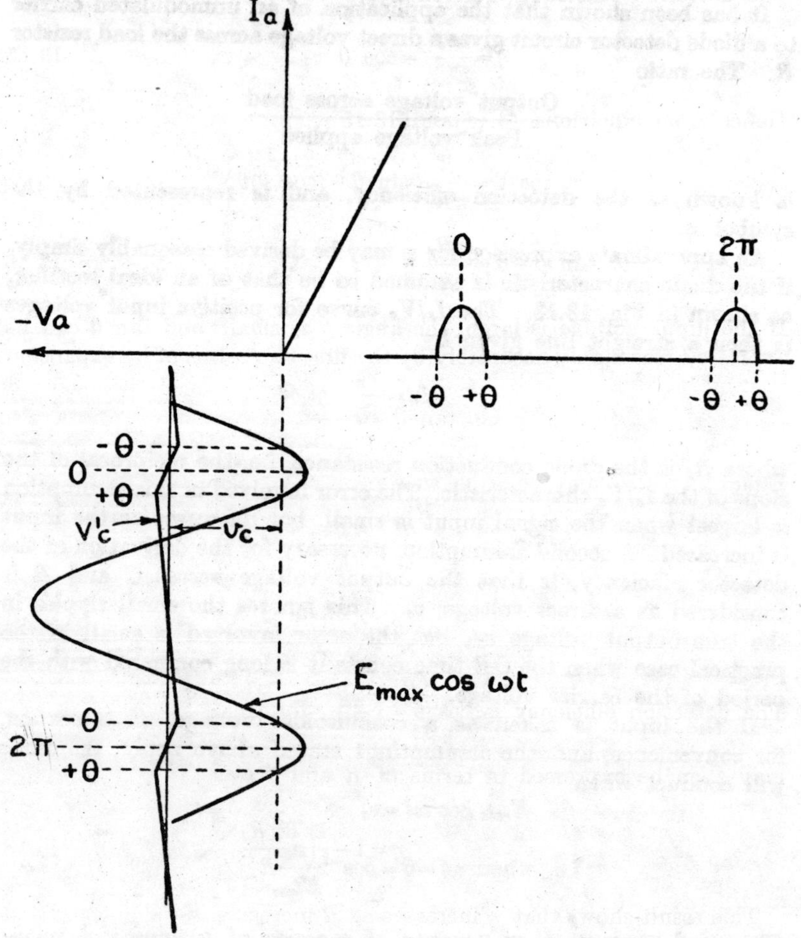

Fig. 13.13.

$$= \frac{1}{\pi}\int_0^{\theta}\frac{(E_{max}\cos \omega t - v_c)}{R_d}d(\omega t)$$

$$= \frac{1}{\pi R_d}(E_{max}\sin\theta - v_c\theta)$$

The output voltage, v_c, is the product of the mean anode current and the diode load resistor R; hence

$$v_c = \frac{E_{max}R}{\pi R_d}\left\{\sin\theta - \frac{v_c}{E_{max}}\theta\right\} \qquad 13.14$$

The detection efficiency is given by

$$\eta = \frac{v_e}{E_{max}} = \cos\theta \quad . \quad . \quad . \quad . \quad 13.15$$

Hence from equations 13.14 and 13.15,

$$\cos\theta = \frac{R}{\pi R_d}\left\{\sin\theta - (\cos\theta)\theta\right\}$$

$$\text{or } \tan\theta - \theta = \frac{\pi R_d}{R} \quad . \quad . \quad . \quad . \quad . \quad 13.16$$

If the input voltage is large, the angle θ is small, and tan θ can be expressed reasonably accurately by the first two terms of its expansion

$$\text{i.e. } \tan\theta = \theta + \frac{\theta^3}{3}$$

Equation 13,16 may thus be written as,

$$\frac{\theta^3}{3} = \frac{\pi R_d}{R}$$

$$\text{or } \theta = \left(\frac{3\pi R_d}{R}\right)^{\frac{1}{3}} \quad . \quad . \quad . \quad 13.17$$

The detection efficiency is $\cos\theta = 1 - \frac{\theta^2}{2}$, for small values of θ, and may then be expressed in terms of R and R_d as

$$\eta = 1 - \frac{1}{2}\left(\frac{3\pi R_d}{R}\right)^{\frac{2}{3}} \quad . \quad . \quad 13.18$$

This result shows that η increases as R increases in value compared with R_d. Thus if $R = 20R_d$, η is equal to 0·77 ; if $R = 200\ R_d$, η is equal to 0·95. With a practical diode, the slope resistance varies, as the I_a/v_a characteristic is in fact curved. The lowest value exists over the linear range of the characteristic, remote from the origin. As a result of this, the detection efficiency varies with the magnitude of the input voltage, and increases with an increase in input. If R is considerably greater than the maximum value of R_d, the detection efficiency approaches unity, and the variation, for change in input is diminished. Diode detectors thus operate most efficiently when furnished with a large input voltage, and with a load resistance very much larger than the slope resistance (for the linear range) of the diode.

Factors Affecting the Value of the Detector Time Constant

It will be realised from what has already been said that the correct operation of a diode detector circuit depends upon the proper values of load resistor and bypass capacitor C. The resistor R should be large compared with the slope resistance of the diode to secure a high detection efficiency. The bypass capacitor C should present a low reactance to the carrier. In particular the reactance of C should be less than the reactance of the inter-electrode capacitance of the diode in order that the whole of the carrier voltage should be applied to the diode. The time constant CR should be long compared with the carrier period to keep the carrier frequency components (i.e. "ripple") in the output small, also the ratio X_c/R must comply with the condition of 13.13 (at the highest modulation frequency) for the maximum depth of modulation.

Diode Detection Characteristics

A great deal of useful information about the operation of a diode detector can be obtained from the diode dynamic characteristics which have the form shown in Fig. 13.14. It has been seen that the application of an unmodulated input to a diode detector circuit

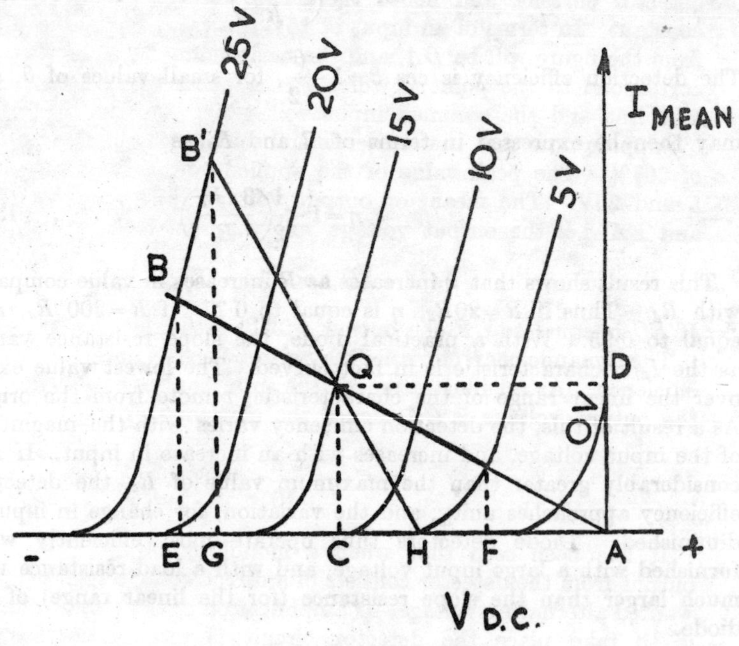

Fig. 13.14.

produces a direct voltage across the load resistance, so that the diode has in effect a direct and an alternating voltage applied across it. The dynamic characteristics can thus be obtained experimentally if a series combination of a direct and an alternating voltage is applied to the diode. If the a.c. source is set to give zero output and the d.c. output is varied, the curve 0V will result. If then the a.c. source is set to deliver an output of say, 5V peak, and the d.c. voltage varied as before, the 5V characteristic will be drawn. By using different values of peak alternating voltage a whole family of characteristics will be obtained. These characteristics can be used in a manner analogous to the use of I_a/V_a characteristics of a triode when it is desired to estimate the amplification for a given load.

If an unmodulated input is applied to the detector circuit the mean current through the valve, I_{mean}, sets up a voltage across the load resistance R of

$$V_{mean} = I_{mean}R$$

The polarity of this voltage is such that the anode is made negative with respect to the cathode. For any given load resistor, a load line such as AB, may be drawn on the characteristics ; the slope of AB is determined by the value of resistor used.

If an unmodulated input of say 15V peak is applied the mean detector current, and hence the mean voltage across the load, is constant. In terms of an input of 15V the value of the mean current from the figure will be DA, and the mean voltage CA, as these values correspond to the point Q which is the point of intersection of the load line and the assumed input voltage.

Suppose now that the carrier is sinusoidally modulated to a depth of $66\frac{2}{3}$%. The peak value of the applied voltage will vary between 5 and 25V. The mean, or output voltage, will vary between FA and EA, i.e. the output voltage will vary between

$$CA + EC \text{ and } CA - CF$$

If EC is equal to CF the output will be free from distortion.

The dynamic characteristics may also be used to obtain the detector efficiency. As an illustration, if the input has a peak value of 15V the output voltage is CA, hence the efficiency $= \eta$ is

$$\eta = \frac{CA}{15} \times 100\%$$

It has been seen that when a modulated input is applied, the output from the detector consists of a direct voltage together with the wanted alternating voltage. If amplification of the alternating voltage is to take place the detector circuit is usually coupled to the

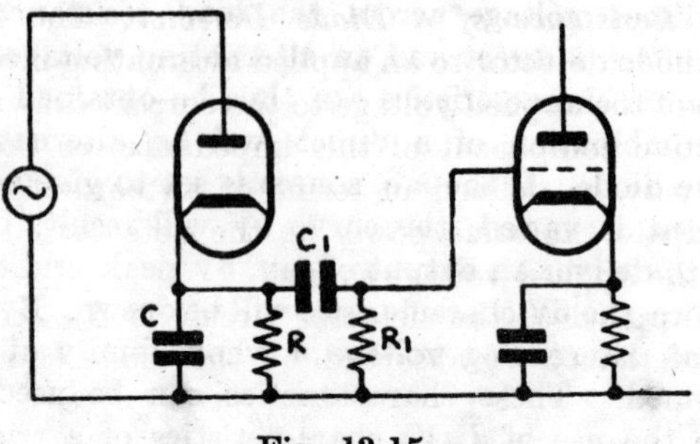

Fig. 13.15.

succeeding valve by the circuit of Fig. 13.15; a blocking capacitor C_1 is used so that the direct voltage developed by the detector load is prevented from upsetting the grid bias of the following valve. R_1 is a grid leak.

The presence of C_1 and R_1 affect the detector operation in the same way as the coupling capacitor and grid leak affect the performance of an amplifier (see chapter 8). C_1 should have a reactance which is small compared with the value of R_1 at the lowest modulation frequency in order that no voltage should be lost across C_1. When the reactance of C_1 is sufficiently small to be neglected, the detector load resistance is R'

$$\text{where } R' = \frac{RR_1}{R+R_1}$$

The load line for a modulated wave is thus the line corresponding to R'. If $R_1 = R$, R' will be equal to $R/2$ and the load line for R' will have twice the slope of AB and will be represented by the line $B'H$ in Fig. 13.14. If the input is a 15V peak carrier sinusoidally modulated to a depth of $66\frac{2}{3}\%$ the output voltage will vary over the range GCH. It is quite evident that under the condition illustrated, distortion exists in the output as the voltage swing GC is not equal to the voltage swing CH. To keep the distortion to a reasonable level, an inspection of the figure shows that the modulation depth would have to be restricted to approximately 33%.

In order to overcome this restriction it is necessary that R_1 the grid leak resistor should be large compared with the diode load resistor so that the d.c. and a.c. load lines (AB and B^1H respectively) do not differ appreciably in slope.

If the capacitor C_1 has not a small reactance compared with R_1 at any modulation frequency, or if the reactance of C is not very much larger than the value of R, the detector load will have a reactive component so that the load line will become an ellipse. (For analogous behaviour in an amplifier see chapter 8.)

Effective Input Resistance of a Diode Detector. The impedance presented by the diode detector to an applied alternating input voltage source is the ratio of the applied voltage to the current drawn from the source. The resistive component of this impedance, or the effective input resistance, may be defined in terms of an equivalent resistor which would dissipate the same power as the detector circuit when connected across the applied voltage source.

If the voltage applied to the detector circuit is $E_{max}\cos\omega t$ then the mean value of the power absorbed by the diode circuit is

$$P=\frac{1}{2\pi}\int_{-\theta}^{+\theta}(I_aE_{max}\cos\omega t)d(\omega t)=\frac{1}{\pi}\int_{0}^{\theta}(I_aE_{max}\cos\omega t)d(\omega t)$$

If the diode characteristic is considered to be rectilinear, as in Fig. 13.13, and v_c is the direct voltage across the load, then,

$$P=\frac{1}{\pi}\int_{0}^{\theta}E_{max}\cos\omega t\left(\frac{E_{max}\cos\omega t-v_c}{R_d}\right)d(\omega t)$$

$$=\frac{E^2_{max}}{\pi R_d}\int_{0}^{\theta}(\cos^2\omega t-\cos\theta\cos\omega t)d(\omega t)$$

$$=\frac{E^2_{max}}{2\pi R_d}\left(\theta+\frac{\sin 2\theta}{2}-2\cos\theta\sin\theta\right)$$

$$=\frac{E^2_{max}}{2\pi R_d}(\theta-\cos\theta\sin\theta)$$

If R_{IN} is the value of the effective input resistance, the power dissipated by this resistance will be $E^2_{max}/2R_{IN}$ so that

$$\frac{E^2_{max}}{2R_{IN}}=\frac{E^2_{max}}{2\pi R_d}(\theta-\cos\theta\sin\theta)$$

and $$R_{IN}=\frac{\pi R_d}{\theta-\cos\theta\sin\theta} \quad . \quad . \quad . \quad . \quad . \quad . \quad 13.19$$

Now the detection efficiency, η, is equal to $\cos\theta$

$$\therefore R_{IN}=\frac{\pi R_d}{\cos^{-1}\eta-\eta\sqrt{1-\eta^2}} \quad . \quad . \quad . \quad . \quad . \quad . \quad 13.20$$

Equation 13.19 can be rewritten as

$$R_{IN}=\frac{\pi R_d}{\theta-\dfrac{\sin 2\theta}{2}}$$

θ is a small angle, so that $(\sin 2\theta)/2 \simeq \theta - \dfrac{2\theta^3}{3}$

$$\therefore R_{IN} \simeq \frac{3\pi R_d}{2\theta^3}$$

Substitution of the value obtained for θ^3 in equation 13.17 gives

$$R_{IN} \simeq \frac{3\pi R_d}{2\left(\dfrac{3\pi R_d}{R}\right)} \simeq \frac{R}{2} \quad . \quad . \quad . \quad . \quad . \quad . \quad . \qquad 13.21$$

As the input voltage is usually coupled to the detector by a resonant circuit the effect of the detector input resistance is to decrease both the selectivity and the dynamic impedance of the tuned circuit (which decreases the gain of the preceding stage).

Other Forms of Detection

In the past, various circuits employing triode and multi-electrode valves have been used as detectors. Most of these suffer from the disadvantage that they only work well on a limited range of input voltage. The diode which is not so restricted, has virtually displaced the other detectors, two of which are shown in Fig. 13.16.

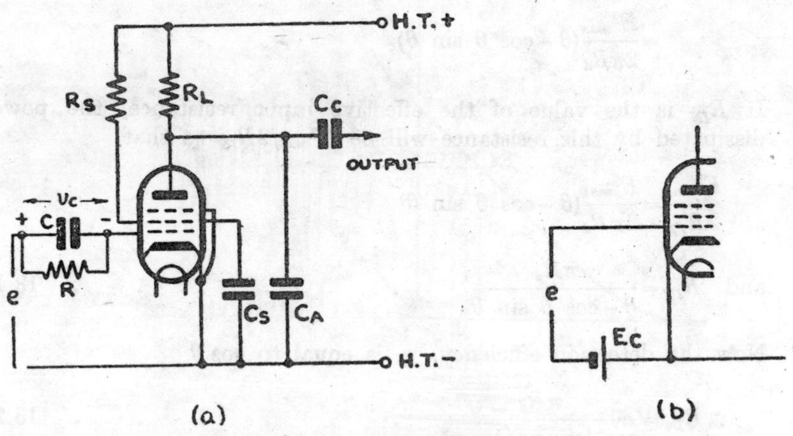

Fig. 13.16 (a) Grid circuit detector
(b) Grid arrangement for anode bend detection.

Grid Circuit Detection

The static grid current/grid voltage characteristics of a triode (or pentode) are similar to the static characteristics of a diode, and the connection of a CR combination in the grid circuit of a valve, as shown in 13.16a, gives a detector arrangement known as a grid leak detector. The grid and cathode of the valve act as a diode so that the application of an unmodulated input gives rise to a direct voltage across the capacitor v_c, with the polarity shown. If the input is modulated, the voltage v_c has a direct component together with a component at the modulation frequency.

As the valve shown is a pentode, variations in grid potential cause variations in anode current which are related by the static I_a/v_g characteristic, as the slope resistance of the valve is much greater than the impedance of the load in the anode circuit.

The direct component of v_c increases the negative bias of the grid so that the anode current of the valve decreases as the carrier amplitude increases. The alternating component of v_c produces variations of anode current at the modulation frequency, and an output voltage at this frequency is produced across the load resistor R_L. The capacitor C_A has a reactance which is small at carrier frequency and high at modulation frequencies ; it serves to bypass the carrier frequency current from the load resistor so that the carrier voltage is filtered off from the output.

Seen in this way, the valve behaves as a diode detector with its

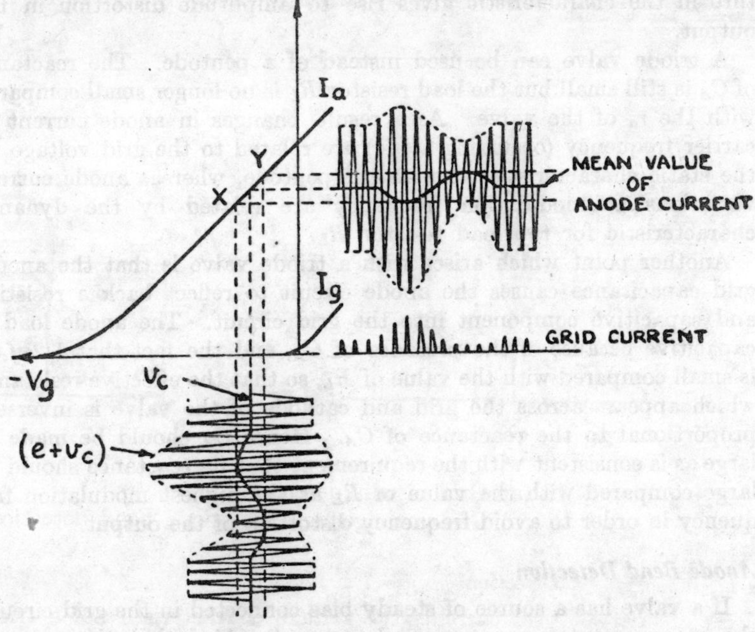

Fig, 13.17.

output connected directly to the grid of a pentode amplifier. This at first sight seems an advantageous arrangement but in practice there are several drawbacks. First of all the valve is not used efficiently as an amplifier. This is evident from Fig. 13.17 which shows that the wanted component of anode current at the modulation frequency is in effect the mean value of anode current. This will reproduce the modulation frequency as long as the total grid excursion, i.e. $e + v_c$, is limited to the linear part of the characteristic. If the grid excursion extends beyond the linear range the mean value of the anode current will change and amplitude distortion will occur. It can be seen that the total grid voltage shown has nearly its maximum permissible amplitude, and so for the depth of modulation considered, the range of the characteristic used as a modulation frequency amplifier is XY. As the valve is capable of handling a larger input than this, the output voltage is not as large as could be obtained if the alternating component of v_c alone was applied to the valve, in such a way as to occupy the whole linear range of the characteristic. Apart from the inefficient use as an amplifier, distortion occurs if the input amplitude is too large; if the input voltage is very small the detector behaves as a square law device which again gives rise to distortion. A variable μ valve does not improve the situation because although an increased value of grid cut-off is obtained, the curvature in the characteristic gives rise to amplitude distortion in the output.

A triode valve can be used instead of a pentode. The reactance of C_A is still small but the load resistor R_L is no longer small compared with the r_a of the valve. As a result, changes in anode current at carrier frequency (occurring alone) are related to the grid voltage by the static characteristic, as with the pentode, whereas anode current variations at modulation frequency are related by the dynamic characteristic for the load resistor R_L.

Another point which arises with a triode valve is that the anode-grid capacitance causes the anode circuit to reflect back a resistive and capacitive component into the grid circuit. The anode load is capacitive because of the presence of C_A, and the fact that $1/2\pi f_c C_A$ is small compared with the value of R_L, so that the effective resistance which appears across the grid and cathode of the valve is inversely proportional to the reactance of C_A. Hence C_A should be made as large as is consistent with the requirement that its reactance should be large compared with the value of R_L at the highest modulation frequency in order to avoid frequency distortion of the output.

Anode Bend Detection

If a valve has a source of steady bias connected in the grid circuit, the arrangement can act as a detector provided that the valve is biased to some point of curvature on its characteristic. The connections for a pentode valve are those of Fig. 13.16a if the grid circuit is modified to that of Fig. 13.16b.

The point of curvature normally selected is the "bottom bend" in the I_a/V_g characteristic somewhere near the "projected cut-off" value. Anode current then flows on positive half cycles of the applied grid voltage and the mean value of the anode current is proportional to the amplitude of the applied grid voltage for moderately large amplitudes of the applied grid voltage (Fig. 13.18).

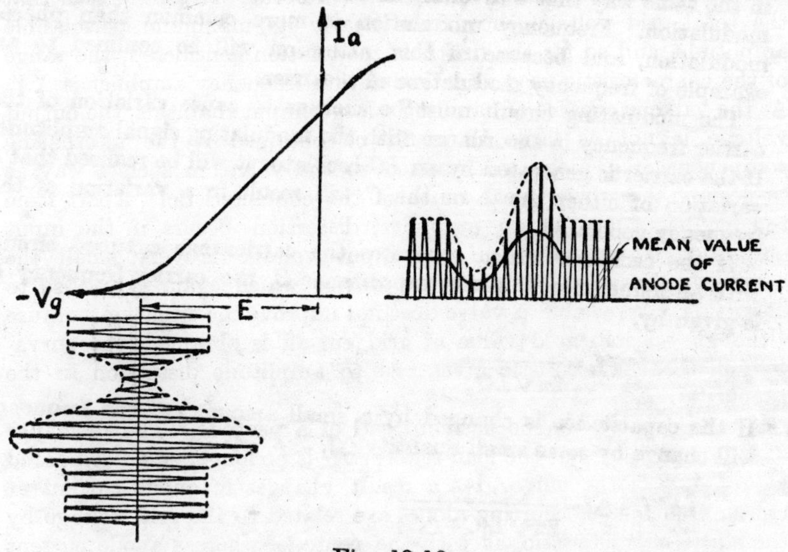

Fig. 13.18.

The component of anode current at modulation frequency gives rise to an output voltage across R_L while the carrier voltage is filtered off by the presence of C_A. Once again the value of C_A is chosen so that

$$\frac{1}{2\pi f_s C_A} \gg R_L \gg \frac{1}{2\pi f_c C_A}$$

where f_s and f_c are respectively the modulation and carrier frequencies.

The maximum amplitude of the applied input voltage should be less than the bias voltage E otherwise the grid becomes positive and the resulting grid current gives rise to amplitude distortion of the output. If on the other hand the input voltage is small the valve acts as a square law detector because of the curvature at the operating point.

For input amplitudes between these extremes the anode bend detector has the advantage of a much higher input resistance compared with a diode detector, as no grid current flows if the grid is maintained at a negative potential with respect to the cathode.

Heterodyne Detection

This method of detection is employed in the reception of some kinds of telegraph signals, and is mentioned in chapter 22.

FREQUENCY MODULATION

A high-frequency carrier can be angle-modulated by several methods in the same way that a diversity of arrangements exist for amplitude-modulation. Frequency modulation is more common than phase-modulation, and because of this, attention will be confined to an example of frequency modulation of a carrier.

The modulating circuit must be such as to cause variation of the carrier frequency in accordance with the modulating signal amplitude. If the carrier is generated by an LC oscillator it will be realised that a variation of either the L or the C will result in a variation of the frequency generated.

If the oscillator which generates the carrier has a tuned circuit with an inductance L and a capacitance C, the carrier frequency f_c is given by,

$$f_c = \frac{1}{2\pi\sqrt{LC}}$$

If the capacitance is changed by a small amount ΔC the frequency will change by some small quantity Δf,

$$\text{i.e. } f_c \pm \Delta f = \frac{1}{2\pi\sqrt{L(C \mp \Delta C)}}$$

$$\text{and so } \quad \frac{f_c + \Delta f}{f_c} = \frac{1}{\sqrt{1 - \frac{\Delta C}{C}}}$$

$$\therefore\ 1 + \frac{\Delta f}{f_c} = \left(1 - \frac{\Delta C}{C}\right)^{-\frac{1}{2}}$$

If $\Delta f / f_c$ is a small quantity, as is normally the case, $\Delta C/C$ will also be small so that if the right hand side is expanded by the binomial theorem, only the first two terms need be considered,

$$\therefore\ 1 + \frac{\Delta f}{f_c} = 1 + \frac{\Delta C}{2C}$$

$$\therefore\ \Delta f = \frac{\Delta C}{2C} f_c \qquad \cdot \quad \cdot \quad \cdot \quad \cdot \quad \cdot \quad \cdot \quad 13.22$$

The frequency change is thus approximately proportional to the change of capacitance, when this is small compared with the total capacitance.

The Reactance Valve Modulator

Frequency-modulation can be produced by means of a "reactance valve". This takes the form of a pentode valve in which the anode voltage is 90° out of phase with the grid voltage. The pentode can be considered as a constant current generator, generating an anode current in phase with the grid voltage, and given by

$$I_a = g_m v_g$$

if the anode load is small compared with the slope resistance of the valve. The valve thus appears as a reactance X, to any external circuit connected across the anode and cathode, where

$$X = \frac{E_a}{I_a}$$

The value of this reactance can be varied by altering the grid voltage if such alteration affects the value of the mutual conductance g_m.

The general circuit arrangement is shown in Fig. 13.19. The impedances Z_1 and Z_2 step down the high-frequency voltage from the anode to the grid and provide the phase shift of nearly 90°.

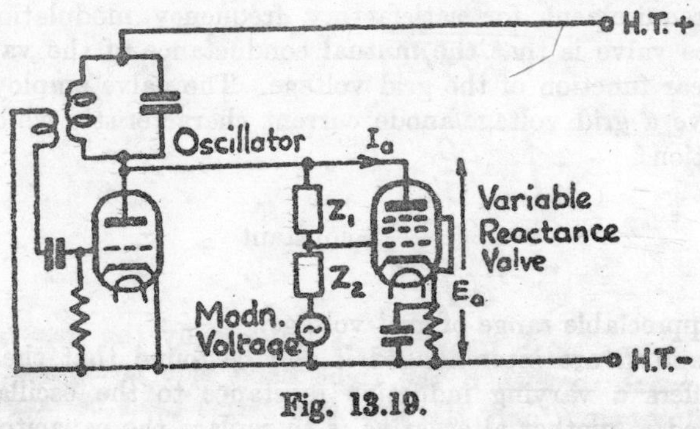

Fig. 13.19.

If steady voltages and currents are neglected, the admittance between the anode and cathode is

$$Y_{12} = I_a/E_a = g_m v_g/E_a$$
$$= g_m Z_2/(Z_1 + Z_2)$$

Suppose now that Z_1 is a capacitance C, and Z_2 is a resistance R, then

$$Y_{12} = \frac{g_m R}{R + 1/j\omega C} = \frac{g_m j\omega CR}{1 + j\omega CR}$$

$$= \frac{g_m(\omega CR)^2}{1 + (\omega CR)^2} + \frac{j\omega CR g_m}{1 + (\omega CR)^2}$$

Hence the impedance at the terminals 12 consists of a resistance R' in parallel with a capacitance C' where

$$R' = \frac{1 + (\omega CR)^2}{g_m(\omega CR)^2} \quad . \quad . \quad . \quad . \quad . \quad 13.23a$$

$$\text{and } C' = \frac{g_m CR}{1 + (\omega CR)^2} \quad . \quad . \quad . \quad . \quad . \quad 13.23b$$

From this it will be seen that variation of the mutual conductance of the valve will cause a variation in the effective capacitance presented by the valve. As the terminals 1, 2 are connected across the tuned circuit of an oscillator, an alteration in g_m due to the modulating signal will cause the desired frequency-modulation of the oscillator. A small amount of amplitude modulation will also occur because of the resistive component of current taken by the valve. This may however be removed subsequently by an amplitude limiting arrangement.

The requirement for satisfactory frequency modulation by the reactance valve is that the mutual conductance of the valve should be a linear function of the grid voltage. The valve employed should thus have a grid voltage/anode current characteristic which satisfies the relation

$$\frac{\partial^2 i_a}{\partial v_g^2} = \text{constant}$$

for an appreciable range of grid voltage.

If C and R are interchanged it will be found that the reactance valve offers a varying inductive reactance to the oscillator to be modulated. Another alternative is to replace the capacitor C by an inductance L.

The modulation is often arranged to take place at some sub-multiple (say $1/n$) of the final carrier-frequency, and the modulated wave is then passed through appropriate frequency multiplier circuits. When this is done the final frequency deviation is n times that which occurs at the modulating point.

Detection of Frequency-Modulated Voltages

The detection of frequency-modulated voltages involves a frequency-to-amplitude conversion so that the amplitude change of the original modulating voltage can be obtained as an output. This may be achieved by the circuit of Fig. 13.20.

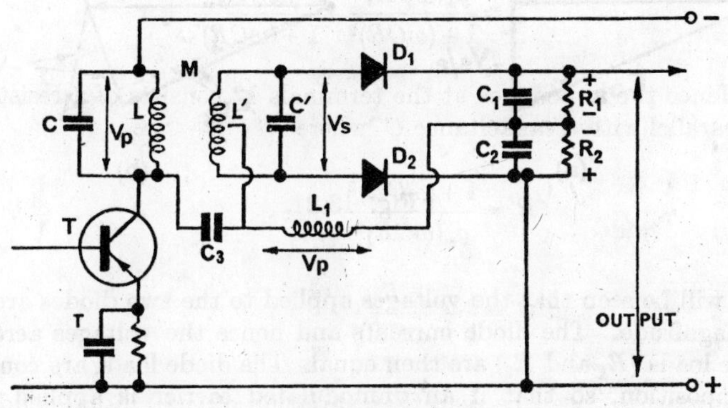

Fig. 13.20.

The frequency-modulated voltage to be detected is amplified to a suitable level and T in Fig. 13.20 may be regarded as the last stage of a high-frequency amplifier. The load for T consists of the parallel LC circuit which is tuned to the carrier frequency, and inductively coupled to the secondary circuit $L'C'$, also tuned to the carrier frequency. In addition to the inductive coupling between the coils L and L' a capacitor C_3 couples the collector of T to the centre tap on the coil L'. Now the capacitors C_1, C_2 and C_3 have negligible reactance at carrier frequency and so it will be seen that V_p the voltage across the primary tuned circuit is also developed across the high frequency choke L_1. It follows that the high-frequency voltage applied to each diode is half the high-frequency voltage in the secondary circuit V_s together with the primary voltage across L_1.

The action of the circuit depends on the fact that at the frequency of the carrier the voltages V_p and V_s are in quadrature. This arises from the fact that the current I_L in L, lags on V_p by 90° while the voltage induced in L' is $-j\omega MI_L$. The circulating current in the resonant secondary circuit is in phase with the induced voltage, and V_s the voltage across the capacitor lags on the circulating current by 90°, if the effect of the diodes and their loads is neglected. V_s is thus in quadrature with V_p.

The voltages applied to the two diodes, D_1 and D_2 are then as shown in Fig. 13.21a.

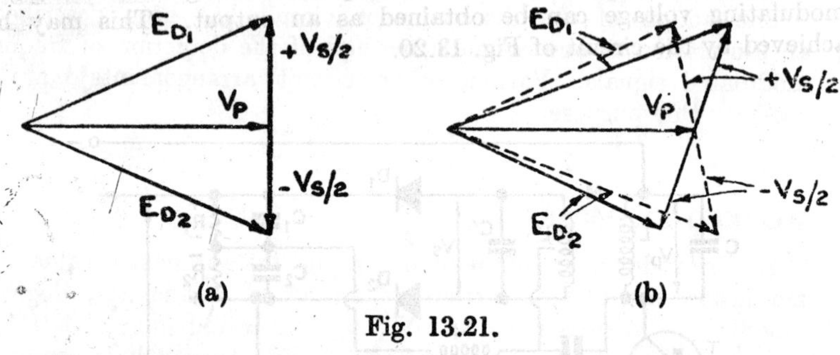

Fig. 13.21.

It will be seen that the voltages applied to the two diodes are equal in magnitude. The diode currents and hence the voltages across the diode loads (R_1 and R_2) are then equal. The diode loads are connected in opposition, so that if an unmodulated carrier is applied to the circuit the output voltage is zero.

If the input voltage has a frequency greater than that of the carrier the voltages are those shown by the solid lines in Fig. 13.21b, which is drawn to illustrate the change in phase of V_s. With an input frequency greater than the carrier, the current through L still lags on V_p by 90°, but the secondary circuit presents an inductive reactance to the induced voltage so that V_s is no longer in quadrature with V_p but leads by an angle which is less than 90°. As a result the voltages applied to the two diodes are no longer equal, and in fact $E_{D1} > E_{D2}$ so that the voltage across R_1 is greater than the voltage across R_2. The difference gives rise to an output of positive polarity with respect to the earth terminal.

When the input frequency is lower than that of the carrier, the opposite conditions prevail. The secondary circuit presents a capacitive reactance to the voltage induced in L' so that V_s leads V_p by an angle which is greater than 90°. E_{D1} is less than E_{D2} and the output has a negative polarity with respect to the earth terminal. These conditions are shown by the dotted lines in Fig. 13.21b.

In this way frequency variations in the input result in amplitude variations in the output.

Fig. 13.21 does not represent the conditions accurately because some amplitude change occurs in the voltages V_p and V_s as the frequency changes, and there may not be exact quadrature between the voltages at carrier frequency because of the presence of resistance in the inductors. Nevertheless the figure illustrates the basic point that the circuit does function by virtue of the change of phase between the voltages V_p and V_s as the frequency changes, and is accordingly referred to as a phase discriminator circuit.[2]

The action of the discriminator circuit has been described as an illustration of one common method of the detection of frequency modulated signals. Various other circuit arrangements[3,4] are also used for this purpose.

WORKED EXAMPLES

1. Write down an expression for the instantaneous value of an amplitude modulated carrier voltage, and define the degree of modulation. A carrier p.d. of 5 V (r.m.s.) at a frequency of 1 MHz and a modulating p.d. of 2 V (r.m.s.) at a frequency of 1 kHz are applied in series to a biased crystal rectifier in which the current on application of a signal of v volts in the range ± 10 V is $i = 5 + v + 0{\cdot}05v^2$ microamperes. Find the degree of modulation of the resulting modulated carrier current, and the frequencies of the components of the total current.

L.U. Ext. Telecomm. 1950.

It has been shown that the instantaneous value of an amplitude-modulated carrier voltage is

$$(A + B \sin \omega_m t) \sin \omega_c t$$

where A is the carrier amplitude prior to modulation, and $A + B$ is the maximum value of the amplitude variation after modulation. The ratio of B/A is defined as the degree, or depth, of modulation. The voltage applied to the crystal is

$$v = 5\sqrt{2} \sin \omega_c t + 2\sqrt{2} \sin \omega_m t$$

where $\omega_c = 2\pi \times 10^6$ and $\omega_m = 2\pi \times 10^3$

The crystal current in microamperes is thus

$$i = 5 + 5\sqrt{2} \sin \omega_c t + 2\sqrt{2} \sin \omega_m t$$
$$+ 0{\cdot}05[5\sqrt{2} \sin \omega_c t + 2\sqrt{2} \sin \omega_m t]^2$$

Expansion and re-arrangement of this expression gives,

$$i = [(5\sqrt{2} + 2 \sin \omega_m t) \sin \omega_c t] + (5 + 1{\cdot}25 + 0{\cdot}4)$$
$$+ 1{\cdot}25 \sin (2\omega_c t - \pi/2) + 0{\cdot}2 \sin (2\omega_m t - \pi/2)$$

The expression in the square brackets is that of an amplitude modulated carrier current, in which the depth of modulation is equal to

$$\frac{2}{5\sqrt{2}} \times 100\% = 28{\cdot}3\%$$

The current contains a component at the carrier frequency of 1 MHz, an upper sideband of 1·001 MHz, and a lower sideband of 0·999 MHz. In addition it also contains a component at the modulating frequency of 1 kHz, together with a second harmonic of this frequency, and a second harmonic of the carrier.

2. A coil A, having a self-inductance of 500 microhenrys and a resistance of 10 ohms is loosely coupled magnetically to a coil B. The latter carries a current having a carrier frequency of 300 kHz, modulated at a frequency of 5 kHz, the depth of modulation being 40%. A variable condenser connected across A is adjusted to give resonance with the carrier frequency. Calculate the ratio of the peak value of the lower sideband to that of the carrier in coil A. With the aid of this result, explain why a sharply-tuned resonant circuit produces distortion of an amplitude modulated wave.

L.U. Ext. Telecomm. 1945.

The coil B carries a modulated current, i_B, such that

$$\begin{aligned} i_B &= I(1 + 0{\cdot}4 \sin \omega_m t) \sin \omega_c t \\ &= I\{\sin \omega_c t + 0{\cdot}2 \cos (\omega_c - \omega_m)t - 0{\cdot}2 \cos (\omega_c + \omega_m)t\} \end{aligned}$$

Now the voltage induced in coil A, by virtue of the current flowing in coil B, is $e = -M\dfrac{di_B}{dt}$, where M is the mutual inductance which exists between the two coils.

$$\begin{aligned} \therefore\ e = -MI\{\omega_c \cos \omega_c t &- 0{\cdot}2(\omega_c - \omega_m) \sin (\omega_c - \omega_m)t \\ &+ 0{\cdot}2(\omega_c + \omega_m) \sin (\omega_c + \omega_m)t\} \end{aligned}$$

The carrier and modulation frequencies are such that ω_c and ω_m are respectively equal to $2\pi \times 3 \times 10^5$ and $2\pi \times 5 \times 10^3$.

$$\begin{aligned} \therefore\ e = -MI\{6\pi \times 10^5 \cos \omega_c t &- 0{\cdot}2 \times 2\pi \times 10^3 \times 295 \sin (\omega_c - \omega_m)t \\ &+ 0{\cdot}2 \times 2\pi \times 10^3 \times 305 \sin (\omega_c + \omega_m)t\} \end{aligned}$$

The coil A is part of a circuit which is resonant at the frequency of the carrier, hence the peak value of the carrier component of current in coil A is given by the peak value of the carrier component of voltage induced in coil A, divided by the resistance of coil A, assuming that the tuning condenser is loss free, i.e.,

Peak value of carrier component of current in coil A

$$=\frac{MI\times 6\pi\times 10^5}{10}=18{\cdot}84MI\times 10^4 \quad . \quad . \quad . \quad . \quad \text{(a)}$$

At the lower sideband frequency, the tuned circuit is no longer resonant, and so the peak value of the lower sideband component of current is given by,

$$\frac{MI\times 0{\cdot}2\times 2\pi\times 10^3\times 295}{\sqrt{10^2+\left\{(\omega_c-\omega_m)L_A-\dfrac{1}{(\omega_c-\omega_m)C}\right\}^2}}$$

Now $(\omega_c-\omega_m)L_A=2\pi\times 295\times 10^3\times 500\times 10^{-6}=926$ ohms

The value of the tuning capacitance C is given by

$$C=\frac{1}{\omega_c^2L_A}=\frac{1}{(2\pi\times 3\times 10^5)^2\times 500\times 10^{-6}}=565\ \mu\mu\text{F}$$

Hence $\dfrac{1}{(\omega_c-\omega_m)C}=\dfrac{10^{12}}{2\pi\times 295\times 10^3\times 565}=956$ ohms

The peak value of the lower sideband component of current which flows in coil A is thus

$$\frac{MI\times 0{\cdot}2\times 2\pi\times 10^3\times 295}{\sqrt{10^2+(926-956)^2}}=1{\cdot}17MI\times 10^4 \quad . \quad . \quad \text{(b)}$$

From equations (a) and (b), the ratio of the peak value of lower sideband to carrier current in coil A is

$$=\frac{1{\cdot}17}{18{\cdot}84}=0{\cdot}062$$

Ideally, this ratio should be 0·2, as the depth of modulation is 40%. The result obtained shows quite clearly that if a resonant circuit is too sharply tuned, the sideband components are attenuated with respect to the carrier; the depth of modulation is decreased, and the modulated wave is distorted.

References

[1] TUCKER, D. G.: "Some Aspects of the Design of Balanced Rectifier Modulators for Precision Applications", *Jour. I.E.E.*, 95, Part III, p. 161 (1948).

[2] FOSTER, D. E., and SEELEY, S. W.: "Automatic Tuning, Simplified Circuits and Design Practice", *Proc. I.R.E.*, 25, p. 289 (1937).

[3] STURLEY, K. R.: " Frequency Modulation ", *Jour. I.E.E.*, 92, Part III, p. 197 (1945).

[4] SEELEY, S. W. and AVINS, J.: " The Ratio Detector ", *R.C.A. Review*, 8, p. 201 (1947).

References for Further Reading

TUCKER, D. G.: *Modulators and Frequency-Changers* (Macdonald & Co., 1953).

SANDEMAN, E. K.: *Radio Engineering* (Chapman & Hall, Ltd., 1953).

HUND, A.: *Frequency Modulation* (McGraw-Hill, 1942).

CAMIES, B. S.: *Principles of Frequency Modulation* (Iliffe & Sons Ltd., 1959).

EXAMPLES

1. Explain what is meant by a " modulated carrier wave " and state briefly the reasons for its use in radio-communication. A signal voltage $e_1 = 2 \sin (5 \times 10^3 t)$ volts and a carrier voltage $e = 5 \sin (5 \times 10^6 t)$ volts are applied simultaneously to the grid of a valve whose anode-current/grid-voltage characteristic under the conditions of operation is $i_a = 10 + 1{\cdot}5 e_g + 0{\cdot}02 e_g^2$ milliamperes. Calculate the frequency and amplitude of the various components of the anode current, and indicate which constitute the " modulated carrier wave ".

L.U. Int. Telecomm. 1949.

2. Describe and compare the two types of modulator commonly used in carrier telephony. Show, using a numerical example, what is meant by an " unwanted sideband ", and how it may be suppressed.

L.U. Ext. Telecomm. 1949.

3. Explain briefly (*a*) what is meant by *amplitude modulation* and (*b*) the function of a *modulator*.

Compare with the aid of sketches the waveforms represented by

$$e_1 = K [\sin \omega_1 t + \sin \omega_2 t]$$

and

$$e_2 = K [1 + \sin \omega_2 t] \sin \omega_1 t \textit{ if } \omega_2 < \omega_1$$

given that $\omega_2 \ll \omega_1$.

If the voltage e_1 is applied directly to an ideal diode, sketch the output current waveform and state the frequencies of the principal components contained therein. What would be the effect on the output waveform if a steady forward bias, of magnitude greater than $2K$, was also applied to the diode?

L.U. Electronics & Telecomm. Part II 1969.

4. Draw the circuit diagram and explain the action of a balanced modulator. In such a modulator a carrier of 1 MHz is modulated at 1 kHz. If the carrier is added to the modulator output with a phase lag of 90 degrees on the position in time for correct amplitude modulation, deduce the nature of the resulting signal.

L.U. Ext. Telecomm. 1956.

5. Describe a typical circuit for the amplitude modulation, by the anode-voltage method, of a high-frequency amplifier and give the equivalent circuit employed in the design of the modulator stage. State the conditions under which the amplifier must be operated to achieve approximately linear response to the modulation and sketch the waveforms of anode voltage, anode current, grid voltage and grid current for the amplifier valve at (a) the peak of the modulation cycle, and (b) the trough of the modulation cycle.

L.U. Ext. Telecomm. 1946.

6. Explain fully the conditions under which a high-frequency amplifier may be modulated by the anode-voltage method. A high frequency amplifier, adjusted for anode modulation, gave results as set out in the following table when operated with fixed bias and input voltage but with various anode voltages throughout the operating range :—

Anode Voltage (V)	40	80	120	160	200	240	280	320
Anode Current (mA)	0·9	1·54	2·15	2·8	3·4	4·0	4·7	5·4

Anode modulation is to be applied by means of a modulator stage employing a modulation transformer and a triode having an amplification factor of 6 and a differential anode resistance of 5,000 ohms. Suggest a suitable ratio of transformation for the modulation transformer if the modulator is to operate under class A conditions.

L.U. Int. Telecomm. 1943.

7. Explain the principle underlying the action of the transformer-coupled anode-modulation system, and show that if such a system is to be capable of 100 per cent modulation, the modulator valve, if run under linear conditions without grid current, must be capable of dissipating twice the unmodulated carrier power input to the modulated valve.

L.U. Int. Telecomm. 1947.

8. Explain, with the aid of a circuit diagram, one method of generating frequency-modulated signals. What is the advantage of frequency-modulated signals as compared with amplitude-modulated signals ?

L.U. Int. Telecomm. 1951.

9. Explain how a pentode valve may be used as a reactance modulator. Show that with certain justifiable assumptions the circuit presents a capacitance

$$C_e = g_m RC$$

where g_m is the mutual conductance of the valve and R and C are the resistance and capacitance respectively of the phase shift circuit. What considerations are involved in obtaining a reasonable linear relation between frequency deviation and g_m when such a circuit is used to obtain frequency modulation?

***L.U. Int. Telecomm.* 1955.**

10. Explain why the time-constant of the resistance capacitance circuit in series with a diode used to demodulate a modulated radio-frequency voltage must not be too large. Draw sketches of the input and output waveforms of a diode operating in this manner.

Discuss the effect of a load resistance coupled to the diode output by a condenser on the demodulation of a deeply-modulated voltage.

***L.U. Int. Telecomm.* 1951.**

11. Explain the action of a simple diode detector in the reception of an amplitude-modulated wave, and show how automatic volume control can be obtained. If the leak resistance is 0·25 megohm and the capacitance is 100 micromicrofarads, find the maximum permissible percentage modulation at a frequency of 8,000 hertz.

***L.U. Int. Telecomm.* 1945.**

12. Make a circuit diagram of a diode detector suitable for use in a superheterodyne receiver. State briefly the use of each component and the factors which determine its value.

Give three reasons why distortion arises if the percentage modulation of the signal being received exceeds certain limits. Discuss *one* of these limiting factors in more detail.

***L.U. Telecomm. Part III.* 1959.**

13. Draw a circuit diagram for an envelope-detector circuit and explain its operation. In such a detector the current through the 0·10 MΩ load resistor is observed to be substantially constant at 0·20 mA when an unmodulated carrier voltage of 18 V r.m.s. is applied, and the diode slope resistance is 1·1 kΩ. Determine (*a*) the maximum value of the current through the diode, and (*b*) the detection efficiency.

L.U. Electronics & Telecomm. Part II 1968.

14. Discuss the statement "in a frequency-modulated system, bandwidth is as significant as power". A frequency modulator consisting of a variable reactance valve is connected across the tuned circuit of a master oscillator operating at 4·5 MHz. The phase-splitting network consists of a capacitance of 5 $\mu\mu$F between grid and anode and a resistance of 5,000 ohms from grid to cathode, and the mutual conductance of the valve (not modulating) is 2 mA/V. If the total capacitance required for tuning to 4·5 MHz is 200 $\mu\mu$F, determine the change in mutual conductance required to produce a deviation of $\pm$ 90 kHz at the final carrier frequency of 90 MHz.

L.U. Ext. Telecomm. **1956.**

15. Explain the action of a reactance valve when used to produce frequency-modulation of a tuned-grid oscillator.

The instantaneous current of a frequency-modulated waveform is given by

$$i = \hat{I} \sin[10^7 t + 50 \cos(2\pi \times 10^3 t)].$$

Calculate the peak frequency deviation.

The current is passed through an inductor: show that the voltage across the inductor is amplitude-modulated, and determine the depth of modulation.

L.U. Telecomm. Part III. **1963.**

14
NOISE

THE output of a communication system may contain, in addition to the desired signal, spurious voltages (or currents) of a random nature. This unwanted output or *noise* may be produced by a variety of causes, and clearly should be at a very low level compared with the wanted signal. If this is not so, the signal will be distorted and the received information subject to error. Amplification after the point of entry of noise into the system will be of no avail, because the noise will be amplified with the signal, and the *signal to noise ratio* will be unchanged. These remarks also apply to amplifiers or radio receivers as well as complete systems. For an amplifier with a noise source at its input, one is led to the idea of a *minimum detectable signal* which is fixed by the noise level, and so the useful sensitivity is limited.

Noise Sources

If all the possible sources of noise are considered, a distinction can be made between sources external to the disturbed communication channel and sources inside the channel.

Noise from an external source is often referred to as interference. This may be produced by radiation from moving electrical contacts, dynamic electrical machinery, fluorescent lamps, power transmission lines and many other causes. Again radiation from electrical discharges in the atmosphere or from distant galaxies may cause interference. In a multi-channel telephony system inter-channel interference is referred to as *cross-talk* and may produce varying amounts of either intelligible or unintelligible speech.

Noise may be produced inside the communication channel itself from intermittent contacts in faulty components. Electrostatic or magnetic fields produced by alternating current power leads may cause hum in signal circuits. When all these sources of noise have been removed, two other types of noise remain, namely *thermal agitation noise* and *shot noise*, collectively called *fluctuation noise.* This arises from a more fundamental cause than the other types of noise mentioned, and unlike them can never be entirely eliminated. Thus the output level of noise picked up from an external source usually depends on the location of the equipment. Such noise can generally be reduced if not eliminated by careful screening of the input circuits. Hum can be reduced to a sufficiently low level by a filtering of the supplies and screening of signal leads. This is especially necessary in the early stages of an amplifier where it is essential that noise, from whatever cause, should be at an extremely low level.

Fluctuation Noise

(*a*) *Thermal Agitation Noise.* The free electrons in a conductor are in continuous motion with a velocity that depends on the temperature of the conductor. The motion of each free electron constitutes a minute current, but over a long time interval the sum total of these currents is zero. At any particular instant, however, there may be a current in one direction or another. This flow of charge creates a random voltage at the terminals of the conductor and the effect, observed by Johnson[1] is called thermal agitation noise or *Johnson noise*. In a resistance, the thermal agitation voltage is given by the relation

$$\overline{e^2_{TN}} = 4kTR\triangle f \quad . \quad . \quad . \quad . \qquad 14.1$$

where $\overline{e^2_{TN}}$ = Mean square value of the thermal noise voltage,

R = Resistance of the component in ohms,
T = Absolute temperature of the conductor,
k = Boltzmann's constant, relating temperature and electron energy $= 1{\cdot}38 \times 10^{-23}$ joule/degree

and $\triangle f$ = bandwidth in hertz, in which the voltage is measured.

This same result was derived theoretically by Nyquist.[2] The relation which may be extended to cover complex impedances where R is the real part of such an impedance, is valid from zero up to extremely high frequencies in the microwave range. At still higher frequencies and near zero temperatures it is modified by quantum effects.[3] For nearly all practical purposes the spectrum of thermal noise may be considered to be flat and independent of frequency.

A practical resistor, R, may be represented, as shown in Fig. 14.1, either by an equivalent noise voltage generator in series with a noise free resistor R, or alternatively a noise current generator in parallel with the noise free resistor R.

It will be noticed that mean square values have been used for noise voltages. Such values (rather than r.m.s. values) have the advantage that if a noise voltage arises from several separate sources the mean square value of the total is the sum of the mean square values of the separate sources, always assuming there is no correlation between the

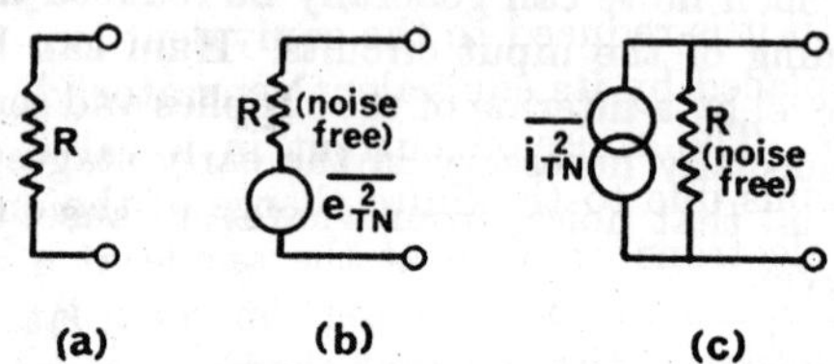

Fig. 14.1 (a) actual noisy resistor
(b) voltage generator $\overline{e^2_{TN}} = 4kTR\Delta f$
(c) current generator $\overline{i^2_{TN}} = 4kT\Delta f/R$

noise from the various sources. In effect the process is equivalent to the addition of power from separate sources. The total power dissipation in a resistor is the sum of the separate power values due to different sources.

If two resistors R_1 and R_2 are connected in series the total mean square noise voltage is

$$\overline{e^2_{TN}} = 4kT\Delta f[R_1 + R_2]$$

for resistors at the same temperature. If the temperatures are T_1 and T_2, then

$$\overline{e^2_{TN}} = 4k\Delta f[R_1T_1 + R_2T_2]$$

If two resistors are at the same temperature T and are connected in parallel (Fig. 14.2) the random noise voltages act independently of each other. The total mean square voltage across the common terminals XY is the sum of the mean square voltages developed across XY by each generator when the other is short-circuited. The output noise voltage at XY is thus

$$e^2 = 4kT\Delta fR_1\left[\frac{R_2}{R_1 + R_2}\right]^2 + 4kT\Delta fR_2\left[\frac{R_1}{R_1 + R_2}\right]^2$$

$$= 4kT\Delta f\left[\frac{R_1R_2}{R_1 + R_2}\right]$$

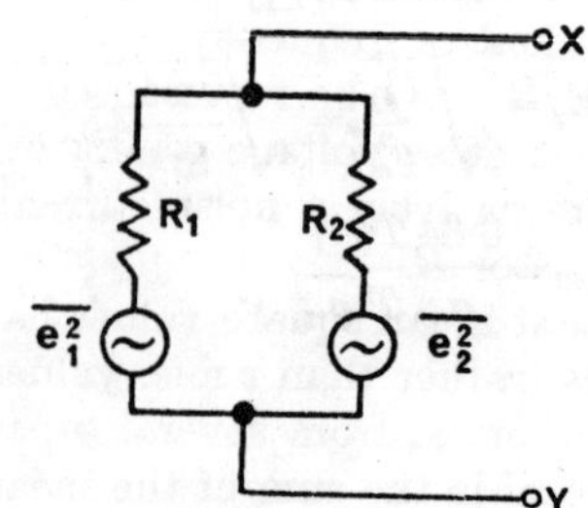

Fig. 14.2.

which is the value for a resistor R equal to the parallel combination of R_1 and R_2. This illustrates that the resultant noise voltage from a two-terminal resistive network may be obtained *either* by replacing each resistor by its equivalent noise generator and noise free source and then using network equations to obtain the solution *or* the network may first be simplified until it is reduced to the equivalent two-terminal resistor which is then replaced by its equivalent generator.

(*b*) *Shot Noise.* The emission current in a valve exhibits minute random fluctuations due to the finite charge of the emitted electrons. The number of electrons arriving at the anode at a given instant of time is not equal to the number arriving a moment later; this is equivalent to a minute alternating current, having an infinite number of frequency components, superposed on the normal current through the valve. There is thus a noise current in the valve and the effect is referred to as *shot noise.* The noise voltage developed across the anode load of a valve due to this cause will be amplified by any subsequent stages, and so the effect may, like thermal noise, set a limit to the possible useful amplification. It is found that valves operated in a space-charge-limited condition give a smaller noise output than valves operating under temperature limited conditions. The space charge smoothing factor in effect relates to the smoothing effect of the space charge on the random emission from the cathode. If the emission rises at some instant, the space charge also increases and tends to return more electrons to the cathode and hence tends to smooth out variations in the anode current.

D. O. North[4] has found that for space-charge-limited triodes the mean-square-value of the noise current in amperes is given by

$$I_{SN}^2 = \frac{0{\cdot}64}{\sigma} 4kT_c g_m \triangle f \quad . \quad . \quad . \quad . \qquad 14.2$$

where σ is a constant depending on the geometry of the valve, with a value between 0·5 and 1. T_c is the absolute temperature of the cathode, and g_m is the mutual conductance in mhos.

It is convenient to treat shot noise in the same way as thermal noise. The anode current fluctuations are expressed as equivalent grid voltage fluctuations which are assumed to be generated in a (fictitious) equivalent grid resistor. Thus the actual circuit of Fig. 14.3a can be replaced by Fig. 14.3b for noise calculations

$$E_1 = \sqrt{4kTR_1 \triangle f}$$

$$E_2 = \sqrt{\frac{I_{SN}^2}{g_m^2}} = \sqrt{\frac{0{\cdot}64}{\sigma} 4kT_c \frac{1}{g_m} \triangle f}$$

$$\text{hence} \quad R_{eq} = \frac{0{\cdot}64}{\sigma} \frac{T_c}{T} \frac{1}{g_m}$$

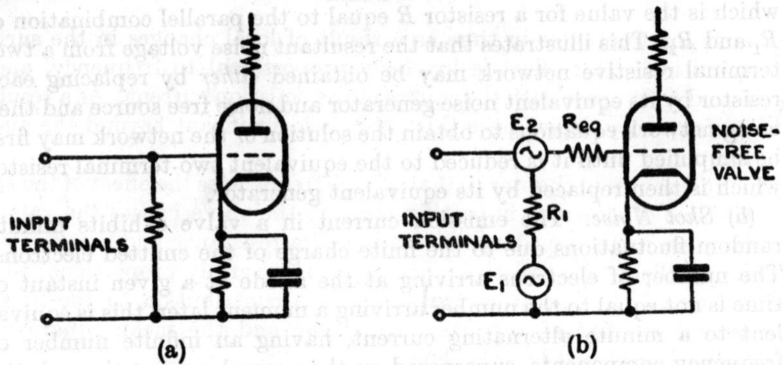

Fig. 14.3. Representation of thermal and shot noise.

If the valve is assumed to be noise free there will then be two noise sources in the grid circuit, namely E_1 and E_2. The former arises from the thermal agitation voltage from the resistor R_1 whilst E_2 represents the voltage from the equivalent grid noise resistor for the valve. The value of the total noise voltage in the grid circuit will be E where

$$\overline{E^2}=\overline{E_1{}^2}+\overline{E_2{}^2}=4(R_1+R_{eq})kT\triangle f$$

Additional Sources of Valve Noise

It is found that multielectrode valves produce a larger noise output than triodes. In say, a pentode, a portion of the current leaving the cathode goes to the screen grid, but this portion is not absolutely constant. There is a small random variation in the division or " partition " of the current from the cathode. This introduces further noise components in the anode current. The effect is referred to as *partition noise.* Values of the equivalent grid noise resistance R_{eq}, have been established for different types of valve operating under normal conditions. W. A. Harris[5] has given the value of R_{eq} for triodes as

$$R_{eq}=2{\cdot}5/g_m \quad . \quad . \quad . \quad . \qquad 14.3a$$

$$\text{and} \quad R_{eq}=\frac{I_a}{I_a+I_s}\left[\frac{2{\cdot}5}{g_m}+\frac{20I_s}{g_m{}^2}\right] \quad . \quad . \quad . \qquad 14.3b$$

for pentodes, where R_{eq} is in ohms. The mutual conductance g_m is measured in mhos and the anode and screen currents, I_a and I_s respectively are measured in amperes. Low noise valves have a comparatively low anode current, a low value of screen current and a high value of g_m. Frequency-changer valves are relatively noisy (and thus have high values for R_{eq}) because of their low effective value for g_m.

A further source of noise is produced by what is known as the *cathode flicker effect* which arises from the fact that at the emitting surface the emission fluctuates in time as a result of local changes in the surface condition. This effect is inversely proportional to frequency, and is found to increase with the square of the emission current. As a result of its frequency dependence this effect is insignificant beyond the audio-frequency range.

It is shown in chapter 10 that at high frequencies the effect of the transit time of electrons in passing through the valve causes the valve to have an input impedance consisting of a resistance and a capacitance in parallel. The resistive component is inversely proportional to the square of the operating frequency. Its contribution to the noise is similar to that of any other resistance and the mean square noise voltage produced by it is thus

$$\overline{e_{TN}^2} = 4kTR_I\triangle f$$

where R_I is the grid-cathode input resistance due to transit time. The noise produced in this resistance, however, is found to be greater than thermal noise in the same value of resistance at room temperature by a factor of five. The mean square noise-voltage for R_I is thus taken as

$$\overline{e_{TN}^2} = 5(4kT_0R_I\triangle f)$$

where T_o is room temperature, commonly taken as 290° A. A further point about this grid-cathode input resistance is that at frequencies at which the effect is significant, R_I is a real resistance which affects circuits external to the valve whereas the fictitious R_{eq} does not. The equivalent noise circuit of a pentode producing shot and transit-time noise is shown in Fig. 14.4.

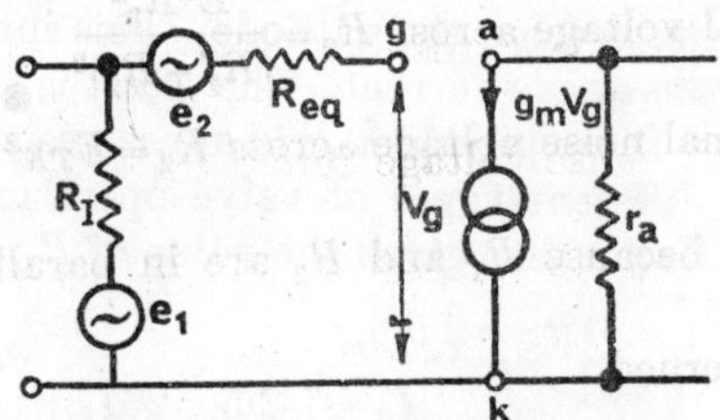

Fig. 14.4. Equivalent circuit for shot and transit-time noise in a pentode.

From Fig. 14.4 the total mean square noise voltage at the grid $\overline{V_g^2}$ is given by

$$\overline{V_g^2} = 4kT_0\triangle f[5R_I + R_{eq}] \qquad . \quad . \quad . \quad 14.4$$

Any external resistance, such as a grid leak connected across the input, would constitute an additional noise source across the input terminals.

Transistor Noise

The movements of the electrons and holes in a transistor produce noise as would be expected. Shot noise is produced by the flow of current carriers across the junctions and thermal noise arises from the resistance of the base, emitter and collector material. Additionally flicker noise is present at low frequencies and because of its inverse frequency relation is sometimes referred to as *1/f noise.* An equivalent circuit for these effects may be produced by the insertion of noise generators in the transistor equivalent circuit. The effect, i.e. the noise produced, varies with the operating conditions so that generalised equivalent circuits tend to become complicated.

In practice it is usual to deal with the effect of noise in transistor (or valve) circuits in terms of the circuit *noise factor*. This is considered later in this chapter.

Sensitivity and Signal Noise Ratio

If an amplifier has a gain such that the fluctuation noise produced at the input circuit appears at the output terminals, it is necessary to state the signal/noise ratio when the sensitivity is quoted, otherwise a statement as to sensitivity of the amplifier is misleading; thus if an amplifier is said to produce an output of one watt for an input of five microvolts this statement has little value if most of the output consists of unwanted noise.

If the circuit of Fig. 14.5 is considered to represent the connection of a generator to the input circuit of an amplifier, then

$$\text{Mean square signal voltage across } R_2 = \frac{E^2 R_2^2}{(R_1+R_2)^2}$$

$$\text{Mean square thermal noise voltage across } R_2 = E_{TN}^2 = 4kTR\,\Delta f$$

where $R = \dfrac{R_1 R_2}{R_1 + R_2}$ because R_1 and R_2 are in parallel as far as noise production is concerned.

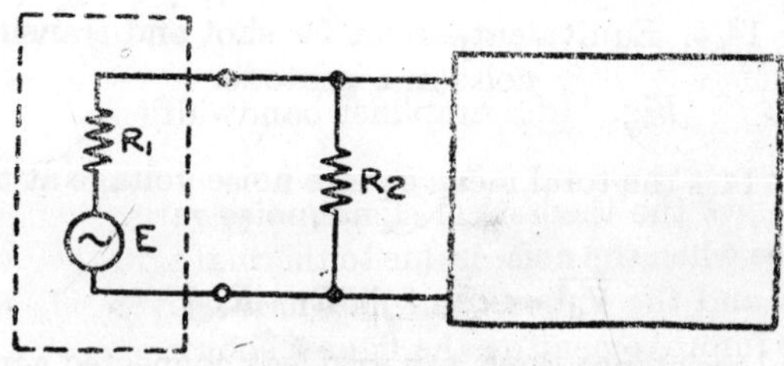

Fig. 14.5.

Hence neglecting shot noise for the moment, the signal/noise ratio is given by

$$S/N = \frac{E^2R_2^2(R_1+R_2)}{(R_1+R_2)^2 4KT\triangle f R_1 R_2}$$

$$= \frac{E^2}{4KTR_1\triangle f} \cdot \frac{R_2}{R_1+R_2} \quad . \quad . \quad . \quad 14.5$$

This last result shows that if the effective bandwidth, temperature, and values of R_1 and R_2 are known, then the theoretical signal/noise ratio for the circuit of Fig. 14.5 may be calculated for any magnitude of input signal.

In the form quoted a ratio of mean square voltages, i.e. a ratio of powers, has been used, and so for signal/noise calculations it will be necessary to obtain a value for the effective power bandwidth of the amplifier. For an ideal amplifier, the frequency response of which is shown in Fig. 14.6a, the effective power bandwidth $B = f_2 - f_1$. For an actual amplifier having a response as shown in Fig. 14.6b the effective bandwidth is defined as,

$$B = \frac{1}{G_{fs}} \int_{f_1}^{f_2} G_f df$$

where G_f is the power response at frequency f, and f_1 and f_2 are the frequencies at which the response becomes insignificant.

G_{fs} is the response at some standard or reference frequency in the amplifier pass band.

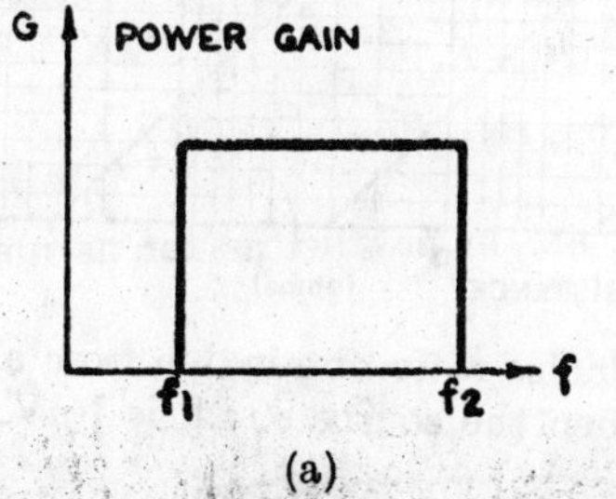

(a)

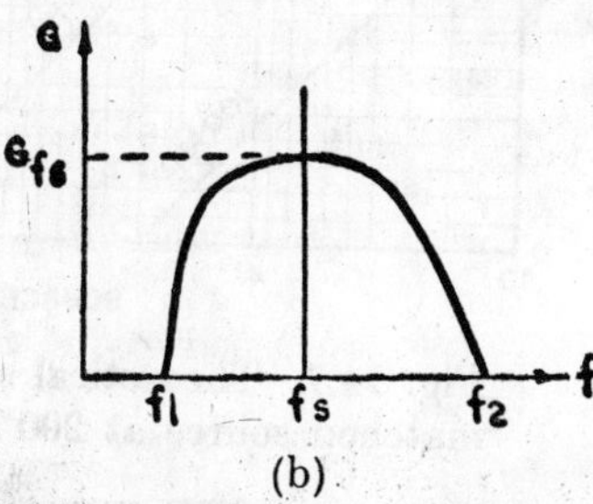

(b)

Fig. 14.6. Amplifier bandwidth.

Fig. 14.7 shows the theoretical signal/noise ratio obtainable from a matched source when the noise is due to thermal agitation at a temperature of 290°K and the source e.m.f. is one microvolt. If $R_2 \gg R_1$ there will be a 3 db improvement on the figures shown.

It will be seen that fluctuation noise gives rise to a voltage which sets a limit to the lowest level of input signal which can usefully be amplified by wideband high-gain amplifiers. For this reason the bandwidth of such amplifiers is restricted to the minimum necessary for the distortionless transmission of the signal. For the same reason the input circuit is usually of low impedance.

Except in rare cases, only the noise from the first stage of an amplifier need be considered, as the noise at the output terminals arising from the second stage will be below the first circuit noise level by a factor equal to the amplification of the first stage. In amplifiers where the input signal is not small the signal/noise ratio will be large and the effects of fluctuation noise need not be considered at all.

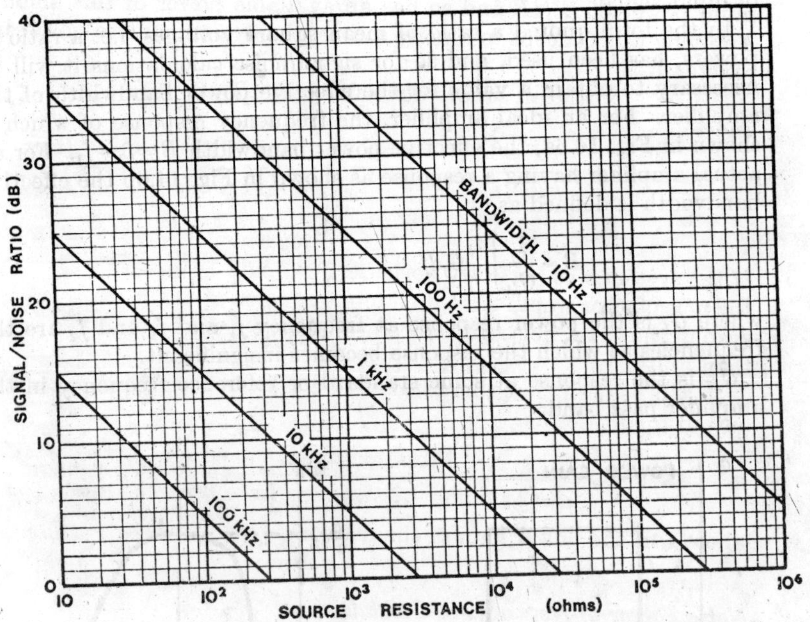

Fig. 14.7. Theoretical signal/noise ratio obtainable from a matched source at 290°K, when the source e.m.f. is 1 μV.

Noise Factor

A quantity known as the *noise factor*, or *noise figure*, is often used to specify the amount of noise introduced by an amplifier, communication channel, or in general terms, a network. The noise factor makes a comparison between the total noise power present and the noise power associated with the signal source resistance which represents a source of noise common to all networks and cannot be eliminated.

The noise factor, F, may thus be defined

$$F = \frac{\text{Available } S/N \text{ ratio at the signal source}}{\text{Actual } S/N \text{ ratio at the output}}$$

If both signal to noise ratios and the noise factor are expressed in decibels, the output signal to noise ratio can be obtained by subtracting the noise factor value from that of the input signal to noise ratio.

If P_N is the amount of noise power, which applied to the input of the system, would give the actual noise at the output with no other source of noise present, then

$$F = \frac{P_N}{\text{Actual noise power from signal source}} \qquad 14.6$$

Now any generator of e.m.f. E and source resistance R gives a maximum power of $E^2/4R$ and so has an available power of this amount. Applying this concept to a noise source, the available noise power in a resistor R is

$$[\text{Mean square noise voltage}]/4R = kT\triangle f$$

and so

$$F = \frac{P_N}{kT\triangle f}$$

$$\therefore \quad P_N = FkT\triangle f \quad . \quad . \quad . \quad . \quad . \quad . \qquad 14.7$$

If the system was perfectly noiseless P_N would be equal to $kT\triangle f$ and the noise factor would have its minimum value of unity. In a practical system the extra noise introduced causes the noise factor to be greater than unity.

It will be seen that the relation 14.6 may be expressed in terms of output quantities as

$$F = \frac{\text{Actual noise output power}}{G[\text{Available noise power from signal source}]} \quad . \qquad 14.8$$

where G is the power gain of the network.

Noise Factor of Networks in Cascade

Suppose two networks are connected in cascade as shown in Fig. 14.8 and that the noise factor and power gain of the first is F_1 and G_1 respectively, while F_2 and G_2 are the corresponding quantities for the second network.

If the input noise power to the first network, i.e. the available noise power from the signal source is N_s, then the output noise power from this network will be $F_1N_sG_1$. If it had been noiseless, the output noise power would have been N_sG_1. The extra noise added by the network is N_1, equal to $(F_1 - 1)N_s$. If the second network produces additional noise N_2, the noise output power from the second network is

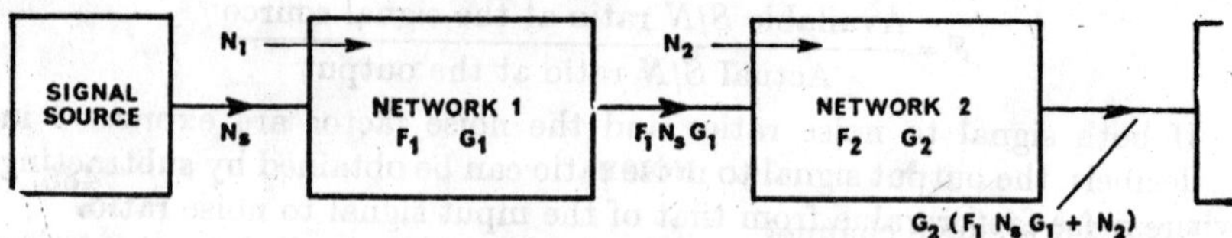

Fig. 14.8. Noise factor in cascaded networks.

$$G_2[F_1 N_s G_1 + N_2]$$

Using the definition of 14.8, the noise factor for the two networks in cascade is thus

$$F_{12} = G_2[F_1 N_s G_1 + N_2]/N_s G_1 G_2 \quad . \quad . \quad . \quad 14{\cdot}9a$$

$$= F_1 + N_2/N_s G_1 \quad . \quad . \quad . \quad . \quad . \quad 14.9b$$

The noise factor of the second network may be determined by making $N_1 = 0$ and $G_1 = 1$. Then equation 14·9a becomes

$$F_2 = G_2[N_s + N_2]/N_s G_2 = 1 + N_2/N_s G_2$$

Hence $N_2/N_s G_2 = F_2 - 1$ and so equation 14·9b then becomes

$$F_{12} = F_1 + [F_2 - 1]/G_1$$

An extension to n networks gives

$$F_n = F_1 + \frac{F_2 - 1}{G_1} + \frac{F_3 - 1}{G_1 G_2} \; . \; . \; + \frac{F_n - 1}{G_1 \; . \; . \; G_{n-1}} \quad . \quad . \quad 14.10$$

If the networks are considered as amplifiers (or the successive stages of one amplifier), these relations show that with appreciable values of gain the noise factor of the first unit is most important, on the assumption that the separate noise factors F_1, F_2, etc., are roughly similar.

Effect of Noise in Cascaded Channels

In many communication applications a number of links, or channels, may exist between the two terminal points. Commonly the links have zero insertion loss, i.e. the transmission loss is made good by an amplifier of suitable gain. When operated in this condition the end-to-end signal level will be independent of the number of links. The signal to noise ratio at the receiving end, however, does depend on the number of links and decreases as the number increases.

If n identical links are connected in cascade and each has zero insertion loss, equation 14.10 becomes

$$F_n = 1 + n(F_1 - 1) \quad . \quad . \quad . \quad . \quad . \quad . \quad 14.11$$

and so the output signal/noise ratio

$$(S/N)_{n\ \mathrm{OUT}} = \frac{(S/N)_{IN}}{F_n}$$

whereas for a single channel

$$(S/N)_{1\ \text{OUT}} = \frac{(S/N)_{IN}}{F_1}$$

$$\therefore \quad \frac{(S/N)_{n\ \text{OUT}}}{(S/N)_{1\ \text{OUT}}} = \frac{F_1}{F_n} = \frac{F_1}{1+n(F_1-1)} \quad . \quad . \quad . \quad . \quad . \quad 14.12$$

The output signal/noise ratio for the channel of n cascaded links is

$$10 \log_{10} [1+n(F_1-1)] \text{ dB}$$

Hence if $F_1 = 4$(6 dB) and $n = 5$, this quantity is $10 \log_{10}(16) = 12$ dB. Thus the replacement of a single link by five will produce a reduction of 6 dB in the S/N ratio at the receiving terminal. If the noise factor of the links is fairly large compared with unity equation 14.12 becomes

$$\frac{(S/N)_{n\ \text{OUT}}}{(S/N)_{1\ \text{OUT}}} \simeq \frac{1}{n}$$

or $(S/N)_{n\ \text{OUT}} \simeq (S/N)_{1\ \text{OUT}}/n$ 14.13

Signal/Noise Ratio Comparisons in Amplitude Modulation Systems

It was mentioned in chapter 12 that an advantage of single sideband transmission compared with a normal double sideband transmission was an improvement in the signal/noise ratio. This may be justified by the following argument which assumes that the noise distribution is uniform throughout the pass-bands considered.

Suppose that the modulation depth in the system is 100%. If now the carrier is suppressed at the transmitter and the levels then adjusted so that the transmitter output power is restored to give the same output before the suppression of the carrier, then clearly the power in the two sidebands is increased by a factor of 3 (equation 12.7). If a local carrier is introduced at the detector in the receiver it is clear that an improvement in the signal/noise ratio by a factor of 3 can be obtained at the receiver output, as the conditions at the detector are the same in the two cases.

Thus for the same total power output from the transmitter in the two cases

$$\frac{S/N_{\text{DSB SC}}}{S/N_{\text{DSB}}} = 3 \ (= 4{\cdot}77 \text{ dB}) \quad . \quad . \quad . \quad . \quad . \quad . \quad 14.14$$

As mentioned in chapter 12, double sideband suppressed carrier working is not commonly used, whereas single sideband transmission, utilising half the bandwidth, is employed in many applications.

In passing, it may be helpful to recall that the frequency spectra at various points in a normal amplitude modulated transmission are as shown in Fig. 14.9.

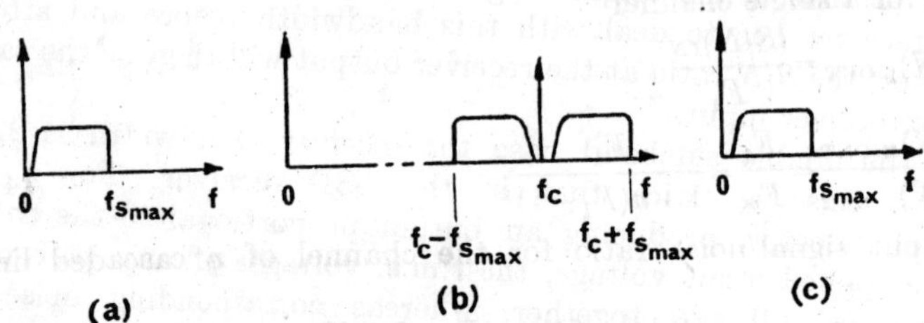

Fig. 14.9 (a) Original signal
(b) Transmitter output
(c) Receiver output.

Amplitude modulation of a carrier by a single sine wave gives a waveform which can be expressed (equation 12.4) as

$$v = A \sin \omega_c t + \frac{k_a A}{2} \cos (\omega_c - \omega_s) t - \frac{k_a A}{2} \cos (\omega_c + \omega_s) t$$

With 100% modulation the waveform amplitude varies cyclically between $2A$ and zero. If for convenience the power is assumed dissipated in a one-ohm resistor, the total sideband power is

$$\left[\frac{A}{2\sqrt{2}}\right]^2 + \left[\frac{A}{2\sqrt{2}}\right]^2 = A^2/4 \text{ watts}$$

If now the carrier and one sideband are suppressed and the remaining sideband voltage increased to the previous maximum voltage of $2A$, the power in this sideband is then $(2A/\sqrt{2})^2 = 2A^2$, that is an increase in total sideband power of eight times.

Having considered the transmitter it is now necessary to turn to conditions at the receiver. The comparison can be taken between the one sideband and the two sidebands of the double sideband system (with carrier). The frequency spectra for a single sideband system are shown in Fig. 14.10.

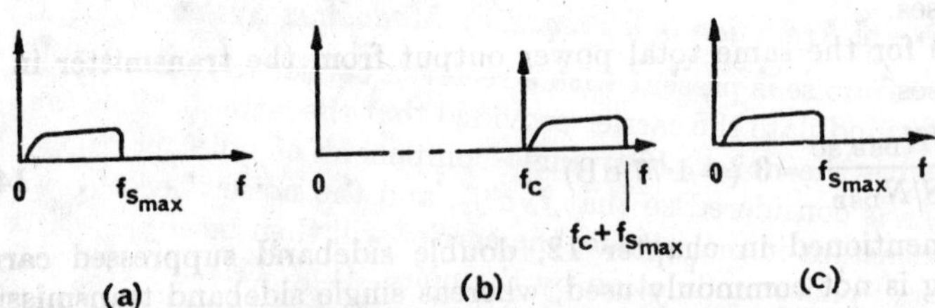

Fig. 14.10. Single sideband transmission
(a) Original signal
(b) Transmitter output
(c) Receiver output.

In the single sideband system the spectrum transmitted has the same width as that of the original signal occupying a bandwidth B. The SSB receiver has to deal with this bandwidth before and after the detector; the S/N ratio at the receiver output will then be the same as at the receiver input.

In the double sideband case the receiver bandwidth is $2B$ and so the noise is twice that in the SSB receiver. For a linear (diode) detector, producing an output proportional to the envelope of the applied input voltage, the r.m.s. voltages of any pair of side frequencies will add together, whereas corresponding noise components will not add coherently and so their mean square voltages will be additive rather than their r.m.s. voltages. The signal/noise ratio at the detector output is thus twice that at the detector input. This is valid at large values of signal/noise ratio. At small values (i.e. small signals) there is an addition to the noise power from interaction between the noise components.

Thus for the same transmitter peak output voltage (or peak power) in the two cases

$$\frac{S/N_{\mathrm{SSB}}}{S/N_{\mathrm{DSB}}}=8(=9\ \mathrm{dB}) \qquad 14.15$$

Single sideband transmission is used in radio transmission and in multi-channel line telephony. Owing to the relative complexity of the receiving equipment, however, it is not employed for broadcast operation, and its use is restricted to point-to-point services which are discussed in chapter 22.

If the conditions of radio propagation are such that the components of the modulated wave do not retain their original phase relationships but have random phase when they arrive at the receiving point the 3 dB gain on detection for the double sideband case is not available so that single sideband operation can then yield a further improvement (to 12 dB) in the signal/noise ratio.

Noise Reduction in a Frequency-Modulated System

If noise is present with a received carrier the noise can be considered to modulate the carrier provided that the latter is fairly large compared with the noise. If a single component of noise voltage of frequency f_N is considered so that $f_N \simeq f_c$, and the noise phasor is assumed to be constant in magnitude, the carrier will then be subjected to amplitude and phase modulation by the noise. (Fig. 14.11a.)

In a frequency-modulation system any amplitude change is suppressed in the receiving equipment so that the noise in the output will be that which arises from the phase modulation. Now it was

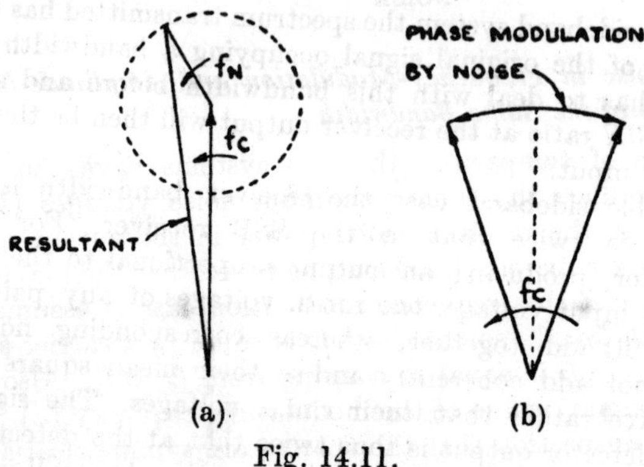

Fig. 14.11.

mentioned in discussing phase modulation that low modulation frequencies produce small frequency deviations while high values of modulating frequency produce large frequency deviations. Hence in a frequency-modulation receiver which gives an output voltage proportional to the frequency deviation from the carrier, the noise components nearest the carrier give the least output, and in general the noise output voltage is directly proportional to its frequency separation from the carrier. The frequency spectrum of the noise output will thus have a triangular distribution as shown in Fig. 14.12a.

In the amplitude-modulation case, the noise output will be that which arises from the amplitude modulation by the noise and this will produce a uniform spectrum as shown in Fig. 14.12b.

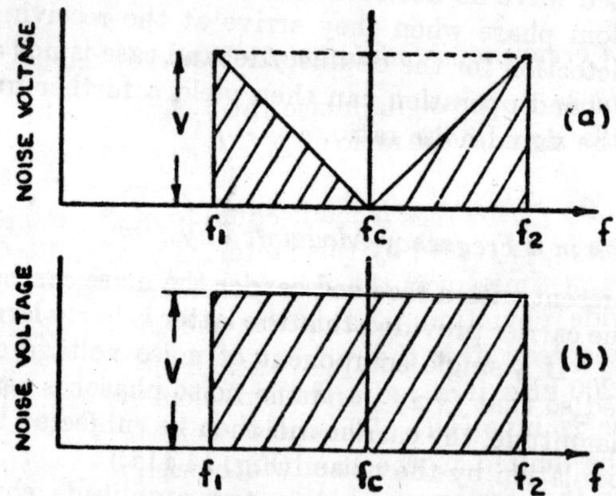

Fig. 14.12 (a) Noise spectrum in FM receiver
(b) Noise spectrum in AM receiver.

Comparison of Noise in Frequency-Modulation and Amplitude-Modulation Systems of the Same Bandwidth

If, for the sake of comparison the two systems have the same bandwidth and produce the same maximum noise voltages (V) as shown in Fig. 14.12, the resulting noise power in the output of the two systems can be compared. (It should be noted that the maximum frequency deviation in the frequency-modulation case is assumed to be equal to the bandwidth, so that $+\Delta f_c$ is equal to a carrier swing from f_c to f_2 and $-\Delta f_c$ is equal to a swing from f_c to f_1. Also Δf_c is equal to the maximum value of the modulating frequency f_s.)

It is obvious by inspection that the spectra are symmetrical about the carrier frequency so that a comparison can be made by considering half the bandwidth involved in either case, e.g. f_2-f_c. In the amplitude-modulation case the noise power between the limits of f_c and f_2 is proportional to

$$\int_{f_c}^{f_2} V^2 df = V^2(f_2-f_c)$$

In the frequency-modulation case the noise power is proportional to

$$\int_{f_c}^{f_2}\left[\frac{V(f-f_c)}{f_2-f_c}\right]^2 df = \frac{V^2}{3}(f_2-f_c)$$

Hence from these results the noise output power in the frequency-modulation case is one third of that in the amplitude-modulation case.

Use of Wide Deviation Frequency Modulation for Noise Reduction

A further improvement in the signal/noise ratio can be obtained if in the frequency-modulation case the ratio of $\Delta f_c/f_{s\,max}$ is made greater than unity.

Thus, suppose the ratio $\Delta f_c/f_{s\,max}$, is made equal to m and the bandwidth of the system is also increased by this factor. The signal voltage will then be increased m times over the case considered above (Fig. 14.12.). With this wide deviation modulation the signal power is carried by frequencies spread over the range $\pm\Delta f_c$ (perhaps a range of the order of 100–200 kHz if a radio transmission system with a high-frequency carrier is involved). The noise contribution in the output will however be limited to the bandwidth within the audible range of the carrier, so that for an aural output the signal/noise ratio will be increased by a factor of m^2. This improvement occurs provided that the carrier is greater than approximately twice the peak value of the noise.[6]

Wide deviation frequency modulation can be regarded as a system which utilises extra bandwidth to obtain an improved signal/noise ratio.

Noise Reduction in Pulse-Modulation Systems

If noise is present at the receiving point, in the form of fluctuation or other noise, a pulse train will have noise superimposed as shown in Fig. 14.13a. (This waveform will appear after the radio frequency carrier has been demodulated.)

If the noise is smaller than the pulse amplitude, the amplitude variation due to noise can be removed from pulse width and pulse position waveforms. This can be achieved by passing the train of pulses through circuits which limit or "slice" the pulse amplitude and establish a new zero reference. The train of pulses then obtained at the output of such circuits will then be free from amplitude variation due to noise (Fig. 14.13b).

Noise will not be entirely eliminated, however, by such limiting action. In addition to amplitude variation, noise causes the position of the pulse edges to vary by small random amounts. Thus if the pulses are width modulated the noise will cause a small variation of width. In pulse position modulation the pulse positions will be varied by the noise. (It should be noted that in practice the edges of the pulses are not vertical as shown in Fig. 13.13b but have sloping sides.)

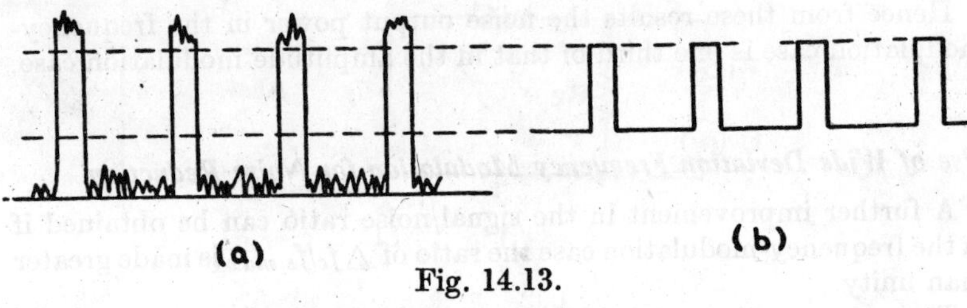

Fig. 14.13.

Pulse-amplitude-modulation cannot be subjected to "slicing" and since such a system does not give an improvement as far as signal/noise ratio is concerned, it is not greatly used. Pulse-code-modulation, does however, yield an appreciable improvement in signal/noise ratio.

This arises from the fact that although the bandwidth is increased (which in itself increases the noise level of the system) the input to the receiver consists of a series of constant amplitude, constant width pulses, and the receiver need do no more than distinguish between the presence or absence of a pulse to give correct operation. Hence relatively error-free operation can be secured even in the presence of high noise levels.

WORKED EXAMPLES

1. An amplifier has an input circuit which has a resistance of one megohm. If the effective bandwidth of the amplifier is 10,000 Hz, calculate the value of the thermal agitation noise voltage at the input terminals. The temperature can be assumed to be 17°C.

$$E^2_{TN} = 4kTR\triangle f$$

In this case, $T = 290°A$, $R = 10^6$, and $\triangle f = 10^4$

Hence $E^2_{TN} = 4 \times 1{\cdot}38 \times 10^{23} \times 290 \times 10^6 \times 10^4 = 1{\cdot}60 \times 10^{-10}$

or $\underline{E_{TN} = 12{\cdot}7\ \mu V}$

2. An amplifier has an input resistance of 100,000 Ω and is connected to a generator which has an internal resistance of the same value. The amplifier has a bandwidth of 10,000 Hz, and the generator has an e.m.f. of 100 μV. If the first valve in the amplifier has an equivalent grid noise resistance value of 40,000 Ω calculate the signal/noise noise ratio appearing at the output if the temperature is 17°C.

Assuming that the noise at the output arises solely from thermal agitation in the input circuit and shot noise from the first valve, the circuit to be considered is that shown in Fig. 14.14.

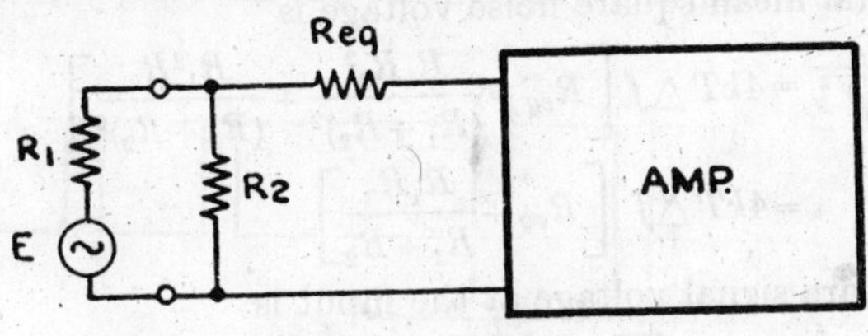

Fig. 14.14.

The signal voltage at the amplifier input will be the same as the voltage across R_2 if the first valve draws no grid current. In this case, the mean square signal voltage at the amplifier input is

$$= \quad E^2R_2^{\,2}/(R_1 + R_2)^2$$

The mean square noise voltage at the amplifier input is, $4kTR\triangle f$

where $R = R_1R_2/(R_1 + R_2) + R_{eq}$

The signal/noise ratio is then

$$= \frac{E^2R_2^{\,2}}{(R_1 + R_2)(R_1R_2 + R_1R_{eq} + R_2R_{eq})} \cdot \frac{1}{4kT\triangle f}$$

$$=\frac{(10^{-4})^2\times(10^5)^2}{(2\times10^5)(10^{10}+4\times10^9+4\times10^9)}\cdot\frac{1}{1{\cdot}60\times10^{-20}\times10^4}$$

$$=174=22{\cdot}4\text{ dB}$$

3. Explain what is meant by the *equivalent grid noise resistance* of a valve, and the *noise factor* of an amplifier.

The input impedance of an amplifier is equivalent to a resistance of 5000Ω. A signal source connected to the input terminals has an internal resistance of 4000 Ω. If the equivalent grid noise resistance of the first valve is 2000 Ω determine the noise factor of the amplifier.

L.U. Telecomm. Part III. 1965.

The circuit arrangement corresponds to that shown in Fig. 14.14. Each of the three resistances contributes a mean square noise voltage at the amplifier input as follows

$$4kT\triangle fR_1\left(\frac{R_2}{R_1+R_2}\right)^2 \text{ from } R_1$$

$$4kT\triangle fR_2\left(\frac{R_1}{R_1+R_2}\right)^2 \text{ from } R_2$$

$$4kT\triangle fR_{eq} \qquad \text{from } R_{eq}$$

and so the total mean square noise voltage is

$$\overline{V_N^2}=4kT\triangle f\left[R_{eq}+\frac{R_1R_2^{\,2}}{(R_1+R_2)^2}+\frac{R_1^{\,2}R_2}{(R_1+R_2)^2}\right]$$

$$=4kT\triangle f\left[R_{eq}+\frac{R_1R_2}{R_1+R_2}\right]$$

The mean square signal voltage at the input is

$$\overline{V_S^2}=E^2R_2^{\,2}/[R_1+R_2]^2$$

If there are no other noise sources in the amplifier the S/N ratio at the output is then

$$\frac{\overline{V_S^2}}{\overline{V_N^2}}=\frac{E^2R_2^{\,2}}{(R_1+R_2)4kT\triangle f[R_1R_2+R_{eq}(R_1+R_2)]}$$

Hence the noise factor F

$$=\frac{\text{Available } S/N \text{ ratio at the signal source}}{\text{Actual } S/N \text{ ratio at the output}}$$

$$=\frac{E^2}{4R_1}\cdot\frac{1}{kT\triangle f}\cdot\frac{\overline{V_N^2}}{\overline{V_S^2}}$$

$$=\frac{(R_1+R_2)[R_1R_2+R_{eq}(R_1+R_2)]}{R_1R_2^{\,2}}$$

$$= 1 + \frac{R_1}{R_2} + \frac{R_{eq}}{R_1}\left[1 + \frac{R_1}{R_2}\right]^2$$

In this question $R_1 = 4000\ \Omega$, $R_2 = 5000\ \Omega$, and $R_{eq} = 2000\ \Omega$. The noise factor is thus

$$1 + 0{\cdot}8 + 0{\cdot}5(1 + 0{\cdot}8)^2 = 3{\cdot}42 \quad \text{or} \quad 10 \log_{10} 3{\cdot}42 = \underline{5{\cdot}3\ \text{dB.}}$$

The alternative approach in terms of numerical values would be as follows.

The mean square noise voltage $\overline{V_1^2}$ due to the source of 4000 Ω alone is

$$\overline{V_1^2} = 4kT\triangle f\,.\,4000\left[\frac{5000}{4000 + 5000}\right]^2 = 4kT\triangle f\,.\,10^5/81$$

The mean square noise voltage V_2^2 due to the source, input, and equivalent grid noise resistances is

$$\overline{V_2^2} = 4kT\triangle f\left[\frac{4 \times 5 \times 10^6}{9 \times 10^3} + 2000\right] = 4kT\triangle f\,.\,4220$$

Hence the noise factor

$$= \overline{V_2^2}/\overline{V_1^2} = 4220 \times 81/10^5 = \underline{3{\cdot}42}$$

References

[1] Johnson, J. B.: "Thermal Agitation of Electricity in Conductors", *Physical Review*, 32, p. 97, (1928).

[2] Nyquist, H.: "Thermal Agitation of Electric Charge in Conductors", *Physical Review*, 32, p. 110 (1928).

[3] Van der Ziel, A.: *Noise* (Chapman & Hall Ltd., 1955).

[4] North, D. O.: "Fluctuations in Space-Charge-Limited Currents at Moderately High Frequencies", *RCA Review*, 4, p. 441 (1939–40).

[5] Harris, W. A.: "Fluctuations in Vacuum Tube Amplifiers and Input System", *RCA Review*, 5, p. 505, 1941.

[6] Crosby, M. G.: "Frequency Modulation Noise Characteristics", *Proc. I.R.E.*, 25, p. 472 (1937).

References for Further Reading

Van der Ziel, A.: *Noise* (Chapman & Hall, Ltd., 1955).

Robinson, F. N. H.: *Noise in Electrical Circuits* (Oxford University Press, 1962).

Rowe, H. E.: *Signals and Noise in Communication Systems* (D. Van Nostrand Co. Inc., 1966).

EXAMPLES

1. Explain why, with high-gain amplifiers, it is desirable to state the signal/noise ratio, as well as the input voltage required for a given output.

A microphone has a resistive internal impedance of 50 Ω and is matched by means of a transformer to the input of a high-gain amplifier. If this amplifier has an effective bandwidth of 20 kHz and the signal/noise ratio at the output is 36 db, find the e.m.f. generated by the microphone. The temperature is 17°C. State any assumptions made. (Boltzman's constant may be taken as $1{\cdot}38 \times 10^{-23}$ joule per degree Kelvin.)

L.U. Telecomm. Part III. 1962.

2. A signal generator has an internal resistance R_S and a resistive load R_L. Compare the ratio of signal/noise power available when R_L is first equal to, then very much larger than, R_S. A valve amplifier has an input resistance of 100 Ω and the first valve has an equivalent grid noise resistance, R_{eq}, of 250 Ω. A signal generator of 100 Ω internal resistance is connected to the input terminals of the amplifier and produces a signal/noise ratio of 20 db at the output. If replacement of the first valve increases R_{eq} to 400 Ω, calculate the new value of signal/noise ratio at the output.

L.U. Telecomm. Part III. 1963.

3. Discuss the effects of fluctuation noise in long-distance cable systems.

A line amplifier has an input impedance of $600\angle 0°\ \Omega$ and the equivalent grid noise resistance of the first valve is 100 Ω. The effective bandwidth of the amplifier is 4 MHz. Determine the necessary level of signal in a 600 Ω source to produce a signal/noise ratio at the output of 30 dB. The temperature may be assumed to be 17°C and Boltzmann's constant is $1{\cdot}38 \times 10^{-23}$ J/degK.

I.E.E. Line Comm. Nov., 1964.

4. Explain the terms *signal/noise ratio* and *noise factor* and discuss the effect of noise in a communication channel.

Derive an expression for the noise factor of two cascaded and matched networks in terms of their individual noise factors F_1 and F_2 and their power gains G_1 and G_2.

I.E.E. Line Comm. June, 1965.

5. State two sources of noise encountered in high-gain amplifier circuits, and briefly explain their origins.

The input impedance of a high-gain amplifier is equivalent to a resistance of 4 kΩ over its operating range. A signal generator is connected to the amplifier by a transformer which matches the internal resistance of the generator to the amplifier. With the generator set to give zero signal output, the noise power is measured at the output terminals of the amplifier. If the output noise power decreases by 4 dB when the secondary terminals of the input transformer are short-circuited, calculate the equivalent grid-noise-resistance of the first valve.

Determine the noise factor of the arrangement under normal operating conditions (i.e. with the short circuit removed from the transformer).

L.U. Telecomm. Part III. 1966.

6. Derive an expression for the overall noise factor of a combination of three two-port networks, connected in cascade, expressed in terms of the individual noise factors and gains of the individual networks.

A receiving system consists of a pre-amplifier connected through a length of cable to a main receiver. The noise factor of the pre-amplifier is 6 dB, while the corresponding values for the cable section and receiver are 8 and 13 dB. The attenuation of the cable is 8 dB, calculate the minimum gain required in the pre-amplifier if the overall noise factor of the system is not to exceed 9 dB.

L.U. Telecomm. Part III. 1969.

15

THE TRANSMISSION OF INFORMATION

IT has already been stated that the transmission of a continuous periodic current or voltage of constant amplitude and fixed frequency does not convey any information of " unexpectedness " between the transmitting and receiving points. In chapter 13 it was shown that modulation of a steady quantity, or carrier, provided a means for transmitting the desired information. For convenience, modulation was illustrated in terms of a sine wave, having a frequency low compared with the carrier. It is important to note however that continuous modulation in this way adds nothing to the received intelligence; one continuous wave has been replaced by three. " Information " passes when an unpredictable change occurs in the transmitted quantity, so that basically information, seen in this way, is a measure of unexpectedness occurring in the received signal. It follows that a waveform conveying information will contain irregular changes, and as a result of this, varying side-frequencies will be produced.

The present chapter presents a short discussion of information and its rate of transmission. This is preceded by a review of the bandwidth required for common types of signal and related topics not so far mentioned.

Phase and Group Velocity

This is an appropriate point to consider the velocity of propagation of the wave envelope of a signal. In chapter 4 the phase velocity for a steady sinusoidal wave was defined as

$$V_p = \frac{\omega}{\beta} \text{ (equation 4.17)}$$

where β is the phase or wavelength constant at the angular frequency ω.

The phase velocity, defined in this way, applies to an infinite sine wave, i.e. for steady-state conditions. In practice, if signals carrying information are to be transmitted, the waveform must consist of at least two, or probably many more component waves, and the quantity that is of interest is the velocity of propagation of the group. Thus, if the signal consists of a pulse, the velocity of propagation of the pulse is of more practical consequence than the velocity of the component sine waves.

If the transmission line, or transmission medium, is such that different frequencies travel with different velocities the line, or medium, is said to be ***dispersive***. In such a case, signals are propagated with a velocity called the group velocity V_g, which in general is less than the phase velocity.

The relationship between the phase and group velocity can be deduced by considering a signal waveform such as that shown in Fig. 15.1b. This waveform arises from the combination of two infinite wave trains as shown in Fig. 15.1a. If the two infinite wavetrains of slightly different frequency travel with the same velocity it is evident that their combination will also travel at the common velocity, so that in this case the phase and group velocities have the same value.

If the two wave trains now travel in a dispersive medium, the change in the value of β with frequency will give them slightly different velocities, V_p and $V_p + dV_p$, and relative movement will now occur between them. The train having the velocity V_p may be regarded as stationary while the other train moves to the right with a velocity dV_p. Now the maximum value of the group occurs when the maxima of the two individual waves coincide, and at the instant shown this occurs at the point P_1. At some short time later the next crest on the faster moving wave train will catch up with the succeeding crest on the slower moving wave train and a maximum will occur at the point P_2 so that in effect the group maximum has fallen back.

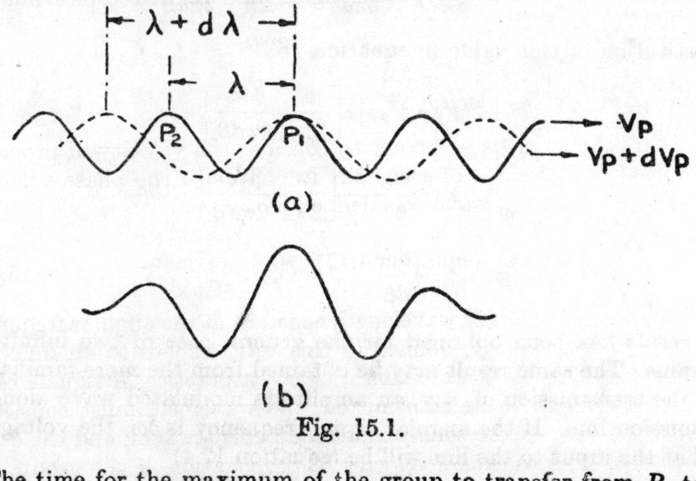

Fig. 15.1.

The time for the maximum of the group to transfer from P_1 to P_2 is $d\lambda/dV_p$. In this time the group maximum has fallen back the distance λ so that the velocity of the group is

$$-\frac{\lambda}{\frac{d\lambda}{dV_p}} = -\lambda\frac{dV_p}{d\lambda}$$

and the absolute velocity of the group V_g is given by

$$V_g = V_p - \lambda\frac{dV_p}{d\lambda} \quad . \quad . \quad . \quad 15.1$$

In a dispersive medium a small frequency change from ω to $\omega + d\omega$ will involve a change of wavelength constant from β to $\beta + d\beta$ so that the wavelength changes from

$$\lambda = \frac{2\pi}{\beta} \text{ to } \lambda + d\lambda = \frac{2\pi}{\beta + d\beta} \quad . \quad . \quad . \quad 15.2$$

As a consequence there is a change in velocity from

$$V_p = \frac{\omega}{\beta} \text{ to } V_p + dV_p = \frac{\omega + d\omega}{\beta + d\beta} \quad . \quad . \quad . \quad . \quad 15.3$$

Equation 15.2 gives $\quad d\lambda = \dfrac{2\pi}{\beta + d\beta} - \dfrac{2\pi}{\beta} = \dfrac{-2\pi d\beta}{\beta(\beta + d\beta)}$

and equation 15.3 gives $\quad dV_p = \dfrac{\omega + d\omega}{\beta + d\beta} - \dfrac{\omega}{\beta} = \dfrac{\beta d\omega - \omega d\beta}{\beta(\beta + d\beta)}$

Hence $\quad \dfrac{dV_p}{d\lambda} = \dfrac{\omega d\beta - \beta d\omega}{2\pi d\beta} = \dfrac{\omega}{2\pi} - \dfrac{\beta d\omega}{2\pi d\beta}$

By substitution of this value in equation 15.1

$$V_g = V_p - \lambda\left[\frac{\omega}{2\pi} - \frac{\beta d\omega}{2\pi d\beta}\right]$$

$$= \frac{\omega}{\beta} - \frac{2\pi}{\beta}\left[\frac{\omega}{2\pi} - \frac{\beta d\omega}{2\pi d\beta}\right]$$

$$= \frac{d\omega}{d\beta} \quad . \quad . \quad . \quad . \quad . \quad 15.4$$

This result has been obtained for the general case of two infinite wave trains. The same result may be obtained from the more familiar case of the transmission of, say, an amplitude modulated wave along a transmission line. If the angular signal frequency is $\delta\omega$, the voltage applied at the input to the line will be (equation 12.4)

$$V_{in} = A \sin \omega_c t + \frac{k_a A}{2}\cos(\omega_c - \delta\omega)t - \frac{k_a A}{2}\cos(\omega_c + \delta\omega)t$$

on the assumption that the modulating signal is a sine wave. If at the carrier frequency the phase change coefficient is β, then the phase change, or carrier phase delay, for a line of length l is βl. For the lower and upper sidebands the corresponding quantities are

$$\left[\beta-\left(\frac{\partial\beta}{\partial\omega}\right)\delta\omega\right]l \quad \text{and} \quad \left[\beta+\left(\frac{\partial\beta}{\partial\omega}\right)\delta\omega\right]l$$

The voltage output from the line is thus

$$\begin{aligned}
V_{out} &= A\sin(\omega_c t-\beta l)+\frac{k_a A}{2}\cos\left[(\omega_c-\delta\omega)t-\left(\beta-\frac{\partial\beta}{\partial\omega}\delta\omega\right)l\right] \\
&\quad -\frac{k_a A}{2}\cos\left[(\omega_c+\delta\omega)t-\left(\beta+\frac{\partial\beta}{\partial\omega}\delta\omega\right)l\right] \\
&= A\sin(\omega_c t-\beta l)+\frac{k_a A}{2}\cos\left[(\omega_c t-\beta l)-\delta\omega\left(t-\frac{\partial\beta}{\partial\omega}l\right)\right] \\
&\quad -\frac{k_a A}{2}\cos\left[(\omega_c t-\beta l)+\delta\omega\left(t-\frac{\partial\beta}{\partial\omega}l\right)\right] \\
&= A\sin(\omega_c t-\beta l)+k_a A\sin(\omega_c t-\beta l)\sin\delta\omega\left(t-\frac{l}{\partial\omega/\partial\beta}\right) \\
&= A\left[1+k_a\sin\omega_s\left(t-\frac{l}{\partial\omega/\partial\beta}\right)\right]\sin(\omega_c t-\beta l)
\end{aligned}$$

The envelope of the modulated waveform, described by the quantity in the square brackets, has a group velocity along the line of $\partial\omega/\partial\beta$.

If $\partial\omega/\partial\beta$ is not constant, i.e. β is not directly proportional to frequency, for the significant frequency band in a transmission system, the various components of a complex wave will be transmitted with different velocities and phase distortion will occur in the system.

MULTI-CHANNEL OPERATION

In any particular communication system the equipment can be arranged to provide efficient transmission with relatively small attenuation over a certain frequency range, or bandwidth. The extent to which this is utilised depends on factors which are mainly economic, namely capital and maintenance costs. The available bandwidth may be used to transmit two or more distinct and separate sets of signals. Any system arranged to do this is called a multi-channel system.

There are two ways in which the available bandwidth may be used for multi-channel operation, namely frequency division and time division.

(a) Frequency Division

A multi-channel system operated on a frequency division basis uses sub-carriers, each of which is separately modulated. The group

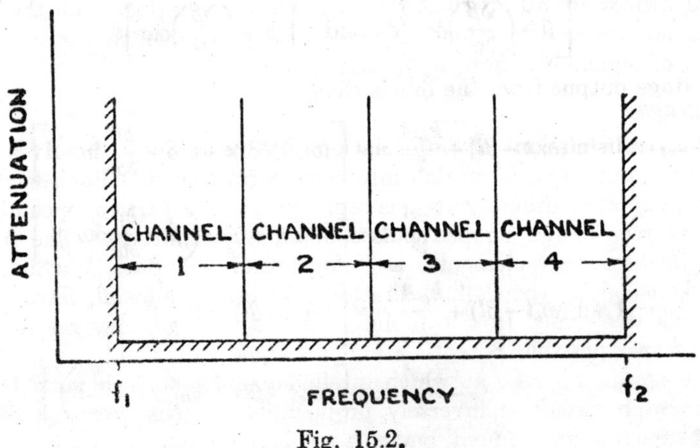

Fig. 15.2.

of sub-carriers is then used to modulate a final carrier of higher frequency so that at least a double modulation process is involved. In effect the total available spectrum of the system is split up into a number of contiguous bandwidths each of which is used as a separate channel. An arrangement of four channels occupying a spectrum between frequency limits f_1 and f_2 is shown in Fig. 15.2.

This method of operation is widely used in carrier current telephony and in voice-frequency telegraphy.

(b) Time Division

An alternative to frequency division is the process of time division. In this case each of the channels is permitted to occupy the full available bandwidth, but only for a fraction of the total time, so that in effect the whole spectrum is allotted to each channel in turn. This process was used in the early Baudot system of telegraphy and is applied to pulse systems of radio communication.[1,2]

BANDWIDTHS USED FOR VARIOUS TYPES OF SIGNAL

The main general requirement for the satisfactory transmission of signals in any system is that the bandwidth should be such that the principal frequency components of the signal are transmitted with little attenuation. Other requirements, which will not be considered here, are a reasonable signal/noise ratio, freedom from interference and crosstalk, together with a certain minimum of phase and non-linear distortion, all of which depend to a varying degree on the type of signal under discussion. The necessary bandwidth for different types of signal will now be considered.

Telegraphy

The transmission of information by telegraphy involves the conversion of the information into some form of code. Each letter of the alphabet, or other symbol, is represented by a particular combination of rectangular shaped pulses of equal amplitude. The morse code utilises two elements, a " dot " and a " dash " which are distinguished by their time duration. In other codes all letters and symbols are formed from combinations of five signal elements having one of two possible potentials and an equal duration.

The maximum rate at which intelligence can be transmitted over a telegraph circuit is inversely proportional to the duration of the shortest signalling element, and as a result telegraph speed is expressed numerically as the reciprocal of the duration in seconds of the shortest signalling element. The *baud* is the name given to the unit of telegraphic speed, so that the telegraphic speed in bauds expresses the number of shortest elements of signal which may occur per second. For a speed of one baud the duration of the shortest element is one second.

In the widely used voice-frequency system of telegraphy (see chapter 18) transmission is by means of an alternating carrier amplitude-modulated by the "telegraph waveform". The minimum theoretical bandwidth is equal to twice the highest sideband frequency used. If in fact only the fundamental alternating component of the telegraph waveform is transmitted this will be the maximum frequency of reversals. If the shortest time element has a duration of say 20 milliseconds, the transmission of a positive pulse of 20 milliseconds followed by a negative pulse of the same duration will give rise to a frequency of reversal of $10^3/40 = 25$ Hz. This will need an overall bandwidth of 50 Hz. The speed of transmission in this case is

$$\frac{1}{20 \times 10^{-3}} = 50 \text{ bauds}$$

so that for a.c. transmission in terms of an amplitude-modulated carrier the required bandwidth in hertz is numerically equal to the speed of transmission in bauds.

If a direct current carrier is used, in effect only one sideband is created so that the speed of signalling can be twice that possible with an a.c. carrier, when both arrangements have the same available bandwidth.

In practice, the voice-frequency system is usually intended to operate at a speed of 50 bauds. Each channel is allocated a bandwidth of 120 Hz to allow for the fact that the necessary bandpass filters do not have a sharp cut-off. If each character occupies $7\frac{1}{2}$ signalling elements and the average word and space is taken as being equivalent to six letters then each word occupies 45 signalling elements. At a speed of 50 bauds this is equivalent to

$$\frac{50}{45} \times 60 = 66 \text{ words per minute.}$$

With the bandwidth of 120 Hz this gives a " message rate " of 66/120 words per minute for each hertz of bandwidth used.

Picture Transmission

(a) *Picture Telegraphy.* The name picture telegraphy, or photo-telegraphy is applied to the transmission of still pictures. Some details of the process are given in chapter 18 and only an elementary consideration of the bandwidth involved will be dealt with at this stage.

In all cases of monochrome picture transmission the picture is analysed at the transmitter into a large number of small elemental areas. This process, referred to as "scanning", involves exploring the picture area in a series of lines, so that the degree of brightness is discovered at each point in succession. At the receiver a small light spot is set up and arranged to move synchronously with the scanning spot at the transmitter. The brightness of the light spot at the receiver is arranged to vary in accordance with the brightness discovered by the scanning spot at the transmitter so that the detail of the received image corresponds with the detail in the picture at the transmitter.

As the scanning takes place in terms of a series of lines (Fig. 15.3a), it is obvious that the resolution is proportional to the number of lines used; the definition along the lines depends on the ability of the system to distinguish between adjacent changes in picture tone. If the resolution along the line is to be the same as resolution from line to line, the transmitting system should be able to distinguish between adjacent dissimilar picture elements when the width of such elements is equal to the distance between the lines. On this basis, equal resolution will be obtained in both directions if a chequer-board pattern of black and white squares can be resolved. The transmission of a waveform corresponding to a light variation as indicated in Fig. 15.3b would involve the transmission of the square waveform of Fig. 15.3c; if only the fundamental component is transmitted the received waveform would be sinusoidal (Fig. 15.3d).

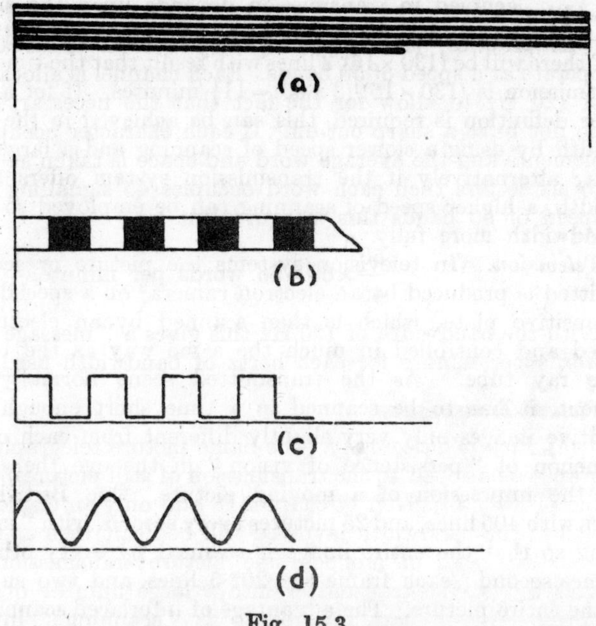

Fig. 15.3.

The picture is mounted on a circular drum which is arranged to rotate at constant speed and is displaced axially by a distance equal to the line width for every revolution ; scanning thus takes place in helical progression. By international agreement, the recommended speed of scanning is one revolution/second, and the index of co-operation (i.e. ratio of drum diameter to line advance) is 352, with a drum diameter of 66 mm (or 88 mm as a preferred alternative). With a drum of 66 mm diameter the standard definition is 352/66 or $5\frac{1}{3}$ lines/millimetre. The time for a reversal from black to white is thus

$$\frac{1}{66\pi \times 5\frac{1}{3}} \text{ seconds}$$

The time for a complete cycle from black to black is then $\dfrac{2}{66\pi \times 5\frac{1}{3}}$ which corresponds to a fundamental frequency of

$$\frac{66\pi \times 5\frac{1}{3}}{2} = 550 \text{ Hz.}$$

For line working, the picture waveform is normally arranged to produce amplitude-modulation of a 1,300 Hz carrier ; on the above basis, the bandwidth necessary is $1{,}300 \pm 550$ Hz.

occupied in transmission depends upon the size of the picture. If the scanning speed is one line/sec then for a picture 13 cm "long" there will be (130 × 16)/3 lines with result that the time occupied in transmission is $(130 \times 16)/(3 \times 60) = 11\frac{1}{2}$ minutes. If for any reason a higher definition is required, this can be achieved in the 1,100 Hz bandwidth by using a slower speed of scanning and a larger number of lines; alternatively if the transmission system offers additional bandwidth, a higher speed of scanning can be employed so as to use the bandwidth more fully.

(b) *Television.* In television systems the picture or scene to be transmitted is produced by an electron camera[3] on a specially formed light sensitive plate, which is then scanned by an electron beam, produced and controlled in much the same way as the beam in a cathode ray tube. As the transmitted scene normally involves movement, it has to be scanned in a time short enough to make consecutive images only very slightly different from each other; the phenomenon of "persistence of vision" in the eye then gives the viewer the impression of a moving picture. One British system[4] operates with 405 lines, and 25 pictures every second, with "interlaced" scanning so that the entire image is scanned by every other line at 50 frames/second; each frame has 202·5 lines, and two such frames cover the entire picture. The advantage of interlaced scanning is that it increases the apparent number of pictures per second and thereby reduces flicker in the received image.

As with the picture telegraph system mentioned above, the larger the number of lines the greater is the detail in the vertical direction; if there is to be as much detail in the horizontal direction as in the vertical, the picture elements must be of the same size as the distance between the lines. The most detailed pattern that can be transmitted is thus a chequer-board pattern of black and white squares as shown in Fig. 15.3b. With an aspect ratio (picture width/picture height) of 4/3 and 405 lines every 1/25 sec, the number of elements to be scanned per second is thus

$$\frac{405 \times 4 \times 405 \times 25}{3}$$

The time for a reversal from black to white in this case is

$$\frac{3}{405 \times 4 \times 405 \times 25} \text{ s}$$

The time for a complete cycle, black-white-black is thus

$$\frac{3 \times 2}{(405)^2 \times 4 \times 25} \text{ s}$$

which corresponds to a frequency of approximately 2·7 MHz. The lowest frequency to be transmitted must represent the slow variation in the general brightness of the transmitted picture. When there is no variation, as in the case of a still picture, a direct component is present. The bandwidth of the signals produced by a high-definition television camera thus extend from zero to about 3 MHz.

As the speed of scanning cannot be reduced in a television system, an improvement in definition can only be obtained by an increase in the number of scanning lines, which increases the bandwidth. It should be noted that the bandwidth is proportional to the square of the number of scanning lines. Applying the argument to a 625 line system gives a figure of 6·4 MHz bandwidth.

Speech

In the production of speech, movements of the mouth, lips and tongue can only occur at a comparatively slow rate, of the order of five movements per second. To secure efficient radiation by the mouth of the sound produced, the articulation movements of the mouth are made to modulate a higher frequency or " carrier " produced in the larynx by the vocal chords on the passage of air from the lungs.

The male voice pitch is normally somewhere between 100 and 150 Hz, whereas that of the female voice is somewhat higher. Differences in the various sounds produced arise from the positioning of the lips, tongue and teeth and also by resonances produced in the oral cavity, which acts as a multiple resonance chamber.

The analysis of speech waveforms shows component frequencies in the range 100 to 10,000 Hz with most of the energy in the lower end of the spectrum. The transmission of high quality speech thus involves a bandwidth of approximately 10 kHz. In multi-channel telephony the spectrum of speech transmitted is, by international recommendation, made sensibly uniform over the range of 300–3,400 Hz. This is located in a channel bandwidth of 4 kHz to allow for the fact that the bandpass filters used do not have an ideally sharp cut-off.

If normal conversation is assumed to take place at the rate of 100 words/min. and the conversation is assumed to be transmitted by a system with a bandwidth of 4 kHz the " message rate " is then 1/40 word/min/hertz of bandwidth used.

Narrow-Band Telephony

It was stated that a telegraph circuit under normal operating conditions can give a message rate of the order of 66/120 word/min/hertz of bandwidth used. Conventional telephony on the other hand, gives a figure of the order of 1/40 w.p.m. per hertz of bandwidth. Viewed in this way, conventional telephony makes less effective use of the bandwidth of the system than a scheme of coding, such as telegraphy. Special systems of telephony have been evolved in which speech may be transmitted in a fraction of the bandwidth which is normally necessary. In "analysis-synthesis" telephony[5], the frequency spectrum of speech is analysed into a number of channels, and only the relatively slow variation of energy which occurs in each channel is transmitted. As a consequence, such a system can be operated in a spectrum approximately one-tenth of the usual bandwidth.

The complexity and cost of terminal equipment of such systems renders them unsuitable for short and medium distances. On very long distance circuits, however, the possibility of more efficient utilisation of the available bandwidth makes narrow-band telephony more attractive.

Music

Some musical instruments produce a waveform which consists of a fundamental frequency with overtones or harmonics to a varying degree, while others produce a transient type of waveform. The harmonics decide by their number and amplitude the quality, or the "timbre" of the sound emitted by the instrument. Accordingly, it is necessary to transmit most of the harmonic frequencies as well as the fundamental tone if the quality of the music at the receiving point is not to be impaired. For high quality music transmission it is necessary to provide a frequency range extending from some 30 Hz up to 10 to 15 kHz. In modern practice in the transmission of music over long lines three speech channels are used, so that a bandwidth of the order of 12 kHz is available.

THE SAMPLING THEOREM

The previous sections have given an indication of the frequency spectra produced by the signal sources, which (except for the telegraph waveform) are assumed to generate continuous time functions. The pulse modulation systems in chapter 12 however are based on the underlying assumption that it is possible to "sample" a continuous time function in such a way that the discrete samples specify the signal completely. Obviously there is a lower limit to the sampling rate; information will be lost if the time varying signal alters between samples. The necessary relationship between the maximum frequency of the sampled signal and the repetition rate of the sampling pulses is given by the sampling theorem which may be stated as follows:

> If a function of time $f(t)$ contains no frequency components higher than W hertz, the time function can be completely specified by determining the ordinates at a series of points spaced $1/2W$ seconds apart.

A waveform period T, having no higher component than W hertz can be represented by a Fourier series with a fundamental component of $1/T$ hertz and a maximum harmonic frequency of W hertz, corresponding to a harmonic number of $W/[1/T] = TW$. As indicated in Appendix E, a Fourier series expressed as a number of sines and cosines, is defined if the coefficients of these terms are known. Two parameters are thus required to specify any particular harmonic,and a total of $2WT$ parameters (excluding the d.c. term) are then required to specify the waveform for each cycle of the fundamental of period T. Hence the minimum number of parameters required per second is $2W$.

A more general form of the sampling theorem for time functions in the spectrum from zero to W hertz shows that the sampling points need not be equally spaced as long as there is one sample located somewhere within each time interval of $1/2W$ seconds.

Reconstitution of the original time function, i.e. the signal waveform, is possible if the sample pulses are passed through a suitable low pass filter. The output obtained is of smaller amplitude than the original waveform $f(t)$ as the sampling with narrow pulses gives only a small fraction of the original energy. A further loss is caused by the removal, due to the filtering, of the high frequencies present in the sampled waveform.

The minimum pulse repetition frequency for the sampling pulses of $2W$ is a theoretical minimum. Practical systems employ a slightly larger value. Thus telephonic speech having an upper frequency of 3400 Hz is commonly sampled at a repetition frequency of 8 Hz.

The process of sampling is of extreme importance in time division multiplex systems. If the sampling rate is increased this decreases the time available between samples and so fewer channels can then be multiplexed.

THE RATE OF TRANSMISSION OF INFORMATION

It has been emphasised that any communication system which is to transmit information from one point to another must have some bandwidth, i.e. there must be a range of frequencies over which the attenuation can be made small. In this connection, a system would have zero bandwidth if it was only capable of dealing with an infinitely continuous sine wave of constant frequency, or even a number of such waves. Such a hypothetical system would not transmit information of any sort. If, however, the system has some definite bandwidth, information can be transmitted by the use of some form of modulated wave ; the amount of information depends on the bandwidth. This question was first considered in general terms by Hartley,[6] who suggested that the product of the system bandwidth and the time of operation might be considered as a measure of the ability of a communication system to transmit information. This is referred to as the *Hartley law*. An elementary illustration of the idea that both time and bandwidth are involved is given by the playing of a gramophone record. If played at its normal speed, the record may require a time of twenty minutes, while the frequencies involved may extend from 50–10,000 Hz ; if played at half speed, the playing time is doubled and the reproduced frequencies are halved, so that the information on the record could be transmitted in a channel of half the bandwidth required for normal playing ; conversely, if the record is played at a rate faster than normal, the information would be obtained in a shorter time but would occupy a greater bandwidth.

The reader should be aware that in recent years a concept has been evolved whereby information can be regarded as a physical quantity and expressed in units. In this sense, the word "information" is applied in rather a different way from that of everyday usage. Whereas one normally thinks of information as referring to ideas, the *information theory*[7] aspect of the word is not concerned with the significance, meaning, or truth of a message, but regards the amount of information on say, a printed page, as a quantity proportional to the total number of words and signs printed thereon. (This restricted interpretation of information will be used for the remainder of this section.) The aspect of information theory which concerns itself with communication, namely *communication theory* regards messages as selections of symbols, which may be classified into two groups. In the first category the symbols are discrete quantities, such as letters or other signs ; the other category of messages involves a sequence of values of some quantity which varies continuously. The irregular voltage waveform obtained from a microphone as a result of speech or music is an example of the second form. Communication theory applies to messages of either type, but is most easily illustrated in elementary terms for the case of messages made up of discrete symbols.

The process of communication of information can be considered as a process of selection ; at the sending end, each symbol is selected in turn from the set of possible symbols ; a series of selections of symbols constitutes a message, which is then itself a selection from all possible messages. At the receiver the message obtained is again a selection from the sets of possible messages. The smallest number of possibilities from which a choice can be made is two, i.e. when a "yes or no" code is involved. The reception of digits transmitted in a binary code is thus an example of a sequence of choices between two possibilities. Four possibilities can be reached by two binary selections, eight possibilities by three binary selections, and so on. In general, if the number of possibilities is a power of two, say n, then the number of binary selections necessary is $\log_2 n$. If the unit of information is taken as one binary selection, then the amount of information defined by the n possibilities is

$$H = \log_2 n \text{ (binary digits)} \qquad 15.5$$

The idea of communication as a selection process, and the use of a logarithmic measure of information was introduced by Hartley[6]. The binary-digit unit is convenient in practice, and the contracted name " bit " is used. The simple idea implicit in equation 15.5 may be extended to deal with messages in which n is not a power of two (also other forms of message), and the reader should consult the references for further reading at the end of the chapter.

No mention has been made of the disturbing effect of noise. As it is always present to some extent, no communication system is capable of reproducing a continuous message with complete exactness; the presence of noise causes a probability of error in the output from the receiver. The effect of noise in communication systems[8,9] has received a great deal of attention in recent work, and Shannon[10] concludes that the greatest quantity of information which may be transmitted in time T, over a system of bandwidth W, in the presence of noise is

$$WT \log_2(1 + S/N)$$

where S and N are the signal and noise powers respectively. The rate of transmission of information may thus approach the value

$$W \log_2 (1 + S/N)$$

A very brief and approximate justification of this result may be obtained as follows. Suppose, in a given system of defined bandwidth, there is a noise power of P_n watts and a signal power of P_s watts. The received signal will thus be $P_s + P_n$ watts and the problem is then to distinguish a signal amplitude of $\sqrt{P_s + P_n}$ volts in the presence of noise having an amplitude of $\sqrt{P_n}$ volts. On the average, the number of distinct amplitudes is thus the ratio of these two quantities so that the average available number of information states is

$$\frac{\sqrt{P_s + P_n}}{\sqrt{P_n}} = \sqrt{1 + \frac{P_s}{P_n}}$$

Any signal variation having an amplitude less than $\sqrt{P_n}$ volts will not then, on the average, be distinguishable from the noise, whereas a signal variation larger than $\sqrt{P_n}$ will probably be distinct. On this basis the maximum possible quantity of information in any interval or selection step will (from equation 15.5) be

$$\log_2 \sqrt{1 + P_s/P_n} = \tfrac{1}{2} \log_2 (1 + S/N)$$

The result of the sampling theorem shows that for a bandwidth W the maximum number of distinguishable intervals is $2W$. Hence during a time interval T the total information which may be transmitted is thus

$$WT \log_2 (1 + S/N)$$

and the average available transmission rate, in bits per second, is

$$W \log_2 (1 + S/N)$$

This indicates that the rate of transmission of information in a channel of communication is determined by the bandwidth of the channel and the signal/noise ratio; the amount of information is unaltered if an increase in W is accompanied by a corresponding decrease in the quantity $\log_2 (1 + S/N)$, i.e. bandwidth may be traded for signal/noise ratio.

References

[1] Bennett, W. R.: "Time Division Multiplex Systems", *Bell System Technical Journal*, 20, p. 199 (1941).

[2] Flood, J. E.: "Time-Division Multiplex Systems", *Electronic Engineering*, 25, p. 2 (1953).

[3] McGee, J. D.: "A Review of Some Television Pick-Up Tubes", *Proc. I.E.E.*, 97, p. 37 (1950).

[4] Wray, D.: "An Outline of the British Television System", *P.O.E.E. Journal*, 46, p. 59 (1953).

[5] Halsey, R. J. and Swaffield, J.: "Analysis-Synthesis Telephony, with Special Reference to the Vocoder", *Jour. I.E.E.*, 95, Part III, p. 391 (1948).

[6] Hartley, R. V. L.: "Transmission of Information", *Bell System Technical Journal*, 7, p. 535 (1928).

[7] Cherry, E. C.: "A History of the Theory of Information", *Proc. I.E.E.*, 93, Part III, p. 383 (1951).

[8] Earp, C. W.: "Relationship Between Rate of Transmission of Information, Frequency Bandwidth and Signal-to-Noise Ratio", *Electrical Communication*, 25, p. 178 (1948).

[9] Tuller, W. G.: "Theoretical Limitations on the Rate of Transmission of Information", *Proc. I.E.E.*, 37, p. 468 (1949).

[10] Shannon, C. E.: "Communication in the Presence of Noise", *Proc. I.R.E.*, 37, p. 10 (1949).

References for Further Reading

Cherry, E. C.: *Pulses and Transients in Communication Circuits* (Chapman & Hall, 1949).

Bell, D. A.: *Information Theory and its Engineering Applications* (Pitman, 1962).

Goldman, S.: *Information Theory* (Prentice Hall Inc., 1953).

Hershberger, W. D.: *Principles of Communication Systems* (Prentice Hall Inc., 1955).

Hancock, J. C.: *An Introduction to the Principles of Communication Theory* (McGraw Hill, 1961).

EXAMPLES

1. Determine by the method of Fourier analysis the harmonic frequency components of a symmetrical rectangular waveform and

show by means of a rough plot the approximation to the true waveform obtained if harmonics above the seventh are neglected.

L.U. Ext. Telecomm. 1945.

2. Explain what is meant by the terms *phase-* and *group-velocity*.

Derive an expression for the phase coefficient of a transmission line in terms of the resistance R, inductance L, and capacitance C per unit length of line. (The leakance is negligible.) Hence obtain expressions for the phase and group velocities in the line. Show that when the quantity Q ($=\omega L/R$) is large both velocities approach a value of $1/\sqrt{LC}$.

L.U. Telecomm. Part III, 1969.

3. Explain what is meant by scanning in a picture-transmission system, and describe the method by which the picture is translated into electrical signals in either (a) a high-definition television system, or (b) a picture telegraphy system. Make an approximate analysis to show how the frequency bandwidth required for picture transmission depends upon the characteristics of the transmitted picture, and give a numerical illustration for each of the two systems mentioned above.

L.U. Ext. Telecomm. 1952.

4. Discuss the frequency bandwidth required in line transmission when each of the following is transmitted:

(*a*) high-quality music,
(*b*) 12 telephone channels,
(*c*) 24 channels of voice-frequency telegraphy, each signalling at 50 bauds,
(*d*) 625-line television picture in which the picture line scan occupies 60 μs, and the aspect ratio is 4/3.

L.U. Electronics & Telecomm. Part II. 1964.

16

MICROPHONES AND SOUND REPRODUCERS

INTRODUCTION

A DETAILED discussion of microphones or sound reproducers involves an extensive consideration of acoustics. Such a digression is not possible because of limitations of space, nor is it wholely desirable in that acoustical engineering is a subject of study in its own right. Accordingly, this chapter will deal only with some definitions of the quantities involved, the analogies between electrical, mechanical and acoustical systems, and some elementary details of the electro-acoustic equipment used in communication work. For further information the reader should consult the references given at the end of the chapter, or any of the large number of works on sound or acoustical engineering.

Sound is the sensation received by the brain through the agency of the ear when a vibrating body sets up a wave motion in air, or in any other material medium; the word "sound" is also applied to the air vibrations, or sound waves themselves. Sound waves in air are longitudinal waves which consist of rarefactions and compressions and have a velocity of about 340 metres per second at normal room temperature.

The more important quantities encountered in the propagation and measurement of sound are as follows:

Sound Particle Velocity **(V).** The particle velocity in a sound wave is the instantaneous velocity of an infinitely small part of the medium, relative to the medium as a whole. Sound particle velocity is expressed in metres per second.

Sound Pressure **(P).** The sound pressure at a point is the alternating component of the total pressure at the point. Instantaneous, r.m.s., and peak values are used, as in the case of electrical quantities. Sound pressure may be expressed in newtons per square metre. With plane sound waves, the sound pressure P, is related to the sound particle velocity V, by

$$P = \rho c V \qquad 16.1$$

where ρ is the density of the medium, and c is the velocity of propagation in the medium.

Sound Energy Density **(E).** The sound energy density at any point is the sound energy per unit volume at that point, and may be measured in joules per cubic metre. For a plane wave,

$$E = \rho V^2 = \frac{P^2}{\rho c^2} \quad . \quad . \quad . \quad . \quad . \quad . \quad . \quad 16.2$$

where P, ρ and c have the same significance as used in equation 16.1.

Sound Intensity. The sound intensity at a point in a progressive wave is the rate of flow of sound energy per unit area normal to the direction of propagation. Sound intensity may thus be expressed in watts per square metre.

Loudness. The loudness of a sound is the magnitude of the auditory sensation produced by the sound.

Equivalent Loudness. It has already been mentioned in connection with the use of the decibel (chapter 4) that the sense of hearing operates on a logarithmic basis, as the ear considers fractional rather than absolute changes of sound energy. As the threshold of audibility varies with frequency it is clear that a simple ratio unit, such as the decibel, is inadequate as a loudness unit. To overcome this difficulty, the unit used is the decibel referred to an arbitrary datum at a specified frequency. The unit of loudness is the *phon*, which is based on a standard tone of 1,000 Hz with an r.m.s. sound pressure of 2×10^{-5} newtons per square metre as the reference level. The loudness of a sound in phons is then numerically equal to the sound intensity in decibels above the reference level, of an equally loud tone having a frequency of 1,000 Hz.

ANALOGIES BETWEEN ELECTRICAL, MECHANICAL AND ACOUSTIC SYSTEMS

When dealing with a transducer* which involves either electro-mechanical or electro-acoustic coupling, or both, it is often convenient and logical to treat the mechanical or acoustic system by the same mathematical methods as are used for the electrical system. The comparison of vibrating mechanical or acoustical circuits with electrical circuits enables equivalent electrical quantities to be determined so that the overall system can be considered in terms of a complete equivalent electrical circuit. Calculations of resonant frequencies, the

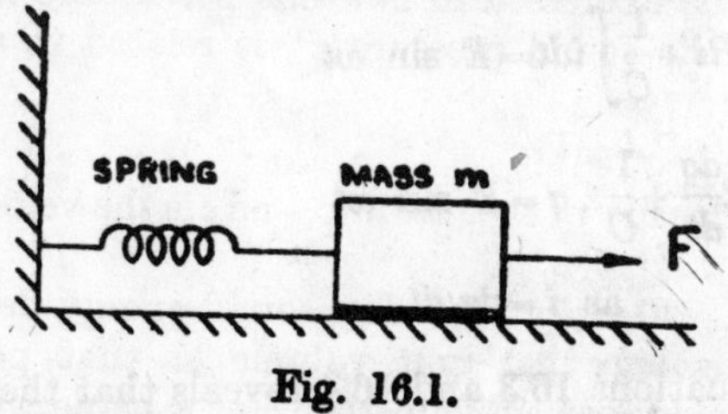

Fig. 16.1.

* *Transducer* is the general name given to a device which enables energy to flow from one system to another.

attenuation/frequency response, and other characteristics may thereby be simplified.

If attention is first of all confined to analogies between electrical and mechanical systems such analogies can be illustrated by the simple mechanical arrangement shown in Fig. 16.1.

If a sinusoidal force $F \sin \omega t$ is applied to a mass m, the latter will undergo sinusoidal displacement. The applied force is equal to the product of the mass and the acceleration, i.e.

$$F \sin \omega t = m\frac{d^2x}{dt^2}$$

If movement of the mass causes resistance to motion in the form of friction which is proportional to the velocity, the force which acts on the mass if then given by

$$F \sin \omega t - r_m\frac{dx}{dt} = m\frac{d^2x}{dt^2}$$

If in addition the mass is attached to a rigid body by a spring as shown in Fig. 16.1 the presence of the spring will exert a force which opposes the motion. If the spring is not stretched beyond its elastic limit, the force exerted by the spring will be proportional to its extension, i.e. to the displacement of the mass.

The complete equation of motion for the system thus becomes

$$F \sin \omega t - r_m\frac{dx}{dt} - s_m x = m\frac{d^2x}{dt^2}$$

where s_m is the stiffness of elastic constraint

$$\therefore\ m\frac{d^2x}{dt^2} + r_m\frac{dx}{dt} + s_m x = F \sin \omega t \quad . \quad . \quad . \quad . \quad 16.3$$

If a simple series circuit of resistance R, inductance L, and capacitance C, has a voltage $E \sin \omega t$ applied, the differential equation governing the behaviour of the circuit is

$$L\frac{di}{dt} + Ri + \frac{1}{C}\int idt = E \sin \omega t$$

$$L\frac{d^2q}{dt^2} + R\frac{dq}{dt} + \frac{1}{C}\,.\,q = E \sin \omega t \quad . \quad . \quad . \quad . \quad 16.4$$

as $i = dq/dt$.

A comparison of equations 16.3 and 16.4 reveals that they have the same general form. The first obvious point is that the mechanical force is analogous to the electro-motive force. The form of the equations shows that mechanical displacement is analogous to electrical charge. On this basis the time rate of change of displacement, i.e. the velocity, corresponds to electric current. Examination of the coefficients in the two equations shows that the elements in the mechanical system namely mass, mechanical resistance and the reciprocal of stiffness, or mechanical compliance, are respectively analogous to the electrical elements of inductance, resistance and capacitance.

In the electrical circuit the ratio of the applied electromotive force to the current which flows, is the complex quantity known as the impedance of the circuit. It follows that in the mechanical circuit the ratio of the applied force and the resulting velocity gives the complex mechanical impedance. For the arrangement in Fig. 16.1 this is

$$Z_m = r_m + j\left(\omega m - \frac{s_m}{\omega}\right) \quad . \quad . \quad . \quad 16.5$$

This consists of a mechanical resistance r_m and a mechanical reactance X_m which is the difference between the mass and stiffness reactances.

In the electrical *LRC* circuit the current which flows is given by

$$i = \frac{E}{Z} \sin(\omega t - \phi)$$

$$\text{where } \phi = \tan^{-1} \frac{\omega L - 1/\omega C}{R}$$

Hence for the mechanical circuit the resulting velocity is given by

$$V_m = \frac{F}{Z_m} \sin(\omega t - \phi_m)$$

$$\text{where } \phi_m = \tan^{-1} \frac{\omega m - s_m/\omega}{r_m}$$

is the angle lag of the velocity on the applied force.

Mechanical resonance occurs when

$$\omega m = s_m/\omega$$

i.e. at the frequency determined by

$$f = \frac{1}{2\pi}\sqrt{\frac{s_m}{m}} \quad . \quad . \quad . \quad . \quad 16.6$$

A mechanical system involving mass, resistance to motion, and compliance can thus be replaced by the electrical analogies of inductance, resistance and capacitance. When the mechanical elements are subjected to the same force the electrical analogies should be connected in parallel; whereas in the case of mechanical elements which suffer the same displacement the corresponding electrical quantities should be connected in series. Mechanical levers have in general the effect of transforming the value of the force (displacement or velocity) applied at one end to a different value at the other end ; the electrical analogue is the transformer. A rigid lever with a frictionless pivot thus behaves in a way which is comparable with an ideal transformer in an electrical circuit.

In the case of acoustic systems one is not so much concerned with the application of forces to rigid bodies, as the application of pressures to compressible fluids, such as air. On this basis acoustic impedance Z_a is defined as the complex ratio of the applied pressure to the resulting volume velocity (i.e. linear velocity multiplied by the area).

The quantities involved in the motion of a volume of gas, are the mass m, the effect of viscosity (and radiation) which produces a resistance to motion (r_a'), and the elasticity or stiffness (s_a). When the gas is subjected to an alternating force $F \sin \omega t$, the equation of motion is

$$m\frac{d^2x}{dt^2} + r_a'\frac{dx}{dt} + s_a x = F \sin \omega t$$

If the gas is assumed to have a cylindrical volume and is contained in a tube of cross-sectional area A so that the instantaneous displacement over any cross-section of gas is uniform (although varying from section to section) then X can be written for xA and P for F/A. The equation of motion can then be expressed as,

$$\frac{m}{A^2}\frac{d^2X}{dt^2} + \frac{r_a'}{A^2}\frac{dX}{dt} + \frac{s_a}{A^2}X = P \sin \omega t \quad . \quad . \quad . \quad 16.7$$

If, as has been suggested, pressure is considered as being analogous to electromotive force this equation has the same form as the equation for the electrical circuit in which an inductance, resistance and capacitance are connected in series (equation 16.4). The quantity X (which has the dimensions of a volume) is described mathematically in the same way as electrical charge in the equation for the electrical circuit. The rate of volume displacement, or volume current as it is sometimes called, is thus analogous to electric current. Comparison of the coefficients of equations 16.7 and 16.4 then shows that the quantities m/A^2, r_a'/A^2 and A^2/s_a are respectively analogous to inductance, resistance and capacitance in an electrical circuit. The quantity $M = m/A^2$ is given the name inertance ; whereas in a mechanical system the effect of inertia is represented by a mass, in an acoustical system inertance is represented by the presence of fluid in a tube in which all the particles move with the same phase when a pressure is applied. Inertance represents the reaction of the medium surrounding a source of sound on the motion of the source. The quantity $r_a = r_a'/A^2$ is the acoustic resistance. Mechanical resistance is caused by friction ; acoustic resistance is caused by viscosity. Hence mechanical resistance can be represented as friction between sliding surfaces and acoustic resistance can be represented by small orifices (which cause dissipation of energy when fluid is forced through them). The quantity $C_A = A^2/s_a$ is the acoustic capacitance. While mechanical capacitance (or compliance) can be represented physically by a spring, acoustic capacitance can be represented by an enclosed volume which acts as a stiffness. The acoustical impedance of the arrangement shown in Fig. 16.2 is given by

$$Z_a = r_a + j\left(\frac{\omega m}{A^2} - \frac{s_a}{A^2\omega}\right) \quad . \quad . \quad . \quad 16.8$$

Acoustical resonance occurs when

$$\frac{\omega m}{A^2} = \frac{s_a}{A^2\omega}$$

i.e. at the frequency determined by

$$f = \frac{1}{2\pi}\sqrt{\frac{s_a}{m}} \quad . \quad . \quad . \quad . \quad 16.9$$

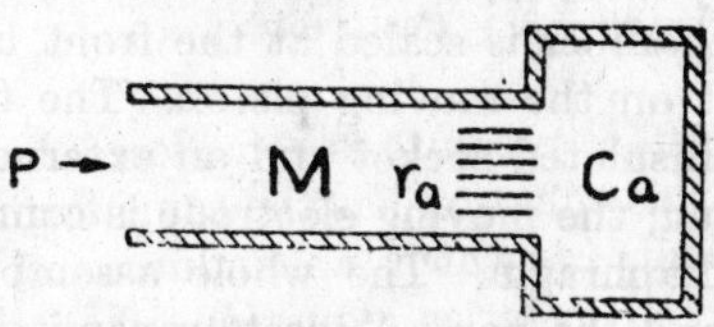

Fig. 16.2.

The mechanical and acoustical quantities which correspond to certain electrical quantities are shown in Table 16.1 below. The resistance in all three systems is the real part of the impedance, while the reactance is the imaginary part.

MICROPHONES

A microphone may be defined as an electro-acoustic device by means of which sound waves are converted into electrical energy ; in telephonic use, the name "transmitter" is often employed. Of all the various types of microphone that have been evolved the carbon microphone is most widely used because of its high sensitivity.

TABLE 16.1

Electrical System	Mechanical System		Acoustical System	
Quantity	*Quantity*	*Dimensions*	*Quantity*	*Dimensions*
Electromotive Force	Force	MLT^{-2}	Pressure	$ML^{-1}T^{-2}$
Charge	Displacement	L	Volume Displacement	L^3
Current	Velocity	LT^{-1}	Volume Current	L^3T^{-1}
Inductance	Mass	M	Inertance	ML^{-4}
Capacitance	Compliance	$M^{-1}T^2$	Capacitance	$M^{-1}L^4T^2$
Impedance	Impedance	MT^{-1}	Impedance	$ML^{-4}T^{-1}$

The Carbon Microphone

The basic features of a carbon microphone are shown in Fig. 16.3a. In effect, two carbon electrodes are enclosed in a chamber almost filled with carbon granules. One electrode is attached to a light metal piston which is fixed to the aluminium diaphragm, while the other electrode is rigidly fixed to, but insulated from, the rear of the granule chamber. This chamber is sealed at the front by silk washers which form a sliding fit on the moving piston. The fixed electrode makes contact with an insulated socket and an external connection is made by means of a plug; the moving electrode is connected to the case via the aluminium diaphragm. The whole assembly is inserted into a moulded casing and the name " inset transmitter " is applied to this particular form of construction.

The force acting on the diaphragm is proportional to the air pressure of the incident sound waves. Movement of the diaphragm gives rise to a variation of pressure on the carbon granules and this causes a change in the resistance of the instrument. The variation of resistance between the electrodes arises from a change in the area of contact between the particles ; the carbon granules have sharp edges and points, and it is the deformation of these edges when pressed into the surfaces of other granules that accounts for nearly all the change in resistance ; in addition there is a very small change of resistance due to the fact that the resistance of carbon decreases with increase of pressure. When an alternating sound pressure is incident upon the diaphragm the microphone behaves as a variable resistance which alternates about a mean value. If a source of direct current (E) is connected in series with a load resistance R, as in Fig. 16.3b, a steady current will flow

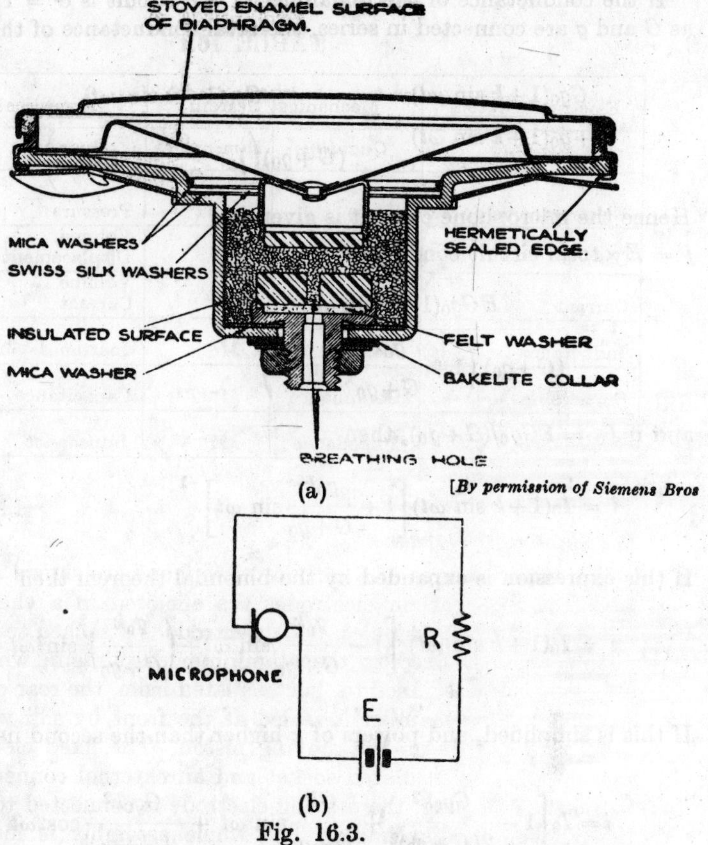

Fig. 16.3.

round the circuit, in the absence of any external pressure on the diaphragm. If an alternating sound pressure is then applied, the microphone resistance will vary, and the current in the circuit will have an alternating component. In effect, the process can be regarded as amplitude-modulation of the direct current by the incident sound waves.

An approximate simplified theory of operation can be obtained if it is assumed that the conductance of the microphone varies sinusoidally with a sinusoidal pressure applied to the diaphragm. This is reasonably true for small displacements of the diaphragm. On this basis, the conductance of the microphone may be expressed as $g = g_0(1 + k \sin \omega t)$ where g_0 is the static conductance of the instrument, and k is a coefficient which is less than unity and depends on the maximum sound pressure applied; $\omega/2\pi$ is the frequency of the applied sinusoidal pressure.

If the conductance of the remainder of the circuit is $G = 1/R$, then as G and g are connected in series, the total conductance of the circuit is

$$\frac{Gg_0(1+k\sin\omega t)}{G+g_0(1+k\sin\omega t)} = \frac{Gg_0(1+k\sin\omega t)}{(G+g_0)\left(1+\dfrac{g_0k}{G+g_0}\sin\omega t\right)}$$

Hence the microphone current is given by
$i = E\times$total circuit conductance

$$i = \frac{EGg_0(1+k\sin\omega t)}{(G+g_0)\left(1+\dfrac{g_0k}{G+g_0}\sin\omega t\right)}$$

and if $I_0 = EGg_0/(G+g_0)$, then

$$i = I_0(1+k\sin\omega t)\left[1+\frac{g_0k}{G+g_0}\sin\omega t\right]^{-1}$$

If this expression is expanded by the binomial theorem then

$$i = I_0(1+k\sin\omega t)\left[1-\frac{g_0k}{G+g_0}\sin\omega t+\left(\frac{g_0k}{G+g_0}\right)^2\sin^2\omega t-\ldots\right] \quad . \quad . \quad . \quad 16.10$$

If this is simplified, and powers of k higher than the second neglected,

$$i = I_0\left[1-\frac{Gg_0k^2}{2(G+g_0)^2}+\frac{Gk}{G+g_0}\sin\omega t+\frac{Gg_0k^2}{2(G+g_0)^2}\cos 2\omega t\right] \quad . \quad . \quad . \quad 16.11$$

The third term is the alternating current which is required, while the last term is an undesired second harmonic component of current.

It will be seen that the amplitude of the fundamental component of current is proportional to the direct component I_0. An increase in I_0 will thus increase the sensitivity. The steady voltage which can be applied to the microphone is limited however by arcing which takes place between the granules. This gives rise to a " frying " noise in the output, and in practice only a few volts can be applied to the microphone terminals. The mean value of the instrument resistance is of the order of 50 ohms and the steady current in normal operation is roughly 50 mA.

If the maximum power transfer theorem is applied to the microphone it may be shown that the maximum power output is obtained when the load resistance R is matched to the static resistance r_0 $(=1/g_0)$. This can be achieved by interposing a transformer between the microphone and load R. If, for purposes of illustration, the microphone is assumed to have a mean resistance of 50 Ω and it is desired to match the microphone to a line of 600 Ω characteristic impedance, a step-up transformer to the microphone to the line would be required with a turns ratio of $1 : \sqrt{600/50}$.

It should be noted that the electrical output may be greater than the sound power applied to the diaphragm. This arises from the fact that the energy is provided by the direct current source, and is only controlled by the sound energy.

A disadvantage of the carbon microphone is the relatively high background noise level, which arises from the random resistance changes which the carbon particles offer to the direct current. Another disadvantage is the limited frequency response of this form of carbon microphone ; the output falls rapidly below 200 Hz and above 3,500 Hz due to the limitations of the mechanical construction. The response between these frequencies is far from uniform if a constant sound pressure of variable frequency is applied. In particular between 100 Hz and 2000 Hz there is a main resonance peak which depends on the values of the mechanical constants of the design. As a result, a considerable amount of frequency distortion occurs. Amplitude distortion is also present as the output does not vary linearly with the applied sound pressure.

Other Microphones

The basic constructional features of some other microphones will now be considered very briefly.

(a) Capacitor Microphone. This form of microphone operates by virtue of a change in capacitance when subjected to incident sound waves. A simplified representation of the instrument is shown in Fig. 16.4a.

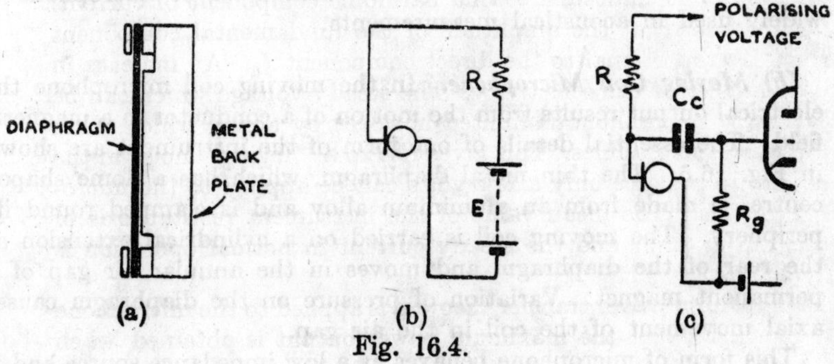

Fig. 16.4.

Essentially the instrument consists of a thin light metal alloy diaphragm and a heavy back plate ; these function as the electrodes of a capacitor. The stretched diaphragm, of circular shape, is clamped round its edge, positioned in front of, and insulated from the back plate so as to leave a narrow air space between. With the circuit of Fig. 16.4b, an alternating sound pressure incident on the diaphragm gives rise to an alternating change of capacitance which causes an alternating voltage to be developed across the microphone, provided that the resistor R is large enough to prevent appreciable change in the charge on the electrodes of the instrument. The voltage changes across the microphone, due to sound pressure changes, are equal and opposite in sign to the voltage changes across the load resistor R. The steady voltage E is of the order of 100 V or more, while the load resistor usually has a value of the order of 10 MΩ.

The capacitor microphone gives a very low output compared with the carbon microphone and the output requires amplification. The connections to an amplifier are as shown in Fig. 16.4c ; the effective load is the parallel combination of the resistors R and R_g. The value of the coupling capacitor C_c is chosen so that its reactance is small at the lowest operating frequency. The effect of shunt capacitance across the load resistance is to increase the total capacitance. As the output is proportional to the change of capacitance with respect to the total capacitance, added shunt capacitance decreases the output ; frequency distortion does not occur as the internal impedance of the microphone, viewed as a source, is capacitive. To avoid loss in sensitivity the amplifier is normally coupled by very short leads ; the first stage is often mounted directly at the rear of the microphone.

The capacitor microphone is relatively free from non-linear distortion and has a fairly uniform frequency response ; a certain amount of harmonic distortion occurs as the increase in capacitance for a given inward displacement of the diaphragm is not equal to the decrease for an equal outward displacement. This form of microphone is widely used in acoustical measurements.

(b) Moving Coil Microphone. In the moving coil microphone the electrical output results from the motion of a conductor in a magnetic field. The essential details of one form of the instrument are shown in Fig. 16.5. The thin metal diaphragm, which has a dome shaped centre, is made from an aluminium alloy and is clamped round its periphery. The moving coil is carried on a cylindrical extension at the rear of the diaphragm and moves in the annular air gap of a permanent magnet. Variation of pressure on the diaphragm causes axial movement of the coil in the air gap.

This form of microphone behaves as a low impedance source and is

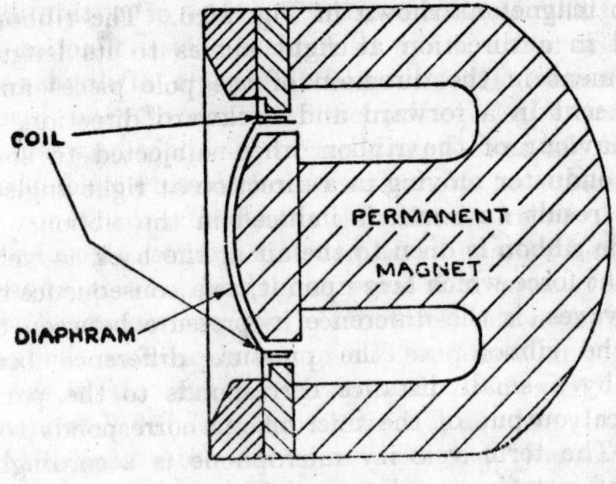

Fig. 16.5.

coupled to external circuits by means of a transformer of appropriate ratio. The sensitivity, while appreciably less than that of the carbon type, is greater than that obtained with the capacitor microphone.

A variation in construction in the moving coil instrument is the use of a paper or metal cone in place of the metal diaphragm shown. With a paper cone the moving coil microphone is very similar in form to the moving coil loudspeaker (see Fig. 16.12) although it is smaller in size.

(c) Ribbon Microphone. In this type of microphone a piece of thin aluminium foil or " ribbon " is suspended between the poles of a

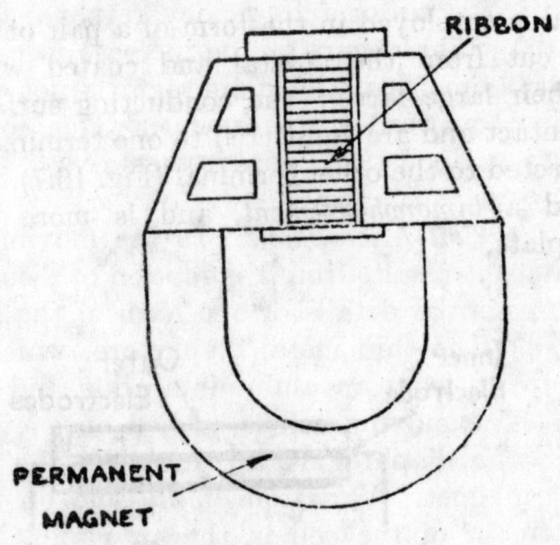

Fig. 16.6.

permanent magnet as shown in Fig. 16.6. The ribbon is normally corrugated in a direction at right angles to its length to prevent side movement in the direction of the pole pieces and yet permit free movement in a forward and backward direction.

The behaviour of the ribbon when subjected to sound waves is that of a conductor moving in a direction at right angles to magnetic flux; as a result an e.m.f. is induced in the ribbon.

When the ribbon is open to the air at the back as well as the front the resultant force which acts upon it, as a consequence of the passage of sound waves, is the difference in pressure between the front and back of the ribbon; as the pressure difference between points separated by a small distance corresponds to the particle velocity the electrical output of the microphone corresponds to the particle velocity. The term velocity microphone is accordingly applied to this type of instrument when both sides of the ribbon are exposed to the air.

Such a microphone has directional characteristics and the plot of the response in a horizontal plane is roughly that of a figure eight. The ribbon microphone is a low impedance source; compared with the moving coil type the high frequency response is improved but the sensitivity is lower.

(d) Crystal Microphone. Crystals of quartz, Rochelle salt and a few other materials exhibit piezo-electric effects whereby the application of mechanical pressure to the crystal gives rise to the production of an e.m.f. between the faces. Rochelle salt (sodium potassium tartrate) is much more sensitive than quartz, and is the material often used in microphones.

The material is employed in the form of a pair of thin plates which are carefully cut from the crystal and coated with a conducting material on their large faces; the conducting surfaces on the inner faces are in contact and are connected to one terminal, while the outer faces are connected to the other terminal (Fig. 16.7). Such an arrangement is called a *bimorph element*, and is more sensitive than a single crystal plate.

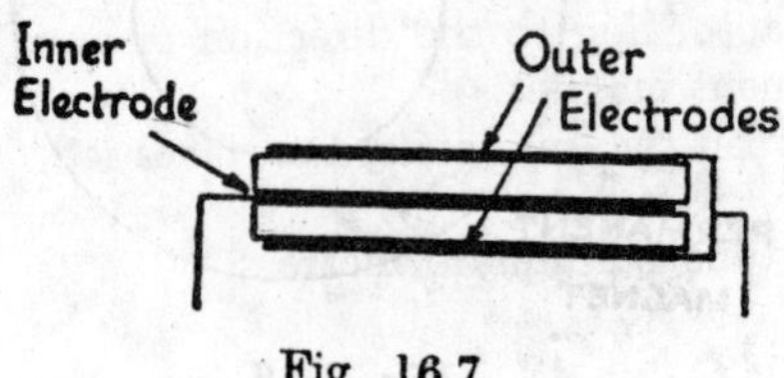

Fig. 16.7.

One form of crystal microphone employs a pair of bimorph elements fixed in a frame parallel to each other with a small distance between them; the inner cavity is airtight and this arrangement is referred to as a sound cell. An alternative form is arranged so that the sound pressure acts upon a diaphragm rather than the crystal unit; this form gives a larger output than the directly actuated type as the diaphragm may be designed as a coupling unit between the relatively low impedance of the air and the high impedance of the crystal.

Crystal microphones have a large capacitive-impedance and may be connected directly to the grid input circuit of an amplifier.

SOUND REPRODUCERS

Sound reproducers comprise the various types of telephone "receivers", and loudspeakers which act as radiators of sound energy. There are basic differences which arise from the fact that the telephone receiver is designed to operate when held close to the ear, whereas loudspeakers are of course required to operate into free air, and are normally designed to produce a larger acoustical output. When held against the ear the receiver is not so much a radiator of sound energy as a generator of sound pressures within a cavity, of dimensions small compared with the wavelength of vibration.

A telephone receiver or loudspeaker may be driven by electromagnetic, electrostatic or piezo-electric means, but in practice the first mentioned type is most commonly employed.

THE MOVING-IRON TELEPHONE RECEIVER

The moving-iron form of electromagnetic receiver is employed in telephone systems and is the only type that will be discussed. In its modern form the instrument is a development of the type invented by Graham Bell. The principle of operation can be illustrated with reference to the magnetic circuit (Fig. 16.8). The receiver consists essentially of a permanent magnet provided with two pole pieces, each of which carries a coil; a circular diaphragm of iron cobalt alloy, about 2 in. in diameter, is positioned in front of the pole faces and clamped round its edges. Two small air gaps are thus formed between the pole faces and the diaphragm. The coils are wound so that the flux, due to a current in them, passes across the air gaps in series and thereby increases or decreases (according to the direction of current) the flux produced by the permanent magnet.

The force acting between two magnetised surfaces is

$$\frac{B^2}{2\mu_0} \text{ newtons per square metre}$$

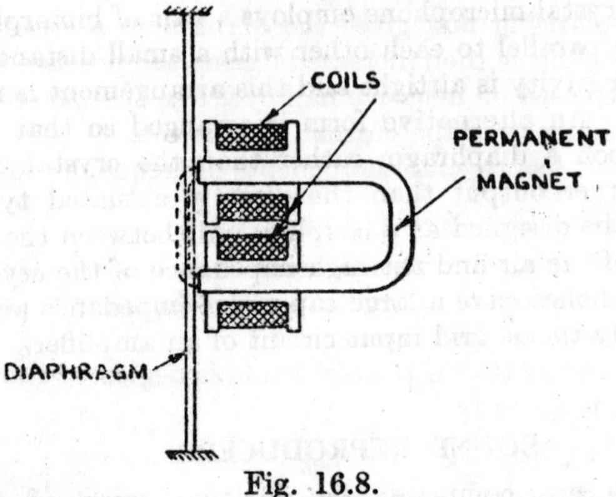

Fig. 16.8.

where B is the flux density, in teslas (webers per square metre), and $\mu_0 = 4\pi \times 10^{-7}$ is the permeability of free space. The force acting on the diaphragm in Fig. 16.8 is thus given by

$$\frac{A}{\mu_0}(B_0 + b)^2 \text{ newtons}$$

where $2A$ is the area of the two pole faces in square metres, and B_0 and b are the flux densities (in teslas) produced respectively by the permanent magnet and the current in the coils.

With a sinusoidal current in the coils, $b = B \sin \omega t$, the force on the diaphragm is given by

$$F = \frac{A}{\mu_0}(B_0^2 + 2B_0 B \sin \omega t + B^2 \sin^2 \omega t) \quad . \quad . \quad . \quad 16.12$$

The second term in equation 16.12 represents the required vibromotive force, and it will be seen that an increase in B_0 increases the sensitivity ; the third term indicates the existence of a second harmonic component of force on the diaphragm. To keep the distortion small it is necessary that the steady value of flux density B_0 be large compared with the peak value of the alternating flux density produced by the coils. A limit is set to the possible value for B_0 however as very large values cause the diaphragm to make contact with the poles ; long before this happens however the excessive pull on the diaphragm causes an increase in its effective stiffness which decreases the sensitivity.

In the absence of any steady flux ($B_0 = 0$ in equation 16.12) a sinusoidal current in the coils would cause the diaphragm to be attracted towards the poles during the positive half cycle ; it would return to the zero position when the alternating flux density is zero, and again be attracted during the negative half cycle. Thus for a current of frequency f in the coils the diaphragm would vibrate at a frequency of $2f$. The addition of the polarising flux gives the diaphragm a steady flexure towards the poles ; this is then increased during the positive half cycle of current and decreased on negative half cycles so that the diaphragm vibrates at the frequency of the current alternation.

If the coil current has several components of frequency so that

$$b=B_1 \sin \omega_1 t+B_2 \sin \omega_2 t+\ \ldots \text{ etc.}$$

the expression for the vibromotive force will contain components which have frequencies equal to the sums and differences of the various frequency components of the current.

Equation 16.12 shows that if the distortion is neglected the required vibromotive force is given by

$$P=2AB_0B/\mu_0 \qquad 16.13$$

where both P and B are vector quantities.

The alternating flux involved is BA, and this must be equal to the m.m.f. of the coils divided by the reluctance (S) of the magnetic circuit to alternating flux. Hence

$$BA=Ni/S$$

where N is the number of turns on the two coils, and i is the value of the coil current in amperes. The insertion of this value for BA in equation 16.13 then gives

$$P=\left(\frac{2NB_0}{\mu_0 S}\right)i=Gi \qquad 16.14$$

where G is a constant of proportionality between the force on the diaphragm and the current in the coils.

Motional Impedance of the Receiver

If, for alternating currents, the coils have a total resistance R, and an inductance L, a measurement of the receiver impedance with the diaphragm clamped so that it cannot vibrate, will give the " clamped " impedance simply as

$$Z_c=R+j\omega L$$

If now the diaphragm is allowed to vibrate, measurement of the current through the coils for a given applied voltage will show that the impedance under this condition is greater than Z_c. This increase in impedance arises from the vibration of the diaphragm, as the vibration produces a change of flux in the magnetic circuit which induces an e.m.f. in the coils. This "back" e.m.f. opposes the applied voltage and thereby reduces the coil current, and so gives rise to an apparent increase in the impedance of the receiver. This additional impedance of the receiver is referred to as the " motional impedance " of the receiver.

The armature of a d.c. motor offers an analogy. When the armature is at rest, voltage and current measurements indicate that the resistance of the armature is small. When the armature is rotated at speed an e.m.f. is induced in the armature conductors and under this condition the *apparent resistance* of the armature is very much greater than the static value.

The value of the motional impedance can be obtained as follows. Suppose that a voltage v is applied to the coils, which have an inductance L and a resistance R, then

$$v = L\frac{di}{dt} + Ri + e' \quad \quad 16.15$$

where i is the current in the coils at any instant of time, and e' is the e.m.f. induced by motion of the diaphragm.

Now movement of the diaphragm towards the poles by a distance x will reduce the reluctance of each gap by $x/\mu_0 A$; as the reluctance S of the whole magnetic circuit can be taken, to a fair degree of approximation, as the reluctance of the air gaps, the inward displacement of the diaphragm may be considered to change the reluctance from

$$S \text{ to } S - 2x/\mu_0 A$$

This reduction in the value of the reluctance will cause the flux to increase by the factor

$$\frac{S}{S - \dfrac{2x}{\mu_0 A}}$$

The total flux is then given by

$$\Phi = B_0 A\left(\frac{S}{S - \dfrac{2x}{\mu_0 A}}\right)$$

$$= B_0 A\left(1 - \frac{2x}{\mu_0 S A}\right)^{-1}$$

If the quantity enclosed in the brackets is expanded by the binomial theorem, the terms involving powers of x higher than the first can be neglected, as x is a small quantity. Hence

$$\Phi \simeq B_0 A\left(1 + \frac{2x}{S\mu_0 A}\right) \quad . \quad 16.16$$

$$\text{Now } e' = N\frac{d\Phi}{dt} = N \cdot \frac{2B_0}{\mu_0 S} \cdot \frac{dx}{dt} = G\frac{dx}{dt}$$

and so equation 16.15 can be written as

$$v=L\frac{di}{dt}+Ri+G\frac{dx}{dt} \quad . \quad . \quad . \quad . \quad 16.17$$

If steady state conditions are assumed and the current and displacement vary sinusoidally so that

$$i=Ie^{j\omega t} \quad . \quad . \quad . \quad . \quad . \quad 16.18a$$

$$x=Xe^{j(\omega t+\varphi)} \quad . \quad . \quad . \quad . \quad 16.18b$$

$$\text{then } V=j\omega LIe^{j\omega t}+RIe^{j\omega t}+j\omega XGe^{j(\omega t+\varphi)} \quad . \quad 16.19$$

The diaphragm of the receiver has distributed mass and stiffness and can resonate *mechanically* in a large number of modes. If for simplification, it is considered to be a concentrated equivalent mass m with a mechanical resistance motion r_m and an equivalent stiffness s the equation of motion is then represented by

$$m\frac{d^2x}{dt^2}+r_m\frac{dx}{dt}+sx=P=Gi \quad . \quad . \quad . \quad 16.20$$

$$\text{then } (-\omega^2m+j\omega r_m+s)Xe^{j(\omega t+\varphi)}=GIe^{j\omega t}$$

which can be expressed as

$$\left[r_m+j\left(\omega m-\frac{s}{\omega}\right)\right]j\omega Xe^{j(\omega t+\varphi)}=GIe^{j\omega t} \quad . \quad 16.21$$

Now GI is the applied force and $j\omega X$ is the vector velocity. The ratio of the force to the velocity gives the vector mechanical impedance which is thus

$$Z_m=r_m+j\left(\omega m-\frac{s}{\omega}\right)$$

If the value for the vector velocity $j\omega Xe^{j(\omega t+\varphi)}$, in equation 16.21, is substituted in equation 16.19

$$v=(R+j\omega L)Ie^{j\omega t}+\frac{G^2Ie^{j\omega t}}{r_m+j\left(\omega m-\frac{s}{\omega}\right)}$$

$$=i\left[R+j\omega L+\frac{G^2}{r_m+j\left(\omega m-\frac{s}{\omega}\right)}\right] \quad . \quad 16.22$$

The quantity $G^2\Big/\left[r_m+j\left(\omega m-\frac{s}{\omega}\right)\right]$ is thus the motional impedance of the instrument. Mechanical resonance occurs at the frequency

$$f=\frac{1}{2\pi}\sqrt{\frac{s}{m}} \quad . \quad . \quad . \quad . \quad . \quad 16.23$$

In deriving the value for the motional impedance, no account has been taken of the eddy current and hysteresis losses which occur in practice. Because of these losses, the flux produced by the current in the coils is not in phase with the current, but lags by some angle. If these losses are taken into account, the impedance of the receiver lags on the impedance derived in equation 16.22.

Frequency Response of the Moving-Iron Receiver

The conventional construction of the moving-iron receiver gives a response curve which exhibits a peak, due to resonance of the diaphragm, in the region of 1000 Hz. Another peak usually occurs in the region of 3000 Hz, after which the response falls off fairly rapidly, as shown in Fig. 16.9. This non-uniform response means that the instrument causes frequency distortion ; the efficiency as an electro-acoustic transducer however increases greatly in the region of resonance.

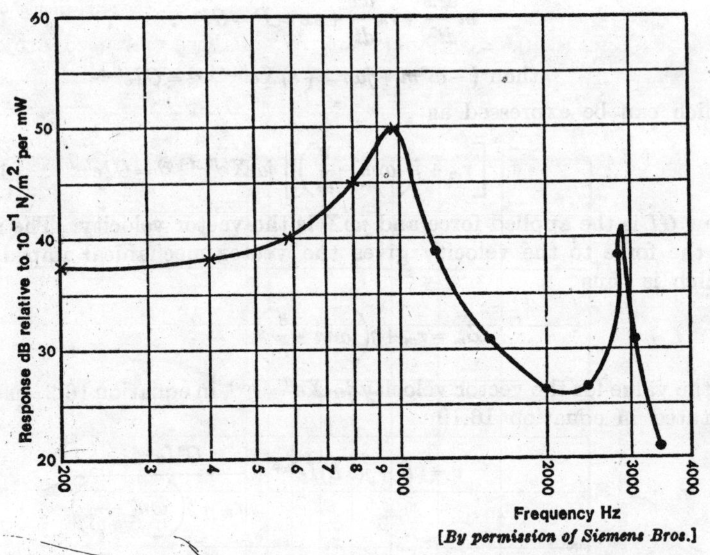

Fig. 16.9. Frequency response of the moving-iron receiver.

The Balanced Armature Receiver

The moving-iron diaphragm receiver as described above has been used in commercial telephone instruments for many years. Recently, improved forms of telephone receiver have been developed, and a sectional view of one such instrument is shown in Fig. 16.10.

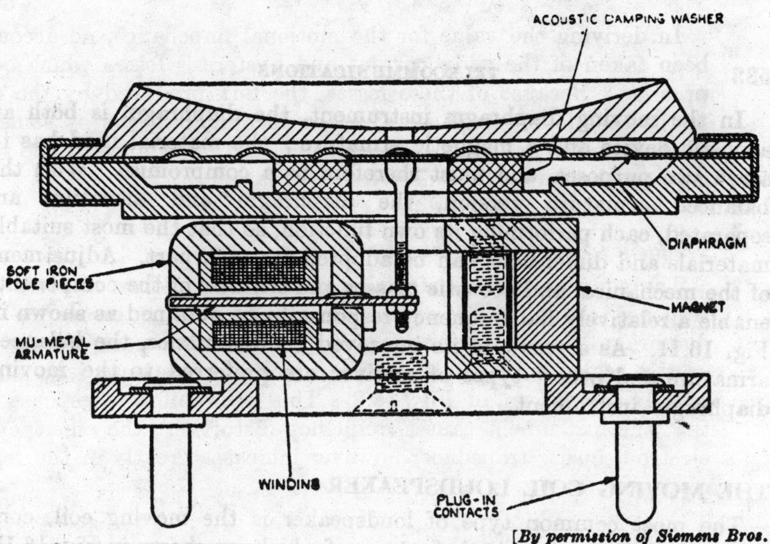

[By permission of Siemens Bros.

Fig. 16.10. Sectional view of equalised balanced armature receiver.

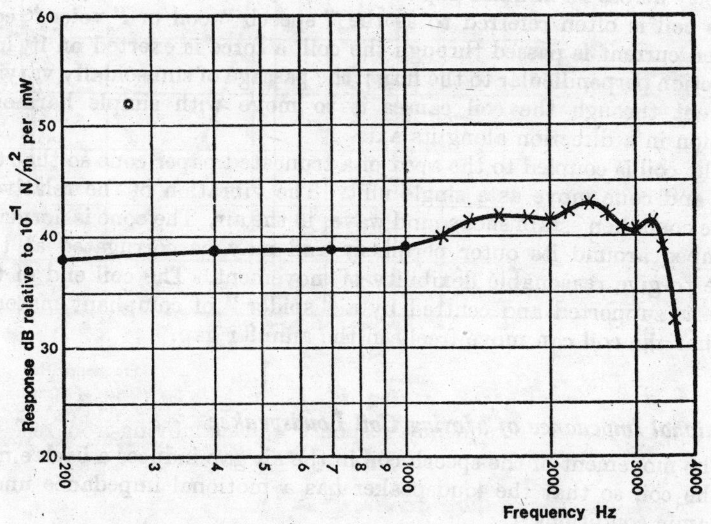

[By permission of Siemens Bros

Fig. 16.11. Frequency response of the equalised balanced armature receiver.

In the moving diaphragm instrument, the diaphragm is both an acoustic device and a magnetic armature; the material used has to serve two purposes, and must therefore be a compromise. With the balanced armature version, the diaphragm and armature are separated, each performing its own function, so that the most suitable materials and dimensions can be adopted for each part. Adjustment of the mechanical and acoustic masses and stiffness of the components enable a relatively flat frequency response to be obtained as shown in Fig. 16.11. As a result of its improved characteristics, the balanced armature and other[1] types of receiver are preferred to the moving diaphragm instrument.

THE MOVING COIL LOUDSPEAKER

The most common type of loudspeaker is the moving coil, cone diaphragm variety, the basic features of which are shown in Fig. 16.12. The operation of this type of loudspeaker is dependent on the force on a current-carrying coil in a magnetic field. As can be seen an electromagnet (or permanent magnet) is arranged to produce a high flux density across an annular gap in which a cylindrical coil is positioned. This coil is often referred to as the "speech" coil or "voice" coil. When current is passed through the coil, a force is exerted on it, in a direction perpendicular to the flux; the passage of sinusoidally varying current through the coil causes it to move with simple harmonic motion in a direction along its axis.

The coil is coupled to the apex of a truncated paper cone so that the coil and cone move as a single unit. The vibration of the relatively large cone then establishes sound waves in the air. The cone is normally clamped around its outer periphery and may be corrugated at this edge to give reasonable flexibility of movement. The coil end of the cone is supported and centred by a "spider" of compliant material so that the coil can move freely in the annular gap.

Motional Impedance of Moving Coil Loudspeaker

The movement of the speech coil in the air gap induces a back e.m.f. in the coil so that the loudspeaker has a motional impedance under dynamic conditions.

If the length of the wire on the speech coil is l metres, the flux density is B webers per square metre, and i is the current in amperes in the coil, the force on the coil in newtons is given by

$$F = Bil = G'i \qquad . \quad . \quad . \quad . \quad . \quad . \quad . \qquad 16.24$$

where G' is the constant of proportionality between the force on the moving system and the current in the coil.

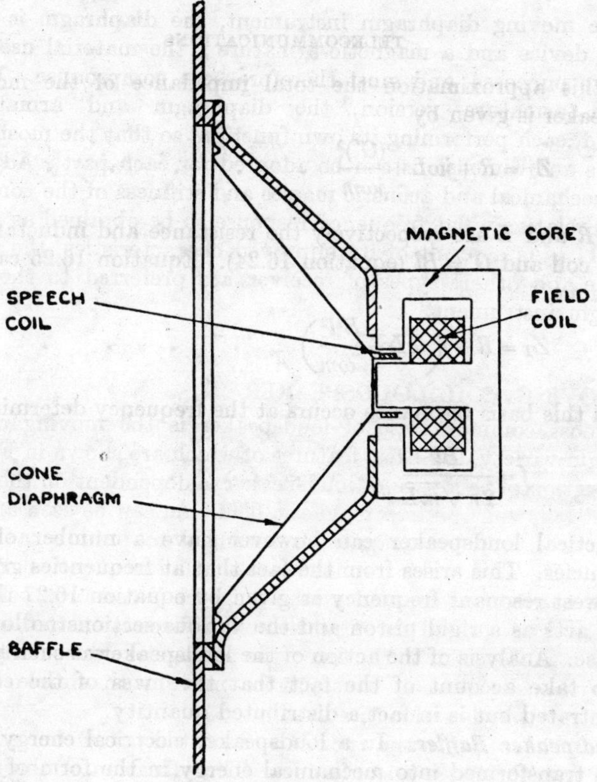

Fig. 16.12.

Now such a coil moving with a velocity v has an e.m.f. induced in it given by

$$e = Blv = G'v$$

It is left as an exercise for the reader to show that if the moving system is regarded as equivalent to a concentrated mass m with a mechanical resistance r_m and a stiffness s_m the motional impedance is

$$\frac{(G')^2}{r_m + j(\omega m - s_m/\omega)}$$

at the angular frequency ω.

One difference between the telephone receiver and the loudspeaker is that the stiffness and mechanical resistance are very much smaller in the case of the loudspeaker and their presence can often be ignored.

With this approximation the total impedance of the moving coil loudspeaker is given by

$$Z_T = R + j\omega L + \frac{(G')^2}{j\omega m} \quad . \quad . \quad . \quad . \quad . \quad . \quad 16.25$$

where R and L are respectively the resistance and inductance of the speech coil and $G' = Bl$ (equation 16.24). Equation 16.25 can thus be written as

$$Z_T = R + j\left(\omega L - \frac{B^2l^2}{\omega m}\right) \quad . \quad . \quad . \quad . \quad . \quad . \quad 16.26$$

and on this basis resonance occurs at the frequency determined by

$$f = \frac{Bl}{2\pi\sqrt{mL}} \quad . \quad . \quad . \quad . \quad . \quad . \quad . \quad 16.27$$

A practical loudspeaker can however have a number of resonant frequencies. This arises from the fact that at frequencies greater than the lowest resonant frequency as given by equation 16.27 the cone no longer acts as a rigid piston and the various sections no longer move in phase. Analysis of the action of the loudspeaker at such frequencies has to take account of the fact that the mass of the cone is not concentrated but is in fact a distributed quantity.

Loudspeaker Baffles. In a loudspeaker electrical energy is applied and is transformed into mechanical energy in the form of movement of the cone, which acts as a coupling unit to give the desired acoustic output. To make the output as large as possible it is necessary that the source be matched to the load, as in the case of purely electrical networks. In the case of the loudspeaker the mechanical impedance of the driving speech coil is much higher than the acoustical impedance of the driven air. A certain amount of matching can be provided if the coil drives a relatively large cone which acts on a large volume of air so that the effective load is increased.

Outward movement of the cone gives rise to compression of the air in front of it with a corresponding rarefaction behind ; the reverse process occurs when the cone moves inwards. If a cone alone is used the compressed air in front of the diaphragm can return to normal pressure by moving round the edge of the cone to the rear where there is a reduced pressure. Under this condition vibrations are set up in the air but they do not produce efficient radiation ; the effect becomes more marked at the lowest frequencies as the time interval between successive compressions and rarefactions is then greatest. This effect can be avoided by the use of some form of " baffle ", the simplest type being a large flat board with a hole in its centre through which the cone operates (Fig. 16.12). Sound waves from the front of the diaphragm are thus unable to interfere with those produced by the back of the diaphragm, and radiation then takes place from the cone into the room. The use of a baffle gives improved radiation at low frequencies and the larger the size of the baffle the lower is the frequency that can be radiated.

Horn Type Loudspeakers. It has already been mentioned that it is necessary to provide the driving system of a loudspeaker with an appreciable acoustic impedance to obtain a large acoustic output economically. The provision of a large freely moving diaphragm is one possibility ; an alternative arrangement is to use a horn. The virtue of a horn resides in the fact that it functions as an acoustic transformer ; it converts the vibrations of high pressure and low amplitude in the region of the diaphragm into vibrations of low pressure and high amplitude at the mouth.

In a horn type loudspeaker the moving diaphragm has often the same general shape as that shown for the moving coil microphone, Fig. 16.5. The diaphragm is thus much smaller than that used in the previous type of loudspeaker considered above. The use of a smaller diaphragm has the advantage that a smaller electrical input is required for a given output, and in general terms horn loaded loudspeakers have a greater overall efficiency than the paper cone type. The improved efficiency makes a saving possible in the power rating and cost of the electrical equipment. An exponential horn, in which the cross section increases exponentially from the initial area at the throat, is found to give good results. Such a horn acts in the same way as a high-pass filter in that it has a cut off frequency, determined by its physical size, below which it does not transmit. The disadvantage in the use of a horn is that it has to be of large dimensions to give good reproduction at the lower frequencies.

WORKED EXAMPLES

1. Describe the construction of a commercial form of telephone receiver and discuss the factors that influence its acoustic output. The flux density in the air gaps of a receiver due to the permanent magnet is 1,000 gauss and the reluctance of the path of the varying flux is 0·8C.G.S. units. If each coil is wound with 400 turns, find the maximum value of the fundamental vibromotive force with an alternating current having an effective value of 20 μA.

This question will first be solved in terms of the C.G.S. units which it employs and then in S.I. units.

The force acting between two magnetised surfaces is

$$\frac{B^2}{8\pi}\text{ dynes/cm}^2$$

when the flux density is quoted in gauss. As a result, equation 16.12 thus becomes

$$F=\frac{2A}{8\pi}(B_0^2+2B_0B\sin\omega t+B^2\sin^2\omega t)$$

where $2A$ is the area of the two pole faces in square centimetres. The fundamental vibromotive force is thus

$$\frac{B_0BA}{2\pi}\sin\omega t$$

and the alternating magnetic flux in the magnetic circuit is BA. Now this must equal the total m.m.f. due to the coils divided by the reluctance of the magnetic circuit, i.e.

$$BA=\frac{4\pi Ni}{10\text{ (reluctance)}}$$

where N is the number of turns on the two coils and i is the current in amperes. Hence substitution of this value for BA in the expression for the vibromotive force above gives

$$\frac{2B_0Ni}{10\text{ (reluctance)}}\sin\omega t$$

The maximum value of the fundamental vibromotive force is then

$$F'_{max.}=\frac{\sqrt{2}\times 2B_0Ni_{max.}}{10\text{ (reluctance)}}\text{ dynes}$$

Now $B_0=1{,}000$, $N=2\times 400$, the reluctance is 0·8, and $i=20\times 10^{-6}$

$$\therefore\ F'_{max.}=\frac{\sqrt{2}\times 2\times 10^3\times 800\times 20}{10\times 0{\cdot}8\times 10^6}=\underline{5{\cdot}6\text{ dynes}}$$

If the question is to be solved in terms of SI units, the quantities given in the question must first be converted into SI values.

A flux density of 1,000 gauss corresponds to 0·1 T, (Wb/m²), and a reluctance of 0·8 C.G.S. units corresponds to

$$\frac{0{\cdot}8\times 10^{-2}}{\mu_0\times 10^{-4}}\text{ A/Wb}$$

$$=\frac{0{\cdot}8\times 10^2}{4\pi\times 10^{-7}}=\frac{0{\cdot}8\times 10^9}{4\pi}\text{ A/Wb}$$

If these quantities are inserted in equation 16.14, the maximum value of the fundamental vibromotive force is given by

$$\frac{\sqrt{2}\times 2NB_0 i_{max.}}{\mu_0\left(\dfrac{0{\cdot}8\times 10^9}{4\pi}\right)} \text{ newtons}$$

$$=\frac{\sqrt{2}\times 2\times 2\times 400\times 0{\cdot}1\times 20}{4\pi\times 10^{-7}\left(\dfrac{0{\cdot}8\times 10^9}{4\pi}\right)\times 10^6}$$

$$=\underline{5{\cdot}6\times 10^{-5} \text{ newton}}$$

(which is in agreement with the previous result as 1 newton $=10^5$ dynes).

2. Compare and contrast the different requirements of a telephone receiver and a loudspeaker. A moving coil loudspeaker has a coil of 3,000 turns of mean diameter 2.5 cm and an inductance of 0·2 H. It moves in a uniform radial field of flux density 0·5 T. It is assumed to be free from all frictional and elastic constraints. A sinusoidal voltage of constant value and variable frequency applied to the coil produced a maximum current when the frequency was adjusted to 500 Hz. If this current had an r.m.s. value of 10 mA, calculate the effective mass of the moving system and its amplitude of motion.

L.U. Int. Telecomm. 1952.

If a coil of resistance R and inductance L moves in a transverse magnetic field, the current which flows in the coil when a voltage V is applied is given by

$$I=\frac{V}{R+j\omega L+\dfrac{(Bl)^2}{r_m+j(\omega m-s/\omega)}} \quad \text{(equation 16.22)}$$

where m is the mass of the coil,

l is the total length of the wire in the coil,
r_m is the mechanical resistance to motion, and
s is the stiffness of the coil.

If, as in the present case, r_m and s can be neglected, the total impedance of the coil becomes

$$R+j\left[\omega L-\frac{(Bl)^2}{\omega m}\right] \quad \text{(equation 16.25)}$$

The impedance will clearly have a minimum value, and the current will be a maximum when

$$\omega L = \frac{(Bl)^2}{\omega m}$$

i.e. when $m = \dfrac{(Bl)^2}{\omega^2 L}$

Now $B = 0{\cdot}5$, $l = 75\pi$, $\omega = 2\pi \times 500$, and $L = 0{\cdot}2$, hence the mass m of the coil is given by

$$m = \frac{(0{\cdot}5)^2 \times (75\pi)^2}{4\pi^2 \times 25 \times 10^4 \times 0{\cdot}2} = \frac{56{\cdot}25}{8 \times 10^3} = 7 \times 10^{-3} \text{ kg.}$$

Reference to equation 16.21 shows that if the coil is assumed to move sinusoidally, and there is no friction or elastic constraint, then

$$(j\omega m)\, j\omega X = BlI$$

so that the displacement X is given by

$$X_{r.m.s.} = \frac{BlI_{r.m.s.}}{-\omega^2 m}$$

Now $I = 10^{-2}$ A, and so

$$X = \frac{0{\cdot}5 \times 75\pi \times 10^{-2}}{4\pi^2 \times 25 \times 10^4 \times 7 \times 10^{-3}} \text{ metres}$$

$$= \frac{7{\cdot}5}{20\pi \times 7 \times 10^3} \text{ metres} = 0{\cdot}017 \times 10^{-3} \text{ metres.}$$

References

[1] ROBERTSON, J. S. P.: "The Rocking-Armature Receiver", *P.O.E.E. Journal*, 49, p. 40 (1956).

References for Further Reading

DAVIS, A. H.: *Modern Acoustics* (Bell, 1934).
OLSEN, H. E.: *Elements of Acoustical Engineering* (Chapman & Hall, 1947).
RICHARDSON, E. G.: *Sound* (Edward Arnold, 1953).
WEST, W.: *Acoustical Engineering* (Pitman, 1932).

EXAMPLES

1. Give a brief description of the principle of operation of each of the following types of microphone :—condenser, carbon, moving-coil and ribbon. Illustrate your description of ONE of these with sketches which show its structure and the materials used for its component

parts. Mention the principal application of each type and explain the reasons for its suitability.

L.U. Ext. Telecomm. 1952.

2. A microphone of resistance 50 Ω is connected in series with a 60 Ω resistance and a 6-volt battery. Two pure tones act simultaneously on the microphone. The first, of frequency 750 Hz, causes a sinusoidal variation of the microphone resistance of amplitude 20%, and the second, of frequency 900 Hz, causes a sinusoidal variation of amplitude of 10%. Find the expression for the alternating voltage across the 60 Ω resistance by applying the binomial theorem and neglecting terms, the power of which is higher than the second.

L.U. Int. Telecomm. 1950.

3. Describe briefly a modern type of telephone receiver used in a subscriber's station apparatus, and explain what is meant by its motional impedance. Describe how the various constants of importance in the receiver theory may be determined experimentally.

L.U. Int. Telecomm. 1951.

4. Describe briefly with the aid of sketches the principle of operation of:

(i) the permanent-magnet loudspeaker;
(ii) the moving-iron telephone earpiece.

Explain why a steady magnetic field is essential in each case and deduce the effect on the harmonic distortion if the field is removed from the telephone earpiece.

L.U. Electronics & Telecomm. Part II. 1966.

5. Derive a purely electrical circuit equivalent for calculation purposes to the electromechanical system of a moving-coil loudspeaker. Explain with reference to this circuit the meaning of the term "motional" impedance.

I.E.E. Radio Comm. April, 1947.

6. Describe briefly the principles of operation of capacitor, carbon and ribbon microphones. State the principal application of each type and explain the reasons for its suitability. A microphone is placed in the field of a plane sound wave which has an r.m.s. particle velocity of 2×10^{-3} m/s. If the internal resistance and the sensitivity of the microphone are respectively 5 Ω and 0·75 mV per N/m^2, determine the maximum power then available at the output terminals. The plane-wave impedance of air is 430 M.K.S. units.

L.U. Telecomm. Part III. 1966.

17

TELEPHONY

INTRODUCTION

A TELEPHONE system is an arrangement of transmitters and receivers with electrical interconnection whereby the communication of speech can be carried on between any two points, which may be close together or remote. Telephone systems may be privately or publicly owned. Private systems are employed for internal communication in a building or buildings, and in addition may provide access to the public telephone system; large organisations such as railways and electricity supply authorities may have their own network of lines to meet their own special needs. In general, all telephone systems must provide for the efficient electrical transmission of speech, together with facilities for signalling and switching.

In the case of a public telephone service, the switching necessary to connect any given talker (commonly termed a "subscriber") to another in the same locality, is carried out at a telephone exchange which also provides circuits and apparatus whereby signalling to and from the exchange can be carried out. The switching may be done manually by the operator, when the exchange is referred to as a manual exchange; alternatively, the switching may be carried out automatically by electro-mechanical or electronic switchgear at an automatic exchange. In the case of a conversation or "call" between distant points, or between different areas of a large city, more than one exchange may be involved, so that lines have to be provided between exchanges. The inter-exchange lines are referred to as "junctions, toll, or trunk lines"; the term "junction" is applied to relatively short lines, whereas the name "toll" or "trunk" is applied to lines of greater length, such as those between large towns. A substantial economy in the number of inter-exchange lines may be obtained if some exchanges are used as route switching centres. Thus the interconnection of six exchanges might well be arranged as in Fig. 17.1b, which is obviously more economical in line plant than the scheme shown in Fig. 17.1a which utilises direct lines between all the exchanges.

As far as the public telephone service in the United Kingdom is concerned, the whole country is divided into Areas or "zones",

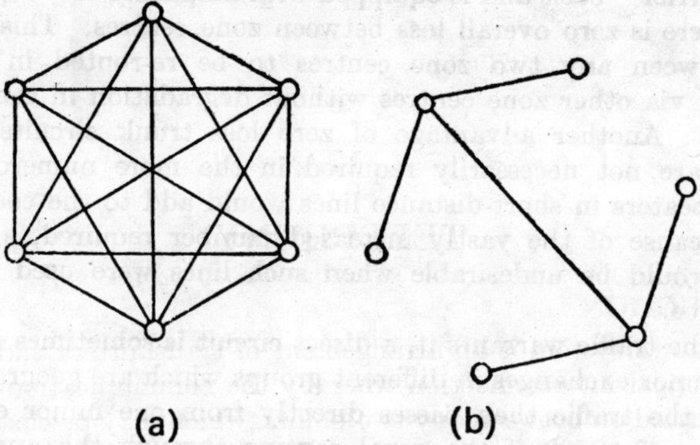

Fig. 17.1.

each zone is subdivided further into smaller areas known as "groups". The geographical extent of any group area depends on the telephone traffic, i.e. on the number and average duration of calls made within a specified period; where the traffic is high the group area is relatively small, while in rural districts where the telephone density is relatively small, the group area is larger. In each group area there may be three types of exchange, namely the main exchange in the group (known as the "group centre"), "minor" and "dependent" exchanges. A minor exchange is provided with direct circuits to the group centre exchange; long-distance calls from or to a minor exchange are then routed through the group centre. A dependent exchange on the other hand has no direct circuits to a group centre (except in the special case when it is located geographically adjacent to a group centre) and so long-distance calls which originate at a dependent exchange normally first pass through a minor exchange and then on to the group centre. Long-distance calls proceed from a group centre to a zone centre which is an exchange in the zone handling all long-distance traffic for, or from the zone. Inter-zone communication then takes place between zone centres.

A call originating in a dependent exchange for a number on another dependent exchange in a remote zone thus proceeds as shown in Fig. 17.2.

Fig. 17.2. Route of a call between two dependent exchanges in different zones.

The greatest distance involved is usually in the trunk circuit between zone centres. This type of circuit is operated on a "multi-channel carrier" basis and is equipped with amplifiers or "repeaters" so that there is zero overall loss between zone centres. This enables traffic between any two zone centres to be re-routed in case of emergency via other zone centres without degradation in the quality of speech. Another advantage of zero loss trunk circuits is that repeaters are not necessarily required in the more numerous local lines. Repeaters in short-distance lines would add to the cost of the service because of the vastly increased number required, also their presence would be undesirable when such lines were used only for local service.

Where the traffic warrants it, a direct circuit is sometimes provided between minor exchanges in different groups which are geographically adjacent; the traffic then passes directly from one minor exchange to the other instead of the usual routing through the appropriate group centres.

In the case of international traffic, the calls are routed from zone centres to the international exchange in London. The call is then connected, via a submarine cable, radio link, or satellite.

It is not possible, nor is it desirable within the scope of this text, to discuss all the apparatus involved, and the various details of operation in the many types of manual and automatic telephone systems. Attention will be confined therefore to an outline of the main principles involved in manual and automatic telephony, together with some details of multi-channel carrier telephony. For further information the reader should consult the references given at the end of the chapter.

MANUAL TELEPHONY

The normal type of transmitter employed in a telephone system is the carbon microphone which was described in chapter 16. This instrument requires a source of direct current, which may be supplied either by a local battery at each telephone, or from a central battery situated at the exchange. One of the simplest arrangements for speech transmission between two points is the local battery circuit of Fig. 17.3.

It will be seen that each of the transmitters T_1 and T_2 is provided with a battery, and is coupled to the line through a transformer which enables the transmitters to be matched to the line. The receivers R_1 and R_2 are connected in series with the line.

Any practical system must incorporate signalling circuits. One of the earliest methods of signalling was the magneto system, which although now obsolescent in the United Kingdom, is still employed

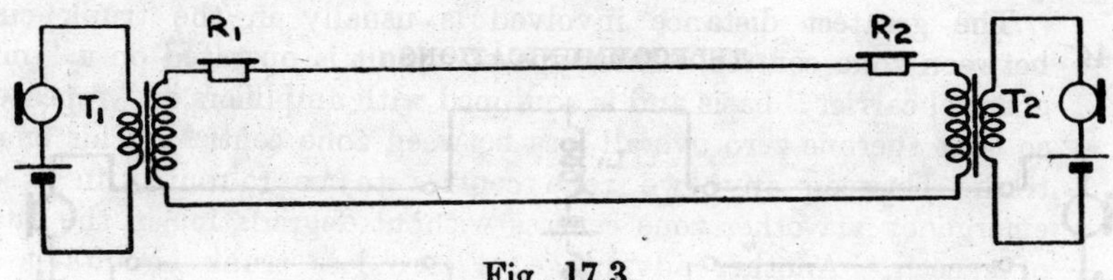

Fig. 17.3.

in remote areas. In the Magneto System a magneto bell and generator are required at each subscriber's telephone in addition to the local battery for speaking purposes. The generator is bridged across the lines to the exchange, and is fitted with switch contacts which connect it to the line when the handle is turned, and also serve to disconnect it when not in use. Local battery working has the disadvantage of a high maintenance cost which arises from the necessity of supplying every subscriber with cells, which need periodic replacement or change of electrolyte. Also, the efficiency of transmission varies with the state of the cells. As a consequence, local battery systems are not favoured, and are only used in exceptional cases where the line to the exchange is so long, and its resistance so high as to preclude the use of a central battery. In some cases central battery signalling is employed in conjunction with local batteries for speaking purposes. Other systems of manual telephony employ the central exchange battery for signalling and speech purposes.

There are thus three systems of manual telephony, namely Magneto, Central Battery Signalling (C.B.S.), and Central Battery (C.B.) working. The last named is the form normally employed in present day practice and the present discussion will be confined to this mode of operation. The capacity of the battery used in a C.B. system depends upon the exchange load, which may have a maximum value of a few thousand ampere-hours per day. Charging plant is used to keep the terminal voltage of the battery within fairly close limits of its nominal value, which may be either 22 or 40 volts in British practice.

One of the simplest possible central battery circuits for speech transmission between two points would be the arrangement of Fig. 17.4a, which shows each transmitter with its associated receiver connected in series at each end of the line. Direct current for the transmitters is fed out over the lines from the common battery.

CENTRAL BATTERY TRANSMISSION BRIDGES

The presence of the inductors L_1 and L_2 in Fig. 17.4a may be questioned, but a moment's reflection reveals the necessity for their presence. As far as speech current is concerned, the battery behaves

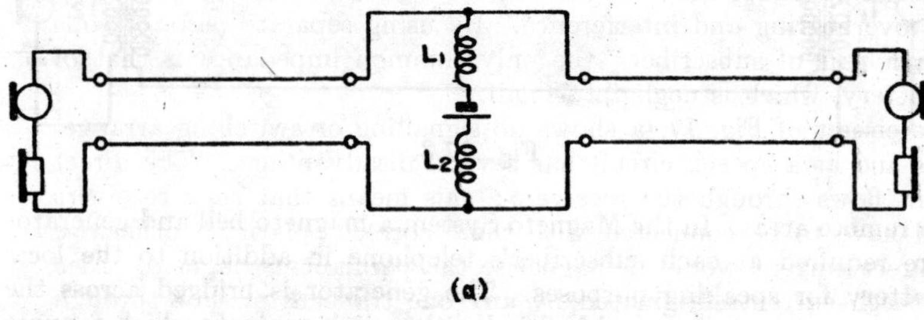

(a)

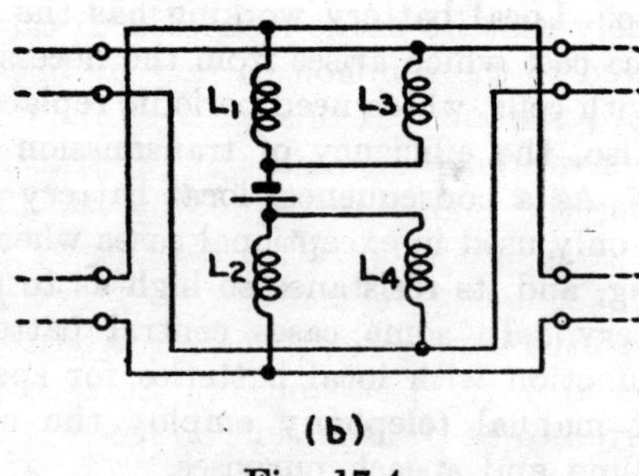

(b)

Fig. 17.4.

as a very low impedance. Direct connection across the line would cause all the transmitted speech to flow through the battery rather than the far receiver. It is thus necessary for the battery path to have a high impedance to currents of speech frequency ; it must also have a low resistance to direct current in order that the transmitter current shall not be reduced unduly. These requirements can be met by the insertion of a suitable inductor in series with the battery. If one side of the battery is earthed, as is normally the case, the inclusion of a single inductor would cause the lines to be unbalanced with respect to earth. Such unbalanced lines are subject to greater interference by induction from other external lines than is the case if the original lines are balanced with respect to earth. Hence in order to reduce the effect of external interference it is desirable to work with balanced lines. This is achieved by the use of a pair of inductors L_1 and L_2, the presence of which also serves to reduce the effect of small changes in the battery p.d. when switching occurs, so that the inductors may also be regarded as " smoothing chokes " in the battery supply.

The connection of a second pair of telephones to the common battery would be as shown in Fig. 17.4b. It will be seen that each line circuit has its own pair of inductors. If only one pair of coils was used for all the line circuits involved, the inductors would act as a coupling impedance between the various sets of lines, and this would cause overhearing and interference. By using separate pairs of coils for each pair of subscribers, the only common impedance is that of the battery, which is negligibly small.

The circuit of Fig. 17.4a shows no signalling or switching arrangements and as a speech circuit has several disadvantages. The direct current flows through the receivers; this means that such receivers would have to be connected with the "correct polarity" otherwise the direct current would demagnetise the permanent magnets. Also the speech currents originated by any one transmitter flow through the associated receiver, thus producing objectionable "sidetone" in that receiver. The simple circuit has another objection which is not quite so obvious, namely that its use is restricted to cases where the telephones are connected to the common battery by lines of approximately equal length, or resistance. If this is not so the direct currents in the two transmitters will not be equal, and the transmitter at the end of the line having the higher resistance may not then obtain sufficient current for satisfactory operation because of the shunting effect of the low resistance line.

This last objection to the simple circuit can be avoided by the use of the circuits shown in Fig. 17.5a and b. Such battery supply arrangements are referred to as transmission bridges.

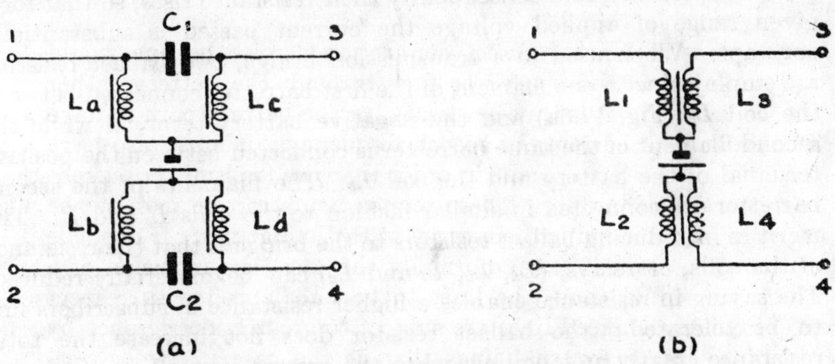

Fig. 17.5 (a) Stone transmission bridge
(b) Hayes transmission bridge.

With the capacitor impedance bridge, or Stone transmission bridge, as it is called, the direct current paths for the two transmitters are split and four inductors are used. The necessary coupling across the bridge for speech transmission is provided by the two capacitors C_1 and C_2. The inductors present a high impedance to currents of speech frequency, whereas the capacitors which usually have a value of 2 μF have a relatively low impedance at speech frequencies. The values of the coil impedance used in practice are such that the loss introduced by the bridge circuit is of the order of 1 db at 800 c/s. In some cases the inductors take the form of relays so that they can be used for signalling duties.

In the case of the Hayes bridge as shown in Fig. 17.5b, the speech circuits are coupled electromagnetically. If an alternating voltage is applied to the terminals 1, 2, the inductors L_1 and L_2 act as a primary winding to induce a voltage in the secondary winding formed by the inductors L_3 and L_4; for voltages applied to the terminals 3, 4, the inductors L_3 and L_4 function as a primary and L_1 and L_2 act as a secondary. With the Hayes bridge, unlike the Stone bridge, currents of speech frequency flow through the battery. To diminish the cross-talk produced by the speech currents in flowing through the battery the inductor connections are normally such that the current in the combination L_1 and L_2 flows in the opposite direction to the currents through L_3 and L_4. For economy and convenience all four inductors may be wound on the same magnetic core.

In recent practice, ballast resistors or " barretters " have been used in the Stone type of transmission bridge. These resistors consist of two tungsten filaments contained in an atmosphere of hydrogen in a sealed glass tube. When the current increases through the filaments, their temperature, and consequently their resistance rises, so that for a given range of applied voltage the current passed is substantially constant. When used in a transmission bridge, two ballast resistors are employed with one filament of the first barretter connected between the coil L_a (Fig. 17.5a) and the negative battery terminal while the second filament of the same barretter is connected between the positive terminal of the battery and the coil L_b. The filaments of the second barretter are connected in similar fashion to the coils L_c and L_d. The merit in introducing ballast resistors to the bridge is that the resistance of the coils, or relays, (L_a, L_b, L_c and L_d) can be materially reduced. The saving in resistance enables a higher resistance of subscribers line to be tolerated; the ballast resistor does not increase the total resistance greatly on long lines when the current is small, but prevents the current rising to an excessive value when a short line is connected to the bridge or when fault conditions occur.

It is important to note that the transmission bridges are not permanently associated with subscribers' lines, but are located in the common connecting circuits which are set up at the exchange to enable any subscriber to talk to any other subscriber. (An exception to this occurs in trunk and automanual exchanges which have the transmission bridge in the line termination.) This practice arises from reasons of economy as the number of common connecting circuits required is far fewer than the total number of subscribers. The actual number of common connecting circuits provided is usually of the order of one-tenth of the number of lines.

Because the transmission bridge is not associated with any particular line it is not possible to maintain the transmitter currents constant at any given value as the feed current depends on the line resistance.

THE MANUAL EXCHANGE SWITCHBOARD

The essential function of an exchange switchboard is to interconnect the telephones of all the exchange subscribers, so that any one of them can converse with a subscriber on that, or any other exchange. The switchboard is required to give signals to attract the attention of the switchboard operator in order that the appropriate connection can be set up ; in addition, supervisory signals are required to advise the operator of the termination of a call so that the connection may be cleared. Facilities are also required for the metering of the calls, to give a record of the traffic.

Each subscriber's line is terminated on a socket or " jack " which appears on the face of the switchboard ; the jack has three connections, two of which are connected to the conductors of the subscriber's line while the third is used as an internal exchange connection for signalling purposes. The connection of the line circuit of one subscriber to that of another subscriber on the same exchange is effected by a cord circuit which comprises two " cords " each having three conductors, interconnected by transmission bridge and supervisory apparatus. Each cord is terminated in a plug, so constructed that when inserted in a jack, three metal sections insulated from one another, permit the flexible conductors to make contact with three connections of the jack.

The detailed sequence of events which takes place when a call is made involves a knowledge of the subscriber's telephone, line, and cord circuits. It is convenient to defer the detailed discussion and consider first of all the simple outline of the steps involved in a local call.

When the calling subscriber lifts his telephone from the rest, the gravity switches in the instrument operate and provide a direct current path across the subscriber's line. The effect of this is to operate a relay in the line circuit at the exchange and cause a calling lamp, associated with the subscriber's jack, to light on the switchboard. The operator on seeing this inserts the plug which terminates one cord (known as the answering cord) of a cord circuit into the jack, and thereby extinguishes the calling lamp. By throwing a switch associated with the cord circuit to the speaking position the operator can then speak to the subscriber and ascertain the number required.

On receiving this information, the operator then inserts the plug which terminates the other cord (known as the calling cord) of the chosen cord circuit into the jack of the called subscriber. The operator then throws the cord circuit switch to the " ringing " position, which action disconnects her telephone and connects a ringing generator across the called subscriber's line to ring the bell in the telephone instrument. When the called subscriber answers, the operator restores the cord circuit switch to the normal position. The two subscribers are then in communication with each other. Two supervisory lamps are employed with the cord circuit; one lamp is associated with the calling subscriber's line and the other with the called subscriber's line. The circuit arrangements are usually such that the supervisory lamp lights when the relevant telephone is replaced on its rest. Consequently, when the operator sees both supervisory lamps alight she is aware that the call is terminated. She then depresses a meter key to register the call and withdraws the plugs from the jacks, thereby extinguishing the supervisory lamps. The cord circuit is then available for any other subsequent call.

When the calling subscriber desires to speak to a subscriber connected to another exchange, the principle involved is the same except that a cord connection is set up between the subscriber's jack and the jack of an outgoing junction line; at the distant exchange the incoming junction is then connected by an operator to the required subscriber in a manner similar to that described for a local call.

Multi-Position Switchboards

The next point to consider is the manner in which the traffic from a large number of subscribers is handled. One operator can deal with somewhere between 100 and 200 subscribers' lines dependent upon the traffic. If the number of lines is greatly in excess of this figure it is obvious that a number of operators are necessary. If an operator is to handle, say, 200 lines, and there are 2,000 lines connected to the switchboard, then ten operators will be required to deal with the traffic. Under a condition such as this, if all the jacks were distributed uniformly over the length of the switchboard any one operator would be unable to reach the jacks of all the lines from her position. This difficulty is overcome by the use of " multiple " jacks, so that each subscriber's line jack is repeated at regular intervals along the switchboard. The " original " subscriber's line jack is referred to as the " local ", " home ", or " answering " jack, while the multiple jacks are the repetitions of the answering jack. Each operator looks after the calling equipment (and associated answering jacks) from which a particular quota of subscribers originate calls. The multiple jacks, which are used only for calls *to* subscribers do not have calling lamps associated with them, and are arranged compactly in the upper portion of each switchboard position in such a manner that any operator is within reach of jacks for all the exchange subscribers. The maximum size of an exchange, normally 10,000 lines, is in fact limited by the possibility of providing jacks for all the subscriber's lines within the reach of an operator.

The jacks of junction lines are also multiplied over the switchboard. As a subscriber's line can be reached from any of a number of jacks, provision must be made to indicate to an operator whether the required subscriber is already engaged or not. The third wire connected to the " bush " or frame of the jack is used for this purpose and carries a warning potential if a plug is inserted into any one of an engaged subscriber's jacks.

Fig. 17.6 shows two sections of the panel and keyshelf of one form of a manual switchboard. The illustration is actually that of the manual switchboard associated with a private automatic branch exchange and not a main manual exchange ; it does, however, give an indication of the general appearance of a manual switchboard.

In the section shown, it will be seen that there are 14 cord circuits, the plugs of which are at the back of the keyshelf. The corresponding speak/ring keys can also be seen together with a second set of keys, known as ring-back keys. These are provided on the basis of one per cord circuit, and enable the operator to recall the originating

[By permission of the G.E.C.

Fig. 17.6. Manual switchboard.

subscriber if required. The supervisory lamps lie between the keys and the plugs of the cord circuits. The keyshelf of the second position is raised to show the wiring of the keys.

The Subscriber's Telephone Circuit

In addition to the necessary transmitter and receiver, the subscriber's equipment must include a bell for signalling purposes, means of matching the transmitter and receiver to the line, and some anti-sidetone device.

Sidetone may be defined as the reproduction of sound in a telephone receiver picked up from the associated transmitter. If the level of sidetone is high the subscriber tends to lower his voice ; if, on the other hand, the level of sidetone is low the subscriber tends to speak louder, which increases the useful transmitter output. As a consequence, modern telephone instruments always have some anti-sidetone circuit.

A simple arrangement which would eliminate sidetone is shown in Fig. 17.7. If the balanced transformer has two equal windings T_1 and T_2 and the impedance Z is made equal to the impedance of the line (which usually has a leading angle), the voltage induced in the secondary winding will be zero, and there will be no sidetone.

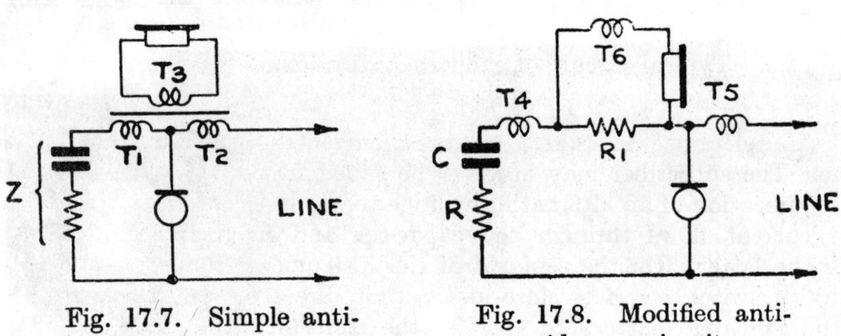

Fig. 17.7. Simple anti-sidetone circuit.

Fig. 17.8. Modified anti-sidetone circuit.

The transmitter must, however, be matched to the line, and this requirement conflicts with equality of the windings T_1 and T_2. In practice the circuit is modified as shown in Fig. 17.8. In this circuit the windings T_4, T_5 and T_6 are coupled magnetically. T_4 and T_5 function as an auto-transformer to step up the impedance of the transmitter to that of the line, while the receiver is also matched to the line. As T_4 and T_5 are no longer equal a voltage from the transmitter is induced in T_6. The resistor R_1 however has a value such that the p.d. across it is equal and opposite in sign to the e.m.f. induced by transformer action in T_6. As a result, the sidetone in the receiver is very much reduced. The complete absence of sidetone is undesirable as it makes the instrument seem "dead".

One practical form of the above circuit is shown in Fig. 17.9. This diagram employs the convention, used in all telephone circuit diagrams, that contacts are shown in the unoperated position.

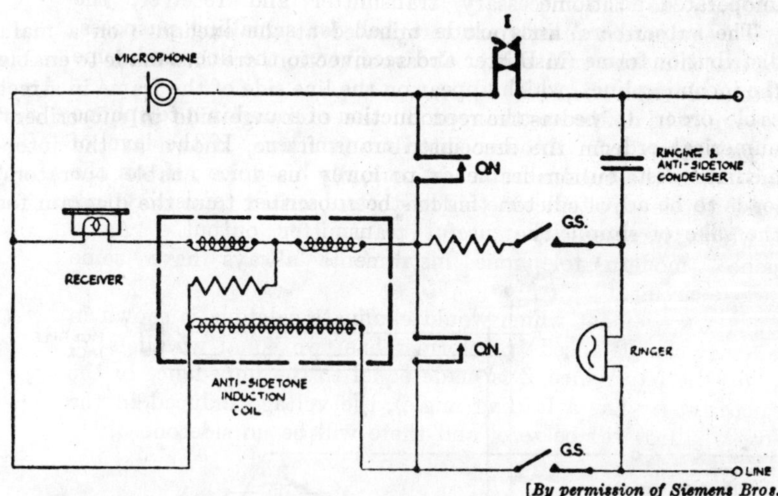

[*By permission of Siemens Bros.*

Fig. 17.9. Typical circuit of modern anti-sidetone telephone.

With the telephone on its rest, no direct current path exists across the line. The subscriber may however be called from the exchange, by the application of an alternating voltage to the line. The resulting ringing current flows through the capacitor and magneto bell to operate the latter. On the removal of the instrument from its rest, the gravity switch contacts close and permit direct current to flow from the exchange battery to energise the transmitter.

The impulsing contacts (I) are used only when the telephone is connected to an automatic exchange. Movement of the dial in the process of dialling causes these contacts to open and close; when the dial is moved from rest the off normal contacts (O.N.) close to prevent the dialling impulses from passing through the transmitter and receiver.

The Subscriber's Line Circuit and C.B. Cord Circuit

The detailed sequence of operations which occurs when a call is made through a manual switchboard may be followed with the help of Fig. 17.10, which shows the subscriber's line circuit, and Fig. 17.11 which shows the cord circuit details. The diagrams are drawn on what is known as a " detached contact " basis ; in this arrangement each relay is designated by a letter (or letters) and a figure, e.g., $\frac{L}{1}$. The letters identify the relay while the figure indicates the number of relay springset combinations. The contacts are drawn in the unoperated position.

The subscribers' lines are terminated at the exchange on a main distribution frame (M.D.F.). Cross connections are then made to enable the incoming lines, which appear on the line side of the frame in street cable order, to be re-arranged on the exchange side in subscribers' numerical order. Another distribution frame, known as the intermediate distribution frame is normally used to enable operators' loads to be adjusted, but this has been omitted from the diagram for the sake of simplicity.

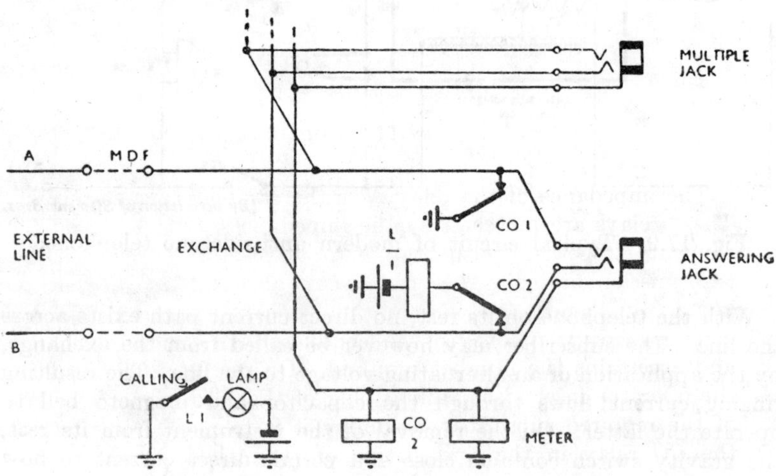

Fig. 17.10. Subscriber's line circuit.

When a calling subscriber lifts his telephone from its rest a d.c. loop is placed on the line and this causes the relay L to operate. A contact of the relay closes the circuit of the calling lamp associated on the switchboard with the answering jack of the subscriber. The calling lamp lights and attracts the attention of the operator who then inserts the answering plug (Fig. 17.11) of a free cord circuit into the jack indicated by the calling lamp. The insertion of the answering plug applies a voltage to the " sleeve " of the jack and this causes the relay CO to operate, contacts of which remove relay L and the earth connection from the A and B conductors. The current fed over the sleeve is insufficient at this stage to operate the calling subscriber's meter.

Meanwhile the insertion of the answering plug causes the relay *M* to operate; the contact of this relay then disconnects the calling supervisory lamp.

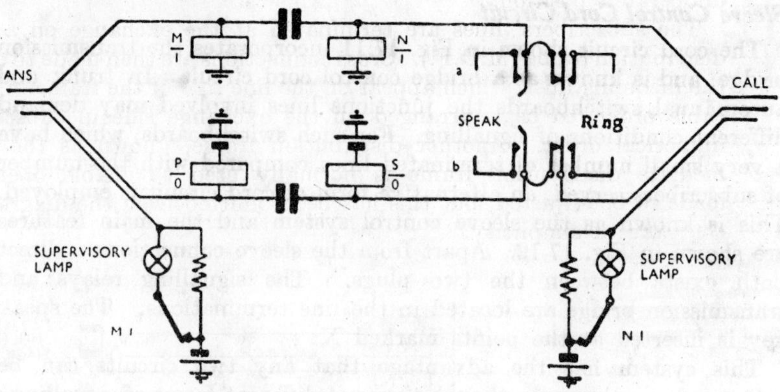

Fig. 17.11. Cord circuit.

The impedance of the relay *N* is the same as that of the relay *M*. These relays are matched by the impedances *P* and *S*, and the four elements together with the two capacitors shown, form the transmission bridge. The cord circuit also contains a multi-contact key. By placing this key in the "speak" position, the operator connects her telephone to the conductors of the calling subscriber and ascertains the number required. On receipt of this information the operator inserts the calling plug of the cord circuit into the jack of the required subscriber, assuming it is free. This action operates the *CO* relay in the line circuit of the called subscriber and the supervisory lamp glows. Ringing of the called subscriber is then achieved by throwing the speak/ring key to the "ring" position.

When the operator has restored the speak/ring key to the normal position (as shown in Fig. 17.11), and the called subscriber has removed his telephone from its rest, a d.c. loop is placed on the called line. This causes the relay *N* to operate, so that the supervisory lamp is disconnected. Both subscribers are then in communication with each other and the equipment connected between the line conductors is removed, except of course the transmission bridge. The circuit is then ready for speech, and remains in that condition until either subscriber replaces his telephone. When this occurs the corresponding relay (*M* or *N*) is restored; this causes the associated supervisory lamp to glow.

When both supervisory lamps glow, the operator is aware that the call has been completed. The call is then registered on the calling subscriber's meter by the depression of a meter key, not shown in the cord circuit, and both answering and calling plugs removed from the jacks. The cord circuit is then ready for use on another call.

Sleeve Control Cord Circuit

The cord circuit shown in Fig. 17.11 incorporates the transmission bridge, and is known as a bridge control cord circuit. In trunk and automanual switchboards the junctions lines involved may demand different conditions of signalling. For such switchboards, which have a very small number of terminated lines compared with the number of subscribers served, an alternative form of cord circuit is employed. This is known as the sleeve control system and the main features are shown in Fig. 17.12. Apart from the sleeve connections a direct path exists between the two plugs. The signalling relays and transmission bridge are located in the line terminations. The speak key is inserted at the points marked X.

This system has the advantage that any two circuits can be connected together even though they use different forms of signalling ; only one type of cord circuit is necessary because the equipment required for diverse forms of signalling is readily incorporated in the relevant line terminations. This simplifies the operating procedure, while greater flexibility in signalling methods is also achieved.

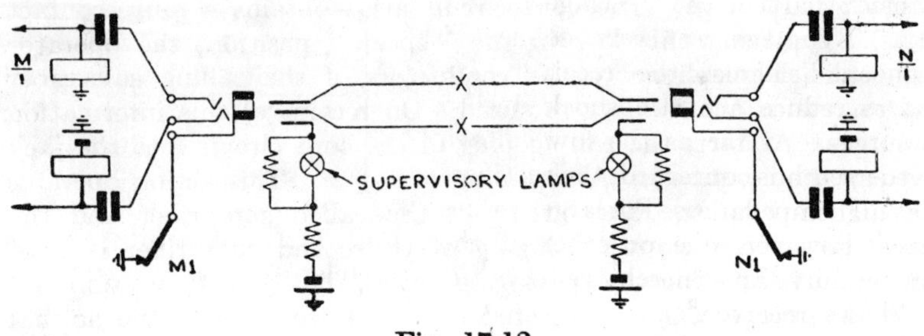

Fig. 17.12.

The simplified diagram Fig. 17.12 shows that the supervisory signalling equipment is associated with the cord circuit and is operated over the sleeves of the jacks. While a conversation takes place the d.c. loops on the subscribers' lines cause the relays *M* and *N* to be operated. The contacts of these relays thus break the supervisory lamp circuits during this period. At the termination of the call, the relays are restored and the supervisory lamps then glow.

Operator's Telephone Circuit

The circuit of the operator's telephone is usually arranged as shown in Fig. 17.13. This circuit is wired to all the cord circuits of the particular operator's position on the switchboard, and is connected to the points *a* and *b*, in Fig. 17.11.

The transmitter and receiver are transformer coupled to the cord circuit as shown. The winding T_1 functions as a primary winding for the transmitter, while T_2 and T_3 act as a secondary winding; the windings T_2 and T_3 serve as an auto-transformer for the receiver, and also act to reduce the level of sidetone.

If the half wave rectifiers connected across the receiver are ignored, it will be seen that the current which flows in the receiver due to transmitted speech, is the difference of the currents i_1 and i_2. When these currents are equal, sidetone is eliminated. As far as received speech is concerned, most of the current passes through the receiver, as it has an impedance which is low compared with that of the winding T_3.

The choke L and capacitor C_1 prevent alternating speech currents from passing through the battery; in addition, stray noise from the battery itself is confined to the path LC_1. The capacitor C serves to prevent direct current, from the cord circuit, passing through the secondary circuit of the transformer. This capacitor also plays an important part in the "engaged test" (see below). The two rectifiers, connected "back-to-back" across the receiver, are provided to reduce acoustic shock due to current surges. As far as the low voltage of received speech is concerned, the rectifiers behave as high impedances. For larger values of voltage, however, one or other of the rectifiers conducts and thereby reduces the current in the receiver.

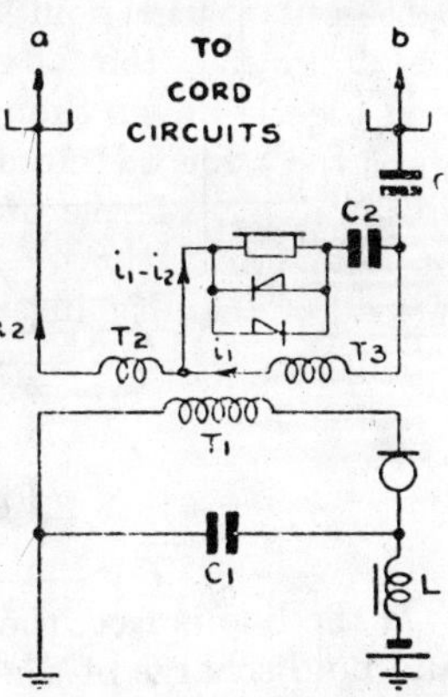

Fig. 17.13. Operator's telephone circuit.

Engaged Test

If a line is engaged it is essential that this should be apparent to all the operators on the switchboard. The way in which a line is tested to check that it is free can be followed with the help of Fig. 17.14, which shows the answering jack of a line engaged.

When the speak/ring key in the cord circuit is thrown to the speaking position, the capacitor C in the operator's telephone circuit becomes charged to the battery potential. The tip of the calling plug of the cord circuit concerned (i.e. the plug connection carrying the conductor *a*) is connected to the positively charged side of the capacitor, which is at earth potential. As the diagram indicates, the sleeves of all the jacks of an engaged line have a negative potential with respect to earth. (The value of this potential depends on the value of the resistance of the cut-off relay in parallel with the meter, compared with the value of the resistor *R*.) Consequently when the tip of the calling plug is tapped on the sleeve of an engaged line, the capacitor *C* is partially discharged. This causes a " click " in the operator's receiver, and indicates that the line is engaged.

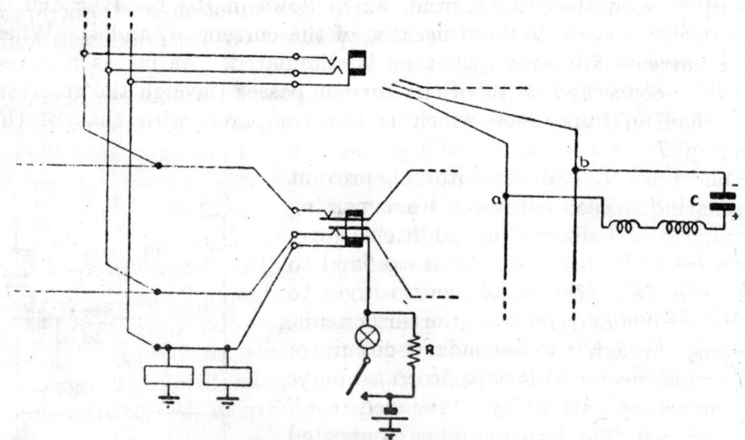

Fig. 17.14. Engaged test.

If the line is free, the sleeve of the jack tested is at earth potential, and no discharge of the capacitor occurs. The operator is then aware that the line is available, and inserts the calling plug into the jack to complete the connection.

Party Lines

In cases where the line plant is inadequate for the connection of further subscribers to an existing exchange, it is possible to accommodate additional subscribers by the process of line sharing. When two subscribers share the same two conductor lines to the exchange, this is referred to as a two-party line. The subscribers have different exchange numbers but only one of them may initiate or receive a call at a particular time.

The bell of one subscriber is connected between one conductor and earth, while the bell of the other subscriber is bridged between the other conductor and earth. By use of the appropriate connections at the exchange, each subscriber may be called independently of the other.

In rural areas where long lines are involved, and the number of subscribers is small, arrangements are made for a number of subscribers to share the same line.

JUNCTION WORKING

The description of the operation of a manual exchange switchboard has so far been restricted to the case of local calls, i.e. when the called subscriber is connected to the same exchange as the calling subscriber. For calls to subscribers on other exchanges junction or trunk lines are involved ; the latter are usually operated on a carrier basis and will be considered later.

When the number of junctions between nearby exchanges is small they are arranged to work in either direction, and are referred to as "both-way" junctions. When a large number of junctions is involved it is usual to arrange for a system of uni-directional working, with the junctions divided into two groups ; one group is referred to as "outgoing" at the originating exchange, and is called "incoming" at the far exchange ; the second group is called "incoming" at the first exchange, and is of course the "outgoing" group at the distant exchange. When junctions terminate on a jack at each exchange, they are called jack ended junctions, to distinguish them from junctions which terminate on a plug at the distant exchange.

Outgoing and both-way junctions are multipled over the switchboard, on the same principle as subscriber's lines, so that any operator can connect a calling subscriber to any junction line. The operations involved at the originating exchange are similar to those involved in a local call. The arrangements are normally such that the first operator has complete control at the outgoing end of the connection, and the supervisory signal on the calling cord is controlled by the action of the called subscriber at the distant end. Incoming junctions are not multipled, but are assembled on special junction positions of the switchboard, where they are dealt with by a "junction" operator.

In one system, the local operator plugs in an outgoing jack relevant to a free outgoing junction, which terminates in a plug at the distant exchange. The operator's circuit at the distant exchange is automatically connected to the line and the local operator notified by the transmission of a signal of two pulses of tone. The local operator then asks the distant operator for the required number. Alternatively, when the distant exchange is automatic, the first operator dials the required number after the receipt of the "pip-pip" signal.

FOUR WIRE REPEATER CIRCUITS

Trunk lines between exchanges separated by an appreciable distance, are equipped with speech amplifiers or repeaters. The circuit may then be operated on what is known as a four wire basis. The two wire lines are converted to four wire lines by means of balanced differential transformers, which are sometimes referred to as hybrid coils. These are shown enclosed inside the dotted lines in Fig. 17.15. The four windings T_1, T_2, T_3 and T_4 are matched, and the windings T_5 and T_6 form the balanced halves of a further winding. The impedance Z_1 is a balancing network, which presents the same impedance as the two wire line West; Z_2 is a line balance for the two wire line East.

Suppose speech is transmitted from the two wire line West. Then if the four windings are in fact equal, and Z_1 has the same impedance as the line, half the speech voltage will be applied to the input of the repeater A_1. If the input impedance of this repeater is the same as the two wire line, the transformer will give rise to a 3 db loss. After amplification by the repeater A_1, the speech is passed to the line, in which additional repeaters may be inserted, as necessary to compensate for line attenuation. The output of the last repeater (A_N in Fig. 17.15) is connected to the windings, T_5 and T_6 of the second hybrid coil. If balance conditions apply, half the power output is delivered to the two wire line East, and half is dissipated in the line balance Z_2. The windings T_3 and T_4 are so wound as to make the equal currents induced in each flow in opposite directions. As a result, no difference of potential exists between the points x and y and no speech voltage is applied to the repeater B_1.

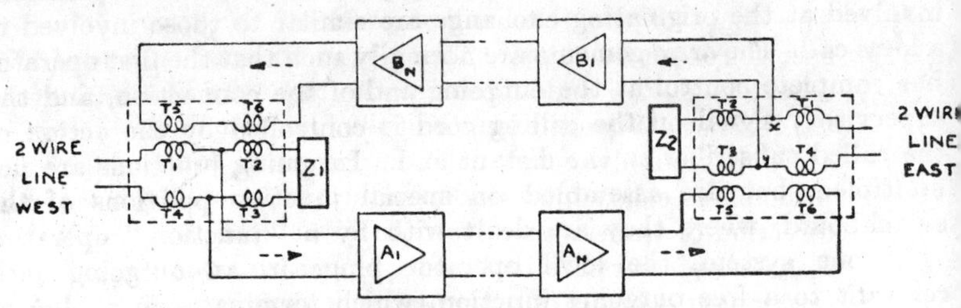

Fig. 17.15. Four wire repeater circuit.

Half the speech voltage arising from the two wire East is passe to the repeater B_1, where it is amplified. The output is then transmitte along the line, and through any intermediate repeaters, to the termin repeater B_N. Half of the output voltage then appears across the tw wire line West. The whole arrangement thus enables uni-direction repeaters to be utilised to transmit speech in both directions between two terminal points.

The spacing of the repeaters depends on the line attenuation ; the length of line between any two repeaters (which operate in the same direction) must be limited so that the signal/noise ratio at the end of that section of line is greater than the minimum permissible value, as the subsequent repeater, or repeaters, cannot improve the signal/noise ratio present at the repeater input.

In practice the terminal two wire lines which may be connected to the hybrid coils, via a switchboard, seldom if ever have the same impedance, and as a result, the line balance network does not always form an accurate balance. When the line balance is imperfect, some fraction of the output voltage of a repeater will be applied to the input of the other repeater connected to the hybrid coil. Some of the output repeater A_N may thus be applied to B_1 while some of the output voltage of B_N may be applied to A_1. If the gain round the " loop " is greater than unity, i.e. zero db, the circuit will oscillate, or " sing " and thereby become unusable. If stability is to be maintained, the total gain of all the amplifiers in the loop must be less than the total attenuation introduced by the four wire lines and terminating transformers.

Echo Suppression

If the line balances are imperfect, speech is transmitted round the four wire loop. Thus, if speech is transmitted from the two wire line West, this will appear at the two wire line East in the normal way ; some of the speech will however be applied to the B_1 repeater and will appear at the two wire line West as an echo of the talker's voice. The delay of the echo will depend on the time of transmission of speech round the loop. The " echo speech " will also traverse the repeaters A_1–A_N and appear at the two wire line East as an echo to the listener. When the length of the four wire line is such as to produce an objectionable echo, echo suppressing equipment is used. In principle an echo suppressor introduces sufficient loss, into the unwanted direction of transmission, to reduce the echo to an insignificant level. Echo suppressors are little used in British practice, except for a very few long-distance Continental trunk circuits.

TWO WIRE REPEATER CIRCUITS

The circuit connections of a repeater unit in a two wire line can be visualised, if in Fig. 17.15 the repeaters A_1–A_N are replaced by a single repeater A, the repeaters B_1–B_N are replaced by a single repeater B and the terminal transformers are assumed to be placed in physical proximity to the repeaters. The two wire line is thus converted to a four wire line at each repeater installation, and amplification of speech can then be obtained for the two directions of transmission. Such an arrangement has several disadvantages as compared with a four wire circuit. First of all, with a two wire circuit every pair of repeaters used need two hybrid coils and two balancing networks ; in addition a low pass filter has to be inserted at the input terminals of each amplifier, otherwise instability may occur if the line balance networks do not have the same impedance as the lines at frequencies beyond the speech range. The amount of amplification which can be obtained is also smaller in the two wire case ; the amplification round the " local loop " must be less than unity, and this means that the gain of the two amplifiers must be limited to a value 12 db above the total of the unbalance loss.

As a result, repeatered lines are usually operated on a four wire basis This means that a smaller number of repeaters of higher gain can be used in the four wire case. The amplifier circuit of one form of telephone repeater is shown in Fig. 17.16. It can be used in either a two wire or four wire circuit.

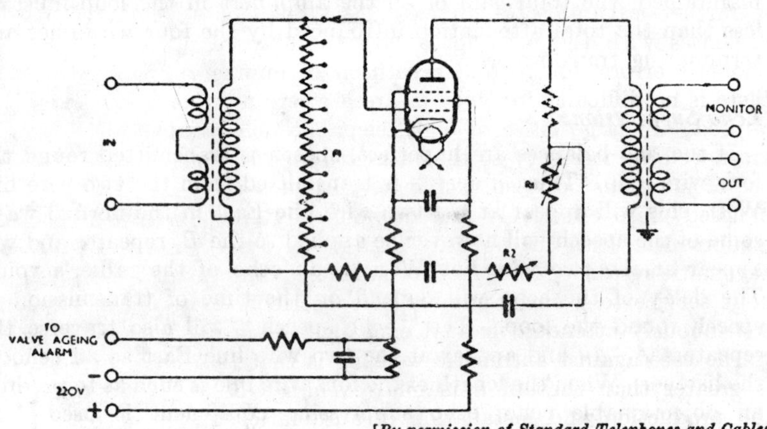

[By permission of Standard Telephones and Cables

Fig. 17.16. Amplifier circuit of telephone repeater.

Increased flexibility in the repeater equipment is obtained by separating the amplifier portion of the repeater from that part of the equipment which is determined by the characteristics of the line. It is therefore possible to substitute one amplifier for another without changing balancing networks and equalisers to suit the conditions on the lines connected to it. Only a small range of fine control of the gain is available on the amplifiers themselves (5 dB, in steps of 0·5 dB) and all lines incoming to one station are built out by means of attenuation equalisers to a standard attenuation which is uniform over the frequency range of interest.

The normal maximum gain of the amplifier shown is 35 dB. Negative feedback is applied to reduce change in gain with changes in supply voltages. The input and output impedances of the amplifier are 600 ohms, and the gain characteristic is flat within $\pm 0{\cdot}5$ dB over the range 300–3400 Hz. The normal output power is $+10$ dB relative to 1 milliwatt into a load of 600 ohms.

AUTOMATIC TELEPHONY

An automatic telephone system in which the connection of the calling and called subscribers' lines is effected automatically by the exchange equipment (on receipt of suitable signals from the calling subscriber), has several advantages over a manual system. First of all, the required connection can be set up and released in a shorter time ; the time required for connection (or disconnection) is substantially constant at all periods of the day, and is independent of the volume of traffic passing, provided always that the number of calls is less than the maximum number which could be handled simultaneously. A further advantage of an automatic telephone system is that it dispenses with the need for a large number of operators. Again, phonetic errors due to oral repetition of numbers are avoided, and there is no difficulty involved in areas where more than one language is used. In large cities of high telephone density several exchanges are normally necessary so that a high proportion of calls involve the use of junctions between exchanges. In such cases the traffic can be handled more effectively and economically by automatic switching equipment. With the opposite extreme of scattered rural areas, the automatic system again is more economic; it can provide a twenty-four-hour service to a small number of subscribers more cheaply than a continuously attended manual exchange.

The case against automatic working is that the initial capital cost is greater than that of a manual exchange of the same capacity ; the production and installation of automatic equipment occupies a longer time than that needed for manual equipment. A further point is that an automatic system demands a higher standard of skill for its maintenance.

As a result, however, of the convenience and economic advantages of automatic working, the trend with all public telephone administrations is to increase the extent of automatic operation. The ideal arrangement is that all subscribers to the system should be able to obtain interconnection by automatic means, and future planning is directed towards subscriber trunk dialling.

In a book of this nature only the outlines of automatic telephony can be discussed. Although several systems of automatic telephony are in current use it would be unwise to attempt to assess the relative merits or points of divergence of the different systems before discussing any of them in detail. Attention will therefore be confined mainly to a description of the fundamental aspects of the step-by-step system used in British practice.

SIGNALLING IN AN AUTOMATIC SYSTEM

Any truly automatic telephone system places the onus of signalling on the calling subscriber. The necessary signalling is usually achieved by means of a mechanical interrupter or dial, the operation of which is shown schematically in Fig. 17.17. Basically, a circular rotatable finger plate with 10 finger holes is fixed to another plate with 10 projections as shown. If the finger plate is turned clockwise the projections will pass the pivoted lever *A* without disturbing the

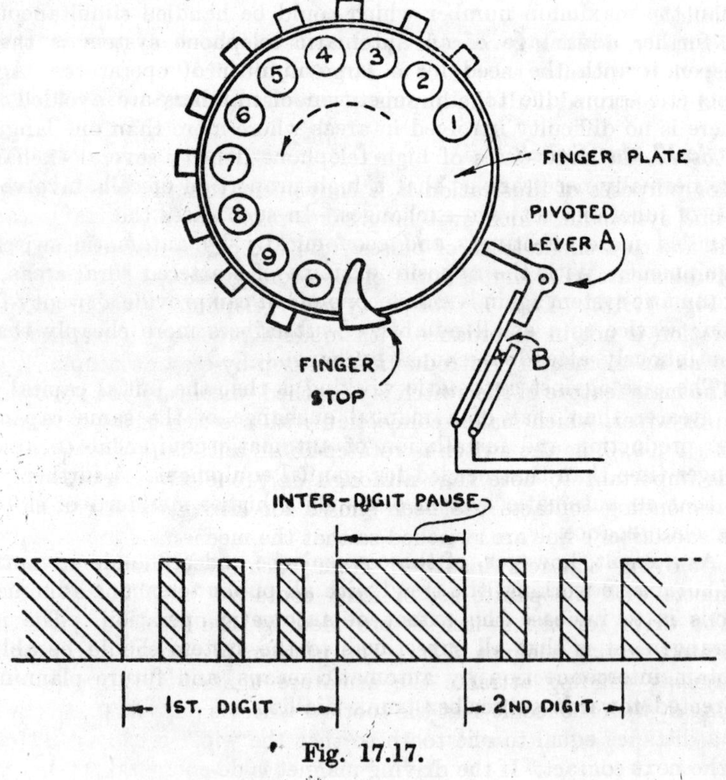

Fig. 17.17.

normally closed contacts *B*. When the plate assembly returns in an anti-clockwise direction to its rest position under the influence of a spring, the contacts *B* will be forced apart by every projection which passes the pivoted lever *A*. Thus if a finger is inserted in the finger hole marked 4 and the plate assembly rotated clockwise to the finger stop, the return movement will cause four interruptions of the contacts *B*.

As the return motion of the dial is controlled by a governor, the interruptions occupy a definite time, and have a definite time interval between them, so that interruptions of fixed duration and frequency are always produced.

If the circuit arrangements are such that when the subscriber lifts his receiver from its rest a d.c. loop is extended from the central battery through the contacts *B*, the operation of dialling will produce a train of impulses. The current in the loop will then have the form shown in Fig. 17.17 if, say, the digits 4, 3 are dialled. The circuit is arranged to provide a minimum inter-digit pause, as in practice certain operations are necessary when more than one train of impulses is dialled.

Normally, dialling is on a decimal basis so that n operations of the dial give 10^n possible selections as opposed to the $10n$ selections which would be obtained if all the impulses were used in an additive manner.

Simple 10 Line Switch

For purposes of illustration it is convenient to start with a simple 10 line system in which switching takes place on receipt of a single digit due to a single train of pulses from the calling subscriber. The basic elements of a simple form of electromagnetic switch are shown in Fig. 17.18. This is not a typical telephone switch and its operation is not in accordance with modern practice ; it is presented here as an elementary introduction to step-by-step switching.

The main feature of the switch is a toothed wheel carrying a movable arm or wiper, which makes connection with a series of fixed contacts 1, 2 . . . 9, 0, as the switch is rotated in an anti-clockwise direction. It is important to note that although only one wiper arm with its corresponding contacts has been shown for clarity, both conductors of a subscriber's line are switched so that the mechanism must provide two moving contacts insulated from each other, each of which connects with a separate set of fixed contacts.

The drive for the switch is provided by the electromagnetically operated driving magnet *DM*. The passage of current through the energising winding attracts the armature against the tension of a spring S_1 with the result that the toothed wheel is pulled anti-clockwise by a distance equal to one tooth so that the wiper is moved forward to the next contact. If the driving magnet is de-energised the toothed

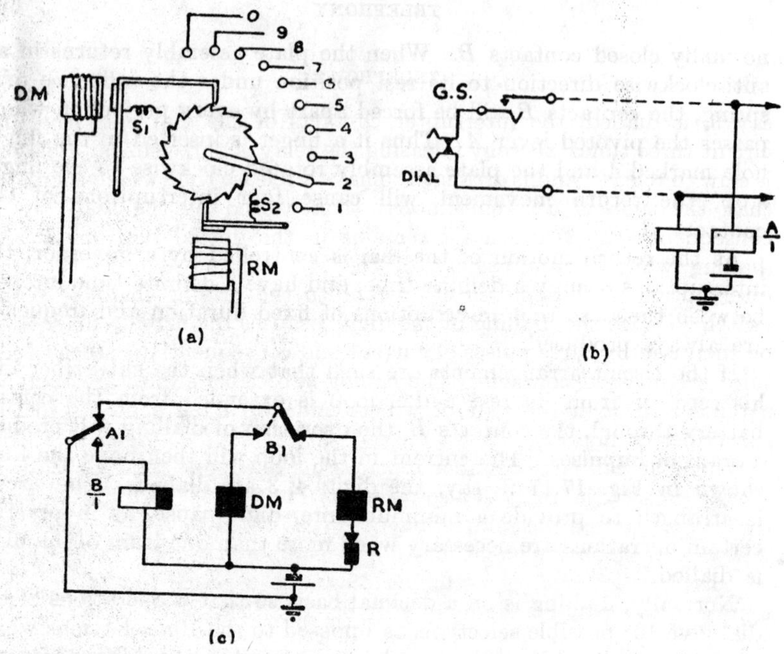

Fig. 17.18.

wheel is prevented from returning to its previous position by the pawl associated with the release magnet *RM*. It will be seen that if a series of pulses of current are applied to *DM* the wiper assembly will move forward from its initial position by a number of steps equal to the number of pulses applied.

If the release magnet *RM* is energised, the associated armature is attracted so that the pawl is disengaged and the wiper system is then free to return to the first position under the influence of a restoring spring (not shown).

Simple 10 Line System

The operations involved in signalling and switching for a 10 line system can now be considered with the help of Figs. 17.18b and 17.18c. The first of these diagrams shows that a line relay *A* and a balancing impedance are connected in series with the subscriber's line. Hence if the telephone is removed from its rest the gravity switch *G S* operates and places a d.c. loop on the line. The line current operates the relay *A* so that the movement of the contact *A* 1 energises the relay *B* and causes its contact *B* 1 to move to the position shown dotted. If a digit, say 3, is dialled, the interrupter contacts of the dial open the line circuit three times, thereby releasing the relay *A* three times. Relay *B* is slow to release, and is arranged to have a release time which is greater than the time of a circuit interruption caused by the dial. As a consequence the *B* 1 contact remains in the dotted position during dialling while the movement of the *A* 1 contact due to the dial interruption applies pulses of current to the driving magnet of the switch. Hence the dialling of the digit 3 causes the driving magnet to be energised by three pulses of current and consequently it steps to the third set of fixed contacts. The calling subscriber's lines are thereby extended through the pair of wipers and two fixed contacts to the subscriber on line 3.

When the calling subscriber replaces his telephone the line relay *A* is released and the relay *B* also releases. The contact *B* 1 then applies the battery across the release magnet *R M* which then operates.

A schematic arrangement for 10 line working is shown in Fig. 17.19. In this and subsequent switching diagrams a single line is used to represent the pair of conductors involved. It will be seen that the

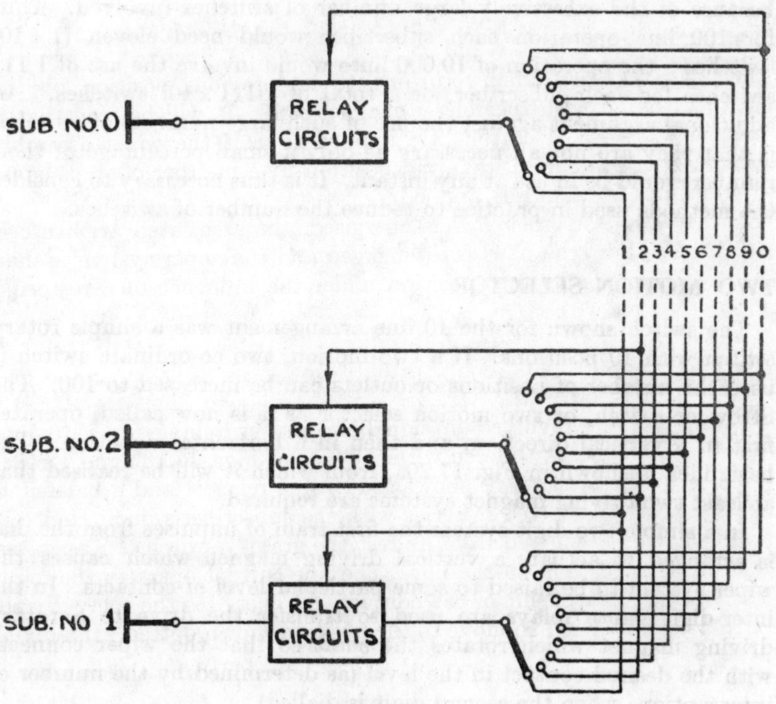

Fig. 17.19.

wipers are connected to the lines of the calling subscribers ; the fixed contacts are connected to the lines of all the subscribers on the system and so the fixed contacts correspond to the multiple jacks in a manual exchange. In Fig. 17.19 the subscriber's lines have been numbered 1, 2, ... 9, 0. Hence the dialling of the digit 0 to reach the last switch outlet involves a train of 10 pulses. This is the arrangement normally adopted in all systems.

The arrangement employed for the interconnection of 10 lines could be extended if a larger number of lines was required. 100 lines could be catered for by the connection of a 10 point switch to each outlet of the original 10 switches ; two ranks of switches would thus be involved, first a group of switches (" group " switches) which would select the appropriate " tens " group, then 100 final switches which would give connection to the subscribers. The system would operate on the signalling of two digits ; the first digit would operate the appropriate group switch and the second digit the desired final switch.

Further extension to a three digit or four digit system to cover 1,000 or 10,000 lines would be possible. While such a scheme is perfectly practicable the economic aspect leaves very much to be desired because of the excessively large number of switches involved. Thus for 100 line operation each subscriber would need eleven $(1+10)$ switches ; the operation of 10,000 lines would involve the use of 1,111 switches for each subscriber, or a total of $1{\cdot}111 \times 10^7$ switches. An additional argument against the use of such large numbers of switches is that they are not all necessary as only a small percentage of their number would be in use at any instant. It is thus necessary to consider the methods used in practice to reduce the number of switches.

TWO MOTION SELECTOR

The switch shown for the 10 line arrangement was a simple rotary switch with 10 positions. If a two motion, two co-ordinate switch is used the number of positions or outlets can be increased to 100. The Strowger switch, or two motion selector as it is now called, operates first in a vertical direction, and then in a horizontal direction. The basic idea is shown in Fig. 17.20a, from which it will be realised that at least two driving magnet systems are required.

In a simple two digit system the first train of impulses from the dial is arranged to actuate a vertical driving magnet which causes the wiper system to be raised to some particular level of contacts. In the inter-digit pause relays are used to transfer the drive to a rotary driving magnet which rotates the shaft so that the wiper connects with the desired contact in the level (as determined by the number of interruptions when the second digit is dialled).

Fig. 17.20a shows one wiper and one set of fixed contacts (or " bank " of contacts). In practice it is usual to have three banks of contacts and three wipers, two of which carry the speech lines while the third is used to hold the switch and indicate whether the particular switch is free or busy.

When the calling subscriber replaces his telephone the release of the selector occurs by additional rotary movement of the wipers until they emerge from the end of the level on which they were employed; the wiper system then drops to a position under the first level and is returned to the original point by spring tension.

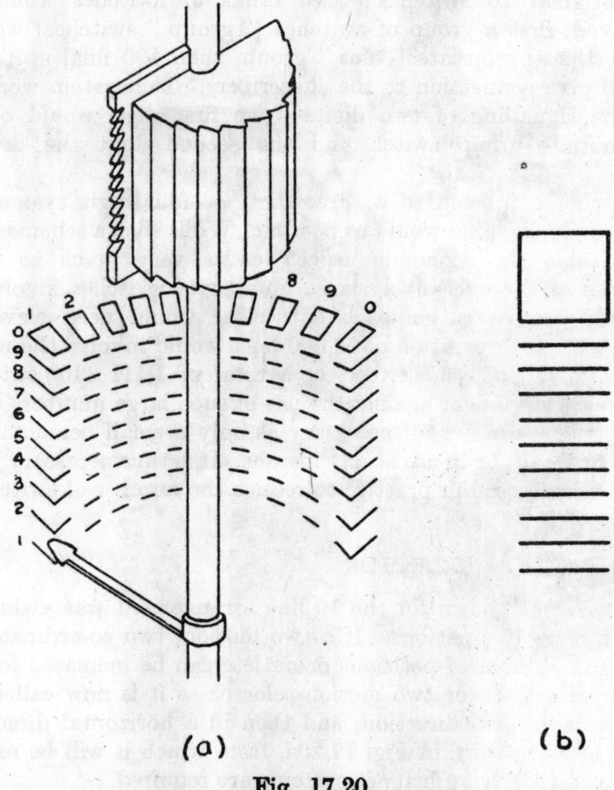

Fig. 17.20.

The connections between switches are normally referred to as " trunks " and a switching diagram is called a trunking diagram. The two motion selector is represented in such diagrams by the symbol shown in Fig. 17.20b; the square represents the relay group and control mechanism, while the 10 lines represent the 10 levels of contacts.

Fig. 17.21 shows an illustration of a modern type of two motion selector fitted with three wipers and three banks of contacts. The relays associated with impulsing of the driving magnets are mounted on the frame of the selector, above the contact system, as shown.

[*By permission of the G.E.C.*

Fig. 17.21.

(This particular switch employs a release magnet, which withdraws the rotary detent to allow the wipers to return across a level and drop to the normal position within a period less than the standard inter-digit pause.)

It is fairly obvious that the replacement of single motion rotary switches by two motion selectors will give a reduction in the number of switches necessary. If two motion selectors replace the 10 point switches of Fig. 17.19, 100 lines can be served with 100 two motion selectors ; 10,000 lines could be handled if each subscriber had one 100 outlet group selector connected to 100 two motion final selectors. Although the number of switches can be reduced in this way, the saving in cost is not so appreciable as might be expected because the two motion selectors are more complicated and more expensive than the simple rotary switch. Again, an arrangement of say 100 lines, each of which uses a two motion selector still results in only a small percentage of the switches being used at any instant.

A substantial decrease in the number of switches may be obtained if they are provided on a traffic basis, i.e. if the number of switches is based upon the maximum traffic which the particular group of switches is required to carry. Statistical investigation may show for example that the probable maximum number of simultaneous calls on a 100 line exchange is 10. Satisfactory operation may then be obtained with the provision of 10 two motion selectors for the common use of all subscribers.

100 LINE SYSTEM WITH COMMON SWITCHING

One possible two digit system for 100 subscribers with common switching is shown in Fig. 17.22. It will be seen that each subscriber is provided with a simple rotary switch ; this form of switch is referred to as a " uniselector ". These switches are shown with 10 outlets and all the corresponding bank contacts are connected together. The outlets from the uniselectors are then connected to a corresponding number (i.e. 10) of two motion selectors, which have their corresponding bank contacts connected together. This is indicated in Fig. 17.22 by the thin lines between the levels.

When any subscriber lifts his telephone from its rest two relays associated with the uniselector cause the wiper mechanism of the latter to rotate to find and seize a free two motion selector in the common group. This hunting takes place automatically, and when a free selector has been found, an indication is given to the caller that the circuit is ready for him to dial. This is achieved by the connection of " dialling tone ". The dialling of the first digit causes the two motion selector wipers to move vertically to the appropriate level, while the second digit causes rotary motion to the required set of contacts.

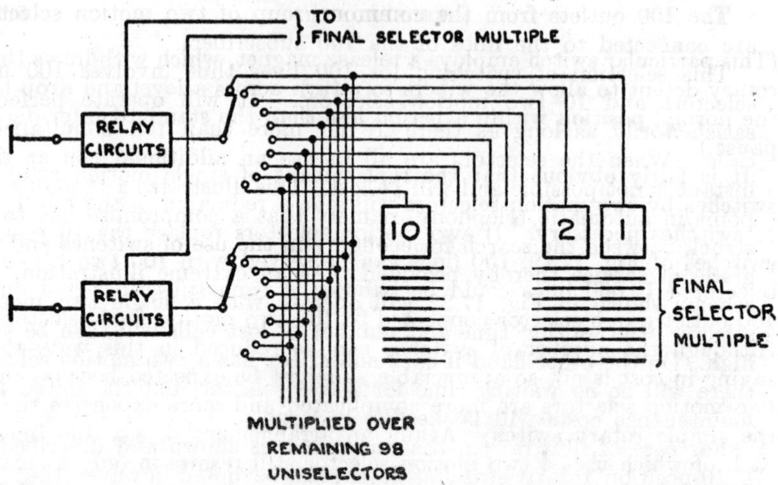

Fig. 17.22. 100 line system with common switching.

[*By permission of the G.E.C.*

Fig. 17.23.

The 100 outlets from the common group of two motion selectors are connected to the lines of the 100 subscribers.

This selection of switching for 100 lines thus involves 100 uniselectors and 10 two motion selectors. It will operate perfectly satisfactorily as long as there are no more than ten simultaneous calls. When the selectors are all in use an additional call at that instant is not possible and will be lost. This illustrates a fundamental point in automatic telephony, namely that a compromise has to be struck between the search for economy in the use of switches and the grade of service thereby provided. As an extreme illustration, the scheme shown in Fig. 17.22 will operate with a single two motion selector ; the waiting time and number of lost calls will then be very high. On the other hand if each subscriber has a two motion selector there will be no waiting time for a free selector, but the initial and maintenance costs will be needlessly large.

For ease of illustration, the uniselector is shown and described as a 10-position rotary switch. It should be noted however that the uniselectors used in current practice have 25 sets of contacts. One form of uniselector which is extensively used is shown in Fig. 17.23.

1,000 AND 10,000 LINE SYSTEMS WITH COMMON SWITCHING

(a) 1,000 Line System

A simple 1,000 line exchange can be considered as ten 100 line systems. To obtain any subscriber, three digits have to be dialled, and three stages of switching are necessary. The first digit selects the appropriate " hundreds " group, while the last two digits give the particular subscriber required. Group selection is achieved by the use of two motion selectors. A two motion final selector is connected to each of the 100 outlets of the group selectors. (In practice the resultant provision of a large number of final selectors would be uneconomic.)

Each subscriber has a uniselector which automatically hunts for a free group selector when the telephone is removed from its rest. The receipt of the first impulse train moves the wipers of the group selector vertically to the required level. On reaching this level the wipers then rotate automatically (in the inter-digit pause) until they find a free outlet to a final selector. This last step is referred to as non-numerical selection. The dialling of the second digit steps the final selector vertically to the required level and the dialling of the third digit causes rotation of the switch wipers to a particular contact in the level of the final selector and so completes the switching.

If the uniselectors have, say, 100 contacts there will be 10 associated group selectors for each hundred of the subscribers. The 10 group selectors have their corresponding contacts connected together so that there are 100 outlets connecting the 100 final selectors. The total numbers of switches used are thus 1,000 uniselectors, 100 group selectors and 1,000 final selectors. Fig. 17.24a shows the outline of the arrangement when the number dialled is 747.

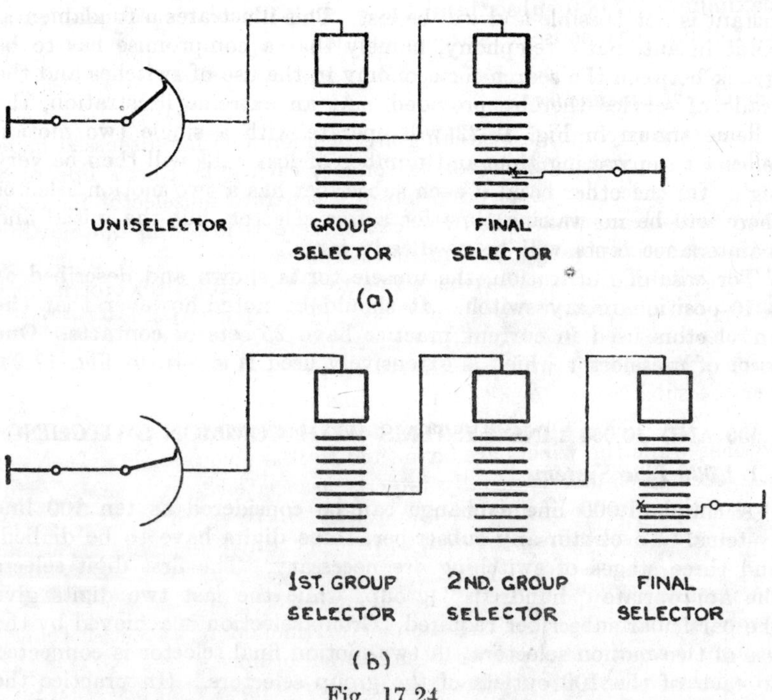

Fig. 17.24.

(b) 10,000 Line System

In a 10,000 line exchange, four digits have to be dialled to perform four stages of switching. In this case the switching path is via the subscriber's uniselector and first group selector where the first digit gives the desired " thousands " level. Non-numerical selection is then used to find a free second group selector in that level. In this selector the second digit gives the desired " hundreds " level and non-numerical selection follows in that level to obtain a free final selector. The third and fourth digits then give vertical and rotary motion to the wipers of the final selector to complete the switching. Fig. 17.24b shows the switching path when the number dialled is 5641.

Numbering Restrictions

It has so far been assumed that a four digit exchange will serve 10,000 subscribers' lines. Such an arrangement is quite feasible but normally there are restrictions on the first selector levels. Thus the first level of the first selector is not employed, as maloperation by a subscriber lifting his telephone from the switch-hook might cause the transmission of a false single impulse which would make the switch wipers search for an outlet in level 1. The tenth or 0 level of the first selector is used to obtain access to the automanual board to obtain the assistance of an operator. Level 9 is conventionally allotted to special services. With these restrictions a four digit exchange would have a maximum of 7,000 subscribers' lines. In particular cases additional restrictions may cause a further reduction.

The Use of Linefinders

The various common switching arrangements so far discussed have utilised a separate uniselector to connect each subscriber's line to a free group selector. This provision of a separate uniselector for each subscriber means that when the calling rate is low, the uniselectors are taken into operation infrequently. This situation can be improved if the switching of a subscriber's line to a free group selector is also placed on a common switching basis. The connection of the subscriber's line to the switching equipment then becomes a process in which a linefinder switch associated with a first group selector hunts over the subscribers' lines to find the line of the calling subscriber.

The subscribers' lines terminate on the bank contacts of linefinder switches while the wipers are connected to first group selectors.

As each linefinder is usually directly associated with a first group selector the number of linefinders required will be equal to the number of first group selectors provided, a quantity which depends upon the traffic.

A linefinder is more costly than a uniselector and so the greatest saving is obtained when the number of linefinders and first group selectors is small compared with the number of lines served. When the traffic is heavy and a relatively large number of linefinders are required, the economic advantage of linefinder operation disappears.

TELEPHONE TRAFFIC DEFINITIONS

The estimating of the switching quantities for an automatic telephone exchange is based primarily on the amount of traffic which it will be required to handle ; calculations of the probable average, and maximum amount of traffic, are necessary to determine the optimum number of switches required in the various switching ranks.

The more important quantities used in traffic calculations are :

(a) *Traffic Unit* (*T.U.*). The traffic unit is used to measure the traffic flow. The number of traffic units carried by a group of switches is numerically equal to the product of the number of calls per hour and the average duration of the calls in hours. The traffic flow in traffic units is equal to the average number of simultaneous calls.

(b) *Busy Hour*. This is defined as the hour of the day in each exchange when the originating traffic carried is the greatest.

(c) *Busy Hour Calling Rate*. This is the average number of calls initiated per subscriber during the busy hour.

(d) *Grade of Service*. The flow of traffic initiated by subscribers varies widely throughout the day, and from one day to the next. If during any traffic peak the number of outlets from a switching stage are all occupied, additional calls at that instant cannot be extended and completed and will thus be lost. The proportion of calls that are lost to the total number of calls in the busy hour determines the quantity known as the grade of service for that particular switching stage. In British practice the grade of service aimed at is one lost call in 500, i.e. a grade of service of 0·002.

(e) *Availability*. The number of trunks to which a switch has access is known as the availability. If a subscriber's uniselector has, say, 25 outlets, each of which is coupled to a first selector, then the availability of the uniselector is 25.

Relationship Between Grade of Service, Average Traffic and Number of Trunks Available

The number of trunks, i.e. the number of connections between one rank of switches and a succeeding rank is determined by the number of switches required in the second rank. A knowledge of the number of trunks required to provide a given grade of service when offered a certain average traffic, is of fundamental importance in all automatic switch quantity calculations. A number of studies have been made of this problem by various workers, and one solution by Erlang[1], for what is known as "pure chance" traffic, is shown in Appendix F, to give the relation

$$\frac{a}{A} = B = \frac{\frac{A^N}{N!}}{1 + A + \frac{A^2}{2!} + \frac{A^3}{3!} + \ldots + \frac{A^N}{N!}} \qquad 17.1$$

where a = Traffic lost, in traffic units

A = Total traffic offered in traffic units

B = Grade of service

N = Number of trunks available

Hence the lost traffic a, is given by

$$a = \frac{\dfrac{A^{N+1}}{N!}}{1 + A + \dfrac{A^2}{2!} + \dfrac{A^3}{3!} + \cdot \cdot \cdot + \dfrac{A^N}{N!}} \quad . \quad . \quad 17.2$$

If a set of N independent trunks is always tested in the same order the traffic offered to each trunk can be calculated with the help of equation 17.2. The traffic offered to any particular trunk is the traffic lost from the preceding trunk. Thus when N is equal to unity in equation 17.2 the lost traffic will be the traffic offered to the second trunk ; the lost traffic from the second trunk will be that offered to the third trunk.

The traffic lost from the first trunk and hence the traffic offered to the second trunk

$$= \frac{A^2}{1+A}$$

The traffic offered to the third trunk

$$= \frac{\dfrac{A^3}{2}}{1 + A + \dfrac{A^2}{2}}$$

and the traffic offered to the Nth trunk

$$= \frac{\dfrac{A^N}{(N-1)!}}{1 + A + \dfrac{A^2}{2!} + \dfrac{A^3}{3!} + \cdot \cdot \cdot \cdot + \dfrac{A^{N-1}}{(N-1)!}} \quad . \quad . \quad 17.3$$

The traffic carried by any particular trunk is the difference between the traffic offered to it and the traffic which is lost from it, or passed on to the next trunk ; the traffic carried by the Nth trunk is thus the difference between the traffic offered to the Nth trunk and that offered to the $(N+1)$th trunk.

The above relations between the grade of service, traffic offered, and number of trunks apply only when the conditions known as Full Availability exist. Full availability occurs between any two ranks of switches when every outlet of the first rank has access to all the switches of the second rank. Thus if subscribers' lines terminate on 25 position uniselectors the bank contacts of which are connected to 25 first selectors conditions of full availability apply between the uniselectors and the first selectors.

Grading

The interconnection of one rank of switches with another has so far assumed what is known as full availability. Thus in Fig. 17.22 10 position uniselectors are shown connected to 10 first selectors. Suppose, however, that the traffic flow is such that 50 first selectors are required. The uniselectors must then either have 50 positions or as an alternative the subscribers must be divided into groups, each of which has access to a proportion of the first selectors. With this last arrangement it would be possible to have five groups of (10 position) uniselectors with each group connected to 10 first selectors; each group would then correspond with the arrangement of Fig. 17.25a. Any given subscriber then has a choice of only 10 first selectors; if these are all engaged his call would be lost. This position would not arise with a 50 position uniselector unless the whole 50 first selectors were engaged; the probability of this happening is less than the probability that the smaller group of 10 first selectors will be engaged.

Hence the subdivision of the subscribers into five groups would give an inferior grade of service compared with the single group case. Alternatively, to maintain the grade of service when the subscribers are divided into five groups the number of first selectors would have to be increased to say, 60. The 60 first selectors could then be served by five groups of 12 position uniselectors. This would then permit each group of subscribers to have access to 12 first selectors.

It would seem worth while to have switches with a large number of outlets. Two factors, however, limit the number of outlets possible. First, the available searching time to find a free outlet should be small, and in the case of first or subsequent selectors this time must not be greater than that of the inter-digit pause. Also the extra cost of the large capacity switches must not be so great as to outweigh the saving effected by reducing the number of trunks and subsequent switches. Another objection to a switch with a very large number of outlets such as, say a 100 position uniselector, is that most of the traffic would be carried by the trunks connected to the first few contacts, while the trunks connected to the later contacts would be used infrequently, as they would be the last choices.

The interconnection between ranks of switches is usually such as to give some form of limited availability, i.e. to limit the number of trunks of a group to which particular selectors have access. This is achieved by "grading" of the trunks. Fig. 17.25b shows a very simple example of the principle of grading. Two uniselectors are shown, each of which is assumed to represent a group of uniselectors (which have all their corresponding contacts connected together). The two groups have 25 outlets or trunks giving access to 25 first selectors. Of these 10 are reached by the first group alone, a further

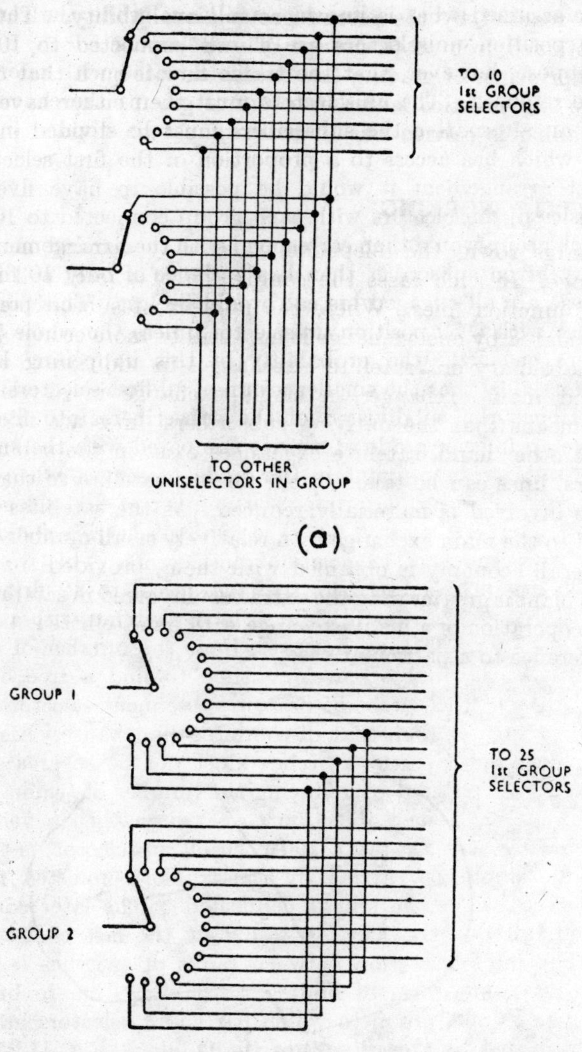

Fig. 17.25 (a) Full availability
(b) Simple grading (limited availabili

10 are reached by the second group alone while the remaining five are obtained from both groups of uniselectors.

The principle of grading has been illustrated with reference to two groups. In practice larger numbers of groups are encountered, and the grading is carried out in more than two steps.

SATELLITE WORKING

In large towns the telephone traffic may demand more than one exchange. In such cases the completion of a local call involves the use of junction lines. Where the number of subscribers can be accommodated by one exchange it may still be more economic to operate with subsidiary or "satellite" exchanges in addition to the centrally situated main exchange. A single exchange in a relatively large town means that the outlying subscribers' lines are fairly long. If, on the other hand, satellite exchanges exist in the suburbs the subscribers' lines can be taken to the nearest satellite so that the length of line involved is materially reduced. As the satellites can be connected to the main exchange by a relatively small number of junctions, an overall economy is obtained with them, provided that the saving in line plant is greater than the extra cost involved in satellite operation.

The operation of a main exchange with its satellites is best discussed by reference to a particular case.

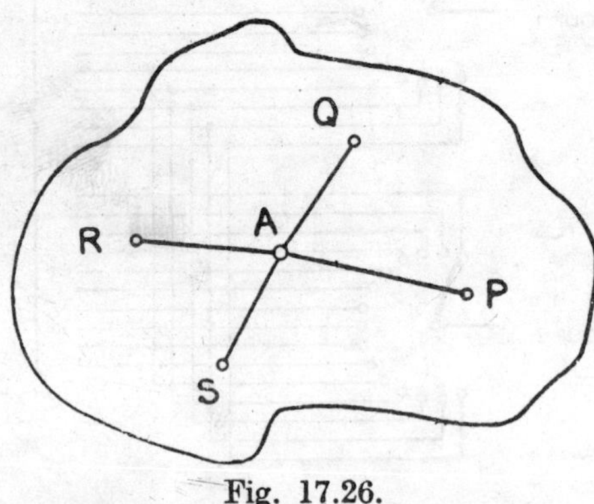

Fig. 17.26.

Suppose for purposes of illustration the area is that shown in Fig. 17.26. This hypothetical area is assumed to have a main exchange A with 4,000 lines and four satellites P, Q, R and S. The satellite P has 1,600 lines while each of the others have 400 lines.

One possible solution of the trunking necessary for an area such as this is shown in Fig. 17.27. Calls to main exchange subscribers proceed by the appropriate level of the first group selector (levels 2 to 5) and then to the particular second group selector and final selector. The final selectors of satellite P are reached via the seventh level of the first group selector and then either by the levels 2–7 of the second group selector or by the first level of this selector and then through a third group selector. In the latter case 5-digit dialling is necessary. The satellites Q, R and S are obtained by 5-digit dialling and all are reached by the sixth level of the first group selector. The satellites can be regarded as detached portions of the main exchange switching plant.

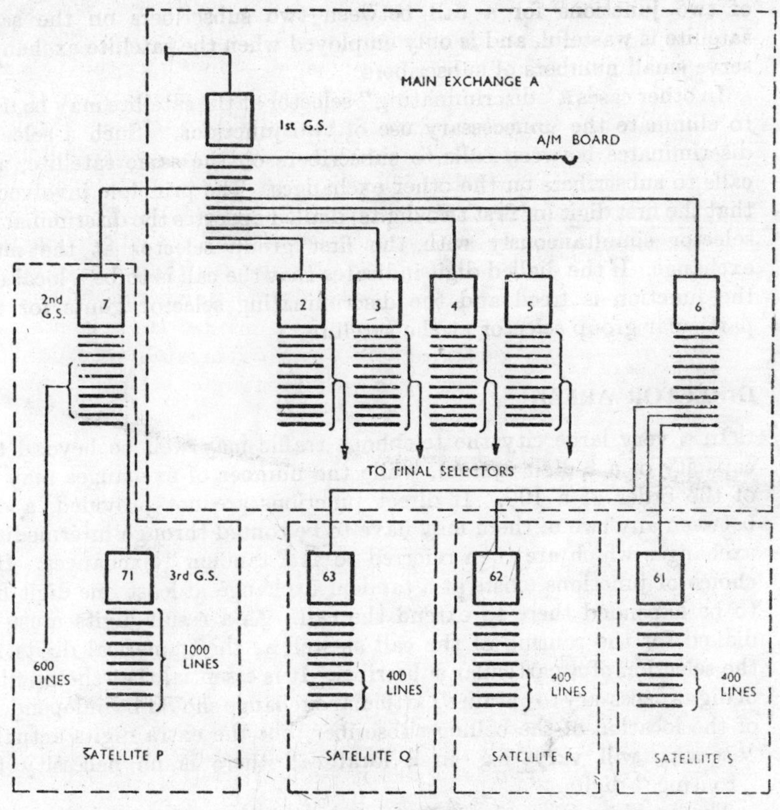

Fig. 17.27.

It should be noted that Fig. 17.27 shows only a single first group selector with a single second group selector connected to each of six of its levels. Any practical scheme would of course have a number of first group selectors with several second group selectors connected to each of the six levels used.

Another point to remember in connection with Fig. 17.27 is that all calls, whether originated at the main or satellite exchanges, will pass through the first group selectors at the main exchange. As a consequence a call between two subscribers connected to the same satellite will involve two junctions, the first will connect the calling subscriber's uniselector or linefinder to the first group selector at the main exchange; the second junction will be required from the appropriate level of a main exchange second group selector (or first selector in the case of satellite *P*) to the third (or second) selector at the satellite. This use of two junctions for a call between two subscribers on the same satellite is wasteful, and is only employed when the satellite exchanges serve small numbers of subscribers.

In other cases a "discriminating" selector at the satellite may be used to eliminate the unnecessary use of two junctions. Such a selector discriminates between calls to subscribers on the same satellite, and calls to subscribers on the other exchanges. The principle involved is that the first digit (or first two digits) dialled operates the discriminating selector simultaneously with the first group selector at the main exchange. If the dialled digit indicates that the call is to be a local one the junction is freed and the discriminating selector hunts for the particular group selector at the satellite.

DIRECTOR AREAS

In a very large city the telephone traffic may well be beyond the capacity of a 5-digit system, while the number of exchanges may be of the order of a 100. If direct junctions are not provided, a call between any two of them may have to be routed through intermediate exchanges which are then referred to as "tandem" exchanges. If a choice of junctions exists at a tandem exchange at least one digit has to be expended there to extend the call. As a result digits must be dialled for the routing of the call as well as the numerical digits for the selection of a particular subscriber. It is essential that the number of digits necessary to obtain a particular exchange should be independent of the location of the calling subscriber, but the extra digits actually necessary will vary, e.g. in a local call there is no necessity for "routing" digits.

The problem of routing calls in such areas is simplified if the digits dialled to obtain a particular exchange can be translated into another set of digits which constitute a code for the routing of the call; the equipment used for the translation of the original digits is termed the "director", and the multi-exchange areas in which it is employed are referred to as "director areas". The dialling system in such areas commonly uses seven digits, the first three of which are used and translated by the director to obtain the particular exchange desired.

The last four digits are then used for the numerical selection of a particular subscriber on a 10,000 line exchange.

The translation equipment is arranged so that the train of impulses from the first digit dialled (referred to as the *A* digit), is applied to a two motion switch, known as an *A*-digit selector. The particular digit which is dialled determines the level to which this selector is stepped; the wipers then search over this level to find a free director. The second and third digits (*B* and *C* digits), then operate a two motion switch in the director circuit. This particular switch, (*B C* switch), has its bank contacts cross-connected to another switch in accordance with the code for the routes to the various exchanges. A set of routing digits are then produced and transmitted by the director back through the *A*-digit selector. The numerical digits forming the exchange number of the called subscriber are stored and then re-transmitted at the end of the transmission of the routing code. The *A*-digit selector and director are then released for subsequent use on another call.

The coding, or routing, digits may vary in number from one, for a local call, up to a maximum of six. The impulse trains of these digits

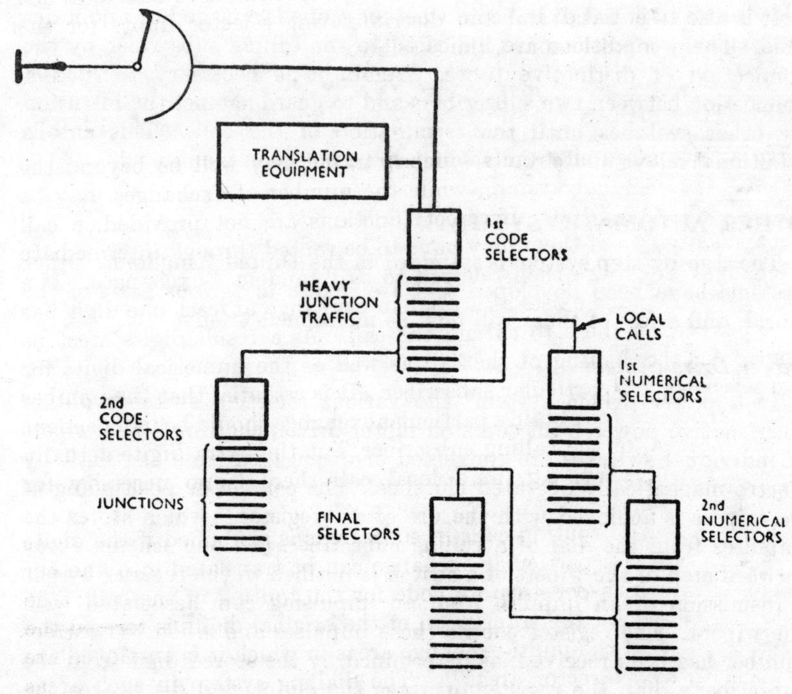

Fig. 17.28.

are applied, step-by-step, to selector switches (known as code selectors) to give the desired route to the distant exchange. Fig. 17.28 shows the schematic arrangement when two code selectors are involved. The junctions which carry a large amount of traffic are allotted levels in the first code selector. Routes which are less frequently used have to pass through the second, and possibly additional, code selectors.

Existing director equipment utilises electromechanical switchgear. Electronic directors have however been produced[2], and will displace present designs in the future.

METERING AND OTHER FACILITIES

The discussion of automatic telephony has been restricted to a bare outline of the main features of step-by-step switching, and on a first approach to the subject this is all that is desirable. It should not be forgotten however that a system of automatic telephony is only practicable if other facilities are provided. It is obvious that a scheme for metering calls is essential. This means that each subscriber must be provided with a meter and circuit equipment for its operation on effective calls.

It is also essential to indicate whether a line is engaged or unobtainable. These conditions are indicated to the calling subscriber by the connection of distinctive tones. Again it is necessary to hold a connection between two subscribers and to guard against the intrusion by other switches until the termination of the call. This entails additional relays and circuits which have not been mentioned.

OTHER AUTOMATIC SYSTEMS

The step-by-step system is standard in the United Kingdom. Other systems have been developed and are in use in various parts of the world, and a few of them will now be mentioned briefly.

Power Drive System

In a power driven system[3] the various selecting switches obtain their motive power from common motor-driven shafting. The wipers of individual switches are connected or disengaged from the shaft by electro-magnetically operated clutches. The control or positioning of the wipers is achieved with the use of a "register" which stores the impulses from the dial of a calling subscriber. In one scheme every forward step of the wipers of a switch is notified to the register by the transmission of an impulse from an impulsing cam associated with the wipers. The register counts these impulses and when the correct number has been received, as determined by the stored digit from the subscriber's dial, the register operates the clutch and disengages the wipers from the driving shaft.

Such an arrangement has the advantage that a relatively high pressure between the wipers and fixed contact can be employed. On the other hand a fault in the common drive equipment may affect a large number of switches.

By-Path System

The outstanding feature of a by-path system[4] is that two distinct " paths " are provided, namely a main path for the speech connection and a " by-path " for switching purposes. The advantage of this is that the switches are not held for the whole duration of a call but are only utilised for the short time required to connect the lines of the calling and called subscriber. The switches can thus be released for further work although the call they have set up is still in progress. The by-path is first set up between one rank of switches and the next, and is then replaced by a speech path. This process is repeated until the speech path is complete.

Crossbar System

This system is based on the use of an electro-mechanical crossbar switch[5], the principle of which is shown in Fig. 17.29.

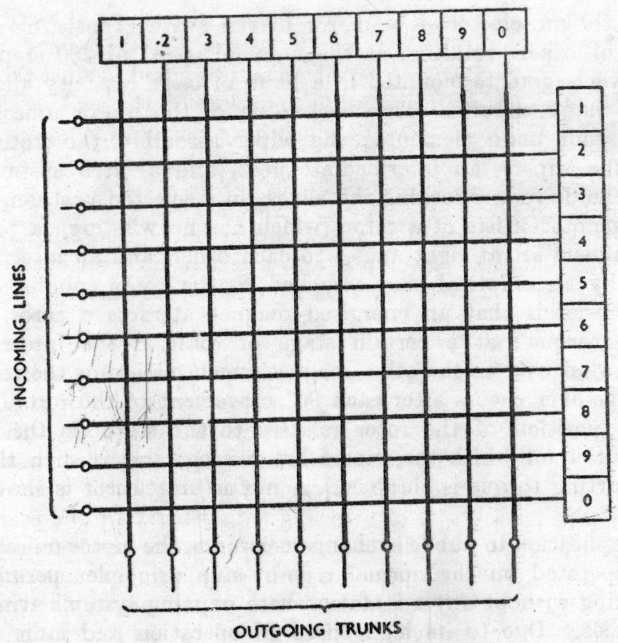

Fig. 17.29.

The crossbar switch has vertical and horizontal bars represented by the vertical and horizontal lines in Fig. 17.29. Each vertical bar has 10 sets of contacts at the crossing points of the horizontal and vertical lines, and the mechanism can cross connect any " vertical circuit " to a " horizontal circuit " by associated electro-magnets. Hence if the horizontal lines in the diagram represent subscribers' circuits and the vertical lines represent trunks, any subscriber can be connected to any trunk.

The common form of crossbar switch has 20 vertical and 5 horizontal bars ; each of the latter has two associated electro-magnets any one of which may be operated at a time to tilt the bar through a small angle on each side of the normal position. The five horizontal bars and ten electro-magnets can thus operate any of the ten sets of contacts on each of the vertical bars, and the assembly is equivalent to twenty 10-point switches.

In addition to the different form of the switchgear, the crossbar system[6] differs fundamentally from step-by-step systems in that the switching is performed by common control circuits. These set up the connections in a manner similar to that used in a by-path system.

Motor Uniselector Switching

The motor uniselector[7] is a motor driven switch consisting of an assembly of wipers rotating, at the nominal speed of 200 steps per second, over segments mounted in a bank of large capacity allowing access to many circuits. The mechanism of the motor uniselector comprises four main elements : the wiper assembly, the motor for rotating the wipers, an intermediate gear, and a latch system for stopping the drive and locking the wipers in a selected position. The motor element consists of a rotor (which has no winding), a pair of electro-magnets set at right angles to each other, and an interrupter actuated by an elliptical cam attached to the rotor spindle. The action in brief is that an energised magnet attracts a rotor pole, producing torque ; at a certain stage of rotation the interrupter switches power over to the other magnet which maintains the torque. This change-over occurs after each 90° movement of the rotor. The stationary position of the rotor relative to the stator is the same for any outlet on which the wipers are resting, and is such that a reliable starting torque is obtained. A motor uniselector is shown in Fig. 17.30.

In its application to public exchange networks, the motor uniselector may be operated on the normal step-by-step principles permitting inter-working without any adaptation with existing systems arranged on this basis. Due to its high speed of operation and large bank capacity, the motor uniselector can sometimes combine the functions of two of the group switching stages into one switch rank, thus

[By permission of Siemens Bros.

Fig. 17.30.

effecting savings in switch requirements. It is also very widely used for the switching of trunk traffic.

Electronic Switching

All large scale automatic telephone systems[8] operate at present by electro-mechanical means, i.e. the switching is performed either directly, or indirectly, by electro-mechanical relays. All the switching produced thereby may however be done by electronic devices, and the trend of development in automatic working is to use electronic switching. This may change the fundamental methods employed in step-by-step switching, because while it is perfectly feasible to replace existing switching equipment by its electronic analogue, the extensive use of transistors is likely to lead to the use of other switching systems.

CARRIER TELEPHONY

BASIC FEATURES OF A CARRIER TELEPHONE SYSTEM

The transmission of speech over long trunk routes is operated on a multi-channel carrier basis employing frequency division multiplex. The usable frequency spectrum of the line or cable used is split into a number of adjacent bands, each of which is then employed as a separate channel ; at least one stage of modulation is essential at the transmitting terminal, in order that the speech should occupy one of the channels ; in some cases three stages of modulation are involved. Modern systems are usually operated on a " four wire " basis, which comprises a " transmit " channel and a " receive " channel ; the two channels then form one circuit.

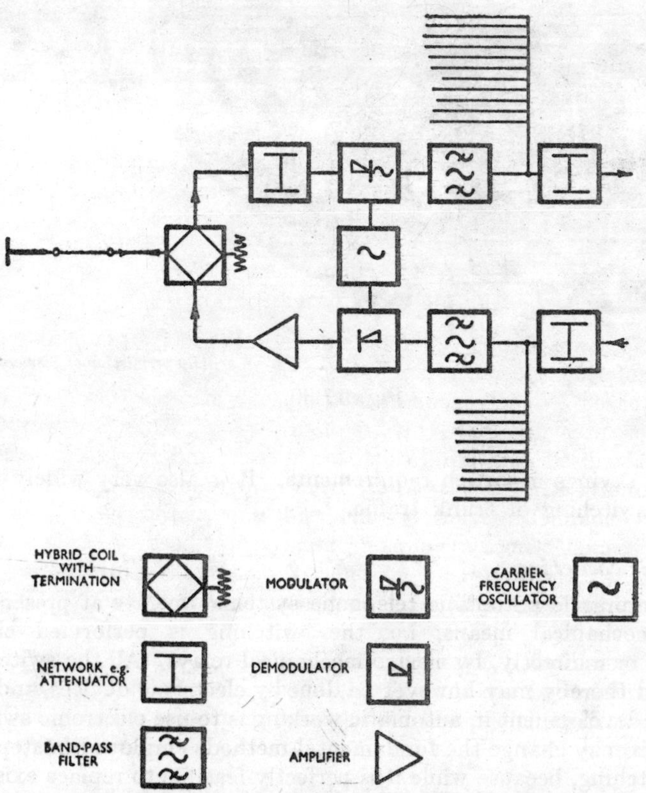

Fig. 17.31. Basic features of channel formation.

If, for purposes of illustration, a single stage of modulation is assumed, the broad sequence of events involved in carrier transmission can be followed with the help of Fig. 17.31.

The speech, fed over two wires, is first of all passed to a hybrid coil at the trunk terminal and the two wire circuit then becomes a four wire circuit. The speech from the hybrid in the transmit channel is passed through an attenuator, to adjust the level to the correct value ; it is then applied to a balanced modulator which is also supplied with a carrier voltage. The original speech and carrier voltages are suppressed and the amplitude modulated sidebands are applied to a band pass filter, which rejects one of the sidebands and passes the other. The outputs from the band pass filters of the other channels are then connected in parallel and passed through an equalising network, the output of which is connected to the line or cable, i.e. to the two conductors which form the transmit half of the circuit.

After transmission through the line, the sequence of events outlined above is reversed in that the channels are separated by band pass filters and then demodulated. Speech is then obtained in a two wire circuit from each of the hybrid coils at the receiving terminal. An amplifier is sometimes connected between the demodulator and terminal hybrid coil, as shown in Fig. 17.31.

In the case of transmission in the opposite direction, i.e. from what has been referred to as the receiving terminal, to the transmitting terminal, a similar process obtains.

Recommendations of the CCITT

Before discussing the details of any carrier system it is worth while considering the recommendations of the CCITT as modern systems are based on such recommendations. It has already been mentioned in chapter 15 that the frequency range 300–3400 Hz has been standardised as a bandwidth for speech, and is accommodated in a channel 4 kHz wide. Apart from low-frequency carrier systems, all multi-channel carrier systems are now based on two alternative 12-channel primary groups. One group utilises upper sidebands and occupies the frequency range 12–60 kHz, while the other group transmits lower sidebands, and occupies the frequency range 60–108 kHz.

Three kinds of systems incorporating these primary groups are now in widespread use throughout the world. (These schemes, which are summarised below, will be discussed in greater detail in the following pages.)

1. 24-circuit systems, on multi-pair cables, transmitted in the range 12–108 kHz. (Some countries only use 12 channels per pair.)

2. 960-circuit systems, on coaxial cables, transmitted as 16 " super-groups " of 60 channels in the range 60–4,028 kHz. A 6 MHz and a 12 MHz system (with a capacity of 2700 circuits) are also used.
3. 12-circuit grouped systems on open wire lines ; agreement on frequency bands has not so far been possible, but maximum frequencies extend to about 160 kHz.

British practice makes use of the first two schemes, but not the third.

MULTI-CHANNEL SYSTEMS

The main features of the more important forms of multi-channel systems will now be considered. Of all the systems in current use, the coaxial cable system is most important, as it forms the basic system for national networks in all industrialised countries. Twelve and twenty-four channel systems are so arranged that they may form part of the coaxial cable system.[9]

(1) COAXIAL CABLE SYSTEM

This multi-channel system is based on the use of coaxial cable. This particular form of cable is discussed in chapter 19. For the present it should simply be regarded as a concentric cable which, in association with suitable amplifiers, enables frequencies up to 4 MHz to be transmitted. This allows 960 channels of 4 kHz bandwidth to be transmitted over the single (two conductor) cable. The use of two cables, one for each direction of transmission, then gives a system of 960 telephone circuits.

In the Standard Telephones and Cables system which follows CCITT recommendation, and is representative of current practice, three stages of modulation are employed. In the first, the channels consisting of voice frequency bands from 300–3,400 Hz are modulated to form a basic group of twelve channels in the frequency range 60–108 kHz. The channel carriers used have the frequencies 108, 104, 100 . . . . 64 kHz. The modulators employ four rectifiers and are of the balanced type described in chapter 14. The speech and carrier voltages are substantially suppressed so that the output consists of the two amplitude modulated sidebands. The output from each modulator is then passed through a band pass filter which transmits the lower sideband.

The second stage of modulation translates five groups (each extending from 108–60 kHz) into positions in the frequency band of a " super-group ", which extends from 312–552 kHz. This is achieved by the use of group modulators, and group carriers which have frequencies of 420, 468, 516, 564 and 612 kHz. The lower sideband from each group modulator is selected for transmission. Fig. 17.32 illustrates the generation of the basic group and super-group.

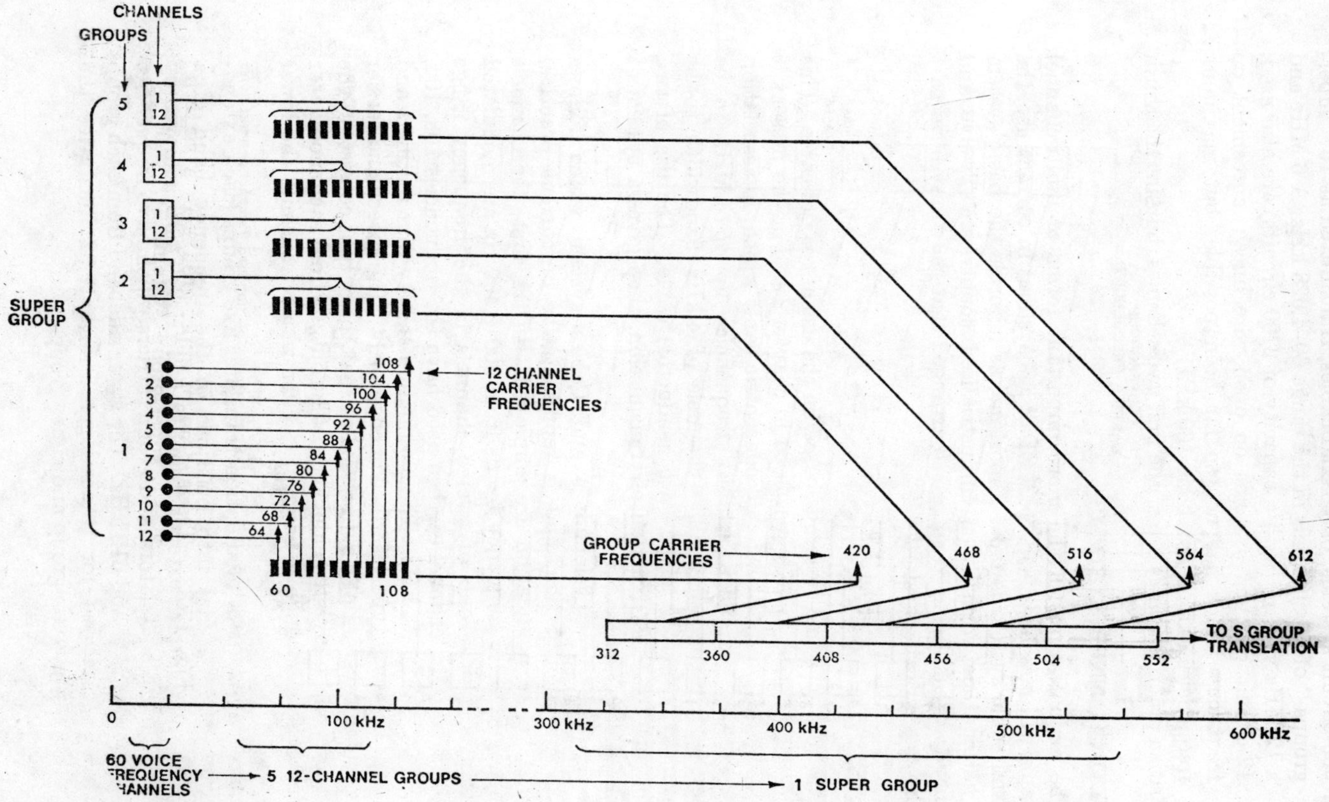

Fig. 17.32. Generation of the basic group and super-group.

[By permission of Standard Telephones and Cables

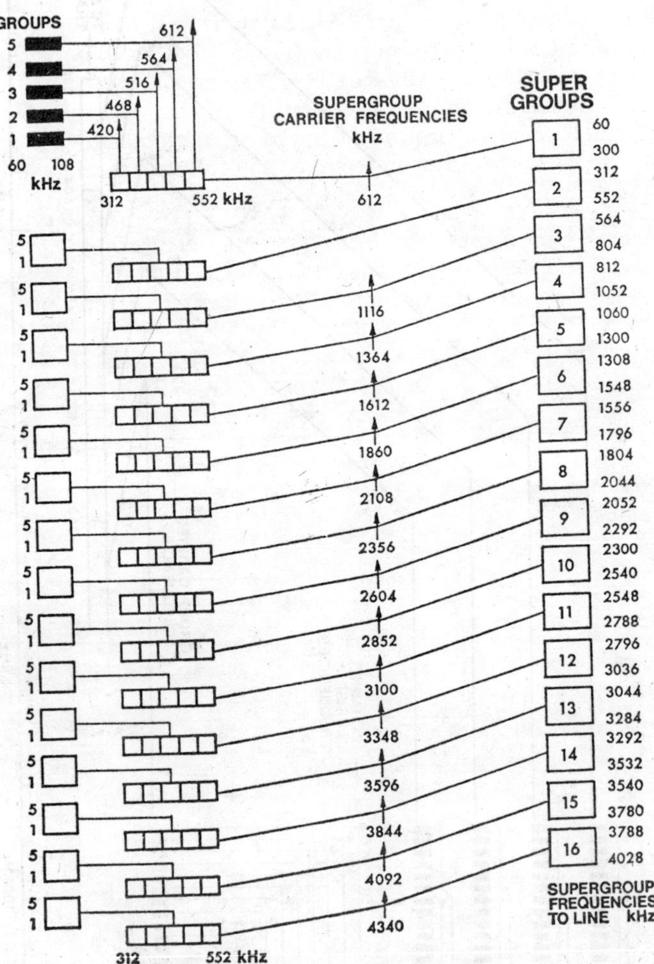

[*By permission of Standard Telephones and Cables*

Fig. 17.33. Translation of super-groups in a sixteen super-group system.

The third stage of modulation translates sixteen super-groups to occupy positions in the frequency range 60–4,028 kHz (Fig. 17.33).

In some cases only ten super-groups (600 channels) are used; the upper frequency limit is then 2,540 kHz. It will be seen in Fig. 17.33 that the second super-group is transmitted to line without any frequency translation. This enables sixty circuits to be used at some point intermediate between the main terminals, without the need for the installation of super-group translation equipment.

The 12 MHz system operates over the frequency range of 300 kHz to 12·5 MHz.

Channel Equipment. The term "channel equipment" in a coaxial cable system refers to the apparatus required to produce the twelve channels of the basic group. The main channel equipment is shown in Fig. 17.34. Speech from the trunk switchboard is passed through a hybrid transformer and variable attenuator to the channel modulator. The output from each modulator is then passed through a band pass filter which is built up of quartz crystals arranged to form two lattice

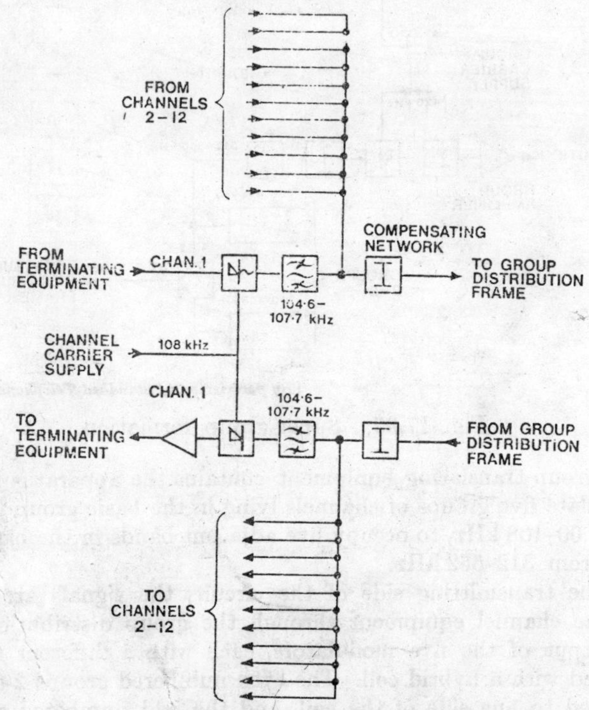

[*By permission of Standard Telephones and Cables*

Fig. 17.34. Channel equipment for group formation.

sections. The output from all twelve filters is then passed through a compensating network which presents a 600 ohm impedance to each filter channel, irrespective of the variation in input impedance of the other parallel connected channel filters. The groups of twelve channels are passed to a group distribution frame which provides a convenient point for the re-routing of blocks of twelve channels.

Group Translation Equipment. This equipment functions in a manner similar to the channel equipment. The schematic arrangement is shown in Fig. 17.35.

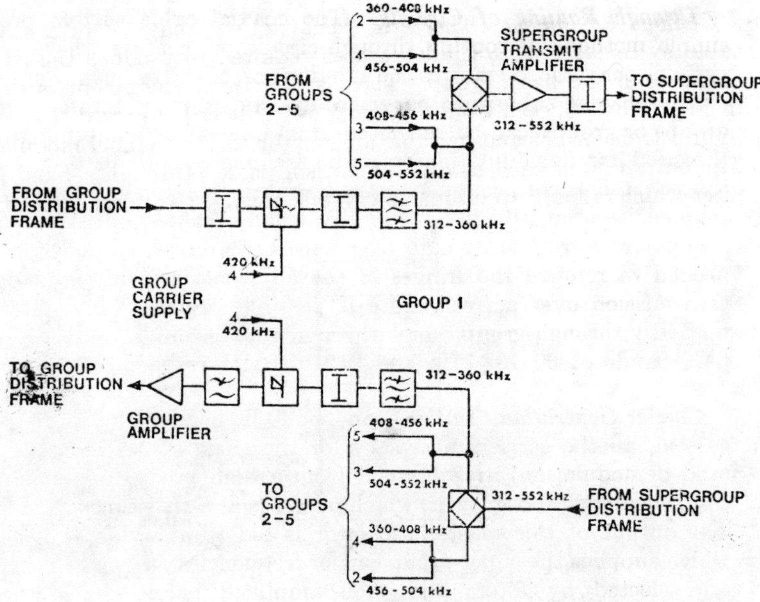

[*By permission of Standard Telephones and Cables*

Fig. 17.35. Super-group formation.

The group translating equipment contains the apparatus necessary to translate five groups of channels lying in the basic group frequency band of 60–108 kHz, to occupy five adjacent bands in the basic super-group from 312–552 kHz.

On the transmitting side of the circuit, the signals are received from the channel equipment through the group distribution frame. The output of the five modulators, each with a different filter, are combined with a hybrid coil. The even numbered groups 2 and 4 are connected to one side of the coil, and the odd numbered groups to the other. This arrangement is used as the rates of cut-off of the filters are such that their pass bands have considerable overlaps. By connecting even and odd numbered filters in separate parallel groups, there is no overlap of pass ranges or variation in the impedance facing each filter.

Super-group Translation Equipment. The output of the group translation equipment is brought to the super-group translation equipment through a super-group distribution frame. This enables through connections of circuits to be made between one system and another in blocks of sixty.

The equipment follows the same general pattern as that described in the formation of the super-groups.

Through Routing of Circuits. The coaxial cable system provides simple methods of routing through-circuits at centres where several systems converge. Owing to the sub-division of the frequency spectrum of the coaxial cable into super-groups and groups, complete super-groups or groups can be re-routed from one cable to another without the need for demodulation to audio frequency. When this is done, the selected super-groups or groups contain portions of the adjacent frequencies originally present in the cable. Where groups and super-groups are re-routed at high frequencies, therefore, special filters are needed to remove the fringes of the adjacent frequencies before re-transmission over a fresh route is possible. Such special filters are termed " through-group " or " through supergroup " filters, and have pass bands of 60–108 kHz and 312–552 kHz respectively.

Carrier Generation. In the Standard Telephones and Cables coaxial system, all the carriers necessary for the three stages of modulation (and demodulation) are obtained from a high precision, temperature controlled crystal oscillator, which operates at a frequency of 124 kHz. The output of this master oscillator is fed to a harmonic generator which supplies the super-group carrier frequencies ; required harmonics are selected by filters and then amplified before distribution to modulators and demodulators.

For the channel and group frequencies, the 124 kHz supply is divided down to 4 kHz and this frequency is then used in odd and even harmonic generators to provide the channel frequencies spaced at 4 kHz intervals, and the group frequencies spaced at 48 kHz intervals.

The terminal equipment also contains frequency comparison equipment. This enables the frequencies generated by the two terminal stations of the system to be compared on a cathode ray oscilloscope.

Line Equipment. It has already been mentioned that all the channels in one direction are transmitted over a single coaxial cable, while a second cable is used for the opposite direction. Both cables are however included in a common sheath so that the "go" and "return" channels are incorporated in a common "cable". Fig. 17.36 shows some of these composite cables. The smallest is a single coaxial cable used for special applications or for lead-in. Two, four and six tube coaxial cables are shown, each with interstice audio pairs for control purposes. The largest cable has four coaxial tubes, with interstice pairs, surrounded by audio pairs. This type is used when circuits to intermediate points have to be extended from the nearest station equipped for access to the high frequency circuits. The audio pairs can also be used for short audio circuits between intermediate points.

[*By permission of Standard Telephones and Cables*

Fig. 17.36. Forms of coaxial cable.

The cable has an attenuation of about 8 dB per mile at 4 MHz and repeaters have a spacing of about seven miles. They are of two types, main and auxiliary. The former normally receive their power supply of alternating current from a public supply undertaking. The auxiliary stations on each side are supplied with power fed through the conductors of the coaxial cable itself from the main repeater station. Power supply frequencies are isolated from the transmission equipment by a combination of filters.

The amplification produced at the repeater stations is of the order of 50 dB, and is controlled as required, by a pilot frequency of 4,092 kHz. This is produced by the carrier supply equipment, and is regulated at the terminal to a standard level. Variable equalising networks are controlled by the level of two other pilot frequencies,

[By permission of Standard Telephones and Cables

Fig. 17.37. Terminal repeater bays (right) and channel modulators and demodulators

one at 60 kHz, and one in the middle range of the frequency spectrum.

Fig. 17.37 shows the form of construction used in multi-channel terminal equipment.

(2) 24-CIRCUIT SYSTEM

This system provides 24 circuits which are obtained as two groups of twelve. The upper group have carriers with frequencies of 64, 68, 72 . . . . 104, 108 kHz. The channels are obtained by direct modulation of the carriers. Balanced modulators are used, and only the lower sideband is transmitted to line. The second group of twelve channels is obtained by a double modulation process. The first stage of modulation again involves twelve carriers spaced at 4 kHz intervals from 64–108 kHz. The twelve channel group thus formed is then used as group modulation of a carrier of 120 kHz, and the resulting lower sideband is selected. Twelve virtual carrier frequencies ranging from 12–56 kHz are obtained and the upper sidebands are transmitted. This second group of 12 channels then extends from 120 minus 108 to 120 minus 60 kHz, i.e. 12 to 60 kHz.

The whole arrangement then gives 24 channels which extend from 12–108 kHz.

Line Equipment. The 24 circuit system is operated on a four wire basis on multi-pair, paper insulated cables. One pair is used to carry the " go " channels, while a second pair, in a separate cable, is used for the " return " channels. Two separate cables are thus essential for this system. Each particular cable is made up of a number of " pairs " so that two cables can carry traffic from several 24 circuit systems.

The cable, normally used, gives an attenuation of 2–3 dB/km at the highest frequencies, and repeaters are installed every 20–30 km. The repeaters, like those installed on coaxial systems, employ negative feedback and have an overall gain of the order of 50 dB.

Carrier Generation. When used independently of a coaxial cable system, the carriers required are generated as harmonics of a 4 kHz oscillator. This in turn is driven from a 1 kHz oscillator, controlled by a 1 kHz tuning fork. As in the coaxial cable system the 4 kHz oscillator is fed to an amplifier and filter system, which has a permalloy cored inductance connected across the output terminals.[10] The 4 kHz sine waveform causes magnetic saturation of the core thereby giving a distorted output which is rich in harmonics ; the odd harmonics are obtained directly from the saturated inductor and even harmonics are obtained from a metal rectifier bridge connected to the saturated coil. The harmonics are selected and used as carriers for the various channel modulators.

(3) 12-CIRCUIT OPEN WIRE SYSTEMS

This type of system is operated over a single pair of overhead open wire conductors. Because of this, different frequencies are used in the "go" and "return" channels. Three stages of modulation are employed, namely channel modulation and two stages of group modulation. Most forms of this system employ the same frequencies for channel modulation, but variations exist in the frequencies used in the group modulation processes.

In some systems the voice frequency bands are individually modulated with carriers spaced at 4 kHz interval from 64–108 kHz, and the lower sidebands are transmitted. The group of twelve lower sidebands then passes to the first stage of group modulation, and is translated from the 60–108 kHz range to 400–448 kHz as the upper sideband of a 340 kHz carrier ; in one form of this type of system the second group carrier has a frequency of 308 kHz. The signals are translated to occupy the range 92–140 kHz. This range is then used for say East to West transmission. For transmission in the opposite direction, the carrier in the second group modulator has a frequency of 484 kHz, so that the signals then extend from 36–84 kHz.

With open wire lines the attenuation is much less than that in multi-pair cables ; the exact value of the attenuation depends on the gauge of wire used, the line construction, and the climatic conditions. The repeaters are spaced at 80–150 km and have a gain of 30–35 dB. In order to compensate for severe changes in attenuation caused by changes in atmospheric conditions, especially when frost and sleet are encountered, a wide range of gain is provided, at terminal and repeater stations. The voltage levels are maintained throughout the system by the transmission of two pilot frequencies.

(4) OTHER CARRIER SYSTEMS

In addition to the systems already described, other arrangements, operating on open wire routes, or multi-pair cables are used. In one system, three carrier channels are used together with a speech channel. The frequency range used for the "go" carrier channels differs from that used for the "receive" carrier channels. The frequency range used for carrier working is approximately 6–30 kHz. This type of system is often used on open wire lines which carry a 12-circuit system.

SUBMARINE TRANSMISSION

As a consequence of the development and widespread use of multi-channel carrier telephone systems over land, it has become desirable to operate submarine telephone cables on a multi-channel basis in order to increase their traffic handling capacity. Carrier operation necessitates the insertion of some form of repeater at relatively frequent intervals along the cable, so that submerged repeaters are necessary for submarine cables of any appreciable length.

Submerged repeaters,[11] incorporating long-life valves, have now been developed for use either in shallow seas or in oceans. The first type is used on submarine routes to Ireland and to Europe, while the second is employed in the Atlantic telephone cable system.[11] Multi-channel carrier operation is used with both types of repeater to increase the traffic handling-capacity of the cable system.

The Atlantic is spanned by two cables to give a separate transmission path in each direction. Armoured coaxial cable with an overall diameter of approximately 3 cm is used; the transmission loss varies from 0·32 to 0·85 dB per km over the service frequency range of 20–164 kHz. The repeaters, which form an integral part of the cable, are at equally spaced intervals and 51 are used in each direction; each repeater provides 65 dB of amplification at the top frequency of 164 kHz.

The system gives one telegraph channel and 35 speech channels. These are assembled as three 12-channel groups in the range 60–108 kHz from standard terminal equipment, and then translated to occupy the spectrum of 20–164 kHz.

WORKED EXAMPLES

1. A total of two traffic units is offered to a full availability group of six trunks. Calculate the grade of service provided, and find also the traffic carried by the first and last trunk. Assume that calls to the group arrive in pure chance order.

The grade of service provided may be obtained directly by the use of equation 17.1. In this case, $N=6$ and $A=2$, hence the grade of service, B, is given by

$$B=\frac{\dfrac{2^6}{6!}}{1+2+\dfrac{2^2}{2!}+\dfrac{2^3}{3!}+\;\ldots\;+\dfrac{2^6}{6!}}$$

$$\frac{\dfrac{64}{720}}{1+2+2+\dfrac{8}{6}+\dfrac{16}{24}+\dfrac{32}{120}+\dfrac{64}{720}}=\underline{0{\cdot}012.}$$

The traffic offered to the second trunk is that lost by the first, and is given by

$$\frac{A^2}{1+A}=\frac{4}{3}=1{\cdot}33.$$

Hence traffic carried by first trunk $=0{\cdot}66$ $T.U.$

Traffic offered to the 6th trunk

$$=\frac{\frac{2^6}{5!}}{1+2+\frac{2^2}{2!}+\ .\ .\ .\ .\ +\frac{2^5}{5!}}=0{\cdot}073$$

Traffic offered to the hypothetical 7th trunk

$$=\frac{\frac{2^7}{6!}}{1+2+\ .\ .\ .\ .\ .\ .\ +\frac{2^6}{6!}}=0{\cdot}024$$

Hence traffic carried by 6th trunk

$$=0{\cdot}073-0{\cdot}024=0{\cdot}049\ T.U.$$

The traffic lost is that offered to the hypothetical 7th trunk. The proportion of lost calls, i.e. grade of service, when a total of two traffic units are involved is then

$$\frac{0{\cdot}024}{2}=0{\cdot}012$$

which agrees with the calculation previously made for B.

2. It is found that, during the busy hour, the average number of calls in progress simultaneously in a certain full availability group of selectors was 15. All the selectors are in use simultaneously for a total period of 30 seconds. Calculate the traffic, in traffic units, offered to the group in the busy hour.

If C = Number of calls per hour

T = Average duration of a call in hours

and A = the traffic flow in traffic units

then $A=C\times T$

The traffic lost will be $=A\times B$ traffic units.

if B = proportion of calls lost

The traffic carried = traffic offered − traffic lost

$$\therefore 15 = A - AB$$

$$\text{or } A = \frac{15}{1-B} \text{ traffic units}$$

$$\text{Now } B = \frac{30}{60 \times 60}$$

$$\text{hence } A = \frac{15}{1 - \dfrac{30}{60 \times 60}} = 15{\cdot}13 \ T.U.$$

Hence the traffic offered to the group of trunks during the busy hour is 15·13 *T.U.*

References

[1] Erlang, A. K.: "Solution of Some Problems in the Theory of Probabilities of Significance in Automatic Telephone Exchanges", *P.O.E.E. Journal*, 10, p. 189 (1917).

[2] Heron, K. M., Baker, H. and Benson, D. L.: "An Experimental Electronic Director", *P.O.E.E. Journal*, 44, p. 97 (1951).

[3] Schreiber, L. and Hatton, W.: "The 7-A2 Rotary Automatic Telephone System", *Electrical Communication*, 11, p. 179 (1933).

[4] Wright, E. P. G. and Baker, J. H. E.: "The Bypath Automatic Telephone System", *P.O.E.E. Journal*, 24, p. 116 (1931).

[5] Reynolds, J. N.: "The Crossbar Switch", *Bell Laboratories Record*, 15, p. 338 (1937).

[6] Davis, R. C.: "The Crossbar System", *Bell Laboratories Record*, 17, p. 173 (1939).

[7] Grinsted, W. H.: "The Motor Uniselector and the Technique of Its Application in Telecommunications", *J.I.E.E.*, 96, Part III, p. 403 (1949).

[8] Flowers, T. H.: "Introduction to Electronic Automatic Telephone Exchanges", *P.O.E.E. Journal*, 43, p. 61 (1950) and *P.O.E.E. Journal*, 44, p. 10 (1950).

[9] Franklin, R. H., and Williams, M. B., "Recent Developments in Line Transmission Systems", Printed Paper No. 213, *P.O.E.E. Journal* (1958).

[10] Peterson, E., Manley, J. M. and Wrathall, L. R.: "Magnetic Generation of a Group of Harmonics", *Bell System Technical Journal*, 16, p. 437 (1937).

[11] "The Transatlantic Telephone Cable," *P.O.E.E. Journal*, 49, Part 4 (1957).

References for Further Reading

ATKINSON, J.: *Telephony* (Pitman, 1950).
BERKELEY, G. S.: *Traffic and Trunking Principles in Automatic Telephony* (Benn, 1949).
BROCKBANK, R. A. and FLOYD, C. F.: " Wideband Transmission Over Coaxial Cables ". Printed Paper No. 190 of *P.O.E.E. Journal* (1946).
COHEN, B. S.: *A Handbook of Telecommunications* (Pitman, 1946).
POOLE, J.: *The Telephone Handbook* (Pitman, 1942).

EXAMPLES

1. Describe briefly the principles of operation of the central battery manual exchange. Explain with the aid of diagrams, how the subscriber calls the exchange and how the connection is cleared at the end of a call.

L.U. Ext. Telecomm. 1952.

2. Describe the apparatus required at the subscriber's end of a line terminating at a central battery manually-operated telephone exchange, and explain the function of each item. Also, explain the arrangements whereby (a) the subscriber calls the operator and (b) the operator makes an " engaged " test on a called subscriber's line.

L.U. Ext. Telecomm. 1945.

3. Show that the principle of the hybrid-coil makes the action of a " 2-wire " repeater possible. What is the essential condition for the prevention of singing, and how is this met in practice ?

L.U. Int. Telecomm. 1951.

4. Draw a circuit diagram for a subscriber's automatic telephone apparatus showing, in particular, how the dial controls the operation of the selector switch. Explain the functions of the line relay and its associated slow-release relay.

L.U. Ext. Telecomm. 1955.

5. Describe, with the aid of a circuit diagram, the speech circuit of a modern subscriber's telephone instrument fitted with an anti-sidetone induction coil. (The dialling connections may be omitted.) Draw attention to the circuit elements which contribute to the suppression of sidetone and explain why this suppression is desirable.

L.U. Ext. Telecomm. 1953.

6. What are the functions of (a) the rotary line switch and (b) the two co-ordinate switch used in automatic telephony ? Describe briefly the operation of these switches which follow the lifting of a subscriber's hand-microtelephone and the first two operations of the dial.

L.U. Ext. Telecomm. 1948.

7. Explain what is meant by the multiple principle in telephone switching and give illustrations of its application in automatic and manual switching equipment. Describe briefly how traffic considerations affect the provision of switching equipment in a simple step-by-step automatic system or a manual system.

L.U. Ext. Telecomm. 1946.

8. Explain in outline how the traffic requirements of a telephone exchange area, having, say, 8,000 subscribers may be met by an automatic switching system operating on the step-by-step principle.

L.U. Ext. Telecomm. 1946.

9. Distinguish between (a) trunking and grading, (b) pure chance and smooth traffic. Calculate the lost traffic and the grade of service provided by five switches arranged in a full availability group when offered 0·90 traffic unit.

I.E.E. Line Comm., April, 1946.

10. State what is meant by *carrier telephony* and explain the difference in principle between frequency- and time-division multiplex telephone systems.
Describe, with the aid of suitable diagrams, the terminal equipment essential for the transmission of speech in a frequency-division system.

L.U. Electronics & Telecomm. Part II. 1966.

11. Describe with the aid of a block diagram the essential features of the terminal equipment for one channel of a multi-channel telephone system.
A 12-channel carrier telephone system has upper sideband channels spaced 4 kHz apart in the range 12–60 kHz. The simultaneous application of pure 400 Hz and 3400 Hz tones at the audio input terminals of the 48–52 kHz channel causes severe overloading in a line amplifier. Determine the audio frequencies of the main intermodulation outputs in the other channels.

L.U. Telecomm. Part III. 1964.

18

TELEGRAPHY

TELEGRAPH TRANSMISSION

THE transmission of information by telegraphy is a process of signalling by some form of code. The letters and characters which form the " message " are first of all translated, at the transmitter, into telegraph signals in the appropriate code ; the coded signals are then transmitted to the receiving point where decoding takes place. The virtue of this process is that it simplifies the form of the signals which the transmission system has to handle, as compared with the complex waveforms which have to be transmitted in a conventional telephone system ; as a consequence a higher rate of transmission of information (in terms of words per minute for a given bandwidth) can be attained.

In d.c. telegraphy, the telegraph signals may be formed by switching a steady voltage on and off in accordance with the code used. Operation in this way is referred to as " single current " working ; in British Post Office practice, the system is said to be " marking " when the voltage is applied, and " spacing " when it is switched off. Fig. 18.1a shows the word " code " in International Morse Code. Alternatively, the telegraph signals may be formed by reversing the polarity of the steady voltage. This system of altering the polarity of the pulses rather than their time duration, is used in the form of Morse Code employed in submarine cable work. Fig. 18.1b shows this scheme used for a seven and a half unit code on which teleprinters are operated. The use of negative and positive impulses is referred to as " double current " working, and the terms " mark " and " space " are still employed.

In a.c. telegraph systems it is usual to produce d.c. telegraph signals, e.g. as in Fig. 18.1b, which are then arranged to produce amplitude modulation of an alternating voltage. The modulated waveform is then transmitted and demodulated at the receiver to produce d.c. telegraph signals. Alternatively two tones (i.e. frequencies) are sometimes utilised, one to " mark " and the other to " space ".

The performance of a telegraph transmission system can be found by an examination of the steady state characteristics of the system for alternating currents. This was discussed briefly in chapter 15 where it was shown that for a.c. transmission, the minimum bandwidth required, in hertz, is numerically equal to the speed of

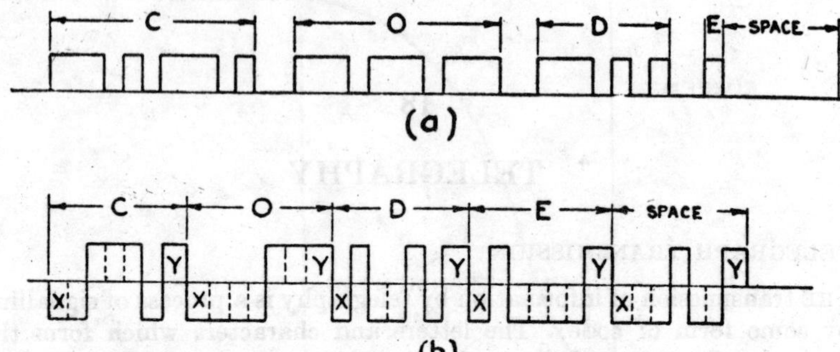

Fig. 18.1 (a) " Code " in International Morse Code
(b) " Code " in seven and a half unit code
(NOTE that X and Y pulses are respectively " start " and " stop " pulses)

transmission in bands ; with d.c. transmission at a similar speed of signalling the minimum bandwidth is half the a.c. value. This bandwidth is much narrower than that required for the exact reproduction of the transmitted waveform at the receiving point. The comparatively narrow bandwidth gives satisfactory operation in the case of telegraphy, because of the simpler function of the telegraph receiving mechanism, which consists essentially of an electromagnetic relay, and consequently can be thought of as a switch which is either open or closed. The meaning of distortion is then somewhat different.

Alternatively, the operation of a telegraph system can be analysed on a transient basis. If, in a d.c. system, the growth of current in the receiving relay occupies a time which is long compared with the duration of the signalling elements, the signals then become a series of transients. Now the way in which the current increases through, say, a simple relay connected across the receiving end of a transmission line is obviously a function of the values of the line constants, the value of the transmitting source impedance, and the impedance of the relay. The effect of these factors can be taken into account in all cases by means of an arrival curve. This is a curve which shows the build up of the current in the impedance at the far end of the line when a particular direct voltage is suddenly applied at the sending end. Fig. 18.2 shows one possible form of an arrival curve.

A quiescent period precedes any current change. Up to the end of this period no component of the transmitted voltage appears at the receiving end of the line. After this time delay the current increases, or builds up ; the time occupied in this process is referred to as the transient time of the system. At the end of the transient time the current has reached its steady state value. The use of an arrival curve

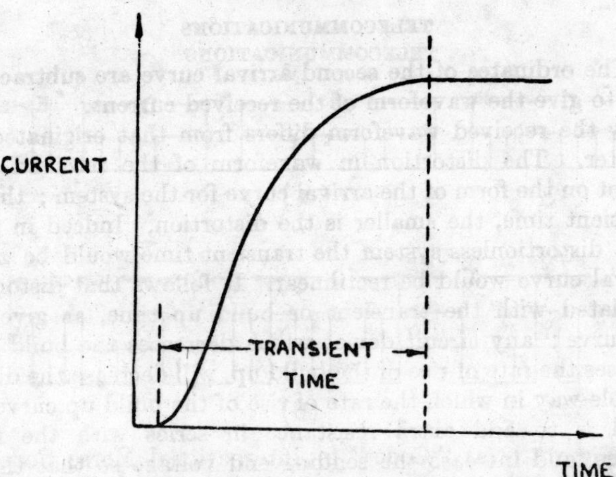

Fig. 18.2. Arrival curve.

is shown in Fig. 18.3. For purposes of illustration a single pulse (Fig. 18.3a) is assumed to be applied to the sending end of the line. The waveform of the current in the receiving end impedance is shown by the full line curve in Fig. 18.3b. This curve is constructed from the arrival curve for the onset of the pulse, and a second similar arrival curve (of opposite sign to the first) due to the cessation of the

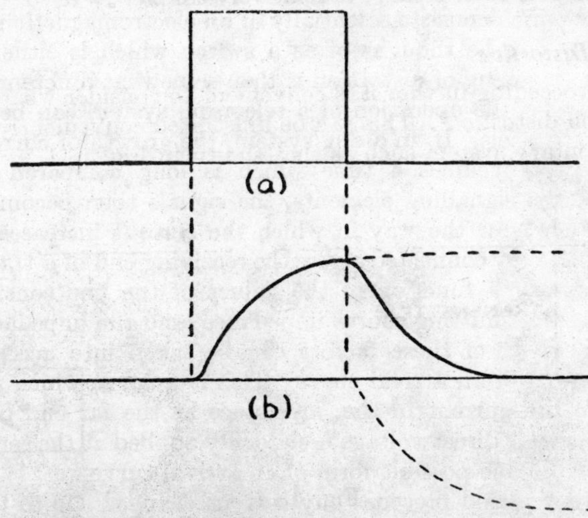

Fig. 18.3 (a) Transmitted pulse
(b) Received waveform from arrival curve for the system.

pulse. The ordinates of the second arrival curve are subtracted from the first to give the waveform of the received current.

Clearly the received waveform differs from that originated by the transmitter. The distortion in waveform of the received signal is dependent on the form of the arrival curve for the system; the shorter the transient time, the smaller is the distortion. Indeed in the ideal case of a distortionless system the transient time would be zero, and the arrival curve would be rectilinear. It follows that distortion can be correlated with the transient or build up time, as given by an arrival curve; any circuit device which decreases the build up time, or increases the rate of rise of the build up, will decrease the distortion. One simple way in which the rate of rise of the build up curve may be increased is to add extra resistance in series with the receiving impedance, and increase the sending end voltage so that the steady state current value is unchanged; in effect the time constant of the system is decreased. A further improvement can be obtained if the added resistor is shunted by a capacitor.

From the foregoing it will be apparent that it is possible to use arrival curves to assess the performance of a telegraph system. The criterion by which the systems are compared is then the rate of rise of the build up of the received current. An arrival curve can be calculated from the steady state characteristics of the system. In practice the calculation is rather cumbersome but the experimental determination of such a curve is relatively simple.

Telegraph Distortion

Before proceeding further it is convenient to consider what is meant by telegraph distortion[1]. This can be illustrated conveniently in terms of an elementary system such as that shown in Fig. 18.4.

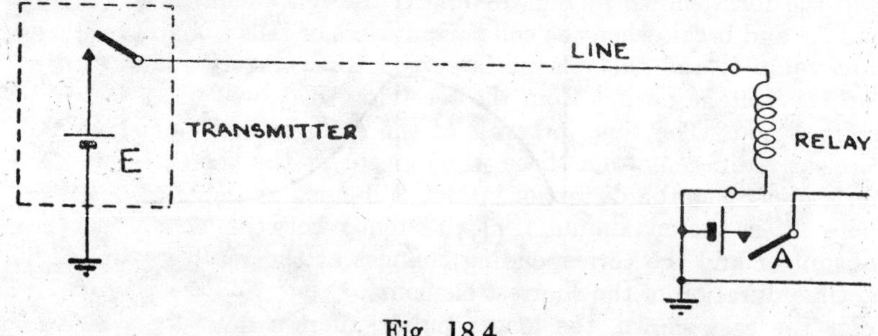

Fig. 18.4.

If the transmitter consists of a simple key, no voltage will be applied to the line when the key is at rest as indicated; a voltage E will be applied when the key is depressed. The received current is assumed

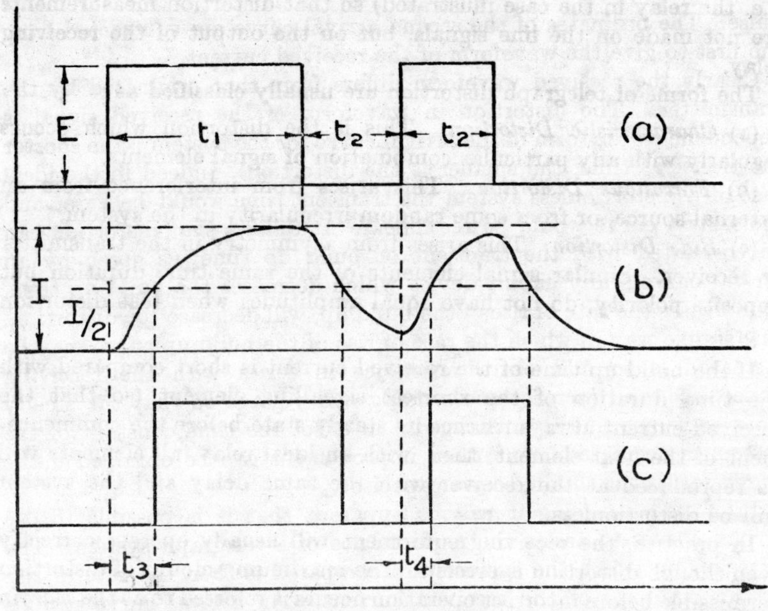

Fig. 18.5 (a) Transmitter voltage
(b) Received current
(c) Output voltage from receiving relay.

to be applied to the operating coil of a relay, so as to make the contact *A* when a certain value of current flows through the coil.

If the transmitter key is manipulated so that the voltage applied to the line is shown as in Fig. 18.5a, the current in the relay coil will have the form shown in Fig. 18.5b. If the relay contact is assumed to make and break when the coil current rises or falls to half the steady state value I, and the relay is assumed to operate instantaneously, then the voltage output from the receiving relay will be as indicated in Fig. 18.5c. The time intervals of the changes of this last voltage are clearly different from those which occur at the transmitter. This constitutes telegraph distortion, which is defined as the ratio of T_1/T_2, where T_1 is the maximum time difference between changes at the transmitter and the corresponding changes at the receiver, and T_2 is the time duration of the shortest element.

For the case shown, the longer pulse suffers a delay t_3, while the shorter pulse has a delay t_4. If the time duration of the shortest signal element is in fact t_2, the percentage distortion is

$$\frac{t_3 - t_4}{t_2} \times 100\%$$

Distortion may be increased or decreased by the receiving apparatus (i.e. the relay in the case illustrated) so that distortion measurements are not made on the line signals, but on the output of the receiving relay.

The forms of telegraph distortion are usually classified as :

(a) *Characteristic Distortion.* This is the distortion which occurs regularly with any particular combination of signal elements.

(b) *Fortuitous Distortion.* This arises from interference from an external source, or from some random irregularity in the system.

(c) *Bias Distortion.* This arises from asymmetry in the transmitter or receiver. Similar signal elements of the same time duration but opposite polarity, do not have equal amplitudes when bias distortion is present.

If the build up time of the received current is short compared with the time duration of the shortest signalling element (so that the received current always reaches its steady state before the commencement of the next element) then, with an ideal relay, all elements will be reproduced at the receiver with the same delay and the system will be distortionless.

In practice, the receiving equipment will usually operate correctly even though distortion is present. The maximum amount of distortion permissible before incorrect operation occurs is referred to as the ***margin*** of the receiver.

Polarised Relays

Polarised relays[2] are extensively used in most telegraph circuits, and are employed in all character printing systems. The magnetic circuit of a polarised relay is shown in Fig. 18.6. An armature, pivoted at its centre has an extension which forms a moving contact. This makes connection with either of two fixed contacts. When the armature lies in a central position all the air gaps have the same reluctance, and the flux in every gap has the same value, so that there is no resultant force on the armature. If the top of the armature is displaced, say towards the left, the flux due to the permanent magnet will be increased in the top left and bottom right air gaps, and will be decreased in the top right and bottom left gaps. This gives rise to a resultant force which will cause the armature to move and rest against the left fixed contact. Under these conditions the fraction of the total flux which passes across the gaps between the yokes without traversing the length of the armature is negligibly small; the flux in the armature can then be taken as the total flux, ϕ_m due to the permanent magnet.

If current is passed through the operating coil, the flux so produced will divide equally between the two limbs of the yoke, as the operating m.m.f. is applied to the two similar magnetic circuits in parallel. If

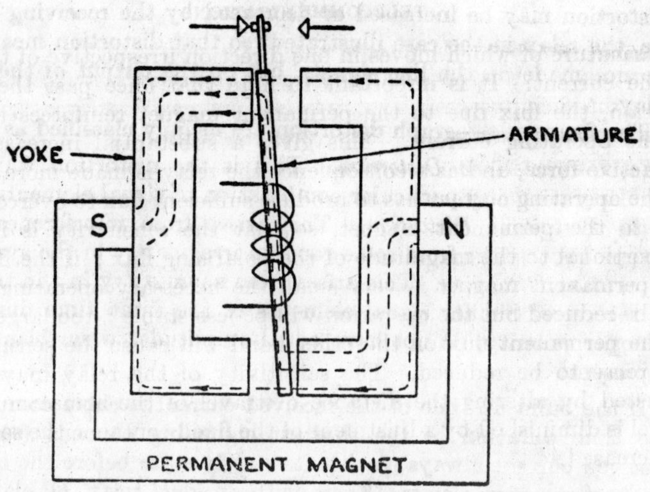

Fig. 18.6. Magnetic circuit of a polarised relay.

the flux produced by the coil has a value ϕ in the armature and acts upwards, the contact will be maintained by a force which is proportional to

$$\left(\phi_m+\frac{\phi}{2}\right)^2-\left(\frac{\phi}{2}\right)^2$$

$$=\phi_m{}^2+\phi_m\phi \quad . \quad . \quad . \quad . \quad . \quad . \quad 18.1$$

on the assumption that magnetic leakage can be neglected.

If the flux produced by the operating coil is reversed in direction as a result of a reversal of the current, the force which tends to move the top of the armature to the right is proportional to

$$\left(\frac{\phi}{2}\right)^2-\left(\phi_m-\frac{\phi}{2}\right)^2$$

$$=\phi_m(\phi-\phi_m) \quad . \quad . \quad . \quad . \quad . \quad . \quad 18.2$$

If the armature is to move, the expression must be positive, i.e. $\phi > \phi_m$. Expression 18.2 shows that the force on the armature is dependent on the flux from the permanent magnet and on the flux ϕ produced by the current. The fact that the operating force is nearly proportional to the current in the operating coil, rather than the square of the current, makes the polarised relay more sensitive to small currents than an unpolarised relay. The direction of movement of the armature of the polarised relay is dependent on the direction of the operating current, unlike the operation of the unpolarised relay the armature of which moves in one direction irrespective of the sense of the current. It is important to note that once past the central position, the flux due to the permanent magnet reinforces that due to the operating current. This gives a substantial increase in the attractive force, and as a consequence the relay is made more reliable.

The operating current has to produce sufficient flux to overcome that due to the permanent magnet, so that the sensitivity is inversely proportional to the magnitude of the polarising flux ; if the flux from the permanent magnet is very small the necessary operating current will be reduced but the operation will be less stable ; too large a value of the permanent flux on the other hand will cause the sensitivity of the relay to be reduced. The sensitivity of the relay may also be adjusted by altering the distance of travel of the armature ; if the travel is diminished by adjustment of the fixed contacts, the sensitivity is increased.

SIMPLE TELEGRAPH CIRCUITS

Most modern telegraph systems employ complex mechanical transmitters and receivers (usually teleprinters, operated on a multi-channel basis). If one considers basic circuits, from which the modern developments are derived, the simplest system would be that represented by Fig. 18.4. With a key and a relay at each end of the line it would be possible to transmit in each direction, though not at the same time. This circuit is referred to as a " single current, simplex circuit ", because the line current is never reversed in signalling, and transmission is limited to one direction at a time. The operation of either relay completes a " local circuit " to operate some device which then gives a visual or aural record of the signals. In the early days of telegraphy the transmitting key was manually operated to give signals in Morse Code.

Simultaneous transmission in both directions can be obtained with

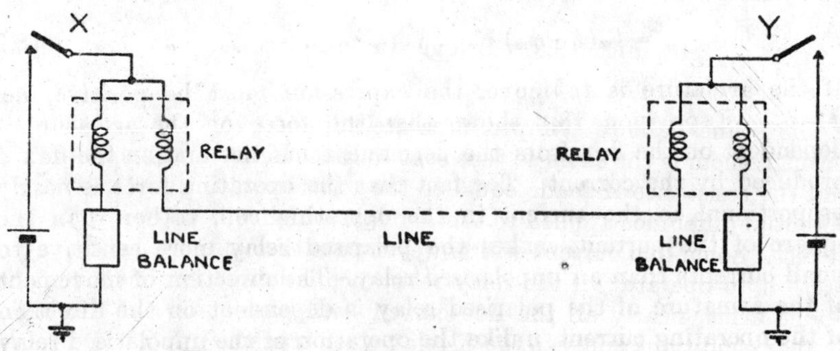

Fig. 18.7. Differential duplex circuit.

a " duplex " circuit. This can be achieved with differentially wound relays, arranged as shown in Fig. 18.7.

If one key is depressed, say that at *X*, current will flow through the two windings of the local relay. The impedance marked " line balance " is adjusted so that the currents in the two differentially wound relay windings are equal. As a consequence the relay at *X* remains unoperated. The line current however passes through both windings of the *Y* relay and causes it to operate. A similar state of affairs occurs if the key at *Y* is depressed instead of the one at *X*. When both keys are depressed, each end of the line is at the same potential with respect to earth, and no line current flows. The currents which flow in the " line balance " circuits then operate the relays.

The system shown in Fig. 18.7 can be used on a double current basis. This can be arranged if two batteries of equal and opposite polarity are provided at each station. The transmitting key then makes contact with one or other of the two batteries, so that the line current when " spacing " is opposite in direction to the " marking " condition. One advantage of double current working is that changes in line attenuation do not upset the relay adjustment, as marking and spacing currents are affected equally.

An alternative duplex scheme is the Bridge Duplex system shown in Fig. 18.8.

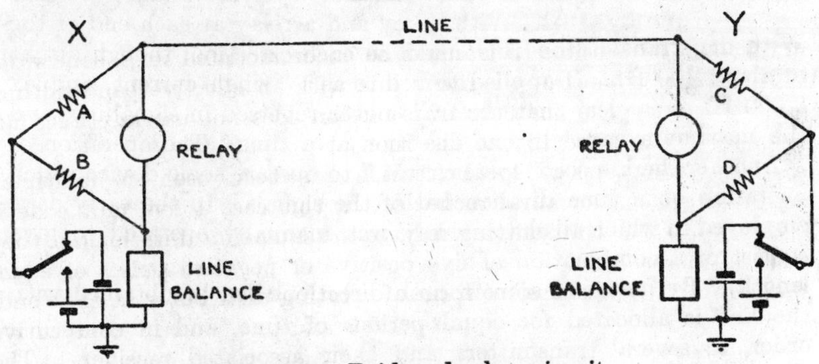

Fig. 18.8. Bridge duplex circuit.

The " line balance " impedances are adjusted so that the current through them is the same as that sent to line. If the *X* key is operated and the resistance *A* made equal to the resistance *B*, there will be no potential difference applied to the *X* relay, which will therefore remain at rest. Some line current will however pass through the *Y* relay and cause it to operate ; if the relay resistance is low compared with the bridge arms, nearly all the line current will pass through the relay. Similar conditions apply to the *X* relay when transmitter *Y* is operated.

HIGH SPEED TELEGRAPH SYSTEMS

If a telegraph circuit is to be used efficiently, the rate of transmission of information should be high, and ideally equal to the theoretical maximum. One of the first steps taken to achieve high speed transmission was the use of mechanical transmitters rather than manually operated keys. This enables signals to be fed to the line at speeds higher than can be achieved by a manual operator. The "message" is first of all prepared by an operator who types on an instrument known as a keyboard perforator. This punches holes in a paper tape, in accordance with Morse Code ; the perforated tape is then passed through an automatic transmitter which may have a maximum operating speed of the order of 200 words per minute. The received signals actuate a relay which controls a reperforator ; this produces a replica of the tape passed to the automatic transmitter. The tape so produced may be used either for retransmission to a further station, or it may be passed through a printer, which translates the signals into Roman characters on a paper tape, or in page form.

If the average number of signal elements involved in an average word of five letters, with one word space, is taken as 50, a speed of 200 words per minute gives a telegraph speed of

$$\frac{200 \times 50}{60} = 167 \text{ bauds.}$$

With d.c. transmission this could be accommodated in a bandwidth of about 100 Hz. If applied to a line with an effective bandwidth of 3,000 Hz it is clear that the transmission does not use anything like the maximum capability of the line.

Another high speed system which has been used, is multiplex operation on a time division basis. In this case a five unit code is employed in which all characters have the same time duration (i.e. they consist of a combination of five positive or negative pulses of equal length). By means of some form of rotating distributor at each end, the line is allocated for equal periods of time, and in consecutive order, to several transmitters and their associated receivers. The rotating brush at the receiving end has to be synchronised with the brush at the transmitter so that corresponding "commutation" segments are always connected to the line.

The most widely used system of telegraphy in modern practice is based on frequency division multiplex. A.C. transmission is employed and the line bandwidth is divided into a number of independent channels. The use of a.c. transmission enables telephone and telegraph networks to be integrated ; normal telephone repeaters can be employed. The interference with neighbouring telephone circuits is also very much less with a.c. transmission.

The Teleprinter

It has been stated previously that multi-channel systems of telegraphy are usually operated in conjunction with teleprinters. It is essential therefore to have some knowledge of the function of these machines before discussing multi-channel systems.

A teleprinter is a complex mechanical device, which at first sight resembles a typewriter in that it has a similar form of keyboard. A teleprinter functions both as a transmitter and as a receiver. A five unit signalling code, operating on a double current basis, is employed so that every character is represented by five equal time impulses of positive or negative polarity. An essential feature of teleprinter working is that it operates on a " start-stop " basis. Every character is preceded by a start pulse and is followed by a stop pulse ; the start pulse sets the mechanism at the receiving teleprinter so that it is ready to print the character transmitted by the following five impulses ; the stop pulse then restores the receiving mechanism. The advantage of such an arrangement is that synchronisation between the transmitting and receiving machines is unnecessary. The stop pulse has usually a length of $1\frac{1}{2}$ units, and the teleprinter code is then referred to as a $7\frac{1}{2}$ unit code. Some machines however use a stop pulse of unit length, and thus operate on a 7 unit code.

[*By permission of Creed & Co., Ltd.*

Fig. 18.9. Page model teleprinter (with cover removed).

When used as a transmitter, the depression of a key actuates a system of cams and levers which cause one lever ("transmitting contact ") to make connection with either of two fixed contacts and in a sequence determined by the signalling code for the character concerned. Two batteries are connected to the fixed contacts so that one has a positive, and the other a negative potential with respect to earth. The movements of the transmitting contact then give an electrical output from the machine of double current pulses, which are made up of a start pulse, five signalling pulses, and a stop pulse, as shown in Fig. 18.1b.

When used as a receiver the received pulses are applied to a form of polarised relay. The signal pulses operate a revolving typehead and type-hammer which gives an impression on paper of the character transmitted.

The actual mechanical arrangement of the machine is too complicated to be described here, but a general view of one form of teleprinter is given in Fig. 18.9.

MULTI-CHANNEL VOICE FREQUENCY TELEGRAPHY

In this system, a.c. transmission is employed and the bandwidth of the line is used on a frequency division basis to form independent channels, in a manner similar to that employed for multi-channel telephony, except that all the telegraph channels occupy one speech channel. The double current pulses from teleprinters are used as the modulating signals and are applied to modulators at the transmitting terminal. These modulators are also supplied with carrier frequencies which lie within the speech range, hence the name, voice frequency. The modulated carrier is transmitted over the line and is demodulated at the receiving terminal. The demodulated signals may then be applied directly to teleprinters, or may be used for re-transmission to some further station.

Factors Affecting the Channel Spacing. It was stated in chapter 15 that the channel bandwidth employed in multi-channel telegraphy is 120 Hz. The main factors which determine the value of channel bandwidth to be employed in any particular system may be listed as follows :

(1) The speed of signalling which is required.
(2) The permissible characteristic distortion.
(3) The permissible level of interference between channels.

The speed of working required of a channel is the main consideration as the bandwidth necessary is proportional to the speed of working. It was shown in chapter 15 that operation at a speed of 66 words per minute was equivalent to a telegraphic speed of 50 bauds, with a

$7\frac{1}{2}$ unit code. This constitutes a reasonable speed of operation of the teleprinter. For a.c. transmission a speed of 50 bauds requires a minimum effective bandwidth of 50 Hz. The nominal bandwidth to be allocated is then determined by the sharpness of cut-off of the bandpass filters. With the type of filter normally used the nominal bandwidth of 120 Hz gives an effective width of at least 80 Hz, so that an appreciable margin is provided for operation at speeds above the normal. The distortion and interference which arises from teleprinter operation at normal speed on a bandwidth of 120 Hz are then reasonably small.

Once the channel bandwidth has been decided, the maximum number of channels obtainable depends on the frequency characteristics of the line. Modern repeatered telephone lines have a fairly uniform characteristic between 300 and 3400 Hz, and can accommodate 24 telegraph channels.

Selection of Carrier Frequencies. All the telegraph channels pass through the various line repeaters. As the valves in such repeaters exhibit non-linearity in their characteristics, some distortion occurs, and sum and difference frequencies (of the various input components) are produced together with other cross-modulation products. The sum and difference components of the carriers are most serious, in that they have the largest amplitudes. A moment's thought will show that if the carrier frequencies are chosen so that they are odd multiples of half the channel bandwidth the sum and difference products of any two carrier frequencies will be even multiples of half the channel bandwidth (i.e. the sums and differences of odd numbers are always even numbers). The sum and difference products will then lie midway between the carriers, i.e. at the edges of the channels, where the bandpass filters offer the greatest attenuation. Alternatively, the products will lie outside the range of frequencies used. The carrier frequencies are thus made odd multiples of 60 Hz, and in the Standard Telephones and Cables 24 channel system, which is representative of modern practice, the carrier frequencies have the values,

420, 540, 660, 780 . . . . up to 3,180 Hz.

The first channel then occupies the range 360–480 Hz, the second occupies the range 480–600 Hz, and the top channel extends from 3,120–3,240 Hz.

Elements of a Multi-Channel System

The basic elements of a multi-channel system of telegraphy are shown in the schematic diagram of Fig. 18.10.

When a large number of channels are used, usually either 18 or 24, the system is operated on a 4-wire basis, i.e. one pair is used for

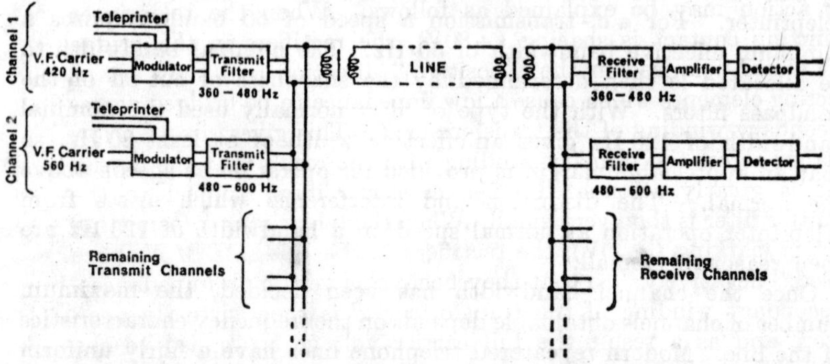

Fig. 18.10. Schematic diagram of a multi-channel telegraph system

transmission in the " go " direction and the remaining pair is used for the " return " direction. Alternatively the system may be operated on a 2-wire basis to give up to a maximum of eight channels in each direction. In this case the frequency range is divided into two parts ; one part of the frequency range is used for transmission in one direction, and the remaining frequency range used for transmission in the opposite direction. The carrier frequencies are derived either directly, or indirectly, from transistor oscillators.

For line transmission, amplitude modulation is employed. One form of modulator which has been used employs four rectifiers arranged in a bridge as shown in Fig. 18.11.

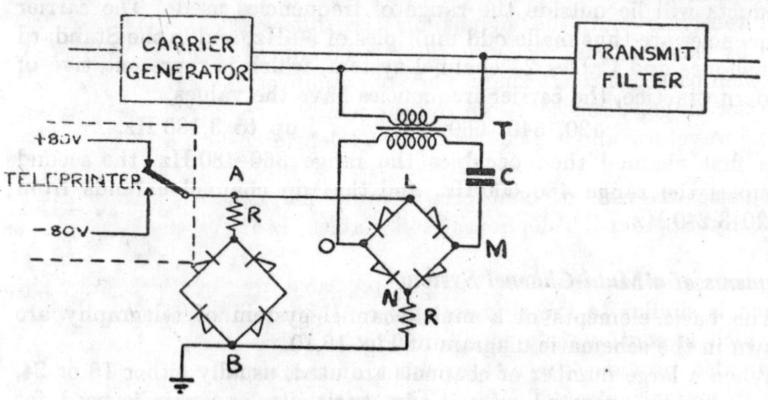

Fig. 18.11. Telegraph modulator.

The action may be explained as follows. When the teleprinter transmitting contact is spacing (+80V), the rectifiers in the bridge *L M N O* are polarised in the "positive" direction and they act as conducting elements which cause a low impedance to be bridged across the secondary winding of the transformer *T*. This gives rise to a low impedance across the primary winding with the result that the carrier voltage is greatly attenuated; the carrier voltage applied to the transmitter filter is then very small. When the teleprinter transmitting contact is marking (−80V), the rectifiers in the bridge *L M N O* are polarised "negatively" so that they behave as very high impedances. The secondary winding of the transformer *T* is then virtually open circuited, and as a result the full carrier voltage is applied to the transmit filter. The rectifiers thus behave as variable impedances controlled in value by the marking and spacing signals from the teleprinter, and produce 100% amplitude modulation of the carrier.

The capacitor *C* serves to block the direct current from the secondary winding of the transformer *T*. The resistor *R* limits the value of the spacing current. The remaining four rectifiers and resistor *R*, connected between the points *A* and *B*, act as a balancing network which makes the mark and space currents equal. It will be seen that if the rectifiers in the bridge *L M N O* are conducting, those in the balancing network are not, and vice versa.

The amplitude-modulated output is passed through the transmit filter, and is then applied to line, through the line transformer. At first sight the transmit filter might appear to be unnecessary. If it was omitted however, the output from one channel modulator would be dissipated in the other modulators, and modulation of any one channel would result in similar modulation of the other channels. The transmit filter also rejects high-order sideband frequencies which would cause interference.

At the receiving end, the signals for the different channels are separated by the bandpass receiving filters. The output voltage from a filter is then passed through single stage of amplification, and applied to a detector stage. This gives an output which corresponds to the modulating waveform and is used to actuate a teleprinter via a polarised relay.

A schematic diagram of one form of amplifier detector circuit, developed by Standard Telephones and Cables Ltd., is shown in Fig. 18.12.

It will be seen that the first valve is preceded by the receiving filter which is similar to the transmit filter. V_1 provides a standing voltage which is continuously monitored by a Valve Failure Alarm Panel; V_1 also provides for measurement of the signal level on a transmission measuring set (T.M.S.). The potentiometer P_2 provides a small adjustment in gain to compensate for individual valve

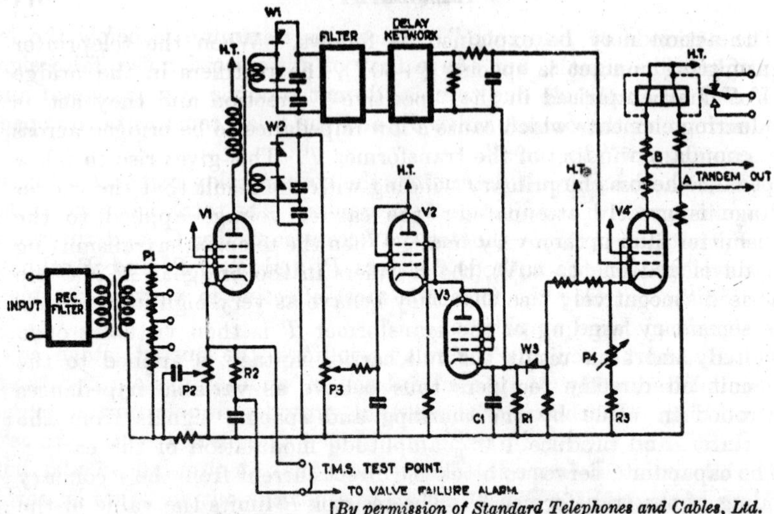

[By permission of Standard Telephones and Cables, Ltd.

Fig. 18.12. Diagram of a V F amplifier detector telegraph circuit.

variation. The output of the amplifier stage is fed through a transformer to two voltage doubler rectifier circuits. The first of these, W_1, passes the rectified signal through a second filter stage to remove residual carrier and harmonics, together with any other unwanted frequencies. The transit time of the signal is increased before it is applied to the grid of the output valve. This signal path, besides introducing delay, makes some correction of phase distortion, and also acts as a limiter. To ensure that the signal is applied to the output valve with a bias appropriate to the signal amplitude, a bias voltage is developed in a signal path which has no such delay feature. This bias voltage is derived from the second voltage doubler W_2, the bias being developed across the reservoir capacitor C_1 which constitutes an integral part of the grid cathode circuit of the output valve.

The two valves V_2 and V_3 in the bias path act as a cathode follower and a diode respectively and ensure that the charging time of the capacitor C_1 is very short. This means that the voltage across C_1 develops very quickly after a long space and will invariably have achieved its correct value before the delayed signal is delivered through the signal path. There is thus negligible distortion of the first signal received. The discharge time constant of $C_1 R_1$ being long, the correct bias, once built up, is maintained over a period of time sufficient for the reception of many characters.

As a safeguard against false operation by line noise, the rectifier W_3 and associated potential divider serve to ensure that the steady voltage across C_1 never falls below a certain minimum even during the periods of "no tone". Since this minimum is below the level of genuine signals, but above that of anticipated noise, false signals of small amplitude due to noise do not produce any change of anode current on the output valve V_4 and the relay remains on its spacing contact on "no tone".

As the bias circuit determines the correct relay response to signals, some form of bias adjustment is essential. The total bias (grid-cathode V_4) is made up from the voltage across capacitor C_1 and the voltage developed on the cathode resistors P_4 and R_3. P_3 and P_4 thus act as bias controls; the former is most effective in varying the bias of signals of large amplitude.

By short circuiting the relay windings, the output stage can be coupled directly to the modulator of another system for tandem working. In this way the output provides double current signals, point A on the circuit being maintained at constant voltage to earth, while point B is made to vary an equal amount above and below the potential of A depending on whether the output valve is marking or spacing.

OTHER A.C. TELEGRAPH SYSTEMS

The multi-channel voice frequency system described above operates on an amplitude modulation basis. Other systems are used in special circumstances.

(a) *Two-Tone V.F. Telegraphy.* When a telegraph system is operated over a radio link, fading of the signals may take place and cause large changes in level of the received signal. Noise may also be present at much higher level than would be encountered in line transmission. These effects may give rise to faulty operation of the receive telegraph relay. An improvement is obtained with the use of two-tone operation[3], in which two adjacent channels are combined to form a single channel. The voice-frequency tone from one channel is transmitted in the marking condition while the tone from the other is transmitted in the spacing condition; the telegraph receiver relay is controlled by the mark and the space channels. The mark and space tones are selected by filters and are then amplified and rectified. The rectified signals then operate a push-pull d.c. amplifier which has the telegraph receive relay connected in its output circuit. The system can operate with a wide range of input levels at the receiving terminal, provided that the difference in level between the mark and space tones is small. The two v.f. tones are transmitted as amplitude modulation of a radio frequency carrier.

(b) *Frequency Shift Telegraphy.* This system[4] is also used for radio transmission of telegraph signals, and, as in the previous case, offers advantages under conditions of fading and high noise level.

With frequency shift telegraphy the "mark" condition of the telegraph code is transmitted at one carrier frequency, and the "space" condition is transmitted at a carrier frequency which differs from the first by an audio frequency referred to as the "frequency shift". In effect, the system can be regarded as a frequency modulation system which employs square wave modulation; the carrier frequency is deviated in one direction to "mark" and in the other direction to "space". Detection may be achieved by the use of a limiter and discriminator, as employed in frequency modulation detection.

(c) *Multi-Channel Frequency Modulation.* Amplitude modulation may be replaced by frequency modulation in a multi-channel system. When a large number of channels are required and the bandwidth of any one must necessarily be relatively small it is found that it is sufficient to employ a bandwidth only slightly greater than the actual frequency deviation of the carrier; the bandwidth occupied by one channel is then the same as would be used for amplitude modulation. Frequency modulation, with its constant amplitude signals, can be used with advantage where the signal level is liable to change in transmission, i.e. in radio circuits. It has the disadvantage however, in that it is subject to distortion when the carrier frequency drifts or changes. Thus in a suppressed carrier telephone system if the local carrier differs from the original the received signals will suffer bias distortion. Detection of frequency-modulated signals is carried out by some form of limiter and discriminator followed by a push-pull d.c. amplifier which controls the telegraph receive relay.

(d) *Sub-Audio Working.* A telephone speech channel does not make use of frequencies below about 200 Hz. As a result it is possible with the addition of the appropriate filters to accommodate one telegraph channel below 200 Hz in a telephone circuit. This is known as sub-audio working.

Operation of Telegraph Systems in Cascade

The widespread use of multi-channel voice-frequency telegraphy has enabled a general telegraph service to be provided, where required, in the associated telephone system. The interconnection between any two terminals may then involve telegraph switching; the output of one telegraph system is then applied as an input to another system and the two systems are then said to be working in cascade. Where cascade operation of telegraph signals is involved, the overall distortion is an important factor, as the distortion produced is cumulative, and if there are several systems so connected the signal elements may be shortened to such an extent as to cause incorrect operation of the terminal teleprinter.

The distortion produced in any system increases as the speed of signalling increases, because the duration of the signal impulses decreases. It follows that the signalling speed of a single system is greater than that of several similar systems connected in cascade. As an example the Standard Telephones and Cables 24 channel system is capable of satisfactory operation at a speed of 75 bauds when two systems are connected in cascade, or at a speed of 50 bauds when eight systems are so connected.

The cumulative effect of distortion in cascade operation may be overcome by the use of regenerative repeaters, which re-create or re-generate telegraph signals with zero distortion. Such repeaters, placed at intermediate points in land-line and radio-link networks, permit a flexible arrangement of teleprinter switching.

PICTURE TELEGRAPHY

The transmission of high definition pictures by means of picture telegraphy has already been discussed in outline in chapter 15. The following brief description of one form of equipment manufactured by Muirhead & Co. Ltd. is given as an illustration of modern practice. Other systems differ in detail but the general features are typical.

Some of the principal characteristics of the equipment used on the Muirhead system,[5] which complies with CCITT recommendations, are :—

Index of Co-operation	352
Drum Speeds	1 or 2 rev/s
Drum Diameter	66 mm
Drum Length	197 mm
Scanning Pitch	5·3 lines/mm
Line Signal	Amplitude-modulated 1,300 Hz carrier
Picture Transmission Band . . .	300–2,300 Hz
Synchronising Frequency . . .	1,020 Hz

The picture to be transmitted is clipped on to the transmitter drum and a lamp (fed with current at high frequency to obviate the risk of hum) is arranged to illuminate a small area of the picture. An image of the illuminated area is focused on to a small aperture pierced in a plate ; after passing through this aperture, the light beam is split into two portions by a half silvered mirror, and each portion falls on one of two photo-electric multiplier cells. The impedance of these photo-cells varies with their illumination, and this effect is used to modulate the carrier with the picture information. Briefly, the photo-cells are used as a balanced attenuator, and an input of carrier frequency is applied to them; as the attenuation produced by the photo-cells is proportional to their illumination, the attenuation of the applied carrier voltage is proportional to the illumination obtained in scanning the picture, i.e. the carrier voltage is varied at picture frequency, and as a consequence the output consists of a carrier which is amplitude modulated. The modulated signal is then passed to line through a line amplifier. The general appearance of the transmitter described above is shown in Fig. 18.13.

[By permission of Muirhead & Co.

Fig. 18.13. Muirhead picture transmitter Type D–601–A.

At the receiving station the apparatus has to convert the received signal waveform into a beam of light of varying intensity. This is arranged to fall on light sensitive paper carried by a drum which rotates in synchronism with the transmitting drum. In the receiver employed in the Muirhead system, the rectified signal waveform is applied to a Duddell type oscillograph unit, the mirror of which is deflected by an amount proportional to the amplitude of the received signal. The oscillograph mirror is illuminated by a fixed lamp, and the beam of light reflected from the mirror is passed through a specially shaped aperture, which is arranged so that the light passed through varies with the displacement of the oscillograph mirror. (The shape of the aperture is determined by the exposure characteristic of the photographic material.) A mirror and lens then gives a spot of light on the receiving drum, with an intensity determined by the point to point density of the light reflected from the picture on the transmitter drum.

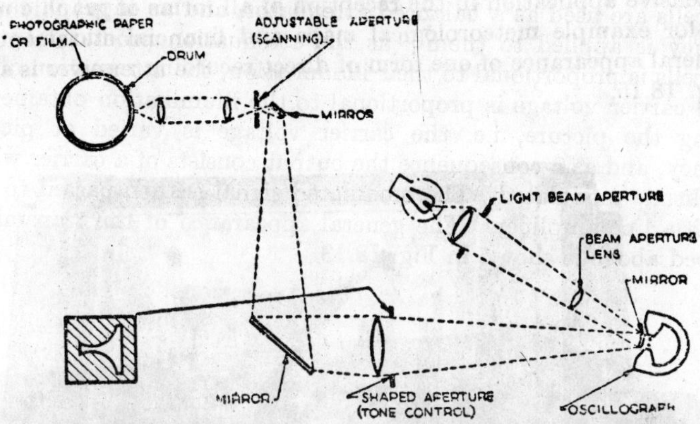

Fig. 18.14. Optical arrangement of picture receiver.

In practice, the sig .l voltage received from the line is first of all passed through a high-pass filter with a cut-off of approximately 300 Hz. This eliminates any spurious low frequency voltages which may be present in the line. The signal is then amplified and subsequently rectified ; the rectified output is passed through an amplifier, which has a low output impedance, and is then applied to the oscillograph coil. It will be realised that it is absolutely essential that the transmitter and receiver drums should rotate in synchronism ; this is achieved by the use of synchronous motors driven by a tuning fork, or some other frequency standard. Means are provided whereby the receiving tuning fork may be matched to the frequency of a synchronising tone sent along the line from the transmitter fork. The phasing signal, which is used to start the receiver drum in the same relative position as the transmitter, is obtained by interrupting the 1,300 Hz carrier signal once per second by a pair of contacts operated from the drum driving gear.

For use over radio circuits, in which frequent fading occurs, the amplitude-modulated signal is converted into a frequency-modulated signal, which is used as a sub-carrier for the radio transmitter. This is in accordance with general practice[6,7]. At the receiver the signal is put through a limiter and then de-modulated to produce an amplitude modulated output. As an alternative to sub-carrier frequency modulation, carrier-frequency-shift working may be employed.

Direct Recording Receiver

The receiver described above uses photographic paper on which to record the received picture, and a delay inevitably occurs in its availability, owing to the necessary processing. This may be obviated by receivers which use electro-sensitive paper. Such receivers find extensive application in the reception of all forms of graphic material, as for example meteorological maps and financial statements. The general appearance of one form of direct recording receiver is shown in Fig. 18.15.

[*By permission of Muirhead & Co.*

Fig. 18.15. Direct recording picture receiver.

This particular receiver is of the continuous recording type, employing electrosensitive paper 11 in. wide. The paper is drawn at constant speed between a stainless steel writing edge and a rotating helix. Current is passed through the paper at the point of contact, causing a chemical action which stains the paper at that point. The tonal density depends upon the magnitude of the current, which is controlled by the received signal. The rotation of the helix and the movement of the paper together cause the point of contact to traverse the paper in a series of horizontal lines, and in this way the picture is built up.

References

[1] JOLLEY, E. H.: "Signal Distortion in Telegraph Circuits", *P.O.E.E. Journal*, 25, p. 259 (1933).

[2] JENSON, K. L.: "The Design of a Polarised Telegraph Relay", *J.I.E.E.*, 83, p. 117 (1938).

[3] BRAY, W. J.: "Single-Sideband Multi-Channel Operation of Short-Wave Point-to-Point Radio Links", *P.O.E.E. Journal*, 45, p. 97 (1952).

[4] RUDDLESDEN, R., FORESTER, E. and JELONEK, Z.: "Carrier-Frequency-Shift Telegraphy", *J.I.E.E.*, 94, Part IIIA, p. 379 (1947).

[5] BELL, J., DAVIDSON, J. A. B. and PHILLIPS, E. T. A.: "Some Recent Developments in Photo-Telegraphy and Facsimile Transmission", *Proc. I.E.E.*, 97, Part III, p. 344 (1952).

[6] COLE, A. W. and SMALE, J. A.: "The Transmission of Pictures by Radio", *Proc. I.E.E.*, 99, Part III, p. 325 (1952).

[7] CARTER, R. O. and WHEELER, L. K.: "A Photo-Telegraph Transmitter-Receiver Utilizing Sub-Carrier Frequency Modulation", *Proc. I.E.E.*, 99, Part III, p. 335 (1952).

References for Further Reading

FREEBODY, J. W.: *Telegraphy* (Pitman, 1963).

COHEN, B. S.: *A Handbook of Telecommunications* (Pitman, 1947).

EXAMPLES

1. Give the essential details of the cable code and the teleprinter code and explain the advantages of such codes over the normal morse code.

I.E.E. Line Comm. October, 1948.

2. Explain what is meant by single-current working and double-current working in telegraphy. Discuss the advantage of the latter over the former.

L.U. Int. Telecomm. 1948.

3. A relay of inductance 20 H is in series with a battery and a switch. The total resistance of the circuit is 10,000 ohms and across the contacts is a capacitance of 4 μF. Determine whether, on opening the switch, there will be a tendency for the relay to release and re-operate. How would you cure this fault if it existed?

I.E.E. Line Comm. October, 1947.

4. Describe the bridge method of duplex telegraphy. Assuming all the circuits to be resistive, deduce an expression for balance under steady conditions. Two similar stations are connected by a balanced bridge duplex circuit. The resistance of each bridge arm is 300 ohms, the receiver resistance is 120 ohms and the line conductor has a resistance of 500 ohms. Calculate the value of each balancing resistance. Also find the line current with a battery having an e.m.f. of 40 V and negligible resistance in circuit at one end. Assume the circuit to have an earth return of negligible resistance, and that all the circuits are resistive.

L.U. Ext. Telecomm. 1943.

5. Enumerate the various systems by means of which more than one telegraph message may be transmitted in a given time over a single wire, and outline the main features and relative advantages of each.

L.U. Ext. Telecomm. 1948.

6. Describe the voice-frequency system of telegraphy, showing diagrammatically the circuit arrangement at both sending and receiving ends. Discuss the factors that determine the most suitable range of frequency and the intervals between the various frequencies used in a given system.

L.U. Telecomm. Part III. 1961.

7. Sketch and describe the main constructional features of a polarised relay suitable for use in high speed telegraphy, and explain the principal factor in the design and adjustment of the relay that enable rapid operation to be achieved.

L.U. Ext. Telecomm. 1950.

19

HIGH-FREQUENCY TRANSMISSION LINES AND WAVE GUIDES

THE basic equations for the impedance, and distribution of voltage and current along any transmission lines have already been discussed in chapter 4. The present chapter will accordingly be devoted to the principal relations which apply to high-frequency lines, together with the special features of such lines.

TRANSMISSION LINES

In the communication field, high-frequency transmission lines are employed in carrier telephony systems, and in the connection of aerials to transmitters or receivers in radio work. In high-frequency circuits short sections of transmission line are employed as circuit elements, e.g. in transistor oscillator circuits, when it is not practical to use lumped circuit elements.

LOSSES IN HIGH-FREQUENCY LINES

In most high-frequency lines, the inductive reactance per unit length is very much greater than the resistance ; susceptance is ordinarily always very much larger than the shunt conductance. As a result, high-frequency lines are in general, characterised by relatively low losses. The error involved in neglecting the presence of series resistance in the conductors, and shunt conductance between them, is insignificant in many calculations, and the treatment of such lines may thereby be simplified.

Before dealing with " loss-free " lines, it should be remembered that there are three possible sources of energy loss, namely copper loss, dielectric loss, and radiation loss.

Copper Loss

The copper loss is the power dissipated as heat in the line conductors as a result of their resistance. The conductor resistance increases as the frequency increases. This is due to the fact that the current tends to increase in density towards the surface of the conductor as the frequency is raised, thus diminishing the effective cross-sectional area. This well known " skin effect " thus causes the high-frequency resistance of a conductor to be much greater than the value obtained for direct current.

The current density can be considered[1] to decrease exponentially into the metal, from the conductor surface. With a flat conductor the current density diminishes to $1/e$, or 37% of its surface value at a depth d, where

$$d = \sqrt{\frac{\rho}{\pi \mu f}} \text{ metres} \quad . \quad . \quad . \quad . \quad . \quad 19.1$$

where ρ = specific resistance of the conductor in ohm-metre units

$\mu = \mu_0 \mu_r$; μ_0 is the permeability of free space ($4\pi \times 10^{-7}$ henrys per metre in S.I. units) and μ_r is the permeability of the conductor material relative to free space and f = frequency in Hz.

This result also holds good for conductors of circular cross-section if the radius of curvature is very much greater than d. In the case of copper, d has a value of 0·0066 mm at a frequency of 100 MHz.

Dielectric Loss

If the dielectric between the line conductors has a finite conductivity an energy loss will occur and appear as heat in the dielectric material. In some cases, e.g. in some forms of coaxial cable, there is a continuous dielectric between the conductors; in other cases the dielectric is mainly air, apart from insulators used for the mechanical support of the conductors.

Radiation Loss

The passage of high-frequency current through an open-wire line gives rise to an electromagnetic field surrounding the conductors, and causes a certain amount of power to be radiated into space. This radiation loss is proportional to the square of the frequency, and increases with the spacing between the line conductors.

DISTRIBUTION OF VOLTAGE AND CURRENT IN LOSS-FREE LINES

It was shown in chapter 4 that the characteristic impedance of a transmission line, expressed in terms of the four primary line constants, is given by

$$Z_0 = \sqrt{\frac{R + j\omega L}{G + j\omega C}}$$

$$=\sqrt{\frac{j\omega L(1+R/j\omega L)}{j\omega C(1+G/j\omega C)}}$$

$$=\sqrt{\frac{L}{C}}\left[1+\frac{R}{j\omega L}\right]^{\frac{1}{2}}\left[1+\frac{G}{j\omega C}\right]^{-\frac{1}{2}}$$

If it is assumed that $R/\omega L$ and $G/\omega C$ are both small compared with unity, and the quantities in the square brackets expanded by the binomial theorem, then

$$Z_0 \simeq \sqrt{\frac{L}{C}}\left[1-j\left(\frac{R}{2\omega L}-\frac{G}{2\omega C}\right)\right] \quad . \quad 19.2a$$

If the line is considered as loss-free, then

$$Z_0=\sqrt{\frac{L}{C}} \quad . \quad . \quad . \quad . \quad . \quad 19.2b$$

The general expression for the propagation coefficient P, is

$$P=\sqrt{(R+j\omega L)(G+j\omega C)}$$

$$=\sqrt{(1+R/j\omega L)(1+G/j\omega C)j\omega Lj\omega C}$$

$$\simeq j\omega\sqrt{LC}(1+R/j\omega L+G/j\omega C)^{\frac{1}{2}}$$

$$\simeq j\omega\sqrt{LC}(1+R/2j\omega L+G/2j\omega C)$$

if $R \ll \omega L$ and $G \ll \omega C$

$$\text{Then } P=j\omega\sqrt{LC}+\frac{R}{2}\sqrt{\frac{C}{L}}+\frac{G}{2}\sqrt{\frac{L}{C}}$$

This shows that the real part of the propagation coefficient, i.e. the attenuation coefficient, is independent of frequency.

If the term due to the conductance is neglected,

$$P=\alpha+j\beta=\frac{R}{2}\sqrt{\frac{C}{L}}+j\omega\sqrt{LC}$$

then by substitution for $\sqrt{C/L}$ from equation 19.2b

$$\alpha=\frac{R}{2Z_0} \quad . \quad . \quad . \quad . \quad . \quad . \quad 19.3a$$

$$\text{and } \beta=\omega\sqrt{LC} \quad . \quad . \quad . \quad . \quad . \quad . \quad 19.3b$$

When it is necessary to consider the effect of attenuation, the relation of 19.3a may be employed. In many cases, however, the effect of attenuation can be neglected. The complex propagation coefficient then becomes an imaginary quantity, i.e.

$$P=j\beta$$

where the wavelength coefficient β has the value $\omega\sqrt{LC}$.

The general expressions for the distribution of voltage and current along a line were given in chapter 4 as,

$$V = V_s \cosh Px - I_s Z_0 \sinh Px \text{ (equation 4.36)}$$

$$\text{and } I = I_s \cosh Px - (V_s/Z_0) \sinh Px \text{ (equation 4.37)}$$

where V_s and I_s are the voltage and current at the sending end of the line respectively.

In the present case $P = j\beta$, and if it is remembered that

$$\cosh j\beta = \cos \beta, \text{ and } \sinh j\beta = j \sin \beta$$

it will be clear that the distribution of voltage and current in a loss-free line, when measured from the sending end, can be expressed by the relations

$$V = V_s \cos \beta x - jI_s Z_0 \sin \beta x \quad . \quad . \quad 19.4$$

$$\text{and } I = I_s \cos \beta x - j(V_s/Z_0) \sin \beta x \quad . \quad . \quad 19.5$$

These relations have been obtained by simplification of the corresponding relations in chapter 4. They could however have been deduced directly from a consideration of the voltage and current in an infinitely short length of loss-free line.

WAVELENGTH AND PHASE VELOCITY IN A LOSS-FREE LINE

It was mentioned in chapter 4 that the wavelength λ of the wave propagation is given by

$$\lambda = 2\pi/\beta$$

In the loss-free case λ is thus given by

$$\lambda = \frac{1}{f\sqrt{LC}} \quad . \quad . \quad . \quad . \quad . \quad . \quad . \quad 19.6$$

The phase velocity is

$$V_P = \omega/\beta$$

so that in the loss-free case

$$V_P = \frac{1}{\sqrt{LC}} \quad . \quad . \quad . \quad . \quad . \quad . \quad 19.7$$

a quantity which is independent of frequency. The loss-free line is thus " distortionless " in the sense that all frequencies are transmitted with the same velocity.

SHORT-CIRCUITED LOSS-FREE LINE

If a loss-free line of length l is short-circuited at the receiving end, equations 19.4 and 19.5 give

$$0 = V_s \cos \beta l - jI_s Z_0 \sin \beta l$$

$$\text{and } I_l = I_s \cos \beta l - j(V_s/Z_0) \sin \beta l$$

The first of these relations gives

$$I_s = -j(V_s/Z_0) \cot \beta l \quad . \quad . \quad . \quad . \quad 19.8$$

$$\text{and } V_s/I_s = X_s = jZ_0 \tan \beta l$$

$$= j\sqrt{\frac{L}{C}} \tan \omega\sqrt{LC} \,.\, l \quad . \quad . \quad . \quad . \quad 19.9$$

In this case the line appears as a pure reactance when viewed from the sending end. When $\tan \beta l$ is positive, the line behaves as a pure inductance; a value of l which makes $\tan \beta l$ negative on the other hand, causes the input reactance of the line to be a pure capacitance.

The current at a distance x from the sending end may be found by inserting the expression obtained for I_s in equation 19.8 in the general current equation (19.5) for the particular value of x thus

$$I_x = -j(V_s/Z_0) \cot \beta l \cos \beta x - j(V_s/Z_0) \sin \beta x$$

$$= -j\frac{V_s}{Z_0}[\cot \beta l \cos \beta x + \sin \beta x] \quad . \quad . \quad . \quad 19.10$$

Similarly, the voltage at any point which is at a distance x from the sending end, is given by

$$V_x = V_s(\cos \beta x - \cot \beta l \sin \beta x) \quad . \quad . \quad . \quad . \quad 19.11$$

An alternative approach to find the current and voltage distribution along a short-circuited loss free line would be to simplify the corresponding equations for the general case. Equations 4.48 and 4.49 give

$$V_x = \frac{V_s \sinh P(l-x)}{\sinh Pl} \text{ and } I_x = \frac{V_s \cosh P(l-x)}{Z_0 \sinh Pl}$$

The replacement of P by $j\beta$ gives

$$V_x = \frac{V_s \sin \beta(l-x)}{\sin \beta l} \quad \text{and } I_x = \frac{V_s \cos \beta(l-x)}{jZ_0 \sin \beta l}$$

which can be rearranged in the form of equations 19.11 and 19.10.

The expression for the distribution of voltage shows that the voltage on the line will always be zero at the points where x has a value that satisfies the relation

$$\cos \beta x = \cot \beta l \sin \beta x$$

$$\text{i.e. } \tan \beta x = \tan \beta l \quad . \quad . \quad . \quad . \quad 19.12$$

For a fixed length of line l the quantity $\tan \beta l$ is constant, and there will thus be a series of values for x which will satisfy equation 19.12. These values occur when $\beta x = \left(\frac{2\pi x}{\lambda}\right)$ is increased by π, i.e. when the distance is increased by $\lambda/2$. The short circuited line, if sufficiently long, thus has a succession of points at which the voltage is always zero ; such points are called *voltage nodes*. The first and most obvious node occurs when $x=l$ i.e. at the end of the line.

There is also a succession of *current nodes*, again separated by a distance of $\lambda/2$. They are determined by the relation

$$\tan \beta x = -\cot \beta l$$

and occur midway between the voltage nodes.

In effect, stationary or "standing" waves of voltage and current are set up along the length of the line as a consequence of the reflections caused by the discontinuity at the end of the line. The voltage and current distributions are shown in Fig. 19.1a.

OPEN-CIRCUITED LOSS-FREE LINE

If a loss-free line has the receiving end terminals free, the voltage and current at the free end are expressed by

$$V_l = V_s \cos \beta l - jI_s Z_0 \sin \beta l$$

$$\text{and } 0 = I_s \cos \beta l - j(V_s/Z_0) \sin \beta l$$

From the second relation

$$I_s = j(V_s/Z_0) \tan \beta l \quad . \quad . \quad . \quad . \quad . \quad 19.13a$$

$$\text{and } \frac{V_s}{I_s} = X_s = -jZ_0 \cot \beta l \quad . \quad . \quad . \quad . \quad . \quad 19.13b$$

The line again has a purely reactive input impedance ; the reactance is inductive when the quantity $\cot \beta l$ is negative, and capacitive when $\cot \beta l$ is positive.

It is easily shown, by a treatment similar to that used for the short-circuited case, that the voltage and current at any point at a distance x from the sending end are expressed by the relations

$$V_x = V_s(\cos \beta x + \tan \beta l \sin \beta x) \quad . \quad . \quad . \quad . \quad 19.14$$

$$\text{or } V_x = \frac{V_s \cos \beta(l-x)}{\cos \beta l}$$

$$\text{and } I_x = j\frac{V_s}{Z_0}(\tan \beta l \cos \beta x - \sin \beta x) \quad . \quad . \quad . \quad . \quad 19.15$$

$$\text{or } I_x = j\frac{V_s \sin \beta(l-x)}{Z_0 \cos \beta l}$$

It will be seen that the voltage in the open-circuited line has the same form of distribution as the current in the short-circuited line, while the distribution of current in the open-circuited case is of the same form as the voltage in the short-circuited line.

The current nodes which occur along the length of the open-circuited line, are determined by the values of x which satisfy the relation,

$$\tan \beta l \cos \beta x = \sin \beta x$$

$$\text{or } \tan \beta x = \tan \beta l$$

A current node exists at the open end of the line, while others are located at points which are $\lambda/2$, λ, $3\lambda/2$, ... $n\lambda/2$, from the open circuit. This is shown in Fig. 19.1b, which also indicates the voltage nodes which occur midway between the nodes of current.

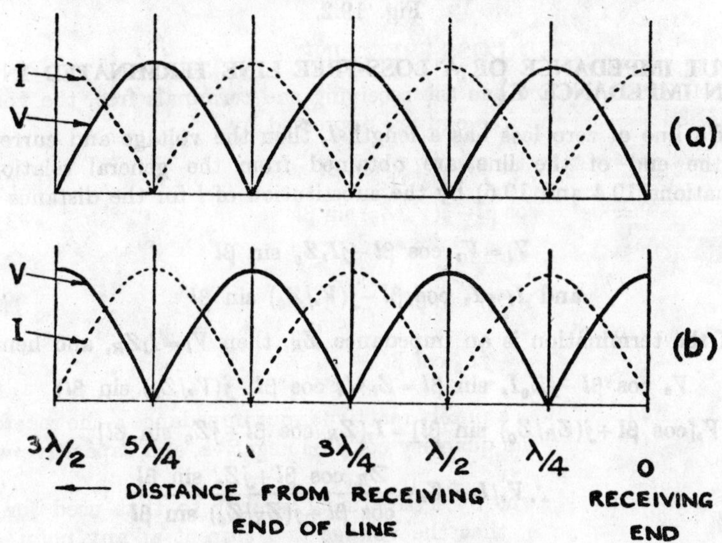

Fig. 19.1. Standing wave patterns on
(a) a short-circuited line
(b) an open-circuited line.

It has already been shown that both short-circuited and open-circuited lines of zero loss present a reactance to the generator at the sending end. The variation of this reactance with line length is shown in Fig. 19.2.

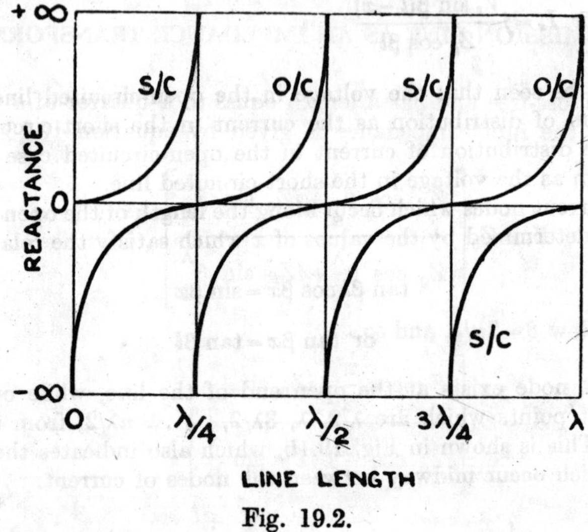

Fig. 19.2.

INPUT IMPEDANCE OF A LOSS-FREE LINE TERMINATED IN AN IMPEDANCE Z_R

If a line of zero loss has a length l, then the voltage and current at the end of the line are obtained from the general relations (equations 19.4 and 19.5) by the substitution of l for the distance x, i.e.

$$V_l = V_s \cos \beta l - jI_s Z_0 \sin \beta l$$

$$\text{and } I_l = I_s \cos \beta l - j(V_s/Z_0) \sin \beta l$$

If the termination is an impedance Z_R, then $V_l = I_l Z_R$, and hence

$$V_s \cos \beta l - jZ_0 I_s \sin \beta l = Z_R[I_s \cos \beta l - j(V_s/Z_0) \sin \beta l]$$

$$\therefore V_s[\cos \beta l + j(Z_R/Z_0) \sin \beta l] = I_s[Z_R \cos \beta l + jZ_0 \sin \beta l]$$

$$\therefore V_s/I_s = Z_s = \frac{Z_R \cos \beta l + jZ_0 \sin \beta l}{\cos \beta l + j(Z_R/Z_0) \sin \beta l}$$

$$= Z_0\left[\frac{Z_R \cos \beta l + jZ_0 \sin \beta l}{Z_0 \cos \beta l + jZ_R \sin \beta l}\right] \qquad 19.16$$

This result should be compared with the input impedance of a line with losses (equation 4.41). It will be seen that the loss-free case can be obtained directly from the general case, as would be expected.

A number of graphical constructions [2,3] have been envolved to determine the input impedance of a line of any length, and with any termination.

THE TRANSMISSION LINE AS AN IMPEDANCE TRANSFORMING DEVICE

If a line is loss-free and has a length equal to a quarter of a wavelength, then the input impedance is given by equation 19.16 as,

$$Z_s = Z_0 \left[\frac{Z_R \cos \beta\frac{\lambda}{4} + jZ_0 \sin \beta\frac{\lambda}{4}}{Z_0 \cos \beta\frac{\lambda}{4} + jZ_R \sin \beta\frac{\lambda}{4}} \right]$$

Now $\beta = 2\pi/\lambda$, and so,

$$Z_s = Z_0 \left[\frac{Z_R \cos \frac{\pi}{2} + jZ_0 \sin \frac{\pi}{2}}{Z_0 \cos \frac{\pi}{2} + jZ_R \sin \frac{\pi}{2}} \right]$$

$$= \frac{Z_0^2}{Z_R} \quad . \quad . \quad . \quad . \quad . \quad . \quad 19.17$$

The input impedance thus varies inversely as Z_R; if Z_R is infinite, i.e. the line is open-circuited, then the line presents a short circuit to the generator, connected to the input end; conversely, if the far end is short-circuited, the input impedance is infinite. Further, if Z_R is resistive, the input impedance of the line is resistive, while a reactive termination gives a reactive input of opposite sign.

A line a quarter of a wavelength long can thus be used to match two lines which have different values of characteristic impedance. This is shown in Fig. 19.3. To effect a match, the characteristic impedance of the $\lambda/4$ matching section is made equal to the geometric mean of the characteristic impedances of the lines between which it is inserted.

If a loss free line has a length of $\lambda/2$ it will be seen that such a line has an input impedance of Z_R, when the termination has a value of

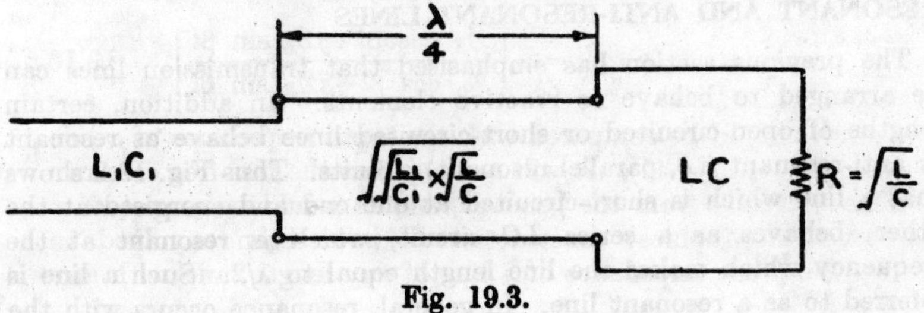

Fig. 19.3.

Z_R. The half-wavelength line thus functions effectively as a one-to-one ratio transformer.

It must be remembered, however, that the impedance transformations given by a section of line only apply at one particular frequency.

THE TRANSMISSION LINE AS A LOW-LOSS REACTANCE

It has already been noted that the input impedance of a loss-free line is a pure reactance when such a line is either short-circuited or open-circuited at the receiving end.

With an open-circuited line the input reactance has been shown to be

$$X_s = -jZ_0 \cot \beta l \quad \text{(equation 19.13)}$$

$$= -jZ_0 \cot \frac{2\pi l}{\lambda}$$

As a consequence, the open line will have a capacitive input reactance when the length is between the limits of 0 and $\lambda/4$ or between $\lambda/2$ and $3\lambda/4$, etc. For example, when $l = \lambda/8$, $X_s = -jZ_0$

A short-circuited loss-free line has an input reactance of

$$X_s = jZ_0 \tan \beta l$$

$$= jZ_0 \tan \frac{2\pi l}{\lambda}$$

Such a line has an inductive input reactance when the length is less than $\lambda/4$, or between $\lambda/2$ and $3\lambda/4$, etc. In this case when l has the value of $\lambda/8$

$$X_s = jZ_0$$

Again, if a loss-free line of any length is terminated in a pure reactance the input impedance will also be a pure reactance, possibly with a change of sign, depending on the length of line involved.

RESONANT AND ANTI-RESONANT LINES

The previous section has emphasised that transmission lines can be arranged to behave as reactive elements. In addition, certain lengths of open-circuited or short-circuited lines behave as resonant or anti-resonant (i.e. parallel resonant) circuits. Thus Fig. 19.2 shows that a line which is short-circuited at one end and energised at the other, behaves as a series LC circuit, which is resonant at the frequency which makes the line length equal to $\lambda/2$. Such a line is referred to as a resonant line. In general, resonance occurs with the receiving end short-circuited when the line is an even integral number of quarter wavelengths long.

When a short-circuited line is an odd integral number of quarter wavelengths it then behaves as a parallel resonant circuit, and is described as an anti-resonant line.

With open-circuited lines, resonance occurs when the line is an odd integral number of quarter wavelengths long; anti-resonance occurs when the line length is equal to an even integral number of quarter wavelengths.

The foregoing relations are summarised in the table below, in which n is zero or an integer.

	Resonance	Anti-resonance
Short-circuited Line	$l=(2n)\frac{\lambda}{4}$	$l=(2n+1)\frac{\lambda}{4}$
Open-circuited Line	$l=(2n+1)\frac{\lambda}{4}$	$l=(2n)\frac{\lambda}{4}$

Hypothetical resonant loss-free lines present a short-circuit to the sending-end generator, while anti-resonant lines present an infinite input resistance. In practice small losses occur, so that resonant and anti-resonant lines have low and high values of input resistance respectively. The actual value of input resistance in any given case can be obtained from the general relations given in chapter 4. For example, the general expression for the input impedance of any short-circuited line of length l is,

$$Z_s = Z_0 \tanh(\alpha + j\beta)l \quad \text{(equation 4.47)}$$

$$= Z_0\left[\frac{\tanh \alpha l + j \tan \beta l}{1 + j \tanh \alpha l \tan \beta l}\right]$$

If the line is to be resonant, its length must be such that $l = n\lambda/2$; βl is then equal to $n\pi$ and $\tan \beta l$ is zero

$$\therefore\ Z_s = Z_0 \tanh \alpha l$$

If the losses are assumed to be small, and the quantity αl is sufficiently small to make $\tanh \alpha l \simeq \alpha l$ then,

$$Z_s \simeq Z_0 \alpha l \qquad 19.18$$

Further if the dielectric loss can be ignored entirely, then $\alpha = R/2Z_0$ (equation 19.3a) and the input resistance of the resonant line is then expressed approximately as

$$Z_s \simeq \frac{Rn\lambda}{4} \quad . \quad . \quad . \quad . \quad . \quad . \quad 19.19$$

It is left as an exercise for the reader to show that a short-circuited low-loss anti-resonant line of length $l = (2n+1)\frac{\lambda}{4}$ has an input resistance which is given approximately by

$$Z_s \simeq \frac{Z_0}{\alpha l} \quad . \quad . \quad . \quad . \quad . \quad . \quad . \quad . \quad 19.20$$

$$\simeq \frac{8Z_0^2}{(2n+1)R\lambda} \quad . \quad . \quad . \quad . \quad . \quad . \quad 19.21$$

if the line has no dielectric loss.

The results of equations 19.18 and 19.20 apply to open-circuited lines as well as short-circuited lines.

It was shown in chapter 3 that the frequency selectivity of a series, or parallel resonant circuit depends on the Q-factor of the circuit, i.e. upon the ratio $\omega L/R$. If dielectric loss is ignored, the Q-factor of a section of line is then $\omega L/R$ where ωL and R may be taken as the series inductance and resistance per unit length of line. With a hypothetical loss-free line the Q-factor is infinitely large. In a practical line of low-loss,

$$Q = \frac{\omega L}{R}$$

By equation 19.3a, $R = 2\alpha Z_0 = 2\alpha\sqrt{\frac{L}{C}}$

$$\therefore Q = \frac{\omega L}{2\alpha\sqrt{\frac{L}{C}}} = \frac{\omega\sqrt{LC}}{2\alpha}$$

$$= \frac{\beta}{2\alpha} \quad . \quad . \quad . \quad . \quad . \quad . \quad . \quad . \quad 19.22$$

This result may be combined with equations 19.18 and 19.20 to express the input impedance of resonant and anti-resonant lines in terms of the characteristic impedance and the Q-factor of the line concerned. The values of Q-factor are much higher than those obtainable with lumped LC circuits.

THE HIGH-FREQUENCY LINE TERMINATED IN ITS CHARACTERISTIC IMPEDANCE

The preceding sections have shown that when the line termination is incorrect, the travelling electromagnetic wave from the generator at the sending end is reflected, partially or completely, at the termination. The combination of the incident and reflected waves then gives rise to standing waves of current and voltage along the line. When the line is correctly terminated, on the other hand, no such standing wave pattern occurs, and energy is conveyed from the generator to the termination where it is absorbed.

If the line has relatively small losses, the characteristic impedance is substantially resistive. When such lines are correctly terminated, they are sometimes referred to as non-resonant lines. The voltage and current are in phase with each other, and are everywhere related by the characteristic impedance, and both decrease exponentially from the sending end by an amount which depends on the losses.

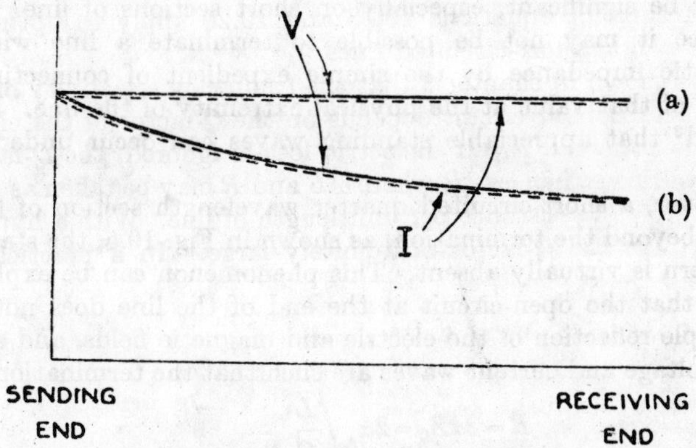

Fig. 19.4. Voltage and current distribution along a correctly terminated line which is (a) loss-free and (b) " lossy ".

When transmission lines are designed to carry appreciable power, it is preferable to operate them in a non-resonant condition. This avoids needless, large dielectric losses which may occur at voltage anti-nodes on resonant lines ; high I^2R losses at current anti-nodes are avoided, and radiation losses are reduced. The absence of any resonant rise of voltage means that the line insulation is subjected to a lower voltage, in proportion to the power transmitted. The limitation on power handling capacity of a line is normally the occurrence of corona round the conductors, and the possibility of flash-over between them.

A correctly terminated line operates at unity power factor, and the transmission efficiency is then highest. Another important point is that the variation of input impedance of the line, with small changes of frequency, is a minimum when the line is terminated in its characteristic impedance.

The use of resonant lines is restricted to applications in which the length of line is short, and the power involved is small.

This is an appropriate point to utter a word of warning about line termination. The line equations used hitherto, have assumed that wave propagation takes place by means of a transverse electromagnetic wave, i.e. one in which the electric and magnetic field components are transverse to the direction of propagation, or energy flow, which is of course along the direction of the line. At discontinuities in the line, a perturbation of the electromagnetic field occurs. When the frequency is low this can be ignored, as the disturbance only exists over a very short length of line ; at very high frequencies, on the other hand, the effect may be significant, especially on short sections of line. As a consequence it may not be possible to terminate a line with its characteristic impedance by the simple expedient of connecting an impedance of that value at the physical extremity of the line. It has been found[3] that appreciable standing waves can occur under such conditions.

If, however, a short-circuited quarter wavelength section of line is connected beyond the termination, as shown in Fig. 19.5, the standing wave pattern is virtually absent. This phenomenon can be explained by saying that the open-circuit at the end of the line does not give rise to simple reflection of the electric and magnetic fields, and so the reflected voltage and current waves are such that the termination does

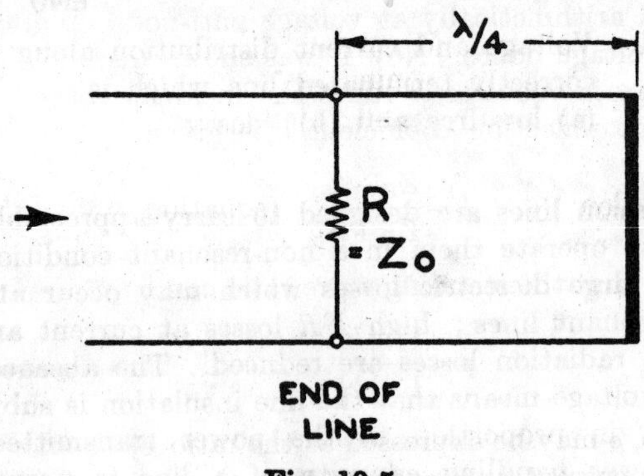

Fig. 19.5.

not correspond with an infinite impedance. Hence the connection of an impedance equal to the characteristic impedance of the line does not terminate the line correctly, and reflections occur.

The presence of the $\lambda/4$ section however gives rise to an infinite impedance at the terminating point. Hence a wave travelling from the left (Fig. 19.5) encounters a termination at the end of the line which is then equal to the characteristic impedance of the line.

The fact that an open-circuit does not necessarily correspond with an infinite impedance at very high frequencies, means that in some cases corrections may have to be applied to formulae for open-circuited lines.

A short-circuit can be arranged more easily. A transmission line can be short-circuited if it is terminated in a conducting surface which conforms to the geometry of the wave front and reflects the incident wave without distortion. An open two-wire line can be short-circuited if the conductors terminate in a large metal plate, rather than a wire which would distort the wave pattern, and behave as a reactive termination.

STANDING WAVE RATIO

When reflection occurs in an incorrectly terminated line, the voltage and current vary in magnitude along its length ; if the line loss is small, all the voltage maxima (or minima) can be assumed to have equal amplitudes. When such conditions apply, the standing ratio ρ may be defined as

$$\rho = \frac{|V_{max}|}{|V_{min}|}$$

where $|V_{max}|$ and $|V_{min}|$ are magnitudes of the voltage at an anti-node and node, respectively. The voltage at any point along the line is equal to the algebraic sum of the incident and reflected voltages. These voltages add arithmetically at voltage anti-nodes and subtract arithmetically at voltage nodes. Now it was shown in chapter 4 that the reflected voltage is equal to k times the incident voltage, where the complex voltage reflection coefficient k is given by the relation

$$k = \frac{Z_R - Z_0}{Z_R + Z_0} \quad \text{(equation 4.30)}$$

It follows from this that the standing wave ratio can be represented by

$$\rho = \frac{1 + |k|}{1 - |k|} \qquad . \quad . \quad . \quad 19.23$$

As an alternative, ρ may be expressed as the ratio of the magnitude of the current at a current anti-node to that at a current node.

It is convenient to represent the degree of mismatch in terms of standing wave ratio as this quantity can be determined readily from measurements.

IMPEDANCE MATCHING IN TRANSMISSION LINES

If the load connected to a transmission line has an impedance which is different from that of the line, it is desirable to employ some impedance matching device, to enable the load to be matched to the line. At high frequencies the necessary impedance matching is usually achieved by one or other of the following methods.

Quarter Wavelength Line

The impedance transforming properties of a quarter wavelength line have already been mentioned. Such a line can only alter the magnitude of an impedance and cannot change its phase angle (except that a positive reactance at one end of such a section may appear as a negative reactance at the other end). The quarter wavelength line is also frequency selective, in that the power transfer varies with frequency. This variation becomes smaller as the impedances at each end of the matching section approach each other in value.

The Tapered Transmission Line

If the spacing of the conductors is varied, the impedance of a line varies; a line in which the spacing varies uniformly from the input provides a gradual impedance transformation along its length. Tapered lines[4] may be constructed so that the characteristic impedance varies exponentially. Impedance matching can be achieved by interposing a suitably designed tapered line between the load and the main transmission line. An advantage of a tapered line is that it is less frequency selective than a quarter wavelength line.

Stub Matching

If a short section of loss-free line is connected across a main transmission line it will introduce at the point of attachment, a reactance, the value of which will depend on the length of the section and on the condition of the end remote from the main line. Such sections of line, referred to as *stubs*, may be used for impedance matching. As a stub is connected in parallel with the main transmission line, it is preferable to treat the question of impedance matching by stubs in terms of admittances rather than impedances; a loss-free stub of variable length should therefore be considered as a device which has zero input conductance and a susceptance which varies with the stub length.

If the terminal load on a transmission line is not equal to th characteristic impedance, then the input admittance of the line w vary with distance from the load. If a stub is placed at a point on tl line where the input conductance at that point is equal to t characteristic conductance of the line, and the stub length is adjust to provide a susceptance which is equal in value, but opposite sign, to the input susceptance of the main line at that point, th the total susceptance at the point of stub attachment will be ze The combination of stub and line will thus present a conducta which is equal to the characteristic conductance of the line, i.e. main length of high-frequency transmission line will be matched. the line is several wavelengths long, there will be a multiplicity points at which the stub may be placed, but it is normally positio at the point nearest to the load. The greatest possible length of is then operated in a matched condition.

Stubs may have the end remote from the main line open-circui or short-circuited ; the short-circuited stub is generally preferred practice as it permits of simpler mechanical construction adjustment.

If a single stub is to be used, as shown in Fig. 19.6, it is first of necessary to find the correct point of attachment, i.e. the valu the distance l. This may be found if it is recalled that the in impedance of a high-frequency line of characteristic resistance

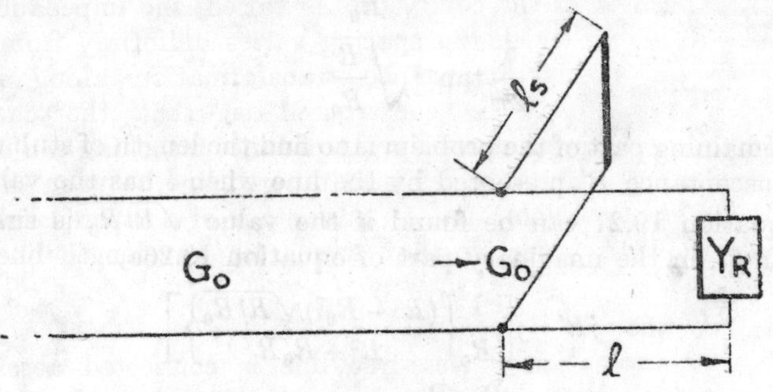

Fig. 19.6.

when terminated in an impedance Z_R is given by Z_{in}, where

$$Z_{in}=R_0\left[\frac{Z_R \cos \beta l+jR_0 \sin \beta l}{R_0 \cos \beta l+jZ_R \sin \beta l}\right]$$

$$=R_0\left[\frac{Z_R+jR_0 \tan \beta l}{R_0+jZ_R \tan \beta l}\right] \quad . \quad . \quad 1$$

If this is expressed in terms of an input admittance Y_{in}, then

$$Y_{in} = 1/Z_{in} = \frac{1}{R_0}\left[\frac{R_0 + jZ_R \tan \beta l}{Z_R + jR_0 \tan \beta l}\right]$$

Suppose now for simplicity that the terminating impedance is a resistance R, then

$$Y_{in} = \frac{1}{R_0}\left[\frac{R_0 + jR \tan \beta l}{R + jR_0 \tan \beta l}\right] \quad . \quad . \quad . \quad . \quad . \quad . \quad . \quad 19.25$$

$$= \left[\frac{R(1 + \tan^2 \beta l)}{R^2 + R_0^2 \tan^2 \beta l}\right] + j\left[\frac{1}{R_0}\left\{\frac{(R^2 - R_0^2) \tan \beta l}{R^2 + R_0^2 \tan^2 \beta l}\right\}\right] \quad . \quad 19.26a$$

$$= G' + jB' \quad . \quad . \quad . \quad . \quad . \quad . \quad . \quad 19.26b$$

If the real part of this admittance is to be equal to the characteristic conductance of the line G_0, $(= 1/R_0)$, then

$$\frac{1}{R_0} = \frac{R(1 + \tan^2 \beta l)}{R^2 + R_0^2 \tan^2 \beta l}$$

$$\therefore RR_0 + RR_0 \tan^2 \beta l = R^2 + R_0^2 \tan^2 \beta l$$

$$\therefore \tan \beta l = \sqrt{\frac{R}{R_0}}$$

The length l may then be determined from the relation

$$l = \frac{1}{\beta} \tan^{-1} \sqrt{\frac{R}{R_0}}$$

$$= \frac{\lambda}{2\pi} \tan^{-1} \sqrt{\frac{R}{R_0}} \quad . \quad . \quad . \quad . \quad . \quad 19.27$$

The remaining part of the problem is to find the length of stub required. The susceptance B' presented by the line when l has the value given by equation 19.27 can be found if the value $\sqrt{R/R_0}$ is substituted for $\tan \beta l$, in the imaginary part of equation 19.26a,

$$\text{i.e. } jB' = j\left[\frac{1}{R_0}\left\{\frac{(R^2 - R_0^2)\sqrt{R/R_0}}{R^2 + R_0 R}\right\}\right]$$

$$\text{or, } B' = \frac{R - R_0}{R_0\sqrt{RR_0}} \quad . \quad . \quad . \quad . \quad . \quad 19.28$$

If the stub is short-circuited, has a length l_s, and characteristic resistance R_0', it will have an input reactance of

$$jR_0' \tan \beta l_s \text{ (from equation 19.9)}$$

which corresponds to a susceptance of

$$\frac{1}{jR_0' \tan \beta l_s} = \frac{-j}{R_0' \tan \beta l_s}$$

If the total susceptance of the stub and the line is to be zero at the point of stub attachment, then

$$B' + \left(\frac{-1}{R_0' \tan \beta l_s}\right) = 0$$

Insertion of the value for B' from equation 19.28 then gives

$$\frac{R - R_0}{R_0\sqrt{RR_0}} = \frac{1}{R_0' \tan \beta l_s}$$

$$\text{from which } l_s = \frac{\lambda}{2\pi} \tan^{-1} \frac{R_0\sqrt{RR_0}}{R_0'(R - R_0)} \qquad . \quad . \quad . \qquad 19.29$$

If the terminal load on the transmission line is a complex impedance Z_R, equal to $R + jX$, rather than a resistance R, the problem may be solved if R is replaced by $R + jX$ in equation 19.25.

The single stub suffers from two disadvantages. First of all the range of terminating impedances which can be transformed is limited. Also, if the terminating impedance varies, it is necessary to adjust the position as well as the length of the stub. This is particularly inconvenient in the case of coaxial cables. Two stubs at fixed points, usually about a quarter wavelength apart, may be used to achieve a wide range of impedance matching; the stub nearest the load (Fig. 19.7) is adjusted to make the real part of the admittance at the points *ab* equal to the characteristic conductance of the line, in the absence of the second stub. This stub is then adjusted to produce zero susceptance at the points *ab*.

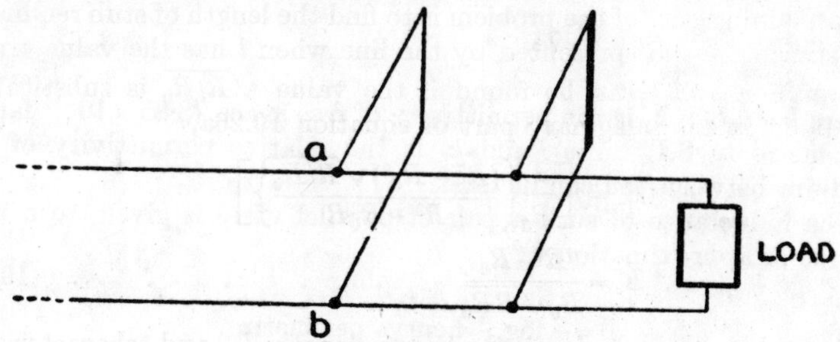

Fig. 19.7. Double-stub matching.

FORMS OF HIGH-FREQUENCY TRANSMISSION LINES

The form of construction employed for a high-frequency line depends on the application for which it is used. In cases where more than one type is suitable, the selection of a particular form then depends mainly a economic factors. The main forms of high-frequency line (in addition to wave guides which are discussed at the end of this chapter) are open-wire lines and coaxial cables.

Open-Wire Lines

These are simple and cheap to construct, and usually consist of two copper (or copper alloy) conductors spaced a few inches apart, and fixed by insulators mounted on poles. As the insulation is almost all air, the dielectric loss is extremely small. An open-wire line also has the advantage that it is balanced with respect to earth.

Radiation loss becomes significant, and makes the use of open-wire lines undesirable above frequencies of the order of 100 MHz.

An alternative open-wire arrangement which is sometimes used, has four conductors instead of two. The four wires are held by insulators at the corners of a square, and the diagonally opposite wires are connected in parallel. Such a line has the advantage that it has a lower characteristic impedance than a two wire line, so that for a given power the line voltage is less, and the insulator losses are reduced.

The characteristic impedance of an open-wire line at high-frequency has been shown to be approximately equal to $\sqrt{L/C}$ where L and C are respectively the inductance and capacitance per unit length. In practice it is more convenient to express the characteristic impedance in terms of the spacing and size of the conductors used.

It can be shown[5] that the capacitance of a pair of parallel wires which have a spacing s, much greater than the radius r of the wires is given by

$$C = \frac{\pi k}{\log_e \frac{s}{r}} \text{ farads per metre}$$

where $k = k_0 k_r$; k_0 is the permittivity of free space ($8{\cdot}85 \times 10^{-12}$ farads per metre in S.I. units), and k_r is the relative permittivity of the medium between the conductors.

The inductance of such a pair of parallel wires is given, to a high degree of approximation by

$$L = \frac{\mu}{\pi} \log_e \frac{s}{r} \text{ henrys per metre}$$

where $\mu = \mu_0 \mu_r$

Hence for an open-wire line

$$Z_0 = \sqrt{\frac{L}{C}} = \sqrt{\frac{\mu_0}{\pi^2 k_0}} \log_e \frac{s}{r}$$

$$=120 \log_e \frac{s}{r}$$

$$=276 \log_{10} \frac{s}{r} \,\Omega \quad . \quad . \quad . \quad . \quad 19.30$$

Coaxial Cables

If one conductor of, say, an open-wire line, is placed inside a larger hollow concentric conductor, the arrangement is referred to as a coaxial cable. It has the merit that the electromagnetic field is confined to the annular space between the conductors, and thereby avoids the radiation loss which would occur on an open-wire line. The outer sheath also acts as an effective shield against external high-frequency interference.

Coaxial cable is made in a variety of forms, and is used to transmit frequencies up to about 3,000 MHz. A cross-section of one type of coaxial cable is illustrated in Fig. 17.36 (composite cables are shown, containing two, four and six coaxial tubes). This form of cable has a solid centre conductor of copper, with a diameter of 2·6 mm ; this is held in position by polythene discs, spaced along its length. The outer conductor has an internal diameter of 9·5 mm and is composed of a spiralled copper tape, 0·25 mm thick, and bound with two layers of steel tape each 0·125 mm thick. These two layers provide an electromagnetic screen and help to strengthen the outer conductor.

Flexible forms of coaxial cable usually have a continuous dielectric ; the inner conductor is stranded and the outer conductor is in the form of braided wire to give the necessary flexibility.

The characteristic impedance of a coaxial cable in terms of the conductor size and spacing can be obtained from the expression for the inductance and capacitance per unit length of cable.

It can be shown[5] that in this case

$$L=\frac{\mu}{2\pi} \log_e \frac{D}{d} \text{ henrys per metre}$$

$$\text{and } C=\frac{2\pi k}{\log_e D/d} \text{ farads per metre}$$

where D is the diameter of the outer conductor and d is the diameter of the inner conductor ; μ and k are respectively the permeability of the conductors and permittivity of the dielectric between the inner and outer conductors. It should be noted that the expression for the inductance of the cable refers to the inductance due to the flux in the annular space between the conductors.

The characteristic impedance of a coaxial cable is thus given by

$$Z_0 = \sqrt{\frac{L}{C}} = \sqrt{\frac{\mu}{4\pi^2 k}} \log_e \frac{D}{d}$$

$$= \sqrt{\frac{\mu_0 \mu_r}{k_0 k_r 4\pi^2}} \log_e \frac{D}{d}$$

$$= 138 \sqrt{\frac{\mu_r}{k_r}} \log_{10} \frac{D}{d}$$

If copper conductors are used and the dielectric is substantially air, then μ_r and k_r are equal to unity and the characteristic impedance of air spaced coaxial cable is then

$$Z_0 = 138 \log_{10} \frac{D}{d} \quad . \quad . \quad . \quad . \quad . \quad 19.31$$

It is interesting to observe that if for economic reasons the diameter of the outer conductor of a coaxial cable is fixed, then there is an optimum size of the inner conductor as far as the attenuation is concerned.

The high-frequency resistance of a coaxial cable in which both conductors are of the same material is proportional to the quantity

$$\left(\frac{1}{D} + \frac{1}{d}\right)$$

where D is again the diameter of the outer conductor and d of the inner conductor.

This follows from the fact that the current flow at high frequencies is confined to a surface layer.

The attenuation, neglecting dielectric loss is given by

$$\alpha = \frac{R}{2Z_0} \text{ (equation 19.3 a)}$$

Now Z_0 is proportional to the quantity $\log_e \frac{D}{d}$ so that the attenuation is proportional to the quantity y, where

$$y = \frac{\frac{1}{D} + \frac{1}{d}}{\log_e \frac{D}{d}}$$

The attenuation is thus a minimum, when y has a minimum value. If $D/d = p$ then

$$Dy = \frac{1+p}{\log_e p} \text{ and if } D \text{ is constant } \frac{dy}{dp} = \frac{\log_e p - (p+1)/p}{(\log_e p)^2}$$

For a minimum value

$$\log_e p = \frac{p+1}{p}$$

The solution of this equation which represents a minimum value is $p = 3{\cdot}59$. Hence the optimum ratio of the radii of the conductors of a coaxial cable to produce minimum attenuation is

$$\frac{D}{d} = 3{\cdot}59$$

provided always that both conductors are made of the same material. This optimum ratio of radii is independent of the diameter and thickness of the outer conductor. It is also independent of the frequency provided that the frequency is sufficiently high for the approximation in the expression for the attenuation to be true.

WAVE GUIDES

GENERAL FEATURES OF WAVE GUIDE PROPAGATION

The term " wave guide " could properly be applied to any system of conductors, or insulators, which serve to confine electromagnetic waves to a particular path. Such a definition would include all types of transmission line. In practice, the term wave guide is usually restricted to a system in which propagation takes place inside a hollow metal tube, and it is in this sense that the term will be used.

The propagation of electromagnetic waves through the interior space of a wave guide can be considered as a reflection phenomenon.

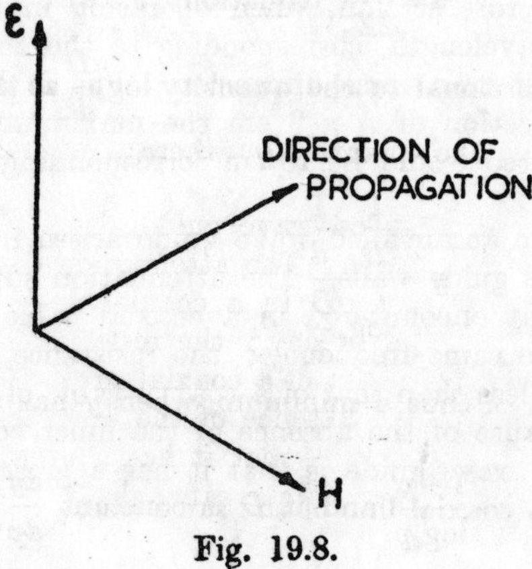

Fig. 19.8.

in which waves are reflected from wall to wall, so that they pass down the tube in a zig-zag path. A uniform plane wave has the electric field E, at right angles to the magnetic field H, and the direction of propagation is normal to the plane containing E and H; the direction of propagation forms a right handed system of axes with the vectors E and H as shown in Fig. 19.8. This mode of propagation is encountered in ordinary transmission lines, and is referred to as a transverse electromagnetic (*TEM*) mode. In a wave guide, the resultant wave travelling longitudinally down the guide, has a component of either the electric or magnetic field in the direction of propagation, so that the transmission is no longer in terms of a *TEM* mode.

If, as a practical approximation, the resistance of the guide walls is ignored, the modes of wave guide transmission may be classified as transverse electric (*TE*) or transverse magnetic (*TM*). In the former case, the electric field lies wholly in the transverse plane, perpendicular to the direction of propagation; while there is a magnetic component along the direction of propagation. This type of wave is sometimes called an *H-wave*. With *TM* modes, the magnetic field exists only in a plane transverse to the direction of propagation, and there is a component of electric field in the direction of propagation. This form of wave is sometimes called an *E-wave*.

A basic feature of wave guide propagation is that it exhibits a frequency characteristic similar to that of a high-pass filter, in that there is a lower limiting frequency below which there is no transmission. At frequencies lower than the cut-off value, the wave is simply reflected backwards and forwards across the guide, and makes no forward progress. The value of the cut-off frequency is related inversely to the transverse dimensions of the guide. This feature restricts the use of wave guides to ultra-high frequencies, as the guides at lower frequencies become inconveniently large. As an example, a guide of rectangular cross section, when operating in its simplest mode, has a cut-off wavelength, corresponding to the cut-off frequency, of twice the largest transverse dimension; thus in a wave guide with a rectangular section of 5 × 2 cm the maximum free space wavelength transmitted would be 10 cm. corresponding to a frequency of 3,000 MHz.

Attenuation in an air-filled wave guide arises from the finite conductivity of the guide walls. The attenuation so produced however is less than that encountered in a coaxial cable of the same size, operating at the same frequency; the resistance of a circular wave guide is clearly less than that of a coaxial cable of the same diameter and length because of the absence of the inner conductor. Another advantage of a wave guide is that it has a greater power handling capacity than a coaxial line of the same size.

PROPAGATION IN A RECTANGULAR GUIDE

The conditions necessary for wave guide propagation can be obtained by considering the process as a reflection phenomenon in which longitudinal transmission occurs as the result of continued reflection of two plane waves. As a beginning, consider a plane wave incident at some angle to a perfect conducting surface as shown in Fig. 19.9

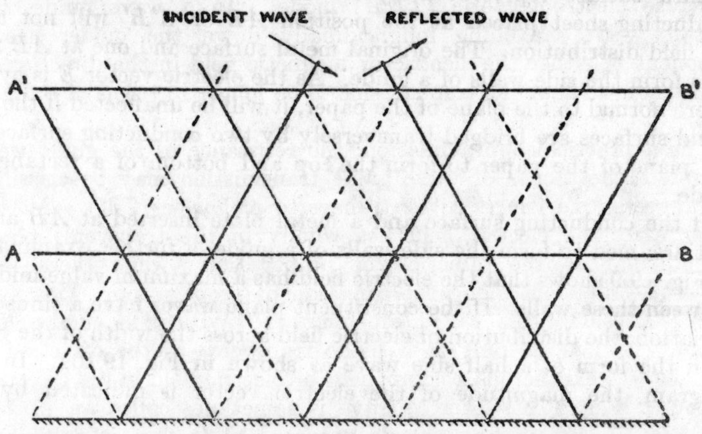

Fig. 19.9. Reflection of a plane wave at oblique incidence on a flat conductor.

Fig. 19.9 is best visualised as a plan view, with the conducting surface vertical. The electric vector is assumed to be normal to the plane of the paper, while the magnetic vector lies in the plane of the paper. The full lines represent wave crests in which the positive electric vector is directed out from the paper ; the dotted lines represent wave troughs in which the electric vector is negative and is directed in towards the paper. The incident wave, travelling towards the bottom right hand side of the page, is reflected by the conducting sheet ; the reflected wave then travels towards the top right hand side of the page.

As the metal sheet is assumed to be a perfect conductor, the component of the electric field tangential to the conducting sheet must be zero. The electric vector must as a consequence change sign on reflection ; incident crests then give rise to reflected troughs, while incident troughs appear as crests on reflection. The addition of the incident and reflected waves then gives the pattern of the electric field. The existence of a (positive) crest and a (negative) trough at any point, as indicated by the crossing of a full and a dotted line, means that the resultant field is zero at that point. The intersection of two full lines indicates a point where the electric field has a positive maximum value; a negative maximum occurs at points of intersection of dotted lines.

An inspection of Fig. 19.9 shows that the value of the resultant electric field is zero at the surface of the metal; it is also zero at a second surface as represented by the line AB in the diagram, or at a third surface represented by the line $A'B'$. It follows that a conducting sheet placed at the position AB or $A'B'$ will not alter the field distribution. The original metal surface and one at AB may thus form the side walls of a guide. As the electric vector E is everywhere normal to the plane of the paper, it will be unaffected if the two metal surfaces are bridged transversely by two conducting surfaces in the plane of the paper to form the top and bottom of a rectangular guide.

If the conducting surface and a metal plate inserted at AB are in fact assumed to form the side walls of a guide, a further examination of Fig. 19.9 shows that the electric field has a maximum value midway between these walls. If the constituent plane waves have a sinusoidal variation, the distribution of electric field across the width of the guide is in the form of a half sine wave as shown in Fig. 19.10a. In this diagram, the magnitude of the electric vector is indicated by the

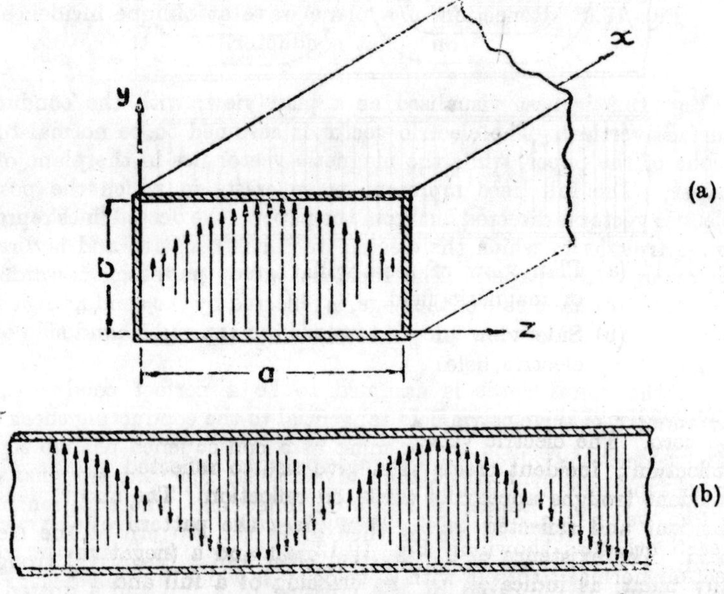

Fig. 19.10 (a) Variation of electric field in yz plane.
(b) Variation of electric field in xy plane.

length of arrow which represents it. The form of the distribution of the electric field applies to all sections of the guide in the *yz* plane. Reference to Fig. 19.9 shows that the electric field alternates in sign along the length of the guide. Fig. 19.10b shows the variation which applies to any *xy* plane inside the guide.

Fig. 19.9 may also be used to obtain the resultant form of the magnetic field inside the guide. The boundary condition for the magnetic field in proximity to a perfect conducting surface is that the field be entirely tangential. Addition of the magnetic components of the incident and reflected waves, bearing in mind the fact that the magnetic vector does not change sign on reflection, gives a series of closed loops, so that the guide has a component of magnetic field in the direction of propagation. The distribution of the magnetic field is shown in Fig. 19.11a which shows the distribution in the *xz* plane. Fig. 19.11b shows the corresponding variation of electric field in the *xy* plane.

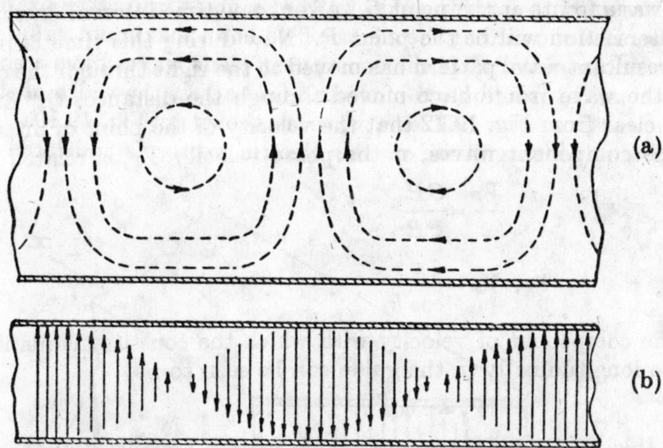

Fig. 19.11 (a) Plan view of rectangular guide showing distribution of magnetic field.
(b) Side view of guide showing the distribution of the electric field.

Phase and Group Velocities

The velocities involved in wave guide propagation may be determined from the pattern of reflected plane waves. If *OQ* and *OR* represent the two wave fronts at some instant of time they will be inclined to each other as shown in Fig. 19.12, and each will advance in a direction normal to itself with a velocity *v* which is the velocity of propagation in free space. The diagram shows the intersection of the

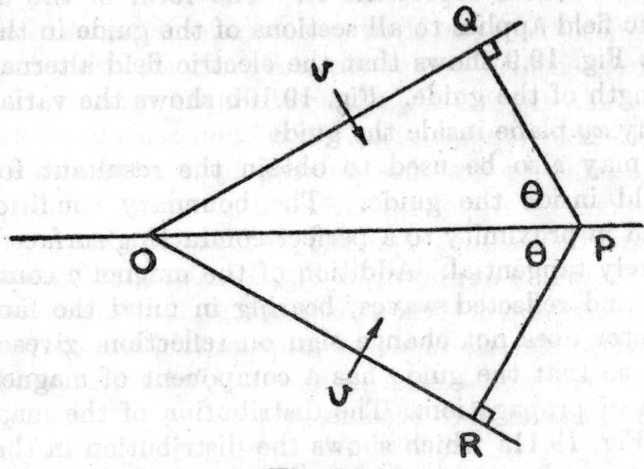

Fig. 19.12.

two wave fronts at the point O. After some time interval δt, this point of intersection will be the point P. Now during this time δt in which the resultant wave pattern has moved to the right through the distance OP the wave fronts have moved through the distances QP and RP. It is clear from Fig. 19.12 that the velocity of the point of intersection of the component waves, or the phase velocity V_P, is related to v by

$$\frac{V_P}{v} = \frac{OP}{PR}$$

$$\text{i.e. } V_P = \frac{v}{\cos\theta} \qquad 19.32$$

The component of velocity with which the constituent plane waves move longitudinally in the guide can be seen to be

$$V_g = v\cos\theta \qquad 19.33$$

and this is the velocity with which energy travels along the guide. Equation 19.32 and 19.33 give

$$V_P \, . \, V_g = v^2 \qquad 19.34$$

ANALYSIS OF WAVE GUIDE PROPAGATION

An attempt has been made to illustrate some features of the distribution of the electric and magnetic fields for propagation in a particular mode in a rectangular wave guide. An alternative approach to the foregoing method of synthesis, is to write down Maxwell's equations and solve them for the particular boundary conditions imposed by the walls of the guide.

For a wave guide of rectangular cross-section, Maxwell's equations are best expressed in the form of rectangular co-ordinates. The electro-magnetic field can then be described in terms of six quantities, namely three electric components E_x, E_y, E_z with three magnetic components H_x, H_y and H_z. The subscripts indicate the co-ordinate along which the component lies. In a homogeneous isotropic medium, these six quantities are inter-related by six equations which have been developed in Appendix G.

It will now be assumed that the co-ordinate axes are disposed with respect to the guide as shown in Fig. 19.10a, that transmission takes place in the direction of the x axis. Further, if attention is concentrated on a transverse electric mode of propagation, the only component of electric field will be E_y, as $E_x = E_z = 0$. Under this condition the six relations of Appendix G become

$$-\mu\frac{\partial H_x}{\partial t} = -\frac{\partial E_y}{\partial z} \quad \text{(a)} \qquad \frac{\partial H_z}{\partial y} - \frac{\partial H_y}{\partial z} = 0 \quad \text{(d)}$$

$$-\mu\frac{\partial H_y}{dt} = 0 \quad \text{(b)} \qquad \frac{\partial H_x}{\partial z} - \frac{\partial H_z}{\partial x} = gE_y + k\frac{\partial E_y}{\partial t} \quad \text{(e)}$$

$$-\mu\frac{\partial H_z}{\partial t} = \frac{\partial E_y}{\partial x} \quad \text{(c)} \qquad \frac{\partial H_y}{dx} - \frac{\partial H_x}{\partial y} = 0 \quad \text{(f)}$$

$$19.35$$

If the six quantities E_x, E_y etc. vary sinusoidally with time so that they contain the factor $e^{j\omega t}$, then the relationships of 19.35 become

$$-j\omega\mu H_x = -\frac{\partial E_y}{\partial z} \quad \text{(a)} \qquad \frac{\partial H_z}{\partial y} - \frac{\partial H_y}{\partial z} = 0 \quad \text{(d)}$$

$$-j\omega\mu H_y = 0 \quad \text{(b)} \qquad \frac{\partial H_x}{\partial z} - \frac{\partial H_z}{\partial x} = (g + j\omega k)E_y \quad \text{(e)}$$

$$-j\omega\mu H_z = \frac{\partial E_y}{\partial x} \quad \text{(c)} \qquad \frac{\partial H_y}{dx} - \frac{\partial H_x}{dy} = 0 \quad \text{(f)}$$

$$19.36$$

Equation 19.36b shows that H_y is zero. Of the six field components only three remain, namely E_y, H_x and H_z.

An equation in terms of E_y can be obtained if equations 19.36a and 19.36c are differentiated with respect to z and x respectively. These operations give

$$j\omega\mu\frac{\partial H_x}{\partial z} = \frac{\partial^2 E_y}{\partial z^2} \text{ and } -j\omega\mu\frac{\partial H_z}{\partial x} = \frac{\partial^2 E_y}{\partial x^2}$$

Insertion of the values of

$$\frac{\partial H_x}{\partial z} \text{ and } \frac{\partial H_z}{\partial x}$$

from these relations in equation 19.36e then gives

$$\frac{\partial^2 E_y}{\partial z^2}+\frac{\partial^2 E_y}{\partial x^2}=(-\omega^2\mu k+j\omega\mu g)E_y$$

If the material inside the guide is a pure dielectric, so that $g=0$ then

$$\frac{\partial^2 E_y}{\partial z^2}+\frac{\partial^2 E_y}{\partial x^2}=-\omega^2\mu k E_y \quad . \quad . \quad . \quad 19.37$$

Clearly E_y must be a function of x and z; $f(z)$ must be such that

$$E_y=0 \text{ when } z=0 \text{ or } a$$

where a is the width of the guide.

It can be shown that a suitable solution of equation 19.37 is given by

$$E_y=Ae^{-Px}\sin\frac{m\pi z}{a} \quad . \quad . \quad . \quad 19.38$$

where A is a constant, m is an integer, and provided that

$$\left(P^2-\frac{m^2\pi^2}{a^2}\right)=-\omega^2\mu k$$

$$\text{i.e. } P=\sqrt{\frac{m^2\pi^2}{a^2}-\omega^2\mu k}$$

Inspection of the expression for E_y in equation 19.38 shows that P is in fact the effective propagation coefficient. If the walls of the guide are assumed to be perfectly conducting, then this fact, together with the previous assumption of a pure dielectric medium inside the guide, means that there will be no loss, and the propagation coefficient will be imaginary, i.e. $P=j\beta$ where β is the wavelength coefficient for the guide. Thus

$$j\beta=\sqrt{\frac{m^2\pi^2}{a^2}-\omega^2\mu k}$$

$$\text{or } \beta=\sqrt{\omega^2\mu k-\frac{m^2\pi^2}{a^2}}$$

β will thus have a real value if

$$\omega>\frac{m\pi}{a\sqrt{\mu k}} \text{ or } f>\frac{m}{2a\sqrt{\mu k}}$$

The limiting frequency f_c is thus given by

$$f=\frac{mv}{2a} \quad . \quad . \quad . \quad . \quad . \quad 19.39a$$

$$\text{and } \lambda_c=\frac{2a}{m} \quad . \quad . \quad . \quad . \quad . \quad 19.39b$$

where $\lambda_c = v/f_c$ and $v = 1/\sqrt{\mu k}$ is the velocity of propagation in free space (see Appendix H).

The particular mode of transmission previously synthesised was such that $m = 1$. Equation 19.39b thus confirms the point previously stated, that with a rectangular guide, propagating in the mode shown in Fig. 19.11, the cut-off frequency corresponds to a free space wavelength equal to twice the width of the guide.

Expressions for the magnetic components H_x and H_z can be obtained by the insertion of the expression for E_y in equations 19.36a and 19.36c. This operation then gives

$$H_x = -\left(\frac{j\pi}{\omega\mu a}\right) A\, e^{-j\beta x} \cos\frac{\pi z}{a} \quad . \quad 19.40$$

$$\text{and } H_z = \left(\frac{\beta}{\omega\mu}\right) A e^{-j\beta x} \sin\frac{\pi z}{a} \quad . \quad . \quad 19.41$$

The magnetic field conforming with these relations is shown in Fig. 19.11.

The foregoing analysis is based on the assumption that a transverse electric mode is involved so that E_y is the only component of electric field. The analysis for a transverse magnetic mode may be carried out on similar lines if the initial assumption is made that H_x is zero. Attention has been confined to guides with a rectangular cross-section. Wave guides with a cylindrical cross-section are also used. To analyse the operation of such guides Maxwell's equations should first be expressed in cyclindrical co-ordinates.

CLASSIFICATION OF WAVE GUIDE MODES

So far, it has been suggested that modes of propagation may be classified as *TE* or *TM*. While this is true, further distinction is necessary as a wide range of modes exist, and suffixes are used. Thus for the TE_{mn} or H_{mn} mode in a rectangular guide, m and n denote the number of half sinusoids in the electric field distribution along the long and short sides respectively of the guide. This applies to transverse magnetic modes (TM_{mn} or E_{mn}) if magnetic field is referred to in place of electric field. It can be shown that the general expression for the cut-off wavelength for a *TE* or *TM* mode in a rectangular guide is given by

$$\lambda_c = \frac{2}{\sqrt{(m/a)^2 + (n/b)^2}}$$

The mode illustrated in Figs. 19.10 and 19.11 has no variation of the electric or magnetic field in the b direction, and one half wave in the a direction so that $m = 1$ and $n = 0$ and the mode is thus TE_{10}. This

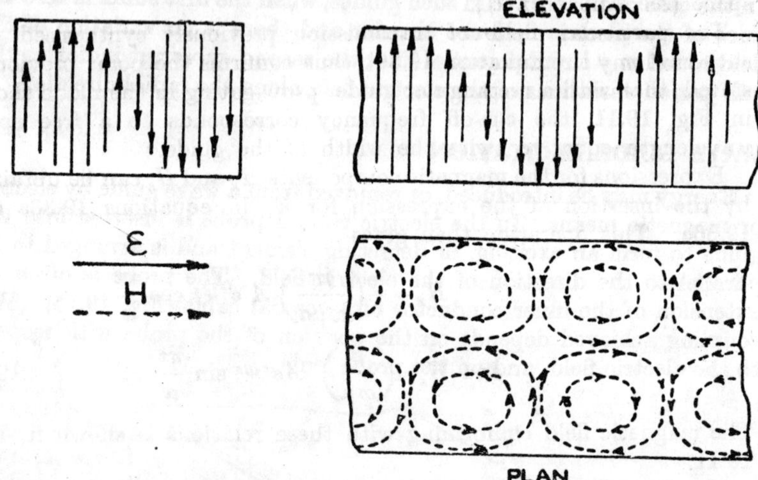

Fig. 19.13. TE_{20} (or H_{20}) mode of propagation in a rectangular guide.

particular mode is referred to as the dominant mode and is important in that it has the lowest cut-off frequency for a particular rectangular guide.

An illustration of a TE_{20} mode is shown in Fig. 19.13. This mode would be produced in place of the TE_{10} considered above, if the metal surface at AB in Fig. 19.9 was replaced by the surface at $A'B'$.

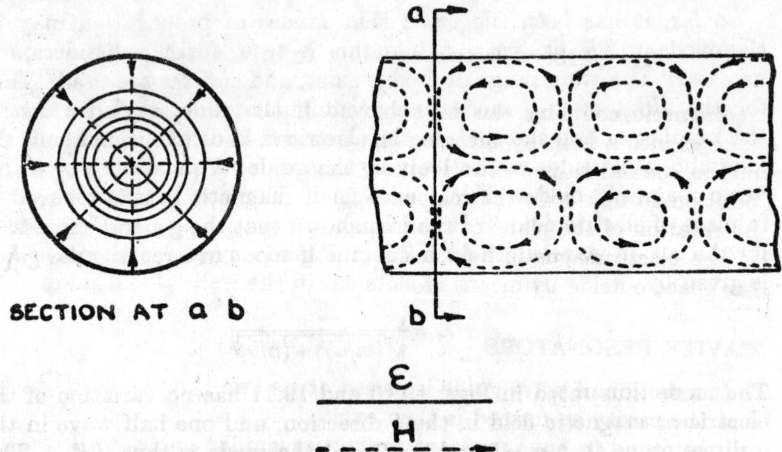

Fig. 19.14. H_{01} mode in a circular guide.

Fig. 19.14 shows an H_{01} mode of propagation in a circular guide. In the case of an H wave in such guides, when the first suffix is zero the lines of the electric field are circular and there is no variation of the field round any circumferential line; the second subscript indicates the half period variations of the electric field along the radial direction.

WAVE GUIDE EXCITATION

Energy may be introduced, or removed from a wave guide by electric or magnetic means. In the electric case, a probe is inserted into the guide to form an exciting, or detecting element and is arranged to lie parallel to the direction of the electric field. The probe is often an extension of the inner conductor of a coaxial cable (Fig. 19.15). The coupling achieved depends on the position of the probe with respect to the electric field, and on the probe length.

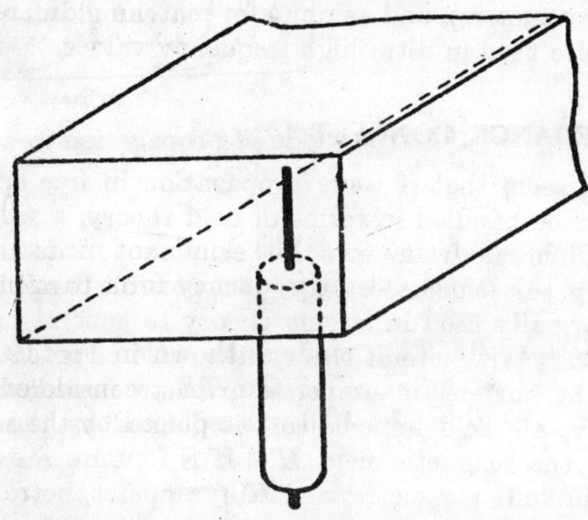

Fig. 19.15. Electric coupling from a coaxial cable.

Magnetic coupling can be achieved if the probe of Fig. 19.15 is formed into a loop by bringing the free end back to the outer screen of the coaxial cable. The loop so formed must then be placed in a position to link with the magnetic field. The coupling can be varied by rotation of the plane of the loop.

The electromagnetic field inside the guide may also be coupled to the space outside by means of slots cut in the walls of the guide.

CAVITY RESONATORS

If a section of wave guide is closed at its two ends by metal plates, and the cavity so formed is then excited by a small probe or loop, it will be found to have resonant properties similar to those of a section of short-circuited transmission line. Most cavity resonators have a large number of resonant modes, each of which corresponds with a definite resonance frequency. If excited at any one of them, a system of standing waves of relatively large amplitude will be set up inside the cavity. When viewed as a section of wave guide, the modes of a cavity resonator may be described by the notation TE_{lmn} or TM_{lmn} where the subscript l refers to the number of half wave variations of the electric field along the direction which corresponds with the x axis of the guide. The shape of cavity resonators need not however be restricted to sections of rectangular or circular wave guides.

In the vicinity of an anti-resonant frequency, a resonant cavity behaves in the same way, and may be considered as equivalent to a parallel resonant circuit of high Q-factor. Cavity resonators find application as frequency selective filters, as wavelength measuring devices (wavemeters), and as units for matching different wave guides. They are also used in ultra-high frequency valves.

THE IMPEDANCE CONCEPT

It would seem that if wave propagation in free space, or in wave guides is to be handled in terms of field theory, a whole technique of analysis, different from that hitherto used, must now be learnt. Fortunately, this is not necessary. It is possible to apply the impedance concept normally used in circuit theory to general problems of wave propagation.[6] With circuit theory, the ratio of potential difference, in volts, to the current, in amperes, gives an impedance in ohms; in field theory, a "field impedance" is defined by the ratio of electric field E to the magnetic field H. If S.I. units are employed, E is measured in volts per metre, and H in amperes/metre. The ratio E/H gives a field impedance, in ohms.

With any particular transmission line, the propagation depends on the primary constants of the line conductors. In the general case of transmission without guiding conductors, the propagation depends on the constants of the medium, i.e. on the values of the conductivity, permeability and permittivity. Any particular medium has an "intrinsic impedance". This is defined as the ratio of the electric to magnetic field for a plane wave travelling through the medium.

It is shown in Appendix H that when the conductivity is zero, i.e. when the medium is a pure dielectric, the intrinsic impedance of such media is given by

$$Z = \frac{E}{H} = \sqrt{\frac{\mu}{k}}\,\Omega$$

where $\mu = \mu_0 \mu_r$

and $k = k_0 k_r$, as previously.

For free space, the intrinsic impedance is

$$Z=\sqrt{\frac{\mu_0}{k_0}}=377\ \Omega$$

For any other pure dielectric,

$$Z=377\sqrt{\frac{\mu_r}{k_r}}\ \Omega$$

The intrinsic impedance of a medium is analogous to the characteristic impedance of a transmission line. In the case of a pure dielectric medium, there is no attenuation, and the intrinsic impedance is a real quantity, which corresponds with the characteristic impedance of a loss-free line. If the conductivity g is not zero, the intrinsic impedance becomes the complex quantity

$$Z=\sqrt{\frac{j\omega\mu}{g+j\omega k}}$$

The concept of the intrinsic impedance of a medium can be applied to the problem of reflection at a boundary surface. If the two media in contact have different intrinsic impedances, partial reflection will occur at the boundary between them ; a wave will be reflected back towards the origin in the first medium, while a wave will be transmitted in the second. The formulae which govern the reflection and transmission are exactly the same as those used in chapter 4 for reflection in transmission lines. The only difference is that intrinsic impedances have to be used in place of transmission line impedances. The same remarks apply to standing waves and the calculation of standing wave ratios.

WORKED EXAMPLES

1. Calculate the characteristic impedance, propagation coefficient and velocity of wave propagation at a frequency of 400 kHz, of a uniform transmission line which has the following constants :

$$L=0{\cdot}5\ \text{mH/mile},\ C=0{\cdot}08\ \mu\text{F/mile}$$

Resistance and leakance negligible.
Derive the necessary formulae from the differential equations for a uniform line which has negligible resistance and leakance.

L.U. Ext. Telecomm. 1951.

As the line can be assumed to be loss-free, equations 19.2b, 19.3b and 19.7 may be applied to find the characteristic impedance, propagation coefficient, and velocity of wave propagation in the line.

$L=0{\cdot}5\times10^{-3}$, $C=0{\cdot}08\times10^{-6}$, and $\omega=2\pi\times4\times10^{5}=2{\cdot}51\times10^{6}$

Equation 19.2b gives $Z_0 = \sqrt{\frac{L}{C}} = \sqrt{\frac{0{\cdot}5 \times 10^6}{0{\cdot}08 \times 10^3}} = 79\ \Omega$

β is given as $\omega\sqrt{LC}$, hence $P = j\beta = 2{\cdot}51 \times 10^6\sqrt{0{\cdot}5 \times 0{\cdot}08 \times 10^{-9}}$

$= 15{\cdot}9$ radians per mile

The velocity of propagation is given by equation 19.7 as,

$V_P = 1/\sqrt{LC}$

Inserting the values quoted above gives,

$$V_P = \frac{1}{\sqrt{0{\cdot}5 \times 0{\cdot}08 \times 10^{-9}}} = 158{,}000 \text{ miles/s}$$

2. Derive from the fundamental differential equations of the uniform line, approximate expressions for the phase and attenuation coefficients applicable where the line is of low loss. A concentric line with air dielectric has a characteristic impedance of 60 Ω. At a frequency of 150 MHz the effective loop resistance per metre of the line may be taken as 0·2 Ω. Calculate, for this frequency, the total phase change along a 100-metre length of line and the ratio of output voltage to input voltage, assuming the line to be correctly terminated.

L.U. Ext. Telecomm. 1947.

The expressions required for the phase and attenuation coefficients of a low-loss line are given by equations 19.3a and 19.3b. If it is assumed that the phase velocity in the line is equal to the free-space velocity c, which has a value of 3×10^8 metres/sec. then the wavelength λ is given by

$$\lambda = c/f = 3 \times 10^8/1{\cdot}5 \times 10^8 = 2 \text{ metres.}$$

The phase change per wavelength is 2π radians, and the total phase change over a length of 100 metres is thus,

$$2\pi \times 100/2 = 314 \text{ radians}$$

Equation 19.3a shows that the attenuation coefficient α is given by

$$\alpha = R/2Z_0$$

where R is the loop resistance of the line per unit length, and Z_0 is the characteristic impedance.
Insertion of the quoted values gives

$$\alpha = \frac{0{\cdot}2}{2 \times 60} = \frac{1}{600}$$

Hence over a metre length of the correctly terminated line,

$$\text{the output voltage} = (\text{input voltage}) \times e^{-\frac{1}{600}}$$

Over the 100 metre length of line

the output voltage = (input voltage) $\times e^{-\frac{1}{6}}$

i.e. $\dfrac{\text{output voltage}}{\text{input voltage}} = \underline{0{\cdot}846}$

3. Show that the input impedance of a transmission line is given by the expression :—

$$Z = Z_0\left(\frac{Z_r \cosh Pl + Z_0 \sinh Pl}{Z_0 \cosh Pl + Z_r \sinh Pl}\right)$$

where Z_0 = characteristic impedance, Z_r = terminating impedance P = propagation constant, and l = length of the line.

Determine the ratio of the conductor diameters for a coaxial quarter-wave transformer for matching a source having an internal impedance of $300\underline{/0°}\,\Omega$ to a load of $20\underline{/0°}\,\Omega$. Assume that the characteristic impedance of a coaxial cable to be $138 \log_{10} D/d$, where D is the internal diameter of the outer conductor, and d is the external diameter of the inner conductor.

L.U. Int. Telecomm. 1951

The general expression for the input impedance of a line has been derived in chapter 4 (equation 4.41).

Equation 19.17 states that the input impedance of a quarter-wavelength section of low-loss line of characteristic impedance Z_0 is given by

$$Z_s = Z_0^2/Z_r$$

where Z_r is the impedance connected to the output end of the quarter-wavelength section. The characteristic impedance of the matching section must therefore be given by,

$$Z_0 = \sqrt{Z_s \,.\, Z_r}$$

Inserting the values in the question gives

$$Z_0 = \sqrt{6{,}000} = 77{\cdot}5\,\Omega$$

and so $\log_{10} D/d = 77{\cdot}5/138 = 0{\cdot}56$

from which $D/d = \underline{3{\cdot}63}$

4. A dipole aerial is to be matched, at a frequency of 100 MHz, to an open-wire feeder having a characteristic impedance of 600 Ω by means of a short-circuited stub, i.e. a length of line, short-circuited, is shunted across the feeder at the appropriate distance from the aerial. Determine the point of attachment and the length of the stub, on the assumption that both feeder and stub are without losses and have

the same characteristic impedance. Assume the input impedance of the aerial to be a pure resistance of 100 Ω. The general equation for the input impedance for a line is :—

$$Z = Z_0\left(\frac{Z_0 \sinh P_x + Z_R \cosh P_x}{Z_0 \cosh P_x + Z_R \sinh P_x}\right)$$

L.U. Int. Telecomm. 1943

The stub must be attached at a distance l from the aerial, at a point where the input conductance is equal to the characteristic conductance of the line. The analysis on page 622 indicates that the distance l is given by,

$$l = \frac{\lambda}{2\pi}\tan^{-1}\sqrt{\frac{R}{R_0}}$$

In this case, $R = 100\ \Omega$, and $R_0 = 600\ \Omega$. If the line and stub are loss-free, the velocity of propagation may be taken as being equal to the velocity of radiation in free space, i.e. 3×10^8 metres per second. Hence, if the frequency of operation is 100 MHz, then the wavelength λ is given by,

$$\lambda = \frac{V_P}{f} = \frac{3 \times 10^8}{10^8} = 3 \text{ metres}$$

$$\text{hence } l = \frac{3}{2\pi}\tan^{-1}\sqrt{\frac{100}{600}} = \frac{3}{2\pi}\tan^{-1} 0{\cdot}408$$

$$= \frac{3}{2\pi} \times \frac{22{\cdot}2 \times \pi}{180} = \underline{0{\cdot}185 \text{ metre}}$$

The stub should therefore be attached at a distance of 0·185 metre from the aerial.

The input admittance of a line which is terminated by a resistance R is given by equation 19·25 as,

$$Y_{in} = \frac{1}{R_0}\left[\frac{R_0 + jR \tan \beta l}{R + jR_0 \tan \beta l}\right]$$

If $l = 0{\cdot}185$ metre then $\tan \beta l = \tan \dfrac{2\pi}{3} \times 0{\cdot}185 = 0{\cdot}408$

$$\therefore\ Y_{in} = \frac{1}{600}\left[\frac{600 + j100 \times 0{\cdot}408}{100 + j600 \times 0{\cdot}408}\right]$$

$$=\frac{1}{600}\left[\frac{6+j0{\cdot}408}{1+j2{\cdot}448}\right]=\frac{1}{600}\left[\frac{7-j14{\cdot}3}{7}\right]$$

$$=\frac{1}{600}-j\frac{14{\cdot}3}{4200}$$

This result shows that the point of attachment is correct, as the input conductance at the point calculated above is equal to the characteristic conductance of the line, i.e. 1/600 mhos. It also shows that at the point of attachment of the stub, the line susceptance is $-j14{\cdot}3/4200$.

The input susceptance of the stub must therefore be $j14{\cdot}3/4200$. Now the short-circuited stub will have a susceptance of

$$\frac{1}{jR_0 \tan \beta l_s}$$

where l_s is the length of the stub.

$$\text{Hence, } \frac{1}{jR_0 \tan \beta l_s}=\frac{14{\cdot}3j}{4200}$$

$$\therefore\quad 600 \tan \beta l_s = -4200/14{\cdot}3$$

$$\therefore\quad \tan \beta l_s = -7/14{\cdot}3$$

$$\text{and}\quad l_s=\frac{\lambda}{2\pi}\tan^{-1}\left(-\frac{7}{14{\cdot}3}\right)=\frac{3}{2\pi}\times\frac{153{\cdot}9\pi}{180}=1{\cdot}28 \text{ metres}$$

The matching stub should thus have a length of 1·28 metres. The reader should check that this length of short-circuited stub presents the necessary susceptance of $14{\cdot}3j/4200$.

References

[1] JORDAN, E. C.: *Electromagnetic Waves and Radiating Systems* (Prentice-Hall Inc., 1950).

[2] SMITH, P. H.: " Transmission Line Calculator ", Electronics, 29, p. 12, (1939) and " An Improved Transmission Line Calculator " 17, p. 130 (1944).

[3] JACKSON, W., and HUXLEY, L. G. H.: " The Solution of Transmission Line Problems by the use of the Circle Diagram of Impedance ", *Jour. I.E.E.*, 91, Part III, p. 105 (1944).

[4] GRANT, A. W., and WALLIS, P. J.: " Impedance Matching by Tapered Transmission Lines ", *Jour. I.E.E.*, 93, Part IIIA, p. 559 (1946).

[5] GOODLET, B. L.: *Basic Electrotechnics* (Edward Arnold, 1951).

[6] BOOKER, H. G.: " The Elements of Wave Propagation Using the Impedance Concept ", *Jour. I.E.E.*, 94, Part III, p. 171 (1947).

References for Further Reading

JACKSON, WILLIS: *High Frequency Transmission Lines* (Methuen & Co., Ltd., 1945).
LAMONT, R. L.: *Wave Guides* (Methuen & Co., Ltd., 1942).
BARLOW, H. M.: *Micro-Waves and Wave Guides* (Constable & Co., Ltd., 1947).
HARVEY, A. F.: *Microwave Engineering* (Academic Press, 1963).

EXAMPLES

1. Derive from the fundamental differential equations, an expression for the characteristic impedance of a radio-frequency transmission line, and an expression for the velocity of a sinusoidal wave along such a line. Why, in the determination of these quantities for the radio-frequency case, is it justifiable to neglect the effect of losses? A concentric cable has a distributed capacitance of 0·037 μF per kilometre and a distributed inductance of 0·75 mH. Determine the approximate characteristic impedance of the cable and the velocity of wave propagation.

I.E.E. Radio Comm. April, 1948

2. Show from first principles that the magnitude of the input impedance of a loss-free transmission line of length $\lambda/8$ terminated by any pure resistance is equal to its characteristic impedance.

L.U. Int. Telecomm. 1955

3. Show that in a low-loss uniform line, of length $\lambda/2$ loaded with a terminal impedance Z_R, the apparent impedance measured at the sending end is Z_R. Give a qualitative physical explanation of this.

L.U. Int. Telecomm. 1947

4. Show that the input impedance of a low-loss line of one quarter wave-length and open-circuited at the receiving end is one half of the line resistance per unit length multiplied by the length of the line. Prove this is in agreement with the conclusion that the current varies sinusoidally along the length of the line.

L.U. Int. Telecomm. 1949

5. Derive from the differential equations of the uniform line, an expression for the phase velocity of propagation of a sinusoidal wave. Assuming the velocity of propagation at radio-frequency to be the velocity of light for a cable with air dielectric, determine the

approximate percentage reduction in velocity, for a cable in which the insulating material has a dielectric constant of 2·25.

I.E.E. Radio Comm. April 1946

6. Derive from first principles, expressions for the attenuation coefficient and characteristic impedance of a uniform, low-loss transmission line when it is used at very high frequencies. Calculate the apparent attenuation, in decibels per kilometre, of a long pair of open wires, at very high radio frequencies, if the characteristic impedance of the line is 400 Ω and the d.c. resistance of the wire is 8 Ω/kilometre of single conductor. Comment on the result.

L.U. Ext. Telecomm. 1949

7. A low-loss uniform line of zero leakance has a resistance of 0·014Ω, an inductance of $7{\cdot}2 \times 10^{-9}$ h, and a capacitance of $0{\cdot}154 \times 10^{-12}$ F per loop cm. If the frequency is 200 MHz, what will be the impedance at the input end if the length is exactly one-quarter wavelength and the receiving end is short-circuited ?

L.U. Int. Telecomm. 1949

8. Assuming that the sending-end impedance of a transmission line is equal to :—

$$Z_0\left[\frac{Z_r \cosh Pl + Z_0 \sinh Pl}{Z_0 \cosh Pl + Z_r \sinh Pl}\right]$$

determine the input impedance at 500 MHz of a short-circuited quarter-wavelength low-loss line having a characteristic impedance of 80 Ω, an effective resistance of 1·6 Ω per loop metre and negligible leakance.

L.U. Ext. Telecomm. 1952

9. Explain why it is necessary to match the impedance of an aerial to that of the feeder and prove that such matching can be obtained with a quarter-wave line. If a feeder having a characteristic impedance of 400 Ω is to be connected to an aerial having an impedance of 70 Ω, calculate the spacing of a quarter-wave parallel wire feeder to be inserted between the two if the diameter of the wire is 3 mm. Assume $Z_0 = 276 \log s/r$, where r = radius of wire and s = distance between centre of wires.

L.U. Ext. Telecomm. 1944

10. Derive approximate expressions for the attenuation and phase-change coefficient of an air-dielectric transmission line, in terms of its primary constants. The characteristic impedance of such a line is 60 Ω and its effective resistance at 100 MHz is 0·2 Ω per loop

metre. Calculate the attenuation of a 100-metre length of cable and the phase-change over this length, when it is terminated by its characteristic impedance.

L.U. Ext. Telecomm. 1955

11. State the conditions under which a load will absorb the maximum power from a source of constant e.m.f. having an internal impedance $R+jX$. A 2 m. length of 70 Ω characteristic impedance cable is employed to connect a high-frequency generator operating at a frequency of 30 MHz to a load. The internal impedance of the generator may be taken as a pure resistance of 200 Ω, and the cable may be treated as loss-free. Determine the resistance and reactance of the terminating impedance which will absorb the maximum power.

I.E.E. Radio Comm. April 1946

12. Plot diagrams of the input reactance of a uniform transmission line, in which both R and G are zero, as the phase varies from 0 to 2π radians, for (a) the receiving end open-circuited, (b) the receiving end short-circuited. Explain the physical conditions prevailing and show how a telescopic line can be used as the equivalent of capacitance or inductance.

L.U. Int. Telecomm. 1951

13. Explain what is meant by (a) a travelling wave, (b) a standing wave, on a transmission line and describe the conditions under which such waves occur. Derive an expression for the input impedance of a loss-free transmission line short-circuited at the far end. Sketch the form of the relation between input impedance and the length of the line.

L.U. Int. Telecomm. 1950

14. Explain why it is important to reduce to a minimum the standing wave ratio on a high-frequency feeder. The characteristic impedance of a high-frequency cable is $60\underline{/0^\circ}\ \Omega$. If this is terminated by an impedance of $55\underline{/20^\circ}\ \Omega$, calculate the standing wave ratio on the cable.

L.U. Ext. Telecomm. 1951

15. Derive from the fundamental differential equations the voltage and current distributions along a uniform transmission line of negligible resistance and leakance. The voltage distribution of such a line terminated in a resistance of 150 Ω is explored experimentally and the voltage is found to vary between 110 and 20 volts. Determine the L/C ratio for the line.

L.U. Int. Telecomm. 1954

16. A certain radio-frequency transmission line, which may be regarded as "loss-free", has a characteristic impedance of 500 Ω and is to supply a resistance load of 300 Ω. Find the position and length of a short-circuited stub (of the same construction as the line) which would terminate the main length of line correctly at a frequency of 50 MHz. The following formula may be assumed :—

$$Z_i = Z_0 \left\{ \frac{R + jZ_0 \tan \dfrac{2\pi l}{\lambda}}{Z_0 + jR \tan \dfrac{2\pi l}{\lambda}} \right\}$$

where Z_i is the input impedance of a line of length terminated in a resistance R, and λ is the wavelength.

I.E.E. Radio Comm. October 1948

17. A loss-free feeder line of characteristic impedance $80\underline{/0°}\,\Omega$ is terminated by a load impedance of $120\underline{/0°}\,\Omega$, the one being matched to the other at 7·5 MHz by a short-circuited stub line of characteristic impedance $80\underline{/0°}\,\Omega$ and length l connected across the feeder at a distance d measured backwards from the load termination. Evaluate d if this length of loaded feeder is to present a conductance of 1/80 mho at the point of stub attachment. Evaluate also the value of l required to annul the susceptance presented by this length of loaded feeder. Derive any formulae used. It may be assumed that the input impedance of a line of length l of loss-free line terminated by Zr may be expressed in the form :—

$$Z_0 \left[\frac{Z_r \cos \beta l + jZ_0 \sin \beta l}{Z_0 \cos \beta l + jZ_r \sin \beta l} \right]$$

L.U. Ext. Telecomm. 1953

18. Give a simple physical description of electromagnetic wave propagation with a single perfectly conducting tube, using as an illustration one of the simplest modes. Sketch the circuit arrangements commonly employed for "launching" and "collecting" the radiation in such wave guides.

I.E.E. Radio Comm. October 1945

19. Define the terms *H waves* and *E waves* in relation to waves propagated in wave guides. Show graphically that by superposition of a pair of plane electromagnetic waves travelling in free space, a field pattern results of such a form that it can be fitted into a rectangular wave guide.

L.U. Int. Telecomm. 1952

20

ULTRA-HIGH-FREQUENCY DEVICES

INTRODUCTION

The term " ultra-high-frequency " is applied to frequencies which range from three hundred to three thousand megahertz, i.e. 0·3 to 3·0 GHz. This range and even higher frequencies are employed in single or multiple-link radio relay systems. In such systems the aerials employed are of high gain, the links are usually less than 60 km long, and the radio paths are unobstructed. As a consequence, transmitter powers of a few watts or less are sufficient to provide the required signal/noise ratio. The transmitter usually consists of a low-power oscillator followed by an amplifier, as a low-power oscillator is more readily stabilised in frequency and modulated than a high-power oscillator. Low-power oscillators are also needed for frequency changing in superheterodyne receivers. Although the power output required from transmitting amplifiers is only of the order of a few watts, it is desirable that the efficiency should be reasonably high, e.g. 10% or more, to reduce the power required from the high-tension supply—an important factor in systems with unattended stations.

As explained in chapter 10, with conventional valves of the space-charge control type, the power output, efficiency and gain decrease as the frequency is increased owing to limitations imposed by (a) the transit time of the electrons, and (b) the effects of the inductance of leads to the electrodes. These limitations can be minimised by using grounded grid, and other triodes with very small clearances between the electrodes; but for practical purposes the useful upper limit of frequency is roughly about 4,000 MHz for amplifiers capable of about a watt output with an efficiency approaching 10%. Although improvements in these figures can be expected, it is apparent that for frequencies much above 4,000 MHz valves of a fundamentally different type are needed to obtain adequate gain, power output and efficiency.

Fortunately, for frequencies above about 2,000 MHz, it is possible to use valves of the " velocity modulation " type, in which use is made of the fact that the electrons take an appreciable time to travel from the cathode to the collector electrode. Such valves may be used as amplifiers, oscillators and frequency multipliers, typical examples being klystrons and travelling-wave valves. In addition to the velocity modulation valves, magnetrons are available as efficient oscillators for continuous wave or pulse-modulation systems.

PRINCIPLE OF VELOCITY MODULATION

All the valves so far dealt with, have operated on the basis of space-charge control. The application of an alternating voltage to an electrode (usually the control grid) caused a corresponding variation in anode current, provided always that the effect of finite transit time could be neglected ; the valve operated on the principle of space-charge variation, or space-charge modulation as it is occasionally termed.

In the case of velocity modulation, the cathode current does not vary, but a density-modulated electron beam is obtained by variation of the velocity of the electrons. This is achieved by passing an electron beam of given velocity through a space where a periodic change of velocity is applied to it by means of a varying longitudinal electric field. As a result, successive electrons in the beam have increments of velocity superimposed on their steady velocity. The magnitude and sense of the incremental velocity is determined by the phase at which the electrons enter the region of the varying longitudinal electric field. The basic principle is illustrated schematically in Fig. 20.1. Suppose electrons leave the cathode with zero velocity, and the two grids G_1 and G_2 have a sinusoidal voltage, $V \sin \omega t$ applied between them as shown. If the alternating voltage can be assumed to be constant during the passage of any one electron between the grids, then the velocity v of the electron on leaving the space between G_1 and G_2 is given by

$$\tfrac{1}{2}\, mv^2 = e(V_0 + V \sin \omega t)$$

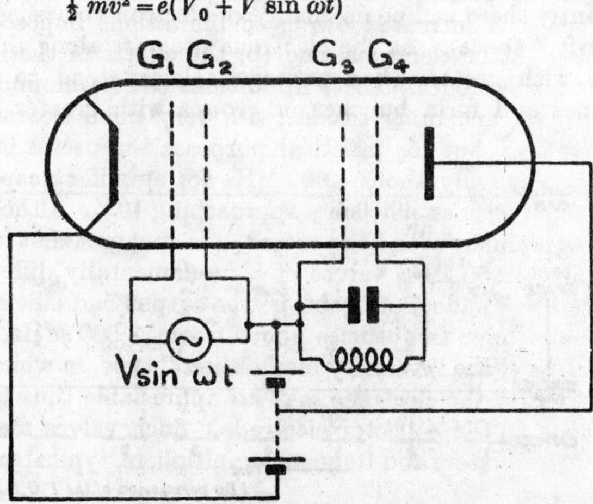

Fig. 20.1.

where e and m denote the charge and mass of an electron, and V_0 is the steady voltage applied between the cathode and G_1.

$$\therefore\ v = \sqrt{\frac{2e}{m}V_0\left(1+\frac{V}{V_0}\sin\omega t\right)}$$

If the steady velocity due to the application of V_0 alone is v_0 then

$$v = v_0\sqrt{1+\frac{V}{V_0}\sin\omega t}$$

Also if $V/V_0 \ll 1$ then this result may be expanded by the binomial theorem, so that

$$v \simeq v_0\left(1+\frac{V}{2V_0}\sin\omega t\right) \quad . \quad . \quad . \quad . \quad 20.1$$

The approximate maximum and minimum electron velocities are then

$$V_{max} \simeq v_0\left(1+\frac{V}{2V_0}\right)$$

$$V_{min} \simeq v_0\left(1-\frac{V}{2V_0}\right)$$

The number of electrons emerging per second from the grid system (G_1G_2) however is equal to the number entering per second, and depends upon the value of the steady voltage V_0.

If the grids G_3 and G_4 in Fig. 20.1, are also maintained at the same steady voltage V_0 with respect to the cathode, the relatively large space between the grids G_2 and G_3 will have no potential gradient, and consequently there will be no change of electron velocities in this space (the " drift " space). As the electrons progress along this region, the electrons with greater than average velocity tend to overtake the slower ones and form bunches or groups with greater than average

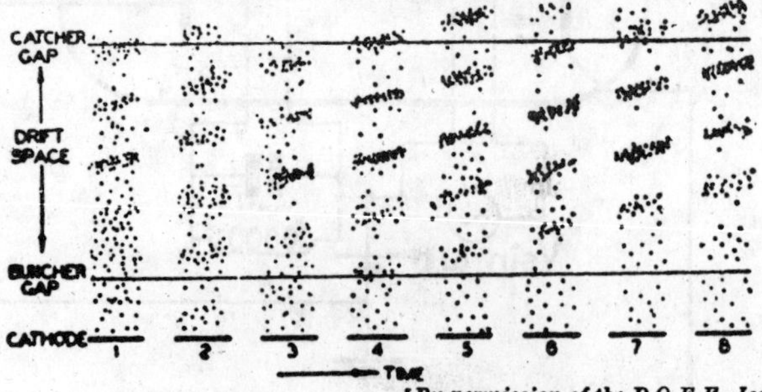

[*By permission of the P.O.E.E. Journal*

Fig. 20.2. Electron bunching.

density, separated of course by comparatively empty spaces. This action is illustrated in Fig. 20.2 for eight equally spaced instants of time corresponding to a total of two and a half u.h.f. cycles.

The time of electron transit between the grids G_1 and G_2 was assumed to be negligibly short in the derivation of equation 20.1. In practice it is a small fraction of the operating cycle. The transit time losses are less than those in conventional negative grid valves, however, because of the higher velocity of the electron beam in the velocity modulation valve. The time of transit through the drift space is comparatively large, and may amount to several u.h.f. cycles in order to obtain effective bunching of the electrons.

The electron beam emitted by the cathode is thus modulated in intensity at a frequency equal to that of the u.h.f. alternating voltage applied between the grids G_1 and G_2. The electron bunches (which correspond to a pulsating current) give rise to an alternating field between G_3 and G_4 which are connected to the output circuit, usually some form of resonant cavity.

THE KLYSTRON

Double Resonator Klystron Amplifier

This form of valve is shown in simplified form in Fig. 20.3 ; it consists essentially of two cavity resonators, *a* and *b*, termed the " buncher " and " catcher " respectively, which are transversed by an electron beam. Each of the resonators shown consists of a toroidal metal enclosure with two plane surfaces separated by a narrow gap (*c*, *d*) at the centre, each surface having a hole in the centre to permit

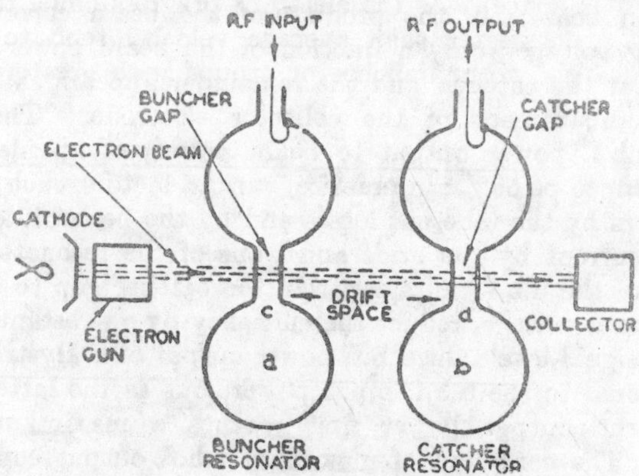

[*By permission of the P.O.E.E. Journal*

Fig. 20.3. Simplified sketch of double-resonator klystron amplifier.

the passage of the electron beam. In practice, however, the resonators may be other than toroidal, and in some valves the holes through which the electron beam passes may be spanned by a rudimentary grid instead of being completely open. When the buncher is excited by ultra high frequency power fed in by means of a suitable coupling loop or probe, a relatively strong alternating electric field is set up across the narrow gap, provided that the applied frequency is close to the resonance frequency of the buncher. Under these conditions, the velocity of the electrons is varied by the electric field as they pass across the gap. Bunching then occurs in the drift space. The average time spent in this space depends on the average velocity of the electrons, and therefore on the direct accelerating potential between the cathode and the cylinder which forms the electron gun. The latter and the resonators are normally earthed and the cathode is usually held below earth potential by some 1,000 to 3,000 V.

The phase relationship between the electron bunches and the field across the catcher gap is dependent on the impedance of the resonator, just as the phase relationship between current and voltage in an ordinary a.c. circuit is dependent on its impedance. When maximum power is abstracted from the resonator, the direction of the field across the gaps is such as to cause the electrons to give up the maximum amount of energy, i.e. the direction of the field must be such as to cause maximum retardation of the electrons. Under suitable operating conditions more ultra high frequency power can be taken from the catcher resonator than is applied to the buncher, i.e. the valve functions as an amplifier. The difference between the u.h.f. output power and the u.h.f. input power comes from the power in the electron beam, i.e. the product of the beam current and the accelerating voltage ; only a fraction of the beam power is however abstracted at the catcher, and the remainder appears as heat due to electron bombardment of the collector electrode. The efficiency (ratio of u.h.f. power output to beam power) of an ideal klystron can be shown to be 58% ; in practice, various factors, such as damping of resonators by the inherent losses and by the beam, interception of the beam current by the grids and walls of the resonators, and the limitation of the u.h.f. voltage across the catcher gap to a value less than the beam voltage, reduce the efficiency by a substantial amount.

For low signal levels the u.h.f. power output of a klystron amplifier is proportional to the u.h.f. input power, but as the latter is further increased the output power first reaches a maximum and then decreases. The condition of maximum u.h.f. output corresponds to optimum bunching of the electron beam ; with smaller u.h.f. inputs the bunching is non-optimum and approaches a sinusoidal variation of the beam current with time ; larger inputs cause the beam to become "overbunched". Overbunching means that instead of the optimum condition in which one narrow bunch of electrons is produced for each ultra high frequency cycle, the bunch spreads and may become in effect two smaller bunches displaced in phase and time from the optimum, so reducing the u.h.f. power obtainable from the electron beam.

Noise in Klystron Amplifiers. The performance of a klystron amplifier with regard to noise is conveniently expressed in terms of the noise factor, i.e. the ratio of the highest signal/noise ratio theoretically available at the source to that obtained in practice at the output of the amplifier. The noise arises chiefly as a result of the inherent fluctuations of current density in the electron stream; he fluctuations of beam current induce voltages in the buncher esonator, which, in turn, give rise to random velocity modulation nd bunching of the electrons and hence amplified shot noise in the tcher resonator; the fluctuations of beam current also excite the catcher directly.

Double-Resonator Klystron Oscillator

If the buncher and catcher resonators of a double-resonator klystron amplifier are coupled by a feed-back path as shown in Fig. 20.4, oscillation will occur if the phase shift round the complete loop is an integral multiple of 2π radians and the small-signal gain through the valve exceeds the loss in the feed-back path. The resonators

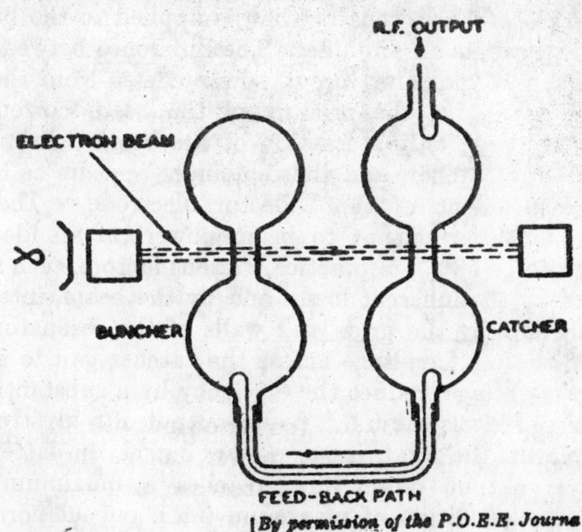

[By permission of the P.O.E.E. Journa

Fig. 20.4. Simplified sketch of double-resonator klystron oscillator.

and the feed-back loop behave as a pair of coupled tuned circuits and the frequency of oscillation adjusts itself until the required phase conditions are satisfied. If the beam voltage is varied the transit time of the electrons and therefore the phase shift in the drift space also vary, and the frequency changes to a new value such that the total phase shift is once again an integral multiple of 2π. If the resonators are under-coupled the frequency of oscillation varies as an approximately linear function of the beam voltage over a limited range; this characteristic may be used for automatic frequency control or for frequency modulation but with the disadvantage, as compared with the reflex klystron referred to below, that appreciable modulating power is required, and the linear range of frequency control is usually limited to a few megahertz. Also there is the additional disadvantage that both resonators must be adjusted if the mean frequency is to be shifted manually, as compared with the one adjustment needed in a reflex klystron.

Reflex (Single-Resonator) Klystron Oscillator

For many purposes the single-resonator reflex (or reflection) klystron oscillator is preferred to the double-resonator klystron

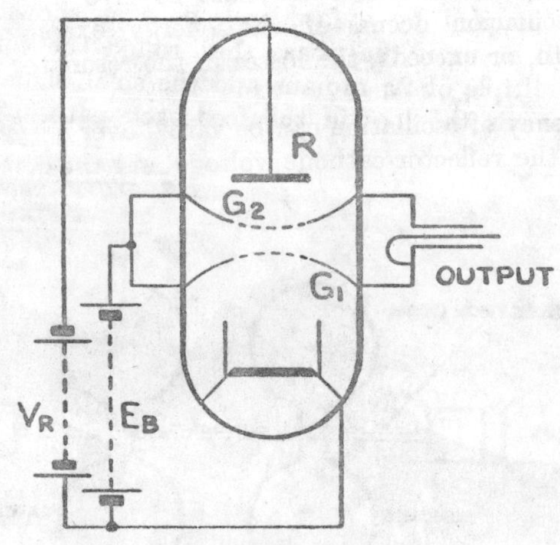

Fig. 20.5.

because of the ease of tuning and simplicity of construction. In a reflex klystron oscillator the electron beam transverses the resonator gap (G_1G_2 in Fig. 20.5) twice, first in a forward direction from the cathode, after which it is returned from a reflector electrode R (held at a negative potential with respect to the cathode), and crosses the gap again in the reverse direction. The beam becomes velocity

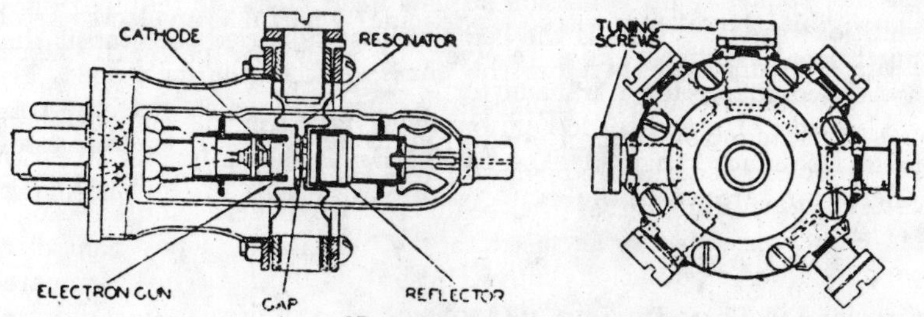

[*By permission of the E.M.I. Ltd. and the P.O.E.E. Journal*

Fig. 20.6. Section of a single-resonator reflex klystron oscillator.

modulated in the first transit and subsequently bunches in the retarding field region around the reflector electrode. The drift time is determined by the resonator voltage E_B and by the reflector voltage relative to the cathode V_R, as the former determines the electron velocities and the latter the distance they travel in the drift space. By suitable adjustment of these voltages the drift time can be made such that each bunch arrives in the correct phase to give up energy to the resonator. Oscillation occurs if the energy extracted from the beam is equal to, or exceeds, the losses in the resonator and the load circuit.

As the frequency of oscillation can be varied over a limited range by adjustment of the reflector-cathode voltage and the reflector current

[*By permission of the E.M.I. Ltd. and the P.O.E.E. Journal*

Fig. 20.7. Reflex klystron oscillator.

is negligible, the reflex klystron is particularly useful as an electronically tuned local oscillator in a receiver, or as a low power frequency modulated source for a transmitter.

A section of a typical low-power reflex klystron, developed for use in the frequency range 3,900 to 4,200 MHz, is shown in Fig. 20.6. The general appearance of the same valve can be seen in the photograph Fig. 20.7.

THE TRAVELLING-WAVE VALVE

The feature of major interest in this device, which was developed by Kompfner[1] during the period 1942–1944, is the remarkably wide bandwidth over which amplification is possible ; bandwidths of some 600 MHz have been obtained in valves designed for use at frequencies of the order of 4,000 MHz.

The construction of the travelling-wave valve is shown in Fig. 20.8. An evacuated glass envelope of circular section has a cathode and electrostatic electron gun assembly mounted at one end, and a helix of copper wire is fixed axially along the length of the tube. A collector electrode, or anode, at the end of the tube remote from the cathode, collects the electrons in the beam. A longitudinal magnetic field is produced by a solenoid carrying direct current. This solenoid is mounted outside the glass envelope and the field produced by it causes the electrons emitted by the cathode to travel in a direction parallel to the axis of the helix ; electrons that move parallel to the magnetic field are unaffected, while those which have a component of motion across the field experience a force which tends to cause them to move in the direction of the magnetic field.

The action of the valve may be explained briefly as follows. The u.h.f. signal to be amplified is impressed upon the helix at the input end and this sets up a current which travels with a velocity approaching the speed of light. The electromagnetic field so created has, as one of its components, a longitudinal wave which travels along the tube with a

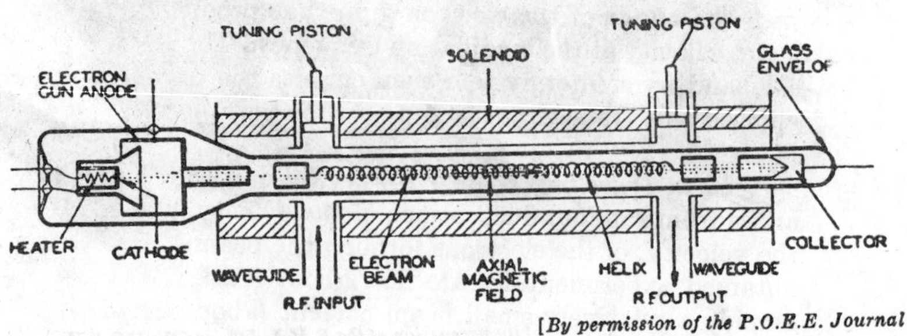

[By permission of the P.O.E.E. Journal

Fig. 20.8. Section of helix type travelling-wave amplifier.

velocity which is determined by the pitch of the helix; if the length of the wire in the helix is n times the axial length of the helix itself, the travelling wave has a velocity which is approximately $1/n$ times the velocity of light. The value of n is usually about 10. The velocity of the electron beam is arranged to be very slightly greater than that of the longitudinal component of the electromagnetic field produced by the u.h.f. signal. Under these conditions a continuous interaction takes place along the length of the helix between the electron beam and the electromagnetic wave. Near the input end of the helix, the intensity of the field produced by the signal is unchanged but as the field passes along the helix it produces signal fluctuations in the electron beam. The beam is travelling slightly faster than the field and, as a consequence, the signal fluctuations build up in amplitude, until after a certain distance they begin to pass energy to the electromagnetic wave. This transfer of energy increases uniformly down the remaining length of the helix and thereby provides an amplified signal at the output end.

The large bandwidth is obtained because the helix acts as a wideband transmission line, and not as a resonant cavity. The coupling elements which join the wave guides to the valve, are usually the factors which limit the operating bandwidth.

The amplification produced by the travelling-wave valve may be about 40 dB in the region of 4,000 MHz. The gain is sometimes limited by the onset of oscillations due to waves reflected back from the output circuit; this difficulty can be minimised by the use of distributed attenuation produced by a film of graphite near the middle of the helix. Such attenuation does not prevent the valve from developing a gain, its main effect is to divide the helix into "buncher" and "catcher" sections as in a klystron, the wave energy being carried in the forward direction by the electron beam and prevented from travelling backwards along the helix by the attenuation due to the film.

In addition to its use as an amplifier, the travelling-wave valve may be used as a phase modulator, or frequency changer.[2] The phase modulation is achieved by injecting the modulating signal in series with the anode of the electron gun, thus producing a variation in the beam velocity at the modulation frequency. The selection of the desired sideband by a filter system then enables the travelling-wave valve to be used as a frequency changing device.

Noise in Travelling-Wave Valves. Noise in travelling-wave amplifiers arises from random fluctuations of the density, and to a less extent of the velocity, of the electrons forming the beam. The best noise factors obtained experimentally are now about 3 dB; these low noise valves employ a relatively small beam current (about 0·2 mA) and require a narrow electron beam of about 1 mm diameter traversing a long narrow helix.

It is essential that the electrons shall travel parallel to the axis of the beam without spiralling and that interception of the beam by the helix shall be very small in order to minimise partition noise.

THE MAGNETRON

The name " magnetron " is applied to valves in which the electrons are controlled by a magnetic and an electric field, and it is thus worth while recalling a few simple facts about the effects of these fields on the motion electrons.

If an electron is given a constant velocity v and then moves in a plane perpendicular to a uniform magnetic field of flux density B, it experiences a force f. This force is related numerically to v and B by the expression

$$f = Bev$$

and always acts at right angles to the electron path so that the electron then moves in a circular track. If this has a radius r there will be a constant acceleration of value v^2/r directed towards the centre.

$$\therefore\ f = Bev = mv^2/r$$

$$\text{and hence } r = \frac{mv}{eB} \text{ metres} \qquad \ldots \quad 20.2$$

if v is expressed in metres/s,

B ,, ,, ,, webers/sq. metre,

and e/m, the ratio of the charge to the mass of an electron, is expressed in coulombs per kilogram.

The angular velocity ω of the electron is given by

$$\omega = \frac{v}{r} = \frac{eB}{m}$$

and the period of rotation is T, where

$$T = \frac{2\pi}{\omega} = \frac{2\pi m}{eB} \qquad \ldots \quad 20.3$$

As far as electric fields are concerned, it is sufficient as a first approach to consider the simple case of the field between a large parallel plane electrode system. If electrons are emitted with zero velocity from one surface, the application of a voltage V between the electrodes causes electrons to travel with a constant velocity v,

$$\text{where } v = \sqrt{\frac{2eV}{m}} \quad \text{(equation 6.21)}$$

In the magnetron the electric and magnetic fields are perpendicular to each other, and the motion of the electrons depends upon the values of both fields. The simplest form of magnetron consists of a cylindrical diode (Fig. 20.9). The anode and cathode are assumed to be concentric cylinders, and a coil is wound round the glass envelope ; the passage of current through this coil produces a magnetic field perpendicular to the plane of the paper.

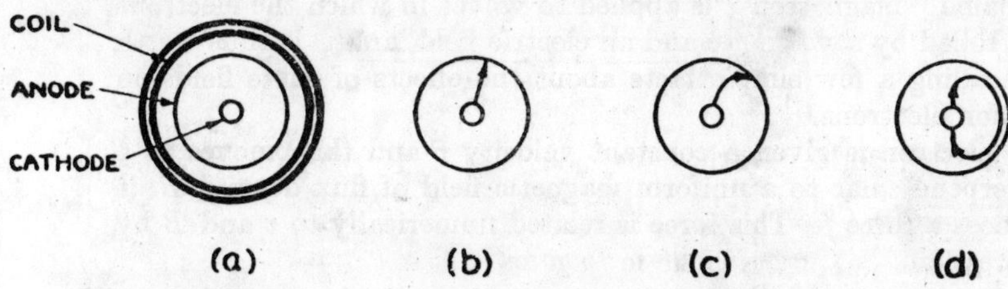

Fig. 20.9 (a) Horizontal section through a cylindrical diode
(b) Form of electron path when $B=0$
(c) „ „ „ „ „ $B<B_c$
(d) „ „ „ „ „ $B=B_c$

If the anode is given a potential which is positive with respect to the cathode, and there is no magnetic field, the path of the emitted electrons will be radial (Fig. 20.9b) ; if a small transverse magnetic field is applied, the electron path will be curved as shown in Fig. 20.9c. An increase in the value of the magnetic field will cause a decrease in the radius of curvature of the electron path, and the condition shown in Fig. 20.9d will ultimately be reached. In this case, the electrons just graze the anode surface and return to the cathode. The anode current is thus cut off with this critical value (B_c) of magnetic field. (Under this static condition, any space charge present will circulate round the cathode with an angular velocity which depends on the anode voltage and the strength of the magnetic field.) Such consideration would predict that the anode current would fall abruptly to zero at the critical value of the magnetic field ; in practice the characteristic of Fig. 20.10 is observed. An approximate expression for the critical value of flux density B_c may be obtained if it is assumed that the electron field between the anode and cathode gives the electrons a uniform velocity v. With this simplifying assumption, the electron paths, under cut off conditions, become circles with a diameter equal to the radius of the anode r_a.

Then from equation 20.2

$$r=\frac{mv}{eB_c}\simeq\frac{r_a}{2}$$

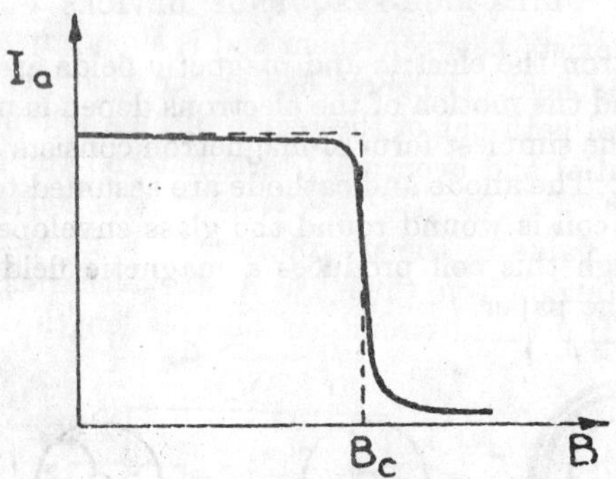

Fig. 20.10. Variation of I_a with B in a simple magnetron.

Substitution of the value for v gives

$$\frac{m}{eB_c}\sqrt{\frac{2eV}{m}} \simeq \frac{r_a}{2}$$

$$\therefore \; B_c \simeq \frac{2}{r_a}\sqrt{\frac{2mV}{e}} \quad . \quad . \quad . \quad . \quad . \quad 20.4$$

This result is an approximation as the electric field is not uniform between the cathode and anode ; the potential gradient is steepest at the cathode surface, and decreases inversely with the distance from the cathode. The exact form of this relation was shown by Hull[3] to be

$$B_c = \frac{\sqrt{8V}}{r_a\sqrt{\frac{e}{m}}} \cdot \frac{1}{\left(1-\frac{r_c^2}{r_a^2}\right)} \quad . \quad . \quad . \quad 20.5$$

where r_c is the radius of the cathode.

The magnetron functions as a generator, and cannot be used as an amplifier. In practice the cavity magnetron is the only type which is now used. The first form, the dynatron oscillator, is included here as an introduction.

The Magnetron as a Dynatron Oscillator

This type employs an anode which is split longitudinally into two parts. When the two anodes have equal positive potentials, the currents which flow to them are equal. If one anode has a higher potential than the other, and the value of the magnetic field is about twice the cut off value, it is found that the anode at the higher potential takes a smaller current. This apparent anomaly is due to the fact that when the two anodes are at different potentials, an electric field exists between them and is superimposed on the existing radial electric field. Kilgore[4] has shown that the emitted electrons follow a spiral path out of the region of high potential into the region of low potential and eventually terminate on the anode at the lower potential.

When the value of the magnetic field is greater than critical, the split anode magnetron thus has a static characteristic of negative resistance. If a tuned circuit, or suitable length of transmission line,

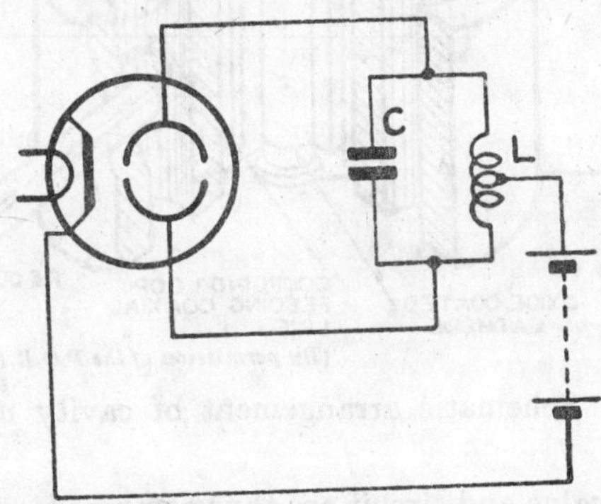

Fig. 20.11. Split anode magnetron oscillator.

is connected between the anodes, as shown in Fig. 20.11, the arrangement functions as push pull dynatron oscillator. The frequency of oscillation in this, as in other dynatron oscillators, is determined by the natural frequency of the $L\,C$ circuit. The operation is unaffected by electron transit time as long as this is small compared with the period of oscillation. At very high frequencies, when this is no longer true, the behaviour of the valve is only partly governed by its static characteristics, and the dynatron action begins to fail. As a consequence of this the upper limit of operation is of the order of a few hundred megahertz.

The Cavity Magnetron

This form of magnetron oscillator. devised by Randall and Boot[5], has a high efficiency compared with other sources of centimetre wave power and can deliver a very large peak-power output (of the order of a megawatt on short pulses). This feature, although of great importance in radar, is of less interest for communication systems as the transmitted power required in such systems is relatively small.

The main feature of this magnetron oscillator is the use of an anode block, consisting of a ring of resonant cavities or slots as shown in

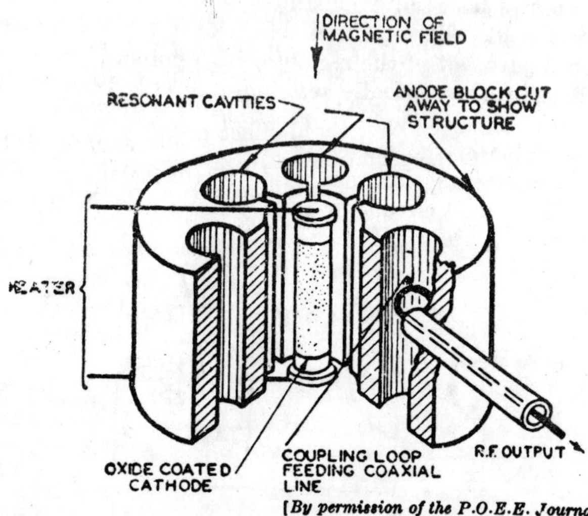

[*By permission of the P.O.E.E. Journal*

Fig. 20.12. Schematic arrangement of cavity magnetron.

Fig. 20.12. The valve and circuit are thus combined. An oxide coated cathode is arranged axially in the centre of the anode block, the whole being enclosed in a sealed off metal or glass envelope forming a vacuum enclosure. An axial magnetic field is provided from an external permanent magnet, or an electro magnet.

The resonant cavities in the anode block are so shaped that when excited, the electric field is mainly concentrated across the gaps, and fringes into the anode-cathode space as shown in Fig. 20.14. The system of cavities can oscillate in a number of modes with different

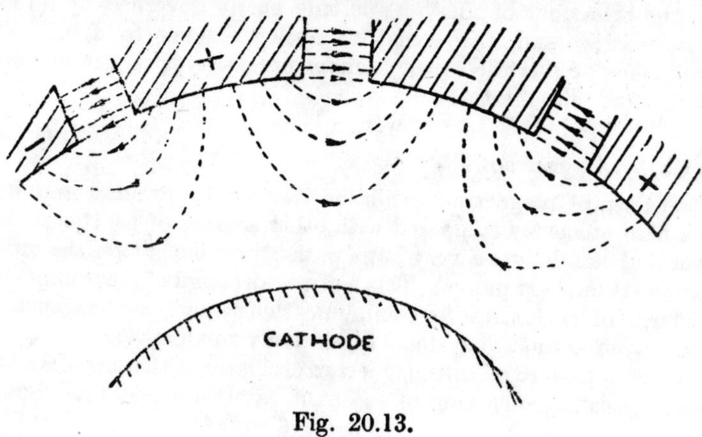

Fig. 20.13.

phase angles between the oscillations in adjacent cavities, provided that the total phase shift round the complete system is 2π (or an integral multiple of 2π) radians. In the normal mode of operation the electric fields across the gaps of the cavities differ by π radians at adjacent gaps as shown in Fig. 20.13. This is known as the π mode. The system of oscillating cavities in effect produces a rotating electric field. Other modes of oscillation can exist and, as they may cause frequency instability, arrangements are often made to inhibit such unwanted modes by strapping together the segments which should oscillate in phase ; alternatively, the dimensions of alternate cavities or slots may be so proportioned that the frequencies of unwanted modes are well removed from that of the wanted modes—this is known as the " Rising Sun " technique from the appearance of the modified anode block.

The simultaneous action of the constant axial magnetic field and the electric field set up by the cavities causes the electrons to follow complex paths as indicated for example in Fig. 20.14. Some electrons

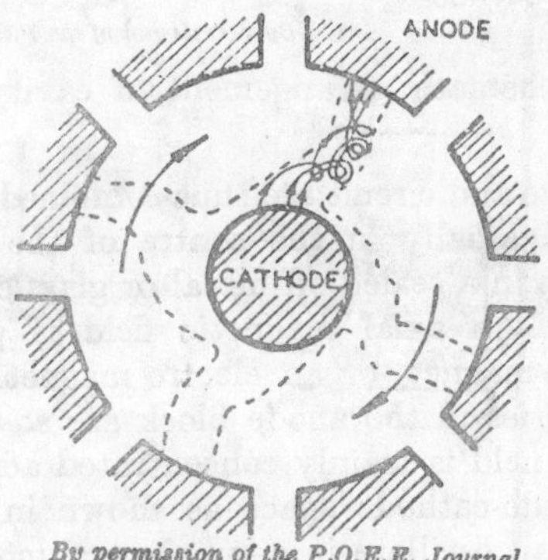

By permission of the P.O.E.E. Journal

Fig. 20.14.

are returned to the cathode and give up their energy as heat, but the majority of the electrons travel towards the anode and transfer their energy to the oscillating system of cavities. The electrons moving across to the anode tend, by the combined action of the direct magnetic field and the u.h.f. electric field of the oscillating system of cavities, to be concentrated in radial spokes of space charge within the limits shown by the dotted lines in Fig. 20.14. These radial spokes of space charge rotate in synchronism with the u.h.f. field, and maintain the state of oscillation by giving up energy to the field.

Power can be abstracted from the magnetron by means of a small loop coupling with the u.h.f. magnetic field within one of the cavities, or by a probe coupling with the u.h.f. electric field.

DISC SEAL TRIODE VALVES

Velocity modulation valves make use of electron transit time. Conventional negative grid valves do not, and are adversely affected by it, so that the problem involved in the design of triode valves for u.h.f. operation is to construct them in such a way that the electron transit time becomes a small fraction of the operating period. Improved performance has been obtained by the adoption of a type of valve construction in which the valve electrodes and their leads are brought out and continued through the glass envelope to the external circuits which consist of lengths of transmission line. The name "disc seal" is given to this type of construction. Such valves are particularly suitable for use with sections of coaxial lines and the electrodes are usually brought out to a ring or disc which fits the line.

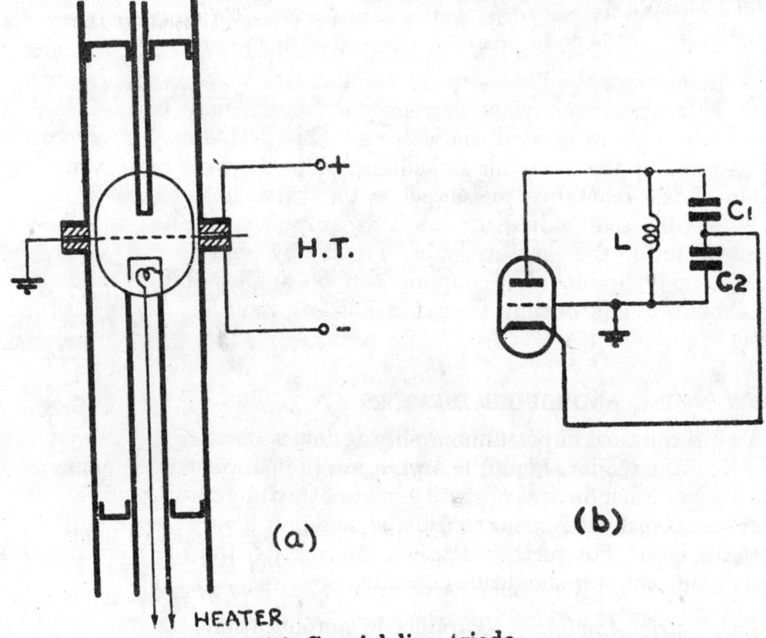

Fig. 20.15 (a) Coaxial line triode
(b) Equivalent "lumped" circuit.

Disc seal triodes operate as oscillators or as amplifiers in the u.h.f. range and may be arranged in a variety of ways. Fig. 20.15a shows a coaxial line triode arranged in a common-grid earthed grid circuit. The grid is in the form of a plane electrode while the cathode is constructed in the form of a cylinder with the heater inside. The anode is continued through the glass envelope to form the central conductor of the grid-anode line. The cathode is continued as the inner conductor of the grid-cathode line. The effective lengths of the two lines are controlled by short-circuiting flanges. The impedance between the anode and grid consists of the anode-grid capacitance C_{ag} in parallel with the input reactance of the grid-anode line. Suitable adjustment of this line length can produce an inductive reactance between the anode and grid. The reactance between the grid and cathode is made up of the grid-cathode capacitance in parallel with the input reactance of the cathode line. This can be adjusted to produce a capacitive reactance between the grid and cathode. The lumped equivalent circuit is then as shown in Fig. 20.15b, in which the inductive reactance represented by the inductance L is produced by the anode line, while C_2 represents the total capacitance between grid and cathode. C_1 is the capacitance between the anode and the cathode. The resulting circuit is then that of a Colpitts oscillator in which the grid is earthed.

In some cases the length of line required to produce the necessary value of reactance may be extremely short and may be such that it should not extend beyond the valve envelope. This may be overcome by extending the line for an additional half wavelength when the value of the reactance presented to the valve is unchanged.

When disc seal valves are used as amplifiers the input signal is injected into the grid-cathode circuit by means of a probe; alternatively, inductance coupling can be employed by means of a small loop. The output from the anode circuit is obtained in the same way.

LOW NOISE AMPLIFIER DEVICES

Two of the most important amplifying devices for microwave systems, of which the reader should be aware, are the parametric amplifier and the maser. Such devices operate in distinctly different fashion from the various valve devices so far considered, and only a very brief comment is possible here. For further detailed information the references at the end of this chapter should be consulted.

Parametric Amplifiers. Parametric amplification derives its name from the fact that the differential equation governing the circuit behaviour contains a reactive parameter which is non-linear or time varying. This parameter is provided by the reverse-bias capacitance of a semiconductor diode, often referred to as a varactor diode.

A parametric amplifier can be thought of as a variable *reactance* modulator, involving at least three frequencies. The input signal provides the input frequency, f_1, to be amplified; a source of high-frequency a.c. power, f_p, known as the *pump* (corresponding to the carrier in modulation terminology) provides the amplification energy;

the amplified power output is at a third frequency, f_2, referred to as the *idler* frequency. This is determined by the pump and input frequencies and the three are related by

$$f_p = f_1 + f_2$$

To achieve fairly large voltages across the varactor diode with small pump power involves a resonant circuit for the pump frequency in addition to the resonant circuits needed for the signal and idler frequencies. Such a system is provided by a resonant cavity arranged so that three of its resonant modes are at the required frequencies. Special arrangements then have to be used to isolate the incoming signal power from the outgoing amplified power. Manley and Rowe[6] have produced relations for the power distribution between the circuits.

The low noise properties of a parametric amplifier arise from the fact that pure reactance does not contribute thermal noise to a circuit. Some residual noise arises from the small loss associated with the variable capacitance. For some applications, such as satellite communication, the noise can be decreased further by cooling the parametric amplifier to a very low temperature.

Masers. The name maser arises from the combination of the initial letters of the phrase " Microwave Amplification by Stimulated Emission of Radiation ".

It was mentioned in chapter 7 that every atomic system has associated with it certain characteristic energy levels. The most likely state of the system is that in which the energy is lowest, namely the ground state. When excited to a higher energy level by the absorption of incident radiation it will subsequently return or relax to its ground state. Suitable material must have levels which are appropriately spaced so that the frequencies involved in excitation or relaxation are in the microwave region. Thus for, say, two levels E_1 and E_2 they must be such that

$$E_2 - E_1 = f_{21}$$

where the frequency f_{21} is in the desired microwave band. For maser action to take place more electrons must be maintained in the higher energy states than would normally exist there. This is achieved by supplying microwave power to " pump " electrons from the lower to the higher states. The signal to be amplified then stimulates the electrons to revert to their original states and produces stimulated emission which is a maximum when the applied electro-magnetic field is a maximum, so that coherent microwave energy is added to the signal.

Crystalline ruby, doped with about 0·05% of chromium, has been the most widely used material. When employed as a low-noise first stage amplifier in a satellite receiver operating at a signal frequency of about 4 GHz, the frequency of the pump source is about 30 GHz.

References

[1] KOMPFNER, R.: " The Travelling-Wave Tube as an Amplifier at Microwaves ", *Proc. I.R.E.*, 35, p. 124 (1947).

[2] BRAY, W. J.: " The Travelling-Wave Valve as a Micro-wave Phase Modulator and Frequency-Shifter ", *Proc. I.E.E.*, 99, Part III, p. 15 (1952).

[3] HULL, A. W.: " The Effect of a Uniform Magnetic Field on the Motion of Electrons between Coaxial Cylinders ", *Phys. Rev.*, 18, p. 31 (1921).

[4] KILGORE, G. R.: " Magnetron Oscillators for the Generation of Frequencies between 300 and 600 Mc/s ", *Proc. I.R.E.*, 24, p. 1140, (1936).

[5] RANDALL, J. T. and BOOT, H. A. H.: " The Cavity Magnetron ", *Jour. I.E.E.*, 93, Part IIIA, p. 928 (1946).

[6] MANLEY, J. M. and ROWE, H. E.: " Some General Properties of Non-Linear Elements ", *Proc. I.R.E.*, 44, p. 904 (1956).

References for Further Reading

BECK, A. H. W.: *Velocity Modulated Thermionic Tubes* (Cambridge University Press, 1948).

LATHAM, R., KING, A. H. and RUSHFORTH, L.: *The Magnetron* (Chapman & Hall, Ltd., 1952).

PIERCE, J. R.: *Travelling-Wave Tubes* (D. Van Nostrand Company Inc., 1950).

SIMS, G. D. and STEPHENSON, I. M.: *Microwave Tubes and Semiconductor Devices* (Blackie & Son Ltd., 1963).

LOUISELL, W. H.: *Coupled Mode and Parametric Electronics* (John Wiley & Sons Inc., 1960).

BLACKWELL, L. A. and KOTZEBUE, K. L.: *Semiconductor Diode Parametric Amplifiers* (Prentice-Hall International Inc., 1961).

SINGER, J. R.: *Masers* (John Wiley & Sons Inc., 1959).

SIEGMAN, A. E.: *Microwave Solid State Masers* (McGraw Hill, 1960).

EXAMPLES

1. Discuss the factors which limit the frequency of conventional feedback oscillators and explain the action of a transit-time oscillator.
L.U. Int. Telecomm. 1951.

2. Discuss the difficulties which arise when trying to use conventional valves and resonant circuits as amplifiers and oscillators at frequencies such as 300 MHz. Mention methods of construction which have partly overcome the difficulties. *I.E.E. Radio Comm.* 1948.

3. Explain why, at very high frequencies, it becomes necessary to employ resonant cavities as oscillatory circuits and to incorporate these cavities in the structure of oscillator or amplifier valves.

I.E.E. Radio Comm. October 1946.

4. Write an account of the principle of operation of an oscillator valve employing velocity modulation of the electron beam.

L.U. Ext. Telecomm. 1950.

5. Describe the construction and operation of either (a) a travelling-wave amplifying valve or (b) a klystron oscillator.

L.U. Ext. Telecomm. 1953.

6. A cylindrical cathode having a finite radius is surrounded by a concentric anode, the assembly being immersed in a uniform magnetic field parallel to the axis of the cathode. Determine the equation of motion of an electron leaving the cathode with zero velocity. Describe how a similar arrangement may be used to generate high-frequency oscillations. *L.U. Int. Telecomm.* 1951.

7. Explain the mechanism of the dynatron, resonance, and travelling-wave oscillation modes of a magnetron. *L.U. Int. Telecomm.* 1955.

8. Derive the relations between the signs of the reactances of the electrodes of a triode necessary for the gyration of oscillations. Describe, with reference to these conditions, the construction of an oscillator operating at about 1,000 MHz.

I.E.E. Radio Comm. April, 1950.

9. Describe the construction of a disc-seal triode and explain its advantages as a high-frequency amplifying valve. A grounded-grid amplifier has a resonant anode circuit with a Q of 100 and a coil resistance of 2 Ω. The valve constants are $\mu = 55$ and $g_m = 11$mA/V. The input voltage is connected between the cathode and earth and has a source resistance of 3000 Ω. Determine from first principles the stage amplification and the input impedance.

L.U. Int. Telecomm. 1954.

10. Explain the principle and describe the constructional form of a travelling-wave tube for amplification at microwave frequencies.

The helix of a travelling-wave tube has 20 turns/in., a diameter of 0·15 in. and an axial length of 9 in. *Estimate* what final-anode voltage must be applied to obtain useful gain. Also calculate the average transit time of an electron through the helix. The ratio of charge to mass for the electron is $1{\cdot}76 \times 10^{11}$ C/kg.

L.U. Telecomm. Part III. 1963.

21

RADIO WAVE PROPAGATION AND AERIALS

INTRODUCTION

RADIO communication is possible because of the fact that energy, in the form of electromagnetic waves, is radiated from a circuit carrying an alternating current. At power supply frequencies this fact is ignored as the effect is insignificantly small. Thus at such low frequencies, the only magnetic flux produced by an alternating current is assumed to be the flux of self-induction, the voltage of which has no component in phase with the current. This assumption, which would imply that no power is radiated into space, is in fact an approximation which does not hold good at high frequencies. It is accepted that the electromagnetic effects of a change in current, and the electrostatic effect of a change in charge, do not take place instantaneously but are propagated in free space with a velocity c, the velocity of light. Thus, if an alternating current flows in a circuit and is represented by

$$i = I_{max} \sin \omega t$$

the magnetic flux at a distance r from the source will not vary as $\sin \omega t$ but will lag behind the current by a time interval of r/c.

A useful analogy on the subject of radiation of energy is provided by the displacement of a solid body floating in water. If the body is depressed slowly, and released equally slowly, the energy expended in sinking the body will be returned when it rises, apart from any loss due to friction. This is analogous to a low frequency electrical circuit containing inductance and resistance; apart from the loss which produces heat in the resistance, the energy absorbed from the supply is returned so that the mean power taken from the supply by the inductive part of the circuit is zero. If the depression and subsequent release of the floating body occurs very rapidly, however, some of the energy supplied by the external force will be expended in setting up a wave motion which will carry energy away from the source of the disturbance. This is analogous to the radiation of energy by an electrical circuit at high frequency.

In the case of a radio transmitter, the radiating circuit, or aerial system, produces one wave for each period of the exciting voltage, and the wavelength of the radiation λ, is related to the velocity of propagation by the expression

$$\lambda = c/f$$

where f is the frequency of the radiation, and c is the velocity of propagation of the wave, a quantity which may be taken as 3×10^8 metres per second. When f is in hertz, the wavelength λ is given in metres.

RADIATION FROM A CURRENT ELEMENT IN FREE SPACE

The simplest possible form of radiator is a thin straight filament of conductor, of very short length, and isolated from all other conductors; the field produced by such an element does not depend on the distribution of current along its length because it is so short that there is negligible phase difference between waves reaching a point in space from different parts of the conductor.

The analysis of the field produced by such a hypothetical conductor is best handled in terms of a set of spherical co-ordinates which have the mid-point of the conductor as origin, and are aligned so that the conductor lies along one axis. If E_r, E_θ, E_ϕ, and H_r, H_θ and H_ϕ are the components of the electric and magnetic fields at any point $P_{(r\theta\phi)}$ due to a current

$$i = I_{max} \sin \omega t$$

in the conductor, then it can be shown[1] that if the element is disposed as in Fig. 21.1, the values of the magnetic field components are

$$\left.\begin{aligned} H_r &= 0 \\ H_\theta &= 0 \\ H_\phi &= \frac{I_{max} l \sin\theta}{4\pi r}\left[\frac{\omega}{c}\cos\omega\left(t-\frac{r}{c}\right)+\frac{1}{r}\sin\omega\left(t-\frac{r}{c}\right)\right] \end{aligned}\right\} \quad . \quad 21.1a$$

where l is the length of the current element. The electric field components are

$$\left.\begin{aligned} E_r &= \frac{2I_{max} l \cos\theta}{4\pi r k_0}\left[\frac{1}{cr}\sin\omega\left(t-\frac{r}{c}\right)-\frac{1}{\omega r^2}\cos\omega\left(t-\frac{r}{c}\right)\right] \\ E_\theta &= \frac{I_{max} l \sin\theta}{4\pi r k_0}\left[\frac{\omega}{c^2}\cos\omega\left(t-\frac{r}{c}\right)+\frac{1}{rc}\sin\omega\left(t-\frac{r}{c}\right)-\frac{1}{\omega r^2}\cos\omega\left(t-\frac{r}{c}\right)\right] \\ E_\phi &= 0 \end{aligned}\right\}$$

$$. \quad . \quad . \quad . \quad . \quad 21.1b$$

where k_0 is the permittivity of free space. If the distances are measured in metres, the value of the magnetic field is in amperes per metre, while the electric field values are in volts per metre.

If the expression for H_ϕ is examined, it will be seen to consist of two terms, one varying inversely with the distance r from the source, and the other varying as $1/r^2$. This second term represents the induction field, while the other represents the radiation field. When r is small, i.e. in regions close to the conductor, the induction term predominates, whereas in regions far distant from the source the radiation term alone is significant. If the expressions for the components of the electric field are examined it will be seen that only the first term in the expression for E_θ varies as $1/r$; the other terms which represent the induction field, vary either as $1/r^2$ or $1/r^3$, and have insignificantly small amplitudes at large distances from the conductor.

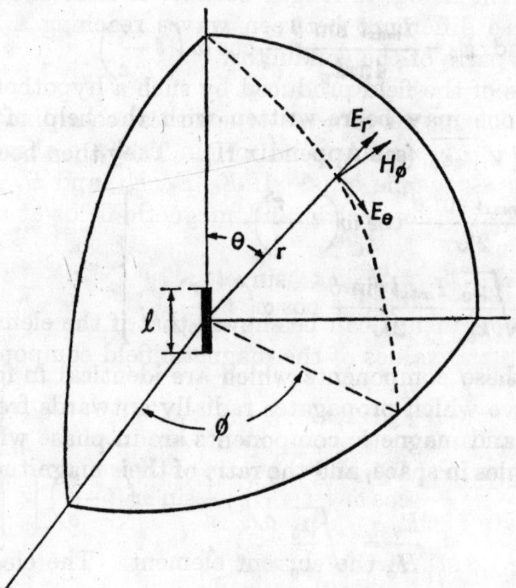

Fig. 21.1.

In the immediate vicinity of the conductor, the magnetic field is in phase with the current in the conductor, while the electric field varies in phase with the charge on either end of the conductor element; in this region the magnetic and electric fields thus have a phase difference of 90°, and are at right angles to each other in space. The radiation component of the magnetic field is produced by the alternating electric field, and the electric radiation component arises from the alternating magnetic field. The flow of current, or movement of charge, in the conductor thus establishes the local induction fields, while the radiation fields exist as a consequence of the changing induction fields.

Equation 21.1a shows that the induction and radiation components of the magnetic field have equal amplitudes at a distance r, such that,

$$\frac{\omega}{c}=\frac{1}{r}$$

i.e. when $r=\lambda/2\pi$, as $c=\lambda f$.
At distances from the source, greater than seventeen wavelengths, the amplitude of the induction field is less than 1% of the radiation field.

The radiation field components are,

$$H_\phi=\frac{I_{max}l\sin\theta}{4\pi r}\frac{\omega}{c}\cos\omega\left(t-\frac{r}{c}\right)$$

$$\text{and } E_\theta=\frac{I_{max}l\sin\theta}{4\pi rk_0}\frac{\omega}{c^2}\cos\omega\left(t-\frac{r}{c}\right)$$

These expressions may be re-written with the help of the relations $c=\lambda f$ and $c=1/\sqrt{\mu_0 k_0}$ (see Appendix H). They then become

$$\left.\begin{aligned}H_\phi&=\frac{I_{max}l\sin\theta}{2\lambda r}\cos\omega\left(t-\frac{r}{c}\right)\\ \text{and } E_\theta&=\sqrt{\frac{\mu_0}{k_0}}\,\frac{I_{max}l\sin\theta}{2\lambda r}\cos\omega\left(t-\frac{r}{c}\right)\end{aligned}\right\} \quad . \quad . \quad . \quad 21.2$$

Taken alone, these components which are identical in form, comprise a spherical wave which propagates radially outwards from the source. These electric and magnetic components are in phase with each other, are at right angles in space, and the ratio of their magnitudes is given by

$$\frac{E_\theta}{H_\phi}=\sqrt{\frac{\mu_0}{k_0}} \quad . \quad . \quad . \quad . \quad . \quad 21.3$$

which, as shown in Appendix H is the impedance of free space. This has a value of 120π or 377 ohms.

The general form of the magnetic and electric field distribution is indicated in Fig. 21.2. The magnetic flux has a circular path centred on the conductor, and the flux density varies in sinusoidal fashion but decreases inversely with radial distance from the conductor. The factor $\sin\theta$ in equation 21.2 is responsible for a variation in the magnetic flux density as the angle of inclination with the axis of the conductor is changed ; the magnetic field is zero along the conductor axis, and has a maximum value in the equatorial plane transverse to the conductor.

The electric field which is everywhere orthogonal with the magnetic field, starts as a field between the ends of the conductor. The collapse

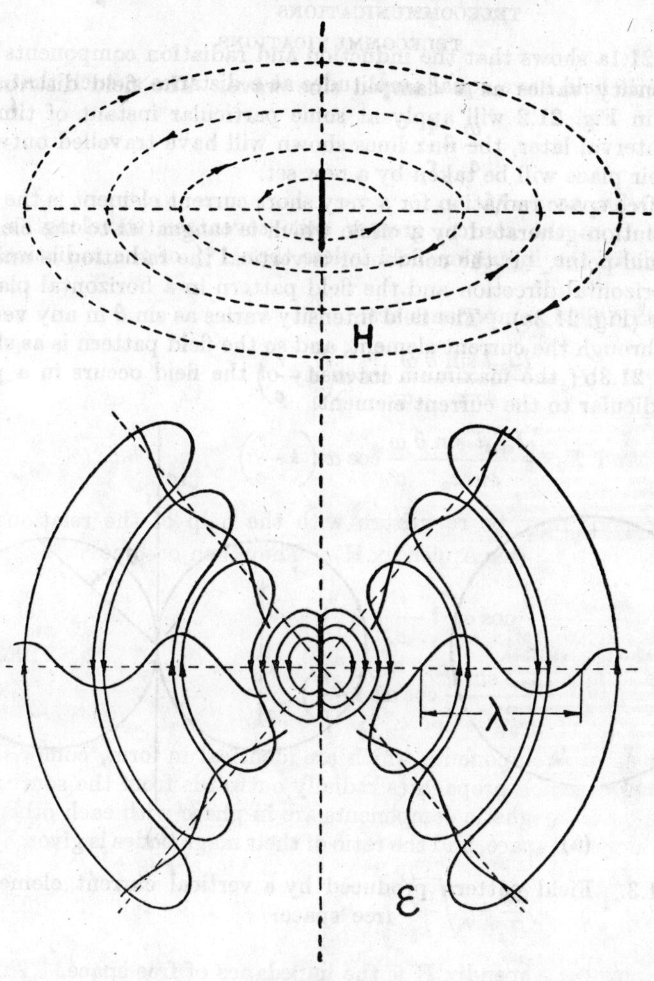

Fig. 21.2.

of this field takes place at a slower rate than the change in potential which produces it ; as a consequence of this, the new electric field starts to build up before the first has disappeared and causes it to be forced outwards, in the form of closed loops as shown in Fig. 21.2. The electric field also varies with the angular orientation from the conductor axis ; at any given radial distance the electric field has its maximum value in the equatorial plane, and minimum value on the axis of the conductor ; this is indicated by the amplitudes of the sine waves drawn in Fig. 21.2. Along any particular radius, the electric flux density varies as a damped sine wave. The field distribution shown in Fig. 21.2 will apply at some particular instant of time; a short interval later, the flux lines shown will have travelled outwards and their place will be taken by a new set.

The free space radiation for a very short current element is the solid of revolution generated by a circle which is tangential to the element at its mid-point. If the conductor is vertical the radiation is uniform in a horizontal direction and the field pattern in a horizontal plane is circular (Fig. 21.3a). The field intensity varies as sin θ in any vertical plane through the current element, and so the field pattern is as shown in Fig. 21.3b; the maximum intensity of the field occurs in a plane perpendicular to the current element.

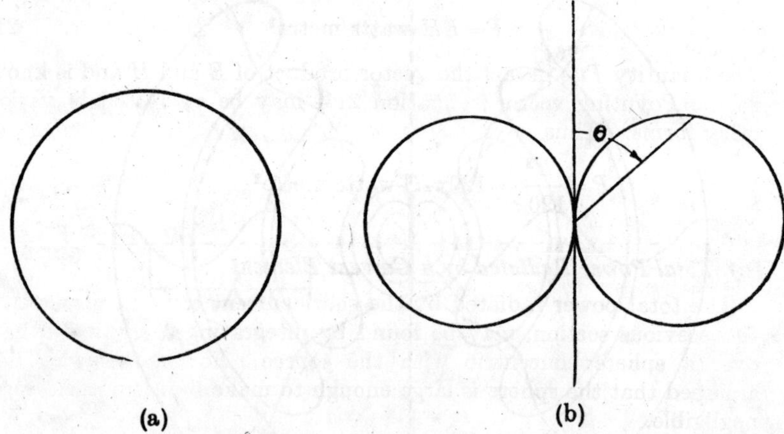

Fig. 21.3. Field pattern produced by a vertical current element in free space.

POWER RADIATED BY SIMPLE AERIALS

Radio waves may be regarded as spherical waves which emanate from the radiating circuit; at large distances from the radiating source a small part of the travelling spherical wave is indistinguishable from a plane wave. The wave front is the plane which contains the E and H vectors, and is at right angles to the direction of propagation and power flow. Such a wave is referred to as a plane polarised wave. The direction of the electric vector is used to indicate the direction of polarisation; thus a vertically polarised wave is one which has the electric vector disposed vertically.

The power, or rate of energy supplied by each square metre of wave front is given by the product of the total energy contained in each cubic metre of space, and the velocity of propagation of the wave. If the electric and magnetic fields E and H are given in terms of S.I. units, so that they are measured in volts per metre, and amperes per metre respectively, then the total energy in a cubic metre of space transversed by such fields is

$$(\mu_0 H^2 + k_0 E^2)/2 \text{ joules}$$

The power density P carried by each square metre of the wavefront is thus

$$P = c(\mu_0 H^2 + k_0 E^2)/2 \text{ watts/metre}^2$$

The quantity c may be replaced by $1/\sqrt{\mu_0 k_0}$ and $E = \sqrt{\frac{\mu_0}{k_0}} \, . \, H$ (equation 21.3) ; these relations enable P to be expressed as

$$P = EH \text{ watts/metre}^2 \quad . \quad . \quad . \quad 21.4$$

The quantity P is in fact the vector product of E and H and is known as the Poynting vector ; equation 21.4 may be expressed in various other forms. Thus

$$P = \frac{E^2}{120\pi} = 120\pi H^2 \text{ watts/metre}^2 \quad . \quad . \quad . \quad 21.4a$$

(a) Total Power Radiated by a Current Element

The total power radiated by the short current element discussed in the previous section, may be found by integrating the power density over a sphere concentric with the source. For convenience it is assumed that the sphere is large enough to make induction field terms negligible.

Equation 21.4a gives the power density as

$$P = 120\pi H^2 \text{ watts per square metre}$$

If the expression for the radiation magnetic field is employed (equation 21.2) then

$$P = 120\pi \left[\frac{I_{max} l \sin\theta}{2\lambda r} \cos\omega\left(t - \frac{r}{c}\right) \right]^2 \quad . \quad . \quad . \quad 21.5a$$

Over a complete period the value of $\cos^2\omega\left(t - \frac{r}{c}\right)$ is 1/2, hence the time average power density is

$$P_a = \frac{120\pi}{8r^2}\left(\frac{l}{\lambda}\right)^2 I^2_{max} \sin^2\theta \quad . \quad . \quad . \quad . \quad 21.5b$$

The power radiated through the element of area da of a sphere of radius r (Fig. 21.4), is thus

$$P_a \, da = P_a \, . \, 2\pi r \sin\theta \, r d\theta \quad . \quad . \quad . \quad . \quad 21.5c$$

The total radiated power is thus

$$P_T = \int_0^\pi P_a 2\pi r^2 \sin\theta \, d\theta$$

$$= \frac{120\pi}{8r^2}\left(\frac{l}{\lambda}\right)^2 I^2_{max} \int_0^\pi 2\pi r^2 \sin^3\theta \, d\theta$$

$$= 30\pi^2\left(\frac{l}{\lambda}\right)^2 I^2_{max} \times \frac{4}{3}$$

$$= \left[80\pi^2\left(\frac{l}{\lambda}\right)^2\right] I^2 \quad . \quad . \quad . \quad . \quad . \quad 21.6$$

where I is the r.m.s. value of the current.

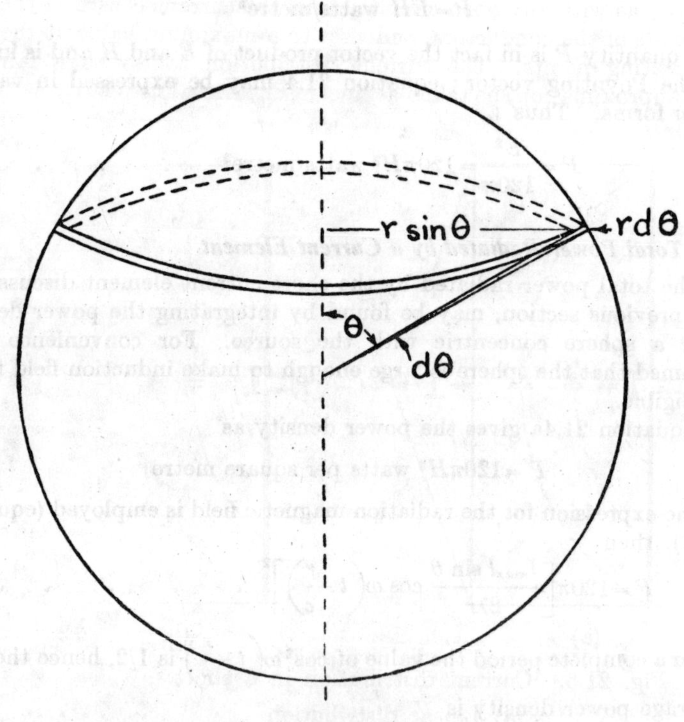

Fig. 21.4.

The power radiated is independent of the radius of the sphere over which the power density is integrated ; this is due to the implicit assumption of a loss free transmission medium.

It is often convenient to regard the radiated power as being dissipated in a fictitious resistance, called the *radiation resistance* R_r. The result obtained above shows that for the very short current element

$$R_r = 80\pi^2\left(\frac{l}{\lambda}\right)^2 \text{ ohms} \quad . \quad . \quad . \quad . \qquad 21.7$$

where l is the length of the element and λ is the radiated wavelength.

(b) *Total Power Radiated by a Short Dipole*

A practical approximation to the hypothetical current element is a dipole which has a length short compared with the wavelength, and is excited at its mid-point as shown in Fig. 21.5a. Such an arrangement may be regarded as an open wire transmission line which has been opened out ; as with any open-circuited line, the current is zero at the "open" ends of the conductors, and rises to a maximum value at the central exciting points. The current distribution can, with a fair degree of approximation, be taken as linear (Fig. 21.5a) or cosinusoidal (Fig. 21.5b).

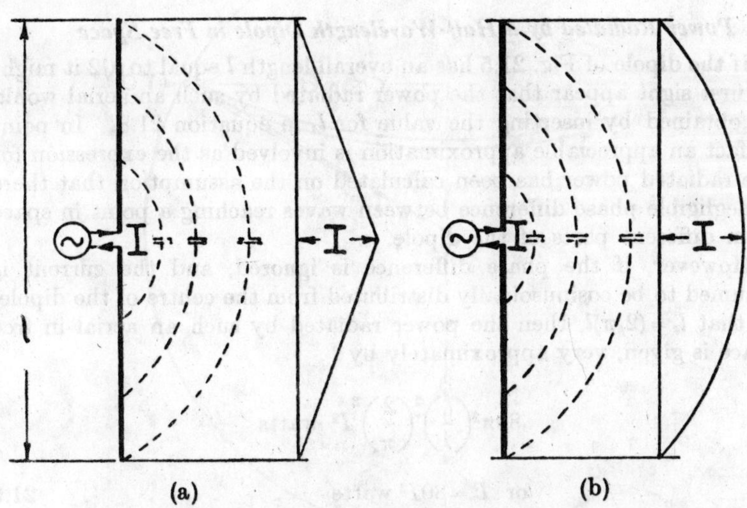

Fig. 21.5. Current distribution in a short dipole.
(a) Linear distribution
(b) Cosinusoidal distribution.

The expression obtained above for the power radiated by a current element was based on the assumption that the amplitude of the current did not change over the length ; clearly, the power radiated by the dipole of Fig. 21.5 will be less than that produced by the current element. This may be taken into account by using an "equivalent length", l_e, for the dipole such that an assumed constant amplitude of current over the equivalent length then gives the same power radiation as the actual distribution of current over the physical length. The current amplitude assumed is that at the exciting points. The power radiated by the electrically short dipole is thus,

$$P = 80\pi^2\left(\frac{l_e}{\lambda}\right)^2 I^2 \text{ watts} \quad . \quad . \quad . \quad . \quad 21.8$$

The radiation resistance is accordingly equal to $80\pi^2(l_e/\lambda)^2$ ohms.

If the distribution of current is assumed to be linear, then $l_e = l/2$ and so the radiation resistance with this assumption is

$$20\pi^2\left(\frac{l}{\lambda}\right)^2 \text{ ohms.}$$

(c) *Power Radiated by a Half-Wavelength Dipole in Free Space*

If the dipole of Fig. 21.5 has an overall length l equal to $\lambda/2$ it might at first sight appear that the power radiated by such an aerial would be obtained by inserting the value for l_e in equation 21.8. In point of fact an appreciable approximation is involved as the expression for the radiated power has been calculated on the assumption that there is negligible phase difference between waves reaching a point in space from different parts of the dipole.

However, if the phase difference is ignored, and the current is assumed to be cosinusoidally distributed from the centre of the dipole, so that $l_e = (2/\pi)l$, then the power radiated by such an aerial in free space is given, very approximately by

$$80\pi^2\left(\frac{l}{\lambda}\right)^2\left(\frac{2}{\pi}\right)^2 I^2 \text{ watts}$$

$$\text{or } P = 80 I^2 \text{ watts} \quad . \quad . \quad . \quad . \quad 21.9$$

as the length $l = \lambda/2$. The radiation resistance is thus approximately 80 ohms.

A more exact value can be obtained by assuming that the dipole consists of short elements of length, each of which contributes to the field in the manner of equation 21.1; the total field is then obtained from the integration of the elemental lengths, which however carry different currents and are at different distances from the point under consideration. An expression for the field then permits the mean power density to be obtained. Integration over a sphere then gives the total power radiated as

$$73I^2 \text{ watts}$$

which of course gives the radiation resistance for the half-wavelength dipole as 73 ohms. The radiation resistance, and consequently the power output, of a dipole when used as a half wavelength radiating element is independent of the physical size of the dipole; if two dipoles are fed with the same current and one has a length of 15 cm. and operates at 1,000 MHz, while the other has a length of 150 metres and is used at 1 MHz, the power radiated will be the same in the two cases.

The field radiation pattern of a half wavelength dipole, set up in free space, is roughly similar in form to that of the current element shown in Fig. 21.3.

(d) Power Radiated by a Short Vertical Earthed Aerial

If the vertical dipole of the previous section was bisected by a large perfectly conducting surface at right angles to the axis of the dipole, the electric field would be normal to the conducting surface which would therefore not disturb the field distribution.

A half dipole, or monopole, on the conducting surface thus produces the same field above the conducting surface as that of the dipole in the absence of the surface. If the earth can be assumed to be a perfectly conducting plane, then a vertical aerial with the excitation voltage applied between the base of the aerial and earth, as in Fig. 21.6a, will thus produce the same field as that due to a dipole consisting of the aerial and its image (Fig. 21.6b).

When the height h_e is very short, i.e. $h<\lambda/10$, then from equation 21.8, the power radiated by the " aerial and image " dipole is

$$80\pi^2\left(\frac{2h_e}{\lambda}\right)^2 I^2 \text{ watts}$$

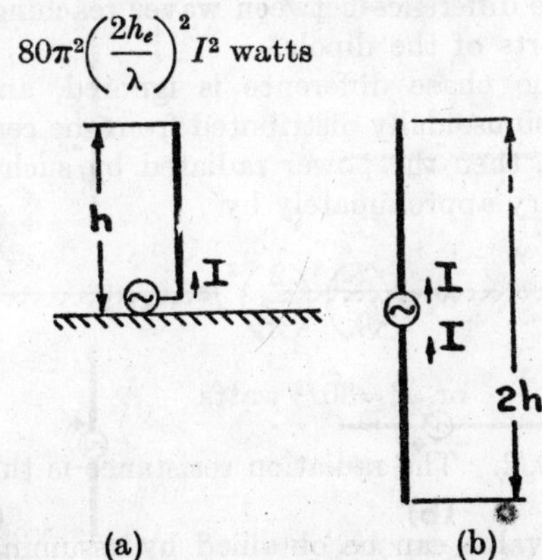

Fig. 21.6 (a) Vertical earthed aerial
(b) Aerial and image.

where h_e is the equivalent height of the aerial. As there is no field below the assumed conducting surface of the earth, the power P, radiated by the short vertical aerial is half that of the "aerial and image" dipole and is thus

$$P = 160\pi^2\left(\frac{h_e}{\lambda}\right)^2 I^2 = 1578\left(\frac{h_e}{\lambda}\right)^2 I^2 \text{ watts} \tag{21.10}$$

If the height of the vertical aerial is $\lambda/4$ the remarks of the preceding section indicate that the power radiated is $36{\cdot}5I^2$ watts and the radiation resistance of this aerial is thus 36·5 ohms.

The Effect of the Earth

Part of the radiation from any aerial will be directed towards the earth (or sea), which will give rise to reflection. The total field at a distant point P may thus be regarded as the sum of a direct wave and a reflected wave (Fig. 21.7a).

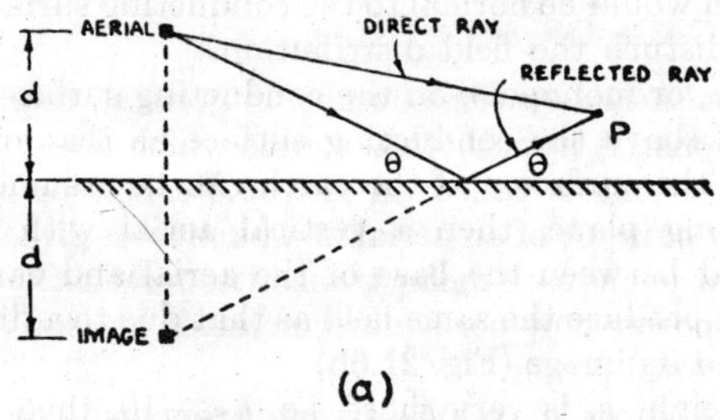

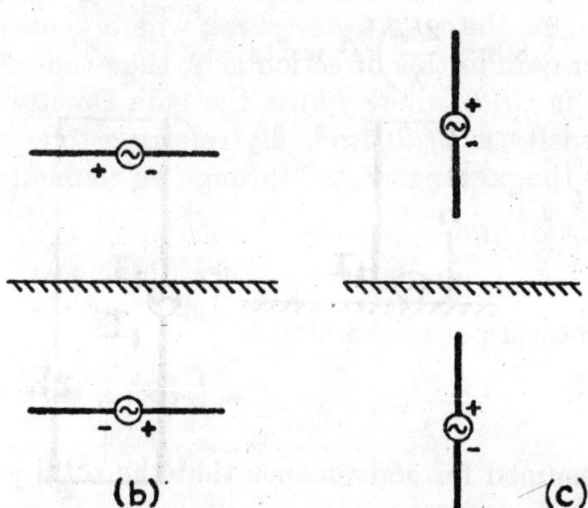

Fig. 21.7 (a) Reflection from the earth
(b) Horizontal aerial and image
(c) Vertical aerial and image.

If, as an approximation, the earth is assumed to present a flat perfectly conducting surface, then at the earth's surface, the tangential component of the electric field must be zero and there will be no energy loss on reflection ; vertically polarised waves may then be assumed to be reflected from the earth without a change of phase, while horizontally polarised waves will be reflected with a phase change of 180°.

With the foregoing assumption the reflected wave can be regarded as originating from an image of the aerial below the conducting surface of the earth. When the aerial is vertical, the currents in corresponding parts of the aerial and image have the same direction and magnitude (Fig. 21.7c) ; a horizontal aerial has an image with current 180° out of phase (Fig. 21.7b).

The total field at a distant point may thus be regarded for calculation purposes as that due to two aerials (with the appropriate phase difference) and accordingly treated as an array.

POWER GAIN OF AN AERIAL

Practical aerial systems do not, in general, radiate power equally in all directions. A hypothetical source which does radiate power equally in all directions is called an *isotropic source* or an *isotropic radiator*. The *power gain*, G, of an aerial in a particular direction is defined as the power flow per square metre transmitted in that direction, as compared with the power flow per square meter of an isotropic source radiating the same total power.

For the short current element previously considered, the power radiated varies with the angle θ to the element (Fig. 21.4) and is a maximum in the equatorial plane where θ has the value of $\pi/2$. If the power gain in this direction is G, then the power gain in any other direction is $Gf(\theta)$ where $f(\theta)$ is the gain function. The corresponding power density is $Gf(\theta)/4\pi r^2$. By referring to equation 21.5c it will be seen that the power radiated through an elemental zone of a sphere is

$$\frac{Gf(\theta)}{4\pi r^2}\cdot 2\pi r^2 \sin\theta\, d\theta = \tfrac{1}{2}Gf(\theta)\sin\theta\, d\theta$$

while the total power radiated is

$$= \int_0^{\pi} \tfrac{1}{2}Gf(\theta)\sin\theta\, d\theta$$

If it is assumed for convenience that the total power radiated is 1 W then

$$\int_0^{\pi} \tfrac{1}{2}Gf(\theta)\sin\theta\, d\theta = 1$$

and so

$$G = 2\Big/\int_0^{\pi} f(\theta)\sin\theta\, d\theta$$

For the current element considered $f(\theta)$ is by equation 21.5b equal to $\sin^2\theta$, and so

$$G=2\Big/\int_0^\pi \sin^3\theta\, d\theta=\frac{2}{4/3}=1{\cdot}5$$

LOW FREQUENCY AERIALS

The term "low-frequency" applied to aerials generally refers to systems which operate at less than 300 kHz. The aerial systems are then normally restricted to vertical radiators of relatively simple form supported by two or more wires or masts and are electrically short.

It was shown in chapter 19 that a loss-free transmission line, a quarter of a wavelength long, presents a short-circuit to a generator if the far end is open-circuited. If one conductor of the line is replaced by the earth (assumed to be a conducting surface) and the other conductor is raised to a vertical position, the former transmission line becomes the earthed aerial system of Fig. 21.8 with a current and voltage distribution along its lengths as indicated.

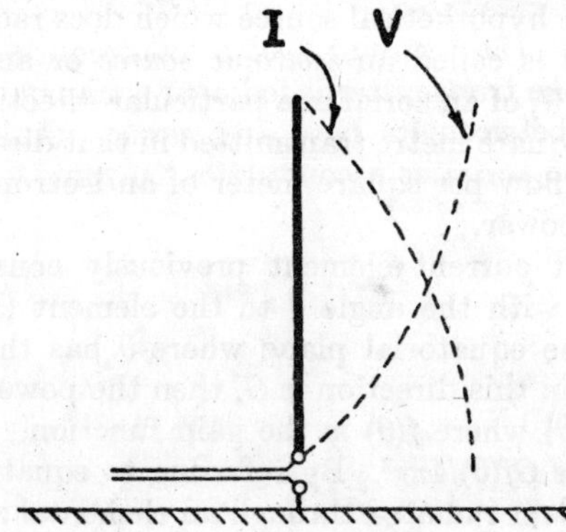

Fig. 21.8. Voltage and current distribution on a vertical aerial.

As far as the input impedance at the base is concerned, the aerial behaves in the same way as a series resonant circuit, and is said to be resonant when its physical height is a quarter of a wavelength. (In practice the effect occurs when the height is slightly less than $\lambda/4$). If the applied frequency is decreased so that the height is distinctly less than $\lambda/4$, the aerial presents a capacitive input reactance, assuming always that the conductor resistance is negligibly small. The general form of the reactance variation is the same as that of an open circuited transmission line as shown in Fig. 19.2, i.e. the base reactance is capacitive for heights up to $\lambda/4$ and inductive between heights of $\lambda/4$ and $\lambda/2$.

If, for economic or other reasons, the conductor height is limited to a value less than $\lambda/4$ (about 800 feet at 300 kHz) the aerial can be "tuned" by the addition of series inductance.

Low-frequency aerials normally have additional capacitance to earth added to the top of the conductor. In its simplest form this is achieved by continuing the vertical conductor horizontally to form an inverted "L"; alternatively, the vertical conductor (or conductors) may be connected to a set of horizontal wires to form a "T" shaped aerial. The added capacitance has the beneficial effect of producing a more uniform current distribution on the vertical wires and so increases the equivalent height of the aerial. As the radiated power is proportional to the square of the equivalent height (equation 21.10), the "top capacitance" is made as large as is convenient. The added capacitance also decreases the capacitive reactance at the input terminals. As a consequence the value of tuning inductance required is smaller. The potential across the inductor, and the losses associated with it are thereby reduced.

Fig. 21.9 depicts the "circuit" of a low-frequency earthed aerial. The output from the transmitter is fed over a transmission line and the aerial is excited between its base and earth. Current flows in the vertical wire of the aerial as a conduction current, through the distri-

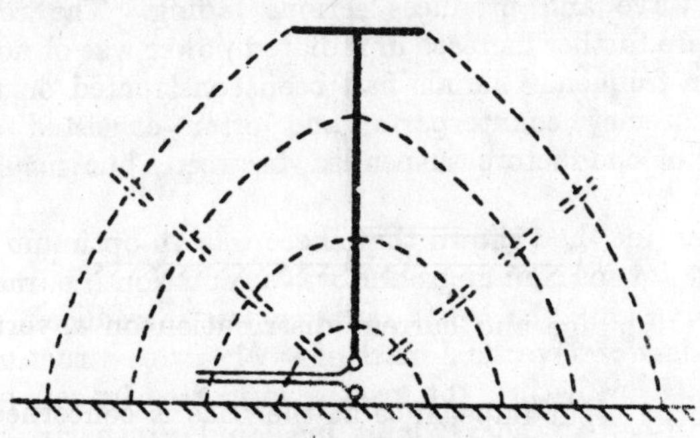

Fig. 21.9.

buted capacitance to earth as a displacement current and, again as a conduction current, in the surface of the earth adjacent to the earthed terminal. Distributed inductance and resistance are also present in addition to the distributed capacitance shown.

Some of the energy supplied to the input terminals is dissipated in the resistance of the actual conductor and the resistance of the earth and earth connection; an additional energy loss arises from dielectric loss in supporting insulators. The efficiency of the aerial as a radiator is defined as

$$\frac{\text{Power Radiated}}{\text{Power Supplied}} = \frac{R_r}{R_r + R}$$

where the quantity R is the total equivalent series loss resistance of the "circuit", and R_r is the radiation resistance.

As the radiation resistance of low-frequency aerials is relatively small, it is essential that the loss resistance be kept as low as possible. Thus, wires are often buried in the soil around the aerial to reduce the earth connection loss; the aerial itself is often constructed in the form of a vertical cylindrical cage of conductors so as to decrease the conductor resistance and increase the capacitance to earth.

MEDIUM-FREQUENCY AERIALS

Medium-frequency aerials may be said to embrace those used between 300 kHz and about 3 MHz; of the various services using this part of the radio-frequency spectrum, the most important is broadcasting in the range 550–1600 kHz.

As broadcasting developed in the nineteen-twenties and transmitter power was increased, it was found that the service area in which reception was reliable, was limited by reflection of high angle radiation from a reflecting layer in the upper atmosphere. This interferes with the ground wave and produces serious fading. The result was a situation where further increase in radiated power was of no assistance. Most medium-frequency aerials had been constructed on the lines of their low-frequency counterparts, and often consisted of a "T" arrangement of conductors suspended between, but insulated from, two towers.

After Ballantine[2] had shown that there was an optimum height of a vertical aerial for maximum ground wave radiation (i.e. radiation in a horizontal direction), the tower radiator was introduced. This form of aerial consists of a vertical mast of steel lattice structure, which is itself used as the radiator; the mast is supported by sets of stays and often rests on a ball and socket joint, insulated from earth.

The variation of the vertical directivity with height for a vertical aerial over a conducting earth surface is shown in Fig. 21.10. When the height is short compared with the wavelength, the polar diagram is approximately semi-circular. (The corresponding three-dimensional solid pattern of radiation is obtained by the rotation of the semi-circle about the axis *aa*.)

As the aerial height is increased up to $\lambda/2$ the radiation is concentrated in a horizontal direction; with a height of about $5\lambda/8$ a secondary lobe of radiation appears. Further increase in height increases the

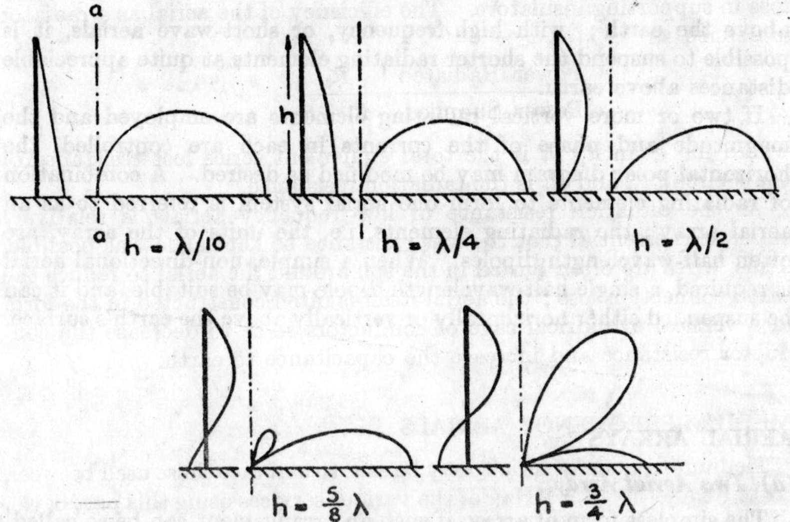

Fig. 21.10. Variation of vertical directivity of a vertical aerial above a conducting earth surface.

high-angle radiation at the expense of that in a horizontal direction.

The height of the vertical tower radiator is made slightly greater than $\lambda/2$ and then has a value which is most favourable for horizontal radiation, while reducing high-angle radiation. The tower radiator thus increases the area of reliable reception by ensuring that the ground wave predominates at greater distances from the aerial ; it also enables the horizontal polar diagram to be more symmetrical as it eliminates the interference produced by the steel masts required to support a suspended wire radiator.

HIGH-FREQUENCY AERIALS

High-frequency aerials may conveniently be regarded as those employed in the frequency range from about 3–30 MHz; the corresponding wavelengths thus range from 100 to 10 metres, and this enables the aerial system to be made comparable in size with the wavelength, a state of affairs which permits directional properties to be produced if desired. Any aerial system could be made to produce directional radiation but the large size and high cost of the structures necessarily involved at lower frequencies normally prohibit the construction of highly directive systems. Fig. 21.10 shows how the height of a vertical aerial affects the vertical polar diagram of the radiated field. The vertical directivity is also affected by the height of the aerial system above the earth; with high-frequency, or short-wave aerials, it is possible to suspend the shorter radiating elements at quite appreciable distances above earth.

If two or more vertical radiating elements are employed and the magnitude and phase of the currents in each are controlled, the horizontal polar diagram may be modified as desired. A combination of radiating elements to form one aerial system is referred to as an aerial array; the radiating elements, i.e. the units of the array, are often half-wavelength dipoles. When a simple, non-directional aerial is required, a single half-wavelength dipole may be suitable, and it can be suspended either horizontally or vertically above the earth's surface.

AERIAL ARRAYS

(a) Two Aerial Array

The simplest form of array, if such an arrangement can be so called, consists of two vertical aerials spaced some distance apart, and energised in phase. At a distant point such as *P* in Fig. 21.11, the difference in strength of the received field from each aerial may be ignored but the phase difference due to the difference in the path length cannot be neglected.

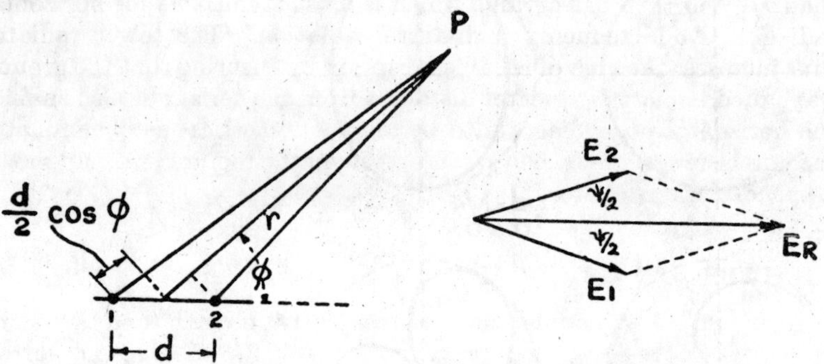

Fig. 21.11. Field due to two aerials.

The total field is the phasor sum of the fields produced by the two aerials. Now, as the diagram indicates, if the distance r of the point P is compared with d the difference in path lengths is $d \cos \phi$ Th gives rise to a phase difference ψ, where

$$\frac{\psi}{2} : 2\pi :: \frac{d}{2} \cos \phi : \lambda$$

$$\text{i.e. } \frac{\psi}{2} = \frac{\pi d \cos \phi}{\lambda}$$

Hence the total field at P is represented by the phasor E_R which is the sum of the equal phasors E_1 and E_2, and so

$$E_R = 2E_1 \cos \frac{\psi}{2} = 2E_1 \cos\left[\frac{\pi d \cos \phi}{\lambda}\right] \quad . \quad . \quad . \quad 21.11$$

This equation thus gives the horizontal polar diagram for the two aerials when they are energised in phase. If the two aerials are supplied with currents, which are out of phase in time, then the resulting phase angle ψ between the two fields will be altered. If there is a phase angle of α radians and the current in aerial 1 lags on the current in aerial 2, then the phase angle involved is

$$\psi + \alpha$$

If, on the other hand, aerial 1 carries a current which leads on aerial 2, then the phase angle becomes

$$\psi - \alpha$$

and it may be shown that equation 21.11 then becomes

$$E_R = 2E_1 \cos\left[\frac{\pi d \cos \phi}{\lambda} - \frac{\alpha}{2}\right] \quad . \quad . \quad . \quad 21.12$$

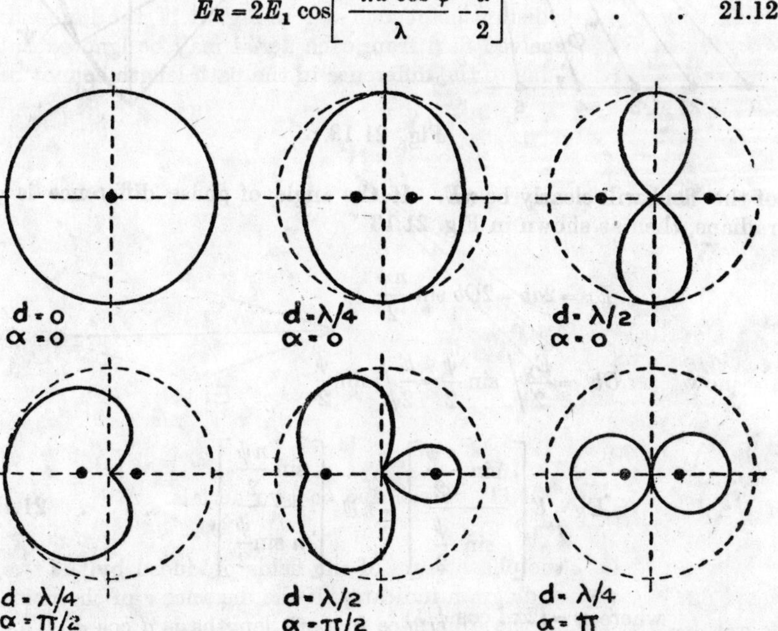

Fig. 21.12. Some horizontal polar diagrams for two vertical aerials.

(b) Broadside Array

Suppose now that there are n vertical aerials, uniformly spaced a distance d apart along a straight line as shown in Fig. 21.13 (drawn for $n=5$) and assume that the currents in all the aerials have the same phase and magnitude.

The resultant field E_R at the distant point P will be given by the phasor sum of the separate fields. $E_1=E_2=E_3$ etc. $=E$. If the separate fields combine arithmetically the resultant maximum value

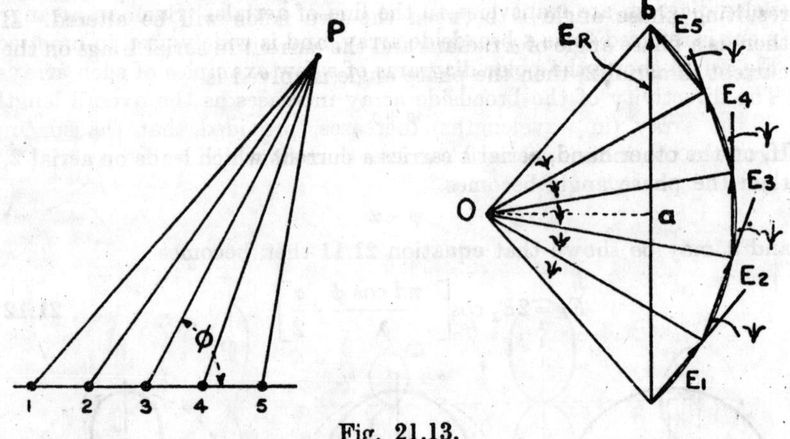

Fig. 21.13.

of the field will clearly be nE. If the angle of phase difference is ψ radians, then as shown in Fig. 21.13

$$E_R = 2ab = 2Ob \sin \frac{n\psi}{2}$$

now $$Ob = \frac{E_5}{2} \Big/ \sin\frac{\psi}{2} = \frac{E}{2} \Big/ \sin\frac{\psi}{2}$$

$$\therefore \quad E_R = E\left[\frac{\sin \frac{n\psi}{2}}{\sin \frac{\psi}{2}}\right] = nE\left[\frac{\sin \frac{n\psi}{2}}{n \sin \frac{\psi}{2}}\right] \quad . \quad . \quad 21.13$$

where $\psi = (2\pi d \cos \phi/\lambda)$

The quantity enclosed by the square brackets is sometimes referred to as the array factor, and has a maximum value of unity. . Equation

21.13 enables the horizontal polar diagram to be drawn. When n is large the value of E_R passes through maximum and zero values as ϕ is varied from zero to 2π. The directions of the maxima may be found by differentiation of equation 21.13 ; the positions of the minima can be found by equating $\sin \frac{n\psi}{2}$ to zero, π, 2π, etc. provided that $\sin \frac{\psi}{2}$ is not also zero, when E_R is indeterminate.

If all the aerials are fed in the same phase, the main " lobes " of the polar diagram are transverse to the line of aerials. Such an arrangement is referred to as a broadside array, and is widely used in practice. Fig. 21.14 shows the polar diagrams of a few examples of such arrays. The directivity of the broadside array increases as the overall length of the array (in wavelengths) increases, provided that the spacing between the individual aerials is less than $3\lambda/4$.

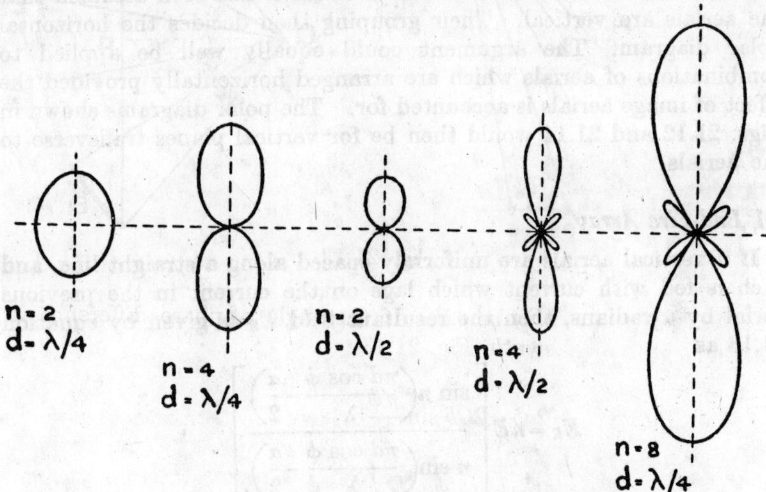

Fig. 21.14. Horizontal polar diagrams of broadside arrays.

Fig. 21.14 indicates that a simple broadside array produces main lobes of radiation normal to itself. As such arrays are usually employed in point-to-point working, the backward radiation is not required and is normally suppressed. This may be achieved by the use of a row of " reflectors " positioned a distance of $\lambda/4$ behind the row of aerials. The reflectors are similar to the aerials but are not excited. Radiation from an aerial excites a reflector a quarter of a period later ; the voltage induced in the reflector lags by a further π radians so that in effect a reflector behaves as a source which radiates with a phase delay of $3\pi/2$ radians at a distance of $\lambda/4$ behind the aerial. The two sources reinforce each other in the forward direction, and produce waves in exact phase opposition in the backward direction. One main lobe of radiation is thus produced in the forward direction.

If the aerials of the array are not fed in the same phase but have a progressive phase difference of α radians from aerial to aerial, the quantity ψ in equation 21.13 becomes ψ', where

$$\psi' = \left(\frac{2\pi d \cos\phi}{\lambda} \pm \alpha\right)$$

The main lobe of radiation is then no longer normal to the line of aerials. It is possible to " swing the beam " of the array through an angle if a suitable progressive phase difference is inserted in the transmission lines coupling the aerials to the transmitter. The desired phase differences are often achieved by using different lengths of transmission line.

In all that has been said on arrays so far it has been assumed that the aerials are vertical. Their grouping then decides the horizontal polar diagram. The argument could equally well be applied to combinations of aerials which are arranged horizontally provided the effect of image aerials is accounted for. The polar diagrams shown in Figs. 21.12 and 21.14 would then be for vertical planes transverse to the aerials.

(c) End-Fire Array

If n vertical aerials are uniformly spaced along a straight line, and each is fed with current which lags on the current in the previous aerial by α radians, then the resultant field E_R is given by equation 21.13 as

$$E_R = nE\left[\frac{\sin n\left(\dfrac{\pi d\cos\phi}{\lambda} - \dfrac{\alpha}{2}\right)}{n\sin\left(\dfrac{\pi d\cos\phi}{\lambda} - \dfrac{\alpha}{2}\right)}\right]$$

where E is the field produced by a single aerial.

If the value of α is equal to $2\pi d/\lambda$ then

$$E_R = nE\left[\frac{\sin\left\{\dfrac{n\pi d}{\lambda}(\cos\phi - 1)\right\}}{n\sin\dfrac{\pi d}{\lambda}(\cos\phi - 1)}\right]$$

The value of E_R is a maximum in the direction of $\phi = 0$; when the aerials are excited to produce this condition, the arrangement is referred to as an *end-fire* array. This form of array may be arranged to give a single major lobe of radiation in the direction of the end of the array which has the lagging phase. Two aerials spaced a distance $\lambda/4$ apart and excited with a phase difference of $\pi/2$ form a simple end-fire array, and have the polar diagram shown in Fig. 21.12. The width of the major lobe of an end-fire array decreases with the array length. A broadside array of the same length produces a narrower lobe of radiation, and because of this and other reasons the broadside form is preferred.

(d) Collinear Array

The arrays so far mentioned have consisted of aerials mounted side by side. An alternative possibility is to arrange the aerials in line with each other. This gives a collinear array.

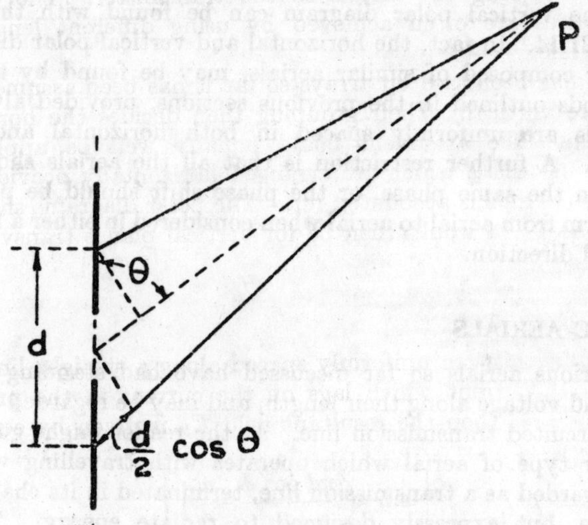

Fig. 21.15. Simple collinear array.

The polar diagram in a vertical plane, or vertical directivity of a vertical collinear array clearly depends upon the length of the individual aerials and their spacing. The field in a vertical plane F_V, may thus be expressed as the product of two factors,

$$F_V = F_1 F_2 \qquad . \quad . \quad . \quad . \quad . \quad . \quad 21.14$$

where F_1 is a function which corresponds to the vertical directivity of one element, and F_2 is another function which depends on the number of aerials and their spacing. When only two aerials are used,

$$F_2 = 2 \cos\left(\frac{\pi d \cos\theta}{\lambda}\right)$$

provided that the currents are in phase. When n aerials are employed, and all carry currents in the same phase, equation 21.13 indicates that

$$F_2 = n\left[\frac{\sin\dfrac{n\psi}{2}}{\sin\dfrac{\psi}{2}}\right]$$

$$\text{where } \psi = \frac{2\pi d \cos\theta.}{\lambda}$$

A practical array may be composed of a number of rows of vertical elements, e.g. several similar vertical collinear arrays side by side. The horizontal polar diagram can then be deduced with the help of equation 21.13; the vertical polar diagram can be found with the help of equation 21.14. In fact, the horizontal and vertical polar diagrams of any array composed of similar aerials, may be found by the use of the methods outlined in the previous sections, provided always that the aerials are uniformly spaced in both horizontal and vertical directions. A further restriction is that all the aerials should carry currents in the same phase, or the phase shift should be progressive and uniform from aerial to aerial when considered in either a horizontal or vertical direction.

RHOMBIC AERIALS

The various aerials so far discussed have had standing waves of current and voltage along their length, and may be regarded as lengths of open-circuited transmission line. As the reader might guess, there is another type of aerial which operates with travelling waves and can be regarded as a transmission line, terminated in its characteristic impedance, but expressly designed to radiate energy. The most important example of this group is the rhombic aerial. As indicated in Fig. 21.16, this consists of four straight wires arranged in the form

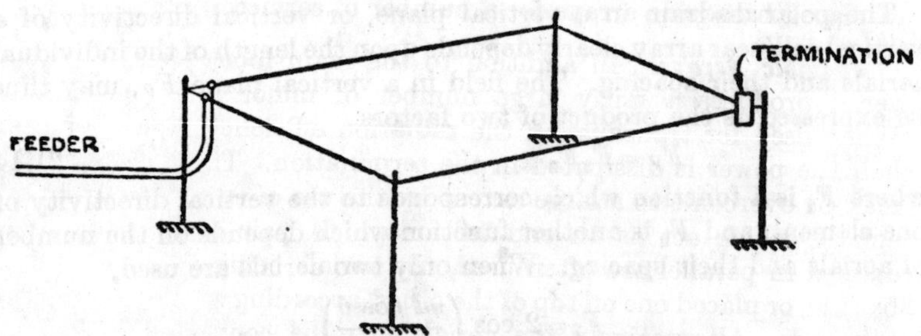

Fig. 21.16. Simple rhombic aerial.

of a rhombus, suspended horizontally above the earth. Such aerials may be used for transmission or reception. In the transmission case the termination is required to absorb relatively large amounts of power and is then usually constructed in the form of a length of transmission line of high dissipation.

Space prohibits a detailed study of the pattern of radiation from a rhombic aerial, but a very brief indication can be made in terms of the radiation produced by a long wire which carries a travelling wave of current. If the minor lobes are disregarded such a wire has a free space radiation pattern as shown in Fig. 21.17. The angle θ decreases as the length of wire increases and is about 20° for a wire six wavelengths long. The lengths of the individual wires of the rhombic are usually several wavelengths long, and if the rhombic angles are correctly arranged, the lobes combine to produce one main lobe of radiation directed along the diagonal of the rhombus from the end connected to the feeder.

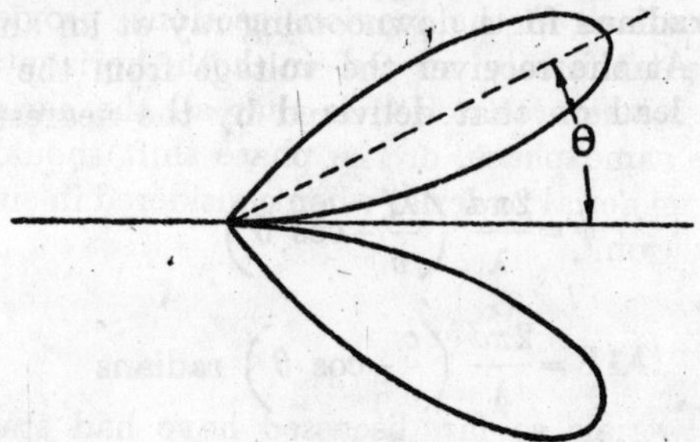

Fig. 21.17. Free space radiation from a wire carrying a travelling wave of current.

The main advantage of the rhombic aerial is that the input impedance and radiation pattern do not change rapidly over a considerable frequency range, as compared with, say, a system of resonant dipoles. For this reason rhombic aerials, or arrays of rhombic aerials have displaced broadside arrays for a number of services.

Rhombic Arrays. In addition to the main lobe, a single rhombic aerial produces a fairly large number of minor lobes of radiation. When used for transmission the radiation efficiency is low, as nearly half the power is dissipated in the termination. These disadvantages may be overcome to a large extent by the use of two or more rhombic aerials, which act as an end-fire array. A pair of rhombic aerials, excited in parallel are often used, the aerials being either placed side by side, or placed one on top of the other, according to the characteristic required. Alternatively the aerials may be connected in series as indicated in Fig. 21.18.

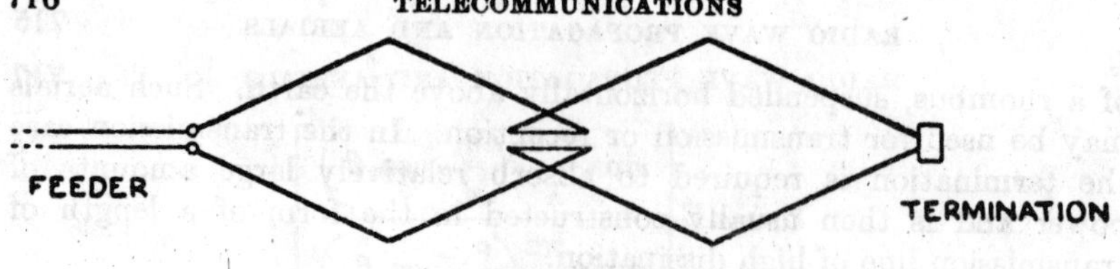

Fig. 21.18.

One form of rhombic array used for receiving purposes, employs a number of rhombic aerials arranged in a straight line and connected to the receiver by individual transmission lines as indicated in Fig. 21.19.

If the difference in length of transmission line connecting two adjacent aerials to the receiver is d metres, this will cause a time delay of d/v seconds, or $2\pi fd/v$ radians, where v is the velocity of transmission along the line. The voltage induced in the aerial nearest the receiver will lag on that induced in the previous aerial by an angle of $2\pi d \cos \theta/\lambda$ radians for a downcoming ray at an angle θ as shown in Fig. 21.19. At the receiver the voltage from the second nearest aerial will thus lead on that delivered by the nearest aerial by the angle ψ where

$$\psi = \frac{2\pi d}{\lambda}\left(\frac{\lambda f}{v} - \cos\theta\right)$$

$$= \frac{2\pi d}{\lambda}\left(\frac{c}{v} - \cos\theta\right) \text{ radians}$$

where c is equal to λf is the free space velocity of the ray.

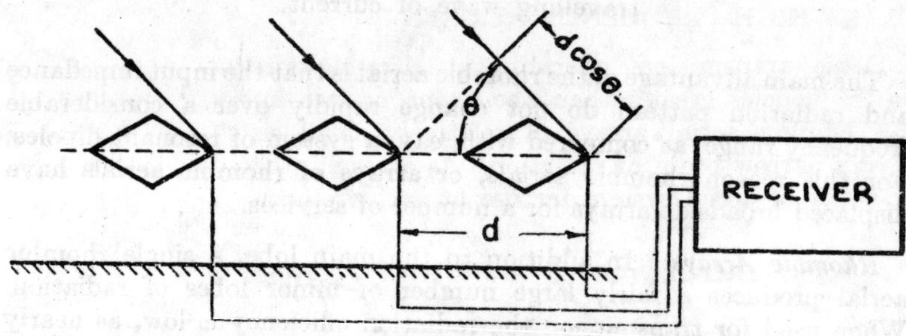

Fig. 21.19. Receiving rhombic array.

If in fact there are n similar, and equally spaced, rhombics the resultant voltage E_R delivered to the receiver will be the phasor sum of equal phasors with an angle ψ between each adjacent pair, hence E_R will be given by equation 21.13 and so

$$E_R = nE\left[\frac{\sin\dfrac{\pi nd}{\lambda}\left(\dfrac{c}{v} - \cos\theta\right)}{n\sin\dfrac{\pi d}{\lambda}\left(\dfrac{c}{v} - \cos\theta\right)}\right]$$

where E is the voltage produced by a single rhombic aerial.

Suppose, in the system shown in Fig. 21.19, phase shifts were introduced in each transmission line, so that all the voltages added up in phase to produce the maximum resultant. The value of the phase shifts would only apply for the particular downcoming angle θ and a change in value would select some other angle. Variation of the phase shifts clearly enables any particular angle to be selected and the vertical directivity of the system altered. In effect, such a variation gives the same results as if the individual aerials were capable of orientation in a vertical plane. This facility of " steering " the aerial system for the optimum angle is extremely useful and enhances the signal/noise ratio when the downcoming angle varies, as it usually does on short-wave transmissions. This form of aerial array is referred to as a *multiple-unit steerable antenna* (MUSA). It is used, with sixteen rhombic aerials connected to a complex version of independent sideband receiver (Fig. 22.4) for transatlantic telephone service. The necessary alterations in phase need not be introduced in the transmission lines themselves as the same effect may be achieved in the receiver by supplying local oscillator voltages which differ in phase, to one of the frequency changer stages in the receiver.

ULTRA-HIGH FREQUENCY AERIALS

Radio transmitters operating at ultra-high frequencies (or even on frequencies greater than about one or two hundred megahertz), can employ aerial arrays of relatively small size, which produce a very narrow beam of radiation. As a result, there is a multiplicity of types of aerial system for use at such frequencies.

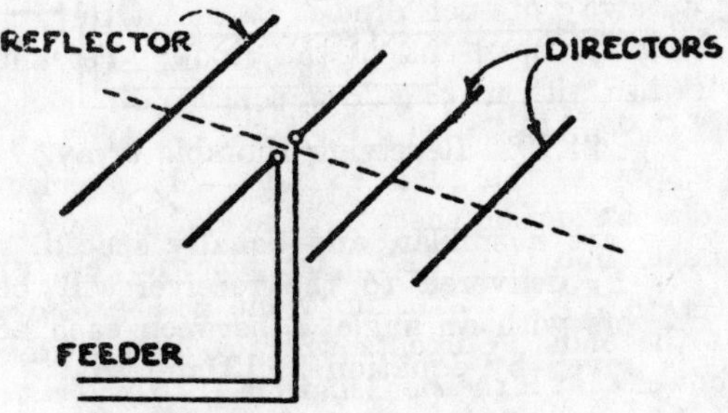

Fig. 21.20. Simple Yagi array.

The nearest approach to the broadside and end-fire arrays previously mentioned for lower frequencies, is a particular form of end-fire array known as a Yagi array. It will be seen (Fig. 21.20) that only one element is excited; the others are parasitic elements excited by the field of the driven element, which is usually a half wave dipode. The single rear reflector is made slightly longer, while the other elements are made slightly shorter than the driven element. The Yagi array produces one main lobe of radiation along the bisector of the element and forward from the reflector. The front elements are referred to as directors and the directivity of the array depends on the number used.

The micro-waves produced by ultra-high frequency sources behave in many respects like light waves, and it is possible to apply some of the principles of optics to u.h.f. radiation[3]. A simple example is the use of parabolic (and other forms) of reflector. The reader will know from elementary optics that a point light source placed at the focus of the parabolic mirror, produces a parallel beam of light. While the wavelength may not always be negligibly small compared with the reflector dimensions, as in the optical case, and some diffraction may occur, a high degree of directivity can be obtained. This may be enhanced by arranging conducting wires or strips, or a dielectric, in front of the excited element to form an electromagnetic lens system[4]. Alternatively dielectric rods[5] may be used as radiating elements in place of metallic conductors.

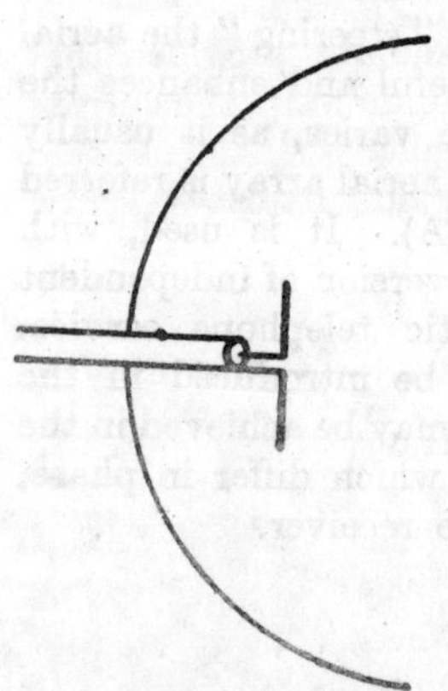

Fig. 21.21. Aerial with parabolic reflector.

The coupling of a u.h.f. transmitter to its aerial system is usually by means of a length of coaxial cable, or wave guide. In the latter case, the radiation may be produced by a dipole fed from a probe in the guide, or an array of such dipoles; alternatively, radiation may be arranged from the open end of the guide. Yet another scheme of radiation, for use with wave guides, consists of a slot (or slots) cut in the wall of the guides[6,7].

As an illustration of this idea, consider a narrow slot, cut in the centre of a large conducting sheet. If the slot is excited at its centre by a transmission line (Fig. 21.22), an electric field will be set up across the slot, having a maximum value at the centre and falling off at zero at the ends. Currents will also flow in the sheet.

It can be shown[8] that if the slot length is $\lambda/2$ it will act as a resonant aerial in a similar manner to a $\lambda/2$ dipole and indeed this is only one example of equivalence between slots in conducting sheets and insulated wires. A comparison of the fields produced by the slot and wire aerials shows that the polar diagrams are the same, but the directions of vibration of the electric and magnetic fields are interchanged, i.e. the slot aerial produces radiation which is polarised at right angles to that of the wire aerial.

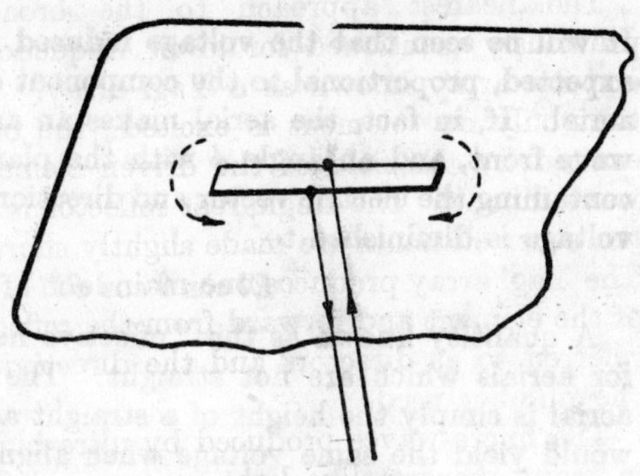

Fig. 21.22.

If the slot is excited by a wave guide it will radiate, provided that it lies across the line of current flow in the wave guide wall ; the current distribution in the presence of the slot is then similar to that indicated in Fig. 21.22. Several slots may be cut in a wave guide to form an array.

RECEIVING AERIALS

(a) Simple Vertical Aerial

The function of a receiving aerial is to abstract power from the electromagnetic field radiated by the distant source. The total power abstracted is that dissipated in the equivalent aerial circuit ; this consists of the power usefully employed by the receiver, together with the power dissipated in the equivalent loss resistance of the aerial, and the re-radiated power. The last quantity is present because the voltage induced by the incident field causes current to flow in the aerial and this gives rise to a local re-radiation of power.

Suppose for the sake of simplicity, that the aerial consists of a short length of thin vertical wire, and that the incident field is vertically polarised, i.e. the electric vector E is vertical. Then, if the height of the aerial is l metres, and E is expressed in volts/metre, the voltage induced in the aerial is

$$El \text{ volts}$$

Alternatively, one can say that the aerial intercepts the magnetic field which moves perpendicularly to it with a velocity c. The magnetic field has a flux density of $\mu_0 H$ so that the voltage induced in the aerial, when calculated in this fashion is

$$(\mu_0 H)lc \text{ volts}$$

This of course gives the same value as that obtained previously as, $c = 1/\sqrt{\mu_0 k_0}$ and $E/H = \sqrt{\mu_0/k_0}$, and therefore $\mu_0 Hlc = El$

It will be seen that the voltage induced in the aerial is, as would be expected, proportional to the component of the electric field along the aerial. If, in fact, the aerial makes an angle θ with the plane of the wave front, and an angle ϕ with the plane of polarisation (the plane containing the electric vector and direction of propagation) the induced voltage is diminished to

$$El \cos\theta \cos\phi$$

A quantity known as the "effective height", h, is sometimes used for aerials which are not straight. The effective height of such an aerial is simply the height of a straight aerial in the same field which would yield the same voltage when aligned parallel with the electric vector.

The resultant voltage which acts in a practical aerial circuit is the vector sum of the separate voltages induced in each element of its length. The aerial system of Fig. 21.23a may thus be represented by an equivalent generator of e.m.f. E and internal impedance Z_a (Fig. 21.23b), where E is the resultant voltage obtained from the aerial, and Z_a is its impedance at the terminals ab viewed from the receiver. The current in the equivalent circuit is thus

$$E/(Z_a + Z_i)$$

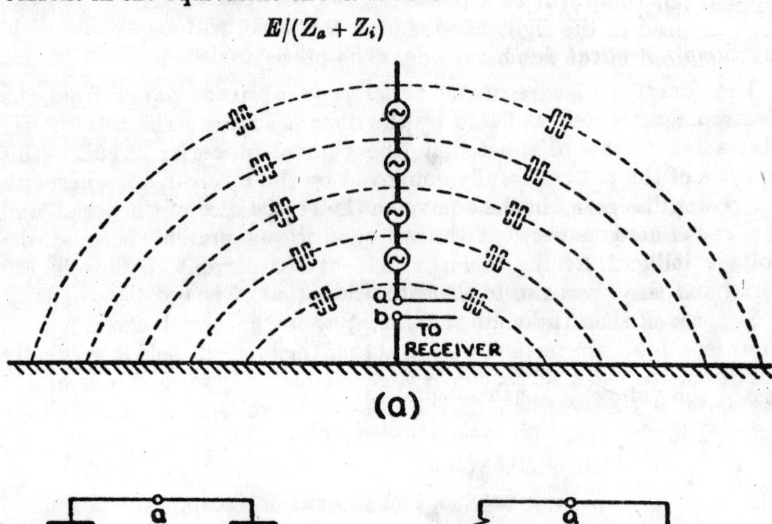

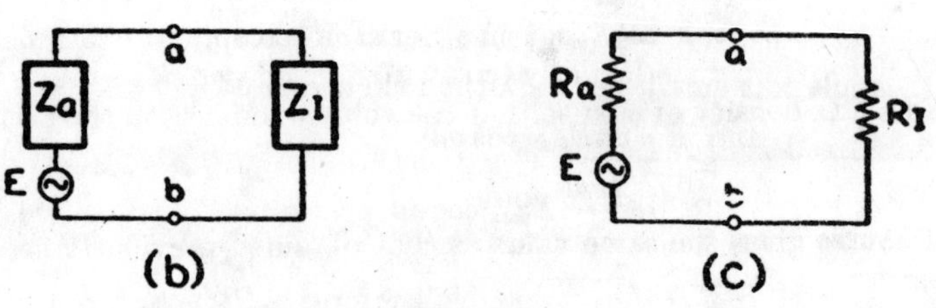

Fig. 21.23.

where Z_i is the input impedance of the receiver viewed from the aerial.

If the receiver input is arranged so that Z_i is the conjugate impedance of Z_a, then the equivalent circuit may be simplified to that of Fig. 21.23c, in which R_a the total resistance of the aerial, is equal to R_i which is the resistive component of the receiver input impedance. The total power absorbed by the aerial is then

$$E^2/2R_i$$

The useful power, as far as the receiver is concerned is half this quantity, i.e.

$$E^2/4R_i \text{ watts}$$

If, as is normally true, the series conductor and insulation loss of the aerial is negligibly small, the aerial resistance is then equal to its radiation resistance.

(b) Loop Aerial

Another form of simple receiving aerial is the loop aerial. If the loop is assumed to be normal to the wave front then a vertically polarised wave, advancing as shown in Fig. 21.24a, will induce voltages in the sides of the loop; the magnitudes of the induced voltages will be equal but there will be a phase angle α between them, as the voltage E_2 induced in the right hand side in this case, will lag on the voltage E_1 induced in the left hand side. The phase angle α is given by

$$\alpha : 2\pi :: d : \lambda$$

$$\text{or } \alpha = \frac{2\pi d}{\lambda}$$

It will be seen that the net voltage E at the terminals of the loop is the difference between the voltages E_1 and E_2 induced in the two sides. (Fig. 21.24c.)

If at any point the electric field is expressed as the quantity $E_{max} \sin \omega t$ then the voltage E_1 is equal to

$$hE_{max} \sin \omega t$$

and the voltage E_2 is thus equal to

$$hE_{max} \sin (\omega t - \alpha)$$

$$\text{Then } E = E_1 - E_2$$

$$= hE_{max} \{\sin \omega t - \sin \omega t \cos \alpha + \cos \omega t \sin \alpha\}$$

If the angle α is small, i.e. $d \ll \lambda$ then $\sin \alpha = \alpha$ and $\cos \alpha = 1$

$$\text{and } E = \alpha h E_{max} \cos \omega t$$

$$= \frac{2\pi dh}{\lambda} E_{max} \cos \omega t$$

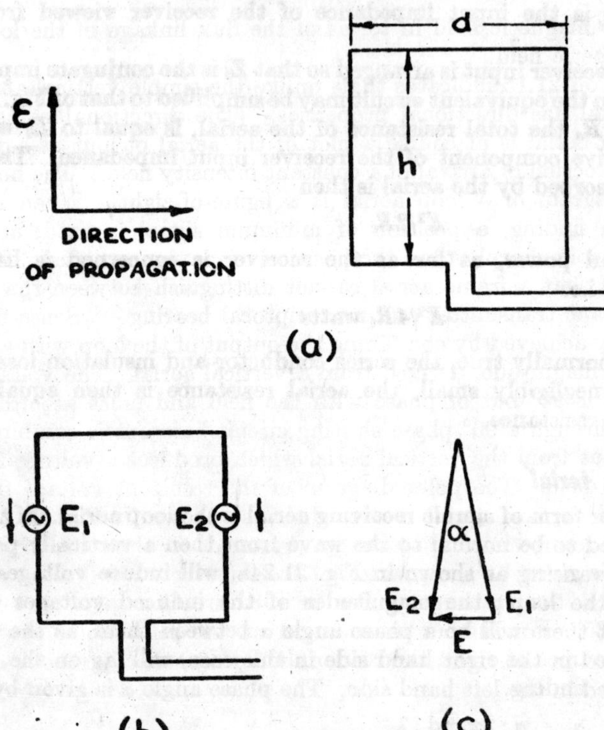

Fig. 21.24.

If the loop is turned through 90° so that the plane of the loop is parallel to the wavefront, the phase angle α is zero and the output from the loop is thus also zero. For an intermediate position when the plane of the loop is at angle θ to the normal to the wave front, the voltage delivered by the loop is then

$$e = \frac{2\pi A}{\lambda} E_{max} \cos \omega t \cos \theta$$

where $A = hd$ is the area of the loop. If the loop has N turns the output voltage is increased N times and the r.m.s. value of the output voltage V is thus given by

$$V = \frac{2\pi EAN}{\lambda} \cos \theta \quad . \quad . \quad . \quad . \quad . \quad 21.15$$

where E is the r.m.s. value of the electric field strength. It is left as an exercise for the reader to show that this value could be deduced from the magnetic field in terms of the flux linkage of the loop with the magnetic field.

Equation 21.15 indicates that, unlike the simple vertical aerial, the loop aerial has directional properties. (The directional pattern of a receiving aerial is of course a plot of the aerial output as a function of the direction of arrival of a constant intensity field.) The horizontal polar diagram of a loop aerial is a figure-of-eight. When used for direction finding, a position of minimum signal is used, as this is defined more sharply than the position of maximum signal. It should be noted that a frame aerial cannot distinguish between the bearing of a distant transmitter and its reciprocal bearing. "Sense-finding" is usually achieved by combining the output of the loop with a voltage of equal magnitude, derived from a vertical aerial. The voltage from the loop is 90° out of phase with the field and must accordingly be passed through a 90° phase shifting circuit before it is combined with the output from the vertical aerial which produces a voltage in phase with the field. The polar diagram of the resultant voltage from the loop and vertical aerial is a cardioid, as shown in Fig. 21.25. The receiver connections are usually arranged so that the transmitter bearing is given by the position of the receiver which gives maximum signal, i.e. the transmitter lies in the direction y, as indicated in Fig. 21.25. For further information on the refinements required to reduce sources of error, the reader should consult a textbook on radio direction finding.

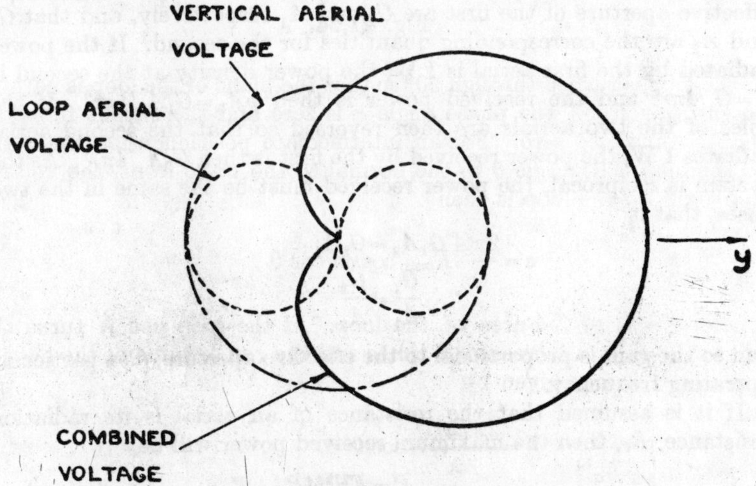

Fig. 21.25. Horizontal polar diagram for a loop and vertical aerial.

The radiation resistance of the loop aerial is relatively low, and such aerials are not used for transmission.

(c) Other Receiving Aerials

The various other types of aerial previously mentioned have been considered from the transmitting point of view. They may also be used for reception. It is unnecessary however to consider them afresh as the reciprocity theorem, mentioned in chapter 2, may be invoked to show that the directional pattern and impedance at a particular pair of terminals of a receiving aerial are unchanged when the aerial is used for transmission.

THE EFFECTIVE APERTURE OF AN AERIAL

The concept of the effective area or *effective aperture* of an aerial is often useful. The effective aperture is defined as the area over which the aerial collects radiation. Hence if the receiving aerial collects a power of P watts from an incident plane wave having a power density of p watts per square metre, the effective aperture of the aerial is $A = P/p$ square metres.

The concept of power gain, G, can be applied to receiving and transmitting aerials and is related to the effective aperture A.

Suppose two very short dipoles are set up in free space, at a distance r apart, and act as a radio link. Assume that the power gain and effective aperture of the first are G_1 and A_1 respectively, and that G_2 and A_2 are the corresponding quantities for the second. If the power radiated by the first aerial is 1 W, the power density at the second is $p = G_1/4\pi r^2$ and the received power is then $pA_2 = G_1A_2/4\pi r^2$. If the roles of the two aerials are then reversed so that the second aerial radiates 1 W, the power received by the first is then $G_2A_1/4\pi r^2$. As the system is reciprocal, the power received must be the same in the two cases, that is

$$G_1A_2 = G_2A_1$$

$$\therefore \quad \frac{G_1}{A_1} = \frac{G_2}{A_2}$$

and so the gain is proportional to the effective aperture, at a particular operating frequency.

If it is assumed that the resistance of an aerial is its radiation resistance, R_r, then the maximum received power will be

$$P = E^2l^2/4R_r$$

where E is the r.m.s. value of the received field strength in volts per metre and l is the aerial length. For a very short dipole it was shown (equation 21.7) that the radiation resistance is $80\pi^2 l^2/\lambda^2$ ohms and so the maximum received power is

$$P = E^2\lambda^2/320\pi^2 \text{ watts}$$

The power density in the wave is by equation 21.4a equal to

$$E^2/120\pi$$

Hence the effective aperture is

$$A = \frac{E^2\lambda^2}{320\pi^2} \cdot \frac{120\pi}{E^2} = 3\lambda^2/8\pi$$

The power gain G for the very short dipole was previously shown to be equal to 1·5. It thus follows that

$$G/A = 1{\cdot}5 \,.\, 8\pi/3\lambda^2 = 4\pi/\lambda^2 \quad . \quad . \quad 21.16$$

This result is important as it can be applied to any aerial or system of aerials.

RADIO TRANSMISSION LOSS IN FREE SPACE

For the system of two very short dipoles spaced a distance r apart the ratio of the received power P_r, to the transmitter power P_t is

$$\frac{P_r}{P_t} = \frac{G_1 A_2}{4\pi r^2}$$

and by applying the result of equation 21.16, this may be written as

$$\frac{P_r}{P_t} = \frac{G_1 G_2 \lambda^2}{16\pi^2 r^2} = \frac{A_1 A_2}{\lambda^2 r^2} \quad . \quad . \quad 21.17$$

Hence the transmission loss in a free space radio link of length such that the wave front at the receiver is plane, is given by

$$\text{Loss} = 10 \log_{10}\left[\frac{16\pi^2 r^2}{G_1 G_2 \lambda^2}\right] \text{ dB} \quad . \quad 21.18$$

where G_1 and G_2 are the power gains of the transmitting and receiving aerials. This, of course, assumes a loss-free medium. At microwave frequencies the loss will be greater because of atmospheric absorption.

THE PROPAGATION OF RADIO WAVES

If a transmitting aerial could be set up in free space, i.e. in an unbounded, uniform, and loss-free dielectric of permeability μ_0 and permittivity k_0, then at large distances from this aerial the electric (E) and magnetic (H) components of the wave would form, with the direction of travel, a right-handed system of axes, while the amplitudes of E and H would diminish inversely as the distance from the aerial. Practical transmitting aerials are not in free space, and the radiation produced by them is affected by the presence of the earth and its atmosphere.

The remainder of the present chapter is concerned with a brief discussion of the factors which affect the transmission of radio waves between the transmitter and receiver. For convenience it will be assumed that the waves travel as rays.

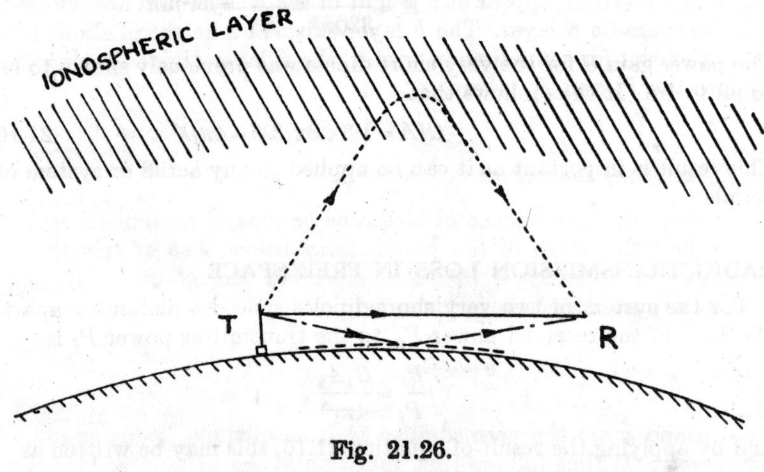

Fig. 21.26.

The energy radiated by an aerial may be divided into sky waves and ground waves (Fig. 21.26). Ground waves remain fairly near the surface of the earth, and are sometimes sub-divided into direct waves which travel in a straight path between the transmitter and receiver, earth-reflected waves which are reflected at the earth's surface, and surface waves which hug the surface of the earth. The sky wave is of interest in that it may be reflected or refracted, by partially conducting layers in the upper atmosphere.

THE IONOSPHERE

It has been found that in the upper atmosphere of the earth the constituent rarefied gases are in a state of ionisation, mainly as a result of ultraviolet radiation from the sun. This ionised atmosphere, extending upwards from heights of about 50 kilometres, is termed the ionosphere. While a state of ionisation exists throughout the whole region, the effect is most marked at particular heights ; these heights of maximum ionisation density are referred to as "layers". The lowest of all, and the most unstable, is the *D* layer, which is found only in the daytime. Because the density of air is relatively large compared with that at higher levels, recombination of the ionised particles occurs fairly rapidly and there is no significant ionisation at night. The next highest layer is the E layer at a height somewhere between 100 and 150 km. Here, the maximum ionisation density is fairly constant throughout the day, but recombination takes place at night and the layer may then almost disappear. Patches, or clouds of abnormal ionisation, appear at a height of the E layer and are referred to as the sporadic E layer. The F layer exists at a height of about 300 km, but except for some time in winter, the F layer divides during the day into the F_1 and F_2 layers.

The Effect of the Ionosphere

One effect of the presence of electrons or ions in an ionised region is to reduce the value of the permittivity below that of free space. It is shown in Appendix H that the velocity of propagation of a plane wave in a pure dielectric is given by

$$v = \frac{1}{\sqrt{\mu k}}$$

where μ and k are the permeability and permittivity of the medium respectively. It thus follows that variation in the value of k produces a variation in the phase velocity, and if the value of k is less than the free space value k_0, the phase velocity of a wave in such a medium must exceed c, the velocity of light. This effect can cause refraction and may be considered as follows.

Suppose that the effect of collisions between electrons is ignored. The ionised region may then be assumed to have N free electrons, each of charge e and mass m, per cubic metre. If this region is traversed by an electromagnetic wave which has an electric field $E \sin \omega t$, the force on an electron is $Ee \sin \omega t$. If v is the average electron velocity in the direction of the electric field, then

$$m\frac{dv}{dt} = Ee \sin \omega t$$

$$\text{and } v = -\frac{Ee}{\omega m} \cos \omega t$$

This corresponds to a current

$$Nev = -\frac{Ne^2E}{\omega m} \cos \omega t$$

and this lags on the applied electric field by 90°.

In free space the displacement current produced by the field $E \sin \omega t$ would be

$$k_0 \frac{d}{dt}(E \sin \omega t) = \omega k_0 E \cos \omega t$$

The total current density in the ionised region thus has the value

$$\omega E \cos \omega t \left[k_0 - \frac{Ne^2}{\omega^2 m} \right]$$

and the permittivity of the ionised space is thus equivalent to

$$k = k_0 \left(1 - \frac{Ne^2}{\omega^2 m k_0} \right)$$

Substitution of the values, $e = 1{\cdot}6 \times 10^{-19}$ coulomb and $m = 0{\cdot}91 \times 10^{-30}$ kg gives

$$k = k_0 \left(1 - \frac{81N}{f^2} \right) \quad . \quad . \quad . \quad . \quad 21.19$$

Suppose now that an electromagnetic wave enters an ionised region from the unionised atmosphere. If the change in electron density is small, the change in phase velocity will be small and the incident wave will undergo refraction in the same way as a ray of light which passes from one medium to another of different refractive index. Snell's law of refraction states in effect that if v_{P_1} and v_{P_2} are the phase velocities in the two media then the index of refraction n is given by

$$n = \frac{\sin \phi_i}{\sin \phi_r} = \frac{v_{P_1}}{v_{P_2}}$$

where the angles ϕ_i and ϕ_r are as shown in Fig. 21.27. If in fact the wave passes from free space into an ionised region, the index of refraction between the two media is

$$n = \sqrt{\frac{k_2}{k_1}} = \sqrt{\frac{k_0 \left(1 - \dfrac{81N}{f_2} \right)}{k_0}}$$

$$= \sqrt{1 - \frac{81N}{f^2}} \quad . \quad 21.20$$

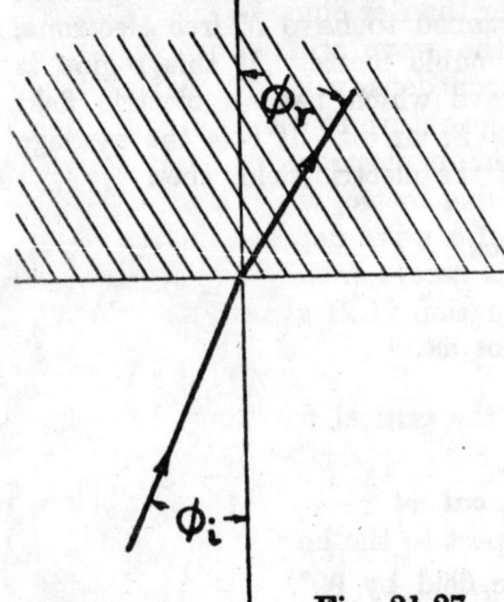

Fig. 21.27.

If the electron density N increases, the wave will travel along a curved path, and if the refraction is sufficient, will ultimately be directed out of the ionised layer back to earth (Fig. 21.28a).

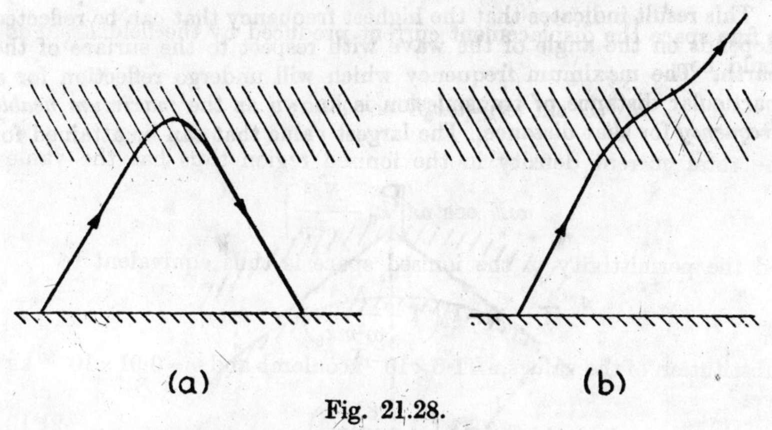

Fig. 21.28.

Critical and Maximum Usable Frequencies

If the electron density in the ionised region increases with height above the earth's surface then the amount of refraction increases; when the index of refraction n has decreased so that

$$\sin \phi_i = n$$

then the angle of refraction ϕ_r will be 90° and the wave will then be travelling parallel to the surface of the earth. The highest point attained by the wave will thus correspond to a height at which the electron density has a value which satisfies the relation

$$\sqrt{1 - \frac{81N_1}{f^2}} = \sin \phi_i \quad . \quad . \quad . \quad . \quad . \quad 21.21$$

Hence if the electron density is greater than or equal to the value N_1 as determined by equation 21.21, the wave will return to earth (Fig. 21.28a). If the maximum electron density is less than N_1 the wave will pass through the layer and not return to earth (Fig. 21.28b).

Equation 21.21 indica es if the maximum electron density in a given layer is fixed at N_{max} electrons per cubic metre, the critical limiting frequency f_c for the return to earth of a wave depends on the angle of incidence to the layer. When ϕ_i is zero, i.e. the wave is directed vertically upwards from the earth, equation 21.21 gives f_c as

$$f_c = 9\sqrt{N_{max}} \quad . \quad . \quad . \quad . \quad . \quad 21.22$$

For any other angle to the vertical, the critical frequency is higher and is given by

$$f = 9\sqrt{N_{max}} \sec \phi_i$$

If α is the angle of the wave with respect to the horizontal, then

$$f = 9\sqrt{N_{max}} \operatorname{cosec} \alpha \quad . \quad . \quad . \quad . \quad 21.23$$

This result indicates that the highest frequency that can be reflected depends on the angle of the wave with respect to the surface of the earth. The maximum frequency which will undergo reflection for a particular distance of transmission is known as the *maximum usable frequency* for that distance. The largest value that can be attained for

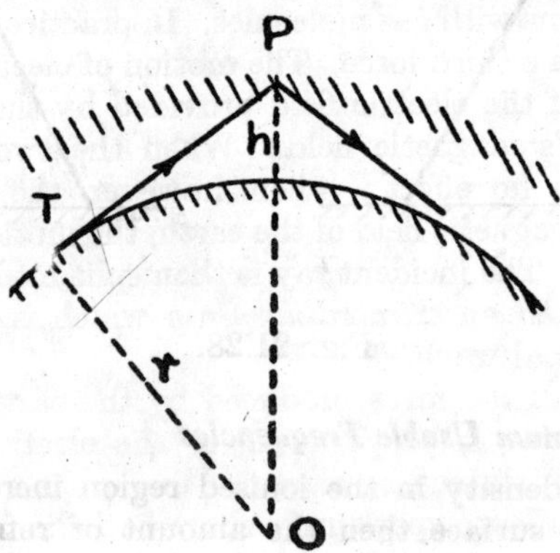

Fig. 21.29.

the angle of incidence, ϕ_i, on the layer is achieved when the wave direction is tangential to the surface of the earth. Neglecting the curvature of the earth, the angle of incidence may be taken as $\sin^{-1} TO/OP$ (Fig. 21.29) or $\sin \phi_i = r/(r+h)$ where r is the radius of the earth and h is the height of the layer above the earth's surface.

Conductivity of an Ionised Layer

It has been shown (equation 21.19) that free electrons in an ionised layer cause the permittivity to be less than the free space value. In practice, the electrons set in motion by the electric field of the passing wave collide with gas molecules and thereby dissipate the kinetic energy which they have acquired from the wave. The effect of collisions thus gives rise to a retarding or damping force on the electrons, and as a consequence the total current produced by the wave has a conduction component, which is in phase with the electric field. This component of current is responsible for the absorption of energy from the wave which then suffers attenuation in its passage through the ionised layer. For purposes of calculation therefore the ionised medium may be regarded as a dielectric with losses, i.e. as a charge-free dielectric with a finite value of conductivity, and a permittivity as expressed by equation 21.19.

The Effect of the Earth's Magnetic Field

So far it has been suggested that there are two forces which act on an electron in an ionised region traversed by an electromagnetic wave. The oscillatory electric field of the wave produces corresponding electron motion, modified to some extent by the damping force which arises from collisions with gas molecules. In practice the magnetic field of the earth acts as a third force. The motion of electrons thus depends on the direction of the electric field provided by the wave relative to that of the earth's magnetic field. When the two are aligned, the magnetic field has no effect; when however the electric vector is transverse to the magnetic field of the earth, the motion of the electrons becomes elliptical. The incident ray is then split into two components, an *ordinary ray* and an *extraordinary ray* which is polarised at right angles to the original wave.[9,10]

The magnitude of the force produced by the earth's magnetic field on a moving electron is proportional to the electron velocity. The maximum velocity attained by electrons under the action of very high frequency waves (of correspondingly short periodic time) is small, and so the earth's magnetic field has little effect at such frequencies. At lower frequencies, the correspondingly longer periodic time of the electric field causes the electrons to attain a greater velocity; the effect of the magnetic field is then increased and the electrons move in elliptic paths; the larger electron velocity gives rise to an increase in the number of collisions and hence of losses. This effect exhibits resonance characteristics and has a resonant, or *gyro-frequency* which is proportional to the ratio of charge to mass of the particle and to the strength of the magnetic field. It can be shown that for a magnetic field strength of $0{\cdot}5 \times 10^{-4}$ T (webers per square metre) the resonance frequency for electrons is approximately 1,400 kHz. At lower frequencies the magnetic field restricts the amplitude of electron motion. This reduces the collisions and causes a relative decrease in the attenuation of the wave.

The mass of any ion is very much greater than that of an electron and the gyro-frequency for such particles falls below any frequency used for radio transmission. The disturbing effect of the earth's magnetic field thus need only be considered in respect of its effect on electrons.

REFLECTION AND REFRACTION OF WAVES IN IONISED LAYERS

It may be as well to emphasise at this stage that ionised layers produce reflection as well as refraction of radio waves. In fact, reflection or refraction or both may take place, depending on the mean ionic density of the layer, the frequency in use, and the angle of incidence.

When conditions are such that the electron and ionic density changes abruptly within the distance of a wavelength, the ionised layer behaves as a reflecting surface, which reflects the incident wave with small loss ; this state of affairs occurs most easily at low frequencies. At higher frequencies, the change in ionisation density is gradual over the shorter wavelength, and refraction occurs, together with some reflection.

Depending on the frequency in use, this wave will undergo either partial refraction with some reflection, or else complete internal reflection in the layer ; in the former case the wave will pass on to higher layers and ultimately into space if the highest layer does not produce sufficient refraction to return the wave to earth.

FACTORS AFFECTING THE PROPAGATION OF RADIO WAVES[11]

The preceding pages have indicated that the ionosphere reflects and refracts radio waves, with a varying degree of attenuation and changes in polarisation. Ground waves are affected by the presence of the earth and suffer varying amounts of attenuation according to the nature and conductivity of the earth's surface ; sky waves reflected from the ionosphere undergo further reflection at the surface of the earth. Conditions in the ionosphere and at the earth's surface are the main factors which influence the propagation of radio waves. Their effect depends to a very large extent on the frequency employed,[12] and can best be summarised with other subsidiary factors by sub-dividing the radio frequency spectrum into a number of frequency ranges, in the manner employed for the discussion of the various types of aerial.

(a) Long Waves

The long, or low-frequency waveband includes transmissions of wavelength greater than 600 metres. As the longest wavelength in use is approximately 20,000 metres, the frequency range extends from 15–500 kHz. At these frequencies the ground wave is propagated with relatively small attenuation, and predominates over the sky wave for distances of several hundred kilometres from the transmitter ; the earth and *E* layer act as conducting surfaces which produce reflection with low absorption, and may be considered to form a sort of spherical wave guide. This is particularly true for the longer wavelengths, generally those greater than 3,000 metres. On such wavelengths, the sky wave is reflected from the lower edge of the *E* layer and the ionospheric absorption is very small. Transmission on these wavelengths provides a reliable means of communication over very great distances.

(b) Medium Waves

This designation may be considered to apply to wavelengths between 600 and 150 metres. The propagation characteristics change gradually from those of low-frequency waves, then differ markedly as the gyro-resonant frequency is approached. Generally, some penetration of the ionosphere occurs and the losses are relatively large, with the result that the sky waves returning to earth from the *E* layer during the day are greatly attenuated. Daytime transmission is restricted to the radial distance covered by the ground wave. This has a shorter range than that of the low-frequency waves on account of the higher ground wave attenuation, which increases with frequency. Consequently, medium waves only give reliable communication over a limited range and are employed for fairly short range services, notably local broadcasting.

At night, a certain amount of ionospheric reflection occurs. On the fringes of the service area the reflected sky wave may have an amplitude comparable with that of the ground wave. When this condition obtains, considerable interference is caused, and the received signal fades and may be distorted.

(c) Short Waves

The term " short wave " is generally applied to wavelengths between 10 and 100 metres, i.e. to transmissions with a frequency between 3 and 30 MHz. In this range the high attenuation of the ground wave causes it to disappear at relatively small distances from the transmitter. Distant transmission on these wavelengths is thus in terms of the sky wave, and is subject to variations due to daily and seasonal changes in ionospheric conditions. Short waves generally penetrate the *E* layer and pass to one of the *F* layers where they undergo refraction if the frequency is less than the critical value for the particular angle of incidence on the layer. For any given frequency there is a minimum distance from the transmitter (along the surface of the earth) at which the reflected wave is first received. There may thus be an area round the transmitter, beyond the limits of the ground wave, in which there are no reflected waves. Such an area is not served by any of the radiations from the transmitter and is called the ***skip-zone*** ; the radial distance across it is referred to as the ***skip distance*** (Fig. 21.30) As the skip distance is decided by the amount of refraction which occurs in the layer it depends on the state of ionisation and the frequency, and is independent of the transmitter power.

Within the short-wave band ionospheric absorption decreases with frequency, and so the frequencies employed for transmission are kept fairly near the maximum usable frequencies for the particular conditions which prevail.

(d) Ultra-Short Waves

The sky wave, from a transmitter operating on a wavelength shorter than about 10 metres, is not returned to earth by the ionosphere,

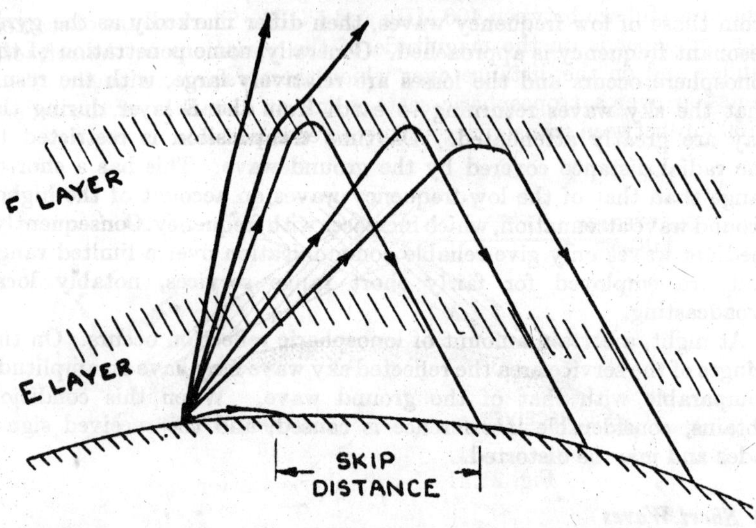

Fig. 21.30.

except under anomalous conditions, and passes out into space. The surface component of the ground wave is rapidly attenuated, and communication takes place in terms of a direct wave from transmitter to receiver. Metric and centimetric radio wave propagation thus has a line-of-sight limitation. Transmission beyond the optical horizon is possible however due to atmospheric refraction and diffraction. In the lower part of the earth's atmosphere, called the troposphere, the temperature and density of the air generally decrease with increasing height, and the permittivity decreases correspondingly. Hence, the radio waves in effect travel slightly faster in the upper atmosphere than they do closer to the surface of the earth ; the result is slight curvature in the propagation path and a consequent increase in the distance of the effective horizon.

SCATTER PROPAGATION

Propagation of radio waves having frequencies greater than 30 MHz is obtained over relatively long distances, i.e. very much greater than indicated above. This arises because the troposphere and the ionosphere are in a continual state of turbulence. This produces local variations in the refractive index of the atmosphere, and causes scattering of radio waves passing through such turbulent regions.

Tropospheric Scattering.[13] Scattering of the energy in a radio wave occurs in the troposphere for a wide range of frequencies of which the most useful are between 400 MHz and 5 GHz. The amount of scattered power depends on the magnitude of the variations in the refractive index and on the distance over which these variations occur. Transmission over a tropospheric scatter link at distances of the order of 750 km between transmitter and receiver is possible.

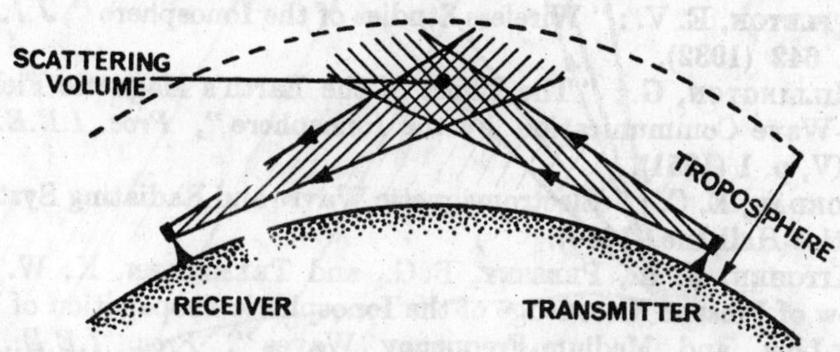

Fig. 21.31. Tropospheric scatter.

The field strength at the receiving end of a scatter radio link indicated in Fig. 21.31, is subject to rapid fading which arises from multipath transmission delay. Slow variations in the received signal level also occur due to variations in the average refraction of the atmosphere. The signal level is, in general, lower than would be obtained over a direct link of corresponding length in free space.

Ionospheric Scattering.[14, 15] Scatter propagation occurs as a result of changes in the ionisation density in the E layer of the ionosphere. The useful frequency range for an ionospheric scatter system is from about 30 to 70 MHz, while the maximum range of such a system is a ground distance of about 2000 km. Random changes in the received signal level occur as in the tropospheric system.

References

[1] Skilling, H. H.: *Fundamentals of Electric Waves* (John Wiley & Sons Inc., 1948).

[2] Ballantine, S.: "On the Optimum Transmitting Wavelength for a Vertical Antenna over a Perfect Earth", *Proc. I.R.E.*, 12, p. 833, (1924).

[3] Ashmead, J., and Pippard, A. B.: "The Use of Spherical Reflectors as Microwave Scanning Aerials", *J.I.E.E.*, 93, Part IIIA, p. 627 (1947).

[4] Kock, W. E.: "Metal-Lens Antennas", *Proc. I.R.E.*, 34, p. 828 (1946).

[5] Halliday, D. F., and Kiely, D. G.: "Dielectric-Rod Aerials", *J.I.E.E.*, 94, Part IIIA, p. 610 (1947).

[6] BAILEY, C. E. G.: "Slot Feeders and Slot Aerials", *J.I.E.E.*, 93, Part IIIA, p. 615 (1946).

[7] WATSON, W. H.: "Resonant Slots", *J.I.E.E.*, 93, Part IIIA, p. 747 (1946).

[8] BOOKER, H. G.: "Slot Aerials and their Relation to Complementary Wire Aerials", *J.I.E.E.*, 93, Part IIIA, p. 620 (1946).

[9] APPLETON, E. V.: "Wireless Studies of the Ionosphere", *J.I.E.E.*, 71, p. 642 (1932).

[10] MILLINGTON, G.: "The Effect of the Earth's Magnetic Field on Short-Wave Communication by the Ionosphere", *Proc. I.E.E.*, 98, Part IV, p. 1 (1951).

[11] JORDAN, E. C.: "Electromagnetic Waves and Radiating Systems" (Prentice-Hall Inc., 1950).

[12] KITCHEN, F. A., PRESSEY, B. G., and TREMELLEN, K. W.: "A Review of Present Knowledge of the Ionospheric Propagation of Very-Low, Low, and Medium-Frequency Waves", *Proc. I.E.E.*, 100, Part III, p. 100 (1953).

[13] BULLINGTON, K.: "Characteristics of Beyond-the-Horizon Radio Transmission", *Proc. I.R.E.*, 43, p. 1175 (1955).

[14] BAILEY, P. K., BATEMAN, R., and KIRBY, R. C.: "Radio Transmission at V.H.F. by Scattering and Other Processes in the Lower Ionosphere", *Proc. I.R.E.* 43, p. 1181 (1955).

[15] BRAY, W. J., SAXTON, J. A., WHITE, R. W., and LUSCOMBE, G. W.: "V.H.F. Propagation by Ionospheric Scattering and its Application to Long Distance Communication", *Proc. I.E.E.*, 103, Part B, p. 236 (1956).

References for Further Reading

MOULLIN, E. B.: *Radio Aerials* (Oxford University Press, 1949).

SCHELKUNOFF, S. A., and FRIIS H. T.: *Antennas* (John Wiley & Sons, Inc., 1952).

KELSO, J. M.: *Radio Ray Propagation in the Ionosphere* (McGraw Hill, 1964).

EXAMPLES

1. Show, from the basic equations of electricity and magnetism that electromagnetic waves can be propagated through free space, and explain what is meant by the terms wave front and polarization. Derive expressions for the velocity of propagation and for the relationship between the magnetic and electric field strengths. State the unit of measurement assumed for each of the quantities appearing in the derived expressions.

L.U. Ext. Telecomm. 1952.

2. Write a brief account of the nature of electromagnetic waves, their production from aerial currents, their propagation round the earth, and their reception by ordinary and by frame aerials.

L.U. Int. Telecomm. 1950.

3. Explain what is meant by the radiation resistance of an aerial. Enumerate the various factors contributing to the total resistance and explain how they can be measured.

L.U. Int. Telecomm. 1955.

4. A transmitting aerial consists of two vertical elements spaced half a wavelength apart. The currents in each element are equal in magnitude, but differ in time phase by one-eighth of a cycle. Plot to scale the horizontal polar diagram in terms of the relative field intensity.

L.U. Int. Telecomm. 1951

5 Why, and in what way, does the radiation polar diagram of a vertical mast radiator of height approximately one half wavelength differ from that of a very short vertical antenna ? In what circumstances is the former diagram the more desirable ?

L.U. Ext. Telecomm. 1949.

6. Derive an expression giving the relative intensity, in the equatorial plan, of the radiated field produced by two short vertical aerials having their mid-points in the plane. Explain, with relation to this expression, the effect of the spacing of the aerials and of the phase difference between the currents. Sketch polar diagrams for typical cases.

I.E.E Radio Comm. October, 1947.

7. Describe the principle of direction-finding by means of a closed-loop frame aerial, and derive the expression for the induced e.m.f. on which the method depends. What means can be adopted for resolving the " sense " ambiguity of 180° implicity in a closed loop direction finder ?

L.U. Ext. Telecomm. 1951.

8. For a plane electromagnetic wave in air, the electric field strength is 10 millivolts per metre. Calculate the rate of transmission of energy per square metre A square frame aerial of 1 metre side and having four turns is placed with its plane parallel to the common plane of the direction of advance of the wave and the direction of

the electric field, two of the sides being in the direction of the electric field. Derive an expression for the effective e.m.f. induced in the aerial and calculate its value if the wavelength is 300 metres.

L.U. Int. Telecomm. 1952.

9. Discuss the advantages and disadvantages of travelling-wave aerials.

An array consists of two identical rhombic aerials, spaced 100 m apart and in line with a distance transmitter. The aerials are connected to individual loss-free coaxial cables whose outputs are connected in series at the receiver. If the difference in length of the two cables is 100 m, determine the total voltage at the receiver when the transmitter produces a down-coming wave at an angle of 50 degrees to the horizontal and induces a voltage of 1 mV at 12 MHz in each aerial. Assume the relative permittivity of the dielectric of the coaxial cables to be unity. *L.U. Telecomm. Part III.* 1962.

10. Write a short account outlining the part played by the ionosphere in long-distance radio communication describing, in particular, what factors govern the selection of the operating frequency for a particular channel at a given time.

I.E.E. Radio Comm. October, 1946.

11. Why is the 3–30 MHz band of frequencies used for long-distance radio communication, and how is the most suitable frequency chosen in a particular case? Explain what is meant by "diversity reception" of signals in this band, and why it is often employed.

L.U. Ext. Telecomm. 1949.

12. World-wide radio communication is possible with very low frequencies (16 kHz for example) or high frequencies (such as 20 MHz). Write a simple account of the propagation phenomena in the two cases, and discuss the reasons which have led to the high frequencies being much more commonly used.

I.E.E. Radio Comm. October, 1948.

13. There are marked differences between the propagation characteristics of radio waves at the frequencies 200, 2,000, 20,000, and 200,000 kHz. Describe and account for these differences. What is meant by the maximum usable frequency of a high-frequency radio link? What factors control its value?

L.U. Ext. Telecomm. 1955.

14. Describe in general outline the equipment of a repeater station in a point-to-point relay chain carrying high-definition signals and operating at a wavelength of about 30 cm. Mention the considerations that would lead to the choice of such a wavelength, with particular reference to the propagation characteristics of 30-cm radiations, and to the types of valves and aerials that can be used at this wavelength.

L.U. Ext. Telecomm. 1951.

15. Explain the distinction between travelling-wave and standing-wave aerials and refer to an example of each type.

Eight co-planar vertical dipoles, with their centres at half-wavelength spacings along a horizontal line, carry currents which are equal in magnitude and phase. Derive an expression for the polar diagram in a horizontal plane in terms of the field strength, E, in this plane due to a single dipole. Hence calculate the angle between the two directions of zero radiation that include the main beam.

What would be the main defect of such an array when used for point-to-point operation? Explain how this could be remedied.

L.U. Telecomm. Part III. 1966.

16. A plane electromagnetic wave is propagated at a frequency of 10 MHz into an ionized but otherwise field-free medium. The electron density increases in the direction of propagation. The positive ions may be regarded as effectively immobile. Taking the electronic mass and charge to be 9×10^{-31} kg and $1{\cdot}6 \times 10^{-19}$ coulomb and the permittivity of free space to be $(1/36\pi) \times 10^{-9}$ farads/metre, determine the electron density at which the phase velocity of the wave tends to infinity and explain what happens physically at this point. Prove any formulae used.

L.U. Ext. Telecomm. 1954.

22

RADIO TRANSMISSION SYSTEMS

Radio transmission systems may be classified in several ways. One may attempt a classification in terms of the character of the information communicated. Such a classification then gives three broad types of system, namely radio-telephony for the transmission of speech and music, radio-telegraphy for telegraph signals and still pictures, and television for the transmission of moving pictures.

It is also convenient to classify radio systems into two groups, one concerned with "broadcasting", and the other with communication between two points. The technical differences between the two groups arise from the different requirements, and while fairly obvious, are worth noting.

BROADCASTING

The provision of information (and entertainment, etc.) for a large fraction of the general public is the basic feature of a radio broadcasting system. In the local form, in which the range does not generally exceed about 150 km, transmitters with fairly high power outputs (up to about 100 kW) are common, and the aerial system is usually omni-directional. The transmitters located in or near densely populated areas have to serve a very large number of receivers. The working field strength at the receiver usually varies somewhere between about 100 microvolts/metre in areas of weak field strength to about 100 millivolts/metre in areas close to the transmitter. Field strengths of such values make normal receiver noise insignificant, and straightforward amplitude modulation is employed. The receivers can thus be of simple design, relatively cheap, and easy to operate.

Frequency modulation at carrier frequencies of the order of 100 M is now used as an alternative for broadcast operation. The improve signal/noise ratio enables relatively low power transmitters to cover a large service area.

Long distance, as opposed to local broadcasting, is carried out between one country and another at frequencies from about 5 to 30 MHz. Such systems employ techniques intermediate between those

used in local broadcasting and those employed in point-to-point working.

POINT-TO-POINT WORKING

The communication networks of many military and civil organisations involve radio links between two points. Such radio systems differ from broadcasting in that two-way communication is usually employed. Another difference is that these radio links may be operated on some form of multi-channel basis, according to the volume of traffic handled. Again, point-to-point systems often employ privacy equipment which makes the information unintelligible when picked up by a receiver other than the one for which it is intended.

(1) ***Long Distance Operation Between Fixed Stations.*** In this case a two-way link comprises two transmitters and two receivers. They have highly directional aerial systems which are arranged to transmit and receive along the great circle path joining transmitter and receiver. The cost of the latter may be high and may approach that of the transmitter, particularly in the case of receivers which use multiple-unit steerable antennas ; an improved service is usually obtained by increasing the sensitivity of the receiver rather than increasing the power output of the transmitter. The receiver in such a system is

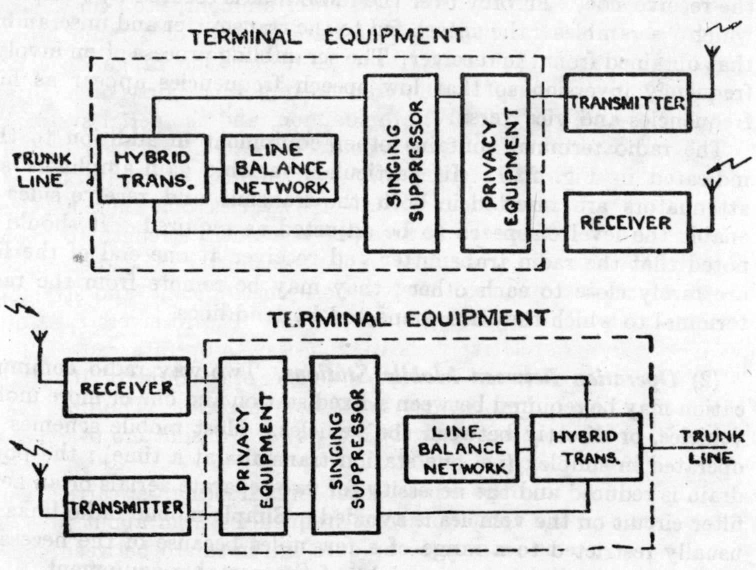

Fig. 22.1. Two-way radio-telephone link.

thus usually much more complex than its broadcast counterpart, and can give a satisfactory output for low values of received field strength, often less than one microvolt/metre. Single-sideband amplitude modulation, with reduced level of carrier on frequencies within the range of 4 – 30 MHz, is commonly employed on transoceanic services[1]; frequency or phase modulation is often used over shorter distances[2].

Fig. 22.1 shows, in block schematic form, a two-way radio-telephone link.

In effect, the two-wire trunk line is converted at the radio terminal, or trunk exchange, to what would correspond to a " four-wire circuit " in line practice. This is done by means of a hybrid transformer and line balancing network. Although speech can pass freely between the two-wire and " four-wire " circuits, the terminal equipment is such that speech signals cannot pass directly from the receiving to the transmitting sides of the radio circuit.

The radio terminal equipment normally includes some form of singing suppressor and privacy equipment. The purpose of the singing suppressor apparatus is to interrupt the receiving side of the radio circuit when the local subscriber is speaking and to interrupt the transmitting side when there is no local speech input. A time delay network is usually incorporated in the transmit path so that when the local subscriber speaks the network delays the speech until the suppressor has operated to give a through connection and has interrupted the receive side. Privacy over the radio link is secured by equipment which " scrambles " the speech fed to the transmitter and unscrambles that obtained from the receiver. The scrambling process often involves frequency inversion so that low speech frequencies appear as high frequencies and vice versa.

The radio terminal contains other equipment in addition to that indicated in Fig. 22.1. In particular, variable gain amplifiers and attenuators are inserted in both the transmit and receive sides to enable the level of speech to be adjusted as required. It should be noted that the radio transmitter and receiver at one end of the link are rarely close to each other; they may be remote from the radio terminal to which they are connected by land lines.

(2) ***Operation Between Mobile Stations.*** Two-way radio communication may be required between a fixed station and one or more mobile vehicles, or directly between the vehicles. Most mobile schemes are operated in simplex (i.e. one station transmits at a time); the power drain is reduced and the necessity for two separate aerials or an aerial filter circuit on the vehicles is avoided. Simple mobile radio links are usually restricted to a range of a few miles because of the necessary limitations on the size and weight of the portable equipment.

(3) ***Multiple-Link Relay Systems.*** Broadband radio systems now form part of the telephone trunk network in many countries. Ideally, the performance of a broadband radio link should be comparable with a coaxial cable system, so that both forms of transmission can be used as links in the trunk network[3]. It follows that the radio system must be designed to accept the same signal band as is used in cable systems. Multi-channel telephony is handled in terms of blocks of 60-channel " supergroups ", each of which has a bandwidth of 240 kHz. Television signals may be transmitted either in place of, or in addition to, telephone traffic.

When handling multi-channel telephony, frequency division multiplex in conjunction with frequency modulation is normally used. Frequency rather than amplitude modulation is preferred as it gives a better signal/noise ratio, also amplitude control of the received signal is easier when fading is present on the radio path. The actual bandwidth occupied by the frequency modulated carrier is larger than the signal bandwidth; 600 telephone channels may require a radio transmission band 15 to 20 MHz wide. Microwave carrier frequencies are used.

Frequency bands allocated for such systems in various parts of the world include 1·7–2·3 GHz, 3·6–4·2 GHz and 5·85–8·50 GHz. Long distance transmission involves a multi-link relay system as propagation of such frequencies is usually line-of-sight, the extreme range of a single link being about 50–100 km, depending on the frequency, the transmitted power and the location of the transmitting and receiving aerials.

The aerials in a microwave link are mounted on masts on high ground. The transmitter is connected by a waveguide feeder to the transmitting aerial, which consists of a metal paraboloid. This may vary from about 1 to 4 m in diameter. Typically, a 4 m diameter aerial used in the 1·7–2·3 GHz band has a gain of 35 dB and a half power beam width of 3°.

At repeater stations the incoming signal is amplified, changed in carrier frequency and retransmitted. Demodulation of the carrier to signal frequency is unnecessary. The retransmitted carrier frequency is altered from the original incoming value in order to avoid feedback to the input. While a frequency change of about 200 MHz may be used between successive links, the same carrier frequencies may be re-employed further along the route.

(4) ***Communication Satellite Systems.*** The most important advantages of satellite systems are: (a) they are able to span extreme distances over the Earth's surface and (b) as a consequence of the particular geometry of satellite links, a satellite repeater may be used simultaneously by a number of Earth stations, thereby enabling each of them to communicate with any of the others. Present objectives assume that

a satellite system should be capable of providing a thousand or more telephone channels and a television channel.

The radio transmitter carried by a satellite delivers only a few watts of signal power. As a result of the long transmission path involved the power level of the signal which reaches the receiver at the Earth station is very low, possibly 10^{-12} watt, or less. One of the main problems is to produce a satisfactory signal/noise ratio for this small signal against the inevitable background of radio noise. The principal sources of noise are three: namely, noise from the sky, thermal noise from the transmission losses in the aerial and feeders connecting it to the first stage amplifier and then the noise generated in the amplifier itself. Noise from the sky originates in radio sources from outer space and in the oxygen and water vapour present in the Earth's atmosphere. For frequencies below about 1 GHz noise from the star galaxy is the predominant source. Above about 10 GHz noise from absorption in the Earth's atmosphere becomes important. The optimum frequency range thus lies from about 2 to 8 GHz.

Noise produced by the losses in the waveguide coupling the focus of the aerial to the first stage amplifier arises from the thermal motion of electrons in the metallic walls of the waveguide which is consequently kept as short as possible.

Two types of low noise amplifier, suitable for the microwave spectrum, are available, namely the maser and the cooled parametric amplifier. The usual temperatures to which both devices must be cooled are in the range from about 77°K (the boiling point of liquid nitrogen) down to 2 or 3°K.

A number of different orbits have been proposed for satellite systems. Circular and elliptic orbits in the equatorial and polar planes of the Earth and elliptic orbits inclined to the equatorial plane are possible. A " synchronous " orbit in which the satellites move in the equatorial plane of the Earth at a height of 36,000 km causes the satellites to appear stationary to an observer on the Earth. Such an orbit has the advantage that with only three satellites, equally spaced, substantially world wide coverage may be achieved.

RADIO TRANSMITTERS

The various kinds of radio system indicate that radio transmitters (and receivers) are required in a diversity of types and sizes. A description of all the various types would fill not one book but several volumes, and so the present section is devoted to a general rather than detailed consideration and is limited to a very brief statement of a few of the elementary distinguishing features which apply to the common types of transmitter.

(a) *Amplitude-Modulated Radio-Telephony Transmitters*

The simplest form of a valve operated telephony transmitter is a single self-oscillating valve, subject to anode choke modulation as described in chapter 13. Such an arrangement does not produce a stable frequency and its use is limited to emergency mobile transmitters of low power. The general form of an amplitude-modulated transmitter capable of a larger power output is shown schematically in Fig. 22.2a.

The carrier is generated by a crystal oscillator operating at a low power level. The output is then fed into a buffer amplifier and a chain of radio frequency amplifier stages to produce the appropriate power output. This chain may involve frequency multiplication, so that the radiated carrier is a multiple of that generated initially. The last amplifier stage is modulated by the speech from the modulating amplifier in the way described in chapter 13, or by some other form of modulation circuit. The modulating amplifier is normally a push-pull stage operating under class B conditions. The required modulated output is then fed to the aerial via a matching network. Modulation of the output stage is referred to as "high-level" modulation; an alternative arrangement is the "low-level" system shown in Fig. 22.2b. As the name implies, modulation is carried out at an earlier point in the transmitter. Technical opinion has long been divided as to which is the preferable arrangement. In the high-level case, the modulating

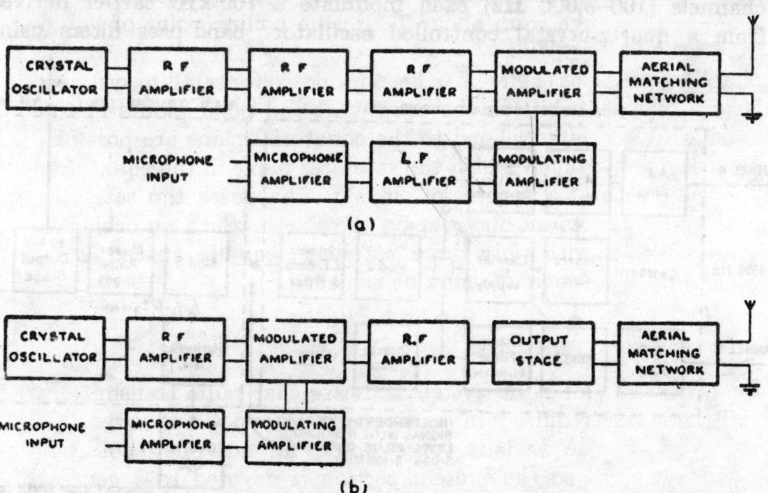

Fig. 22.2. Schematic diagram of a radio-telephony transmitter using (a) High-level modulation and (b) Low-level modulation.

amplifier has to produce a large amount of power ; the radio-frequency amplifier stages however have to amplify only the single frequency of the carrier and may thus be operated at high efficiency under class C conditions. With low-level modulation, the modulating power required is small, but this advantage is offset to some extent by the fact that the succeeding radio-frequency amplifiers have to amplify the modulated waveform and must therefore be linear, and are usually operated under class B conditions.

(b) *Independent-Sideband Transmitters*

The previous remarks applied to double-sideband amplitude modulated transmitters, such as are used for local broadcasting. Independent-side band transmitters, employing amplitude modulation are used in point-to-point working. Such a system is a development of single-sideband operation capable of transmitting two independent channels on each side of the carrier frequency. Each channel has a bandwidth of approximately 6 kHz and may itself be subdivided into two 3 kHz speech channels, or even a combination of speech and telegraphy channels. The block schematic diagram of an independent-sideband transmitter as used by the British Post Office, and typical of current practice, is shown in Fig. 22.3. The equipment is made in two units, a low power drive unit, and the main transmitter.

At the transmitter, the audio-frequency signals from the *A* and *B* channels (100–6,000 Hz) each modulate a 100-kHz carrier derived from a quartz-crystal controlled oscillator ; band-pass filters using

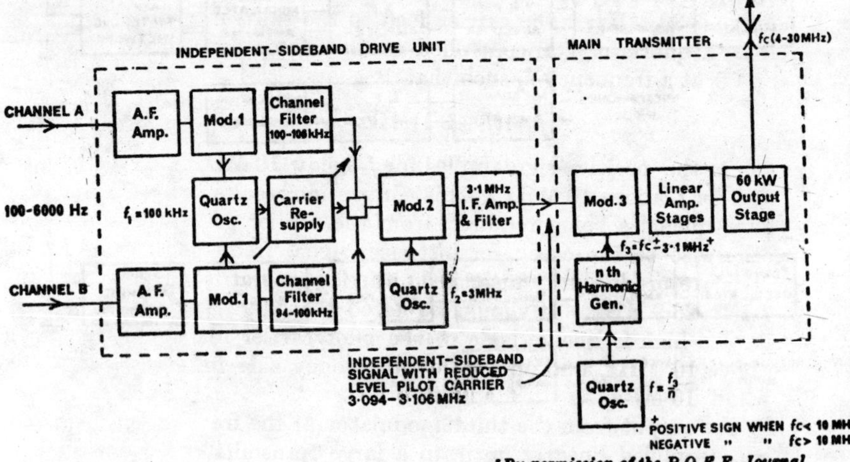

[*By permission of the P.O.E.E. Journal*

Fig. 22.3. Block schematic diagram of independent-sideband transmitter.

quartz-crystal resonators then select the upper sideband (100–106 kHz) in one case, and the lower sideband (94–100 kHz) in the other. The modulators (MOD. 1) used are nominally balanced; if the balance were perfect no 100 kHz carrier would be present in the output, but in practice the balance is not perfect and a small amount of carrier leak occurs. The *A* and *B* channel sideband signals are combined and passed through a narrow-band 100-kHz stop filter (not shown) to remove the residual carrier without attenuating the sidebands. A 100-kHz carrier at a level of 26 dB below the peak sideband power (the "pilot" carrier) is then added. The residual carrier is removed to ensure that the pilot carrier shall remain at a fixed level relative to the peak sideband level, even though variations in the balance of the modulators occur. As the automatic gain control of the distant receiver is operated by the pilot carrier, any changes in the pilot carrier level, relative to the peak sideband level, would result in unnecessary changes in the gain, and therefore in the audio output of the received signal.

The composite signal in the range 94–106 kHz is translated in frequency by a second modulator (MOD. 2), using a 3-MHz carrier, to the range 3·094 MHz–3·106 MHz; it is then amplified to a peak power of about 0·25W. The equipment used up to this point is termed the transmitter "drive unit"; it serves as a constant-frequency feed to the main transmitter.

The output of the drive unit is then passed to the main transmitter, where it is translated in frequency by a third modulator (MOD. 3) to the frequency f_c allocated to the service, f_c usually being in the range 4–30 MHz. The carrier feed to the third modulator is derived from a quartz-crystal-controlled oscillator, via a harmonic generator, and is at a frequency f_3 such that

$$f_3 = (f_c \pm 3{\cdot}1)\,\text{MHz}$$

where the positive sign applies for f_c below 10 MHz and the negative sign for f_c above 10 MHz. This convention results in a narrower range of frequencies being required from the carrier generator than would otherwise be the case; for instance, signal frequencies from 4 to 30 MHz are produced by means of a carrier generator covering the range 7·1 to 26·9 MHz. It should be noted that the *A* channel is radiated on the high-frequency side of the pilot carrier for signal frequencies above 10 MHz, and on the low frequency side for signal frequencies below 10 MHz.

The output from the third modulator at the frequency f_c is selected and amplified linearly until, in a large transmitter, a peak power of some 60 kW may be obtained for application to the transmission line and aerial; for many services, however, peak powers of about 20 kW, and even 4 kW in certain cases are sufficient.

(c) *Frequency-Modulated Telephony Transmitters*

A simplified block schematic diagram of one type of frequency-modulated transmitter suitable for telephony is shown in Fig. 22.4. A carrier is generated by a master oscillator and modulated with speech by means of a reactance modulator. The frequency-modulated output is then multiplied to give the final frequency radiated.

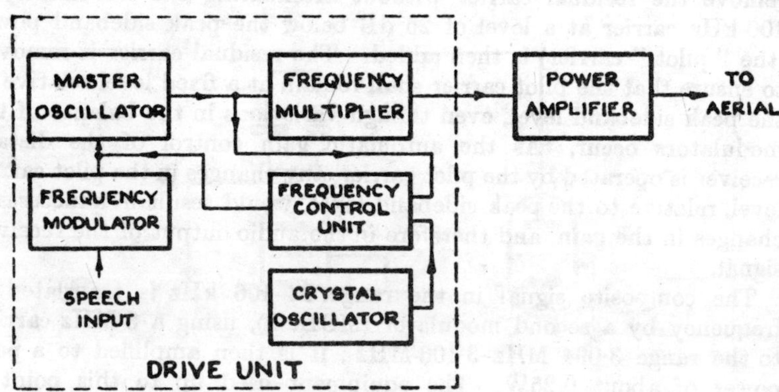

Fig. 22.4. Block schematic diagram of frequency-modulated telephony transmitter.

Multiplication of the carrier frequency η times causes the final frequency deviation at the output to be η times that produced by the modulator.

In order that frequency modulation may be produced, the carrier is necessarily generated by some form of oscillator other than a crystal oscillator. A high degree of stability of the mean, or unmodulated, carrier frequency is necessary however and this may be achieved in the manner indicated in Fig. 22.4. A fraction of the frequency-modulated signal is compared with the output of a crystal oscillator and arranged to produce a control voltage which regulates the frequency generated by the master oscillator. The low-power, frequency-modulated output, from the final frequency multiplier stage, is applied to power amplifier stages which increase the power to the desired level. All the power amplifier stages handle signals of constant amplitude and therefore operate under class C conditions at high efficiency.

(d) *Radio-Telegraphy Transmitters*

In modern practice telegraph signals are very often transmitted over a radio link on a multi-channel basis. The equipment normally operates on a two-tone basis in which two adjacent tones are required for each channel, the tones being keyed by static relays so that one tone indicates " mark " and the other " space ". Such an arrangement may be employed to modulate any transmitter used for telephony, such as the independent-sideband type of transmitter mentioned above. Another development is the frequency shift system[4], in which

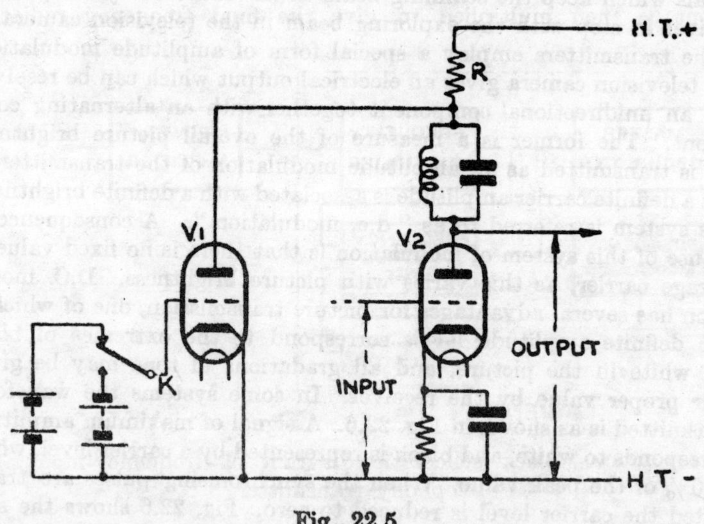

Fig. 22.5.

the " mark " impulse of the telegraph code is transmitted at one carrier frequency, and the " space " pulse is transmitted at a carrier frequency which differs from the first by an audio frequency, referred to as the " frequency shift ". This may be between 200 and 1,200 Hz.

If a radio transmitter is required only to produce simple telegraph signals, a scheme of " on and off keying " can be produced in a variety of ways. Normally the power supply to one of the low-power amplifier stages subsequent to the carrier generating oscillator is interrupted by a key. One way of achieving this is shown in Fig. 22.5 When the key is depressed, the keying valve V_1 is biased negatively so that it draws no current. When the key K is released V_1 is given a positive bias and draws a relatively large current which flows through the resistor R. The voltage drop in R is then such that the output from V_2 is small and the valve of the subsequent (class C) stage remains cut-off. Under this condition the transmitter does not radiate. The depression of the key permits the normal anode voltage to be applied to the anode of V_2 which then produces a large output voltage. This is subsequently amplified to produce the full transmitter output.

(e) *Television Transmitters*

The waveform radiated by a television transmitter is complex as it consists of the vision signals, which contain the information of the picture transmitted, together with line and frame synchronising signals which keep the scanning beam in the cathode ray tube of the receiver in step with the exploring beam in the television camera.

The transmitters employ a special form of amplitude modulation. The television camera gives an electrical output which can be resolved into an unidirectional component together with an alternating component. The former is a measure of the overall picture brightness and is transmitted as an amplitude modulation of the transmitter so that a definite carrier amplitude is associated with a definite brightness. This system is referred to as " d.c. modulation ". A consequence of the use of this system of modulation is that there is no fixed value of average carrier, as this varies with picture brightness. D.C. modulation has several advantages for picture transmission, one of which is that definite amplitude levels correspond to the extremes of black and white in the picture, and all gradations of tone may be given their proper value by the receiver. In some systems the waveform transmitted is as shown in Fig. 22.6. A signal of maximum amplitude corresponds to white, and black is represented by a carrier level, which is 30% of the peak value. When the synchronising pulses are transmitted the carrier level is reduced to zero. Fig. 22.6 shows the synchronising signals between each line. Additional synchronising pulses (not shown) are employed at the end of each frame.

Alternatively " negative d.c. modulation " may be employed, so that the synchronising pulses represent the maximum carrier amplitude ; in effect, as far as the general form is concerned, the waveform radiated is that of Fig. 22.6 inverted.

A high-definition television system gives rise to a large bandwidth somewhere about 6 MHz. As a result of this, vestigial or asymmetric sideband transmission is often employed. In this system one sideband is largely eliminated by means of a filter at the transmitter so that the frequency spectrum radiated has the form shown in Fig. 22.7. The

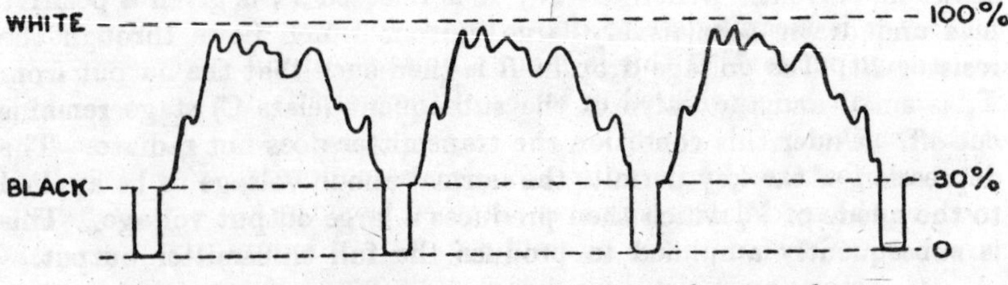

Fig. 22.6. Envelope of television line waveform.

vestigial sideband method thus economises in bandwidth and is really a double sideband system for low frequency modulation components, merging into a single sideband system for the high frequency modulation components.

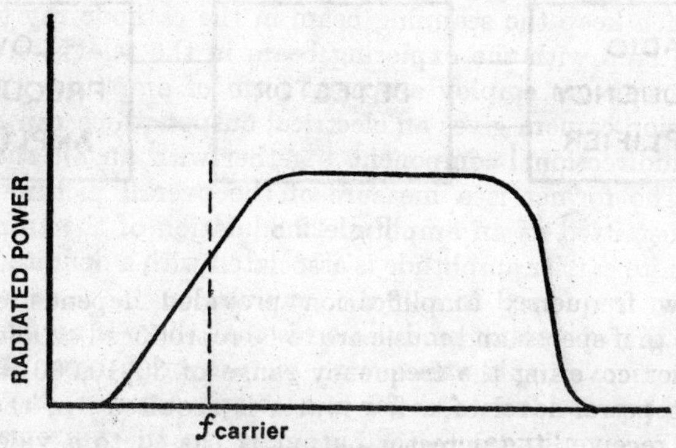

Fig. 22.7.

RADIO RECEIVERS

A radio receiver is required to operate over a certain range of carrier frequencies, and must produce as an output, a signal which is a faithful reproduction of the original modulation applied to any desired carrier. The receiver must thus be able to select the desired carrier (and sidebands) to the exclusion of others ; in the ideal case, the selectivity of the receiver should be such that when " tuned " to any desired carrier that carrier and its sidebands alone are accepted, and all other input frequencies rejected. Tuning of the receiver is brought about by variation in the value of the capacitors in the resonant circuits in the high-frequency amplifier section of the receiver.

The sensitivity of the receiver refers to the voltage required at the input terminals to produce the desired output. With high-gain receivers, capable of dealing with very small input voltages, it is essential to know the signal/noise ratio as well as the sensitivity, because it is meaningless to quote input voltages which will give the desired output level if this is mainly noise. Alternatively, the effect of noise can be considered in terms of the noise factor (see page 482) of the receiver.

A basic feature of any radio receiver is some form of detector circuit in which the modulating signal is obtained from the applied modulated waveform. Most detector circuits require a minimum input voltage for satisfactory operation and it is usually necessary to provide some pre-detector amplification. The output from the detector usually requires further amplification to operate the output device, e.g. loudspeaker, telephones, cathode ray tube, or other equipment. All the common forms of radio receiver may thus be represented schematically as shown in Fig. 22.8.

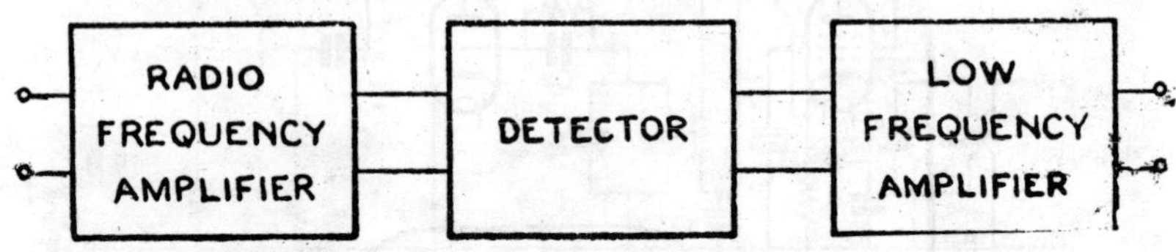

Fig. 22.8.

The low frequency amplification provided depends on type of receiver, e.g. if speech and music are to be reproduced on a loudspeaker, an amplifier covering the frequency range of 30–10,000 Hz and with an output power level of a few watts is required ; in the case of a television receiver the detector output is passed to a video amplifier which has a bandwidth of several megahertz, and must produce a peak-to-peak output voltage of the order of 100V.

There are three main types of radio receiver used in practice ; the straightforward tuned radio-frequency receiver was originally the type most commonly used, but has now been displaced for most applications by the supersonic-heterodyne type. A third variety, the super-regenerative receiver, is occasionally used, particularly at vei high frequencies.

(a) TUNED RADIO-FREQUENCY RECEIVER

This type of receiver is simple in that the pre-detector amplification is performed at the frequency of the desired carrier. An example of a simple tuned radio-frequency receiver, suitable for there production of speech or music on a loudspeaker, is shown in Fig. 22.9, which is thus a detailed illustration of the block schematic diagram of Fig. 22.8.

In the receiver shown in Fig. 22.9, the aerial is transformer coupled to the tuned circuit (*LC*) in the grid circuit of the pentode radio-frequency amplifier valve. The anode of this valve is transformer coupled to the second valve which functions as a grid leak detector. Selection of the wanted transmission is achieved by adjustment of the variable tuning capacitors (*C*) which are usually mechanically coupled together. The grid and cathode of the second valve, together with C_2 and R_2, function as a diode detector system to produce the desired low frequency voltage across R_2. This voltage is amplified and passed by the resistance-capacitance coupling to the output valve, which is transformer coupled to the loudspeaker.

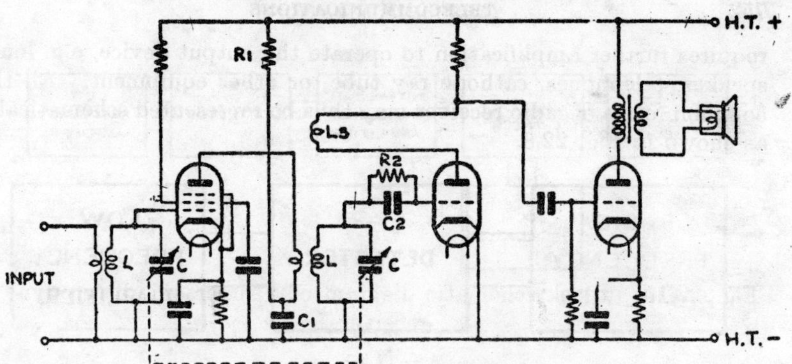

Fig. 22.9. Simple tuned radio-frequency receiver.

The coil L_3, which has a negligible impedance at audio frequencies is coupled to the coil L in the grid circuit and produces "reaction". Briefly, a component of radio-frequency current flows through the detector valve and L_3, and induces a voltage in the grid coil L in such a sense as to produce positive feedback which increases the gain of the stage. Increase of reaction gives increased gain at the expense of stability and leads ultimately to sustained self-oscillation.

Fig. 22.9 shows one form of t.r.f. receiver. A diode detector without reaction is often used; two or more stages of high-frequency amplification may be used when the input voltage is small. The low-frequency amplifier may be modified in a variety of ways, e.g. a stage of amplification may be inserted between the detector and the output valve, or a pair of valves arranged in push-pull may be used for the output stage.

(b) THE SUPERSONIC HETERODYNE RECEIVER

The existence of a large number of high-power radio transmitters in a given frequency band demands a very selective receiver, if each transmission is to be received satisfactorily. Quite often it is necessary to employ three or more variable resonant circuits, as opposed to the two shown in Fig. 22.9. In such circumstances it is no easy matter to arrange that the receiver has a fixed selectivity or bandwidth at any point in its operating range. The supersonic heterodyne (or "superhet") receiver disposes of this problem by translating all incoming signals so that the carrier frequency is, in effect, changed to a new value, which is constant for all carriers. Most of the pre-detector amplification is then carried out at this frequency, which is referred to as the intermediate frequency (i.f.). The basic features of a supersonic heterodyne receiver are shown in Fig. 22.10.

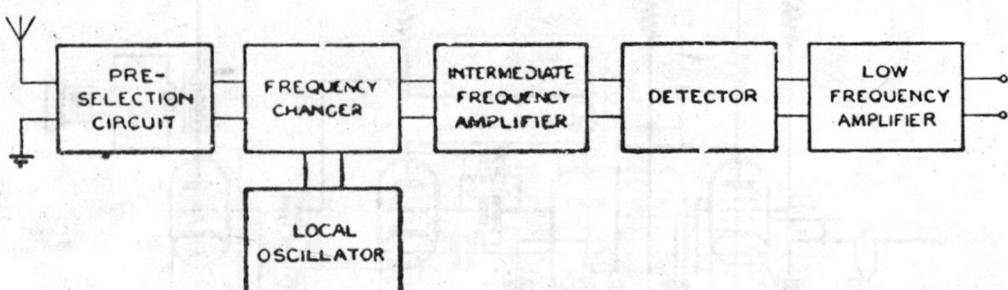

Fig. 22.10. Block schematic diagram of a supersonic heterodyne receiver.

In the superheterodyne receiver the radio-frequency voltage obtained from the aerial is first passed through a pre-selection circuit. In its simplest form this often consists simply of a parallel resonant circuit, tuned to the frequency of the wanted transmission. This part of the circuit is then the same as the grid circuit of the first valve in Fig. 22.9. If greater selectivity is required, at this stage, the pre-selection circuit may consist of a complete stage of radio frequency amplification, with a parallel tuned circuit connected between grid and cathode, and a similar circuit, transformer coupled to the anode, as shown in Fig. 22.9.

The Frequency-Changer Stage. The frequency-changing section of the receiver is required to translate the frequency of all incoming carriers to the intermediate frequency value, and so it acts as, and may be regarded as, a form of modulator. The signal voltage supplied by the pre-selector circuit is one input which can for the moment be regarded as a single frequency, f_s. The second input is supplied from a local oscillator which supplies a frequency f_o. The output current of the frequency changer then has the frequency components

$$f_s, f_o, f_o + f_s \text{ and } f_o - f_s$$

as one might expect. In practice the output load for the frequency changer is a resonant circuit, tuned to the intermediate frequency, and the local oscillator is arranged so that the component $f_o - f_s$ is always equal to the intermediate frequency. The fact that the input signal consists of a carrier and sidebands rather than a single frequency does not upset the argument. A variety of frequency changing circuits exists; the form employing a triode-hexode valve is shown in Fig. 22.11.

The triode section of the valve acts as the local oscillator, while the hexode section acts as radio-frequency signal amplifier, the gain of which is varied at the local oscillator frequency. Reference to Fig. 22.11 shows that the wanted signal voltage is developed across the parallel resonant circuit LC and is applied to the control grid of the

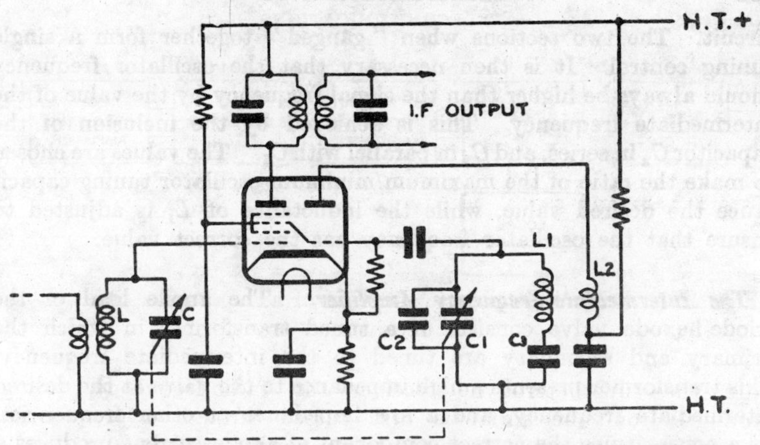

Fig. 22.11. Triode-hexode frequency-changer stage.

hexode section of the valve. The local oscillator shown is a tuned-grid type with anode coupling. For the moment, the components which determine the oscillator frequency may be taken as L_1 and C_1. The variable capacitors C and C_1 are "ganged".

Ganging the Local Oscillator. It has already been mentioned that the local oscillator frequency must always differ from that of the signal by the value of the intermediate frequency In theory, the local oscillator frequency could be either greater or less than the signal frequency by the necessary amount. In practice it is more convenient to choose the former condition as the frequency range over which the oscillator has to operate is then smaller.

The general operation can best be illustrated in terms of a numerical example. Suppose that the signal frequency range for which the receiver is to be designed is 500–1,500 kHz, and that the intermediate frequency is to be 450 kHz. The value of L, and the minimum of the capacitor C together with all stray capacitance must be chosen to give resonance at 1,500 kHz. Then, if the maximum/minimum capacitance ratio of C when stray capacitance is included, is 9 : 1, the signal circuit will tune from 500–1,500 kHz. If the local oscillator is to be higher in frequency than the signal then the local oscillator frequency must vary between 950 and 1950 kHz, i.e. a frequency ratio of 2·05, which means a variation in the value of the total oscillator tuning capacitance of $(2{\cdot}05)^2 : 1$, i.e. 4·2 : 1. A local oscillator lower in frequency than the signal in this case would require a variation in total oscillator tuning capacitance of 441 : 1.

The normal practical arrangement of the local oscillator circuit is to choose a capacitor-section, similar to that which tunes the signal circuit. The two sections when "ganged" together form a single tuning control. It is then necessary that the oscillator frequency should always be higher than the signal frequency by the value of the intermediate frequency. This is achieved by the inclusion of the capacitor C_3 in series, and C_2 in parallel with C_1. The values are chosen to make the ratio of the maximum/minimum oscillator tuning capacitance the desired value, while the inductance of L_1 is adjusted to ensure that the oscillator frequency has the correct value.

The Intermediate-Frequency Amplifier. The anode load of the triode-hexode valve consists of a tuned transformer in which the primary and secondary are tuned to the intermediate frequency. This transformer presents a high impedance to the valve at the desired intermediate frequency, and a low impedance at other frequencies. As a consequence the correct component of anode current produces a relatively large output across the terminals of the secondary winding of the intermediate-frequency transformer. The i.f. output (Fig. 22.11) is connected to the grid and cathode of an i.f. amplifier stage which has a further i.f. transformer as an anode load. The amplified signal is then amplified by a further stage or passed to a detector circuit.

It is important to appreciate that in a superheterodyne receiver most of the selectivity (and amplification) is produced in the i.f. amplifier. This operates as a "fixed-tune" amplifier and has the advantage that the response curve can be adjusted to give a suitable compromise between selectivity and reduced sideband level. This overall response curve is the same for all transmissions received.

The choice of the value of the intermediate frequency depends on several factors. Low values assist in discriminating between adjacent carriers and reduce the "adjacent channel interference". Thus, if the i.f. is say, 450 kHz and two carriers at the receiver input terminals have frequencies of 1,000 kHz and 1,010 kHz, a local oscillator frequency of 1,650 kHz will produce an output of the lower frequency carrier and some of the other (translated to 440 kHz), depending on the frequency response characteristic of the intermediate frequency amplifier. An intermediate frequency of say 100 kHz on the other hand, will clearly improve this situation. However, with an i.f. of 100 kHz and the local oscillator set at, say 1,650 kHz, an output will be produced if there are signal inputs of either 1,550 or 1,750 kHz. Thus a wanted transmission on 1,550 kHz will suffer interference from an unwanted one on 1,750 kHz, and vice versa. This effect is known as "second channel interference"; such interference may be reduced to a large extent if a stage (or stages) of high frequency amplification is used before the frequency-changer stage.

Domestic radio receivers employ an intermediate frequency of about 450 kHz. Freedom from both adjacent channel interference and second channel interference is achieved in double superheterodyne receivers which have two intermediate frequency amplifiers, one operating at a high value of intermediate frequency and the other at a relatively low value.

Automatic Gain Control. On many occasions the input voltage to a receiver varies or " fades ", particularly so when indirect ray propagation is involved between the transmitter and receiver. The resultant annoying variation in output level may be reduced somewhat by the use of automatic gain control. This necessitates the use of a diode detector, on account of the relatively large values of signal voltage required at the detector by such a system ; the direct component of the output, which is a measure of the carrier amplitude, is used to bias back the preceding amplifying valves, so reducing their gain, provided always of course that they have variable-μ characteristics. A receiver so controlled is less sensitive to changes in the input voltage, and if the a.g.c. circuit is properly designed, can handle large input signals without serious overloading.

A simple form of automatic gain control is illustrated in Fig. 22.12. The pentode intermediate frequency amplifier stage is shown coupled to a diode which functions as a detector and a.g.c. source.

The application of a signal to the diode causes the end of the load resistor R, remote from the diode cathode, to become negative, with respect to the H.T.-line by an extent which is nearly equal to the peak value of the applied intermediate frequency voltage. This " negative " voltage is fed back to the grid of the pentode valve (and also any others which may be controlled). The filter consisting of C_1 and R_1 is used to prevent low frequency and carrier voltages from being fed back to the controlled valves.

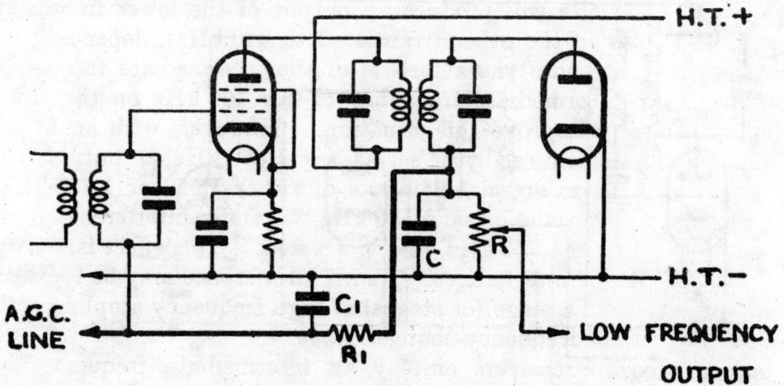

Fig. 22.12. Simple a.g.c. circuit.

Most practical automatic gain control circuits incorporate refinements not shown in Fig. 22.12. This does however illustrate the basic principle.

(c) THE SUPER-REGENERATIVE RECEIVER

This form of receiver makes use of the principle that a small voltage induced in a resonant circuit increases enormously in amplitude if the circuit becomes oscillatory, i.e. if the series resistance, or the equivalent shunt conductance of the circuit, becomes negative. The oscillation in the regenerative circuit is stopped, or " quenched " at a frequency which is small compared with the signal radio frequency, but large compared with the frequency of modulation. In the linear mode of operation, the circuit arrangements are such that the oscillations built up during a quench cycle do not attain the maximum possible steady state amplitude (as determined by the characteristics of the maintaining valve) ; the peak amplitude of such oscillations is then proportional to the magnitude of the signal voltage at the commencement of oscillation.

The basic features of one form of super-regenerative receiver are shown in Fig. 22.13. The regenerative circuit LC, is maintained by the valve V_1, but arranged so that it does not oscillate when there is no injected quench voltage. V_2 functions as a generator of a quench frequency voltage which is injected into the anode circuit of V_1. As a result, the regenerative circuit oscillates for a fraction of each period of the quench voltage. The resulting pulses have a duration which is small compared with the period of modulation, and their amplitude is proportional to the amplitude of the signal voltage at their initiation. Rectification of the pulses by a conventional diode detector then gives

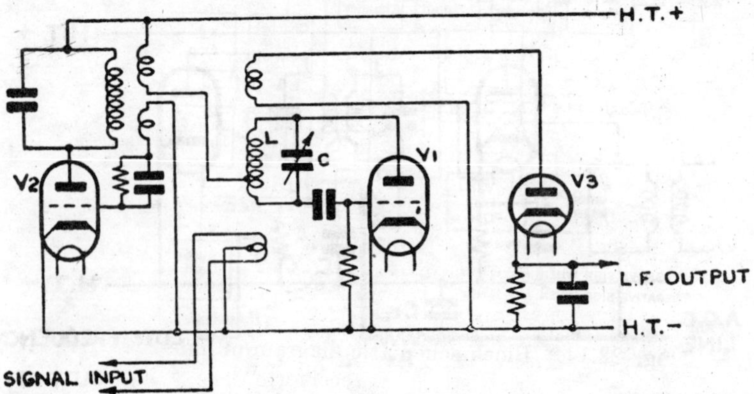

Fig. 22.13. Basic features of one form of super-regenerative receiver.

the desired modulation; quench frequency components are also present in the output from the diode and must be removed by some form of filter.

Super-regenerative receivers are often arranged to be self-quenching and provide direct detection of modulated signals; such a receiver would then simply have one valve instead of the three shown in Fig. 22.13. Super-regenerative receivers are compact, economical in space and weight, and yet extremely sensitive. As a result they are used as portable receivers for frequencies above about 50 MHz.

SPECIAL FORMS OF RADIO RECEIVER

As already remarked, the superheterodyne receiver is the type most favoured for general use. The particular form, or degree of complexity necessary in the design of the circuits depends on the purpose for which the receiver is to be used. The simplest form is the transistorised sound broadcast receiver; this may or may not have a radio-frequency stage before the frequency changer. This is then followed by one or two stages of i.f. amplification, leading to a detector, a.g.c. source and low-frequency amplifier. The "double superheterodyne" is a more complex form which is highly selective.

Independent-Sideband Receiver. An example of a complex double superheterodyne receiver is the independent-sideband receiver shown schematically in Fig. 22.14. This is operated in conjunction with transmitters of the type shown in Fig. 22.3.

The received signal, which will usually be in the range 4–30 MHz,

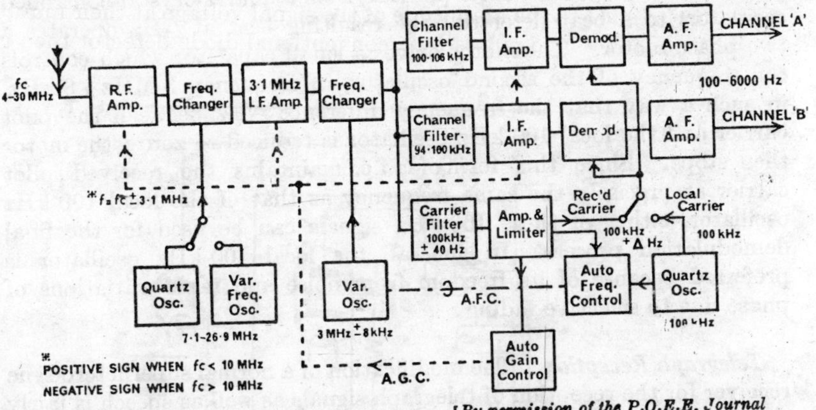

[*By permission of the P.O.E.E. Journal*

Fig. 22.14. Block schematic diagram of independent-sideband receiver.

is first amplified by a tuned *R.F.* amplifier and is then translated in frequency to 3·1 MHz (see Fig. 22.14). The first frequency-change oscillator is quartz-crystal-controlled, or a stable variable-frequency oscillator when suitable crystals are not available. Since the standard independent-sideband transmission has channel A above the carrier frequency when the latter exceeds 10 MHz, and below the carrier frequency when it is below 10 MHz, it is arranged that the frequency of the first oscillator in the receiver is below the carrier frequency when the latter exceeds 10 MHz, and above the carrier frequency when the latter is below 10 MHz, in order that a given channel may always be identified with a given audio output of the receiver.

After amplification at 3·1 MHz the signal is again translated in frequency, this time to 100 kHz, the complete two-channel signal then occupying the band 94–106 kHz.

Channel filters, similar to those used in the drive unit, select the *A* and *B* channel sideband signals which are then amplified and passed to the *A* and *B* channel demodulators ; the carrier supplied to the demodulators is at 100 kHz and the audio-frequency output is thus 100–6,000 Hz.

A narrow-band 100-kHz filter using quartz-crystal resonators selects the 100-kHz pilot carrier which is amplified and, after detection, operates the automatic gain control (a.g.c.) in the receiver. The amplified pilot carrier, after limiting to remove fading, is also used for automatic frequency control (a.f.c.) i.e. to synchronise the frequency of the received pilot carrier with that of a locally-generated 100-kHz oscillation, in order that the latter can be used for demodulation purposes. The pilot-carrier frequency (100 kHz +△Hz) is applied with the local 100-kHz carrier (derived from a quartz-crystal-controlled oscillator) to a beat detector ; the resulting beat at △Hz operates a two-phase motor. The motor drives a small capacitor which controls the frequency of the second oscillator, of frequency 3 MHz ± 8 kHz, in such a way that the frequency difference △Hz between the pilot carrier and the local 100-kHz oscillator is reduced to zero ; the motor then stops. Since this form of a.f.c. maintains the received pilot carrier at precisely the same frequency as that of the local 100-kHz oscillator, either of these 100-kHz signals can be used for the final demodulation process. In general, the local 100-kHz oscillator is preferred because of its freedom from noise and rapid variations of phase due to selective fading.

Telegraph Reception. The modification of a normal superheterodyne receiver for the reception of telegraph signals as well as speech is fairly simple, and is mentioned here not because the point is particularly important, but because it is an application of the principle of heterodyne detection which has not so far been mentioned.

When two sinusoidal voltages, of approximately the same frequency are superimposed, the envelope of the resultant waveform varies in amplitude at a frequency which is equal to the difference between the two original frequencies. This difference frequency, referred to as the " beat frequency ", always arises as a consequence of heterodyning, or mixing, one frequency with another. The heterodyne waveform when rectified produces a current which varies in amplitude at the beat frequency, and this constitutes the principle of heterodyne reception as applied to telegraph signals. The process operates as a form of frequency changing and is used to convert the carrier frequency of a radio-telegraph signal to a low-frequency which will operate a loudspeaker or headphones.

Suppose two voltages v_1 and v_2 are heterodyned. Then if $v_1 = V_1 \sin \omega t$ and $v_2 = V_2 \sin (\omega + \triangle\omega)t$, the resultant voltage is given by

$$v = V_1 \sin \omega t + V_2 \sin (\omega + \triangle\omega)t$$
$$= [V_1 + V_2 \cos \triangle\omega t] \sin \omega t + [V_2 \sin \triangle\omega t] \cos \omega t$$
$$= \sqrt{V_1^2 + V_2^2 + 2V_1V_2 \cos \triangle\omega t} \quad \sin(\omega t + \phi) \qquad . \quad . \quad 22.1$$

$$\text{where } \tan \phi = \frac{V_2 \sin \triangle\omega t}{V_1 + V_2 \cos \triangle\omega t}$$

Equation 22.1 shows that the resultant waveform may be regarded as having an amplitude which varies at the beat frequency $\triangle\omega$, but is clearly not sinusoidal in shape.

In practice a superheterodyne receiver may be adapted to provide heterodyne detection if a second local oscillator, or beat frequency oscillator (b.f.o.) is fitted. This oscillator is arranged to deliver a voltage to the detector at a frequency which differs from the intermediate frequency by about 1,000 Hz. Thus, with an i.f. of 450 kHz, the b.f.o. could operate at 451 or 449 kHz to provide an audio output of 1,000 Hz. It is customary to inject a fairly large b.f.o. voltage into the (diode) detector circuit. Under this condition linear detection is obtained and the output is approximately proportional to the weaker signal voltage.

Television Reception. A simplified block schematic diagram of a television receiver is shown in Fig. 22.15. The unit marked SOUND RECEIVER may consist of a high frequency amplifier stage (or stages) tuned to the sound carrier, followed by a detector circuit, low frequency amplifier and output stage. The unit marked VISION RECEIVER consists of a number of high-frequency (wideband) amplifier stages followed by a detector and a video amplifier. Alternatively, the receivers may be of superheterodyne form. The signal voltage produced by the latter is then fed to the cathode ray tube. A synchronising signal separator stage is fed from the vision receiver and delivers line

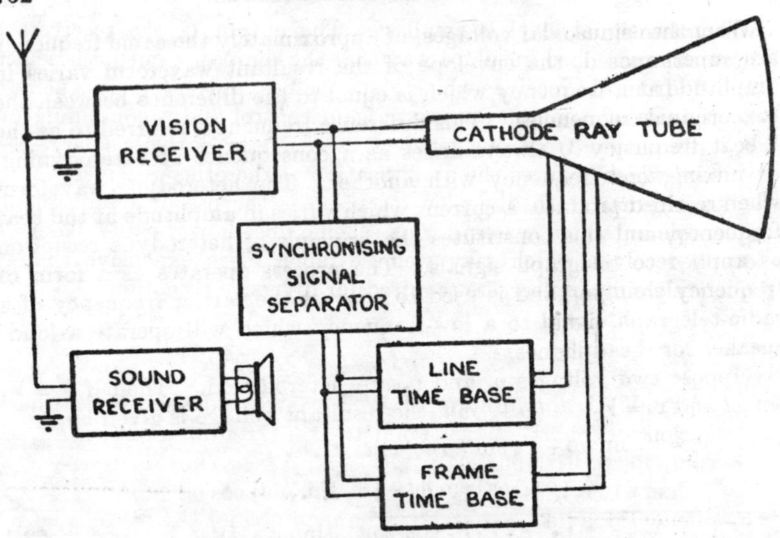

Fig. 22.15. Simplified block schematic diagram of a television receiver.

and frame synchronising pulses to the line and frame time bases. These units then produce output currents which when applied to deflecting coils on the neck of the cathode ray tube cause the beam to trace out a " raster " or pattern of lines. The picture information, delivered by the vision unit, then modulates the brightness of the spot and so reproduces the transmitted picture. For further information the reader should consult the references at the end of this chapter.

Diversity Reception. Long-distance short-wave radio transmission (in the frequency range 4–30 MHz) and scatter propagation systems operating at higher frequencies suffer from the disadvantage that the received signal changes in magnitude and phase as a consequence of changes in the transmission path. This fading cannot be entirely counteracted by automatic gain control in the receiver. It is found that at a given frequency, the signal strength may fall at a given site, and yet remain unaffected, or even increase in level, at a point a wavelength or more away. As a consequence, diversity reception schemes are employed in which the signals from two or more aerials spaced some distance apart, are passed through similar receivers and then combined.

The simplest arrangement, namely the parallel connection of the low frequency outputs of the receivers is not used as this collects noise (and distortion) from each, irrespective of whether it is producing any signal or not, and the noise output of course is unfortunately greatest when the signal level is smallest. The output of the receivers are normally combined in such a way that the composite output is selected mainly from the receiver which gives the best output ; this is achieved by the use of common automatic gain control and a combining unit. A large output from one receiver causes it to develop a large a.g.c. voltage which reduces the amplification of the other receivers.

An alternative to diversity reception is the use of a multiple-unit steerable antennae system. This scheme does however involve a very costly receiver which may well be much more expensive than the relatively simple receivers required for diversity reception.

References

[1] BRAY, W. J. and MORRIS, D. W. : " Single-Sideband Multi-Channel Operation of Short Wave Point-to-Point Radio Links "; *P.O.E.E. Journal*, 45, p. 97 (1952).

[2] MERRIMAN, J. H. H. and WHITE, R. W. : " The Application of Frequency Modulation to V.H.F. Multi-Channel Radio Telephony " ; *Jour. I.E.E.*, 94, Part IIIA, p. 649 (1947).

[3] BRAY, W. J.: "The Standardisation of International Microwave Radio-Relay Systems"; *Proc. I.E.E.*, 108, Part B, p. 180 (1961).

[4] SMALE, J. A. : " Some Developments in Commercial Point-to-Point Radiotelegraphy " ; *Jour. I.E.E.*, 94, Part IIIA, p. 345 (1947)

References for Further Reading

TERMAN, F. E.: *Radio Engineering* (McGraw Hill, 1947).

LADNER, A. W. and STONER, C. R. : *Short Wave Wireless Communication* (Chapman & Hall, 1950).

STURLEY, K. R. : *Radio Receiver Design*, 2 Vols. (Chapman & Hall, 1949).

WHITEHEAD, J. R. : *The Super-regenerative Receiver* (Cambridge University Press, 1950).

KERKHOFF, F. and WERNER, W. : *Television* (Philips Technical Library, 1952).

AMOS, S. W. and BIRKINSHAW, D. C. : *Television Engineering* (Iliffe & Sons, Ltd., 1953).

WENTWORTH, J.: *Colour Television Engineering* (McGraw Hill, 1955).

KRASSNER, G. N. and MICHAELS, J. V.: *Introduction to Space Communication Systems* (McGraw Hill, 1964).

MUELLER, G. E. and SPRANGLER, E. R.: *Communication Satellites* (John Wiley & Sons Inc., 1964).

GATLAND, K. W. (Ed.): *Telecommunication Satellites* (Iliffe Books Ltd., 1964).

EXAMPLES

1. A multi-stage, amplitude-modulated, radio transmitter may be modulated at a low power level or in the final stage. Compare the merits of the two methods. Explain with the aid of a circuit diagram how anode modulation of a class C amplifier may be achieved.

The unmodulated output of a class C carrier amplifier is 150 W and the valve has an anode efficiency of 75%. Anode modulation is applied from a class A modulator valve with an anode efficiency of 40%. Estimate the anode dissipation required for each valve, if the signal is sinusoidal and the modulation depth is 100%.

L.U. Telecomm. Part III. 1964.

2. Describe, with the aid of a block diagram, the principle of operation of a superheterodyne radio receiver and state its advantages over a tuned r.f. receiver.

A superheterodyne receiver has a signal-frequency range of 500 to 1500 kHz and an intermediate frequency of 450 kHz. Determine the tuning range of the frequency-changing oscillator and hence the ratio of the maximum to minimum tuning capacitance required for this oscillator.

L.U. Electronics & Telecomm. Part II. 1965.

3. Explain, with the aid of a block diagram, the main features of a superheterodyne receiver.

A receiver having an intermediate frequency of 450 kHz is required to tune over the range 550–1650 kHz. The ganged variable capacitor has a capacitance variation of 455 to 15 pF in each section. Determine, for the r.f. circuit, the value of (*a*) the shunt trimmer capacitance and (*b*) the tuning coil inductance.

What maximum to minimum ratio will be required for the tuning capacitance of the local oscillator?

L.U. Electronics & Telecomm. Part II 1969.

4. Explain how the design of the inter-valve coupling circuits of the i.f. amplifier in a superheterodyne receiver may be used to control the selectivity. The anode circuit of a pentode amplifier stage is tuned to resonance at 1 MHz by an effective capacitance of 200 $\mu\mu$F. The effective series resistance of the tuned anode circuit is 20 ohms at the relevant frequency. The valve has a mutual conductance of 3·0 mA/V and its anode slope resistance may be assumed to be very high. Calculate the maximum gain of the stage.

L.U. Ext.-Telecomm. 1952.

5. Show how a diode rectifier circuit can be arranged to provide automatic gain control in a superheterodyne radio receiver, and explain the action of the controlled variable-*mu* valves. What factors determine the efficiency of control?

L.U. Ext.-Telecomm. 1949.

6. Write a short account of the principles underlying the transmission and reception of television. Illustrate your answer with a block diagram of a typical television receiver and explain briefly the function of each unit.

L.U. Telecomm. Part III. 1958.

7. Explain the principle of single-sideband, suppressed carrier transmission. What are its advantages for (a) carrier telephony on lines, and (b) long-distance radiotelephony? Why is the system not used for broadcasting?

The current in the aerial of a radio transmitting station as measured by a thermal ammeter, is 15A when a 1 MHz carrier only is being transmitted and rises to 17A when sinusoidal, amplitude modulation at 2 kHz is applied. The carrier and both sidebands are being transmitted.

Determine the percentage modulation, and the frequencies and values of the component currents which make up the aerial current.

L.U. Telecomm. Part III. 1958.

8. Describe the superheterodyne principle as applied in radio receivers and explain what is meant by the term *image-channel interference*.

A superheterodyne receiver has an intermediate frequency of 3·1 MHz and the oscillator frequency is higher than that of the signal. A tuned circuit with a Q-factor of 100 precedes the frequency-changer. Calculate the relative attenuation (in dB) of an interfering signal at the image-channel frequency when the receiver is tuned to a wanted carrier at 78 MHz.

L.U. Electronics & Telecomm. Part II. 1966.

APPENDIX A

PARAMETERS OF THE FOUR-TERMINAL NETWORK

THE circuit performance of any four-terminal, or two-port, network may be specified in terms of the general four-terminal network parameters which relate the input and output currents and the voltages at the four terminals. Fig. A.1 shows the network connected to a voltage source and a load, and indicates the sign convention for the general case.

Fig. A.1. The general four-terminal network.

With the sign convention shown, the source and load are related to the input and output voltages by the equations

$$v_1 = V_s - i_1 Z_s \quad \text{and} \quad v_2 = -i_2 Z_L$$

Of the possible sets of parameters, the three most commonly used are, the open-circuit impedance or z parameters, the short-circuit admittance or y parameters, and the hybrid or h parameters.

Open-circuit Impedance Parameters

If the input and output voltages are expressed in terms of the currents, the four-terminal network may be described by the equations,

$$v_1 = z_{11} i_1 + z_{12} i_2 \qquad \text{A.1}$$

$$\text{and} \quad v_2 = z_{21} i_1 + z_{22} i_2 \qquad \text{A.2}$$

If now the output terminals are open-circuited as far as a.c. is concerned, so that $i_2 = 0$, then

$z_{11} = v_1/i_1 = z_i$ the input impedance

$z_{21} = v_2/i_1 = z_f$ the forward transfer impedance

With the input terminals open-circuited as far as a.c. is concerned, so that $i_1 = 0$, then

$$z_{12} = v_1/i_2 = z_r \text{ the reverse transfer impedance}$$
$$z_{22} = v_2/i_2 = z_o \text{ the output impedance.}$$

These four quantities, the z's, the small-signal impedance parameters, relate small changes of voltage and current. When the four-terminal network is an active device, such as a transistor, they are commonly partial derivatives of the corresponding steady quantities. Thus for example, $z_{11} = \partial V_1/\partial I_1$ for $i_2 = 0$, where V_1 and I_1 are the steady values of input voltage, and input current.

Short-circuit Admittance Parameters

If the currents i_1 and i_2 are assumed to be the dependent variables, the four-terminal network may be represented by the equations

$$i_1 = y_{11}v_1 + y_{12}v_2 \quad . \quad . \quad . \quad . \quad \text{A.3}$$
$$\text{and} \quad i_2 = y_{21}v_1 + y_{22}v_2 \quad . \quad . \quad . \quad . \quad \text{A.4}$$

If now the output terminals are short-circuited to a.c. by say the connection of a suitable capacitor across them, so that $v_2 = 0$, then

$$y_{11} = i_1/v_1 = y_i \text{ the input admittance}$$
$$y_{21} = i_2/v_1 = y_f \text{ the forward transfer admittance}$$

With the input terminals short-circuited to a.c. so that $v_1 = 0$, then

$$y_{12} = i_1/v_2 = y_r \text{ the reverse transfer admittance}$$
$$y_{22} = i_2/v_2 = y_o \text{ the output admittance}$$

These four quantities, the y's, are the small-signal admittance parameters.

Hybrid Parameters

The previous representations of the four-terminal network have been in terms of impedances or of admittances. A mixture of these gives a third set, the hybrid parameters. These are defined by the equations

$$v_1 = h_{11}i_1 + h_{12}v_2 \quad . \quad . \quad . \quad . \quad \text{A.5}$$
$$i_2 = h_{21}i_1 + h_{22}v_2 \quad . \quad . \quad . \quad . \quad \text{A.6}$$

If now the output terminals are short-circuited to a.c. so that $v_2 = 0$, then

$$h_{11} = v_1/i_1 = h_i \text{ the input impedance}$$
$$h_{21} = i_2/i_1 = h_f \text{ the forward transfer current ratio, or forward current gain}$$

With the input terminals open-circuited to a.c. so that $i_1 = 0$, then

$$h_{12} = v_1/v_2 = h_r \text{ the reverse transfer voltage ratio, or reverse voltage gain}$$
$$h_{22} = i_2/v_2 = h_o \text{ the output admittance}$$

APPENDIX B

THE HYBRID-π CIRCUIT

As far as a.c. equivalent circuits for a transistor are concerned, neither simple-T nor the hybrid parameter circuits (Figs. 7.16 and 7.17) are suitable for use other than at low frequencies. Both circuits are entirely resistive and omit capacitive effects, so that for an extended frequency range the circuit has to be modified. The hybrid-π circuit shown in Fig. B.1 is generally satisfactory and widely used.

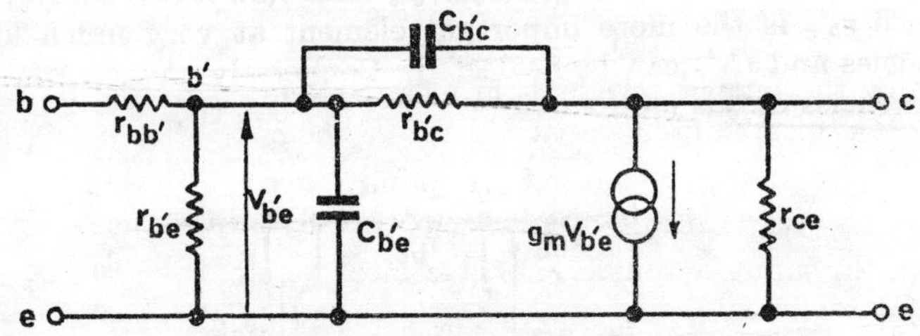

Fig. B.1. Hybrid-π circuit.

In the circuit of Fig. B.1 the standard notation for the components has been used.

The resistance $r_{bb'}$ connected between the external base terminal b and the active part of the base b' accounts for the resistance of the base material. The value of $r_{bb'}$ is usually about 100 Ω or less, but does of course depend on the type of transistor involved.

The resistance $r_{b'e}$ represents the base to emitter junction resistance and has a value of about 1000 Ω.

The capacitance $C_{b'e}$ represents the depletion layer and diffusion capacitances across the base-emitter junction. In an alloy junction transistor the value of $C_{b'e}$ may be about 1000 pF but much less in a silicon planar type.

The resistance $r_{b'c}$ represents the resistive component of the feedback from the output to the input and has a value of from 1–3 MΩ.

The capacitance $C_{b'c}$ represents the collector-base capacitance. In an alloy junction transistor this may be about 10 pF or half this in a silicon planar type.

The resistance r_{ce} represents the equivalent parallel resistance from collector to emitter and has a value ranging from about 100 kΩ to 20 kΩ.

The current generator $g_m V_{b'e}$ generates a current β times that in the input resistance $r_{b'e}$. The value of the mutual conductance, g_m, may be about 40 mA/V.

The complete equivalent circuit of Fig. B.1 may be simplified if required according to the frequency of operation and it is convenient to consider low, medium and high-frequency ranges.

Low-Frequency Range. This is defined as the frequency range over which the capacitances $C_{b'e}$ and $C_{b'c}$ can be neglected. The circuit then reduces to that shown in Fig. B.2. Suppose as an approximate illustration of numerical values, $C_{b'c}$ and r_{bc}' are respectively 10 pF and 2 MΩ, then the frequency at which the capacitive reactance is equal to the resistance is $1/2\pi C_{b'c} r_{b'c} = 10^{12}/(2\pi \times 10 \times 2 \times 10^6) \simeq 8$ kHz. Hence $r_{b'c}$ is the more important element at very much lower frequencies and $C_{b'c}$ can be neglected. Conversely at very much higher frequencies $C_{b'c}$ is more important and $r_{b'c}$ can then be neglected.

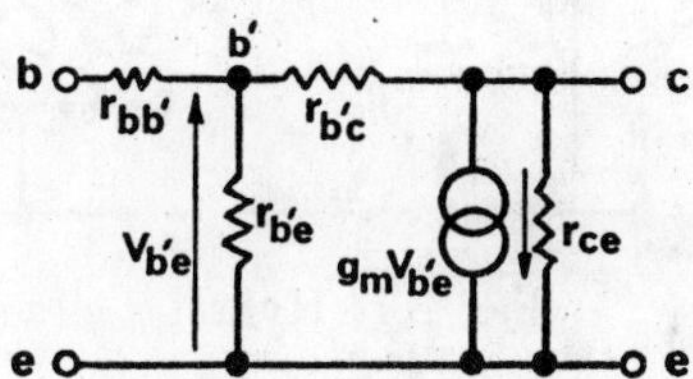

Fig. B.2. Approximate low-frequency circuit.

If $C_{b'e}$ and $r_{b'e}$ are assumed to be respectively 1000 pF and 1 kΩ, the capacitive reactance is equal to the resistance at $10^{12}/(2\pi \times 10^3 \times 10^3) \simeq$ 160 kHz.

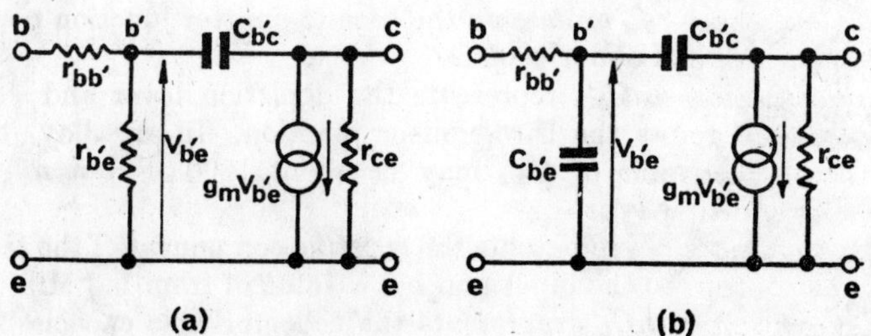

Fig. B.3 (a) Medium-frequency approximate circuit
(b) High-frequency circuit.

Medium-Frequency Range. **This is defined as the frequency range over which the presence of $r_{b'c}$ and $C_{b'e}$ may be ignored, thus giving the approximate circuit as shown in Fig. B.3a.**

High-Frequency Range. **It follows from the argument above that for still higher frequencies**

$$1/\omega C_{b'c} < r_{b'c} \quad \text{and} \quad 1/\omega C_{b'e} < r_{b'e}$$

and so both $r_{b'c}$ and $r_{b'e}$ can be neglected. The resulting high-frequency circuit for the transistor is then as shown in Fig. B.3b.

A further approximation is sometimes made by omitting the resistance $r_{bb'}$ from the input circuit. The value of the mutual conductance g_m is then modified.

APPENDIX C

MATHEMATICAL FORMULAE

(a) *Binomial Theorem*

This theorem enables powers of a binomial to be expressed in the form of a series, and may be stated as,

$$(1+x)^n = 1 + nx + \frac{n(n-1)}{\lfloor 2}x^2 + \frac{n(n-1)(n-2)}{\lfloor 3}x^3 + \ldots$$

If n is a positive integer, this is true for all values of x ; if n is fractional or negative, the expansion holds if x is a positive or negative quantity which is less than unity. It is often useful to remember that if $x<1$, then

$$(1+x)^n \simeq 1 + nx$$

(b) *Maclaurin's and Taylor's Theorems*

If a function $f(x)$ can be represented by a series

$$a_0 + a_1x + a_2x^2 + a_3x^3 + \ldots$$

then $f(x) = f(0) + xf'(0) + \dfrac{x^2}{\lfloor 2}f''(0) + \dfrac{x^3}{\lfloor 3}f'''(0) + \quad \ldots$ C.1

This is called *Maclaurin's series*. If it is desired to expand a function $f(x)$, the successive derivations of the function $f'(x), f''(x)$, etc., must first be found.

$$f'(x) = \frac{d}{dx}f(x)$$

$$f''(x) = \frac{d}{dx}f'(x) \text{ etc.}$$

The substitution of $x=0$ then gives $f(0)$, $f'(0)$, etc. The insertion of these values in equation C.1 then gives the expansion.

If it may be assumed that, for all values of h,

$$f(x+h) = a_0 + a_1h + a_2h^2 + a_3h^3 + \ldots$$

then $f(x+h) = f(x) + hf'(x) + \dfrac{h^2}{\lfloor 2}f''(x) + \dfrac{h^3}{\lfloor 3}f'''(x) + \ldots$

This is called *Taylor's series*.

(c) ***Exponential and Logarithmic Functions***

$$e = \underset{n \to \infty}{\text{Limit}} \left(1 + \frac{1}{n}\right)^n = 1 + 1 + \frac{1}{\lfloor 2} + \frac{1}{\lfloor 3} + \frac{1}{\lfloor 4} + \cdots = 2{\cdot}71828$$

$$e^x = 1 + x + \frac{x^2}{\lfloor 2} + \frac{x^3}{\lfloor 3} + \frac{x^4}{\lfloor 4} + \ldots$$

$$+ a^x = 1 + x \log_e a + \frac{x^2}{\lfloor 2}(\log_e a)^2 + \frac{x^3}{\lfloor 3}(\log_e a)^3 + \ldots$$

$$+ \log_e(1 + x) = x - \frac{x^2}{2} + \frac{x^3}{3} - \frac{x^4}{4} + \ldots \text{ when } |x| < |$$

$$+ \log_e \frac{m}{n} = 2\left[\frac{m-n}{m+n} + \frac{1}{3}\left(\frac{m-n}{m+n}\right)^3 + \frac{1}{5}\left(\frac{m-n}{m+n}\right)^5 + \ldots\right]$$

(d) ***Trigonometric Functions***

$\sin(-\alpha) = -\sin\alpha$; $\cos(-\alpha) = \cos\alpha$

$\sin\alpha = \cos\left(\frac{\pi}{2} - \alpha\right)$; $\cos\alpha = \sin\left(\frac{\pi}{2} - \alpha\right)$

$\cos^2\alpha + \sin^2\alpha = 1$; $\sec^2\alpha = 1 + \tan^2\alpha$; $\text{cosec}^2\alpha = 1 + \cot^2\alpha$

$$\sin(\alpha + \beta) = \sin\alpha\cos\beta + \cos\alpha\sin\beta$$

$$\sin(\alpha - \beta) = \sin\alpha\cos\beta - \cos\alpha\sin\beta$$

$$\cos(\alpha + \beta) = \cos\alpha\cos\beta - \sin\alpha\sin\beta$$

$$\cos(\alpha - \beta) = \cos\alpha\cos\beta + \sin\alpha\sin\beta$$

$$\tan(\alpha + \beta) = \frac{\tan\alpha + \tan\beta}{1 - \tan\alpha\tan\beta}$$

$$\tan(\alpha - \beta) = \frac{\tan\alpha - \tan\beta}{1 + \tan\alpha\tan\beta}$$

$$\sin\alpha\sin\beta = \tfrac{1}{2}[\cos(\alpha - \beta) - \cos(\alpha + \beta)]$$

$$\cos\alpha\cos\beta = \tfrac{1}{2}[\cos(\alpha - \beta) + \cos(\alpha + \beta)]$$

$$\sin\alpha\cos\beta = \tfrac{1}{2}[\sin(\alpha + \beta) + \sin(\alpha - \beta)]$$

$$\sin\alpha + \sin\beta = 2\sin\frac{\alpha + \beta}{2}\cos\frac{\alpha - \beta}{2}$$

$$\cos\alpha + \cos\beta = 2\cos\frac{\alpha + \beta}{2}\cos\frac{\alpha - \beta}{2}$$

$$\cos\alpha - \cos\beta = -2\sin\frac{\alpha + \beta}{2}\sin\frac{\alpha - \beta}{2}$$

$\sin 2\alpha = 2 \sin \alpha \cos \alpha$; $\cos 2\alpha = \cos^2\alpha - \sin^2\alpha = 2 \cos^2\alpha - 1$

$\sin 3\alpha = 3 \sin \alpha - 4 \sin^3\alpha$; $\cos 3\alpha = 4 \cos^3\alpha - 3 \cos \alpha$

$$\sin^2\alpha = \frac{1 - \cos 2\alpha}{2}; \quad \cos^2\alpha = \frac{1 + \cos 2\alpha}{2}$$

$$\sin \alpha = \alpha - \frac{\alpha^3}{\underline{|3}} + \frac{\alpha^5}{\underline{|5}} -$$

$$\cos \alpha = 1 - \frac{\alpha^2}{\underline{|2}} + \frac{\alpha^4}{\underline{|4}} -$$

$$\tan \alpha = \alpha + \frac{\alpha^3}{3} + \frac{2\alpha^5}{15}$$

$$a \cos \alpha + b \sin \alpha = \sqrt{a^2 + b^2} \sin \left(\alpha + \tan^{-1}\frac{a}{b} \right)$$

$$\sin \alpha = \frac{e^{j\alpha} - e^{-j\alpha}}{2j}; \quad \cos \alpha = \frac{e^{j\alpha} + e^{-j\alpha}}{2}$$

$$(\cos \alpha + j \sin \alpha)^n = (e^{j\alpha})^n = \cos n\alpha + j \sin n\alpha$$

(e) ***Hyperbolic Functions***

$\cosh^2\alpha - \sinh^2\alpha = 1$; $\operatorname{sech}^2\alpha = 1 - \tanh^2\alpha$; $\operatorname{cosech}^2\alpha = \coth^2\alpha - 1$

$$\sinh (\alpha + \beta) = \sinh \alpha \cosh \beta + \cosh \alpha \sinh \beta$$

$$\sinh (\alpha - \beta) = \sinh \alpha \cosh \beta - \cosh \alpha \sinh \beta$$

$$\cosh (\alpha + \beta) = \cosh \alpha \cosh \beta + \sinh \alpha \sinh \beta$$

$$\cosh (\alpha - \beta) = \cosh \alpha \cosh \beta - \sinh \alpha \sinh \beta$$

$$\tanh (\alpha + \beta) = \frac{\tanh \alpha + \tanh \beta}{1 + \tanh \alpha \tanh \beta}$$

$$\tanh (\alpha - \beta) = \frac{\tanh \alpha - \tanh \beta}{1 - \tanh \alpha \tanh \beta}$$

$$\sinh \alpha + \sinh \beta = 2 \sinh \frac{\alpha + \beta}{2} \cosh \frac{\alpha - \beta}{2}$$

$$\cosh \alpha + \cosh \beta = 2 \cosh \frac{\alpha + \beta}{2} \cosh \frac{\alpha - \beta}{2}$$

$$\cosh \alpha - \cosh \beta = 2 \sinh \frac{\alpha + \beta}{2} \sinh \frac{\alpha - \beta}{2}$$

$\sinh 2\alpha = 2 \sinh \alpha \cosh \alpha$; $\cosh 2\alpha = \cosh^2\alpha + \sinh^2\alpha$

$\sinh 3\alpha = 3 \sinh \alpha + 4 \sinh^3\alpha$; $\cosh 3\alpha = 4 \cosh^3\alpha - 3 \cosh \alpha$

$$\sinh j\alpha = j \sin\alpha\ ;\ \sin j\alpha = j \sinh\alpha$$

$$\cosh j\alpha = \cos\alpha\ ;\ \cos j\alpha = \cosh\alpha$$

$$\cosh\alpha + \sinh\alpha = e^{\alpha}$$

$$\sinh\alpha = \frac{e^{\alpha} - e^{-\alpha}}{2} = \alpha + \frac{\alpha^3}{\underline{|3}} + \frac{\alpha^5}{\underline{|5}} + \frac{\alpha^7}{\underline{|7}} + $$

$$\cosh\alpha = \frac{e^{\alpha} + e^{-\alpha}}{2} = 1 + \frac{\alpha^2}{\underline{|2}} + \frac{\alpha^4}{\underline{|4}} + \frac{\alpha^6}{\underline{|6}} + $$

$$\tanh\alpha = \alpha - \frac{1}{3}\alpha^3 + \frac{2}{15}\alpha^5 -$$

$$\sinh(\alpha + j\beta) = \sinh\alpha\cos\beta + j\cosh\alpha\sin\beta$$

$$\sinh(\alpha - j\beta) = \sinh\alpha\cos\beta - j\cosh\alpha\sin\beta$$

$$\cosh(\alpha + j\beta) = \cosh\alpha\cos\beta + j\sinh\alpha\sin\beta$$

$$\cosh(\alpha - j\beta) = \cosh\alpha\cos\beta - j\sinh\alpha\sin\beta$$

(f) *Differentiation*

$$\frac{d}{dx}e^x = e^x$$

$$\frac{d}{d\theta}\cdot\sin\theta = \cos\theta\ ; \qquad \frac{d}{d\theta}\cdot\cos\theta = -\sin\theta$$

$$\frac{d}{d\theta}\cdot\sinh\theta = \cosh\theta\ ; \qquad \frac{d}{d\theta}\cdot\cosh\theta = \sinh\theta$$

If $y = f(x)$ and $x = \varnothing(y)$, $\dfrac{dy}{dx} = \dfrac{1}{\dfrac{dx}{dy}}$

If $y = uv$, where u and v are functions of x, $\dfrac{dy}{dx} = u\dfrac{dv}{dx} + v\dfrac{du}{dx}$

If $y = \dfrac{u}{v}$, where u and v are functions of x, $\dfrac{dy}{dx} = \dfrac{v\dfrac{du}{dx} - u\dfrac{dv}{dx}}{v^2}$

If $y = f(u)$, where u is some function $\varnothing(x)$ of x, $\dfrac{dy}{dx} = \dfrac{dy}{du}\cdot\dfrac{du}{dx}$

(g) *Table of Derivatives and Integrals*

(The constant of integration is omitted from the values of the integrals.)

$$\frac{d}{dx}\cdot x^n = nx^{n-1}, \qquad \int x^n dx = \frac{1}{n+1}x^{n+1}$$

(except for $n = -1$)

$$\frac{d}{dx}\cdot\frac{1}{x} = \frac{-1}{x^2}, \qquad \int\frac{dx}{x} = \log_e x,$$

$$\frac{d}{dx}\cdot e^{kx} = ke^{kx}, \qquad \int e^{kx}dx = \frac{1}{k}e^{kx},$$

$$\frac{d}{dx}\cdot\sin(ax+b) = a\cos(ax+b), \qquad \int\sin(ax+b)\,dx = -\frac{1}{a}\cos(ax+b),$$

$$\frac{d}{dx}\cdot\cos(ax+b) = -a\sin(ax+b), \qquad \int\cos(ax+b)\,dx = \frac{1}{a}\sin(ax+b),$$

$$\frac{d}{dx}\cdot\tan x = \sec^2 x, \qquad \int\tan x = \log(\sec x)$$

$$\frac{d}{dx}\cdot\cot x = -\operatorname{cosec}^2 x, \qquad \int\cot x = \log(\sin x)$$

$$\frac{d}{dx}\cdot\tanh x = \operatorname{sech}^2 x, \qquad \int\tanh x = \log(\cosh x)$$

$$\frac{d}{dx}\cdot\coth x = -\operatorname{cosech}^2 x, \qquad \int\coth x = \log(\sinh x)$$

$$\frac{d}{dx}\cdot\sin^{-1}x = \frac{1}{\sqrt{1-x^2}}, \qquad \int\sin^{-1}x, = x\sin^{-1}x + \sqrt{1-x^2}$$

$$\frac{d}{dx}\cdot\sin^{-1}\frac{x}{a} = \frac{1}{\sqrt{a^2-x^2}}, \qquad \int\sin^{-1}\frac{x}{a}, = x\sin^{-1}\frac{x}{a} + \sqrt{a^2-x^2}$$

$$\frac{d}{dx}\cdot\cos^{-1}\frac{x}{a} = -\frac{1}{\sqrt{a^2-x^2}}, \qquad \int\cos^{-1}\frac{x}{a} = x\cos^{-1}\frac{x}{a} - \sqrt{a^2-x^2}$$

$$\frac{d}{dx}\cdot\tan^{-1}\frac{x}{a} = \frac{a}{x^2+a^2}, \qquad \int\tan^{-1}\frac{x}{a} = x\tan^{-1}\frac{x}{a} - \frac{1}{a}\log\sqrt{a^2+x^2}$$

$$\frac{d}{dx}\cdot\sinh^{-1}x = \frac{1}{\sqrt{x^2+1}}, \qquad \int\frac{dx}{\sqrt{x^2+a^2}} = \sinh^{-1}\frac{x}{a},$$

$$\frac{d}{dx}\cdot\cosh^{-1}x = \frac{1}{\sqrt{x^2-1}}, \qquad \int\frac{da}{\sqrt{x^2-a^2}} = \cosh^{-1}\frac{x}{a},$$

$$\frac{d}{dx}\cdot\tanh^{-1}x = \frac{1}{1-x^2}, \qquad \int\frac{dx}{a^2-x^2} = \frac{1}{a}\tanh^{-1}\frac{x}{a}.$$

APPENDIX D

S.I. UNITS

THE SI (Système International d'Unités) system of units was adopted by the International Electrotechnical Commission in 1960. The relations between SI and C.G.S. units are shown in the table below.

Quantity	Symbol	SI unit	Equivalent in C.G.S. units	
			Electromagnetic	Electrostatic
Mass	M	1 kilogram	1000 g	1000 g
Length	L	1 metre	100 cm	100 cm
Time	T	1 second	1 second	1 second
Force	F	1 newton	10^5 dynes	10^5 dynes
Work	W	1 joule	10^7 ergs	10^7 ergs
Power	P	1 watt	10^7 ergs/s	10^7 ergs/s
Current	I	1 ampere	0·1 unit	3×10^9
Charge	Q	1 coulomb	0·1 unit	3×10^9
Potential	V	1 volt	10^8 units	1/300 unit
Resistance	R	1 ohm	10^9 units	$(1/9\times10^{-11})$
Inductance	L	1 henry	10^9 units	$(1/9\times10^{-11})$
Capacitance	C	1 farad		9×10^{11} units
Magnetising Force	H	1 amp-turn/metre	$4\pi\times10^{-3}$ oersted	
Magnetomotive Force	NI	1 amp-turn	$4\pi\times10^{-1}$ gilberts	
Magnetic Flux	Φ	1 weber	10^8 maxwells	1/300
Magnetic Flux Density	T	1 Tesla	10^4 gauss	
Electric Force	E	1 volt/metre		
Electric Flux Density	D	1 coulomb/metre^2		$1/(3\times10^4)$ unit/cm
Permeability of free space	μ_0	$4\pi\times10^{-7}$ unit	1 unit	
Permittivity of free space	k_0	$8{\cdot}85\times10^{-12}$ unit		1 unit

APPENDIX E

FOURIER ANALYSIS

THE analysis of a linear electrical network is relatively simple if the applied voltages are harmonic quantities, such as sin ωt, cos ωt, etc. In communication engineering many of the voltages encountered are not simple harmonic quantities, and such voltages (or currents) are said to have a complex waveform. The analysis of networks subject to the action of non-harmonic forces may however be treated by the application of Fourier's theorem, which states that any single-valued periodic function (i.e. a function which can have only one value for any given value of the independent variable) can be resolved into a fundamental periodic function and a number of harmonics. Thus a periodic function $y=f(t)$ having a period 2π, may be expressed as,

$$y=a_0+a_1 \sin \omega t+a_2 \sin 2\omega t+a_3 \sin 3\omega t$$

$$+b_1 \cos \omega t+b_2 \cos 2\omega t+b_3 \cos 3\omega t+\ldots \qquad 1$$

$$\text{or } y=a_0+\sum_{N=1}^{\infty}(a_N \sin N\omega t+b_N \cos N\omega t) \qquad 2$$

$$\text{where } a_0=\frac{1}{2\pi}\int_0^{2\pi} y\, d(\omega t) \qquad 3a$$

$$a_N=\frac{1}{\pi}\int_0^{2\pi} y \sin N\omega t\, d(\omega t) \qquad 3b$$

$$\text{and } b_N=\frac{1}{\pi}\int_0^{2\pi} y \cos N\omega t\, d(\omega t) \qquad 3c$$

Hence, if a periodic non-harmonic voltage (or current) is applied to a network the distribution of currents and voltages in the network may be obtained in three stages. First, the input voltage is analysed into its various components by means of the Fourier theorem ; the action of each component is then calculated separately in accordance with steady-state alternating current theory ; finally, the total voltage across, or the current in each branch of the network is obtained by the application of the superposition theorem to the voltages or currents produced by the separate components of the applied input voltage.

In any application of the Fourier series it is first of all necessary to determine the coefficients a_0, a_N and b_N of equation 1 ; the values have been given above (equation 3) and it is now proposed to show how these results are deduced. Briefly, the coefficients a_0, a_N and b_N are obtained by multiplying both sides of equation 1 by a suitable factor and integrating between the limits of 0 and 2π. If the multiplying factor is correctly chosen, all terms vanish except those which give the required coefficient. In this process use is made of the following values of integrals.

$$\int_0^{2\pi} \sin nx \, dx = -\frac{1}{n}[\cos nx]_0^{2\pi} = -\frac{1}{n}[1-1] = 0$$

where n is any integer.

Likewise $\int_0^{2\pi} \cos nx \; dx = 0$.

$$\text{Also, } \int_0^{2\pi} \sin mx \cos nx \, dx = \int_0^{2\pi} \{\tfrac{1}{2} \sin (m+n)x + \tfrac{1}{2} \sin (m-n)x\} dx$$

$$= 0$$

where m and n are any integers.

$$\int_0^{2\pi} \cos mx \cos nx \, dx = \int_0^{2\pi} \{\tfrac{1}{2} \cos (m+n)x + \tfrac{1}{2} \cos (m-n)x\} dx$$

$$= 0 \text{ if } m \text{ is not equal to } n.$$

$$\int_0^{\pi} \sin mx \sin nx \, dx = \int_0^{2\pi} \{\tfrac{1}{2} \cos (m-n)x - \tfrac{1}{2} \cos (m+n)x\} dx$$

$$= 0 \text{ if } m \text{ is not equal to } n.$$

$$\text{and } \int_0^{2\pi} \sin^2 nx \, dx = \int_0^{2\pi} \cos^2 nx \, dx = \pi$$

If the results quoted above are borne in mind, and equation 1 is integrated throughout with respect to ωt, between the limits of 0 and 2π, all the terms on the right-hand side vanish except a_0 ;

$$\therefore \; a_0 \int_0^{2\pi} d(\omega t) = \int_0^{2\pi} y \, d(\omega t)$$

$$\therefore \qquad a_0 = \frac{1}{2\pi} \int_0^{2\pi} y \, d(\omega t)$$

which is the result given in equation 3a above. It will be seen that a_0 is the mean value of y between the limits of 0 and 2π.

To find a_N, the right-hand side of equation 1 must be multiplied by a factor such that integration between the limits of 0 and 2π causes all terms to vanish except the one containing a_N; this can be achieved if sin $N\omega t$ is used as the multiplying factor. Then, as a result of the values of the integrals quoted above.

$$\int_0^{2\pi} y \sin N\omega t \, d(\omega t) = a_N \int_0^{2\pi} \sin^2 N\omega t \, d(\omega t)$$
$$= a_N \pi$$

and so
$$a_N = \frac{1}{\pi}\int_0^{2\pi} y \sin N\omega t \, d(\omega t)$$

which is the result given in equation 3b.

To determine b_N, equation 1 must be multiplied throughout by the factor cos $N\omega t$ and integrated with respect to ωt between the limits 0 and 2π. Then,

$$\int_0^{2\pi} y \cos N\omega t \, d(\omega t) = b_N \int_0^{2\pi} \cos^2 N\omega t \, d(\omega t)$$
$$= b_N \pi$$

which gives the result

$$b_N = \frac{1}{\pi}\int_0^{2\pi} y \cos N\omega t \, d(\omega t)$$

Example of Fourier Analysis

As a simple example of the application of Fourier analysis, suppose that a voltage has the waveform shown in Fig. E. 1. The function y in this case is such that

$$y = 1 \text{ (in the range } 0 < \omega t < \pi)$$
$$y = -1 \text{ (in the range } \pi < \omega t < 2\pi)$$

Now equation 3a states that

$$a_0 = \frac{1}{2\pi}\int_0^{2\pi} y \, d(\omega t)$$
$$= \frac{1}{2\pi}\int_0^{\pi} d(\omega t) + \frac{1}{2\pi}\int_{\pi}^{2\pi} - d(\omega t) = 0.$$

Also,
$$a_N = \frac{1}{\pi}\int_0^{2\pi} y \sin N\omega t \, d(\omega t)$$
$$= \frac{1}{\pi}\int_0^{\pi} \sin N\omega t \, d(\omega t) + \frac{1}{\pi}\int_{\pi}^{2\pi} - \sin N\omega t \, d(\omega t)$$
$$= \frac{2}{\pi N}[1 - \cos N\pi]$$

hence when N is odd, $a_N = \frac{4}{\pi N}$

and when N is even, $a_N = 0$.

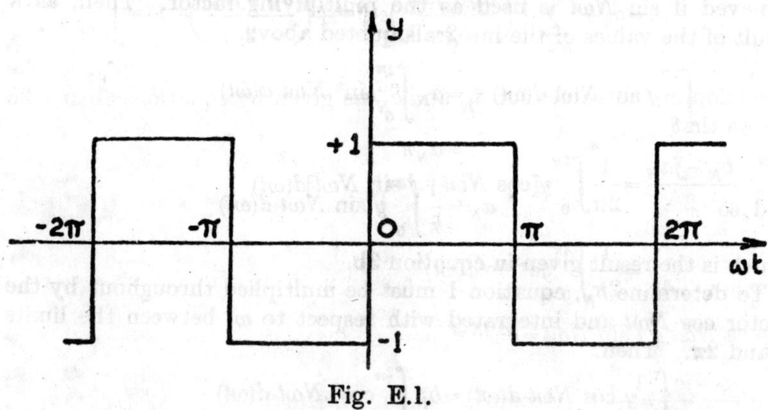

Fig. E.1.

Equation 3c gives,

$$b_N = \frac{1}{\pi}\int_0^{2\pi} y \cos N\omega t \, d(\omega t)$$

$$= \frac{1}{\pi}\int_0^{\pi} \cos N\omega t \, d(\omega t) + \frac{1}{\pi}\int_{\pi}^{2\pi} -\cos N\omega t \, d(\omega t)$$

$$= \frac{1}{\pi N}[\sin N\omega t]_0^{\pi} - \frac{1}{\pi N}[\sin N\omega t]_{\pi}^{2\pi}$$

$$= 0.$$

The required equation for the function y in this case is thus given by

$$y = \frac{4}{\pi}\left[\sin \omega t + \frac{1}{3}\sin 3\,\omega t + \frac{1}{5}\sin 5\,\omega t + \frac{1}{7}\sin 7\,\omega t + \ldots\ldots\right]$$

The voltage waveform represented as a time function in Fig. 1 may thus be resolved into a fundamental alternating component and an infinite series of odd harmonics.

Complex Fourier Series

The Fourier series is given in equation 1 as a series of sines and cosines. Some simplification can be achieved if an exponential form is employed. Thus equation 2 can be rewritten as,

$$y = a_0 + \sum_{N=1}^{\infty}\left[a_N\left(\frac{e^{jN\omega t} - e^{-jN\omega t}}{2j}\right) + b_N\left(\frac{e^{jN\omega t} + e^{-jN\omega t}}{2}\right)\right]$$

$$= a_0 + \sum_{N=1}^{\infty}\left[\left(\frac{b_N - ja_N}{2}\right)e^{jN\omega t} + \left(\frac{b_N + ja_N}{2}\right)e^{-jN\omega t}\right]$$

Insertion of the values for a_N and b_N as given by equations 3b and 3c shows that

$$\frac{b_N - ja_N}{2} = \frac{1}{2\pi}\int_0^{2\pi} y[\cos N\omega t - j\sin N\omega t]d(\omega t)$$

$$= \frac{1}{2\pi}\int_0^{2\pi} ye^{-jN\omega t}d(\omega t)$$

as $\cos N\omega t \pm j\sin N\omega t = e^{\pm jN\omega t}$

also $\dfrac{b_N + ja_N}{2} = \dfrac{1}{2\pi}\displaystyle\int_0^{2\pi} y[\cos N\omega t + j\sin N\omega t]d(\omega t)$

$$= \frac{1}{2\pi}\int_0^{2\pi} ye^{jN\omega t}d(\omega t)$$

while equation 3a gives

$$a_0 = \frac{1}{2\pi}\int_0^{2\pi} y\, d(\omega t)$$

It will be seen that the three formulas of equation 3 are now all of the same form. If $(b_N - ja_N)/2$ and $(b_N + ja_N)/2$ are written respectively as a_{-n}, and a_n then only one expression is required for all the coefficients, namely

$$a_n = \frac{1}{2\pi}\int_0^{2\pi} ye^{-jn\omega t}d(\omega t)$$

provided that n takes on all positive and negative integral values, including zero.

The series expressed in equation 2 may thus be written, as

$$y = \sum_{n=-\infty}^{n=+\infty} a_n e^{jn\omega t}$$

This equation is referred to as the complex Fourier series and may be used in place of equation 2. The manipulation of the complex form of the Fourier series is, in general, easier than the trigonometric form as the problems of differentiation and integration are simpler.

APPENDIX F

THE RELATION IN AUTOMATIC TELEPHONY BETWEEN THE GRADE OF SERVICE, THE TRAFFIC AND THE NUMBER OF TRUNKS

It was stated on page 574 that the relation between the grade of service (B), the traffic offered (A), and the number of trunks (N) is given by the Erlang formula

$$B = \frac{\frac{A^N}{\underline{|N}}}{1 + A + \frac{A^2}{\underline{|2}} + \frac{A^3}{\underline{|3}} + \frac{A^4}{\underline{|4}} + \cdot \cdot \cdot \cdot + \frac{A^N}{\underline{|N}}}$$

This relationship was deduced by Erlang after making certain simplifying assumptions, and assuming that the system was in a state of *statistic equilibrium.* The main assumptions involved may be listed as follows :—

(*a*) The system is assumed to be such that if a connection is required when all the trunks are engaged, then that call is lost ; the holding time of all such attempted calls at that stage is also assumed to be zero.

(*b*) The calls are assumed to be distributed quite accidentally throughout the time in question (i.e. the busy hour) so that a call is as likely to originate at one moment as the next. This constitutes *pure chance* traffic. In precise terms this is only possible if the number of subscribers (or switches in the previous stage) is infinite, but a large number gives a fairly good approximation.

(*c*) A very large number of groups of trunks (or lines) is assumed and these are considered during periods in which, roughly speaking, the average traffic is neither rising nor falling. If at some moment a count is made of the number of calls in progress in all these groups, some would have just begun, and others would be ending. A further examination of the number of calls after a very short time dt would then reveal that some calls had ended while others had been initiated. The assumption of a very large number of groups of trunks gives the characteristic property that, in spite of individual alterations, the general state remains unaltered, as the alterations of the different kinds balance each other. This property is called ***statistic equilibrium.***

Suppose now that each group has N trunks and carries an average traffic A. If the proportion of groups with zero trunks engaged is S_0, the proportion with one trunk engaged is S_1, and the proportion of groups having N trunks engaged is S_N, the total proportion of groups is equal to unity, and so

$$S_0 + S_1 + S_2 + S_3 + \ldots\ldots + S_N = 1 \quad . \quad . \quad . \quad (1)$$

The assumption of statistic equilibrium implies that the proportions S_0, S_1, S_2, etc. remain constant, although there will be changes in any one group.

If a group has 0 trunks engaged and is designated as an S_0 group, then in a time dt which is so short that it allows only for the termination, or the origination, of a call, the group may receive a call which will convert it into a group with one trunk engaged (an S_1 group).

The chance of a call originating in a group in time dt is

$$A.dt$$

hence the proportion of groups changing from S_0 to S_1 in time dt is

$$S_0 \;.\; A.dt$$

In a group which has one trunk engaged, the connection must terminate within a period equal to the holding time (considered as unit time), and so the chance of it finishing within the time dt is

$$1.dt$$

and therefore the proportion of groups which change from S_1 to S_0 in the interval dt is

$$S_1.1.dt$$

The proportion of groups changing from S_0 to S_1 must balance those changing from S_1 to S_0, and so on

$$S_0.A.dt = S_1.1.dt$$

$$\therefore S_1 = S_0.A \quad . \quad . \quad . \quad . \quad (2)$$

A group with one trunk engaged may either lose a call, in the time dt and so become an S_0 group, or it may receive a call and thereby become an S_2 group. The change to an S_0 group has already been considered, and the possibility of change to an S_2 group has to be balanced against the possibility of a loss of a call by an S_2 group.

As the chance of a call originating in a group in time dt is

$$A.dt$$

the proportion of groups changing from S_1 to S_2 in time dt is

$$S_1.A.dt$$

In a group with two trunks engaged, the two calls must end within a period equal to the holding time, so that the chance of a call finishing in the short time interval dt is

$$2.dt$$

The proportion of groups changing from S_2 to S_1 is thus

$$S_2.2.dt$$

The proportion of groups changing from S_1 to S_2 must balance those changing from S_2 to S_1 and so

$$S_1.A.dt = S_2.2.dt$$

$$\therefore S_2 = S_1\frac{A}{2} = S_0\frac{A^2}{2} \quad . \quad . \quad . \quad . \quad (3)$$

Applying the same argument to groups with 3, 4, ... N trunks engaged gives

$$S_3 = S_0\frac{A^3}{\lfloor 3}$$

$$S_4 = S_0\frac{A^4}{\lfloor 4}$$

$$S_5 = S_0\frac{A^5}{\lfloor 5}$$

and $$S_N = S_0\frac{A^N}{\lfloor N}$$

By means of these relations and equations 2 and 3, equation 1 may be rewritten as

$$S_0\left(1 + A + \frac{A^2}{\lfloor 2} + \frac{A^3}{\lfloor 3} + \; . \; . \; . \; . \; . \; + \frac{A^N}{\lfloor N}\right) = 1$$

$$\therefore S_0 = \frac{1}{1 + A + \frac{A^2}{\lfloor 2} + \frac{A^3}{\lfloor 3} + \; . \; . \; . \; . \; . \; + \frac{A^N}{\lfloor N}}$$

and so $$S_N = \frac{\frac{A^N}{\lfloor N}}{1 + A + \frac{A^2}{\lfloor 2} + \frac{A^3}{\lfloor 3} + \; . \; . \; . \; . \; . \; + \frac{A^N}{\lfloor N}}$$

The quantity S_N was taken as the proportion of groups with N trunks engaged, and is the proportion of time in which all N trunks are engaged in a particular group. The proportion of lost calls, or grade of service B is thus

$$B = \frac{\frac{A^N}{\lfloor N}}{1 + A + \frac{A^2}{\lfloor 2} + \frac{A^3}{\lfloor 3} + \; . \; . \; . \; . \; . \; + \frac{A^N}{\lfloor N}}$$

APPENDIX G

MAXWELL'S EQUATIONS IN RECTANGULAR CO-ORDINATES

ELECTROMAGNETIC fields may be described mathematically by Maxwell's equations. These are based on the fundamental laws of Gauss, Faraday, and Ampere, together with Maxwell's conception of displacement current. If SI units are employed, these relations take the following form :—

(a) *Gauss's Law*

When applied to electric flux, this states that the net outward flux through any closed surface is equal to the charge enclosed by that surface. In the case of a magnetic field, the net outward magnetic flux through any closed surface is zero, i.e. lines of magnetic flux are continuous and form closed loops, as North and South magnetic poles cannot be dissociated.

(b) *Faraday's Law*

This states that the electromotive force induced in a closed loop is equal to the negative time rate of change of the magnetic flux linking that loop ; or the line integral of the electric force round the loop is equal to the rate of change of the magnetic flux through the loop, i.e.,

$$\oint E dl = -\frac{d\Phi}{dt}$$

It should be noted in passing that the loop or path over which the electric force is integrated may lie in a dielectric, a conductor, or in free space. In effect, any changing magnetic flux is encircled by an electric field, the lines of which are endless closed curves.

(c) *Ampère's Law*

This states that the line integral of the magnetic force round a closed path is equal to the total current linking that path, i.e.,

$$\oint H\,dl = i_{total}$$

The current must include both conduction and displacement components.

The displacement current, suggested by Maxwell, arises from the time variation of an electric field in a dielectric. A simple illustration of displacement current is provided by a capacitor connected to a source of alternating voltage. Conduction current flows in the wires connecting the voltage source to the capacitor ; this current is then continued in the dielectric between the plates by the displacement current. The current, as always, forms a closed path; where the conduction current stops the displacement current begins, and conversely the conduction current starts where the displacement current ends.

The electric flux D, per unit area, in a dielectric is related to the electric force E, by

$$D = kE$$

where $k = k_0 k_r$; k_0 is the permittivity of free space, and k_r is the relative permittivity of the dielectric. The electric force E is in volts per metre, and D is in coulombs per square metre. The displacement current density, j_d, is then given by,

$$j_d = \frac{dD}{dt} = k\frac{dE}{dt}$$

The foregoing relations may be expressed in terms of rectangular co-ordinates for a homogeneous, isotropic medium, i.e. a uniform medium with the same properties in all directions.

Thus, consider an elementary rectangular area, lying in the yz plane, with sides $\triangle y$ and $\triangle z$ as shown. If there is a component of the magnetic flux density B_x, directed from the origin along the x axis, then the flux linking the rectangle is

$$\Phi_x = B_x \triangle y \triangle z = \mu H_x f \triangle y \triangle z$$

where $\mu = \mu_0 \mu_r$; μ_0 is the permeability of free space, and μ_r is the relative permeability of the medium.

By Faraday's law, the line integral of the electric force E, is equal

to $$-\mu \triangle y \triangle z \frac{\partial H_x}{\partial t}$$

The line integral of the electric force round the rectangle, in the right-handed sense round B_x, is given by,

$$\left[E_z + \frac{\partial E_z}{\partial y}\triangle y\right]\triangle z - \left[E_y + \frac{\partial E_y}{\partial z}\triangle z\right]\triangle y - E_z \triangle z + E_y \triangle y$$

$$= \left[\frac{\partial E_z}{\partial y} - \frac{\partial E_y}{\partial z}\right]\triangle y \triangle z$$

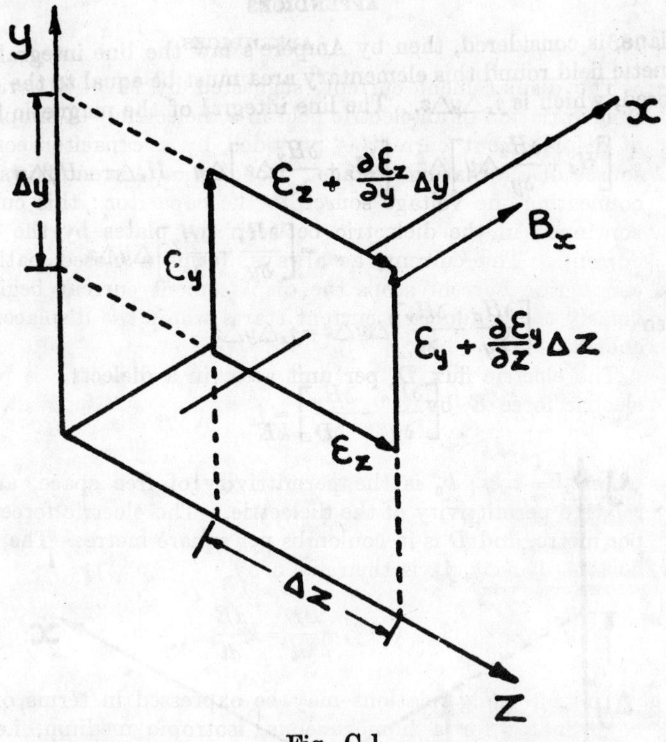

Fig. G.1.

Hence it follows that

$$\left[\frac{\partial E_z}{\partial y} - \frac{\partial E_y}{\partial z}\right]\triangle y\triangle z = -\mu\triangle y\triangle z\frac{\partial H_x}{\partial t}$$

or
$$\frac{\partial E_z}{\partial y} - \frac{\partial E_y}{\partial z} = -\mu\frac{\partial H_x}{\partial t} \quad . \quad . \quad . \quad . \quad (1)$$

Two other equations may be obtained in similar fashion for the other components, namely

$$\frac{\partial E_x}{\partial z} - \frac{\partial E_z}{\partial x} = -\mu\frac{\partial H_y}{\partial t} \quad . \quad . \quad . \quad . \quad (2)$$

and
$$\frac{\partial E_y}{\partial x} - \frac{\partial E_x}{\partial y} = -\mu\frac{\partial H_z}{\partial t} \quad . \quad . \quad . \quad . \quad (3)$$

Suppose now that there is a component of current density j_x in the x direction. If an elementary rectangular area, lying wholly in the

yz plane, is considered, then by Ampère's law the line integral of the magnetic field round this elementary area must be equal to the current enclosed, which is $j_x \Delta y \Delta z$. The line integral of the magnetic force is

$$\left[H_z + \frac{\partial H_z}{\partial y}\Delta y\right]\Delta z - \left[H_y + \frac{\partial H_y}{\partial z}\Delta z\right]\Delta y - H_z\Delta z + H_y\Delta y$$

$$= \left[\frac{\partial H_z}{\partial y} - \frac{\partial H_y}{\partial z}\right]\Delta y\Delta z$$

and so
$$\left[\frac{\partial H_z}{\partial y} - \frac{\partial H_y}{\partial z}\right]\Delta y\Delta z = j_x\Delta y\Delta z$$

or
$$\left[\frac{\partial H_z}{\partial y} - \frac{\partial H_y}{\partial z}\right] = j_x$$

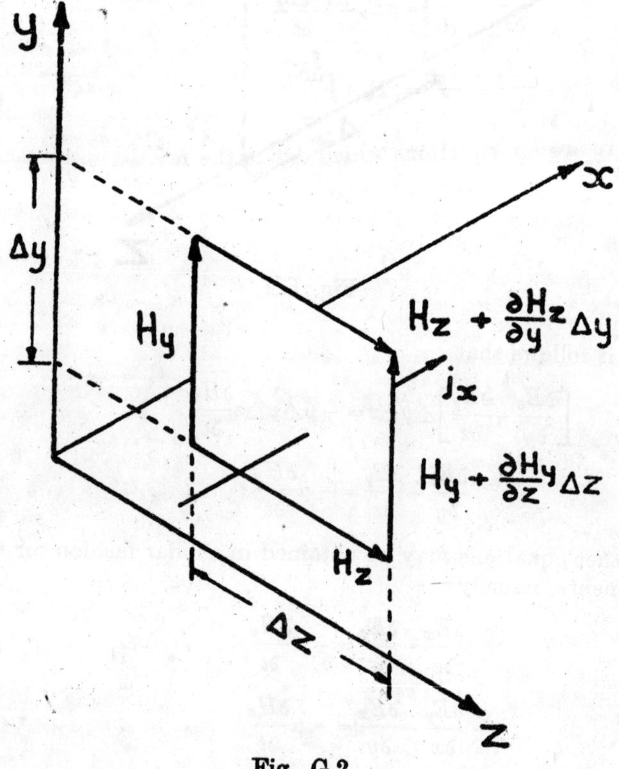

Fig. G.2.

If the current density has a conduction component j_c, and a displacement component j_d, then

$$j = j_c + j_d$$

$$= gE + k\frac{\partial E}{\partial t}$$

where g is the conductivity of the medium.

The result obtained above may thus be expressed as

$$\frac{\partial H_z}{\partial y} - \frac{\partial H_y}{\partial z} = gE_x + k\frac{\partial E_x}{\partial t} \quad . \quad . \quad . \quad (4)$$

The other components give two other equations, namely

$$\frac{\partial H_x}{\partial z} - \frac{\partial H_z}{\partial x} = gE_y + k\frac{\partial E_y}{\partial t} \quad . \quad . \quad . \quad (5)$$

and

$$\frac{\partial H_y}{\partial x} - \frac{\partial H_x}{\partial y} = gE_z + k\frac{\partial E_z}{\partial t} \quad . \quad . \quad . \quad (6)$$

so that there are six equations which define the relationships between E and H.

APPENDIX H

THE PROPAGATION OF A PLANE WAVE

PLANE waves are important because at large distances from a radiating source most waves approximate to plane waves when they are considered over an area which is small compared with the distance from the source ; plane waves are also the simplest type of wave from the viewpoint of analysis.

If a uniform plane wave is assumed to be travelling in the x direction, and the plane of the wave lies in the yz plane, there will be no variation in a direction normal to the direction of propagation of the wave, and so $\partial/\partial z = \partial/\partial y = 0$. The six equations of Appendix G for the electric and magnetic intensities thus become

$$0 = -\mu\frac{\partial H_x}{\partial t} \quad . \quad . \quad (1) \qquad 0 = k\frac{\partial E_x}{\partial t} \quad . \quad . \quad (4)$$

$$-\frac{\partial E_z}{\partial x} = -\mu\frac{\partial H_y}{\partial t} \quad . \quad . \quad (2) \qquad -\frac{\partial H_z}{\partial x} = k\frac{\partial E_y}{\partial t} \quad . \quad . \quad (5)$$

$$\frac{\partial E_y}{\partial x} = -\mu\frac{\partial H_z}{\partial t} \quad . \quad . \quad (3) \qquad \frac{\partial H_y}{\partial x} = k\frac{\partial E_z}{\partial t} \quad . \quad . \quad (6)$$

if the medium is a pure dielectric of zero conductivity.

Equations (1) and (4) show that H_x and E_x must be either zero or constant quantities ; the latter are not involved in wave motion, and so $H_x = 0$ and $E_x = 0$.

If the electric force is taken as parallel to the y axis, then $E_z = 0$ and from equation (2) or (6) $H_y = 0$. The only equations remaining are then the pair (3) and (5). Differentiation of equation (3) with respect to x, and (5) with respect to t gives

$$\frac{\partial^2 E_y}{\partial x^2} = -\mu\frac{\partial^2 H_z}{\partial x \partial t}$$

and $$-\frac{\partial^2 H_z}{\partial x \partial t} = k\frac{\partial^2 E_y}{\partial t^2}$$

from which $$\frac{\partial^2 E_y}{\partial t^2} = \frac{1}{\mu k}\,\frac{\partial^2 E_y}{\partial x^2} \quad . \quad . \quad . \quad . \quad . \quad (7)$$

The corresponding relation for H_z is

$$\frac{\partial^2 H_z}{\partial t^2} = \frac{1}{\mu k} \frac{\partial^2 H_z}{\partial x^2} \quad . \quad . \quad . \quad . \quad . \quad . \quad (8)$$

This is obtained by differentiating equations (3) and (5) with respect to t and x respectively.

If E_y and H_z have a sinusoidal time variation, so that E_y can be written as $E_y e^{j\omega t}$ and likewise H_z written as $H_z e^{j\omega t}$

then $$\frac{\partial^2 E_y}{\partial x^2} = -\omega^2 \mu k E_y e^{j\omega t} \quad . \quad . \quad . \quad . \quad . \quad (9)$$

and $$\frac{\partial^2 H_z}{\partial x^2} = -\omega^2 \mu k H_z e^{j\omega t} \quad . \quad . \quad . \quad . \quad . \quad (10)$$

If the medium considered is homogeneous, there will be an outgoing plane wave, but no reflected wave. The variation of E_y and H_z with distance along the x axis may then be expressed in similar form to that used for the distribution of voltage and current along an infinite loss-free transmission line, i.e.

$$E_y = Ee^{-j\beta x} \quad . \quad . \quad . \quad . \quad . \quad (11)$$

and $$H_z = He^{-j\beta x} \quad . \quad . \quad . \quad . \quad . \quad (12)$$

where β, the wavelength constant, is given by

$$\beta = \omega\sqrt{\mu k} \quad . \quad . \quad . \quad . \quad . \quad (13)$$

E_y and H_z vary with time and space and may be expressed as

$$E_y = Ee^{j(\omega t - \beta x)} \quad . \quad . \quad . \quad . \quad . \quad (14)$$

$$\text{and } H_z = He^{j(\omega t - \beta x)} \quad . \quad . \quad . \quad . \quad . \quad (15)$$

These expressions for E_y and H_z then satisfy the general equations (7) and (8) respectively. At any point in space the electric and magnetic fields have a sinusoidal time variation, and are in phase with each other; at any instant of time, the electric and magnetic field intensities vary sinusoidally with distance along the direction of propagation of the wave.

Equations (14) and (15) may be expressed in their equivalent trigonometrical form as

$$E_y = E[\cos(\omega t - \beta x) + j \sin(\omega t - \beta x)]$$

and $$H_z = H[\cos(\omega t - \beta x) + j \sin(\omega t - \beta x)]$$

From this form it can be seen that at any fixed time, the value of E_y (or H_z) repeats itself whenever the distance is increased by a value

x', where $x'=2\pi/\beta$. This special distance x' is the wavelength λ, and is related to the velocity of propagation of the wave v, by

$$v=\lambda f$$

where f is the frequency of variation of the fields. Hence

$$v=\frac{\omega}{\beta}$$

and from equation (13)

$$v=\frac{1}{\sqrt{\mu k}} \quad . \quad . \quad . \quad . \qquad (16)$$

It follows that the velocity of propagation of a plane wave in a pure dielectric medium is determined by the permeability and permittivity of that medium. For free space,

$$\mu=\mu_0=4\pi\times10^{-7}$$

and
$$k=k_0=\frac{1}{4\pi\times9\times10^9} \text{ in SI units,}$$

so that the velocity of propagation in free space is very nearly equal to 3×10^8 metres per second.

The relation of the electric field intensity to the magnetic field intensity may be obtained from equations (3), (14), and (15). If the value of E_y and H_z, as given by equations (14) and (15) are inserted in equation (3), then

$$\frac{\partial}{\partial x}[Ee^{j(\omega t-\beta x)}]=-\mu\frac{\partial}{\partial t}[He^{j(\omega t-\beta x)}]$$

or
$$-j\beta Ee^{j(\omega t-\beta x)}=-j\mu\omega He^{j(\omega t-\beta x)}$$

and hence
$$\frac{E}{H}=\frac{\mu\omega}{\beta}=\sqrt{\frac{\mu}{k}}$$

ANSWERS TO EXAMPLES

CHAPTER 2

3. $E' = \dfrac{E(1 - j\omega CR)}{1 + \omega^2C^2R^2}$ $\quad Z' = \dfrac{R - j\omega CR^2}{1 + \omega^2C^2R^2}$
4. 1·8 mA.
5. Each T-circuit should be converted to an equivalent π. If Z'_e is equal to the parallel combination of the two series impedances (Z_e in Fig. 2.3b), the condition for zero output voltage is that Z'_e should be infinite. This occurs at the frequency of 636 Hz.

CHAPTER 3

1. 1·589 MHz.
2. (i) 0·031% low.
   (ii) 0·12% low.
   (iii) 0·00016% low.
3. $Q = 150$: parallel resonant impedance 106,000 Ω.
4. (a) 36,000 Ω (b) 16,000 Ω.
8. $27 - j\,36{\cdot}1\ \Omega$: Q-factor $= 9$.
9. An increase of 22 $\mu\mu$F.
11. 0·0124 volt.
12. 513 Ω.
13 An inductive reactance of 135 Ω and a capacitive reactance of 304 Ω.
14. 0·03 mH.

CHAPTER 4

1. Attenuation coefficient = 0.0098 neper : wavelength coefficient = 0·051 radian: $Z_0 = 520\underline{/-1C^\circ 51'}\ \Omega$: velocity of propagation = 98,400 miles/s.
2. $290\underline{/-25{\cdot}6^\circ}$: 65,000 miles/s.: 3·5 dB: 44°.
3. 31·4 dB : 12·3V.
4. (a) 15·05 dB, 17·32 dn, (b) $I_s = 9{\cdot}8\underline{/45^\circ}$ mA, $I_r = 1{\cdot}73\underline{/-54^\circ}$ mA
5. (i) 4·1 mA (ii) the received current leads the voltage by 23·8°.
6. (a) $5{\cdot}01\underline{/-44^\circ}$ (b) $7{\cdot}09\underline{/-22^\circ}$: $P = 0{\cdot}069 + j0{\cdot}077$. Velocity of propagation = 66,000 mls/s.

7. (a) $36\angle -180°$ (b) $0{\cdot}12\angle -172°$A.
8. $I_s = 5{\cdot}72\angle 38{\cdot}5°$mA : $I_r = 15{\cdot}15\angle -85{\cdot}5°$mA.
9. Attenuation coefficient = 0·045 neper/mile, wavelength coefficient = 0·059 radian/mile : velocity of propagation = 85,100 miles/s.
10. **$141\angle 16{\cdot}2°\,\Omega$. (*a*) 12·3 mls. (*b*) 123,000 mls/s. 25·6 db.**
12. 0·2.
15. Each series arm contains a resistance of 110 Ω in series with an inductance of 2·71 mH : the shunt arm consists of a resistance of 83 Ω in series with a capacitance of 0·603 μF.
16. Series arms $500\angle -11{\cdot}4°\ \Omega$: shunt arm $226\angle -29{\cdot}8°\ \Omega$.
17. $Z_0 = 613\angle -27°\ \Omega : P = 0{\cdot}086 + j0{\cdot}82$.
18. $Z_0 = 396\angle -9°\ \Omega$.
19. $81\angle -10{\cdot}8°\ \Omega$.
21. Coil spacing 1·06 miles: attenuation coefficient 0·01 neper per mile: velocity of propagation 13,000 miles/s.
22. 0·7 mile : 0·016 neper per mile.
23. 4·7 nautical miles.
24. 15·9 kHz : 52 mH : 1·42 mls. : 74 mH,

CHAPTER 5

1. Iterative impedances, $Z_{11} = 460\ \Omega$, $Z_{22} = 260\Omega$:
   Image impedances $Z_{01} = 400\ \Omega$, $Z_{02} = 300\ \Omega$.
2. Series arms 210 Ω : shunt arm 220 Ω.
3. Series arms 491 Ω : shunt arm 121 Ω.
4. 392 Ω ; 8·4 dB.
5. Series arms 200 Ω : shunt arm 803 Ω : error in attenuation 0·5dB.
6. Series arms 350 Ω : shunt arm 184 Ω.
7. 1·8 H.
8. 5·5 dB.
9. 0 and 1,000 Hz.
11. Series arms of 32 mH : shunt arm 0·177 μF.
12. (a) 3,000 Hz (b) 19·1 dB.
13. Cut-off frequency 1,500 Hz : infinite attenuation at 1,800 Hz.
14. 42°. 500 Hz is in the passband.
15. 23 dB.
16. 300 Hz and 3,000 Hz.
17. The requirements can be met by a constant-K T-section with an m-derived half section at each end. The T-section should have series arms of 32 mH, and a shunt arm of 0·177 μF. For the m-derived sections, $m = 0{\cdot}25$, and so the series arms should contain an inductance of 8 mH, and the shunt arm should have an inductance of 60 mH in series with 0·044 μF.
19. Series capacitor 0·25 μF : shunt capacitor 0·33 μF.
21. 592Ω. j678Ω.

CHAPTER 6

5. 950 mW.
6. Approximately 1 W : with an input voltage of 14 V peak : cathode bias resistor 350 Ω : transformer ratio 18 : 1.
11. Sensitivity decreased by $1/\sqrt{2}$ with magnetic deflection.

CHAPTER 8

1. 930Ω
2. 45: 2·2 and 5·8V: 1V.
3. The working point is determined by the anode supply voltage available and the permissible dissipation for the valve. A suitable operating point is $V_a = 275$V, and $i_a = 90$ mA ; this needs a bias voltage of -16V, and a peak input signal of 16 V. r_a is 1,000 Ω, and if the load resistance is made 2,000 Ω, the power in the load is then 2·4 W. The maximum dissipation of the valve must not be exceeded even if no signal is applied, hence to limit the current to 90 mA under this condition the choke must have a resistance of (300–275)/0·09 Ω, i.e. 280 Ω.
4. −295
5. 2600: 2600.

CHAPTER 9

1. $\mu = 158$, $r_a = 45{,}000\ \Omega$, $g_m = 3{\cdot}5$ mA/V : output power 0·49W. : 2nd harmonic distortion 7·1%.
2. The phase shift/frequency characteristic is non-uniform over the range 30–300 Hz : the phase shift is 46·7° at 30 Hz, and 6·2° at 300 Hz.
4. 909 : 865.
5. $-27{\cdot}5 - j\,131$: negative feedback.
6. 3%.
9. $\beta = 0{\cdot}004$: 5.
10. (a) 35·6 to 59·5 (b) 7·8 to 8·6.
12. 462 Ω.
13. (a) 1·3 MΩ (b) 2,300 Ω.
14. Gain reduced by a factor of 0·306.
15. 0·87 : 381 Ω : 3·3pF.
17. 25: 5·6 Ω.

CHAPTER 10

1. 111 : 32 Hz and 61·3 kHz.
2. 60 : 32 Hz and 57·4 kHz.
4. 61.
5. 236.
6.

Grid voltage	= −15	−9	−7	−5	−3 volts
Gain	= 6	25	27·5	62·5	62·5

7. (a) 398 and 252 V: (b) 190.
10. 17.
11. 344×10^{-6} mho.
12. 11·6.

CHAPTER 11

2. 1/35 of output voltage fed back in anti-phase to the grid.
4. 3·4 mA/V.
5. 2·6 μH.
11. 74%.

CHAPTER 12

1. 12·5%.
10. (a) 2·12 V: (b) 1·91 V.

CHAPTER 13

1. The carrier has a frequency of $(5/2\pi)$ MHz, from which the side-bands are spaced by $(5/2\pi)$ kHz. In addition to the d.c. component, there is a component of twice carrier frequency, and one of twice signal frequency : depth of modulation 5·4%.
6. 3·6 : 1.
11. 62%.
13. 5mA : 79%.
14. g_m should change by ± 0·016 mA/V.
15. 50 kHz. 3·14%.

CHAPTER 14

1. 11·4μV.
2. 18·3 dB.
3. 160 μV.
5. 1300 Ω : 5·2 dB.
6. 19·3 dB.

CHAPTER 15

1. $x = \frac{4}{\pi}\left[\sin x + \frac{1}{3}\cos 3x + \frac{1}{5}\sin 5x + \quad . \quad . \quad . \quad . \quad . \right.$
4. (a) 12 kHz. (b) 48 kHz. (c) 2880 Hz. (d) 7 MHz.

CHAPTER 16

2. The voltage across the 60 Ω load is

$$V = 3{\cdot}27 + 0{\cdot}298 \sin 1500\pi t - 0{\cdot}0135 \cos 3000\pi t + 0{\cdot}149 \sin 1800\pi t - 0{\cdot}0034 \cos 3600\pi t + 0{\cdot}0135 \cos 300\pi t - 0{\cdot}0135 \cos 3300\pi t$$

6. 0·02 μW.

CHAPTER 17

9. Lost traffic 0·0018 *T.U.*: Grade of service 0·002.
11. 1·4 kHz in 44–48 kHz channel and 2·2 kHz in 52–56 kHz channel.

CHAPTER 18

3. When the switch opens a series *LCR* circuit is formed. This will produce oscillatory current if $R<2\sqrt{L/C}$, but may be avoided if the circuit resistance is increased so that $R>2\sqrt{L/C}$. The circuit is non-oscillatory.
4. Balancing resistance 656 Ω : line current 42 mA.

CHAPTER 19

1. 142 Ω : 190,000 km/s.
5. 33%.
6. 0·17 dB/km.
7. 177,000 Ω.
8. 53,400 Ω.
9. 6 mm.
10. $V_{out}=0{\cdot}846\,V_{in}$, hence attenuation = 1·6 dB. Phase change is 209 radians.
11. $R=26\ \Omega$: $X=20\ \Omega$.
14. 1·43 : 1. 15. 27.
16. The stub should have a length of 1·96 metres, and be positioned 0·63 metre from the termination.
17. $d=5{\cdot}6$ metres, $l=7{\cdot}5$ metres.

CHAPTER 20

9. Stage gain of 1·6. Input impedance 179 Ω.
10. 2·84 kV. 0·0072 μs.

CHAPTER 21

8. $0{\cdot}266 \times 10^{-6}$ watt per square metre : 0·84 mV.
9. 0·45 mV. 15. 29°. 16. $N = 1{\cdot}2 \times 10^{12}/m^3$.

CHAPTER 22

1. Modulator valve 250 w: carrier amp. valve 75 w.
2. 4·25.
3. 40 pF : 170 μH : 4·41.
4. 95.
7. 75·5% : 1·0, 0·998 1·002 MHz : 15 5·65, 5·65A
8. 24 dB.

INDEX